eADOPTION AND THE KNOWLEDGE ECONOMY: ISSUES, APPLICATIONS, CASE STUDIES

Information and Communication Technologies and the Knowledge Economy

Volume 1

An associated publication by IOS Press:

2003 P. Cunningham, M. Cunningham, and P. Fatelnig (Eds.), Building the Knowledge Economy: Issues, Applications, Case Studies

ISSN 1574-1230

eAdoption and the Knowledge Economy: Issues, Applications, Case Studies

Part 2

Edited by

Paul Cunningham

and

Miriam Cunningham

IIMC International Information Management Corporation Ltd, Dublin, Ireland

IOS
Press

Amsterdam • Berlin • Oxford • Tokyo • Washington, DC

ISBN 1 58603 470 7
Library of Congress Control Number: 2004113875

Publisher
IOS Press
Nieuwe Hemweg 6B
1013 BG Amsterdam
The Netherlands
fax: +31 20 620 3419
e-mail: order@iospress.nl

Distributor in the UK and Ireland
IOS Press/Lavis Marketing
73 Lime Walk
Headington
Oxford OX3 7AD
England
fax: +44 1865 750079

Distributor in the USA and Canada
IOS Press, Inc.
4502 Rachael Manor Drive
Fairfax, VA 22032
USA
fax: +1 703 323 3668
e-mail: iosbooks@iospress.com

PRINTED IN THE NETHERLANDS

Preface

While much progress has been made in building the Knowledge Economy, many challenges remain. This requires ever-greater transparency of public and private initiatives, whether commercial, legislative, political, social or technical in nature.

It is important that human, cultural and technological issues related to eAdoption and the Digital Divide are constantly in the public eye. Sharing problems encountered and lessons learnt helps inform national and international policy, as well as avoiding expensive mistakes and providing a framework for replication of successful implementations.

This book brings together a comprehensive collection of over 230 contributions on commercial, government or societal exploitation of the Internet and ICT, representing cutting edge research from over 30 countries. The issues, applications and case studies presented facilitate knowledge sharing, which is key to addressing global eAdoption issues and the Digital Divide. It can be used to benchmark regional and national developments, avoid previous mistakes and identify potential partners and exploitation opportunities.

The contributions reflect state-of-the-art research initiatives funded privately, nationally and regionally, as well as at European level. The increased emphasis on close cooperation and collaboration between end users and commercial and academic researchers is very welcome, and augurs well for the continued development of the European Research Area

Reflecting the breadth and depth of the ICT related research undertaken by the contributors, the contents are broken down into eight broad thematic areas. These are: Broadband and Mobility; eBusiness; eGovernment and eDemocracy; Knowledge Management; Networked, Smart and Virtual Organisations; New Working Environments; SME Issues; and Training and Education. Papers within each thematic area are in turn grouped under the subheadings of Issues, Applications and Case Studies, reflecting their primary focus.

We would like to acknowledge the valuable contribution of the Advisory Committee who provided authors with actionable feedback in finalising their papers for publication, and the encouragement and support of Alcatel and the European Commission.

Paul Cunningham
Miriam Cunningham

Advisory Committee

Contents

Part 1

Preface v
Advisory Committee vi

Section 1: Broadband & Mobility

Section 1.1: Issues
WiFi vs. UWB - Present and Future Hot Spot Technologies for Open Mobile Networks, *J. Wylegalla* 5
4G Mobile in Europe: Business Scenarios and Implications for Research Policy, *P. Ballon and E. Bohlin* 12
Using Dynamic Service and Network Discovery to Stimulate eBusiness over Composite Radio Environments, *N. Koutsouris, L. Papadopoulou, V. Stavroulaki, P. Demestichas and M. Theologou* 20
Infrastructure Requirements for Smart Spaces and Managed Zones, *M. Ó Foghlú and E. De Leastar* 28
Integrated Management of Smart Spaces, *S. van der Meer and B. Jennings* 35
Managed Person-Centric Adaptive Services for Smart Spaces, *D. Lewis, A. Brady, K. Carey, O. Conlan, K. Feeney, S. Higel, T. O'Donnell, D. O'Sullivan, K. Quinn and V. Wade* 42
Customer Needs in Mobile Rich Media Markets, *T. Brodt and M. Heitmann* 50
Mapping of Customer Needs for eEurope 2005, *M.-L. Viherä and L. Viukari* 58
Opportunities, Threats and Critical Success Factors of the ASP Business Model, *L. Hansen* 65

Section 1.2: Applications
Mobile Technologies: Paving the Way for Achieving eInclusion, *M.F. Cabrera, J.L. Villalar, M.T. Arredondo and J.C. Naranjo* 75
Indoor Wireless Location Management System for Smart Space Applications, *R. Mathur, M. Klepal and D. Pesch* 80
Supporting eBusiness Activities In Multi - Service and Network Provider Environments, *N. Koutsouris, V. Stavroulaki and N. Mitrou* 87
Supporting eLearning and eHealth in a Broadband Network Environment, *V. Chionsini and S. Giordano* 94
Mobile Biometric Person Identification System on the Basis of Pattern Recognition Software and GSM Cellular Networks, *A. Yudashkin, I. Danilushkin, S. Kolpaschikov, A. Maslennikov and R. Demyanenko* 102
Breaking the High-Speed Barrier: Inhibitors to Broadband Exploitation by SMEs, *A.J. Davies, D. March and B. Evans* 109
A Collaborative Framework for Distributed Winter Testing, *P. Törlind* 116

Section 1.3: Case Studies

The Internet Goes Mobile – SMS Usage by Austrian Students, *A. Dickinger and J. Murphy* 127
Organizational Consequences of E-mail Adoption and Diffusion: Theoretical Issues and Empirical Results, *L. Biggiero, A. Sammarra, C. Muzzi and R. Dandi* 134
Science Game: Mobile Gaming in a Scientific Exhibition, *F. Bellotti, R. Berta, A. de Gloria, E. Ferretti and M. Margarone* 141
Designing Business Models for Location Based Advertising, *B. Kölmel* 147
Exploring Business Opportunities with Intelligent Mobile Redirect Service, *D. Buyse and R. Hemmerich* 155

Section 2: eBusiness & eCommerce

Section 2.1: Issues

Multicultural Commercial Websites: When Translating Might Not Be Enough, *J. Nantel and E. Glaser* 167
Challenging Web Design and Cultural Issues in International E-commerce Sites, *K.S. Kang* 174
Reputation Systems and Data Protection Law, *T. Mahler and T. Olsen* 180
Cyber-Trust, *J. Cave and L. Valeri* 188
Trusted eBusiness Services in Social Housing, *S. Robinson and S. Mathews* 196
BioSec: Biometrics and Security Towards Trust and Security, *O. Sanchez* 203
Foreseeing the Single European Electronic Market - Information Collection and Study, *R. Jardim-Goncalves, H.M. Vieira and A. Steiger-Garcao* 211
Choosing Channels - Exploring the Effects of Consumers' Use of Multiple Channels, *D. Osterlund* 217
Interoperability in the Model Accelerated Society, *J. Goossenaerts* 225
Business Model Interoperability using Enterprise Model Integration, *H. Kühn, M. Murzek and F. Bayer* 233
The Third Estate – The Role of SMEs in ICT Standards Setting, *K. Jakobs* 241
Towards the Development of Standards for Electronic Business in Services, *G. Gudergan, H. Hoeck and H. Behrens* 249
Effectiveness of Governance Structures for 3G Standardization and Implications for China's 3G Policy, *K. Reimers and M. Li* 256
A Taxonomy of Service Standards and a Modification for E-Business, *K. Blind* 264
The xNAL Based Method of Postal Address Management in e-Commerce, *D. Trninic* 271
Knowledge-Based Business Process Re-engineering for e-Business, *N. Mekras* 279
The Adoption of Standardised Technology in the Automotive Industry, *M. Gerst and R. Bunduchi* 287
Enabling Business Opportunities in the Post Block Exemption Era - MYCAREVENT, *A. Garg, H. Dirlenbach and A. Quadt* 295
Emerging Issues at European Airports, *C. Stockhammer and J. Pfister* 303
The Analysis of Rising Private e-Money Based on Business Model: Korean Cases, *S. Park and J. Han* 311
New Financial Support Strategies for eTechnology Companies, *U. Meyer-Reim, A. Hussla, I. Hussla and H. Bechmann* 319
The Peer-to-Peer Dilemma, *L. Eriksson and N. Enlund* 327
Online Music and Competitive Actions in the Music Industry, *S. Mäkinen and M. Aunola* 335

P2P, "Legal" Downloading Sites and the Future of Music Distribution, *A. Edström-Frejman* 343
Television Content Online - eBusiness Strategies for AV-Archives, *M. Grill and A. Hecht* 351

Section 2.2: Applications
EUPKI, the Libre Software Public Key Infrastructure, *E. Tric* 359
A Practical Solution to the Interoperability Challenge in PKI related Online Services, *A.K. Möller, P. Boscolo and S. Topham* 365
Electronic Content Publication, Certification and Verification System, *I. Pigulevsky* 372
ASP Solutions for XML Archives Management and Exploitation, *F. Nahum and C. Bruno* 379
Business Interoperability Based on e-Documents with Embedded Workflow, *M. Garuti* 386
Automating Business Process Integration - Pilot Findings, *H. Hinderer, E. Folmer and J. Vlachakis* 394
Semantic Integration in eCommerce, *X.A. Navarro, A. del Río Rodríguez and J.I. Mirad* 400
Next Generation Mediation Service for the eTourism Market, *M. Hackl and O. Fodor* 407
Managing Copyright on Cultural Heritage, *R. Gagliardi, C. Prandoni and S. Boi* 414
Hermes - The Trans-European Hybrid Mail Service, *L. Merlo and S. Zamboni* 422
Customer Relationship Management and Service of Capital Goods at Remote Locations, *K. Jansson and J. Hemilä* 429
Situation-Aware Service Selection from Large Offers, *B. Holtkamp, R. Gartmann, N. Weissenberg, Y. Han and G. Li* 437
Towards a Platform Enabling Grid based Application Service Provision, *S. Wesner, L. Schubert, T. Dimitrakos, D. Mac Randal, M. Gaeta, P. Ritrovato and G. Laria* 445
The FairsNet System in the European Trade Fair Market, *F. Barbini, M. Contenti, A. D'Atri and O. Strignano* 453
SEEM-Enabling Technologies, *J. Vlachakis, S. Abels, S. Campbell and P.D. Monari* 460

Section 2.3: Case Studies
Transforming Research Activities to Product Offerings, *O. Terzidis* 469
A B2B Architecture for Goods Distribution in Urban and Metropolitan Areas, *G. Ambrosino, M. Boero, F. Logi, A. Liberato and B. Wild* 478
Economic Impact of E-Business, *P. Verhoest, C. Huveneers and R. Hawkins* 485
Bifurcation - Improving the Effectiveness of Personalized Web-based Systems, *B. Lennstrand, C. Persson and E. Wallin* 491
The Swedish Newspaper Industry's Changing Business Strategies for Multi-Channel Publishing 1995 – 2004, *T. Uppgård, A. Jonsson and E. Appelgren* 499
Electronic Banking in Estonia: Development Aspects and Risks, *D. Sokolov* 507
Physical-Virtual Back-and-Forth: Lessons Learned from the FlyAway Travel Case, *S. Wikström and S. Värlander* 514
SATINE Project: Exploiting Web Services in the Travel Industry, *A. Dogac, Y. Kabak, G. Laleci, S. Sinir, A. Yildiz and A. Tumer* 522
The Future of Mobile Payment: Quest for Standards, *A.S. Lim* 530
Electronic Data Interchange: Efficient ICT Use in Agriculture, *V. Jucevičienė, V. Aleknevičienė, D. Zinkevičienė and D. Jatkūnaitė* 537
Towards a Global Integration of the Portuguese Wine Cluster Information – The INFOVINI Project, *H. Nóvoa, M. Fernandes, N. Ramos and J. Falcão e Cunha* 543

An Interoperability Testing Study: Automotive Inventory Visibility and Interoperability, *N. Ivezic, B. Kulvatunyou, S. Frechette, A. Jones, H. Cho and B. Jeong* 551
Organisational Alignment and Managing Innovation with In-Company Incubators, *K. Kutsikos and A. Warr* 559

Section 3: eGovernment & eDemocracy

Section 3.1: Issues

Innovation 2010 – Towards More Coherent Policies for Europe, *R. Zobel and E. Filos* 571
eGovernment and the Feasibility of Going Online, *N. Monks* 582
E-Delivery – Based on the Austrian eGovernment Law, *P. Reichstaedter* 590
eGovernment Learning Journeys: Knowledge Management in Action, *C. Lowe* 597
eGovernment for Businesses: Lessons Learned from a Trajectory for Standardization of Business Information, *J. Verhoosel and V. Akkersdijk* 604
Putting the User at the Centre – Implications for the Provision of Online Public Services, *K. Gareis, K. Cullen and W.B. Korte* 611
The eUser in a Universally Accessible Information Society, *C. Stephanidis and M. Antona* 619
Policy Approaches to Involve Societal At-Risk Groups in European eServices, *L. Kubitschke and K. Cullen* 624
From Teleworkability to eGovernmentability – Telework in Public Administration, *I. Götzl* 631
New Public Management and the Use of Distance Work, *W. Knudsen, M. Bjørnholt and T. Lissner* 639
Systematic Design and Realization of Security-Critical Inter-Organizational Workflows, *R. Breu, M. Hafner, B. Weber and A. Nowak* 646
A Research Roadmap for Sustainable Information Cities, *S. Curwell, M. Deakin, A. Hamilton, K. Paskaleva-Shapira, S. Soubra and J. Turner* 654
Towards Virtual Governance Architecture - A Perspective on Information Technology as a Transformer of Public Institutions and Governments, *T. Zwahr and M. Finger* 662
QUALEG Quality of Service & Legitimacy in eGovernment, *N. Benamou, D. Guarnieri, S. Mantovani and A. Savoldelli* 670
An Experience of Transition to Open Source Software in Local Authorities, *P. Zuliani and G. Succi* 678
In Principle: Towards an Open Architecture for eGovernment Identity Management, *B.R. Katzy, J. van den Hoven and G. Igl* 685
Strategies Used to Reach eGovernment Interoperability: An Initial Evaluation, *A. Busson and A. Keravel* 693
TERREGOV: Collaborative Practices among Civil Servants, *S. Filipazzi and A. Savoldelli* 700
Implementing Adaptive Collaborative Telework in Public Administration, *M. Hori and M. Ohashi* 708
Resolving Interoperability Issues for eGovernment Identification Systems, *A. Ni Fhloinn* 715
Identity and Relationship Management – The Key to Safe, Secure ICT Infrastructure, *G. Montaletti, M. Martin and N. Fröschle* 724
The Evolution of an eGovernment Identity Management Architecture, *GUIDE Consortium and L. Borthwick* 732
eVoting: Who Controls the eElectoral Process?, *A. Xenakis and A. Macintosh* 739
Implementing eDemocracy: eVoting and eParticipation, *M.A. Biasiotti and R. Nannucci* 745

Regulatory and Legal Challenges for eVoting and eDemocracy, *A. Kosmopoulos* 751
The Cure for the Ills of eDemocracy is More eDemocracy - Networked Governance in the Information Society, *J. Cave* 760
Democracy in Action - Open Source in eGovernment, *S. Simmons* 768

Section 3.2: Applications
The Virtual Dossier (from the Paper Dossier to the Virtual Dossier), *E. Fenoglio* 777
E-Procurement: On-Line Public Administration Purchasing, *A. Leli and L. Milone* 785
Circuit Infrastructure for Multi-Functional Card-Based Citizen Services, *A. Battaglino* 793
Selling an eTax Service Revenue Commissioners, Ireland, *M. Whelan* 801
The Regione Piemonte Ability Passport – A Regional Service Network for Disabled Citizens, *P. Raviolo, M. Oberto Tarena and S. Sinigaglia* 809
RISER: Trans-European Access to Resident Registers for Business and Citizens, *H. Tamm* 817
SITAD: Building a Local Spatial Data Infrastructure in Piedmont (Italy) within INSPIRE Perspective, *P. Cipriano and L. Garretti* 825
Enabling Interoperability between Public Administrations - A Pan-European Approach, *D. Werth, F. Zangl and O. Adam* 833
eEpoch Interoperable Electronic Identity Management, *V. Sebastian, A. Marques and M. Torres* 841
Knowledge Representation and Sharing for European Values based Identity Management, *A. Kő, M. Biró, A. Gábor and R. Vas* 847
The 3SI Framework: Assessing ICT Development Initiatives, *E. del Hoyo-Barbolla and M.T. Arredondo* 854
eService Co-Design Platforms, *O. Forsgren* 862
Net Readiness Perception Index, *M. Goliński* 869

Author Index 877

Part 2

Preface

Advisory Committee

Section 3: eGovernment & eDemocracy (continued)

Section 3.3: Case Studies
The Austrian eGovernment Initiative – Good Practice in European eAdministration, *C. Rupp* 885
Emilia-Romagna Regional Strategy on ICT, *S. Lotti and K. Shahin* 893
Uptake of eServices in Danish Municipalities, *H.Z. Henriksen* 901
Experiences from Formulating Recommendations for a National Interoperability Strategy, *E. Tambouris, A. Stefanou, V. Peristeras, G. Fragidis and K. Tarabanis* 909
Local Data Sharing and Co-Branding to Better Serve Citizens, *N. Conso* 917
Born to Co-Operate: New Communication Approaches for eGovernment, *J. Tepandi* 924
Open Applications and Solution Sharing for Governments, *D. Rowe* 932
An Evaluation Methodology for Innovative Mobility Services: The MEROPE Cities, *P. Frosini, S. Gini, G. Ambrosino, J. Barceló and G. Ostyn* 940
Enterprise Workflow in a Public Sector Context, *P. Jackson* 947

vCRM - Vienna Citizens' Request Management, *J. Wustinger* 955
Kommunalnet.at – The Intranet for Local Authorities in Austria, *P. Parycek, W. Seboeck and N. Edelmann* 961
Personal Identity and Proxy Identities Austria's eGovernment, *A. Hollosi, L. Naber and M. Liehmann* 968
Towards Intelligent Cities, *S. Curwell, A. Hamilton, A. Marshall-Ponting, S. Soubra and R. Vankeisbelck* 974
PAPÁS, Advanced Services for the Educational Community, *M. Camacho, V. Fernández, A. Conde and J. Mena* 982
Mapping the Law: Knowledge Support for Business Development Enquiry, *F. Wilson and R. Peters* 990
Argument Visualisation to Support Democratic Decision-Making, *A. Macintosh and A. Renton* 997
A Method for Decision Support in e-Democracy, *M. Danielson and L. Ekenberg* 1004
DEMO*sfera*: A Laboratory for eCitizenship in Sicily, *J. Marsh and F. Passantino* 1009

Section 4: Knowledge Management

Section 4.1: Issues
A National Programme Perspective on ERA Challenges for Semantic Systems and Services, *E. Prem* 1021
Knowledge Management in 2010 - Business Needs and Market Prospects, *J. Sage, P. Stanbridge and E. Husmann* 1029
The Role of a Semantic Engine in an Information Management System, *A. Zamolotskikh, M. Cunningham and P. Cunningham* 1035
Knowledge Transfer from Researchers to Businesses - eXperience and EUREXIS, *B. Sigrist, M. Göckel and P. Schubert* 1044
P2P Interactions for the Support of Knowledge Sharing in Networked Enterprises, *R. Ratti, A. Bokma, K. Ginty, D. Tektonidis and A. Koumpis* 1051
Introduction of Value and Cost Centres in the Management of European RTD Projects, *I. Pavlou and A. Koumpis* 1059

Section 4.2: Applications
Johanna: A Knowledge Centered Infrastructure for Teleorganizations, *M. Gaspari, D. Guidi, A. Petrucci and L. Picci* 1069
ICONS based Knowledge Management in the Structural Funds Projects Preparation, *E. Staniszkis and B. Nowicki* 1077
Content Engineering for Conversational Advisory Systems, *M. L'Abbate, T. Kamps and U. Thiel* 1085
Natural Language Access and Intelligent Service Discovery in e-Business, *M. Simonov, M. Soroldoni and A. Gangemi* 1093
Experimental Design of the Text Identification Language within the ELIS Instrumental Testing System, *V. Gorbunov* 1101
Building Community Mirrors with Public Shared Displays, *M. Koch* 1108
InnovationEnterprizer: System for Evaluating and Managing Corporate Innovation, *I. Bitran, S. Conn and M. Torkkeli* 1115
Learning User Preference Models and Business Strategies for E-Commerce, *M.J. Viamonte, C. Ramos, F. Rodrigues and J. Cardoso* 1123

Section 4.3: Case Studies

Ontology-Enabled Knowledge Asset Trading, *D. Apostolou, P.-P. Georgolios, K. Kafentzis, M.-F. Schäfer and P. Jones* 1133

Managing Knowledge in Networked Product Creation Organisations, *P. Pöyry, M. Johnson and J. Meriluoto* 1140

Customisation of Information in the Manufacturing Industry, *C. Persson* 1148

Facilitating Knowledge Exchange and Decision Making within Learning Networks, *D. Apostolou and S. Papadopoulou* 1156

Section 5: Networked, Smart & Virtual Organisations

Section 5.1: Issues

The Co-Existence of Communities of Practice and Virtual Organisations, *F. Sturm and P. Wolf* 1169

Building Knowledge Driven and Dynamically Networked Communities within European Healthcare Systems, *S. Bettoni, L. Gadda, V. Perdoni and A. Savoldelli* 1175

Enforce Engineering Collaboration, *M. Callot, L. Saint-Marc, P. Nowak and B. Eynard* 1183

Enabling Dynamic Security Perimeters for Virtual Collaborations, *T. Dimitrakos, I. Djordjevic, D. Mac Randal, M. Gaeta, G. Laria, P. Ritrovato and N. Romano* 1191

Towards a Trust and Contract Management Framework for Dynamic Virtual Organisations, *T. Dimitrakos, D. Golby and P. Kearney* 1199

Web Services Security for Trustworthy Business Processing in Dynamic Virtual Organisations, *J. Claessens and C. Geuer-Pollmann* 1208

Autonomic Privilege Management - Extending PERMIS to Contribute to the TrustCoM Objectives, *D. Chadwick* 1216

Integrating the Hybrid PKI Model into Trust Relationship Lifecycle for Dynamic Virtual Organizations, *J. Haller, Y. Karabulut and P. Robinson* 1223

Decision Support and Strategy Formulation in Supply Chain Management *M. Schnetzler, A. Nobs and A. Sennheiser* 1231

Profiling for Supplier Selection in the Context of the Extended Enterprise, *K. Dunne and J. Browne* 1239

The Role of ICT in Reverse Logistics: A Hypothesis of RFID Implementation to Manage the Recovery Process, *A. Payaro* 1247

E-Solutions for Planning Lifecycle-Oriented, Flexible Production Systems, *G. Schuh, C. Schleyer and N. Wemhoener* 1254

GRID Based Virtual Laboratory for Scientific and Industrial Collaboration, *G.R. Meijer and L.O. Hertzberger* 1262

Section 5.2: Applications

Competence Profiling and Problem Solving in Virtual Networks, *C. Edelmann and K. Wagner* 1271

Guidance in SCM Configuration – The PRODCHAIN Toolbox, *M. Weidemann, V. Stich and A. Nobs* 1278

e-HUBs: e-Engineering Enabled by Holonomic and Universal Broker Services, *G. Augenbroe* 1285

Implementation of an Integrated Organisation and Process Tool for Engineering Design Co-Ordination, *C. Merlo, R. Michel, P. Girard, P. Nowak and L. Roucoules* 1293

Specifications of a Collaborative Tool for Product Design, *B. Rose, M. Lombard, L. Gzara, L. Lossent, P.-A. Claudon and P. Leboeuf* 1301
A Comprehensive XML-Based Approach for Trust Negotiations, *E. Bertino, A.C. Squicciarini, E. Ferrari and L.D. Martino* 1309
New Working Environments for Product Development - A Component Framework for CAx Application Development, *M. Richter* 1316

Section 5.3: Case Studies
Enhancing Presence and Context Awareness in Collaborative Settings, *H. de Poot, J. Kort and D. Langley* 1325
Learning through Online Communities - A Study of Health Care Sites in Europe, *Å. Smedberg* 1333
Virtual Organisations in Healthcare: Organisation, People and Technology, *M. Grootveld, J. Swaak, R. Brussee, R. Huis in't Veld and M. Michel-Verkerke* 1340
Managing Virtual Projects – A Benchmark Study of Collaboration Tools, *B. Katzy, G. Sung and C. Serrano* 1347
Fostering Innovation in Extended Enterprises, *M. Sorli, D. Stokic, Á. Gorostiza, A. Correia and A. Campos* 1354
Virtual Integrated Design in an Intranet Environment, *Z. Weiss and J. Diakun* 1362
Digital Engineering and Supply Chain Management for Enhanced Toyota System, *S. Kuroiwa* 1368
Applying Collaborative e-Business in the Automotive Electronics Industry, *J. Eschenbaecher and N. Meyer* 1376

Section 6: New Working Environments

Section 6.1: Issues
Getting Organisation and Human Ready for Information Systems, *I.-S. Fan, N. Wognum and H. Buhl* 1387
Challenges of Work/Home Boundaries and User Perceptions for Ambient Intelligence, *R. Ellis* 1395
Natural Multimodal Interaction for Design Applications, *E. den Os and L. Boves* 1403
Ambient Intelligence Vision: Exploring the Social Risks of its Construction, *I. Lopez de Vallejo* 1411
Organisations as Multilayered Networks: The 'Space Syntax' of Ambient Intelligence, *A. Penn* 1418
Building Context Awareness into Physical Service Environments, *G. Cortese and F. Davide* 1426
Understanding Innovation in the Mobile Workplace, *H. Schaffers* 1433
Wearable Mobile Computing - A Paradigm for Future European eWork, *M. Boronowsky, L. Gong, O. Herzog and I. Rügge* 1441
EDEL: Developing a Second Generation Night-Vision System, *C. Bellotti, F. Bellotti, A. de Gloria, L. Andreone, D. Kooss and M. Mariani* 1448

Section 6.2: Applications
Mobile Support for Communities of Practice, *E. Hinrichs and W. Prinz* 1457
Sustainable eWork: An Online Self-Assessment Tool for Organisations, *W.B. Korte and N. Kordey* 1464
COMBINE-for-PACE: Performance Assessment of a Complex Enterprise, *N. Yarushkina and I. Semoushin* 1472

Gesprecons: An eSafety and Risk Prevention Platform, *J. Molina, M. Martinez and I. García* 1480
Spin-3D: A VR-Platform on Internet ADSL Networks for Synchronous Collaboration, *D. Pavy, A. Bouguet, P. Le Mer, S. Louis Dit Picard, L. Perron, G. Saugis, C. Chaillou and S. Degrande* 1486
Useful Semantic Product Properties in Virtual Worlds, *R. Malkewitz and G. Gadda* 1494
Virtual Reality Applications in the Energy Industry, *R. Salve* 1502

Section 6.3: Case Studies
Visiting eWorkers' Homes - Three Stories for Designing eWork Homes and Furniture, *K. Virtanen, T. Mattelmäki and S. Heinonen* 1511
Evaluation of an AmI Workplace, *A. Harrison and P. Steggles* 1519
Citizen-Centric Network of Professionals: Well-Being Services @ Work, *N. Saranummi* 1527
How to Speed-Up the Implementation of eWork in the Health Care Sector, *U. Kirchhoff, D. Stokic and H. Sundmaeker* 1534

Section 7: SME Issues

Section 7.1: Issues
Using Enterprise Models to Define a Web Based Collaborative eEngineering Environment for SMEs, *D.C. Amaral, G. Augenbroe, R.K. Scalice, L.D.V. Ribeiro, R.G. Dias Netto and H. Rozenfeld* 1547
Enabling Internet-Based B2B Transactions through Application Interconnection, *Y. Charalabidis, V. Karakoidas, S. Androutsellis-Theotokis and D. Spinellis* 1554
Roadmap for SME Sustainable Profitability, *J. Fradinho Oliveira, A. de Oliveira and E. Fradinho* 1562

Section 7.2: Applications
e-Services for Support of Robot Applications in SME-Networks, *R. Berger, G. Schreck and C. Willnow* 1571
Traceability Service Centres Supporting Agri-Food SMEs, *P. Onesti, M. Mattioli and M. Garuti* 1579

Section 7.3: Case Studies
Results from an e-Business Strategic Framework Deployment in Micro-SMEs, *R. Patrício, A. Silva, G. Ramalhão and L. Castilho* 1589
Is There an e-Business Digital Divide Among Firms? Evidence from a Multinational Pilot Study, *H. Schedl* 1597
Coaching High-Growth Start-Ups: Integrating Online Intelligence Solutions and In-Depth Support, *E. Chatard and D. Vian* 1604
Understanding the Dynamics of e-Business Adoption by SMEs, *G. Lee* 1611
Collaboration and Enterprise Networks: What About SMEs?, *M. van Leeuwen and K. Cormican* 1618

Section 8: Training & Education

Section 8.1: Issues
eInclusion of Sign Language Users, *F. Dotter* 1629
eEurope-Plus: Digital Divide or Digital Inclusion?, *N. Kligiene* 1637
Initiating Transformational Change in Dynamic Environments, *T. O'Keeffe* 1645

Developing European eSkills and Qualifications Frameworks, *B. Sellin* 1653
Driving Informatics Competence in Europe: The EUCIP Programme, *P. Schgör* 1658
eLearning in European SMEs: The Challenge for Policies and Practice, *G. Attwell* 1665
From Hands-on Experience to e-Learning, *I. Popova and O. Popov* 1672
A Methodology for Developing Quality e-Learning Systems, *K. Papanikolaou, S. Mavromoustakos and A.S. Andreou* 1679
Development and Implementation of a Collaborative Environment for Education, *I. Rivilla, M. Castro, M. Arjona, M. González and J. Peire* 1686
ORGANIC - Continuous Organisational Learning in Innovation and Companies, *R. Messnarz, R.V. Horvat, K. Harej and E. Feuer* 1693
Future Educational Needs for Manufacturing Strategy, *A. Rolstadås and B. Moseng* 1700
The Suitability of an Irish Third-Level Blended e-Learning Programme for Lean Competitiveness Training in SMEs, *L. Brown, E. Murphy, E. McQuade and M. Pauli* 1708

Section 8.2: Applications
From Continuous Medical Education to Continuous Professional Development, *R. Nardi, G. Ventriglia and J. Heyrman* 1719
MetaCampus Marketplace and the Challenge for Next Generation eLearning Platforms, *S. Le Goff and S. Ristol* 1727
Pilot Implementation of an Intelligent e-Learning Environment, *P.D. Cristea and R. Tuduce* 1734
The Virtual Laboratory as an Active Learning Environment, *M. Morozov, A. Tanakov, A. Gerasimov, D. Bystrov and V. Cvirko* 1742

Section 8.3: Case Studies
The Impact of Low Computer Literacy in the Information Society, *F. Sala* 1751
The Employability of ICT Professionals - A Study of European SMEs, *D. Scholarios, E. van der Schoot and B. van der Heijden* 1758
TRAIN-IT: Turning e-2004 Technologies into Business, *I. Hussla and H. Bechmann* 1766
Noisy Reform or Silent Revolution in Higher Education? A Hungarian Overview, *A. Gábor and Z. Szabó* 1774
Adopting Groupware for Collaborative E-Learning: A Blackboard '*Groups*' Case Study, *A. Hogarth* 1781
eLearning Knowledge Representation by Interactive Formal Models & Virtual Worlds, *O. Moukhine and K. Mukhin* 1789
eChallenges in International Education, *H. de Ruiter and B. Ding* 1796
A Client-Server System for Mass Recruitment to Secondary Schools in a Metropolitan Area, *C. Mazurek, M. Stroiński and A.P. Urbański* 1801

Author Index 1809

Section 3

eGovernment & eDemocracy

(continued)

Section 3.3

Case Studies

eAdoption and the Knowledge Economy: Issues, Applications, Case Studies
P. Cunningham and M. Cunningham (Eds.)
IOS Press, 2004

The Austrian eGovernment Initiative – Good Practice in European eAdministration

Christian RUPP
Federal Executive Secretary eGovernment, Austrian Federal Chancellery, Ballhausplatz 2, Vienna, 1014, Austria
Tel: +43 1 53115-6130, Fax: + 43 1 2697861, Email: Christian.Rupp@bka.gv.at

Abstract: The Austrian Federal government launched a broad eGovernment initiative (2003 – 2005) at the Austrian eGovernment conference in June 2003. It was established by the Council of Ministers of the Federal government in May 2003. A series of measures, coordinated with regional and local authorities, is intended to place Austria among the European Top 5 in the area of electronic administration by 2005. Within only 12 months, Austria has already improved its ranking within the eGovernment benchmarking of the European Commission from No. 11 to No. 4.

1. Organisational Structures

In May 2003, the Council of Ministers of the Austrian Federal government established an "eGovernment Platform" [1], which is chaired by the Chancellor Dr. Wolfgang Schüssel. This demonstrates the high priority given to the implementation of eGovernment. Members include the Vice-Chancellor, Federal Minister of Finance, Federal Minister of the Interior, Federal Minister of Justice, the State Secretary in the Federal Chancellery, governors of the Federal provinces, the president of the association of Austrian cities and towns, the president of the Austrian association of municipalities, the business sector (Presidents of the Federal Chamber of Commerce, of the Austrian Social Security Institutions and of the National Conference on Liberal Professions), the Federal Chief Information Officer, several external experts and the Federal Executive Secretary for eGovernment [2].

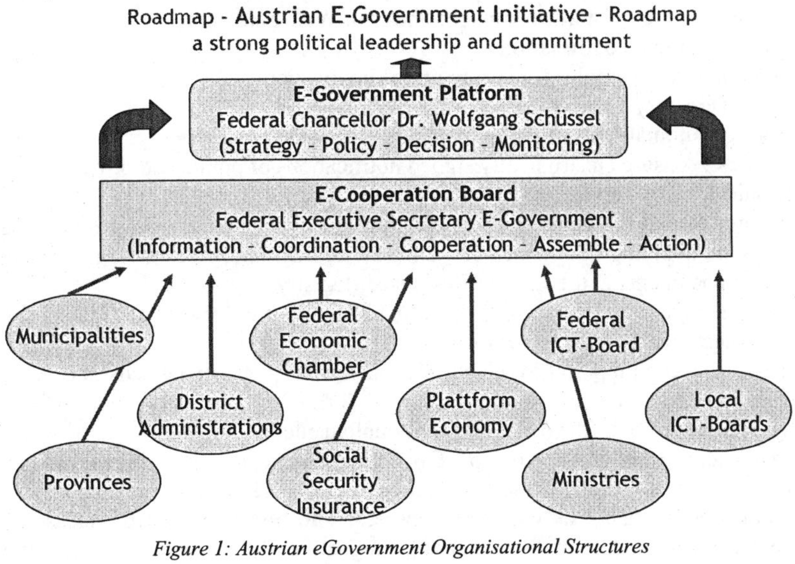

Figure 1: Austrian eGovernment Organisational Structures

This platform has to agree on an “Austrian eGovernment Roadmap” (nearly 100 projects until 2005) and to ensure the overall coordination of its implementation.

An “eCooperation Board” chaired by the Federal Executive Secretary for eGovernment, is responsible for the preparation of the Roadmap and monitoring of ongoing activities. In this board each ministry, each Federal province; experts from the associations of municipalities, cities and towns are represented as well as experts of chamber organisations. A separate business platform involves nearly 150 companies in the eGovernment field.

Establishing an “eGovernment Platform”, “eCooperation Board” and a business platform guarantees necessary communication between all stakeholders and political parties, as well as representation of the interests of everyone concerned.

2. Strategy of the Austrian eGovernment Initiative

The crucial points of the initiative are summarised in this section of the paper.

2.1 Consolidate and Expand What has been Achieved to Date

The initiative is based on a two-folded approach. On one hand new initiatives shall lead to an innovative eGovernment in Austria. On the other hand existing activities that have already started to bring public administration services online will be intensively continued. In the future it should be possible to carry out complete administrative procedures and transactions online. All activities are guided by the principles of quality over quantity, transparency, open interfaces and sustainability. Information- and network-security, data protection and accessibility are preferred over quick to implement but short-lived solutions.

2.2 Basic Services

A nationwide eGovernment must be built on a standardized basis. The development of common solutions means cost savings for all participants, and more efficient use of resources. As a contribution to the overall architecture, the Federal government provides central concepts that have been developed with the provinces, cities and municipalities:

- Style-guide for administrative forms in line with WAI-guideline
- Electronic payment confirmation
- Specifications and modules for secure online applications
- Common Directory services
- Methods of automatic assimilation of data in electronic processes
- Procedures to ensure electronically signed notifications of public authorities
- Electronic delivery services
- The Central Residence Registry (Zentrales Melde Register) as an eGovernment registry
- Methods of avoiding supplementary enclosures facilitating the storage of the most important documents in the Central Residence Registry
- Companies registries (registration of organizations, etc.) that are suitable for both eGovernment and the business world.
- help.gv.at as a central portal for electronic transactions between citizens/ businesses and public administrations.

Many of these concepts have already been implemented:

The main component of the Austrian eGovernment strategy is the “citizen card” concept [3]. It contains fundamental elements required for safe electronic transactions between administrations and citizens as well as businesses. The first citizen cards released by the private sector in combination with an electronic signature [4], are already in circulation. By Q4 2004 all new maestro bankcards will also serve as citizen cards [5]. An alternative to the secure signature - the so-called administrative signature, is offered for eGovernment transactions. Service cards (e.g. student cards) carrying a certificate, as well as mobile phones [6], can be used to interact with the Austrian eGovernment. Therefore eGovernment is also accessible with technologies that are familiar to most of the Austrian population. Above all, there is no need of any software installation.

A Form Style Guide ensures that the public administration Internet forms are designed in a uniform manner. Thus, the entire public administration presents itself with a uniform look and feel, which improves accessibility and usability. The implementation of eGovernment activities is based on close cooperation with regions, provinces, cities and municipalities. Spot solutions have been replaced by a nationwide, uniform approach. Concepts, guidelines and specifications are developed in working parties with the participation of all stakeholders. A common working-website has been established where draft documents can be discussed. As outlined in the action plan, eEurope tools developed to implement eGovernment are made freely available to public authorities and entities [7].

In many cases the delivery of public services is connected with the payment of fees. In order to facilitate the reliability of payment transactions, an electronic payment confirmation has been designed in collaboration with the Austrian banks [8]. The interface will be implemented by all public administrations. At present electronic payments can be made with credit card (certificate of criminal record) or with mobile phone (confirmation of residence). Payment using online banking methods will be implemented soon.

Electronic delivery is an important element of a modern, service-oriented administration. For citizens it means time savings and increased comfort. Having to collecting registered letters from the nearest post office can be avoided. Beyond that the proof of delivery guarantees both the receiver and the sender that the delivery actually took place. The delivery itself is conducted by an electronic delivery service, which makes documents of public administrations available for registered recipients and informs them electronically of the availability of new documents [9].

For efficient eGovernment it is necessary to automate and optimise organisational processes within the administration. By introducing electronic files on a Federal level, the Federal administration will achieve fast reaction and processing times [10].

2.3 Framework Consolidation

The current legal framework for electronic services was completed on 1st March 2004, when an "eGovernment Law" came into force. This is designed specifically for electronic communication between citizens, the business community and public administrations [11].

The eGovernment Law will create the legal frame for the following subjects:

- Unambiguous electronic identification
- Standard electronically documents
- Data protection in eGovernment
- Citizen Card and administrative signature
- Network of administrative portals
- Directories and Registries
- Electronic delivery
- E-Governance and citizen participation
- Certificate register

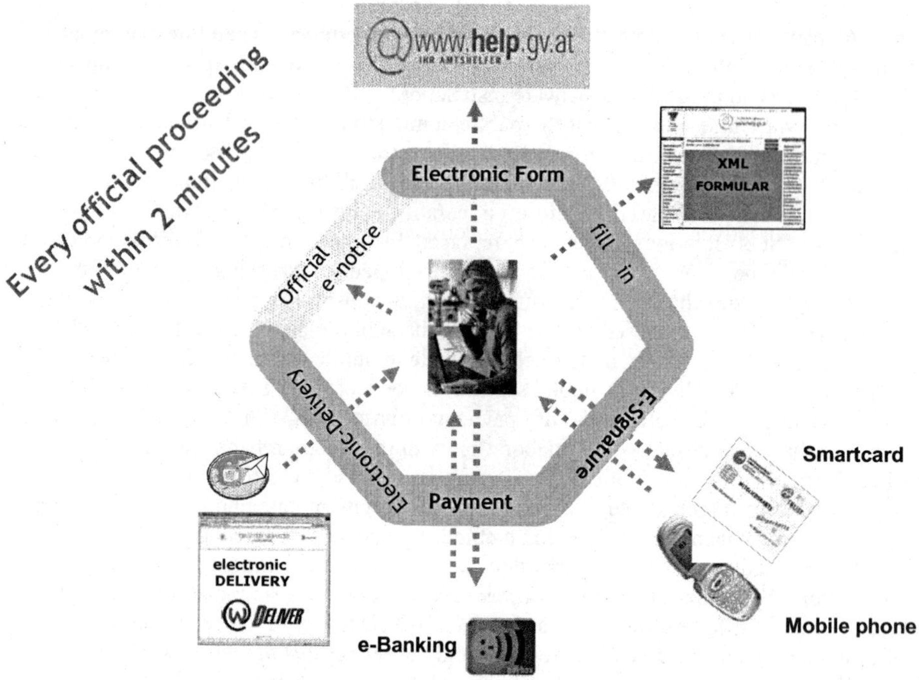

Figure 2: eGovernment in Austria

2.4 Encouraging infrastructure measures

Within the scope of the eGovernment initiative, infrastructure measures in the areas of broadband will be promoted, as well as the provision of PIAPs (Public Internet Access Points) and WiFi hot-spots. In line with pan-EU measures to support the expansion of broadband infrastructure the Federal government has decided to boost the spread of broadband connections with the 2004 tax reform.

2.5 eGovernment for municipalities

Selected municipalities of different sizes will demonstrate how online services can be implemented at municipality level, integrating new eGovernment building blocks such as digital signature, e-payment and electronic delivery into existing IT systems. The experience gained and the know-how produced will serve as the basis for a virtual competence centre for regional and local eGovernment suppliers [12].

2.6 Network of Administrative Portals

By interconnecting administrative portals on the Federal, provincial and municipal level, the databases of individual authorities become accessible to all participants of the network. This makes parallel directories obsolete and enables the common use of existing services. The allocation of access rights is decentralized, and the responsibility of every network participant [13].

2.7 ICT Board (Information and Communications Technology Board)

The Austrian ICT Board was established in June 2001 as the central governing body responsible for the integration and synchronisation of IT technologies on a Federal level. It is managed by a Federal Chief Information Officer appointed by the government.

2.8 Success is Guaranteed with the eGovernment Quality Mark

A number of directives, guidelines, and specifications have been worked out for the application of online processes. Forms, modules for online applications and electronic delivery are only a few examples. The Austrian "eGovernment Quality Mark" [14] provides a guarantee for the quality of services, software and hardware in line with established eGovernment standards and concepts. It gives citizens and businesses the certainty that they are dealing with serious providers of public services, and standard conforming products. This fulfils the consumers' demands of a modern and secure eGovernment.

3. Help.gv.at – Virtual Guide to Austrian Authorities

HELP was launched in 1997 as an Internet information platform. Today it is a comprehensive service platform for citizens. HELP [15], which supports official Internet channels, describes the related official procedures, starting from life situations (over 200) such as pregnancy, birth or marriage. It offers information on administrative processes, required documents, fees and deadlines. In addition, forms can be printed or downloaded, individual requests can be made, and official procedures can be handled electronically.

HELP is the electronic interface in Austria between 12 Federal ministries, 9 provinces, 80 district administrations and 2359 municipalities. As the virtual guide through the world of Austrian administration, HELP has made the step from a pure information medium to a communication and interactive medium for users, successfully supporting electronic processing of official procedures (transactions). "Official Proceedings Online" gives visitors the opportunity to complete their official procedures (over 1,000) online with the Austrian partner cities and municipalities as well as

- integration of e-signature and e-payment
- interface to the government back office
- life situations also for disabled people
- and for foreign citizens(English, Czech, Slovakian, Hungarian, Slovenian)
- interactive dictionary for governmental terms
- high service quality for individual request.

4. eEurope 2005 – EU eGovernment Benchmarking

At the beginning of 2004, Cap Gemini Ernst & Young released the most recent results of their ongoing survey on the adoption of electronic Public Services across Europe. Undertaken on behalf of the European Commission the report looks at the progress that Europe is making in providing online services at both the citizen and business level across the 15 EU member countries plus Norway, Iceland and Switzerland.

While the adoption of eGovernment continues to grow, the pace of growth slowed between 2002 and 2003. The level of online sophistication grew by 7% to 67%, compared with 60% in 2002 and 45% in 2001. Austria has made the most progress of any one country in the 12-month period.

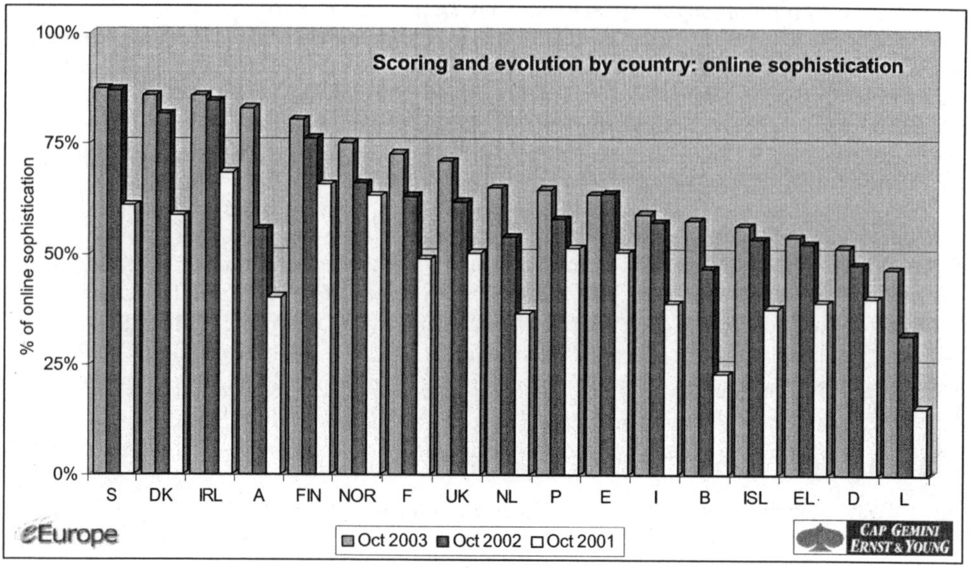

Figure 3: eGovernment Benchmarking I

In 2003 significant progress was made. This allows the research to focus on the number of public services that are truly fully transactional online. Based on this indicator of Europe's overall progress, only 45% of services are fully available online. In this area Denmark, Austria and Sweden currently lead the way.

While in the 2002 study, only Denmark, Sweden, Ireland and Finland showed progress towards two-way interaction, today almost all the countries surveyed have improved the average level of online sophistication of their public services beyond one way interaction, from the government to the users, towards two-way interaction.

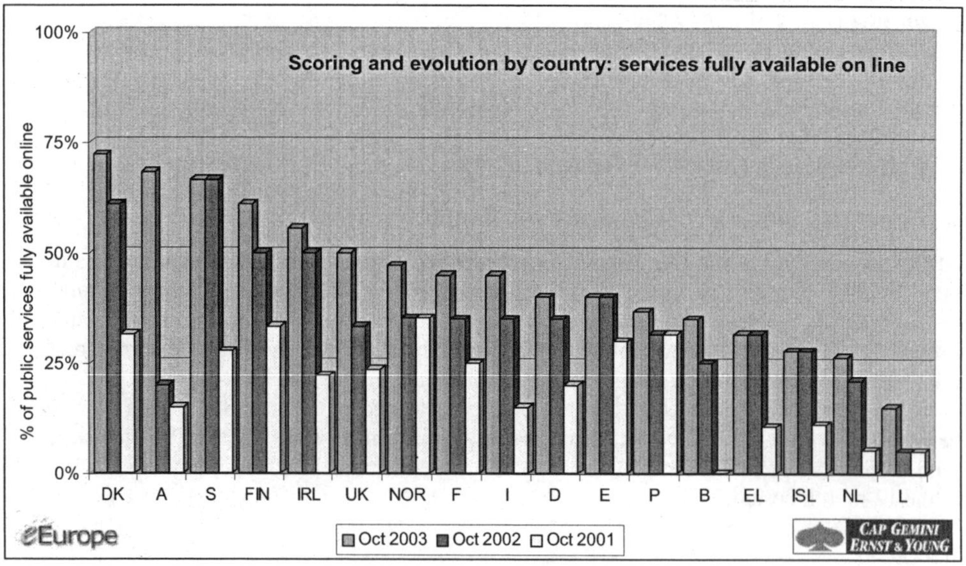

Figure 4: eGovernment Benchmarking II

Twenty basic public services have been identified, eight for citizens and twelve for business. The level of interaction, ranging from online information to full electronic transactions, was measured. The public services have then been clustered in four key areas:

- Income-generating: services where payment flows from citizens and businesses to the government (mainly taxes and social contributions)
- Registration: services related to recording data based on administrative obligations (births, deaths, marriages)
- Returns: services provided by government to citizens and businesses in return for taxes and contributions (e.g. public libraries)
- Permits & licences: documents provided by governmental bodies giving permission to build a house, to run a business etc.

Once again in almost every country, more progress was made by online services for business than those for citizens. Services for business achieved an overall score of 79% for online sophistication, and 63% for full availability online. The services for citizens remain at 58% for online sophistication, and only 32% for fully available online. However, services enabling the collection of taxes from citizens and businesses are more sophisticated than services the government is required to provide to the recipient (e.g. permits, registrations).

5. eAustrian Facts and Figures

In Q1 2003 more than 96% of Austrian enterprises were using computers. While almost 100% of all central and large-scale enterprises (with 50 or more employees) use computers, this is only the case with 96% of small businesses. The level in 2002 was 94%. In 35% of all enterprises, an enterprise-internal Intranet is used. 50% of all enterprises have a LAN, and 8% a wireless LAN (WLAN). 40% of all enterprises have special computer-systems for orders or purchases. In the trade sector, this is higher at 61%. 27% of all enterprises link these computer systems with accounting and payment systems.

In Q1 2003 nearly 91% of the Austrian enterprises are using Internet, compared with 85% in Q1 2002. 58% of Austrian enterprises with Internet access have a broadband connection. 87% of large enterprises have broadband. Internet banking and financial services are used by 71% of enterprises. 74% of enterprises use eGovernment offers from public places to downloading forms. 20% of enterprises already complete official procedures electronically. In 2003 71% of all enterprises had their own Website (2002: 65%). There are almost 21.000 ICT companies in Austria today. In 2001, e-commerce sales (i.e. sales via Internet and/or electronic data interchange [EDI]) by Austrian enterprises was 22.8 billion Euro. Those accounts for almost 7% of total sales, an enormous increase over the 2.5% of total sales achieved in 2000.

Internet based sales in 2001 were worth 6.3 billion Euro (c. 1.9% of gross income). Most eCommerce sales were made by EDI (16.5 billion Euro or c. 5.1% of gross income). In 2001, 21% of all enterprises received orders over the Internet. Most buyers of goods and services from Austrian enterprises over the Internet are from Austria: 82% of Internet sales are to domestic buyers, with 11% elsewhere within the European Union. Special order production accounts for 10.4 billion Euro of eCommerce sales. The trade sector converted 2001 8.4 billion Euro in Austria. Electronic purchasing by Austrian enterprises accounted for 12.2% of all purchases in 2001, worth 23.7 billion Euro (17.9 billion Euro over EDI).

In March 2003 49% of all Austrian households had a computer. This compares with only 45% in June 2002. There was at least one mobile phone in 75% of all households (June 2002: 69%) and 16% of all households have at least one Internet-enabled mobile phone. Around 1.2 million households (36% of all households) had Internet access in March 2003, compared with 31% in June 2002. Dial-up Internet access is still used by 70% of all households with Internet access, while 27% of households with Internet access already use a broadband connection. The remaining 3% access the Internet via a LAN.

35% of all Internet users have already obtained information from public authorities web sites and 26% stated that they had already downloaded official forms.

6. Conclusions

This paper illustrates that much progress has been made in Austria in relation to the adoption of eGovernment to support citizens and business. This is due to strong political leadership and commitment, and close cooperation between all stakeholders. We look forward to building on this foundation to make eGovernment a beneficial reality for all.

References

[1] www.eGovernment.gv.at
[2] www.bka.gv.at
[3] www.buergerkarte.gv.at
[4] www.a-trust.at
[5] www.europay.at
[6] www.mobilkom.at
[7] www.cio.gv.at
[8] www.stuzza.at
[9] www.zustellung.gv.at
[10] www.elak.gv.at
[11] www.cio.gv.at/egovernment/law/E-Gov_Act_endg_engl_Fassung1.pdf
[12] www.weikersdorf.at, www.inzersdorf.at, www.kremsmuenster.at, www.steyr.at, www.wien.at
[13] www.portal.gv.at
[14] www.guetesiegel.gv.at
[15] www.help.gv.at

Emilia-Romagna Regional Strategy on ICT

Sandra LOTTI [1], Kussai SHAHIN [2]
[1] *Direzione Generale Organizzazione, Sistemi Informativi e Telematica, Regione Emilia-Romagna, Viale Aldo Moro 18, Bologna, 40127, Italy*
Tel: +390516397908, Fax: +390516397914, Email: progeur@regione.emilia-romagna.it
[2] *ASTER S. Cons. p. A., Via Gobetti 101, Bologna, 40129, Italy*
Tel: +390516398099, Fax: +390516398131, Email: kussai.shahin@aster.it

Abstract: The objective of the paper is to give an overview of the Regional ICT plan of the Emilia-Romagna Region (Italy) and its structure. In particular, the paper will focus on the three main actions areas of the plan, namely, the telecommunications infrastructure, the eGovernment projects and the support to IT research. Actually, the Emilia-Romagna Region has produced a Regional ICT plan for 2002-2005, which provides a strategic framework for the construction of the regional information society of the future. The paper is intended as the presentation of a best practice in the field of regional programming instruments in the area of Information Society that could be replicated by other European regions. This is made even more possible by the extensive benchmark exercise that was started together with the plan (using the e-europe indicators) and is now more aimed at regional policies by means of an European project on regional benchmarking of Information Society.

1. Introduction

The Regional ICT Plan is a public action plan designed to maintain and promote the leading position of the Emilia-Romagna region (4 million inhabitants, surface of 22.120 square kilometres, per capita GP € 25.733) while safeguarding the principles of democracy, social cohesion and social solidarity for which the region is noted.

The regional government drew up the action plan of the Emilia-Romagna Region with contributions from the Telecommunications Advisory Group (composed mainly of experts from regional universities and research centres) and the Regional Technical Group for eGovernment and the Information Society (made up of representatives from provincial local authorities, municipal government, and their associations). The Regional ICT Plan is based on a yearly Operational Programme, which aims to review the actions undertaken in the previous year, and to decide on the actions necessary to maintain and consolidate the progress made. It should be emphasised that the definition of the projects, included within the annual Operational Programme, involved all levels of regional government in the definition and implementation of actions.

In effect this approach has created a system or institutional framework that has proved to be a successful formula in winning the first Itàlian call for bids for eGovernment. This collaborative approach is being continued in the implementation of the series of integrated projects, which will form the basis for truly effective regional eGovernment.

The main difference from previous approaches is that previously each province was allocated a budget to be used on local projects/priorities; this was due to the fact that all territories had to be stimulated towards the concept of Information Society. This phase produced very different results and levels of accomplishments. The present strategy was aimed at defining the priorities that were common to all territories and at working together to a common result, uniform achievements and avoiding digital divides.

We believe that this type of co-operation between the various levels of regional government has proved to be the winning approach in the second stage of implementing eGovernment – as defined by the National plan for eGovernment - when the solutions adopted will be made available to the largest number of local authorities possible. The solutions have been developed by local government administrations as part of the Nuova regione – New Region framework where eGovernment is seen as an integral part of governance as a whole and where the intention is to ensure that products can be effectively integrated into the organisational processes of other public administrations (PA) at the local level. The natural target of this initiative is therefore the regional PA system to start with, as service provider to citizens and enterprises.

The Regional ICT Plan 2002-2005 of the Emilia-Romagna Region provides a framework for the construction of the regional information society of the future. Its purpose is to bring together all those components that go to make up an Information Society. Components include investments in infrastructure, public administration on-line services, research, training and education. Training is necessary to turn these investments into a concrete reality. Training and research, because we are convinced that our region must have the innovative local talent needed to make our region competitive and enable it to play a leading role on the global stage.

In recent times, eGovernment has become a major public policy driver in the development of the Information Society (IS). This is clearly shown by the fact that one of the most important activities in 2003 was the negotiation of a framework agreement on e-government with central government's Ministry of Innovation and Technology (MIT).

The Ministry of Innovation and Technology and regional governments are working towards the shared vision necessary to take eGovernment forward. This joint commitment has led to the creation of the eGovernment Regional Competence Centres (CRC). CRCs have two main objectives. Firstly, to enable and facilitate the creation of regional eGovernment systems: they do this through the organisation of training courses for Public Administration employees on the themes connected to the implementation of e-government but also making information available on best practices in this field (i.e.: via the creation of a regional observatory on IS [1]).

Secondly, to provide a channel for interaction between regional CRCs and central staff which co-ordinates the initiative, so that expertise and excellence at the local level can be incorporated in the national strategy.

2. Objectives

The Regional ICT Plan is accompanied by a regional law on "Regional development of Information Society". This law gives the regional government the role to activate infrastructures and telecommunication networks; it also identifies the management model of the ICT development in the regional territory: it has designed a governance structure composed by a scientific committee, a legislative-economic committee and a committee for the definition of the policies and co-ordination with all local authorities.

This paper is not intended to provide a description of the technological solutions in detail but rather to show the methodology used in Emilia-Romagna to define priorities and build the Information Society of the future based on a political shared framework into which single initiatives are included.

For this reason the plan focuses on both the development of infrastructure and online services, in the belief that once the services are ready they need a suitable infrastructure that makes them available to everybody, reaching all territories.

With regards to the realisation of the telecommunications infrastructure the plan concentrated on the creation of a "private broad band network for public administration" (called LEPIDA) that starts from a process of aggregation of "virtual" demand for communication and tries to foresee and anticipate the future.

The main goals of the broadband diffusion initiative are:

1. to create a modern communication network for local public administrations to allow for the appearance of innovative information systems with a technology life of (at least) 30 years and the availability of advanced services;
2. to promote a one-stop-shop approach for communication services for all local PA within the region;
3. to make the region as a whole more competitive by improving and easing access to broadband services for businesses and citizens as well - having the telecommunication operators extend the infrastructure (last mile);
4. to reduce the risk of geographical digital divide.

In the infrastructure area special attention was given to the creation of a new multi-services digital radio network for the emergency services, which covers all regional areas.

With regards to services, the Plan is implementing services that were agreed upon and considered priorities by all local administrations; more than this all local PAs are either actively involved in the development of the projects or have already expressed their interest in implementing the solutions once they are made available. Some PAs in particular are going to be pilot users and their feedback will be fundamental for final tuning the solutions.

Other European regions could use the methodology developed in Emilia-Romagna. Certainly the model adopted in the area of infrastructure is of more immediate interest to other regions and reflects an overall European interest in this field testified also by the recent guidelines on the use of structural funds for infrastructure developments.

But what do we mean by the model adopted in the area of broadband infrastructure? The regional government decided to involve all local authorities - as they have the best knowledge on their territories' strength and weaknesses – so as to act as a whole (not locally) and to identify the assets present in each territory to implement the plan in an efficient way.

3. Methodology

The Operational Programme has mainly covered the following areas of activity:

- Telecommunications infrastructure;
- eGovernment projects; and
- IT research.

We have also implementing a monitoring and benchmark activity to monitor the quality of results and evaluate the efficiency of the policies, which gives us a precise idea of where we stand and of future perspectives.

3.1 Telecommunications infrastructure

Like all local authorities, the regional government of Emilia-Romagna was faced with a dilemma – which do we provide first, infrastructure or services? The Regional government of Emilia-Romagna took a long-term, strategic decision to equip the region with the very best telematic infrastructure designed to meet medium-term future needs rather than just present day requirements. In practice this objective takes the form of two projects: a broadband network for local authorities and a regional mobile radio network for the emergency services. The projects shared the same two aims:

- To provide public administrations with infrastructure that will facilitate the creation of truly innovative, leading edge applications and advanced organisations.

- To promote local initiatives and to stimulate the supply side of the market offering services to citizens and businesses and thus give the regional area a competitive advantage.

The implementation of these initiatives will require agreements at the institutional level, the creation of technical and scientific working parties, skills in the management of large projects and, above all, the investment of much effort in change management.

Institutional agreements and change management will be the joint responsibility of the regional government, local authorities and local authority groupings.

3.2 eGovernment projects

The distinctive feature of the eGovernment projects already started is that they involve the entire regional area. The regional government is central to the process, integrating, co-ordinating and supervising activities. But at the same time none of the projects could exist without the initiative and direct continuous participation of the local authorities involved. Ever-closer collaboration between regional government and provincial, municipal and health service authorities will continue to be a feature of these projects. The Regional Technical Group plays an important role in this collaboration for eGovernment and the Information Society (as described in the introduction).

3.3 IT research

The Region of Emilia-Romagna intends to co-fund research projects in the areas described in this section. These projects will be partnerships between the universities and businesses located in the Region of Emilia-Romagna.

The policy to support research projects is based on two primary considerations:

- Regionally-based research is a fundamental to the spread of new technology.
- ICT research, both pure and applied, is typically software oriented. It is therefore labour intensive and requires people and management rather than capital intensive investment in plant and equipment.

The policy objective is therefore to support IT research and development at the regional level within a mixed public-private sector framework and to create the trust of local industry in the regional plan for the information society. The basic idea is to aid several research groups, which will each have the critical mass necessary to deliver products of excellence.

In practice this will be done using calls for bids and following the negotiating procedure. The procedure consists of two stages:

1. Selection. Applicants will be judged on the basis of the procedural principles and the bid specifications. The bid specifications define the areas for which research and development projects can be proposed as follows:
    - Multimedia systems.
    - Wide band technologies and applications.
    - Development of applications for ambient intelligence.
    - E-learning platforms and content.
    - Applications for network organisations and for industrial districts.

2. Negotiation. This stage consists of in-depth analysis of the projects selected in the first stage and the modification, where necessary, of the original project. The analysis will lead to the drafting of a classification ranking the project participants.

The bid was issued in September 2003 and the negotiation phase is at the end at the time of writing (June 2004). Projects should be able to start in autumn 2004.

This initiative will be funded for two years and the results expected at the end of this period will include a combination of the following:

- Initiatives for local business and the production of innovative products destined, in particular, for use by public administrations.
- Research spin-off including methods for implementing the Regional ICT Plan actions and for the establishment of new research centres by Italian and foreign companies in our region.
- Consolidation of research networks with the major involvement of research institutes, universities and businesses.

4. Technology Description

As mentioned before, the Regional government of Emilia-Romagna took a long-term, strategic decision to equip the region with the very best in telematic infrastructure designed to meet medium-term future needs rather than just present day requirements.

In practice this objective takes the form of two projects: a broadband network for local authorities and a regional mobile radio network for the emergency services. We are going to concentrate on the infrastructure initiative, which at the moment pools the majority of our investments giving an overview of the process but no in depth technical details.

4.1 Private broadband network for public administrations

The general idea is to develop a data network with an entry point of 100 megabit/sec gradually passing to speeds of one gigabit/sec or faster as soon as costs become acceptable; this development is planned for the period running up to 2007. One of the planned results is the delocalisation of processing equipment in service centres with a consequent greater emphasis on applications and services.

It is important to emphasize that the project's stakeholders are: Regional administration, 9 provincial administrations, 341 municipalities, health care system and 5 universities.

The technical and administrative operations required for the first stage of the private broadband network for local authorities have been finalised and represent the structure that has been followed also in the other areas.

The first stage of the project has commenced, covers the provincial local authority areas of Bologna, Forlì-Cesena, Rimini and Ravenna and is based around four agreements:

- A framework agreement between the Region of Emilia-Romagna and the local authorities (provinces, municipalities and mountain communities) in the designated areas where the parties to the agreement indicate the Hera multi-utility company as the company responsible for the construction and management of the sub-network.
- A contract with Romagna Acque S.p.A. for the extraordinary maintenance of civil engineering works and for the purchase of fibre optic equipment to be used in the construction of the network primary infrastructure.
- A contract with Hera S.p.A. for works to complete the primary infrastructure, for making network connections (with fibre optics, xDSL or satellite, whichever is most convenient) and for managing the network.
- A contract with the University of Bologna for the connection of the Romagna local centres to the central office and for the construction of a metropolitan area network (MAN) at the towns of Cesena and Ravenna.

The same route has been followed in the province of Modena (second stage) the mountain area (third stage, mostly covered via satellite) and the fourth (Ferrara). At the time of writing the further stages (Reggio Emilia, Parma and Piacenza) are being finalised.

The institutional and administrative framework is planned for completion within the next 10 to 15 months.

Studies are also underway to develop new technical-organisational models to be implemented for the network nodes, those parts of the network covering provincial local authorities and municipalities.

Once the network is fully operational, a “Centre for the development of regional ICT” will be set up with responsibility for the technical control of the network and for managing the organisational changes involved.

4.2 Regional mobile radio network - R3

The other major ICT initiative in the Region of Emilia-Romagna is the construction of a digital radio network for the emergency services. This brings together the existing, separate radio networks for the ambulance service, civil defence and municipal police into a single, unified network. The objective is to provide centralised services and the best technology that the market has to offer.

The general idea is that the Region builds the infrastructure, with funding from the Ministries of Civil Defence, Health and the Interior, coordinate the information system and provide support in the form of the Telecommunications Advisory Group. Studies are planned into a management system that will pass some of the project costs onto users and thereby enable partial recovery of investment costs.

Specifications have already been drafted and a call for bids has been issued. The call is for the design of the entire network and the construction of the first stage, which will provide mobile radio cover throughout the regional area.

At this stage the call has been completed and the next tasks include: set up the works management; proceed with the funding and order of the second stage, which will provide portable equipment cover throughout the regional area.

Seminars for the first groups of users have already been started; seminar participants are from the ambulance service, civil defence and municipal police forces. In-depth technical, organisational seminars are planned. These will be focussing on the central, and perhaps most difficult, part of the project – the management of the transfer from the existing old systems to the new system. The transfer should take place within two years of the start of works, i.e. between the end of 2005 and the beginning of 2006. Once the network is fully operational (with between 6,000 and 7,000 users) it will be developed and extended to serve additional users.

5. Developments

The Regional ICT plan of Emilia-Romagna is closely linked to the national plan: in particular as far as the Broad band infrastructure is concerned we are considered as a best practice in Italy and are following the guidelines provided by the national government, in the framework of e-Europe.

The region’s strategy in the broadband area has two main goals that we are going to pursue in the next few years:

1. To create a modern communication network for local public administrations able to:
   - ease the start of innovative information systems;
   - promote new forms of associated management of services;
   - be so technologically advanced to have a life of (at least) 30 years.
2. To encourage the start up of local operators that can offer the market (be it citizens or enterprises) telecommunication services of high performance, at affordable costs - as a competitive advantage for the whole regional territory.

Once the backbone is completed (first phase) two further phases are foreseen. A second phase to build the MAN that will cover municipal territories; a third phase to complete with fibre the primary network so as to reach all municipal territories, consistently with availability of resources that will be sought at local, national and European level.

The same goes for the online services that are going to be developed with co-financing from the national government and will answer to a second call on reutilization form other PAs (which also means customisation of present solutions to new customers).

The "Centre for the development of regional ICT" which is described above will have the responsibility for the technical control of the network and for the interface with the national public connectivity system foreseen at the Italian national level to guarantee the quality of services and security of all networks of public administration.

To ensure that the development of our strategy is going to fill in gaps or provide answers to particularly less developed issues, we have set up a benchmark exercise that has already produced analysis on the main eEurope indicators. We are going to fully implement this research through a European project, the UNDERSTAND project, co-ordinated by Emilia-Romagna Region. The projects involves ten partners from seven European states, and has the support of Eris@, the European association of regions developing information society. The project is co-financed by the Interreg IIIC programme.

UNDERSTAND's main objective is to compare and evaluate regional development of the Information Society by defining and applying a set of common regional e-indicators on Internet usage by citizens and business, e-government and broadband infrastructure. This will enable policy-makers to better understand the impact of Information Society investment and readdress their policies [2].

The main specific objectives are:

- To evaluate the eEurope indicators through the proactive involvement of regional policy makers;
- To define common indicators and methodologies (the benchmarking tool-kit), for at least 4 e-domains (government, companies, families/individuals, broadband);
- To create a network of Regions that benchmark on the development of the information society and thereby to provide policy-makers in these regions concrete support to investment decisions;
- To build on hard data to detect HOW and WHY some regions perform better then other;
- To disseminate guidelines, methodologies and tools among all EU regions in order to create a common standard of regional e-indicators;
- To provide to EC and Member States with a regional perspective on benchmarking eEurope.

6. Conclusions

The paper has presented the Emilia-Romagna strategy on the implementation of the Information Society at a regional level.

In particular major relevance was given to the activities related to the broadband infrastructure implementation since its approach can be re-utilised by other regions and since it is a fundamental step in the development of the Information Society.

The region's goals regarding broadband are reached through finding the right implementing subjects, based locally and therefore able to link all the regional public administrations; normally they have an in depth knowledge of the territory, with special focus on local economy. They are entrusted with carrying out and management of the network for the public administration.

Due to public intervention, access will be guaranteed in an homogeneous manner to all areas, including remote and poorly populated ones. The network of the public administration will act as the driving force for the commercial offer, contributing to the avoidance of the digital divide. Besides, this strategy is believed to create the conditions for the competition between local and national operators, promoting a virtuous circle between an offer at reasonable costs and a widespread demand. This - in the medium-long period – should act as a stimulus and also as an advantage for other operators.

References

[1] http://osservatorio.regionedigitale.net/Osservatorio/Home/index.jsp
[2] http://www.understand-eu.net

eAdoption and the Knowledge Economy: Issues, Applications, Case Studies
P. Cunningham and M. Cunningham (Eds.)
IOS Press, 2004

Uptake of eServices in Danish Municipalities

Helle Zinner HENRIKSEN
Center for Research on Information Technology in Policy Settings (CIPS), Copenhagen Business School, Howitzvej 60, 2000 Frederiksberg, Denmark
Tel: +45 38152452 Fax: + 45 38152401, Email: hzh.inf@cbs.dk

Abstract: Among the European countries Denmark is ranked high with respect to on-line services. This paper presents a preliminary, exploratory analysis of factors supporting the diffusion of electronic services (eServices) in Danish municipalities. The objective of the study is to perform an explorative search for explanatory variables, which make municipalities adopt eServices, and specifically to gain an understanding of why some municipalities embrace eServices more extensively than others. Based on an analysis of quantitative data it is found that the degree of urbanization, the population density, the educational level of citizens, and the increase in employment in the municipality appears to be the most significant explanatory factors supporting a high level of eService adoption.

1. Introduction

Denmark ranked as number one among eighteen European countries with respect to being "Fully available online" according to a recent study prepared by Cap Gemini Ernst & Young for the European Commission [1]. The parameter "Fully available online", is defined as the public sector institutions' capability to offer complete electronic case handling. The same study reports that Denmark ranked as number two, only surpassed by Sweden, with respect to "Online sophistication" of electronic services offered to citizens and businesses. The Cap Gemini Ernst & Young study presents a picture of the state-of-the-art with respect to the level of electronic service offered at the national level, and it indicates that Denmark provides a relatively high level of electronic services to its citizens and businesses. One initiative which contributes to the high ranking is the NetCitizen self-service portal (NetCitizen.dk, the English equivalent of the Danish "NetBorger.dk").

The NetCitizen service portal is developed and supported by KMD. KMD is one of the leading providers of IT solutions in the public sector in Denmark. Based on decades of experience of providing IT solutions to the public sector this company has highly specialized insights into the particular needs of public sector institutions. KMD is not the only provider of eServices in Denmark. Some municipalities have chosen to develop their own eService solutions or they have subscribed to alternative off-the-shelf applications. However, KMD is by far the largest eService solution provider to Danish municipalities.

The NetCitizen services have been on-line since the beginning of 2000. During its first four years of existence KMD has continuously increased the number of off-the-shelf eServices available for municipalities. By December 2003 a total of 32 eServices were available. Some of the listed links to the eServices actually represent several services at the deeper levels and the services vary in degree of interactivity and sophistication. Some offer information while others provide more interactive services such as calculation of pensions or payment of debts. A number of studies have discussed the nature of eServices and have presented extensive categorizations of eServices, see for example [2] and [3]. These categorizations based on innovation attributes provide a good overview of the level of sophistication of eServices.

However, in the present study of the diffusion of eServices in Danish municipalities focus is shifted from the attributes of the innovation and thereby also the particularities of the eServices provided by NetCitizen. The present focus is municipalities as adopting units and an examination of the underlying processes that make municipalities adopt eServices. The overall assumption of the study is that the value of this type of insight can guide and help policymakers in their dissemination efforts. Given that there is considerable attention to dissemination of eGovernment in for example, the eEurope 2005 Action Plan, it is useful to understand which mechanisms support the diffusion of eGovernment initiatives. In particular to understand how to operationalize and fulfil the goals outlined in the policy statements. The objective of the present study is therefore to perform an explorative search for explanatory factors, which make municipalities adopt eServices, and specifically to try to understand why some municipalities embrace eServices more extensively than others.

2. Adoption and Diffusion of eServices in Public Sector Institutions

Given that other considerations than profit typically drive public institutions to adopt innovations, other factors than those traditionally studied in the adoption of innovations among individuals [5] or among organizations [6] should be included. Public services are contrary to private services either offered universally or provided to specific eligible groups such as disabled or elderly. Public services have to be accessible for those living in rural and remote areas as well as those living in urban areas and most important, they are not based on a citizens' capability or willingness to pay for the services [7].

Though there might be competition among municipalities to adopt innovations, the driving force is not merely efficiency. Berry and Berry [4] suggest that the incentive for adoption of innovations in the public sector is dual: to achieve competitive advantage and to avoid being disadvantaged. Berry and Berry illustrate this situation by the following examples: municipalities may decrease welfare benefits to match the levels of their neighbours to avoid being a welfare magnet for the poor, or municipalities may adopt economic development incentive programs already present in other municipalities to prevent an exodus of businesses from the area. Another factor, which drives the diffusion process in the public sector, is the fact that most elected officials would like to stay in office for another term. Therefore, public pressure to adopt a popular policy programme might influence the adoption of innovations, which voters favour.

In their review of dominant theories of government innovation in the public policy literature, Berry and Berry [4] claim to have found two dominant explanations for the adoption of a new program of a state: internal determinants and diffusion models. Berry and Berry base their study on American research and focus on state level not municipality level. It should be stressed that there are important differences between American states and Danish municipalities e.g., with respect to size and even more important to governance. However, there are also similarities especially due to the significance of elected representatives and their manoeuvrability due to voters' judgment at the end of the councillor's term.

Explanations driven by internal determinants models focus on internal conditions of the adopting unit. Factors related to political, economic or social characteristics in the municipality explain a given adoption behaviour. Diffusion models in contrast are driven by inspiration from peers. Municipalities often imitate other municipalities, which have already adopted a given innovation. According to this view diffusion of innovation happen due to emulation of politicians [8].

In this first phase of the search for explanatory factors for the diffusion of eServices among Danish municipalities, focus is on the internal determinants leading to adoption. The present study focuses thus on characteristics of the adopting unit rather than on possible influences from change agents or from trends in the social system. In the following section the variables included in the study are presented in more detail.

3. Empirical Model: Variables and Measurement

In order to identify possible patterns of adoption and reasons for the different levels of adoption of the NetCitizen eServices by the 271 municipalities in Denmark, a number of variables were included in the exploratory analysis of adoption patterns.

When studying internal determinants for diffusion of innovations the traditional approach is to measure how early a programme or policy has been adopted by a given unit compared to other units [4]. In the case of adoption of eServices a slightly different approach was chosen. The dependent variable of the study is defined as the level of adoption of services from the NetCitizen portal. Just by browsing through a few municipality sites at NetCitizen, it is obvious that there is a great variation in the number of eServices the 271 Danish municipalities offer their citizens. Of the 32 different services provided by December 2003 by NetCitizen, the largest municipality in Denmark, Copenhagen, only offered 9 eServices from the NetCitizen portal to its citizens, whereas three other municipalities offered 28 different eServices from the portal to their citizens.

Previous studies of the diffusion of policy initiatives suggested two overall groups of explanatory factors: political and demographical [9; 8]. In this study the overall groups are expanded to four groups of explanatory factors: political, demographical, geographical, and economic.

3.1 Political explanatory variables

Two overall variables related to the political characteristics of the municipality were included in the dataset: political affiliation of elected representatives and voter turnout. Voter turnout is used as a measure of the political involvement of citizens. Citizens' involvement in political processes can be used as an indicator in the sense that elected representatives might feel pressure to adopt eServices, which can ease the life of their voters. It is therefore expected that municipalities with a high voter turnouts tend to adopt more eServices.

The variable representing political affiliation of elected representatives is related to the political affiliation of the council members. As pointed out by McNeal et al. [8] political factors are not straight forward with respect to adoption of innovations. Adoption behaviours are rarely driven solely by political ideologies. In the Danish political scene social democrat-left wing parties tend to argue in favour of administrative reforms to support improved citizen participation in democratic processes. Liberal-conservative parties on the other hand are in favour of reducing the costs of administration thereby implicitly focusing on efficiency. While the incentives for adoption are strong across political ideologies the argumentation differs. Given the inherent expectation that adoption of eServices can lead to increased efficiency in the public administration, municipalities governed by liberal-conservative majority might be more likely to adopt eServices.

3.2 Demographical explanatory variables

The Internet adoption-rate is high in Denmark. According to Statistics Denmark (www.dst.dk) about eighty percent of the population had access to the Internet at home or at work by mid-2003. A larger share of citizens with higher education has access to the Internet compared to citizens with a relatively lower level of education. In the 16 to 59 age-group, the adoption rate varies from 87 to 95 percent, whereas only one out of two persons in the +60 age group have adopted the Internet.

Given that Internet access and in particular use of the Internet is a prerequisite for using services, it is found prudent to look at the age distribution and educational level of the population in the different municipalities. It could be expected that decision-makers would consider whether or not their citizens are among the population typically those using the Internet. This assumption rests on the expectation that the pay-off of the investment will be better the larger the share of the population is that uses the eServices provided, thereby freeing resources from municipal call centres and offices. In order to explore this proposition, the impact of age distribution and educational level of the municipality's inhabitants were included in the analysis of the level of adoption of eServices of a given municipality.

3.3 Geographical explanatory variables

The degree of urbanization has been suggested to be an explanatory variable for adoption of innovations [8; 9]. With respect to the adoption of services, variables related to the areas of the municipalities were included. Given that municipalities with large areas/ distances must be expected to have more logistic challenges in servicing their citizens, access to services via Internet might be a solution worth pursuing.

Furthermore, it is found plausible that the population density of a municipality influences the incentive to adopt eServices. Given that sparsely populated areas require the same services as heavily populated areas but that sparsely populated areas have fewer inhabitants to cover the expenses, a low population density could be expected to favour eService adoption. The third and final geographical variable included in the dataset is related to the metropolitan, rural or urban status of the municipality.

3.4 Economical explanatory variables

Slack resources are an important factor when innovations are adopted [10]. The economic resources were measured as the relative wealth of the municipality. Two variables were used to measure economic resources: growth in employment and tax level. The variable employment growth was measured as number of full-time employed workers during the period 1997-2002. Employment growth was defined by calculating the municipality's share of the total employment in Denmark for each year and by calculating the average employment growth for each municipality for the period 1997-2002. This variable is based on the assumption that growth in employment in a region attracts investments and tax payers. The second economic variable, taxation level, indicates the relative level of expenses of a municipality compared to its income.

4. Data Collection

The number of eServices provided by the 271 Danish municipalities was gathered from the NetCitizen eService portal. The procedure followed was to use the entry to the portal available to citizens. Data from the individual site of each municipality in the portal was registered separately. All data from the NetCitizen portal were gathered from the portal during December 2003. Data related to political affiliation of the mayor, first vice-mayor, second vice-mayor and the council members were collected from the 2002 Handbook of Municipalities [11]. The gender of the mayor, first vice-mayor, and second vice-mayor, voter turnout, municipal tax rate, and the area and population size of the municipality were also collected from the same source. The remaining data concerning socio-economic status and age distribution of citizens from each municipality were obtained from Statistics Denmark (www.dst.dk).

5. Results

In the following results bi-variate relationships between number of eServices offered and the political, demographical, geographical, and economic variables are presented.

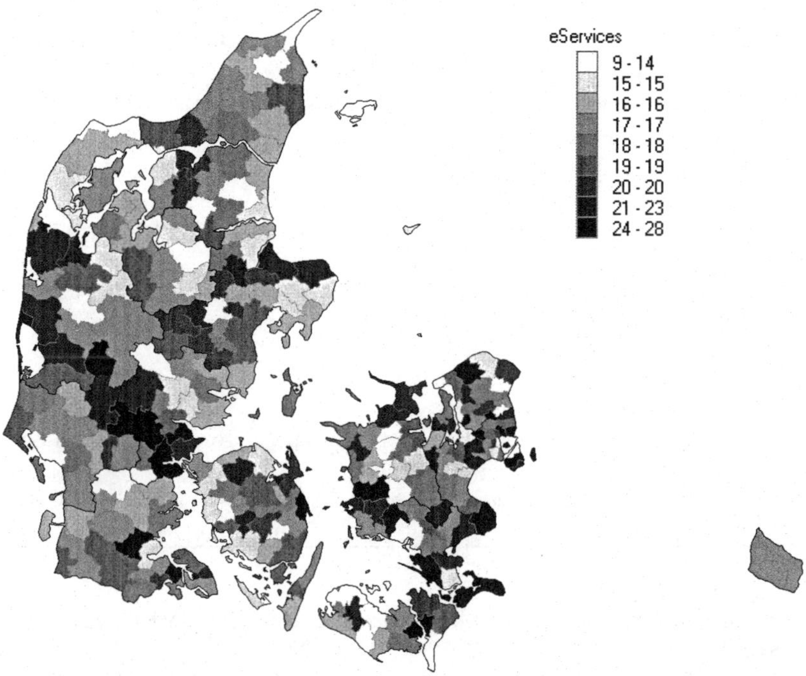

Figure 1: Distribution of eServices in the 271 municipalities in Denmark

Figure 1 depicts the number of eServices offered by the 271 municipalities in Denmark. The darker the colour of a given municipality the more eServices the self same municipality offers to its citizens. As the legend shows the level of eService adoption is categorized and is grouped into nine classes. In the bi-variate statistical analysis of the number of eServices, the total number of NetCitizen eServices for each municipality was grouped to form a categorical variable with three ordered categories: 1-16, 17-20, and 21 and more eServices. The first category represents approximately the lower quartile and the third category represents approximately the upper quartile.

5.1 Bi-variate analysis of eServices by quantitative variables

Table 1: Bivariate analysis of eServices by three quantitative variables

Variable	Statistics	DF	Chi-Square	Probability
Voter turnout	Kruskal-Wallis tests	2	0.2821	0.8685
Taxation level	Kruskal-Wallis tests	2	1.0737	0.5846
Population density	Kruskal-Wallis tests	2	7.5673	0.0227*

Legend: * p<= 0.050; ** p<= 0.010; *** p<= 0.001

Table 1 presents the values for the Kruskal-Wallis tests for the analysis of eServices by voter turnout, eServices by taxation level, and eServices by population density.

5.2 Bivariate analysis of number of eServices by categorical variables

Table 2: Bivariate analysis of number of eServices by categorical variables

Variable	Statistics	DF	Value	Probability
Mayor's gender	MHC	1	2.2886	0.1303
First vice mayor's gender	MHC	1	0.5731	0.4490
Second vice mayor's gender	MHC	1	3.1488	0.0760
Urbanization, 3 categories: metropolitan, urban, rural	Chi-sq	4	8.8329	0.0654
Urbanization, 2 categories: urban, rural	MHC	1	7.1060	0.0077**
Percentage of citizens with higher education. 3 categories: 1-14, 15-19, 20+	Chi-sq	4	12.0365	0.0171*
City council's party affiliation, 3 categories: left, right, other	Chi-sq	4	2.0442	0.7276
Mayor's political affiliation. 3 categories: social democrat and left-wing, liberal and conservative, all other	Chi-sq	4	5.2177	0.2657
City council's majority 3 categories: social democrat and left wing, liberal and conservative, all other	Chi-sq	4	1.5446	0.8187
Percentage of elderly in the municipality, 3 categories: more, average, fewer	Chi-sq	4	6.5853	0.1595
Employment increase, 3 categories: fewer, average, more	Chi-sq	4	11.2516	0.0239*

Legend: * p<= 0.050; ** p<= 0.010; *** p<= 0.001

Table 2 presents the chi-square or the Mantel-Haenszel chi-square (MHC) values for each bivariate analysis.

6. Discussion and Conclusion

The exploratory search for explanatory factors supporting the adoption of eServices provided by the NetCitizen portal in Danish municipalities resulted in four explanatory variables being statistically significant.

Two variables related to geography were found to be statistically significant. It was found that the higher population density the more eServices a given municipality provides. This is also reflected in the bi-variate analysis of eServices by urbanization, where the MHC test shows a highly significant relationship ($p = 0.0077$). What is surprising is, that inclusion of the metropols in the analysis reduces the statistical significance ($p = 0.0654$). This suggests that municipalities with larger cities, but not metropols, are eager to adopt eServices. This result contradicts the assumption that long distances to public service institutions would stimulate the adoption of eServices. One interpretation of this finding is that adoption of eServices might not be driven by considerations related to the needs of the citizens in the municipality, but rather as a source of achieving savings internally in the administration.

Another finding from the statistical analysis is related to a demographical explanatory variable. The statistical analysis shows that the higher educated the population is in a given municipality the more eServices are provided ($p = 0.0171$). This could indicate that decision-makers consider whether or not the citizens living in the municipality belong to the group identified by Statistics Denmark as frequent users of the Internet. If this line of thought is pursued then considerations related to efficiency could be one of the drivers for the adoption of eServices in the Danish municipalities. Implicit in this reasoning is an expectation that there is a positive return on investment given that a larger number of users will use the eServices provided.

The fourth variable, which turned out to be statistically significant in the analysis was categorized as an economical explanatory variable in the research model. Growth in employment during the period 1997-2002 turned out to be statistically significant at the two-percent level ($p = 0.0227$). One interpretation of this result is that municipalities, which have experienced growth in employment have more slack resources, which generally have been found to stimulate adoption of innovations [10]. Another interpretation is that growth in employment means that the municipality has more citizens engaged in active employment who demand various public services. In order to attract and especially keep employees (and in particular tax payers), an increased level of services is therefore crucial. Given that most public offices have opening hours similar to normal working hours eServices might a good solution to keep them to stay in the municipality.

The exploratory search indicated that other factors than direct pressure from voters influence the decision to adopt eServices. The variable voter turnout was not found to have any statistical significance in relation to the level of eService adoption. One reason for this result might be that the last election for offices at municipality level took place in year 2001. At that time the NetCitizen initiative was still in its infancy and voters might not have been aware of the possible convenience of eServices. The other political variable, political affiliation, which was included in the analysis, was similarly found not to bear any statistical significance when related to the level of eService adoption. This trend that political ideology does not determine adoption of innovations at the public sector level corresponds to findings by McNeal [8] and Walker [9]. A recent study of eService adoption in Switzerland [12] confirms the same trend.

The study of internal determinants as diffusion mechanisms point towards the conclusion that demographic, geographic, and economic variables rather than political variables stimulate the diffusion of innovations in Danish municipalities. The study indicates that municipalities with a well-educated population, with a high population density, and with an economic growth above average are more willing to adopt off-the-shelf eServices. One practical implication of this finding is that policy makers should consider these results in their dissemination efforts. Governments throughout the world have used action plans as an instrument for supporting the diffusion of ICT and its usage in the form of eCommerce and eGovernment during the past decades [13]. Using Denmark as an example, it is evident that the preferred instrument used to support the diffusion of e.g., eGovernment has been information campaigns (contrary to economic incentives in the form of subsidies or direct normative intervention in the form of rules determining exchange of information electronically). There is no reason to believe that this pattern changes in the near future.

One major challenge in the context of designing information campaigns aiming at supporting the diffusion of technological innovations is to identify how to address potential adopters [5]. The study has identified a possible profile of municipalities ready to adopt eServices without further support from policy makers. Based on the findings of this study, it is recommended that the addressee of future information campaigns aiming at supporting the diffusion of eGovernment should be the rural and sparsely populated municipalities with economic growth below average rather than the urban and densely populated municipalities with economic growth below average. This could serve as a useful scenario when operationalizing action plans such as eEurope in a local context.

One limitation of the study is that it focuses solely on the internal determinants and thereby only on the characteristics of the municipality. Municipalities do not operate in isolation. Influence from peers and opinion leaders may also influence decision makers at municipal level. As illustrated in Figure 1 it looks like the adoption of the NetCitizen eServices have happened in clusters. This is especially evident in the lower left part of the graphics where there is a "dark belt" of municipalities, which have adopted more eServices than their neighbouring municipalities. This effect of communication and interaction with others should be addressed in future research. Another limitation of the study is the focus on a single provider of eServices. Though KMD is the largest provider of eServices in Denmark, a more complete picture of eService adoption among the Danish municipalities should to be mapped in future research.

References

[1] Cap Gemini Ernst & Young. *Online Availability of Public Services: How is Europe Progressing?* Report prepared for European Commission DG Information Society. 2003.

[2] Stamoulis, D. and Gouscos, D., "Revisiting Public Information Management for Effective e-government Services," *Information Management & Computer Security*, vol. 9, no. 4, pp. 146, 2001.

[3] Layne, K. and Lee, J., "Developing Fully Functional E-government: A Four Stage Model," *Government Information Quarterly*, vol. 18 pp. 122-136, 2001.

[4] Berry, F. S. and Berry, W. D., "Innovation and Diffusion Models in Policy Research," in Sabatier, P.A. (ed.) *Theories of the Policy Process.* Oxford: Westview Press, 1999, pp. 169-200.

[5] Rogers, E. M., *Diffusion of Innovations*, Fourth ed. The Free Press, 1995.

[6] Tornatzky, L. G. and Fleischer, M., *The Process of Technological Innovation* Lexington Books, 1990.

[7] Teicher, J. and Hughes, O., "E-government: A Route to Public Sector Quality," *Managing Service Quality*, vol. 12, no. 6, pp. 384, 2002.

[8] McNeal, R. S., Tolbert, C. J., Mossberger, K., and Dotterweich, L. J., "Innovating in Digital Government in the American States," *Social Science Quarterly*, vol. 84, no. 1, pp. 52, 2003.

[9] Walker, J. L., "The Diffusion of Innovations among the American States," *The American Political Science Review*, vol. 63, no. 3, pp. 880-899, 1969.

[10] Downs, G. W. and Mohr, L. B., "Conceptual Issues in the Study of Innovation," *Administrative Science Quarterly*, vol. 21, no. December, pp. 700-714, 1976.

[11] Mostrup, *Kommunalhåndbogen 2002* Denmark: Eniro, 2002.

[12] Schedler, K., "Local and Regional Public Management Reforms in Switzerland," *Public Administration Review*, vol. 81, no. 2, pp. 325-344, 2003.

[13] Andersen, K.V. and Henriksen, H.Z. "B2B E-Commerce Diffusion: The Efficacy of Institutional Discourse", in Doukidis, Mylonnopoulos and Pouloudi (eds.) *Social and Economic Transformation in the Digital Era.* IDEA group publishing, London, 2004, pp. 56-75.

eAdoption and the Knowledge Economy: Issues, Applications, Case Studies
P. Cunningham and M. Cunningham (Eds.)
IOS Press, 2004

Experiences from Formulating Recommendations for a National Interoperability Strategy

Efthimios TAMBOURIS[1], Antonios STEFANOU[1], Vassilios PERISTERAS[2], Garyfallos Fragidis[2], Konstantinos TARABANIS[2]
[1]*Archetypon S.A., 236 Sigrou Av., Athens, 176-72, Greece*
Tel: +30 210 9536410, Fax: + 30 210 9536411,
Email: tambouris@archetypon.com; astefano@archetypon.com
[2]*University of Macedonia, 156 Egnatia Str, Thessaloniki, 546-38, Greece*
Tel: +30 2310 891578, Fax: + 30 2310 891544, Email: {per, garyf, kat}@uom.gr

Abstract: This paper presents the experiences from conducting a study aiming to evaluate citizen satisfaction with respect to the citizens centers, to investigate the interoperability requirements between the citizens centers and back offices at various public authorities, and finally to formulate recommendations for a national strategy towards interoperability. The Citizens Centers are institutions, running under the supervision of local municipalities in the Greek public sector, realising a flexible citizen-centric mechanism and increasing the flexibility and efficiency of the way citizens interact with the public sector. Our study focuses on the organisational (rather than technical) aspects of interoperability with an emphasis on take-up by public authorities wishing to provide their services via the Citizens Centers.

1. Introduction

It is only in the last few years that the importance of citizen-centered, online one-stop public service provision has been recognized [1]. eGovernment is one of the first priorities of the eEurope2005 policy of the European Commission [2]. Furthermore, the Interchange Data between Administrations (IDA) initiative [3] supported by the European Commission has prepared the first draft of a European interoperability framework following the recommendations of eEurope2005 policy.

The Greek Government, realising the need for improved provision of public services to the citizens, introduced the Citizens Centers as the first step in a chain of changes aiming to establish the basis for effective eGovernment service provision. The Citizens Centers are autonomous institutions established in most of the Greek cities that act as an intermediate between the Citizen and the Public Authorities. Consequently, Citizens Centers provide a homogeneous interface Citizens can use and rely on for their transactions with the Public Sector, formulating a citizen-centric 'one-stop' shop.

The main objective of this paper is to describe the outcome of the third phase of a project concerning the evaluation of the Greek Citizens Centers with respect to interoperability. It presents the experiences from conducting a study aiming to investigate the interoperability requirements between the Citizens Centers and back offices and to formulate recommendations for a national strategy towards interoperability. The outcome of the study could be beneficiary for the interoperation of the Public Sector and consequently for the citizens.

This paper is organized as follows. In section 2 we briefly describe the Greek Citizens Centers concept. In section 3 we present the statistics collected concerning the main services offered by the Citizens Centers and the corresponding Public Authorities with respect to interoperability aspects. In section 4 an overview of interoperability eGovernment frameworks around the world is presented. Section 5 presents a number of recommendations towards a national strategy for interoperability, while section 6 concludes the paper.

2. The Citizens Centers

The Citizens Centers formulate a large-scale attempt of the Public Sector to introduce the "one-stop" shop concept in the Greek reality. Citizens Centers are service intermediates distributed all over the country that citizens can visit in order to request both information and public services. Citizens Centers form a big evolution in the Citizens to Public Sector relationship and a major modernization in the way Greek Government visualizes the way citizens should be treated. The responsibilities of Citizens Centers could be summarized in the following list:

- They maintain an updated list of all the actions required by the citizen for the completion of each supported transaction.
- They are responsible for collecting the official request form of the citizens.
- They check the validity and correctness of the requests done by the citizens and inform them about possible mistakes or missing information.
- They assist the citizen in the collection of the required papers and wherever possible they undertake the responsibility of collecting these papers for them.
- Upon completion of paper collection, they deliver the whole package to the responsible authority and monitors the procedure up to the point the final document is returned to the citizen as requested.

Furthermore Citizens Centers are also responsible for the provision of less importance services, such as the validation of public certificates photocopies, certification of citizens' signature on photocopies as well as the provision of financial statement through the use of the corresponding information system (TAXISnet) provided by the Ministry of Finance.

The direct benefits to the citizens of the introduction of the Citizens Centers can be summarized as follows:

- Citizens can be accurately and efficiently informed about the exact process steps and possible certificates required for the provision of the service
- Citizens Centers undertake the coordination effort required for service provision
- Citizens advance from the one-stop shops (visit one place for provision of all services)
- Citizens Centers are located close to citizens' place of residence.

At the beginning of 2004, 786 Citizens Centers are established and operate all over the county, while the number is anticipated to reach the maximum of 1,052 by the end of the year. At the same time, the Citizens Centers are authorized to provide 851 certified services (services that require interaction with Public Authorities) to the citizen. The number of certified services is expected to increase in the near future and will exceed 1,000 different services. In addition to that, the Citizens Centers are also responsible for the provision of 26 more services that do not require an interaction with a public authority (e.g., official validation of photocopies of public certificates) and are not examined in this paper.

3. Evaluation of interoperability between Citizens Centers and Public Authorities

The analysis presented in this section is based on a sample of more than 600.000 citizen transactions, which were retrieved from the data repository of the Citizens Centers' production information system and on the answers provided on assessment questionnaires delivered to all Citizens Centers around Greece.

A first observation of the study is the difficulty in locating a national strategic plan envisaging the role, importance and future plan of Citizens Centers. The existence of such a plan is essential for the success of the project since its absence could mislead its evolution within time. Despite the lack of a strategic plan, citizens realize the significance of technology and its impact in their daily life and are willing to try alternatives in the way they used to interact with the public sector. More than 700.000 transactions undertaken within a period of 6 months is a proof for the validity of the aforementioned statements.

Moreover, the statistical analysis of findings from the dissemination of questionnaires revealed that the employees of the centers are very familiar with the use of computers and information systems. On average, five out of six employees working in the daily production per Citizen Center are very familiar with the new technologies. The exact percentage can be seen in Figure 1.

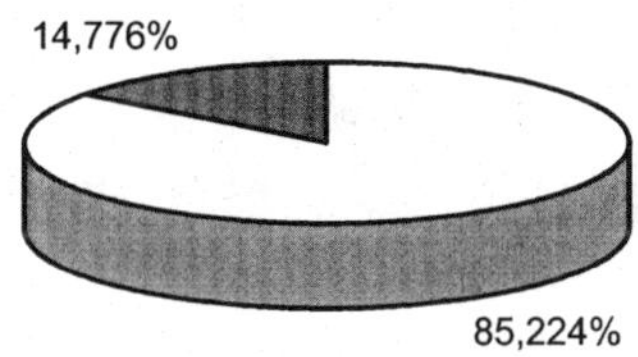

Figure 1: Employees familiar with computers in Citizens Centers

The aforementioned is the proof that the selection of employees in the Citizens Centers was based on know-how criteria and that the importance of the information technology was realised on time. In addition, 95% of the employees stated that they are very satisfied with the facilities and the majority believes that the information system (e-kep) responsible for the daily production in Citizens Centers fulfils their requirements (Figure 2).

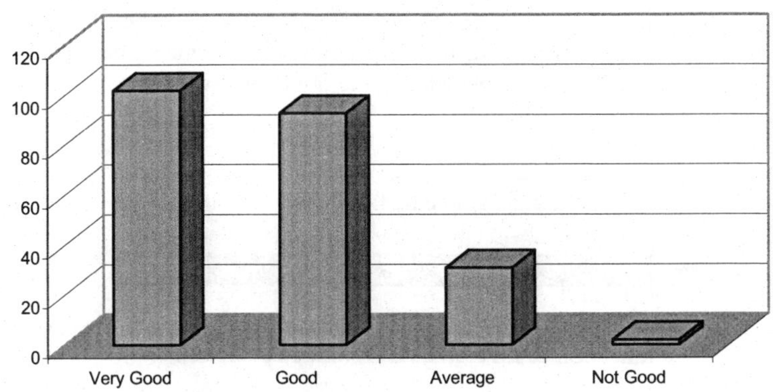

Figure 2: What is your opinion about the e-kep information system?

All the above indicate that Citizens Centers have the appropriate infrastructure to form the basis for a "one-stop" shop service and that the importance of technology has been realised on time. Unfortunately, this does not seems to be the case when the issue of electronic interaction between Citizens Centers and Public Authorities (or among Public Authorities) for service provision is raised. All communication is done via paper exchange mechanisms and the lack of interoperable information systems that could mutually exchange electronic information, data and services is more than obvious. This is depicted in

Figure 3, which presents the ways Citizens Centers exchange information with the Public Authorities.

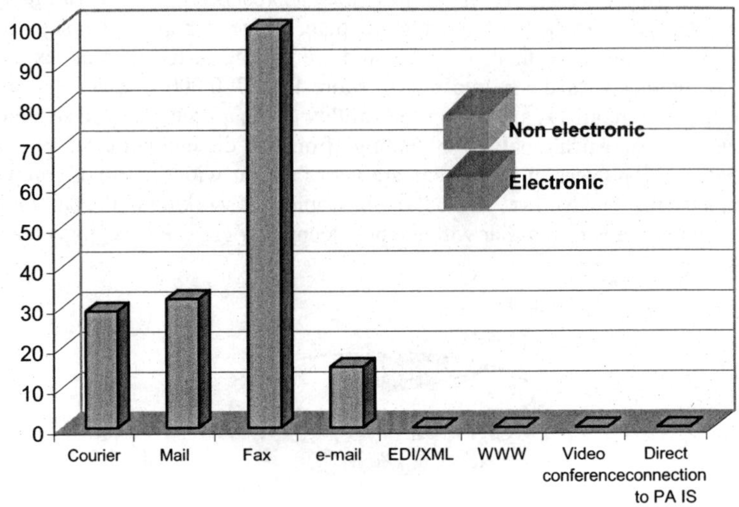

Figure 3: Average number of transactions between Citizens Centers and Public Authorities

The above figure states clearly that although Citizens Centers have an information system developed to serve their needs the Public Authorities are not equipped with interoperable system which could advantage from that. Furthermore, apart from not being able to exchange electronic information with the Citizens Centers, Public Authorities are also not able to communicate electronically with other Public Authorities. Once a certification from Public Authority A is required for the provision of a service in Public Authority B, B is not able to ask the provision of service directly from A. Instead, the employee in Citizen Center is informed, to either request the service from A or ask the citizen to do so. The aforementioned is depicted in the figure below.

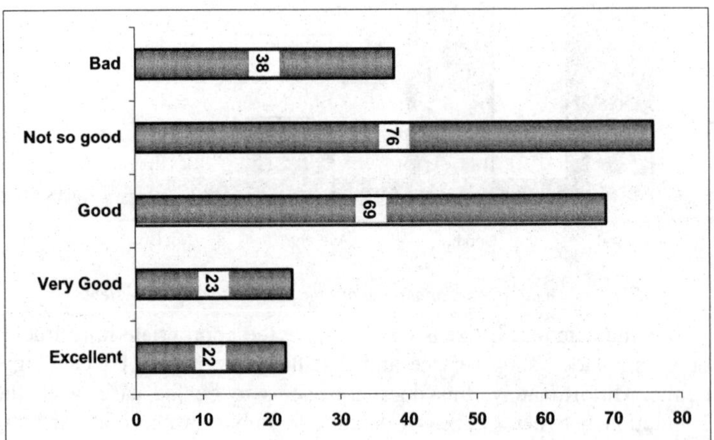

Figure 4: Maturity level of back office information systems as far as interoperability is concerned

It also explains the hesitation of citizens in trusting Citizens Centers for the provision of composite services i.e. services where more than one authorities are involved. Citizens are mainly using the Citizens Centers for the provision of simple services. Figure 5 below presents the most frequently asked services by the Citizens.

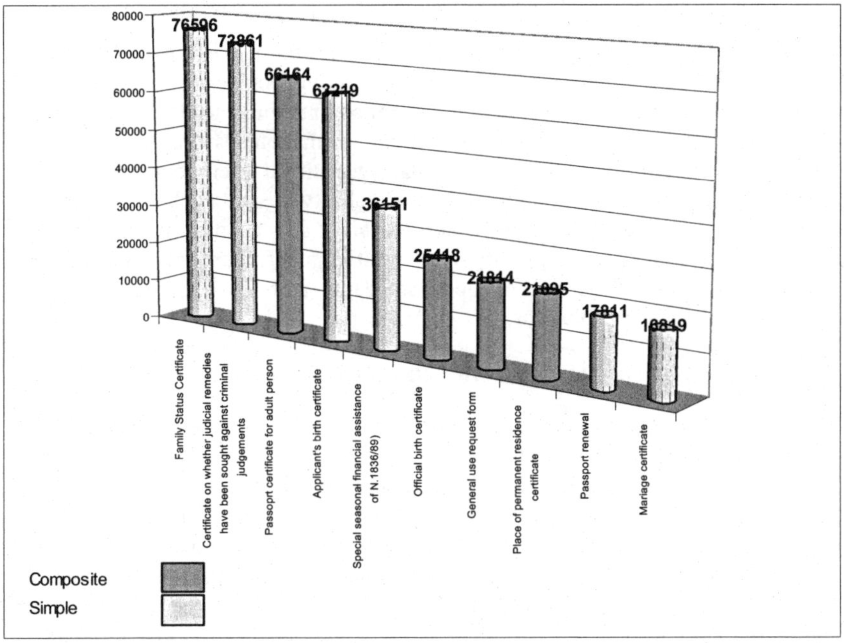

Figure 5: Top requested services

In the survey conducted in a sample of Public Authorities, the outcome was the obvious absence of interoperability standards in most of the developed information systems. The lack of a strategic interoperability plan led each authority to operate autonomously, trying to develop information systems that could serve their daily needs and could not envisaged themselves as part of a unified eGovernment system in which standards and rules (allowing the mutual exchange of information among the various parties) exists.

It is this absence that limits the ability of Citizens Centers to provide electronic services to Citizens. This was obvious during the study of the Citizens Centers' portal. The portal has proven unable to catch up to the modern eGovernment standards, since it is limited to provision of services of level 2. The Citizen cannot interact with the actual back office on his own and is limited in collecting information and downloading paper applications.

Consequently, the need for a strategic plan concerning interoperability that will extend the existing eGovernment Interoperability Framework [4] (which however is strictly limited to technical aspects) and will allow the Public Authorities to catch up with the modern standards and implement a functionable and interoperable back office which is a requirement in all modern eGovernment architectures.

The benefits from the existence of an interoperable back office include the following:

- Decrease the required number of (average) 6 days the citizens has to wait for the provision of the service
- Allow authorities to interact without the need of Citizens Centers' coordination
- Provide electronic services of level 4
- Increase the satisfaction of the citizen against the Public Sector.

4. Interoperability eGovernment frameworks all over the world

4.1 The European Interoperability Framework (EIF)

The EIF defines a set of recommendations and guidelines for eGovernment services, so that public administrations, enterprises and citizens can interact across borders, in a pan-European context. It addresses information content and recommends technical policies and specifications for joining up public administration information systems across the EU. The EIF focuses on supplementing, rather than replacing, national interoperability guidance, by adding the pan-European dimension. Key interoperability areas that should be covered are organizational interoperability, semantic interoperability and technical interoperability. EIF is based on the principles of accessibility to all, multilingualism, security, privacy (personal data protection), subsidiarity, use of open standards and Open Source Software and development of multilateral solutions.

4.2 The electronic Government Interoperability Framework (e-GIF)

e-GIF defines the necessary policies and technical specifications for the electronic integration across government and the public sector in United Kingdom. The framework is specifically designed to cover the exchange of information between government systems as well as the system's interactions between government and citizens, businesses, other government organizations and other (foreign) governments. e-GIF covers interconnectivity, data integration, e-services access and content management. Its key features are the adoption of Internet and WWW standards, the use of XML as the primary means for data integration and presentation, the use of a browser interface as the key interface to the system and the use of metadata for content management.

4.3 Standards and Architectures for e-government Applications (SAGA)

SAGA, the German initiative for eGovernment interoperability, focuses on four directions: the definition of technical normative references, standards and architectures, process modelling, data modelling and the development of basic components. SAGA pursues interoperability, re-usability, openness, cost and risk reduction and scalability.

The architecture model aims at facilitating communications about IT technologies and e-government structures, identifying and evaluate technologies and providing uniform standards. The basic component of the Architecture is the Reference Model of Open Distributed Processing (RM-ODP). According to it, the analysis of applications is broken down into different viewpoints: the enterprise viewpoint, the information viewpoint, the computational viewpoint, the engineering viewpoint and the technology viewpoint

4.4 Federal Enterprise Architecture

The Federal Enterprise Application Framework (FEAF), the United States' initiative for eGovernment interoperability, provides various approaches, models, and definitions for communicating the overall organization and relationships of architecture components required for developing and maintaining the FEA. The FEAF defines a four layer, segmented structure for defining the Federal Enterprise Architecture, consisting of: a) Business Architecture, b) Data Architecture, c) Application Architecture and d) Technology Architecture.

5. Recommendations towards a national strategy

Based on the experiences collected from other countries, a set of recommendations towards a national strategy for interoperability has been included in our study. For the purpose of this paper, we present three critical issues:

- A proposal for the introduction of a Governmental Central Interoperability Unit (GCIU)
- Recommendations for enhancing the capacity of individual agencies to design and implement interoperable systems
- The need for creating the Interoperability Application Infrastructure

5.1 The Governmental Central Interoperability Unit (GCIU)

The Governmental Central Interoperability Unit is proposed to be responsible for:

- The analysis and prioritization of interoperability needs,
- The definition of standards about information, processes, structures, human resources and technology
- The formulation of the general strategy for the expansion and improvement of interoperability.

GCIU is proposed to consist of a Steering Committee and seven functional Departments. The Steering Committee consists of the CIOs from the Ministries and representatives from other public authorities. Its main task is the formulation of the interoperability strategy and the definition of the interoperability standards and guides, which should be adopted by any initiative/ project for the development of information systems in public administration.

Among the proposed Departments, four have "productive" role (Department of Metadata Definition and Semantic Interoperability, Department of Institutional Interoperability, Department of Technical Interoperability, Department of Organizational Interoperability and Human Resources) and the rest are supportive (Department of Documentation and Technical Support, Secretariat, Department of Finance). Their main tasks are the development of standards, guides and frameworks, the support to other public agencies that adopt public interoperability standards and the development and maintenance of the central metadata warehouse.

From an organisational point of view, the introduction of GCUI does not seem to be a difficult task. Key issues for the successful operation of GCUI though, are the extent of its political legitimacy (how well-approved it will be and how it can be functionally and smoothly incorporated into the public administration environment) and operational competence (resources availability).

5.2 Recommendations for enhancing the capacity of PA agencies to design and implement interoperable systems

Two recommendations are included in relation to this topic:

- Creation of CIO positions in all PA organizations.

The importance of CIOs both in private and public organizations has been a popular topic in recent literature. Currently, there is a severe lack of qualified personnel inside the Greek administration who possess a business perspective to information management.

- Upgrading the capacity and scope of existing IT Departments.

The traditional IT department cannot meet the complex requirements posed by contemporary PA agencies. Their view remains parochially technological. Under the supervision of the CIO, we propose the operation of three new sub-units with horizontal perspective to information and process. These are:

1. The Technology Unit (actually close to the existing IT departments)

2. The Process and Workflow Management Unit
3. The Knowledge Management Unit

5.3 The Interoperability Application Infrastructure

The proposals of this part refer to systems that could create a supportive infrastructure for ensuring the interoperability amongst public administration information systems. This recommendation has been derived mainly out of a shortage of the Greek national strategy for public administration information systems development. According to the later, each ministry proposes the development of the information systems needed for covering its functional domain, in a bottom-up fashion. There has been no attempt to align all these ministerial proposals at a global level. Thus, inevitably this situation led to severe duplication (e.g., almost all ministries proposed systems for HR management) and shortage of a global (or federal) view to the overall public administration enterprise architecture (e.g., no ministry alone could propose a common governmental library for geographical information to be used by all administration).

In this line, we envision two types of supportive systems:

- Horizontal systems.
- Generic systems.

The horizontal systems could be used as infrastructure by other systems. We actually need just one instance of each type of these systems. More specifically, in the study we proposed the following horizontal systems/studies:

- Creation of a shared services layer (e.g. directory services, e-forms, systems for authorization, authentication, digital signature and payment)
- Creation and maintenance of the Governmental Metadata Repository
- Drafting the Greek Governmental Enterprise Architecture

The generic systems could be designed and implemented once, and then multiple PA organizations could use them as prototypes and install them with minimum customisation. These may include:

- Systems for A2C communication (e.g. generic CRM system)
- Portals
- A system for supporting the Citizens Centres
- Back-Office systems (e.g. HR management, logistics, document management)

6. Conclusions

The introduction of Citizens Centers is a major modernization for the Greek Public Sector since it forms the first attempt to realize the concept of "one-stop" shop where citizens could apply for all transactions with the Public Sector. The paper examines the Citizens Centers reality based on a broad range of statistical findings and proceeds to a set of recommendation towards a national strategy for interoperability.

References

[1] Tambouris E. and Wimmer M. (2004) "Online one-stop government: a single point of access to public". Chapter of the book *Digital Government: Strategies and Implementations in Developed and Developing Countries*, which has been scheduled to be published by Idea Publishing Group, USA in 2004 (ed. Dr. Wayne Huang).

[2] European Commission, eEurope 2005 Action Plan, [online] http://europa.eu.int/ information_society/eeurope/2005/all_about/action_plan/index_en.htm

[3] Interchange of Data between Administrations, [online], http://europa.eu.int/ISPO/ida/

[4] Information Society, "Greek eGovernment Interoperability Framework", http://www.infosociety.gr/

Local Data Sharing and Co-branding to Better Serve Citizens

Nicolas CONSO
Caisse des depots et Consignation, 137 rue de l'université, Paris, 75013, France
Tel: +33 158507349, Email: Nicolas.conso@caissedesdepots.fr

Abstract: The paper will describe the subject of one of the e-Forum learning journeys: Service-Public, in France. This platform delivers centrally-produced content to enable local authorities to build a local one-stop e-government portal centred on their users. It enhances local e-government service provision by enabling local authorities to develop a local single source of integrated e-government services that has multi-channel access (Internet, kiosk, telephone, counter etc.) and it provides ubiquitous, accurate & timely local content across a whole country by the sharing of e-government information and e-government services between local authorities of different levels and central government, in order to give users the best services. In particular, the paper will cover the insights that the various presentations to e-Forum generated and will show how the ensuing discussions generated new ideas that helped the team further to improve their service

1. Introduction

Service-Public Local is a solution to a pressing public sector problem: allowing national, regional and local government to cooperate to deliver seamless public services. This learning journey brought together participants of different European countries to share key learning points and examine how replicable the application might be elsewhere in Europe.

The Service-Public Local platform enhances citizen-centred local one-stop-shop portals developed by local authorities by organizing data exchange between national, regional and local public bodies. It is a co-branding and information sharing data platform allowing:

- regional and local authorities to build a local unique access point to e-government services on their web site by co-branding with www.service-public.fr, the French national one-stop government portal
- sharing of relevant local, regional and national data, to be able to answer citizens' principal queries (e.g. administrative information, access to forms and online services).

Note that all data exchanges are based on XML published schemes

This platform was launched in Q4 2002 and is now used by over 450 local authorities and cities (from Paris to Aubazine, which has with just 700 inhabitants).

2. Objectives

The first objective of Service-Public Local is to enhance the quality of local e-government by enabling the local authorities to develop a local single access point to e-government services with multi-channel access (telephone, counter). For most people in France, the city hall is still the place where you go when you have an administrative question (Which part of the public sector can help me? What do I have to do? What is the public service I need? Who provides it? Where? When is it open?) The city website is the natural place where you would expect to find a one stop e-government portal; it allows improvement of the quality of services delivered on line to French citizens by being closer and thus more relevant.

If the local e-government portal is good, it can also support people delivering face: face or telephone service. For instance this front end is used in the Saint-Etienne city call centre. In the city of Cergy, the service centre people use a Service-Public Local-based portal to inform people and will soon be able to print a document or a form from it to give to citizens

This benefits users by having all the information and services they need, with full national, regional and local integration, on local websites. They therefore save a lot of time.

The benefit for local authorities is a better quality response from users and saving in building their on line e-government service by using national and regional information, on line forms and services already provided, and kept updated, by others at no cost to them.

The second objective of Service-Public Local is to organise the sharing of e-government information and services between local authorities of different levels to give users better services. For instance in a Département (about 300 towns), the Préfecture provides information about the services for which it is responsible (eg opening hours of counters, on line service for cars registration). All the towns can use this information and service directly on their web site. The Service-Public Local platform allows the decentralised co-production of relevant information for citizens and organisation of its exchange in XML, to use the potential of new technology to give a relevant response to citizens' needs on local web sites

The third objective is to homogenise the quality of services provided by different levels of government and offer local access to a personalised and seamless e-government service.

3. Methodology

Different methods are used to promote the use of this service

3.1 Institutional and Official Communication

The ministers in charge of e-government in France encourage in their local authorities communications the use of co-branding with www.service-public.fr.

3.2 Partnership with Regional Agency

Some Régions or Départements have put in place a regional ICT agency in order to promote and accelerate the use of co-branding with www.service-public.fr. For instance the ICT agency in Région Midi-Pyrénées encouraged the putting in place of co-branding with www.service-public.fr using the Service-Public Local platform for 200 small towns in 2003. At the moment 3 other regions are developing a similar strategy.

3.3 Partnership with Private Sector

The Private sector is a key player for developing local e-government. Specific conditions have been proposed to allow all the players in the local e-government solution market to include the use of co-branding in the solutions they provide to local authorities. More that 20 companies are integrating access to the platform in their products, including IBM.

3.4 Managing Change

In order to assure the success of the services proposed on local authorities' websites, it is important to explain the potential of this tool and teach the people serving the public how to use the service co-branded with www.service-public.fr. Equally, it is important to stress its value for by call centres and counter staff, as well as for web portals.

For that purpose we encourage each local authority by giving them guides and learning tools to train their staff. We support this by encouraging best practice through a monthly newsletter, a mailing list and of course a dedicated website for member organisations. We also organize a meeting four time a year to:

- organise exchanges on the Service-Public Local platform,
- discuss local content and national content, and how to make them complementary in order to serve users better
- debate local e-government projects.
  It is a powerful way to design the future of the platform with the members.

3.5 Business Model

Service-Public Local is a service platform for local authorities. An innovative economic model has been put in place:

- all the exchanges of data are free for those who contribute and give access to data
- a very low membership fee for local authorities who use the platform for co-branding (from 150€/year for a town with less than 3500 inhabitants to 4000€/year for Paris)

4. Technology Description

One has to decide where this service will be accessible by users from the local web site and then integrate very easily a JavaScript code in the corresponding web page.

Local authorities add, using the platform tool, the data (counter address, opening hours, services on line, call centre…) corresponding to the services it delivers to its citizens (for instance for a city, on line form to obtain a birth certificate…).

Local authorities check the data coming from other public content providers (national, departmental, local) that are going to be displayed on its web site. At the end of this process, local authorities have a comprehensive local e-government one-stop shop service, personalised with data and services relevant to its own inhabitants.

La Documentation Française has put in place a server, which contains www.service-public.fr data in XML. This is a reference server where the data is updated and accessed by the Service-Public Local platform. XML has been chosen to make easier the use of structured sub-items of the service-public.fr files. The application has been developed in java (J2EE) and SQL. At the moment, four servers are used (one for the database, three for the co-branding front office. These developments have been using well known and open standards to assure compatibility and re-use.

For data management, XML has been chosen to allow exchange of information between different IT applications in the different local and regional e-government environments.

Specific and generic data exchange models in XML have been developed conjointly by Caisse des dépôts and La Documentation française and are openly published on the national XML schema (http://les.schemas.service-public.fr). An extract of the schema is added. This schema is very general and can be used by other European countries to exchange data on local services useful to citizens. The first XML schema describes the data of www.service-public.fr that are the basis of the application. The second scheme deals with the local data corresponding to services to users complementary to the www.service-public.fr files, for which all data can be exchanged.

These services are linked to files in www.service-public.fr (e.g. driving licence document) for a specific geographic area (town, group of town or departement)

The Service-Public Local platform is accessible from the web when it is used as a co-branding server by local authorities' web sites. The use of XML allows local authorities to co-brand information with different techniques:

- for the majority of local authorities' web sites not using XML, a simple JavaScript included in the local web site calls the Service-Public Local platform and the XML data (service-public.fr + local data relevant coming from different sources) into html through an XSL sheet which is read by the user browser.

- for those using XML, they can do the XSL transformation in their servers

The use of JavaScript allows fast service development without expecting all local authorities to manage XML development. The platform is accessible from the web by local authorities and e-government agencies using authentication with login password and then SSL sessions to update, extract, send local data or customise their co-branding diffusion.

Of course, local authorities can exchange their data directly in XML, even if the majority prefer to use the user friendly interface of the Service-Public Local platform and then extract the data for other uses than co-branding with service-public.fr.

Using the power of web co-branding in e-government is seen by local authorities as a major breakthrough in developing e-government services. They are able to use national and local data to personalise a service on their own website, using their own graphic charts. Meanwhile, the user sees – and credits – their local authority as offering the service.

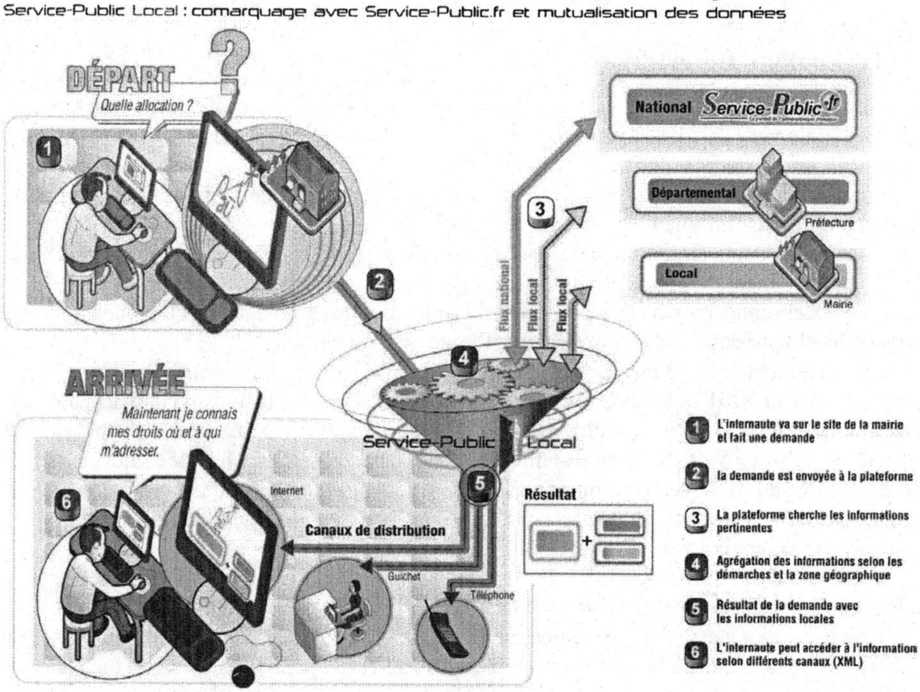

Figure 1

5. Results

5.1 Improvement of Quality of www.service-public.fr due to Local Authorities

The overall impact is a better service to the public for all the services covered by www.service-public.fr (about 2700) that include relevant local information. The municipality offers a one stop shopping e-government portal more relevant than www.service-public.fr on its own website!

450 local authorities are now members of the Service-Public Local platform. These serving over 20 millions inhabitants, which is very good for a 18 month old service. (Local government delay in engaging eGovernment projects is generally quite long.)

The quality processes used for Service-Public Local platform impose a systematic form for completion by local authorities on the data and services of www.service-public.fr. As they use it to serve their citizens and are closer to them than La Documentation Française, the initial responses from local authorities have led to important changes that have improved the usability of the national portal:

5.2 Re-organisation of Database Update in Local Authorities (Paris)

For most members it has been an occasion to reorganise the process of updating the existing databases (for instance Paris) or to create coordination with public local bodies to harmonise the quality of the services proposed by the city website to users.

5.3 Better Service to the Public and Better Image for the Local Administration

Perhaps the most important result is the improvement of the service offered to users by local government web sites that are members of the Service-Public Local platform. They have, via the website of their local administration, both the centrally produced (and maintained) official answer to their questions combined with access to the administration and the on line services relevant to where they live. For instance the connection to Niort website, one of the first members, has had an increase of 50% in visits thanks to co-branding with www.service-public.fr. A large number of local authority members see this service as a way to modernise the image of local authority activity to citizens.

5.4 Higher Confidence in eGovernment due to Service Quality

A very big impact is the increase in confidence in e-government versus traditional government service delivery. The information provided via the Service-Public Local platform is date-stamped. So, for instance, in the example described above, the user can see that the general information comes from service-public.fr together with the date of the most recent update, and knows that the local information and on line service comes from the town of Agen also with the date of that most recent update.

5.5 Better Application of the Law and Coherence of Public Websites

The information in www.service-public.fr is considered the best reference for administrative procedures. Having the local authority using this data to build their e-government service improves the homogeneity of the public web site and helps the local authority to follow better the changes of law and procedure.

5.6 Better Access to eGovernment Services by Multi-channel

It is a key point that e-government breakthroughs improve traditional government services. Saint-Etienne is using the platform to answer citizens by phone and the town of Parthenay has trained all the people working in counter services to use the one-stop shop portal available on the Parthenay website. Using the town web sites they can for instance download a form and fill it in for users coming to the counter. All citizens can take advantage of e-government: not just internet users.

5.7 Strength Local Cooperation between Local Public Services

When a town uses the Service-Public Local platform to build a one stop shop portal, it is advised to involve all the local public bodies. For instance the city of Pau took the opportunity of using the Service-Public Local platform to involve local employment agencies and welfare bodies in the construction of the one-stop shop service of the website of the city.

6. Learning Points from the Learning Journey

The debate between participants drew out some especially valuable learning points that can also be used in other European e-government projects.

6.1 Co-branding with Local Authorities Increases the Audience for National Services

When a one-stop shopping portal or a national service is set up, co-branding is a solution to widen its audience by being seen by users via their natural portal, which is often the local authority web site.

6.2 Managing an Exchange Data Platform and Producing Content are Different Skills

It is critical to build partnerships with complementary public players. A limited experimentation phase, led by La Documentation française, followed by an ambitious generalisation project managed by the Caisse des Dépôts, have in combination resulted in a very powerful platform. Experimentation and generalisation are very different projects. Experimentation is necessary to analyse user needs and technical feasibility of projects. For generalisation, sustainability and development planning needs an "industrial" approach.

6.3 Method of Generalising Innovation to Local Authority

Small local authorities generally cannot afford research. Innovation has to be brought in by their natural partner: either a regional IT agency or private companies in charge of their information system.

6.4 Citizen Centric Project is Key for Local-National Cooperation.

It is when you focus on citizen need that it is easier to analyse what each level of government can bring to build a solution. It is a way to overcome competition between each government body. In our experience the most information comes from the national level because it is a transcription of national law, and customisation is done by each competent level because it is where it is more relevant to users.

6.5 Turnkey Solutions are Necessary for Small Local Authorities

When you build a exchange data platform, one of the service has to be turnkey to deal with local authority which have no IT skills.

6.6 Private Sector Cooperation is Mandatory for Significant Generalisation.

The private sector plays an important part in e-government innovation. A public solution must have the possibility of being imbedded in the private sector solution in order to accelerate local e-government improvement.

6.7 XML is not enough for Data Exchange

XML normalisation is mandatory to build long-term information systems. But to effectively organise data exchange, each actor must be interested (e.g. local authorities are interested because the data exchanged are published on their own web site). We enclose an extract of a freely available XML schema that can be useful for other European public bodies.

6.8 Local Authorities are Key to Developing eGovernment

Our experience shows that, even in very centralised a country, local authorities are very often the best level to deliver e-government service, mainly because it is where equivalent counter service are delivered.

6.9 Quality of Service Increases Confidence

The first results show that quality of service is very important to develop internet use. If the information or service first found on the web is not good, most citizens will be reluctant to use e-government services for a long time. It is very important to provide solutions to local authorities that help them to offer a high quality level of service, first time, to their citizens.

7. Conclusions

The debate initiated at the Learning Journey proved to be extremely valuable in challenging assumptions and suggesting new avenues to consider. This journey re-enforced the need to emphasise the topic of central-local cooperation in building e-government in Europe following the e-Europe 2005 objectives.

The next step is to build common authentication and personal data schemas between national and local e-government projects. Thanks to the outcome of this Journey, the Local Service-Public platform is developing on the same basis access to co-branded interactive and personalised services.

Born to Co-operate: New Communication Approaches for eGovernment

Jaak TEPANDI
Tallinn University of Technology, Ehitajate tee 5, Tallinn 19086, Estonia
Tel: +372 50 290 28, Fax: + 372 6202 308, Email: tepandi@cc.ttu.ee

Abstract: Interoperability of services and systems is an important prerequisite for creating eGovernment applications that support co-operation and best practice sharing. The paper compares several promising approaches aimed at achieving these objectives: interoperability (standard) frameworks, web services, intelligent software agents, and semantic web. These approaches are on various levels of readiness and require different resources. A case study is proposed, involving interoperable digital signatures for cross-border electronic services. Development of such services includes dealing with incompatibility problems on all levels of digital signature infrastructure, making agreements between service stakeholders, and implementing projects involving various services. Use of interoperable digital signatures can best be implemented through the web services approach.

1. Introduction

eGovernment infrastructure and services help citizens to be better informed, to do everyday tasks more efficiently, and to enjoy to a larger extent their citizens' rights. Examples from Estonia include the portal for citizens, electronic application for parents' compensation, and electronic provision of proposals for new and amended laws. People feel motivated by being able to acquire competitive skills and investors prefer areas with contemporary information technology infrastructure.

New possibilities create new risks and problems:

- Dependency of people, economy, and the whole state on new technologies creates risk of interruption for important services
- Important information may be altered or destroyed in an unauthorized manner
- Confidential information may be revealed
- eGovernment systems may be incompatible
- Those who have (computers, software, communications, etc) may gain more with introduction of electronic services, while those who do not may become even poorer
- Due to their wide scale and novelty, eGovernment solutions may be expensive and the percentage of successful projects may be low - although it is difficult to say whether the situation is better in other areas, such as e-Business

These perspectives must be taken into account while developing new services. One of the risks is potential incompatibility of systems and services. Interoperability on the otherhand, improves co-operation and best-practice sharing when developing eGovernment solutions, and enables development of systems that require less human intervention.

Although there are many important examples in many countries both in the European Union and outside, the focus will be on examples from Estonia - first, because we have a good overview of this area and second, because this country is known to have achieved relatively good results with rather limited resources.

2. Objective

The objective of the paper is to compare, in the context of a wider digital commons framework [1], several promising approaches aimed at achieving improvements in co-operation: interoperability (standard) frameworks, web services, intelligent software agents, and semantic web. These approaches complement each other, but are at various levels of readiness and require different resources. Based on the comparison, a case study is proposed. We hope this analysis will help designers of eGovernment systems to enhance interoperability and usability of new applications, thus delivering better quality systems.

3. Methodology: Investigating Co-operation and Interoperability

Co-operation may have different content (e.g., co-operation in building eGovernment applications or in providing specific services), occur between different stakeholders (e.g., human-human, human-system, or system-system), and take different forms (e.g., exchange of good practices, development of a joint project, providing automated services).

Interoperability is important in all these cases. In a technological sense, software interoperability is the capability of the (software) product to interact with one or more specified systems [2]. From a broader perspective, interoperability means the ability of information and communication technology systems and of the business processes they support to exchange data and to enable sharing of information and knowledge [3].

Interoperability includes legislative, organizational (collaboration of administrations, interoperability between business processes, and the like), semantic (the meaning of exchanged information is understood between all parties involved), technical (interoperability of hardware and software infrastructure, communication protocols, messaging and other), and even psychological aspects. The organisational interoperability may be the most difficult to achieve, followed by semantic and technological properties.

Taking again an example from the Estonian public sector IT project experience, interoperability of systems and services is greatly enhanced due to application of the X-road project and over 50 translated/ accepted international IT standards. The X-road project is intended to develop software, hardware and organisational methods for standardised usage of national databases. Currently 26 most important Estonian registers, such as the population register, the business register, buildings register, land register, and many others, have been joined with the X-road environment.

At the same time, many problems remain. The basic systems and standards underlying the eGovernment infrastructure, such as the address register, classifier registers, geodesy system, and security standards, are insufficiently developed. Many public sector databases are still separated, duplicated, or inaccessible to the public. Common standards for public sector IT projects are not widely accepted; quality requirements are not sufficient.

To aid in solving these problems, we compare several widespread approaches towards interoperability and propose a case study.

4. Comparison of Four Approaches Towards Interoperability

Interoperability becomes important when different systems from various organisations must work together. This is why in the not so distant past, this concept was not of much concern - organisations were satisfied with their legacy systems that operated in isolation. From recent developments, four approaches to interoperability have been particularly promising.

4.1 Interoperability Frameworks

An interoperability framework can be defined as a set of standards and guidelines that describe the way in which organizations have agreed, or should agree, to interact with each other [3]. Interoperability frameworks provide recommendations on architectures, best practices, and standards for eGovernment. They represent readily available and low cost solutions for enhancing co-operation and best-practice sharing in development of eGovernment processes and applications.

The European Interoperability Framework provides a generic model for national frameworks. Based on the EU model, several EU countries have developed their interoperability standards. The problem is that it may be difficult to enforce such frameworks. They are also not easy to use in already existing applications. Still such frameworks may be recommended as the first and very cost-effective step towards services and applications interoperability.

A government ICT architecture and interoperability framework has been developed for Estonian public sector. As a solution for a small country, it integrates architectural and interoperability recommendations. It is based on the European interoperability framework and takes into account relevant standards and frameworks of other countries, as well as the Internet Engineering Task Force and the W3C recommendations and standards.

The framework comprises relevant practices of Estonian public sector organisations and various Estonian interoperability initiatives, such as the X-road and others. To avoid non-realistic expectations, the framework does not include standards marked as "Mandatory" - the strongest level of recommendation is "Strongly suggested", followed by "Suggested", "Allowed", and "Becoming obsolete".

Some of the risks associated with this approach are as follows:

- The interoperability frameworks may become too technology driven. To avoid this, the organisational and semantic aspects have to be taken into account
- The interoperability frameworks may become too public sector oriented. Future shows how enthusiastic the private sector will be to follow this initiative
- Wrong standards may be enforced. This risk may be reduced by keeping the framework flexible and avoiding enforcement of non-mature standards
- Right standards may be enforced in a non-effective way. To avoid this risk, one should calculate the costs and improvements, working case by case especially when attempting to enforce new standards for legacy systems
- Preferences to open standards may be inserted so as to favour or eliminate certain suppliers or products. Complying with principles of non-discrimination and equal treatment would reduce this risk. The goal is to provide organisations and individuals with a ability to choose between options, not to insist on using certain kind of standards

In summary, this approach may be recommended as mature for using in eGovernment applications. When cautiously applied, the costs associated with interoperability frameworks are reasonable.

4.2 Web Services

Web services technology has had interoperability as a significant goal from the beginning. There are several web services models. One of the popular models includes the following main components of the web services architecture: actors (the service provider, the service requester, and the service registry), objects (the service and the service description), and operations performed by the actors on the objects (publish, find, and bind) [4].

The provider creates a web service and publishes its description with a service registry based on the Universal Description, Discovery, and Integration (UDDI) specification. The service requester finds the service via the UDDI interface, receives a description of the service in the Web Services Description Language (WSDL), and obtains a uniform resource locator pointing to the service. This information can be used to bind and invoke the service.

Web services implementation comprises a collection of predefined layers. The number and content of these layers as proposed by different sources is varying. A widespread model comprises six layers: the three core ones (network, XML-based messaging, service description) and the three optional ones (service publication, service discovery, and service flow). All the layers must address the security, management, and quality of service needs.

The web services architecture, albeit not yet heavily used, is commonly agreed between the major information technology players. A number of implementation platforms have been proposed, such as .NET from Microsoft, Java Web Services Developer from SUN, WebSphere Application Server from IBM, and others. The Web Services-Interoperability Organization has proposed a high level definition of a Supply Chain Management application to demonstrate various web service interoperability scenarios.

Several businesses, such as Google, Amazon, and others, provide both web services as well as a possibility to define and apply new web services. The number of real eGovernment implementations of web services is not high. As an example from Estonia, the latest version of the X-road project is partially implemented using the web services architecture. At this moment this solution is not fully documented and the WSDL descriptions of the services are not sufficient for automated use of the services.

The following risks may be highlighted in connection with the web services approach:

- Common standards will not emerge, there will be several partially incompatible solutions from major vendors
- The users are not willing to introduce new services, or are reluctant to use the web services architecture
- Sufficient level of web services security may be hard to achieve. As a result, the threats to privacy may be increased due to interconnection of databases and registers that include various kinds of data about individual persons To reduce this risk, interoperable digital certificates may provide a way to safely link together chains of services
- Payment models for web services may be insufficiently elaborated. The payment models are currently under development

In spite of these risks, the web services may be considered as mature enough for implementation, and may become the next viable and cost-effective approach for eGovernment services.

4.3 Intelligent Agents

The concept of an intelligent software agent is not yet uniquely established. It has been proposed both on a design and implementation level. On the design level, agents represent high-level communicating entities performing tasks meaningful form the system users' viewpoint. On the implementation level, the concept of an intelligent / software agent varies from a mobile entity travelling in networks and performing tasks on behalf of its sender, to an image on the screen responding to questions from the users.

There are several desirable features towards which all such agents seem to be oriented - an ability to perform meaningful tasks, to take responsibility and act on behalf of its owner, to communicate with humans and other software agents, to have some competency, to learn, etc. The Foundation for Intelligent Physical Agents [5] is a non-profit organisation aiming to produce standards for the interoperation of heterogeneous software agents.

Web services and intelligent agents may complement each other in the future, providing architecture to develop end-to-end services and integrate these in a standardized and efficient way. As an example, a personal intelligent agent may search for and make use of available web services while solving tasks on behalf of its manager. In the case such a perspective will occur, integration of semantic web and intelligent agents will offer a good platform for interoperable eGovernment applications.

At the current state of art, the software agent standards and architectures are not so well established as those behind the web services. Therefore it may be worthwhile to be careful developing an eGovernment framework based on that architecture.

4.4 Semantic Web

Semantic web [6] provides uniform treatment of huge amounts of relational and semi-structured data and smart queries. The basic layers of semantic web, XML and the Resource Definition Framework, are ready for use. The next layer - the ontology and logic languages, allowing for creation of world descriptions and execution of smart queries over the data in the web - is also improving.

Efficient use of these tools requires development of commonly accepted world descriptions given e.g. in the Web Ontology Language and agreed by all stakeholders. Such descriptions are evolving in web search engines, but this may be the most time-consuming activity of semantic web development. Therefore using the data provided by semantic web, for example by web services and / or intelligent agents, is potentially very useful, but currently it may be too early to attempt to widely use this approach in eGovernment.

The basic features of the approaches are summarized in Table 1.

Table 1. A Summary Comparison of the Four Approaches

	Interoperability frameworks	**Web services**	**Intelligent agents**	**Semantic web**
Idea	Agreed interoperability standards	Services and their descriptions in the web	High-level communicating entities performing meaningful tasks	Information in the web is given a well-defined meaning
Example	EU and national frameworks	e-Business applications	A prototype travel agent	Ontologies for web search engines
Main co-operation focus	Human-system; System –system	System- system	Depending on definition	Human-system; System -system
Opportunities	Interoperable applications and data	Machine-machine communication	Intelligent services on the web	The web as a big database with meaningful data
Risks / problems	Unbalanced or poor frameworks; non-efficient implementation	Incompatible standards, security, privacy, payments	Incompatible solutions, running ahead, security, privacy	Incompatible solutions, running ahead, privacy
Maturity	Mature	Early mature	Developing	Early developing
Recommendation	Use	Prototype	Experiment	Be aware, participate in R&D

5. Case Study: Digital Signatures for Cross-Border Electronic Services

As discussed above, interoperability frameworks and web services are sufficiently mature approaches for co-operation oriented eGovernment applications development. As a case study, we consider a web services application that will provide interoperable digital signatures for cross-border electronic services.

The demand for such services is high. The eEurope initiative requires numerous public services both for citizens and businesses, such as declaration of income taxes, job search services, customs declarations, public procurement, and other [7].

The Directive of the European Parliament on a Community framework for electronic signatures [8] has provided a basis for development of national regulations. Digital signature legislation is in use in most EU countries and useful applications are available.

As an example, the ID card implemented in Estonia as the primary document for identifying citizens and alien residents living in the country, facilitates secure authentication and legally binding digital signature, in connection with nationwide online services. By 17.05.2004, 500,000 ID cards had been issued in Estonia (1.4 million population). Many applications, including handling data in state registers, ID tickets in public transport, and communicating with the Estonian Tax Board are available. These examples indicate that the spreading of digital signatures and the level of existing services has reached the point where extending the services over the borders is becoming meaningful and realistic.

The task of introducing cross-border services is not trivial and requires a substantial amount of resources. Recent initiatives in this area in EU, US, and Northern eDimension are under development. Example scenarios for the pilot projects may include exchange of digitally signed cross border agreements and other documents, accessing social security and healthcare data for a foreign person needing medical help in another country, a policeman having a fast access to personal data for a foreigner, simplifying and fastening custom procedures with direct access to customs and company data, using ID cards when crossing borders, etc. In general, extending them over the borders will enhance most of the public services for citizens and businesses requested by the eEurope initiative.

The service interoperability is currently best supported by the web services architecture. As an example, a query about the legal status of one's real estate property may require services from the real estate register, land cadastre, population register, authentication service, as well as from other component services (Figure 1).

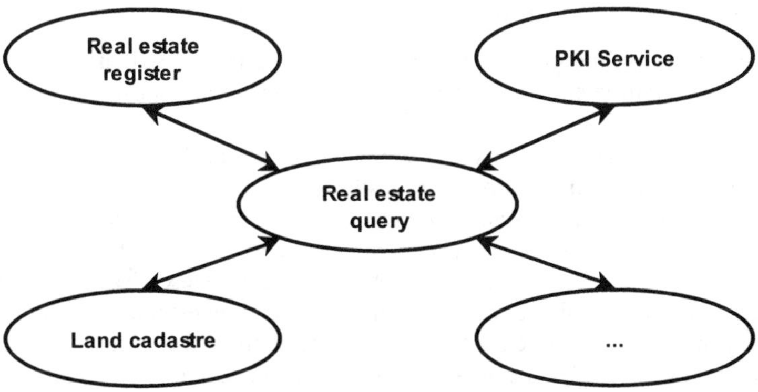

Figure 1. A Complex Service

A number of incompatibility problems have to be solved before such cross-border services will become a reality [9]. The electronic signature legislation in various countries may vary to a large extent in all aspects, including cross-border issues. As an example, the Directive of the European Parliament on a Community framework for electronic signatures [8] and the UNCITRAL (United Nations Commission on International Trade Law) Model Law on Electronic Signatures [10] differ in several aspects related to interoperability.

On the PKI level, the services proposed by the service providers may be incompatible. The PKI Forum [11] has proposed a PKI Interoperability Framework involving three layers: Component-Level Interoperability, Application-Level Interoperability, and Inter-Domain Interoperability. Significant initiatives in the PKI interoperability area are underway both in EU and in US. In EU, the European Bridge-CA is a public-private partnership lead by TeleTrusT. It is focused upon the Bridge Certification Authority (BCA) concept [11]. This concept enables corporations and public administration units to communicate with one another on a secure and authentic basis. Existing PKIs of individual organizations are linked together by incorporating previously issued certificates into the Bridge-CA network. A neutral board decides which existing PKIs will be connected to the European Bridge-CA.

Development of cross boarder electronic services using digital signatures has been initiated within the Northern eDimension framework [9]. The main objective is to show the use of interoperable digital signatures in cross-border electronic services in the Northern Dimension countries. The initiative has three main components: understanding the status of interoperability between digital signatures across borders in the participating countries, specification of the requirements for interoperability, and demonstration of interoperability in real life, across borders with several countries involved using one or more applications.

6. Business benefits

Interoperability approaches provide more effective and efficient human-system and system-system interactions. As an example, interoperability frameworks may provide for reuse of eGovernment applications, make the system development life cycle shorter and cheaper, and enhance co-operation and exchange of information. Web services may eliminate human intermediaries in the value chain, replacing them by interoperable services and providing considerably faster and cost-effective results. Intelligent agents improve human-system co-operation making work both more efficient and less stressing. More precise web search results due to semantic web will make the web a truly integrated source for information.

7. Conclusions and Summary Recommendations

It is important to select the most appropriate architecture that would enhance co-operation and best-practice sharing in development of eGovernment solutions. The above analysis gives the following suggestions for such a decision:

- Interoperability frameworks may be recommended as the first and cost-effective step towards services and applications interoperability
- A number of risks may be highlighted in connection with the web services approach, such as possibly incompatible standards, reluctance of users to introduce new services, and problems with security and payments. In spite of these risks, the web services approach may be considered as mature enough for implementation, and may become the next viable and cost-effective approach for eGovernment services
- Web services and intelligent agents may complement each other in the future, providing architecture to develop end-to-end services and integrate these in a standardised and efficient way. In the case such a perspective will occur, integration of semantic web and intelligent agents will offer a good platform for interoperable eGovernment applications
- Semantic web provides uniform treatment of huge amounts of relational and semi-structured data and smart queries. Efficient use of semantic web requires development of commonly accepted world descriptions. This may be the most time-consuming activity of semantic web development. Currently it may be too early to attempt to widely use this approach in eGovernment

As a case study, we have considered a web services application that will provide interoperable digital signatures for cross-border electronic services. Significant work is needed to deal with incompatibility problems on all levels of digital signature infrastructure, to make agreements between service stakeholders, and to implement projects involving various services.

Acknowledgements

This paper was partially supported by the ESF Grant No. 5645.

References

[1] O. Forsgren. Digital commons – Theory, challenges and a framework model. Proceedings of eChallenges 2004 (to be published)

[2] International Standard ISO/IEC 9126-1:2001. Software engineering – Product quality – Part 1: Quality model

[3] European Interoperability Framework for pan-European eGovernment Services. IDA working document - Version 4.2 – January 2004

[4] K. Gottschalk, S. Graham, H. Kreger, and J. Snell. Introduction to Web services architecture. IBM Syst. J., Volume 41, Number 2, 2002

[5] Foundation for Intelligent Physical Agents - http://www.fipa.org/

[6] Semantic Web - www.w3.org/2001/sw/

[7] eEurope 2005: An information society for all. Brussels, 2002

[8] Directive 1999/93/EC of the European Parliament and of the Council of 13 December 1999 on a Community framework for electronic signatures

[9] J. Tepandi. Digital signatures in interoperable electronic services. Baltic IT&T Review, Nr.3 (30), 2003, pp. 62-65

[10] UNCITRAL Model Law on Electronic Signatures With Guide to Enactment 2001. United Nations Publications 2002

[11] PKI Forum. PKI Interoperability Framework. 2001

[12] Polk, W. T. and N. E. Hastings. "Bridge Certification Authorities: Connecting B2B Public Key Infrastructures", National Institute of Standards and Technology, http://csrc.nist.gov/pki/rootca/

Open Applications and Solution Sharing for Governments

David ROWE
Microsoft EMEA (Europe Middle East and Africa)
Microsoft Campus, Thames Valley Park, Reading, RG6 1WG, UK
Tel: +44 (0)118 909 4508, Email: davrowe@microsoft.com

Abstract: The growth of effective information technology (IT) solutions in Government is often challenged due to the nature of eGovernment solutions, which – like all large-scale IT systems and solutions – are typically complex, have high implementation costs and involve inherent production risks. Furthermore, while many governments may be facing similar service requirements, the trend is to develop new systems and solutions from scratch (thereby 'reinventing the wheel'). In considering these challenges, this paper presents a number of examples (featuring award-winning solutions and real-world case studies covering both Western and Eastern Europe) where eGovernment development is accelerated by the reuse of existing solutions, thereby reducing cost and risk. This paper also investigates more programmatic application sharing initiatives that provide a community/collaborative environment facilitating the sharing, rework and enhancement of government solutions. Findings, learnings and recommendations are presented as points of departure for further discussion.

1. Introduction

The mission of Government is to provide information, protection, programs and services to their citizens, create an environment that fosters a growing economy, proper healthcare and educational systems, plentiful jobs and an overall improved standard of living. Coupled with the broad aims of modernisation (e.g. the EC's eEurope initiative), governments often pursue their mission utilising IT solutions that meet a broad range of citizen and organizational needs, from local government portal to data-centre management.

However, eGovernment solutions – like all large-scale information technology (IT) systems and solutions – typically have high implementation costs and inherent production risks. While many governments may want to implement similar services (e.g. child benefits) the trend is to develop new systems and solutions from scratch (thus 'reinventing the wheel'). This does nothing to reduce risk or costs – both of which are barriers to effective eGovernment development in the face of failing projects and falling budgets.

In addressing these challenges, the concepts of open standards, open source, solution reuse and collaborative solution development promise to help. This paper investigates that promise by illustrating a number of examples where eGovernment development has been accelerated by the effective and efficient reuse of applications and solutions, thereby reducing cost and risk. Projects featured include the UK Government's GovTalk initiative (www.govtalk.gov.uk), Italy's eGovernment Competence Centre (www.egovcenter.it) and the award-winning Romania Gateway (www.e-guvernare.ro).

This paper also investigates mechanisms by which government bodies or associations may cooperate to reuse applications and solutions for a common constituency. The aim of such associations/organisations is to provide better solutions for their governmental constituents at a more affordable cost (often sharing the development cost) with reduced risk (as others have already implemented, used and enhanced the solutions on offer).

Examples include the Dutch municipality of Deventer (www.kennisportaaloverheid.nl) and Ireland's Local Government Computer Services Board (www.lgcsb.ie).

These discussions tie into the concept of 'digital commons' – where the sharing of eGovernment experiences, knowledge and solutions is encouraged. The content of this paper will be further augmented by more recent developments and lessons learnt in the months leading up to the eChallenges Conference, with a consolidated view to be presented during the e-Challenges Workshop for review, reflection and discussion.

2. Reuse of Open Standards, Application Code and Solutions

Based on our experience in providing software solutions for governments both in Europe and internationally, we observe the following as both a global corporate citizen and a software solution provider:

- Duplication of solutions and effort is common. Many governments IT solutions are 'bespoke', being built separately, several times over by different agencies even within a single jurisdiction, let alone within a single country or between friendly nations.
- Yet… the spirit of sharing does exist amongst peers. Government departments routinely share information, IP and ideas with their peers. Despite that, the sharing of actual solutions is not common.
- And… commercialised sharing of IP is difficult. Governments often have rules governing commercialisation of publicly funded IP. Sometimes it happens, but commercialising of government solutions (often world-leading) is rarely a focus.
- At the same time… budgets for IT are not growing. Budgets for IT projects are not growing around the world yet the reliance on IT for service delivery and demand for greater system agility is growing strongly.

In considering these challenges, we explore the concepts of open application sharing, open standards and solution reuse in the following sections.

2.1 Open Solution Sharing – Another 'OSS'

Open Source Software (OSS) is a software development model in which the source code of applications and tools is 'openly' available to be used, copied, extended and redistributed with or without modifications [14]. Open source software may be offered either with or without a fee. The combination of source code access, open licensing models and an active, collaborative community allows developers and practitioners to benefit from this model.

Despite the typically controversial commentary about OSS [3, 7, 12] there are many advantages to the open source model as it broadly applies to the development of standards, applications and solutions [4]. Recognised benefits include:

- The ability to view, modify and redistribute the source code of applications.
- Lower costs from reduced rework and the leveraging of collaboration.
- A community of peers and experts providing help and support.
- Increased flexibility in vendor and procurement arrangements.

Now 'source' can reside at many levels in a solution: it constitutes the 'operating system', 'application code' and 'glue code'. However, access to the all the source code may not be required all of the time, and it may be argued that the greatest benefit of open development and software reuse comes at the solution or application level. This is the level that addresses critical organization needs while delivering true business value, rather than implementing (yet another) system tool such as a text editor or file sharing mechanism.

Further, we highlight that the open software model can thrive on a commercial (or 'not free') software platform [4]. In fact, when referencing the eighty thousand or so projects on Sourceforge.net [15] – one of the largest open source repositories/work spaces on the

Internet – there are roughly as many projects/solutions based on commercial operating systems as non-commercial. Another way to look at it is that there roughly as many solutions based on Microsoft's Windows platform as Unix-related operating systems.

It is in this context that we propose the term 'Open Application Sharing' as a valuable permutation of the typical 'open' debate. (In this paper, we choose 'Open Application Sharing' instead of 'Open Solution Sharing' to get a distinctive term and acronym – OAS.) Rather than thinking in terms of low-level code reuse utilising 'free and open source software', we focus on the benefits of the 'open' model as applied to the development and reuse of eGovernment solutions and applications – regardless of platform. Those benefits relate to efficiencies in solution and experience reuse, access to the core solution (whether it be documents, schemas or source code), collaboration amongst peers and incremental enhancement. This point is highlighted in the experiences illustrated below.

2.2 Open Standards Enabling Broad Interoperability – UK's GovTalk

Modern eGovernment demands joined-up information, communication and technology (ICT) systems. The necessary result is interoperable systems working in a seamless and coherent way across the public sector to provide better efficiency and services tailored to the needs of citizens and businesses at a lower cost. However, the reality of today is the emergence of 'islands' of eGovernment that are frequently unable to interoperate due to fragmentation resulting form uncoordinated efforts in developing services and implementing technologies (as observed by the EC IDA workgroup [9]).

Within Europe, there are many notable projects focusing on standards and policy frameworks for ensuring interoperability. The UK Government has implemented the eGovernment Interoperability Framework (e-GIF) which defines policies and specifications for interoperability, information management and e-services access across government, ensuring connection to external entities (including citizens and businesses) and alignment with global IT trends. e-GIF is a key component in the UK's modernisation strategy.

At the centre of e-GIF is GovTalk [13] — an industry-endorsed XML specification for all government services. The use of GovTalk and other industry accepted open standards (including SOAP and UDDI) allows the connection of best-of-breed players and service providers. To facilitate this process, the GovTalk website enables the Public Sector, Industry and other interested parties to work together to develop and agree policies and standards for effectively delivering on the UK's eGovernment agenda.

Embracing open standards and providing an open development model (for both eGovernment frameworks and service specification) has allowed the UK Government to gain broad buy-in from industry as well as government bodies and organisations. An illustration of GovTalk's success is that there are now over 12 accredited UK Software Suppliers (including Sage Software, Paladin Solutions and CINTRA Payroll services) that supply their business payroll solutions with an integrated Filing By Internet (FBI) mechanism that allow for direct submission of payroll data to the Inland Revenue. In addition to creating value in the ISV community, such solutions help spread the usefulness of eGovernment services and drive uptake.

2.3 Access to Source Code and Solution Building-blocks – Italy's e-Gov Initiative

In the face of wide-spread modernisation goals, the Italian Government launched their eGovernment strategy in June 2000, entitled the "E-government Action Plan" [11]. The Ministry of Technology and Innovation (www.innovazione.gov.it) has been instrumental in carrying this initiative forward.

The software industry's response was to rapidly translate the Ministry's Action Plan into concrete projects. One key initiative headed by Microsoft (in conjunction with other industry partners including Accenture, Bull, Getronics, HP, Saga and Etnoteam) aimed at providing an eGovernment solution kit, the key elements of which include:

- Italian focused: This is a local initiative with specific local investments & contributions.
- Solution acceleration: Helps the market speed up and meet eGovernment challenges.
- Open components: eGovernment building-blocks are based on accepted standards such as XML, SOAP, etc. and open to all IT operators

At the core of the initiative is the EASI solution kit (E-government Acceleration Solutions for Italy), which consists of technical building-blocks (including web portal, authentication and integration components), documentation and specifications, processes particular to the Italian e-government scenario as well as training material (including an eGovernment competence framework). Support is provided to Public Administrations (municipalities, aggregations of municipalities, regions and their technology partners) and IT vendors via industry training events and the content is openly available via an online-Government Competence Center (www.egovcenter.it).

The success of this program is highlighted by the attendance of over 700 people for training in the solution, active participation of over 22 partners, uptake by Italian municipalities (including the Province of Naples – highly regarded for their eGovernment thought leadership) and the proliferation of successful projects based on the EASI toolkit (including a number of identity, case management and ERP solutions as well as successful project references such as the Italian Ministry of the Environment's National Mapping Portal (ww3.atlanteitaliano.it/atlante/Consultazione/Main.asp).

2.4 Sharing Solutions and Facilitating Reuse – Romania's Gateway

The benefits of software reuse (whether at the source, component or application level) have long been discussed [2, 8], with the key benefits being reduced cost and risk (subject of course to effective processes and management [10, 5]). An open model involving shared source components (or entire solutions) can be critical in delivering such benefits. An example of this success is Romania's WSIS award winning National Electronic System).

A core component of the Romanian National Electronic System is a sophisticated authentication and integration eGovernment Gateway (https://secure.e-guvernare.ro/). The gateway was implemented utilising intellectual property, source-code and design principals directly drawn from the UK's Government Gateway (www.gateway.gov.uk). The UK Gateway's 200+ thousand lines of bespoke code were shared with the Romanian Government to enable and accelerate their eGovernment programs and projects.

Statistics from the Romanian Gateway project highlight the benefits of open solution sharing. When comparing implementation effort, the Romanian gateway was implemented with less than $1/10^{th}$ of the UK project's man-days (including language translation and integration of three simple services). Similarly, the cost of the project was dramatically reduced, reflecting not only the fraction of effort required but also the relatively low cost of local partners and operations. Risks were mitigated by reusing an already successful solution, while subject-matter experts and solution support was provided as required from the UK-based Gateway implementation partners.

The Romanian Gateway is a prime example of what can be achieved when the public and private sector work together to leverage already-successful solutions and exploit the potential of new technologies. Since the Romanian experience, the UK Gateway has also been replicated in the Czech Republic and utilised in the Taiwan eGovernment activities.

3. eGovernment Collaboration and Open Application Sharing

These project references and case studies demonstrate there is already considerable collaboration and solution sharing across Europe. However, it is still relatively difficult to find good examples of successful collaboration and solutions sharing across a broader region and/or community. The following subsections explore a number of community-based collaboration initiatives and highlights the successful experiences and practices.

3.1 Mechanisms to Support Open Application Sharing

The project references and case-studies cited above illustrate that there is already a degree of collaboration and sharing amongst eGovernment practitioners and implementers. In addition to sharing, there is also open acknowledgement of great projects and solutions such as the WSIS Award (as mentioned above) and the eEurope Award for eGovernment. The Stockholm Challenge Awards is also a well recognised award at the international level.

Another key mechanism for facilitating eGovernment solution sharing are programmes such as the EC's IDA [9] which also identify and catalogue great eGovernment solutions via their published solution catalogues and the online 'eGovernment Observatory'. An important point to note about the IDA's catalogue/observatory activities is that they are aimed at the senior decision maker, addressing an audience that is not necessarily technical.

Such awards and peer-acknowledgement help drive the progress of eGovernment as well as connect practitioners internationally. Often one government or agency will approach another and wish to replicate their success. This often leads to a 'point-to-point' collaboration whereby a solution originator shares the intellectual property associated with a solution with a benefactor. An example cited above was the replication of the UK Gateway in the Czech Republic, and a pleasing side note drawing from this experience is that the originator can also benefit from modifications and enhancements that are the result of the reuse process. In this case, Czech-based enhancements were folded back into UK Gateway code base and redeployed in the UK. Such is the benefit of collaboration!

Point-to-point collaboration has its weaknesses, particularly in terms of reach and the number of entities who can benefit. A wider model would include a consortium of entities that can co-develop concepts and solutions and collectively benefit from the experience. An example of such a project is Avanti (www.avantiproject.org), a European Commission co-funded FP5 project aimed at addressing e-service delivery and digital inclusion. Within the Avanti project, four city governments from four different European countries worked together with two industrial partners to implement a solution that formed the back-bone of a number of different project implementations and uses across Europe. The resulting Avanti Toolkit has won a number of industry awards [17] – thereby demonstrating the effectiveness of this consortium-driven collaboration model.

Looking more broadly than a structured consortium sharing solution development leads to the typical 'open community' model as demonstrated at open source development sites such as Sourceforge (www.sourceforge.net) and Freshmeat (www.freshmeat.net). Such sites host thousands of source projects. The challenges with government entities using these sites is that the communities are not focused on the subject of government (exhibiting many projects from a broad range of sectors) and the projects themselves are rarely at the application (or solution) level, rather comprising application tools or source snippets (for example, over half of the 53,000 Freshmeat projects are directly related to system applications/tools and development tools). This reduces their effectiveness at addressing the eGovernment market's specific needs.

3.2 Building eGovernment Communities around Open Application Sharing

At present, there is no 'Sourceforge.net' equivalent for a government-focused open source community development. There is the similarly named Government Forge (governmentforge.org), but its site is more a project page hosting very few solutions yet promoting the use of Linux to the exclusion of other platforms (as Government Forge is affiliated with the Open Source Software Institute). At least Sourceforge seems to be politically neutral: it hosts open applications on any platform including Microsoft's, two examples of which are UNESCO's Greenstone library management application and UWC's Knowledge Environment for Web-based Learning (KEWL) system.

Despite the inevitable religious or political zeal that comes from technology debates, the most important thing in an open, collaborative community is delivering better solutions with reduced cost and risk for the constituents of that community. It is primarily this shared goal – as well as the facing the same problems and needing similar solutions – that drives eGovernment communities together.

There are many examples of such communities across Europe, often clustered around a government body or organisation that delivers eGovernment services or has the energy to provide thought leadership. Some prominent examples of online communities include:

- The Dutch Municipality of Deventer (www.kennisportaaloverheid.nl): The CIO of Deventer hosts an online community for sharing eGovernment solutions amongst the 10 or so neighbouring municipalities. Many users of the site are internal municipality employees who also appreciate the online collaborative environment.
- Ireland's Local Government Computer Services Board (www.lgcsb.ie): LGCSB provide eGovernment solutions and services to Ireland's local authorities, supporting 35 municipalities and engaging with over 35,000 users. An extranet site hosts a discussion board and solution sharing site with over 1000 regular users and contributors.
- UK's Local Authority Software Consortium (www.lasc-online.co.uk): The LASC is a subscription-based organisation that promotes eGovernment and champions solution reuse. The LASC's flagship solution is a CRM application that has been implemented in 12 other UK local authorities (with 20 more to adopt it by the end of 2004).

A key point to note of the sites listed here is their focus on the topic of eGovernment. The communities band around the problems of government (such as library management, or geographical information systems) and hence solutions shared are focused on the needs of the community. Furthermore, what is shared is not always 'source code'. In a departure from Sourceforge, the eGovernment communities often share learnings via discussion, whitepapers illustrating concepts, design documents... and sometimes code. The communities are necessarily much broader than just considering source code.

3.3 Principles of Effective Open Application Sharing in Collaborative Communities

Based on the observations drawn from a number of eGovernment application and solutions sharing projects (many of which are discussed herein) – this author proposes a number of critical success factors for eGovernment solution sharing communities:

- Face a common (eGovernment) goal: Collaboration is most effective when the stakeholders face the same goal (or problem). This stands true for all community activities and explains the success of smaller, focused community collaboration sites.
- Embrace thought leadership: Government bodies also suffer competitive behaviour (and ego – the 'not built here' syndrome). This needs to be managed culturally.
- Allow collaboration to grow organically. While higher-level decision makers may not consciously discuss or share solutions across borders, an online community can collaborate and grow from the ground-up, helping to break down barriers.
- Promote good solutions: The success of a community is built on the success of the solutions. Having good solutions creates momentum and credibility. However, this also raises the question of solution evaluation and how it may be done most effectively and fairly.
- It is not just about source code: The process of solving problems requires more than source code. Solutions may come in the form of ideas, whitepapers, etc.

- Ensure there is incremental enhancement: A solution that is enhanced through reuse should be offered back to the originator – hence creating a virtuous circle.
- Incentive mechanisms need to be explored: How can someone benefit from contributing their hard work?! Also, how can someone ensure they aren't harmed or criticised?!

It is not possible to explore these points further within the context of this paper. However, these points will be presented during the eChallenges Workshop to provide a firm basis for further discussion and avenues of collaboration.

4. Conclusions

This paper covers a broad range of concepts related to eGovernment solution development and reuse. A number of eGovernment projects that were successfully accelerated by the effective and efficient reuse of applications and solutions are presented. Drawing from the open source community and focusing on the needs of eGovernment practitioners, the term 'open application sharing' is offered as a broader concept (broader than just 'source code') supporting the collaboration of eGovernment practitioners.

Also drawing from the open development paradigm, different models of collaboration are explored. At one level, recognition and peer-acknowledgement (such as IDA's eGovernment Observatory) are key to the sharing of best practices (and perhaps more importantly – not making the same mistakes). More extensive collaboration models are also presented were communities of like-minded stakeholders could share, reuse and enhance a number of solutions (as well as best practices). The mechanisms supporting these communities are explored and success factors posed for further discussion within the context of the e-Challenges workshop and ongoing collaboration.

Visualize an extensive cross-European (or global) network of free government applications, architectures, white papers, studies, plans, references and developers. This paper highlights the success stories and the success factors necessary to achieve this vision of effective application sharing amongst governments.

5. Acknowledgements and Disclaimer

The information in this paper is gleaned from public sources and represents the personal view of the author on the issues discussed and may not necessarily represent the view of Microsoft or organisations referenced. Microsoft is a registered trademark of Microsoft Corporation in the United States and/or other countries. The names of other companies and products mentioned herein may be the trademarks of their respective owners.

References

[1] Albinsson L. & Östevik S.A., "Collaboration networks in Governments", *Workshop on Public Sector in Common Europe – Trends and Fashions*, 6-8 June 2004, Lofoten, Norway
[2] Boehm B.W., *Software Engineering Economics*, Prentice-Hall, 1981
[3] Bonaccorsi A. & Cristina R., "Altruistic individuals, selfish firms? The structure of motivation in Open Source software", *MIT Open Source Research Community Papers*, October 2003
[4] Brown A.W. & Booch G., "Reusing Open-Source Software and Practices: The Impact of Open-Source on Commercial Vendors", *Information and Computer Science Readings (ICSR-7)*, pp. 123.136, 2002.
[5] Favaro J., "What Price Reusability: A Case Study", *Ada Letters*, Spring 1991, pp. 115-124
[6] Forsgren O. et. al, "e-Service co-design platform(ECP) - an outline for an e-service exchange and development platform", *The First Scandinavian conference on e-Government*, Örebro, Sweden, 2004.
[7] Gabriel R.P. & Goldman R., "Open Source: Beyond the Fairytales", *Perspectives on Business Innovation (Issue 8)*, Cap Gemini Ernst & Young, 2003
[8] IEEE, *Proceedings of the 4th International Conference on Software Reuse (ICSR '96)*, April 23 - 26, 1996
[9] Interchange of Data between Administrations (IDA), *Linking up Europe: the Importance of Interoperability for e-Government Services*, Commission Staff Working Paper, Commission of the European Communities, 2003 [http://europa.eu.int/ISPO/ida/]
[10] Poulin J. & Carlson B., "The business case for software reuse", Computerworld, February 2004

[11] Prime Minister's Office / Italian Department of Public Services, *e-Government action plan*, 22 June 2000 [www.innovazione.gov.it/eng/soc_info/politiche_governo/egovernment_00.pdf]
[12] Meyers B.C. & Oberndorf T. *Open Systems: The Promises and the Pitfalls*, Version 1.3, Carnegie Mellon University/Software Engineering Institute, 1997
[13] UK e-Government Interoperability Framework (e-GIF), UK GovTalk Website (Library), February 2003 [http://www.govtalk.gov.uk/documents/e-GIF_v5_part1_2003-02-07.rtf]
[14] Note that there are many definitions for 'open source'. There is actually a common definition as used by the open-source community (www.opensource.org/osd.html). However, it is rather narrow in scope, referring most particularly to the kind of licensing used in a released product, and the rights of third parties to be able to extend, customize, and reuse that product.
[15] Numbers approximate as based on a project snap-shot taken from the Sourceforge web site (http://sourceforge.net/) on 29 April 2004
[16] "The Romanian National Electronic System was the only European e-Government application that received the World Summit Award (WSA) at the World Summit for Information Society (WSIS), hosted in Geneva between 10 and 12 December 2003." MCIT of Romania, December 30, 2003.
[17] The Avanti Toolkit won the IM2002 award for best CRM solution (http://www.elanconf.co.uk/im2002winners.php) as well as the Nabarro Nathanson Technology Industry Award for the Most Innovative Use of Technology: http://uk.fujitsu.com/news/awards/

An Evaluation Methodology for Innovative Mobility Services: the MEROPE Cities

Paolo FROSINI[1], Saverio GINI[1], Giorgio AMBROSINO[2], Jaume BARCELÓ[3], Gilles OSTYN[4]
[1] *Regione Toscana, Via S. Gallo 34/a, Florence, I-50129, Italy*
Tel: +39 055 4382427, Fax: +39 055 4382426, Email: {p.frosini, s.gini}@regione.toscana.it
[2] *MemEx srl, Via Cairoli 30, Livorno, I-57123, Italy*
Tel: +39 0586 211646, Fax: +39 0586 211777, Email: memex@tin.it
[3] *Universitat Politecnica de Catalunya, Pau Gargallo 5, Barcelona, E-08028, Spain*
Tel: +34 93 4016947, Fax: +34 93 4015881, Email: barcelo@tss-bcn.com
[4] *CETE Méditerranée, BP 37000, Aix-en-Provence Cedex 3, F-13791, France*
Tel: +33 4 42248314, Fax: +33 4 42607975, Email: gilles.ostyn@equipement.gouv.fr

Abstract: The main objective of this paper is to define a general methodological framework to support Local Public Administrations and other involved stakeholders in the planning of innovative urban mobility integrated services. Starting from the clustering identified amongst MEROPE pilot sites and secondly according to the typology, objectives, available data and resources of the planned intervention, the methodology acts as a guideline highlighting the steps to follow in each case. It also provides the appropriate evaluation schemes in order to measure the impacts of the planned services under different perspectives. The approach is based on the assumption that the most appropriate evaluation of these type of projects has to be quantitative in nature and therefore based on models. Application of this methodology will be provided in Lucca and Piacenza case studies.

1. Introduction

MEROPE (Telematic instruments for innovative services for mobility and logistic in urban and metropolitan areas) is an INTERREG III B MEDOCC (Western Mediterranean area) project which started in September 2002 and ends in September 2004 [1].

MEROPE addresses the use of ICT tools to support mobility and logistics innovative integrated services in urban and metropolitan areas and the development of related evaluation models facing logistics, accessibility and public transport problems from the perspective of the possibilities that ICT offers to improve their impact on sustainable mobility [2]. The goal is to reach a better awareness of opportunities and services in which ICT would be able to bring real benefits.

The main objective of MEROPE is to activate, in several urban and metropolitan areas, study projects, analysis and simulation for the use of ICT in innovative services for mobility and logistic [3]. At a local level MEROPE carries out the implementation of 5 studies and 8 demonstrative pilot projects in 14 cities or urban areas; most aiming to improve logistics freight distribution in urban areas, others addressing ICT support services to urban public transport. In the sites where the approach and solutions to these issues are more mature, demonstrative projects are realized concerning:

- the application of integrated systems of communication as a support to urban logistics;
- the development of centres for the remote traffic control and to direct vehicles to parking areas;
- the use of communication networks and telematics system to optimise services and information to end users;

- remote control of tourist buses and online system for booking parking areas;
- intelligent platform for freights distribution.

2. Context and Objectives

Goods distribution in urban and metropolitan areas is not often taken into account by local authorities, though it is one of the main sources of energy consumption, noxious gas emissions and noise jointly to private traffic flows.

Underestimating the freight distribution brings about not only a deterioration of the quality of life and a damage of the environment but also a reduction of city/metropolitan area competitiveness because of delays and high costs caused by traffic congestion.

The lack of efforts on the freight distribution and urban traffic management system is mainly due to the complexity of urban mobility and interrelated city management issues: institutional, city regulatory and mobility policies, political, social and citizens consensus, city operational and business processes, infrastructural/technological service organization.

Nevertheless the local pilot projects foreseen in MEROPE are in line with the set of answers that urban policy makers need. Above all the effort to apply ICT tools and to define integrated service platform is coming out.

From the IC technologies point of view, several projects have been started in many European cities to introduce and develop urban logistics platform systems oriented towards the freight distribution at urban, regional or urban/regional levels but the technical solutions have often an experimental and step-wise nature.

What is missing is a coherent and general-purpose methodology to be followed as a guideline by Public Authorities that are planning innovative services in urban mobility and traffic management. It is clearly a very ambitious objective to define such methodology. Nevertheless starting from the analysis of its wide range of sites, MEROPE aims to contribute to the discussion with this framework that had been developed jointly by Universitat Politecnica de Catalunya (UPC) and CETE Méditerraneé.

The methodological approach is mainly focused on urban freight distribution systems as well as the examples that will be provided.

3. Methodology

The evaluation of transportation systems, and in particular of City Logistics systems, requires quantitative and qualitative modelling of the processes in order to assess the related impacts. This is especially true for MEROPE actions, feasibility studies and pilot projects, where the system is planned or only implemented as a prototype.

The basis is the information gathered from the feasibility analysis of each site reviewed with the most recent references in the field. Objectives related specifically to ICT were highlighted, then appropriate approaches for the evaluation of each site typology have been defined and a cross-correlation between objectives and methodological guidelines have been also identified. MEROPE pilot site projects can be clustered as follows: city logistic feasibility study projects; logistic demonstration projects; projects combining city logistic objectives with more general traffic management; projects with the objective of implementing Information Systems.

The methodological proposal is based on an identification of the involved applications, the appropriate models for each application and a well-defined framework integrating the various models involved in each project.

The criteria are multiple and conflicting since there are numerous stakeholders involved; in particular:

- Public sector tries to alleviate traffic congestion and environmental problems;
- Private shippers and freight carriers are aimed to reduce their freight costs;

The MEROPE methodology, proposed also in literature [4], is built on key steps:

- Problem definition: identification and quantification of the problem to be addressed at each site is necessary to provide an objective basis;
- Evaluation criteria: identification of the multi-objective evaluation techniques must be used to compare the performance of alternative schemes (social, economic, environmental, energy consumption, etc.);
- Model selection: a set of ad hoc models for location of logistic centres, routing and scheduling vehicles, measuring the performance indices for the various evaluation criteria are available.

3.1 City logistics feasibility studies and pilots

As previously mentioned, the main focus of this work is on City Logistic related projects. In the case of the study projects, the proposed evaluation methodology for MEROPE sites should be based on a simulation study, thought the use of a software platform integrating the various models.

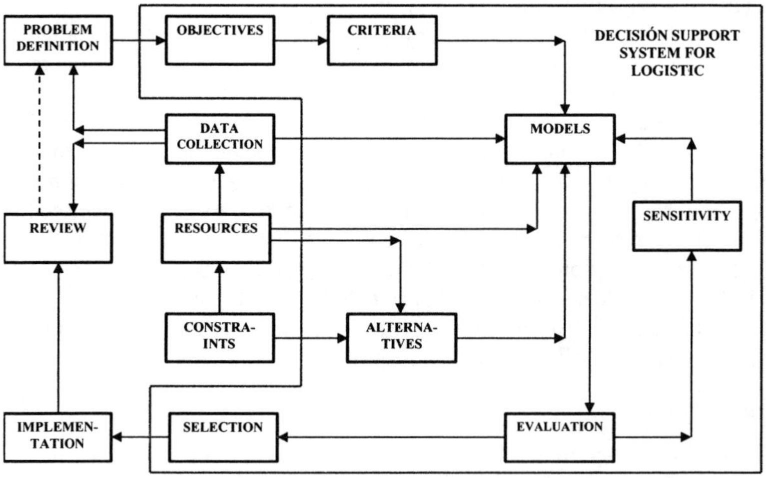

Figure 1

The highlighted area in Figure 1 corresponds to functions to be integrated in a Decision Support System platform, providing the user with utilities to analyse logistics applications. This methodology is based on the proposals of Taniguchi et al. [5] and Kohler [6].

The main components of a Decision Support System are the graphic user interface, Geographic Information System, database and related management system, model base and related management system. Models concerns plant location, vehicle routing and traffic assignment and simulation. Taking into account that many proposed local projects deal with goods distribution in urban areas, involving fleet management aspect based on the ability of a real time tracking and dispatching of the vehicles, the simulation models should be of microscopic type to allow the tracking of the individual vehicles. The evaluation platform should then integrate the vehicular traffic simulation with the models for vehicle routing and scheduling, as depicted in the conceptual diagram in Figure 2.

Vehicle Routing and Scheduling (VRS) provide the core technique of this approach in both case as when customers specify a time-window to be visited by the pick-up/delivery trucks and when the vehicle routing and scheduling has to be dynamic based on real time information. The information changes whilst vehicles are distributing goods and a sequential updating of routes should occur when new information is received.

The results from the traffic assignment can provide the basis for an accessibility analysis in terms of average travel times between origins and destinations or a support in the operational restructuring of the city logistics.

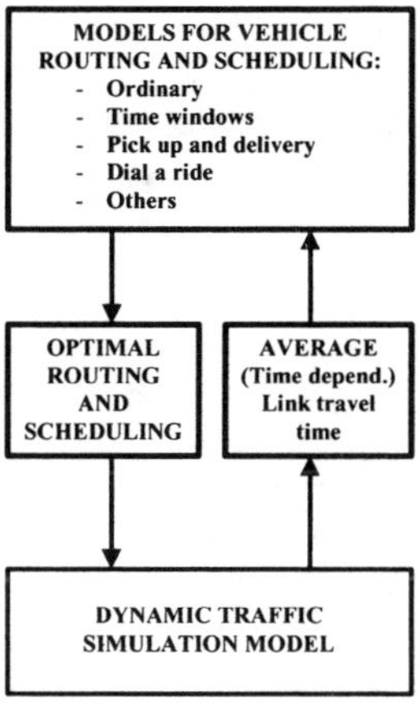

Figure 2

This methodology requires:

1. Build and validate a dynamic traffic simulation model of the site importing automated building of the graph representation of the road network thorought "shape files", digital maps, road maps, etc.;
2. Develop the model of the logistic application to be tested;
   I. Location of the city logistic centres
   II. Fleet management system
      a. Real-time tracking of the fleet vehicles;
      b. Decision rules for dispatching;
      c. Dynamic assignment of routes to the fleet vehicles;
      d. Client location: demand, service time, access time, costs (user defined/distance based);
      e. Other data: arc capacities,time windows, etc.;
   III. Performance indices
      a. Operational costs
      b. Delivery times
      c. Load factors
      d. Environmental indices
3. Integrate the logistic application into the site microscopic simulation model;
4. Choose an algorithm;
5. Design and conduct the simulation experiments to collect the data for the evaluation;
6. Evaluate the proposed system on the basis of the performance indices values estimated with the simulated data.

In most cases the strict application of this methodology can be difficult due to the intensive data requirements, not always available in the sites. In these cases the recommendation is an approximation of the requirements. A static traffic model, with average travels instead of time dependencies, replaces the dynamic simulation model. In a similar way the VRP is solved in terms of average travel times [7].

4. Results

The above methodology has been applied on Piacenza and Lucca pilot sites. Both cities have provided a digitalized background geometry of the map of the city and other ancillary information as the direction of circulation on the road sections, the number of lanes of each section and the lane width. In some cases data were provided in printed or graphic format since there was no availability of such data in a digital format.

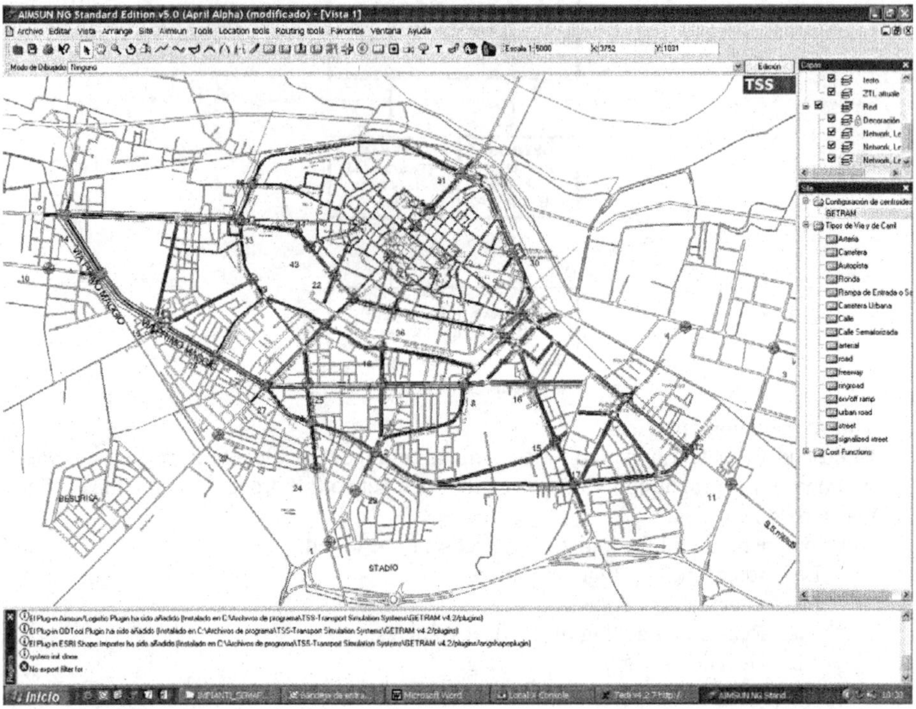

Figure 3

Traffic flows on a road network are conditioned by the traffic management schemes establishing allowed movements, and allocating timings to each set of compatible movements according to signal setting procedures. To ensure an appropriate microscopic model building allowed turning movements have to be defined for all intersections in the network. Controlled intersections phases and timing of the signals settings have been provided (traffic light timing, give way and stops rules, allowed turnings).

The model set up phase has been really complex due to the lack of appropriate data, and interaction difficulties among technical research partners and local public administrations such as municipalities and provinces. Thanks to the strong commitment coming from the MEROPE project rules and deadlines, many problems have been solved efficiently.

Piacenza simulation (Figure 3: snapshot of Piacenza model) results were compared with a local survey output and presented to Provincial decision maker for further conclusions.

Lucca outputs (see Figure 4: snapshot of Lucca model), included in a complete feasibility analysis about economic and social consequences of a logistic platform realization, have convinced local authorities to push this project development and start the deployment phase.

Figure 4

5. Conclusions

MEROPE project, through the interaction among the heterogeneous partners (regional governments, municipalities, universities, public transport societies and research centres), demonstrates that is possible to transfer and validate innovative ICT tools from the research community to the public and private stakeholders.

The outcome of this methodology leads to a better understanding of impacts and strengthens of local projects operations, producing best practices on ICT services applications in city logistic.

Acknowledgements

MEROPE (Telematic instruments for innovative services for mobility and logistic in urban and metropolitan areas) is an INTERREG III B MEDOCC (Western Mediterranean area) project started September 2002 and ending September 2004 [1].

Interreg III is the initiative of the European Community for the period 2000 – 2006, financed by the ERDF (European Regional Development Fund). The section "B" regards the cooperation among countries and it allows the realization of projects that aim a lasting, harmonious, and balanced development and to a better territorial integration in particular within the Western Mediterranean area, that includes regions of the south of Spain, France, Portugal and west Italy.

MEROPE project complies with objectives of axe 3 measure 4 promoting the use of ICT tools on the transport field and encouraging the telecommunications operators to act following the territorial development policies contributing to foster competitiveness and the economic, social and territorial cohesion of the area.

MEROPE addresses the use of ICT tools to support mobility and logistics innovative integrated services in urban and metropolitan areas and the development of related evaluation models facing logistics, accessibility and public transport problems from the perspective of the possibilities that ICT offers to improve their impact on sustainable mobility [2]. The goal is to reach a better awareness of opportunities and services in which ICT would be able to bring real benefits.

The MEROPE consortium, leaded by Regione Toscana, Innovation and research area, includes 12 partners from 3 European countries and 1 partner from South Mediterranean area (Morocco). The partners belong to a wide range of typologies: municipalities, universities, public transport companies and associations for research. The partners and cities involved in the initiative are listed below:

1. Regione Toscana: Firenze, Siena, S.Gimignano and Lucca;
2. Regione Emilia Romagna: Piacenza and Modena;
3. Regione Umbria: Terni;
4. Regione Calabria: Cosenza;
5. Comune di Genova: Genova;
6. Compagnia Trasporti Pubblici SpA: Pozzuoli (Napoli);
7. Federtrasporto: Roma;
8. AICIA: Sevilla;
9. Universitat Politécnica de Catalunya;
10. Govern de les Illes Balears: Palma de Mallorca;
11. Centre de Recherche Armines - LGI2P;
12. Centre de Recherche CETE Méditerranée;
13. Communaute Urbaine de Marrakech.

References

[1] Fiche projet, MEROPE Interreg III B project, n 2002-02-3.4-I-091

[2] P. Frosini, G. Ambrosino et al., Urban Mobility and Freight Distribution Service: the 14 Cities of MEROPE Interreg III B Project, CESURA '03, Gdansk, June 4 – 6, 2003

[3] G. Ambrosino et al.: The role of ITS in urban freight transport: The ALIFE project in Siena, 2nd ITS in Europe Congress 20-23 June, 2001 - Bilbao, Spain.

[4] E. Taniguchi, R.G. Thompson, T. Yamada and R. Van Duin, City Logistics: Network Modelling and Intelligent Transport Systems, Pergamon 2001.

[5] E. Taniguchi and R.E.C.M van der Heijden , An Evaluation Methodology for City Logistics, Transport Reviews, Vol. 20, No. 1, pp. 65-90, (2000)

[6] U. Kohler, An innovating concept for City Logistics, Proceedings of the 4th World Congress on ITS, Berlin, 1997

[7] The Vehicle Routing Problem, Edited by P. Toth and D. Vigo, SIAM Monographs on Discrete Mathematics and Applications, 2002.

eAdoption and the Knowledge Economy: Issues, Applications, Case Studies
P. Cunningham and M. Cunningham (Eds.)
IOS Press, 2004

Enterprise Workflow in a Public Sector Context

Paul JACKSON
Institute of Public Finance, NLA Tower, Croydon, CR0 0XT, UK
Tel: +44 208 6671144, Fax: +44 208 6818058, Email: paul.jackson@ipf.co.uk

Abstract: This paper describes the use of workflow technology in a public sector context. It reviews the experience of eight local authorities that contributed to the UK Government's National Project on Enterprise Workflow (in which the author's organisation was a key partner) and outlines the main business outcomes and project learning that resulted from the exercise. The paper shows that major process redesign may be needed to exploit the potential of enterprise workflow, leading to a general rethink on departmental roles and relationships. The paper concludes with two case examples that demonstrate organisational processes that were particularly ripe for enterprise workflow enabled change.

1. Introduction to the Enterprise Workflow National Project (EWNP)

This paper is concerned with the use that public sector organisations can make of enterprise workflow technology (the software tools that support the management and execution of work processes). It draws on the experiences of eight local authorities that participated in the UK Government's Enterprise Workflow National Project (EWNP). The author's own organisation – the Institute of Public Finance (IPF) – played a number of key roles in this initiative, including quality assurance, learning support and 'toolkit' development. The findings below represent the distillation of this work and bring together the partners' experiences over the 12 months of the project.

1.1 Background to the project

The UK Government approved the EWNP in March 2003 as part its Local Government Online programme (which also included initiatives on Customer Relationship Management (CRM), knowledge management and e-procurement, among others). Work started in April 2003 and ran for 12 months. The Project was intended 'to facilitate the development of enterprise workflow in a local authority context', and in so doing deliver: '...a range of published products designed to give practical guidance and support to the wider Local Government Community on Enterprise Workflow Methodologies' [1].

The Project was delivered by a partnership, led by Knowsley Metropolitan Borough Council in the north west of England and included 8 case study sites:

- London Borough of Bromley
- Harlow District Council
- St Helens Borough Council
- London Borough of Tower Hamlets
- North Wiltshire District Council
- Sedgemoor District Council
- London Borough of Croydon
- Poole Borough Council

The main 'user site' for the Project was Sedgemoor District Council, in Somerset.

1.2 Methodology

Apart from Sedgemoor, all the partner authorities were seen as 'proof of concept' sites. In other words, their role was to apply enterprise workflow technology to specific business areas (such as debt recovery and social care) and identify lessons that could be codified and shared for the benefit of other authorities. Particular solutions used as part of this included Staffware, W4, Anite, Oracle and Comino.

IPF performed the key role in data collection and analysis. This included site visits and interviews, and the creation of a set of web-based 'learning logs', which allowed partners to record their own thoughts and experiences, as well as share project documents. The categories for this repository were developed in workshops with project partners, who provided vital input in identifying classes of data.

Following completion of the individual 'proof of concept' projects, case study and interview data were combined with learning logs and secondary literature to produce an overall narrative and 'toolkit'. The toolkit provides a systemic methodology, intended to guide other authorities through the process of workflow decision-making and implementation. In compiling this, recognition was also given to the range of stakeholders that would need to be addressed by any methodology/toolkit – from senior managers deciding on the strategic virtues of workflow, to the IT manager needing to understand issues around technical standards.

2. Understanding Enterprise Workflow

It is important to remember that while the national project was concerned with workflow systems generally, it was particularly charged with the use of 'enterprise' applications. But to begin, let us look at a couple of more generic definitions.

2.1 Workflow - in general

> Workflow ... encompasses both a business approach and a range of technologies that enable the transformation and automation of processes through the electronic receipt, processing and management of work based on the underlying business rules and data needs [1]

This definition, while it does mention the 'business' issues, perhaps underplays the human element. To balance this, let us also look at a second definition that was used in the project:

> Simply put, workflow is about getting the right work to the right people at the right time – time after time (and knowing you have done so). [2]

Workflow thus involves human, technical and business process elements. It is also helpful to think in terms of the different 'dimensions' of workflow, and thus the different meanings that people employ when they talk about the subject. In total, three were identified: (1) workflow 'software tools', which operate as part of a broader (2) workflow 'system' (or technical architecture), to improve the way (3) 'business processes' (or workflows) are organised and managed. (See also [3] for a discussion on the important links between Workflow Management and Workflow technology.)

Workflow tools, so described, enable rules related to business processes to be written in to work systems, thus representing to rules or 'logic' of the process [4]. Such tools also allow for greater automation, both of work itself (the execution of tasks) and the transmission of work elements (such as an application form or report). A number of specific benefits flow from this:

- More responsive services
- Less manual processing
- Improved efficiency and effectiveness
- Greater transparency and monitoring of work
- Improved consistency and quality

2.2 Enterprise Workflow

To understand what enterprise workflow is we first need to understand what it is not. Most local authorities in the UK already use workflow functionality to support their operations; however, this is usually 'embedded' within 'line-of-business' applications, such as those used for processing tax payments. These allow work to be automatically routed and processed within a specific task group, and for work queues and other management data to be generated.

Applications with embedded workflow, while useful in themselves, are often poor at talking to other applications: for example, they may not allow for automatic links between the applications used by different task groups and departments. As a consequence, work is handled in a fragmented way across the organisation.

In contrast, enterprise tools and methods help join people and applications up across the organisation. This requires – and supports – enterprise-wide process management, something that helps to overcome the shortcomings of fragmented, 'silo' type approaches to management. Indeed, in a survey of existing workflow use by local authorities, carried out as part of the National Project, 56% said that their authorities already had initiatives involving multiple departments.

The benefits of enterprise workflow, over an above those of embedded systems, include the following:

- Enabling e-Government
- Straight through, enterprise-wide processing
- Fewer manual hand-offs (between departments)
- Process transparency at an enterprise level
- Easier organisational change

Enterprise workflow systems are intended to combine with (and 'leverage') other parts of an organisation's IT architecture, such as CRM and Electronic Document Management Systems (EDMS). Here, workflow can be described as 'sitting on top of' other applications - supporting integration between such systems and managing the flow of work and data between them (see Figure 1). Indeed, without workflow behind it, CRM solutions are in danger of being little more than 'message-taking' systems. In other words, in the absence of workflow, the front office (a call centre, website or one-stop-shop) may not be able to kick-off – or 'trigger' – processes or services, but merely log requests and pass details on (to the back-office departments that deal with them). For this reason, EDMS, CRM and workflow initiatives will need to be carefully co-ordinated.

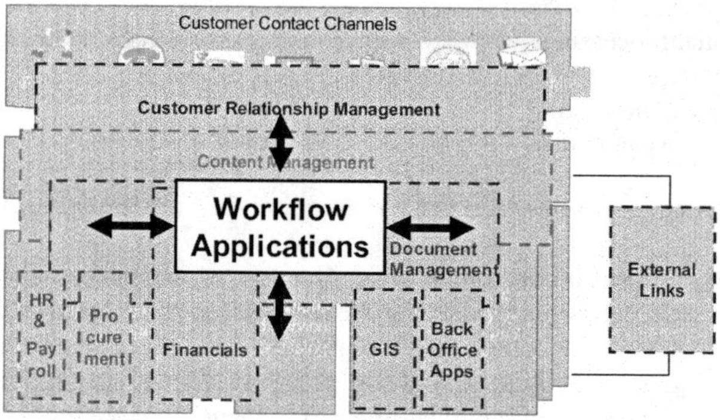

Figure 1: Workflow sitting on top of other applications

Enterprise workflow not only provides end-to-end (cross-department) support for process management, it also makes changes to those processes much easier. Embedded workflow systems, in contrast, present a range of difficulties when it comes to changing the underlying processes and rules. In a sense, these are 'hardwired' into the application, making it difficult for business users to easily perform amendments (who instead have to call upon the IT department to make any changes).

Enterprise workflow operates on a different premise. Here, a given application/user still carries out the work, but some or all of the process rules (the 'business logic') are programmed into an independent, enterprise layer of logic (within the workflow tool). This may even help to link together the embedded workflow in different (line of business) applications! Because such tools are intended to be configurable by 'non-techies', managers themselves should be able to instigate changes to process designs and operating rules. This makes continuous process improvement more straightforward and leaves IT specialists to concentrate on more technically complex and strategically important tasks.

3. Improving Business Process Management

Experience in the EWNP has underlined the roles of workflow in 'modernising' the execution and management of business processes (or workflows).

3.1 Workflow initiatives support BPR initiatives and principles

As the project found, workflow methods reflect important principles behind business process re-engineering (BPR). Firstly, BPR recognises that many process do not serve the wider ends of the enterprise (which may be slow and ineffective in responding to customer needs). Secondly, it addresses the fact that processes may also be inefficient, consuming unnecessary resources and being subject to low levels of productivity.

One reason why BPR has become necessary is to correct a lack of process design in the first instance. In many organisations, ways of working (who does what and how) have 'evolved' over time. The rationales behind such developments are often forgotten and may have become inappropriate. As a result of such 'implicit' design, processes are often fragmented, sub-optimal and even redundant. Certainly they are likely to reflect local, departmental needs more than enterprise and customer requirements.

To correct this, BPR exercises seek to redesign processes with process-wide goals and customer needs in mind, unencumbered by existing structures and ways of working. Having redesigned a process, workflow tools offer ideal support: work items can be logged and automatically forwarded according to the new process rules. You could even say that without workflow support, BPR initiatives are only 'half done'. The result will often be a quite different set of processes – more streamlined and with a different set of (horizontal) organisational structures to support them.

3.2 The horizontal organisation

It was recognised early in the project that the organisational dimensions of workflow would feature heavily in findings and recommendations. The conceptualisation of the 'horizontal' organisation – as an 'ideal type' structure in contrast to the classic 'hierarchy' – provided a powerful means describing the broader structural changes that would need to take place (see also [2]).

Figure 2 provides a diagrammatic representation of this change. It illustrates the problems caused by hierarchical/functional approaches – where processes are strewn across a range of departments and workgroups, with no one person having a single view of the overall process. This fragmentation of roles and responsibilities is ameliorated significantly in the horizontal approach, in which there is a clear view across processes (and sub processes), and who works on what (and when). And with workflow, of course, the journey of an individual case can be tracked through the organisation.

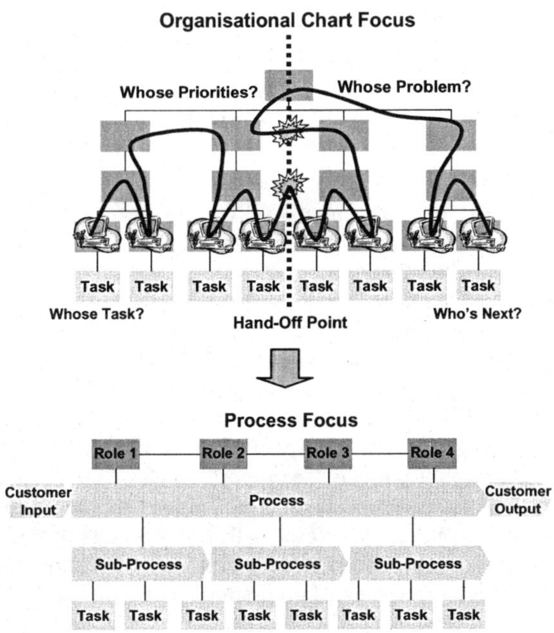

Figure 2: Moving towards the horizontal organisation

3.3 Workflow enhances visibility and control

Because particular jobs (or 'cases') are electronically logged, there is much greater visibility as to where something is in the system and when it is likely to be completed. This makes the flow of work, the productivity of individuals and groups, and peaks, troughs and bottlenecks, much more transparent (and in real-time). Such transparency is a boon to management control - and not just for tactical adjustments. Because workflow applications capture data on workflows (when/where/how items come in, when they are processed, by whom work is done, and how long it takes), it is easier to fine-tune process designs and resource allocations.

This feature of workflow proved particularly attractive in one of the partner authorities, Sedgemoor. In its case, a lack of transparency in its Debt Recovery work - caused by a combination of manual systems and isolated spreadsheets – made performance management extremely difficult. But before we look at that particular example, let's review the overall process of prioritising particular processes for workflow-enabled change.

4. Scoping and Prioritising Enterprise Workflow Projects

As mentioned earlier, one of the key products from the EWNP was an overarching methodology (which included the following advice and supporting diagrams) for guiding managers through the process of workflow decision-making.

4.1 Understanding workflow impacts and critical success factors

Despite the temptation to 'champion' its methods and technologies, we were also keen to ensure that enterprise workflow would be used appropriately by authorities; as such we sought to develop a range of management heuristics to underpin decision-making. At its simplest, this meant reminding managers that investment in technology-supported change is usually best approached by first understanding which areas are critical to corporate success.

Firstly, this means ensuring that workflow initiatives are closely aligned with corporate plans and priorities (such as CRM, as mentioned in 2.2). Fortunately, most authorities these days are required to keep performance plans and corporate strategies, which also help to identify the critical success factors (CSFs) to which a workflow programme could be linked.

Secondly, thought needs to be given to those organisational problems and opportunities that are best addressed through enterprise workflow. Typical characteristics here would include:

- A reliance on manual working
- Multiple 'hand-offs' (especially manual ones) between departments
- Poor management data on workloads and work items
- Bottlenecks occurring at key points in a process
- Missed opportunities for automation and parallel processing

Depending on the significance of a process to the organisation's CSFs, and the scale of impact on process quality that enterprise workflow is likely to make, it's possible to identify a short-list of potential projects (see Figure 3). Of course, such decisions should also be accompanied by risk assessments, and evaluations into the state of organisational preparedness for the projects in question (especially the readiness of the IT infrastructure to support workflow systems). To address these points – and ensure effective governance decision-making and change – a system of programme oversight is also required, as we will see next.

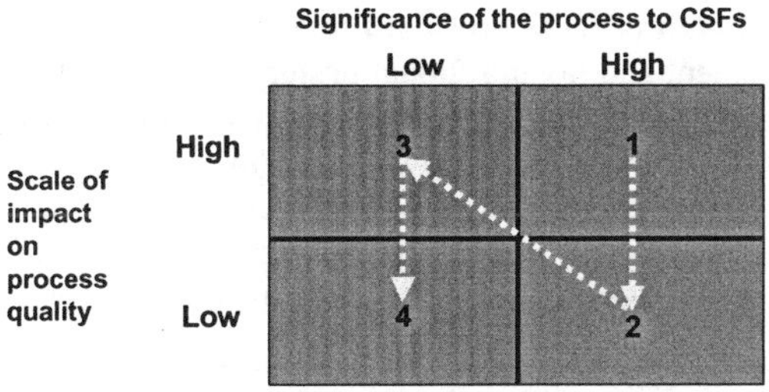

Figure 3: Short-listing workflow projects

4.2 Workflow changes in a programme management context

The approach adopted by the EWNP reflects best practice in programme management, in which there is a separation of responsibilities between the day-to-day management of individual initiatives and their executive oversight (see also [5]). This ensures that decision-makers of sufficient seniority are involved – and so give projects the authority and resources they need, as well as aligning them with corporate plans generally. It also means that project managers are free to concentrate on the substantive aspects of preparing for and implementing change, reporting to a senior management team (or programme board) at key decision points during change.

These principles are reflected in Figure 4, which shows activities and roles when prioritising and scoping workflow initiatives. This recognises the various constraints on decision-making, with the outcome being (1) a short-list of projects and (2) an overall vision, which are then put to senior management for approval.

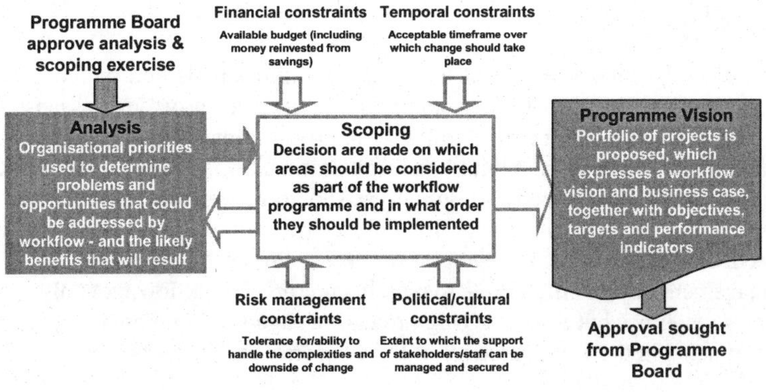

Figure 4: Roles and responsibilities in scoping and approving workflow projects

5. A Case Study Example

Having gone through the process described above (which very much reflects the project's toolkit), the main user authority – Sedgemoor District Council – identified two projects/processes as the most suitable starting points for enterprise workflow enabled change. These addressed (1) Corporate Debt Management and (2) dealing with Planning Correspondence. The shortcomings of these before workflow, and the plans for and objectives of change, can be seen in Figure 5.

Prior to the project, both of these processes reflected some of the classic symptoms of poor workflow management and organisational design. There was little use of IT, resulting in manual processing and paper chasing – including manual hand-offs between a range of departments. The use of enterprise workflow, linked in the Planning case to a Document Management system, allowed for a major improvement in performance. In the Debt Recovery case this also involved a centralisation of roles (with the number of people engaged in debt recovery predicted to fall by more than 50%).

	Corporate Debt Management	Planning Correspondence
Prior to the change	• Debt collection dispersed throughout a number of departments • No clear lines of ownership, and difficult to set corporate Service Level Agreements (SLAs)	• Manual process supported by Excel spreadsheets • Hard to measure individual performance or tie together related items of correspondence
After the change	• Form a corporate debt recovery team supported by workflow	• Use workflow linked to scanning technologies to automate document management
Objectives of change	• Reduce staffing requirements • Reduce amount of debt being write off • Quicker debt recovery	• Management visibility • Ability to set SLAs & targets • Automation of letter creation • Demonstrate link to Customer Services

Figure 5: Case Study Examples

6. Conclusions

This National Project has shown that enterprise workflow tools and methods can indeed bring improvements in a public sector setting. It also provides lessons for other organisations. These include the need to focus on process improvement across departments – something that demands a rethink on organisational roles and responsibilities. For workflow to be used most effectively, initiatives should concentrate on processes that have most impact on corporate performance. In addition, process modeling across the enterprise will be needed, with work being re-engineered accordingly. As with many such ventures, senior management have a critical role to play in enterprise workflow, not only in providing the necessary resources but also in giving project managers the authority needed to operate across departments in the wider interests of the enterprise and its customers.

References

[1] PA Consulting, Enterprise Workflow: From Automation to Transformation. Office of the Deputy Prime Minister, 2003.
[2] G. Docherty, Workflow from a Business Perspective. Office of the Deputy Prime Minister, 2003.
[3] W. van der Aalst and K. van Hee, Workflow Management – Models, Methods and Systems, ISBN 0-262-01189-1. MIT Press, 2002.
[4] L. Fischer (Ed), 2004 Worflow Handbook, ISBN 0-9703509-6-1. Future Strategies Inc, 2004.
[5] J. Ward and J. Peppard, Strategic Planning for Information Systems, ISBN 0-470-84147-8. John Wiley & Sons, 2002.

eAdoption and the Knowledge Economy: Issues, Applications, Case Studies
P. Cunningham and M. Cunningham (Eds.)
IOS Press, 2004

vCRM
Vienna Citizens' Request Management

Josef WUSTINGER
Vienna City Administration - MD-KS, Rathausstrasse 1, 1083 Vienna, Austria
Tel: +43 1 4000 75202, Fax: +43 1 4000 99 75202, Email: wus@mks.magwien.gv.at

Abstract: The paper describes the main aspects and functionalities of the workflow based system, which deals with citizens' complaints and requests. The name "Vienna Citizens' Request Management" (vCRM) was chosen to allow for the expansion of the idea and the development of a system for citizen participation. The paper outlines the development of the system and the reasons behind it. It shows the actual status and the benefits for an administration when applying such an interactive tool to enhance the Citizen to Administration (C2A) transparency as needed in a large city like Vienna. The system was chosen for exhibition at the Brussels e-Government Congress in November 2001 and for an award by the Pan European "Global Award for Excellence in Workflow" in San Francisco; it was a finalist at the Global Stockholm Challenge and was the subject of various presentations (e.g. in Lisbon).

1. Introduction

Austria's federal capital Vienna has approximately 1.8 million inhabitants. Like all administrations of large cities, the Vienna City Administration is also strictly task-oriented and structured in a total of about 70 Municipal departments with approximately 120 subordinate organisational units. Under the Vienna City Statutes, the departmental structure is grouped into several Administrative Groups, each headed by a politician, i.e. an Executive City Councillor.

Vienna is divided into 23 political districts also headed by politicians. In all these topic-oriented and politically structured areas there are contact points for citizens, who have the possibility to voice their worries and concerns, their wishes and ideas.

In 1978 the "Bürgerservice der Stadt Wien" (Citizens' Services of the City of Vienna) was set up as a central contact point for all matters of interest affecting the citizens. In 1979 this central service point was split into a mobile and a central "Bürgerdienst der Stadt Wien" (Community Services of the City of Vienna) to locate these contact points as close as possible to the citizens and to guarantee a quick response to citizens' requests through special mobility. Even at this stage it become clear that these different access possibilities for the citizens were an important boost to deal efficiently with citizens' requests, as the competences divided into different external offices and specialised departments represented a major impediment to co-ordination in dealing with these matters.

The continuous adaptation processes in the City Administration as well as the overlapping or changing competences of the individual administrative areas made real connections or networked treatments very complicated. The evaluation of these issues on an even basis was very difficult in practice.

2. Objectives

Therefore the following objectives were defined:
- Coordinated complaint management

- Identification of parallel cases
- Availability of information independent of location
- Similar complaints – one file
- Cross-departmental system with only one continuous reference number!
- Electronic saving of all data and documents (protocol, word processing, e-mail, scanning, etc.)
- Electronic workflow
- Usability for handicapped users
- Multi-language approach for minorities

3. Target group

The vCRM's main target group are the Viennese citizens and in particular those with requests, wishes or complaints, which do not match defined administrative legal procedures [1], such as "the traffic light is broken", or "our street is very noisy". A second target group is the entire administration in order to enhance the intercommunication between the different special departments (i.e., the department for citizen services and department for public lighting).

4. Methodology

In 1999, after several failures, an adequate IT system (ELAK – short for electronic file, Fabasoft Components) was finally set up and the decision was taken to create one systematic platform to process all issues, wishes, ideas, and complaints submitted by the citizens following one standard and to forward them in the electronic workflow as well as to communicate with the citizens on this level.

The networking of four departments of the City Administration, more or less represented a cross-section of the municipal hierarchy structure as a short-term goal. In 2001, after the analysis of all experiences, the City Administration began to implement its final objective: the vCRM integration of all departments of the City Administration, all areas of the city government, all district councils of the City of Vienna, as well as of parts of the federal administration (especially the federal police), the Vienna public transport system (Verkehrsverbund), the Vienna hospital system. This process is to be completed by 2005.

The networking also provided for the direct integration of citizens into the system offering them the possibility of directly accessing the documentation process with a status query. It was therefore necessary to develop a web-based application.

At the time it was already clear that it is of little importance to the citizens how competences and responsibilities are defined within the City Administration. Questions such as where, at what location and how do citizens submit their requests and in what form do they expect a reply to their requests must be adjusted to the citizens' wishes and are not to be defined by the needs of the City Administration. This, however, should not mean that open transparency in the system impedes the necessities of the administrative processes, which cause problems to the speedy processing of the respective case.

5. Technology Description

5.1 Technological Infrastructure

Software: Fabasoft Components
3 WEB servers, of which
2 WEB servers with 2.2 GB CPU each, Windows 2000 Server 5.0.2195 service pack 4,
2 CPU X866, 8,3 with 664 MHZ each
1 WEB server with 2 GB CPU, Windows 2000 Server 5.0.2195 service pack 4,

	2 CPU X866, 11,1, with 1396 MHZ each
1 Backend server	1 CPU 1263 MHZ, 135GB HD with 3 partitions storing the vCRM domain and the content data (Word, EXCEL, Images)
1 AIX server with	a vCRM domain, Oracle Database (for the storing of metadata of the Fabasoft Components i.e. citizen's address etc.)

5.2 Transferability

Our project is based on an object-oriented software product called Fabasoft Components. It provides basic functionality like Workflow and special functionality adapted to the requirements of the Viennese Municipal Council. The product offers the functionality of an individual adaptation of a project-based expansion respectively of the required functionality.

As a result of this implementation model it is possible to "deliver" the customised project as a solution package that can easily be installed on any Microsoft server with a preinstalled database environment. In 2003 this was done to support Vienna's Municipal Department 53 - Press and Information Services in carrying out its project "Wien spricht anders" to develop modern language and communication standards to replace the "Officialese" language of the Vienna City Administration. The replication can be compared to any server-application and is only limited by the Fabasoft Components license agreements. Our experience with the replication process is based on our internal test-, prototyping- and quality management-processes. Our product was the first web-based project implemented with the product Fabasoft Components in the public area. UNISYS undertook the customisation in cooperation with the Vienna City Administration.

6. Solution

Zentrales Bürgeranliegenmanagement (vCRM - Vienna Citizens' Request Management) is a multiple-access platform for citizens, government, staff and politicians. All organisational units included within the vCRM platform in an open system have access to all the data. Access authorisation in the system is defined through an adequate access authorisation and the definition of the access scale in the system for every organisational unit, user group, or individual. Citizens can submit their queries via Internet access and identify themselves using an ID number without having to reveal their personal data. The system can be accessed via public access points or by submitting the matter to any department of the City Administration - even though it might not be competent in this specific case. Replies can also be obtained via the same channels.

6.1 Interoperability within and between Government Agencies

This aspect is one of the most important strategic objectives of vCRM. Processes between and within the individual organisational units are handled by electronic workflow. This also includes the possibility of defining processes in advance, or, particularly in the area of *vCRM light*, to kick off workflows in pre-defined categories, which are automatically allocated to the respective area of competence for completion. The case officer can either keep the responsibility for a process and request a completion notice, or transfer the responsibility for completion or contacts with the citizens to other organisational units via the "allocation" function.

6.2 vCRM light

vCRM light will mostly be applied in smaller, easily realisable areas in which pre-defined keyword codes are used. *vCRM light* cases are structured in an easy acceptance process (automatically dispatched to the competent organisational unit with a click on a code list).

The case is registered in a pre-defined vCRM hub, checked for possible parallel cases, and automatically routed to the competent department. The department then writes a simple completion notice and routes it through an automatic workflow on to the vCRM hub, which saves the entire administrative process. The department can simply forward the cases to the next available possibility, which provides a simple solution for potential multiple competences.

6.3 Full vCRM Version

The full vCRM version currently only generates ad-hoc workflows. This means that the unit which accepts the case from the citizens collects and registers the citizens' request checks for prior or parallel cases, and forwards the file to be completed by an expert department or transfers the responsibility for the file and allocates it. This procedure, which is minutely defined for every administrative area, is jointly determined with the new vCRM partners in the introduction phases. The existing processes are therefore analysed in every organisational unit and, if necessary, are adjusted to the requirements of ELAK and vCRM.

7. Practical Results and Impact

7.1 Practical Results

Since the establishment of the vCRM we have seen major progress, particularly with regard to productivity gains. The automatic combination of various local observations submitted to different departments provided for the analysis and evaluation of large areas.

For example, if there are several separate complaints regarding smell nuisance in a particular district, the actual source causing the smell nuisance can soon be identified. Consequently the source can promptly be investigated. Public officials can find the causes faster and more competently because they are able to easily identify problematic areas.

Decisions can be made promptly. It is only due to the introduction of the vCRM that the Vienna City Administration has been able to act in a far more targeted and networked way, following four steps: Collecting, Identifying, Deciding, Acting. The citizens input their requests via the Internet at an Access Point or at home. These requests will be collected in a database (collecting). The cases will be identified in the back office and clustered into a classification tree (identifying). The decision will be made as to which municipal service is in charge of solving the requested problem (deciding). After forwarding the case to the municipal department in charge, the case will be handled and a solution will be found (acting). After finalising the request, the system sets the status to ready (workflow).

7.2 Some Figures

- 15 departments, 97 vCRM groups and 330 users were integrated.
- Volume of transactions processed annually: 50,000
- Processing time: improving throughput time from 12.8 days/file to 7 days/file (i.e. a reduction by approx. 42%)
- Effect on reducing administrative costs: EUR 317,000 in 2003 and 469,000 in 2004
- This platform ranks 3rd among all the Vienna City Administration platforms.

The number of transactions (50,000 without previous advertising or public announcements) shows that the citizens appreciate this communication instrument, and it can serve as a valuable feedback for the project team.

8. Problems perceived during Implementation

- The pilot phase was too long: it took a long time to convince the municipalities to participate.

- It took several very exhausting attempts to start implementation.
- The strategic decision to use it area-wide was taken only 4 years after the start-up (good for the quality of the system but aligned with more efforts for the implementation).
- We realised the necessity to develop a web-application (Win 32) after the roll-out.

9. Lessons learned

The implementation of such an overall system with defined standards for all, the simultaneous implementation of an electronic act, direct access of the citizen to inquire the status of the case, common statistics and starting to set standards for completion of the requests up to the financing breakdown demands exhaustive activities from all participants and the project team.

Most of the departments interested in participating in the project had already internally considered topics such as CRM, Change Management, etc.

Staff expressed certain fears concerning increased control through the display of the workflow, while managers were afraid that certain basic information was transparent in the system.

In depth roll-out was only possible after a pilot phase in one department and required intensified information activity (relatively elaborate).

Often only an in depth roll-out can convince the heads of the departments of the advantages. Only the conviction that the new ways also provide advantages allows for a meaningful participation.

10. Objectives realised / not yet realised

+ Cost reduction
+ Quality improvement
+ Equal standards for different areas of tasks
- Development of interfaces for many special information systems: the transfer is still not supported
- Very different standards and high costs

11. Innovation

The innovation of vCRM is that a system for collecting, processing, and evaluating data was created with completely equal standards on the same basis. On the one hand this allows for the fast acceptance, forwarding, and efficient assessment of the joint standards and on the other hand for a large degree of universality through the use of the jointly established reference code catalogue for each department to be able to deal with the citizens' concerns in the vCRM.

The respective cases can be shown online in the GIS (Graphic Information System) and can therefore also be presented visually.

The new advantages for the citizens are equal treatment of similar cases, shorter processes because easy cases are forwarded to the responsible experts, round-the clock submission of citizens' requests as well as faster and more systematical investigation of problem zones.

12. Conclusions

The vCRM (Vienna Citizens' Request Management) is the basic interface for informal requests embedded into the Vienna portal [2], which are submitted by the citizens to the Public Administration It has been designed to deal with individual complaints and wishes more swiftly, to recognise similar cases and thus increase efficiency, and to provide for the visualisation of problem areas in a system as complex as a city.

The application is being prepared for future Web integration following the WAI-guidelines. In the future, communication and interaction between the Vienna City Administration staff and citizens will be possible independent of time and place. The Web browser represents a homogenous user interface making the vCRM (Vienna Citizens' Request Management) application independent of the operating system due to its improved workflow. Citizens can submit their complaints anonymously and query the status of their case via the Web anytime. This enables citizens to submit their requests or complaints via home PCs but also via so-called ACCESS points (kiosk systems) accessible to all citizens at several locations in the entire city. In the future there will also be development and improved statistics by using the OLAP-Cognos Reports. Interfaces will be standardised and connections to call centres are to be established.

We are also considering the use of intelligent tools such as automatic routing systems, visualisation support for local problem areas, and personalisation tools for individual access demands.

The implementation of the vCRM, Vienna Citizens' Request Management, is a step forward to the extended idea of a CRM, Citizen Relationship Management, a system in which citizen participation is a matter of fact.

References

[1] Access to the system and further description http://www.wien.gv.at/english/vcrm/
[2] Main portal of the VCA (Vienna City Administration)
http://www.wien.gv.at/english/ (English version)
http://www.wien.gv.at/ (German version)

Kommunalnet.at – the Intranet for Local Authorities in Austria

Peter PARYCEK[1], Walter SEBOECK[2], Noella EDELMANN[3]
Danube University Krems, Dr. Karl Dorrek Strasse 30, 3500 Krems, Austria
[1]Tel: +43 2732 893 2312, Fax: + 43 2732 8934300, Email: peter.parycek@donau-uni.ac.at
[2]Tel: +43 2732 893 2317, Fax: + 43 2732 8934304, Email: walter.seboeck@donau-uni.ac.at
[3]Tel: +43 2732 893 2303, Email: noella.edelmann@donau-uni.ac.at

Abstract: The Kommunalnet.at intranet platform provides a "central-decentral" e-Government solution for all the local authorities in Austria. The platform provides horizontal and vertical communication, acts as an interface to other platforms, portals and business, and aims to support and provide a nationwide communication network for the Austrian local authorities. The intranet platform is based on a study conducted in 2002 by the Danube University to establish the needs of the employees working in the local authorities, and in October 2003, the CEO of the Austrian Federal Union agreed to the implementation of the Kommunalnet.at intranet. In this paper we describe the concept of a platform, which can satisfy both national and regional needs, its framework, the advantages for users and the long-term aims.

1. Introduction

The European Commission provide guidelines to all EU countries in relation to the provision of e-government services to its citizens. In federal countries this raises the problem as to where the real and virtual interface between the citizen and public sector is. Increasingly, it seems that the local authority can provide this interface, as they are locally and virtually nearest to the citizen. This is an important issue in a country such as Austria, which consists of 2,359 local authorities, a situation which could lead to the argument of not using the local authority as the interface. The same situation is found in Germany. Local authorities are also faced with increasing demands and tasks, some of them from changes in technology, which cannot be dealt with adequately. The intranet Kommunanlnet.at aims to provide a more direct form of communication, and to merge the information and services relevant to the local authorities.

In order to achieve this, a central perspective has to be adopted. The Austrian Association of Municipalities (AAM) has been aware of this since 2001, so a study was conducted [1] to investigate the Austrian local authorities' needs. The results (based on a 41% response rate from 2,359 local authorities) from this study were used to develop the concept of an intranet platform, which would offer employees working in local authorities the information and services necessary to complete their work.

The aim of this project is to develop an intranet solution, which provides a closed information and transaction system available to all employees of the local authorities in Austria. The vision is that Kommunalnet.at will be the local authorities' employees working space – one portal which provides all information, communication, services and applications required to complete all work.

2. Strategy

To implement this vision, it is necessary that each of the necessary dimensions - political, economic, socio-cultural and communication dimensions - are considered and have their own strategy.

Information and communication technologies (ICT) provide citizens with a new way of approaching and dealing with local authorities, so the very first priority is to ensure that the employees of the local authorities also know how to work with these ICTs.

eGovernment is based on organisational and technological change, and implies change for the employees of the local authorities. Citizens' requests will be dealt with quicker, information can be provided faster, processes are more transparent and the relationship between citizen and local authority will improve in quality. This means that the employees of the local authorities need to have the competences and the organisational, technical and social skills. Economic and political strategies are necessary to ensure the development of these competences. The political strategy will play the key role.

2.1 Political Strategy

Most eGovernment solutions have focused on the interface between citizen and business, the main aim being to achieve a process and method of transporting information without a break in the media used. These processes have not changed in the last hundred years; they have survived different political systems, industrial change and the beginning of the new era of technology. It is the Internet that has offered the possibility of fundamentally changing administration. The Internet medium means that entire processes can be changed, and intermediary steps either reduced or deleted. Extensive networks mean that eGovernment can increase efficiency that goes beyond simply reducing costs: it is the reorganisation of the countries' administrative structure and processes. eGovernment is not simply a technological component, rather, it is the heart of Government administration.

The eGovernment roll-out demands extensive changes in the processes and structures found in public administration, including a service orientation towards the citizen, an increase in motivation and efficiency of the civil servants, and a measurable decrease in the financial costs. eGovernment can also be used as a planning and organisational tool. But the political strategy can only be achieved by integrating it with the other strategies.

2.2 Economic Strategy

The implementation of eGovernment also needs to be considered from the perspective of the national economy. This new form of organisation will change processes and lead to synergies, which will obviously lead to a reduction in costs. But in order to develop a strategy, it will still be necessary to decide what criteria should be used to measure economic advantages.

A reduction in the number of employees is contra-productive, as local authorities are already confronted with problems resulting from understaffing. eGovernment does not mean a reduction in employees, as this would only lead to further problems and to difficulties in the implementation of quality service.

2.3. Socio-cultural and Communication Strategy

In recent years there has been an increasing need for networked and parallel communication and interaction, which reflects the one-stop-shop or one-stop-government approach. New electronic communication processes can reduce the amount of redundancy and maintain "knowledge pools" and ensure that "more time is spent with the citizen". It is important that the communication process be user friendly and that they can be understood intuitively.

3. Kommunalnet.at: the Aims

The aim of the Kommunlnet.at platform is twofold, on the one hand providing horizontal internal communication between the local authorities, and on the other hand, providing and ensuring vertical communication between the local authorities, the organisations belonging to the Austrian regions and the Federal Union. The success of the platform depends on quality of the information, service and usability provided, but above all, the extent to which it is accepted by the target groups (the users). This means that all the main content providers, such as the federal regions and their representatives, should be integrated into the intranet portal solution as partners.

3.1 Regional

The regional representatives are involved from the beginning, as they already provide information and services, as part of the platform or by linking their regional websites into the protected area of the kommunalnet.at portal. All partners and service providers are placed in the relevant areas of the portal and are to be clearly portrayed as such, to protect copyright. Regional differences are included to ensure that the regional representatives' and the regional identity are maintained.

The AAM guarantees the involvement of the local authorities and the municipalities. Local authorities trust the AAM, and given that the AAM recommends the use of the intranet platform Kommunalnet.at, the local authorities are likely to use it. The platform is also developed in cooperation with the local authorities, so their ideas and needs are included. The future user is integrated in the development, which means that the user will accept and adopt the platform. Similar projects have shown that if the users not involved in the development of an innovation will probably resist its implementation and use.

3.2 Personal

The portal automatically adapts to the user and the user's region following authentication and identification (sign-on). This means that the portal's layout is modified, for example, according to regional content and user requirements, thus reducing confusion and guaranteeing that the right information can be accessed. The user is able to access information and services at the federal level as well as information and services specific to the region. The intranet platform therefore follows a "central-decentral" approach, which provides relevant information at both the federal as well as the regional level.

4. Target Groups

The target groups and the advantages of this portal are described in detail. The main target group are the employees in the 2,359 local authorities, but there are further groups who could also use the platform. There are advantages for other groups as well, who will be able to provide information and services through the portal. The portal therefore also mediates offer and demand. The 2,359 local authorities will be the main group requiring services and information, and two main groups will provide these services: the public sector and the business sector.

4.1 The Public Sector

The Kommunalnet.at intranet provides the first opportunity for the AAM and the Austrian Ministries to communicate directly with all the local authorities in Austria. Until recently it was not possible to guarantee that all the information from the AAM and the ministries would actually reach the local authorities. The information available on the AAM's and the ministries' websites is often not ideal, has no context, is difficult to find and is generally not an ideal source of information. There is no "help.gv.at" equivalent provided by the AAM for the local authorities. Although the Government has reserved all the local authorities' web addresses (recognised by the ".gv"), only 15% of the local authorities actually use their web-addresses. Another option, also rarely used, is access to the Central Registration Office, which can cover most of the smaller local authorities' needs. Often, the local authorities are simply not aware of these options, so there is obviously a need for the AAM to be able to directly contact the local authorities. Kommunalnet.at gives the AAM the opportunity to provide information and applications, which will lead to an increase in cooperation and efficiency between public offices and the local authorities.

The Austrian ministries will work with the Kommunalnet.at platform, integrating their information and services into the portal to the extent they see as necessary. The first relevant sources of information will be the eGovernment services offered by the Austrian ICT Unit, so that the Austrian eGovernment strategy can be directly communicated to the local authorities. Services from the Ministry for Interior (Home Office) and the Ministry for Finances will be included in the platform.

4.1.2. Regions

Regional Governments will provide content and services, so it will not be necessary to build an intranet for each region. The regional Governments will be able to use the intranet as their own regional intranet to directly access and transact with the individual local authorities. The extent to which the regional Governments will use the Kommunlanet.at platform is difficult to establish at present, as this depends on the regions' prerequisites and needs.

The Vorarlberg and Upper Austria regions already have extensive intranets, while other regions in Austria either have a small or no intranet solutions. Each region decides on their own the extent to which they want to implement the Kommunalnet.at platform. The main advantages for the regions are that they will not have to set up their own intranet, and that a local authority can access a number of services from one platform. The regions mainly fear that they will loose their identity within the Kommunalnet.at platform. To counter this fear, the intranet retains the region's local identity – each region can, if it so desires, access the portal through the regional website and present the information and services in the way typical for the regional.

4.1.3 Austrian Association of Municipalities (AAM)

The Austrian Federal Union (AAM) is the main political force in this project, as it sees the intranet platform as a way of servicing its members. The Kommunalnet.at platform will make the Austrian local authorities the forerunners of eGovernment and provide a valuable contribution to the national eGovernment strategy. Without the support of the 2,359 Austrian local authorities, there will be no extensive eGovernment in Austria. The Kommunalnet.at platform provides its members a unique, innovative and future-oriented service.

As a central platform, Kommunalnet.at will provide local authorities with new procurement and purchasing opportunities. Kommunalnet.at will therefore also be a business portal with a market orientation and will be able to provide members with goods and services at better conditions. This strengthens the AAM's basis for business negotiations.

All eGovernment and business services will be available to all the local authorities. The AAM will use the technology presently available to contact the Regional Representatives and the local authorities directly, and help speed up the decision-making process. Interactive elements and services such as discussion groups, Internet shops, download areas, etc. provided by Kommunalnet.at and the AAM will be available on the platform.

4.2 Business

Through the Kommunalnet.at platform, business partners will have a central spokesperson and a communication and transaction system with which to contact all the Austrian local authorities. The portal is open to all business services. The services offered must provide the local authorities with an advantage though, such as financial benefits and it must be legal. The returns from this PPP business model could be used to cover the running and development costs of the intranet.

4.3 Local Authorities

The main target group are the 2,359 local authorities in Austria. The first step is to ensure that all local authorities decrease their information deficits. Information would be provided by the AAM, the Regional Representatives and other content providers – and be edited by a specialised team. The employees of the local authorities would have access to relevant and up-to-date information on a regular basis.

The services provided by the AAM and the regions, which are to be accessed by the local authorities, would be bundled and integrated onto the platform. These would be easy to find, following a single login. The single-sign-on identifies the user and the user's role and allows access to the relevant services and information.

The information available on the platform can come from a number of sources, for example, the AAM, the Austrian regions, etc. but information and services may also be generated by the platform itself. The main advantage for the user is that all information and services can be accessed from one site.

The intranet adapts to the regional and personal needs of the user, i.e. each user is attributed a role. The roles given to the users are the central element of this intranet solution. It is a platform that adapts to the regional and personal needs of the user, so that it merges different types of information and applications, yet at the same time recognizes the individual needs of the target user, thus avoiding information overflow. Different employees at different levels in the local authority may have different roles. The services to be accessed would include:

- Cross-regional communication platforms accessible to employees of the local authorities only (e.g. discussion groups)
- All relevant information to be found at one glance
- Special offers for members
- Access to the platform association
- Electronic balloting
- E-learning tools and expert discussion groups for new and old applications
- Electronic shopping groups

In addition to the free services offered, there will be services offered at a special price by business partners, such as project management tools, resource management tools, and e-learning tools. The aim is to provide these services on a transaction basis, as they may be developed according to the size of the local authority, and thus provide an eGovernment solution that even small local authorities can afford. All local authorities should be guaranteed the same possibilities to implement such solutions, so that eGovernment does not become a solution that only the bigger local authorities can afford to implement.

5. Implementation

In October 2003 the CEO of the AAM agreed to the implementation of the Kommunalnet.at platform. At the same time, the project became part of the official Austrian eGovernment Roadmap. This project is to be completed by 16 September 2004.

The first step is the internal development of the platform and the development of efficient processes for the employees of the local authority. They work with eGovernment on a daily basis and will be confronted with the different applications, so they must be able to work with the new tools. Thus, during the first step, the platform focuses on the employees of the local authority.

The second step will involve the national economy, and includes developing both mass and individual electronic administrative procedures. The main aim here is to provide new and faster processes. It is important to integrate the business sector, as there is regular contact between business and the local authorities.

The implementation of the Kommunalnet.at platform will provide a horizontal and a vertical solution, and an interface to other platforms and portals. It uses technologies, information and services already available, yet at the same time it increases the value of the Austrian local authorities and ensures the establishment of an Austrian-wide communication architecture.

The two industrial partners who will implement the technical part were chosen on the basis that they best fitted into the overall and the technical strategy of the project. They both have experience in developing and hosting platforms. The strength of this platform lies with the powerful user administration, which is responsible for the identification, authentification and personalisation of content and applications. The implicit OR attributes (these describe the hierarchy of the organisational structure) are: federal state, political region, municipality, and function (politician, mayor, administration). It is these attributes that are responsible for the regionalisation and personalisation of the Kommunalnet.at platform. The user administration also provides the management of the different applications available. In the next step, the explicit AND attributes will enable an even stronger personalisation of the user.

The further technical details, such as linking the regional websites to the platform, the provision and generation of content are defined in cooperation with the project partners (public and business sector).

6. Conclusion

The first phase of the project, as described in this paper, is political rather than technical. The technical concept is based on state-of-the-art intranet services and user administration, which can be designed and managed by experienced IT companies. The first, main difference to other, similar projects is that the target groups were asked in advance to provide information about their technical and administrative difficulties. The Kommunalnet.at platform is therefore based on data gained from the study conducted during 2002, where 41% of the questionnaires were returned. The second difference, which probably has the major impact on the project as a whole is AAM's support, who owns 50% of the company which will run the platform. There are two issues associated with this. The first is AAM's political power, which, with the Danube-University's know-how on intranet portals, could identify and satisfy the needs in the administration of local authorities. The AAM can use its political power to convince the federal republic and the 8 federal states of Austria that they adopt the Kommunalnet.at platform. Political power is also very important for the coordination of this project with other projects in the area of eGovernment. The second issue is AAM's recommendation of the platform, an important factor given the municipalities' trust in AAM.

In conclusion, it can be said that the critical success factors for IT projects in public administration, are primarily political and only secondarily technological.

References

[1] Parycek, P. and Seboeck, W (2002): Internet needs in Local Authorities in Austria. Unpublished study.

[2] Lenk, K., Traunmüller, R., Öffentliche Verwaltung und Informationstechnik, Heidelberg, Decker, 1999.

[3] Lenk, K., Elektronische Bürgerdienste im Flächenland als staatlich-kommunale Gemeinschaftsaufgabe, in: Verwaltung und Management, 4-10 S., 1 B. , 2002.

[4] Stabsstelle IKT-Strategie des Bundes, http://www.cio.gv.at/.

[5] Kooperation Bund / Länder / Gemeinden, http://reference.e-government.gv.at/

Personal Identity and Proxy Identities in Austria's eGovernment

Arno HOLLOSI[1], Larissa NABER[2], Michael LIEHMANN[3]
Federal Chancellery, Federal Staff Unit for ICT-Strategies
Ballhausplatz 2, Vienna, 1014, Austria
Tel: +43 1 53115 0, Fax: +43 1 2697861
Email: [1]arno.hollosi@cio.gv.at, [2]larissa.naber@cio.gv.at, [3]michael.liehmann@cio.gv.at

Abstract: The notion and definition of identity of individuals and of legal entities is essential for eGovernment. Although the area of identity of individuals is well researched and diverse solutions for a broad field of applications exist, acting by proxy for legal entities is still in its infancy. Even the comparatively simple case of identification of individuals, legal ramifications can add complexity to available technical solutions. In this paper we address the issue of proxy identities, signed authorizations (mandates), and partial identities for privacy and outline ways to bridge the gap between privacy and strong identification. We also present Austria's current status in personal and proxy identities.

1. Introduction

Like many European countries, Austria is marked by strong privacy and data protection laws [17][18][19]. While citizen rights and privacy laws are landmarks of our society, technological implementation of eGovernment is complicated by these very same qualities. Nevertheless we want to show, that basic ingredients of eGovernment, like citizen identification, can be compatible with privacy laws. Besides citizen authentication and identification we will touch upon acting by proxy, which will be a driving force for economic development.

2. Objectives

First we define identity in the context of eGovernment. Then we discuss why names or electronic signatures are not enough to uniquely identify citizens.

We next discuss how European and especially Austrian privacy/data protection laws are a diametrically opposed to unique identification of citizens. This leads us to the introduction of fractional (context dependant) identities.

Then we look at acting by proxy and discuss the three roles in that scenario, namely the proxy person (representative), the authorizing body, and the original holder of the powers to be mandated. Taking general conditions into account we define a data structure for certificates of authority and look at the life cycle of such a mandate, from creation, delivery, and usage to withdrawal and destruction.

3. Technology Description

3.1 Identifying citizens

An identity comprises a uniquely defined and maintained set of data that can be well distinguished for each person and that can be aligned with procedures - ideally without prior registration to these procedures. Such identities should work cross application and cross border.

Based on that data set, a unique personal identification number or base number can be issued. Many such numbers are known, for example social security numbers, tax numbers, or numbers of a central population register. Identifying individuals by such numbers proves to be more efficient and better suited for the electronic world than the name of an individual, as names may change (for example by marriage).

Before we can securely identify citizens, we will have to securely authenticate them. Section 3.2 shows how to use electronic signatures for authentication. Section 3.3 shows why signature certificate are not sufficient for identification and what to change to allow for unique identification. As the easiest solution is illegal, at least in Austria, we will have a look at how the identity link and fractional identities can solve legal drawbacks in section 3.4 and 3.5.

3.2 Signatures for authentication

Digital Signatures have all the properties that make them an ideal authentication vehicle. Based on strong asymmetric cryptography, it is certain beyond doubt that only the person possessing the private key matching the public key in the certificate was able to create the signature. Furthermore, the private key is protected from read-out in an SSCD (secure signature creation device, e.g., a smart card) [9][10] and can only be activated by some password, effectively providing a two-factor authentication method.

Having tied the signature to the certificate, we now have to tie the citizen to the certificate.

3.3 Signature certificates are not sufficient for identification

Qualified certificates, which are issued according to the European signature directive [1], contain at most first name and surname. They may even contain a pseudonym instead of the name. Furthermore, the same individual may have any number of public keys associated with him/her. Granted, the certificate authority which issued the certificate knows the identity of the individual, but this information is not available online. It is only available by a manual request procedure that may require a court order to reveal the identity.

Electronic signatures or more precisely the public keys for the electronic signature can be revocated or become otherwise invalid. Even accounting for this, the information provided by a certificate may not suffice to uniquely identify the person.

Numbers on the other hand have a 1:1 relation and usually have a very long lifetime. The simplest solution is adding a unique identity number to the signature certificate. This way the best of both worlds can be combined, namely high quality, long-lived identity and strong authentication. Indeed in some European countries it is implemented this way.

However, in Austria (and other countries as well) data protection laws effectively forbid the administration to use one and the same identification number throughout different databases. If applications are in different domains, they have to use different identification number systems. This means that the certificates cannot be stored in conjunction with the signed documents, which in turn could mean that the administration may be unable to verify signatures after a certain time, which is unacceptable.

The solution to this problem lies in separating the identification information from the signature. That way we have one data structure containing the individual's unique number and another one to hold the certificate information.

3.4 Identity Link

We call the link between the unique identification number and the authenticating signature the identity link [7] [8]. The data structure of the identity link contains the public keys of the signature and the personal identification number (base number) and is signed by a federal authority (or trusted third party). We have defined this data structure as SAML XML, although it can be viewed as an attribute certificate as well. One advantage of this construct is that it can also be issued for foreigners using their certificate authorities and numbers. The process of authenticating an individual therefore contains the following three steps (see Figure 1):

1. verify the signature and check the signature certificate
2. verify the identity link (check federal signature and federal certificate)
3. check that identity link is linked to the certificate

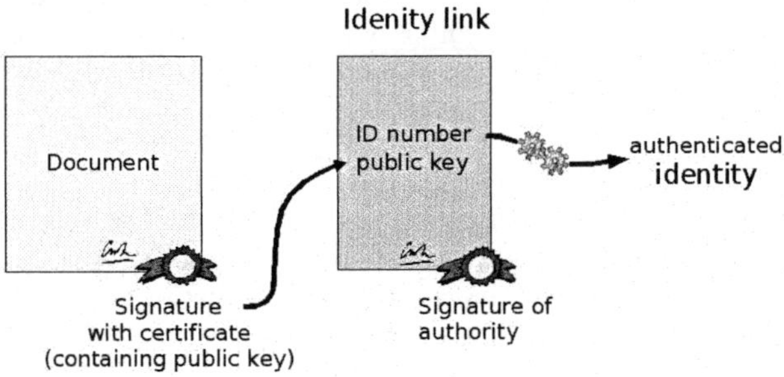

Figure 1: Authentication with identity link

3.5 Fractional identities

As mentioned, in some countries (like in Austria) unique identification numbers cannot be used across all administration, because of data protection laws. Therefore fractional context dependant identities are needed. Fractional identities are derived by using secure cryptographic one way functions which take as input the base number and the name of the context (domain) for which the identity should be generated [4]. The result is a fractional identity that can be calculated given the inputs, but where deriving the base number from one fractional id, or deriving one fractional id from another fractional id is impossible. These fractional ids can then be stored in databases without the possibility of correlating database entries based on these ids. Figure 2 illustrates the concept.

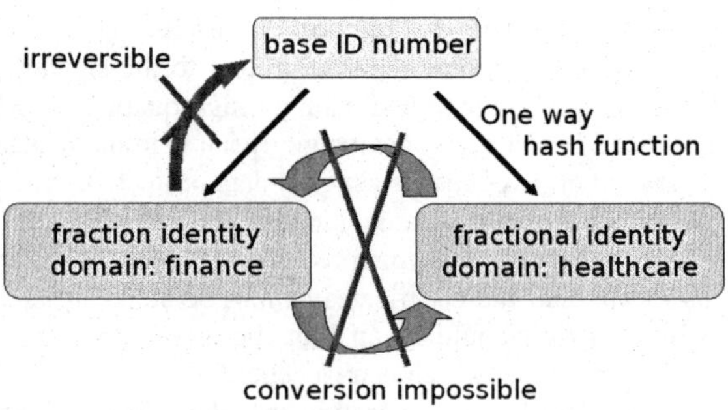

Figure 2: Deriving domain specific fractional identities from one base ID number

3.6 Acting by proxy

While the domain of single identities is well understood, we did not find much relevant research on the topic of acting by proxy, i.e. someone is acting on someone else's behalf. In the real world, mandates are used for this purpose.

When talking about mandates or certificates of authority we usually separate two roles, namely the proxy person and the original individual. In the real world, the individual mandates (authorizes) the proxy by means of signing a sheet of paper. The electronic equivalent would be electronically signing some kind of data structure. The data structure contains the identities of the proxy and the individual. However, such a simplistic model does not solve all issues relevant for Austrian eGovernment.

For one, what if the individual is in fact a legal entity? Legal entities cannot by their very nature act or sign themselves, but always act through a proxy. This is a catch-22. Another problem arises when the individual has no means of making electronic signatures. For example, how should Bob (who does not have a signature creation device) authorize Alice (who has a signature creation device) so that she can act on his behalf within eGovernment?

The solution is to differentiate the role of the original individual into the individual whose powers are delegated and into an authorization body that asserts that a certificate of authority is in fact authentic. By introducing this third role the authorization body can now be a trusted third party, such as the federal administration or a notary.

The data structure thus contains the identities of the proxy and the original individual and is electronically signed by the authorization body. Note that neither the proxy nor the individual actually need an electronic signature. This is relevant for the proxy when the proxy is an intermediary and does not act itself but by using another proxy. Furthermore the data structure contains restrictions such as area and time of validity etc. If the mandate is restricted by context, the identity of the roles can be further protected by using fractional identities instead of their base numbers.

As with all public key infrastructures, one main issue (and indeed its Achilles' heel) is revocation. Several solutions exist for this problem, none without drawbacks.

White listing, which corresponds to an online check, whether a given mandate is still valid seems like the best approach for high transaction systems. Credit card companies have proved this. The drawback is that one needs to be online when checking.

Black lists, which correspond to revocation lists, can be used for offline transactions, but they have severe drawbacks, mostly distribution issues and time delay.

Taking into account the cost of running such white or black list services, it needs to be decided on a case by case basis if the risk of using revoked mandates is worth the cost of these services. The responsibility for white listing can be shifted on to the represented person by including an URL under which the validity of the mandate can be checked. As running a web-server is out of bounds for a majority of represented persons, this is not a likely solution as of now.

A third method is to issue mandates with a short lifetime or even one-time mandates. No final conclusion has been reached on this issue in Austria. Currently our XML data structure is able to hold data for all three cases by way of precaution.

3.7 Creating the mandate

The following use case represents the case, where both represented person and proxy, can make use of digital signatures. Parties without digital signatures require intermediaries, e.g. notaries.

- The represented person prepares the mandate for the proxy. To identify the proxy he/she needs their name and birth date. Additionally the scope of the mandate, the period of validity and more information can be added to the mandate.
- The mandate is encrypted and transferred over secure lines to an authority.
- The authority internal signs the mandate.

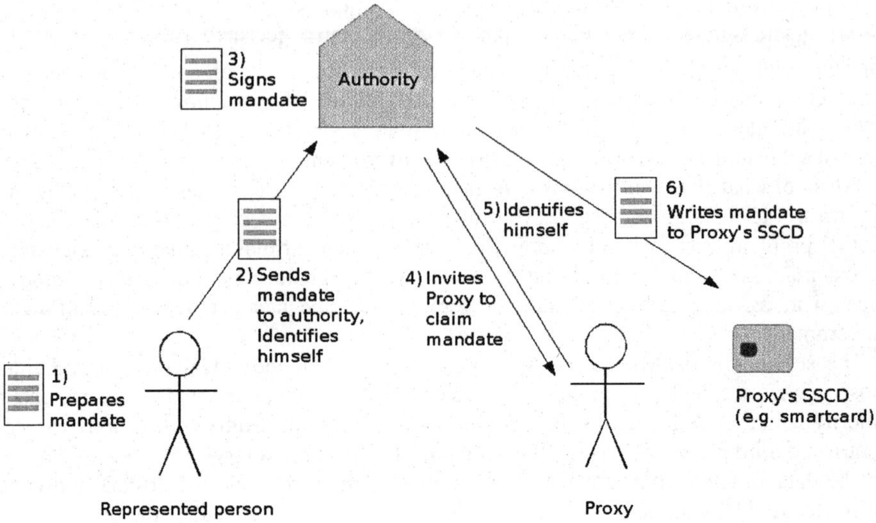

Figure 3: Mandate creation

- The authority checks the identity of the represented person and in doing so the authenticity of the mandate. Furthermore the proxy can be identified by using the transmitted information.
- The proxy is informed by the entity that a mandate is waiting for him/her to be claimed.
- After an authenticity-check for the proxy, he/she claims the mandate from the entity.
- The mandate is transmitted to the SSCD of the proxy.

4. Developments

Recently Austria made substantial progress with the coming in force of the eGovernment Law [5] on April 1st 2004 paving the way for widespread use of digital signatures. In addition to the conventional setup using smartcards and card-readers, a new type of SSCDs has been introduced, which relies on GSM mobile phone technology. While the usage of digital identities is still in an early stage, we are confident that the phone based identification and acting by proxy combined with interesting e-government applications (e.g. electronic delivery) to be rolled out this summer, will boost the numbers of citizens choosing e-government over traditional administration.

5. Conclusion

Identity management for large user groups such as the population of a nation is still a daunting task. Adding privacy and proxy mechanisms adds further complexity. In this paper we discussed the Austrian solution which is used in its eGovernment framework and which is coded into Austria's eGovernment Law, which came into force in 2004. We have shown how fractional context dependant identities can be created based on a unique personal identification number to enhance privacy and data protection.

Based on this system we have discussed the structure for encoding certificates of authority. We have shown that for an effective framework the role of authorizing body has to be differentiated from the original holder of the rights. This differentiation allows for mandates where either the original holder or the proxy person or both have no means to act within the electronic world.

The described framework will be implemented within Austria's eGovernment. Issues of revocation and further privacy enhancements still need more research, but we are confident that our research will proof to be viable in practice.

References

[1] Directive 1999/93/EC of the European Parliament and of the Council of 13th December 1999 on a community framework for electronic signatures.
[2] Arno Hollosi, Gregor Karlinger, Reinhard Posch: "Security-Layer for the Austrian Citizen Card", November 2001, http://www.buergerkarte.at/konzept/
[3] Reinhard Posch et al: "Weißbuch Bürgerkarte" ("Whitebook Citizen Card"), May 2002, http://www.buergerkarte.at/konzept/
[4] Arno Hollosi and Rainer Hörbe: "Bildung von Stammzahl und bereichsspezifischem Personenkennzeichen (bPK)" ("Algorithms for the generation of base numbers and fractional identities"), June 2004, http://www.cio.gv.at/
[5] Austria: E-Government Law, BGBl. I Nr. 10/2004.
[6] Germany: Gesetz über Rahmenbedingungen für elektronische Signaturen und zur Änderung weiterer Vorschriften vom 16. Mai 2001, BGBl. I, S. 876; veröffentlicht am 21. Mai 2001.
[7] Arno Hollosi and Gregor Karlinger: "XML-Definition der Personenbindung" ("XML specification of the identity link"), February 2004, http://www.buergerkarte.at/konzept/
[8] OASIS: Assertions and Protocol for the OASIS Security Assertion Markup Language (SAML). Version 1.0, April 2002, http://www.oasis-open.org/committees/security/
[9] International Organization for Standardization: "Information technology - Security techniques - Evaluation criteria for IT security", ISO/IEC 15408-1 to 15408-3, 1999.
[10] CEN/ISSS WS/E-Sign Workshop: Security Requirements of Secure Signature Creation Devices (SSCD-PP), CWA 14168 and CWA 14169, 2002.
[11] ETSI SEC: Electronic Signature Formats, v.1.2.2, Technical Specification ETSI TS 101733, 2000.
[12] ETSI SEC: XML Advanced Electronic Signatures (XAdES), Technical Specification ETSI TS 101903, 2002.
[13] ETSI SEC: Policy requirement for certification authorities issuing qualified certificates, v1.1.1, Technical Specification ETSI TS 101456, 2000.
[14] Efthimios Tambouris and Maria Wimmer: "Online one-stop government: a single point of access to public services". In W. Huang, K. Siau, K.K. Wei (Eds.), Digital Government: Strategies and Implementation from Developing and Developed Countries. Idea Group Publishing, Hershey, PA
[15] Roland Traunmüller and Maria Wimmer: "E-Government: The Challenges Ahead", in R. Traunmüller (Ed.), EGOV 2004, 3rd International Conference on E-Government, Springer Verlag, Heidelberg et al, September 2004
[16] M. Casassa Mont, S. Pearson, P. Bramhall: "Towards Accountable Management of Identity and Privacy: Sticky Policies and Enforceable Tracing Services", HPL-2003-49, 2003
[17] Austria: Datenschutzgesetz 2000 (DSG 2000), BGBl. I Nr. 165/1999, January 2000
[18] Germany: Bundesdatenschutzgesetz BDSG, BGBl. I 2003 S.66, August 2002
[19] Great Britain: Data Protection Act 1998, 1998 Chapter 29, ISBN 0-10-542998-8
[20] Rössler Thomas and Hollosi Arno: "Privacy and Trust in Distributed Networks", Proceedings of CMS 2003, Torino, Italy, ISBN 3-540-20185-8
[21] Leitold H., Posch R., Rössler T.: "Identification in cross-border e-Government", 4th European Conference on e-Government (ECEG 2004), Dublin, Ireland, June 2004
[22] Posch R. and Leitold H.: "Identification and Confidentiality for e-Government", Proceedings of IFIP World Computer Congress, Stream 10 - Security
[23] Leitold H., Hollosi A., Posch R.: "Security Architecture of the Austrian Citizen Card Concept", Proceedings of 18th Annual Computer Security Applications Conference (ACSAC'2002), pp. 391-400, IEEE Computer Society, ISBN 0-7695-1828-1, ISSN 1063-9527.
[24] Birgit Pfitzmann: "Privacy in Enterprise Identity Federation Policies for Liberty Single Signon", 2002
[25] Thien-Loc Nguyen: "National Identification Systems", Master Thesis at Massachusetts Institute of Technology, 2003
[26] Clemens H. Cap and Nico Maibaum: "Digital Identity and its Implications for Electronic Government"
[27] Roger Clarke: "Human Identification in Information Systems: Management Challenges and Public Policy Issues", Information Technology & People 7,4 (December 1994) 6-37, http://www.anu.edu.au/people/Roger.Clarke/DV/HumanID.html
[28] A.Fiat, A.Shamir, "How to prove yourself: Practical solutions to identification and signature problems", Advances in Cryptology: Proc. Crypto'86, Lecture Notes in Computer Science 263, Springer, (1987), pp. 186 -- 194

Towards Intelligent Cities

Steve CURWELL[1], Andy HAMILTON[2], Amanda MARSHALL-PONTING[3], Souheil SOUBRA[4], Rémi VANKEISBELCK[5]
[1,2,3] Research Centre for the Built and Human Environment (BUHU), University of Salford, the Crescent, Salford, M7 1NU, United Kingdom
[1]Tel: +44 161 295 4622, Fax: + 44 161 295 5011, Email: s.r.curwell@salford.ac.uk
[2] Tel: +44 161 295 5366, Fax: + 44 161 295 5011, Email: a.hamilton@salford.ac.uk
[3]Tel: +44 161 295 7056, Email: a.j.marshall-ponting@salford.ac.uk
[4,5] CSTB, BP 209, 06 904, Sophia Antipolis, France
[4]Tel: +33 4 93 95 67 23, Fax: +33 4 93 95 67 23, Email: soubra@cstb.fr
[5]Tel: +33 4 93 95 64 15, Fax: +33 4 93 95 67 23, Email: remi.vankeisbelck@cstb.fr

Abstract: This paper reports on the ongoing IntelCities (Intelligent Cities - IST no. 507860) integrated project, which commenced in January 2004, that seeks to integrate e-governance and e-urban planning. IntelCities is still at a formative stage and the paper seeks to explain the background, the research questions and preliminary design of prototyping studies to be carried out in the cities of Marseille, Siena, Helsinki, Rome, Leicester, Dresden, Berlin and Manchester. These prototypes are to be linked together to demonstrate an integrated open system city platform. The main business opportunities for IST companies and in terms of increased efficiency in e-urban planning are explored. The main outcomes are anticipated, which include a new public asset in terms of a city-wide intelligent information system.

1. Introduction

Internet access is expanding rapidly, with penetration into households across the whole of the EU likely to exceed 50% in the near future. As over 70% of Europeans live in cities, visions of the knowledge society (KS) are largely framed in an urban context in the form of information and computer technology (ICT) enabled, intelligent communities. EU policy has explicitly cast cities in the role of engines for change for regional, national and European economic progress. Hence, from an EU policy perspective, the interaction between cities and ICTs is expected to act both as the key driver and as the primary location for the delivery of the knowledge economy and society.

In this context the main objective of INTELCITIES – developed from the Intelcity Roadmap project in FP5 [1] – is to create a new and innovative set of interoperable eGovernment services to meet the needs of both citizens and businesses. This will provide interactive citywide on-line applications and services for users that will make all aspects of what is "going-on" in the city available to all, which will support:

1. the everyday needs and requirements of citizens and business through 24 hour access to enhanced transactional city services;
2. more efficient city management and administration by integrating functions and services across city authorities, regional and national governmental agencies, utility and transport system providers and citizens/NGO networks;
3. much more innovative and effective approaches to urban planning through more reliable electronic city modelling, using advanced visualisation and predictive techniques, which will enable citizens and businesses to play a far more participative and inclusive role in influencing how planned changes in the city will affect their lives.

2. Objectives

The main objectives of the project which address the broad requirements of an "integrated project" as a new form of EU research instrument include [4]:

1. RTD in terms of interoperability and advanced visualization for e-local Government and e-Planning services, including open system architecture, data mapping and integration, and indicators and benchmarks;
2. Prototyping and demonstrations in a number of EU cities in terms of e-Local Government Services, including enhanced Information Services, e-Transport Information and Mobility, e-Land Use and e-Regeneration, and issues of e-Inclusion and e-Participation;
3. Knowledge Management in terms of capturing good practice in the participating cities and development of e-Learning and capacity building modules for city officials, business and citizens;
4. Innovation and transformational changes in e-Local Governance for more effective exploitation and implementation in Cities and business opportunities for ICT companies particularly SMEs.

3. Methodology

The new forms of electronic governance are at an experimental stage in which learning by doing in cities is the key, especially for developing and utilizing best practice. In the project, prototype system development will test interactive forms of electronic service delivery over different technology platforms, e.g. iDTV, PC based and mobile, in diverse socio-economic environments. The underlying objective is to ensure that all the applications and services can be made to work together in a seamless and interoperable manner. At the same time the project is addressing key human factors in order to ensure that these approaches maximize support for social inclusion so that all citizens, regardless of gender, age, ethnicity and disability, will be able to use the applications and services in ways which will increase their knowledge of, and involvement in, the city. Ultimately the aim is to ensure that people can use these to enhance their lives and to participate more fully in the information society and the knowledge economy.

The five main areas of activity structuring the project – technology development (city prototyping activities), ICT research, technological development and innovation; knowledge transfer and capacity building; governance and business development and innovation; and project management and communications – will be integrated to develop the Integrated Open System City Platform (IOSCP). Stakeholder participation plays a central role in the project and is the major factor that drives the research design. The consortium's construction and structure reflect this and the cities will be considered as social learning laboratories in which iterative action research experiments will take place. Each will develop modules of the IOSCP through technology implementation and the re-engineering of administrative and planning processes that seek new e-solutions for advancing the relations between citizens, public administration and business.

The work is divided into three phases: development requirements and specifications, implementation of the prototype studies and final evaluation. The main project outcome is a prototype of the IOSCP and a detailed specification for the development and deployment of it in cities. Figure 1 shows the overall logic and interactions within the iterative process anticipated within Work Packages (WPs) 1-5. This is mediated by the current state of the art and maturity of ICTs and the possibilities presented by RTD in terms of the content and concept development of the prototyping studies to be undertaken. The user-needs must also drive the benchmarking tool that is to be developed and used in the assessment and evaluation of the prototyping pilot studies. Together this will ground the proposals in terms of realistic appreciation of needs and outcomes with all stakeholders and identify feasible development paths from the current situation in cities towards the IOSCP prototype. Each of the cities hosting a study is at a different stage of development in terms of eGovernment administrative and planning systems.

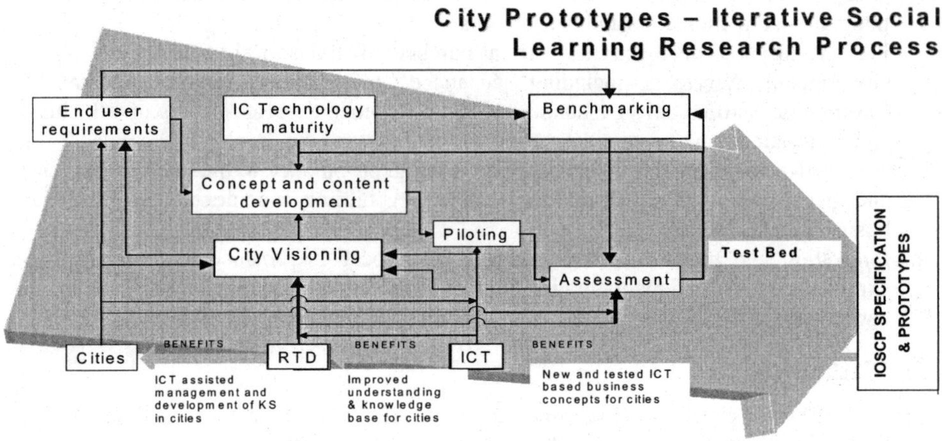

Figure 1: Iterative social learning research process

The evaluation points, at six-month intervals, address human factors in city and business process re-engineering as well as technological developments and integration problems identified from all the WPs. This evaluation is dependent upon the Benchmarking Model and associated indicators developed in WP8. Evaluation will include a review of development experience in order to identify and understand the development paths from each host city's "legacy" system towards the IOSCP.

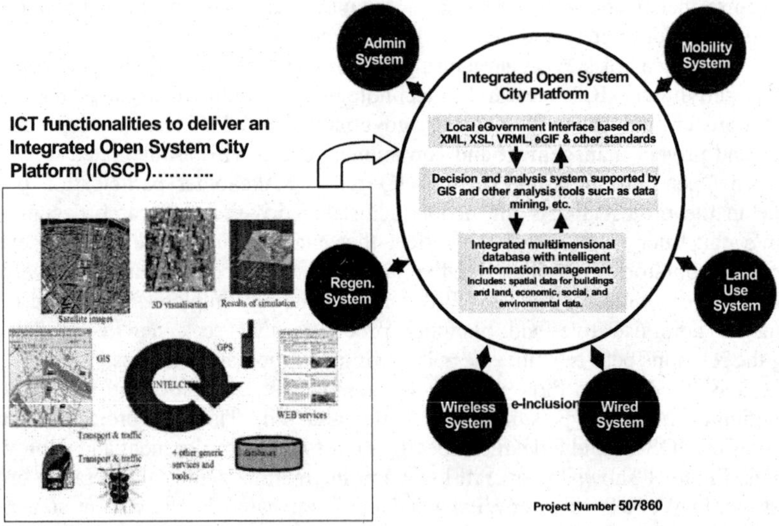

Figure 2: ICT functionalities to deliver an Integrated Open System City Platform (IOSCP)

4. Technology Description

The IOSCP will link local e-Government interfaces based on XML, XSL, URML, eGIF and other standards with decision and analysis systems using GIS and other analysis tools such as data mining supported by an integrated multi-dimensional database with intelligent information management. In this interoperability questions form the main technical challenges.

The overall system architecture is based on state-of-the art technologies for multi-tier distributed architectures. Innovation lies in the way these various technologies are integrated and used to meet the end-users needs. The challenge also relates to the federation of different domains and fields of interest (represented by the "prototype applications" in Figure 2) and integrated in the IOSCP. The architecture proposed is based on multi-tier distributed business components architectures (e.g. Sun's Enterprise Java Beans and OMG's CORBA Component Model) and takes into account Intelcities end-users requirements namely:

- Services distribution. IntelCities vertical services will be distributed over the network. End users will access the applications through a web browser, Wi-Fi enabled PDA, etc. Also, the services themselves could make use of distribution (e.g. parallel super computers).
- Heterogeneous environments. Services will be developed using various languages and technologies, and that they will sometimes make use of platform-specific resources. Thus, the IntelCities integration framework needs to support virtually any kind of application running on any kind of platform.
- Transversal features. The vertical applications will make use of transversal features that should be provided by the framework. These features concern IT-specific, "low-level services" (e.g. support for transactions, security, etc.) as well as "domain-specific facilities" (GIS, nD modelling, etc.).
- Deployment facilities. Applications will be "deployed into" the IntelCities framework to be made available to end-users. Some procedures and tools will be defined for the prototype applications designers to allow easy deployment of applications (Component Deployment Toolkit).
- Scalability, Quality of Service. The IntelCities framework should improve the citizen's quality of life. What if the system crashes or provides poor performance level? This issue is crucial, and has to be considered at the earliest stage in the project. The IntelCities system needs to provide quality of service and scalability features.

4.1 The "proxy container" approach

The proposed architecture can be described as a "proxy container" that relies on container-based environments, with the introduction of an additional level of indirection. The IOSCP needs to be able to integrate remote heterogeneous vertical services, and allow them to rely on our container to provide low-level and transversal features. The idea is to represent the services in a container, allowing them to make use of container-provided features, and let the services run remotely. All IntelCities vertical applications/services could then run somewhere on the network and publish their API, with no considerations for the underlying implementation, and be represented by a "proxy" in the IOSCP. The proxy would be the only gateway to the service, and would handle security, transactions and so on.

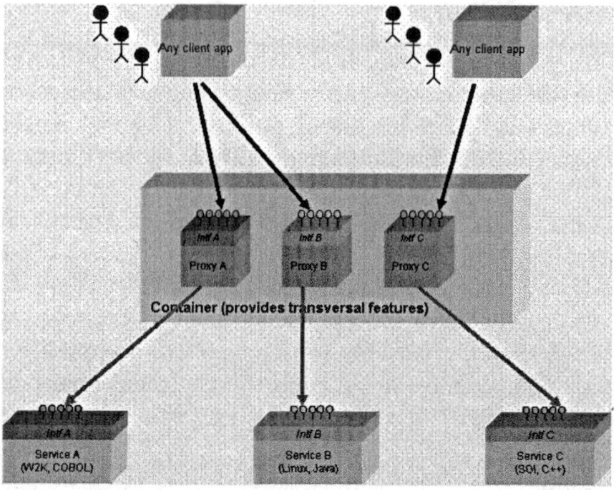

Figure 3: Proxy container – the big picture

In figure 3, one can see, starting from the bottom:

- The services developed in city prototypes (grey boxes). They are running on different platforms, and implemented using various programming languages. Nevertheless, they all have a common "property": they expose their business methods through an interface. The implementation is encapsulated in a non-intrusive way under this interface, and no one needs to know what's going on below. The three interfaces may of course be different since they address different business domains. What is common is that they are all expressed using a common standard interface definition language (e.g. IDL, WSDL, etc.), which allows the container to manipulate them.
- The red arrows show invocations of the services by proxies in the container. At the moment, the only thing that has to be noticed is that these invocations should be done in some "private" and "secured" networks, enforcing that only the container can invoke them.
- The yellow box in the middle represents the container. Its role is to manage the proxies for each service and allow their invocation by client applications. It also provides the proxies with transversal features.
- The three boxes in the container represent proxies. Each service proxy exposes the service's interface to the outside world (client applications). This allows the client to use the proxy as if it was the service itself, transparently. The proxy will handle the calls from clients and react in consequence. It could do security checks before the real method is invoked, start/end transactions, etc. The code for doing this is not in the service, but in the proxy, therefore this specific code is in no way intrusive in the code of the service itself. Last but not least, access policies to some of the transversal features could be done declaratively at deploy-time, "à la EJB!" The code of the proxy itself is not hand-written but is generated by container-provided tools (i.e. Component Deployment Toolkit).
- Last (upper) level is where client applications come into the scene. These end-user applications could be web-based (accessed through a web browser), running on PDAs or whatever. They are "client" applications in the sense that they use the services (transparently through their proxies) of the IntelCities framework. Typically, these applications will be Graphical User Interfaces and more generally they will concern the presentation layer of multi-tier applications, business logic and resources being handled by the service itself.

5. Developments

As already explored in the methodology section above the project will carry out a number of prototyping studies as shown in Table 1. Due to limited space the development of one of these – No. 5 e-Regeneration (the Manchester case) is explored in more detail below.

Table 1: Nature of the prototyping studies in WPs 1-5.

WP	Main City location	Main Focus	ICT Platform & Development	Main Questions	Anticipated Outcomes
1. e-Admin	Marseille	Nature and provision of Local Administrative Services	Enhanced Web systems and formats	Future possibilities of advance web based services	Development and migration routes from existing web services
2a e-Inclusion (wired)	Siena	New and more inclusive ways of working – expanding use of existing wired system	Technical enhancement of existing broadband multi-media system	Steps towards expanding use and e-participation	Detailed understanding of economics and use factors of TV/ set-top-box potentialities.
2b e-Participation (wireless)	Helsinki	Initial community experiments via mobile interaction	Development of mobile devices and software	Role of mobile interfaces in local participation	Preliminary understanding of mobile devices for e-participation
3. e-Mobility & Transport	Rome & Leicester	Real-time mobility information services	Technical integration of transport information systems	Possibilities+ functionality of mobility information service	Understanding of technical integration problems and solutions
4 e-Land Use Information	Dresden + others	e-Broker land use information system	Integration of and open access to GIS systems and data.	Development towards open GIS system(s)	Understanding role and potential of urban GIS
5 e-Regeneration	Manchester	e-planning (Inclusive strategic planning and development control)	Integrating nD data bases + GIS/VR & Internet	Appropriate systems and ways of working for community decision-making	Development of stakeholder ownership of plans and programmes

5.1 Manchester Prototype

From the perspective of Intelcities there are 2 significant factors in the Manchester experience. Firstly, Manchester has a long and strong tradition of support for the non-statutory sector and encourages community involvement. The means of undertaking community engagement and the success of these initiatives has varied but it is politically encouraged. Secondly there is an equally strong tradition of supporting the use of ICT in business and community development. This goes back over 13 years with the launch of the Manchester Host – the UK's first ever public access integrated email, bulletin board and online database service in 1991, through the launch of the Electronic Village Halls in 1992, the Manchester Community Information Network in 1994 and the Manchester Digital Development Agency (MDDA) in 2003.

Workpackage 5 focuses on urban regeneration in Manchester as it relates to the post industrial city moving into the knowledge economy, including physical, social and economic aspects together with their interdependencies and how emerging ICTs can be configured to support this. The Manchester Regeneration Statement [2] places the council policy within a strategic framework and explains how that policy will be executed. This takes an holistic approach, encompassing relatively rapid and large-scale change across the physical, economic and social landscape of an area. Potentially there are multiple impacts to factor into any decision-making structure and a range of issues to be addressed in developing regeneration programs and evaluating their success. Thus involving stakeholders in the decision-making process is a challenge. The e-Regeneration systems will be designed and tested to support stakeholder decision-making with a particular emphasis on the support of citizens. Issues such as strategic planning, development planning and accessibility are also being addressed.

Development planning is both an analytical and visual process. Also there is a need for communication within the design team and between the design team and all other stakeholders. These requirements can be met by systems that closely link analytical modelling (based on GIS technology) and visual modelling (based on VR technology) accessible over the Internet. In research work over the last 6 years at the University of Salford a system has been specifically designed to support public participation in urban planning via the Internet by integrating VR and GIS technologies. The prototype study involves the deployment of this system in a regeneration area in East Manchester.

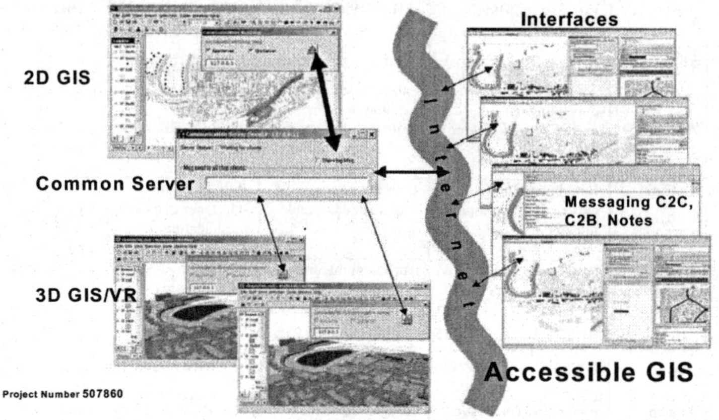

Figure 4: GIS and VR integrated and delivered over the Internet

Strategic planning systems for the City will be provided by Manchester University and will incorporate aspects considered important by the City. The model will be used to predict possible city futures. The city will work with CISCO to identify and evaluate technological and social solutions to support social and economic inclusion covering access in the home (via PC and iDTV) and in community locations.

Individuals and community groups will use the e-planning system to explore proposed redevelopment (e.g. a new school or some shops) in both 2D and 3D environments (3D is especially suitable for the lay person). They will be able to discuss issues about the plans with other residents, community leaders, and planners using email, chat, web discussion, etc. A feature will be the ability to leave messages in the 3D environment (e.g. controlled road crossing needed here for new school). These messages will be represented by icons in the 3D environment (and stored in the system database) to be read by all future visitors to the e-Planning system. Other systems have been developed that address some of the issues discussed in this paper but none provide the holistic view for all stakeholders in the same way as Intelcities. In this way the Manchester prototype study will examine the potentials and impacts of the system.

6. Business Benefits and Challenges

In order to address the challenges referred to in this paper the project brings together 18 cities, led by Manchester and Siena, with 20 ICT companies including Nokia and CISCO and 36 research groups to pool advanced knowledge and experience of electronic government development, interoperability, virtual planning systems and citizen participation from across Europe. This critical mass of partners will enable the project to explore new forms of public private partnerships in the development and provision of the IOSCP as the basis for the intelligent city of the future.

The integrated e-planning system(s) described above support complex multi-stakeholder problem-solving linking environmental science, city society, industry and businesses. They harnesses nD modelling, visualisation and simulation and knowledge management resources from cities and researchers across Europe and bring them to the desktop or mobile interface of any planner, politician, architect, engineer, utility and transport service provider and most importantly to each citizen. This provides important business opportunities for ICT companies, including the established players and SMEs, in terms of new interfaces and software as well as extending the market for current and close to market devices. Also, because of the complexity of the urban planning problem, development control is often characterised by protracted and adversarial decision-making processes that provide significant disincentives to inward investment, undermining business confidence and competitiveness. The e-planning processes and ICTs under development will re-engineer urban re/development planning in order to accelerate urban development control decision-making. In this way the social learning experiments underway will start to address the uncertainties over community reaction to proposals and how inward investment can be secured for more sustainable growth, urban regeneration and improved competitiveness of cities, and their constituent businesses components.

The exploration of user needs has highlighted that fact that use of eGovernment portals is not the first place that citizen's turn to solve urban problems or express their views on local planning issues. There is a need to define and populate the local "virtual space". Thus the broader societal challenges of e-Participation and of "trust and confidence" and individual rights are emerging as the most significant barriers. This means that the knowledge management dimensions of the project through the creation of a "learning city" environment will have to supply a deeply supportive and very user-fiendly interfaces for e-skills learning and development.

7. Conclusions

The IOSCP will enable a more intelligible and intelligent city, directly related to the major eGovernment drivers aimed at supporting achievement of a Knowledge Society by 2010 [3]:

1. Delivery of a more streamlined city government, city management and urban regeneration processes, aimed at achieving more efficient use of city facilities and resources and improve the economic competitiveness of cities.
2. Improved experience and good practice over "virtual" interaction between business, developers, local administration and citizens – the 'e-Agora' [1], to promote social inclusion, extend citizenship and "ownership" of plans and proposals.
3. Promoting the concept a NEW form of public asset – not just as the basis for delivery of a wide range of integrated services but as a 'one-stop' intelligent metropolitan information infrastructure as the platform to secure institutional and government knowledge, that citizens value and are prepared to pay for (e.g. through pay on demand and/or through local taxes)

References

[1] www.scri.salford.ac.uk/intelcity/
[2] www.manchester.gov.uk/regen/statement
[3] Zobel, R., Director: Components, Sub-systems and applications, DG INFOSOC, European Commission at eGovenment Information Day, 7th February 03.
[4] www.intelcitiesproject.com

eAdoption and the Knowledge Economy: Issues, Applications, Case Studies
P. Cunningham and M. Cunningham (Eds.)
IOS Press, 2004

PAPÁS, Advanced Services for the Educational Community

Miguel CAMACHO[1], Victoria FERNÁNDEZ [2], Ana CONDE[3], José MENA[4]
SADIEL, S.A., C/ Isaac Newton s/n, Seville, 41092, Spain
Tel: +34 95 5043600, Fax: +34 95 5043600 Email: [1]mcamacho@sadiel.es, [2]vfernandez@sadiel.es, [3]aconde@sadiel.es, [4]jmena@sadiel.es

Abstract: PAPÁS, PArtnership of PArents and Schools, is a web-based application that allows Public Administrations to play a key-role in the advent of e-Society. PAPÁS makes it possible for EU Citizens to interact with the Educational Administrative Bodies on a one-to-one basis, allowing a comprehensive follow-up of their children's education in a ubiquitous, interactive and multilingual manner. This goal is achieved thanks to a wide portfolio of services, including e-Administration, educational follow-up and socio-educational services, that are accessible through the PAPÁS platform. PAPÁS is the key element for the implementation of an Advanced Management Model of Web-based Educational Services, that benefits not only the Educational Administration, but also Schools and Homes. This paper gives an overview of PAPÁS' success story, from its initial conception, closely related to the Spanish case, to its current implementation status, after the internationalisation of the solution and its customisation. The services offered, the technical approach and the benefits for the education network will be specially highlighted.

1. Introduction

The PAPÁS project focuses on optimising the relationship between Public Administration and Citizens in the field of Education, by means of making the most of the new Information Society Technologies. This is achieved by the development of a common platform that not only manages information and administrative processes, such as applications for admission or for grants, but also enables alternative means of communication between schools and homes, via Internet or mobile telephony (SMS and WAP).

1.1 State of the Art

The Education Network is a complex system involving a wide amount of actors (students, parents, teachers and staff belonging to departments at different levels of the Public Administration), which altogether represent a significant percentage of the population. For this reason, the quality of the Educational Services as perceived by all the actors involved has a very strong impact in our Society.

The management of schools and educational centres and the immediate availability of detailed and reliable information on their status are two of the main concerns of the Educational Administration since their planning capacity depends directly on them.

The current technological situation in the educational domain in Europe shows that back-office applications are being developed and are being initially deployed, although most only address a limited set of internal managerial tasks and services. Nowadays, the objectives of applications such as the one that PAPÁS is proposing are considered by many as R&D, since fully established back-office services need to be running with a full infrastructure in order to be able to provide optimal Front-Office Services.

Traditional school management systems are based on a distributed infrastructure, with local databases and applications that result in a very heterogeneous scenario. This implies that many schools are using several management systems, with very different user interfaces, for their different needs. The use of local systems also implies problems caused by software distribution and updating. The usability of these solutions varies depending on the human and material resources available and on the technical maturity reached by each school, thus producing a digital gap.

Besides, the compilation of data and its analysis for statistical purposes is currently very expensive and time-consuming, due to the fact that data related to academic management is distributed among different systems, the information sources are not synchronised and the transfer of information between School Centres and the Administration takes place by means of disks and paper files.

The development of the ICT allows the evolution from the above described situation into a new scenario, in which Advanced Services for Educational Management are being developed, making it possible the creation of Integrated/Centralised Systems, avoiding hence problems related to the information's updating, distribution and consolidation, and making it possible to count on high quality information that allows for a better knowledge of the citizen's needs.

1.2 The need for a solution

Due to the dimension and the complexity of the community it serves, the Administration is spending a huge amount of resources to guarantee the provision of services to all the agents of the Educational Community (that is, parents, students, teachers and managing and administrative staff), and to ensure the homogeneity and the reliability of the services provided. This makes the need of a continuous internal optimisation process, to achieve top efficiency on the one hand and higher standards in education on the other.

In the meantime, Internet is no longer a futuristic vision, it is a common element in many people's everyday life and the number of homes connected to it is increasing constantly. Citizens are taking advantage of the current ICT sector development status, and they are increasingly demanding for alternative access to the services, and for immediate availability of reliable information, that will help them to combine their family and working lives without neglecting one of them. In the above-described scenario, Internet is becoming an alternative communication vehicle between school and home.

It is therefore of utmost importance for the Public Administration, and for any other body providing educational services, to improve their internal management systems (Back-Office), to provide citizens with complementary services and support tools (Front-Office), and to give access to their services via Internet or mobile telephony. The new services must be easily accessible, available from any location and at any time and allow a fluent communication between the school's staff and the parents and student to whom they provide their services.

This need can be summarised by implementing a model for the provision of Advanced Services for Educational Management via the Internet. The new paradigm supported by web-based advanced management services, prevents problems related to the updating, distribution and consolidation of data, increasing its quality and allowing the Administration to have a better understanding of the Educational Community and its needs.

To move from this situation to a new paradigm a few requisites must be fulfilled:

- First, the Educational Network (schools and homes) must have the infrastructure, material and software necessary for promoting the use of Internet and of the new technologies.
- Second, the internal management processes must be improved. This is achieved by optimising and rationalising the natural flow of documents and information related to

the administrative, economic and academic management of the schools, which are usually comprised by the Back-Office Systems. The internet-based centralised management model has been identified as one of the most cost-effective manners of deploying a solution since it grants the same level of quality of service to all citizens and reduces overheads at schools.

- Last, once a centralised back-office system running the internal management processes is available, it can be said that there is an appropriate basis to provide support to the applications designed to offer Advanced Services to the Educational Community.

2. The Spanish Example: SENECA and PASEN

In 1998, the main goals of the Regional Ministry for Education of Andalusia were to provide schools with a corporate integrated information system, that would help the optimisation of the educational management tasks at schools, and would also improve the decision making processes at the Educational Administration, thanks to a unique, real time and reliable database. The centralised management system envisaged would set up the basis for a scalable service platform, which would guarantee the provision of the same level of services to all citizens.

The Regional Government of Andalusia (Spain) decided to lay the foundations for a brand new, citizen-oriented network, which would facilitate the communication among all the actors involved in child education in Andalusia (around 2 million people). As a result, SÉNECA was born (http://www.juntadeandalucia.es/educacionyciencia/seneca).

SENECA is the web-based service for the management of the Regional Ministry of Education's School Centres. It has created, for the first time, an integrated real-time repository that centralises all types of information about students and their academic progress (curricular programs, students and teachers information, marks, groups and timetables, absences control…), and that supports the academic and administrative management of the educational processes (evaluations, pre-registration, registration, etc). It has been conceived as a working tool that allows the interaction of all the Schools with the Administration. The system centralises all information about students and centres. It was developed by SADIEL and all Public Education professionals in Andalusia are using it.

Based on the experience built up during the development and implementation of SENECA, the Andalusian Back-Office system, SADIEL started, in 2000, a research project with the aim of building a Front-Office application. The resulting application, called PASEN, enables parents to communicate with the school and with the Administration Services and to monitor and to participate actively in the education of their children.

PASEN (www.juntadeandalucia.es/educacionyciencia/pasen) is a highly interactive tool available to all actors, which provides a fast and efficient reply channel to all the inquiries and needs that usually arise in the relation between the Administration and Citizens in the educational field. PASEN is currently being used in Andalusia, where it will support over 1.200.000 Students and their 1.500.000 Parents and about 80.000 Teachers, distributed along more than 4000 Schools. The deployment process has been planned in two steps, so that over 100 schools (and its students and families) are using PASEN during the 2003-2004 school year, and the take-off will be complete during the 2004-2005 school year. Besides this, e-Administration facilities have been accessible to all the Andalusian Educational Community from April 04.

3. PAPÁS, Advanced Management of Web Educational Services

3.1 The PAPÁS Project: Internationalisation of a Solution.

PAPÁS was conceived as a natural continuation of the PASEN Project, a R&D initiative funded by the Spanish Government. The objective of the PAPÁS project is to explore the possibilities of the already developed system (PASEN) to suit the needs of different European educational environments. In order to do this, the PAPÁS Platform is being validated at different administrative levels and locations.

In general terms, the model of unified management of education services through Internet implies a series of advantages:

- The services are open to all the School Centres and all Educational Community actors.
- The services offered are integrated with Public Administration's management tools.
- The use of a common infrastructure and resources guarantees equal access opportunities and minimisation of the digital exclusion effects.

The use of the PAPÁS platform involves the interaction of many actors in the Educational domain: citizens to which the service is addressed (parents, students, parent's associations…); and organisations providing the service and their staff. For all of these actors, the implementation of the PAPÁS platform will bring significant benefits.

There are four organisations in the PAPÁS Consortium. On the technical side, SADIEL, S.A. (Spain), Oy Media Tampere Ltd (Finland) and TSD Projects Srl (Italy). On the public education side, the Regional Ministry of Education from Castilla-La Mancha in Spain. External collaborators (City of Tampere in Finland and Istituto Professionale Statale in Pavia, Italy) have committed to take part in the system's piloting and evaluation.

Figure 1: PAPÁS Platform Customised

As a result of the previous project phases and thanks to its flexibility and modularity, that make the customisation process very easy, PAPÁS is currently a multilingual application, available in English, Spanish, Italian and Finnish, and in a near future also in German and French languages.

The application is accessible using any W3C compliant browser, from different platforms. Although the main access mean will be the PC, some functionalities such as registering absences, are available for teachers through PDA devices and WAP mobile phones. Concerning security issues, PAPÁS is SSL compliant and can be integrated in any organisational security environment.

The platform is integrated with the existent Back-Office systems thanks to XML based communication mechanisms, and this guarantees the availability of reliable information. In fact, it currently gets the school related information from Procapita (Finland), Wincare (Italy), Delphos (Spain) and Seneca (Spain).

As an example of its success, it can be pointed out that the services in Andalusia are being used in 80 schools, upon request, by 5000 teachers, 1500 parents and 3800 students. In Finland, the results of a preliminary analysis of the user feedback currently being collected shows a positive acceptance of the systems by 84% of the parents using PAPÁS, after a validation period of about one month.

3.2 Services Offered by the Platform

The PAPÁS Platform offers a wide range of services to all the members of the Educational Community, which can be extended as per the customers needs (Public Administration or private school organisation). The platform and its services are conceived to be accessible 24 hours a day, 365 days a year, from any place based on a variety of user profiles.

3.2.1 Students

PAPÁS provides students with monitoring tools to perform a comprehensive follow-up of their own academic progress. It offers updated details on the school timetables, absences, dates of exams, homework and assignments submitted or pending, and a communications module, which allows them to contact the schoolteachers.

An Agenda is available where the student can insert exams, deadlines for assignments, appointments with teachers or other relevant events. Additionally, students can view the historical record of marks achieved during previous years at school. PAPÁS also provides information on the School, News and allows students to change their password.

3.2.2 Parents

Parents and legal guardians can access the same services as their children. Additional services are available in order to optimise the follow-up of their children's progress and to improve their communication with other parents, school staff and the Administration.

Parents are able to subscribe to alert services through which they will be able to receive SMS messages or emails regarding their child's performance or attendance to school as well as other types of information (events, news…).

The platform allows parents to interact with the rest of the Educational Community through the PAPÁS Fora and Students Parents Associations (SPA) module where parents will be able to exchange their views and learn and participate in the SPA's activities.

From an administrative point of view, PAPÁS offers parents all the relevant information regarding procedures and deadlines related to the services offered by the Administration. In addition to this, it is also possible to use PAPÁS to send their pre-registration, admission application or grants forms, and to follow up the progress of their requests online.

3.2.3 Teachers

Teachers can manage daily follow-up of students through the allocation and marking of homework and assignments, management of exam dates and control of school attendance. Moreover, teachers are able to contact students and parents, making communications between them fluent and timely, thus improving the overall results of their work.

3.2.4. Public Administration / Private Educational Organisations

PAPÁS provides all the tools necessary to guarantee the successful provision and maintenance of the services offered to the citizens and employees aforementioned.

The platform includes management modules for the system's users, the Bulletin Boards, Discussion Fora and for the Notices received by the different user profiles.

In general terms, the Public Administration's staff will be able to interact with the citizen through the system, opening an alternative to the traditional channels of dealing with communications and administrative processes.

4. Technical Approach

PAPÁS is a centralised web-based application that brings to this Advanced Educational Services management model all the benefits derived from the utilisation of a single application and a unique real-time database.

The PAPÁS system is based on a standard open physical infrastructure supporting a scalable JAVA architecture. The purpose is to facilitate maintenance and operation tasks (the most costly parts of any information system). The system consists of one WEB server accessed by the user via Internet/Intranet from fixed or mobile platforms and containing HTML and WML pages. Support for email and SMS is also included.

The PAPÁS Platform is organized along the Model-View-Controller (MVC) architecture. The MVC architecture is a widely used architectural approach for this kind of web-based applications that separates functionalities among application objects so as to minimize the degree of coupling between the objects.

The platform's three-layered architecture allows the modification of the graphic interface, allowing its adaptation to the corporate identity of the relevant public administration, without touching the logic part of the system.

Figure 2: PAPÁS three layer architecture

The hardware infrastructure necessary for this architecture (web server, application server, reports server, database server and communications module) will vary depending on the mass of population addressed in each case, which will influence the required services' capacity of the PAPÁS platform in a specific environment. If the services are being provided to a large educational community, the use of separate machines for each of the servers is recommended.

Among the optimisation criteria followed for the design and development of the platform, it is worth to highlight the following:

- Security - users authentication and security requirements when invoking any services.

Concerning the access to the system, user authentication is carried out through either the username and password method, or by means of the user's digital certificate, at the application's home page. This homepage is protected through the SSL protocol, guaranteeing the password's confidentiality during the authentication process.

In order to achieve the necessary security level for providing e-administration services, a combination of SSL, digital signature and time-stamp service will be used. The digital signature guarantees the integrity of the data entered by the user in the application form and the non-repudiation on both sides, user and administration, of the service requested.

It is necessary to guaranteeing data security for data handled by the PAPÁS Platform (e.g. data about school children and their academic and family situation). The rules defined to this aim are strictly followed in each new implementation of the PAPÁS Platform.

- Multilinguality – provided by internationalisation and local adaptation functionalities.

Internationalisation guarantees the ability to support several languages. A web-application uses a single version of the pages served to show the information in all available languages. All language sensitive resources of PAPÁS are stored in a single resources file.

Local adaptation consists in providing the necessary information to an already internationalised program or set of programmes so they can show the resources in a specific language. To extend the set of available languages in PAPÁS, it will only be necessary to translate the web site resources file into the new languages, without changing a single page of the system. This makes the maintenance and the addition of new languages much easier and faster, allowing a customer's request for it to be satisfied in a short time.

Additional optimisation criteria relate to Usability and the Accessibility of the Platform.

5. Customisation Process

Customising the PAPÁS Platform can be summarised as follows:

- The first step entails an intensive Requirements analysis of the educative system. This involves mapping structures, concepts and actors to those pre-defined in PAPÁS.
- The next step is defining user profiles, and associated PAPÁS functionalities. Possible profiles includes different levels of administrators, teachers, health-care personnel, parents and students, depending on the allocation of responsibilities in the Network.
- Once the profiles and functionalities have been determined, the platform must be localised, which consists of translating the platform to the relevant language/s (if not already available) and of further adaptations (cultural factors, corporate identity…).
- PAPÁS must be connected to the back-office system managing the educational core information. This requires analysis and mapping of information stored in the B.O. database with the one needed by PAPÁS, and necessary data exchange mechanisms.

The customisation process has been already validated, and the system has been successfully installed in Finland, Italy and Castilla-La Mancha, in a very short period of time.

6. Lessons Learnt

The success of advanced web-based services like those offered via the PAPÁS Platform, must not rely solely on the suitability of the platform. Based on many years experience of implementing advanced management services in Education, two lessons have been learnt:

1. Citizens must be both aware of e-services, and educated about their advantages. The promotion of e-services among its users should emphasize that the electronic channel:

- Is as valid as the traditional channel and that both channels can coexist. Citizens are given an alternative way of doing things that makes services more flexible than before.
- Enables a personalised dialogue with the Public Administration, which is otherwise not always possible through the traditional channels.
- Is secure and complies with Personal Data Protection Regulations

2. The challenge is not the technology but the perceived service quality and efficiency. A significant change in service provision is essential. Public Administration should play a pro-active role and adopt a citizen-oriented approach towards the services being provided.

To gain acceptance, e-services must be very user-friendly in terms of agility and efficiency. In most cases, this requires considerable redesign of processes and procedures, and as a consequence of this, the definition of a change management plan through which the staff of the Public Administration is duly trained and prepared for providing e-services.

The implementation of e-services must be supported by appropriate technologies and a sound strategic plan addressing the issues presented above through adequate mechanisms.

7. Conclusions

PAPÁS was conceived as a national RTD initiative, and became a fully operational and successfully implemented system. Based on the system in use in Andalusia and developed to suit specific end-user requirements, PASEN has evolved to a customisable platform, PAPÁS, which has been adapted to the requirements of further educational models.

Information management needs are similar in all Public Administration Bodies working in Education, whether at local, regional or even national level. The platform can be customised to meet the requirements of individual schools, school associations, the private sector (primary/secondary/higher education), language institutes or vocational/commercial training schools. In addition to covering their administrative and communication needs, the portfolio of services offered through the PAPÁS platform can be seen as a competitive advantage in front of other organisations not offering advanced e-services.

In spite of technical infrastructure differences (access to Internet, PC's...) and the Back-office systems being at different stages of development and implementation, the needs and requirements of the agents belonging to the Educational Community are the same in all the environments analysed (e.g. absence control and further follow-up mechanisms).

The feedback from project presentations in multiple scenarios across Europe indicates that the PAPÁS approach fits the needs and expectations of the educational community in different countries and regions, especially with regard to the follow-up of child education and encouragement of Home-School Collaboration. Many organisations have demonstrated interest in the platform, which is promising in terms of commercial deployment.

Finally, it is important to highlight that, though the PAPÁS project was conceived to foster the active participation of actors involved in the field of Education, its open and modular architecture makes possible its exportation to other sectors. For example, in the case of Health, Social Welfare or Financial Departments, the need to access the information and services managed by the Public Administration is similar, and the relationship between citizens and Public Administration is a key element to be considered. Only the information and service requirements and the profiles related to them would need to be redefined following the specific procedures of the relevant section of the Public Administration.

Acknowledgements

PAPÁS is a market validation project co-funded by the EC through the eTEN programme.

References

[1] Camacho M., Conde A., Fernández V., Mena J., 'PAPÁS, Advanced Management of Web Educational Services'. In Proceedings of the 4th European Conference On E-Government, 2004.

[2] Cook M.E., 'What Citizens Want From E-Government', Technical report, Center for Technology in Government, University at Albany, 2000.

[3] G8 GOL Democracy Team, 'Democracy and Government On-Line Services', www.statskontoret.se/gol-democracy, 2000.

[4] Jerez, Henry N. 'WEB Based Education Opportunities and Challenges'. Distance Education Workshop. Patzcuaro Michoacan, México, 2002.

[5] Jeff Chamberlain and Tanya Castleman 'EGovernment Business Strategies and Services to Citizens: An analysis of the Australian e-tax system'. Presented at IFIP WG 8.4, 2nd Conference on E-business: Multidisciplinary Research and Practice, Copenhagen, Denmark, June 2002.

[6] Preston, M., 'E-Government US-Style', New Statesman, Vol. 129, No. 4517, 2000.

[7] Becta, 'How learning is changing: information and communications technology across Europe - ICT in education policy'. Coventry: British Educational Communications and Technology Agency, 1998.

[8] Conway, P., 'Schools Information Technology (IT) 2000: Technological Innovation and Educational Change'. Dublin: Irish Educational Studies, 2000.

Mapping The Law: Knowledge Support for Business Development Enquiry.

Frank WILSON[1], Rob PETERS[2]
[1]*Interaction Design Ltd (IDL), 13 Stonehills House, Welwyn Garden City, AL8 6NH, UK.*
Tel: +441707338751, Email: fwilson@i-d.co.uk
[2]*Leibniz Centre for Law, University of Amsterdam, Oudemannehuispoort,*
Kloveniersburgwal 82, Amsterdam, 1012 CZ, Netherlands.
Tel: +31627015002, Email: Rob.Peters@lri.jur.uva.nl

Abstract: The Add-Wijzer project set out to demonstrate the business value of public sector information exploitation by making 'law information' more accessible in support of business planning by professionals who are not lawyers. The public-private partnership formed for this task have shown that integration of various business-relevant data sources along with geographical information and tools can increase business planning capacity and can reduce time and costs associated with planning. The extension of the approach to wider usage by citizens and professionals in further usage cases is identified.

1. Introduction and Background to Add-Wijzer

While it was probably our 'earliest federalist' Johann Althuis [1] who first tried to organise our view of Law as a set of meaningfully related rules, rather than a scattered collection of the whims of people in power, it was probably Gottfried Leibniz [2] who laid a foundation for treating law and its embedded rules and intentions as something open to more formal relationship, explanation and operation. Yet despite the passage of 300 years we are still working towards widespread 'knowledge support for legal enquiry' [3].

In recent years many attempts have been made to improve access to, and usage of, laws information. Early exploitation of ICT saw large scale transfer of laws to CD-ROM format for lawyers (e.g. by Context in London) and this was later replaced by online access via Internet to reduce costs and speed-up access to new information [4]. During collaboration between Context and IDL in 1999-2000 on improvement of this kind of service for non-lawyers, it was identified that a wide range of professionals have reliance on law information but lack support either for their non-lawyer status, or for their specific professional tasks. Modern business development and operation involves constant reliance on legal knowledge, and may involve expensive legal representatives (experts). Apart from the enormous complexity of law in Europe, the reliance on experts is also driven by the highly specialised nature of the content, both in terms of its specific technical language, and in terms of the knowledge required for interpretation in a specific case. Current work in this area mainly targets lawyers [5] more than business managers, and less support is available for the many 'intermediaries' (advisors who are not lawyers, such as business planners). This situation led to the formation of the Add-Wijzer group to investigate ways to improve access to law, and to improve usage of law information by business professionals who are not trained in law. The research is supported by the CEC eContent programme, under its action to promote better use of Public Sector Information (PSI).

Early in our work, a specific concern was raised by the Province of South Holland (PZH) and FramFab around spatial and environmental planning, where regulations emanate from different levels of society (e.g. local, regional, national, European), as well as from different types of regulatory authorities (e.g. water, food and hygiene, public safety, transport, building, etc.). This often means relying on different types of legal experts to combine the required specialisations. Furthermore, law texts referring to spatial domains do not easily support reasoning about 'place'. The problem of understanding both 'where this law applies', and 'where can I do this business activity' may therefore require both expert legal consultation and negotiation with regional authorities. Business trying to develop in this way can face time-consuming processes, which may provide a negative result – drawing a blank. It was clear that business managers and advisors required knowledge support for enquiry where they themselves could prepare a 'viable' case before taking it to a legal expert for completion. This would allow reduction of cost, speeding of process, and the flexibility to test numerous possible cases before selecting some targets for more serious consideration. For the above reasons, 'spatial planning and environmental law' became the primary focus for Add-Wijzer soon after project initiation.

2. Objectives

The objectives of Add-Wijzer are to show how existing PSI can be exploited for wider business and social benefit through partnerships and arrangements between public authorities, developers, service providers and end-user groups. The target PSI content includes maps, GIS data, legal texts and other regulatory instruments, combined with population data, environmental data, economic data, and numerous other sources of information relevant to solving business problems. The integration of these to support visual display and reasoning about planning problems for business and legal intermediaries is the single development objective, and is already realised as a demonstrator available at http://www.addwijzer.com

The remainder of this paper briefly describes the initial results and lessons learned in what has been described by the Public Data Group as a 'flagship eContent project' [6].

3. The Add-Wijzer Approach, Technology, Business Case, and Results to Date

The business case, as previously described in the background section, is improved access to law information and decision support for planning where law is critical, but where legal expertise is expensive and time consuming.

3.1 Studies of Users of Existing Legal Databases

To inform the initial design of Add-Wijzer, a set of studies were conducted at Queens University Belfast [7, 8] to examine how people with some level of legal knowledge, or experience in fields using law information deal with existing law information systems. This was intended to provide a baseline for improvements over current practice. The evaluation used scenarios from an earlier requirements study clearly showed that typical users start with a domain-specific task-support requirement, and then transform this to an information-seeking strategy, and finally secure relevant information to use in satisfying a task (work) need. Each scenario had a set of known problems relating to how people develop an information-seeking strategy, how they find the necessary information, and how they then understand and make use of it in a satisfactory way. The set of scenarios and related problems was used to design an enquiry using interviews of experts, plus protocol analysis of observations of users carrying out example tasks. Tests were then carried out with seven non-lawyers who came from a planning or environmental background, but who had no specialist experience in law, and five professionals who had a background in law but were not necessarily fully qualified lawyers.

Significant examples of problems for users with no legal experience included making sense of the legal texts found (understanding), knowing which documents were relevant to their problem, completing search forms in a way that conforms to system requirements, targeting relevant information inside lengthy legal texts, identifying 'amendments' to law, and finding the 'commencement date' and 'extent' of laws. In addition, numerous usage problems were seen which derived from poor interface design in the systems observed. A set of design guidelines were then derived to address both classes of problem [9].

A key finding was the need to provide summary data and interpretation for all legal instruments to ensure that the barriers of 'specialist language' and 'complex document structure' were overcome. It was noted that the user interface problems could be remedied through good interface design practice following current standards and good practice guides [see 9 for examples].

3.2 Studies of Business Users of Add-Wijzer Prototypes

The evaluation study [7, 8] also included demonstrations of prototype interfaces under development for Add-Wijzer, and these were provided to candidate business users who were interviewed to ascertain their perceptions of the designs offered and their knowledge of likely problems in law information usage.

Prototype 'document search' interface: Tests were conducted with seven candidate users. Example problems related to structure of search forms for non-lawyers, categorisation of information and terminology, labelling of results in lists, and highlighting of 'target' information in displays of finds.

Prototype 'scenario enquiry' interface: A group of specialists were interviewed/tested and included coverage of the areas of event organising, architecture, geographical information system usage, environmental planning, soil science, notaries, planning enforcement, and placement of 'liquid petroleum gas' (LPG) stations. Example problems and benefits identified for these types of users were quite varied, as may be expected from the wide area of professions covered. For example, the event organiser found it very useful that 'prohibited' areas were masked on the map, but could not see why some 'explanation' could not be provided. He also found it very attractive that all of the relevant information could be provided via a single interface.

In the case of the architect, he found it particularly useful that the system would allow him to identify archeologically sensitive areas, since the Treaty of Malta places specific requirements on architects in this regard. Another attractive feature for architects was the 'standardisation of municipal information' in Add-Wijzer, plus the ability (e.g. when making zoning plans) of being able to access many different types of PSI (e.g. pollution, noise, traffic, etc.) in a single interface.

The LPG specialist also noted the significant advantage of being able to access many kinds of information in a composite model of planning space, built environment and applicable laws. He emphasised the complexity of gathering data on zoning plans, historical information (archaeology), soil, cables, piping, sanitation, etc. Normally an enquiry with municipal authorities can take a long time, and the instant results of an Add-Wijzer system would show significant business benefits.

The results of our tests illustrate significant differences in usage characteristics between the user types, but show business experts can adapt to law as well as law experts can adapt to business issues with the help of an appropriate interface backed up by PSI content. A key finding in our business user studies was the need to introduce new GIS objects (geographical information system objects) to deal with legal instruments and other data necessary for addressing business problems. It was noted that the essential model of GIS was expandable to allow inclusion of any data that could be meaningfully linked to the core concept of spatial representation, and this is currently done in Add-Wijzer.

3.3 Technical Challenges

Development of Add-Wijzer has addressed a number of significant technical challenges. A set of candidate technologies is considered in detail elsewhere [10] and here we consider the rationale for selection of the elements implemented in the Add-Wijzer platform. It was planned that Add-Wijzer would operate within a web-service model, importing well defined data sets from a diversity of sources marked up via extensible mark-up language (XML). For our purposes, the information had also to be contained within well defined metadata sets, while at the same time leaving the maintenance of the data where it belonged.

The Dutch national information model for spatial planning (IMRO[11]), which was derived from the Dutch real estate standard (NEN 1878/3610), did provide the basic principle for data set import and export, but many municipalities struggled with their first attempts to apply these standards in the real life planning process. There is a clear need to support migration to new standards in user constituencies not familiar with this approach (process change).

It was also seen that the software packages used by the municipalities were not up to the task of handling the new standardisation process in planning. Some of the functional variation was seen to provide a potential impact for business because the new data model is inclusive of specific detail (mark-up and coding of information objects) derived from a municipal planner perspective, while ignoring some requirements of 'business planners'. Solving this problem will be crucial even at the European level of Dublin core interpretations for eGovernment archives (see also eGMS and EGCL for the UK [12]) if eGovernment is to fully support exploitation of PSI for business usage. For example, when the municipalities together decide to leave the 'maximum allowed weight' out of the coding system for 'roads' because the 'speed limitations' is perceived as a more relevant category for them, some businesses depending on road transport (logistics) could lose important 'business inquiry value' in the future. We therefore recognise that if technical experts fail to inform 'domain experts' about the consequences of such categorisation choices for the data model, or fail to work with domain experts to develop a common view of such consequences, then the limitations of the system will only be seen later, in early usage, when an array of design decisions may have rendered the system/software either inflexible or expensive to adapt.

A critical challenge in achieving the Add-Wijzer technical architecture has been the enormous complexity generated by inclusion of the finer information (requiring mark-up) derived from a broad range of business themes, related information sources (documents), maps and space-related data items for visual presentation. This mass of otherwise unstructured data included different formats (such as Word files, PDF's, geographic shape files, spreadsheets, etc.) relating to quite diverse content (such as laws, policies, subsidies, traffic flows, populations, etc.), and all had to be 'mapped' to the thematic layers of the GIS system as the display vehicle. The visitor to the website must also be able to conjoin relevant documents/data-sources related to the commercial enquiry at the right regional 'scale' and within an appropriate business 'context'. For these reasons our information architects had to identify/define suitable layers of policy documents deduced from the anticipated needs of business people.

A series of interviews with potential business users helped to develop a range of detailed scenarios that such professionals actually follow in real life. This allowed identification and understanding of the complexity of bringing together and analysing 'business relevant' information and data sources in real life planning problems. Examples showed interrelationship (co-relevance) of sources as diverse as (i) traffic density on national, regional and local roads, (ii) documented descriptions of planner intentions within environmentally protected areas, and (iii) the considerations required in planning the relocation of Liquid Petroleum Gas (LPG) stations. Such complexity greatly influences the navigational requirements of the solution – the task support that must be provided to the end user.

In traditional GIS systems the user manipulates the interface by activating or de-activating thematic map layers (show and hide spatial features). However, as identified in Add-Wijzer, solving real business problems requires the integration of both geographic features and geo-related information that is not simply a feature of either the built environment or the natural environment. This means that traditional GIS interaction techniques cannot easily support business planning enquiry beyond simple 'geographic' queries, and could not relate relevant documents (such as legal texts) to enquiries with a spatial component.

The company ISIS (now part of Bentley) had produced a shell around a map engine, which enabled flexible formulation of SQL queries on the objects in the database to solve parts of this class of problem [13]. We wanted a visitor to be able to enter queries related to otherwise diverse topics such as 'water' and 'building' and retrieve documents relevant to any issues involving both these planning areas. The text query had to be 'map sensitive' and the maps had to be 'document sensitive' through an information architecture that supported semantic relationships between information domains not normally related in a single system. The ISIS navigation shell, 'Flexiweb', delivered the major part of that functionality, and as part of the public-private partnership in Add-Wijzer they embarked on extending it to solve our new class of problem. With their support, the core engine was extended to handle multiple document types derived from multiple information domains where content was tagged within a common information architecture.

Despite the aforementioned challenges, Add-Wijzer has been able to demonstrate PSI exploitation via an enhanced set of tools that allow data owners (public authorities) to easily 'tag' documents and other information sources for geographical relevance. An added benefit is the removal of duplication in the meta-tagging effort.

3.4 Partnerships for Service Delivery

A key aspect of the success of Add-Wijzer has been the very successful public-private partnership. The role of the Province of South Holland (PZH) has been key to our success so far. PZH have fully embraced the need for digitalisation of plans at municipal and regional level, and have organised a very large group of municipalities to collaborate on the adoption of the new standards/approaches necessary to support future PSI exploitation in this area (IMRO, DURP). This collaboration ensures exchange of data and acceleration of local digitalisation plans to meet the project schedule, and feedback from participating public authorities suggests this was partly due to the attractiveness of the Add-Wijzer solution and the wider recognition that this approach will meet both Governmental as well as business and eventually citizen needs. In addition to the organisation of content through their collaborative activities, PZH have also worked very closely with FramFab, the main system developer, and have shown that a public-private partnership can satisfy both the needs of commerce (users of PSI) and the needs of public authorities - data holders with a duty to facilitate best usage of data for planning purposes. PZH estimate that a planning process of six-months can be reduced to three-months or less by using digital access approaches such as Add-Wijzer.

3.5 Public Demonstrator

The Add-Wijzer project is now in its demonstrator phase, and full public access is given to selected operational scenarios (http://www.addwijzer.com). The demonstrator can be used to solve problems within those selected scenarios, or indeed within any scenarios relevant to real business problems in the geographical areas described (PZH – including Den Haag, Rotterdam, etc.).

The early feedback from the demonstrator suggests that a general purpose 'planning advisory' system offers significant potential business benefits. The principal advantage is the ability to access a wide range of information critical to planning tasks within a unified interface that supports many different types of users. Their business needs may vary enormously, but their requirements for support are in common. They need to be able to reason about the spatial domain via maps and additional graphical representations, and at the same time be able to discover the implications of existing planning and legal instruments that may impact upon their business objectives (non-map and non-image data relevant to spatial planning and business planning enquiry).

In parallel with the public demonstration, we are now examining the transferability of our results to other European states and law systems. We have already completed an initial study of law information availability across Europe [14], and these results already show, in principle, that Add-Wijzer can provide benefit in the wider European context. We will complement this with the results of a further study (now being conducted by Queens University Belfast) addressing the fitness of the Add-Wijzer solution for use in other Member States, and any apparent needs for localisation or adaptation to meet local requirements.

4. Key lessons learned and future perspectives

The key lessons exposed in the body of this paper provide a firm basis for proceeding towards a pan-European adoption of planning support based around visualisation of spatial and other image data in association with non-spatial and non-image information such as laws, regulations, policies, etc.

Intermediaries and managers can reason about business development problems and law, but they need support that is sensitive to their information and task needs. Focusing on one province in one country has helped integrating the information and task requirements, but extension to a European scale will require adaptation and elaboration. This could be better supported by common eGovernment approaches and standards.

Business operators can take account of laws, regulations and other instruments in business planning activities, but the special language, document formalities and variety of sources and types brings new complexity. Tools such as ISIS Flexiweb+ can support these new user tasks, as can provision of summary information to support improved user understanding of content, and provision of usable interfaces.

Public sector agencies have substantial reservoirs of content but do not always realise the value for the outside world. While we have shown how such content can be made more accessible and usable for business benefit, the problems related to tagging of highly heterogeneous data sets, and the need for an intermediate metadata architecture, suggest that increased standardisation among public data owners would be of significant future benefit.

Professionals involved in business planning can develop cases to a high level, sometimes even answering the problem completely, before recourse to expensive legal expertise. The time frame can also be shortened considerably (e.g. 50%), and so savings in time and costs are easily possible.

Provision of knowledge support for legal enquiry relies on a partnership between public authorities, business, and value-added service providers. In the case of Add-Wijzer this benefited from a pro-active and progressive regional authority (PZH) but a wider adoption may not be easy unless agreements between authorities are forthcoming, especially in the area of PSI information standards (e.g. IMRO), and standard approaches to allowing PSI exploitation (e.g. UK Information Fair Trade scheme [14]).

Add-Wijzer users uniformly identify the wider set of opportunities beyond business support, especially in improving public authority relationships with citizens (eGov-Citizen). Future developments in Add-Wijzer will examine how to take account of technical needs to support this interaction area.

Add-Wijzer has provided a first value-added service in business development addressing the relationship between regulations, population statistics, built-environment data, natural environment data, economic data, and real business development problems. The intense interest in the project emphasises the need for better access to PSI, and also for better tools to make such access and professional tasks possible.

Elaboration of the Add-Wijzer approach beyond the business development arena could show a broader scope for exploitation of public sector information through an enquiry and representation method (graphical / maps) that is usable by, and beneficial for, a wide set of citizens, professionals and experts alike.

References

[1] Johann Althuis; on Roman Method of Jurisprudence – 1581; on Political Method - 1601; cited in Thomas O'Hueglin 'How We Studied the Wrong Authors? On the relevance of Johannes Althuisius', in Studies in Political Thought (Winter 1991-1992).

[2] Gottfried Leibniz, 'Leibniz: New Essays on Human Understanding', 1996, G.W. Leibniz, Edited by Peter Remnant, Jonathan Bennet, Cambridge Texts in the History of Philosophy, Cambridge, England.

[3] Project 'Add-Wijzer'; CEC eContent Programme 2003-2004; online at http://www.addwijzer.org and at http://www.addwijzer.com

[4] Service http://www.justis.com

[5] Service http://www.justcite.com

[6] Response of the Public Data Group meeting to the invited Add-Wijzer presentation, 28th November, 2003, Luxemburg.

[7] Philip Leith and Karen McCullagh, 2003, 'Developing European Legal Information Markets based on Government Information; First findings from the Add - Wijzer project', in procs. BILETA Conference, London, April 2003.

[8] Ursula Doherty and David Newman, 2003, 'Initial Evaluation and Evaluation Methods for the Demonstrator Phase', CEC eContent Programme, Add-Wijzer project, Project report D603, (available from the authors)

[9] Frank Wilson, 2003, 'Design Guidelines V0.6', CEC eContent Programme, Add-Wijzer project, Project report D603-b, (available from the authors)

[10] Eriks Sneiders, 2004, 'Tool Support for Legal Enquiry: Focus on Spatial-Planning Law'. In Proceedings of the 6th International Conference on Enterprise Information Systems (ICEIS), Porto, Portugal, April 14-17, 2004.

[12] http://www.govtalk.gov.uk/schemasstandards/metadata_document.asp?docnum=768

[11] http://www.ravi.nl/standaardisatie/imro/imro_startpagina.htm

[13] ISIS and Flexiweb - http://www.isis.nl

[14] Philip Leith and Ursula Doherty, 2003, 'Laws structuring: laws affecting public sector content across Europe', CEC eContent Programme, Add-Wijzer project, Project report D403, (available from the authors)

[14] UK Information Fair Trade Scheme at http://www.hmso.gov.uk/copyright/regulation/ifts.htm

Argument Visualisation to Support Democratic Decision-Making

Ann MACINTOSH and Alastair RENTON
International Teledemocracy Centre, Napier University, 10 Colinton Road, Edinburgh, EH01 5DT, Scotland, UK
Tel: +44 131 455 2545, Fax: + 44 455 2282, Email: itc@napier.ac.uk

Abstract: This paper investigates the extent to which technology can be designed to constructively inform and encourage debate on public policy issues. The research is innovative in that it aims at moving away from text-based information provision and consultations to a representation based on visualisation of arguments, providing graphical support for information and deliberation. Whether the public can benefit from, or is indeed willing to use, such visualisation techniques is very much a debate in itself. The development of policy can be described, in the terms of Horst Rittel, as a wicked problem. These types of problems require deliberative discussion. The purpose of this paper is to explore how Computer Supported Argument Visualisation (CSAV) can relate to parliamentary debates in order to assess the extent by which they affect the public's understanding of, and participation in, policy-making.

1. The Need for Deliberation and Informed Debate

Much of the work of parliament and government relates to preparing policy that requires widespread discussion and engagement with civil society organisations and citizens as individuals. Over the last decade there has been a gradual awareness of the need to consider new tools for public engagement enabling a wider audience to contribute to the democratic debate and where contributions themselves are both broader & deeper. Enacting democratic principles, building the enabling infrastructures, and engaging citizens in democratic decision-making is expected to lead to more active citizenship and good governance.

Two OECD (Organisation for Economic Co-operation and Development) publications are relevant to the online engagement of citizens. The first, a report, "Citizens as Partners: Information, Consultation and Public Participation in Policy-making"[1], discusses the government-citizen relationship in democratic decision-making and argues that bringing together top-down government-led approaches and bottom-up community-led approaches can enable a strong partnership that results in a strengthening of representative democracy and a more active citizenship. It defines three types of democratic participation, namely:

- Information: a one-way relationship in which government produces and delivers information for use by citizens.
- Consultation: a two-way relationship in which citizens provide feedback to government. It is based on the prior definition of information.
- Active participation: a relationship based on partnership with government in which citizens actively engage in defining the process and content of policy-making.

This OECD publication lays out the ground rules for best practice citizen engagement, but it does not consider in detail the consequences of applying ICT to support the processes.

The second OECD publication [2] considers online citizen engagement. The report specifically looks at how ICT could be applied to enhance citizen participation in the policy process. The report provides an analytical framework for e-participation. Importantly for this research, it provides the overarching objectives for applying ICTs to the democratic decision making processes. These are:

1. reaching a wider audience to enable broader participation
2. supporting participation through a range of technologies to cater for the diverse technical and communicative skills of citizens
3. providing relevant information in a format that is both more accessible and more understandable to the target audience to enable more informed contributions
4. engaging with a wider audience to enable contributions and support deliberative debate.

Democratic political participation must involve both the means to be informed and the mechanisms to take part in the decision-making. Our work in CSAV addresses these issues.

Firstly, considering information, OECD [1] guiding principle 5 on 'objectivity' states: Information provided by government during policy-making should be objective, complete and accessible. All citizens should have equal treatment when exercising their rights of access to information and participation. (p.15)

One of the objectives of technology enabled information dissemination is to provide relevant information in a format that is both more accessible and more understandable to the target audience to enable more informed participation and acceptance of policy. To move towards this many government agencies are providing Web portals for citizens to gain access to information. Due to the expected diversity of users, the aim should be, wherever possible, for text to be written clearly and simply with the avoidance of jargon and legalistic terms. There is a need to ensure that citizens have access to relevant, complete, timely and understandable information on the basis of which they may then formulate their own opinions and proposals for policy. Therefore there is a need to move away from purely text-based information provided by government to a situation where information may be 'visualised' in different ways to cater for diverse audiences.

Secondly, e-consultations have generally taken one of two forms that correspond with different stages of the policy making life-cycle [2]:

- Issue-based discussion forums, i.e. organised around policy issues that have been formulated by policy-makers, interest groups or 'experts', and presented as the heading of one or more discussion 'threads'. Responses are sought in order to gauge opinion or solicit ideas. Position statements, links to topic-related websites and other background information may also be presented. Such forums can be considered appropriate at the policy agenda setting, analysis and monitoring stages of the policy life-cycle.
- Policy-based discussion forums, i.e. organised around themes/issues that relate to a draft policy meant to address these, and where discussion threads are intended to solicit responses from those affected. Participants might be encouraged to submit alternative ideas and suggestions but the format implies that what is being sought is an indication of how far the participants agree (or not) with the proposals, and why. Such forums can be considered appropriate at the policy creation stage of the policy life-cycle.

Since 1999 we have designed and conducted a number of e-consultations on policy-issues on behalf of government agencies [3]. Through this work we have started to develop an evaluation framework to support the analysis of contributions and usefulness of the approach [4]. A major difficulty is that the current online discussion forums were originally developed for IT literate newsgroups. The discussion is structured via a variety of links to previous messages that merely provide a threaded discussion where messages are linked by simple association. This typically results in an unsorted collection of vaguely associated comments. Such discussion threads were not designed for use by a broader public.

Discussion forums were not designed to encourage citizens into thinking about public issues and listening to, and engaging in argument and counter arguments. They are thus not likely in their current from to support e-participation. Coleman and Gøtze [5] argue the need to move from current forms of citizen engagement to more deliberative forms. They define deliberative engagement as:

Methods of public engagement can be described as deliberative when they encourage citizens to scrutinize, discuss and weigh up competing values and policy options. Such methods encourage preference formation rather than simple preference assertion.

Fishkin [6] states: a major part of the problem of democratic reform is how to promote mass deliberation - how to bring people into the process under conditions where they can be engaged to think seriously and fully about public issues. (p.41)

From our work to date, there is a clear need for more research in how to design technology to support deliberation and informed debate. This implies a major shift from online discussion forums to forums designed to visualise arguments and counter arguments.

Van Gelder [7] in his discussion on how CSAV could enhance deliberation, highlights the subtle differences between argumentation and deliberation. He describes deliberation as a process aimed at deciding whether some claim can be achieved by considering the relevant arguments.... Thus deliberation often involves considering an extended hierarchy of arguments.(p98)
Whereas argumentation is defined by van Eemeren [8] as A verbal and social activity of reason aimed at increasing (or decreasing) the acceptability of a controversial standpoint for the listener of reader, by putting forward a constellation of propositions intended to justify (or refute) the standpoint before a rational judge. (p5)

Therefore van Gelder argues that deliberation by contrast is aimed at determining one's own attitude. However he concedes that forms of deliberation are like argumentation in that they are often a collective activity and essentially involve reasoning and argumentation.

2. Supporting Deliberation and Informed Debate

Policy decision-making falls into the category of wicked problems. In the 1970's Horst Rittel termed problems characterised by indeterminacy and complexity as "wicked" problems [9, 10]. These types of problems require deliberative discussion where alternative options and competing interests can be exposed. Buckingham Shum [11] suggests that wicked problems, as opposed to tame problems have a number of distinct characteristics. For policy decision making these can be translated as:

- not easily defined in such a way that all stakeholders agree this is the problem to solve
- has no clear stopping rules, it is only the time limits on consultation that mark the end of a problem solving period
- there is no clear cut right or wrong approach, instead there are better or worse solutions
- difficult to provide objective measures of success
- policy making is an iterative process
- solutions and/or options have to be discovered
- although policy options may be similar, each are unique
- the level of detail necessary to define the problem is a matter of judgement
- there is strong moral and political pressure against failure.

To support solving such problems Rittel developed IBIS (Issue-Based Information Systems) – a language and graphical representation scheme for visualising argumentation.

Much research has been conducted on argumentative discourse; for example, Lueken [12] took a philosophical perspective where argumentation is considered as a way of theory formulation. On the other hand, Heidrich [13] considered support through speech act theory and discourse analysis. A comprehensive study is given in [8].

The area of computer supported argument visualisation (CSAV) offers the potential to support deliberation and informed debate in democratic decision-making. Recent, research in CSAV [11] has resulted in such techniques being used in resolving industrial conflicts and supporting strategic gaol setting in businesses. It has been shown that the application of CSAV techniques makes it easier for participants in a debate to follow where lines of thought have taken them, rather than having to look back through pages of notes. Once a decision has been taken, the argument visualisation constitutes a readily accessible justification for the resulting actions. This allows those affected to see whether their concerns were taken into account and how those concerns fitted into the overall debate.

As such CSAV has the potential to provide a readily accessible medium by which citizens can follow and join in online public debates on policy issues, can see how others react to their concerns and can appreciate the issue in its entirety not just from their own individual viewpoint. If organisations have experienced an improvement in employee relations with less dissatisfaction being expressed at policies, then such CSAV techniques have a potentially important role to play in engaging citizens in democratic decision-making leading to better policy-making and a more engaged citizenry.

The development of systems to support argumentation is a growing research and development area. For instance, one of the original tools, QuestMap by Conklin [14] captured the key issues and ideas during face- to-face meetings and created shared representation of the arguments, decision and rational. The more recent tool, Compendium, is based on QuestMap. Also, Belvedere [15] uses a rich graphical language to support arguments and their relationships in a debate. This system was originally designed for students debating critical science issues. Our research has used the Compendium tool for visualising political debates as it is the result of 15 years experimentation and is freely available for downloading from www.compendiuminstitute.org/tools/compendium.htm.

3. Using CSAV to Understand Political Debates

This case study involves the provision of information by the Scottish Parliament (www.scottish.parliament.uk). The Parliament publishes the Official Report of the Parliament's meetings in the Chamber by 7am on the following day. Unfortunately, these are typically the verbatim, text-based debates of the MSPs. They can be both complex and verbose- making it difficult for citizens to easily appreciate the main arguments arising. Our work concerns these verbatim, text-based debates of the Parliament. The work started in October 2003 and has involved modeling complex debates and re-presenting them using argument visualization techniques using the Compendium tool.

Compendium is a very sophisticated tool, but basically icons representing 'questions', ideas' supports', and 'contests' can be used to represent the relevant concepts in a debate and these are positioned as nodes on a map. These nodes can be connected by arrows to show different types of relationships between the concepts. The nodes have a roll-over feature that can be used to add additional properties such as to indicate the names and political party of the person making a statement. Other node icons such as 'note' and link' can be used to point to further information, such as reports mentioned in the debate. It should be noted that Compendium has much more to offer than outlined here, but our purpose was to assess the extent by which CSAV techniques affect the public's understanding of political issues and not to assess Compendium as a CSAV tool.

The Compendium tool was used to represent two recent topics discussed by the Parliament: a lengthy and emotional debate concerning anti-social behaviour; and a shorter technical debate concerning terrestrial trunked radio masts (TETRA). The Antisocial Behaviour debate is an especially long debate lasting for four and a quarter hours with 32 speakers and running over 2 sessions of Parliament. It is also a debate that is likely to be of interest to citizens and give rise to an emotional response from them. However, its length and structure make reading it a daunting prospect. Therefore it was possible to explore whether the visualisation of the debate could improve the ability of citizens to understand what was happening. On the other hand the TETRA debate is relatively short lasting 45 minutes and with only 8 speakers. However it contains technical jargon that is unlikely to be understood by a layperson. Therefore it was possible to explore the possibility of representing a debate that assists in the clarification of technical terminology and the ability to see the development of arguments on a complex, technical issue.

Two visualisation maps for the TETRA debate are shown in Figure 1 and Figure 2. The first figure shows only part of the debate but usefully indicates how the icons are used as nodes in the map to represent concepts and how these can be related to one another. The purpose of Figure 2 in this paper is not for readers to be able to read the arguments, but rather to indicate the complexity of debates that have to be represented.

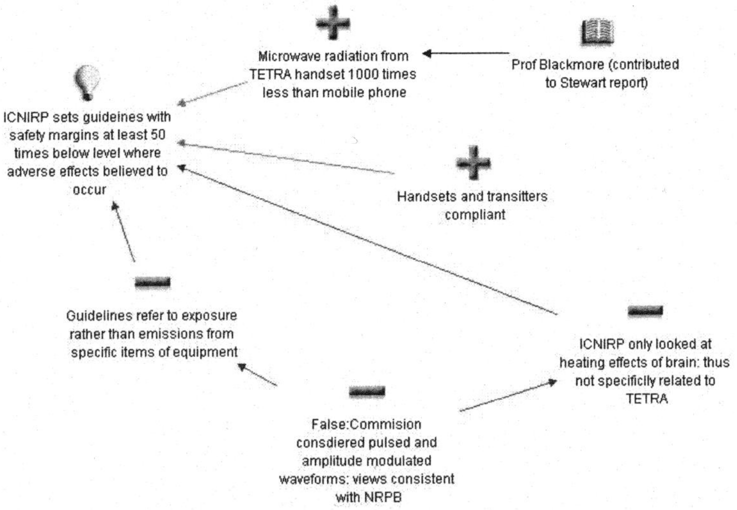

Figure 1: Small section of the TETRA debate

The Scottish Parliament and the Scottish Civic Forum have been involved in evaluating the usability of the visualisation maps using structured interviews. This allowed for comments on the comparison between the verbatim reports and the maps and also on how CSAV techniques could be used in the future. Overall the maps were judged to be a definite improvement upon the verbatim reports. However it was felt that they could not replace verbatim reports entirely. The verbatim report is necessary when in-depth research is being conducted into the debate issue. On the other hand the map wins when easy access to the main issues of the debate is required, such as when someone needs an overview of a particular issue. There is potentially more benefit to be gained from the map in situations where the debates are long. Other positive statements made during the evaluation include:

- Maps provide interesting representations with the style of text in the nodes well suited to providing information concisely.
- Maps give a better feel for the issues.
- Maps make it easier to appreciate the complexity of an issue.

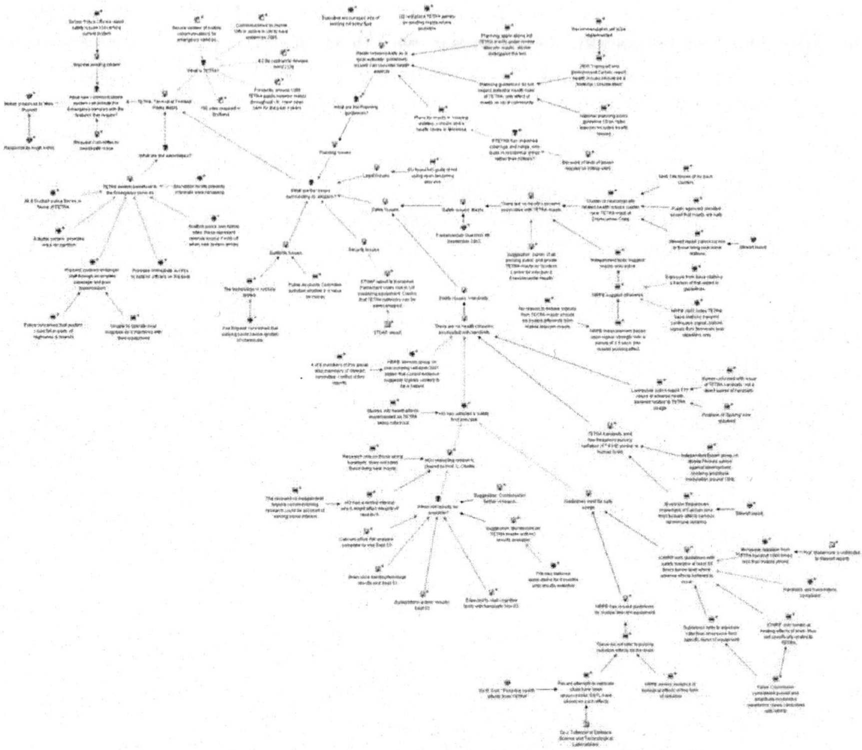

Figure 2: The complexity of debates from the Scottish Parliament

A tentative conclusion we draw is that it is possible to create valid representations of political debates using CSAV and that these visualisations enhanced the user's appreciation of the issues covered in the debates, as compared with reading the verbatim reports. However, it should be stressed that this small project should only be regarded as providing a stimulus for pursuing the application of CSAV techniques further in supporting public engagement in policy-making. Also, the feedback collected indicates a number of ways in which the visualisations could be improved and used under different circumstances.

4. Conclusions

Being an innovative technology it lacks robustness and most people are unfamiliar with its properties. More research is required to build up a culture that enables CSAV to be utilised with little trouble. Buckingham Shum [11] remarks: The process of learning the representational notation inculcates a useful new ability to attend to the underlying structure of arguments and debates…in the terms of that particular notation. An important consequence of this, however, is that until one has had some practice…argument mapping initially feels like learning a new foreign language, and the temptation is to lapse back into more familiar languages…We are, in short, talking about a new *literacy* in being able to read and write in the new medium, and a new fluency in using these conversational tools (p.19).

Our application of CSAV techniques to parliamentary debates is directed towards providing the public with an additional way of accessing information, thereby increasing their understanding of the policies being developed on their behalf. CSAV has the potential to provide a socio-technical approach to addressing online provision of information and consultation, providing the opportunity for:

- supporting deliberation by explicitly showing emerging arguments
- using diagrams to improve comprehension
- visualising potentially large amounts of information.

CSAV has the potential to make it easier for citizens to follow where lines of deliberation have taken them, rather than having to read through screens of text. Once a debate is over, the argument map provides a visual representation on what has been agreed and the extent to which consensus has been reached.

In conclusion, democratic political participation must involve both the means to be informed and the mechanisms to take part in the decision-making. CSAV techniques have the potential to deliver e-participation activities which address these joint perspectives of informing and participating. However, research into CSAV techniques in general is relatively new; there has been limited opportunity to apply such techniques in the real world; and the domains in which they have been used are predominantly 'business' and 'academia'. Our research starts to investigate whether similar successes can be achieved in the field of politics.

References

[1] OECD *Citizens as Partners: Information, consultation and public participation in policy-making*: OECD, Paris. 2001.

[2] OECD *Promises and problems of e-democracy; Challenges of Citizen on-line Engagement.* OECD, Paris. 2004

[3] Macintosh, A. and Smith, E.; Citizen Participation in Public Affairs; In: R.Traunmuller and K.Lenk (Eds); Electronic Government, First International Conference; proceedings / EGOVS 2002, Aix-en-Provence, France, September 2002. Springer (Lecture Notes in Computer Science; Vol. 2456). pp256-264

[4] Whyte, A. and Macintosh, A. Analysis and Evaluation of e-consultations; e-Service Journal; Volume 2, No 1 "e-democracy in Practice"; Indiana University Press; 2003.

[5] Coleman, S.. and Gøtze, J. *Bowling Together: Online public engagement in policy deliberation.* Hansard Society and BT. 2001

[6] Fishkin, J. S. *The voice of the People. Public Opinion and Democracy.* Yale University Press. 1995

[7] van Gelder, T., 2003, Enhancing Deliberation Through Computer Supported Argument Mapping. In P.A. Kirshchner, S.J. Buckingham Shum, & C.S. Carr (Eds.), *Visualizing Argumentation*, London: Springer.

[8] van Eemeren, F. H., Grootendorst, R. and Snoeck Henkemans, F.; *Fundamentals of Argumentation Theory*; Erblaum, Mahwah, NJ, 1996.

[9] Kunz, W. and Rittel, H. Issues as Elements of Information Systems. Technical Report, 0131. Universitat Stuttart, Institut fur Grundlagen der Planninung, 1970.

[10] Rittel, H. and Webber, M. Dilemmas in a General Theory of Planning. Policy Science, 155-169, 1973.

[11] Kirshchner, P. A., Buckingham Shum, S.J., & C.S. Carr, (Eds.), *Visualizing Argumentation*, London: Springer, 2003.

[12] Lueken, G. L.; Incommensurability, Rules of Argumentation and Anticipation. In F.H. van Eemern, R. Grootendorst, J.A. Blair and Ch. A. Willard (eds) Proceedings of the 2nd International Conference on Argumentation, Amsterdam the Netherlands, 1991)

[13] Heidrich, C. H.; Montague-grammars for Argumentative Dialogues. In Barth and Martens (eds. Argumentation approaches to Theory Formulation. John Benjamins, Amsterdam, The Netherlands, 1982.Toth, J. A., Suthers, D. and Weiner, A. Providing Expert Advise in the Domain of Collaborative Scientific Inquiry. In Proceedings of the 8th World Conference on Artificial Intelligence in Education (AI-ED'97), Kobe, Japan. August 1997.

[14] Conklin, E. J.; Designing Organisational Memory: Preserving Intellectual Assets in a Knowledge Economy. GDSS working paper, 1996. Available at www.gdss.com/wp/DOM.htm

A Method for Decision Support in e-Democracy

Mats DANIELSON[1], Love EKENBERG[2,3]
[1] *Dept. of Informatics / ESI, Örebro University, SE-701 82 Örebro, Sweden*
Email: msdn@esi.oru.se
[2] *Dept. of Computer and Systems Sciences, Stockholm University,*
Forum 100, SE-164 40 Kista, Sweden Email: lovek@dsv.su.se
[3] *The Institute for Public Information Systems, Mid Sweden University,*
SE-851 70 Sundsvall, Sweden

Abstract: In this paper, we discuss the ADL method for integrating decision methods with democratic processes. The method consists of an interaction part and a decision process part. We demonstrate how the method can be used for enhancing transparency and efficiency in public decision processes. We also discuss a set of three complicated decisions made by the politicians in a medium-sized municipality near Stockholm. The experience from this project has been that the ADL method is a useful analysis tool, even in complicated political decision processes involving several stakeholders.

1. Introduction

The need for decision support methods in e-democracy projects has been recognized for some time now [1]. There is, for example, a pan-European consortium created to promote the use of decision theoretic and analytic tools and methods for enhancing the democratic aspect of electronic (primarily web-related) democracy projects [3]. This paper presents a case in the same tradition, integrating decision methods with democratic processes with the aim of enhancing transparency and efficiency in public decision processes.

The case discussed in this paper is a set of three complicated decisions made by politicians in a municipality of 75,000 inhabitants just outside of Stockholm, "Muni-X". The entire decision project, "Project Q", was on the Web, accessible for all citizens within (and outside of) Muni-X. The project was a joint collaboration effort between the municipality of Muni-X, a consulting company, and researchers from the DECIDE Research Group (Örebro University, Stockholm University, and Mid Sweden University).

2. Objectives

The purpose of this paper is to present a framework for decision support in democratic processes together with a case. The framework has been tested in real-life government decision projects in society, both on regional and national levels.

Muni-X consists of several parts (sub-municipalities). There was a disagreement between proponents from the parts and from Muni-X at large regarding infrastructure in a sub-area A1. Many inhabitants of A1 desired to have their own proposals implemented, while the centralized Muni-X government feel another solution was appropriate. Project Q was concerned with making decisions regarding the following issues in A1:

- A new water and sewage system
- A new road plan
- A new commuting harbour

The decisions had been postponed on several occasions and were labelled "infected" by some of the stakeholders. The purpose of Project Q was to take the decision process from start to finish without unnecessary interruption or hesitation. This required determined participants and a strong belief in the capabilities of the process.

3. Methodology

The Analytic Decision Layer (ADL) method consists of the interaction part (ADL InterCom) containing communication channels to the stakeholders and the decision process part (ADL Process), which consists of a three-layered working process model carrying the decision from problem issue to solution in a supposedly transparent and cost efficient way.

3.1 ADL InterCom

Project Q has been run in conformance with practices in Muni-X. This allowed any citizen to access information from the municipality, reading council board reports, a.s.o. This is also in accordance with the Swedish law of public information in which almost every authority's written documentation is public.

The InterCom part allowed any citizen to access information from the governmental body, reading government board reports, a.s.o. This openness is one of the cornerstones of the methodology. In addition, an ADL project was highly visible on the web. Stakeholders and other citizens were encouraged to submit material to the process. The submitted material was used in the decision process and was also displayed on the website. All intermediate results of the project group, such as consequence analyses or sets of criteria selected, were continuously published on the web.

Having been "infected issues" for several years, the Muni-X Council Board decided to try a structured decision process to resolve them. Such a process contains at its heart an analytic decision method. In the Q case, the entire method implementation consisted of:

- A web site for all documents.
- E-mailboxes for interaction with stakeholders and citizens.
- A newsletter continuously reporting all progress and problems.
- The ADL Process for preparing and carrying out the decision.

This paper mainly discusses the ADL Process, which is at the core of the decision method.

3.2 ADL Process

The guiding purpose of the overall ADL decision process is to provide:

- A description of the alternative options available.
- A description of the criteria (perspectives) under which to view the alternatives.
- A description of the consequences of each alternative with respect to each criterion.
- A procedure that evaluates & compares alternatives, taking account of relevant criteria.

At the same time, the process is supposed to maintain transparency and cost efficiency. The ADL Process is designed to meet those requirements. It contains a proven decision analytic method as its core and a layered process to execute the decision steps appropriately. The decision method used in ADL has been used on a number of occasions, notably in a big decision problem involving a large number of stakeholders, viz. the design of a public-private flood insurance system for Hungary [4]. That project involved IIASA (International Institute for Applied Systems Analysis) and the Hungarian Academy of Science. It was a multi-stakeholder policy decision problem. The stakeholders included, among others, the inhabitants in high-risk and low-risk areas, the insurance companies, and the government. Partly from this project, the ADL process has been derived.

The ADL process is based on the Delta decision method [2]. Delta has been used and validated in several decision projects ranging from deposition of spent nuclear fuel in Sweden, over large purchasing decisions at the Swedish Rail Administration (around 1 billion Euros) and investment analyses [5], to the aforementioned Hungarian project. The method has been packaged into a decision tool that accompanies the ADL process [6].

4. Technology Description

The work is carried out at three different levels (layers) in the method. There is an outer, semi-political stakeholder process, a middle layer investigation process, and an inner loop containing the decision process. There is continuous interaction between the process layers.

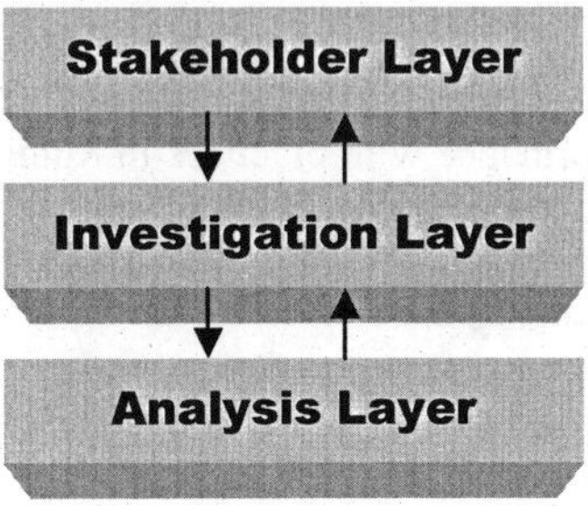

Figure 1: ADL Process Layers

The stakeholder layer contains the political process and the interaction with the citizens. Often, the political process itself is rather traditional, including preparation of material in working groups and involving representatives from the political parties elected to the local parliament. The strong interaction with the citizens through Internet communication channels is a novel component, not previously tried in this setting. This is the layer where the goals are set and later measured.

The investigation layer consists of employees of the local government performing the investigations and assessments necessary for carrying the process further. They are responsible for processing the information from the stakeholder layer, i.e. the views of the citizens and of the political governing council. Further, they take all facts available into account, ranging from environmental reports to laws controlling the various ways plans can be implemented. This is the layer where most of the structuring takes place along with the processing of the information obtained into decision data.

The analysis layer consists of a decision analytical process carried out in a number of steps. The steps are supported by the decision analysis tool DecideIT [6]. The investigation layer gathers the initial information from different sources. Then it is formulated into statements and entered into the analysis layer. Following that, an iterative process commences where step by step the process participants gain further insights. The inner loop process in the analysis layer that drives the ADL Process is shown in Figure 2.

Thus, the ADL Process can be seen as a model and process driven multi-level information process comprising citizens, politicians, and government investigators.

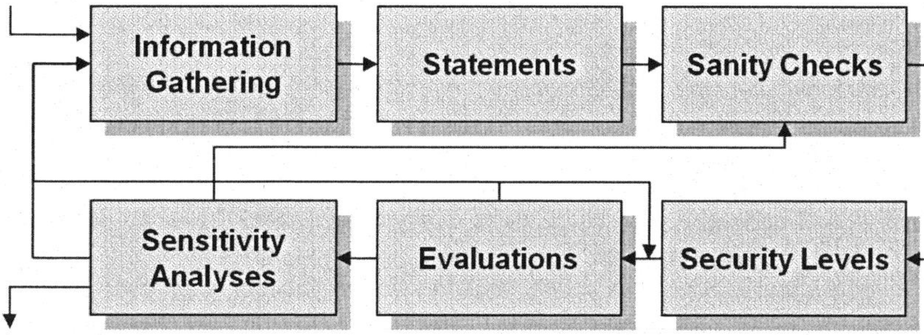

Figure 2: The ADL analysis Layer Steps

5. Developments

The first data collection phase in ADL is a large step when the problem is complex or different views are hard to obtain in a common format. For Project Q, it took several man-months to perform. The project web, "Q-Web", had to be designed and deployed. Information from citizens had to be collected by all available conventional means, but was also collected from politicians. The project goals and guidelines were given by the political agenda of the Council. This was received by the investigation layer and transformed into plans and schedules. Data from citizens was taken into account when collecting information on the various possible alternatives and consequences.

After the information collection phase, a modelling task commenced at the investigation layer, where the participants structured and ordered the information in Project Q. The first subtask was to describe all feasible solutions to each decision problem. The descriptions of the alternatives had to be comparable with each other. There is no requirement in ADL for the alternatives to have the same number of consequences. However, within any given alternative, it is required that the consequences are exclusive and exhaustive, i.e. whatever the result, it should be covered by the description of exactly one consequence. If not, a residual consequence is added to take care of unspecified events. The alternatives considered at this stage were from the following categories:

- The Council's centralized solutions
- The Council's localized solutions
- The alternatives from lobby groups in Area A1
- A zero action alternative – no decision made

The alternatives were not described in detail at this stage. The primary goal was to ensure most interested citizens understood the alternatives. At this stage, it was not a requirement that the alternatives could be implemented in detail. Interactive maps of the proposed alternatives were presented through the communication channels of the stakeholder layer. This was key to reach an understanding among the citizens for the proposed alternatives and their consequences. During the entire decision process, citizens were encouraged to submit views and supply additional information into the process.

6. Results

Each decision option has a number of consequences. During the process, these consequences were bundled together into criteria. For each of the three options, criteria were collected, communicated, and iterated with all parties involved. Examples of such criteria included:

- Cost
- Environment
- Health

- Real estate value
- Fairness

Project Q was analyzed through the evaluative phases, viz. Sanity Checks, Security Levels, and Evaluation in Figure 2. After several iterations, each decision problem as well as its proposed solution(s) in the form of preferred courses of action was well understood and documented. The decision analysis could then continue, involving all relevant criteria, consequences, and preference orderings under consideration. The final analyses were also made available to the Government Council for discussions and as a basis for decision The analyses were primarily based on a generalization of maximization of the expected and weighted utilities together with a security analysis, cf. [2], but since we want to discuss the non-technical components of the ADL method, the technical details have been omitted.

7. Conclusions

This paper has discussed the non-technical components of the ADL method for decision support in e-democracy projects. The method is integrating decision methods with democratic processes with the aim of enhancing transparency and efficiency in public decision processes. The case discussed in this paper is a set of three complicated decisions made by the politicians in a medium-sized municipality near Stockholm.

This project has shown that the ADL method is a useful tool in complicated political decision processes involving several stakeholders. The decision problems could be evaluated using the available background information in an efficient way. Despite the complexity of the issues involved, the method also facilitated the communication processes by increasing the visibility and clarifying the objectives and consequences involved.

The analysis results were provided as advice not decisions. The purpose was not to replace but to support the political process in a structured, analytical way. Anyone interested and with access to the data can later check, verify (and criticize) the decisions based on the output documentation. As all consequences are clearly presented, it shows how all the alternative courses of action were valued. Also, during the decision process, the analysis was open for comments and could become the basis for further discussions. The political element will always be present in the uppermost layer, and this is in accordance with the ADL model. This is not a deficiency of the method but rather a path to gaining wide-spread acceptance for this way of working with a democratic decision process.

From this successful pilot case, we are now in the process of further developing the entire decision process and we are currently investigating the possibilities to provide templates for typical decision problems and how the use of such can be integrated in the method for speeding up various sub-processes during the analyses. We will, in the near future, implement these in collaboration with other Swedish municipalities.

References

[1] Grönlund, Å.: "e-Democracy: in Search for Tools and Methods for Effective Participation", in *Journal of Multi-Crit. Decis. Anal.*, vol.12, pp.1-8, 2003.

[2] Danielson, M., and Ekenberg, L.: "A Framework for Analysing Decisions under Risk", in *European Journal of Operational Research*, vol.104, pp.474–484, 1998.

[3] Towards Electronic Democracy – Internet Based Complex Decision Support. bayes.escet.urjc.es/ted/

[4] Ekenberg, L., Brouwers, L., Danielson, M., Hansson, K., Johansson, J., Riabacke, A., and Vári, A.: Flood Risk Management Policy in the Upper Tisza Basin: A System Analytical Approach – Simulation and Analysis of Three Flood Management Strategies, IIASA Report IR-03-003, 2003.

[5] Danielson, M., Ekenberg, L., Johansson, J., and Larsson, A.: "Investment Decision Analysis – A Case Study at SCA Transforest," in *Proceedings of the 2003 International Conference on Information and Knowledge Engineering*, CSREA Press, 2003.

[6] Danielson, M., Ekenberg, L., Johansson, J., Larsson, A.: "The *Decide*IT Decision Tool", in Bernard, J M, Seidenfeld, T., & Zaffalon, M. (eds.), *Proceedings of ISIPTA'03*, pp.204-217, Carleton Scientific, 2003.

eAdoption and the Knowledge Economy: Issues, Applications, Case Studies
P. Cunningham and M. Cunningham (Eds.)
IOS Press, 2004

DEMO*sfera*: a Laboratory for eCitizenship in Sicily

Jesse MARSH[1], Francesco PASSANTINO[2]
[1]*Atelier Studio Associato, via XX Settembre 70, Palermo, 90141, Italy*
Tel: +39 091 6253378, Fax: +39 091 6253378, Email: jesse@atelier.it
[2]*iTeam5.net, via Angelo Poliziano 40, Palermo, 90145, Italy*
Tel: +39 347 6195970, Email: francesco@iTeam5.net

Abstract: This paper presents a case study of a local, citizen-driven e-Democracy initiative under way in Palermo (IT). The background scenario is first described, primarily in terms of the digital divide separating those with civic and/or political interests and those with IST competencies. The DEMO*sfera* project aims to overcome these barriers so people can work fruitfully together to develop new solutions. The first experiments – DEMO*news* and DEMO*dai* – are briefly described together with their development potential and technical implications. Considerations are also offered regarding the business case/survival potential of such an initiative in terms of a balance of actual and perceived cost/benefit exchanges. Finally, lessons learned and suggestions for future work are put forward.

1. Introduction

1.1 Background: eDemocracy Challenges and Citizen Groups in Palermo

While there is currently much discussion on "eDemocracy" and "eCitizenship", it is still very far from addressing the key concerns of citizens. The large part of related policies under eEurope 2005 and the IST program treat it as a sub-set of eGovernment, with an emphasis on technical solutions for current practices such as voting [1]. As the limits of traditional paradigms – "efficiency" as the driving benefit of IST, or the product-driven distinction between "provider" and "client" – become evident however, many experiments are beginning to explore new ways of balancing the human and the technological, new forms of collaborative and collective development, and new approaches to political organisation and the practice of democracy. [2][3][4]

Within a domain that is still so open to definition and experimentation, an interesting example of a bottom-up exploration of the problems and opportunities for eDemocracy is the DEMOsfera project, launched in early 2004 in Palermo (IT). This spontaneously organised initiative aims to meet needs and fulfil requirements of its participants as they arise without any formal structure, workplan or external funding.

The DEMOsfera constituency includes a broad range of local citizen movements, anti-mafia groups, and voluntary associations that have been co-ordinating efforts over the last few years, more or less in parallel with the rise of the no/new-global and anti-war movements. The first experience of active cooperation among these groups proposed primary elections to choose the centre-left's candidate for the race for the President of the Province of Palermo in early 2003. This proposal involved an organisational innovation supported by a Web-based service for the registration of voters and votes, as reported in [5], and awoke the politically active to the potential impact of ISTs for eDemocracy.

Following that experience (and its mixed outcomes), an enthusiastic but chaotic use of basic Internet services flourished. Mail lists for each group expanded as citizens provided email addresses on every occasion: only afterwards did they realise that this meant receiving all sorts of announcements, petitions, etc. often several times. “Communication groups” were thus set up to coordinate these efforts, aiming unsuccessfully to set up a single portal onto the varied world of political groups, movements and associations. [6]

1.2 Objective

The main objective of this paper is to follow the story of DEMOsfera from this point onwards. The approach is principally a narrative one and the insights set forth are mostly speculative, since communication and negotiation processes have been determining the project's development path more than pre-defined methodologies or benefits to be gained by one or more of the parties involved. In the end, DEMOsfera attempts to exploit new tools but in a way that puts the human, social and political dimensions first.

Nonetheless, by describing the DEMOsfera approach and some of its first experiments, we also aim to highlight concrete outcomes and ultimately demonstrate the broader potential of the approach. These implications imply a process whereby industrial innovation follows and is determined by social innovation, making it difficult to go beyond the extrapolation of weak signals at this stage. In this context, possible developments can be suggested along three axes:

- DEMOsfera as an exemplar of a truly participative and collaborative development methodology, broadening current trends in shared software development to involve technicians and non-technicians on an equal basis.
- DEMOsfera as an original and effective means of generating frameworks and specifications for the full-scale development of ISTs.
- DEMOsfera as an initiative whose potential sustainability is based on a balance of actual and perceived cost/benefit exchanges for a variety of stakeholders in a network, rather than a “business case” for a single company/industry sector.

2. Barriers to eDemocracy

2.1 The eCitizenship Divide

The DEMOsfera idea primarily addresses two barriers that appear to block a positive interplay between people and technologies for the development of appropriate IST tools to support citizens movements. The first involves the profound differences in culture and practice between those whose interests are mainly technical and those more involved in the political dimension. Some of the issues involved here are summed up in Table 1 below.

Issue	**Technical culture**	**Political culture**
Awareness of IST potential	Enthusiasm for latest, most sophisticated tools	Aware of widely diffused tools, critical view on rest
Emphasis of interest	What technology makes theoretically possible	Technology as a cure for political apathy
Emphasis of practice	Conformity of behaviour to norms and standards	Inclusion of the technically less aware
View of information	Expressiveness of multimedia	Importance of editorial validation of knowledge
View of communication	Idealised peer-to-peer interaction	Diffusion of own ideas

Table 1: Issues in the eCitizenship Divide

In practice, these differences lead to a substantial gap in the status of eCitizenship that applies equally to both sides of the equation. The technical culture is unable to fully understand the values driving political participation, while the politically involved continue to see IST people and tools as something extraneous to their way of doing things.

Visible signs of this gap were evident in a series of meetings in late 2003 and early 2004, where the aim was to bring together the technically competent and the politically involved in order to define a common strategy. When the majority of participants were the leaders of the citizen groups, discussion focused on organisation of an editorial board, thematic division of content, or the links between a portal of the movements and off-line information channels and events. Technical discussion, if any, would be based on generic visions of common electronic calendars, unified mail lists, etc. To the technicians, these appeared to be boring discussions that did not produce any concrete results.

When the majority of participants were technically competent, discussion shifted to application scenarios, technical architectures, demonstrations of new technologies, etc. With only a little integration, miracles could happen if only people were to, say, format their messages in the proper manner. To the politicians, this all appeared irrelevant, they were more interested in using the technology in any way so long as the objective is reached.

2.2 The Limitations of Free Service Provision

A second barrier to eCitizenship consists, ironically, in free service provision. Modem connectivity and email are provided by local and global services alike at no cost. In addition, most of the larger providers offer further services such as forums, mail lists or even blogging. While this trend has had a significant impact on the democratisation of IST – indeed, these services constitute the initial platform for many spontaneous global citizen movements – it has also set significant limitations on the socially-driven development of new services. Some concrete examples from our experience help illustrate this point.

- The introduction of (paid-for) ADSL has re-introduced a bandwith differential that had all but disappeared with the diffusion of 56K modems. A video clip sent from the office in seconds takes time to download at home; this can be particularly important when people access the Internet for non-work reasons from different places.
- The diffusion of free email has raised the uncertainty of using email at all. A single individual or voluntary group may have several mail addresses, some for different purposes or simply created when a password was forgotten. In addition, the storage limit (normally 3 MB) assigned to free mailboxes can quickly fill up and it is impossible for the sender to tell whether this is a temporary or permanent situation.
- Other added value services generally supporting "communities" of users have the main limitation of being closed. In the social sense, the community in question is seen as a self-contained world in contrast with the arena of overlapping citizen movements we are dealing with. The services are also technically closed, in the sense that it is impossible to know exactly what features are implemented and how, or to make any modifications.

3. The DEMOsfera Scenario

3.1 Addressing the eCitizenship gap

The DEMOsfera approach addresses precisely the barriers identified above. To overcome the limitations of service providers, the project aims to set up all required services "in-house" to the community, by interlinking different resources via a local VPN. To avoid the main pitfalls of the gap between the technical and political cultures, a range of discrete modular project/services are proposed rather than an integrated site.

This approach enables a DEMOsfera scenario designed not as an IST service for a given set of users, but rather as a collective laboratory to openly explore new approaches to eDemocracy and eCitizenship. The scenario brings together the volunteer efforts of programmers, ISPs, webmasters, active citizens, political parties, elected representatives, etc. all sharing the desire to contribute according to their competence and interests, and to mutually benefit from the contributions of others.

At the heart of DEMOsfera is an on-going dialogue between different types of actors with different levels of technical competence. The collective efforts of those with connectivity, those with available hardware and those with programming and systems integration experience, aim to provide a platform that empowers the technical neophyte as much as the expert hacker. Since all hardware and software are open source or "on loan", all DEMOsfera services can be offered at no cost.

3.2 Services and platforms

We have thus been setting up an open, multi-site VPN platform offering whatever is appropriate and freely available: from a simple, configurable mail/conferencing system to a fully-configured Windows FrontPage server to more challenging Linux servers with blogging, streaming, etc. The idea is to proceed by open fragments – audio and video streaming for recordings of workshops and events, a city councillor blogging reports of council meetings, an RSS feed from a common calendar of planned events, etc. – leaving their selection and assembly to the choice of specific groups who can freely integrate these fragments into Web sites whose editorial approach reflects their values and views.

To support these initiatives, a basic set of services is envisaged for the start-up phase, to be enhanced over time. The main elements include:

- A shared calendar that can be edited by the responsibles of different groups to add events and related documents and also to plan the use of shared resources such as meeting facilities.
- An open database of mail lists, that integrates the lists belonging to different groups while maintaining their original integrity, as well as allow for individuals and groups to signal the kind of information they are interested in receiving.
- Both public and private conferences for uses ranging from open forums for public debate to restricted group workspaces for distance collaboration.
- Specific services to be developed such as: a service to distribute a petition and collect signatures, a simple opinion poll service, ready-made RSS feeds, etc.
- In-house installations of open source versions of specific service platforms, e.g. peer-to-peer networking, audio and video streaming, and web logging.

Implementation of the DEMOsfera services occurs in three main platform environments. The first consists of the Microsoft Web Server complete with all FrontPage extensions. While this is not in our opinion an ideal platform, there are two main advantages: a) many members of the technical community are most comfortable programming on the Microsoft platform, using e.g. ASP pages; and b) due to the diffusion of the Microsoft Office environment, this platform is the most accessible to a non-expert interested, say, in maintaining a simple Web site with FrontPage. The second platform environment is Linux, which beyond the well-known advantages of security and openness is also the ideal platform for running many innovative freeware services. Again, a good part of the development community has more fun programming for Linux than working with Windows. The third platform is the less-known FirstClass groupware environment, already licensed to Atelier (the organisation hosting most of DEMOsfera's activities) and selected in part because of its effectiveness combined with ease of use and distributed administration. This environment offers the basic mail, conferencing and calendar services required as well as a flexible programming interface to Web services. Due to its proprietary nature, however, this may all be replaced with freeware modules over time.

The physical architecture is primarily defined by the availability of contributions from different individuals and organisations participating in the DEMOsfera initiative. Thus, Atelier provides connectivity and a set of IP addresses left over from a package subscription, as well as the above-mentioned FirstClass server. The ISP providing the connectivity also includes full Windows hosting as part of its package, while another organisation participating in DEMOsfera has offered use of its Linux server. These servers will in the short term be connected via a VPN, but over time replaced by servers running on old machines donated by other participants and directly hosted on Atelier's premises.

4. The First DEMOsfera Experiments

The DEMOsfera concept includes not only the above-mentioned suite of services and platforms for experimentation, but also specifically targeted projects that integrate these services in a new way. While the platforms described above make anything possible (at least in theory; empowerment is a higher priority than reliability) the main emphasis remains on meeting the expressed requirements of the citizen groups, associations, politicians etc. participating in the initiative.

In the following, we describe the first projects undertaken in DEMOsfera, with particular emphasis on illustrating how the methodology of starting with ad-hoc fragments and working along a gradual interoperability and integration path can throw up new and otherwise unexpected requirements for eCitizenship services.

4.1 DEMOnews: What's Happening in Sicily

One of the first problems highlighted by different citizen groups and movements was the proliferation of mail lists and chaotic distribution of emails. Different announcements and documents distributed, all follow their own logic and format, from the scanned (nearly illegible) image of a printed conference invitation to a richly formatted html mail document that comes out in surprising ways on anything but the latest version of Outlook.

From the analysis of this problem, the DEMO*news* project was born, as a simple email-based update of what is going on politically in Sicily. The concept is closer to a relay service (receive, synthesize and forward) than a newsletter, where the need for an editorial board would have taken us back to the eCitizenship gap. Indeed, simply putting together a synthesis of all messages received at the mail address demonews@atelier.it (actually a FirstClass conference) and sending it out each week has a political impact of its own. From the first feedback received, DEMO*news* has been successful in stimulating civic participation simply by raising awareness of the richness and variety of activities taking place and by fostering interaction between and among different interest groups.

The first implementation of DEMO*news* (launched in early March 2004 and continuing weekly since) required a group to meet weekly and read messages sent to the email address, synthesize the contents and add links for further information (all attachments such as petitions or seminar programs are stored in a common library and linked from the body text), and send the weekly summary off to the collective mailing list (currently just over 2,000 addresses coming from different lists).

In parallel, technical brainstorming identified the possibility of integrating this approach with blog and group calendar services and an RSS feed that would make DEMO*news* available as a service to be integrated into the Web site of any participating group or association. Interoperability would primarily be based on re-coding the incoming mail envelopes as XML tags, so as to (nearly) automatically generate the blog environment that, in turn, would generate the group calendar and news summary through RSS.

The "manual" process originally implemented mimics this potentially IST-based procedure. The current organisation uses a web log to transfer different messages to a common format and library during the week. This makes weekly editing much simpler, allows the group to better distribute responsibilities and maintain an archive of DEMO*news* items. In addition, it helps us understand what enhancements to Blogger's standard tags and template would be required to automate the whole process as in the long-term scenario.

The concrete experience of producing DEMO*news* over the last few months has thrown up other unexpected twists. For example, the mail lists coming from different groups and associations have far less overlapping listings than expected. Rather than a core group of active citizens, the community is driven by discrete groupings with well-defined interests and only exceptional (through very visible) cases of cross-participation. Secondly, the material coming in is dishomogeneous by both type (events, petitions, briefing papers) and media (e.g. the scanned image of a workshop program). Such evidence, taken as expressions of real needs rather than people not following instructions, raises interesting new bottom-up requirements for a semantics of democracy – an e-demXML?

4.2 DEMOdai: Transparency in Fund Raising

A second DEMO*sfera* experiment was linked to the June 2004 European Parliament elections, where citizen groups faced an interesting challenge. In recognition of the important contribution they make to the renewal of participatory democracy, leading members were called on to take up the responsibility of candidacy. However, most were anxious to avoid the trap of being sucked into the political parties' structures and methods and thus lose a detached position held important to continuing in their role as watchdog.

Encounters with potential candidates explored the terrian for some kind of initiative that could distinguish their role from that of career politicians and perhaps even challenge some of the less transparent aspects of political practice. The issue of campaign financing seemed a natural candidate: leaving aside actual vote-buying, fund raising in even the best of circumstances is a haphazard process leaving little guarantee to the giver that his or her money will end up being used for the intended purpose.

The DEMO*dai* ("dai" in Italian means "give" or "come on") initiative was proposed as an alternative fund-raising service providing increased transparency in managing contributions. The concept is that any individual could choose to which party(ies) and/or candidate(s) their money shall go to and in what proportion. For each target it should be possible to exclude its use for television advertising. The DEMO*dai* service would provide for the collection of money based on these criteria and credit the appropriate accounts once the donation is registered. It addition, it would publish the overall accounts of donations and withdrawals in order to demonstrate that the intended usage has actually occurred.

The DEMO*dai* proposal was backed up by a design for a Web-based service that would parallel the flow of real money with a virtual currency accounting system. This would occur by keeping track of the purpose money is destined to and checking process synchronisation with the flow of real money at the appropriate intervals, such as when collected donations are actually given over to a candidate or deposited in a bank account. The implementation architecture foreseen is similar to that set up for the primary elections in early 2003 [7].

Our experience – DEMO*dai* was not actually implemented in time for the 2004 elections – showed however that the implications of the idea are far more political than technical. In terms of ethical commitment, in order to appear in the list of possible choices a candidate or political party would have had to sign up to certain principles and methods of transparency in the handling of money. What became clear was that beyond the initial support and enthusiasm (inversely proportional to the political experience of the candidate), DEMO*dai* indeed touched upon very sensitive issues. As we carry forward this project with a core group of interested parties for the next (planned) elections in 2005, the hidden rules of campaign financing will have to be dealt with.

5. Conclusions and Recommendations

5.1 Is there a Business Case for DEMOsfera?

One of the key questions concerning the potential significance of the DEMO*sfera* experiment is its ability to survive over time. Normally, this question is answered by examining the business case for a given IST service, with the potential benefits for both the product or service provider and the market and its user/client/consumer groups. In our case, however, the issue is not so simple: democracy and citizenship are not (yet) business sectors, and the initiative in no way leads itself to commercial exploitation as a whole.

If the concept of business case risks being irrelevant for a situation such as DEMO*sfera*, its sustainability can still be investigated with other approaches. Indeed, it may be more appropriate to think of a multi-actor "cooperation survival plan". In this case, an organic system – albeit a small one – is taken into account as "containing" all the main actors and thus their transactions, rather than emphasizing each transacting pair of actors singly through a purely monetary filter. This approach thus analyses the point of view of each of the different types of stakeholders involved, particularly with regards to the different "transaction currencies" implicit in their cost/benefit reasoning: for some it may indeed be money, but for others it may include prestige, visibility, participation, social capital, etc.

On the basis of the DEMO*sfera* experience to date, we suggest a first idea of what such an analysis might look like in the following table.

Stakeholder	Currency	Perceived costs	Benefits seeked
Political activist	Power	Learning	Citizen consensus
Association leader	Social mobilisation	Sharing	Increased reach
Active citizen	Participation	Increased involvement	Increased impact
Platform provider	Quality system usage	Facilitation, assistance	Enhanced offer
Developer/integrator	Hacker-type prestige	Dealing with politicians	Widespread usage
Big solution provider	Market share	Dealing with ad-hocism	Innovative solutions

Table 2: A Multi-actor Analysis for DEMOsfera

A short and long term "balance sheet" could be drawn up for each stakeholder in their own "currency" and for the initiative as a whole in terms of percentage of added value.

5.2 What Further Research is Required to Tap the Potential Benefits in Other Contexts?

DEMO*sfera* represents a case study with a potential for broader significance in the search for methods and services that can appropriately respond to citizens' increasing dissatisfaction with current forms of participation, democracy and the expression of citizenship. While the initiative is still in its youth, the issues discussed in this paper appear to promise interesting developments for the future. In particular, however, the following aspects are likely to require further investigation:

- In order to promote the transferability of the DEMOsfera approach, and thus enable comparative case studies across political and cultural contexts, the laboratory approach will require a more formalised representation allowing to highlight local specificities with respect to generic rules of thumb.
- Further development of a possible e-demXML would require linking bottom-up requirements from experiments such as DEMO*news* with a top-down analytical approach that exploits experience gained in more mature domains such as e-commerce.
- The idea of a "cooperation survival plan" also requires further formalisation, that could equally benefit from examples in other application areas such as open source software development, collaborative e-music composition, etc.

Finally, if approaches such as DEMOsfera are considered to make a positive contribution towards collective policy goals related to democracy and citizenship, the question arises as to how public entities can promote such initiatives. At issue is not only the absence of a single beneficiary as the potential recipient of support, but also the potentially negative imbalances that could be introduced into the equilibrium of the cooperative network. Yet if current industry-led or government-led approaches are inadequate to fully address citizens' desires and demands for participation in a balanced way, the need to broaden the scope of the policy tool-kit becomes all the more urgent.

References

[1] A good example is the eTen E-Poll Project http://www.e-poll-project.net
[2] The 2-part workshop "eDemocracy and Participation" held at the eChallenges 2003 conference in Bologna presented case studies in Finland, France and Italy. See www.echallenges.org/2003/default.asp
[3] Further examples of participatory and political eDemocracy experiments include www.moveon.org in the US, the UK-based www.voxpolitics.com or www.france.indymedia.org (and other Indymedia sites in Europe and the world).
[4] Finally, for an excellent updated overview of the challenges and potential of eDemocracy in Italy, including a rich set of national and local case studies, see AA.VV., "Linee guida per la promozione della cittadinanza digitale: e-democracy" (in Italian), published by the Italian Ministry of Innovation and Technologies and available at http://www.crcitalia.it/UserFiles/1691.pdf
[5] J. Marsh and F. Passantino, "Primary Elections in Palermo: Case Study of an eDemocracy Service", in *Building the Knowledge Economy: Issues, Applications, Case Studies*, IOS Press, Amsterdam (NL), 2003.
[6] Based on models of integrated political portals such as www.centomovimenti.it or www.attac.info
[7] See [5] above.

Section 4

Knowledge Management

Section 4.1

Issues

eAdoption and the Knowledge Economy: Issues, Applications, Case Studies
P. Cunningham and M. Cunningham (Eds.)
IOS Press, 2004

A National Programme Perspective on ERA Challenges for Semantic Systems and Services

Erich Prem
eutema, Dr.-Karl-Lueger-Ring 10, Vienna, A-1010, Austria
Tel: +43 1 5245316, Fax: +43 1 5245396, Email: office@eutema.com

Abstract: In this paper we report on the design of FIT-IT, a novel Austrian national IT research programme focusing on semantic systems research. FIT-IT addresses a particular challenge of the Austrian innovation system. The programme concentrates on RTD projects with a medium term market perspective. It addresses the challenge of pushing industry players towards earlier development of truly novel technologies. The area of semantic systems provides a particularly interesting challenge for such a programme as the field has only recently found a substantial market in specific application areas. The programme is embedded in the policy framework of the European Research Area (ERA) that poses novel problems for designers of national research and innovation programmes. The paper summarizes the author's views concerning design implications for novel national programmes in the ERA.

1. European Research Challenges for Semantic Systems

1.1 Introduction

The growth of information stored in electronic databases worldwide in combination with the accessibility of this information through the Internet offers both enormous opportunities and challenges. The exploitation of the full economic and social potential of the newly available data and services has only started. But it has already become clear that much more research will be necessary to tackle problems related to the sheer size of the databases, interoperability issues, security aspects, and – most notably – issues related to the meaning of all the information stored on the web. Consequently, researchers, companies, and policy makers show increased interest in research into questions relating to semantic systems and web services – by many considered essential for the next generation of the web.

In this paper we report on the design of FIT-IT, a new Austrian IT research programme with a strong focus on semantic systems. We will outline the importance of semantic systems as a European research topic, describe the design of our national initiative and show that the advent of the European Research Area adds another level of complexity to the design of such programmes. It is argued that further European co-operation will be vital to fully exploit the potential of the semantic web.

1.2 The Demand for Semantic Systems Research

The Semantic Web is based on the vision of describing and linking data on the web so that it can be used by machines for display, automation, integration and reuse across various applications. The potential economic impact of this vision is fascinating. For example, IDC (www.idc.com) estimates that by 2008 companies will spend US$11 billion for web service software alone. The direct exploitability of this potential for EU enterprises is not evident, however. The field has only recently found a substantial market in highly specific application areas. It is still very much driven by university-type research and players who are university spin-offs. Real-world examples of business cases using semantic web technologies are confined to small application domains or limited numbers of sites and services.

A preliminary analysis shows that only a few companies are active in the core areas of semantic services and systems. These are mostly spin-off type enterprises, e.g. active in ontologies, XML editing, natural language and artificial intelligence (AI) techniques. With their relatively weak customer base and in many cases only marginal revenues these companies may not yet be good candidates for state intervention due to the low expected impact. However, on second glance Semantic Web (semweb) and related technologies (including AI, cognitive systems, new web-based services) are an area of activity of many mature enterprises covering a broad range of industries from automotive to steel. Semantic aspects are also an area of research for the larger, more traditional IT vendors and service providers as they offer to open up new markets for novel value-added service.

The current economic promises combined with the technological challenges also suggest that semantic systems are an area with a high potential for radical innovation. This is one of the reasons why research and research policies have recently focused on the area.

1.3 Embedded Systems Research in Europe

Today, there are a number of national semweb activities in Europe. Consider Ireland which gained first experiences in its "Informatics Research Initiative". The UK has been running CoAKTinG (Collaborative Advanced Knowledge Technologies in the Grid) and the JISC and the Engineering and Physical Science Research Council (EPSRC) have undertaken to fund projects to progress the development of a Semantic Grid and Autonomic Computing. Germany included "Intelligent Systems and Knowledge Processing", "Knowledge Networking" and "Internet-based Business Processes" in its IT2006 programme. Austria's programme "FIT-IT Semantic Systems and Services" is described below.

Apart from this interest of a number of EU member states, the European Commission has also recognized this potential through research programmes. In the Framework Programmes, semantic issues were already addressed in the 5th FP by IST and are currently covered by the strategic objective on "semantic-based knowledge systems". Of course, similar interest exists at international level, e.g. by NSF programmes in the US.

It may be argued that semantic technologies lend themselves very well to application areas of particularly European interest. Examples include domains such as eTourism and Cultural Heritage; but also strong EU industrial sectors such as automotive or telecommunications. Even European expansion and its challenges address issues related to semantic systems: European cultural diversity calls for investments in technology with the potential to support trans-national integration or offering of services. The fact that semantic technologies support precisely this sort of integration irrespective of human language makes them a promising opportunity to address the challenges in the enlarged EU and to fully exploit its economic potential. It is evident that projects in this area will only benefit from co-operation with new member states and across linguistic boundaries.

However, the relatively weak penetration of the IT and internet market with semantic technologies (including in particular intelligent services in the telecom sector) calls for more European co-ordination. While the EU's activities in FP6 are certainly interesting, much more needs to be done to co-ordinate research programmes and policies in this area.

1.4 The European Research Area (ERA)

Co-ordination and co-operation of European national research has been recently addressed by the term "European Research Area", the latest major EU RTD policy development. The ERA initiative aims to address three weakness of research in Europe: insufficient funding, lack of an environment to stimulate research and exploit results, and the fragmented nature of activities and dispersal of resources. Consequently, the objective of the ERA initiative combines three related and complementary concepts, cf. EC (2000):

- the creation of an "internal market" in research, an area of free movement of knowledge, researchers and technology;
- a restructuring of the European research fabric, in particular by improved coordination of national research activities and policies;
- the development of a European research policy which takes account of all relevant aspects of other EU and national policies.

The development of this common European Research Area (ERA) is ongoing and the current 6th Framework for Research and Technological Development (FP6) plays an important role in bringing the different players in Europe closer together. FP6 also provides funding opportunities at the level of national research programmes by offering support for the networking of national programmes. The fact that 422 funding agencies, programme managements, ministries and the like participated in a first call for ERA-NET projects gives an impression about the inherent difficulties related to this task [2].

The ERA [1] also poses novel problems for designers of national research and innovation programmes. National programmes until recently were designed without giving consideration to aspects of European co-operation and co-ordination of research. With the advent of the ERA as a core guideline of European innovation policies this situation has changed. In the following we report about the design of FIT-IT as a novel Austrian national IT research programme with a focus on semantic systems and services.

2. FIT-IT Semantic Systems and Services

2.1 Principles of FIT-IT

FIT-IT is a new IT research programme designed to address a particular challenge of the Austrian innovation system. While there is a long tradition of both funding scientific research and more industrial development-type innovation, the funding of truly innovative and co-operative research from industry and academia is not common. This characteristic of the Austrian innovation system is, of course, generally true in Europe. It is symptomatic for a situation in which IT industry tends to innovate rather incrementally as opposed to more radically. FIT-IT focuses on RTD projects with a time-to-market in the 3 to 8 years range to address the challenge of pushing in particular industry players towards earlier development and consequently earlier exploitation of truly novel technologies.

The design of FIT-IT used a logic chart approach to clarify programme mission, goals, instruments, outputs, and outcomes. While the overall mission is characterized as pushing Austrian companies towards longer-term radical innovation, its goals are the development of innovative technologies, opening of future application areas and markets, improving the qualification of IT research personnel, and increasing the international and European visibility of Austrian IT research in semantic systems and services.

Instruments to reach these goals include co-operative research projects, scholarships, and accompanying measures (e.g. conferences, networking activities, etc.). The largest budget is reserved for cooperative research between industry and academia. Such projects are funded at a maximum rate of 75% of project costs, if the research institute costs are at least 80% of total costs. An international jury of experts propose the projects to be funded.

2.2 Experiences from the Test Phase

From 2002 on first experiences were gained with a two-year test phase during which 28 projects were funded in the area of "Embedded Systems". This area is of high economic relevance in the EU and while it shares the high potential for innovation with "Semantic Systems and Services", its maturity and market size are quite different. Figure 1 depicts project sizes (funding over costs) for the test phase.

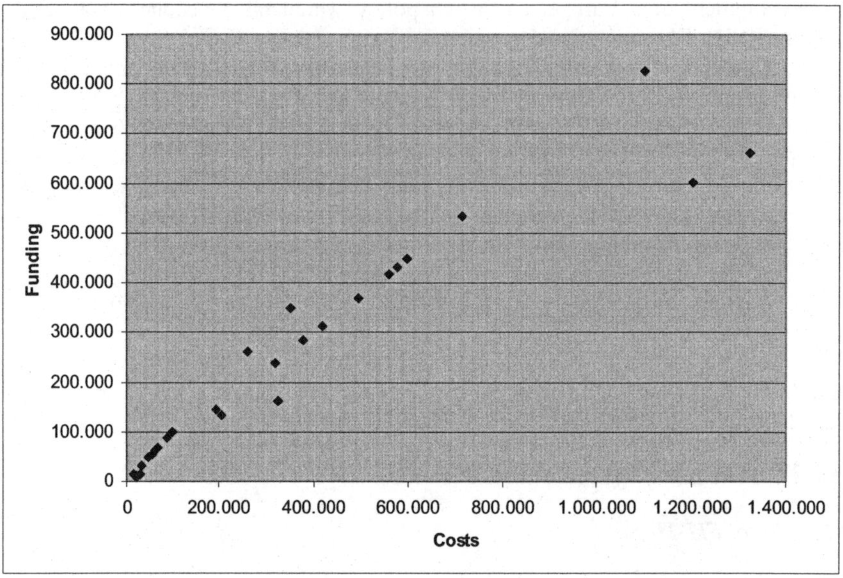

Figure 1 Total project costs and funding of projects selected for funding during the first two years of FIT-IT in the programme line "Embedded Systems".

First experiences with the test phase made it clear that despite of a high funding rate of up to 75% of project costs, companies are reluctant to move towards longer-term high-risk projects. However, the percentage of truly challenging projects increased over the three calls and shows that companies accept the push towards longer-term projects. An important side-effect of the new instrument was a process of reinforced community-building and even self-awareness. As an important lesson for the design of FIT-IT Semantic Systems, this means to foster on communicating the target time-to-market of 3 to 8 years.

As one of the expected drawbacks of FIT-IT, the introduction its new instruments impacted negatively on the number of projects submitted to the more traditional funding institutions. This is, however, acceptable as the total number of projects in this area increased. For semantic systems, this aspect is negligible since the total number of projects in this area submitted to traditional funds is marginal only.

2.3 Focussing the Topic Area

It is a general principle of FIT-IT to continually monitor areas of information technology and evaluate their suitability for new programme actions. There are three fundamental requirements for starting a new line in FIT-IT: a high potential to create economic impulses in Austria, a sufficient number of companies, and excellent academic research in this field.

Starting with the last of these requirements, a review of the research scene performed during programme design showed that high-quality research activities in the area exist in

Austria. The core research competencies include semi-structured data, XML processing, logic and knowledge based techniques for data analysis, AI and agents, and web services. The international activities of these groups range from close co-operation with institutes abroad to several EU projects. Interestingly, the groups are not solely located at technical faculties, but also at business schools and privately organized research institutes that combine industry and academia, e.g. in the areas of telecommunication, electronic commerce, and knowledge technologies (ftw, EC3, Know-Center [5]).

An existing company base with future economic potential in Austria is the second requirement for setting up a new programme line. A first analyis showed that a number of smaller, but active enterprises operate in the core areas of semantic systems. These include leading companies in XML editing (Altova), knowledge management and groupware (CarambaLabs, Hyperwave, PunktNetServices), visualisation (Holomey, Uma), information extraction and data integration (Lixto, Niwa, Widhalm), agent technologies (Netdynamics, Sysis) and tourism services (Lovo, Tiscover, Tourismhotline). While many of these are small companies, their technological excellence is often secured through close co-operation with universities. Indeed, many of the above companies are really spin-offs from academia.

Thirdly, we had to estimate the potential for a new programme line on semantic systems to create significant economic impact. Apart from an excellent penetration of internet technologies and broadband communication services in companies, there is a strong interest in relevant application areas such as eTourism, content and cultural heritage, and in general, activities towards new EU member states. Austria's geographic location at the border of four new member states and its leading position in (e-)tourism were major drivers in the creation of a new research programme for semantic services.

With Austria being a small country and the area of semantic systems potentially very broad, we performed a survey on research in semantic (and cognitive) systems and services to focus on the most promising technology areas with respect to academic and company interest. The survey included topics such as cognitive systems, agents and AI, natural language technologies, web services and adaptive systems. These fields are characterized by a wide variety of types of organizations active in research on semantic systems.

A total of 41 persons representing 37 organizations submitted questionnaires. They include both industrial (14) and more academic (23) research areas related to semantic (and cognitive) systems in Austria. When taking a look at the activity areas of respondents to the questionnaire (which are also similar to the activity areas of their organizations) it turned out that people in academia have in the past been involved with "agents and AI" and "web services" (20%), "semantic web" (18%), cognitive systems (16%), adaptive systems (14%) and natural language technology (10%).

Interestingly, the figures are significantly different for industry: "semantic web" (30%), "web services" (24%); "cognitive systems", "agents and AI", "adaptive systems" (13%), and "natural language technologies" (9%). The companies active in these areas are mostly SMEs with annual turnover of under €2 million. Research organizations are mostly university institutes but there are also two larger co-operative research organizations.

Most interesting for the programme designer is the topic area ratings for future expected developments (Figure 2). Note the difference in responses between companies and research institutes and the overall appraisal of the areas of "semantic web" and "web services".

Since FIT-IT is designed as a co-operative research programme fostering industry-academic links it was important to analyze the existing co-operations and potential for further collaboration in these areas. In the past, 21% of companies and institutes co-operated with partners from academia and companies, respectively, in semantic systems, these figures are 23% and 19% for web services. All the other areas show relatively little co-operation levels below 15% (with 10% as the smallest percentage for institutes that in the past co-operated with companies in the area of natural language).

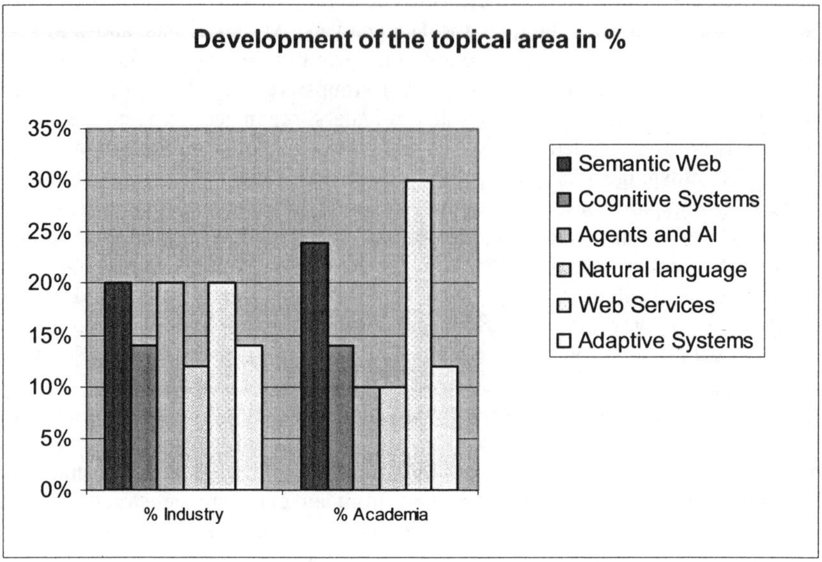

Figure 2 Development of topical sub-areas in %. (Which of the following areas is currently undergoing the greatest dynamics or will be most productive in the near future?)

When asked which areas are likely to hold the greatest potential for further co-operations, companies respond relatively uniformly (15-20%) in relation to "cognitive systems" while institutes find co-operation in the area of "web services" the most attractive (27%). Web services is seen as the most promising candidate for further co-operation.

An important indicator for the selection of a topic in relation to the expected economic impact is the relative importance of an area for the organization in the future. Organizations were asked about the role of semantic systems for the organization. The results (Table 1) express the expectations connected with the area. Note that the sample for the questionnaire included mostly organizations active in the area of semantic systems. Consequently, 26% of the industrial organizations rate "semantic systems" as a core competence. It is, however, interesting that the area is seen by the industry as truly opening up new markets while at the same time offering the potential for improving competitiveness in traditional markets.

Table 1 Responses to the role of "semantic systems" for the organization. (How important are semantic systems for your organization? Multiple answers possible.)

	Total	% Total	Industry	% Ind.	Academia	% Acad.
Core competence	18	26%	9	23%	9	30%
Experimental	14	20%	4	10%	10	33%
Complement our technology offer	6	9%	3	8%	3	10%
Improve our competitiveness in traditional markets	16	23%	13	33%	3	10%
Have the potential to open up new markets	15	22%	10	26%	5	17%
Sum	**69**	**100%**	**39**	**100%**	**30**	**100%**

2.4 FIT-IT Semantic Systems

As a result of the above considerations and interviews with experts, FIT-IT has launched a new programme line that focuses on semantic technologies for systems and services but does not particularly emphasize AI technologies, natural language or the like. These technologies are all regarded as important means to realize semantic systems but not an aim of the initiative as such. In 2004, FIT-IT will have a budget of € 4 million for this area.

"Semantic systems and services" is very different from the first programme line of FIT-IT, embedded systems, with respect to maturity of the field, economic exploitation, and constituency. The question thus arose whether the same instruments suitable for funding radical innovation in "Embedded Systems" should also be applied to "Semantic Systems and Services". Interviews with experts in principle supported the existing co-operative research projects as the major tool for funding truly innovative research in semantic systems. The importance of academic research in this area means that it may also be worthwhile to allow for purely academic partnerships with a clear economic orientation of the research (so-called targeted basic research). This is currently under design.

3. FIT-IT in the ERA

In addition to these goals, international networking and relating the programme to EU policies was a requirement based on previous Austrian experiences with EU research [4]. For a small country, co-operation with international partners is of particular interest and a necessity to achieve high-quality results at an international level [3]. While straightforward at the level of ambitious research projects, it is probably less obvious for industry. Today's partnerships of Austrian companies operating in the area of semantic systems clearly show the importance of internationalization. While companies such as Lixto find most customers abroad, others such as Altova base their research in the US. The same is true for researchers. For example, Dieter Fensel took a chair at the University of Innsbruck, Austria and is now the scientific director of the Digital Enterprise Research Institute (DERI) at the National University of Ireland, Galway. Thus, internationality for projects is a fact.

Internationality as a requirement at national programme level is, however, much less obvious and not only driven by international research projects. Recent activities in networking national programmes (ERA-NET activities) show that the mere existence of a topical national programme is essential for playing a substantial part in the design of co-operation of EU national programmes. International co-ordination requests clear interfaces which are naturally defined and often supported through topical programmes. In the case of FIT-IT the programme management also actively interfaces with policies at the EU level. The existence of a research programme with a well-defined topical focus facilitates policy discussions at trans-national levels, e.g. in the definition of EU strategic objectives.

Despite of the difficulties to fund non-Austrian organizations from national budgets, FIT-IT remains explicitly open for co-operation in this direction. FIT-IT is particularly open to bi-lateral co-operation with regions and countries in the EU and elsewhere. Currently, FIT-IT projects already involve partners from Germany, however without funding. In some cases, FIT-IT can also fund research organizations not located in Austria.

Extrapolating from our analysis of the Austrian research and industry co-operations it follows that ERA-NET type activities would be particularly useful in the area of semantic systems. The international character of the World Wide Web and the cross-border nature of services offered via the internet are important arguments for international co-operation and co-ordination in this area. Looking at US dominance in the area, the expected economic impact, and the challenges of the EU enlargement it is worthwhile to seriously consider even stronger efforts for co-ordinated trans-national research activities, even if the total number of companies may not currently justify a European Technology Platform.

4. Conclusions

Semantic systems and services are a particularly interesting topic for IT research in the EU: at the level of national programmes, but also at EU level due to the inherently trans-national characteristics of both applications and research. In this paper we have presented design considerations for the new Austrian initiative on semantic systems research. Analyses of the company base, the research organizations, and the potential economic impact through application areas supported the creation of the programme line. A survey of RTD interests served to carve out core issues of semantic systems as special topics. Technologies such as AI, agents, cognitive and natural language technologies will be considered as important contribution to semantic technologies, but not funded without such reference.

Researchers in the area of semantic systems clearly request international co-operation and regard it as essential for the future. FIT-IT was designed with a certain built-in flexibility to allow for trans-national co-operation. However, national regulations, organisational issues, and budgets, naturally limit the options for funding non-national research projects. More co-ordination is thus needed and can only be realised in a truly European framework, be it trans-national or multi-national. It remains to be seen whether the proper framework will develop into bi- or multi-national co-operation, ERA-NET activities, or simply the continuation of framework programmes.

References

[1] Communication from the Commission: "Towards a European research area" COM (2000) 6 - 18.01.2000. Brussels: European Commission, 2000.

[2] Countering the Fragmentation of European Research. IP/03/1707. Brussels: European Commission, 2003.

[3] Erbschwendtner J. et al., "IKT in Österreich." (ICT in Austria). Wien: IWI, 2003.

[4] Prem E., "Measures Driving SME Participation in the 'Information Society Technologies' Program of the EU". Melbourne, 5th Int. and 8th Nat. Res. Conf. on Quality and Innovation Management, 2001.

[5] www.ftw.at, www.ec3.at, www.know-center.at

eAdoption and the Knowledge Economy: Issues, Applications, Case Studies
P. Cunningham and M. Cunningham (Eds.)
IOS Press, 2004

Knowledge Management in 2010 - Business Needs and Market Prospects

Jonathan SAGE, Peter STANBRIDGE, Elmar HUSMANN
IBM Business Consulting Services,
Avenue de Woluwe 22, B 1932 Woluwe St Stevens, Belgium
Tel: +32 473 910 380 Fax: + 32 2 4165099 Email: jonathan.sage@be.ibm.com

Abstract: This paper discusses the general framework of our findings from the Study on Business Needs and Technology Trends in Knowledge Management (KM) recently completed for the European Commission (www.km2010.org referred to as the KM study) and apply it to the requirements of ground level knowledge management consulting. We emphasise the importance for practicing management consultants to have a solid foundational knowledge of academic and theoretical perspectives underlying the subject. We illustrate this with a perspective framework developed in the KM study and show how embracing a multiple perspectives view will promote more informed guidance to client implementation engagements.

1. Introduction

A particularly intriguing characteristic of knowledge management is that it has not faded as a serious management concern despite its shortcomings as a discipline in failing to provide organisations with all it has promised. Another characteristic of knowledge management is the diversity of approaches and technologies associated with it alongside its evolution.

On the one hand, the strategic importance of the subject area of knowledge management is widely acknowledged – given, for example, the growing demand for innovation and the increasing knowledge-intensity of many business sectors. However, the connection with concrete management practices or technologies is still fuzzy.

For some time interest in knowledge management has been carried by the hype-wave of the virtual or networked organization in the context of electronic business. However, KM has not benefited from this connection or from being regarded as a technology-centric discipline. We perceive knowledge management as neither a tool nor a trend. Instead, in its core it relates directly to a fundamental and fascinating discipline of organizational behaviour: the building and learning of organizational capabilities and the mechanisms by which these capabilities are stored and transferred into organizational action.

As a factor that determines business success, organizational capabilities are fundamental and universal. Studies on the evolution of organizational capabilities sometimes take examples from early industrialisation to show striking similarities with today's business world. What is new today – and called knowledge management - is the explicit attempt to influence and manage these processes.

As a rule of thumb, management practitioners typically care little for management theory. They are interested in concrete tools and action advice and often skip the step of a more profound understanding of organizational reality that management theory could offer. They also often skip the step of detailed organizational analysis that would allow for a better understanding of the characteristics and specifics of their own organization. Hence, knowledge management tools and approaches have often been over generalized.

2. Knowledge Management Theory Matters

We claim that part of the confusion and frustration associated with the knowledge management domain is linked to this overgeneralization of approaches and missing understanding of the diverse theoretical backgrounds that have led to them. In the context of practical application, it pays out negatively that knowledge management is one of the most multi-facetted areas in management theory.

In the recently published study (www.km2010.org), we show how much a theory-based perspective on knowledge management helps to clarify the maze of knowledge management approaches and technologies – at least where highly advanced programmes as the European Commission 6th Framework Programme (FP-6) are concerned. We claim that a number of perspectives have dominated the knowledge management industry, but at the client engagement and product vendor level, little attention is given to these multiple perspectives, let alone the engaging history of the problem of knowledge within philosophy, cognitive science, critical theory, hermeneutics, psychology and sociology. Our recommendations in the study urge more attention be given to the potential of the emerging study of social complexity has on innovation and knowledge management. We further claim that it is rather the evolution of a better understanding of organizational knowledge that will drive technological and management practices evolution than vice versa.

Therefore, instead of using technological- or application-scenarios, we have based our study on five different perspectives for the main academic directions that determine underlying assumptions and insights into knowledge management.

We were able to show how closely these are connected with specific organizational approaches and technological solutions. We also showed from the history of knowledge management that the discipline has not developed in a linear way in a single direction but has instead already diversified into multiple directions. Being an early adopter or research sponsor in the field of knowledge management therefore is a probe and learning game based on a portfolio of different activities that have to be pursued in parallel.

Our analysis reveals a blind-spot area of FP5 (EC 5th Framework Programme) portfolio of funded research projects touching on or dealing with KM. Interestingly, this blind spot is precisely the development direction which we argue has the potential to become key to European competitiveness in Knowledge Management. It is furthermore rooted in an area of European academic strength that seems currently little connected to technological product development and specific management practices. In the study, we underline our findings by a competitiveness analysis of the European position in knowledge management research and products in comparison to the US and the rest of the world.

However, the approach of our study is not limited to those shaping innovation and future technology policies on a European level. It is also particularly interesting for the knowledge management practitioner who is searching for strategic directions in the ongoing discussion on knowledge management. Thereby we discourage the hope for easy and transferable best practices that could fit any corporate environment.

We strongly recommend that engaging in knowledge management should not happen by bypassing the underlying theory and searching for easy to apply tools and technologies. In fact, applying them without understanding might turn out to be a waste of effort.

We argue the importance of an individual approach to knowledge management, based on a deeper understanding of the specifics and history of a given organization's characteristics of learning and transferring knowledge and an understanding of the underlying theoretical perspectives of the management discipline [1]. There is no simple way to design these capabilities into an organization or to renew them instantly. Instead they have to be build-up over a longer period in time. This makes successful knowledge management a long-term strategic programme not a short-term improvement activity.

3. World Views and Multiple Perspectives

In any area of business or information technology consulting, the various approaches adopted by practitioners are typically grounded in high-level theory (Figure 1).

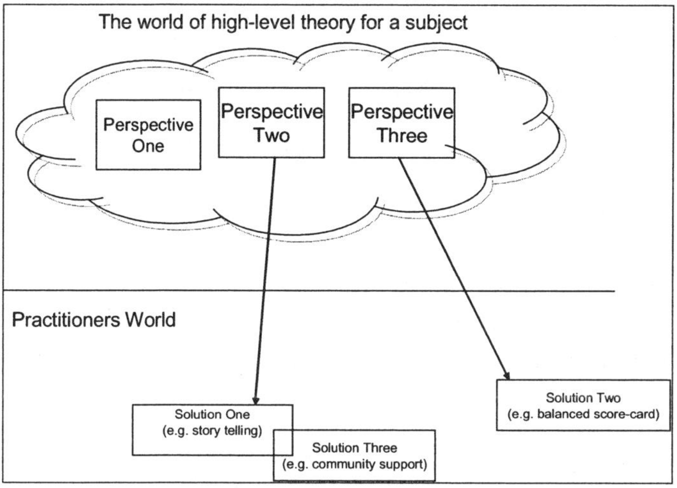

Figure 1 Multiple Views and Perspectives

We make the following additional explanations about the diagram:

- A consultant's perspective is based on his experience and those of his colleagues.
- This experience is frequently piecemeal, and specific to the particular engagement
- The technologies available to the consultant are frequently prefabricated and are often responsible for the intellectual substantiation of the specific perspective followed
- An implementation solution typically has its roots in some particular high-level theory. This is not surprising, given the easy access to academic publications and the academic background of many of the practitioner "gurus" in the marketplace.

Table 1. Examples of Typical Bifurcations Found in Knowledge Management Discussion

Natural-Science Perspective Terminology	Social-Science Perspective Terminology
Technology focus	Cultural/human focus
Natural sciences approach	Social sciences approach
Knowledge as a thing	Knowledge as a process
Knowledge can be classified, structured and shared	Knowledge is build through evolutionary processes and organizational learning
Information/knowledge described mathematically	Information/knowledge considered constructively
Technology impact inevitable (essentialism)	Technology in human control (if used at all)
Knowledge embedded into formal processes and organisational functions	Knowledge embedded in informal processes and chance encounters
Knowledge management as a separate discipline or as part of IT	Knowledge management as an essential part of organizational capabilities (but difficult to isolate in terms of actors, routines and objects)
Knowledge management as specified initiatives and programs, standards and technologies	KM as an organic knowledge enabler based on creative encounters, constructive activity and social behaviour
Knowledge management as a program managed and implemented by executives	Knowledge management as an all embracive activity central to strategy and the tasks/outlook of senior executives themselves

- It is not easy for practitioners to see the picture of multiple perspectives being developed in the world of high-level theory. Practitioners defending positions on the bottom level frequently argue for single perspectives. Engaging in bifurcations of positions is common, whereas a dialectical engagement would typically be more profitable. A set of examples of this bifurcation of views is illustrated in table 1 above.
- Academics in the high-level world tend to specialise. While acceptable in academic circles and seen as necessary for scientific rigor, this specialisation gives the impression of single perspectives. For the practitioner, the situation should be seen as a foundation for workable solutions based on the multiple approaches developed at the high-level.

4. Fundamental Perspectives in Knowledge Management

In the study, we identified five general perspectives (also referred to as scenarios) on knowledge management shown in Figure 2.

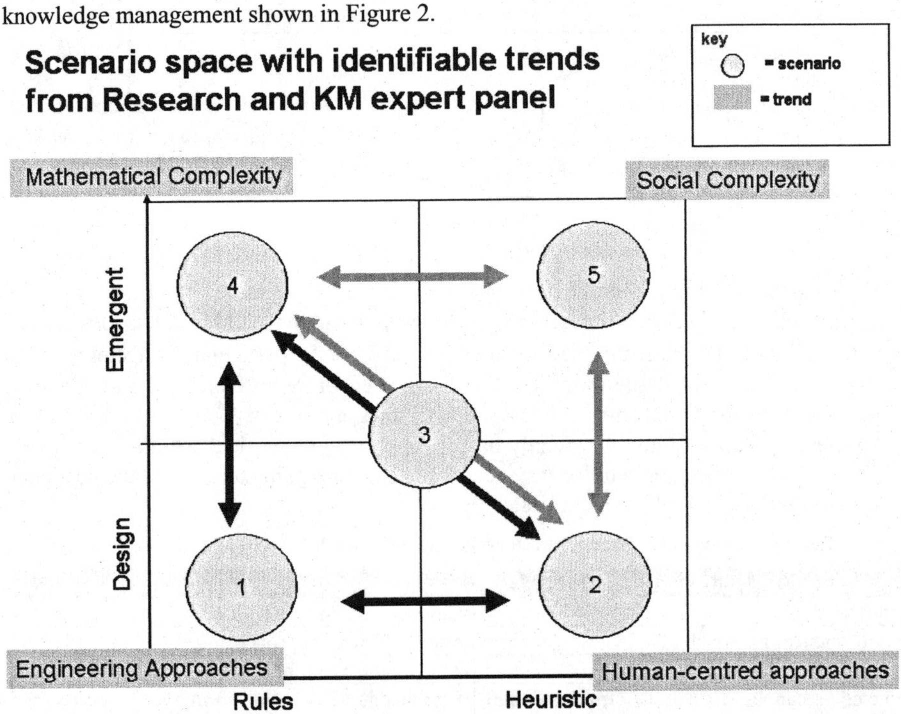

Figure 2: Knowledge Management Trends and Scenarios

The first perspective, which we called the engineering perspective, was an early perspective adopted in knowledge management. Technology developers but also implementation-oriented consultants have – somewhat unintentionally - found it most easy to deal with knowledge management based on a classical design metaphor. This also corresponded widely to "traditional management thinking" or "scientific management" over the last decades. Knowledge in this understanding is an entity or "thing" that can be isolated, processed and transferred like other fixed assets. Implementations in this perspective are most likely to be concerned with knowledge bases, document storage, data warehousing, workflow management and also in certain areas of CRM.

This method has strengths. Initiatives are clearly defined, easy to measure success and adapted to well-defined problem areas. KM applications in the engineering perspective draw on the foundations of previous IT generations covering such aspects as the application life-cycle, project management, technical and architectural design and implementation strategies. However, the approach cannot in most cases deliver on its own in the less well-defined and strategic areas of organisational innovation. But the KM practitioner can see in this perspective interesting quick-win solution ideas that can provide significant benefit provided expectations are managed. Also, at a tactical level, there are many solutions defined in this perspective that have significant contributions to make to business processes improvement and various types of organisational knowledge capture. Many of the other perspectives build on the technologies implemented in the engineering perspective.

Two important alternative development routes were taken in recent years. The first is equally rule-based but increased the mathematical complexity (4) of modelling knowledge representations (e.g. by complex ontologies), and retrieving information from distributed sources. It is promoted by IT experts and data analysts. The second route is human-centred (2) and based on an understanding of knowledge as being mainly tacit thus bound to concrete persons as knowledge holders. This second route underlined collaborative aspects and the importance of identifying and linking knowledge holders. It has found widespread acceptance among HR professionals and organizational consultants.

Both routes have also been reflected on the technology side (e.g. people search engines, collaboration tools or business modelling languages). The human-centered perspective has also provided well-established methodologies and approaches that can be applied by practitioners (such as storytelling [3]). However, both have their inherent limitations. Whereas the mathematical complexity approach tends to underestimate the tacitness and diversity of social knowledge, the human-centred approach tends to overemphasize it thereby neglecting ways to make knowledge explicit and increase manageability.

A fourth route has emerged that centres on the social complexity (5) and the dynamics underlying organizational learning, knowledge creation and exchange. The basis for this thinking is rooted in research on complexity theory, as provided by the Sante Fe Institute [2] and evolutionary economics. It also draws on the wider research areas of organizational learning, capabilities building and emerging strategies. It widened the toolbox of analytical techniques applied in knowledge management to add narrative or anthropological methods.

In Europe, research has been conducted into how complexity relates to Knowledge Management, by initiatives led in Catalonia / Spain under Max Boisot [4], the Cynefin research centre in Cardiff, Wales led by David Snowden [5], the eBMS Management School in Lecce, Italy, the Finnish Futures Research programme in Helsinki, Finland, the Complexity Science Research Centre at the Open University founded by Elizabeth McMillan [6] and by Ralph Stacey, director of the Complexity and Management Centre at the Business School of the University of Hertfordshire [7]. This perspective provides an important balance to the rules and "knowledge as thing" approaches of the other two schools mentioned, but for the practitioner, it represents the greatest risk area. Firstly, because it is currently still an emerging area of research that itself has multiple perspectives. While some examples can be found of practical implementations using social complexity, much of the current research remains in the high-level area. Secondly, the social complexity approach by definition requires new skills and approaches to the consulting task itself and will always require considerably more dexterity of skill by the practitioner than the other approaches. But all this remains to be seen.

Our fifth perspective captures much current management consulting. Resulting from a lack of orientation over the many theoretical perspectives, recent corporate knowledge management activities supported by the large consulting groups have therefore frequently adopted a consensus approach (3). In many ways, this is not a perspective – it is the anti-perspective. In this perspective, methodological approach is adopted by best practice, past experiences and packaged solutions designed to be replicated across consulting engagements. The advantage of the consensus approach is that it engages multiple perspectives, but it does so blind to the high level theory the techniques are taken from.

Our solution to the problem of knowledge management effectiveness is in the recognition of multiple perspectives based on a clear understanding of the high-level theory that has shaped knowledge management. This theory lies in the fundamental research in engineering, mathematical complexity, human-centred research and social complexity. Practitioners need to ground their work in these underlying theories, making themselves more aware of different opportunities, risks and approaches available when serving their clients. Sufficient knowledge management literature to gain access to all these perspectives, but we recognise that reference material covering a specialised overview survey of these perspectives is missing and currently needed for the knowledge management community.

5. Conclusions

Knowledge management is a complex area of organizational concern. While its subject matter, knowledge, has been debated since man has philosophized, considerable literature on knowledge management exists covering a wide range of approaches we have broadly classified into five different perspectives. Our study emphasized the need for European research to increase focus on social complexity as a major contributor to improved European organizational competitiveness. But we show recognition in this paper that current practice must intelligently apply techniques, tools, technologies and approaches developed from all of the various perspectives. Intelligent adoption means understanding the nature of these perspectives, how they can be applied to different organizational contexts and a sober realization of their strengths and weaknesses. But current consulting practices seldom provide space for such an understanding, yet we believe this is essential if organizations are to receive the quality and diversity of implementations they need.

More work is needed in providing more depth and empirical support to the perspectives we have identified. Practicing consultants also need to refer to reference material that provides them with a solid but unbiased grounding in the alternative approaches, but to our knowledge, no such work currently exists. We also believe that more research is needed to provide a more holistic approach to knowledge management perspectives, not only placing them alongside other general management perspectives (such as for strategy, marketing and innovation) but also within general philosophical perspectives.

References

[1] Clayton M. Christensen, Michael E. Raynor, "Why Hard-Nosed Executives Should Care About Management Theory", Harvard Business Review, Sep 1, 2003

[2] See John Casti, "Complexification" Harper Collins 1994.

[3] One could compare the anecdotal and experiential approach (based on work in the World Bank) of Steven Denning (see "The Springboard: How Story Telling Ignites Action in Knowledge-Era Organizations", Butterworth Heinemann, 2001) coming from the bottom of the line, with Yiannis Gabriel (see, for example, "Storytelling in Organizations: Facts, Fictions, and Fanticies", Oxford University Press, 2000) who is working in the high-level theory space. It is interesting to see Denning quote Gabriel. As mentioned, practitioners representing a viewpoint on the bottom frequently gain inspiration from the top.

[4] Max Boisot, "The Creation and Sharing of Knowledge" in Choo and Bontis, "The Strategic management of Intellectual Capital and Organizational Knowledge", Oxford University Press, 2002, pg 65-78

[5] See Dave Snowden, "Complex Acts of Knowing: Paradox and Descriptive Self-awareness, Special Edition, Journal of Knowledge Management, Vol 6, No. 2, May 2002.

[6] See Elizabeth McMillan, "Complexity, Organizations and Change", Routledge, 2004

[7] See Ralph D. Stacey, "Complex Responsive Processes in Organizations", Routledge, 2001

[8] The Study: Jonathan Sage, Dave Snowden, Rod Shelton, Peer Stanbridge, "Business Knowledge Management: A study on market prospects, business needs and technology trends", Final report to the European Commission

eAdoption and the Knowledge Economy: Issues, Applications, Case Studies
P. Cunningham and M. Cunningham (Eds.)
IOS Press, 2004

The Role of a Semantic Engine in an Information Management System

Anton ZAMOLOTSKIKH[1], Miriam CUNNINGHAM[2], Paul CUNNINGHAM[3]
IIMC International Information Management Corporation Limited,
128 East Wall Road, Dublin 3, Ireland
Tel: +353-1-8170607, Fax: + 353-1-8170606
Email: [1]anton@iimg.com; [2]miriam@iimg.com; [3]paul@iimg.com

Abstract: The paper describes some of the requirements to support semantic queries and rule-driven workflow in a modern information system. It proposes the introduction of a server-side Semantic Engine software module to meet these requirements. Such a Semantic Engine will support the mapping of different kinds of data stored in corporate relational databases to an ontological representation, querying such data using this ontological representation and handling workflow events. The combination of the Semantic Engine's event and rule-driven workflow capabilities and its support for queries, offers considerable benefits for adopters.

1. Introduction

Modern corporate networks are overloaded with information contributed and stored in a variety of different document and database formats. Finding relevant information in a timely fashion is increasingly difficult, thus impacting on organisational productivity. Incorporating some formal representation of the semantics or meaning of such information that would allow humans and software systems alike to understand the content of such information would reduce information overload and increase efficiency. While the systematic introduction and use of a corporate ontology and standards based tools such as OWL and DAML+OIL facilitate the introduction and management of semantic representation, interrogating and interpreting this representation is a major software challenge. It is important to provide a unified, but still flexible way to exploit the semantic knowledge stored in the system because of the diversity of software modules implemented and integrated over the lifetime of a typical corporate system. This paper proposes the concept of a server-side Semantic Engine, designed to providing semantic-based functionality to other software modules within or between corporate information systems.

2. Requirements

This section outlines a number of key requirements primarily related to information search and workflow support that the proposed Semantic Engine aims to cover.

2.1 Information Search

The most obvious application of semantics in distributed systems is finding relevant information, i.e. a search engine. Historically two different approaches have been applied to information searching: taxonomies and textual searching. The first one presumes that content is somehow pre-categorized by contributors or editors, thus facilitating user browsing through a tree-like structure of categories and sub-categories. Where documents sets are compact and well maintained, such an approach is very efficient. The second approach is based on using a textual sub-string or set of words to find a subset of relevant documents within a closed document universe. Indexing is used to increase performance.

The effectiveness of this latter technique is very dependent on the document content of interest, the vocabulary used to represent it and the vocabulary (language or key words) used to find it. The meaning or semantics of a document may be well or badly represented either by a single word or combination of words in certain circumstances. Using either technique, experienced users of information systems are more likely to find relevant documents because they are better equipped to select appropriate search patterns.

It is clear that both approaches have serious potential limitations. A key challenge for researchers and software developers is to design a more sophisticated way of both representing and finding relevant information. The goal is to provide accurate definitions of the meaning of different piece of information by using ontologies and provide a mechanism to extract semantics automatically from the content of documents and facilitate applying a number of "finding" strategies to the content. Such strategies must include browsing, text-searching and more complex (or multi-axis) queries.

The Ontologies produced tend to have a more complex structure than taxonomies. The constructed queries used to find relevant information cannot be expressed simply as named calls, parameterised by constants. As a result, a search engine must be able to efficiently parse logical expressions and ontology patterns with both bound and free variables.

As relational databases are still the industry standard for data storage in business and government, any Semantic based search engine must fulfil the following functions:

- store ontology information about different pieces of content into a relational database
- extract this information back into ontology representation
- pose complex semantic queries against the relational data for such extraction
- serve requests of different software modules, including remote modules

Any module supporting such features, can be called a Semantic Search Engine.

2.2 Rule-driven Workflow Support

Any information system imposes the requirement to support specific workflow. The more complex the information system becomes, the more complex the workflow support required. The minimum level of workflow support in any corporate information system is that all user privileges are defined by and limited by their rights, thus limiting what actions they can perform. In this case, every user is responsible for locating whatever information they need to process, defining what they will do and informing other relevant parties about the results achieved and any problems encountered.

As information flows get more intensive and complex, more explicit workflow support is required. The next level of workflow support is hard coded and heterogeneous. Individual software modules within the system are responsible for providing task related information and dispatching content to users. However, workflow is implemented in a module-specific way, and there is no common framework to control and manage workflow processes.

The next level is unified hard coded workflow support. This approach defines data structures describing the current state of each object and actor of workflow, the roles of actors and how content is dispatched. However, as the workflow rules are still hard coded in different software modules, it is not possible to define or change actual workflow rules. This approach only works well as long as a system remains static.

Rules-driven workflow requires a system module specifically designed to execute workflow rules that are defined outside the code. It can be part of the system configuration, or can even be dynamically changed as data, depending on the implementation.

The main objects of content-oriented workflow rules are content objects, actors, events, tasks, conditions and actions. As specific events occur, connected rules can be fired and related conditions checked. Based on rules, tasks may be assigned to actors in respect to content objects and other actors, and some automated actions may be invoked on content objects. New events may arise as a result of either automated or user actions.

While events are atomic objects, actors and actions are black boxes. Conditions must be interpreted and content objects may be partially "understood" by the workflow support module. This content needs to be represented as machine-readable semantics.

The internal representation of such semantics is likely to be a relational database. However, to be able to express the conditions it must be visible as ontology-type data (e.g. – a semantic network). This can be achieved by the introduction of a Semantic Workflow Engine, which handles conditions expressed as ontology patterns and logical expressions much like the Semantic Search Engine described above. This workflow engine must be event driven as well as directly responding to the actions of users.

As there is a high level of intersection between the functionality of the search and workflow engines described above, it is reasonable to propose to utilize a common Semantic Engine, which can handle both complex information searching as well as event and rules-driven workflow support.

3. Technology

3.1 Semantics Representation and Relational Databases

Within most of modern information systems, data available for interpretation is usually represented in the form of relational databases. This makes it possible to utilize the power of SQL and database interfaces for all platforms to extract and manipulate data from traditional applications.

However, relational database structures are not naturally mapped to semantic networks for example, the most popular theoretical model for semantic representation. Meersman (2002) discusses some reasons for such mapping [2], while Decker discusses related problems in [3]. On the other hand, not all the data within the database structure may require such a mapping, and the effectiveness of the relational database approach is worth retention.

This suggests that the existing data storage should be retained, while the information structures in the database(s) should be mapped on the semantic network. As mentioned above this is one of the functions of the proposed Semantic Engine.

Representation in a semantic network consists of a set of nodes, representing real world entities and a set of relations between those nodes defined by triples (i.e. object-subject-verb). Resource Description Framework (RDF) defines both the schema and formats (including XML-based RDF/XML) used for such representation.

As this representation is by its nature very basic, a number of higher-level languages have evolved above RDF, such as OWL and DAML+OIL, which distinguish between classes and instances, properties and associations etc.

Without going into the fine details of syntax, the following rules may be applied on mapping a relational database structure to an ontological representation:

1. Every relational database table corresponds to some class of the resulting ontology. Let us call such classes "table-level classes". This is useful as the entities reflected by records of one table are supposed to be of a similar nature and to have similar features.
2. Some table-level classes may be derived from more common classes, if corresponding entities express useful similarities. For example, XML documents and binary documents may be stored in different tables, but have common features like title and publishing date and relations of the same type (e.g. relation to users as authors). Let us call such more common classes "database structure generalizations".

3. Each record in a table represents an instance of some class or a number of classes. The table class is always included.
4. Both table and generalization classes are in some sense static. They stay unchanged as long as database structure is unchanged. There can also be dynamic classes as well as static classes there can also be dynamic classes. A record in a classification table represents each dynamic class. Such classification tables may hold a set of categories from a particular domain (e.g. groups of users), or even on a more generic level – a set of common categories with the domain affiliation explicitly mentioned in each record. As a result, the dynamic classes system may actually be changed by a user without any intervention into the code or the database structure.
5. All scalar fields are defined as simple properties of corresponding table classes (and all their instances), while relations between tables can express either aggregation (containment) or association. For example, the authorship of the document is an association between the instance of class "document" and an instance of class "person", while relations between chapter and whole document implies that an instance of class "document" contains an instance of class "chapter" as part of its inner structure.

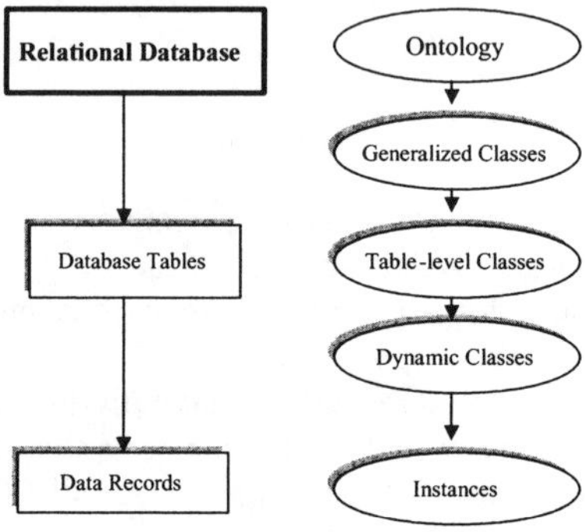

Figure 1

This way of constructing an ontology on an existing relational database produces a restricted subset of ontologies. For example table-level classes do not intersect in any way, generalized classes always include entire table-level classes, and dynamic classes are always entirely included in generalized classes, but not necessarily in table-level classes.

There is also a duality of dynamic classes present. This, means that a dynamic class is a class in the sense that a number of instances may belong to it (e.g. a number of users may belong to a group "Administrators"). On the other hand, the same dynamic class is an instance of some table class (e.g. "Administrators" group is an instance of the class "group") as reflected by a record in the corresponding table. Despite these limitations the method allows the creation of an ontological view of real data and the extraction of OWL or other RDF-based representation by applying simple rules.

It is important to note, that the database structure by itself cannot be mapped to such a view without some knowledge of the semantics of this structure. For this reason, it is proposed to introduce a corresponding mapping language in the Semantic Engine to describe the way a relational database maps to an ontology-like information structure.

3.2 Derived Association and Classification

Not every relation between entities is explicitly expressed in relational database. For example if some document is contributed by a user, which, as an employee of the organisation, belongs to a particular department, it may mean that the document is contributed by this department. This association of document with department may be useful for some workflow rules and as such must be reflected in the ontological view.

It is proposed to extract such information by including the ability to build derived association (and classification) in the configuration of the Semantic Engine. For the sake of computability and performance, this ability should not include recursive definitions and some other restrictions may apply.

3.3 Querying Semantics

As discussed in the Requirements section, the core functionality of the proposed Semantic Engine is the ability to execute semantic queries for the purpose of finding relevant information and testing conditions. It should be possible to express such semantic queries in a formal language within the structure, which allows their construction through a user interface (UI). The basic element of the proposed semantic query syntax is an ontology pattern. For example (in OWL/XML syntax – please refer to [1]):

```
<owl:Thing rdf:ID="MyDocument">
    <rdf:type rdf:resource="#NewsStory" />
    <author rdf:resource="#JDoe0001" />
</owl:Thing>
```

Figure 2: Proposed Semantic Query Syntax

This expression defines that MyDocument is a news story and its author is someone known as JDoe0001. Assuming that MyDocument is actually a free variable, this may be read as "find all news stories written by John Doe".

It is then possible to bind a set of free variables to a set of instances for which the condition becomes a true statement in our constructed ontology. All possible bindings of that kind will represent the result of searching, while binding to particular instances may check the condition in the case of workflow.

Unlike relational databases, ontologies do not pretend to contain complete information about the real world. If something does not exist in a relational database, it is interpreted as not existing in the real world. When it does not exist in an ontology, it can only be interpreted as lack of knowledge. On the other hand, it is possible to explicitly declare in an ontology that a particular entity does not exist.

Basic ontology patterns are not sufficient to construct complex queries. Logical constructs are required, including basic logical operators and quantifiers. The quantifiers are particularly important when constructing complex queries. Compare for example: "find documents which have been read by all members of the international programme committee" and "find documents, which have been read by at least one member of the international programme committee". In this case the universal quantifier is used in first query, but the existence quantifier is used in the second.

3.4 Handling Events

As discussed in the Requirements section, the proposed Semantic Engine must be event driven to support workflow. Any event must be represented by an event type and a set of associated instances of some classes in some roles. Events by themselves are instances of "Event" class and its subclasses. Based on such representation, events are described in exactly the same way as any other entity of the system.

The only specific feature of events is that they form a stream consumed by the Semantic Engine. The configuration of the engine should describe which conditions have to be checked if a particular event occurs and which actions should then be taken.

As all the actions are external to the Semantic Engine, it is only capable of checking the condition and invoking the action passing the parameters, and cannot track any results unless the action fires another event.

3.5 Security

As the Semantic Engine is a server application, it is important to manage the identification of users and apply user rights when processing queries and handling events. All communication in a distributed environment must also be secure.

We propose to solve the identification task by using either encrypted user-password pair identification or digital certificate-based identification. The identification of actual users of client software, not of the client software instance, must be passed to the engine as the rights of users are calculated inside the Semantic Engine itself.

Having identified the digital rights of the user, the query is constructed in such as way that any search results, which should not be accessible for a particular user are automatically filtered out. Events may also have additional security conditions attached to them depending on the rights of the user.

4. Architecture and Implementation Overview

4.1 General Architecture Layout

As discussed earlier, the Semantic Engine must be able to serve remote requests and invoke remote actions. To support interaction with a variety of distributed software modules, IIMC is implementing its proposed Semantic Engine within its web services enabled data provision server architecture. This server architecture already supports a number of data providers in handling SOAP-formatted requests. These include simple relational database data provider, HTTP and SOAP data collector and dispatcher, UI functionality implementation modules, UI rendering engine and, now, the Semantic Engine.

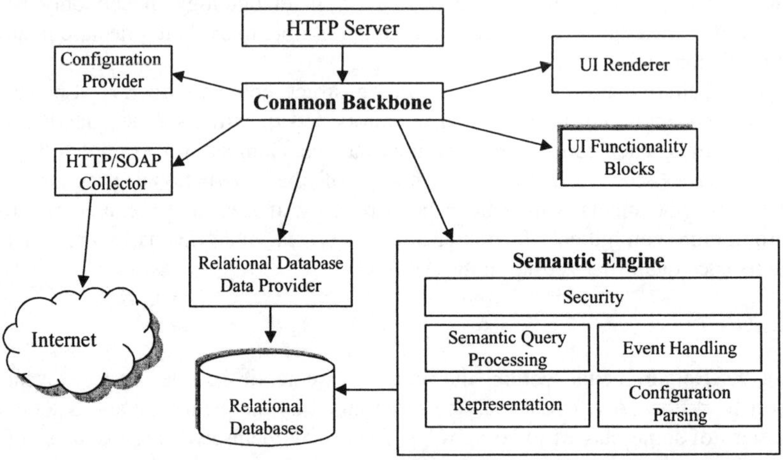

Figure 3: General Architecture Layout

The HTTP/HTTPS and inner requests are placed on the common server backbone and dispatched across a number of data providers, each running in multiple threads. Responses are dispatched in the same way with external responses returned to remote parties using HTTP/HTTPS.

4.2 Inner Structure

The Semantic Engine itself is currently being implemented as a number of Java classes, exposing the same interface to the common backbone as any other data provider within our architecture. It contains the following code modules:

- Configuration Parsing Module is responsible for processing configuration provided in XML form (either as file or as an extraction from a relational database), including classification, properties, aggregation and association mapping, derived classification and association definitions, pre-composed queries and event handling definitions.
- Representation Module is responsible for mapping relational data to an ontological representation and back. It is used for extracting data as well as for storing it.
- Query Processing Module handles both search and condition checking. It uses processed configuration to map logical statements on ontology patterns to SQL queries. The module uses the representation module for actual data extraction.
- Event Handling Module uses the Query Processing Module to check conditions attached to incoming events and to invoke remote or internal actions accordingly.
- Security Module handles user identification (either a software agent or an actual user using the client application) and attaching user rights filters to all queries created.

By combining these modules as wel as a scheduler embedded into the overall web services server, the desired Semantic Engine functionality of is achieved.

5. Applications

5.1 Pre-configured Information Search

Such a Semantic Engine makes it possible to build highly efficient, pre-configured search queries that can be easily parameterized by end users. For example, it is possible to easily construct a query "find all issues of the journal and all papers that contains the word X in the title and were published between Y and Z dates". The UI forms for invocation of those queries may then be placed in appropriate places of the portal or intranet site and the user will only have to enter X, Y and Z to extract the results. The key thing to remember is that journal issues and papers are quite different entities. An attribute "to be published on D date" for an issue is a direct attribute, but for a paper it is actually an attribute of the issue with which it is associated. The Semantic Engine makes it easy to construct such context relevant pre-configured queries.

5.2 Advanced UI-based Information Search

A more advanced use of the Semantic Engine is proposed for knowledge workers or those who spend a lot of time trying to find information relevant to their tasks,. A UI will be developed that allows such power users to construct semantic queries on the fly by selecting search axes and then parameterising those axes from sets of possible values. The actual process of query construction in this case actually involves using a set of queries to different domains within the system to obtain possible parameter values. This is complex, as such values may include instances of some classes within the ontology, or even classes themselves, not only simple values (such as strings and dates).

5.3 Pre-configured and Customisable Workflow

As in the case of queries, workflow rules may be pre-configured inside the semantic engine and only parameterized as necessary. Such an approach makes sense in the case of more or less static workflow, which may need only occasional modification. It is also very useful for typical workflow scheme libraries, which may be used in, for example, ASP solutions. In such a situation users can select whatever workflow scheme applies to their tasks and can then parameterise it as necessary.

More advanced customisable workflow requires extensive effort in designing and implementing an appropriate UI and validation mechanisms. These have not yet been built. However, an administration UI that enables the ability to easily construct workflow rules, and design the entire workflow scheme and then identify and correct any problems, can be of particular value for organizations that change their rules more frequently.

Semantic engine is also considered to be useful within a distributed workflow implementation, where software agents carry out processes based on changing local and global ontologies as described in [4].

5.4 Automatic and Semi-automatic Classification

The view on the data provided by the Semantic Engine can also create a good interface for an automatic classification tool. Based on machine learning principles, such a tool may learn how to categorize objects (e.g. documents) based on a pre-categorized training set, and construct a classification for other documents not yet categorized. In the context of the Semantic Engine, such a tool can operate purely in ontological terms, free of implementation details. In addition, this tool may rely on additional available semantic information, such as categorization along other axes.

Semi-automatic applications of such a tool with the Semantic Engine would allow subject experts to fix machine-learning errors, while still reducing the amount of man-hours required. For example, let us look at dispatching an inbound flow of documents (e.g. customer requests) into an organization. The documents arrive and are stored with some additional metainformation already attached, such as identity and location of contributors, simple (often misleading) classification, how they contributed the documents etc. Then the automatic classifier analyses the text of these documents and associated metadata, identifies the appropriate employee to deal with each document, and dispatches the documents accordingly. If the employee receiving a document decides that a mistake has been made, they redirect the document back to the classifier with instructions in relation to appropriate person to receive the document. The classifier not only re-sends the document to a correct person, but also learns on this experience, thus reduces similar errors in the future.

Over time, most incoming documents will be forwarded to the appropriate individuals and only a little minority of such documents will require manual intervention. The tool may even dispatch the documents more appropriately than a single individual, as it accumulates the knowledge of number of employees who actually process the documents and may even first query who is logged onto their computer or who may be on holidays, because it is tied into the overall corporate information system.

The machine learning techniques may be also used on the stage of ontology construction for existing relational data. Such an approach is suggested in [6]. If implemented, it may be used in semi-automatic fashion for extracting hidden dependencies and validating the resulting mapping.

6. Conclusions

These types of potential applications would complement existing content management, digital rights management or knowledge management initiative in any large organisation.

The Semantic Engine approach described is a way to build a compact, powerful solution for advanced information retrieval and complex workflow support within corporate information systems, intranets, portals and ASP services. It relies in concept on mapping existing relational databases to an ontology-based representation for these particular applications, while keeping the underlying data intact. The ontological information used by such a system may be enriched by use of machine learning methods. Event-driven condition checking and a black box approach to invoked actions provide a firm foundation for workflow rules definition. The suggested implementation is in a form of web services server, combining the Semantic Engine with other data providers. This makes it easy to utilize the engine in combination with a variety of existing distributed information system components.

References

[1] OWL Web Ontology Language Reference. 2004 W3C www.w3.org/TR/owl-ref

[2] R. Meersman. Semantic Web and Ontologies: Playtime or Business at the Last Frontier in Computing? 2002 http://lsdis.cs.uga.edu/SemNSF/Meersman.doc

[3] S. Decker, Semantic Web and Databases: Relationship and some Open Problems http://lsdis.cs.uga.edu/SemNSF/Decker-Position.pdf

[4] T. Barrett, D. Jones, J. Yuan, J. Sawaya, M. Uschold, T. Adams & D. Folger, RDF Representation of Metadata for Semantic Integration of Corporate Information Resources, International Workshop Real World RDF and Semantic Web Applications 2002 www.cs.rutgers.edu/~shklar/www11/final_submissions/paper3.pdf

[5] J.W. Shepherdson, S.G. Thompson and B.R Odgers, Cross Organisational Workflow Co-ordinated by Software Agents http://more.btexact.com/projects/ibsr/papers/wacc99.pdf

[6] A. Maedche, S. Staab, Ontology Learning for the Semantic Web http://www.aifb.uni-karlsruhe.de/WBS/sst/Research/Publications/ieee_semweb.pdf

Knowledge Transfer from Researchers to Businesses - eXperience and EUREXIS

Barbara SIGRIST[1], Matthias GÖCKEL[2], Petra SCHUBERT[3]
University of Applied Sciences Basel, Peter Merian-Str. 86, Basel, CH-4002, Switzerland
[1]*Tel: +41 61 279 17 66, Fax: +41 61 279 17 98, barbara.sigrist@fhbb.ch*
[2]*Tel: +41 61 279 17 92, Fax: +41 61 279 17 98, matthias.goeckel@fhbb.ch*
[3]*Tel: +41 61 279 17 90, Fax: +41 61 279 17 98, petra.schubert@fhbb.ch*

Abstract: Researchers depend upon business people and vice versa. They profit from each other by means of knowledge exchange: business of all sizes learn by reading about successful and unsuccessful projects and researchers gain insights through sophisticated research activities around aggregated case studies. There are various efforts in Europe directed to support these activities, of which two are discussed in this paper. eXperience is a Swiss project aimed at Swiss researchers and businesses deploying an operational case study platform. EUREXIS is an international Network of Excellence combining research agendas with local businesses and research institutions in Europe. Both projects build upon a common understanding of the e domain: the e business navigator. The e-business navigator is an approach for a common terminology that serves the specific purpose to foster structured storage and accessibility of knowledge about e-business best practice.

1. Introduction

eXperience is a national database for e-business case studies set up by the University of Applied Sciences Basel, Switzerland (FHBB) and mandated by the Swiss State Secretariat for Economic Affairs (seco). eXperience is a national project and results are made available to the public. It is a success story that is going to be transferred to an international level by means of EUREXIS (EURopean EXperience In e-businesS) and enhanced with a research agenda supported and carried out by international research institutions in collaboration with European businesses. This envisioned network is already in the making and partners are lined up. However, there are several issues related to the launch of an international network of this size and reach, and this paper addresses the issues and tasks that (1) were successfully mastered and (2) are still pending. These issues are of rather different sorts than those compared to networks of practice or communities of interest as described in [1].

Both project and network activities are focused on case-based research on one hand, and managing knowledge to support innovation and business strategies through sharing, exchanging, and quality control of knowledge and intellectual capital in the area of e-business/e-government on the other hand. More specifically, it involves establishing relationships with SMEs and government agencies in order to collect case study material and good practice in Europe, NAS, and EU-affiliated countries; authoring and translating case studies in research institutions; editing case studies written by research institutions in other countries; integrating international research in the areas of e-business and e-government; and networked researching amongst SMEs and research institutions.

Figure 1 provides an overview of the concepts:

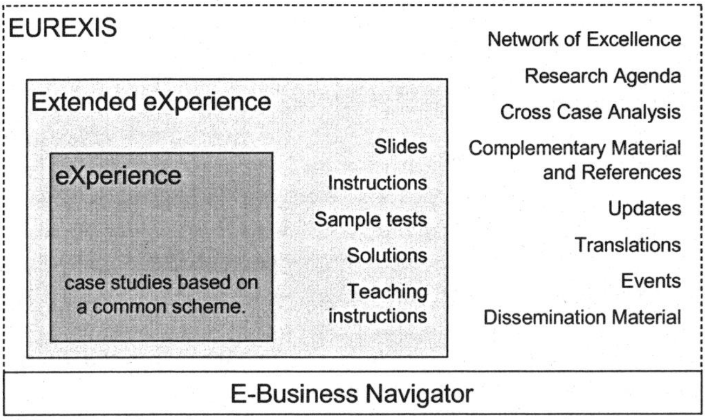

Figure 1: Nesting of concepts

2. Objectives

Case studies are "an intensive, detailed description and analysis of a single project, program, or instructional material in the context of its environment" [4]. A case study can be applied in almost any setting where the curriculum spans parts of real world phenomena. Case studies foster online and offline collaboration on problems discussed and therefore lend themselves to being used in traditional and blended learning. Researchers can get easy access to case experts and the tacit knowledge that otherwise remains undocumented.

For many years, researches in these fields have recognized shortcomings of traditional research strategies in dealing with the high complexity and richness of phenomena in real world business scenarios. Today, case study research goes far beyond portraying isolated pieces of evidence, but has become an established methodology of theory building (for an early, but very comprehensive review see [3]). Especially European research with its tendency to a more qualitative analysis has extensively embraced the case study approach.

There are various efforts under way trying to consolidate research efforts in Europe. One is built upon the preliminary work of eXperience and goes beyond the borders of a single University expanding to a network: EUREXIS (see [7] for the full proposal; related efforts include e.g. EBRN). Joint research efforts such as EUREXIS are only possible if all involved academic constituencies agree to a common understanding of the e-business landscape. Therefore, the e-business navigator has been proposed as the common thematic ground of both eXperience and EUREXIS [8]. The objectives of this paper are threefold:

1. To outline and comment the concept and lessons learned from the eXperience project;
2. Summarize and comment on the lessons learnt from the onset of the idea of a network to the actual problems and tasks at hand;
3. Describe the idea of an e-business navigator.

3. Methodology: From the Raw Material to the Case Studies

Within the context of this broad range of existing activities and traditions, eXperience takes a clear position described by three points of view. First, it is necessary to have a clear focus on e-business / e-government. This is a field characterized by rapid development, a wealth of innovation, a high demand of consulting and advice in the corporate sector, a strong need of up-to-date teaching material in the educational sector, and a lack of theory in research and academia. Moreover, it is important to pave the way for strong integration of business / governmental activities and research in the case development phase plus business research and education in the case exploitation phase. Last, the above two mentioned goals will only be achieved if a symbiosis of efficient case representation and retrieval mechanisms is built in addition to the invaluable contribution of human experts who actively carry case knowledge into practice, teaching, and research. The core of such representation and retrieval mechanisms is an integrated and scalable case study database.

The case study database eXperience themed "sharing success" is the leading case study offering in the German speaking area. Experts deliver insight into their solutions to specific and broader problems. As of June 30th 2004, there are 193 case studies in German, sixty in English, and twelve in French. The University of Applied Sciences Basel (UAS Basel) developed the concept, the technical architecture, the application design and programming, and the editorial processes, thus effectively reducing costs by deploying existing know-how and the technical framework of the Institute of Business Economics at the UAS Basel.

The process for preparing and editing the case study is established and well documented for the Swiss platform eXperience, which is the precursor for the European platform EUREXIS. It starts with authors submitting case study material online. An editor classifies the content and checks if the eXperience requirements are met. These requirements are:

1. Is the solution realistically described and portrayed in detail?
2. Are the following questions answered sufficiently according to the case study scheme [6]: Who? What? When? Why?
3. Are the solution providers named?
4. Do the authors provide diagrams and charts?
5. Is there a management summary?
6. Is the online and offline publication right explicitly granted?

In a next step, the assigned editor coaches the author in the writing and wrap-up process. Furthermore, the editor assigns keywords to the case study and then classifies the content according to the four dimensions "economy and management"; "functions and processes"; "technology"; and "design and interaction".

The last step is to insert information about the author, solution provider and solution partner. The combination of all information allows for specific database searches, such as by keyword (e.g. value chain), sector (e.g. Catering Trade/Leisure/Tourism/Culture/Sport), operational area (e.g. e-procurement), focal point (e.g. functions and processes), technology (e.g. UN/EDIFACT), IT products (e.g. IPEC), or by IT contractors (e.g. Triamun). These preprocessed listings combined with a comprehensive full text search including selected indexed words are the key requirement of the database sponsor seco, to which the described editorial activities pay a significant contribution sine qua non.

Setting up of a European network focused on case study acquisition, processing (editing and research), and dissemination has related issues in terms of its core content (i.e. case studies), but the administrative, research, and support tasks are much broader and on average more difficult to put under one roof. This entails member acquisition, scientific and organizational objectives of a research network, and finding relevant funding sources.

Member acquisition was not particularly difficult and a matter of a short period of time. The idea of a European Research Network of Excellence (NoE) was very well received among its current members and the number quickly exceeded twenty institutions. The definitions of the scientific and organizational objectives on the other hand were more difficult to agree upon. This process is in fact not yet finished and probably will never be, as these issues need adaptation as the network adapts to the changing requirements of the time being. The set-out is the work packages defined in the proposal submitted to the European Commission in 2003 (details see [7]).Yet by far the most difficult task is the funding process. A first attempt in the IST priority of the Sixth Research Framework (FP6) of the European Commission was promising, but not yet successful. Other activities in the direction of COST did not yet yield positive results either as of April 2004.

The two above-mentioned objectives reach onward to and are at the same time based on a common understanding of the underlying e-business concepts. The proposed navigator (see Figure 2) is a chart subdivided into three layers: management, applications, and technology, each of which contains terms with defined notions [8]. Actors comprise business partners, customers, administration and agencies, citizen and companies, procurement and sales, research and development, and operations.

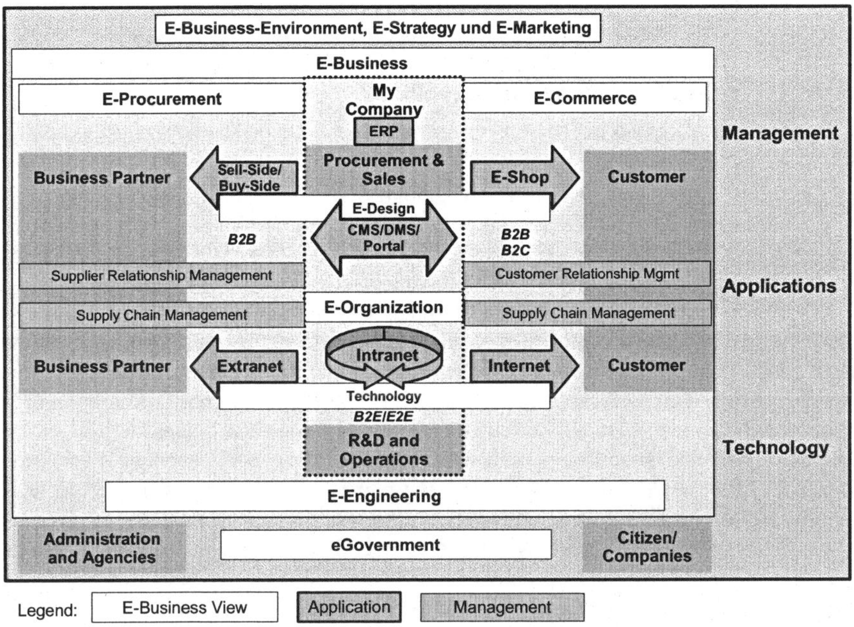

Figure 2: E-Business Navigator

The common classification scheme structures relevant knowledge and make it available to interested researchers and practitioners. One of the objectives is the creation of a common language for stakeholders. EUREXIS is in the making and will advance the discussion about the common e-language and e-understanding. This network will work with the classification scheme and validate its use and implementation in the time to come.

4. Technology Description: Case Study Platform

The eXperience platform is based on Lotus Notes Domino and is the prototype for the EUREXIS platform. This will be extended as presented in Figure 2. An intermediate step is the extension of eXperience using didactical material. The "Extended eXperience" adopts the basic source database set-up and has additional material attached. The Web front end (see "Relevant Web Sites") informs the visitor about availability of slides, instructions, sample tests, solutions and teaching instructions (how to write teaching material is described in [2]). Information about target markets, language and year of publication are displayed. The extended material encompasses discussion possibilities and update/feedback services. The Web front end has a powerful back-end input interface. Currently, this is realized using a Lotus Notes client. Editors and selected authors provide their input via an elaborate form segmented into different sub sections: general information; information about authors and editors; details about providers and operators; the case study text and its meta data; change history; the case study classification; and teaching material uploads.

To illustrate the path of a possible user query, take the example of a teacher looking for a case study with supplemental class instructions and test questions / solutions. The average case study focuses on implementation of an e-business application. Via the extended eXperience homepage, the teacher may look for the keyword that closely matches his focus:

e.g. "e-shop". He clicks on the word on the chart displayed on the homepage and is directed to a list of possible case studies with detailed classification and meta information for each list entry. He chooses the best match to his needs in terms of content and availability of didactical and dissemination material. He can print and/or download the material and use it in class. The copyright of eXperience is included in the material and must not be removed (user agreement). The copyright remains with the platform operators & case study authors.

5. Results: from eXperience to EUREXIS

eXperience as the precursor to EUREXIS, offers valuable insight in relation to larger scale requirements to be considered. However, the opportunity costs are very high, if not too high, for many micro-enterprises. Even though they have presentations and project documentation of success stories at hand, integrating them into a case study is usually too expensive. SMEs often have the necessary means and material to publish case studies in the eXperience sense. Marketing budgets are frequently allocated and texts and figures come in publishable form and shape. As a rule of thumb, every one out of ten enterprises contacted by the eXperience team submits one or more case studies. In most instances, solution partners are the primary applicants who submit their implementation examples.

Another result of eXperience is that the editorial work takes up more resources and time than planned. The more practically oriented case study authors are, the less willing to invest into verbalization and submission of a case study they seem on average. Furthermore, authors most often neglect or underestimate the complexity and efforts needed to write a case study. Collaboration between editor and author requires much time and it takes up to eight weeks to publish a case study, whereby the overall case study quality varies to a great degree. The mere case study recording into the database typically takes up two to three hours. The subsequent editorial work depends upon the type of a case study:

1. The quality of university case studies is usually good. The overall work from input to publication is about three and a half hours. Half of the time is spent on editorial work.
2. Case studies written by specialists are less problematic. The overall work from material input to publication is about four hours. Half of the time is spent on editorial work.
3. The quality of company case studies varies depending on the authors' qualifications. One out of five studies will be withdrawn. Editorial work involves three to four hours.

E-business projects can contain confidential information (e.g. security concepts). Such information must not reach the public and the editors offer authors a customized publication of their case study. Before such a case study will be published, a detailed agreement is set up listing which content may be used and the parts that will not be published. A specific solution operator may for example not be named but "company X" will be used instead.

If a company cannot provide the resources to write a case study, the editors recommend approved and reliable authors. They document a project, complying with the eXperience requirements and specifications and charge CHF 2000 – CHF 2500 per case study.

The database and the website content including sixty existing case studies were translated from German to English in September 2003. The French and German websites were updated. Two factors determined the success of this transfer project. First, the quality of the case study translations influenced significantly the work of the case study entry by the editors. A rigid project management solved most of these issues in order to comply with the tight schedule. Second, technical terminology is commonly an issue with regards to linguistic quality assurance. An English lecturer (native English speaker) of the University helped with the process. In a first step, the key word list and the synonym catalog were translated. Secondly, the editors wrote the translation guidelines (i.e. order of submitted material, etc.). Last, the editorial team controlled the translated material on a regular basis in cooperation with the lecturer issuing a written quality control report. All material was made available to the translators promptly upon completion.

The project ended successfully in February 2004. The overall costs for the English website including the entry of sixty translated case studies amount to roughly CHF 40'000. The effective translation costs for the sixty case studies added up to about CHF 100'000.

6. Business Benefits

There are no numbers and figures about direct business benefits for case study providers or authors. At best, the influence can be estimated indirectly and is directly attributable to the marketing effect by enhancing name recognition. Case studies by definition do not offer a silver bullet to foolproof business cases, but rather provide access to structured knowledge. Therefore, the primary goal of the described project and network activities are geared towards optimized material acquisition and case study dissemination.

The constituencies of eXperience and EUREXIS in the dissemination process, the most important process in the value chain from a company's point of view, are the dissemination partners, academic partners, and small and medium enterprises. Each of them interacts with the database in a defined yet unrestricted way. As illustrated in Figure 3, all partners have access to the database, though dissemination actors fulfill a more prominent role than the dissemination partners: they help SMEs to understand and apply relevant information to their specific situations and needs. Dissemination actors may in turn get access to further case study raw material, consequently fueling the case study acquisition process.

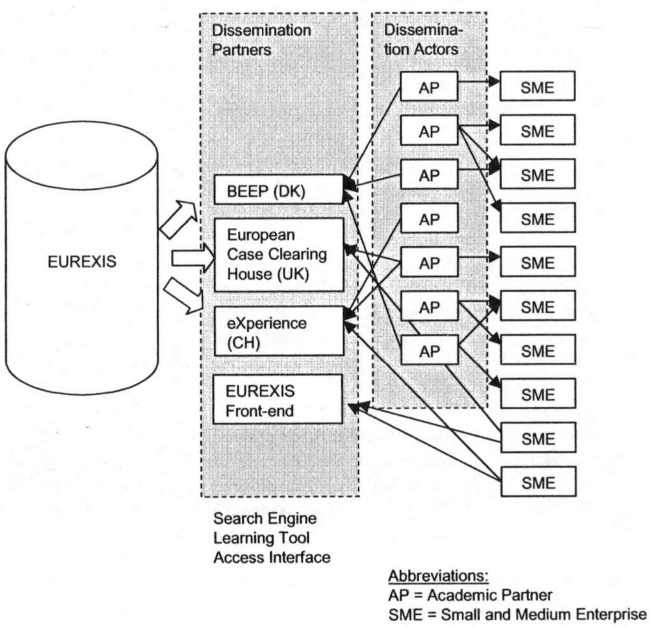

Figure 3: Dissemination: Integration and Interaction of the EUREXIS Constituencies

7. Conclusions and Lessons Learned

The e-business navigator is an approach for a common terminology that serves a specific purpose: to foster structured storage and accessibility of knowledge about e-business best practice. Representatives of the Ecademy member schools in Switzerland are already using the classification scheme on a national level in classes and projects (for a description of a project see [5]). Furthermore, the eXperience project successfully implemented the e-business navigator as an access interface to case studies [8]. The growing number of case study queries to the database gives evidence of its usefulness for research and practice.

The navigator approach will be taken a step further into the European research agenda through EUREXIS, which will carry out meta-research on case studies and cross-analyze the accumulated knowledge, for which the e-business navigator lays out the structured core. This is the basis for further discussion & refinement of the proposed classification schemes.

A very important goal of the Swiss project and the EUREXIS network activities lie in the socio-economic objectives: the transfer of experiences in an optimized form from industries and universities across the boundaries of European countries. This goal is met for the Swiss market, but it has not yet been met on a European level.

There are a few lessons the project teams learned the hard way. The most difficult part is finding funding sources. The IST Priority in the current Sixth Framework Programme (FP6) is very difficult to address as a funding source because the definition of "Network of Excellence" (NoE) remained rather fuzzy for the consortium, setting the ground for long and not fully resolved discussions. In addition, a very large number of NoE applications overwhelmed the European Commission, setting the threshold at an extremely competitive level. Another issue is network management: without reimbursement, upfront initiatives are kept low amongst network members. However, most discussion partners at agencies and research institutions readily acknowledged that knowledge imparted by the local research institutions will help companies, agencies, and academics to build the necessary IT infrastructures for the support of organizational networking (e.g. virtual organizations), design process integration (e.g. linking legacy systems with modern e-business applications), and enable the sharing of resources (databases and applications). Also, the integration of business processes between government and small business has been identified as a key area of interest (see for example the two European projects COCONET and VOOMAP), which is a great encouragement for the teams despite all obstacles.

References

[1] Cox, Andrew; Morris, Anne: Information Dynamics and Discourse in a Distributed Professional Community, in: Proceedings of the 37th HICSS Conference, Hawaii, 2004

[2] Farhoomand, Ali: Writing Teaching Cases: A Quick Reference Guide, in: Communications of the Association for Information Systems (CAIS), Vol. 13, 2004, pp 103-107.

[3] Eisenhardt, Kathleen M.: Building Theories from Case Study Research. In: Academy of Management Review, 14 4, 1989, pp. 532-550

[4] National Science Foundation: Division of Research, Evaluation & Communication (REC), User-Friendly Handbook for Mixed Method Evaluations, www.ehr.nsf.gov/EHR/REC/pubs/NSF97-153/CHAP_9.HTM

[5] Schubert, Petra; Sigrist, Barbara: Ecademy Competence Profiles: an Internet-based Application for the Acquisition & Dissemination of Distributed Knowledge, „Ecademy Kompetenzprofile: Eine Internet-basierte Applikation zur Erfassung und Abfrage von verteiltem Wissen", Basel: Fachhochschule beider Basel (FHBB), Institut für angewandte Betriebsökonomie (IAB), Arbeitsbericht E-Business Nr. 10, 2002

[6] Schubert, Petra: Introduction to E-Business Terms, original title: „Einführung in die E-Business-Begriffswelt", in: Schubert, Petra; Wölfle, Ralf (Hrsg.) (2000): E-Business erfolgreich planen und realisieren - Case Studies von zukunftsorientierten Unternehmen, München, Wien: Hanser Verlag, 2000, pp. 1-12

[7] Sigrist, Barbara; Schubert, Petra: EUREXIS – European Experience in E-Business. Proposal submitted to the European Commission under the Sixth Framework Programme (FP6), April 2003

[8] Sigrist, Barbara; Schubert, Petra: The E-Business Navigator: Implementing a Classification Scheme for the E-Domain, in: Proceedings of the 17th International Bled Electronic Commerce Conference, Bled, Slovenia, June 21-23, 2004.

Relevant Web Sites

eXperience (http://experience-en.fhbb.ch)
Extended experience (http://experience-en.fhbb.ch/cases/caseteach.nsf
EUREXIS (www.eurexis.net)

eAdoption and the Knowledge Economy: Issues, Applications, Case Studies
P. Cunningham and M. Cunningham (Eds.)
IOS Press, 2004

P2P Interactions for the Support of Knowledge Sharing in Networked Enterprises

Roberto RATTI[1], Albert BOKMA[2], Kevin GINTY[2], Dimitrios TEKTONIDIS[3], Adamantios KOUMPIS[3]
[1]*TXT e-solutions, Via Frigia 27, Milan, 20126, Italy*
Tel: +39 02 25771230, Fax: + 39 02 2578994, Email: roberto.ratti@txt.it
[2]*University of Sunderland, St. Peter's Campus (Rm DM401), Sunderland, SR6 0DD., U.K*
Tel: +44 191 515 3233, Fax: + 44 191 515 3236, Email: albert.bokma@sunderland.ac.uk
[3]*ALTEC Research Programmes Division, M. Kalou 6, GR 546 29 Thessaloniki GREECE*
Tel: +30 2310 595 659, Fax: +30 2310 595 630, Email: akou@altec.gr, dte@altec.gr

Abstract: The paper presents results from NOPIK, a current IST project, which is in its final stages. A number of tools to support team-based problem solving activities have been developed and evaluated with the project users with overall positive results. The toolset also supports a distributed architecture where separate installations and their content can be synchronised with a central server. This in principle provides an architecture enabling collaboration and sharing in a relatively static environment. In an open world where ad hoc connectivity is required, a peer-to-peer architecture is needed and this is proposed and discussed in this paper. Our research has shown that organisations are usually sensitive to letting documents be stored off their premises and thus solutions such as P2P offer the potential to overcome these barriers and provide an ad hoc connectivity otherwise not easily achievable.

1. Introduction

The aim of our work is to develop tools to create and manage open personal knowledge spaces that can be connected to provide shared network resources. Information is growing at an alarming rate and exists in a variety of formats and locations. This requires a variety of tools to access and navigate it. Users typically develop a considerable amount of knowledge about the collections of information with which they engage in their daily interaction, and what is useful to record either for personal use or to be shared in a collaborative situation and to help in the correct interpretation of these information resources.

Knowledge Management systems have typically been presented as subsystems of enterprise applications like Customer Relationship Management. The NOPIK system is a standalone information system that supports the creation and organisation of information and knowledge inside a company and can communicate with 3rd party applications to classify and retrieve information. To create and organize knowledge is a very general concept and we have implemented this through the use of three specific knowledge management methodologies for creating and organizing knowledge:

1. Support for remote access to process support environments: This supports mobile workers through web-based access to task lists through an e-work environment, where the user can download new jobs to perform and to upload the jobs completed.

2. Corporate Problem Solving: This is related to an e-management of non-conformity reports, where the user (employee or external expert) needs to report some anomaly or non-conformity occurred on a plant or on an application managed by the system.
3. Web-based Corporate Information Management Environments: Supporting the creation of semantically structured and graphically navigable repositories of documents used by individual workers in the organisation and shared by workgroups and their annotation with knowledge records.

2. Objectives

In the emerging area of P2P computing, the concept of a "service" or an "interaction" is used in several ways. An important operational aspect of this relates to the perception of the final customer of that service. Only by the usage of such a service, is its operational relevance established; that is to say, the P2P network can be implemented either at the system architecture level, as has historically been the case, or at the user interface level which affords P2P functionality to the user without necessarily being implemented as P2P components.

The relevance of a P2P service at an operational level depends on the coherence of the constituent components. Breaking these barriers shall lead to true innovations in P2P service provisioning, but its success strongly depends on the basic architecture to be developed and its integral manageability. The aim of the work presented in the paper therefore is to derive a reference model for a dynamic networked enterprise consisting of communities (work groups), who share their de-centralized intelligence with other communities, thus creating a Virtual Community. Using plug-and-participate-technology, each one of the actors will be able to combine, share and manage their own resources and those found in community environment they are part of.

Finally, a key consideration is to keep centralized control to a minimum. The only "supervision" will arise from corporate Enterprise Resource Planning (ERP) systems that are concerned with the management of tangible assets and extend this to a new generation of systems that will enable the management of intangible assets to be included.

2.1 Remote Access to the Process Support Environment

The remote process support methodology requires the existence of processes, more or less structured, which users are required to participate in and can take different forms:

- **Brainstorming**, a Name, Description, Keywords, List of People involved, where just a free Contribution form is required to be filled in. The first case could also be a consequence of Problem Solving or Innovation reports, where the system decides to open a discussion about a report, involving one or more experts.
- **Desktop**, where we can find a pool of diverse activities without any precedence relation, but each one associated to some precise application (i.e. tool + template) available for giving contributions (Office tools, Diagnostic Tools, etc.).
- **Project**, where each activity is part of a plan and has a start/end date, resources' planned/actual efforts, identifiable input/output documents, a precise application (optional) necessary to perform it.

In such a situation (see Figure 1), the user connected to the system has to carry out the required tasks. Through the Middleware layer or connecting directly using the web GUI the user retrieves his TO-DO list. The TO-DO list can be thought of as a set of brainstorming, Desktops and Projects the user is required to give contributions to. In Brainstorming, the user is just required to fill in a web (or local) form with his contribution; in Desktop, he can use different tools (one or more) that are initialised to some standard template; in Project, he has to produce specific outputs as required, using inputs coming from previous activities.

All the material necessary to produce the above GUI has to be downloaded from the system at the beginning of a working session; all the results produced have to be uploaded to system at the end of a working session.

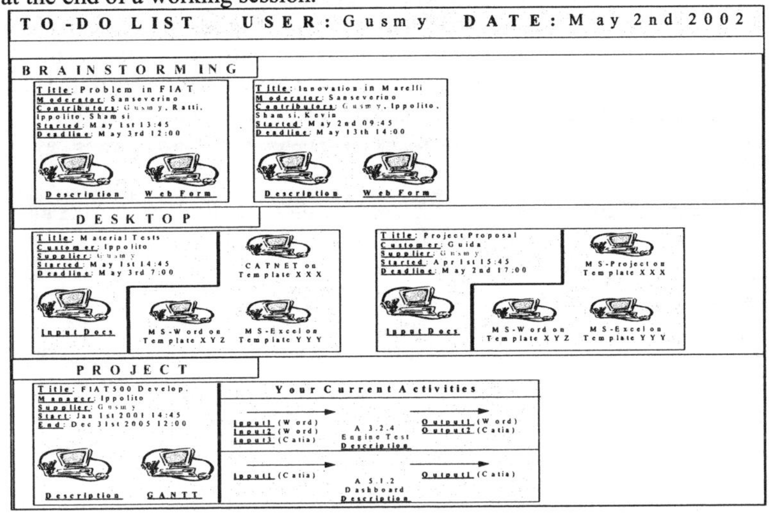

Figure 1: GUI for To-do List.

2.2 Problem Solving

In order to accomplish this task, the system module (accessed via a browser) is able to detect anomalies and to report an anomaly or non-conformity to one of the assigned servers. This module works independent of the pre-defined tele-working environment that organises user input through the brainstorming, desktop or project framework, however the user can access it and initiate problem analysis using a dedicated case based reasoning environment.

A new "Problem" can be input into the case based reasoning (CBR) tool using a web-form, where all the parameters needed are presented to the user. The CBR tool is set up for a particular application domain by specifying a domain specific ontology that in the case of non-conformity analysis contains details about products, customers, faults and alarms. The ontology also contains a number of different types of relations such as IS-A relations in the case of Customers, Faults or Alarms, or PART-OF as in Product. Each ontology description contains structured fields, unstructured fields and attachments.

3. The Use of Ontologies for Information Management

In terms of managing information and information retrieval in a flexible and semantically sensitive way, there are important recent developments in the area of the Semantic Web that are relevant here as well as results from past and current framework projects. Thus work has been done on automated information extraction and classification techniques using ontologies as a classification principle currently developed in association with the SHOE and Parka projects [1] [2] [3] and others in the ontology community [4] including KAON, to name but a few. The basis of the work on integrated information and knowledge management paradigms developed as part of the Burma-X and NOPIK FP5 projects is reported in [5].

Ontologies are increasingly being used to underpin information systems but have in the main been used in the background to facilitate information storage retrieval and manipulation tasks or to provide thesauri for example in information retrieval systems.

One practical problem is how to arrive at useful ontologies for this purpose in the first place. Falling short of users generating them from scratch there have been a number of proposed approaches for the automatic generation of ontologies based on typical samples of information from the domain in question such as typical documents. A considerable amount of work has been done on the techniques and tools are emerging such as [6]. A more comprehensive survey of available techniques was carried out in the course of the OntoWeb project and which highlights a considerable number of techniques and tools [7].

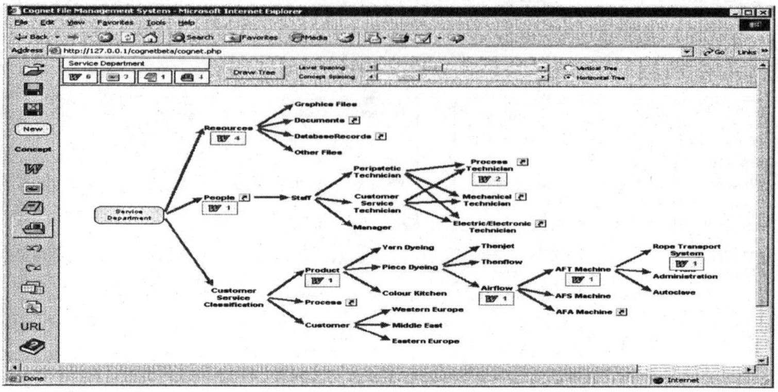

Figure 2: The Main Cognet User Interface

However, specific ontologies are usually constructed by analysts or ontology experts for a given use case and then used in an application and where the applications can vary in how they accommodate changes in the ontology as the application domain evolves over time.

Typically, the detail of the ontology is hidden from the end user or only parts of it are made visible. Furthermore users are usually not able to subsequently change these ontologies to suit their needs and the evolution of the domain or application in question. The work carried out in the NOPIK and Burma-X projects aims to reverse this trend and offer the user more control over these matters and to use them as the navigation principle. Thus the focus is on the use of ontologies at the user interface level, where users interact with the ontology not just to view results but evolve these ontologies to customize the tools to their domain of application. The evaluation of this approach to date has shown that the users are quite capable of devising meaningful ontologies and to use them to associate documents with them. Users have also responded positively to the use of graphical representation and navigation techniques that were chosen because they were expected to be more intuitive to the user than tabular representations. Figure 2 illustrates this and shows the main user interface with the graphical representation of the ontology used as a classification principle to which documents can be associated. Some of this innovation has therefore already being piloted in the Burma-X and NOPIK projects but work needs to be completed to provide a deeper use of ontologies and the more flexible use to manage a wider range of information types and additionally to record knowledge about the documents in question and their relations and make this fully navigable.

3.1 Ontology Impact

The proposed approach strongly relies on bringing ontologies to the user interface level and allowing users to engage with the ontologies and in particular with their visualisation in order to browse, store and retrieve content in a variety of formats and locations as well as knowledge records that exist about this content and to evolve the ontologies as the organisation or application domain changes.

As such, there is a strong element of using ontologies at a user level and on interactive visualisations. Amongst the currently available approaches and technologies there is still a lack of support of exactly this type of use. Plenty tools for ontology editing exist and which can be usefully re-employed and there are a variety instances where visualisations are emerging such as OntoViz for Protégé (http://protege.stanford.edu) or hyperbolic graphs and 3D graphs now in use in commercial products such as OntoBroker and SemanticMiner from Ontoprise (www.ontoprise.de). Visualisations are also emerging elsewhere such as VisioDAML (www.daml.org) and Aidministrator, to name but two. However the visualisations are either too complex to be easily navigated by the average user or usually do not allow the user to interact with the visualisations other than to browse and retrieve; thus not supporting editing of them and using them to record and store. As for the support of ontologies at the user level there is still a large gap in the available technologies that continue to be aimed at the domain expert or expert user to build applications that use ontologies heavily as their backbone but not at the user interface level. In this respect the proposed environment will continue work undertaken in Burma-X (GRDI-2000-25560) and Pikon (renamed as NOPIK IST-2001-33487) and will provide a much needed solution also for the semantic web if it focuses substantially on the human user level rather than the automated processing level.

3. Developments

Conceptually the NOPIK toolkit can be divided into a client and a server part, without necessarily implying a centralized architecture. The important aspect is that the users should have off line capabilities. However the existence of a server for the coordination and the synchronization of the content is considered useful and important.

Users access the environment and individual tools via a browser and the integrated environment offers a set of functionalities to the user for creating and organizing information and knowledge as well as problem solving related services and activities. The toolkit consists of seven components under an integrated user interface [8] including the following components:

1. Cognet (Ontology based information management environment)
2. Case Based Reasoning Module (CBR) for problem solving
3. A Search Module
4. Performance Indicator Module
5. Messaging Client
6. Problem Solving Process Manager
7. Office and OS automation components

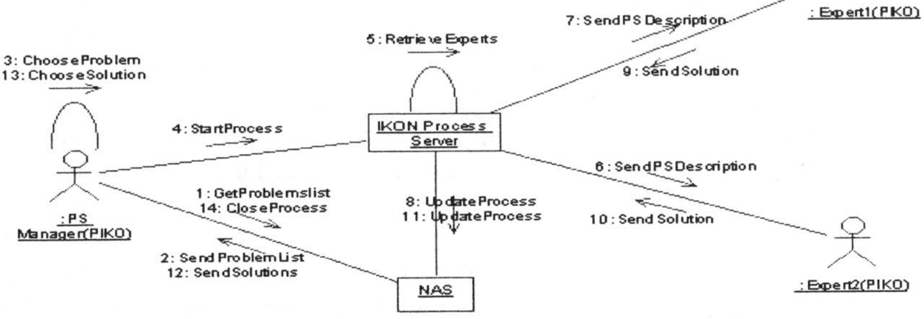

Figure 3: Problem solving accomplishment for the single server case.

All of these seven components use a common repository where the information is gathered. This repository serves as database and document repository for the PIKO client (Personal Information and Knowledge Organiser). The client provides off-line support intended mainly for individual users to ensure that their personal resources are always accessible even when working on the move. The IKON server (Information and Knowledge Organiser Network) consists of the Network Application Server (NAS) the Messaging server and the central repository of shared information resources. The NAS is the central module responsible for the synchronization between the different user environments and the individual servers. Figure 3 shows in a collaboration diagram the communication between the users and one server instance in a Problem Solving scenario.

4. Adoption of the System

In a majority of enterprises or organisations considerable collections of information exist in document form but in many cases no systematic care is taken for managing information and knowledge as well as the flow of knowledge. Thus there are a considerable amount of under-utilised resources that can be potentially turned into commercial value if only the means existed to exploit them more proactively. However these collections of information are frequently under the control of individuals who have accumulated them often over a period of years. As these collections are growing they become unmanageable even for the user who accumulated them (let alone as a resource for the organisation). In the course of the NOPIK project an environment was developed that allows the user to use self-generated or imported light ontologies, that represent domain specific taxonomies to manage such collections and attach documents to them with the use of an automatic classifier and where associations can in addition be customised individually by the user. This has created nodes or islands of information and sense-making, but where the focus is largely on individuals or groups working with their shared taxonomies and shared collection of documents. This is designed for more explicit collaboration and which is supported by the tools developed in the course of the project. However, there are in addition frequently occurring situations where other users from within or without the organisation would want to gain access to this information in an ad hoc fashion and which is not easily supported in the current framework – a situation which will be typical of a semantic web world where the individual user may search for information he does not necessarily know (or wants to know) where it resides nor how it can be accessed.

The most appropriate architecture for open, ad hoc exchange of information is a peer-to-peer architecture where nodes that hold resources in a distributed fashion can connect to other nodes to allow access to their own resources and seek information from other nodes. Peer-to-peer networks have attracted a lot of criticism and mistrust because of copyright violations and a consequent reluctance of the commercial world to work with them. The question arising is therefore how we can harness them to ensure proper use and to ensure that privacy and access is properly managed. The key here lies in providing principle universal connectivity while restricting access to and transfer of content based on authentication and permissions. While in the case of Napster, users were prepared to infringe copyright of music tracks in exchange for getting access to someone else's tracks, there is a difference with respect to personal and organisational collections of information in that there is on one hand a much more keen sense of ownership as individual users tend to be more protective of the information they consider key to their work and role in the organisation. In addition, there are ways and means of exerting control and auditability and this would be greeted with more enthusiasm by prospective users that can thus exert control over the access and proliferation of their personal collections and to be able to audit and demonstrate the utilisation and hence utility of their resources and the added value they create. In this view the P2P platform will be the place where thematic features and spaces for the exchange of ideas and creative activity will be combined, and the needs of teleworkers and teams catered for. We refer to these islands as Basic Independent Knowledge nodes (BIKs). Each BIK is able to carry out the task for which it has been trained, within a given context of work, and without explicit in collaboration with other BIKs. At any time a new BIK or some new functions of a BIK may be integrated into the system without any changes to any other BIK in a plug-and-participate fashion. Each BIK brings to the P2P network an added and innovative value, in terms of specialised services provided to the community.

There are several innovative things coming along with our system compared to existing solutions in the arena of Knowledge Management systems or approaches. First of all, our system is not only a toolset, but also a methodology. This methodology will ensure that the base for a successful KM environment within a company will be given namely by providing organisational methods in order to implement relevant organisational changes, which finally results in an environment where Knowledge is accepted as a value that has to be shared between people, whereas the intention here is not to force people but to convince them to share their knowledge with others.

The second innovative point is a technical one, namely the integration of an ontology-based approach for the modelling and representation of knowledge, with a Case-Based Reasoning (CBR) component in order to support the user while solving a specific problem. Although CBR could be seen as a method to represent knowledge on his own, the ontology-based approach combined with graphical tools for modelling, representing and browsing through the knowledge base, is more user-friendly and suitable for domain experts.

However, for day-by-day activities, employees do not just need methods for the retrieval of knowledge, but also support for problem solving or decisions making. This should be based on the past experience of users in order to guarantee best results. However, this more "process-based" knowledge will be kept within the CBR component and therefore, both approaches will complement each other.

In addition, there are some other differentiating features of the system. The web-based architecture will ensure that the tool is applicable in arbitrary IT environments, and furthermore reflects the distributed enterprise of today. The resulting system is composed of different components, which addresses issues regarding scalability and the cost to developer and eventual user and that is of key importance especially for SMEs. Finally, the solution also addresses the needs of domain experts, which means that every user (a blue- or a white-collar worker) will be able to use this tool in a user-friendly way in order to share his knowledge and to improve the competitiveness of his company.

5. Conclusions

The material presented is based on tools that are being developed in the course of the NOPIK project and represents a proposition for how this could be extended in future through a true P2P architecture and the benefits that can be expected. The experience with the basic problem solving architecture in the course of the project has been positive and its capabilities to substantially support problem solving activities has been demonstrated in user trials. A number of lessons have been learnt, including that the analysis need for the introduction of customisable solutions needs careful attention not because the customisation per se would be problematic but because it requires active input from the eventual user who may not be accustomed to analysing the way business processes are carried out or to changing them readily even though in principle it would be beneficial to the organisation due to organisational constraints. However though the tools need customisation test users have largely been able to develop categorisations for the Cognet tool, for instance, with relative ease but unfortunately at the time of writing, the ontology learning techniques available cannot be applied automatically.

The work of Cognet has been to evaluate the ability of ordinary users of engaging with ontologies and has been a success. The technology including the CBR tool and several other tools has been tested with three main users in the course of the project and with a number of additional voluntary users. The use cases include managing business consultancy services of a regional development agency, a customer complaints handling process from a construction sector supplier and anomaly handling in the automotive sector.

Problem solving is a time and resource consuming activity in organisations, for example, in complaints handling and customer service and where concrete economies can be achieved by utilising suitable information management and decision support techniques as well as streamlining the involvement of experts. The P2P concept presented is a proposition of how to extend the functionalities of the NOPIK toolset and to further exploit the knowledge management and open interchange and sharing paradigms that allow more ready connections between distributed nodes in an environment where participants may need to connect in an ad hoc fashion and where current typical technical incompatibilities readily limit interoperability. Consequently the material presented in this paper, while based in part on existing work, will be the basis for future work in order to generate the P2P platform that will need to be superimposed on the existing technology. Early work in relation to the distributed architecture and the development of a networked application server has been undertaken, but will need to be extended to generate the full functionality that has been outlined here. Proposals for extension of the work as a whole and commercial exploitation avenues of individual tools are currently under investigation. At present an advanced demonstrator web based toolset is available as the NOPIK project is in its final stage and includes the synchronisation of distributed installations but on a static basis rather than in a dynamic, ad hoc fashion as would be the case in a true P2P scenario.

The proposed approach aims to contribute to the research and innovation in the field of open integrated management of information and knowledge using ontologies and semantic web technologies that and P2P computing. More specifically, the proposition is to introduce a novel P2P platform for facilitating rapid service creation and maintenance, so that networked enterprise processes can be established on an ad hoc manner, i.e. dynamically and on demand.

Acknowledgements

This work has been partly funded by the European Commission IST Programme. The authors wish to gratefully acknowledge their support as well as the contribution of the NOPIK project partners.

References

[1] J. Heflin, J. Hendler, In: "Dynamic Ontologies on the Web", Proc of the 7th Int. Conf on Artificial Intelligence (AAAI-2000), Menlo Park CA/Cambridge MA, AAAI/MIT Press

[2] J. Heflin, J. Hendler, In: "Searching the Web with SHOE", in Artificial Intelligence for Web Search. Papers from the AAAI Workshop, WS-00-01, Menlo Park CA, AAAI Press

[3] J. Heflin, J. Hendler, In: "Semantic Interoperability on the Web", Proc of Extreme Markup Languages 2000, Graphic Communications Assoc. AlexandriaVA

[4] S. Staab, J. Angel, S. Decker, M. Erdmann, A. Hotho, A. Maedche, HP. Schnurr, R. Studer, Y. Sure, In: "Semantic Community Web Portals", 2000, Computer Networks 33(1-6) pp. 473-491

[5] A. Slade, A. Bokma, In: "Ontologies within Extended Enterprises", Proc of the 35th Hawaii Int. Conf on Systems Science, Hawaii Big Island, January 2001, Computer Society Press

[6] Maedche, A. and Staab, S.: The Text-To-Onto Ontology Learning Environment. Software Demonstration at ICCS-2000 - Eight International Conference on Conceptual Structures. August, 14-18, 2000, Darmstadt, Germany.

[7] A. Gomez-Perez and D. Manzano-Macho, "Deliverable 1.5: A survey of ontology learning methods and techniques"

[8] D. Tektonidis, R. Ratti, N. Solomon, A. Bokma, L. Rabe, In: "NOPIK Generic Integrated System: Software Concept, Architecture", Deliverable D3.6, Thessaloniki, Greece

eAdoption and the Knowledge Economy: Issues, Applications, Case Studies
P. Cunningham and M. Cunningham (Eds.)
IOS Press, 2004

Introduction of Value and Cost Centres in the Management of European RTD Projects

Ioanna PAVLOU, Adamantios KOUMPIS
ALTEC S.A., M. Kalou 6, Thessaloniki, GR 546 29, Greece
Tel: +30 2310 595 646, Fax: +30 2310 595630, Email: pavi@altec.gr; akou@altec.gr

Abstract: A novel approach to research work is presented, in which all financial and resource-related reports are expanded into comprehensive disclosures, portraying not only the consequences of past transactions, but also a fair representation of the activities of the project participants, the obligations undertaken (whether implemented or not), and the particular risk profile. Furthermore, our approach proposes an internal evaluation of the project partners work progress, together with a financial audit. Using this approach, work is organised into a set of Value Centres, which are directly related to specific tangible results that are reflected in the project Deliverables. Direct labour and any other costs are in turn assigned to a set of corresponding Cost Centres, all of which are related to the aforementioned Value Centres. The cost centres are also responsible for organisation of the research work and for any replanning of the activities.

1. Introduction

European RTD projects are expected to reflect the way trans-European multi-stakeholder consortia should move forward to seize opportunities provided by the technology they develop. Yet, the reality is that projects find that their good intentions in this respect are disabled by the Project Management procedures, which in practice are too inflexible. This is mainly due to the fact that the Framework Programme patterns and practices still reflect the weaknesses of earlier Framework Programmes, from a time when the involved actors were not so fast changing, nor involved in such complex networks of alliances and partnerships, as well as linkages to other related schemes.

Furthermore, the traditional project "accounting" system and its major outward expression, the much unloved Cost Statements and financial reports, essentially only reflect already completed transactions (usage of resources, purchases and expenses of various categories, etc). Such a narrowly-based, backward-looking reporting mechanism is ill-suited to providing the information really needed by the Project Management Board.

In this paper, we shall be presenting a novel new approach that shows all resource-related and financial reports fully expanded into comprehensive disclosures. These will portray not only the consequences of past transactions, but also a fair representation of the activities of the project participants, the obligations undertaken by them (whether executed or not), and the particular risk profile. Furthermore, our approach proposes that a project internal evaluation of the partners work progress is conducted, together with a financial audit.

If applied, the results of such a procedure should be communicated to the Commission and to any other party such as the Management Boards of participating organisations. This internal project procedure should be regarded as complementary to any carried out by the Commission and by each individual partner's internal auditing units.

The analysis, proposals and suggestions outlined in the paper are not just aimed at preventing future sub-optimalities in projects although, considering the increase in budgets for Integrated Projects, such failures would pose a massive threat. More broadly and importantly, they are aimed at enhancing project effectiveness, by ensuring they are better suited to a fast growing economy, well-functioning markets, and ethical and equitable behaviour. The pursuit of these high level goals is the major purpose of our novel approach.

In the following section we describe in more detail the means we employ to support the above principles.

2. Concepts

Building on lessons from past projects that involved trans-European research collaboration, in which we have been actively involved as either Coordinator or partner/Contractor, we have devised a new and more effective structure for organising and conducting work in research projects. This takes into account the structural inefficiencies that we faced in a number of such projects, that generally tended to lead to sub-optimal satisfaction of the goals originally set down. Ongoing improvement of a high level is really essential, when having in mind the costly project structures that are an inherent feature of much of the 6th Framework Programme.

Within this new approach, work is organised into a set of Value Centres that are directly related to specific tangible results reflected in the project Deliverables. Direct labour and any other costs are assigned to a set of corresponding Cost Centres, all of which are related to the aforementioned Value Centres. The Value Centres are in turn responsible for organisation of the research work and for any replanning of the project activities.

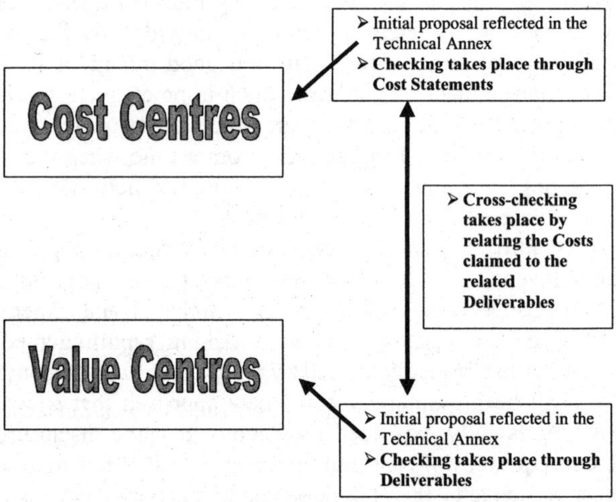

Figure 1: Cost- and Value-Centre correspondence

Our approach also provides a two-level model for checking the project progress and the work quality :

- Checks carried out at the first level cover:
  - for each Value Centre: work carried out with respect to the Deliverables, and
  - for each Cost Centre: project costs claimed in the cost statements, while

- At a second level cross-checking occurs of the Deliverables produced against the Cost Statements provided (i.e. claimed).

This procedure enables the proper monitoring of effort (and costs) expended on the project, disabling (or at least minimising) any opportunities for ex post facto adjustment of work items.

It should be noted that the above model should not increase communication overheads; on the contrary, the authors firmly believe that it will increase communication efficiencies, as well as the overall project work quality. It will obviously necessitate continuous (i.e. at least monthly) monitoring of progress, based on appropriately adapted time sheets by the project participants.

3. Contrasting the proposed future approach with the current one

3.1 Situation As-is

The current situation is that the organisation of work within the RTD project takes place within WorkPackages. Each WorkPackage then leads to certain results, which are identifiable (and auditable) by means of Deliverables. However, slackness occurs for, amongst others, the following reasons:

- Work taking place within a WorkPackage may be further broken down into a set of tasks;
- These Tasks may lead to discretely identifiable Deliverables; or they may not.
- In the latter case, it may be difficult to check whether expenses (i.e. "costs") claimed against such a Task have actually been incurred and therefore whether the claim is just;
- This may, of course, be regarded as a responsibility of the Co-ordinator; or at the final level of the Commission, who both have to audit the claimed resources for each "cost item";
- A frequent and therefore indicative example of this is the case of consortia that do not feel it necessary to allocate resources (typically in the form of person-months) to individual Tasks, thus limiting their oversight to just the overall budgets per WorkPackage. (A wise move, a cynic might add, if the entire reporting edifice lies within the sphere of virtuality.)

Currently, to the best of our knowledge, reviewing usually takes place at a high level that does not deal with such discretely identifiable "cost items". Of course there are (historical) reasons for this approach; people experienced with the idiosyncratic elements of research work per se – even where this is of the most applied nature - would argue that it is difficult to foresee the final results one or more years ahead or to firmly commit oneself to them. They would argue that at the macro level a fair balance occurs between the swings and the roundabouts of project resource consumption. But this is an insufficient argument for separating the value created within a particular WorkPackage or Task from the costs that have been claimed for its execution.

On the other hand, however, it is not difficult to provide a level of transparency that helps people work to the highest ethical standards while also encouraging them to safeguard basic principles of integrity, both at the personal and at the corporate levels.

In a relatively recent Commission Note of February 2004 [1] it was recognised that "Multi-contractor instruments in FP6 apply the principle of collective technical responsibility and most such instruments also apply collective financial responsibility." This opens the road to consortia so that "if a contractor breaches the contract and the consortium does not make good this breach by continuing to carry out the project, the Commission may, as a last resort and if all other approaches have been explored, hold the other contractors liable for the debt of that contractor under certain conditions."

There is no doubt that moral responsibility is individual by its very nature. However, in today's world, perception matters more than ever. And in these post-Enron times of meta-modern accounting, with confidence and trust having been significantly shaken, it is important that European Research should meet the highest integrity standards and not be hindered by the existence and operation of an old-fashioned and marginally efficient reporting system.

Paraphrasing what Baruch Lev, Professor of Accounting in the Stern School of Business at the New York University and a legendary figure in the area of Intangibles and their reporting, identified in his 2002 testimony on "the reform of corporate reporting and auditing" to the U.S. House of Representatives, one can say that currently, and in the "As-Is" situation being discussed here, we have:

- Financial reporting that is "too narrow" as it is based on already executed transactions, as reported in the periodic cost statements, and without reference to the unexecuted obligations of each party;
- Auditing that is "too cosy" as it mainly uses the same already executed transactions as its inputs for checking the validity of these claims;
- Reviewing that usually takes place in a quasi-academic and/or quasi-industrial style, and that in a majority of cases fails to address the money-for-value principle.

And though it seems transcendental, it is also a practical finding that better cost reporting shall lead to higher research results; some obvious reasons for this are that:

- If a well-defined pathway for documenting an activity is in place, and this is also traceable with the costs that this activity is incurring, people shall not (be able to) inaccurately estimate their efforts, while
- If the path is enabling tactical machinations and roundabouts, then it is only a matter of time (and not of the location) that creative or inventive accounting practices shall be grown and unfolded – which shall of course diminish the value and kill the potential of the research work.

3.2 Proposed Situation

Day one of our proposed approach starts with abolition of the concept of WorkPackages as an artefact that drives the planning and organisation of work within RTD projects. An outmoded relic of an approach lingering on from previous Framework Programmes, WorkPackage-centric organisation of project work and commitments has reached (or significantly bypassed) its limits.

Within this new concept, consortia shall in future develop their proposals on the basis of Value Centres. Work will be organised, reported, reviewed, and audited around these value centres. Each Value Centre shall have associated with it a corresponding Cost Centre.

In this approach, Value Centres are assigned a projected initial cost. This should be seen as a purely nominal cost for kick-off purposes that need not necessarily be exactly met in practice; in many cases it may be exceeded, while in others it shall not be met at all.

This approach enables re-allocation of initial project resources from value centres 'in the black' to other Value Centres that have moved into the red, based on appropriate judgements and as needed by the project. For some cases, the consortium may decide to create a new Value Centre for some need that was not initially identified, in order to use resources for some justified activitiy that was not given sufficient importance at the beginning, or even in specific cases to not use the entire budget. Is it an oxymoron or a paradox that in times where companies or organisations are trying to downsize and cut spending on almost everything, co-funded projects seem to meet budgets – sometimes even with an excess? Does this drive us to cynical conclusions about research project accounts?

Having disposed of WorkPackages, it is possible to now focus on the Value Centres, including their outcomes, which are Deliverables. These can be either of discrete nature, notifying the completion of some task, or of continuous nature (as is usually the case for management activities).

All developments and outcomes during the entire project lifecycle will thus be tracable as a consequence of their interaction with each other. For example, it shall be possible to use a Deliverable of a Value Centre X related to User Requirements for work on a system design, that in turn devolves into some other Deliverable. We use this case as it is suitable for demonstrating why our approach is so much better than following an approach based on the structure of WorkPackages. The answer, again, comes in two parts:

- The first part relates to the existence of the capacity to cross check work done as part of a Value Centre with costs incurred as part of the corresponding Cost Centre. Is there any doubt of the necessity for this? In answer, one might consider the example where an analysis report which could be purchased for 100 Euros (overnight!) from the Internet, is submitted as the outcome by one or more partners of a WorkPackage that has allegedly cost 20 person-months and for which the remainder of a consortium has been waiting 7 months;
- The second part, which is equally important, concerns the current lack of procedures for tracing the actual give and take that occurs between the project parties, and which brings transparency to the process of results creation. (We should not forget that consortia running multi-party RTD projects derive their value solely from the existence, the volume and the quality of such transactions: no transactions, no value; too few good quality transactions, little value, etc).

To create any type of value, one builds on ones existing legacies. In the case of RTD projects, these are mostly intangible assets, such as skills and tacit knowledge, corporate or organisational values and norms, technology and any other type of explicit knowledge, the particular Management Processes, and finally any other endowments that can be of use [3]. It is on these assets that core project competencies shall be improved or created within the project lifetime, and it shall also be possible to quantify the project results with respect to their particular contribution margins for each involved party and the market.

In contrast, with the current system nobody knows exactly how to measure the value created by a project. The introduction of Value Centres facilitates documentation of the initial assets within the consortium at the time of kick-off, and thereafter monitoring is possible to take place in a consistent and stable way. Of course, disagreements may appear in the selection of the system to be adopted for the valuation of these resources. Our opinion is that any system should in principle be welcome, though our own recommendation is for an adaptation of that developed by Andriessen as reported in [3].

More specifically, the central improvement – or extension - we would propose to this would be related to its use not only as a valuation tool but as a project management method. Such a valuation method would also help improve the existing templates for representing exploitation plans; we consider that the existing TIP (Technology Implementation Plan) may be counter-productive, by actually generating a certain degree of confusion and an enhancement would serve the interests of all stakeholders.

Last but not least, we propose the disassociation of the notion of project time with this of real life time; it is not unusual that tasks which have been planned to consume 4 manmonths over a period of 4 months, need to expand their lifetime over two or even more additional months. This rather 'spatial quality' of project time forms an important issue that has been addressed in a highly acute way in [4]. We all know that in the as-is situation, projects are unnecessarilly urged to timely completion of the various tasks and WorkPackages, while a re-assessment of the real time needed is not supported as it may in general cause unwished bureaucratuc overheads. Except from the ability to support predictable and foreseeable monetary inflows that stem from the processing of the corresponding Cost Statements, this linearity should rather make us feel uncomfortable and also feel the need to question the value that is related with respect to the associated costs.

3.3 Myths and realities of the approach

Criticisms are needed of the proposed approach in respect of its capability to account for the idiosyncracies of multi-party research work, of being too commercial or realistic for actions that aim to "increase innovation and competitiveness in European businesses and industry and to contribute to greater benefits for all European citizens", as the latter are expressed, amongst others, in the objectives of the IST 2003-2004 Work Programme.

We shall now seek to look at some myths that can be found in the proposed approach and some realities that may underlie it.

A first myth is that too many aspects of RTD projects are dealt with on the fly for strong controls to apply and, as time goes by, some decisions mature and get better by, inter alia, improvements in the intra-consortium communications. This implies that a chance factor necessarily exists. The proposed approach can be claimed to disable these essential characteristics of RTD. This is a myth. The approach neither disables nor enables someone to better carry out his or her research work. It merely improves all round transparency for all parties. As far as the research work in an RTD project is concerned, we face two general cases:

- Those cases in which it is known what should be built but the knowledge is lacking of how to do it; for this category it is essential for the partners responsible to create new process knowledge besides the planned Deliverables. And it is also obvious that the costs will be justified not only by the final outcome but also by the means that were utilised, including also all efforts expended on documentation, exploration of possible approaches, etc.
- Those cases where it is known what should be built and where it is also known which methods should be employed to achieve this. For this, it is clear that cost claims are easier to plan in advance and commitments can be made to them with greater proximity.

For both case types, our approach only calls for a linkage of the two worlds and how reporting takes place within them.

A second myth is that the approach would be difficult to employ in view of the disparity between the accounting systems used by different actors, whether companies, organisations, or institutions. We believe this again is not a valid concern as the plethora of different methods and practices does not impact on the approach we propose. It is rather in much better semantical and operational proximity with many of the established practices in the field.

Having looked at some myths, let us now look at the unavoidable consequences of this approach.

A reality is that in the new approach many projects would find that the consortia themselves, as well as their individual participants would no longer be able to justify spending and / or costs in the way they have done up to now. As the linkage to the created value will be tighter and of a more direct nature, the opportunity to support undue inflationary RTD economies will vanish. The worst that might happen (from a cynic's perspective), is that projects might cost less and produce more.

A second reality is that it shall become more difficult to use methods that are sub-optimal in terms of both the value and the cost they create. A concern we have experienced is in recognising that, by their nature, not all activities within an RTD project will be value added. It is not reasonable to say yes; in many cases the uncertainties inherent in RTD mean that a project only partially consists of value added activities. Certainly threre is need for activities of a supporting nature, or activities that are prerequisites for others that themselves create the value sought by the project. Even here, our approach aids transparency as it is now easy to make distinctions between value-added and non-value-added activities; and who would now dare to claim inflated costs for an activity that itself clearly creates no value at all?

In this way, we believe, that various reporting inaccuracies of RTD projects will in future become more difficult or will lose their raison d'etre. And the creation of core competencies and other types of intangible assets will become easier.

4. Conclusions

In a recent article questioning whether the auditing profession can do more to identify potential problems, David Devlin, president of the Federation des Experts Comptables Europeen's (FEE), which is the umbrella body for European accountants, has recognised that "[the standard on fraud] should require [auditors] to be more sceptical of management's explanations and audit evidence. It needs to emphasise 'prove it to me' rather than 'tell me'" [2].

A main postulate of our work is that by improving the system, project participants will develop their proposals and organise their work reports in a way that is closely (if not directly) linked to the actual costs of carrying out the work. Substantial improvements will also then emerge in the quality of the conducted research.

Replacing the as-is situation of WorkPackages with Value Centres, and linking the latter with Cost Centres improves the transparency of the cost claims made by consortia, while the resultant enhanced visibility makes it easier to check the quality of the conducted work with respect to the incurred costs.

This is obviously not a novelty for the business world – but it is our firm belief that it is a serious measure that will result in a drastic improvement for European RTD projects.

In this direction, the authors are working towards the formulation of an analytical scheme that shall be possible to support the described functionality in terms of a combined methodology and software system, and in direct linkage with a project intangibles accounting infrastructure. The goal of such an implementation is the convergence to a cross-entry accounting practice in European RTD projects with the use of Value and Cost Centres.

References

[1] European Commission Note "Financial collective responsibility in FP6 contracts", DG Research, Directorate A - Coordination of Community actions, Regulatory and cross-cutting matters, February 2004.
[2] David Devlin "A superiod armoury for the war on fraud" in Financial Times, February 26 2004, p. 13.
[3] David Andriessen "Making sense of intellectual capital: designing a method for the valuation of intangibles", Burlington: Butterworth-Heinemann 2004.
[4] Frederick Brook "The Mythical Man-Month", Addison-Wesley, 1975.

Section 4.2

Applications

Johanna: A Knowledge Centered Infrastructure for Teleorganizations

Mauro GASPARI[1], Davide GUIDI[1], Andrea PETRUCCI[3], Lucio PICCI[2]
[1]*Dipartimento di Scienze dell'Informazione, University of Bologna, Via Mura Anteo Zamboni, 7, Bologna, 40127, Italy*
Tel: +390512094875, Fax: +390512094510, Email: gaspari@cs.unibo.it
[2]*Dipartimento di Scienze Economiche, University of Bologna, Strada Maggiore, 45, Bologna, 40100, Italy*
Tel: +390512092608, Fax: +390512092664, Email: lucio.picci@unibo.it
[3]*CSP s.c.ar.l., Via Livorno 60, Torino 10144 Italy*
Tel: +390114815176, Fax: +390114815001, Email: Andrea.Petrucci@csp.it

Abstract: We have developed an open framework within the Johanna project to support organizations with collaboration technologies in information technologies - rich environments. Its main features are represented by compliance with the Semantic Web guidelines, usability, attention to users' needs, and the use of open source technologies. In this paper we describe the project's goals, its architecture, its current status, and a roadmap for future developments.

1. Introduction

Johanna is an open framework providing organizations with knowledge-centered communication and collaboration technologies.

Knowledge is playing an increasingly important role within an Internet that, under the Semantic Web research agenda, is evolving towards an open and services-oriented architecture. Within this context, services are being extended with semantic information, and sophisticated methods for retrieving and composing them are under development. Organizations aiming to operate within this framework should consider knowledge not only as a tool to manage their internal competences and procedures, but also as a key feature of their interface with respect to the outside world.

Johanna provides a set of tools to do that. Its core includes a knowledge-based description of an organization that automatically turns into running programs: databases, Web interfaces, and Web services. E-mail and Web services are the basic mechanisms to enable the integration of other collaborative technologies. E-mail is the basic tool for communication, and Web services provide both human readable information and machine-understandable information, according to the principles of the Semantic Web.

From a methodological point of view, Johanna's basic philosophy is best described by a simple motto: "usability and users' feedback". Usability is achieved following a non-invasive approach. While the knowledge coded into the system could support a variety of synchronous and asynchronous communication tools, at the current stage of development, e-mail is the main communication tool, and the user is not constrained to any particular e-mail program, desktop environment and/or application program. More generally, Johanna supports collaborative work by providing the "glue" to integrate a set of collaboration components, without requiring a fixed working environment. Thus Johanna differs from tools such as Lotus Notes [1] or Novell Groupwise [2], that constrain the user to adopt a set of groupware, and often proprietary, tools.

"User's feedback" is seen as a key element for success. Too often collaborative environments that are successful from a technological perspective, ultimately fail because users do not materialize. Users' feedback helps in securing the consensus of potential users, and it is guaranteed by the continuous monitoring of users' needs, as already experimented in a field test - the first Johanna based site has been delivered to an academic organization. Such a monitoring is carried out on the technology, and on the users reactions to the technology, in order to improve features, interfaces, etc.

In the following sections, we first describe what Johanna does, rooting our analysis to an analytical framework based on the theory of complex organizations. We then present its architecture, its current status, and a roadmap for future developments.

2. Objectives: Organizations, Teleorganizations and the role of Johanna.

We provide two different arguments to explain Johanna's objectives. We start with a bottom-up view, to show that in the "belly" of many organizations some current practices would be carried out more easily by means of collaborative tools of the type that we propose. After that, we'll look at matters from the top, by defining the concept of "teleorganization". We will show that the concept of teleorganization is useful both to highlight the requirements for using Johanna, and also to provide a broader framework for its analysis.

Let us consider a generic organization, where all its members regularly check e-mail and have access to the Web. Within similar organizations, where there is an expectation that anybody can be reached by e-mail, such messages are used for activating procedures that are part of the functioning of the organization. That is, e-mail is used not just in semi-official contexts, such as within work groups or advisory committees, but also in official communications, and this is true regardless of the presence of digital signatures[i].

A large part of modern life, it has been remarked, is spent in meetings. This piece of popular wisdom reflects the fact that, in any complex organization, there are many organs: boards of directors, committees, working groups, etc. Within the organizations satisfying the requirements that we have specified, e-mail is widely used today for the purpose of making these organs work. At a simpler level, it is used for scheduling purposes. It is also used to exchange documents and opinions, and for preparatory work that a face-to-face meeting is then called to refine or, sometimes, just to ratify. Moreover, e-mail is used massively to organize and implement communication with the outside environment. Contacts with vendors, customers, even the press, are increasingly carried out in this way.

How does all this happen in real life organizations? Typically, in a very decentralized and inefficient manner. When sending an e-mail message to many people, most times people use the "cc" (or "carbon copy") field of the header of their e-mail message. More refined users have learned the use of so called "aliases", and group aliases, that allow the copying of many addresses once and for all (as long as the list does not change). In both cases, different people needing a given list of e-mail addresses are responsible for setting it up and for its upkeep.

A further level of refinement is the use of mailing lists software such as Majordomo, Mailman, or Listproc, to name a few popular choices. Such software centralise the list of addresses for a given mailing list, thus avoiding the duplications that we have described. Also, they typically provide useful features, such as Web archives, easy management of subscriptions, and monitoring of malfunctioning. These operations are typically carried out by a so called "list master", a person who is in charge of the upkeep of the mailing list, and who typically is in power to decide who is in, and who is out.

However, mailing lists software, while being a very useful tool, are only a partial solution to the problem. Let us consider an example to clarify the point. Suppose that at "We Do It, Inc.", a private firm where everybody has frequent access to e-mail, there are 50 mailing lists, and that Mr. Smith – an employee - as part of his work duty, is a member of 20. Now suppose that Mr. Smith leaves his job. He then has to be cancelled from 20 mailing lists, possibly by 20 distinct list masters.

The solution to this problem in principle is quite simple: "We Do It, Inc." should put the information about the people who work there, appropriately structured, in a database, and the 50 mailing lists should be the result of appropriate queries to that database. When Mr. Smith leaves "We Do It", he also leaves the database, and, by such an act, he automatically does not satisfy the query for any mailing list. Quite obviously, the same database can be queried in order to publish desired personal information on a Web site, such as a directory of people.

Although some mailing list managers, for instance Sympa [3], provide facilities to retrieve users information and mailing lists from a database, the integration of the mailing list services with the underlying database is loose. The database is seen just as an external data repository and is not fully integrated with the provided communication facilities. And, vice versa, a database is not aware that the mailing list manager exists. A better solution would be a framework where a database is fully integrated with the mailing lists manager. As soon as "We Do It" database schema is designed, all the necessary relations would be “automatically" generated, and, vice versa the mailing list manager should be (automatically) tailored to the specific "We Do It" needs.

From a bottom up perspective Johanna organises information in a database that is tightly integrated with a mailing list manager (and, in principle, to a host of other communication tools). The design of a database schema automatically generates a connection with a mailing list manager, and appropriate queries decide who should receive a given message. Part of the story, then, is about tightly integrating databases, mailing list managers and eventually other Web services into a unifying framework.

Before we move on to the next part of the story, it is useful to consider the matter further: the issue is not just to allow people in organisations to be more efficient, by centralizing several repositories of information, structuring information appropriately and, in this way, avoiding duplication of effort and guaranteeing a better upkeep of the information itself. With Johanna, the people in the organisation are allowed to do things that they could not have done before. In order to see that, let us proceed with our example, to consider the interaction of the organization with its outside environment.

Mr Smith does not leave "We Do It" (maybe because its employer finally decided to adopt Johanna). He is in charge of sales and, following the opening of a new local branch, wants to offer a rebate to the people in that area. "We Do It" owns a vast list of e-mail addresses, maybe from people who accessed its Web side and that declared some interest. Mr. Smith contemplates writing to the people who live nearby the new branch. If the information about them were not collected for that purpose, it may prove impossible, or very costly, to do it (maybe the right information are there, but are held by Mr Jones, who does not like Mr Smith, and querying the database is not straightforward anyway). On the other hand, if the information was collected within the Johanna framework, Mr Smith could send the desired message to the appropriate people with a few clicks of his mouse.

Johanna is not just a way to rationalize e-mail (and other communications tools) usage. In fact, the basic idea is much more general, and has to do with the construction of a structured repository of information that is relevant for an ample set of organizations' procedure, and of the tools to use such information appropriately. Johanna is a "machine" to entertain relations within the organization, and between the organization and its outside environment.

We have mentioned "an ample set of organizations' procedure", but so far we have come short of declaring that the purpose of Johanna is to describe the whole organization.

The scope of Johanna is an important issue when we define the domain of application of the project. We clarify it by means of a "top down" approach.

Researchers have long studied the impact of new technologies on organizations. While it can be safely said that the nature of an organization is never neutral to technological change, there is a presumption that change and innovations in the field of information technology are of particular relevance, given that they have an impact on an essential feature of organizations - the flow of information, so much so, that an organization can be seen, and described, from the point of view of the information flow within it, and between it and its external environment [5].

While there is a wide consensus on the fact that the new information technologies are already shaping a new organizational world, it is not easy to describe any definite pattern, besides a general increment in "interconnection" among the different atoms of the organizational world. [6]. Here we need not take a stand in this debate, and we simply describe such a process of technology adoption, using the term "virtualization", that we define as the process by which, within an organization, more and more activities are carried out without the need for-face-to meetings. We also introduce a terminal point for such a process, by defining the concept of "teleorganization": an organization where all transactions are carried out thanks to the Internet. A teleorganization is obviously an "ideal type", that is, an abstraction.

As we mentioned, an organization can be described in terms of the information flows within it, and between it and the outside environment [5]. A teleorganization can also be seen as a schema describing a flow of information, both within its boundaries, and with its outside environment. In a teleorganization, we assume that such information flows are all Internet based: e-mail messages, Web services, etc., and they are implemented, and accessed, in a variety of ways: from desktop computers, personal digital assistants, mobile phones, etc.

Within such a teleorganization "ideal type", Johanna represents the technology that allows such information flows to be effectively managed. Since the description of this flows is a description of a given teleorganization, Johanna represents the organization and its working, and, in a sense, Johanna is the teleorganization at a given point in time, or, more to the point, the teleorganization is the knowledge representation allowed by Johanna.

However, organizations evolve in time. In particular, at a given point in time, organizations are a sort of combination of traditional components, where face-to-face interactions matter, and of a teleorganization components – their virtual part. A "virtualization strategy" represents the process by which an organization becomes more similar to a teleorganization. This is what we mean when we observe real life organizations investing in Internet technologies and trying to modify their oganizational practices accordingly. We plan to extend Johanna so that it will also serve such change in time.

Within this framework Johanna's role will then be twofold. At a given point in time, Johanna already represents that part of the organization that is already virtual and it describes the set of "teleorganizational practices" already in place. Moreover, Johanna will also constitute the set of technologies and practices needed for a given virtualization strategy. The set of practices, and not just technologies: behind Johanna there is an idea of how technology enabled change management works. That is, Johanna will also be a methodology, supported by a set of technologies, to implement what has become fashionable to call "change management".

3. The Johanna Framework

The delivery of a Johanna based site to an organization follows a knowledge-centered approach aiming to speed-up the development process. First, we must define an ontology, providing a formal description of the entities involved in the organization, together with their properties and mutual relationships. Such an ontology describes the working of the organization, and provides a frame for the desired flows of information, within the organization, and between the organization and its outside environment. In this sense, it is an "organization ontology", as defined in [9]. An advanced knowledge-based editor (Protégé-2000 [4]) provides an easy-to-use graphical user interface for a high level description of the organization ontology. This description is then exported into the Ontology Web Language (OWL) [8] to ensure compliance with the Semantic Web guidelines. The OWL description contains several Johanna specific classes, objects and relations, and constitutes the "Johanna Meta Language" (JML).

Given the JML description, an interactive installation process generates the "glue procedures" integrating Johanna's main components. These are an easy-to-use graphical user interface - the Johanna GUI - running on a Web server (Apache-Tomcat), using a database (Postgres or Mysql) for storing information on the users and the entities of the application domain, and a mailing-list manager (Sympa [3]). Both the Johanna GUI and the mailing-list manager use the database as their source of information.

Johanna exploits a modular architecture. A core, "the Johanna core", provides the glue to integrate other collaborative technologies. The core is based on the integrated use of e-mail and Web services and on JML, and it allows the user to easily configure and customize a Johanna application. This infrastructure is the basis for the integration of other tools supporting different forms of collaboration.

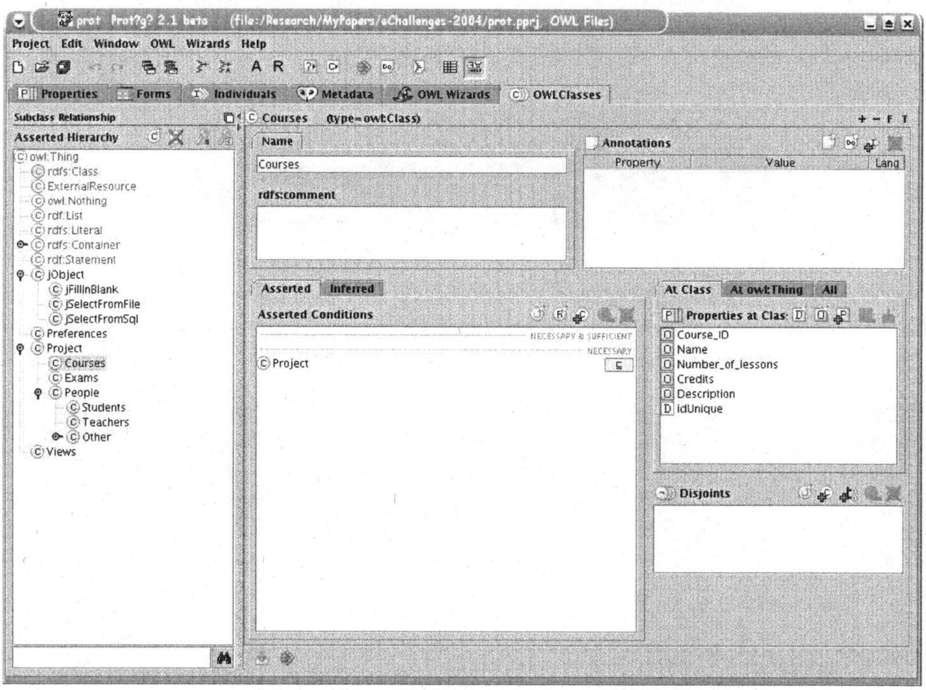

Figure 1: Snapshot of Protégé-2000 working on a generic organization

3.1 The Johanna Meta Language

The JML allows the designer to customize the main components of Johanna with the information relevant to a particular application domain in a machine-understandable format. To simplify the modelling task of an organization, a generic template is included in the

Johanna distribution. The designer should extend this template with all the information related to the particular domain, using the namespace provided with it. A snapshot of Protégé-2000 working on a generic organization is shown in Figure 1.

The left part of Figure 1 shows some class describing an example organization. The *jObject* class and all its subclasses (*jFillInBlank, jSelectFromFile* and *jSelectFromSql*) are provided by the namespace. These three classes refer to object types - use for storing data in the database - that are treated differently by the Johanna GUI: *jFillInBlank* means that any content can be entered in this field, *jSelectFromFile* means that a drop down menu will appear, whose values are retrieved from a file, one per line. Finally the *jSelectFromSql* will show another drop-down menu, whose values are grabbed from a query of a database table.

Any object created by the designer must be an instantiation of a subclass of *jObject*. Every object has different properties that describe itself. Those properties may be related to the database (i.e. if a specific field represents a primary key) or to the Johanna GUI (i.e. a regular expression associated to an input field that control user input). The *Preferences* class stores some preference related to the project, like the backend used for the database: Mysql or Postgres. The Project class stores all the information about the specific organization. The *courses* object is selected, and all its properties are shown in the right part: *Course id, Name, Number of lessons, Credits, Description, [idUnique]).* Finally the *views* class is used to store different profiles for creating several layers of visibility of the database.

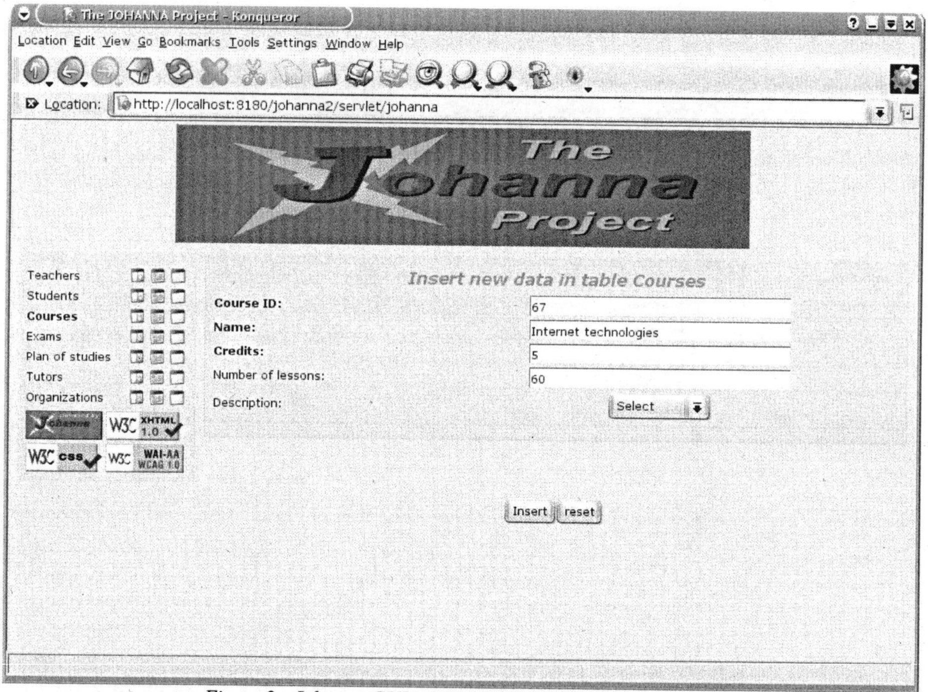

Figure 2: Johanna GUI – Insertion of data for course object

3.2 The Johanna Graphical User Interface

Both the database and the graphical user interface are automatically generated from the JML. Thanks to Johanna's GUI, the user can administrate the content of the database and manage Johanna's configuration. Built upon the Apache Web server, the Johanna GUI is still reachable from any host connected to the Internet. However, permission to view only selected information is achieved through the "views" configuration. Different profiles might be created, and any registered person can be associated to one or more profiles.

A snapshot of the Johanna GUI when inserting data for the *course* object is shown in Figure 2. In the left part of the figure, the structure of the organization that refers to the previous example is shown, meanwhile in the right part all the properties of the courses object are displayed. The three icons in the Main Menu allows the user to insert, modify/search and delete instances of object in the database. In the Insert Course menu the *Description* field is an instance of *jSelectFromFile*, where all others are instances of *jFillInBlank*. The green dot near *Number of lessons* means that this field is optional, while a red dot means that the field is required.

3.3 The Johanna Web Services

Johanna provides a set of Web services. Although the role of Web services is to make the Johanna functionalities accessible to external agents, they also constitute an application programming interface to extend Johanna with new functionalities. As an example, any functionality provided by the Johanna GUI can be exploited as a Web service. Useful public services, currently under development, enable the search for particular information over a portion of the database.

4. Results

As a way to illustrate the benefits provided by Johanna, we briefly illustrate its more coherent application to date. In 2000, the University of Bologna started a new three-year Bachelor Degree in Internet Economics ("Corso di laurea in Economia di Internet", http://www.ei.unibo.it). Over the last three years, Johanna has been used – and in fact, it was originally developed – to serve the needs of such an organization.

Such needs can be easily summarized. The main actors involved are: instructors, students, administrative personnel, potential students, and firms (where students are required, in their third year of study, to do an internship). An appropriate coding of the information has allowed for easy communications between instructors and their students (each course has a corresponding mailing-list, where all students who are enrolled and have not yet passed the final exam are automatically subscribed). Such mailing lists are sometimes used for simple purposes, such as class rescheduling, etc.; some instructors are using them for what we could dub "soft e-learning": discussions on material covered in class, etc. Other mailing lists are used to deal with other organizational needs: communications among instructors, various committees, and communication with the listed actors.

There are around 300 students enrolled in the program, and 25 instructors, 10 administrative personnel, currently actively using the system. A measure of Johanna's success is in the simple fact that people are really using it, because they find it useful and because it is simple: for example, an instructor knows that in order to communicate to his/her students he/she only has to write an e-mail message to a mailing list, whose name derives from the official denomination of the course he/she is teaching.

Additional functionalities are realized exploiting the Web services interface using the encoded information in other ways. For example, the administrators of the Degree in Internet Economics are provided with a particularly useful Web-based system providing a host of descriptive statistics on grade averages, students progresses, etc.. Such a system is widely used for monitoring and planning purposes.

5. Conclusions

Johanna has been delivered and successfully used in a few academic organizations and projects. The last Johanna distribution is available and can be downloaded from http://johanna.sourceforge.net. All the Johanna components are open source software systems, and the Johanna interfaces are distributed under the GPL agreement themselves. Such a licensing arrangement should facilitate the dissemination of the program. At the current stage, no commercial exploitation of the program is expected; however, in the future, and particularly when Johanna fully meet our expectations of becoming a "change management methodology" (and set of technologies), we could think of a possible commercialisation, by private third parties, of Johanna-based consulting services.

Future development will integrate other collaborative technologies and tools, such as a chat manager or a SMS messenger. We also plan to enhance Johanna by investigating several directions: the integration of a distributed authentication procedure (based on LDAP), and the addition of new modules, such as a content manager and the integration with a Geographical information system (GIS).

An important issue concerns the analysis of the organizational needs that are expressed by the users, which we perform by using the analytical tools of the theory of complex organizations, in order to guarantee the necessary consensus to the organizational change that Johanna helps in delivering. To this respect, we emphasize that Johanna is expected to become a technology that enables organizational change, where by "technology" we do not only mean the software, but also the set of codified practices that allow for the planning of the information flow and for the continuous monitoring of users' need.

More work is needed to fully reach this goal. Such a methodology will require an appropriate considerations of what each Johanna's user is allowed to do within the system, and on how, at any given time, it can contribute to the changing of the onthology. We are currently working to address this problem that requires flexibility and granularity of users' rights.

References

[1] M.Falkner. How to Plan, Develop and Implement Lotus Notes 5.0. JohnWiley&Sons, 2000.

[2] S.B.Rogers. Novell's Groupwise 6 User's Handbook. JohnWiley&Sons, 2001.

[3] S.Aumont, O.Salaun. Smime and sympa mailing lists manager. Linux Expo Paris. 2001.

[4] J.Gennari, M.A.Musen, et al. The Evolution of Protégé: An Environment for Knowledge-Based Systems Development. Technical Report SMI-2002-0943. Stanford Medical Informatics.

[5] G.Morgan. Images of Organizations, Sage Publications. 1986.

[6] L.Picci. La Sfera Telematica, Baskerville, Bologna. 1999.

[7] E.Visani. La valutazione della didattica nell'università italiana. Il caso del Corso di Laurea in Economia di Internet. Dissertation in Political Science. University of Bologna 2004.

[8] S.Bechhofer, et al., editors M.Dean, G.Schreiber OWL Web Ontology Language Reference. http://www.w3.org/TR/2004/REC-owl-ref-20040210. 2004.

[9] MS.Fox, M.Barbuceanu, M.Gruninger, J.Lin. An Organization Ontology for Enterprise Modelling. In *Simulating Organizations: Computational Models of Institutions and Groups*, M.Prietula, K.Carley & L.Gasser(Eds) Menlo Park CA: AAAI/MIT Press, pp.131-152. 1998.

---

[i] As an example, and as an anticipation to the application that will be described in a further section, at the University of Bologna official Faculty's meetings used to be called by means of closed envelope traditional messages signed by the Dean. Today, such meetings are regularly called using email, with no (digital) signature, that is, based on the good faith of the senders and of the receivers, and on a degree of trust on the security of the communication channel employed (or, more to the point, to the consideration that the stakes are not high enough to encourage unlawful violations of the integrity of the network or of the messages).

eAdoption and the Knowledge Economy: Issues, Applications, Case Studies
P. Cunningham and M. Cunningham (Eds.)
IOS Press, 2004

ICONS based Knowledge Management in the Structural Funds Projects Preparation

Eliza STANISZKIS, Bartosz NOWICKI
Rodan Systems SA, ul Puławska 465, 02-844 Warszawa, Polska
Tel: +48 22 6439208, Fax: +48 22 6439210
Email: eliza.staniszkis@rodan.pl, bartosz.nowicki@rodan.pl

Abstract: The Structural Fund projects represent a vital opportunity for the new Member States to close the social and economic gap between these countries. The structural funds implementation process may fail to bring the expected results, however, due to stringent standards for project proposal eligibility and generally poor documentation quality of project proposals. The presented Structural Fund Project Knowledge Portal aims to fill the gap within the existing IT infrastructure pertaining to early support in project proposals preparation process. The domain that requires browsing of vast amounts of documents (formal guidelines and success stories), intensive collaboration of applicants, and external expert support under time pressure is a sensible demonstration of the ICONS knowledge management platform capabilities. This work has been supported by the ICONS Intelligent Content Management System IST project, www.icons.rodan.pl.

1. Introduction

The Structural Fund projects represent a vital opportunity for the new Member States that joined the European Community in May 2004 to close the social and economic gap between these countries and the European Community. The challenge recognized by all new Member State Governments is to create conditions for the best possible use of the funds made available to them. The prime concern of most newly accessed countries, and indeed an important political priority, is to promote the sufficient number of high quality eligible project proposals to ensure the highest possible usage of the structural funds.

The current efforts of the new Member States governments concentrate on setting up the management structure and the legal framework matching the EC requirements as well as on deploying national systems responsible for registration and assessment of submitted proposals and monitoring the realisation progress of the selected projects. Tracking and reporting on the structural fund utilisation level as well as the projects impact on national statistics is another realm of the system functionality. This infrastructure is, however, to the same extent indispensable as inadequate, as it does not solve the intrinsic problem of structural funds acquisition – providing effective access to previous experiences, lessons learned, templates, success stories, identified risk patterns, current regional statistics values, rules and expertise that altogether allow achieving the sufficient level of formal and essential knowledge to obtain funding.

The goal of the Structural Fund Project Knowledge Portal (SFP) is to support organizations and individuals involved in the process of proposals preparation to achieve the highest possible number of high quality eligible project proposals meeting the stringent EC criteria. The secondary goal is to provide access to the structural funds benchmarking data to be used in the project proposal preparation to support the planning and cost estimation, as well as the cost-benefit and the risk analyses. The only way to achieve those objectives is to accumulate an appropriate amount of knowledge: both explicit (encoded in documents) and implicit (provide by externally hired experts), and to equip applicants with the effective methods of knowledge access [1].

In view of the past experience of such accessing countries as Spain, Portugal, and Greece, meeting an acceptable threshold of the structural fund usage, in particular during the initial period, is a difficult, if not impossible, task. Even small improvements in project proposal development processes resulting from application of the advanced knowledge management techniques and methodologies will have a substantial economic impact on the regional development of the accessing countries. Indeed a 1% improvement in the structural fund project proposal acceptance level would mean additional €138 million to be invested in the Polish regional economy alone in years 2004-2006. The figure for all new Member Countries for the period 2004-2006 amounts to €30 billion. Hence, the potential value of a 1% improvement of the SF project acceptance rate increases to €300 million. Clearly the above figures exemplify a strong economic motivation of the accessing countries to invest in ICT solutions pertaining not only to monitoring of the SF projects but also to improvements of quality and acceptance rate of the SF project proposals.

The paper presents the structural funds domain challenges and associated risks. Then, the SF Portal environment and its interfaces with other elements of the structural funds system infrastructure are introduced. System functions that support applicants in the proposal preparation process are described in details. Both static (data) and dynamic (proposal development process) aspects are addressed. Special focus is put on the underlying ICONS platform knowledge management generalized services that turned out to be indispensable in the development of the SF Portal. Finally, a thorough discussion on knowledge management aspects of the application is incorporated.

2. System Environment

In order to create the critical-mass of knowledge and to support the seamless work over project proposal, SFP interoperates with external systems (see Figure 1).

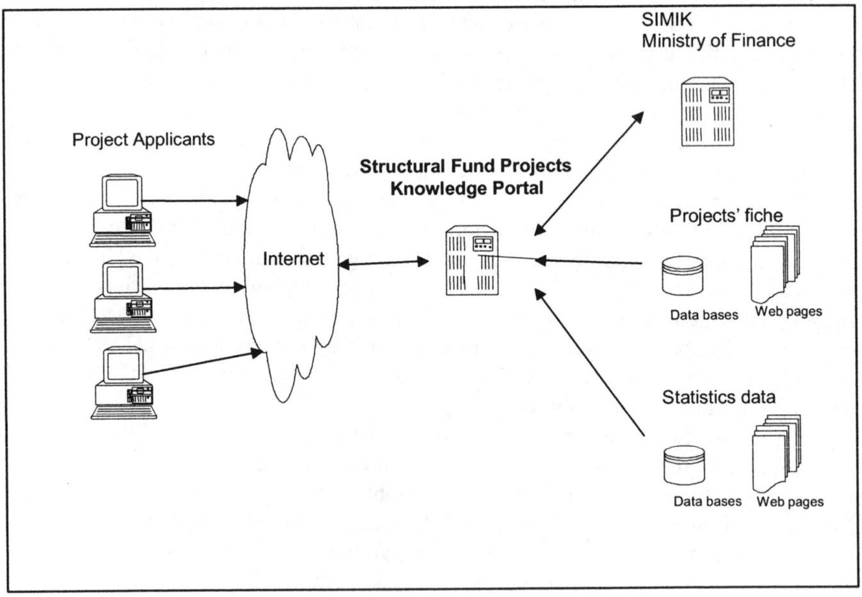

Figure 1: Context of the System

SIMIK [2] is an example of the national system for structural fund system monitoring and control starting from project proposal registration, up to aggregation of evaluation data and financial clearing with EC. Whereas SFP is designed to support project proposal development process, starting from bringing forth an idea, up to generating the proposal in the xml form compatible with SIMIK. The essential parts of the projects proposal documentation, as well as the fiche with projects' results are of great importance as the source of inspiration for the prospective structural funds applicants. SIMIK will become a valuable source of such information within the next few years, while today it is possible to take advantage on the projects' data from the current EU Member States. SFPKP realizes this idea by integrating data from heterogeneous external databases and web pages (e.g. InfoRegio).

The same mechanism of data integration is deployed to obtain the current value of the statistics (e.g., economical indicators as unemployment rate for a given region). The indicators are essential in the project argumentation, as one of the structural fund objectives is the pursuit to minimize the disparities in the European Community. The statistical data come from databases of regional or national statistical offices, SIMIK, New Cronos, or Eurostat web pages.

The end-users of the SFP (applicants, experts, knowledge engineers responsible for knowledge base, etc.) will interact with the system through the Internet web browser.

3. System Architecture

SFP is a prototype realised as a demonstrator of ICONS research project results. A schematic view of the system architecture is presented in Figure 2.

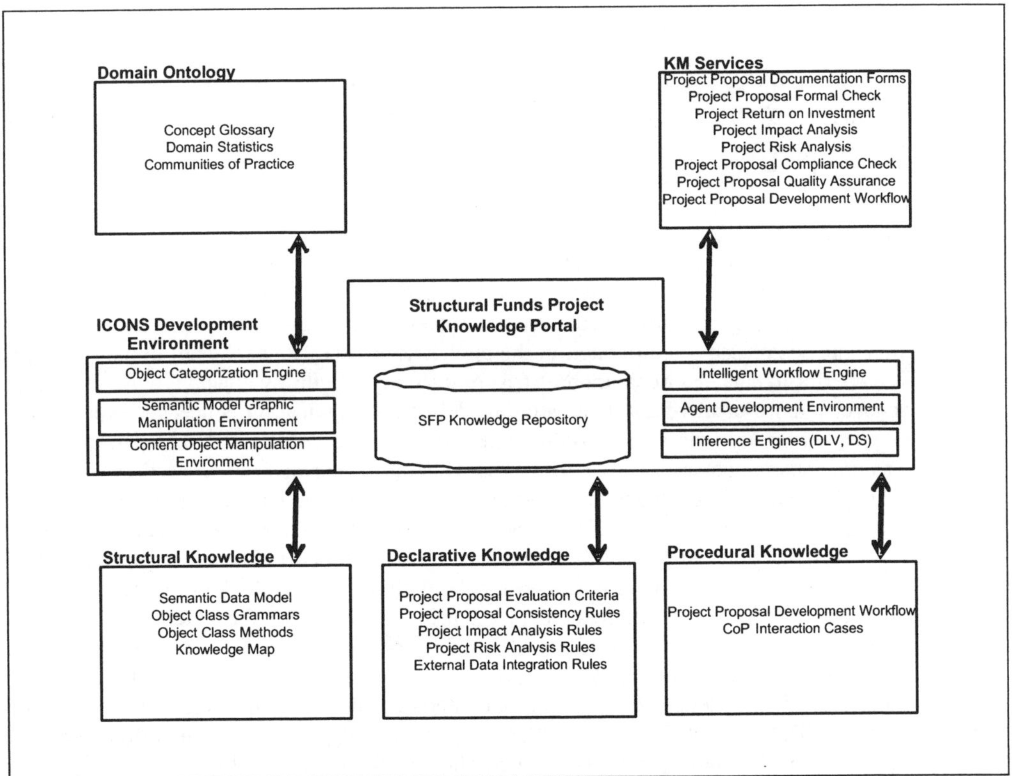

Figure 2: The SF Project Knowledge Portal architecture

The SFPKP knowledge services are supported by three complementary knowledge representation paradigms: declarative knowledge, structural knowledge and procedural knowledge representation. The declarative knowledge represents the application domain ontology and business rules valid within the system. The structural knowledge represents the content objects classes, as well as its structure and behaviour, associations between content objects and hierarchical organizations of those objects. The procedural knowledge represents the business processes in a given application domain.

The Domain Ontology provides the conceptual foundation for all other areas of the SFP system architecture. The principal part, typical for all knowledge management applications, is the Concept Glossary defining the Structural Fund terminology and providing support for both expert and non-expert use of the underlying knowledge representations and knowledge management services. Creation of a coherent domain model for the Structural Fund projects domain ontology is the very first step in the SFP system conceptual design. It entails identifying and extracting terms from information sources within the system terms of reference and gradually, with the use of a stepwise refinement procedure, organising those terms into partial ontologies to be finally integrated into the SFP ontology represented by the system Concept Glossary.

The SFP Domain Statistics are required to provide the basis for evaluation of macroeconomic information to be used in SFP proposal argumentation. Domain statistics are to be organised following the territorial structure used for the structural funds strategic planning and allocation.

The Project Proposal Development Workflow Service is to provide workflow process classes corresponding to the identified types of the SF project proposal development lifecycles. System users will organise their proposal development work according to the predefined proposal development process invoking required roles, both automatic and/or human expert, and generating knowledge artefacts to be stored in the system knowledge repository. Work assignment may involve human expert selection and service negotiation following a predefined expert interaction model and supported by the ICONS intelligent agent management environment. To increase the contextual awareness of the activity performer, the graphical representation of process instance according to [3] was applied.

The Communities of Practice cluster human experts playing key roles in the knowledge management lifecycle of the SFP system. The Communities of Practice ontology provides information regarding the classification of knowledge and skills required within the system knowledge processes and links into rosters of human experts providing knowledge services and contributing tacit knowledge into the system knowledge repository. The external experts are seamlessly incorporated in the applicant project proposal team by delegating a task to perform, such as preparation of feasibility study, eligibility check, etc. Additionally, whenever a more creative and innovative model of communication is needed, experts may be contacted through discussion forum, where the issues are discussed. The persistence of the forum content enables reuse of elaborated strategies, decisions and scenarios.

The Knowledge Management Services represent the functionality of the SFP system embedding all knowledge processes support provided within the realm of the SFP proposal and evaluation processes. The knowledge processes supported within respective KM Services utilise knowledge artefacts available within the system knowledge repository represented by the ICONS content objects, and extended with the external information resources integrated with the system as defined in the Knowledge Schema. Results of KM Services performed on the SF project proposals constitute an important body of the SF project related knowledge to be stored and rendered available in the system knowledge repository. The Project Proposal Documentation Forms Service is supporting assorted templates and electronic forms required by the EC or national institutions as the project proposal documentation standards. The use of electronic forms and the associated data mapping functions is the precondition for most of the proposed services of the system. The Project Proposal Formal Check Service entails completeness and syntactic validation of project proposal documents, in particular those parts of documents that are developed with the use of electronic forms, and that may to a large extend be performed automatically. The Project Proposal Compliance Check Service entails both automatic proposal evaluation and the manual proposal evaluation. In the first case, respective compliance rules may be used to evaluate the quantitative aspects of the project proposal versus the stated evaluation criteria and the corresponding domain characteristics provided as the domain statistics. The latter case requires intervention of human experts, who should confront the qualitative project proposal aspects with the corresponding evaluation rules and guidelines of the EC or national institutions, proceeded by a semi-automatic expert selection and service negotiation process. Experts will be supported by an appropriate set of electronic evaluation sheets to enforce a uniform and predictable proposal review process. The Project Proposal Return on Investment and Project Proposal Impact Analysis Services are developed as a set of financial analysis and economic analysis models, corresponding to wide project classes identified in the system, to be used by human experts to assess economic feasibility of the proposed initiative. The Project Proposal Risk Analysis Service is based on a set of generalised risk models corresponding to the identified SF wide project classes and based on probabilistic reasoning under the conditions of uncertainty. The Project Proposal Quality Assurance Service will support the inherently manual quality assurance processes providing electronic evaluation sheets and appropriate checklist to the human experts performing the manual quality control checks.

The contents of the system knowledge repository are organised according to the multiparadigm Knowledge Schema syntactic and semantic rules [4,5] and rendered to the system users via the knowledge portal HCI (human-computer interaction) interface based on the advanced graphic models for accessing and manipulation of knowledge. The innovative graphical navigators are powerful tools supporting the atrribute-based and full-text search functionality of a system. The Knowledge Map Model provides facilities to represent content object categorisations in three different modes, namely value-based categorisation, providing the principal mechanism for dynamic materialisation of categorisation tree control structures, the manual categorisation, supporting information-bearing relationships between a categorisation tree and the corresponding set of content objects, and the automatic text.

The conceptual view of the system knowledge schema is formally defined with the use of an unattributed UML Class Association Diagram, the UML process models, as well as selected examples of declarative knowledge specifications. The SFP Semantic Data Model as well as detailed specification of SFP services is presented in [6].

4. Knowledge Management in SFP

The ICONS platform addresses the most essential needs of knowledge workers in learning organisations. Information redundancy and lack of pertinent information, a flood of uncategorised documents, poor integration with external sources of information, lack of uniform, user-friendly or personalised interfaces, huge amount of various stimuli overwhelming direct communication of individuals and groups, low level of exiting knowledge reuse, flat learning curve, etc. that is to mention just few symptoms hampering contemporary knowledge organisations. The primary objective of the ICONS platform based applications is to create conditions, in which "the right person carries out the right task at the right time based on the pertinent and comprehensive information". However, the focus is not only on content and processes. The underlying premise is that knowledge management is to the same extent concerned with tacit, as with explicit knowledge.

By knowledge management we understand support for all activities pertaining to knowledge creation, publication, shearing and exploitation. The knowledge base, in turn, comprises of persistent and widely accessible knowledge representation. The primary knowledge management objective is to increase organisations' productivity through shortening the knowledge lifecycle without compromising quality of the resulting knowledge. The SFP system supports its users both with respect to knowledge base access as well as knowledge management facilities. The system offers functionality meeting the requirements of so-called "First Generation Knowledge Management" (FGKM) or "supply-side KM" systems [7], that provides a natural link into the realm of currently used content management techniques, such as groupware, information indexing and retrieval systems, knowledge repositories, data warehousing, document management, and imaging systems. Moreover, SFP provides comprehensive IT support for accelerating the production of new knowledge, focusing on enhançing the conditions in which innovation and creativity naturally occur, that exemplifies so called "Second Generation Knowledge Management" (SGKM) systems. The high potential of the SFP system follows form the nice balance between FGKM and SGKM feature requirements.

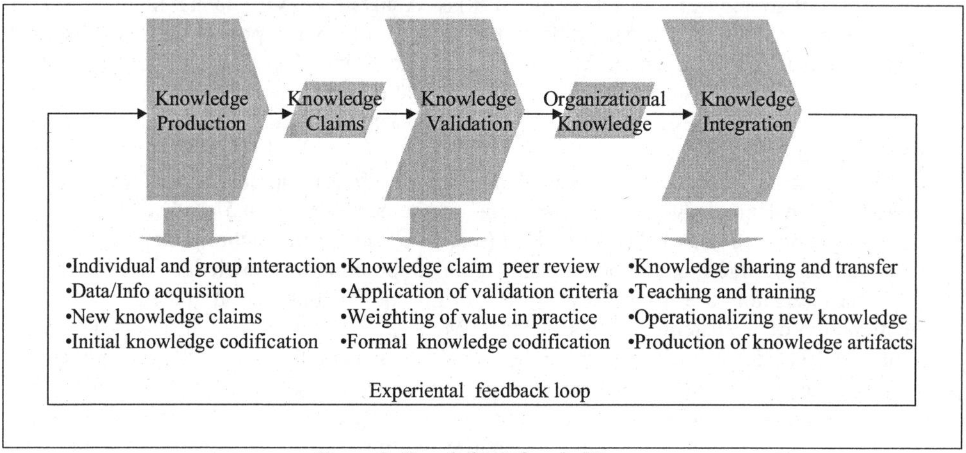

Figure 3: Knowledge Lifecycle [7]

The Knowledge Lifecycle (see Figure 3) is implemented both on the level of a particular project proposal preparation processes as well as on the level of the global system definitions. KLC presence in a particular proposal elaboration is evident: early project proposal versions (claims) are validated by independent experts at three mile points, namely eligibility check, feasibility check and risk analysis. The final validation takes place during the formal evaluation in the SIMIK system. The genuine benefit from the KLC comes, however, from the experiential feedback loop as information on accepted and rejected proposal (statistics, publicly available parts of proposal, evaluation reports) are made available and may be exploited during preparation of consecutive proposals.

Dynamics applied to global SFP system definitions could be considered as a meta-process of knowledge life cycle as it results in improvement of the system functionality and performance. Modifications are carried out on schema level of particular knowledge representations defined in the underlying ICONS platform: the structural knowledge (e.g., changing the semantic data model by adding a new content object class), the declarative knowledge (changing business rules, extending domain ontologies, etc.), the procedural knowledge (modifying definitions of business processes, e.g., adding a new control point in the proposal preparation process).

5. Underlying ICONS Platform

Development of any system of the SFPKP size and complexity is a non-trivial task. Hence it was based on generic and powerful services of the ICONS platform for knowledge management intensive portals development [5]. One of the crucial points was to map application relevant services to generic services of the platform and fill in the gap between what is generic and what is specific. We found the experience of the SFPKP demonstrator development to the same extent valuable and important, as the experiences and competencies gained during the development of underlying ICONS platform.

Technologically, the ICONS platform provides a well-balanced set of innovative multimedia and content technologies implemented into fine grained and encapsulated modules (see Figure 5). Detailed information may be referred at ICONS project site [8].

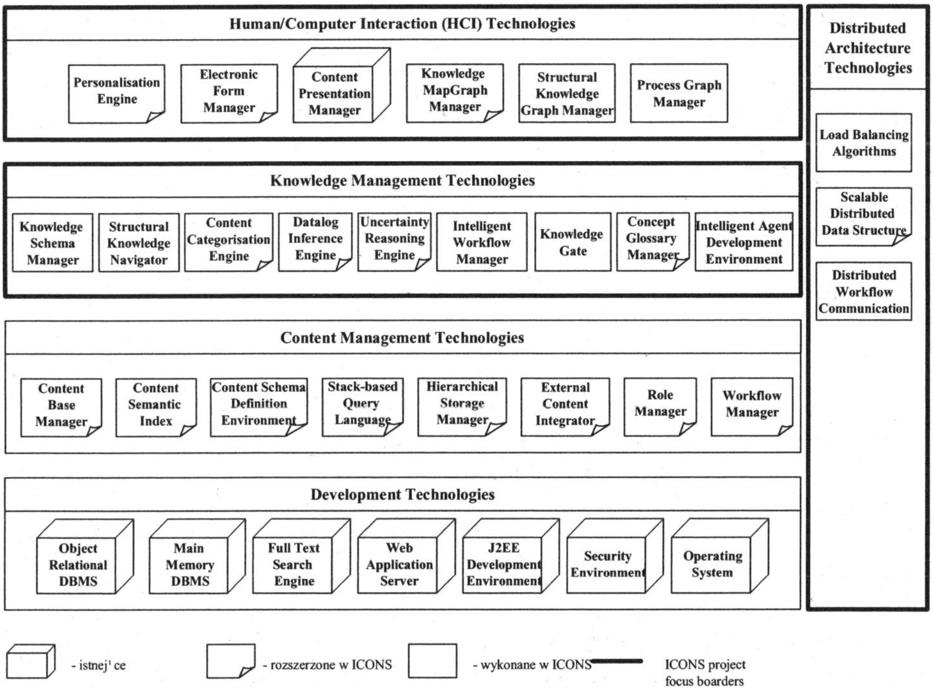

Figure 4. Abstract architecture of the ICONS platform

6. Conclusion

In April 2004 the ICONS project was completed and resulted in a stable working prototype version of the Structural Fund Project Knowledge Portal build upon the ICONS platform. The consortium carried out a systematic user oriented assessment of the SFP to check to what extent the vision and its implementation meets the end-users' expectations. The assessment and other dissemination activities confirmed the clear need of a system of this type. Various organizations that will play different, yet complementary, roles in the SF projects (government offices representing global objectives of the SF project and responsible for registering and evaluations of project proposals as well as their progress monitoring, consultancy companies willing to support proposers, financial institutions providing resources for unfounded part of SF projects and organizations interested in operating and maintaining the system) expressed their full support for the initiative (acknowledged by 8 Letters of Interest). The effort to commercialise the SPF KP has been continued after official project completion. The consortium is well motivated as it envisages the forthcoming benefits for national economics and the consortium.

References

[1] Staniszkis, W., Staniszkis, E., Intelligent Agent-based Expert Interactions in a Knowledge Management Portal, Proc. of Electronic Government, Second Int. Conference, EGOV 2003, Prague, Czech Republic, September 2003.

[2] System informatyczny monitorowania i kontroli finansowej funduszy strukturalnych i funduszu spójności – SIMIK, www.mf.gov.pl, January 2003.

[3] Business Process Management Initiative, Business Process Modeling Notation, working draft, version 1.0, August 2003.

[4] The Multi-Paradigm Integrated Knowledge Schema, www.icons.rodan.pl, IST-2001-32429 ICONS Consortium, January 2003.

[5] The ICONS Software Technical Design Manual, www.icons.rodan.pl, IST-2001-32429 ICONS Consortium, August 2003.

[6] Technical Design for Structural Fund Project Knowledge Portal, www.icons.rodan.pl, IST-2001-32429 ICONS Consortium, October 2003.

[7] Firestone, J.M., Enterprise Information Portals and Knowledge Management, Butterworth-Heinemann, October 2002.

[8] www.icons.rodan.pl.

Content Engineering for Conversational Advisory Systems

Marcello L'ABBATE, Thomas KAMPS, Ulrich THIEL
Fraunhofer Integrated Publication and Information Systems Institute (IPSI), Dolivostr. 15, 64293 Darmstadt, Germany
Tel: +39(0)61518694945, Email: {labbate, kamps, thiel}@ipsi.fraunhofer.de

Abstract: In this paper we analyze the application of a conversational system as a virtual assistant in the finance and insurance domain. The aim is to extend a risk management expert system with an electronic advisor, guiding the user during the interaction, and offering support and advice in problematic situations. The standard dialogue management is enhanced with the access to external information sources, such as a domain ontology and a case based reasoning process.

1. Introduction

The Internet has changed the way of communicating, doing business, and even playing games. Many people now use the Internet for banking, retail, entertainment, and business-to-business document and service exchanges. The growth of the Internet (and e-commerce applications) is changing the way companies interact with customers. With the new era underway, companies must prepare for the web-based communication and develop a new competitive landscape. According to Forrester Research, there is an increasing need to upgrade the efficiency of application specific conversations. It is necessary to improve new-word-detection/learning capability during the interaction, and the system's ability to identify the customer's intention clearly, in order to provide accurate information and respond quickly with user-friendly interaction. Moreover, for the final presentation of precise and trustworthy content as a result of a customer's request, domain specific knowledge has to be collected systematically and made available to the application's internal filtering and retrieval processes.

To meet these requirements, in this paper we focus on natural language based systems and the improvement of their underlying contents and knowledge. By the use of a conversational interface, specific learning efforts are not required from the user, and the grammar of a natural language provides enough expressive power for formulating interaction steps in many different alternative ways. For this aim, the application must be built on a robust dialogue management approach, capable of effectively recognizing the intention and contents of the user's utterance. Moreover, it must rely on a comprehensive range of knowledge sources involved in the generation of a system's response. As an application framework, we present specific aspects of the work carried out in the frame of the VIP-Advisor EU co-funded project whose objective was the development of a virtual insurance and finance assistant capable of natural language interaction. In particular we describe and discuss the engineering steps undertaken for the achievement and integration of the content and knowledge sources, which mainly consist of a domain ontology and a repository of successful subdialogues. By means of a modified case based reasoning approach [2], the dialogues (i.e. cases) are accessed and used as a source for solving dialogue problems that may arise during the interaction with the system.

Common conversational systems such as chatterbots or other more sophisticated conversational agents frequently rely on the same technology [3]: user utterances are interpreted and, by means of a pattern matching approach, an applicable rule is selected from a predefined rule base. The chosen rule also defines the system response to be delivered back to the user. If no relevant rule can be found, a standard answer like “Please reformulate your input” is given. By strictly following this approach, the entire “knowledge” of the information system has to be coded within the rules. This process appears particularly cumbersome, especially if the system’s knowledge is often modified or updated. For this reason, conversational systems are usually enhanced with retrieval engines in order to access external databases or knowledge bases for the completion of the system response [1]. In our approach, we use this solution for accessing the underlying knowledge sources. Instead of delivering the standard system response, an unrecognized user utterance is used as input to a problem identification module, which is responsible for the recognition of the kind of dialogue problem to be solved and the appropriate knowledge source to use for the achievement of a solution.

2. VIP-Advisor

The key objective of the VIP-ADVISOR project (IST-2001-32440) was to develop a virtual personal insurance and finance assistant capable of natural language interaction. This personal assistant is specialised towards risk management counselling for Small and Medium sized Enterprises (SMEs) but can be extended for general insurance counselling for private persons. The interface supports speech recognition and synthesis in order to make the electronic advisor easier and more convenient to use. Through online translation mechanisms it is possible to use the advisor in German and in English. The project builds upon an existing tool (the Risk Manager Online, accessible at http://www.winterthur.ch) provided by Winterthur Insurances. The Risk Manager Online takes the user through a Q&A session with predefined questions before producing a risk analysis matrix. The first steps of the Risk Manager Online (RMO) target the generation of an enterprise profile. For this aim, the pertaining business sector is identified out of a list of 15 entries.

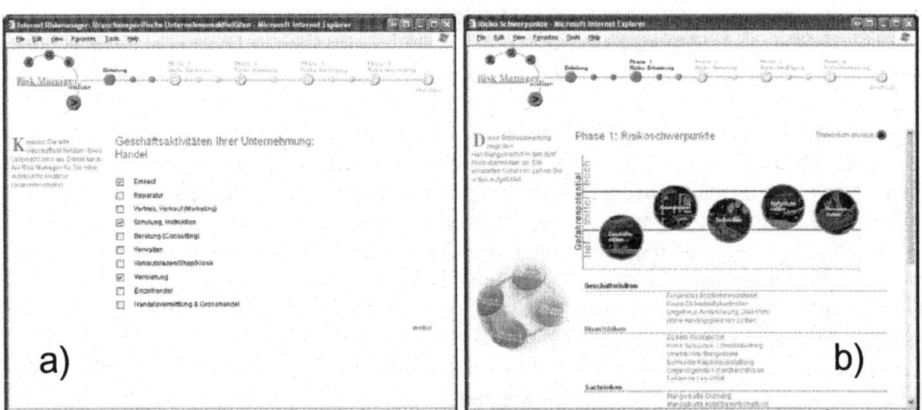

Figure 1: Screenshots of the Risk Manager Online

Afterwards, the main business activities have to be selected. For every business sector a different set of activities is generated (Fig. 1a). On the base of the produced profile, the system generates a list of generic assertions, which are evaluated by the user according to different levels of appropriateness. For instance, the user may have to provide the level of dependency on its suppliers (in the case of a business pertaining to the “retail trade” sector and exercising the activity “purchasing”). Finally, the evaluated sentences are used for the generation and visualization of a risk portfolio. The identified risks are grouped to five main categories and their weighting is shown by means of a diagram (Fig. 1b). In the successive steps of the RMO the user can view and select appropriate measures to counter the presented risks and, finally, build a personalized risk management plan.

For the prototypical implementation within the VIP-Advisor project, only the steps up to the presentation of the risk analysis are considered. The standard interaction means of the RMO are augmented by the usage of natural language for both input and output. The virtual assistant guides the user during the elicitation of the needed data and provides help in unclear or problematic situations (Figure 2). Therefore, the user can always take over the initiative, by asking questions or expressing his uncertainty while performing a specific task.

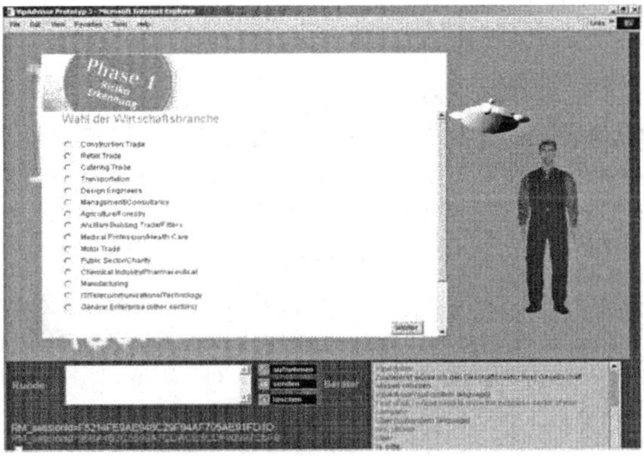

Figure 2: A Screenshot of the VIP-Advisor system prototype

The Interaction Manager component is responsible for coordinating and synchronizing the multi-modal interaction with the system [7]. The user can simultaneously talk via a microphone and make selections directly from the Risk Manager Forms via the pointing device and keyboard. The dialogue management is based on predefined dialogue plans monitored by the Interaction Manager. A plan consists of the realization of a strategy for guiding the interaction through a predefined sequence of dialogue steps. The default plan used every time a new session starts aims at guiding the user through the sequence of interaction steps defined by the RMO. Whenever a user's intervention causes a deviation from the current plan (i.e. by means of an unexpected question or clarification wish), the case based retrieval module (cf. section 3) and/or the domain ontology (cf. section 4) are accessed and a suitable answer is generated (also including contextual information [6]). Four problem classes in which the system recognises the need to apply a new dialogue plan are identified: concept definitions, process descriptions, concept clarifications and arbitrary knowledge requests. A concept definition may consist of a straightforward question from the user seeking a definition e.g., "What is a fire risk?". Process descriptions entail the user asking for explanation of a process, e.g., "How can I prevent a fire risk?". In both of these cases a direct answer to the question usually suffices so that FAQ-like dialogue plans (consisting of one question and a related answer) are used for solving the problem. Concept clarification is more complex than the first two problem classes since the solution consists of more than a straightforward sequence of questions and answers. A user may, for instance, ask "Why should I prevent a fire risk?". Such a question can only be answered in a satisfactory way, if the specific situation of the user is known to the system. Therefore, more information needs to be elicited from the user so that the system can present the user with a process as its answer. The dialogue cases here are manual-like (troubleshooting) rather than FAQ-like. Finally, an arbitrary knowledge request may be part of the dialogue, for example, a user may enquire possible payment modes or ask for the location of an office. The solution is provided by general information retrieval, information sources being either the enterprise portal or the Web, whereas the Case Based Retrieval Module handles problems of the first three classes.

3. The Case Based Retrieval Module

The main aim of the Case Based Retrieval Module (CBR) is to retrieve a dialogue sequence from a set of predefined ones (the case base) which can be used by the interaction manager component for reacting appropriately to a problematic user utterance. The CBR is invoked by the Interaction Manager by passing an XML representation of the identified dialogue problem definition in terms of communicative acts, which are part of a semantic language used for describing both system and user actions (based on the speech act theory [4]). The communicative acts represent both the meaning and the intention of an interaction step. They are extended by a set of parameters that specify the meaning and contents. The received dialogue problem definition is first parsed by a wrapper and then forwarded to a Retrieval Engine (in our case we use HySpirit - Hypermedia System with Probabilistic Inference for the Retrieval of Information, [5]). The CBR also accesses available contextual information in order to provide a more suitable response.

In Vip-Advisor cases are structured recordings of previous successful dialogues including the dialogue rules/plans used. Particular care has been taken in the design and implementation of the case base, which now contains about 500 different problem definitions and related solutions. For collecting the cases, different knowledge sources have been used. For instance, an interview with 4 professional advisors was carried out at the Winterthur offices in Switzerland. The aim was to recognize problems and questions that users normally have during a risk management advisory session. A questionnaire was prepared in advance and the whole interviews recorded digitally in order to ease the post-processing task. The recordings have been transcribed and formatted within Excel sheets. Furthermore, Winterthur has released a CD-Rom containing a risk management application. This tool is used directly by both final customers and professional advisors in support of the risk management procedure. It is based on the four-phase model, similar to the Risk Manager Online, which is the underlying application of VIP-Advisor. The CD-Rom contains numerous help texts explaining the meaning of used concepts and procedures. The help files have been analysed and several cases extracted. The WWW has also been used as a source for cases. For instance, the Credit-Suisse Portal has been analysed and generic business and financial web sites have been browsed, with the aim of finding explanations and definitions of business sectors and activities. Finally, laws and other legal material applicable to the insurance domain have been found and used as a source for cases.

As a final step all generated cases have been coded in XML, in order to be processed within the VIP-Advisor Application. The XML Case Base is divided into seven Categories, as described below:

- Laws – This set of cases contains problems and solutions related to legal questions that customers might have during a risk management session.
- The RMO Phases – While using the Risk Manager Online, users may request the explanation of how to carry out specific processes or functions. Cases in this Category are intended to offer some support and/or instructions.
- The Quick Tour – At the beginning of an RMO session, the system offers to show the quick tour, which is a short introductory movie explaining the four phase model and providing some instructions. These cases address technical issues and other details about the quick tour.

- Risk Factors – Cases explaining the meaning of property, business, financial, liability and personal risks that may occur are contained in this category. Sometimes, details about consequences and measures for avoiding them are also provided.
- RMCD-Definitions – Generic financial and insurance concepts are defined and explained by the cases of this category. Moreover, several insurance types, used to cover a variety of risks are also explained.
- Business Sectors and Activities – During a risk management online session, the user is required to provide information about his/her company in terms of affiliation to a business sector or specification of performed business activities. Questions related to these concepts are handled here.
- Interview Transcripts – This category contains the cases generated from the interviews carried out with risk management advisors (see explanation above).

```
<?xml version="1.0" encoding="UTF-8"?>
<!-- edited with XML Spy v4.2 U (http://www.xmlspy.com) by Marcello L'Abbate
(Fraunhofer Gesellschft) -->
<!DOCTYPE case SYSTEM "case.dtd">
<case>
        <problemType>process description</problemType>
        <problemDefinition>
                <ComActList>
                        <request>
                                <type>explanation</type>
                                <matter>process</matter>
                                <subject>deal</subject>
                                <content>measures catalogue</content>
                        </request>
                        <the text>How do I process the measures catalogue?</text>
                </ComActList>
        </problemDefinition>
        <problemSolution>
                <ComActList>
                        <inform>
                                <type>explanation</type>
                                <matter>process</matter>
                                <subject>deal</subject>
                                <content>measures catalogue</content>
                        </inform>
                        <text>The measures stated in the catalogue are general
instructions how entrepreneurs can reduce risks. They shall serve as an inspiration
because the realisation of the measures is always business specific.</text>
                </ComActList>
        </problemSolution>
        <contextualData>
                <avPair>
                        <attribute>priority</attribute>
                        <value>2</value>
                </avPair>
        </contextualData>
</case>
```

Figure 4: An example of a case

Normally, a case consists of 2 distinct parts, the “problem definition” and the “problem solution” (Figure 4). Both parts contain one or more sentences as well as their representations in terms of communicative acts. The first part also contains an example question that a user may post for describing his/her problem. Questions are normally coded by the communicative act “request” and the parameters used here express the user’s wish for an explanation of a process, dealing with the catalogue of risk measures. Answers are described by the act “inform” which uses in this case the same set of parameters as the request. The solution offered in the second part can be delivered also in case of questions formulated differently. It is the task of the Interaction Manager to interpret a question, and assign it the right communicative act representation. Some cases also contain a third part, describing some contextual circumstances that may possibly apply. This information is also used by the CBR for determining the suitability of the case to an arisen Problem. For instance, a frequently appearing contextual parameter is the priority value. It is used in the case of users requesting for further explanation to an already occurred problem (possibly by using a reformulated question about the same problem). The aim is to avoid providing the same solution again, as the user may not be satisfied with the given answer. We distinguish three levels of priority: the value 1 pertains to a definition of a concept, 2 is used for a deeper explanation and 3 for an example. The lower the value is, the higher the priority is set. As another example for contextual information, some cases include the indication of a country name. This can be used especially for determining the suitability of a case containing legal aspects: the solution will be offered only if the user's country matches the one of the case.

After the processing phase of the CBR, the result is returned using the same description format. In this way the Interaction Manager can include and process the new dialogue plan arrived at in the ongoing dialogue session.

4. The Domain Ontology

The VIP-Advisor domain ontology models the risk management domain implicitly represented by the Risk Manager Online tool (RMO) using a DAML + OIL-like storage model. The primary source of both class and instance data for the ontology were the contents of the RMO and the RM CDs.

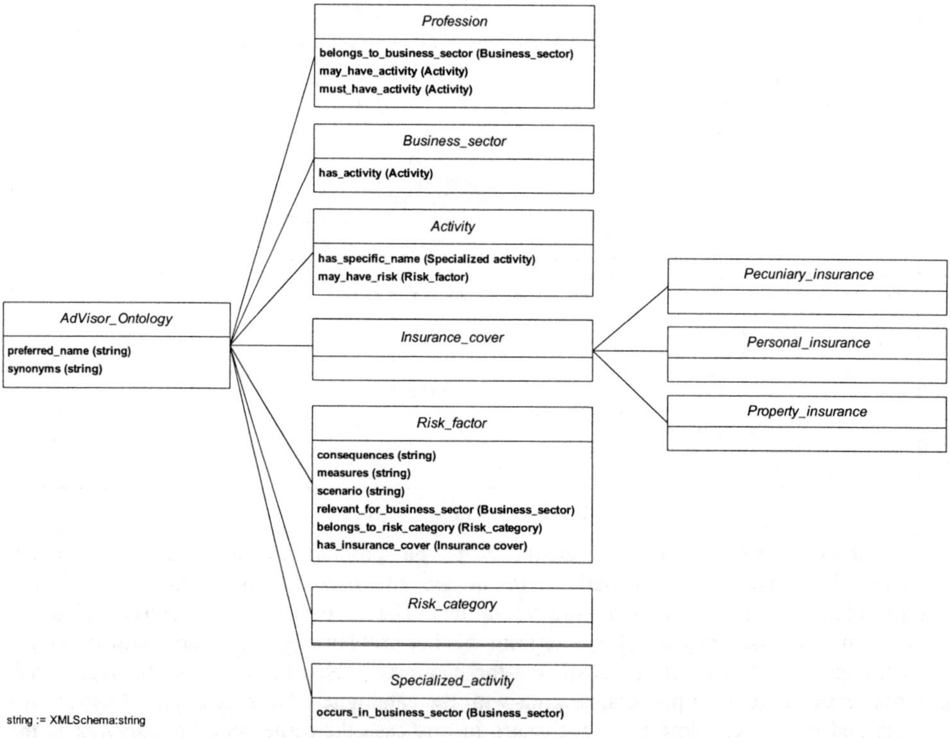

Figure 5: The schema used for the VIP-Advisor Domain Ontology

The different categories (e.g. types of risk or types of insurance cover) contained in the tables as well as the implicit relations between the tables or columns have been imported into the ontology, by adding explicit relations. Since manual entry of instance data would have been time-consuming and error-prone, a semi-automatic process was preferred. Figure 5 contains a visual representation of the schema file used for the Ontology. Classes are represented by rectangles. The slots pertaining to each class are listed in lower case in the bottom half of each rectangle – the range of each (i.e. what the class maps onto, either another class or a string) is given in brackets. These slots represent the relations that may exist between classes. Apart from the top-level class, AdVisor Ontology, the class names are taken from the RMO file and can be described as follows:

- Profession - this class contains the 152 occupations within the scope of RMO; note that the names of the instances are not always those denoting a person carrying out a profession.
- Business sector – this is a broader category than profession and denotes the sector that a profession may be assigned to. There are 15 distinct sectors, for example construction trade, motor trade, chemical industry.
- Activity – this class denotes the activities relevant to a business sector. Examples include auditing, accounting, education/training.
- Specialised Activity – this class denotes the more specialised activities that exist, which are strongly dependent on Business Sector. Examples include Training as a more specialised aspect of education/training.
- Risk category – this class has 5 direct instances, business, financial, liability, personal and property risk. Note that the risks themselves are assigned to these categories but are not regarded as sub concepts of the risk category.
- Risk factor – this class has 100 instances of risks, which are grouped according to their membership of a risk category.
- Insurance cover – this class has 3 sub-classes, pecuniary, personal and property insurance. There are 30 instances of insurance cover, such as fidelity insurance, accident insurance, and livestock insurance, respectively types of pecuniary, personal and property insurance.

The slots denote relations that exist, mainly between classes. For instance, there is a slot called "Belongs_to_business sector" which maps the class Profession to its relevant business sector; the slot "May_have_activity" expresses which activities are potentially relevant for a given Profession; "Belongs_to_risk_category" maps the Risk Factor onto its relevant Risk Category and so on.

5. The use of the information sources

By means of some excerpts from an example dialogue with the VIP-Advisor system prototype, in this section we will show how the described information sources are used during the dialogue management. As a generic scenario, we consider an owner of a petrol station who is interested in an analysis of his business risks. He connects to the VIP-Advisor Website and first gets welcomed. After the introductory phase, in which the user is asked if he is willing to watch a short movie about the RMO, the profile specification phase starts. During the selection of the appropriate business sector, some needs for advice may arise. For instance, a definition of one of the appearing sectors may be asked. Since the standard interaction management only expects a selection at this time, the request for clarification is recognized as a dialogue problem, and passed to the CBR. The Case Base contains an answer to the user's question, which is included in the current dialogue plan, satisfying the user's wish. If he still isn't sure about which sector to choose, the system offers the user also the possibility to input his performed profession. At this time, a case is retrieved which accesses also the ontology. The slot "Belongs_to_business_sector" is used for finding a link between the inputted and the list of business sectors.

Also during the business activities selection phase both the ontology and the case base can be used for solving dialogue problems. Consider the user asking: “Which ones and how many activities should I select?”. A standard answer can be of course provided by the CBR, explaining the aim of this selection phase and mentioning activities often selected by previous users. But since the user’s profession is known, a more personalized answer can be provided. By using the “May_have_activity”-relation of the Ontology a list of activities selected by other petrol station owners in previous sessions can be provided.

Some cases contained in the case base have a more complex structure providing a subdialogue for the solution of a problem rather than only a direct answer. For instance, a user asking for advice about his measure plan against possible financial risks will be engaged in a subdialogue in which he is asked to provide more details about his economic assessment including for instance his cash flow.

6. Conclusions and Future Work

In the framework of the project activities several functionality and usability tests were performed. Real users with different levels of expertise were involved in the evaluation, carrying out risk management sessions on the basis of predefined scenarios. While improvements to the interface components such as the voice recognition and the translation engine are still needed, the outcome of the tests showed a positive impact of the system’s problem solving capabilities. About 70% of user requests were answered positively.

Discussions with Winterthur following the project confirmed the potential benefits of a conversational advisory system. Even if human-like advisory still remains a cumbersome goal to reach, the implemented problem solving capabilities can be regarded as a useful improvement to form-based interfaces, providing users with helpful assistance during their task. Moreover, within a one-year time frame, the effectiveness and stability of the additional interaction means (such as the speech recognition and the online translation) can surely reach a more satisfying level. Especially the interfaces between the involved modules can be enhanced, with the aim of improving synchronisation and integration.

As regards the components described more closely in this paper, future activities will concentrate on a deeper involvement of the external sources. For instance, synonyms and homonyms will be considered during the interpretation process of the user’s utterances. Moreover, subsumption relations will be also used for improving the identification of contextual information, used in the response generation task.

References

[1] L'Abbate, M.; Thiel, U.; Andersen, H.H.K.; Andersen, V., Improving agent technology: An intelligent search for product information. In: Challenges and achievements in Ebusiness and E-work. E-2002; E-Business and E-Work annual conference, Prague (CZ), 16-18 Oct 2002. Stanford-Smith, B.; Chiozza, E.; Edin, M. (eds.), (IOS Press, Amsterdam, 2002) pp. 772-779

[2] D. Leake, CBR in context: The present and future. In: Leake, D. (ed), 1996, Case-based Reasoning: Experiences, Lessons and Future Directions. Menlo Park: AAAI Press/MIT Press, 1996.

[3] Wilks, Y. (editor): Machine Conversations. Kluwer Academic Publishers, Dordrecht, 1999.

[4] J.R. Searle, Speech Acts: An Essay in the Philosophy of Language. Cambridge University Press, 1969.

[5] N. Fuhr and T. Roelleke, HySpirit - A probabilistic inference engine for hypermedia retrieval in large databases. International Conference on Extending Database Technology (EDBT), Valencia, Spain, 1998.

[6] M. L'Abbate, U. Thiel: Use of Contextual Information in a Proactivity Model for Conversational Agents. In P. Blackburn, C. Ghidini, R. M. Turner, F. Giunchiglia (Eds.): Modeling and using Context, Proceedings of the 4th International and Interdisciplinary Conference, Stanford, CA, USA, June 2003, Springer LNAI.

[7] Correas J., Bueno F., Teruel D., García-Serrano A.: An agent based architecture for multi-user applications. In Proc. of "Challenges in Open Agent Systems". Workshop at AAMAS'02 in Bologna, Italy, July 2002.

eAdoption and the Knowledge Economy: Issues, Applications, Case Studies
P. Cunningham and M. Cunningham (Eds.)
IOS Press, 2004

Natural Language Access and Intelligent Service Discovery in e-Business

Mikhail SIMONOV[1], Massimo SOROLDONI[2], Aldo GANGEMI[3]
[1, 2]Nomos Sistema S.p.A., Viale Monza 259, Milan, 20126, Italy
Tel: +39 02 252901, Fax: +39 02 27006614
Email: [1]simonov@nomos.it; [2] soroldoni@nomos.it
[3]LOA ISTC-CNR, Viale Marx 15, Rome, 00137, Italy
Tel: +39 06 86090249, Fax: +39 06 824737, Email: a.gangemi@istc.cnr.it

Abstract: NLP and Ontological engineering play an important role in industrial systems by enabling access to remote services; both of them can be used for service discovery. We have created an enterprise framework embracing various aspects (Soft computing, Ontology Engineering, Advanced Data Mining, NLP, Information Retrieval, etc.) offering a natural language, web-based access to distributed Legacy systems or web services in Banking, Insurance and ICT. Our Business Case has been co-funded by the Eureka program and it illustrates some lessons learnt from National R&D programs. The core system implements an ontology-driven filtering of user queries in order to discover the intended Legacy or Web service. The application implements functionalities for information retrieval, knowledge extraction from free texts, semi-structured and structured documents, automated reasoning, service location, and dynamic invocation. The solution is RDF and XML-compliant according to recommendations given by the W3C Consortium.

1. Introduction

This paper outlines some of our experiences in the IKF[i] project, concerning the implementation of a system for Natural Language access and Intelligent Legacy or Web Service Discovery in e-Business (e-Insurance, e-Banking, Internet Service providing).

Many traditional business applications rely on Legacy applications, while some new applications have started using Web Services. Both classes of applications require a solution enabling natural language based access in order to offer customers a value-added support. Accessing a system from anywhere and in different languages is not an option anymore for virtual organisations. Unfortunately there are no suitable "universal" solutions, since the correct service discovery must be performed locally. Conforming to that, IKF-IES is an enterprise Business Information System, including a knowledge management system and a domain ontology offering a solution to this problem [10]. Semantic parsing techniques are used in order to obtain basic lexical disambiguation capabilities for Italian and English[ii]. Our Business Case is in the area of web-based self-help and semantic support for Call Centres.

In this paper, we explain how we have adopted knowledge technologies in order to facilitate the transition of traditional business into e-Business supporting e-Work, e-CRM and e-Content. We also explain the multi-disciplinary mix of technologies that we have employed: typical domain corpora, ontology-related issues, integration issues, Legacy service discovery and invocation, business support offered by fuzzy logic, DSS-related issues, and self-learning capabilities offered by genetic algorithms. We summarise lessons learnt from the Business Case, from national R&D programs, and we draft the possible future use of the technology involved.

2. Objectives

Our Business Case comprises three different vertical applications for Banking, Insurance, and ICT. The main functionalities required are:

- Enterprise integration with Knowledge Technology and Advanced Data Mining
- Semantic capabilities and Natural Language Processing (NLP)
- Language independent knowledge representation, usable in a mobile context
- Language independent eContent generation
- Semantic query answering
- Legacy and web service discovery and secure invocation
- Security/protection of Code base, personal data, information and knowledge

Our objectives have been pursued in the context of an industrial research and prototypal development EU co-funded project. Our prototype is a proof-of-concept in order to demonstrate the possibilities offered by the technology and to show a transformation path from traditional business into e-Business.

3. Methodology

We have applied methodologies from ontological engineering and W3C standardisation efforts (e.g., related to RDF, XML, OWL etc.). Traditional and novel NLP techniques are also employed to process user queries. Business modelling is done in UML. We also use guidelines and methods concerning the transition to new forms of work organisation: e-Work, virtual organisation, anywhere, anytime mobile access. Multi-disciplinary approach is the main fingerprint of the technology. "Proof by example" is adopted.

The first step in our methodology includes the analysis and reengineering of existing resources: document corpora, existing Q-A systems, and the informal glossaries and terminologies already exploited in the three domains [10].

Text analysis is performed both at development time in order to create a lexicon and to feed the ontology library, and at runtime to process the queries or to manage the documents that enter the lifecycle. We perform three kinds of processing:

- Free text processing by means of natural language parsers supported by a lexicon and an ontology-driven link elicitation allowing semantic reasoning
- Semi-structured data processing by means of pattern matching and link elicitation
- Structured data processing by means of fuzzy rules generation.

The synchronisation of real time reports generated by the Information Retrieval System (IRS), by the Knowledge Subsystem (KS), and by remote components (e.g. a given Legacy or Web Service) is performed through a specific communication channel.

The main challenge consists in a semantic processing of the query, formulated in a natural language. In the following, we detail our application design and functionalities.

4. The Application

4.1 Knowledge Management Framework

The Knowledge Management Framework (KMF) is the core of the system. It is responsible for the natural language based query parsing, since a semantic parser is wrapped into this system. KMF is responsible for inference engine invocation (an automated reasoning is performed), for Legacy or web service discovery and communication, for the interaction with the ontology server, and for the query tunnelling towards the Knowledge Repository. The last process is an asynchronous one: it is well known that the time of query processing is different since the remote call is synchronous; partial results coming from IRS are quickly available, while knowledge retrieval is time consuming. The overall design of IKF is illustrated in Figure 1 below:

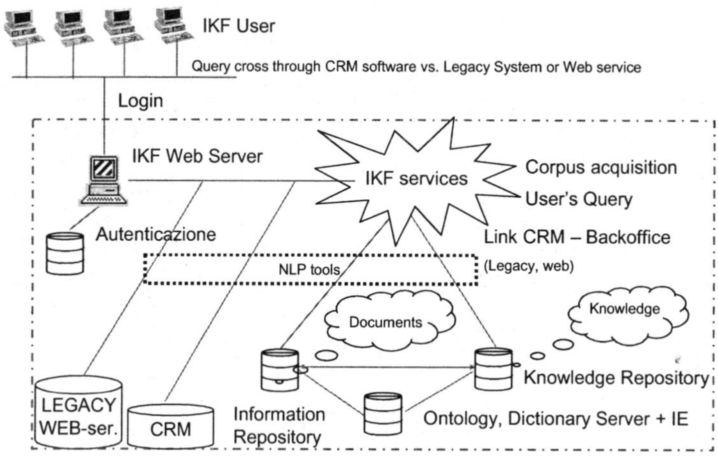

Figure 1: IKF Architecture

In brief, users can login to the IKF Web Server that provides access to possible legacy servers, to the CRM module (or the other modules that can be plugged in the system), and to the knowledge services: document corpus management and linkage to back office and query engines for access to the repositories: information (documents), ontology (metadata), and knowledge (ontology-encoded data). In order to process the corpora, a semantic parser for Italian and English is used in conjunction with the ontology server and the inference engine, which allow a link elicitation process with recall and precision suitable (customized) to the domain addressed by the IKF plug-in (CRM in the figure). The processing is also based on some heuristics able to increase the precision.

4.2 NLP tools and techniques

We use two natural language parsers (one for English and one for Italian), both developed by Expert System, Italy. This commercial solution uses an embedded lexicon called Sensigrafo®[iii], an enhanced dictionary originally based on WordNet [6]. The core of this disambiguation system is a set of deeply interconnected semantic nets that contain a huge amount of information about linguistically-oriented semantic aspects and that are used during the whole process. The disambiguation system works through consecutive text analyses and can be split into three main operation blocks: i) part of speech tagging (includes morphological analysis) that includes collocations recognition (taken from the Sensigrafo or matching heuristic rules) and locutions matching; ii) sentence analysis; iii) semantic disambiguation.

A fundamental feature of the system is the fact that these three analyses are interwoven in a way that, for example, the part of speech tagging is influenced by the sentence analysis in the same way the recognition of the subject is influenced by the semantic disambiguation: the whole process is recursive and the depth of recursion depends from the minimum acceptable performance in the different contexts of use.

In the first step (part of speech tagging), the text is cleaned and modified so that it can be easily analysed (trim of spaces, mapping of characters, intelligent management of caps) and then processed by the parser. The parser makes several passages on the text to improve, with heuristic and statistical algorithms, equivalent recognitions (for example, ambiguous sequences like the ones with noun and adjective in Italian or noun and verb in English) and then moves to complex phrase recognition.

In the second step (sentence analysis), grammatical elements are grouped into logical objects to prepare the best input for the following step.

In the third step (semantic disambiguation), information taken from the Sensigrafo® is heavily used. The possible senses for each element are associated, sorted by frequency and mixed with possible root form ambiguities (for example, in Italian the word “conti” is an inflection of both “conto” and “conte” having different meaning), filtering them on the recognised grammatical characteristics. Once this process is done, everything is ready for the real disambiguation that is implemented with successive refinements executed through multiple passages on all elements, which (in brief) exploit: i) frequency order, ii) the domains of the meanings (taken from the synsets and processed based on frequency, grammatical type and thematic role), and iii) the relevant contexts for the different meanings by checking the surrounding elements and weighing the possible match both on the distance and semantic relevance of the link.

Another key feature of this system is the optimisation of all steps for the maximum speed of execution without seriously compromising the final quality of disambiguation. The result is a set of XML parsing trees delivering different meanings to be disambiguated manually, suitable for the post-processing or for other use. An intuition of the design and functionalities of NLP tools in IKF is given by Figure 2:

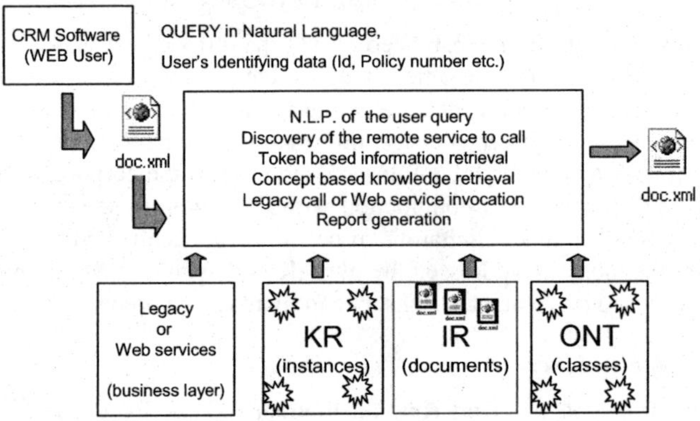

Figure 2: Use of NLP tools

We also show some sample results coming from the above-mentioned NLP tools adopted in our Business Case. The first example (Figure 3) illustrates the Italian and the second (Figure 4) one illustrates the English language NLP.

Notice that the semantic parser allows not only the recognisation of the syntactic structure, but also performs a lexicon entry for the relevant phrases. For example in Figure 3 the concept "surrender value" is recognised as a whole during this stage. The next stage will manage the thematic role used in the following pattern that will help us to answer the question: "Insurer" - calculates the - "surrender value".

By means of semantic parsing, IKF can elicit a basic knowledge from free text, semi-structured, and structured documents. The lexicon includes a taxonomy of synsets ("synonym sets": equivalence classes of word senses), and the typical WordNet-oriented relationships among synsets (e.g.: noun synset - hypernym (is a), noun synset - meronym (part-of), verb synset – subject, adjective synset – quality, synset disjointness, etc.).

Since the semantic parser is lexicon-driven, but not ontology-driven[iv], and even though Sensigrafo currently has one of the best coverings of the Italian language [8], specialised terminology and conceptual models must be represented into specialised ontologies. To this purpose, IKF uses an additional module named Link Elicitor that performs knowledge elicitation by exploiting the IKF ontology.

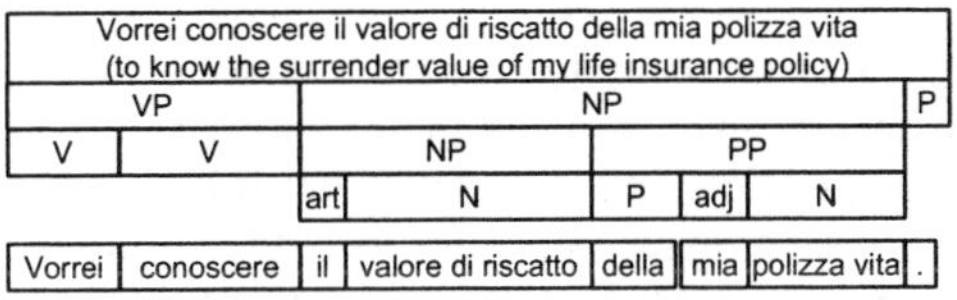

Figure 3: Parse tree for Italian

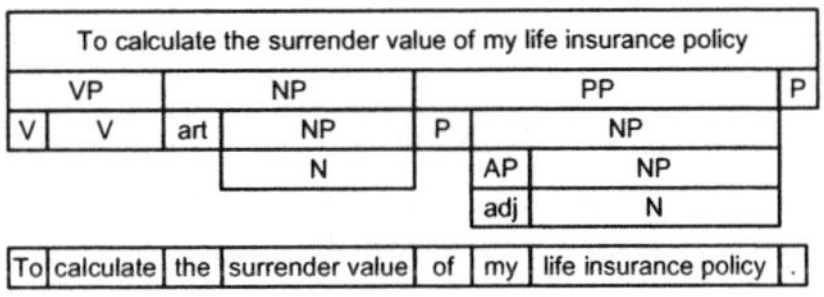

Figure 4: Parse tree for English

The Link Elicitor component manages uncertain knowledge by means of fuzzy rules (more information about the process is available in [11] and [12]. Link Elicitor produces RDF(S) triples by querying the ontology server, and stores the extracted triples in a dedicated Knowledge Repository, represented in an XML/RDF compliant frame-based language. An analysis of the parsed syntactical structures is adopted in order to establish the degree of plausibility of triples retrieved by means of the ontology. A plausibility=1 is equivalent to the presence of a qualified semantic relation.

The results of link elicitation allow us to perform some reasoning. For example, we are able to discover semantic relations between concepts by applying patterns coming from the ontology. Elicited links are needed for semantic discovery of the Legacy or Web services. For example, a user formulates the query: "[I want] to know the surrender value of my life insurance policy". The expected net contains [someone, an actor having the following role "Insured"] - [wish to know] - [the surrender value] - [of the own instance] - [life insurance policy]. Ontology-enriched lexicon gives us the following substitution: [to know] - isInterpretedAs - [to calculate]. The domain ontology tells us that an allowed (conceptual) triple is: [the Insurer] - [calculates] - [values], and [surrender value] IS-A [value]. At this point we can match and call a descriptor for a Legacy or Web service named [Calculate_Surrender_Value] with some parameters to be replaced with actual values.

We have developed two separate modules belonging to the IKF technological framework, named MetaDiscoverer, responsible of the service discovery, and Invoker, responsible for the correct service invocation and parameters calculation. The collection of instances of life insurance contracts belonging to an actor is used at the right time in order to allow the disambiguation of "my life insurance policy". Therefore, we have the possibility to query the Legacy system for the whole collection of the life insurance contracts. The situation retrieved can be summarised as follows:
[Object = Insured, Name = Mikhail Simonov, Id = 123, Sex = M, ...], Today = 01-04-2004
[Object = Life Insurance Policy, Id = 987654321, Start = 01-01-1992, Duration = 10, ...]
[Object = Life Insurance Policy, Id = 987654322, Start = 01-01-2093, Duration = 10, ...]
[Object = Life Insurance Policy, Id = 987654323, Start = 01-01-2003, Duration = 10, ...]
Query = "to know the surrender value of my life insurance policy".

In the worst case we have to call the service Calculate_Surrender_Value() three times.

4.3 Ontologies

The core functionality of our system is ensured by its ontological component, which is customisable, reusable, and is still growing to cover other subdomains of the insurance domain. IKF presently uses domain ontologies for Banking, Insurance and ICT. All three are linked to the DOLCE-Lite-Plus foundational ontology, at the time being using version 3.5. The main peculiarity is the use of the specific Description & Situation design pattern [4] allows us to detect the given situation and to trigger it by acting according to the pre-programmed behaviour expected by e.g. the Insurance Company. Formal specification of domain-specific workflow, by using the D&S design pattern, allows a formal matching between procedural domain knowledge and the system components. This peculiar use of ontologies is exploited in related work carried out within the IKF project for different domains, e.g. anti-money laundering regulations in the banking domain [2], an evidence support in Insurance and service-level agreements in ICT.

The ontology per se cannot match specific needs of a given Insurer, but it allows the rules coming from the Italian legal system to be followed. For example, the Insurance Domain Ontology is used in order to perform link elicitation, i.e. to discover relations between concepts or individuals referred by terms within documents or records in databases. Link elicitation is performed by deriving a set of relevant RDF(S) triples out of the ontology. Triples constitute a "lightweight" semantic network that is then translated into a suitable Legacy service invocation of the Meta-discovery module.

Our Core and Domain Ontology are currently expressed in the Loom-Ontosaurus knowledge representation system [7] that implements a very expressive description logic, but they will be ported to both KIF and OWL (whose versions already exist for DOLCE-Lite+), in order to benefit from both logical programming engines, and Semantic Web inference engines. The assertional part of the knowledge containing textual occurrences has been encoded in a specific knowledge repository specified in a dedicated frame-based knowledge representation system. For further details cf. the web portal of the IKF project. More information about the Insurance Domain Ontology and CRM ontologies, and the specific design pattern adopted can be found in [10].

4.4 Other components

4.4.1 Metadiscovery and remote calls (Legacy and Web service)

The Metadiscovery module is ontology-driven and performs a brokering service between the conceptual model of the ontology and the business model adopted in the Legacy database. It performs reasoning and unification between the part of the semantic network coming from the user's query and the object model of the Legacy part of the enterprise application. After Metadiscovery has resolved the Legacy or Web Service, this module physically performs the call and handles marshalling data vs. remote system and viceversa. Some special heuristics are used in this process that are a protected industrial know how.

Legacy/web calls are performed after the correct service was discovered accordingly the semantics and the marshalling components are properly initialised with correct values. This process is ontology-driven, since the correspondence between slots and values comes from the knowledge frames represented in RDF(S).

4.4.2 Query answering

When a domain-related corpus is loaded on the system, knowledge extraction is performed for each introduced document. Since the relationship between **information objects** and **documents** is used during the query answering, the knowledge elicitation process creates links between both of them, and populates the Knowledge Repository with instances of classes describing domain relevant objects. The query answering adopted involves three separate answers: the first one comes from a Knowledge Retrieval component, the second one from an Information Retrieval one, and the last, most interesting one from the remote system (Legacy or Web service based). Since the enterprise system is constrained by some legal issues, a human must control the Corpus introduced into the Information Repository.Once the Information Repository is populated with documents, and the extracted Knowledge is loaded into the Knowledge Repository, the query can be answered through query expansion and disambiguation, meta-discovery, legacy call, and report generation.

4.4.3 User interface

Our system is web-based and the user interface consists of a set of JSPs and Servlets.

Let us assume that a customer is 37 years old, the policy N. 987 in the only one managed contract (otherwise we will be invited to disambiguate), and the current Tariff is RX. We know also that "Today" is 10th December 2003 and the next renewal or surrendering will be at the end of the year, i.e. on 31st December 2003. The remaining duration of the policy can be calculated and will give us the remaining duration = 6 years. The above-mentioned customer can now post a natural language question through the web interface: "Vorrei conoscere il valore di riscatto della mia polizza vita", i.e. "to calculate the surrender value of my life insurance policy". We will handle NPs, VPs and links between them according to the ontology.

Now query processing performs stages of (1) Semantic parsing, (2) Disambiguation, (3) Query expansion. The next step is the SERVICE discovery: (1) Semantic Discovery, (2) accessing the Service descriptor, (3) Translation vs. Legacy or Web service call, (4) Service Invocation at a correct location.

The above-mentioned query looks like the following one:

CALC. VAL. RISCATTO Is-a <LEGACY SERVICE>, <Invoked by INV07> <from CICS03> <on server \\urano>. It has 6 parameters:

1st Cust.Id, 2nd Age, 3rd PolicyNumber, 4th TariffId, 5th Date, 6th Duration

The binding between actual and formal parameters will be performed in order to ensure the correspondence between the service required and the available Legacy (Web) Service so that Invoker will call the correct code base. Furthermore, marshalling and call invocation are performed. Hence the following natural language query: "to know the surrender value of my life insurance policy" is translated into a procedural call similar to this one: GetVRisc(Id=123, Age=37, Pol=987, Tar=X, From=31-12-2003, Years=6).

This is possible because thematic roles model situations like "in order to know X" "to calculate Y". The calculation of "surrender value" is then available as a service.

5. Conclusions

The paper treats a crucial problem involving NLP and Legacy or Web service intelligent discovery. The Business Case illustrates the concrete possibility to create an enterprise system allowing a natural language based access to remote Legacy and web services. Our solution includes the definition of a suitable Domain Ontology for each business case and links to lexicalisations managed by Lexicon component. A range of technical, practical, socio-political and socio-economical problems can be solved by the described solution. The proposed approach can be adopted in a wide range of scenarios since Ontology-based systems are reusable across many domains and application classes.

Further developments of insurance ontology and related applications will include the matching between legal insurance regulation and policy enactment. We also expect to apply outlined technologies in order to manage the Corpus related to e-Health domain from within the solution to be developed in the DOC@HAND[v] research project.

We recommend the outlined solution for wider use in most social domains, which share many reusable ontologies for organisations, workflows, planning, regulations, etc.

6. Acknowledgements

Some of achievements described in this paper come from the HPPC/SEA and IKF projects co-funded under Eureka. The work described in this paper draws upon the contributions of many people, to whom the authors are indebted. The authors would like to thank the IKF Consortium for their support. We hope that the work performed by this inter-disciplinary international team of professionals is a real demonstration of Integration of the European Research Area.

References

[1] E.Terenzi, B. Di Eugenio, Building lexical semantic representations for Natural Language instructions. HLT-NAACL03, Human Language Technology Conference, Edmonton, Canada, 2003.

[2] Gangemi A., Pisanelli DM., Steve G., A Formal Ontology Frame-Work to Represent Norm Dynamics. Proc. of *Second International Workshop on Legal Ontologies,* Amsterdam, 2001.

[3] Gangemi A., Guarino N. Masolo C. Oltramari A., Schneider L. "Sweetening Ontologies with DOLCE", Gomez-Perez & Benjamins (eds.), Proceedings of EKAW02, 2002.

[4] Gangemi A., Mika P. 2003, *Understanding the Semantic Web through Descriptions and Situations,* Meersman R, et al. (eds.), Proceedings of ODBASE03, Springer, Berlin, 2003.

Gruninger M. and Fox M.S., "*The Logic of Enterprise Modelling*", in Modelling and Methodologies for Enterprise Integration, pages 140--157, 1996.

[5] Jarrar M, Verlinden R, Meersman R, Ontology-based Customer Complaint Management, Proceedings of WORM03 Workshop at ODBASE03, Springer, Berlin, 2003.

[6] Miller G.A., Beckwith R., Fellbaum C., Gross D. & Miller K., "Introduction to WordNet: An On-Line Lexical Database", http://www.cosgi.princeton.edu/~wn; 1993.

[7] Swartout B., Patil R., Knight K. and Russ T., "Toward Distributed Use of Large-Scale Ontologies", in *Proceedings of the Tenth Knowledge Acquisition for Knowledge-Based Systems Workshop*, Banff, Alberta, Canada, 1996.

[8] R. Meersman, K. Aberer, Dillon T.In, (eds). *Semantic Issues in e-Commerce Systems, IFIP TC2 / WG2.6 Ninth Working Conference on Database Semantics (DS-9)*, Boston/Dordrecht: London, 2002. Kluwer Academic Publishers.

[8] López-Ostenero, F., Gonzalo, J., Peñas, A., and Verdejo, F. (2002) Noun Phrase Translations for Cross-Language Document Selection In Cross-Language Information Retrieval and Evaluation, Lecture Notes in Computer Science 2406, Springer-Verlag.

[9] Fernández-Amorós, D., Gonzalo, J. and Verdejo, F. (2001) The role of conceptual relations in Word Sense Disambiguation. In Proceedings of the 6th International Workshop on Applications of Natural Language for Information Systems (NLDB-01).

[10] M. Simonov, M. Soroldoni, A. Gangemi, Ontology-driven Natural Language access to Legacy and Web services in the Insurance Domain, Proceedings of BIS 2004 Conference.

[11] M. Simonov, L. Sammartino, M. Soroldoni, A. Tettamanzi, M. Beretta, Self learning Environment for Life Time Value calculation of customers in Insurance domain, Proceedings of GECCO 2004 Conference.

---

[i] IKF project, Hwww.ikfproject.comH, is an European research project co-funded by EUREKA authorities.

[ii] Other languages can be handled, using appropriate tools, e.g. available from the Natural Language Understanding Consortium, known as NLUC.

[iii] Sensigrafo® is a trademark of Expert System S.p.A., Italy: Hwww.expertsystem.itH. Expert System is a member of NLUC.

[iv] Although Wordnet are sometimes considered ontologies, we distinguish here on the basis that current wordnets are not formal, axiomatic theories [cf. Gangemi et al. 2002.].

[v] DOC@HAND is a Sixth Frame-Work Program (Priority eHEalth) co-funded project named "Knowledge Sharing and Decision Support for Healthcare Professionals"

eAdoption and the Knowledge Economy: Issues, Applications, Case Studies
P. Cunningham and M. Cunningham (Eds.)
IOS Press, 2004

Experimental Design of the Text Identification Language within the ELIS Instrumental Testing System

Valery GORBUNOV
Bashkir State Pedagogical University
Oktyabrskaya Revolucia Street, 3a, Ufa, 450000, Bashkortostan, Russia,
Tel: +7 (3472) 226023, Fax: +7 (3472) 226023, Email: valmigo@bspu.ru

Abstract: At present a lot of different programmes exist, which use the procedures of text identification. For example, computer users look for a required document using keywords, teacher automated the examination of learner knowledge by comparing it with some etalons. Nevertheless, Internet users could receive a list of thousands of useless documents in response to his request, as computer text control cannot exactly separate the set of possible correct answers from incorrect. The ELIS programme (erudition, logic, intuition and sharpness) overcame this by presenting the computer user with a specific tabular language to analyse the elements of text answers based on programmable testing models of word positions. Groups, orders and search intervals, reflexes and virtual words in a testing dialogue allow the use of logical accuracy in the identification of the text answers as well as to assess the knowledge of the examinees. This approach could be applied to other problems.

1. Introduction

Identification of texts is successfully used in automated translation, spelling, and document searching as well as in other tasks. The problems of identification of the text draw the most steadfast attention of numerous researchers. Experimental models of the text have been investigated in structural linguistics for a long time. J.D.Apresjan advocates the following operations: addition of elements to the given language form; omission of elements from the given language form; replacement of one element with another; rearrangement of elements and transformation of the given form in another [1, p. 22].

The researchers' attention is focused on concepts of "Truth", "True", "Sincerity", "Correctness" and "Lie" as the parameters of conformity / discrepancy of the contents of the offer idea and the validity [3, p. 31]. These are the most important positions for computer analysis of text.

In computer systems different decisions of tasks of identification of texts are possible. In the most common case this task is solved with the help of intellectual systems. Experts of different fields of knowledge are forming the actual and logic components of the analysis of the text. The known lack of such decisions is gradually overcome by the creation of more powerful and perfect systems. Another examples represent special cases of the decision of tasks of identification (search of the text, automatic replacement of words, etc.). One of these examples is the expert method digital text structure in tool system of testing ELIS. In this system the identification of the text is carried out with the help of experimentally established typical block diagrams, which are set by operators of identification and key words in verifying models. The set of operators forms logic part of check, key words - actual. Such a combination is well known, but the ways and structure of representation of verifying models that are clear to usual users of a computer have faciliated one of possible decisions of tasks of the automated identification of the text.

Potentially this task can be solved in a search system with the advanced language of commands and patterns, but to program difficult verifying conditions consisting of hundreds of operators of comparison, are beyond the power of the most computer users Usually, such users use a simple kind, within the limits of several operators of the comparison, not providing efficiency of identification of texts. That is why the ELIS analyser of text was developed to receive more exact comparisons of texts due to the curtailed structures of the analysis considerably not complicating appearance of conditions of identification. It is necessary to mention, that during the computer testing of pupils' knowledge there are optimum, well controllable conditions of studying the processes of identification. On the other hand, in contrast to the search tasks the conditions of identification here are more rigid. It is necessary not only to define similar messages, but also to define its abnormality due to the incorrect order of elements of the text or misuse of words in the message. That is why it is necessary to mention that identification of text answers in tool systems of educational achievements testing has its specificity and demands the special programming language of checking systems. Firstly, it is a narrow, specialized, expert problem in a context "the task (question) - the answer". Secondly, there is higher responsibility for legitimacy of the automated decision-making, demanding, as high semantic accuracy of possible (probable) correct and wrong texts answers distinction. Thirdly, this system should provide the ability to undertake high speed checking of the correctness or incorrectness of each current answer of the examinee on a personal computer.

The ELIS automated testing tool system, as well as many other similar systems, was worked out by comparison of logic models of the key words positions [2], set by the composer of test tasks, with logic model of positions of the words found in the answer of the examinee allocated from the text answer. At the same time, this system has original decisions, allowing the ability to program the automated check of more complex text answers in the comparison with the opportunities of known versions (SuperTest v2.4, SunRav, TestOfficePro, etc.) of instrumental systems of testing. ELIS does not use generally accepted substitution marks ('*', '?' etc.), which make reading of check models difficult, and lead to an unnatural view of the text. At complication of verifying conditions they look bulkily and do not allow to see check structure. Another example is that the table of inquiry for similar comparisons compels the user to carry out difficult transformation of arbitrary text to the fields of inquiry. Verifying logic expressions with operational brackets are bulkily and inaccessible for understanding general logic of comparison. The necessity in more comfortable functions of semantic comparison of verifying model of identification and arbitrary text are shown in both examples. Such functions are in the ELIS verifying system. Even more important, features of the new system include compactness, simplicity and presentation of programming comparison texts.

2. Objectives

This paper aims to raise awareness among project managers of educational test or search systems to the possible application of experimentally approved algorithms of texts identification and participation in joint projects. The author has been creating such algorithms in an experimental research since 1987 in various programming languages of transformation procedures and in processing of text arrays with the use of symbolical functions and logic expressions. The system could be useful for teachers in universities and secondary schools as an instrument for self-depended composition of tests with different forms of tasks and test conducting.

3. Methodology

The methodological basis of research has been the theory of information, the theory of artificial intellect, the theory of educational activity, and also logic, linguistics, combination theory, the theory of probability and statistics. Studying the theory and distributed testing systems shows the difference between real and expected results. The creation of this system for testing was based on the requirements of universities and secondary schools. On the base of analysis of ELIS instrumental system' protocols, we studied experimentally the difficulties facing teachers while translation of the text in electronic version and difficulties facing students while testing in classes. The testing system becomes open for development.

4. Technology Description

The ELIS analyser of texts was created not as the linguistic processor [4], but as a system programmed by the user for identification of natural symbolical structures by the authorities experts. "Word" is understood in this verifying system as any number (within the limits of a field of the answer) of printed symbols, including each sign (for example, a punctuation mark). The degree of the detailed elaboration is defined by the compiler's expert knowledge of tasks and allows the export to adjust, in his/her opinion, accuracy and discrepancy of the answer within the limits of preservation of correct sense of the answer.

The system of decision-making on correctness of the answer of the examinee consists of three levels (Figure 1), controlled by operators and parameters of logic models of test tasks compiler's answers. Each level has an arbitrary set of entry points, set by the compiler (results of the analysis in the subordinated systems) and one output (decision). The top level is formed by the current set of verifying models connected by attitudes AND, OR, NOT (Figure 2). The structure of such verifying models of each task of the current test is indistinguishable from models from the common bank of all system of testing ELIS. The volume of each model, the common number of used models is determined by the potential complexity of checking the current task answer. Each current model of the set of one task verifying models forms the second level. Its structure includes operators of the third level the checks that carry each verifying word to one scheme of groups of words and scheme of word orders or carry out the reference to external, filled up bank of models.

The same operators carry each word to the basic word, synonym or antonym. Others – are the set of intervals, virtuality of words, reflexes. The length of a word, a distance in symbols, unity of words or randomness of a distance are used in definition of intervals of search of the following words concerning the current found word in the ELIS verifying system. Virtual words for which, as well as for other words of the answer the logic of positions is checked, but their absence in the text of the answer does not result in denying identification. The item logic of operators allows to set most compactly and evidently parameters of check for identification of semantic set of allowable positions of words in text answers is used in verifying models.

Convergence of semantic correctness of the answer is provided by several ways. Firstly, it is special conditions and restrictions in the text of the test task (question). Secondly, programmed reflexes (reaction of verifying system) at the words and reflexes at the model of words positions, are found out in the text of the examinee's answer and declared during the check. It allows to divide the long check into stages, if necessary. Thirdly, it is checked in the form of dialogue with a tested and possible (probable) output to the qualifying (within the limits of a verifying continuance) unequivocal answer as the selective, crossword or coordinate answer in the picture.

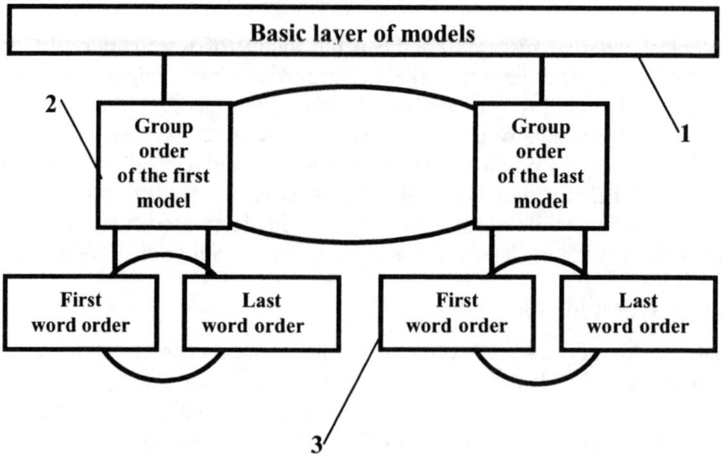

Figure 1: The general circuit of level identification of the text for one answer.
1 – upper level of group of models, 2 – average level of group order, 3 – lower level of word order.

The dialogue form is also used for improvement of verifying models with the help of bank of answers created during check and reports of check. With same purpose autotune of weight factors of difficulty of tasks and auto detection of factors of complexity of tasks are used. Productivity of system of decision-making is provided with rational sequence of check and switching-off in the program of analysis lines not semantic circuits of positions of words in a hierarchical tree of the analysis of possible positions of words of the answer.

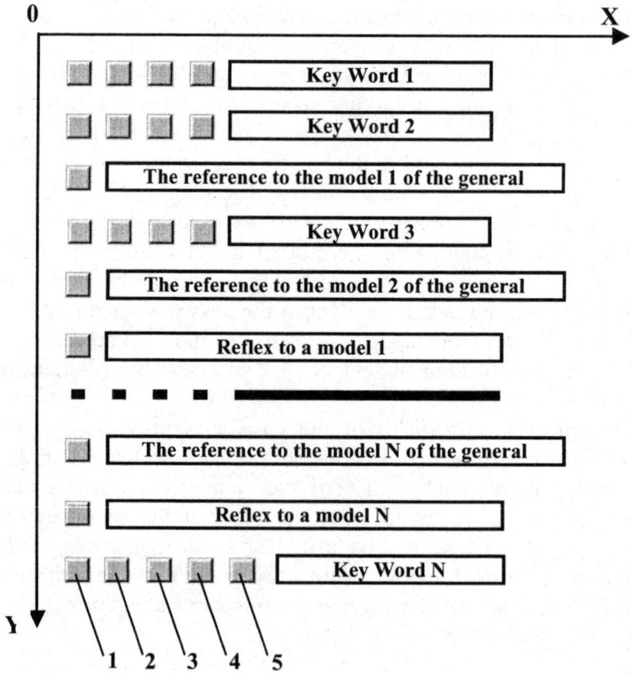

Figure 2: External, basic layer from a set of models.
1 – Type of a line (number of group of word, logical or service line of model), 2 – Scheme of orders, 3 – Distance or relative position, 4 – Virtuality words, 5 – Reflex to a word from the general base of reflexes.

Groups, orders, intervals of search, reflexes and virtual words allow to receive semantic accuracy of identification, to establish correctness of answers and (or) presence of the examinee's knowledge. These are the main means of check of answers programming in the used analyzer of texts. Other decisions have also been experimentally studied according to relative positions of words and interpretation of their meanings.

It is established in the given research, that the greatest external presentation and simplicity of perception of complex checks possess not bulky expressions with the use of operational brackets, but compact models on the basis of hierarchy of syntax tables of language of checking answers is set with its structure. The main table of the models, the subordinated groups of words and separate tables of the common bank of the verifying models, are caused from any current model of any task form the hierarchy of tables (Fig 3).

Evolution of systems of verifying models occurs at addition of lines on an axis Y (Figure 1). It is a usual methodical task of composers of verifying models. Evolution of the verifying system occurs at addition columns on an axis X. It is a technological problem of the programmer. It is necessary to note, that task with input of text answers demand long expenses of time and the greater effort of examinees in comparison with a choice from variants of answers. The programming language of check of text answers in the ELIS tool system allows the checking not only open text, but also the closed selective answers (choice of variants, an establishment of conformity, an arrangement under the order, etc.). That is why in the ELIS tool system it is possible to use any of verifying forms (the selective answer, a crossword puzzle the answer, the coordinate answer and the text answer) in one window, that allows the composer to reduce time by testing the use of mainly selective forms of answers, and as not numerous, difficult tasks - open text answers.

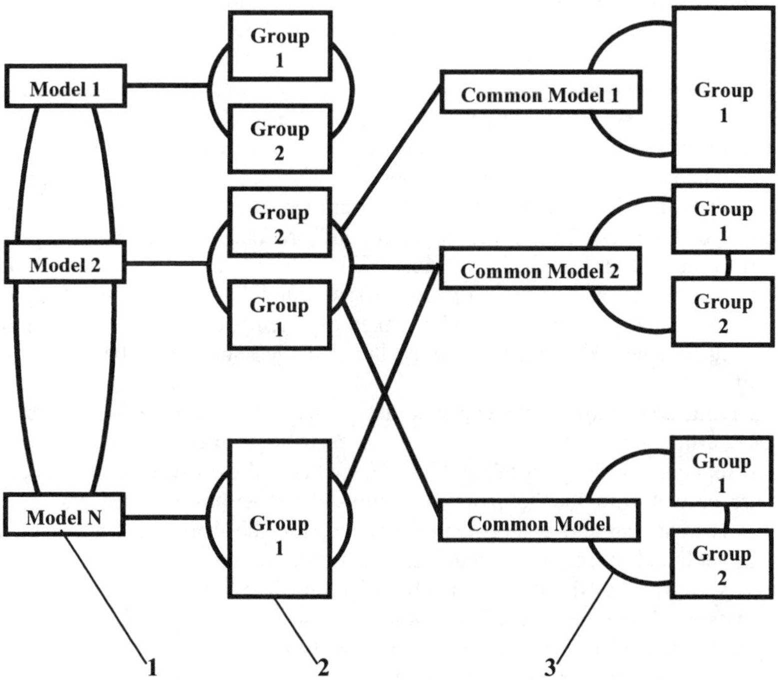

Figure 3. The general circuit of identification models for one answer
1 – An external, basic layer of set of models, 2 - Groups of words in models of check possible answers, 3 – Common bank of additional models.

Correctly made questions and check verifying models allow successfully checking of such answers in the ELIS analyser of texts. At the same time, computer comparison of text messages in such system has both advantages and weaknesses. Advantages include the opportunity to develop computer-verifying models up to a condition of effective check in typical verifying situations. The weaknesses include the impossibility of the analysis beforehand unpredictable messages.

It is necessary to note, that the task of identification of two identical messages in sense (semantic identity) which will consist of various and identical words, various and identical orders of elements of the text in some cases unequivocally cannot be solved even by a commission of experts. That is why various receptions of identification and special decisions for overcoming existing lacks are used in the ELIS verifying system. The use of various receptions of identification of texts depends on the opinion of the expert (commission of experts), a stage of development of system of verifying models, restrictions on time of check and volume of the checked text. The rough, exact and combined comparisons are different. The rough comparison, allowing the expert to judge mainly about basically knowledge of tested, uses (usually unchangeable) parts of words in view of possible syntax of sentence. In the exact comparison the result of the morphemic analysis of words is in addition taken into account. A limiting case of exact comparison is the comparison on the individual symbols forming morphemes. The most effective on volume and speed of the checked text is the combined way, when in the prospective message areas for exact (the basic semantic loading) and rough check (minor semantic loading) confidently are defined.

Features of the analysis of the text can be considered in separate examples. So, for the task "Considering forces of pressure upon a body in a liquid or gas, briefly explain the reason of occurrence of force Archimed". It is possible to show some examples of correctly determined answers at the basis of rough comparison: "The difference of forces of pressure", "Pressure below is more", "The upper force of pressure is less, than lower ", "Unequal forces of pressure" and others. The text analyser quite successfully distinguishes possible wrong arrangements of words from possible correct. Use of figure to the task allows more exactly to set sense for the supposed examinee's answer. For example, in the case of the question "What are the name of the main sentence parts?" the answers can be various. Some of them can be such as: “Subject and predicate”; "It is cubes – predicate, subject”, "It is subject and predicate"; "Most likely it is not subject and not predicate"; "They are named subject and a predicate". In verifying model of the analysis of the text the first answer at the expert's discretion can be ranked to a right answer. The same can be told about the second answer knowing, that the teacher at the lessons used cubes with names of sentence parts.

The verifying system allows the expert to define the denying right answer as the wrong answer (the fourth answer). At the same time it is possible to present a situation of use of even or odd sequence of denying of right answer, which will be difficult to identify. Such problems are solved with the help of instructions - restrictions for answers. The most difficult part is treatment and acceptance of a decision to the words of the answer, which has not been included in verifying model. In local comparison of two texts this problem cannot be solved. That is why during the check by the ELIS analyser for the superfluous text the message above percent of incomprehensible text or the message "It is not everything clear for me in your answer». Unambiguity of acceptance of a decision in the case of the wrong answer is provided with additional exact question with the unequivocal answer. This simple decision simultaneously allows the accumulation of material for the development, perfection of verifying model by the methodologist. Accumulation of the perfect, successful models of comparison is a valuable material not only for the methodologist, but also for research of processes of identification of texts.

5. Developments

The worked out language of texts identification is applicable in other cases. For example, it can be used in tasks of export, import of test tasks for compatibility of the ELIS tool system with other tool systems of testing. Research of produced and dynamic models of recognition in the ELIS tool system, on which the first simple experiments are carried out, is the most perspective continuation of the given experiment.

6. Results

The ELIS tool system was successfully applied for testing of students in educational institutes in Ufa. The results of experimental research of the analysis text knowledge answers were submitted at conferences and then published [2, 5, 6 and etc.]. In spite of getting the practically suitable results, we plan to continue the experimental work since received results will lead to new, more complex problems. Bashkir State Pedagogical University has comfortable conditions for research work, but for commercial use of its results it is essential to have European partners, specialized in such tasks.

7. Business Benefits

The results of the carried out experiments, the developed circuits of identification of text answers can be applied in tool systems of testing for remote training in some cases requiring more exact search of the text information in control systems of databases or in search servers in Internet. Developed technology for text analysis could be presented to the market with the help of software producers.

8. Conclusions

The value of the given research consists of the following: it has created a working program system, which really takes into account opportunities of a computer and the user. Complexity of solved problems is that systems of checking text and selective answers in the ELIS tool system are coordinated with mechanisms of standardisation of test points, factorial diagnostics of the level of examinees' knowledge, by means of test system protection and other subsystems. The examples listed do not exhaust all aspects of identification of texts in test systems. In this experiment the author has carried out the researches of other methods of text identification. Steady scientific interest to the given problem allows the author to express readiness for realization of the further researches within the framework and in the united projects.

Acknowledgement

This paper was submitted with the support of ADMIRE-P EU project (№ IST-2001-35449).

References

[1] Apresjan JU.D. Experimental research of semantics of Russian verb. Moscow: Nauka, 1967. pp 251.
[2] Gorbunov V. Comparison of texts on models of positions of words / Magazine "Computer science and education". Moscow, 1990, №4, pp. 45-49. ISSN 0234–0453.
[3] The logic analysis of language. Cultural concepts. Moscow: Nauka, 1991. pp. 204. ISBN 5-02-011055-8
[4] Yu.D.Apresjan, I.M.Boguslavskij, L.L.Iomdin and others, A linguistic processor for complex information systems. Moscow: Nauka, 1992. 256 pp. ISBN 5-02-006928-0.
[5] Gorbunov V. Logic models of check of answers in computer pedagogical tests // Information technologies in education. Conference proceedings. Part V. ISBN 5-7262-0460-3. MEPI, Moscow, 2002, pp.25-27.
[6] Some lines of logic-semantic transformation of the data in computer systems of testing // New communication technologies: achievements, problems of prospect. The international forum. September, 23-24, 2003. Novosibirsk, 2003.

eAdoption and the Knowledge Economy: Issues, Applications, Case Studies
P. Cunningham and M. Cunningham (Eds.)
IOS Press, 2004

Building Community Mirrors with Public Shared Displays

Michael KOCH
Technische Universität München, Germany
Tel: +49 89 289-18690, Fax: +49 89 289-18657, Email: kochm@in.tum.de

Abstract: Community support is gaining increasing importance in all areas from knowledge management to customer support. This paper addresses the use of non-desktop user interfaces, namely public shared displays, as an additional interface to community support applications. By displaying information from within the community such Community Mirrors can support insiders and outsiders gaining awareness of the community. We present an overview of how such devices can be used for community support, and describe three applications we have designed.

1. Introduction

Starting from early studies on computer-supported collaborative work, the role and potential of community support is gaining more and more importance in the development of new applications for information and communication technologies.

The success of community support applications depends on the active participation of a significant percentage of the community members. Hence, the availability and modality of access to the community support application can be considered a major issue. However, experience so far demonstrates that the common user base of community support applications is mainly composed of computer literate individuals, accessing the systems with desktop computers at home or at the workplace. In fact, community support applications are often based on large bulletin boards, and the main user interface usually is a Web browser.

Ubiquitous Computing and mobile computing, i.e. new user interfaces that are emerged in the real world, may address the boundaries of community support and offer possibilities for enlarging the reach of community support applications.

One field, where new user interfaces for community support might prove especially useful is awareness support, i.e. visualizing the activity in the community, the relationships and interactions among the community members, and presenting this information at locations and in situations where the community members meet.

We call such awareness applications for communities "Community Mirrors". Community Mirrors provide information about the community and its activities for community members to support interaction and matchmaking in the community.

In this paper we first discuss some basics on communities and community support to derive possible application areas for Community Mirrors, then summarize existing work, and finally present three Community Mirror applications we are currently developing.

2. Community Support and Community Mirrors

We began our project on Community Mirrors with revisiting basic work on community support. The goal of the task was to answer the question, what communities are and in which tasks they can be supported, in order to derive possible application areas and requirements for the usage of public Community Mirror displays.

2.1 Communities

In general a community is a group of people who share some interest, identify with a common idea or more generally belong to a common context. Thus, a community can be seen as a descriptive identity for a set of people.

Early sociological work points out that communities always need a locality and interaction [9]. While the demand for a common physical locality is no longer seen necessary, the demand for interaction is still valid. While no active interaction among community members is required, they must have the ability to interact with the rest of the community. The ability to interact implies the existence of a common communication medium, common protocols and awareness of existence and membership in the community.

Other characterizations highlight the need for mutual community collaboration, e.g. the will to exchange knowledge or to help each other [10]. A community is not just a set of people with something in common and the ability to communicate, but rather as a set of people who are willing to help each other, and collaborating to the advantage of all.

Besides the collaboration among the members itself, the main activities in communities are communication and finding people to communicate with. Hence, community support can be seen as "communication and matchmaking/awareness support".

2.2 Community Support

The use of networked computers to support communities can be traced back to the beginnings of the Internet: The second service in the initial Internet, the file transfer service was soon "misused" to transfer messages from one person to another – email was invented [8]. Quickly mailing lists followed and Newsgroup services were available – both on the Internet (Arpanet) and on alternative networks formed of loosely connected computers (e.g. the FidoNet). These first community support services of the Internet still exist. Additionally, different (Web-based) platforms emerged, that provide virtual places for communities. Such solutions are labelled as platforms for community support (community platforms).

However, community support did not start with computers. Support for the building and the maintaining of communities can be classified in classical approaches like private letters, leaflets, magazines, paper whiteboards, specialized radio and TV programs, and approaches based on networked computers (bulletin board systems, MUDs, MOOs).

Both support types, the classical and the electronic ones, provide a medium that can be used for member interaction. Both have advantages and disadvantages. For classic media the advantages are availability, familiarity, and ease of use. For electronic media the advantages are dynamicity, speed, ease of replication, and distribution; disadvantages are barriers to usage, problems with access, and lack of availability.

Generalizing the functionalities of different electronic community support tools and matching them with the basic characterization of communities presented in the previous section one can identify the following basic concepts of community support applications:

- Providing a medium for direct communication and for indirect exchange of content and comments within the common scope of the community.
- Providing awareness of other members and helping to discover relationships (for matchmaking). This can help to find possible cooperation partners for direct interaction.

2.3 Public Shared Displays for Community Support

Support of informal communication and awareness is important for teams and communities as it helps to establish the common ground necessary for meaningful conversations and relationships. Clark in "Using Language" [5] defined common ground, as information that two parties share and are aware that they share. According to Clark, "Everything we do is rooted in information we have about our surroundings, activities, perceptions, emotions, plans, interests. Everything we do jointly with others is also rooted in this information, but only in that part we think they share with us". Information on how the concept of common ground can be used to design collaboration technology can be found in [2].

Closely related to common ground is the concept of awareness, which has been researched intensively in the collaboration support domain. Dourish and Belotti define awareness as "an understanding of the activities of others, which provides a context for your own activities" [6]. Context for own activities can be different types of information, ranging from the availability of co-workers to notifications about people or information that might be relevant to your own work or leisure activities. Schlichter et al. regard providing awareness as the most common dominator in collaboration support [19]. They list contact facilitation and collaborative usage of knowledge as the main activities in communities to be supported by awareness. While groupware focuses on workspace awareness, community support focuses on people/presence awareness (due to the lack of a common workspace).

Common ground and awareness suggest that providing a detailed and aggregated view of a community, a Community Mirror, can help community members in their activities. From the theories one can classify different types of information that can be useful for the individual community members: awareness of community members, information contributed by community members, and activities in the community information space.

Awareness of community members – Information about known community members can help to coordinate activities. For unknown community members this information serves contact facilitation. As well as information about specific community members, aggregated information of community membership can be helpful for insiders and outsiders.

Information contributed by community members – Communities cluster people with similar interests. Thus, information contributed by community members in the context of the community is potentially interesting for other members. This information also provides hints about the interests of the contributing users, thus supporting contact facilitation. In this category the display of detailed and aggregated information is possible and useful.

Activities in the community space – A special type of information contributed by community members implicitly are activities they are performing in the community space. These events, again in detail or aggregated, can help other community members in identifying information or people that can help them in their activities.

2.4 Application Architecture

The displays we are envisioning for presenting this information should be public, shared, interactive, and personalized:

- Public display: The display can be used by anyone with access to its public location.
- Shared display: The display can be viewed/used by more than one user at once.
- Interactive display: The users can interact with the display.
- Proactive/Personalized display: The display can react to users without direct user interaction (e.g. recognizing users by RFID & adapting the information displayed [14]).

In our work we first concentrated on public shared displays – i.e. displays placed in a (semi-)public space and can be accessed by several users at once – and thereby constitute a social place where people can meet. This feature (social place) can further enhance the pure information distributing effect for the single user of the display. Interactivity and (automatic) personalization are considered as optional features in our designs [11].

In contrast to existing solutions for (community) awareness support consisting of single applications dealing with information gathering, storing and visualization, we focus on connecting Community Mirrors to existing community support platforms. Web-based community support platforms can be enhanced by additional shared displays or kiosks. This architectural consideration also suggest including mobile devices for information display and interaction. We consider this in our projects, but do not address it further in this paper.

For implementing such hybrid systems different applications have to be integrated. Based on this need we have built Cobricks, a modular toolset for building community platforms that easily can be accessed from other platforms or from external applications like Community Mirrors (see www.cobricks.org for more information).

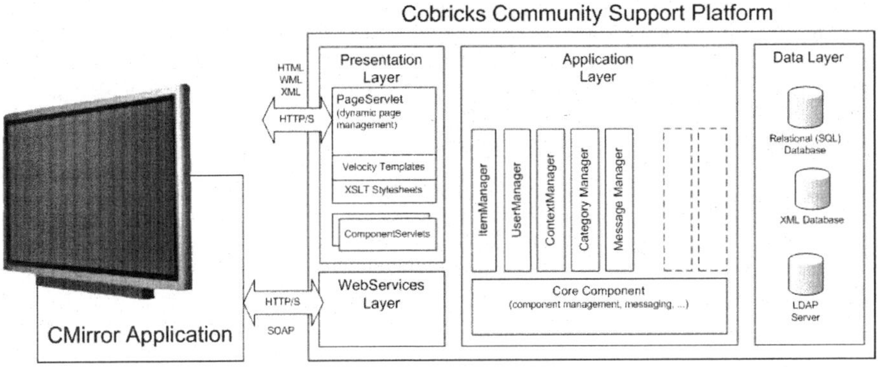

Figure 1: Cobricks Overall Architecture

One part of Cobricks is the CMirror application framework. Using this framework, Community Mirror applications can be built that display different information from a Cobricks platform. The framework provides all functionality for screen layout and for communicating with the community platform.

3. Related Work

Public shared large screen user interfaces are not a new concept, having been pioneered in the 1970's by Myron Krueger [12]. Recent work has mainly focused on supporting collaboration between co-located or distributed users. For the co-located support the central concepts are to provide an interface, which can be used simultaneously by more than one person, and to provide a large working area that can fill the field of view.

An example of using large screens to support collaboration is the DynaWall [7], developed at GMD/Fraunhofer-IPSI. This is a large screen display with an active area of 4.5 x 1.1 meters and a resolution of 3072 x 768 pixels. It is formed by three networked, back-projected electronic whiteboards each which its own controlling PC. User interaction is by hand-gesture and pen input.

Only recently a trend investigating large screen displays for publishing and matchmaking in communities has started to emerge, specifically addressing settings like conferences and exhibitions. Some public displays have been created that attempt to address the issue of providing common ground to inspire conversation. McCarthy's Groupcast is a peripheral display that recognizes passers-by and posts content of interest to at least one of the users [13]. The Silhouettell system [17] also uses large screens to project information of common interest to people meeting before the shared display.

More examples for current systems supporting communities can be found in [16], e.g. Plasma Poster from Fuji Xerox Palo Alto Laboratory [3][4], Magic Wall from Accenture Research, and CWall from Xerox Research Lab Europe [1][20]. In most projects the development was for office environments, i.e. communities sharing the same physical work location. The Plasma Poster is intended for knowledge sharing at the workspace and has also been extend to conference usage in CHIplace and CSCWplace by Churchill et. al. [4].

Outside of research, several large, interactive shared displays have also been deployed. For example BBCi has built street-level window displays that allow passersby to not only see and hear interviews in progress, but also to submit their own questions using SMS text messaging. Likewise, the Vodafone Lisbon office contains a giant cube display on which passersby can request news, short animations, and games, again using SMS text messaging. See [18] for more information on these examples.

The main shortcut of existing applications is that they usually are self-contained. The full potential of Community Mirrors however can only be made available when connecting large screen displays to existing (community) platforms. Additionally, it would be ideal if existing large screen displays could be used for more than one community platform.

4. Application Areas and Prototypes

Based on the theoretical considerations and possible functionalities we have started to build Community Mirror applications for several application areas. In this section we will briefly describe three projects that are nicely covering the possibilities for Community Mirrors.

4.1 Library Mirror / Engramm

For identifying interesting topics or people to contact it is useful to have peripheral awareness of what other people (in the community) are working on or looking for.

We have implemented a Community Mirror application for the main library of our university, which anonymously visualizes what library users (both in the physical library and via the Internet search engines) are searching for. This visualization is displayed on a large screen projection in the entrance area of the library and optionally on mobile devices.

The design of the library mirror includes the real-time visualization of queries, the visualization of aggregated query information (Figure 2), and the display of announcements of the library. We also address how users can interact with the visualization to obtain additional information. See [15] for more details on this application.

Figure 2: Library Mirror

4.2 Meeting Mirror

An important activity in communities of practice is attending (physical) community meetings, i.e. events during which members of the community come together for communication and for exchanging information.

While much effort has gone into creating online spaces for people to meet, network, share, and organize, relatively little effort has gone into creating awareness of online social activities in physical community places [4]. Support for awareness and matchmaking during such physical events currently is limited to simple badges and printed participant lists. These tools usually cannot be influenced a lot by the community members whose information is distributed through them.

We took these observations as a starting point to look closer into possibilities to support community meetings and designed a Community Mirror application for supporting matchmaking during such community meetings [11]. The Meeting Mirror application provides an interactive visualization of the participant list of the meeting. In addition to the visualization this application also addresses issues of identity management for managing the access rights to a user's personal information. We envision the Meeting Mirror in the form of a pillar (see Figure 3), the current implementation however uses flat screens only.

4.3 Announcement Mirror

The third application being evaluated is an announcement mirror, i.e. an application that visualizes the content that members publish on a community platform for other members.

We have implemented such an Announcement Mirror displaying selected contents from the community platform of a university department on a large screen display.

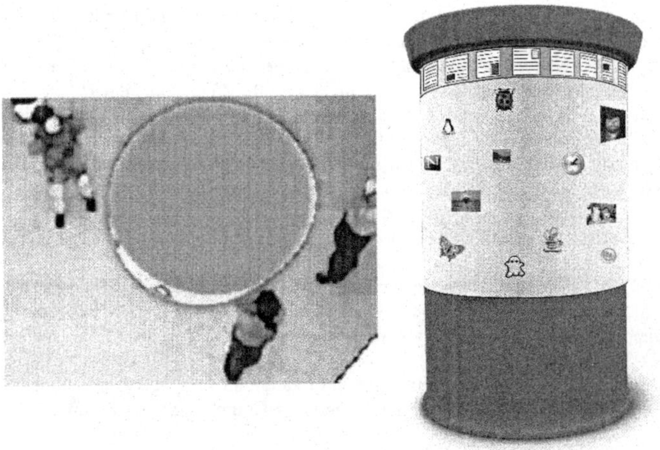

Figure 3: Meeting Mirror

5. Conclusions

In this paper we have presented the concept of Community Mirrors, discussed some possibilities for their application, and presented three applications of such community awareness visualizations. These examples offer both applicable solutions for different community support scenarios, and provide inspiration for new developments in this area.

The most important message of this paper is that different user interfaces should be used to provide access to existing and new community support platforms. Large screen displays are especially effective for providing an overview of what is going on in the community (awareness). Mobile devices might be added to the setup for interaction with the platform – this is something we are also planning to address in the future.

References

[1] A. Agostini, V. Giannella, A. Grasso, M. Koch, D. Snowdon, and A. Valpiani (2000): Reinforcing and Opening Communities through Innovative Technologies. In: M. Gurstein (ed.): Community Informatics – Enabling Communities with Information and Communication Technologies, Idea Group Publishing.

[2] O. de Bruijn, and R. Spence (2001): Serendipity within a Ubiquitous Computing Environment: A Case for Opportunistic Browsing. In: Proc. Ubicomp 2001: Ubiquitous Computing, Third Intl. Conf., Vol. 2201 of Lecture Notes in Computer Science, Springer, pp. 362-369.

[3] E. Churchill, L. Nelson, and L. Denoue (2003): Multimedia Flyers – Informal Information Sharing with Digital Community Bulletin Boards. In: Proc. Communities and Technologies, Amsterdam, Kluwer Publishers.

[4] E. Churchill, A. Girgensohn, L. Nelson, and A. Lee (2004): Blending Digital and Physical Spaces for Ubiquitous Community Participation. Communication of the ACM, Feb. 2004, 47 (2), pp. 39-44.

[5] H. H. Clark (1996): Using Language, Cambridge University Press.

[6] P. Dourish, and V. Belotti (1992): Awareness and Coordination in Shared Workspaces. In: Proc. of the Conf. on Computer-Supported Cooperative Work, pp. 107-114.

[7] J. Geissler (1998): Shiffle, throw or take it! Working efficiently with an interactive wall. In: Proc. CHI'98, Los Angeles, LA.

[8] K. Hafner, and M. Lyon (1996): Where Wizards Stay Up Late: The Origins of the Internet. Simon and Schuster.

[9] G. A. Hillery (1955): Definitions of Community: Areas of Agreement, Rural Sociology, 20, pp. 111–123.

[10] T. Ishida (1998): Community Computing. John Wiley and Sons.

[11] M. Koch, S. Monaci, A. Botero Cabrera, M. Huis in't Veld, and P. Andronico (2004): Communication and Matchmaking Support for Physical Places of Exchange. Proc. Intl. Conf. On Web Based Communities (WBC 2004), Lisbon, Portugal, Mar. 2004, pp. 2-10.

[12] M. W. Krueger (1991): Artificial Reality III, Addison-Wesley.

[13] J. F. McCarthy, T. J. Costa, and E. S. Liongosari (2001): UniCast, OutCast and GroupCast: Thre Steps Toward Ubiquitous Peripheral Displays. In: Ubicomp 2001: Ubiquitous Computing, Third Intl. Conf, Vol. 2201 of Lecture Notes in Computer Science, pp. 332-345.

[14] J. F. McCarty, D. H. Nguyen, A. M. Rashid, and S. Soroczak (2002): Proactive Displays and the Experience UbiComp Project, SIGGROUP Bulletin, Dec. 2002, 23 (3), pp. 38 – 41.

[15] M. Ngo (2004): Erfassung und Visualisierung eines Community-Gedächtnisses für eine Universitätsbibliothek, Master Thesis, Institut für Informatik, Technische Universität München.

[16] K. Ohara, M. Perry, E. Churchill, and D. Russel (Eds.) (2003): Public and situated displays: Social and interactional aspects of shared display technologies. Kluwer, London.

[17] M. Okamoto, H. Nakanishi, T. Nishimura, and T. Ishida (1998): Silhouettel: Awareness Support for Real-World Encounter. In: T. Ishida (ed.): Community Computing and Support Systems – Social Interaction in Networked Communities. Springer. Lecture Notes in Computer Science 1519, pp. 316-329.

[18] J. Scanlon (2003): If walls could talk, streets might join in. New York Times, September 18th.

[19] J. Schlichter, M. Koch, and C. Xu (1998): Awareness - The Common Link Between Groupware and Community Support Systems. Community Computing and Support Systems (Toru Ishida eds.), Springer Verlag, pp. 77-93, Jun. 1998

[20] D. Snowdon, and A. Grasso (2002): Diffusing information in organizational settings: learning from experience. Proc. ACM CHI'02 Conf. on Human Factors in Computing Systems, pp. 331-338.

InnovationEnterprizer: System for Evaluating and Managing Corporate Innovation

Iain BITRAN[1], Steffen CONN[2] and Marko TORKKELI[3]
[1] *S3 International Ltd, PO Box 18, Worsley, Manchester M28 1XP, UK*
Tel: +44 161 703 9411; Email: ibitran@s3inter.net
[2] *ISPIM: International Society for Professional Innovation Management; c/o Innovation Management U3, Vesterbrogade 149, DK-1620 Copenhagen V, Denmark*
Email: conn@ispim.org
[3] *Lappeenranta University of Technology; Department of Industrial Engineering & Management, Prikaatintie 9, FIN-45100 Kouvola, Finland*
Tel: +358 40 7611 223; Email: marko.torkkeli@lut.fi

Abstract: As traditional product and service lifecycles shrink in their turbulent markets, managers are placing greater emphasis on the timely and efficient development of new products, processes and services. This paper relays the development, methodology and application of a systematic method for assessing and promoting innovation best practice in corporations: innovationEnterprizer. This method provides the framework for a software-based knowledge system, which also contains comprehensive support materials for manager and business consultant training. Subsequent to the short introduction, an overview of the concepts and issues relating to the field of corporate innovation is given. Thereafter, the innovationEnterprizer methodology and algorithm are relayed as are the software functionalities. The conclusion highlights the benefits of innovationEnterprizer.

1. Introduction

It has been widely observed that business growth and long-term profitability are related to, and probably largely dependent on, successful corporate innovation. This is because traditional product and service lifecycles are shrinking in their turbulent markets. Thus greater emphasis is placed on the timely and efficient development of new products, processes and services cf. [1] to meet this capricious demand and to compete against evolving competition.

Due to the perceived importance of innovation, academics and practitioners have devoted significant energy to understanding the benefits, impediments, catalysts and conditions that might promote innovation both amongst individual employees and organisations as a whole. This paper contributes to this end by relaying the development, methodology and application of a specific approach to assessing and promoting innovation best practice in corporations: innovationEnterprizer.

innovationEnterprizer is positioned as an action-oriented, method-driven managerial support system with a scientific basis. Its two main modules facilitate the assessment of an organisation's product or service development process and its management thereof. It provides a common, categorical framework, which allows the explication and measurement of both tangible and intangible factors, which best practice research suggest are critical for successful, repeatable innovation. In short, the system measures and benchmarks an organisation's innovation competency and provides prescriptions for procedural and managerial improvement. Accompanying the managerial support system is extensive learning and support materials for managers and business consultants alike.

The analytical core of innovationEnterprizer is defined by three inter-related parameters: stakeholders, best practice success factors and performance measurement inputs. The definition of successful innovation depends on the viewpoint that is taken. As such, innovationEnterprizer employs the multi-perspective approach of organisation-specific stakeholders, each with weighted importance. The best practice success factors are the core of the system and are organised into three parsimonious, coherent dimensions. These success factors, and the way in which they combine, have been developed from primary and secondary best practice research.

Finally the performance measurement inputs are provided in a facilitated environment within the organisation in question. These make explicit the organisation's current performance levels, benchmarked against best practice. They allow for group discussion and the development of feasible plans for improvement. As such, algorithms can be used to generate what-if scenarios that represent potential future improvement strategies. These key functionalities are supported by embedded innovation expert help. This scientifically-based online advice provides context-specific assistance and suggestions for further reading and learning for facilitators and managers alike.

Following a short introduction, this paper provides an overview of the concepts and issues pertinent to stimulating and managing corporate innovation. Next, the structure of the individual modules is described within the context of the innovationEnterprizer methodology and algorithm. Subsequently, the functionalities of the innovationEnterprizer software are briefly relayed. Finally, a short conclusion draws out the essence of the paper and the benefits of innovationEnterprizer are detailed.

2. Innovation

Innovation is a new idea, method, or device. Innovation can be defined as the act of creating a new product, service or process. The act includes invention as well as the work required to bring an idea or concept into final form [2].

Innovation and product development are now even more critical to the success of organisations and companies than before. Information technology has played an important role in facilitating innovation. In this changing environment, networking, co-operation, and effective group work are of growing importance for innovation. Human capital and knowledge management appear to be key factors in today's effective innovation processes [3]. Also from the global perspective, innovation and technological progressiveness are commonly considered as being among the most important drivers of economic growth.

As innovation and product development have become more important to business, and competition has increased [4], organisations seek to obtain more results from their R&D expenditure [5], and pressures to develop products more rapidly have increased. In this complex arena, where companies cannot afford to be wrong, the importance of decision-making concerning innovation has increased [6].

2.1 Success Factors

In order to identify the success factors for corporate innovation, a number of criteria must be defined by which a project's success can be measured and which can be used to make an objective distinction between successful and less successful or failed innovations.

In innovation management literature, some major trends have prevailed during the last ten years. Competition is harder when more companies are competing for the same markets [4]. Market conditions are changing rapidly while product/technology life cycles are becoming shorter [7]. Many studies on (new) product development practices and principles give ideas for and confirm the need for effective innovation management. Customer involvement in product development activities is increasingly important for market success [8]. [9] has identified four main approaches to project evaluation. He emphasises that the problem is usually about resource allocation among a number of projects or technologies and there is no one best way to solve the problem. Cooper's four approaches include benefit measurement, economic, portfolio selection and market research models.

The need for innovationEnterprizer can be conducted from the perspectives of innovation, conditions affecting innovation, challenges and fundamentals, success factors, measures, benchmarks, and criteria. The main argument is that corporate innovation is a challenging area that must be supported from the organisational point of view. The organisation has to take the changes in the dynamic, competitive environment into account and attempt to, proactively, innovate a new product or service matching the market need.

The criteria involved in innovation management decisions can vary greatly, depending on the characteristics of the product and the organisation. Regardless of the criteria used, the selection process must meet some basic requirements. [10] has proposed some common characteristics of successful selection methodologies (see Table 1). These success factors should be carefully considered when developing and carrying out innovation management.

Table 1. Characteristics of successful methodologies [10]

Procedure • Well defined stages • Easy-to-use tools and techniques • Producing written records	**Project Managing** • Adequate resourcing • Agreed timescales
Participation • Individual and group • Workshop style meetings • Decision making leading to action	**Point Of Entry** • Clearly defined expectations • Ways to establish understanding, agreement and commitment

[11] tested the Schumpeterian Hypothesis (large firms are more innovative, imperfect competition promotes innovation) in their study. They found that large firms are more innovative when those firms are in markets characterised by imperfect competition. Significant variables in explaining the difference in innovation rates between large (500+ employees) and small firms are: capital output ratio, advertising intensity, concentration, unionisation, and percentage of industry accounted for by large firms.

[12] discussed how to measure the return on research and proposed the profit from projects in the last five years divided by the cost of all projects in the last five years. He suggested that one should compare profit from older operations to profit from more recent operations. Profit results from: 1) the selection of research problems, 2) the solution of the problem, and 3) subsequent commercialisation of the research results. According to [13] firms' spending on R&D makes them more able to absorb technological knowledge.

[8] focused their empirical study on companies' performance rather than project performance. They began with ten performance measures factor-analysed into two factors: program profitability and program impact (sales, success rate, technical success, etc). They categorised four groups of companies: 1) solid performers, 2) low impact performers, 3) high impact technical winners, and 4) dogs. Finally, they determined what distinguishes the solid performers from the dogs. According to [8] drivers of performance were:

- high quality new product process

- clear and well-communicated new product strategy
- adequate resources (senior management attention, R&D, necessary people)
- senior management commitment
- entrepreneurial climate
- senior management accountability
- strategic focus and synergy
- high-quality and cross functional development teams

Next, the structure of the system is described within the context of the innovationEnterprizer methodology and algorithm.

3. The innovationEnterprizer Methodology

innovationEnterprizer is an intelligent tool driven by S3i's Enterprizer software platform. The innovationEnterprizer tool contains an "expert-shell", a software front end and an "assessment engine". An expert shell represents an enterprise's business and operational environment, and includes a baseline of all the relevant success factors, stakeholders, relationships and weightings. The expert shell is divided into three distinct dimensions each with a unique set of critical success factors. These three dimensions are: 1) Organisational environment, 2) Operational procedures, 3) Human processes. They deal with enterprise-wide strategic issues related to innovation, the day-to-day processes and decision-making regarding innovation, and micro inter-personal and cultural level. This baseline of success factors is based on scientific research and provides a starting point for best practice.

Throughout innovationEnterprizer, stakeholders are given an important role. Using a stakeholder approach to make decisions is becoming increasingly effective as networks of enterprises become the norm, and collective agreement is necessary to successfully execute business decisions. Therefore, innovationEnterprizer requires the views of relevant stakeholders to be inputted against all success factors on the three dimensions.

Having been guided through this structured reflective process, the assessment engine calculates the overall innovation scores for the enterprise on the three dimensions (See Figure 1). It does so by transforming each stakeholder's rating of each factor into a utility score, and then calculating a weighted average, based on the relative importance of each stakeholder. The system then offers prescriptions for improvement or adjustment of the enterprise's management of and potential for innovation, by identifying the success factors that have the greatest impact on the final innovation score.

Online materials support the user in every entry made to the system. This is available through an html advisor (innovationExpert) that offers contextually pertinent best practice and conceptual tools. The methodology and components described in this section are clarified in the following section, where the usage scenario is relayed.

$$\sum_{i=1}^{i=I} \left[\frac{\left[\sum_{j=1}^{j=J} \left[\frac{a_j \cdot b_i \cdot c_{ij} \cdot d_{ij}}{\sum_{i=1}^{i=I} c_{ij}} \right]_{ij} \right]_i}{\left[\sum_{i=1}^{i=I} \left[\sum_{j=1}^{j=J} \left[\frac{a_j \cdot b_i \cdot c_{ij} \cdot d_{ij}}{\sum_{i=1}^{i=I} c_{ij}} \right]_{ij} \right]_i \right]_i} \right]_i \cdot \frac{1}{\sum_{j=1}^{j=J} a_j}$$

Where:
a_j = importance of stakeholder
b_i = importance of success factor
c_{ij} = importance attached by stakeholder_j to success factor
d_{ij} = utility function of stakeholder_j per success factor

Figure 1. Generation of Success Scores

4. innovationEnterprizer Usage Scenario

It is important to understand that innovationEnterprizer can only be used by trained experts acting as facilitators. This is due to the nature and complexity of the subject matter. These "experts" must be trained not only in the technical aspects of how to use innovationEnterprizer but also in the underlying methodology. For this purpose, innovationEnterprizer includes both technical training and learning and support materials (innovationExpert) that gives context specific methodological advice and examples.

A facilitator could either be internal, in the case of larger companies, or external (consultants and business advisors) in the case of smaller companies. In both cases this person must be able to effectively administer innovationEnterprizer, drive the development process, guide the assessment and optimisation process and interpret the results generated by the optimisation process. The facilitator must also be able to generate meaningful output. It should be noted that the target client-users of innovationEnterprizer include both large enterprises and small and medium sized businesses.

4.1 Usage Process

The facilitator works with innovationEnterprizer in workshops and small-groups interacting with the target beneficiaries and stakeholders. The first step is for the facilitator to help the client group define the deliverables that they wish to assess. These deliverables are typically products, services, projects or occasionally policies. In each case, the level of innovation will be assessed and then optimised. For each deliverable, the user must enter assumptions, research findings and data, based on collective knowledge and experiences.

More precisely, inputs to innovationEnterprizer will be provided before, during and after the workshops, for each specific deliverable. This is done through a series of in-built questions and required inputs for multiple innovation-specific parameters. These include:

- relative importance of stakeholders
- stakeholder preferences for success factor performance (utility functions)
- relative importance of success factors per stakeholder (relationships)
- performance measurements against standard success factors (from expert shell)
- innovation management objectives, strategies, plans and actions.

Review of these inputs during workshops ensures that they are relevant and acceptable to the participants. Numerous sources may be consulted to give the optimal picture including research findings, assumptions, and other inputs provided by subject matter experts and stakeholders whose knowledge can be solicited and used. Any input is possible with findings from innovation-specific research, such as competitive studies, represented in innovationEnterprizer as textual inputs, and can be captured via the hypertext link facility.

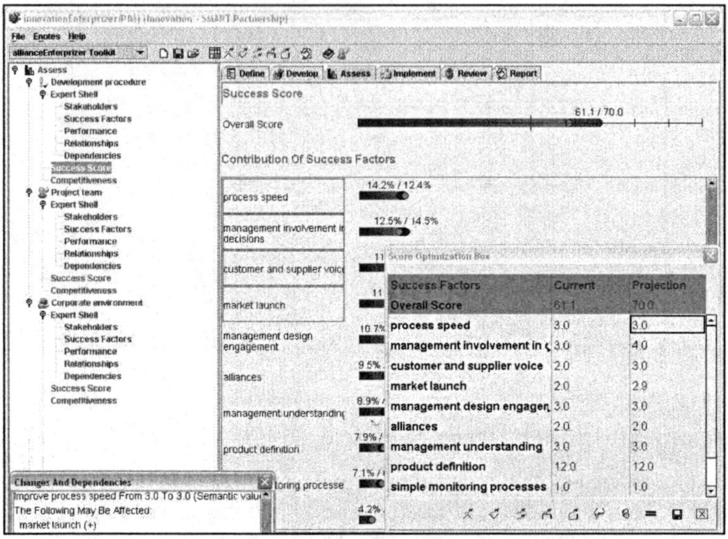

Figure 2. innovationEnterprizer Optimisation Screen Shot

Following the entry of these data, the facilitator or nominated system administrator will be able to use innovationEnterprizer's inbuilt assessment and optimisation functionalities to drive multi-parameter "what-if" and impact analyses to set new goals and generate optimised prescriptions for reaching these goals (see Figure. 2).

Links to Gantt charts and budgets (see Figure 3) will enable implementation of the analyses via defined tasks and actions. The results can also be used for subsequent review, refinement and enhancement. Indeed, these plans as well as the assumptions, and data upon which they are based, will be reported by the facilitator using the fully-configurable reporting facility in HTML with graphics that allow users to generate any type of report required. Users can decide whether to include all data relating to a specific deliverable or simply modify a report to include specific data. Users can also choose whether or not to include detailed graphics or simply to have textual output.

With the fully populated innovationEnterprizer model in place, the facilitator may choose to continue the dialogue with stakeholders though the eNotes facility that allows users to communicate in context. Each eNote includes the user's identification details and the facilitator retains administrator privileges over the communication. At this point, innovationEnterprizer can be made available either as a stand-alone version or a networked multi-user version and can be accessed via various user access privileges. Typically there will be three user access privileges, Administrator (allowing changes to both the embedded expert shell and user environment), Author (allowing user input), Reviewer (restricted to review and comment only). It should be noted that access is restricted to licensed users only, with other user access combinations configurable as required.

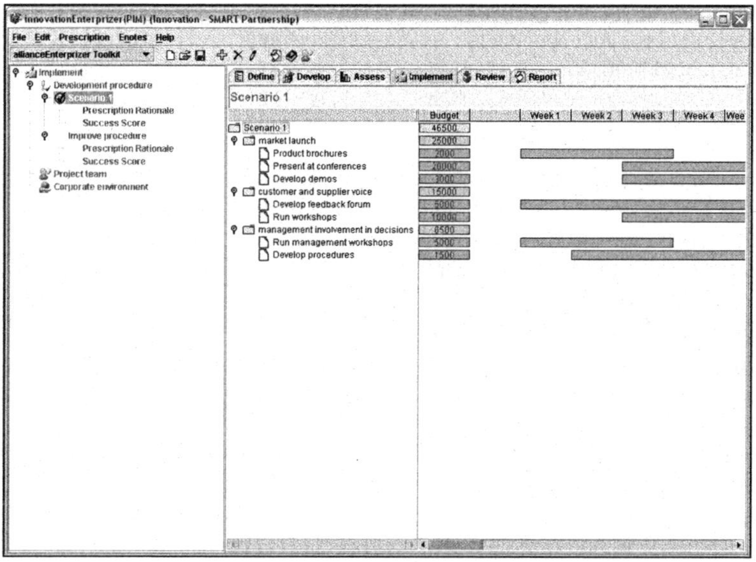

Figure 3. innovationEnterprizer Gantt Chart Screen Shot

As a dynamic model, innovationEnterprizer should be regularly updated. Depending on the nature of the update these may be done collectively, in workshops facilitated by experts and/or the trained system administrator, while others may be entered directly by trained innovation managers.

4.2 Implementation of innovationEnterprizer

The following describes the typical process for training and licensing the target users and for integrating or interfacing innovationEnterprizer with existing business processes:
Step 1: Facilitator Training: Train-the-facilitator program (training of in-house trainers in methodology and usability aspects)
Step 2: Adaptation: Adapt innovationEnterprizer (more industry-specific; stakeholders, success factors, relationships, dependencies; terminology & language)
Step 3: Testing: Testing in a simulated or actual project by fully populating innovationEnterprizer to ensure correct use
Step 4: Licensing & Report Generation: Define the licensing arrangement including number of Licenses, any potential networking requirements and user privilege assignment.
Step 5: Installation: Install innovationEnterprizer on the enterprise's network and on any designated laptop computers ensuring multi-user accessibility.
Step 6: Integration with Existing Business Processes: Develop procedures and software interfaces to existing processes to integrate innovationEnterprizer with existing business.

5. Conclusion

The importance of speedy, effective, repeatable innovation has generated the need for innovationEnterprizer. The configuration of innovationEnterprizer, which is a knowledge-based software support system is based on the unique scientifically-researched best practice methodology. The methodology contains three distinct dimensions that represent organisational, operational and human critical success factors. These factors, and the way in which they combine have been developed from primary and secondary best practice research conducted during the development of innovationEnterprizer.

By way of a trained facilitator, stakeholders give contextual background to the situation, evaluate pertinent parameters in each dimension. The facilitated process allows the various stakeholders in the innovation process to be taken into account, and can calculate success scores, based upon the three aforementioned dimensions. Ultimately, innovationEnterprizer offers prescriptions for "innovation score improvement" and managerial action, with associated budgets and Gantt charts.

5.1 Benefits

Throughout the development and validation process, feedback from managers and domain experts has highlighted the following major benefits of using innovationEnterprizer.

- Crisp visualisation of factors that impact success : "makes the invisible visible"
- Clear insights into complex scenarios: "unexpected results that otherwise would have been missed"
- Optimal and financially grounded paths to improvement and implementation
- Rapid, in-context decisions : "collective wisdom for sophisticated decision-making"
- Consensus and stakeholder buy-in: "I walked in with individuals and walked out with a team"

In addition, the following benefits, which are specific to consulting firms were received:

- Unique value proposition for "report-weary" market
- Own innovation-specific consulting tool
- Increased opportunities for integrated strategy and implementation-support projects
- Higher productivity & profitability due to more efficient consulting performance, with improved client participation and acceptance
- New sources of revenue from client adaptation and software.

References

[1] Cooper, R. (2000). Product innovation and technology strategy. *Research Technology Management*, **43**, 1, 38-41.
[2] Rosenau, M., Jr., A. Griffin, G. Castellion, and N. Anschuetz (1996), *PDMA Handbook of New Product Development.*
[3] Nonaka, I. and T., Hirotaka (1995). *The knowledge-creating company*. University Press, New York.
[4] Hayes, R., Wheelwright, S. and K. Clark. (1988). *Dynamic manufacturing*, The Free Press, New York.
[5] Hatfield, G. (2002). R&D in an Eva world. *Research Technology Management*, **45**, 1, 41-47.
[6] Carneiro, A. (2001). A group decision support system for strategic alternatives selection, *Management Decision*, **39**, 3, 218-226.
[7] Bayus, B. (1994). Are product life cycles really getting shorter? *Journal of Product Innovation Management*, **11**, 4, 300–308.
[8] Cooper, R. and E. Kleinschmidt (1995), Benchmarking the firm's critical success factors in new product development, *Journal of Product Innovation Management*, **12**, 374-391.
[9] Cooper, R. (1993). *Winning at New Products: Accelerating the Process from Idea to Launch. Reading*, Addison-Wesley, USA.
[10] Platts, K. (1994). Characteristics of methodologies for manufacturing strategy formulation. *Computer Integrated Manufacturing Systems*, **7**, 2, 93-99.
[11] Acs, Z. and D. Audretsch (1987). Innovation in large and small firms, *Review of Economics and Statistics*, **69**, 567-575.
[12] Bachman, P. (1972). The value of R&D in relation to company profits, *Research Management*, **15**, 58-63.
[13] Cohen, W. and D. Levinthal (1989). Innovation and learning: The two faces of R&D, *Economic Journal*, **99**, 569-596.

eAdoption and the Knowledge Economy: Issues, Applications, Case Studies
P. Cunningham and M. Cunningham (Eds.)
IOS Press, 2004

Learning User Preference Models and Business Strategies for E-Commerce

Maria João VIAMONTE[1], Carlos RAMOS[1], Fátima RODRIGUES[1], José CARDOSO[2]
[1]*GECAD - Knowledge Engineering and Decision Support Research Group,*
Institute of Engineering Porto, 4200-072, Portugal
Tel: +351.22.8340500; Fax +351.22.8321159; Email: {viamonte, csr, fr}@dei.isep.ipp.pt
[2] *Department of Electrical Engineering, University of Trás-os-Montes e Alto Douro,*
Vila Real, 5000, Portugal
Tel: +351.259.9350300, Fax: +3512599350300; Email: jcardoso@utad.pt

Abstract: We forecast a future in which the global economy and the Internet will host a large number of interacting software agents. Most of them will be economically motivated, and will negotiate a variety of goods and services. It is therefore important to consider the economic incentives and behaviours of economic software agents, and to use all available means to anticipate their collective interactions. This paper addresses this concern by presenting a multi-agent market simulator designed for analysing agent market strategies based on a complete understanding of buyer and seller behaviours, preference models and pricing algorithms. The system includes agents that are capable of increasing their performance with their own experience, by adapting to the market conditions. The results of the negotiations between agents are analysed by data mining tools in order to extract rules that give agents feedback to improve their strategies.

1. Introduction

As the result of technological developments E-Commerce (EC) is emerging as the new way of doing business. We believe that, over the course of the next decade, the global economy and the Internet will merge into a global market with a large amount of autonomous software agents that exchange goods and services with humans and other agents.

Agents will represent consumers, producers, and intermediaries. Interactions among agents will be supported by a number of efforts that are already under way, including standardisation of agent communication languages, protocols, and infrastructures. When interactions among agents become sufficiently rich, a crucial qualitative change will occur. New classes of agents will be designed specially to serve the needs of the other agents. The agents we are envisaging will not be just assistants to business process. They will be economic software agents: independent, self-motivated economic players, endowed with algorithms for maximizing utility and profit on behalf of their human owners. They will add value to their activities by synthesising, filtering, translating, and mining. However, it would be dangerous to assume that theories and intuitions based on centuries of experience with human economic agents will be directly applicable to understand, anticipate, and control the behaviour of markets in which software agents participate.

To study electronic markets behaviour and evolution, we developed ISEM, a multi-agent market simulator [1,2,3], designed for analysing agent market strategies. This simulator has been selected to be included in a book about the application of agents in EC in Europe [4]. The main objectives will be described as follows.

First, ISEM addresses the complexities of online buyers behaviour by providing a rich set of behaviour parameters. Second, ISEM provides available market information that allows sellers to make assumptions about buyer's behaviour, and preference models. Third, the different agents customise their behaviour adaptively, by learning each user's preference models and business strategies. The learning agent capacity is achieved through data mining techniques applied online during the market sessions.

This paper describes the characteristics of the ISEM simulator, focusing specially on the performance of the seller and buyer agents. The negotiation model and the interaction between agents are also detailed and a special highlight is given to seller and buyer agent's strategies, decision algorithms and data mining techniques used.

2. ISEM Concept

The underlying structure of ISEM is that a simulation-based approach can model more diverse and complex scenarios, rather than the general case. By using a simulator prior to conducting marketing experiments, suppliers and consumers can develop an intuitive understanding of the theoretical findings and use this knowledge to develop a more sophisticated strategy implementation.

The simulator probes the conditions and the effects of market rules, by simulating the participant's strategic behaviour. ISEM is flexible; the user completely defines the model he or she wants to simulate, including the number of agents, each agent's type and strategies. Moreover, they can adapt their strategies as the simulation progresses on the basis of previous effort's success or failure.

Our market simulator is related to the finite markets where resources and capabilities are finites; further, seller agents make assumptions about buyers behaviour and preference models based on available market information.

These ideas seem very promising and innovative, when compared to other approaches that study dynamic market strategies for finite markets, such as the work of Gallego and van Ryzin [5], Biller et al. [6], and J. M. DiMico et al. [7]. Gallego and van Ryzin, addressed the challenges of dynamic pricing in markets with a finite time horizon and inventory, but from a theoretical standpoint. They examined a deterministic version of the problem by making the assumption that consumers demand curves do not change over time, but what our analysis of pricing strategies emphasises is that we cannot assume perfect knowledge of the demand curve. In a recent analysis of the automotive industry, Biller et al., designed a theoretical model for applying dynamic pricing to a market with unknown changing demand levels, they demonstrate that under fluctuating demand there is always a dynamic pricing strategy which is more successful than a fixed-price strategy; but their model does not account for constraints in inventory. Very relevant is the work of J. M. DiMico et al., with the Learning Curve Simulator, a market simulator designed for analysing agent pricing strategies in a market under finite time horizons and fluctuation demand. This perspective on dynamic pricing focuses on how a seller can take advantage of the fluctuations in cumulative buyer demand over time; however they are interested in analysing only agent pricing strategies for sellers. The results obtained with these approaches can be duplicated in the ISEM system and in addition our simulator works as a tool for buyers and sellers analysing dynamic agent market strategies, enriched by the inclusion of data mining techniques for discovering new knowledge.

3. ISEM Simulator

ISEM works like an open market where suppliers and consumers meet (Figure 1). Agents represent market entities such as buyers, sellers, market facilitator, and new participants such market information provider. The architecture adopted for the market is by now prepared to support new classes of agents. The increased competition creates opportunities for new players or agents to enter the market, such as traders. Traders are intermediaries between consumers and suppliers. They can act as retailers, brokers, aggregators, or marketers.

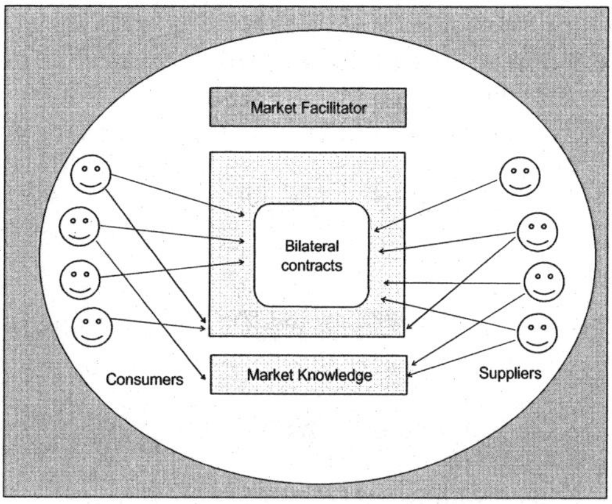

Figure 1 Multiple agents in ISEM

The market facilitator coordinates the simulated market and ensures that it functions correctly. It knows the identities of all the agents in the market, regulates negotiation, and ensures the market operates according to established rules. Before entering the market, agents must first register with the market facilitator, specifying their role and services.

Sellers and buyers are the two key players in the market, so we devote special attention to them, particularly to their business objectives and strategies to reach them.

The market knowledge is a special agent, which plays the role of "power" agent. This agent has access to market knowledge, which contains information about the organisational and operational rules of the market, as well as information about all different running agents and historical information. The market previsions and agent models behaviour are achieved with data mining techniques. The market knowledge is a kind of information provider; moreover the other agents can request its services.

The user completely defines the number of sellers and buyers in each scenario and must specify their intrinsic and strategic characteristics. "Intrinsic characteristics" refers to the agent's individual knowledge related to product list, limit prices, preferred prices, profile and available capacity or consumption needs. "Strategic characteristics" refers to the strategies the agent will use to reach the objective of selling the available inventory at the best price (if a seller) or buying the needed items with minus costs (if a buyer). Sellers will compete with each other because they are all interested in selling their inventory at the highest possible values. On the other hand, sellers will cooperate with buyers to establish an agreement that is profitable for both. This is a rich domain for which it is possible to develop and test several decision algorithms and strategies for cooperation and competition.

The ISEM facilitates agent meeting and matching, besides supporting the negotiation model. In order to have results and feedback to improve the negotiation models and consequently the behaviour of user agents, ISEM simulates a marketplace for a fixed period of time, and it considers that this limit is composed by a regular number of negotiation periods, which can represent one day, for example. At a particular day, each agent has an objective that specifies its intention to buy/sell a particular product and on what conditions.

3.1 Negotiation model

The negotiation model used in ISEM is bilateral contracting where buyer agents are looking for sellers that can provide them the desired products at the best price (Figure 2). Bilateral contracts are established through a series of requests for proposals (RFP) distributed by buyers. In response, a seller agent analyses its own capabilities, current availability, and past experiences and formulates a proposal (PP). Seller agents can formulate two kinds of proposals: a proposal for the product requested or a proposal for a related product, according to the buyer preference model. Buyer agent evaluates the PP's received and will accept an offer that satisfy the user request; otherwise it formulates a counter-proposal (CP), based on the user profile (see Agents Strategic Behaviour section for details).

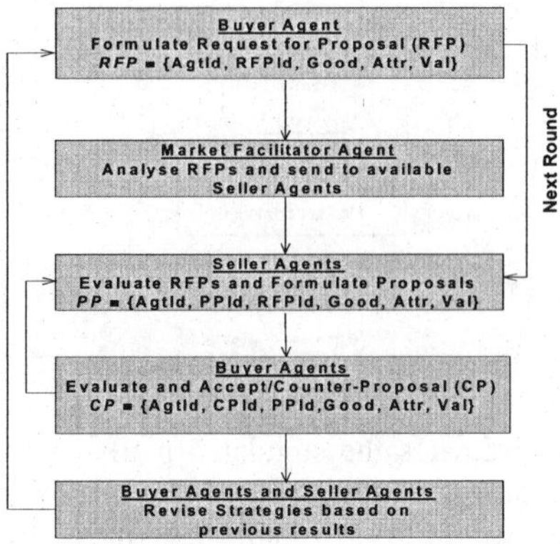

Figure 2 Sequence of bilateral contracts

On the basis of the bilateral agreements made among market players and lessons learned from previous bid rounds, both agents revise their strategies for the next negotiation rounds and update their individual knowledge module.

3.2 Data mining functionality

Online companies can quickly segment their customers by drawing upon multiple sources of information, from click stream data on the current online session to customer buying histories tracked in databases. Once a retailer can identify an online customer segment, he can immediately offer a segment-specific product or price. Unfortunately, this causes the explosive growth of data, which requires a more efficient way to extract useful knowledge.

On the other hand, people have gradually noticed that data mining can not only offer very meaningful knowledge about customer shopping behaviours by analysing the transaction data in the past, but also can improve the efficiency and quality of managerial decision making.

The ISEM system has the advantage that all agent interactions are logged at a transaction level of detail, which provides a rich source of business insight that can help to customise the business offerings to the needs of the individual buyers. Data from multiple agent negotiations are manipulated to create "basket" records showing product purchases with data behaviour of each buyer agent. This data is combined and manipulated with the APriori algorithm [8] to discover associations between buyer details and purchases. The best association rules, those with a strong support and confidence, are extracted and transferred to the market knowledge agent. With this kind of knowledge it is possible to provide insight to the sellers about the profiles of buyers with certain purchase propensities, showing associations between price, style, etc.

The ISEM system also allows sellers to define targeted marketing strategies. This entails systematic analysis of buyers behaviour. For that, a Two-Step clustering algorithm [9] designed to handle very large data sets, with both continuous and categorical attributes, is used to target buyers with similar characteristics in the same agent group. After agent clustering a rule-based modelling technique, C4.5 algorithm [10], is used to analyse those clusters and to obtain descriptions based on a set of attributes collected in the individual agents knowledge module. These models offer a set of market information, like, preferred sellers, preferred marks, favourite products and reference prices, which support the process of strategy implementation. Only players with more sophisticated behaviour will take advantage of this new knowledge by requesting the services provided by the market knowledge agent.

4. Agents Strategic Behaviour

Seller and buyer agents have a strategic behaviour to define their business actions. Agents use time-dependent strategies to change the price according to the remaining time until the end of the negotiation period; and behaviour-dependent strategies to define parameters for the next negotiation period according to the results obtained in the previous ones.

Buyer and seller agents develop their behaviour and strategies based on a combination of public information, available through requesting for market knowledge agent services; and private information, available only to the specific agent at their individual knowledge module. It is expected that each agent develops the individual knowledge module with historical information. On the basis of results from ISEM simulations, the agents can build a profile of the other agents with expected proposed prices, limit prices, needs and capabilities. The maintenance of an individual knowledge module is extremely important since the negotiation model used in ISEM is bilateral contracting; the results of the bilateral transaction are not public. On the other hand, requests for market knowledge agent services also provide a great support for agents that have more sophisticate behaviours.

4.1 Buyer agents

Over the course of the market, the collective behaviour of buyer agents is defined by three variables: the lifetime, the màximum price, and their strategy; the lifetime parameter indicates how many days they are disposed to wait in the market, continuously looking for the best deal. Indirectly, the lifetime of buyers determines the number of buyers in the market each day. Pre-existing buyers return if they were unable to purchase in the previous days and their specified lifetime has not expired.

Each buyer has a set of products to buy, and for each one it has information about attributes and alternative products, if any. Buyers will analyse the sellers proposals with an advanced algorithm, which analyses the different proposals, evaluates the expected returns and then apply a decision method (decision buyer algorithm) to decide when accept a bilateral contract or formulate a counter-proposal.

The advanced algorithm, first sorts the proposals for the requested product by price and then selects the best one, which will be compared to its own values. If it finds a seller proposal satisfactory; the buyer will contact directly the seller in question; otherwise if the buyer has a preferred "seller" then it increases the reserve price (e.g. plus 10%); finally it analyses the proposals for related products, if it finds proposals for alternative products accordingly to the user preference model, then it will start a similar analysis.

Buyer agents can choose from four different time-dependent tactics: Determined, Anxious, Moderate and Gluttonous [1]. These strategies differ depending on both the point in time when the agent starts to modify the price and the amount it changes; and can use two complementary behaviour-dependent tactics: the Modified Goal Directed for Buyers (MGDB) and the Fragmented Demand (FD).

The MGDB strategy [1] is based on two consecutive objectives; the first one is buying the consumption needs and then reducing payoff. Following this strategy, buyers will offer a higher price if they did not meet their consumption needs in the previous period and offer less if they succeeded in meeting their needs.

The FD strategy [3], adjusts the demand per day by attempting to reach the goal of buying its entire needs by the last day of the market, and not before; this strategy paces its purchases over the market, with the goal of buying all the units needed but with less costs. This strategy allow buyers to save money, however, sometimes buyers are not capable of buying all the needed units, because while waiting to buy till the last day of market they lose the chance of buying.

4.2 Seller agents

The user defines the behaviour of the sellers in the market, both in terms of their behaviour over time, business objectives and agent risk characterisation; and their behaviour on a per day basis, negotiation strategies.

Every day each seller has a set of products to sell. The seller will analyse the request for proposals received and formulates a proposal (PP) with an advanced algorithm.

Two kinds of PP's are possible: a PP for the requested product, if the seller sells the requested product or a PP for a related product. The seller agents should be pro-active, by asking for the services provided by the market knowledge agent to suggest a feasible alternative product. A seller formulates an alternative proposal, supported by an overall utility function, which reflects the business objectives of the user that it represents and the agent risk characterization, which will determine how the seller will behave [3].

To change the price during a negotiation period, sellers can use the same time-dependent strategies (Determined, Anxious, Moderate and Gluttonous).

To define the next period parameters according to the results obtained in the previous ones, sellers can choose among two different behaviour-dependent strategies: the Modified Goal Directed for Sellers (MGDS) and the Derivative Following (DF) strategy that can be weighted by Seller Satisfaction (DFWS) or by the Previewed Demand for a specific product (DFWPD).

The MGDS strategy [3] adjusts its price by attempting to reach the goal of selling the entire inventory by the last day of the market, by lowering prices when sales in the previous day are low and raising prices when the sales are high.

The DFWS/P strategy [3] adjusts its price by looking to the amount of revenue earned on the previous day as a result of the previous day price change: if in the previous day, the price change produced more revenue, then the strategy makes a similar change in price, otherwise the strategy makes an opposite price change. This strategy calculation is an adjustment of the Derivative Following strategy analysed in [11]. We modified the DF strategy for a finite market by attempting to reach the goal of selling the entire inventory by the last day of the market, instead of adjusting the price each day, the change is scaled by a ratio based on the progress through the market and can be based on the percentage of Buyers that we expect to satisfy or based in the value for Previewed Demand. Seller agents can obtain these values through requesting for market knowledge agent support.

5. Dynamic Strategies Analysis

We use the strategies previously outlined to present the following example, which illustrates some differences in the performance of the behaviour-dependent strategies. Consider a simple scenario with a few sellers and few buyers using time-dependent and behaviour-dependent strategies. In every trial we present, the market has 10 days, each seller has 200 units and each buyer wants 150 units of the same good (e.g., a digital camera). We test the strategies under a comparison-shopping and with preferences for certain sellers over others. All sellers start with the same price and each buyer is able to pay different prices. Moreover, all of the agents have the last day of functioning of the market as the deadline to do their transactions. We pretend to analyse which behaviour-dependent strategy is appropriate under these specific conditions.

In a competitive market, the adaptive pricing strategies react to the others strategies in the market in addition to the buyers demand. As we can see in figure 3 all the sellers achieve their goal, to sell almost everything.

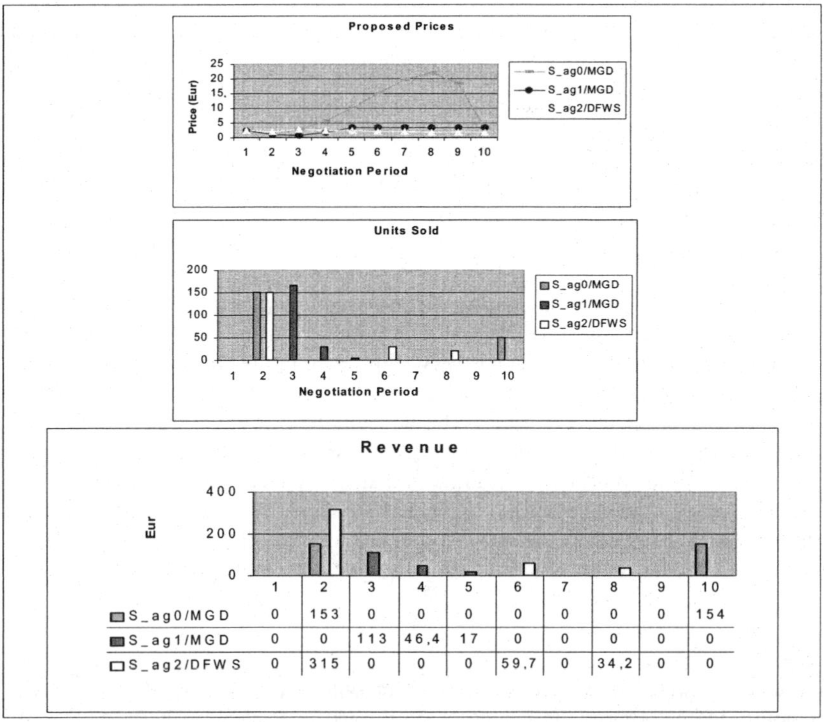

Figure 3 The modified goal directed for sellers and derivative following weighted by satisfaction strategies

After carefully analysing the results, we can observe that the DFWS strategy produces a high amount of revenue and often sells more units than the others seller agents using MGDS strategy. The success of a DFWS depends on the starting price it chooses, and the percentage of buyers satisfied. When DFWS sells approximately the same amount of inventory as MGDS, it usually produces more revenue than the MGDS strategy, and frequently occurs that, even DFWS sells less amount of inventory, it usually produces more revenue than MGDS, since this one makes a dramatic price changes. This occurs because the MGDS strategy spreads out its sales, including selling on the last days when prices approaches the minimum. Another important issue is that MGDS does not take into account the percentage of buyers that are satisfied when making price changes. Furthermore, we can conclude that when the demand is less than the most competitive sellers available capacity, the seller will lose money when using the MGDS; the seller will decrease the price and try to sell more, which could not be possible because of insufficient demand. However, the MGDS strategy can be valuable, particularly to increase market share when two or more sellers are competing directly because of similar proposed prices. In general DFWPD has the same behaviour of DFWS; nevertheless sometimes projections for demand are subject to uncertainty. This uncertainty arises from such factors as weather forecast errors, inaccurate projections of type and number of future customers. It would be interesting to develop another strategy that combines the two described seller strategies. This way, an agent could select the most suitable strategy for each negotiation period on the basis of market conditions and business objectives: if a seller concludes that the demand is lower than its available capacity and it intends to increase the profit, it will use DFWS/P; otherwise, if it intends to increase the market share, it will use MGDS; moreover, if it concludes that a competitor has similar prices, and it intends to increase the market share, it will use the MGDS, otherwise it will use DFWS/P.

Buyers using time-dependent strategies always try to buy all units as soon as possible what is equivalent to have more expenses. On the other hand, buyers using the FD strategy, frequently, bought the requested units and with less costs. However, sometimes they are not capable of buying all the needed units, because while waiting to buy till the last day of market, buyers may lose the opportunity of buying.

Although these strategies are computationally straightforward, they are surprisingly robust under extremely different market conditions.

6. Conclusion

In the near future, agent market strategies will be a common competitive manoeuvre for EC. The multi-agent technology enables easy future improvements and model enlargement. Market participant's strategic behaviour is very significant in the context of competition. In addition, the availability of new market knowledge obtained with data mining techniques is vital for supporting marketing and sales. The development of agent-based tools that will help suppliers and consumers in understanding what kinds of electronic market strategies are appropriate are also important. Although we implemented some valuable promising strategies, we must enlarge the portfolio of agent's strategies and behaviours. Directions of our future work include evaluating additional dynamic market strategies; based on different value-added services, for sellers and more sophisticate behaviour-dependent strategies for buyers.

References

[1] M. J. Viamonte, C. Ramos, J. C. Cardoso. "ISEM – An Intelligent System for Electronic MarketPlaces", In Challenges and Achievements in E-business and E-work, B. Stanford-Smith, Enrica Chiozza and Mireille Edin, editors, IOS Press, pp. 560-567, 2002.

[2] M. J. Viamonte, C. Ramos, F. Rodrigues, e J. C. Cardoso. "A Simulation-Based Approach for Testing Market Strategies in Electronic MarketPlaces", Proceedings of the International Conference on Web Intelligence -WIC, Halifax, Canada October, pp. 490-494, 2003.

[3] M. J. Viamonte, C. Ramos, F. Rodrigues and J. C. Cardoso, "A Market Simulator for Analysing Agent Market Strategies". In Building the Knowledge Economy: Issues, Applications, Case Studies. Paul Cunningham, Miriam Cunningham and Peter Fatelning, editors, IOS Press, pp. 284-291 2003.

[4] M. J. Viamonte, C. Ramos, "A Model for an Electronic MarketPlace", Agent Mediated Electronic Commerce, European AgentLink Perspective, Lecture Notes in Artificial Intelligence 1991, Frank Dignum and Carlos Sierra, editors Springer, pp.115-125, 2001.

[5] G. Gallego and G. V. Ryzin, "Optimal Dynamic Pricing of Inventories with Stochastic Demand Over Finite Horizons". Management Science, Vol. 40 No.8, pp. 999-1020, 1994.

[6] S. Biller, L. M. A. Chan, D. Simchi-Levi and J. Swann, "Dynamic Pricing and the Direct-to-Customer Model in the Automotive Industry". GM Research & Development Center, 2000.

[7] J. M. DiMico, A. Greenwald, P. Maes, "Learning Curve: A Simulation-based Approach to Dynamic Pricing". Electronic Commerce Research Journal: Special Issue on Aspects of Internet Agent-based E-Business Systems, 2001.

[8] R. Agrawal, H. Manilla, R. Srikantand, H. Toivonen, I. Verkamo, "Fast discovery of association rules". AAAI Press, 1996.

[9] T. Zhang, R. Ramakrishnon,, and M. Livny. "BIRCH: An Efficient Data Clustering Method for Very Large Databases". Proceedings of the ACM SIGMOD Conference on Management of Data, Montreal, Canada, pp. 103-114, 1996.

[10] J. Quinlan, "C4.5: Programs for Machine Learning "Morgan Kaufmann Publishers, San Francisco, USA, 1993.

[11] Greenwald, J.Kephart and G. Tesauro, "Strategic Price-bots Dynamics". Proceedings of the First ACM Conference on Electronic Commerce, Denver, USA, pp. 58-67, 1999.

Section 4.3

Case Studies

eAdoption and the Knowledge Economy: Issues, Applications, Case Studies
P. Cunningham and M. Cunningham (Eds.)
IOS Press, 2004

Ontology-enabled Knowledge Asset Trading

Dimitris APOSTOLOU[1], Panagiotis-Petros GEORGOLIOS[2], Kostas KAFENTZIS[2], Marc-Frédéric SCHÄFER[3], Paul JONES[4]
[1] *Planet, Apollon Tower, 64 Louise Riencourt Str., Athens, 11523, Greece*
Tel: +302106905000, Fax: + 302106981885, Email: dapost@planet.gr
[2]*National Technical University of Athens, 9 Iroon Politexniou Str., 15780 Zografou, Greece*
Tel: + 30 2107723895, Fax: + 30 210 7723895, Email: {panos, kkafe}@softlab.ntua.gr
[3]*Universität St. Gallen, CH-9000 St. Gallen, Switzerland*
Tel: + 41 71 224 3488, Fax: + 41 71 224 2771, Email: marc-frederic.schaefer@unisg.ch
[4]*TW, Granta Park, Abington, Cambridge, CB1 6AL, UK*
Tel: +44 1223 891162, Email: paul.jones@twi.co.uk

Abstract: INKASS ("Intelligent Knowledge Asset Sharing and Trading") is an intelligent Internet-based marketplace for knowledge assets. At the core of the technological approach of INKASS stands a case-based reasoning approach for ascertaining knowledge assets for relevant user contexts and a comprehensive metadata description of information objects that represent tradable knowledge products. The research approach, the metadata description and the initial evaluation results of two running pilots (for a research & technology organisation and a management consultancy) are discussed in this paper.

1. Introduction

Internet-based marketplaces that support buying and selling of knowledge–intensive products, such as information-based goods or professional services, have recently emerged worldwide [1]. Existing approaches vary in their focus on the type of knowledge exchanged (tacit or explicit), business model used, pricing mechanisms supported, and technical infrastructure used to manage content and support matchmaking between demand and supply. An in-depth review of existing implementations [2] identified the following points of consideration for the development of knowledge marketplaces:

1. A knowledge product is not just a document to be described & retrieved with a simple keyword. Its complex context and content features determine its applicability & usefulness in a situation;
2. For electronic knowledge trading one can not simply copy ways of working known from traditional business (e.g. catalogue-based), but in exploiting the strength of manifold synchronous and asynchronous communication means, as done in conventional knowledge provision services (e.g. professional service provision);
3. There should be a focus on developing the necessary technical, business and organisational mechanisms for managing and maintaining an electronic knowledge marketplace. These include quality assurance mechanisms, content editing and reviewing processes, appropriate pricing mechanisms for different kinds of knowledge, etc.

INKASS is a European research project that has developed an electronic knowledge marketplace toolkit. The toolkit includes a software platform and a methodology addresses these challenges. This paper focuses on the metadata required to describe and retrieve knowledge products in electronic marketplaces. It also describes how the INKASS metadata model is utilised in the INKASS software platform, which aims to support the trading lifecycle of a knowledge product. Finally, initial evaluation results, lessons learned and implications for developing similar initiatives are discussed.

2. Existing Theories and Work

An active research community has been working on intelligent methods for eCommerce solutions for several years. Most of this work has focused on intelligent agents for trading and negotiation processes [3][4][5][6] and has not considered which kinds of goods are traded. Almost no work has explicitly addressed the particularities of knowledge as a tradable good. Hence, resulting solutions neglect many efforts made in the Knowledge Management, Digital Library and e-Learning areas, which address the issue of how knowledge-intensive products such as Lessons Learned, Expert's Skills, Intellectual Property Rights (IPR), or Consulting Services are best described. Normally, the few existing knowledge marketplaces treat knowledge similarly to other tangible goods. Knowledge-intensive products are represented by simple, static metadata schemas, content is described by referring to a taxonomy of subjects and few other attributes, beyond simplistic quality assessments, such as simple Amazon-like five-star ratings, are provided.

A survey of existing knowledge marketplaces [2] highlighted issues with marketplace metadata:

1. Representation of knowledge content is interesting, but usually weak as references to potential usage context are seldom considered. Usage context is quite different from content description (e.g. the difference between 'aspirin' as a descriptor & 'headache' as a usage context).
2. Many other aspects (e.g. evaluation of knowledge quality) are purpose-built or neglected.
3. None of the marketplaces attempt to make information objects more self-contained to allow them to be traded beyond their home-marketplace.
4. No effort to move towards reusable, standardised metadata schema sets is evident. Existing metadata standards or e-Commerce ontologies seem not be used or integrated.

These shortcomings are addressed by the INKASS Information Ontology. Four sources were used in its design: First, taxonomies and thesauri already in place for internal content management purposes in the two pilots: (a) TWI Ltd– selling technology documents, specifically configured knowledge packs and consulting services in the area of welding and joining technology.; and (b) Planet – a management consultancy. Second, prior research and customer projects done by project participants. Third, the state of the art in the scientific literature, in particular the Dublin Core initiative and the IEEE Learning Object Metadata standard (LOM), as well as solutions for specific problems, such as IPR representation or contract representation. Fourth, WordNet [7], which helped the project to group structure certain aspects of content and context descriptions.

3. Research Approach

The concept of an Information Ontology was introduced by [8] in the knowledge management area and normally applicable as a metadata schema in the Digital Library and the e-Learning areas. It provides a specification of the knowledge representation schema used and describes the knowledge products themselves and related background concepts. It supports content-type specific characterisations of knowledge products enabling better search & retrieval. It will support powerful new services such as collaborative filtering or elaborated versioning and evaluation mechanisms, and allow the interchange of knowledge product descriptions between trading platforms.

A full-fledged Information Ontology in the ideal knowledge trading system comprises:

1. A specification of all the attributes an Information Object for trading knowledge may possess.
2. The value ranges of attributes used and if necessary supplementing this with related ontologies.
3. A specification of links and relationships that may exist between information objects, (indicating that some products could provide prior knowledge to help better understand other products).
4. A specification of knowledge products, if required. These comprise aggregated information objects and context specific tacit knowledge.
5. All other supporting data structures required to supporting knowledge trading, such as contractual and transactional aspects. .
6. Ontologies may contain additional supporting information used by the marketplace such as the similarity between concepts required for assessing corresponding demand and offer representations in a case-based retrieval approach, such as developed by the INKASS project.

This paper will only discuss the top-level of the INKASS Information Ontology. It comprises eleven facets and indicates how the description of information objects can be organized meaningfully. These facets are: content, context, community, domain, history, evaluation, method, transition, business, legal, and security. This top-level structure is discussed in detail in [9].

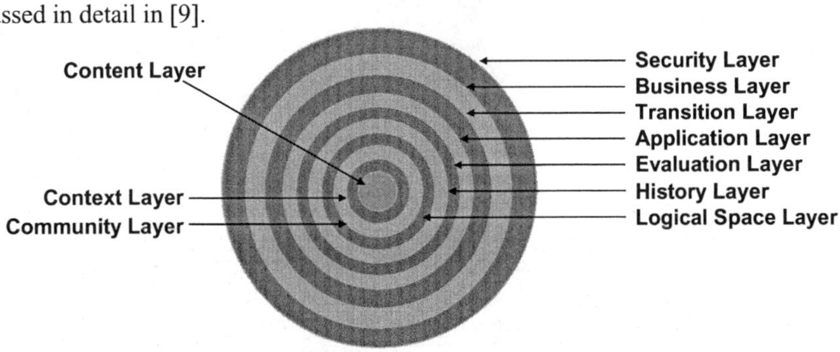

Figure 1: INKASS Information Ontology facets

The intention of this faceted description is that if all the facets are sufficiently described, it should be possible to assess comprehensively the content, potential usage and value of an Information Object (IO). This description will support all the transactions and modifications during the lifetime of an IO. It makes each IO self-contained, allowing its complete creation and modification history to be transferred from one marketplace to another, without loosing any descriptive information or legal commercial integrity. The Information Ontology forms the basis of the knowledge-buyer/knowledge-seller matchmaking scheme developed in the INKASS project.

4. The INKASS Software Platform

The INKASS system is based on eKMS, a content management and e-commerce middleware offered by Empolis (www.empolis.com). Using Case-Based Retrieval (CBR) and the underlying Information Ontology, INKASS matches supply and demand among market participants. This section outlines how this matchmaking is achieved in INKASS. According to the Business Media Framework [10] (a foundation for designing business media and supporting software platforms) the trading lifecycle of a knowledge product (in fact of any product), from creation to consumption, can be considered as a sequence of 4 phases, namely Information, Intention, Contracting and Settlement.

In INKASS, the Information Phase refers to the identification of the best-suited knowledge product for the buyer's need. This phase is more important in knowledge marketplaces than in traditional marketplaces, because the buyer's need is often vague and can't be clearly expressed. In this phase, the buyer is able to retrieve information about the documents and consulting services by using natural language queries (Figure 1). The use of vague terms in the queries is mitigated by the Information Ontology: if no exact term is found in the content description, content tagged with similar keywords is retrieved. The description of the retrieved content gives the buyer sufficient knowledge to decide whether further interaction with the seller is necessary.

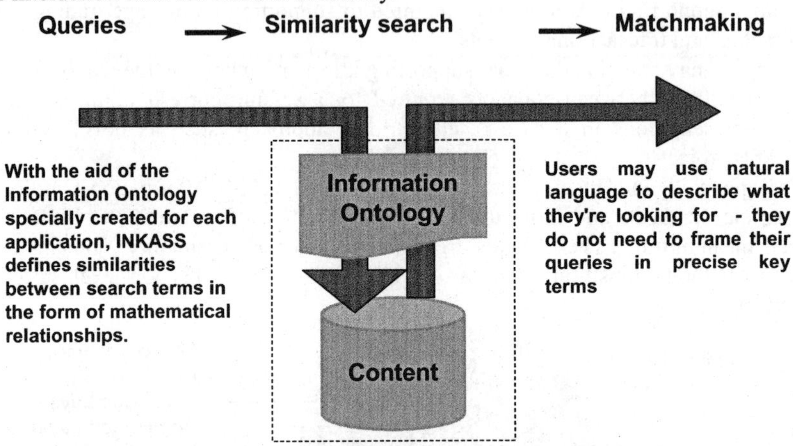

Figure 2: Matchmaking between knowledge supply and demand

As INKASS is based upon the CBR paradigm, Information Objects become Cases in the software realisation. The Information Ontology describes a class hierarchy, where each instance can be treated as a case in the CBR paradigm. In reality, the case base is a collection of use cases for information objects. Taxonomic structures and relations are translated into similarity measures for retrieval and augmented by adaptation rules that enable actions such as the transferral of an information object to a new use context. In operation, each successful INKASS marketplace transaction becomes a new case in its case base. Users specify their knowledge need by describing an information object that would meet their requirements. INKASS then retrieves those information objects that are most similar to the specified need. The object finally selected, together with the new use context, will form the new case. The INKASS platform thus captures knowledge on the use of its information objects and thereby enhances retrieval quality and user guidance. The latter is achieved by a dynamic user interaction strategy, formed on the basis of an information-gain calculus. For example, the system asks the buyer about aspects of the situational context that they have not specified, but which helps to distinguish between potentially useful information objects.

In the Intention Phase, the buyers and sellers signal their intentions based on knowledge obtained in the information phase and their desires and goals. In the intention phase, the INKASS system provides a variety of workflows to be executed by provider and client. (e.g. the Request for Quotation workflow facilitates iterative negotiation, ending in agreement between buyer and seller.

In the Contracting Phase, and in cases where new knowledge is to be created, the buyers and sellers create contracts based on the agreement reached in the intention phase. In INKASS, the contracting phase comprises a separate interoperable e-contracting model using XML and Java, which has flexibility to adjust to any participating company's operational needs. The result of this phase is a legally binding contract of the obligations of supplier and buyer.

In the Settlement Phase the buyers and sellers carry out the contract, including payment and delivery of the products. At the completion of this phase, a knowledge transaction has been completed or has been mutually cancelled. INKASS provides a shared workspace for submitting deliverables and communicating messages related to the work specified in the contract.

5. Comparative Analysis of Evaluation Results

The empirical evaluation of the INKASS platform was performed through a first test phase of the system, where buyers and sellers had access to the platform to perform transactions. Following this phase, users completed a questionnaire that captured impressions of the system's performance. The survey was designed according to the Goal Question Metrics (GQM) approach [11]. All answers were collected and measured by a Likert-scale where the participants answered on a scale from 1 to 5, where 5 meant "I completely agree" and 1 meant "I completely disagree". For each of these questions the average, minimum, maximum and variance were computed. (For simplicity reasons we present only average values herein). Further feedback was gained through telephone interviews with test participants. . The questionnaire had two parts: evaluation of the system and evaluation of the business model applied. TWI had a third set of questions that compared its existing text retrieval knowledge service, JoinIT, with INKASS. In total 35 questionnaires were completed (20 from TWI customers and 15 from Planet customers).

The preliminary test phase for TWI users lasted 2 weeks and two months for Planet. As a result, significant differences in results between TWI and Planet occurred. As Planet customers had more time to become familiar with the system, comparisons of the two tests must be handled carefully.

Overall, TWI and Planet customers had a positive first impression of INKASS. TWI customers perceived INKASS to have superior functionality than JoinIT. Other features that received positive ratings from TWI customers were:

- The results tree, a visualization feature that presents content objects in a hierarchical way, compared to the full text-search (average rating 3.7).
- The table view, where the user can navigate through the search results using tables based on the Information Ontology (average rating 3.7).
- Dialogue questions (average rating 3.6) where customers could narrow down search results by answering questions automatically generated by the system based on the Information Ontology.
- In both the survey (average rating 3.6) and direct feedback, TWI customers rated INKASS search results better than JoinIT.

Planet customers rated highly the results of the full text search, which analyses natural language ontology-based queries (average rating 4.9). The he table view (average rating 4.5), the result tree (average rating 4.5) and the dialogue questions (average rating 4.1) were also highly rated.

Throughout the survey the users perceived the ontology (graphical concept tree) as being very helpful in classifying the question (average rating TWI: 3.3; Planet: 4.3). The quality of the problem solution provided by the INKASS system was perceived as high, in terms of information quality measured in relevance of the document provided in the context of the question asked.

By using the INKASS ontology it is possible to relate documents. TWI and PLANET customers found it very helpful to get background information on the question asked, even if it was not directly related to the question (average rating TWI: 4.0; PLANET: 3.7). They also found it helpful to learn about similar kinds of problems other customers faced (average rating TWI: 4.2; PLANET: 4.1).

Regarding the business relevance of INKASS, this was evaluated through pre-identified generic business situations, upon which knowledge products were gathered and aggregated. For PLANET two cases were deemed as most relevant by users: the "Library case", where the customer is looking for specific information on a well known subject (average rating 4.1); and the "Option Planning" case, where the customer is looking for several options which are usable to solve a problem (average rating 4.5). With TWI, the generic case is "Problem Solving" and customers use INKASS to find a solution to a technical (average rating 3.9) or materials related problem (average rating 3.9).

6. Conclusion

The main technical considerations addressed in developing the INKASS software platform were to:

1. Integrate e-commerce with knowledge management software technology: INKASS has built on Empolis' e:kms, which is an e-Commerce middleware solution for intelligent retrieval and assistance. It has been enhanced with e-commerce transaction and workflow functionality needed to implement services such as Request for Quotation.
2. Focus on the critical questions that distinguish knowledge trading from other e-commerce areas; for this the project developed: (i) A powerful, knowledge-based matchmaking mechanism comparing supply and demand, utilising the information Ontology. (ii) Flexible, intuitive interfaces and intelligent assistance, helping users to express their demands and interactively search for appropriate solutions. These include system-initiated dialogue-based retrieval, visualised topic-map navigation, clustering of retrieved results providing a combination of query-based search and navigation, and finally, human-initiated feedback on user queries.
3. At the operational level, focus on how to cost-effectively use the platform for the novel problem of trading knowledge. In order to do this, the project developed: (i) The very basic ontological foundations for the utilization of e-commerce systems for knowledge trading, plus cost-effective methods for up-front knowledge engineering. (ii) An overall Business Engineering and configuration of existing mechanisms (e.g. different pricing mechanisms) which take into account the particularities of knowledge trading in each case. (iii) Appropriate business models, roles, processes, and revenue models for installing and running knowledge trading platforms.

   In relation to the INKASS Information Ontology, the distinction between a content facet and a facet for describing potential usage context opens the possibility for an extremely powerful retrieval approach. This reflects the situation that the customer often may not know the solution to their problem but can specify the problem details. The INKASS Information Ontology is derived from a broad range of scientific and practical inputs, which guarantee a good application coverage. However, this is work in progress that requires much thought and experimentation. Eventually, the layered INKASS ontology will turn out to be an exploitable asset in itself. The fact that Information Objects are modelled in a way that represents different levels of generality significantly increases the level of re-use of ontologies. The development phase of ontological engineering is shortened and using the Information Ontology achieves cost-effectiveness.

The INKASS pilots at TWI and PLANET have shown that tacit as well as explicit knowledge can be traded over the Internet. With careful planning, the trading of tacit knowledge could be established manifesting as offerings of expert advice through physical or virtual channels, such as selling consulting time or online collaboration. Consequently, a well-designed system, based on a stable model of knowledge tacit and explicit resources will result in service improvements In addition to the pilot knowledge e-marketplaces, there are two further exploitable results that together comprise the holistic INKASS solution for inter-organisational knowledge sharing and trading:

a) The generic INKASS e-marketplace technological platform. It is suitable for both closed user communities (1- or few-sellers to many buyers) and open markets (many sellers to many buyers). The platform comprises all tools necessary to setup and maintain a knowledge e-marketplace.

b) A business engineering services pack, to provide implementation support for the creation and/or participation in an electronic knowledge marketplace. Support involves guidance, in terms of tools and methods, in all stages of INKASS deployment, from strategic planning to actual rollout.

The target markets for the INKASS solution are internal knowledge markets in large corporations, such as Siemens and companies that sell technological know-how, such as TWI and PLANET and publishers of professional information, e.g. Wolters-Kluwer or Bertelsmann.

Acknowledgements

We would like to thank the European Commission for co-funding the INKASS IST project.

References

[1] Skyrme, D. J. (2001) "Capitalizing on Knowledge: From e-business to k-business", Butterworth-Heinemann, London.
[2] K. Kafentzis, D. Apostolou, and G. Mentzas, Knowledge marketplaces: strategic issues and business models, to appear in Journal of Knowledge Management, 8(2), 2003.
[3] Dignum, F., Sierra, C., eds. (20001): Agent Mediated Electronic Commerce - The European AgentLink Perspective. Springer LNAI 1991.
[4] Moukas, A., Sierra, C., Ygge, F., eds. (2000): Agent Mediated Electronic Commerce II - Towards Next-Generation Agent-Based Electronic Commerce Systems. Springer LNCS 1788.
[5] Dignum, F., Cortés, U., eds. (2001): Agent-Mediated Electronic Commerce III. Springer LNCS 2003.
[6] Liu, J., Ye, Y., eds. (2001): E-Commerce Agents, Marketplace Solutions, Security Issues, and Supply and Demand. Springer LNCS 2033.
[7] Miller, G. (1990): WordNet: An On-line Lexical Data- base. International Journal of Lexicography, 3(4), pp. 235- 312.
[8] A. Abecker, Towards a Technology for Organizational Memories. IEEE Intelligent Systems, 13(3), May/June 1998.
[9] A. Abecker, D. Apostolou, J. Franz, W. Maass, G. Mentzas, C. Reuschling, and S. Tabor, Towards an Information Ontology for Knowledge Asset Trading, in Weber, Pawar, Thoben (Eds) Proceedings of the 9th International Conference on Concurrent Enterprising, Espoo, Finland, 2003, 187-194.
[10] B. Schmid, and M. A. Lindemann, Elements of a Reference Model for Electronic Markets, in Proceedings of the 31st Hawaii International Conference on Systems Science (HICCS'98), Hawaii, January 1998, 193-201.
[11] Victor R. Basili, Gianluigi Caldiera, H. Dieter Rombach: "The Goal Question Metric Approach, Encyclopedia of Software Engineering. Wiley 1994.

Managing Knowledge in Networked Product Creation Organisations

Päivi PÖYRY[1], Mikael JOHNSON[1] & Jouni MERILUOTO[2]
[1]*Helsinki University of Technology, Software Business and Engineering Institute*
P.O.Box 9210, FIN-02015 HUT, Finland. Tel. +358-9-4511, Fax: +358-9-4514958
Email: Paivi.T.Poyry@hut.fi, Mikael.Johnson@hut.fi
[2]*Nokia Research Center, P.O. Box 407,FIN-00045 Nokia Group, Finland*
Tel.+358-50-4837366, Fax: +358-50-84837366, Email: Jouni.Meriluoto@nokia.com

Abstract: This paper presents the results of a case study conducted in a network of product creation organisations. The paper focuses on the consequences of new organisational structures, distributed collaboration and knowledge work in a virtual, networked organisation. The purpose of this paper is to describe from the employee's perspective how the new forms of inter-organisational collaboration affect product creation work. The results indicate that successful virtual work requires that the partner companies have designed the network carefully and have defined ways of collaboration. Moreover, the information systems supporting collaboration have to be chosen and developed with this in mind. In addition, sharing a history of collaboration supports the formation of rather uniform work practices or even a virtual organisation culture.

1. Introduction

The organisational structures have been changing towards new forms - such as networks, strategic alliances and virtual organisations - while an increasing amount of the product creation work is done in global, distributed organisations. At the same time the creation and use of knowledge is today argued to be one of the major building blocks of an organisation. However, the new ways of functioning and the new organisational structures require new support mechanisms, such as IT tools for communicating, storing and sharing information and knowledge. New ways of knowledge management (KM) are needed in order to collaborate efficiently, when both people and knowledge are dispersed in terms of time, physical distance, and organisational structures.

This paper presents the results of a case study carried out as a part of the WISE project. WISE (Web-enabled Information Services for Engineering), a European Commission co-funded IST (Information Society Technologies) research project, studied knowledge management within distributed product creation engineering environments. The goal of this case study was to understand and describe how people working in product creation experience new ways of organising work, when the borders between different organisations are diminishing due to outsourcing, dynamic project work, and close inter-company collaboration. The case study also addressed the design of the collaboration networks and the ways of collaboration as well as the information systems supporting the collaboration.

2. New forms of organisation and working

During the last decade, co-operation between companies in the field of high technology has increased significantly. The R&D sector's ability to produce innovations efficiently in the rapidly changing competitive environment has become dependent on the inter-organisational networks. The reasons for creating connections between organisations include for example, striving for increased revenue or cost reduction, and accessing the complementary resources or crucial competences of the partner company [4]. The new organisational forms have been developing in an environment that is characterised by global competition and globalisation, fragmentation of the markets, international decentralisation of production, and the demand of customised products. The organisations have responded to these challenges by outsourcing, flexible manufacturing, and innovating fast. Work has become complex, and it requires cross-functional teamwork, continuous learning and knowledge-intensive skills, abilities to collaborate with expert colleagues, and capability to adapt to constant change [6]. Ebers [4] identifies several forms of networking between companies, e.g., joint ventures, strategic alliances, subcontracting relationships, networks, virtual organisations etc. Even though the forms of co-operation vary, some common factors in the networks can be found. These factors include repeated resource and information flows, mutual expectations, and governance or coordination structures, and also factors related to the human interaction within the networks. One example is trust that enables people to communicate, collaborate, and finally innovate efficiently. The fundamental benefit of inter-organisational networking is the competitive advantage produced by the utilisation of wide spectrum of competences, sharing of risks, and informational synergies. [4]

Managing organisational knowledge has become increasingly attractive in economic life as the companies' potential for success is closely tied to their ability to innovate and to develop their ways of production; all this is based on the knowledge assets possessed by them [5]. KM focuses on facilitating and managing knowledge-related activities, such as systematic, explicit and deliberate building, renewal and application of knowledge in order to maximise an enterprise's knowledge-related effectiveness and returns from its knowledge assets [8]. However, for the inter-organisational networks KM should include a process enabling successful collaboration [9].

The development of information and communication technologies for its part has contributed to the creation of new forms of working. It has become possible to distribute the work not only between different offices but also between different companies. People may belong to several teams or work groups that more often are formed on an inter-organisational basis. Virtual work is usually done in virtual teams that are created to serve a specific purpose; the teams are dissolved as soon as the goals have been met [17]. In the virtual teams the social processes are relatively similar to the ones in traditional teams, but the distance and the use of technology as a mediator of information and communication creates challenges [2]. This kind of complex, distributed or virtual work requires specific technologies providing support for efficient communication [17].

The emergence of virtual work also demands improved KM activities, while at the same time the virtual way of working makes KM more complex than before. The internet-based technologies may offer one solution supporting the communication of knowledge between co-operating organisations or colleagues [16]. Various kinds of technologies and information systems have been developed and adopted for supporting KM, but the technology alone does not offer a solution; an extensive change is needed at behavioural, cultural and organisational levels in order to make KM successful. Moreover, concerning the process of knowledge creation, information systems fail to fulfil their promises [5]. Most of the current IT tools for KM are merely information management tools, in the sense that they are only able to process information, which is inherently different from knowledge that is deeply embedded in action and context [14].

Organisational culture, according to Schein [15], has been defined as a property of a group of people, which includes the shared assumptions, attitudes, values, beliefs, and simply the common ways of doing things. Most of the culture of an organisation is invisible; it is a shared mental model or a mindset that manifests itself in the daily actions and behaviour of the members of the organisation. The culture affects significantly the ways people act and interact in the organisational contexts. [15; 5] In virtual work the perception of organisational culture may become extended so that it incorporates the whole virtual organisation resulting in a feeling of cultural "globalness" among the employees [3].

3. The case study framework

In this study, the focus was on the inter-organisational networks formed by partner companies, on the various effects of new organisational forms, and on the distributed ways of work from the product creation engineers' perspective. Work practices, work culture, and the ways of collaboration were investigated. The research questions were:

- The design of the inter-organisational networks: How is the collaboration organised between the networked companies?
- The tools of knowledge work: Is the networked nature of work reflected in the information systems used in the daily work?
- Describing the work practices in the new inter-organisational networks: How do the individual product creation employees experience the networked mode of product creation work?

In this case study an applied or a "rapid" ethnography was used, that is a lighter version of the traditional ethnographic approach intended for doing research in industrial settings [11]. The basic research method was thematic ethnographic interview that is characterised by its emphasis on understanding the interviewees from their own perspectives [7]. Thus the interviews were carried out in the workplace of the interviewees, as the aim was to understand their work and its contexts. As Kvale [10] states, the interview situation consists of interaction and exchange or co-construction of meanings between the interviewer and the interviewee. This is why the content of each interview varied a little, and the question lists we had prepared served as checklists in order to make sure that all the central issues were discussed with the interviewees. A group of four, consisting of two representatives of the focal company and two university researchers, prepared the interview themes and questions, and analysed the interviews in co-operation.

People from both the focal and partner companies were interviewed, and the interviewees were principally engineers or technical writers. Five of them were working for the partner companies and nine for the focal company. The interviewees were chosen on the basis of being involved in inter-organisational collaboration, but they did not represent one particular product creation project. Instead they were involved in the focal company's product creation in different activities, such as testing or documentation. The 14 interviews, which were all held in Finland during the Spring of 2003, were recorded, transcribed and finally analysed with qualitative content analysis techniques. Two researchers carried out the interviews and transcribed the tapes. All four members of the group first read through and analysed the interviews individually, after which a group session was organised so that the individual interpretations could be discussed and a consensus could be reached.

4. Results of the case study

In this section the results of the case study are presented. The names of the companies involved in this study have been omitted, and they are referred to as "focal company" or "partner companies". Excerpts from the research material have been added in order to illustrate the findings.

4.1 The design of the inter-organisational networks

Usually the focal company did the innovative work related to the product creation. Partners carried out very limited, and pre-defined parts of the product according to the requirements and specifications of the focal company. This kind of collaboration can be seen as an extended enterprise that consists of a focal company and several collaborators that participate substantially in the operating of the focal company.

> "... we usually implement the knowledge the other company [the focal company] has created. It's a clear division of work. They make the innovation and we do what we are asked to support them."

This division of work functioned well in most cases, but was challenging when the product changed during development. It was considered normal to put the technical development on hold, while business representatives renegotiated the deals concerning schedules, resources, and money. These "project freezes" required the partner companies to be very flexible and re-allocate resources within very short timeframes, e.g., with a week's notice. Some focal company interviewees wished that they could get more feedback from the partners, who they thought did not report their problems early enough. Insufficient communication of trouble in understanding the requirements may increase the uncertainty of the estimated work efforts, which then increase the risk of project delays. Little if any collocated work was done between the focal company and its partners. Instead, there were short working visits to the partner site, but the work was done at each partners' own premises.

> "Quite little [collocated work] as far as I've understood. ...There are this kind of information transfer situations. Then they come to Espoo [town in Finland] for a visit and then they go back to India."

Training was offered to the partners regularly, as well as familiarisation to the product and processes used during the product creation, and a contact person was defined with a responsibility of the partnership collaboration. Usually the partners followed the focal company's process models, which framed the partner's own internal processes. The information systems were usually shared to some extent: not all documents were shown to the partners, but the partners were given access to all documents they needed in their work. However, these practices varied considerably between different projects and partners.

> "As far as I understand, all information systems are available to the partners."
> "We use the focal company's product creation process model. In general it is very clear and well defined. It makes it easier for us to work."

The processes, practices, and interfaces of collaboration were in the process of development. Two of the interviewees had been in a position where they had to create new project organisations. It was supported by the existing processes, but they reported that there had been some "fighting" to get their process innovations included in the official processes.

4.2 The tools of knowledge work

In this chapter the findings concerning information systems in the networked knowledge work are briefly presented The results represent two groups of interviewees: the employees of the focal company and the partner companies. The common factor between these two compared groups is the attitude to information systems in the knowledge-intensive cooperative work, and little if any difference was found.

Extended organisational networks between collaborators require new kind of management. A holistic view of processes is necessary, not only in the focal company, but among all collaborators as well. The information systems supporting knowledge work easily remain unchanged and rooted in the practices before the outsourcing. The holistic view of the process is based on the fact that collaboration works best when systems are not the only channel for information and knowledge sharing. None of the respondents denied that certain knowledge is dynamic and generated during discussions - even the topics are basically work process related. To some extent informal communication based on personal and organisational relationship is needed. Information systems and documentation are not enough. During the knowledge creation phase, interaction is more important than documentation. Even later, in a formalised process, at some point documentation – without supporting interpersonal relationship – begins to contribute more to confusion than comprehension.

"When we were working in the same room with designers, the unofficial information search was easy."
"Informal knowledge sharing is crucial in the beginning of the project"
"In principle everything is available from the system, but if you have something to ask, it's easier to contact directly"
"Draft documents are commented in discussions, by on-line meetings or by e-mail"

Discussions are more than information sharing – they generate new knowledge. However, information systems can be used to optimise the correct mix of documentation and interaction to convey understanding, because their role is twofold: they are used for documentation storing as well as for communication. All interviewees of this research mentioned e-mail as a crucial supporting channel of documentation process. A document management system is used for storing formal releases. The basic features, like version management, workflow, document lifecycle, check-in and check-out, compound documents etc. were considered to be important, but only for the inspected documents.

Before the formal documentation process there are more informal storing methods, such as file servers, web servers and groupware. These phases depend even more on communication technology and culture. These more informal document sharing platforms – as well as the formal systems – need a responsible key user: a person who knows about the technology but also about the content of the document bases. Of course there can be standard roles for the users, like administrators, managers, authors, designers, readers, editors or depositors, but the specification is not clear cut when talking about a temporary, working storage used in collaboration with external partners. The roles are not formal, the users and their roles are changing, and the user can act in multiple roles. It is crucial that the information systems support dynamic roles when the organisations and the processes change continuously. Otherwise, static roles only reinforce the practices from the time when the information systems were built and new process innovations have to struggle against the system. This discussion of flexibility of information and knowledge systems has also been dealt with in research under other topics like elastic interfaces [1], tailorability [12], and end-user computing [13]. Hopefully these impressions of user agency will influence the designers of process-oriented information and knowledge management systems, which currently cannot handle emergent processes very well.

When selecting the right system for each collaboration case, one problem is that multi-purpose systems have the best features for one purpose only: a groupware system is not the best document management solution, while the document management system does not have good enough support for communication, and so on. Even within the document management category there are discrepancies, like differences between inadequate new

XML based systems and "too mature" SGML based systems, neither of which are best for PDF or other publishing purposes. Therefore it is not possible to define a unique new system for engineering documentation management in cooperative work. For example, some of the respondents considered audit trails or tracing important for a new system, but none of them said that this feature is used in the existing systems.

The selection of the right system also depends on the phase of the project and process. Then there are other supporting systems, like project management, metadata management, reporting etc. As a summary the networked characteristics of collaboration is reflected in the information systems on three levels:

1. Both traditional documents and new document formats can be managed well in collaboration, after they have been inspected and imported to the formal product creation process. This includes also other documentation specific features, like reporting and publishing.
2. In between the step 1 storing and step 3 communication is the layer of groupware, metadata, project management; portals, dynamic file servers, and other extranet servers. This layer can include data about the persons and their roles in the project as well.
3. The systems for communication are needed in every phase of the collaboration. This includes e-mail and on-line meetings, but also some features of the document management systems, such as notifications. The informal relationships give another means to support cooperation between organisations, and should not be ignored.

All the systems need some amount of communication. For example, when a product update is released, the learning curve is crucially lower if there is personal training supported by self-studies and on-line exercises. The communication is very critical – and most difficult – between collaborators with different educational background. Then there are time restrictions and linguistic and cultural gaps as well when we are talking about a global company. However, these should be seen as challenges and enrichment of collaboration. All in all, the question is not to select documentation or interaction exclusively, but the right mixture of documentation and right kind of interaction to create extended organisational knowledge.

4.3 The work practices in the new inter-organisational networks

Most teams investigated were professionally homogenous, i.e. at the focal company they consisted of mostly engineers. In contrast, the technical writers at the partner companies were usually professionals of linguistics or humanistic fields. Therefore consulting technical support was needed in documentation teams. However, there were no significant difficulties between different professions' representatives, as the corporate culture was the connecting factor creating a relative uniform way of working, even if the different sites also had unique characteristics depending on location and function. Corporate culture was perceived similar in the partner companies as a result of close collaboration with the focal company, or in some cases the partner being a former part of the focal company. Moreover, there were some persons with hybrid-skills that bridged the gap between the engineers and humanists.

> "Most of us are engineers. There may be some other educational backgrounds, too… But the engineers may represent many different fields of engineering."
> "We need many kinds of people, many kinds of personalities, but I'm not sure if we need people with different professions. …and this [work] requires a certain mindset."

In contrast, one of the technical writers reported that the culture was not as relaxed now that the focal company had become the customer, compared to when everyone were working for the same company. This new organisational independence that had occurred two years before the interviews, was still very present in the discussions with all technical writers. On the one hand, it had brought about a centralisation of the technical writers away from the designers into their own offices, and facilitated closer collaboration between technical writers. This change had mixed reactions within the technical writers, of which some felt an increased hesitation to call the engineers being afraid of disturbing them, while others were very pleased with the strengthened technical writing culture. In addition to these dilemmas of project continuity and whether to work with engineers or technical writers, another outer threat emerged in almost all interviews: scarcity of time. Some said that they have to manage with the available resources; others blamed time to be the reason why the communication sometimes did not work very well.

Formal communication included the pre-defined progress meetings, audits, and kick-offs, and informal communication included emails, telephone calls, and occasional meetings that were arranged for solving a specific, urgent problem. Both virtual and face-to-face meetings were arranged, but more face-to-face interaction was needed, because not all problems could be solved via email. If there was a problem that required discussion or hands-on approach, there was an evident need for face-to-face meetings. When people got used to the virtual meeting system, it was not seen as an obstacle for communication. However, it was seen as extremely useful that the people met at least once in the beginning of the project: this improved the communication significantly. Communication was seen as successful if there were enough personal contacts between the partners. People wanted to know the person with whom they are talking to or sending emails to.

Informal feedback and networks for personal information exchange were considered of utmost importance. A technical issue could serve as a reason to call or to visit a person, and many other important matters were discussed during the call or visit as well. The interviewees felt that sharing knowledge was a value at the focal company, and in practice, some managers encouraged people to share knowledge. However, there was no uniform practice in sharing knowledge. Instead, the ways varied a lot from unofficial coffee-table discussions to more official newsletter-like forms of distributing the lessons learned.

> "…it's hard to find out about the experiences of the others, because we don't meet these people and nobody writes down the lessons they have learned…"

5. Conclusions and discussion

In this case study, the inter-organisational network was designed to support a flexible product creation process, which was divided between the focal and partner companies so that the main responsibility for the innovation remained in the focal company. The ways of collaboration were clearly defined, which was a critical factor for the success of distributed working. The IT supported tools of knowledge work, however, have to be chosen carefully, and there has to be a good balance between documentation and communication.

The work processes, ways of working and even organisational cultures were in this case study - if not the very same, at least very close to each other creating a sense of a virtual organisation and common way of doing things. The factors that enabled and facilitated virtual collaboration included direct personal contacts and meetings in person in the beginning of projects requiring extensive virtual communication between distant sites. The results also show examples of the new dilemmas that emerge in networked product creation. People ponder on where and when to work when colleagues and collaborators are dispersed in time, location, and organisational structures. Great flexibility from the partners' side is needed when the focal company's processes, products, and projects change during product creation. These flexibility issues in the organisational structures are reflected in the tools of the knowledge work, and designing flexible, and tailorable tool architectures becomes increasingly important.

The results of this case study have been utilised for process development within the companies involved in this study. The lessons learned may also be useful for other companies facing increasing requirements for inter-organisational collaboration and networking, and this case study also makes a contribution to the research in the field of KM. This case study opened up topics that are being studied in more detail in a new research project about technology mediated knowledge services for industrial settings. Further research including new interviews concentrates on the virtual collaboration of experts and online communities of practice, and it aims to develop a process model for improved sharing of tacit knowledge in distributed knowledge work.

References

[1] Andersen, P.B. (1999). *Elastic Interfaces. Maritime instrumentation as an example.* Proceedings of the CSAPC'99, Université de Valenciennes, Valenciennes, France, pp. 35-41.

[2] Blanchard, A.L. & Markus, M.L. (2000). *Sense of Virtual Community – Maintaining the Experience of Belonging.* In: Proceedings of the 35th Hawaii International Conference on System Sciences 2002. IEEE Computer Society.

[3] Burn, J.M. & Ash, C. (2000). *Managing Knowledge for Strategic Advantage in the Virtual Organisation.* In: Malhotra, Y. [ed.] (2000). Knowledge Management and Virtual Organizations. Idea Group Publishing. Pp. 144-161.

[4] Ebers, M. (ed.) (1997). *The Formation of Inter-Organizational Networks.* Oxford University Press.

[5] Davenport, T.H., & Prusak, L. (1998). *Working Knowledge: How Organisations Manage What They Know.* Cambridge MA: Harvard Business School Press.

[6] Hatch, M.J. (1997). *Organisation Theory Modern, Symbolic, and Postmodern Perspectives.* Oxford University Press.

[7] Heyl, B.S. (2001). *Ethnographic Interviewing.* In: P. Atkinson, A. Coffey, S. Delamont, J. Lofland & L. Lofland (eds): Handbook of Ethnography. Sage 2001, pp. 369-383.

[8] Kemp, J., Pudiatz, M., Perez, P., & Ortega, A.M. (2002). *KM Framework (2nd Release).* European KM Forum (IST 2000-26393): D1.1. Final report.

[9] Klueber, R., Alt, R. & Österle, H. (2000). *Implementing Virtual Organizing in Business Networks: A Method of Inter-Business Networking.* In: Malhotra, Y. [ed.] (2000). Knowledge Management and Virtual Organizations. Idea Group Publishing. Pp. 43-62.

[10] Kvale, S. (1996). InterViews. *An Introduction to Qualitative Research Interviewing.* Sage Publications.

[11] Millen, D.R. (2000). *Rapid Ethnography: Time Deepening Strategies for HCI Field Research.* Proceedings of DIS'00, pp. 280-286.

[12] Mørch, A.I. (1997). *Method and tools for tailoring of object-oriented applications: an evolving artifacts approach*, PhD dissertation, Department of Informatics, University of Oslo.

[13] Nardi, B.A. (1993). *A Small Matter Of Programming: Perspectives on End User Computing*, Cambridge, Massachusetts: MIT Press.

[14] Nonaka, I., Reinmöller, P., & Toyama, R. 2001. *Integrated information technology systems for knowledge creation.* In: M. Dierkes, A. Berthoin-Antal, J. Child, & I. Nonaka (Eds.), Handbook of Organizational Learning and Knowledge Management, Vol. Paperback Edition. Padstow, UK: Oxford University Press. Pp. 827-848.

[15] Schein, E. (1999). *The Corporate Culture Survival Guide – Sense and Nonsense About Culture Change.* Jossey-Bass Publishers.

[16] Schwartz, D., Divitini, M. & Brasethvik, T. (2000). *Internet-Based Organisational Memory and Knowledge Management.* Idea Group Publishing.

[17] Watson-Manheim, M.B. & Belanger, F. (2000). *Exploring Communication-Based Work Processes in Virtual Work Environments.* Proceedings of the 35th Hawaii International Conference on System Sciences 2002. IEEE Computer Society.

Customisation of Information in the Manufacturing Industry

Christian PERSSON
Høgskolen i Gjøvik, PB 191, 2802 Gjøvik, Norway.
Tel: +47 61 13 51 00, Fax: +47 61 13 51 70, Email: chpersson@telia.com

Abstract: The production and distribution of information in connection with products and services is one of the most important functions in today's business world. The ability to produce and deliver information to the right place on time is often crucial for the company's reputation and sales. This paper address questions about how companies can establish a dynamic information system with the help of digital media technology and customisation of information. Customisation of information is a process where information is adapted and distributed on different media platforms. A case study of a manufacturing company with global information activity is presented. The case describes a renewal of the company's information strategy in relation to its customer's preferences. The case demonstrates how multi-channel publishing, including electronic online medias, combined with digital printing can offer efficient tools to reach out to the customers with customized information.

1. Introduction

The ability to produce and distribute information in connection with products and services is one of the most important functions in today's business world. A company's ability to produce accurate information and deliver it to the right place on time is often crucial for the company's reputation and sales. Today's often-global business activities necessitate a global responsibility for service and maintenance. This is the case for companies active in the service industry as well as the manufacturing industry.

This paper addresses questions on how companies can establish a dynamic information system with the ability to adjust information with the help of digital media technology. The focus is on the possibility to access information related to specific products in a way and on media platforms that best suit the users' preferences. The process where digitalised information is adjusted to a specific product or a user is often referred to as customisation of information. A customized information distribution process makes a one-to-one relationship possible [1] between the sender of the information and the receiver.

There are two main factors behind the extended use of online electronic media and multi-channel publishing. One is the digitalisation of the content and information technology. Another factor is the integration of the computer with the telecom system that makes it possible to carry information in a digital format around the world. The result is often referred to as the development of convergence in media.

The Internet is especially important for the media convergence phenomenon. The Internet makes it possible to establish presence for text, sound, pictures and video through the same media system [2]. The Internet is also a media system that provides an opportunity for interaction, i.e., the media consumers' ability to interact with the distributed content and to choose and activate preferred parts of it.

The shift to a digital representation of information has brought dynamics into the distribution and publishing process of information [3]. The content can now be presented directly as digital documents using online sources such as screen displays and digital discs or it can be published as printed matter.

The ability to publish information as an electronic document is important. Before the digitalisation of information, text and pictures were normally produced and distributed as printed matter. The distribution and the spread of the Internet have dramatically influenced the shift to the use of digital documents. The development of the Internet is the single most important factor in the development of publishing information as an electronic document. It is evident that most of the earlier printed information is today produced and distributed electronically. The Internet is, in most cases, the first choice of distribution method. Printing as a distribution channel is becoming a sub-set of the Internet and hence a secondary channel. Still, printing has an important role to play in many situations. Paper is a well-known and robust mediator of information and is superior in many situations. This paper describes how electronic documents can be used together with printed documents to produce customized information and how both media formats are a result of the information digitalisation process.

2. Objectives

The ability to present information, upgrade information in real time, distribute information on-demand and distribute information on different media platforms are crucial tasks for companies. The objective of this paper is to demonstrate how a company can make use of multi-channel publishing, including online electronic information distribution, together with digital printing technology in an effort to extend its customer and service information systems.

3. Method

Customisation of information is discussed within the context of a case study, which describes how a manufacturing company with global information responsibility is renewing its information strategy and information system. The case study shows how it is possible to meet a challenging information task by restructuring the management of information with a system that supports a customized information structure where digital documents are presented on-screen in combination with information presented with the help of digital printing technology.

4. Business Case Description

The following case is presented in a master thesis work at the Department of Media Technology and Graphic Arts, Royal Institute of Technology, Stockholm [4].

The manufacturing company studied produces trucks for a global market. The future aim of the company is to be able to adjust all service information connected with the products on an individual basis. The company uses a module system in its manufacturing process to decrease production costs and at the same time establish conditions for customised production. Each truck produced consists of several modules that are put together. There are different engine modules, gear system modules, wheel system modules, interior parts modules, and so on. The module systems can be combined to produce an almost unlimited number of different trucks. The module system has advantages. For example, it makes it possible to customise each truck, i.e., each truck can be adjusted to a customer's individual preferences and demands. Very few trucks produced by the company are identical. Estimation is that there are around 1 million possible truck combinations from which to choose. Another advantage is that the stock and production costs can be reduced due to an efficient production process.

The module system also implies a challenge to the company. One of the most important challenges is linked to the information system that supports the truck and service systems. Customized production also implies a need to customize the information material. Generalized information material covering all aspects of the product assortment would be extensive because of the many possible module combinations. It would not be easy to find relevant information on a specific truck in such extensive material. The challenge to the information system would be especially strong in relation to the aftermarket of the trucks covering maintenance and information support.

To deal with the difficulties connected with the present information system, the company has started a process to change the information structure from its present static one with six different output channels - electronic as well as printed - to a database system with the ability to produce customized information on-demand distributed on different channels.

4.1 The present information system

One of the main publishing channels in the present information system consists of a user's manual that is produced and distributed with each truck. It contains necessary information about the everyday use of the vehicle. The user manual has information such as driving instructions, automatic gearbox instructions, oil-change instructions and a maintenance schedule. Different folders are put together to build the user manual. Each folder has its own table of contents. The user manual in its present shape is partially customised for different truck models. However, the information is not customised for each specific truck. Part of the content in the user manual is common for all truck models. This is the case, for example, for the driving instructions folder. The folder contains both relevant and irrelevant material depending on the specific solutions chosen for the actual truck model. A manual process is used to produce the parts of the user manual that are customised. Different information folders are put together manually and placed in a cover. The finished user manual consists of about twenty different compiled folders. The user manual is then distributed together with the vehicle.

Another important part of the information system is the service manual used at the service centres. The company's unique module production system that customises every truck to individual customer demands also means that the information has to be upgraded when new functions and parts are introduced into the trucks. Service manuals must be updated when new parts or functions are developed. The service manual is presently produced as both a text version and an electronic version. The information in the service manual is saved as a text document and is not stored in a database structure. The same text and pictures are therefore presented at different places in the manual. It is not possible to perform an automated search for information in its present structure. The information structure in the service manual also makes it difficult to update the information.

A technical newsletter is distributed regularly to the service centres to inform them of production changes. This information is paper-based. Another information system is a computer-based version of the service manual combined with a chassis number database and a spare parts catalogue. The information in the electronic service manual system is PDF-based. The manual also has a search function based on chassis numbers where it is possible to find the original configuration of each truck. However, this information is not connected with any information on the specific parts defining the truck. Hence, the digital service manual is no easier to navigate than the paper-based one. One problem with the electronic service manual is keeping it updated. It is not uncommon for different versions to be installed on different computers at the same service centre simultaneously.

4.2 The information flow in the present information system

Technique informants and illustrators manage the present information system by producing information for the different information channels. The information in the system is static and linked to each specific channel. The same work has to be done several times to produce the information separately for each distribution channel, i.e., a component description is made for each channel and a translation is carried out for each language.

The structure of the present information system is as follows:

1. A developing engineer develops a component
2. A method engineer develops work instructions for the component
3. A technique informant describes a work procedure for the part; a unique information text is produced for each distribution channel
4. The texts are translated for each channel
5. Each text is published in its respective channel

4.3 The future information system

There are different reasons behind the decision to change the present information system to a new data based one. One important reason is the company's wish to establish a more direct dialogue with its customers and service workshops. With the help of an improved dialogue, the company expects to get, among other things, feedback that is more precise on the provided information. It is, for example, important that the company receive feedback if something in the information material is erroneous or can be misinterpreted.

The future information system is based on a multi-channel publishing strategy [5]. The method to achieve multi-channel publishing is based on a central database structure where all information types (text, pictures, videos, drawings, etc.) are stored in an XML format. The strategy behind publishing information in several channels is that it will increase the possibility to reach the individual receiver more precisely than if only one single channel is used. The information structure in the future information system makes it possible to publish information in different channels without any extra production effort. The strategy is to re-use the basic information that is produced and structure it in accordance with every single channel that is in use. The ability to use different information channels is also an advantage because of the characteristics of the different channels and their suitability for different tasks. If, for example, an animation is needed in the information process, a screen presentation is better suited for this task than a printed channel.

The future system is characterised by its version handling ability. This will eliminate the present problem of different versions in parallel use. The future system is based on a multi-channel publishing structure and supports workflow management. The workflow management ensures that the right person has access to the relevant information. It also facilitates the handling of the information flow between the technique informants, illustrators and translators. There is also an authorization system, which gives different users access to different areas in the information system.

It is possible to search for information in the future system. The importance of the search function is expected to increase with the future technological development of the trucks.

4.4 The structure of the future information system

Information is dynamic in the future information system. The information is produced one time and re-used in each channel.

1. A developing engineer develops a component

2. A method engineer develops the instructions on how the component should be handled by the technicians
3. A technique informant describes the work procedure for the component; a common information text is produced to be used in every distribution channel
4. The common text is translated
5. The common text is published in each channel

4.5 The information flow in the future Information system

The information flow in the future system is built on a structuring of the information into different information elements. The information flow is illustrated in Figure 1.

1. The source for the future information system is the text and picture descriptions of all the truck parts. This information consists of several thousands of pages.
2. Each information element is defined according to one of six content categories. The categories are "term", "aim", "explanation", "function", "placing" and "consists of". Each element is also marked according to which trucks it belongs.
3. Each text element is stored in XML [6] format in a database.
4. The XML coded information is linked to a DTD (Document Type Definition) that defines the rules that are valid for the information objects in the XML documents.
5. The verified XML document is linked to a XSL document (eXtended Stylesheet Language). The XSL document contains information on the layout of the information in relation to the channels. The adjusted information is presented on each output channel.
6. Different channels are hence linked to different XSL documents.

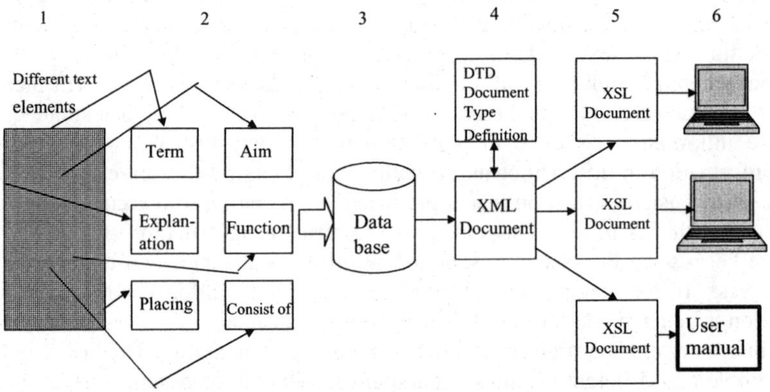

Figure 1: Information flow in the future system [4]

5. Print on demand

One important information issue for the truck manufacturing company is the ability to distribute information both as a digital document and as printed matter. Combined production of digital documents distributed via electronic medias, e.g. a computer screen, in parallel with the production of personalized printing on paper is carried out with the help of digital printing through digital presses [7].

5.1 Personalized printing

One important advantage with digital printing compared to e.g. offset printing is the possibility to use variable data in the documents [8]. Printed matter based on variable data and produced by a digital printing press can be customized in accordance with an individual's requirements. It can also be used to produce customized information intended for a specific product, e.g. an instruction manual. This process is often referred to as personalised printing.

Specific input about the customer's wants and needs, or specific product knowledge is needed to produce personalised printed information. A personalised document can be more or less personified from the individual address of the receiver to a situation where every text and print element is adjusted to the individual customer's preferences. Studies that have compared the communication ability between traditional mass distributed prints with personalised printing have shown that customised documents have better communication ability and are hence able to improve business opportunities. Ordinary direct-mail campaigns usually have a response rate of about 1-2%. A personalized direct-mail campaign has in comparison a response rate between 10-20% [4]. The digital printing process also improves the possibility to produce printed information on demand. Print on demand means a cost reduction because no items have to be kept in stock. It also ensures that the information material asked for will be accessible as long as the information is stored in a database.

The main strategy behind personalized printing is to reach those users that are genuinely interested in the information. This is especially important since the production costs for digitalised prints are higher than those for traditional offset printing. It is therefore important in personal printing to have knowledge about who will use the information since the success of the personalised information material is dependent on how well it reaches its target users.

The truck manufacturing company has traditionally produced most of its information material as printed matter. This has, for example, been the case with the user manual distributed together with each truck. Printed information has traditionally also been the framework for the service documentation used at the service centres. The printing process must work in conjunction with the overall digital information structure where the information is stored in a database. It must be possible to produce printed matter down to a customised level as part of the information distribution. The present system of manual customisation of the user manual will be replaced in the future with a workflow where a unique document is printed and delivered together with each truck.

5.2 Workflow for personalized prints

The workflow necessary to produce personalized prints includes more process steps than an ordinary printing process without variable data. The following steps are typical for the personalized process:

- Form an idea and objective for the personalization activity
- Collect data from different data bases and structure these data in a database
- Design the layout of the personalized document
- Analyse the database and control that necessary data is available
- Link the data from the database onto the layout and prepare the file for printing
- Make a test print to ensure that the personified parts are in place
- Rip the file and print it in a digital printer
- After-treatment process
- Distribute and follow-up the results

6. Discussion

Information is a core asset in most products today. The activities that have been described in the truck manufacturing case, where a dynamic information production and distribution process is replacing a static process, is an example of how customisation of information can be used to increase both the customer and producer benefits in the manufacturing industry. The production of customised information and distribution on demand is an optimisation of the information process. This process aims to increase the value of the information and, at the same time, reduce costs in the production process of the information [9].

The value increase is achieved on different levels. Some are related to the reduction of costs. The customised user manuals will reduce the printing costs since fewer pages have to be printed. The information search at the service centres will also be more efficient and the information-gathering precision will be higher when the future system is in place. This implies shorter stops for the trucks at the service centres, something that will save money for everyone. The information in the service manual will be distributed as a digital document. This will reduce printing costs since printing will be on demand. Postage costs will also be reduced when digital documents and print on demand are implemented. The continuous update of the information in the database and hence, the different output channels, will also increase the value to the product user and at the same time reduce costs at the service centres. However, the future system can also generate costs. The purchase of the future system will imply costs. This is also the case in connection with the training of the staff at the truck company and the service centres.

The demand for an information distribution process that supports production on demand and can be customised to individual products is an answer to the increased competition on the market where customers evaluate the extended product, including the information material.

One challenge for the truck company in relation to the future information system is to coordinate all the information published on different media platforms. In the present system where all of the information is static, the production process is rather easy to control. The problems have to do with the redundancy in the information and the difficulties to navigate the information. The future system with its dynamic generation of information provides the users with easier accessible information, but also demands new quality control systems adjusted to the dynamic environment.

Another challenge is the learning process on the production and use of the information. New routines are necessary both on the production and user sides. This will be especially sensitive in the future for the service organisation when the information will only be accessible through digital media and not as printed instruction manuals. Traditionally, the service technicians have used paper-based information in their work. The future digital information system at the service centres will distribute the information primarily via computer screen; however, it will also be possible to print the information from this system.

7. Conclusions and Summary, Recommendations

This case study demonstrates how multi-channel publishing including electronic online media, combined with digital printing, can provide a manufacturing company with new tools to reach out to its customers and service partners with customised information. However, to create a better understanding of the capacity in multi-channel publishing technologies, the recommendation is for more in-depth analysis and evaluation of the experiences that have been accumulated up to now. It is especially important to analyse how multi-channel publishing can be used in different branches to increase value to both the company and their customers. In this connection, it is important to carry out a careful cost benefit analysis in relation to the company's need for customisation of information. There will obviously be different strategies to choose from depending on the company and branch.

Important questions that remain are: How can the communication process between the involved parts in the information process be designed? How can knowledge about the potential in customized information be transferred to the information users? What methods can be developed to better evaluate the effects of customized information? Where are the economical gains in the customisation of information? It is necessary to answer these questions through future research before the potential of multi-channel publishing can be fully realised.

References

[1] D. Peppers, M. Rogers, The one-to-one future. Building Relationship One Customer at a Time. New York, Currency/Doubleday, 1993.
[3] S. Rasmussen, Mediernes sammensmeltning. CFJE Rapport nr. 3, 2000
[2] M. Lister, J. Dovey, S. Giddings, I. Grant, K. Kelly, New Media. A Critical Introduction, Routledge, 2002.
[4] M. Ericsson, Personalization and Multimedia Publishing. Master Thesis at The department of Media technology and Graphic arts, Royal Institute of Technology, 2003.
[5] C. Huusko, *Publishing in Multiple Media*, Masterthesis, Royal Institute of Technology, 2001.
[6] E. H. Rusty, S. Means, *XML in a nutshell*, O'Reilly & Associates Inc. Sebastopol, 2001
[7] I. Lundin, A study of the production flow for digital printing. Master Thesis at The department of Media technology and Graphic arts, Royal Institute of Technology, 2003.
[8] D. Broudy & F. Romano, *Personalized & database printing, The Complete guide.* Gama, Salem,1999.
[9] D. Remenyi, A. Money, M. Sherwood-Smith, Z. Irani, *The effective measurement and management of IT costs and benefits*, Butterworth Heinemann, Oxford, 2000.

Facilitating Knowledge Exchange and Decision Making within Learning Networks

Dimitris APOSTOLOU, Soumi PAPADOPOULOU
PLANET S.A., 64 L. Riencourt, Apollon Tower, Athens, 115 23, Greece
Tel: +30 210 690500, Fax: + 30 210 6981885, Email: dapost@planet.gr, soumi@planet.gr

Abstract: The Learning Network (LN) is an innovative scheme that has been introduced recently in several countries in Europe. This paper introduces a conceptual model for LNs and presents an integrated tool-set for supporting knowledge sharing and decision making in LNs that consists of a software system and a methodology. It also presents how the tool-set has been piloted and evaluated by an automotive cluster. Finally it provides a constructive set of recommendations for leveraging the operation of the main functions of LNs using Information Technology.

1. Introduction

Learning Network (LN) is an innovative scheme that has been introduced recently in several countries in Europe. The term learning network does not refer to networks where learning simply happens as it is the case with Communities of Practice – groups of people who share a concern, a set of problems, and who deepen their knowledge and learn by spontaneously interacting on an ongoing basis [1]. On the contrary, Learning Networks are inter-organisational structures, formally established to increase the participants' knowledge and innovative capability [2]. Previous research suggests that learning networks [3]:

- are formally established and defined;
- have a structure for operation with boundaries defining participation;
- have a primary learning target;
- have formally developed processes that can be mapped on the learning cycle;
- have practical learning outcome than can be measured.

This paper introduces a conceptual model for Learning Networks and presents an integrated tool-set for supporting knowledge sharing and decision making in LNs that consists of a software system and a methodology. It also presents how the tool-set has been piloted & evaluated by an automotive cluster. Finally it provides a constructive set of recommendations for facilitating the operation of the main functions of LNs.

2. Existing Theories and Work

2.1 Learning in Groups

Although much of the discussion on learning is concerned with learning at the individual level, there is an emerging strand, which deals with the theme of group learning. In particular the active participation of others in the process of learning and support is recognised as a powerful enabling resource and was developed into a widely used approach termed 'action learning'[i] [4]. The whole idea of action learning is based on the combination of personal example (the action dimension) with the notion of learning community. This concept stresses the value of experiential learning and the benefits, which can come from gaining different forms of support from others. Part of the vision of Revans [5];[6], one of the pioneers of the concept, involved the idea of 'comrades in adversity', working together to tackle complex and open-ended problems.

Arguably self-learning within a group has much to offer to organisational learning. The experience of regional clusters of small firms provides one important piece of evidence in support of this. In the case of an Italian furniture cluster, for example, a dominant position in world trade has been achieved and sustained over 15 years, yet the average firm size is less than 20 employees [7]. In a similar vein, large corporations have managed to develop world-class competencies and products by allowing the formation of "communities of practice" within their organisation (i.e. communities of people with alike interests who interact with and learn from each other) [1]. It has been increasingly recognised that organisational knowledge results from complex and multi-faceted interactions among different individuals [8], [9].

However, learning has not been without problems:

1. First, learning requires the transfer not only of explicit and codified knowledge but also of tacit knowledge, which is usually associated with experience and practice.
2. Secondly, learning can be out of context reducing significantly its potential; it is important to remember that context is what converts information into knowledge.
3. Thirdly, despite the obvious benefits, learning can be expensive preventing especially the individuals within smaller firms from upgrading their skills and the relevant organisations from developing their capabilities.

2.2 The Role of Information Technology in Learning Networks

The new knowledge-based economy necessitates increasingly the collaboration between different organisations. For example, within supply chain work environments, there is a growing recognition that the next step after moving from confrontational to co-operative relationships within supply chains is to engage in a process of shared development and learning [10]. Despite the recent upsurge in e-learning and knowledge management systems, the vast majority of these systems focus on either individual users or individual organisations [11].

It can be argued that self-learning within groups and inter-organisational learning has largely been ignored by the latest systems. However, Information and Communication Technologies (ICT) have a significant potential for networks of individuals and companies. Multimedia, groupware and the Internet in general are stimulating the emergence of new models and systems aimed at improving the efficiency and quality of knowledge creation and diffusion processes [11], which are being gradually adopted by educational institutions and corporations worldwide. In the context of a Learning Network, new technologies can have an impact by leveraging:

- the intensive interaction of the people (broker/network moderator and/or members) with decision making authority;
- the interaction of the members to share knowledge and exchange experiences;
- the diffusion of captured knowledge within the organisation, by allowing all people to access the learning content in order to benefit a wider set of people and enable the conversion of learning outcome to specific changes in organisational routines.

All three functions are restrained by the usual time and travel limitations of the involved actors, if physical meetings are required. Apparently there is a tremendous potential for Information and Communication Technologies to support all three aspects, enhancing significantly the efficiency of the learning process.

3. Objectives

Knowlaboration (KNOWLedge Application for collaBORATIve Organisational Networks) is a European research project that has developed a tool-set that aims to enhance learning, knowledge sharing and decision-making in LNs in five ways:

- Firstly, improve decision-making, as this process is critical for the success of learning since this process results to the specification of a variety of issues related to learning process and content.
- Secondly, address one of the most usual problems of LNs, which is the restriction of learning during the formally organised learning sessions of the network (due to time and travel limitations).
- Thirdly, support participants that have been in a relevant learning session, but have no way to re-access the content of the learning session once they go back to their organisation. (i.e. organisation & availability of resources)
- Fourthly, raise a very important barrier for increasing the efficiency of LNs, which is related to the difficulty of the individual members who participate in the learning sessions to pass the captured knowledge in the rest of the organisation.
- Finally, support members that join a LN at a certain time to benefit from previous learning that has taken place in the network, missing a valuable part of the learning trajectory.

This paper presents a conceptual model that has been developed for Learning Networks and outlines how the aforementioned objectives have been achieved by the Knowlaboration tool-set.

4. A conceptual model for Learning Networks

In order to understand the conceptual context of the Knowlaboration tool-set, a conceptual model has been developed presenting the key terms and assumptions employed. Based on literature review and findings from a market research of 20 LNs across Europe, LN activities take place at three different organisational levels (Figure 1):

- The first level is the level of a single actor (a company or an individual representing a company) taking part in the various activities of the network in order to satisfy some learning needs.
- The second level of analysis is the learning group, which represents the core of the learning network because it is where the actors commit themselves into the main learning activities.
- The third level is the learning network as a whole representing a dynamic entity, which reconfigures its processes and resources over time.

  Moreover, the key elements of a LN's infrastructure are identified as follows:

- Actors & roles: key actors that are typically involved in learning network processes, such as LN moderator / manager, learning group facilitators, LN members (these terms may vary among LNs) etc.
- Processes/ activities: the processes vital for learning & knowledge sharing. Four key processes are identified as vital in all learning networks: Decision Making Process, Collaborative Learning, Learning Dissemination and Harvesting Learning
- Resources: sources of information and material that are necessary for the performance of the network's processes
- Systems: methods of work and IT systems that currently support the network's operation & learning processes

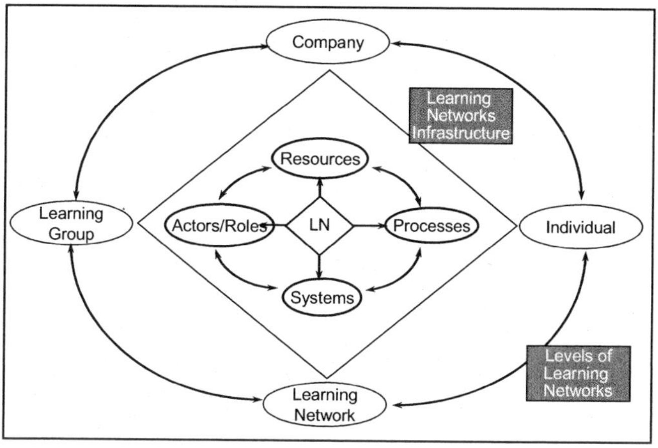

Figure 1: The Learning Network Conceptual Model

5. An IT Platform and a Supporting Methodology for Learning Networks

5.1 The Knowlaboration IT Platform

The Knowlaboration IT platform support all key elements of a LN - actors & roles, processes, resources and systems -, at all organisational levels of a network – individual, learning group, network.

In more detail, the Knowlaboration IT platform is designed to support the following key processes/activities of a Learning Network:

- Decision-making: the system supports decision-making through forums, chats and voting forums. For example network board members can create a private group area and take decisions through group forums & chats. Network members can also participate in decision making through voting forums. For example, the network moderator or a network member can suggest a new learning event. The network members post their votes for this suggestion and the system automatically generates the results.
- Collaborative learning: the Knowlaboration system supports collaborative learning by supporting both online learning sessions as well as offline/physical learning sessions (in this case the pre-session & post-session activities). The system enhances sharing of experiences, knowledge and resources through document management facilities, dynamic search, forums, chats, instant messaging, SMS, e-mail & /mailing lists.
- Learning dissemination: the Knowlaboration system supports the dissemination of learning and knowledge to the other network members as well as non-network members through the: network news section, network calendar (where events are published), forums, chats, instant messaging, sms, e-mail & /mailing lists.
- Harvesting learning: the Knowlaboration system supports the assessment of the learning impact on the network and its members with voting forums (as presented above) and an online evaluation tool through which the network moderator and group facilitators can post questions and see the aggregated results.

5.2 The Knowlaboration Methodology

The Knowlaboration methodology incorporates guidelines for deploying the Knowlaboration system in a LN. It intends to assist the external consultant, network manager or appointed change agent (within a LN) to plan and successfully deploy the

Knowlaboration system in a network. The Knowlaboration methodology is designed to be modular so that a network can choose to start at different levels depending on its readiness and requirements.

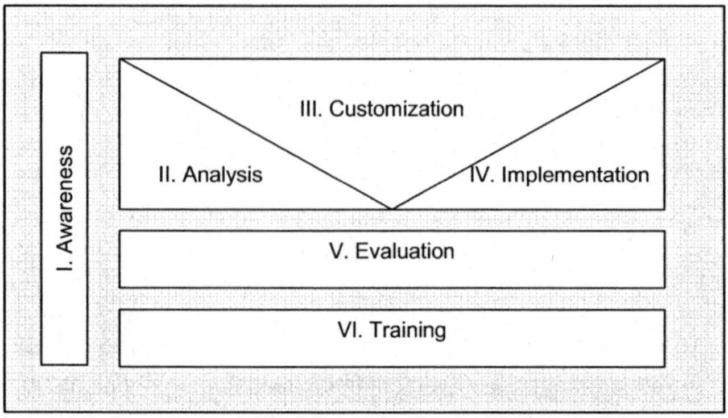

Figure 2: Phases of the Knowlaboration Methodology

The basic phases of the Knowlaboration methodology are the following:

- Phase I - Awareness & Understanding:. The main purpose of this starting phase is to create awareness and common understanding about the Knowlaboration toolkit and its value to Learning Networks.
- Phase II - Organisational Analysis: this is a critical preparatory phase for understanding the learning network's specific needs/requirements and its readiness to introduce the KLB system. This analysis is performed in terms of the network's processes and activities, structure, actors/ roles, resources and network learning culture.
- Phase III - Customization: The KLB system is customised based on the identified network needs and requirements derived from Phase II. Specifically, the system can be tailored to support the specific processes & activities of the Learning Network, its actors and roles.
- Phase IV - Implementation: this phase involves the deployment of the Knowlaboration system throughout the network. This deployment is carried out in a step-wise approach, starting from the pilot-use by a selected learning group within the network, and gradual roll-out throughout the network.
- Phase V - Training: the objective of this horizontally running phase is to provide a set of guidelines and pedagogical material aimed at facilitating the gradual and successful introduction of the concepts and tools developed in the Knowlaboration Project within a given Learning Network.
- Phase VI - Evaluation: the objective of this phase is to assess the impact of deploying the KLB system on the learning network. In other words, to assess the extent to which the system has facilitated the needs of the network.

6. Pilot-testing the Knowlaboration tool-set and lessons learned

In this section we will briefly describe the lessons learned from the pilot use of the Knowlaboration toolkit (platform and methodology) by an Austrian automotive cluster - ACStyria. Auto Cluster (AC) Styria, is a network of some 180 small to medium sized automotive suppliers in south central Austria who have come together to support the region and themselves. In what is essentially a classic inter-organizational learning model, ACstyria facilitates learning primarily through face-to-face meetings/sessions, in which knowledge exchange occurs primarily in an informal way (tacit to tacit knowledge). Moreover, ACStyria has created working/learning groups that group members by their major concerns (e.g. Controller Group, Quality Management Group, Future Factory club etc). These learning groups meet on a regular basis, in order to discuss a specific topic and exchange ideas.

In order to pilot test the Knowlaboration platform in the ACStyria network, the Controller Group was selected as a pilot case study. The Controller Group comprises of 15 members (each member is in the position of controller in their respective companies) and a Group Leader coordinates its activities. The group meets on a monthly basis, in order to solve problems of individual members through the transfer of knowledge among members. Occasionally experts are invited to present specific topics.

The Controller Group members used the online Knowlaboration platform for a period of three months. The platform supported the planning and evaluation of their monthly meetings/learning sessions mainly through the platform's dynamic calendar (that can make a link to meeting agendas and presentations), the news section, as well as the online forums. Specifically, the members used the platform in order to learn about forthcoming meetings, propose topics for a meeting and obtain meeting agendas. After a meeting took place, members had access to the presentations made during the meeting (from the documents library) and had the possibility to evaluate the meeting (through the online forums).

Main lessons learned from the pilot use of the Knowlaboration platform are as follows:

- The pilot group members used the platform mainly near (before and after) the scheduled group meetings took place in order to obtain relevant information. In other words, the Knowlaboration platform can effectively support the organization and planning of events.
- The platform offered effective communication tools (mass mailing lists, instant messages) for the Group leader as well as among group members.
- Another tool that met the needs of this group was the documents library functionality. The Group leader was able to publicise documents produced in the meetings (presentations etc) in an organized and easily accessible manner.
- On the other hand, the forum and chat functionalities did not become part of the users' daily "habits". Perhaps, this was due to the lack of time to invest in such activities or even the lack of interest to interact in an online manner.

The key lesson learned is that the Knowlaboration platform in order to be effectively deployed in a network has to meet the specific needs of the network. In some networks, certain aspects of the platform are destined to be used more or less than in another network. The crucial factor is to identify the specific needs of a network and customize the platform in a way that meets these.

7. Recommendations

From our experience and interaction with LNs in the Knowlaboration project we have derived a constructive set of recommendations for effectively deploying Information Technologies in LNs. These design principles are not recipes, but rather embody our understanding of how modern IT can help LNs.

The first recommendation highlights the need to support three main LN management processes: (i) The initiation phase that concerns itself with the setting up of the LN. The IT tools should provide a detailed checklist with potential network-initiators and mechanisms to identify the type of members that such a network would require. (ii) Facilities during the operation phase should monitor if the individual members can see benefits for themselves and their business and provide ways for measuring the impact of the IT tool on their individual learning as well as the improvement of the network. (iii) During the maintenance and improvement phase, IT tools should provide facilities to support the maintenance and growth of the network and member management facilities that will help users' integration in the main activities of the network. (e.g., synchronization of calendars). Other useful facilities aiming at promoting and marketing the network to relevant stakeholders include invitations, minutes of recent events and hot topics.

The second recommendation refers to the integration of the system with existing business processes. Participation in a LN usually competes with other priorities in the lives of members. It is crucial to make participation as easy and efficient as possible. IT tools should therefore make participation easy, provide time and attention management, through functionalities such as personalized knowledge/application portals, subscriptions, tours of new activities and archiving of interactions, integration with work systems.

The third recommendation clarifies that the LN system should address the issues of presence, visibility and motivation. Personal identities are a crucial aspect of participation. Members bring their identities to the community and their participation both develops and shapes their identities. IT can help with features such as member profiles, ranking and preferences and presence awareness. The use of personal profiles in the IT system can reveal relationships, support private interactions and interpersonal and mentoring relationships.

Fourthly, a LN should thrive to deliver value both to their members as well as to the stakeholders and the network as a whole. Preserving the time of experts within the network is for instance an important concern. The IT system should provide mechanisms for asking questions, lists of Frequently Asked Questions, databases of answers, intelligent access to experts and brainstorming facilities.

The value of belonging to a LN derives not only from having access to peers, but also from having access to the leading edge in the broader world. Therefore as a fifth recommendation, we stress the need for IT facilities that assist in the direction of providing connections to the world include: what is happening, what is hot in the field, new developments, new technologies, evaluation and reviews, external experts, reference material, news and announcements of external events, directory of external experts, links to other sites and library of references.

LNs usually have members who take an active role in cultivating the community and may participate in the decisions that affect the operation of the network. The sixth recommendation related to offering a variety of administrative tools to monitor and configure the use and effectiveness of the network space. Typical features of this kind include: logs and statistics for monitoring, polling and voting facilities, assessment tools and surveys, performance indicators.

8. Conclusions and further work

The main industrial significance of Knowlaboration is the offering of a holistic solution (system, practice guide and services) that supports in an integrated and methodical way the deployment and customisation of IT tools for the needs of learning networks. Eventual benefits of Knowlaboration can be summarized as follows:

- It provides integrated e-learning modules to develop higher-order skills of learning network participants.
- It enables networks to create online communities in a networked world where traditional communication methods based on proximity in terms of time and space may no longer be feasible or applicable.
- It combines functionalities that support learning, knowledge management, communication and decision-making, whereas other knowledge management and e-learning systems focus on one (or some of the above) feature.

- It enables broad member participation in decision-making processes, such as the planning and management of learning activities. Competitive systems do not support decision-making through broad member participation.

Regarding commercial exploitation of Knowlaboration, the initial focus will be on small and medium learning networks, with a pricing policy that takes into consideration the needs and limited resources of these networks. Provided a niche in this market segment is established by attracting a significant number of clients with relatively low risks, inter-organisational & corporate networks will be targeted, but at the same time further development will take place to accommodate their more complex needs and requirements. In order for Knowlaboration to be deployable in corporate networks, issues of interoperability with internal IT systems as well as ownership of content need to be effectively addressed. To this end we aim to make use of the latest Internet standards related to Web Services. Web Service technology can enable the Knowlaboration tool to offer controlled but open resource sharing especially in situations where we have to deal with well-defined and possibly structured knowledge sources. Indeed, in such cases the learning network architecture can be directly translated into a Web Services based distributed and decentralised infrastructure, where network partners are in control of their own resources and are given discretionary access to resources of other members.

References

[1] Wenger, E.; McDermott, R.; Snyder, W.: "Cultivating Communities of Practice"; Harvard Business School Press (2002).

[2] Bessant, J.; Francis, D.: "Using learning networks to help improve manufacturing competitiveness"; Technovation 19 (1999), 373–381.

[3] Project ION, EPSRC/UK 2000

[4] McGill, I. and S. Warner Weil (1989). Making sense of experiential learning. London, Open University Press.

[5] Revans, R. (1983). Action learning 2. Buckingham, G. Wills/ IMCB.
Angehrn, A.; Gibbert, M.; Nikolopoulou, K.: "Collaboraiton, Governance, and Technology in Inter-Organisational Learning Networks: Evidence from a Cross-Case Analysis"; Proc. 4th Triple Helix Conference (2002).

[6] Pedler, M., T. Boydell, et al. (1991). The learning company: A strategy for sustainable development. Maidenhead, McGraw-Hill.

[7] Best, M. (1990). The new competition. Oxford, Polity Press.

[8] Cook, S. and Seely Brown, J. (1999), Bridging Epistemologies: The Generative Dance Between Organisational Knowledge and Organisational Knowing, Organisation Science/, Vol. 10, No 4, July-August, pp.381-400.

[9] Nonaka, I. and Takeuchi, H., (1995), The Knowledge Creating Company, Oxford University Press

[10] Hines, P. (1994). Creating world class suppliers: Unlocking mutual competitive advantage. London, Pitman.

[11] Angehrn, A.; Nabeth, T.: "Leveraging Emerging Technologies in Management Education: Research and Experiences"; European Management Journal, 15, 3, 1997, 275-285.

---

[i] Action learning involves a group of managers facing broadly similar problems, who come together to discuss real life problems. Each group has a facilitator, whose job is to develop the group into a learning team so that managers learn primarily with and from each other -by reflecting on their own experiences- rather than from a professional educator.

Section 5

Networked, Smart & Virtual Organisations

Section 5.1

Issues

The Co-Existence of Communities of Practice and Virtual Organisations

Flavius STURM[1], Patricia WOLF[2]
Fraunhofer IAO, Nobelstraße 12, Stuttgart, 70569, Germany
[1]*Tel: +49 711 9702040, Fax: + 49 711 9702299, Email: flavius.sturm@iao.fraunhofer.de*
[2]*Tel: +49 711 9702096, Fax: + 49 711 9702299, Email: patricia.wolf@iao.fraunhofer.de*

Abstract: There are a significant number of publications treating the issue of collaboration in Communities of Practice (CoP). Simultaneously, there are a lot of activities in the area of collaboration in networked organisations, especially in Virtual Organisations (VO). The authors contend that looking at these two types of organisational forms, which have resembling elements, but are traditionally being looked at from different perspectives, delivers new insights into collaboration practices, especially from a Knowledge Management (KM) point of view. The underlying assumption is that the emergence of CoP can be considered to be a relatively new trend - but also a new challenge - within KM research, stressing especially its 'human-centered' aspects. Responding to this challenge, i.e. the purposeful creation and management of CoP, requires the consideration of a number of factors, which will be highlighted in this paper.

1. Introduction

The acceleration of business processes, new technological developments and the emergence of more information and knowledge-intensive markets has lead to new opportunities, but also to new requirements that organisations have to face. The emergence of networked structures goes hand in hand with this development as today's organisations can hardly respond to the new challenges on their own. Especially in fast-moving markets, organisations are forced to focus on their core assets (including knowledge) in order to maintain their competitiveness. Generally speaking, a stronger need for collaboration occurs, leading to a broad spectrum of multi-organisational constellations. Out of these different collaborative organisational forms, the Virtual Organisation (VO) and Communities of Practice (CoP) have gained substantial recognition in recent years.

Current management practices, however, do barely respond to the needs that arise from collaboration, whereas the authors contend that the increasing disaggregation of today's organisations with its emphasis on temporary co-operative arrangements will result in greater demands on all organisational levels. Looking closer at the collaboration processes, one will find that a central issue for network organisations - whose competitiveness is based on the existence of specific knowledge and competencies - is the one of sharing knowledge.

So far, the potential risks associated to knowledge transformation and transfer in a network context have been largely excluded in KM research. As tacit knowledge is transformed into explicit knowledge, it becomes vulnerable to replication, implying a potential loss of a firm's competitive advantage. The dilemma for KM on an inter-organisational level now becomes obvious: A naive attempt to share knowledge could threaten an organisation's knowledge advantage, yet the level of network performance, in turn, depends on the amount and quality of information and knowledge exchange.

While researchers tend to focus on discovering the KM practices within a specific organisational form, for instance in VO, they run the risk of overlooking alternate and complementary forms of knowledge exchange. In a networked economy, individuals are often part of more than one organisational form and a thoughtful combination of different collaborative organisational forms, in this case VO and CoP, can compensate for any shortcomings a particular organisation has. A thoughtful consideration of collaboration options is therefore necessary to exploit the full problem-solving potential that collaborative networks offer. We expect insights from this paper to be useful for practitioners that deal with organisational design as well as competence and business development.

2. Objectives and Methodology

This paper aims at clarifying the relationship between CoP and VO from a KM perspective. It will show that CoP represent an option for the conservation and further development of knowledge that is created in other organisational contexts. The creation and maintenance of CoP, however, requires a substantial amount of efforts and hence needs to be managed consciously. Some insights on the barriers and enablers that are critical for creating and running CoP will be highlighted, based on the investigation of two particular cases:

- The "KnowledgeBoard" Community, to date Europe's largest KM community, built up and supported by the IST Project "European Knowledge Management Forum",
- The "cross-functional CoP" at DaimlerChrysler, which were subject of a PhD study.

3. Theoretical Background and Case Description

3.1 Virtual Organisations from a Knowledge Management Perspective

As VO are being researched by a number of different disciplines, definitions of VO vary strongly (Sabeel et al. 2002). However, they "can be understood as a special form of a network community" (Kahler/Rittenbruch 1997). In order to distinguish VO from other organisational forms, researchers tend to agree that a typical VO is

- an alliance of legally independent firms, mostly SME,
- that come together for a limited period of time to share their resources in order exploit a specific market opportunity and,
- as they are often geographically dispersed, they coordinate and communicate using ICT.

The essential challenge for a VO is to master the flexible aggregation of individual competencies to such an extent that it remains competitive. A specific danger for organisations involved in VO is the protection of their core assets (especially their specific knowledge), as these represent their individual source of competitiveness. Once these specific assets are absorbed by a certain partner within the VO, this partner could exploit the newly acquired skills in a future VO venture and substitute the originator. However, the creation of complex products and services requires the sharing and transfer of information along the value chain. Until now, few researchers have tackled the management of information and knowledge in a collaborative context and especially in virtual organisations (e.g. Bosch-Sijtsema 2002, Becker 1999, Buxmann 2001, Malhotra 2000, Mertens/Faisst 1998, Weissenberger-Eibl 2000). As Schmalz/ Hagenhoff point out along a KM process model ranging from knowledge identification to knowledge conservation, knowledge management within a network of independent companies has to overcome substantial hurdles along all process stages. These hurdles are not only related technical problems (e.g. integration of different standards and applications), but also to managerial issues (e.g. the potential loss of competitive advantage). BOSCH-SIJTSEMA shows that the lack of physical proximity and personal contact in VO is a major reason for the lack of knowledge transfer. In an investigation on learning within VO, STEIL/BARCIA/PACHECO conclude that the degree of knowledge sharing is strongly related to the dominant organisational culture. Intensive socialisation techniques (e.g. story-telling), that bring together all VO members, are necessary to create the required ambiance for knowledge exchange. As a result, knowledge exchange within VO is likely to remain a time-consuming issue that cannot be resolved with generic recommendations, but is subject to individual solutions.

Apart from the question how knowledge is managed during the lifecycle of a VO, there is also a growing interest in the destination of the commonly created knowledge after a VO is dissolved. Typically, large companies have a standardised process for finishing bigger projects, in which they document project outcomes. These findings are a valuable factor for the design of future projects, especially consulting companies are known to be eager to capture this type of knowledge. For VO, there doesn't exist an equivalent institution or procedure yet, a factor that – not only from a macro-economic point of view - can be a disadvantage since this knowledge won't be at the disposal of future VO.

3.2 Communities of Practice and Business Benefits with regard to Knowledge Exchange

Looking at the KM issues VO have to deal with, it seems that the lack of re-use of generated knowledge is a challenge for networked organisations and that even large networks such as regional clusters, for instance, could strongly benefit from the avoidance of knowledge loss. As the previous paragraph has shown, the "KM dilemma" of the VO is rooted in its very nature, hence it is seems to be promising to look for alternate forms of inter-organisational knowledge exchange. In this respect, the authors contend that local and virtual Communities of Practice (CoP) can be a deliberate means for KM, not only for addressing the potential loss of knowledge after collaboration, but also for enhancing existing knowledge and for the initiation of new collaborative projects.

CoP have been defined as "[…] informal groups of people bound by a shared practice related to a set of problems" (Snyder and Wenger 1999). The members of a CoP typically solve problems, discuss insights and share information. They mentor and coach each other, generate plans for future activities and develop shared knowledge frameworks as well as methods and tools for solving common problems. Over time, these mutual relationships enable CoP members to define certain forms of interaction and develop a sense of identity.

In fact, CoP are quite similar to VO: For good collaboration, they require mutual trust, a manager takes care of interaction and communication, and they usually use ICT tools for communication purposes and have a dynamic structure (Wolf/Wunram/Vallejos 2004). The difference between these two collaborative forms is that they have essentially different, but complementary objectives: Whereas VO put the emphasis on reaching a commonly defined goal, namely the provision of a product or service within a limited period of time, CoP tend to aim at continuously enhancing individual and organisational capabilities.

Despite the relatively short research period spent on CoP, they have already proven to be an efficient instrument to support cross functional knowledge sharing and collaboration in organisations. This insight seems to be common sense among CEOs and members of management boards: The World Bank characterised its so-called 'Thematic Groups' as "[…] the heart and soul of World Bank Knowledge Sharing" Lessner and Prusak, 1999), and Dr. Josef Hofer-Alfeis, Senior Consultant in Knowledge Management at Siemens, stated "CoPs are the heart of KM systems" (Hofer-Alfeis 2002). The cross-functional CoP that DaimlerChrysler implemented two years ago have been one of the most important driver for organisational learning. They empowered the organisation to help each other solving cross functional problems and to coordinate activities and decisions (Wolf 2003). They soon delivered perceivable business benefits, as they helped

- to avoid redundancies and double work by making use of synergies,
- to build expertise for the organisation in critical knowledge areas,
- to save time, e.g. through providing access to available knowledge and experts,
- to keep up with latest ideas and technology developments,

- to enable the CoP members to build skills, relationships and reputation by
  - providing opportunities for experts to connect across the network,
  - inviting newcomers to participate in expert discussions,
  - making recommendations for formal trainings and promotions.

With regard to the sharing of knowledge in collaborations, it is important to recognise that CoP do not only support knowledge sharing within single organisations, they are also wide-spread as professional networks evolving around a specific topic of interest. Such professional networks are common in professions that use a lot of ICT, such as developers.

The KnowledgeBoard (www.knowledgeboard.com) is an example of a virtual thematic CoP: Developed by the EC funded project "European Knowledge Management Forum" in January 2001, the goal was to build a pan-European web based platform to distribute, share and integrate lessons learned and best practices concerning KM, to establish a network of experts from different branches, to define common European KM standards in terms of terminology, methods, concepts etc., as well as to stimulate the building of a European KM-Community. The KM community accepted the KnowledgeBoard (KB) very quickly as community platform, with c. 6000 registered users presenting, exchanging and discussing their knowledge and KM case studies in 26 Special Interest Groups and Language Zones.

The results of the latest KnowledgeBoard member survey (February/March 2004) underline the importance of the knowledge sharing facilitation provided by KB: 70 persons answered to the survey and stated that they use the KB primarily as a platform for sharing knowledge. This helps them to learn from other users (66%) and to get useful feedback (26%). Interaction on the KB usually happens around articles and presentations that feature other research projects or individual research interests related to KM. 33% of the users have published one or more articles, whereas 48% haven't done so, but would like to do it.

Over 50% of the survey participants feel they receive a perceivable benefit from KB, even though it is entirely based on voluntary contributions. Only 9% of all survey participants have the impression of giving more than they get in return. In addition, users seem to succeed in building relationships among each other. 60% of the users know at least three other KB users and almost half of the participants have already collaborated with other KB users in some way. Experience even shows that several new research projects have been initiated after users had found other individuals with common interests.

3.3 Critical Success Factors and Pitfalls for CoP Creation and Development

There are many general critical success factors in the implementation and development of Communities of Practice. According to Snyder and Wenger (1999), who were also involved in the CoP creation at DaimlerChrysler, the most important requirements are:

- A CoP needs to create value for both members and the organisation
- A CoP needs leadership that appreciates the nuances
- A CoP must be supported by an energetic core group
- The CoP members need enough interaction to build relationships
- Participation and contribution in a CoP has to be recognised at an organisational level.
- The organisation needs to build up a culture that promotes initiative and collaboration to build expertise

Concerning the pitfalls of CoP, SNYDER/WENGER (Snyder and Wenger 1999) consider the following point as the biggest mistakes:

- To start with technology and documentation before convening the community
- To give the task of documenting the knowledge to outsiders
- To underestimate the skill and effort required to realise the potential of a community
- Members do not see concrete value in their CoP work

- Insufficient attention to community leadership and performance problems

Another important pitfall is to underestimate the role language plays. As CoP are basically driven by communication, the need for integration and personal contacts requires a language spoken and written by all Community members. There is no common way to overcome language barriers (Wolf et al. 2003). In an interview, WENGER (Wolf 10/2003) tackled the problem of the language, which is a very big issue in global, international communities. He stated "the only solution that seems to work is the same as the solution addressing size: sub-groups connected by brokers". Brokers shouldn't translate everything, but they can convey the most important elements. Making English the official language is a solution chosen by a lot of organisations, but it tends to marginalize certain participants.

Successful CoP are bringing a real value to the organisation, yet they need a lot of support. These insights are especially crucial for virtual CoP: At the KnowledgeBoard (KB), one of the most important co-operation supporting feature is the discussion forum facilitated by moderators. These moderators are the so-called Special Interest Group (SIG) leaders, professional volunteers who are enthusiastic enough to tackle the issues in their KM area of interest for free. The facilitation has been characterized as 'just right' by most of the participants (83%). Without the facilitation and guidance of the SIG editors, the KnowledgeBoard would have been a virtual but no vital Community of Practice.

Looking at the group of KB users who do not participate in the discussions, there are various reasons for their hesitance: First of all, discussions sometimes seem to be "too high level", which makes participants not confident enough to participate (48%). For virtual collaboration this implies that especially a virtual CoP needs to stimulate its members by ensuring that discussions are striking the right note, while keeping a high level of quality.

4. Results

The performance of virtual CoP depends on a variety of different factors and requires the consideration of a few pitfalls, which can put the CoP to an early end. The main results drawn from our observations are:

- (Virtual) CoP can be used as an additional deliberate means for KM. With regard to knowledge conservation, CoP seem to have the potential to serve as a bridging element to address inefficiencies of other transient organisational structures (such as the Virtual Organisation) through the provision of an organisational framework, in which knowledge can be stored and transferred through simple written or oral conversations.
- (Virtual) CoP are not only a source of knowledge, but also a place where knowledge is transformed and "up-dated". The posting of articles on KnowledgeBoard usually results in discussion, and authors will get constructive feed-back. It was observed that Special Interest Groups lead to the initiation of new projects and new knowledge creation.
- A step-wise approach seems to be necessary to create an ambience that motivates community members to contribute to the (virtual) community. It is necessary to look closely at different stages that lead to the creation of trust and identity, prerequisites for successful virtual CoP. A number of issues have been identified as pitfalls (e.g. language) and critical success factors (e.g. to start with a critical mass of active community members).

5. Conclusions

By comparing Virtual Organisations and Communities of Practice with regard to their effectiveness concerning knowledge exchange, the authors have contributed to a clearer positioning of these two prominent networked organisational forms from a KM point of view. It was shown that knowledge and information exchange is a prerequisite for a high performance of these two organisational forms and that both face challenges if they want to implement KM practices. Apparently, knowledge exchange is an especially delicate issue in VO due to the potential loss of competitive advantage for VO members. This doesn't mean that knowledge creation and transfer has slowed down in general, but it seems that new channels are and mechanisms are more adequate for these purposes. The example of the KnowledgeBoard has shown that a CoP can tremendously facilitate cross-organisational knowledge exchange in several respects through the implementation of relatively simple communication mechanisms, if the pitfalls for CoP creation and management are avoided.

CoP are just one way to support knowledge exchange. As mentioned earlier, the emergence of the "knowledge economy" goes hand in hand with new organisational forms and new KM measures. Inter-organisational collaboration is likely to give KM a boost, as individuals will increasingly be part of several organisational structures, partly virtual and local and partly formal and informal. Consciously fostering and designing such networked structures, while knowing their strengths and limitations, will continue to be a growing research field, as well as a distinct (knowledge) management task for the years to come.

References

[1] Becker, C.(1999): Informationsmanagement innerhalb der Lebenszyklus-Phasen des virtuellen Unternehmens, Würzburg

[2] Buxmann, P.(2001): Informationsmanagement in vernetzten Unternehmen: Wirtschaftlichkeit, Organisationsänderungen und der Erfolgsfaktor Zeit, Wiesbaden

[3] Bosch-Sijtsema, P.M. (2002), Knowledge Management in Virtual Organisations: Interorganisational and interproject knowledge transfer, presented at the Organizational Knowledge, Learning and Capabilities Conference 2002

[4] Hofer-Alfeis J. (2002): "Knowledge for Success": Knowledge Management at Siemens - Overview, Presentation at the Siemens Workshop on Knowledge Management for the KnowledgeBoard theme 1 "What business problems can you solve with KM?", Munich http://www.knowledgeboard.com/doclibrary/knowledgeboard/intro_j_hofer_alfeis.pdf, last visited on 02.04.2004

[5] KnowledgeBoard 2.0 Team, KnowledgeBoard member survey, online available at http://www.knowledgeboard.com/survey/, last visited 30.04.2004

[6] Lessner E.; Prusak, L. (1999): Communities of Practice, Social Capital and Organizational Knowledge, White Paper, online available at http://openacademy.mindef.gov.sg/OpenAcademy/Central/HTML%20Folder/KM/bcp/downloads/copsc3.pdf, last visited 02.04.2004

[7] Malhotra, Y.(2000): Knowledge management and virtual organizations, Hershey, PA

Mertens, P.; Faisst, W.(1998): Virtuelle Unternehmen und Informationsverarbeitung, Berlin

[8] Probst, G.; Raub, S.; Romhardt, K. (1999): Wissen managen: Wie Unternehmen ihre wertvollste Ressource optimal nutzen, Frankfurt/Main.

[9] Saabeel, W., Verduijn, T.M.; Hagdorn, L.; Kumar, K.(2002): A model of virtual organisation: A structure and process perspective, in Electronic Journal for Organizational Virtualness, Vol.4, No.1, www.virtual-organization.net/files/articles/Saabeel-Verduijn-2002.pdf, last visited on 28.04.2004

[10] Schmaltz, R.; Hagenhoff, S. (2003): Wissensmanagement in unternehmens-übergreifenden Kooperationen, Arbeitsbericht 09/2003, Universität Göttingen, Göttingen

[11] Snyder, W.; Wenger, E. (1999): Communities of Practice. Lessons learned from Auburn Hills. DaimlerChrysler Corporate University, Stuttgart

[12] Steil, A. V., Barcia, R. M., Pacheco, R. C. S. (1999): An Approach to Learning in Virtual Organizations. In: Organizational Virtualness and Eletronic Commerce ed.Berlin, pp. 67-85., Bern

[13] Wolf, P. (2003): Erfolgsmessung der Einführung von Wissensmanagement. Eine Evaluationsstudie im Projekt „Knowledge Management" der Mercedes-Benz Pkw-Entwicklung der DaimlerChrysler AG, Münster

[14] Wolf, P. (10/2003): Interview with Etienne Wenger on Communities of Practice, Interview for the KnowledgeBoard theme 8 "Communities of Practice and other networked organisations – How to organise our work and life", http://www.knowledgeboard.com/cgi-bin/item.cgi?ap=1&id=119473&d=pnd&dateformat=%25o-%25B, last visited on 02.04.2004.

[15] Wunram, M.; Wolf, P.(2003): Barriers to KM between Organisational Cultures in the Face of Concurrent Enterprising: How to Overcome them?; in: Proceedings of ProVE 2003, Lugano

[16] Wunram, M., Wolf, P.; Vallejos, R.V.(2004): Uncovering the difference: Management of Collaboration in Communities of Practice and in Virtual Enterprises/Virtual Organisations, Presentation at ICE Conference 2004 Seville, Spain

Building Knowledge Driven and Dynamically Networked Communities within European Healthcare Systems

Silvia BETTONI[2], Lara GADDA[1], Valentina PERDONI[2], Alberto SAVOLDELLI[1]
[1]Politecnico di Milano, 20133 Milano, Piazza Leonardo da Vinci 32, Italy
[2]Fondazione IARD, 20123 Milano, via Soncino 1, Italy

Abstract: Medical errors and diagnostic and therapeutic risk management are critical issues in the European healthcare system. A national health information infrastructure is needed to provide immediate access to complete patient information and decision support tools for healthcare professionals. Capturing patient safety information as a by-product of care will make it possible to design even safer delivery systems. Better management of health information is a prerequisite to achieve patient safety as a standard of care: this represents the main pillar on which the researches presented in this paper will be based. This paper aims at elaborating a new approach to diagnostic and therapeutic risk management in healthcare by building knowledge driven & dynamically adaptive networked communities within European healthcare systems. The goal is to create a system that both prevents errors and learns from them when they occur. The starting point is a multi-directional investigation of healthcare in Europe, focusing on four specific areas that will serve as Pilot Context. Even if the research is conducted in different ambits (technological, socio-economical, demonstration activities), the crucial part is the unification of these different visions under a single and complete approach to the risk management. The consortium of research centres and technology partners will focus on analysis of the knowledge supporting the health care professional's work process and the associated procedures and human factors connected with the risk event deepening the studies already carried out. These results will then be merged in order to start at defining, which are the main features and peculiarities of a knowledge driven & dynamically adaptive networked communities within European healthcare systems.

1. Introduction

Medical error is one of the most important issues in the European healthcare system to be faced in the coming years. As a matter of fact, a lot of effort has been invested in the healthcare system in the areas of prevention and non-intrusive treatments.

Risk management for a healthcare professional is related to their responsibilities in patient diagnosis and treatment processes. The growth of patient judgment autonomy and the level of information, together with the assessment of cost/benefit before deciding intervention actions, are three important factors that force the healthcare professional to pay much more attention in providing the right answer to the patient problem [1].

The increase in the last 5 years of both juridical trials (ten fold), and the healthcare insurance costs for the HC professional, in the measure of (five fold) [2], for covering medical error effects, are important indicators of the scale of the problem at European level.

The side effects of this problem consist of [3]:

- increasing the cost for the patient in all care processes (diagnosis; treatment; intervention); in fact a medical error could bring the patient in paying for more diagnosis, for longer treatment, for not required intervention;

- increasing the cost of the social healthcare system for the local authorities as well as for the national government and the EU – more longer the patient stays in the care process, more cost the public authorities in general have to pay;
- increasing external impact. For example the longer a patient stays in care, the less time he can dedicate to employment activities, his family or even personal hobbies.

The enabling technology, the healthcare professionals association forms as well as treatment and diagnosis methodology are not enough for bridging the gap; every day European citizens live with the risk of medical error, misdiagnosis or mistreatment.

Those of us who live in wealthy countries with well-developed medical services generally assume that medical problems will be dealt with promptly and effectively. Up to now, most of us were looking forward to continuing improvements in this art as scientific understanding of diseases and their management continued to grow rapidly, and expected this to get a further stimulus with the explosion of new knowledge in the post-genomic era.

Unfortunately, the provision of top quality care is not uniform, even in wealthy societies, and the unprecedented growth in our understanding of diseases and their management is not matched by equivalent abilities to apply that knowledge in practice. The main reasons for these problems are lack of uniform access to new knowledge, and insufficient resources to deliver its benefits to all.

Socio-economic and organizational factors are a primary cause of unequal access to the best medical care. In modern, science-based medicine, the traditional process of care - one clinician looking after one patient - is being replaced by one in which the patient is managed by a multidisciplinary team of health care professionals, such as oncologists and cardiologists working with general practitioners and home-care nurses [4]. The effectiveness of such shared care depends on the ability to share patient specific information and medical knowledge among care providers. It is widely recognized that the inability to coordinate information and services across organizations represents one of the major impediments to quality care and that we need to take a more process-oriented view of health care delivery with appropriate organizational and information infrastructures.

One solution is to increase the knowledge of healthcare professionals facing diagnostic and therapeutic risk. It is necessary to develop a specific method in order to enhance healthcare professionals' knowledge, performance and efficiency [5]. Technological innovation and web-oriented technology are the necessary starting point for developing an innovative toolset for healthcare risk management.

The aim of this paper is to show the main results of the new organisational and technical methods for risk and knowledge management to be developed by the COCOON Integrated Project co-funded under the IST programme, which aims to define a new approach to diagnostic and therapeutic risk management in healthcare by supporting knowledge driven collaborative practices in Networks of Healthcare Professionals. The goal is to minimise medical errors in diagnosis and treatment and raising quality of care.

2. The new approach to the diagnostic and therapeutic risk management

The new approach to the diagnostic and therapeutic risk management is guided by four factors [6]: low capacity for sharing experience due to the lack of methodological uniformity in identification and measurement, low confidentiality of data due to the fear of professional liability, weak information system and limited understanding and knowledge of the epidemiology of adverse events – frequency of occurrence, causes, determinants and impact on patient outcomes, and of effective method for preventing them.

A large part of the literature about risk management deals with the analysis of the factors that contribute to errors [7]. A general consensus does not exist due to the lack of a standardised taxonomy for reporting adverse event, errors and risk factors. An interesting taxonomy is related to the activity in which an error occurs distinguishing among diagnostic error, treatment error, preventive error, or other errors [8].

Preventing errors means redesigning the healthcare system at all levels to make it safer. Not enough is known about what errors are occurring, the causes of those errors, the processes or procedures that can be changed to improve safety, and what actions can be taken by the public, purchasers and others to raise performance expectations for providers and healthcare systems [9]. It is critical to analyse different components of the problem including root causes, informatics, role of human factors, role of the healthcare institutions.

Human factors require study of the interrelationships between humans, the tools they use, and the environment in which they live and work. It is important to understand where and why systems or processes break down. This approach starts by examining the role of General Practitioners as the first medical contact within the health care system, dealing with all the health problems of clients regardless of age, sex, or other characteristics. As such, they are exposed to diagnostic and therapeutic risk. It continues by looking at causes of errors (e.g. circumstances, conditions, associated procedures and devices and other factors).

The goal is to support the GPs in avoiding "system errors" by providing them with a new methodology of work focused on the following philosophies:

- **Patient centred medicine**. The concept and it's ethical foundations are closely related to humanistic psychology and the person-centred therapy [10] .The traditional, one-dimensional biomedical paradigm must be replaced by a new, patient centred, bio-psycho-social paradigm [11]. Doctors classified as having a patient-centred style tend to be the most flexible. They focus almost exclusively on description and classification of physical symptoms to reach a diagnosis and prescribe appropriate treatment.
- **Evidence-Based Medicine**: the aim of the EBM is to encourage clinicians to make decisions that are fully informed by available scientific knowledge. The main methodology of EBM is regularly carry out and publish rigorous and comprehensive reviews of international clinical research, setting out recommended clinical practice together with the justification for those recommendations [12]. While EBM represents a vital contribution to improving the consistency and quality of care, as it depends on traditional methods of disseminating medical knowledge, it risks adding to the already intolerable burden of information on doctors and other healthcare professionals. The technological research aim at creating a platform for sharing new specific knowledge, creating a statistical dynamically adaptive system dedicated to the patient profiling which will help physicians in performing the best possible service for their patients at the right time. The advantage is that the doctor can compare the data of his patient with the ones stored in the this system and can add new and better information; thanks to the push modality is the system itself which alerts the GPs about the new available information.
- **Clinical governance** is a framework making HC organisations accountable for continuously improving the quality and safety of local health services and promoting excellence in patient care [13]. The socio-economic researches of the project will approach the clinical governance issue by analysing the following:
    - Managing risks: Providing systems, processes and procedures to ensure diagnosis monitor and minimise the risks to patients and to learn from mistakes.
    - Clinical audit: Regular systematic review of procedures to address any problems.
    - Use of information: the approach to the collection and interpretation of clinical information and its use, to monitor, plan and improve the quality of patient care.
    - Education, training and continuing professional development: this aspect covers the support available to enable staff to be competent in doing their jobs.
    - Clinical effectiveness: Ensuring approaches and treatments used are appropriate.

- **The use of Information Technology** is widely expected to make a vital contribution to helping doctors and other medical professionals. New information technologies include:
  - Electronic patient records: up to date, easier to access, more complete than paper;
  - Standardized medical terminologies and languages;
  - Methods and tools to support faster dissemination of new understanding of diseases;
  - Timely, reliable methods and tools to support team communication & coordination.

By themselves, these technologies do not directly help in the retrieval and application of the right knowledge at the right time with the right result. The technological research of the project define models and tools able to become the medical knowledge available for the professional of the healthcare sector, due to the use of a push driven modality, so taking into consideration individual and specific needs of the single healthcare professionals.

This new approach to the risk management will reduce the direct and indirect costs related to medical errors and increase efficiency by reducing "backend" administrative tasks, redundant laboratory tests, enhancing the safety in drug prescription and dosing, the effectiveness of intervention and thus positively influence the quality of medical care.

The development of IT infrastructures is essential to improve the safety of the safety of the healthcare system. Computer-based reminder systems for patients and HC professionals can improve compliance with preventive service protocol [14]. The availability of complete patient health information at the point of care delivery, along with clinical decision support system can reduce human error. Computer assisted diagnosis and treatment management programs can improve clinical decision-making and adherence to clinical guidelines.

3. The methodology and proof of concept approach

The methodology used is very similar to those for software design, based on the users early involvement and the continuous enhancement of the existing technologies, through an inter-disciplinary approach. The methodology will be divided in the following steps:

- concept - specification: conceptual models and basic methods relevant to the Research area are addressed at this level through an inter-disciplinary approach. Results will be supported by early prototypes implementing possible approaches for experiments. Socio economic research will provide input as well user requirements analysis;
- early development: as a proof of concept of the research direction activities an early prototype will be developed and tested within the main pilot site (Lombardy, Aquitaine, Epirus, European Medical Association). This represents the core of the research since the users requirements have to be necessarily gathered on field. An AS IS Analysis of the situation existing within the different healthcare system involved in the Demonstration actions carried out in the four Pilot contexts was performed. This step enable to recognise which are the common needs of these organisation, to build a complete picture of the environment and to define a restricted area in which the model will be firstly applied and tested. From this analysis, it will be possible to elaborate some TO BE Situations for the Pilot Contexts, which will represent the starting point for the creation of a more general paradigm of reference.
- concept improvement, in parallel with the toolset development will be maintained a certain attention on the foundational research directions. The goal is to highlight possible improvements of the risk management concept that arise;
- proof of concept improvement development: for any possible concept improvement a proof of concept will be organised. These proof of concept will be tested in the field trials and the most promising will be included in the toolset refinement. Each level will be addressed through a first stage of studies followed by a second validation stage aiming at integrating into the research feedback from users.

4. The System Architecture

To support the diversity of networked communities foreseeable in healthcare, the technological perspective of the research unfolds on the applicability of the community of practice mechanisms to HC professionals to achieve two scientific objectives. The first consists of assessing risk management processes in the variety of healthcare network, defining "Community and Knowledge Management" models and tools for supporting healthcare professionals in their daily practices, reducing risks of medical errors. The second objective is defining decision support methods for implementing the most adequate "Community and Knowledge Management" practices in a given healthcare network.

In this framework a careful set of studies on the field of risk management process will be carried out. One of the most challenging technical questions the technological research will face is the set-up of an efficient architecture able of guarantee the main mission of this project "providing the right information to the right place at the right time to the right person". This impacts on the overall architecture because it implies three basic concepts:

- quality of Service (avoid bottle necks and maintain high uptime statistics);
- trace-ability of the end-users (multi-modal access to information);
- correct classification of information (web ontology, smart search engines).

The most important element on which COCOON will be based is its Infrastructure. On top of services offered by this Infrastructure, it will be built all the knowledge related services, collecting information from already existing peers, nodes, which are the real knowledge repositories, which integration is the COCOON target. The figure below gives the vision of how Smart Search Engines, K.M. Services, and Multi-channel delivery are connected to the Infrastructure and knowledge repositories.

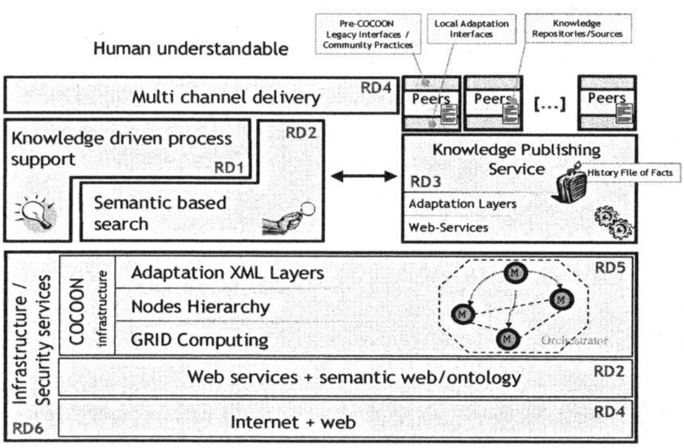

Figure 1: Overall Vision of how the different Technologies will be used in COCOON

The knowledge is built through the connection of different levels, each one giving more information, deriving from a larger collection of data sources. In this vision a shared structure of collaborating peers and the semantic/ontology information will help to make results extremely effective and to reduce the number of false results.

In the following table the six RDs are explained in terms of metrics and measurable objectives; state of the art [15] and expected progress made by COCOON researches.

RD	Metrics for the measurable objectives	State-of-the-art in the area concerned	Progress beyond current state of the art
1. Knowledge driven process support	Evaluation test of system knowledge support related to human critical building of knowledge, through relevance matching	**Content organization** (taxonomy/ontology) via attribute and metadata management. **Search & Retrieve** engines, **Patterns recognition, Profiling**	Dynamic of the web service mutual understanding, related to interoperability of tagging, automatic taxonomy generation improvement and pattern recognition.
2. Semantic based search & semantic interoperability	Full interoperability test and evaluation of functional semantic layer over inferential search engine through smart search operating test	**Web-Services, GRID Computing, Web-Semantics/Ontology and the Personalization of Internet Services**	Harmonization of most used protocols, letting their semantics to be integrated into a unique architecture
3. Knowledge publishing service	Test of the retrieval middleware NLU based and analysis of matching on the expected knowledge	**Semantic interoperability standards** (web services standards, RDF)	An ontology management system (OMS) able to 'translate' the user's intention (natural language input) to the expert's system expectation.
4. Multi—channel delivery	Full access test coherent with the actual state of the art	**Full devices range over WPAN ,WLAN, WWAN, related access architectures and standards**	Improve open wide network access through full development of devices capabilities and optimization
5. Decision support systems for risk management	Benchmark on the functional features on the three levels (research, technology and integration)	**DSS core structure that is related inference engine standards**	Development of a completely modular, standards-based medical Decision Support System based on an automated learning process
6. Security Research and Security Technological Research	Test on security middleware using common attack strategies	Password synchronizing, SSO,restoring password, PKI, smart cards, biometric, VPN, RC4/WEP, DSSS, Network name, ACL , RBAC	Realization of a full integrated security system over the business processes

Table 1: State of the art of the main technological researches

5. The main benefits for the healthcare sector

The adoption of the COCOON solution will improve the efficiency and cost effectiveness of the European HC system. Adverse events directly affect patient outcomes and indirectly impact upon healthcare budgets.

Patients will be able to decrease the number of contacts necessary in arranging care services and avoid repeating unnecessary medical examinations, thus reducing costs, time and effort spent for healthcare services that requires cross-sectors communication.

By providing health care professionals with a medical decision support toolset, the proposed solution will reduce "backend" administrative tasks, redundant laboratory tests, enhance safety in drug prescription and dosing, the effectiveness of intervention, thus improving the quality of medical care. Wide adoption will dramatically contain the cost of medical malpractice insurance, which since 2000, has consistently risen [16]. Related premiums contribute about 1 percent to the overall cost of health care.

The aim of the project to minimize health care professionals' risk of medical errors in their daily practices, can have an enormous impact on the welfare of the addressed community by rising the quality of care and minimize the events of medical malpractice.

Within the changing scenario of the Heath Care system, COCOON may help physicians in adapting to those transformations. Sharing new specific knowledge will help physicians in performing the best possible service for their patients in a cost effective way.

Finally, the COCOON project will create a statistical system, dedicated to patient and healthcare professional profiling as well as the least 100 new protocols on different more frequent pathologies definition (in particular for cardiopathies; abdominal pain, cess to pain, lumbar pain, headache, migraine; allergy test; dizziness; fatigue; viral diseases; skin problems), accepted and recognised by the most important health care associations.

6. Business Benefits: exploitation strategy

Commercialisation will be focused on prototypes produced within the project. All prototypes will be used as basic elements to develop and produce marketable results: as in-house developments by each partner and in collaboration with project partners. A quick process of research transfer in production will provide Consortium partners with competitive advantage for a further consolidation of the respective positions on the market. The specific techniques implemented in the project will be used by most of the Partners to enhance the techniques already in use, contributing to consolidate a competitive advantage.

The use and exploitation of project results will be ensured inside and outside project Consortium, following two axes of use and expansion.

6.1 Internal use:

The strong commitment of industrial partners to deployment and exploitation of results is testified by the fact that COCOON pursuit objectives are fully compliant with their organisational strategies and planned activities.

The Regions, clinical operators and Multiplier partners are deeply interested in take up and extracting the most from the developed solution. All those actors are implementing innovation plans focused on addressing problems to which COCOON can give a proper solution or are giving priority to the specific objectives our research is addressing.

6.2 External expansion:

The industrial partners are very credible, and their international business relationships increase the opportunity to promote international take up of the COCOON solution. The project partnership offers the potential to achieve market penetration across Europe.

In this framework, a three-phase strategy has been planned for the development and commercialisation of COCOON products and researches:

- in a *first* phase, on a national basis, each industrial partner will exploit the researches starting from the developed prototypes in its own industrial association, enlarging then the market base to reach the whole national market.
- in a *second* phase, still on a national basis, each industrial partner will extend their market segment by taking into consideration the work done by the other partners, namely, the specialisation of the pilots developed by the other partners.
- In the *third* phase, partners will offer services on a European basis. It is foreseen that this phase can start only and will depend on:
    - commercial results obtained in the national market;
    - support from the other industrial partners in the Consortium through the creation of a joint venture for this specific purpose.

7. Conclusion

The innovation of the research of the COCOON project consists of supporting knowledge driven collaborative practices in Networks of Healthcare Professionals in dealing efficiently with complex case, in order to minimize medical errors in diagnosis and treatment and raising quality of care and to join knowledge driven and dynamically adaptive learning communities in which healthcare professionals and citizens are fully knowledge driven in taking promptly the best possible decision for prevention, diagnosis and treatment. The research goal consists of increasing collaborative practices amongst the healthcare communities, supporting knowledge sharing and transfer. This should be one of the major evolutions that characterises healthcare in Europe in the coming future [17]. The rationale is that since healthcare is the archetype of a knowledge intensive sector, providing the right information to the right place at the right time to the right persons is a critical quality factor.

Future challenges include the collection and analysis of the social literature on the role of healthcare professionals in the HC community as well as the "state of the art" of the involved technical research directions. Moreover an extensive user requirement analysis in the three regions directly involved in the project started, in order to define the needs for COCOON toolset and related methodology, support the technological Research Directions in addressing the real user needs, sustain the functional requirement of the toolset definition and outline the business model. To support the objectives of healthcare delivery that is free of errors and the implementation of robust safety reporting system a broad range of patient data will be needed, included sign and symptoms, test results, diagnosis, therapies and outcomes; the involvement of the other 10 European regions in the project has been planned in order to store the platform with as much as possible data.

References

[1] Lesar TS, Briceland L, Stein DS. Factors related to errors in medication prescribing. JAMA (1997).

[2] Vincent C., Neale G., Woloshynowych M. Adverse Events in British Hospitals: Preliminary Retrospective Record Review, BMJ (2001).

[3] Pit Salute, Italian Patient Right Court - Annual Study, (2000).

[4] Brennan, T.A. The Institute of Medicine Report on Medical Errors- Could It do Harm?, New English Journal Medicine, (2000).

[5] Coile R., Quality pays: A case for improving clinical care and reducing medical errors, Journal of Healthcare Management, Chicago, May/June (2001)

[6] Alberti KMMG, Medical errors a common problem. BMJ Research (2001).

[7] Leape, L.L. Errors in medicine, JAMA, Vol.272. (2000)

[8] Cathy Buck, Application of Six Sigma to reduce medical errors, Quality Congress – Annual Quality Congress Proceedings, Milwaukee, (2001)

[9] Coulter A. The future. In: Edwards A, Elwyn GJ, eds. Evidence-based patient choice. Oxford: Oxford University Press, (2001)

[10] McCracken EC, Stewart MA, Brown JB, McWhinney IR. Patient-centred care: the family practice model. Can Fam Physician (1993)

[11] Levenstein JH, McCracken EC, McWhinney IR, Stewart MA. The patient centred clinical method. A model for the doctor-patient interaction in family medicine.(1986).

[12] Dawes, Martin G. On the need for evidence-based general and family practice. Evidence-based Medicine (1996)

[13] Louise Simpson and Paul Robinson, "e-Clinical Governance" Radcliffe Medical Press, Oxford, (2002)

[14] M. E. Johnston, K. B. Langton, B. Haynes, & A. Matheu, "Effects of computer-based clinical decision support systems on clinician performance and patient outcome. A critical appraisal of research". Annals of Internal Medicine, (1994).

[15] European Health Telematics Association, Green Paper: Legal aspects of health telematics (2002).

[16] Johnson, W.G., Brennan, T.A., et al., The economic consequences of medical injuries, JAMA, Vol.267, N.18, (2002).

[17] Eisemberg, John M., Meyer Gregg, Foster Nancy, Medical errors and patient safety: A growing research priority, Health Service Research, Chicago, (2000).

eAdoption and the Knowledge Economy: Issues, Applications, Case Studies
P. Cunningham and M. Cunningham (Eds.)
IOS Press, 2004

Enforce Engineering Collaboration

Martine CALLOT[1], Laurent SAINT-MARC[1,3], Pierre NOWAK[2], Benoît EYNARD[2]
[1]*EADS CCR, 12 rue Pasteur, 92150 Suresnes, France*
Tel: +33 1 46 97 38 43, Fax: + 33 1 46 97 32 59, Email: martine.callot@eads.net
Tel: +33 5 61 18 87 47, Email : laurent.L.SAINT-MARC@airbus.com
[2]*Troyes University of Technology, BP 2060, 10010 Troyes Cedex, France*
Tel: +33 3 25 71 56 71, Fax: +33 3 25 71 56 71, Email: firstname.lastname@utt.fr
[3]*LAP-GRAI, UMR 5131 CNRS, University Bordeaux 1, France*

Abstract: This paper presents an approach in order to manage engineering data exchanges between multi-disciplinary designers working in a collaborative way. The goal is to address in a unique and common understanding a collaborative design process modelling for enhancing project and engineering performance. Process modelling is described using three views as design process modelling, discipline process modelling and collaborative process modelling. A performance indicator describing the maturity of engineering data is defined. A business case concerning the development of the aircraft pylon is under construction and future research work is detailed. This work was carried out in the IPPOP Project, a research project labelled and supported by the French government.

1. Introduction

Aircrafts are complex systems to define and assemble. Their development through concurrent engineering [1] requires cooperation of thousands of engineers and technicians.

Due to the complexity of aircraft and the workload, several design teams were created to define the main parts to assemble (i.e.: wings, landing gear, fuselage nose, central and rear fuselage, propulsion, etc.). This is the classic example of the engineering breakdown structure developed in Airbus. The activities of design within a process are made in a convergent way as well for the integration of products, as for the design of each part.

In Concurrent Engineering, design activities are performed by multidisciplinary team of experts with different roles and objectives [2]. They collaboratively contribute to the design activities by making decisions and sharing engineering data with each other [3].

The engineering stakes can be summarized in the three following topics:

- How to help designers from different disciplines having to produce/use engineering data in delocalised location?
- How determinate if an engineering data is an hypothesis, if it is incomplete, consolidated or validated?
- How validate and manage data exchanges between disciplines in order to converge through a common goal?

2. Context and Objectives

2.1 Economic Environment

Improving design performance is essential due to economic and technological pressures. It is not any more enough to lower production costs, it is necessary to elaborate quality products satisfying the needs of the customer in optimal economic conditions. This imposes better management of expenses, and control of activities that create expense without any direct added value. The implementation of the design project in integrated Product teams implies numerous exchanges of data (drawings, calculations, procedures, methods, means, etc.) between the designers to end in a compromise. It is at the same time acceptable for them and it also meets the requirements of the customer. The concurrent engineering certainly brought a reduction of delays and a better dynamic of the design. But the demands of improvement are more and more growing in order to reduce Engineering cycles through Engineering data availability and quality management [4].

2.2 Discipline Collaboration Environment

In relation to the daily tasks of the designer, there is a lack of common processes and rules for data exchanges and sharing between disciplines, and this wastes resources and time. The consequence is that the data may not be appropriate or available at the right time.

Concerning the engineering data management, access is often only possible through local tools & procedures. There is no common method and tools across Engineering (Specific Design – Non Specific Design – Partners - Suppliers) to notify the disciplines impacted by a change. For historical reasons, a large number of Repositories & Vaults exists and an important number of skill Applications are deployed.

2.3 Business Objective

The main objective of this work is to enforce collaboration in Engineering by supporting Discipline and Collaborative Processes complexity, by enhancing collaboration work through data availability and quality control. The final objective is to decrease rework of designers due to non-mature information or over information.

3. Design process characteristics

Design activities are fairly different from production activities. The design process of a product can be characterized in the following way [5]:

- It contains iterations contributing to the consolidation of the engineering data supplied by some or such activities,
- Because actors are based on several sites, communication and coordination is complex.
- The disciplines in the design process are numerous and diversified

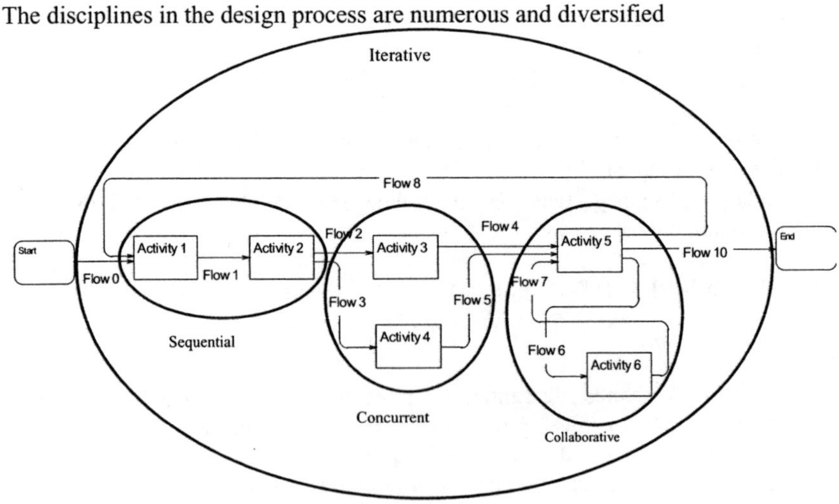

Figure 1 : Engineering types in a Design process

The major characteristic of a design process is that there are strong interactions between the activities performed by many Disciplines (Aerodynamic, AeroElasticity, Stresses, Systems, etc.) with important exchanges of engineering data. The activities take place either in a sequential way but often in a parallel way; the exchanges participate in the building of a common knowledge (sharing of the information generated between the actors belonging to various disciplines). In fact, a design process can be made of a scheduling of activities from different engineering types: sequential, concurrent, collaborative, and iterative.

4. Methodology of Process Modelling

The method of process modelling used shall be represented by multi-views models. A model or a view is always a partial representation of the reality. So three views as Product Design Process, Discipline Process and Collaborative Process are necessary to represent the complexity of an engineering domain [6]. One of the fundamental difference between them is that Discipline Process and Product Design Process are activities driven, Collaborative processes are exchanges driven [7].

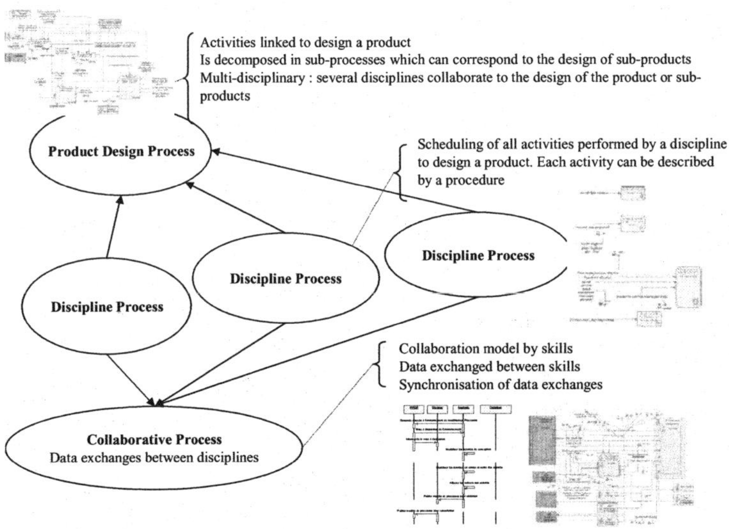

Figure 2: 3-views process modelling

4.1 Product Design Process View and Contribution to the End-User

The product design process view describes all the activities contributing to the design of the product. This process could be decomposed in several sub-processes corresponding at the design of sub-products. This type of process is multi-disciplinary: several disciplines contribute to the design of the product.

The advantage is that this model gives a product-oriented view and allows the understanding of the global behaviour of the process. In return, the inconveniences are that several levels are required in order to describe the overall process: this has for consequence the complexity of the representation and the difficulty even the impossibility to represent the loops. This model starts from a classical approach of the process modelling. It follows a logic of downstream hierarchical breakdown level of which most is reduced to a macro activity and to an identification of the product to be designed as well as inputs necessary for the design of this product. In this model, several disciplines can realize or contribute to the same activity: we then can speak about collaborative activities.

4.2 Discipline Process View and Contribution to the End-User

The Discipline process view describes all the activities a discipline performs to design the product. This type of process could also be decomposed in several sub-processes depending of the level of detail the discipline wants to represent. The advantage is that this model gives a discipline-oriented view, focusing of internal work of a discipline.

4.3 Collaborative Process View

The Collaborative process view describes all the exchanges between disciplines contributing to the design of the product. At each exchange, the engineering data corresponds to a certain delivery state, which is called the maturity of the engineering data.

The advantage is that this model gives an exchange-oriented view, focusing of interfaces between discipline processes where activities are considered as black boxes.

5. A performance indicator: the maturity of engineering data

At AIRBUS, fourteen milestones cover the design process from the first idea up to end of the development phase of the aircraft. These milestones help designers to define a controllable concurrent engineering design process. For each milestone, designers implement and conduct program reviews to evaluate their progress as well as to solve problems and to freeze the different solutions, ratify the development of the aircraft.

Between two milestones, teams and designers exchange engineering data. They also exchange engineering data with their partners (engine or nacelle manufacturers for example) or subcontractors that are usually located in distant engineering offices.

At each exchange, the engineering data corresponds to a certain delivery state. This can be seen as the level of confidence in the data by the provider: we call it Engineering data Maturity [8]. The engineering data exchanged will be used by different Disciplines. Knowing the maturity will allow them to make decision if they can use the engineering data for their work or if it is better to wait for an other release and then avoid rework.

The maturity of Engineering data between two milestones is evaluated as follows:

1. "Absolute Maturity" (Ma) identifies the current maturity level evaluated by the provider and the receivers of the data. At the beginning of the design, the absolute maturity is null, then absolute maturity increase to reach the objective maturity level.
2. "Objective Maturity" (Mo) characterizes the maturity level that data must reach at a given milestone (program, product) and represents the objectives pursued by the designers. Mo is defined at the start of the collaboration.
3. "Relative Maturity" (Mr) is the global maturity indicator. It highlights the gap between Mo and Ma. This indicator is a ratio between the absolute and objective maturity. So "Mr" stands between 0 (at the design beginning) and 1 (when Ma reaches Mo).

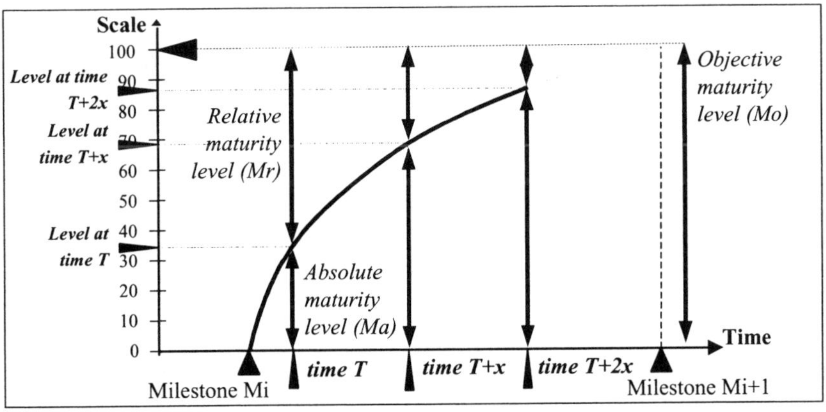

Figure 3: Engineering data Maturity between two milestones

6. Business Case

6.1 Business Case Description

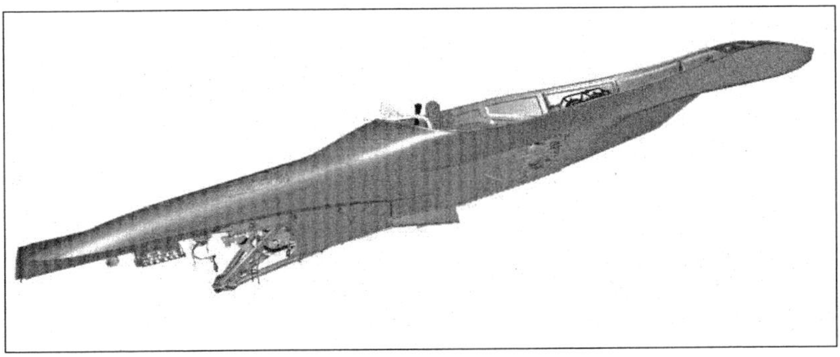

Figure 4: Pylon

The business case is issued from the aeronautic field: the design of the pylon. The pylon is a product being a key link for the aircraft by connecting the engine with the wings. Many systems cross the pylon and are essential (fuel distribution, hydraulics, air, electricity). The pylon can be described by a structural point of view, by the systems which cross it, and finally by the collaborations on the interfaces with the engine and the wing.

6.2 Implementation

The design process and discipline processes are well known and then the implementation has concerned the definition of the collaborative process. A method has been developed to help designers for characterizing their collaborative process. It has three main steps :

First step: Define Disciplines who exchange during a given phase or between two milestones. Aircraft main phases are Feasability phase, Concept phase, Definition phase, Development phase. We can determinate teams of designers working together intensively called "Collaborative clusters". A Collaborative cluster is a means to structure et address the complexity of the collaboration all along the Aircraft life cycle.

Second step: In a Collaborative cluster, we define engineering data needed by each Discipline. For example, if a Discipline "D" has to deliver an engineering data at a given Milestone, for that, he needs engineering data as inputs from other Disciplines "A","B" and

"C". Then we can say that Discipline "D" is seen as a Customer for Disciplines "A","B" and "C" and Disciplines "A","B" and "C" are seen as Providers for the Discipline "D".

Third step: For each engineering data, we define the awaited maturity for corresponding customers. The maturity evaluation of engineering data is subjective and each actor generally defines its own indicators in order to estimate his design work relative to his point of view: each designer has his own decomposition and understanding of the maturity.

Table 1: Example Engineering data "Aerodynamic Reference Shape" maturity states

1. Global Shape without winglet
2. Global Shape with uncertainty on winglet positioning
3. Shape with accurate winglet positioning but not validated
4. Shape with MOD on accurate winglet positioning

This maturity is local to a given Discipline and understood by internal actors, but understanding can vary for the other disciplines. Moreover, the maturity is not always sharable or IT implementation compliant. It is necessary to define an Information System (IS) point of view global to Engineering through standard Product Life Cycle Management (PLM) implementation [9], [10]. It shall be common and shared for all the actors of Engineering. This IS point of view needs to make sense to be efficiently used by disciplines and must represent a consensus across the Engineering data owner and other disciplines using that Engineering data There exits a need for a method defining a maturity mapping between disciplines-oriented maturity definition and IS proposed definition in order to determine standardized maturity levels. Those levels shall be defined and fixed with flexibility for disciplines to use selected levels. Maturity is complementary to codification versioning for Engineering data but could be a basis for versioning rules.

Table 2: Example Engineering data "Aerodynamic Reference Shape" standard maturity distribution

1. Maturity Rough: Global Shape without winglet
2. Maturity Prelim: Global Shape with uncertainty on winglet positioning
3. Maturity Reliable: Shape with accurate winglet positioning but not validated
4. Maturity Release: Shape with MOD on accurate winglet positioning
5. Maturity Validated : Shape with accurate winglet positioning validated

The maturity states distribution is defined from previous experiences on Aircraft Programs and can be considered as a delivery state agreement between Disciplines.

6.3 Feedback and Lessons Learned

The maturity states definition is a most critical step of this method. It allows a common understanding for all actors but it is time consuming. So, this common understanding of the maturity is clearly done on a selection of engineering data according to some criteria's. Otherwise the maturity analysis will be too much expensive with regard to the product program performance. Those selection criteria's can be defined for engineering data often exchanged during a phase or engineering data as an important deliverable for a gate review (for main milestones or in between) or part of certification

The application has shown that a fourth view is then necessary to show all the maturity states that follows an engineering data. An engineering data has a life cycle with different states and it is necessary to identify these different states and the corresponding milestones.

Collaborative agreements can be built taken into account all the information collected in the previous steps. All the Disciplines belonging to a collaborative agreement will exactly know what they have to provide, for who, at what time, and the corresponding maturity state. Al designers are aware of their position of customer and/or provider.

A discipline who is a customer for a given collaborative agreement becomes a provider for other collaborative agreements. Then we can envisage a follow-up of theses collaborative agreements and this corresponds to a management not only by the task follow-up but also by the engineering data content follow-up.

7. Business Benefits

7.1 Business benefits for the Discipline

The Disciplines will have a view of their business organization and will better forecast resources and deliverables. They will have a guarantee for the availability and quality of needed engineering data availability through a capitalization from their practices.

7.2 Business benefits for the collaboration

Collaboration in engineering will be enhanced by the availability and conformity of engineering data exchanged. A common understanding between the provider and customers of engineering data will facilitate an exchange protocol with rules and constraints.

All collaborative processes description represents a fundamental view to understand and represent what are the collaborations all along the Aircraft program

7.3 Business benefits for the Project

Project manager will have at his disposal means of anticipation for preparing critical Design Reviews and move from "On time delivery" to "On time on quality delivery - every time".

The engineering data quality will be controlled and optimised across the aircraft life cycle phases through a strong relationship between disciplines and program management.

8. Conclusions and Future Research

Four views were defined for modelling processes in a concurrent engineering environment: Product design process view, Discipline processes view, Collaborative processes view, Engineering data life cycle view.

The Collaborative Processes are the glue between Discipline Processes, leading to a set of consistent engineering data characterizing the final product with all Disciplines views.

A performance indicator has been defined: the maturity of the engineering data. This maturity can be local to a given discipline and mapped to standardized maturity states to be common and shared.

The next research step will focus in the three following aspects:

- To define a method of building dependency tree on engineering data exchanged on along the Aircraft lifecycle. On these dependency trees, the objective is to build impact analysis and calculate critical path on engineering data exchanged.
- To define dashboards adapted to the role of the user (designer or program manager) allowing him to take decisions in an anticipative and corrective way.
- Deploy these concepts in a multi-project environment.

References

[1] Dunyach, J.C., CE in Aeronautics, Proceedings of the 6th International Conference on Concurrent Enterprising - ICE 2000, Toulouse, June 28-30, 2000.
[2] Sohlenius G., 1992, Concurrent Engineering, Annals of the CIRP, 41/2, 645-655.
[3] Girard P., Deschamps J.C., Zolghadri M., "*Collaborative engineering design spaces*", 10th ISPE International Conference on Concurrent Engineering: Research and Applications CE'03, Madeira, Portugal, July 26-30, 2003.

[4] Hubel H., Colquhoun G.J., « A reference Architecture for Engineering Data Control (EDC) in capital plant manufacture », Computers in Industry, n° 46, pp 149-165, 2001.
[5] Eynard B.. "Modélisation du produit et des activités de conception - Contribution à la conduite et à la traçabilité du processus d'ingénierie", PhD thesis of the University of Bordeaux 1, France, 1999.
[6] Nowak P, Rose B, Saint-Marc L, Callot M, Eynard B, Gzara-Yesilbas L, Lombard M. "Towards a design process model enabling the integration of product, process and organization", *Proceedings of the 5th International Conference on Integrated Design and Manufacturing in Mechanical Engineering - IDMME'2004*, Bath, UK, April 5-7, 2004,
[7] Moly M., Callot M., Saint-Marc L., Trebucq B., "Collaborative processes enabler", Proceedings of the INCOSE 2004, Toulouse, June 20-24, 2004.
[8] Moly M.,. Callot M, Reyterou C., Saint-Marc L., Girard P., Deschamps J.C., "Toward a data maturity evaluation in collaborative design processes" , Proceedings of DESIGN 2004 Dubrovnik, May 18-21, 2004.
[9] Eynard B., Gallet T., Nowak P., Roucoules L., UML based specifications of PDM product structure and workflow, *Computers in Industry*, in press, 2004.
[10] Xu, X.W., T. Liu, 2003, A web-enabled PDM system in a collaborative design environment, Robotics and Computer Integrated Manufacturing, 19/4, 315-328.

Enabling Dynamic Security Perimeters for Virtual Collaborations

T. DIMITRAKOS[1], I. DJORDJEVIC[1]*, D. MAC RANDAL[1],
M. GAETA[2], G. LARIA[2], P. RITROVATO[2], N. ROMANO[2]
[1]*Central Laboratory of the Research Councils, Rutherford Appleton Lab., OX110QX, UK*
Tel: +44 1235 446387, Fax: +44 1235 445831, Email: theo.dimitrakos@rl.ac.uk
[2]*CRMPA, Università di Salerno, Italy*

Abstract: This paper summarises an emerging solution enabling the federated management and distributed enforcement of dynamic security perimeters for virtual communities of services and resources that span across administrative and enterprise boundaries. We highlight how this architecture, realised in a European research project exploring a Grid infrastructure for application serviced provision, addresses outstanding challenges that underpin automation of trust and security management in scalable, multi-institutional, dynamic Virtual Organisations.

1. Introduction

Application Service Provision (ASP) is a business model, originally derived from the idea to use the Internet or other wide area networks to provide online application services on a rental basis—commercially delivering computing as a service. The ASP model takes advantage of several technological breakthroughs that have made it feasible to sell computing as a service rather than a product. The traditional ASP model can be understood as an evolution of outsourcing. Clients enjoy the benefit of offloading complex and expensive IT to the ASP while maintaining control and visibility of business processes. However, performance, security, reliability and maintenance are still bound to constraints of solutions that have been originally designed for specialized in-house implementations.

More recently, a new form of ASP has emerged (called IBSP [13]), based on a Business Model that better exploits the wide adoption of the Internet and the Web. The IBSP model focuses on ASPs providing applications that are Internet-enabled by design and network-centric (e.g. being themselves a bundle of loosely coupled Internet-enabled services). IBSPs and ISVs target economies of scale, in addition to economies of skill, they run their services in a multi-tenancy model, they support thousands of customers on a single code basis, they reduce hardware and administration cost by partitioning and distributing resources, and they reduce client-side development and maintenance investment by using standard Web technology at the client side interface. Utility computing has also emerged as a paradigm where shared infrastructure can be provided on demand to multiple customers [16]. That business model lets companies pay for IT services as needed, charge customers per-use or metered use. Supporting this charging model requires dynamic allocation of resources and integration of services. Finally, the concept of the Grid has emerged as a new approach to a high-performance distributed computing infrastructure for supporting Virtual Organisations (VO), defined as any dynamic collection of individuals and organizations required to share resources to achieve certain goals [12]. Following this, hybrid Grid Computing, Web Services and Peer-to-Peer solutions are being promoted for commercial applications such as in distributed collaborative design and engineering, or distributed supply chains [11],[12]. Leveraging on this convergence, we anticipate new business and scientific computing paradigms based on dynamic VO that span across Organisational boundaries and enable the enactment of collaborate processes that integrate services, resources and knowledge in order to perform tasks that the VO partners could not undertake on their own [11].

Although such a dynamic and complex structure may be able to support future hybrids of IBSP, ISV and Utility computing [16], it opens several challenging problems relating to VO security. (See [11] for an indicative overview of these challenges.) Such a dynamic and complex structure opens several issues related to the security that need to be considered:

- collaborating services and resources may be based in different security domains;
- on-demand collaboration implies trust has to be established in real time on a P2P basis;
- collaborators need protection from other VO members, as well as from outsiders;
- the same service or resource may participate in different VOs, and hence different (potentially conflicting) security policies may apply;
- security conditions for a service or resource may differ throughout the life of the VO;
- no centralised administrative point implies a devolved policy management scheme combined with distributed enforcement at a peer level.

A suitable architecture must provide a security and trust management infrastructure that meets these requirements. We will introduce the basic elements of such an architecture, the underlying model of which has been analysed in [5],[6], and gradually explain how it aims to address the above requirements, by means of dynamic security perimeters. For an overview of the advanced ICT infrastructure upon underpinning scenario and architecture, see [15] in this proceedings and [8],[10] which provide further insight on the platform

2. Overview of a security perimeter solution for Grid ASP

Before presenting the dynamic security perimeter solution, we provide a simplified overview of the context and Grid environment within which it is realised, focusing only on the services of interest for the purpose of this presentation. For a further description of this environment including services for service location, orchestration, contract performance monitoring, and accounting, the reader is referred to [8] and to [15] in this proceedings.

Consider an Application Service Provider (ASP) that is part of a VO encompassing itself and other Service Providers (SP) on which it can call. Each SP (and ASP) can be considered an independent Hosting Environment (HE); a single administrative domain (integrating several hosts) whose security is administered locally by its own Local Security Manager (LSM). To deliver an application instance, the ASP composes different services provided by SPs, which it discovers from a Locator service (LOC) running in the VO. The service instances (SI) required for the application are created on request by a Service Instantiator (INS) service running in each HE, which selects an appropriate host within the HE and instantiates the service. Host selection is based on criteria related to local security policy, SLA obligations and resource availability information [15]. The SIs making up the application are grouped into a virtual community (SIG) spanning across multiple HEs, protected by

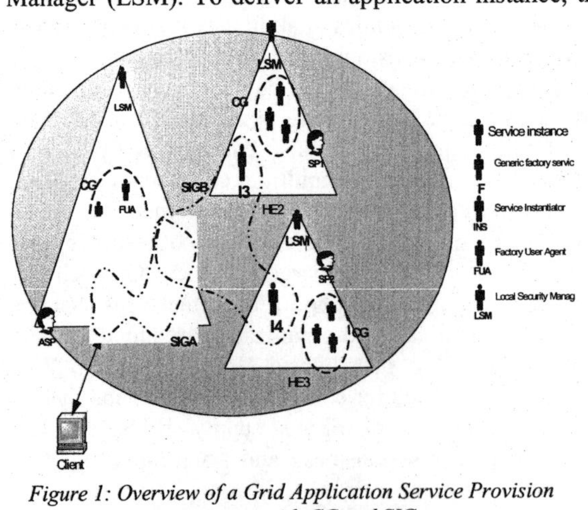

Figure 1: Overview of a Grid Application Service Provision environment with CG and SIGs

an agile security perimeter encompassing only these SIs.

This perimeter can be virtualized as an aggregation of security enforcement components, each of which is attached to the SI it protects and permits only interactions within the security perimeter. Each SIG has its own administrative service, supported by the involved LSMs. The purpose of the security solution presented this paper is to realise such agile, dynamic security perimeters by firstly segregating the administrative services managing each HE and the rest of its resources from the service instances it contributes to the enactment of a specific collaborative task, and secondly allowing control aggregation of service instances performing the collaborative task from different Hosts across multiple HE.

We distinguish two types of communities differing in purpose and kind of entities they bring together: A Core Group (CG) includes all administrative services of a single HE. These are distinguishable from services offered by HEs to virtual collaborations. A Service Instance Group (SIG) includes all instances contributed by several HE for the purpose of enacting a collaborative task. Figure 1 shows three HEs each of which has a CG and contributes to some SIG (i.e. [UA,I1,I2], [I2,I3,I4]), to enacts distinct collaborative tasks.

2.1 Logical structure of the dynamic security perimeter architecture

This security architecture is being developed with two main goals in mind:

- Enabling communication within dynamically created communities, that is secure, scalable, accountable, robust and independent of network topology.
- Enforcing dynamic security perimeters, which adapt to the evolution of a virtual community (in terms of membership, performance and security policy).

These goals are addressed through the following means:

- Attribute Certificates to manage community membership and privileges.
- Role based security policies describing permissions, prohibitions and obligations within the collaboration teams, set by, and negotiated between, the community mangers.
- Mechanism for distributed enforcement of the security policies at each service instance that protects individual members within a community and the community as a whole.

The logical structure of the security architecture distinguishes several roles and interaction modes that capture the required functionalities (Figure 2). These include:

Community-peers (or Peers) are the service instances that are created within a HE for the purpose of contributing to the enactment of a collaborative task. Each Peer possesses a security token (resembling a Public Key Certificate) issued by the LSM as a proof of registration with the HE. This is presented whenever basic authentication of the Peer is required, and the key-pair itself may be used for encrypting or signing parts of the messages it may exchange. A Peer can interact with other Peers by creating a new community (SIG) or joining an already existing one (therefore becoming a SIG member). At any time a Peer can be a member of one or more SIGs. Introduction of a Peer to a SIG has to be agreed by both its LSM and the corresponding Community Manager.

Local Security Managers (LSM) are responsible for the population of Peers within a HE. They define the basic organisational policy containing constraints that must be met by every entity under that LSM's administration, irrespective of any subsequently defined collaboration policy for specific SIGs. They do this by assigning one or more organisational roles to each Peer and providing it with attribute certificates (AC) as a proof that it can assume these roles. Such roles define the Peer's default security settings, bound to the administrative domain of its HE; they are not necessarily recognised outside that HE.

Community Managers (CM) are responsible for managing community membership, and coordinating the internal level of security. They define the collaboration policy for their community, and coordinate enactment of such policies; in practice they must negotiate with the LSMs of the contributing HEs, as organizational policy is primary. Actual enforcement of collaboration policies is delegated to the corresponding LSMs, who control the security enforcement agents of corresponding Peers. CMs are realised as dedicated functionality exposed by the security administration of selected a HE to the VO environment. A selected LSM may be authorised to assume such a role or a selected HE may be able to provide CM factory services. Note that CM is not a member of the community it manages.

Community Members are Peers that have joined a specific community (i.e. the CG of a HE or a SIG; a CG can be considered as a local SIG). In addition to possessing AC to prove the organisational role that they may assume within their HE, for each community the corresponding CM assigns one or more collaboration roles to each SIG member, and provides it with attribute certificates (AC) as a proof that it can assume these roles in interactions with other members of that community. Such collaboration roles are bound to a community: they are recognised only by the HEs that contribute Peers to that community and only within the scope of interactions in the context of that community; they are not necessarily recognised in any other HE or in relation to different transaction contexts. All communication from community members with their CM is channelled via the LSM of the member's HE, as it is responsible for endorsing the community management actions that apply to the Peers of its HE and may refuse to forward any message encapsulating interactions that violate the organizational policy of its HE.

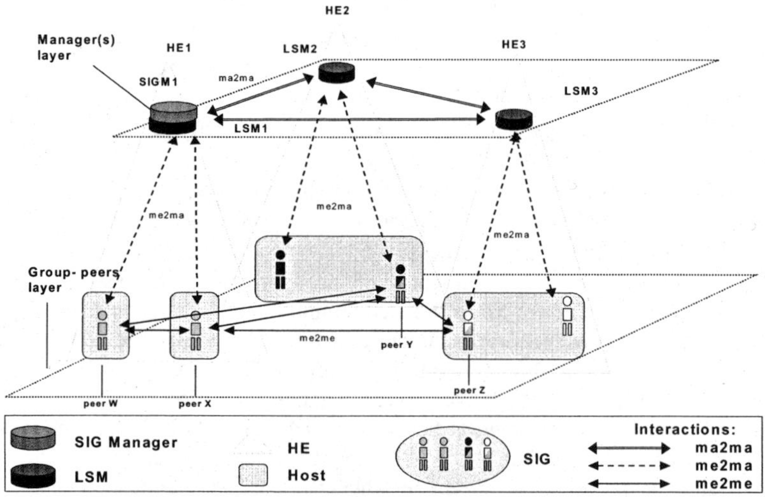

Figure 2: Main roles and interactions of the dynamic security perimeters architecture

Basic Interactions: Once a Peer joins a SIG, it interacts directly with other SIG members, without the manager's involvement. SIG members are informed of each other's identity and location and interact on a peer-to-peer basis through message exchange (e.g. SOAP). Depending on the purpose of each interaction they are required to embed different kind of certificates in the messages they interchange. Occasionally, interactions between managers may take place in order to support creation of SIGs across multiple HEs. Figure 2 illustrates the roles and main types of interactions in the SIG environment:

- me2me (member-to-member): direct p2p communication between Peers. This requires a (unique) community certificate, which is issued by the CM.
- me2ma (member-to-manager): community management related interactions between a member and its LSM (e.g. local distribution of community policy updates, request to create a new community or join/leave a community) require a member's security token.

- ma2ma (manager-to-manager): direct p2p communication between managers (including CM and LSM) about security management (e.g. membership management, policy negotiation, policy update, etc.). They require a ma2ma certificate.

2.2 Overview of the dynamic security enforcement architecture

Security policy enforcement takes place at each end-point by means of a multilayer shell that protects each Peer. Security Enforcement Agents (SEA) virtualise security enforcement mechanisms attached to each Host (Network layer) or Peer (Application layer) within a HE [5]. Conceptually, this extends the notion of a distributed firewall [1] by introducing further layers of control for member authentication and fine-grained role-based access control to service instance data and operations that are enforced by dedicated SEA at each peer.

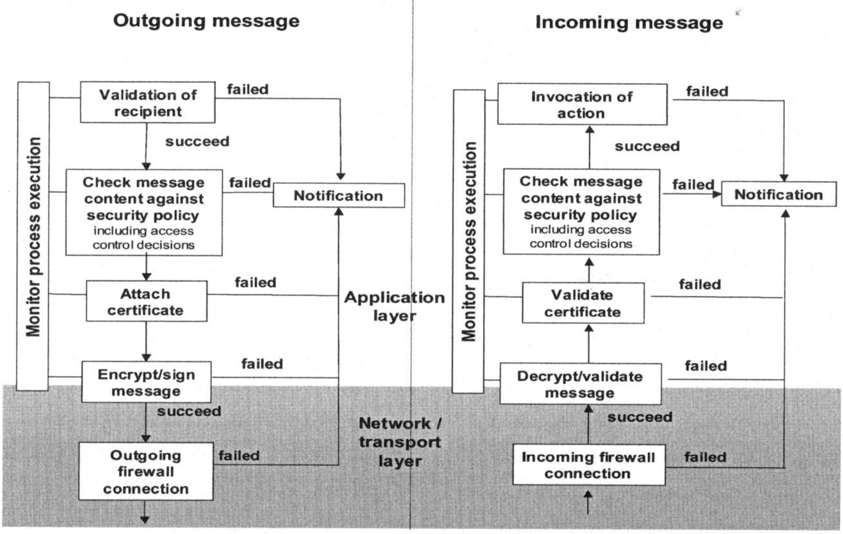

Figure 3: Overview of security enforcement activities

A Host-SEA virtualises the Host-instance of a distributed firewall that protects the whole HE and is administered by LSM. A peer-SEA virtualises the security enforcement mechanisms of that Peer. For every interaction between Peers, the following per-message security checks are performed at a distributed security perimeter instance (Figure 3). The use of Web/Grid services technology entails that all interactions reduce to message exchanges between peers and that all actions including method invocations are encapsulated as data in the messages exchanged.

For an outgoing message, the corresponding context is identified and the recipient's identifier and the intended action (e.g. encapsulated by a SOAP-RPC) are checked against the security policies associated with the sender's roles in that context. If compliance fails, the intended action is replaced by a failure notice and the LSM is notified, otherwise the appropriate certificate proving the Peer's role is attached to the message and any encryption or signing required by the corresponding security policy is carried out. Finally, the message is sent via the distributed firewall instance protecting the Host accommodating the sender.

For an incoming message, at first the packet stream is examined by the distributed firewall instance protecting the Host that accommodates the recipient. Then, the context of the corresponding interaction is identified, and the sender's certificate is validated. If validation fails, the message is destroyed and the LSM notified. Then the message content is analysed against the security policies associated with the role and context claimed. Each intended action (e.g. encapsulated by a SOAP-RPC) is checked prior to its execution. Invocations corresponding to authorised actions are realised; unauthorised actions are skipped, a fault is logged and the LSM is notified.

In addition to the network layer (packet monitoring) and service/application layers of the security perimeter (reflected in the functional separation between SEA explained earlier), a final third layer monitors the process execution (via "monitors" distributed to each service, which communicate events of interest to their CM, or to a trusted third party, where analysis can be performed based on evidence/data collected by all SIG members).

For more details on the enforcement architecture see [3],[5],[6]. Note the differentiation between of policy specification and policy enforcement is a key feature that brings flexibility and scalability. Furthermore [7] explains how obligation policies that underpin electronic contracts can be deployed, and proposes a related monitoring scheme.

2.3 Security perimeter dynamics: Overview of the community life-cycle model

In this section we further explain the security perimeter solution presented by focusing on the basic interactions and security functionalities that underpin its dynamic behaviour. To simplify presentation we describe the main interactions in the life cycle of a community:

Creation and expansion can be initiated by any Peer (wishing to join a SIG) or by the CM. Peer-to-peer interactions at the Peer level are permitted only within already established communities. All legitimate communication between Peer and CM is channelled via the Peer's LSM. Interactions between Peer and CM can be understood as happening within a secure channel with two end-points (Peer, CM) and a single intermediary (Peer's LSM). The LSM is able to check, endorse or object and forward or reject any request from the Peer to the CM. However the LSM cannot change the original content of the Peer's message as these messages are digitally signed by the Peer.

Operation: When a community is formed, community members engage in peer-to-peer interactions. These interactions are restricted to community members and do not require or entail any involvement of the CM or LSM. Communication is performed by means of (typically SOAP) messages which may be encrypted with session keys exchanged between SIG members at the beginning of a session. Legitimate messages must have embedded a (me2me) community certificate. Changes to security policies, as well as the introduction of new Peers and the departure or expulsion of existing Peers, necessitate interactions between the CM and some LSMs. These are peer-to-peer interactions between peers at management level. In analogy to the interactions between SIG members, interactions among the CM and the corresponding LSMs require using a ma2ma certificate and may be encrypted.

Shrinkage occurs when a member leaves the community. This can be caused by (i) a Peer that has reached the end of its operational life-time and is about to be destroyed, releasing the resources it occupies; (b) a Peer that is forcefully destroyed (e.g. a user logs off); (c) a Peer is expelled from the Group (reasons may include: underperformance, unavailability, hostile behaviour, etc., as well as completion of required tasks before the end of the Service instances lifetime.). In any of the above cases, an update of the community membership is issued by the CM, and the corresponding LSMs are instructed to update the SEA configuration so as to ensure that any interaction in the context of that community (between Peers that have left the community and remaining Peers) is blocked.

Dissolution: This is effectively the departure of the last remaining member of a community or the expulsion or destruction request of all remaining community members. It can be requested by the CM or any LSM (potentially acting upon the request of some Peer in their HE). As with all community management actions, enforcement of community dissolution can only be initiated and coordinated by the CM; it is enacted by the corresponding LSMs that have ultimate control over the SEA of each Peer.

3. Status of existing implementation

A variant of the proposed security solution is being implemented within the European project GRASP [8],[10],[15]. This implementation builds on top of a realisation of OGSA on Microsoft .NET. The GRASP Security Infrastructure (GRASP-SI) [9] is currently being implemented in the Microsoft C# Programming Language as a collection of Grid Service port types and administrative tools to configure the running environment. Much of the features are realized using the WS-* security specifications (e.g. WS-Security, WS- Secure Conversation), leveraging on their implementation provided by Microsoft in Web Service Enhancements (WSE) v2.0. The overall infrastructure is included in an OGSI compliant middleware developed on top of the OGSI.NET framework released by the University of Virginia [17]. The communication model is realized using SOAP on HTTP and the messages are managed by the Microsoft SOAP pipeline, modified through dedicated SOAP handlers which are provided by the OGSI.NET framework and by the GRASP platform.

The VO model supported by GRASP is divided in independent HE as presented previous sections of this paper. Each HE comes together with a LSM service, which is implemented as a persistent Grid service that is able (among) others to provide operations for controlling access to the active services and (in/out-bound) communication flow for the HE it administers. LSM sets the local security policy for the HE (including the Core Group of all persistent services that support the administration of the GRASP platform at the HE) and manages the registration of any services operating in its HE. Registration is proved by the possession of a specialised WS-security token that is issued and signed by the LSM.

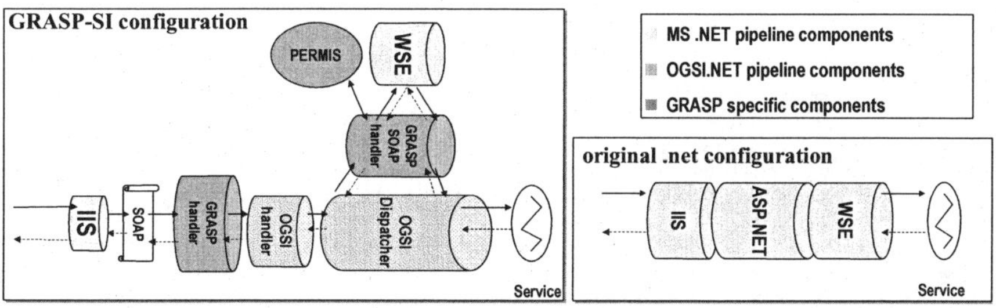

Figure 4: SOAP message pipeline extension to support enforcement in a .Net setting

Security enforcement takes advantage of the data-encapsulation of procedure calls within the SOAP messages and the possibility to automatically adapt the control of the .Net SOAP pipeline. We have extended the default SOAP pipeline of .Net as shown in Figure 4. The GRASP handlers leverage on the flexibility of WSE, in order to use the WSE pipeline for verifying security tokens, and the SOAP dispatcher of OGSI.NET for enforcing the related security perimeter access policies, based on the access control decision of a separate Policy Decision Point (PDP) with which the GRASP handler interfaces. (Presently, a PERMIS [3] module is cloned at each Host in a HE, acting as a local PDP. In general, GRASP handler can interface with external third party PDP via SAML message exchange.)

4. Conclusion and further work

The emergence of agile security solutions that enable dynamic integration of services and resources across multiple administrative and execution environments that may be owned and controlled by different Organisations is an essential prerequisite for the realisation of a global economy where networked businesses and governments are able to integrate their processes, services and resources within dynamic Virtual Organisations in response to a business opportunity or a market demand.

In this paper we presented a novel solution enabling the dynamic formation and self-management of security perimeters protecting communities of users, services and resources. The interaction model of the proposed architecture integrates a layered peer-to-peer model (between the managers administering network entities and between the administered entities), with a centralised community management model (between community members and their local security managers) and a master/slave model (between security managers and enforcement agents). It supports on-demand creation and management of dynamic virtual collaborations in the form of secure communities of peers (user agents, services, resources, etc.) that are independent of network topology and span across multiple administrative domains, execution environments and enterprise boundaries.

Additional flexibility and protection of the SIG perimeters could be achieved by introducing elements of trust, as means of assessing confidence in a network entity on the basis of evidence accumulated by observing behaviour in different SIGs and by integrating and co-using the process execution monitoring and enforcement mechanism with other subsystems or specialised applications focusing on SLA administration and accounting. Related research has been initiated in [7]. Future work includes: to integrate a variant of this security solution into a comprehensive trust and contract management framework in the context of the TrustCoM European Integrated Project [11] (www.eu-trustcom.com); to extend this solution with a federated policy specification framework in the context of the DyCom UK project [3], to fully integrate application and network level security policy enforcement in the context of the Akogrimo European Integrated Project [1].

References

[1] Akogrimo project pages: www.akogrimo.org and www.mobilegrids.org
[2] Bellovin S.M. – Distributed Firewalls. login, pp.37-39, Nov 1999., www.research.att.com/~smb/papers/distfw.pdf
[3] David Chadwick, Theo Dimitrakos, Kerstin Kleese-Van Dam, Damian Mac Randal, Brian Matthews, Alexander Otenko "Multilayer Privilege Management for Dynamic Collaborative Scientific Communities" UK Workshop on Grid Security Experiences, Oxford 8th and 9th July 2004
[4] T. Dimitrakos, I. Djordjevic, B.M. Matthews, J.C. Bicarregui, C. Phillips. *Policy-Driven Access Control over a Distributed Firewall Architecture*. (Proceedings of the IEEE Policy Workshop 2002. IEEE Press, 2002
[5] Djordjevic I., Dimitrakos T., Phillips C. *"An Architecture for Dynamic Security Perimeters of Virtual Collaborative Networks"* IFIP/IEEE NOMS 2004.
[6] Djordjevic I., Dimitrakos T., "Towards Dynamic Security Perimeters for Virtual Collaborative Networks" in Proceedings of iTrust2004: the 2nd International Conference on Trust Management. Springer-Verlag LNCS 2004
[7] Dimitrakos T., Djordjevic I., Milosevic Z., Jøsang A., Phillips C. - *Contract Performance Assessment for Secure and Dynamic Virtual Collaborations*, to appear in Proc. of EDOC'03, 7th IEEE International Enterprise Distributed Object Computing Conference, September 16-19 2003, Brisbane, Australia
[8] Dimitrakos T., D. Mac Randal, F. Yuan, M. Gaeta, G. Laria, P. Ritrovato, B. Serhan, S. Wesner, K. Wulf, *An Emerging Architecture Enabling Grid-based Application Service Provision.* Proceedings of the 7th IEEE International Enterprise Distributed Object Computing Conference, IEEE Press 2003.
[9] Dimitrakos T., I. Djordjevic, D. Mac Randal, M. Gaetta, P. Ritrovato. *"Dynamic Security Perimeters for Grid-enabled Collaboration"*. UK Workshop on Grid Security Experiences, Oxford 8th and 9th July 2004
[10] Dimitrakos T., D.MacRandal, G.Laria, N.Romano, P.Ritrovato, B.Serhan, S.Wesner, *Trust, Security and Contract Management Challenges for Grid-based Application Service Provision.* ITrust2004 Springer-Verlag LNCS, 2004
[11] Dimitrakos T. and Kearney P., "Towards a Trust and Contract Management Framework for dynamic Virtual Organisations". eChallenges Conference e-2004.
[12] I. Foster, C.Kesselman, J. Nick, S. Tuecke. Grid Services for Distributed System Integration. Computer, 35(6), 2002.
[13] Summit Strategies. Market Analysis Report, Out of the Box: Top Nine Net-Native Software-as-Services Design Differentiators. June 2002. http://www.summitstrat.com/
[14] S. Tuecke, K. Czajkowski, I. Foster, J. Frey, S. Graham, C. Kesselman; *Grid Service Specification.* Open Grid Service Infrastructure WG, Global Grid Forum, Draft 3, July 2002.
[15] Wesner S., Sehran B., Dimitrakos T, Mac Randal D., Laria G., Ritrovato, P., Towards a platform enabling Grid based Application Service Provision. eChallenges Conference e-2004.
[16] Vijay Machiraju, Jerry Rolia, Aad van Moorsel, Quality of Business Driven Service Composition and Utility Computing, Software Technology Laboratory, HP Laboratories Palo Alto, HPL-2002-66, March 15th , 2002
[17] Wasson, G., Beekwilder, N., Morgan, M. and Humphrey, H. 2004. OGSI.NET: OGSI-compliance on the .NET Framework. ccGrid '04. http://www.cs.virginia.edu/~gsw2c/OGSIdotNet

* Research carried out during the tenure of an ERCIM fellowship (www.ercim.org) at CCLRC.

eAdoption and the Knowledge Economy: Issues, Applications, Case Studies
P. Cunningham and M. Cunningham (Eds.)
IOS Press, 2004

Towards a Trust and Contract Management Framework for dynamic Virtual Organisations

Theo DIMITRAKOS[1], David GOLBY[2], Paul KEARNEY[3]
[1]*Central Laboratory of the Research Councils, Rutherford Appleton Lab., OX110QX, UK*
Tel: +44 1235 446387, Fax: +44 1235 445831, Email: theo.dimitrakos@rl.ac.uk
[2]*BAE Systems Advanced Technology Centre, Sowerby Building, Bristol BS34 7QW, UK*
[3]*BT, Antares Building pp2/4, Adastral Park, Ipswich IP5 3RE, UK*

Abstract: TrustCom is an European co-funded Integrated Project that aims to develop a framework for trust, security and contract management in dynamic Virtual Organisations. The framework will enable the secure enactment of collaborative business processes in self-managed, and dynamic value-chains of businesses and governments. It will leverage and extend the emerging convergence of open-standards, and in particular Web Services, and open Grid Services architectures. Validation will take place within industrial strength test-beds in the areas of collaborative design engineering (CE) and provision of ad-hoc, dynamic processes (ADP) for the on-demand provision of aggregate electronic services. This paper provides an overview of the TrustCom vision, objectives and anticipated results.

1. Introduction

Recent years have seen an unprecedented acceleration in the evolution of the Internet as the technological vehicle underpinning the expansion of service provision and inter-/intra-enterprise integration in all market sectors. This brings about the prospect of ad hoc integration of systems across organisational boundaries to support collaborations that may last for a single transaction or evolve dynamically over many years. This sets new requirements for scalability, responsiveness and adaptability that necessitate the on-demand creation and self-management of dynamically evolving virtual organisations (VO) spanning national and enterprise borders, where the participating entities (enterprises or individuals) pool resources, information and knowledge in order to achieve common objectives. The objectives may be short term - e.g. to deliver a one-off service in response to a specific customer demand - or long-lasting. In the latter case, the VO's structure, business processes and operational infrastructure must adapt as the goals of the collaboration, the participating entities, the business context and the technologies employed, change.

Emerging ICT paradigms such as Autonomic computing, Utility computing and Grid computing are making the formation and operation of virtual organisations easier by providing dynamic management of the distribution of computational processes across available resources. However, the malleability of the digital medium that makes this possible is also a liability: a major limiting factor is a well-founded concern about exposure to fraud or misuse of the technology. Today, concerns about trust and security are acknowledged to be significant barriers to providing access to outsiders. Notwithstanding the major ICT breakthroughs of the last two decades, protecting one's assets while integrating services, processes and resources, remains a major ICT challenge. Overcoming such challenges requires the development of disruptive technology realising innovative ideas over widely acceptable interoperable platforms. The required scalability, responsiveness and adaptability for on-demand created and dynamic virtual organisations, makes the provision of cost effective trust and contract management solutions for VO environments, the most demanding and timely research challenge in this field. Effective solutions require interdisciplinary approaches integrating tools from law, cognitive and social science in addition to telecommunications and computing. The successful deployment of secure and trusted dynamic VOs requires converging strategic research at a European level, coupled with mechanisms for integration of existing experimental results and the rapid dissemination, realisation and take-up of new research outputs.

1.1 The TrustCom project

In response to this challenge, the European Commission and a consortium of end-users, major software vendors and telecom operators, national research institutes and Universities, are implementing the new Integrated Project TrustCom. TrustCom will conduct multidisciplinary research in order to deliver:

1. A novel trust and contract management reference architecture that will enable collaborative work within on-demand created and self-managed dynamic VOs leveraging on the emerging convergence of Web Services and Grid technologies.
2. A set of conceptual models explaining the fundamental concepts, principles and methods underpinning the above architecture. Effectively these provide the meta-model of any new architectural constructs that may result from TrustCom research.
3. A set of profiles, that bring together and potentially extend selected Web/Grid Services specifications at specific version levels, along with conventions about how they work together to support potential implementations of the TrustCom framework.
4. A reference implementation of the above integrating and extending already established or emerging interoperability standards for autonomic security, trust and contract management based on Web and Grid services technology.
5. System and software engineering tools and methods analysis the VO life-cycle and offering a library of design patterns and generic software components implementing selected services that offer the core functionalities of the VO.
6. Testbeds exhibiting instantiations of the above architecture and reference implementation into two classes of realistic application scenarios, namely collaborative engineering (CE) and provision of ad-hoc aggregated services (ADP).
7. Selected demonstrators exhibiting the business value and benefits of the TrustCom framework in the abovementioned application domains.
8. Studies analysing selected aspects of the legal and socio-economic context that underpins such Virtual Organisations.

2. Examples of Virtual Organisations in Collaborative Engineering

The development, production and support of modern products such as ships, aircraft etc are highly complex processes that often involve great risk including technical complexity and changing customer and market requirements. The ability to manage these and other risks is a distinguishing feature of competitive organisations in the engineering sector. A strategy for managing this complexity is to form partnerships or Joint Ventures (JVs) in order to exploit new markets and opportunities through Collaborative Engineering (CE). In a JV partners focus on particular aspects of the product through its lifecycle, enabling more focus on core business capabilities. Emerging technologies such as web and grid computing may facilitate the evolution of JVs into Virtual Organisations (VOs), where organisations quickly come together to share resources without requiring the development of new facilities, and systems- a common feature of JVs at present. The CE scenarios described here attempt to cover most of the phases of the product lifecycle within a CE VO through development, production and in-service product upgrade.

The first of the scenarios focused on the collaborative design of a product in order to win a customer contract. The VO included principal partners who supply major subsystems collaborating together to deliver a design that meets customer requirements and will lead to the award of a production contract. Customer requirements are negotiated and constantly refined and re-negotiated based on the results of the collaborative design activities. The VO also includes other collaborators who provide technical capabilities from High Performance Computing through to highly specialised engineering analysis services. Capabilities that currently reside within monolithic enterprises, and which are expensive to support, are outsourced and yet can still be integrated closely with the product development process within the VO. The benefits to the VO from this sharing of design data are improved understanding of customer requirements and reduced risk by more extensive design investigations using external specialist services. The interaction between partners' security policies that control access to the design data and collaborative agreements, defined at the business level, is an important issue in this scenario.

The second scenario focused on the management of complex engineering processes associated with the production phase. These processes span enterprises, potentially in different countries or economic zones and are possibly subject to export restrictions. Each partner providing a major sub-system (eg, engine, fuselage of a civil aircraft) also has a network of component suppliers and logistics support. These production processes are complex and may require re-scheduling in the case of delays in deliveries, etc. This may necessitate the sharing of process information (so-called 'process visibility') across the VO, entailing flexible security systems that control access to internal information. Other issues include the identification of trustworthy suppliers who can deliver components to time and specification in accordance with service level agreements.

The third scenario looked at the upgrade of an in-service airliner to include an in-flight entertainment system. The VO reconfigures to admit a new sub-system provider responsible for delivering this system. The new partner is also a member of other VOs, possibly competing with the current VO. An important business decision concerns the trustworthiness of the product data - the new partner must establish the completeness and accuracy of the product data before it can plan its activities. A possible consequence is their possible withdrawal from the VO if this data is of poor quality and poses unacceptable contract delivery risks. The new partner also wishes to monitor the in-service system performance using the customer's operations data. The security system of the new partner must be trusted by the VO to not allow sensitive product data to be accessible to competitors and by the customer to not disclose operations data to its own competitors.

In summary, the three scenarios have highlighted the importance of effective and flexible security system for building confidence in more integrated collaborations that VOs offer over conventional JVs. Security policies should be correlated both with collaborative agreements established between partners at the business level and with agreements established within other collaborations as well. The benefits from an effective security and contract management framework are the ability for engineering collaborations to be quickly reconfigured in order to expose the assets that need to be shared to achieve the business goal. Service level agreement monitoring is important for ensuring that suppliers (of components, services etc) perform according to contracts. Benefits here possibly include the automation of processes between clients and suppliers that are usually repetitive. Finally, trust frameworks are required for supporting collaborations. The first of these concerns managing the reliability and trace ability of engineering data, ensuring that greater confidence can be given to it and that it can be relied on in major engineering tasks. The second of these Trust frameworks should facilitate the search for new partners/suppliers of components or services that were previously unknown to the VO. This should include some assessment of the trustworthiness of the security systems and its security policies.

3. Examples of VOs for Next Generation Service Providers

We are interested here in VOs that are formed through ad hoc aggregation of component services offered by different 'real' service providers. Increasingly, enterprises are using web services and related technologies to provide their customers, suppliers and partners with direct access to their services and business processes. Motivations include reducing costs and speeding up processes through automation. However, the vision behind the web services oriented architecture revolution is that distributed applications can assembled as needed by connecting together pre-existing services. Services selection takes place through a 'discovery' process. As well as connecting the services together into a supply chain capable of fulfilling a customer order, the business process of the enterprises involved must also be interfaced. Furthermore, contracts need to be agreed establishing the the mutual rights obligations of the participating service providers. When connections at the these three levels can be established on demand, we can truly say we have an and hoc dynamic VO.

We are already seeing services being 'disaggregated', that is, in addition to offering 'complete' services, simpler constituent services are offered separately. Other organisations can then make use of these constituents in combination with their own service elements to offer composite services to their customers. Motivations for disaggregation include regulatory / anti-trust factors, advantages arising from focus on core competences, business agility (ability to launch new services / enter new markets rapidly), a desire on the part of the individual SPs to retain the advantages of small scale (or conversely to avoid the overheads and inertia of large organisations. New services may also be created specifically for use as constituents of larger services offered by other enterprises. This could offer opportunities for specialist start-up companies to enter a market. Benefits of dynamic aggregation include provision of services that are precisely tailored to a specific customer need. The need to offer a wide range of tailored services could arise from a wide range of preferences or requirements among the targeted customer base, or because the specifics of the service depend on the circumstance of the customer, e.g. current location, the task currently being undertaken, and other context specific variables. The ability to participate in dynamic VOs greatly increases the range of services a provider can offer to its customers, and also the number of end-customers it can reach indirectly via partners.

Five such 'Aggregated Services' (AS) scenarios have been defined and analysed as part of the TrustCoM problem definition: The first takes uses one of the ISTAG Ambient Intelligence scenarios: 'Maria the Road Warrior'. This follows a near-future business traveller through her day, during the course of which she makes use of various services provided collectively by the many devices and systems making up the pervasive computing environment. We can see these services as being provided by virtual organisations forming in response to Maria's needs. The second scenario was similar, but less futuristic. A business traveller in a foreign city wants something to do in the evening. He calls into a WLAN-equipped café, and requests a personalised multi-media city tour guide to be shown using a combination of his personal computing equipment and the café's facilities. This service is provided by a VO consisting of the café, content providers / aggregators, the users 'home' service provider, and other network operators. The detail of the scenario focuses on the use of trust service providers representing the interests of the various parties. In the third scenario, a small software company wants to bid for a new contract, which under normal circumstances would be beyond the scope of its resources. The company has involved itself in a network of similarly placed small companies and is able rapidly to form a VO to compete with larger corporations in the development of new technologies. It is interesting to note that analogies can be drawn between this scenario and the TrustCoM project itself, raising the possibility that TrustCoM could be used as a test-bed for its own technology developments. The fourth scenario concerns experiential e-learning that may take advantage of a combination of semantic-based content selection, personalization of learning activities and integration with high-performance capabilities for virtual experimentation. Here, VOs providing highly personalised educational services are formed within a community of service, content and resource providers. A learner is assisted in defining a personalised training session, which is then enacted by the VO for the benefit of the Learner. The fifth scenario examines how a national or international incident (e.g. an environmental crisis) could be handled through collaboration among organisations that are selected according to context and must agree on a way of sharing and managing resources. As each organisation manages its resources and services, a decentralised command and control system will be advocated to synchronise their efforts and their use of the resources.

In summary, the five scenarios have highlighted that dynamic VOs inevitably incur a management overhead compared to real organisations, and indeed to static VOs (formal consortia). There is a requirement for additional services to provide the glue that enables the VO to function as a viable entity (e.g. to provide overall coordination of activities while retaining flexibility). We expect these services can be defined to be independent of the particular application domain. Furthermore, there is a requirement for services to replace the trust inherent in operation within an integrated real organisation (trust in colleagues even when not known personally, trust in procedures and processes, etc.), and the trust between customer and an established service provider with a clear legal identity and brand / reputation. This last class of service is a main ingredient of the TrustCoM Framework. Without such a framework, it is likely that enterprises will judge that the risks participating in dynamic VOs will out-weigh the benefits. Similarly, end-customers will be reluctant to buy from dynamic VOs. There are substantial commercial opportunities for enterprises offering the trust, security and contract management services instantiating the TrustCoM framework. The TrustCoM project will prototype implementations of potentially useful classes of service, drawing on the scenarios mentioned above for requirements.

4. An emerging common vision of Virtual Organisations

Based on the experience of the scenarios summarised in the previous sections, here we sketch the Virtual Organisations that TrustCoM innovations will help bringing about, emphasising some of the fundamental common characteristics that distinguish such emerging forms of VO from more traditional enterprise networks.

4.1 Virtual Organisations versus Enterprise Networks

A Virtual Organisation is understood as a temporary or permanent coalition of geographically dispersed individuals, groups, organisational units or entire organisations that pool resources, capabilities and information to achieve common objectives. Virtual Organisations can provide services and thus participate as a single entity in the formation of further Virtual Organisations. This enables the creation of recursive structures with multiple layers of “virtual” value-added service providers. The parties that form a virtual organization are typically part of a larger enterprise network of which a selection of partners is made. This phenomenon is known as “network activation” in VO modelling theory (See for example [18] and [13]). The entities in the Universe of such networks share some broad characteristics, e.g. belonging to the same economy or market sector, and their participation indicates a disposition to work together in a future market opportunity.

4.2 A common VO life-cycle model

The following life-cycle model emerged as a reference, although it was noted that not all of these phases would necessarily fit the specifics of all VO variants considered in the project. A similar model was used as a reference by the VOmap roadmap project “Roadmap Design for Collaborative Virtual Organisations in Dynamic Business Ecosystems”.

- VO Identification. This involves opportunity identification, evaluation and selection.
- VO Formation. This phase involves partner identification, evaluation, selection and partnership formation, including binding selected candidate partners into the actual VO.
- VO Operation & Evolution. This phase is characterised by the controlled integration of the services and resources, offered by the VO partners in VO-wide collaborative processes leading to the achievement of shared business objectives. Membership and structure of VOs may evolve over time in response to changes of objectives or to adapt to new opportunities in the business environment. Changes of VO context may necessitate contract amendment or adaptation of policy and business process enactment.
- VO Dissolution. This phase is initiated when the market opportunity is fulfilled or has ceased to exist. The major decision processes operation termination and asset dispersal.

4.3 Targeted Virtual Organisations

This emerged as a characteristic of VOs that are formed and exist for a purpose [15] and in response to a market opportunity or to fulfil a market demand [10]. Consequently, the VO focuses on a target market segment or group. Targeted VOs are characterised by goal-specificity [14], i.e. activities and interactions of constituents are coordinated to achieve explicitly defined goals that provide unambiguous criteria for selecting among alternatives, and by deliberate cooperation [14], i.e. the relations between VO partners and the services and resources they contribute is explicit and can be "deliberately reconstructed".

4.4 Dynamic Virtual Organisations:

Membership and structure of such a VO may evolve over time to accommodate changes in requirements or to adapt to new opportunities in the business environment. While the VO as a collective collaborates towards a common objective, parts of the VO capacity and capabilities are owned by different independent partners with their own (partly overlapping, partly conflicting) interests. When the goal of a partner is met or the partner feels its own objectives no longer align with the goal of the VO, it can step out of the VO. Partners collaborating in order to perform a task in a phase of a VO may leave and join a different, potentially competing VO within the life-time of the former. The ability to self-organise is a key attribute of cost-effectiveness for dynamic VOs. A specific kind of dynamic VO are those with the ability to unite quickly to exploit an apparent opportunity or common goal. We refer to this as "on-demand formation of a VO". Dynamic VOs are particularly useful when faced with market incentives for responsiveness, dynamic service delivery, and charging based on usage. Beyond technological innovation, cultural adaptability in the organisation is essential for achieving an adequate degree of responsiveness.

4.5 Self-management of Virtual Organisations:

Self-managed VOs are characterised by the ability to manage their operation and evolution without necessitating explicit intervention from VO partners or other outside parties. Self-management necessitates a form of integration that is enabled by the presence (or ability to form) an "autonomic" inter-organisational information system (IOIS) that supports the:

- Negotiation and agreement of the conditions of involvement of VO participants by means of electronic contracts whose operation is monitored and enforced by the IOIS;
- Membership management and trust establishment between the collaborating entities, be they the VO participants or the services and resources offered by the VO participants;
- Specification, negotiation and distribution of policies that control the sharing and aggregation of services and resources of VO partners in compliance with their

agreement. Such policies need to be enforceable by the IOIS, and allow for adaptation (in real time) in response to changes of the context of interactions;
- Specification, distribution and enactment of business processes, which orchestrate the aggregation of information, services and resources in accordance to the consolidation of agreements between VO partners, VO-wide policies, and local (organisational) policies.
- Resolution of conflicts or adaptation of VO operation in response to alleviating the impact of violations of agreement or conflicts between policies, agreements, and business processes – both on the basis of their static description and their enactment.

The efficiency and effectiveness of self-management also depends on the extent that a VO achieves security and integration and in particular organisational transparency, shared leadership, and separability in VO operation and management.

4.6 Scalable Virtual Organisations

Scalability refers to the ability of the VO framework to be realised in different scales depending on its objective and the kind of the parties involved (e.g. large corporations, SMEs, solitary entrepreneurs). Scalability also allows the multiple interdependent layers of outsourcing as manifested by the constitution of recursive VO structures where similar VO formations may appear in micro- and macro- levels. This can be the case for example of a federation of providers offering high-performance end-to-end aggregate processes, where some activities are realised by aggregations of services provided by smaller-scale nested VOs and enacted over virtual execution environments which are also understood as VOs of execution hosts that federate resources in order to realise the enactment a service component.

4.7 Integrated Virtual Organisations

This characterises VO structures that comply with the typology of "dynamic networks" [16] [17], while they also support the following extreme aspects of an organisational network:
- Organisational transparency – meaning that although frequent and fine-grained interactions with customers are supported in order to facilitate mass-customisation, the co-operation of VO partners may not be visible to customers.
- Cost-effective inter-organisational information system (IOIS). A cost-effective IOIS requires the virtualisation of information and computation services and resources (at different levels of granularity) and their "just-in-time" integration across the boundaries of the VO partners. The formation of such a IOIS to accommodate the secure enactment of a collaborative business process within the VO should ideally take place at the time of demand. Its operation should respect the agreements between VO partners, the policies of the services and resource providers (who may maintain overall governance of the assets the provide to the VO) and the service and resource distribution should be transparent to the consumer both within and outside the VO;
- Shared control – meaning that while every partner contributes to the operational management of the VO, it does not automatically control the whole VO, although it effectively maintains high-level control within its own local administrative domain;
- Shared leadership – meaning that while every partner maintains control of their own assets and serves their own interests, these must relate to, and may be partly overlapping with, the interests of the collective.
- Shared access to resources and services – VO member may consume shared resources or services of other members for the purposes of enacting a collaborative task;
- Shared loyalty – entities within a VO constituency contribute to the common objective of the VO but also serve the specific objectives of their own organisation.

- Mission overlap & co-destiny – there may be partners that are also doing business outside of the context of the VO (and have a partial mission overlap) in addition to those (having a complete mission overlap) that all business is conducted within the VO context. In either case, the mutual dependencies due to the sharing or resources, services and knowledge and the shared risks make the VO partners also more dependent on each other, therefore necessitating collaborations based on a sufficient level of trust;
- Separability – meaning that VO management is characterised by clear distinctions between specification and deployment, and between a VO-wide "global" strategic management and a "local" operational management.

To achieve the desired economical performance, "integrated" VOs require a functional efficient corporative network. VOs may be embedded in a larger network of corporations, from which certain members are recruited to deliver the required performances.

5. Anticipated Innovation

TrustCom innovation in supporting VOs will be centred around the following main themes:
- Establishing trust relationships using digital identities, certification, reputation, and inspection to ensure the security, dependability and competency of business partners,
- Autonomic security, including specification, automated management and enforcement of policies controlling fine-grained access to the services and resources contributed by the VO constituents and assuring confidentiality / privacy, integrity, availability and accountability at VO level, while self-adapting to contextual changes within the VO.
- Contracting, focusing on the provision of trusted services to support the management of electronic contracts, the incorporation of guarantees to facilitate trustworthy collaboration, and performance assessment at the enactment of electronic contracts.
- Business Process Enactment, focusing on securing the enactment of collaborative business processes invoking services and consuming resources contributed by the VO partners in compliance with their security policies and agreements, and on self-adaptation to changes on the agreements contextual changes within the VO, including changes to the VO membership, security policy or agreements.

Research and technological innovation in the above themes will be informed by analyses investigating the legal and socioeconomic context of VOs:
- Socio-economic Context. Based on an empirical analysis of the market needs, TrustCom aims to develop new socio-economic models underpinning the establishment of digital economies within which VOs can evolve and generate profit. These will identify methods for creating incentives for engaging in trustworthy electronic collaborations and sharing services, resources information and knowledge within VOs in order to achieve common objectives in a way that multiplies their productivity and allows for the achievement of results that participants could not produce on their own.
- Legal Context. TrustCom will study selected legal and regulatory issues of collaborative work in VOs, focusing on privacy, data protection, and international issues. Analysis will also assess the expected impact of technological innovation in light of these issues and some legal and regulatory factors that could influence its exploitation.

6. Conclusion

In this paper we presented an overview of the motivation, objectives and approach of the TrustCom European project. Paper [1] analyses indicative application scenarios, [11] refers to relevant legal aspects, [3] focuses on the use and extension of Web Services Security technologies to achieve TrustCom objectives. Papers [4][12][2][7] present partial solutions that may be reformulated and integrated in the context of TrustCoM. The project started in February 2004 and is expected to deliver the first version of its framework during 2007.

Acknowledgements

The TrustCom consortium partners are: AtosOrigin (prime contractor), BAE SYSTEMS (leading the CE application area), BT (leading the ADP application area), CCLRC (responsible for technical management and scientific coordination), ETH, HLRS, IBM (leading analyses of the business and economic context), Imperial College (leading dissemination), King's College London, European Microsoft Innovation Center (leading standardisation), NRCCL (leading analyses of the legal context), SAP (leading exploitation), SICS, SINTEF, the University of Milano, and the University of Salford. For more information about TrustCom see www.eu-trustcom.com

References

[1] Bernhard Katzy, Gordon Sung, "State-of-the-Art of Virtual Organisation Modelling". In P. Cunningham et al (Eds) Building the Knowledge Economy, IOS Press Amsterdam, 2003

[2] Chadwick David et al Extending/Adapting PERMIS to contribute to the TrustCoM objectives. eChallenges Conference: e2004.

[3] Claesens Joris et al Investigating the Web Services Security framework as an enabling and extensible technology for trustworthy business processing in dynamic Virtual Organisations eChallenges Conference: e2004.

[4] Theo Dimitrakos et al. Dynamic Security Perimeters for Virtual Collaboration Networks. eChallenges Conference: e2004.

[5] Stefan Wesner , Theo Dimitrakos et al. Towards a platform enabling Grid based Application Service Provision. Challenges Conference: e2004.

[6] Dimitrakos T., Valles J., Wesner S. The Grid for e-Collaboration and Virtual Organisations. In P. Cunningham et al (Eds) Building the Knowledge Economy, IOS Press Amsterdam, 2003

[7] Karabulut Yuecel Integrating a Unifying Trust Management Approach into Dynamic Virtual Organizations eChallenges Conference: e2004 (submitted).

[8] Bernhard Katzy: Design and Implementation of Virtual Organizations. IEEE HICSS (4) 1998

[9] Katzy, B.; Obozinski, V. Designing the virtual enterprise, Proceeding of ICE'99, 5thInt. Conf. On Concurrent Enterprising, The Hague, Netherlands, 15-17 Mar 99

[10] Kotler, Philip. 1994. Marketing Management. Englewood Cliffs, NJ: Prentice Hall

[11] Mahler Tobias et al. Reputation Systems and Data Protection Law. eChallenges 2004.

[12] Martino Lorenzo et al. eChallenges Conference: e2004 (submitted).

[13] Saabeel, W., Verduijn, T.M., Hagdorn, L., Kumar, K. (2002), A Model of Virtual Organisation: A Structure and Process Perspective, Electronic Journal of Organizational Virtualness, 4: 1. 2002

[14] Scott, W.R. (1998), Organizations: Rational, Natural and Open Systems, Prentice-Hall.

[15] Shao, Y.P., Liao, S.Y. and Wang, H.Q. (1998), A model of virtual organisations, Journal of Information Science, 24: 5, pp. 305-312.

[16] Snow, C.C., Miles, R.E. and Coleman. Managing 21st Century Network Organizations, Organizational Dynamics, Vol. 20, No.3, pp. 5--20. 1992

[17] Anne Powell, Gabriele Piccoli, Blake Ives. Virtual teams: a review of current literature and directions for future research. ACM SIGMIS 35(1). 2004

[18] Wassenberg, A.F.P. (1995), Netwerken: organisatie en strategie, Amsterdam: Boom Meppel.

[19] Wildeman L (1998), Alliances and networks: the next generation, International Journal of Technology Management, 15: 1/2, pp. 96-108.

Web Services Security for Trustworthy Business Processing in Dynamic Virtual Organisations

Joris CLAESSENS[1], Christian GEUER-POLLMANN[2]
European Microsoft Innovation Center, Ritterstr. 23, 52072 Aachen, Germany
[1]*Tel: +49 241 9978419, Fax: +49 241 9978477, Email: jorisc@microsoft.com*
[2]*Tel: +49 241 9978418, Fax: +49 241 9978477, Email: chgeuer@microsoft.com*

Abstract: Virtual Organisations (VOs) are coalitions of individuals and organisations each bringing in their resources and expertise in order to achieve a common business objective, such as the collaborative engineering of a highly complex product, or the provision of a composed, aggregated service. The EU FP6 project TrustCoM will develop a framework for trust, security and contract management, providing the basis for trustworthy collaborative business processing in dynamic VOs. This paper investigates the Web Services Security specifications as an enabling and extensible framework in this context. It provides an initial analysis on how the specifications can support the TrustCoM framework, and how they can complement specific tools and technologies for trust, security and contract management within this framework.

1. Introduction

Virtual Organisations (VOs) over open distributed systems have been proposed as a mechanism for supporting collaborative working across enterprises. VOs are coalitions of individuals and organisations using their resources and expertise to achieve a common business objective. VOs are dynamically established for the collaborative engineering of a highly complex product, for the provision of a composed, aggregated service, etc. This vision will only come about if enterprises and individuals are confident that services will be delivered 'as advertised', not only in terms of functionality, but also in the behaviour of participating entities. The VO should in particular comply with the security and privacy requirements of all participating entities. These requirements must be expressed in mutually agreed security policies based upon the VO collaboration contracts. The EU FP6 project TrustCoM [1] will develop a framework for trust, security and contract management, providing the basis for trustworthy collaborative business processing in dynamic VOs.

Web Services provide an interoperable framework between software components that can communicate between different companies and organizations, while possibly residing on different platforms and infrastructures. As such, Web Services constitute the ideal framework for collaboration within a VO across enterprises. It is however essential that these services are provided in a secure and reliable way, and that they support transactions. Specifications for secure, reliable, and transacted web services [2] have been and are being developed by IBM, Microsoft, and others. This paper investigates the Web Services Security specifications [3] as an enabling and extensible framework for trustworthy collaborative business processing in dynamic VOs. It provides an initial analysis on how these specifications can support the TrustCoM framework, and how they can complement specific tools and technologies for trust, security and contract management within this framework. The paper intends to bring together ongoing academic research in trust and security on one hand with the emerging business-driven security specifications on the other.

1.1 Outline of the Paper

The paper is structured as follows. The next section discusses VO-enabled collaborative business scenarios in more detail, and trust and security requirements to be addressed. Section 3 then gives an overview of the current Web Services Security specifications. Subsequently, section 4 investigates how the specifications can enable and support trust and security in dynamic VOs, where they could be extended, and how they can complement specific tools and technologies for trust, security and contract management.

2. Trustworthy Collaborative Business Processing in Dynamic VOs

In the scope of the TrustCoM project, two main use case domains for collaborative business processing in dynamic VOs are considered. Dynamic VOs can for example be established for the collaborative engineering of highly complex products, or for the provision of composed, aggregated services. Collaborative engineering is about the design, production, and maintenance of highly complex products (e.g., an aircraft). To be able to manage the complexity, such products are engineered by several companies forming a VO, each focusing on specific parts, and each bringing in their assets and expertise. An aggregated service is a service composed by several simpler services operated by different service providers forming a VO. An example is a travel agent who provides a travel booking service, composed by a flight booking service, a hotel booking service, car rental service, etc. We refer to [4] for an in-depth discussion of these dynamic VO use-case domains.

TrustCoM will develop a framework for trust, security and contract management in these scenarios. The TrustCoM framework should ensure that the security policies (e.g., confidentiality of design documents) of each of the participating companies are enforced. This is for example the confidentiality of the design documents in the collaborative engineering scenario, or the privacy of the customers in the aggregated service scenario.

Generally, a VO has a life-cycle with 5 different phases [5]: identification, formation, operation, evolution, and dissolution. As outlined in the table below, each of these phases has specific trust and security issues that need to be addressed.

Table 1: trust and security issues in the VO life-cycle

VO Identification	discovery of potential trustworthy and reliable partners
VO Formation	trust and contract establishment security policy consolidation based on contract
VO Operation	membership and trust maintenance autonomic security policy deployment and enforcement secure service orchestration
VO Evolution	membership and security policy adaptation
VO Dissolution	termination of trust relationships maintenance of trust knowledge and reputation

3. Web Services Framework and Web Services Security Specifications

Web Services enable a service-oriented architecture paradigm. They offer an interoperable framework for stateless, message-based and loosely-coupled interaction between software components. These components can be implemented on different platforms, spread across different organisations & reside in different computing infrastructures.

There are many and broad definitions of the Web Services concept. We here refer to Web Services as services that expose useful functionality on the Internet via XML messages which are exchanged through a standard protocol, called SOAP [6]. The interface of a Web Service is described in detail in an XML document using WSDL [7]. Finally, a Web Service is registered at a UDDI [8] server, and is as such discoverable.

Figure 1 presents the complete Web Services specifications "stack". Web Services provide XML-messages-based interaction between components. Messages are exchanged via a messaging framework using SOAP, which can run on top of different transport protocols (http, but email and others are possible). In addition to the basic features of Web Services, three different sets of specifications ensure that messages are exchanged in a secure, reliable, and transacted way [2]. Messaging, security, reliability, and transactions specifications make extensive use of metadata. Metadata specifications allow to describe and communicate various and necessary properties of a web service, such as its messaging interface, its owner and business description, (security) policy, etc. To bootstrap Web service communication, WS-MetadataExchange [20] allows the retrieval of three types of metadata: the policy associated with a web service, the WSDL associated with a web service, and the XML Schema associated with a target namespace. On top of the framework for secure, reliable, and transacted messaging, business processing can be performed [23].

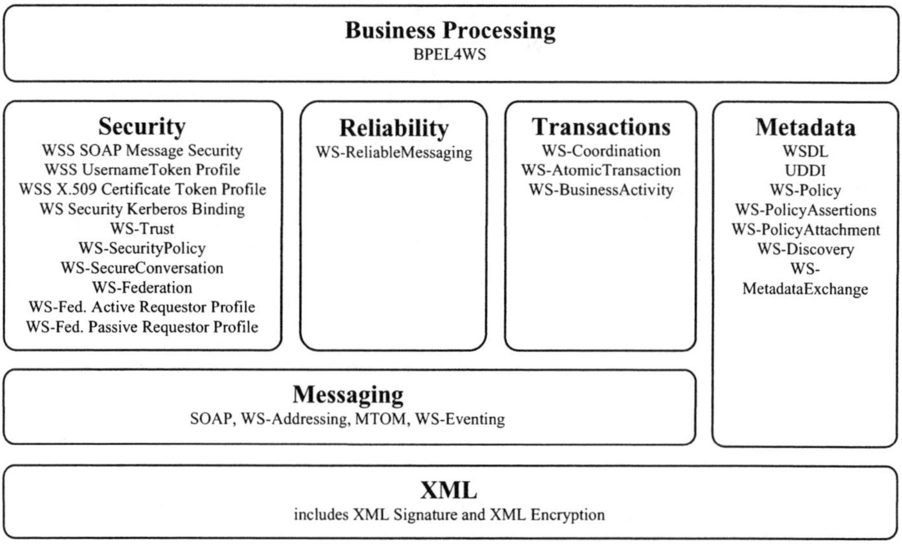

Figure 1: the Web Services specifications stack

Web Services are currently standardised in different bodies. The core underlying messaging related technologies (e.g. XML, SOAP and WSDL) are standardised within the W3C. Other mechanisms (e.g. UDDI and WS-Security) are standardised within OASIS. The more recent specifications are industry initiatives by IBM, Microsoft, and others.

3.1 Web Services Security Specifications

The main technologies under investigation in this paper are the Web Services Security (in the remainder of the paper referred to as WSS) specifications, as proposed by IBM and Microsoft in the architecture and roadmap of April 2002 [3]. These specifications provide a comprehensive security framework for SOAP-based web services, supporting and integrating various security models, mechanisms, and technologies in a way that enables a variety of systems to securely interoperate in a platform- and language-neutral manner. The WSS roadmap consists of different, flexible and extensible specifications, each addressing specific parts of the security framework, including WS-Security, WS-SecureConversation, WS-Trust, WS-SecurityPolicy, WS-Federation, WS-Authorization, and WS-Privacy.

The architecture supports the secure exchange of SOAP messages as follows.

WS-Security [11] specifies how to apply XML Signature [9] and XML Encryption [10] within a SOAP message in order to provide single-message authentication (origin authentication and integrity) and single-message confidentiality. It also specifies how to attach, or refer to, the associated security tokens in a SOAP message.

WS-SecureConversation [17] specifies how to establish, and how to reference to, a security context, and supports a secure conversation with multiple messages.

WS-Trust [15] specifies how to request, issue, validate, and exchange security tokens. Security tokens are cryptographically protected claims (e.g., identity or authorization assertion) and/or cryptographic keys. Security tokens may be forwardable, delegatable, or proxiable. Security tokens are issued by a Security Token Service (STS). Security token requests may be secured using WS-Security (when exchanging one security token for another), or are secured with an explicit challenge/response or other negotiation protocol (when the requestor does not have a WS security token yet). The WSS framework can in fact support any type of security token. However, security tokens that are to be used across different domains should be interoperable. The following tokens are currently standardized and explicitly supported: username/password combinations [12] and X.509 certificates [13]; binary security tokens, such as Kerberos tickets [14]; and XML security tokens, such as SAML assertions [21] and XrML tokens [22].

WS-Policy [19] provides a framework that allows Web Services to describe and communicate (publish) policies to Web Service requestors. WS-SecurityPolicy [16] specifies security policy assertions to be used. The security policy assertions state requirements on the security tokens used and whether or not a message has to be signed etc.

WS-Federation [18] describes how to manage and broker trust relationships in a heterogeneous federated environment including support for federated identities, attributes, and pseudonyms. A federation consists of multiple Web Services domains, each with their own STS and security policy. WS-Federation specifies scenarios using WS-Trust to allow requesters from one domain to obtain security tokens in the other, and subsequently to get access to the services in the other domain. Additionally, mechanisms are defined for single sign-in and sign-out, sharing of attributes based on authorization and privacy policies, and integrated processing of pseudonyms (aliases used at different sites/federations).

WS-Privacy will describe a model for how Web services and requesters state privacy preferences and organizational privacy practice statements, while WS-Authorization will describe how to manage authorization data and authorization policies

3.2 Interoperability and Implementation Notes

The complete Web Services framework consists of an extensive set of flexible individual specifications. Although these specifications are (being) standardized, it may be difficult to effectively build interoperable applications, due to the many options that can be taken during implementation and that are supported through the flexibility of the specifications. Therefore, in addition to the various individual Web Services standards, WS-I [24] is developing a core collection of profiles that support interoperability for general purpose Web services functionality. A Profile is a named group of Web services specifications at specific version levels, along with conventions about how they work together. The WS-I Basic Profile covers aspects of SOAP, WSDL, UDDI, and HTTPS. The WS-I Security Scenarios define the requirements for and scope of the WS-I Basic Security Profile.

The Web Services Enhancements toolkit (WSE) [25] provides an implementation of the WSS specifications for .NET. It currently supports WS-Security, WS-SecureConversation, WS-Trust, WS-SecurityPolicy, username/passwords, X.509 certs and Kerberos tokens.

4. Supporting Trust and Security, Complementary Tools & Technologies

Web Services provide a standardized framework for interoperable, secure, reliable and transacted messaging. They are an ideal underlying service-oriented messaging framework for collaboration within dynamic VOs across enterprises. This section investigates to what extent the WSS specifications can address some of the VO life-cycle related trust and security issues identified in Section 2, how the specifications can support trust and security in dynamic VOs as a flexible and extensible underlying technology, and how they complement specific tools and technologies for trust, security and contract management.

4.1 Trust Establishment (VO Formation)

How trust is established or determined, is outside the scope of current WSS specifications. Federations across different organisations are setup assuming mutual trust. From a WSS technical perspective, organisations trust their respective Security Token Services correctly map between an identity, a role, or an access right, and the associated public key. These statements need to be securely communicated, so the organisations need to establish trust in the cryptographic root keys with which the authenticity of the tokens and assertions can be verified. Trust management and secure exchange of root keys happens entirely out-of-band.

Dynamic VOs would benefit from trust establishment through mediation with trusted services. These trusted services act as roots of trust, reputation services, or recommendation services. Trust and reputation statements could also be communicated in between peers directly. The WSS specifications can complement trust management frameworks (e.g., Sultan [32]) in terms of the secure communication of trust statements, and the support of specific trust-related security tokens. Particularly, trust and reputation statements and recommendations could be published in UDDI; WS-Trust can be leveraged to request, issue, and validate trust and reputation statements/assertions and recommendations; and trust/reputation can also be seen as a WS-Federation attribute service. Trust in the cryptographic key themselves, with which trust statements can be verified, can be seen as a recommendation service, similar as in the "web of trust".

The WSS specifications can support maintenance of trust knowledge (VO Dissolution), whereby organisations can securely push trust knowledge, and provide recommendations.

4.2 Security Policy Consolidation based on a Contract (VO Formation)

The WSS specifications allow to describe and to publish the security policy associated with a web service. The security policy can be retrieved in various ways. The formation and negotiation of the security policy is however out of the scope of the WSS specifications. Without automated support for security policy consolidation, WSS policies will be fairly static, and will not easily allow for very dynamic VOs.

The WSS specifications should be complemented with a contract negotiation framework. The contract defines the rights and obligations of each organisation in the dynamic VO, related to the overall business process. The WSS policies should be derived from the negotiated contracts. A higher level policy language, in between WS-Policy and the contract could be introduced (e.g., Ponder [26]). WS-(Security)Policy may need to be extended to capture all high-level dynamic VO policy semantics into low-level WSS terms.

When forming the VO, the contract should be negotiated. The security policies and trust knowledge of the participating organisations give input to this process. The WSS specifications can support secure contract negotiation and secure communication of the policy and trust inputs. A negotiated contract can be stored in UDDI.

Trust and contract negotiation may require interactive and selective disclosure of policies and credentials, such as offered by Trust-X [27]. This is not supported within the WSS specifications. As WSS policy is derived from trust and a contract, direct negotiation of web service policy and security token usage – requiring an interactive protocol between requester and web service – does not seem to be needed. Negotiation may be an interesting feature when requesting security tokens (e.g., trust recommendations) through WS-Trust.

4.3 Security Policy Deployment and Enforcement (VO Operation)

The WSS specs only deal with security on the level of web services, and for example assume that SOAP nodes are accessible on the network layer; this assumption cannot be made in a dynamic context. Security policy enforcement must be done in a consistent way across different layers (business process, web service, and network). This requires the WSS specifications to be complemented with a higher level policy (see above) and authorisation framework (e.g., PERMIS [28]) which drives policy and authorisation at different levels, including WSS. At the WSS level, this can be realized if the authorization framework foresees the necessary WS-Trust interface.

In a typical WSS scenario, security policy enforcement is based on looking at a single web service request. Security policy enforcement should also take into account the business process and context related to a specific web service request. In a dynamic VO, the context is typically determined by the contract associated with the VO and the business process.

Federations of organisations do not need a single PKI anymore, but traditionally still have a limited number of central security token services, across which trust is brokered. Dynamic VOs require further security decentralization (cfr. GRASP [29] and Hybrid PKI [31]) and explicit authorisation delegation (e.g., Delegent [30]). Dynamic VOs also need to be able to cope with peer-to-peer and "off-line" (i.e., no central security token service available) scenarios. The WSS specifications in principle support any type of (XML) security tokens. Aspects such as delegation can be properly addressed by adding explicit support for the appropriate, delegatable security tokens. Peer-to-peer and off-line scenarios in WSS means that end nodes should be able to play the role of security token service.

4.4 Security Policy Adaptation (VO Evolution)

During the lifetime of a VO, security policies may need to be adapted (e.g., to reflect leaving, joining, or re-assessing trust of members). The WSS specifications do not include a standardized way to push policy updates (new policies can be published, but need to be polled by the requesters). As dynamic policy updates should reflect contract amendments, WSS policy updates should be pushed from the contract management, rather than directly across the web services. Interaction should happen at the trust and contract management.

Trust management frameworks deal with quantified trust. This allows more granular statements (as opposed to Boolean) about trust in partners, which may be re-assess during the lifetime of the VO. How does this influence security policy adaptation? Quantified trust has definitely an impact during contract negotiation, and consequently indirectly an impact on the VO security policies (e.g., more restrictive policy with more extensive auditing is applied with partners who are less trusted). A good approach seems to be that in the scope of a contract (which can be updated), the security policy is fixed and partners are "fully trusted" (under the rights and obligations specified). Trust re-assessments lead to contract changes, which subsequently are then pushed down into updated WSS policies.

It is not clear whether it is a good idea to allow trust to be a direct parameter in the WSS policy itself. Autonomic security decisions should for example not become unpredictable.

Direct trust-based authorization would require trust assertions to be attached to web service requests and validated by the service. WS-Policy would need to be extended with rules that can interpret and make access control decisions based on the trust claims in the tokens. This is less straightforward to realize, and may be better left to a higher-level policy language.

5. Conclusions

We have identified many ways in which the Web Services Security specifications can support a framework for trust, security and contract management meeting the security requirements of dynamic Virtual Organisations. This paper provides an initial assessment of how the specifications can be extended and how they can complement existing and future tools and technologies for trust, security and contract management within this framework.

Support and complementarity can particularly be realized through the extensibility in terms of new XML security tokens, and the flexibility in using these tokens. Metadata can be associated with Web services in different ways and for different purposes. Metadata allows to describe the interfaces of web services, to register web services, to discover web services, and to formulate and attach policies to web services. The overall web services messaging framework and the generic metadata mechanisms has as such been shown to support and enable technologies for interoperable trust and contract management in VOs.

This paper provided an initial analysis of the WSS specifications in the context of trust and contract management. Many ways of support and complementary have been identified. Future work, carried out in the scope of the TrustCoM project, will investigate these ways more thoroughly, and will result in actual tools and specifications for trust and contract management, complementing, and supported by, the WSS specifications.

References

[1] TrustCoM. A Trust and Contract Management framework enabling secure collaborative business processing in on-demand created, self-managed, scalable, and highly dynamic Virtual Organisations. http://www.eu-trustcom.com/.

[2] IBM and Microsoft. Secure, Reliable, Transacted Web Services: Architecture and Composition. September 2003. http://msdn.microsoft.com/webservices/?pull=/library/en-us/dnwebsrv/html/wsoverview.asp.

[3] IBM and Microsoft. Security in a Web Services World: A Proposed Architecture and Roadmap. April 2002. http://msdn.microsoft.com/webservices/?pull=/library/en-us/dnwssecur/html/securitywhitepaper.asp.

[4] Paul Kearney et al. Trust in Dynamic Virtual Organisations: Defining the problem in terms of scenarios. eChallenges 2004.

[5] Theo Dimitrakos and Paul Kearney. Towards a Trust and Contract Management Framework for dynamic Virtual Organisations. eChallenges 2004.

[6] W3C. SOAP Version 1.2. W3C Recommendation 24 June 2003.

[7] W3C. Web Services Description Language (WSDL) 2.0. W3C Working Draft 26 March 2004.

[8] OASIS. Universal Description, Discovery and Integration. UDDI Version 3.0.1. 14 October 2003.

[9] IETF/W3C. XML Signature Syntax and Processing. W3C Recommendation 12 February 2002. IETF RFC 3275. March 2002.

[10] W3C. XML Encryption Syntax and Processing. W3C Recommendation 10 December 2002.

[11] OASIS. Web Services Security: SOAP Message Security 1.0. March 2004.

[12] OASIS. Web Services Security: UsernameToken Profile 1.0. March 2004.

[13] OASIS. Web Services Security: X.509 Certificate Token Profile 1.0. March 2004.

[14] IBM, Microsoft. Web Services Security Kerberos Binding. December 2003.

[15] IBM, Microsoft, et al. Web Services Trust Language (WS-Trust). Version 1.1. May 2004.

[16] IBM, Microsoft, et al. Web Services Security Policy Language (WS-SecurityPolicy). Version 1.0. December 18, 2002.

[17] IBM, Microsoft, et al. Web Services Secure Conversation Language (WS-SecureConversation). Version 1.1. May 2004.

[18] IBM, Microsoft, et al. Web Services Federation Language (WS-Federation). Version 1.0. July 8 2003.

[19] IBM, Microsoft, et al. Web Services Policy Framework (WS-Policy). Version 1.1. 28 May 2003.

[20] IBM, Microsoft, et al. Web Services Metadata Exchange (WS-MetadataExchange). March 2004.

[21] OASIS. Security Assertion Markup Language (SAML). http://www.oasis-open.org/committees/tc_home.php?wg_abbrev=security.
[22] OASIS. eXtensible Rights Markup Language (XrML). http://www.oasis-open.org/committees/tc_home.php?wg_abbrev=rights.
[23] IBM, Microsoft, et al. Business Process Execution Language for Web Services Version 1.1. 5 May 2003.
[24] Web Services Interoperability. http://www.ws-i.org/.
[25] Microsoft Web Service Enhancements 2.0 for .NET. http://msdn.microsoft.com/webservices/building/wse/.
[26] N. Damianou, N. Dulay, E. Lupu and M. Sloman. The Ponder Policy Specification Language. Workshop on Policies for Distributed Systems and Networks. 2001. Bristol, UK.
[27] Elisa Bertino, Anna Cinzia Squicciarini, Elena Ferrari, Lorenzo D. Martino. A Comprehensive XML-based Approach for Trust Negotiations. eChallenges 2004.
[28] D.W. Chadwick, A. Otenko, E. Ball. Implementing Role Based Access Controls Using X.509 Attribute Certificates. IEEE Internet Computing, March-April 2003, pp. 62-69.
[29] T. Dimitrakos, I. Djordjevic, G. Laria, D. Mac Randal, N. Romano. Enabling Dynamic Security Perimeters for Virtual Collaborations. eChallenges 2004.
[30] Erik Rissanen. Server based application level authorisation for Rotor. IEE Proceedings Software, 150(5):291-295, October 2003.
[31] J. Haller, Y. Karabulut and P. Robinson. Integrating the Hybrid PKI Model into Trust Relationship Lifecycle for Dynamic Virtual Organizations. eChallenges 2004.
[32] T. Grandison. Trust Management for Internet Applications. PhD thesis, Imperial College London, July 2003.

Autonomic Privilege Management - Extending PERMIS to Contribute to the TrustCoM Objectives

David CHADWICK
University of Salford, The Crescent, Salford, M5 4WT, UK
Tel: +44 7796 44 7184, Fax: + 44 161 295 5351, Email: d.w.chadwick@salford.ac.uk

Abstract: This paper briefly describes the existing PERMIS privilege management infrastructure (PMI), the new TrustCoM European Integrated Project, and autonomic security. It then provides the business case for an autonomic PMI, and looks at the issues that will need to be resolved in order to make PERMIS more autonomic. In addition, it addresses the issues that TrustCoM will need to solve in order to maximise its use of an autonomic PERMIS.

1. Introduction

1.1 PERMIS

PERMIS [1] is a standard's based Privilege Management Infrastructure (PMI), built according to the ISO 10181-3 Access Control Framework [2] and X.509 [3] standards. It utilises X.509 Attribute Certificates (ACs) [3] to store user privileges (roles), and XML data structures to hold the authorisation policy. PERMIS makes its decisions by being passed the name of the subject, the name of the target, the action the subject wants to perform, and optional environmental parameters such as time of day. PERMIS then fetches the roles of the subject, which are typically stored as X.509 ACs in LDAP directories, to use in its decision making process. PERMIS implements the NIST role based access control (RBAC) model [4], and its XML policy states which roles subjects must have in order to perform which actions (e.g. project managers can update project files and team members can read project files). Because PERMIS supports hierarchical RBAC, then superior roles inherit the privileges of subordinate roles, for example, project managers could inherit the ability to read project files from team members. Optionally, additional conditions can be placed on access permissions. These conditions must be fulfilled in order for the role to be granted access, for example, grant access if the time of day is between 9am and 5pm.

A recently completed development project, in collaboration with Argonne National Laboratory, USA, has been to integrate PERMIS with Globus Toolkit v3 [5], using the GGF specified SAML interface [6]. This will allow Grid applications, often used by virtual organisations (VOs), to seamlessly use the PERMIS RBAC infrastructure to control which users, from which organisation, are authorised to do what.

1.2. TrustCoM

The TrustCoM Integrated Project [7] aims to develop a framework for trust, security and contract management in dynamically evolving VOs. This will enable secure collaborative business processing within on-demand created and self-managed, dynamic collaborative networks of organisations built on top of the emerging convergence of Web Services, agent and Grid technologies. This will allow the VOs to tackle collaborative projects that their participants could not undertake individually, and to collectively offer enhanced services to customers that could not be provided by any of the individual enterprises.

Innovations expected from TrustCoM include: mechanisms for establishing of trust, autonomic security, electronic contract management and business process enactment. PERMIS is one of the many middleware components and services that will be needed by TrustCoM in order to realise its vision. However, PERMIS will need to become more autonomic, so that the overhead of managing this security component of the trust, security and contract management framework will be lessened.

1.3. Autonomic Security

Autonomic computing has been defined by IBM as an approach to self-managed computing systems with a minimum of human interference. The term derives from the body's autonomic nervous system, which controls key functions without conscious awareness or involvement [8]. According to IBM, there are eight crucial elements in an autonomic computing system [9]: it must maintain comprehensive and specific knowledge about all its components; it must have the ability to self-configure to suit varying and possibly unpredictable conditions; it must constantly monitor itself for optimal functioning; it must be self-healing and able to find alternate ways to function when it encounters problems; it must be able to detect threats and protect itself from them; it must be able to adapt to environmental conditions; it must be based on open standards rather than proprietary technologies; and it must anticipate demand while remaining transparent to the user.

An autonomic security system will therefore have knowledge about all of the components that make up its trusted computing base. It will know which parts of the overall system can be trusted and which parts cannot. It will be able to monitor its environment and reconfigure itself with different policies and components according to the current environment and existing threats. It will be constructed from standard's conformant components so that reconfiguring is possible.

PERMIS is a standard's conformant PMI that can already make access control decisions based on the environmental conditions, so it forms a solid basis from which to build an autonomic authorisation system. What additional features will a fully autonomic self-managing, self-healing, self-configuring, self-monitoring, threat-detecting, adaptable PERMIS contain? And how will these relate to the trust and contract management infrastructure that is to be provided by TrustCoM? These are the issues that are to be (at least partially) addressed in this paper.

The rest of this paper is organised as follows. Section 2 provides the business case for an autonomic PMI such as PERMIS, its industrial significance and potential benefits. Section 3 describes the existing autonomic features of PERMIS that already contribute to the overall TrustCoM vision. Section 4 describes additional features that are required to make PERMIS more autonomic, and that we plan to provide during the TrustCoM project. Section 5 describes how it is proposed to integrate PERMIS into the TrustCoM trust management infrastructure. Finally section 6 provides a conclusion and summarises where extensions to PERMIS are needed in order to fulfil the TrustCoM objectives.

2. The Business Case for an Autonomic PMI

Attribute certificates and Privilege Management Infrastructures have been researched for more than a decade. The SESAME project [12], co-funded by the EC RACE programme in the early 1990s, was a notable milestone, and first defined privilege attribute certificates. PMIs have a significant number of advantages over traditional access control lists. These include: reduced management costs, delegation of authority, scalability, and homogeneous access control policy enforcement over a whole domain of resources. The latter ensures that "holes" do not exist in the access controls, which can often be the case with complex access control lists. PMIs allow managers who control resources to set the access control policy for the resource, while other managers are responsible for allocating user privileges. This significantly reduces the administrative workload of managers, and allows those who are know the users, to set their privileges in signed attribute certificates. Delegation of authority allows these managers to delegate their rights to subordinates, further simplifying the allocation of user privileges. Such a system is infinitely more scalable than requiring an administrator to set the access control list for all users of a resource, who must be known in advance. Policy based controls do not require this. Any user who has the necessary privilege attribute certificate will be granted access by the policy. Now that Internet use has become widespread, supporting millions of users, policy based controls become essential. Further, where short term business relationship (VOs) are continually being formed and re-formed, we need an agile system that can instantly be reconfigured to cater for the new environment. Re-setting the access control policy of a PMI is one way of achieving this.

Despite their advantages, PMIs have not yet made their way into mainstream commercial security infrastructures. Why is this? Part of the reason is that companies in the past did not have the need for such a sophisticated solution, since access controls list were quite adequate for their requirements. The cost of migration to a PMI could not be justified. But now, with the creation of virtual organisations, where resource owners wont even know all of the VO members, setting access control lists is not viable. Even if it were, they would be too time consuming and expensive to maintain. Consequently, it makes much more sense to migrate to a PMI, and to delegate the allocation of privileges to the managers in the collaborating organisations. An autonomic PMI further increases the business benefits, since it will be able to react to its environment and reconfigure itself, whilst simultaneously reducing the overall management costs.

3. Existing Autonomic Features of PERMIS

The existing PERMIS access control decision function is policy controlled, and thus PERMIS is already capable of making decision according to the prevailing environmental conditions. The PERMIS policy can contain rules, which state that access may only be granted if certain environmental parameters fall within preset values. Time of day is the most common example of this, but environmental parameters can also refer to such things as: a user's creditworthiness, a user's bank balance, a user's calling IP address etc. The implementer will need to define these environmental parameters, e.g. say what data type they are (integer, string etc) and configure the interface to pass the actual values across to PERMIS at decision time. PERMIS will then compare the actual values against those in the policy to determine if access should be granted.

PERMIS comes pre-configured with a set of operators (e.g. EQ, GT, GE, LE, LT etc.) with which to make the comparisons. It also has a plug-in capability that allows the implementer to add new operators (e.g. logically equivalent to ⇔). The Java object performing this new operation is called by the PERMIS decision engine at the appropriate time. This allows PERMIS to be adapted to changing environments and applications.

PERMIS also has the ability to continue to make access control decisions when things start to fail. For example, if a denial of service attack is under way, which prevents PERMIS from accessing a user's X.509 ACs, then PERMIS will revert to granting default access rights to the user, rather than denying the user access altogether. At the moment this functionality is rather basic, and requires the user to actually ask for services that are protected by default rights whilst (s)he is denied access to more protected services, but a future version might be expected to return the default services (as hints) if a more protected service is asked for and denied.

PERMIS can already be configured with knowledge about all its components. These comprise: the targets that it is protecting, the subjects who may be granted access, its roots of trust, and the locations of the various LDAP repositories where user attribute certificates (ACs) and attribute certificate revocation lists (ACRLs) may be obtained. It has a well defined trust model that allows it to compute its trusted computing base.

Subjects and targets are specified as domains, so that if new ones spontaneously arise within a known domain, they will already be catered for and access control decisions can be made for them. If new subjects arise from unknown domains, then they will be denied access (actually an exception is thrown). If known subjects attempt to access targets in unknown domains, they are also denied access (again, an exception is thrown). We intend in a future version to categorise different exception classes so that the processing of different exceptions classes can be handled automatically by the calling application.

Different types of targets within the same naming domain can also be selected e.g. all printers at the University of Salford, or all cluster servers at Rutherford Laboratory. This allows sites to reconfigure, add to, and subtract from their resources without having to change the access control policy for the domain.

PERMIS recognises two different types of root of trust, namely the authorisation root of trust and the PKI root of trust. The PKI root of trust is the root CA or CAs trusted to validate all the X.509 ACs that PERMIS encounters. The actual specification of the PKI root or roots of trust is left up to the configured PKI to determine, and as such is viewed as out of scope of the PERMIS policy. In other words, the configured PKI is trusted to manage itself. The authorisation root of trust configured into PERMIS at initialisation time, is the name of the manager who sets the PERMIS authorisation policy, and it is (s)he who is ultimately responsible for defining who is allowed access to which resources controlled by the policy. PERMIS allows the manager to delegate trust down to authorised subordinates, who then become part of the trusted computing base. Delegation is however tightly controlled, in that the policy states what privileges the authorised subordinates are allowed to assign to which subjects. This delegation of authority is currently static, in that the policy must be changed if new subordinates are to be authorised. A more autonomic PERMIS will allow dynamic delegation of authority to take place, and this is needed to support dynamically evolving VOs. Consequently dynamic delegation of authority is one essential feature that needs to be added during the lifetime of the TrustCoM project.

LDAP repositories are modelled as a Java subclass of a more generic repository object class, so that in future different types of repositories can be added e.g. web pages (similar to the VeriSign certificate store accessible via the HTTP protocol), file stores etc. In addition, new LDAP repositories can be dynamically made known to PERMIS at decision time, which allows the system to respond to a changing environment without reconfiguration.

4. Future Autonomic Features of PERMIS

However, PERMIS's current knowledge about and use of repositories is rather basic. They either exist or they do not, and if they exist they will be contacted. PERMIS has no ability to be configured with alternate types of repositories, backup repositories, or the detailed characteristics of its repositories, such as their performance, throughput, hours of operation etc. It has no ability to choose between different repositories according to the prevailing conditions. These are future enhancements that will need to be added in order to make PERMIS more autonomic.

Other areas in which PERMIS needs enhancements, in order to lessen the management load, are in the areas of self-healing and threat detection and protection.

PERMIS currently has the ability to be configured with different policies for different occasions e.g. a red policy for times of high alert and a green policy for low risk periods. But human intervention is required to tell PERMIS when to switch between policies. A more autonomic PERMIS will be able to automatically switch between policies when it detects threats/incidents to itself or to the environment. For example, if PERMIS detects that ACRL repositories that should be available are not available, it might decide to switch to a higher security policy, or if unusually many access requests are being denied, this could indicate an attack. If PERMIS detects that an attacker is trying to gain unauthorised access to resources, it could reduce the attacker's existing access rights, or notify a manager, or both. When PERMIS is linked to the trust infrastructure (see later), if it detects a user has become less trustworthy it could reduce their existing access rights, or conversely, if a user becomes more trustworthy they could gain access rights.

More sophisticated decision-making is required in order to enforce the mutual exclusivity of roles. Mutual exclusivity mandates that a user be not allowed to hold conflicting roles, for example, buyer and seller, or examiner and pupil. In the context of TrustCoM, mutual exclusivity could refer to membership of competing VOs that access common resources. If a user does posses conflicting roles, then they should be denied access to all actions that require any of the conflicting roles. Implementation of this feature will require an upgrade to the PERMIS policy and decision engine, but also may require knowledge of role memberships to be remembered by the decision engine.

Several of the more advanced autonomic features require PERMIS to keep an historical record of past access attempts and role memberships etc. in order to inform future access decisions. This feature is referred to as Retained ADI in [2]. In order to implement Retained ADI, PERMIS will need to have access to a secure transaction database, in which all past access decisions are logged. Fast searching of this database will be essential if the authorisation decision-making is not to be unduly slowed down as a result. We intend to implement this feature during the lifetime of the TrustCoM project.

5. Linking PERMIS to the Trust Infrastructure

The TrustCoM framework will establish a trust infrastructure, in which entities reputations are computed and shared between all the entities in VOs. As entities participate reliably in contracts, one might expect their reputations to increase, and conversely, if they default on contracts, one might expect their reputations to diminish. By adding a new condition to the PERMIS policy, namely the trustworthiness (or reputation) of a subject, the policy will be able to state that subjects are only allowed access to perform certain actions on certain targets if their trustworthiness is greater or equal to a particular value, and if not, that they are only to be granted lower access rights. (We note that a subject's inherent trustworthiness is manifest through interactions with the subject, but that it is the subject's reputation that is transferred between third parties and is thus measured. We use the terms interchangeably in the discussion here.) Below a certain trustworthiness, a subject could be denied access completely. There are however particular difficulties with this model, which have to be overcome, before it can be fully implemented in PERMIS.

Firstly, trustworthiness or reputation is linked to entities (individual, organisations, trusted third parties etc.) but the PERMIS infrastructure currently makes access control decisions based on the roles of the entity. Just because one role holder acts in an untrustworthy manner does not mean that all role holders should be trusted less. Therefore PERMIS will need to be modified to include the identity of the subject in its decision making process (which means that the decision making process will no longer be pure RBAC). In the TrustCoM project we will determine the best way of achieving this. One possible solution is that the conditional IF statement supported by PERMIS could be enhanced to include the identity of the subject, for example, IF trustworthiness of <subject> GE <some value> THEN grant access.

Secondly there is the issue of apportioning responsibility in order to determine who is to be held accountable when a contract is breached in some respect, and as a consequence, whose reputation should be decremented. We need to clearly distinguish between the various actors such as employees, role issuing authorities and organisations. When an employee, assigned roles by an Attribute Authority (AA), participates in a contract on behalf of their organisation, and fails to fulfil the obligations of the contract, is it the organisation that is less trustworthy as a result, or the employee acting on behalf of the organisation, or the AA that issued privileges/roles to the individual? At what point should the organisation audit the actions of its employees and make recompense? When should an AA revoke the privileges/roles of the holders who abuse them? When should all three entities be held accountable in some way and all three have their reputations decreased? These are some of the issues that the TrustCom consortium must resolve since the outcomes will affect the trust information feeding into the decision making process of PERMIS.

Thirdly, the TrustCoM framework assumes that trustworthiness or reputation can be measured and given a value to be used in comparison operations. The metrics of trustworthiness are something that will need to be developed within the TrustCoM project.

Fourthly we need to consider the trustworthiness of the reputation broker that issued the reputation statement about the subject. What if the reputation broker itself is not that trustworthy? We thus have a recursive problem, in that in order to determine the trustworthiness of a subject we need to first determine the trustworthiness of the reputation broker that issues reputation statements about subjects. This recursive process can only stop with the trustors themselves, who ultimately will have to decide how much they trust certain reputation brokers or trusted third parties that act as trust anchors or roots of trust in the trust computing chain. This is sometimes termed plausibility considerations in the literature [10]. An interesting alternative scenario has recently been proposed by Philipp Obreiter [10] who suggests that rather than having plausibility considerations about reputation brokers, instead the transacting parties themselves could provide digitally signed evidences that show they have participated faithfully in transactions. We thus no longer need to trust the reputation brokers themselves. We only need to trust the roots of trust in the PKI (i.e. the Certification Authorities) that provided identity certificates to the transacting parties (to ensure that masquerade is not taking place) and the parties providing the evidences to ensure that collusion is not taking place (i.e. making up false claims between themselves).

Previous research by the author [11] addressed the former problem by computing trust quotients for Certification Authorities, trust quotients taking values being between 0 and 1 (where 0 represents completely untrustworthy and 1 represents completely trustworthy). The system also had a TrustCheck server that polled the network retrieving information upon which the trust quotient was based, so that dynamic trust quotient calculations could be made. Extending this work could provide some of the autonomic features of the trust infrastructure that we are looking to provide in TrustCoM. However, the knowledge involved in deciding whose trust-quotient to alter, and by how much, and under which conditions, and indeed what elements of trustworthiness are involved, is complex and highly ill-structured. Furthermore, it will be important to explore the juridical ramifications of such trust-altering decisions, and to build these into the knowledge base. To acquire such knowledge to a degree that is commensurate with normal juridical practice will require considerable knowledge acquisition expertise. Such a knowledge base could potentially be generated during the TrustCoM project.

6. Conclusions

We have shown that the PERMIS authorisation infrastructure already contains a number of features that constitute autonomic computing. However, in order to make the PERMIS authorisation infrastructure fully autonomic, and to better integrate it into the TrustCoM framework, addition enhancements are needed such as: the ability to grant default rights automatically if a user's requested rights are denied; dynamic delegation of authority which will allow new managers to be automatically included in a VO; the addition of new types of repository such as web pages and file stores; the ability to select between different repositories according to the prevailing access conditions; automatic switching between access control policies according to the changing security environment; implementing mutual exclusion of roles to prevent users abusing their privileges; adding a secure historical database/audit function so as to base future decisions on past ones; and making decisions based on the trustworthiness or reputation of the accessing subject. The latter PERMIS enhancement places a number of requirements on the TrustCoM infrastructure, namely: how to measure the trustworthiness/reputation of subjects, how to determine the trustworthiness of reputation brokers, how to apportion responsibility between the various actors when a contract fails to be fulfilled, and how to collect and use evidences on which trustworthiness/reputation calculations are based. Whilst it may not be possible to solve all of these challenging problems during the lifetime of the TrustCoM project, we certainly intend to make significant progress towards doing so.

References

[1] D.W.Chadwick, A. Otenko, E.Ball. "Implementing Role Based Access Controls Using X.509 Attribute Certificates", IEEE Internet Computing, March-April 2003, pp. 62-69.

[2] ITU-T Rec X.812 (1995) | ISO/IEC 10181-3:1996 "Security Frameworks for open systems: Access control framework"

[3] ISO 9594-8/ITU-T Rec. X.509 (2001) The Directory: Public-key and attribute certificate frameworks

[4] The NIST RBAC Standard can be downloaded from http://csrc.nist.gov/rbac/

[5] A.Otenko, D.W.Chadwick, Von Welch "Integrating PERMIS with GT3" – in preparation

[6] Von Welch, Frank Siebenlist, David Chadwick, Sam Meder, Laura Pearlman. "Use of SAML for OGSA Authorization", Jan 2004, Available from https://forge.gridforum.org/projects/ogsa-authz

[7] The TrustCoM website is at http://www.eu-TrustCoM.com/

[8] http://www.research.ibm.com/autonomic/glossary.html#ac

[9] http://www.research.ibm.com/autonomic/overview/elements.html

[10] Philipp Obreiter "A Case for Evidence-Aware Distributed Reputation Systems" in Proceedings of the 2nd International Conference on Trust Management, 2004

[11] E.Ball, D.W Chadwick, A. Basden. "The Implementation of a System for Evaluating Trust in a PKI Environment" in *Trust in the Network Economy*, Evolaris vol 2. Eds Otto Petrovic, Michael Ksela, Markus Fallenbock, Christian Kitti. Pp 263-279, SpringerWein, 2003. ISBN 3-211-06853-8. (also available from http://sec.isi.salford.ac.uk/Papers.htm)

[12] SESAME project. See https://www.cosic.esat.kuleuven.ac.be/sesame/

eAdoption and the Knowledge Economy: Issues, Applications, Case Studies
P. Cunningham and M. Cunningham (Eds.)
IOS Press, 2004

Integrating the Hybrid PKI Model into Trust Relationship Lifecycle for Dynamic Virtual Organizations

Jochen HALLER, Yücel KARABULUT, Philip ROBINSON
SAP Research, CEC Karlsruhe, Vincenz-Priessnitz-Str. 1, 76131 Karlsruhe, Germany
Tel: +49 721 690284, Fax: +49 6227 7843082
Email: Jochen.Haller@sap.com, Yuecel.Karabulut@sap.com, Philip.Robinson@sap.com

Abstract: Virtual Organizations (VOs) are proposed as the future of collaborative business systems. For dynamic VOs, specification and enforcement of permissions can be based on a public key infrastructure, with its foundations in asymmetric cryptography. In our initial work, we identified the trust relationship planning as feature that could serve trust management in the context of dynamic VOs, and proposed a trust relationship lifecycle. In this paper we make a contribution to the trust management layer of dynamic VOs by suggesting how a trust relationship planning approach could be technically supported by a hybrid PKI model. This has been analysed to the point where VO members reach a phase of commitment.

1. Introduction

A VO is understood as either a temporary or permanent coalition constructed from heterogeneous and autonomous business units or organizations that pool resources and capabilities to achieve a common goal. Dynamic Virtual Organizations, which are formed on-demand, share services and resources across enterprise boundaries in order to tackle collaborative projects that their participants could not undertake individually, or to offer composed services that could not be provided by individual enterprises. The formation of VOs is driven by several partially overlapping objectives: opening new markets, risk reduction, overcoming trade barriers, linking complementary competences of the partners in a value system, achieving synergy effects, etc. Such VOs will be based on new forms of collaboration in which participants can specify and negotiate their own conditions of involvement by means of electronic contracts. The collaborations can be established only by using a secure computing infrastructure. In such collaborations, the credentials of the involved participants, along with their respective roles and permissions, can be specified and enforced using a public key infrastructure (PKI). Previous trust management approaches to credential based access control are classified as based on trusted authorities with licensing or based on ownership with delegation. As reported previously, these approaches have been extended and integrated into a novel hybrid PKI model [2][3][5][6][7].

The state of the art in trust management provides support for verifying and maintaining trust between parties by way of specifying authorization policies, codifying digitally signed digital credentials, and evaluating credential chains. We refer to these as "live" operational issues that reflect the pending and somewhat basic access control needs of the partners rather than their strategic objectives. Strategic objectives are more concerned with the *control of the process* rather than of the data accessed. We suggest that a trust management solution adequate for the needs of a VO should support strategic forecasting, process optimization, service and resource selection, monitoring and decision support. In our previously published work [14], we identified trust relationship planning as a feature missing from trust management in the context of dynamic VOs and proposed a novel trust relationship lifecycle as a model upon which this planning is based.

We argue that a trust management infrastructure as needed by dynamic VOs may employ the hybrid PKI model in order to fulfil the trust management related requirements of involved business partners. In this paper we make a contribution to the trust management aspect of dynamic VOs by evaluating our trust relationship-planning concept against the hybrid PKI model, and hence proposing the hybrid PKI model as a basis for the underlying support of the trust relationship lifecycle. While this evaluation justifies that the trust relationship planning approach is applicable and foreseeable in dynamic VO environment, the integration shows that the hybrid PKI model is a comprehensive trust management approach that operates on strategically defined trust parameters.

This paper is structured as follows. Section 2 discusses why dynamic VOs need a strategic relationship centric approach to trust management. Section 3 outlines the trust relationship lifecycle. Section 4 presents characteristics of a concrete informational environment (4.1) associated with a aggregated services scenario (4.2), revisits the hybrid PKI model (4.3) and shows the evaluation of trust relationship planning against the hybrid PKI model. Finally, Section 5 presents conclusions and future work.

2. Strategic Trust Relationship Management for Virtual Organizations

A popular scenario that exploits a VO model is found in Collaborative Engineering. For example, designers, manufacturers and testers are not only disparate in terms of their physical location, but also in terms of their view with respect to the requirements of the product to be built [15]. The process of transferring requirements and results between these groups includes a number of quality controls, as the meaning of requirements and expectations of the different production groups is generally not clear. Trust management should therefore be considered as a means of optimising the processes by justified reduction in the number of controls between steps in the process. Note that in the absence of trust concerning a particular interaction between parties, a contract may be specified in order that an operational control or monitor is not required, as the implications of low quality or failure to deliver are specified but not immediately controlled. However, our emphasis in this paper remains with the management of trust relationships, as contractual relationships are another theme beyond the scope of this paper. Trust is an accepted “social energy” that binds parties together, yet a comprehensive technical understanding and representation of this energy within computer system interactions is to this date not entirely existent – how is it created, measured, preserved and transferred? In the Collaborative Engineering Scenario, it is foreseen that future collaborations may be between smaller organizations without any prior interaction, more reliant on Information Computer Technology (ICT), and dynamically formed as the result of a client’s circumstance or specification e.g. current location, specialized quality controls and conditions, existing partners and legal restrictions. Some of the questions that we continue to deal with include: when does trust begin to play a role in the advancement of the relationship? How do the responsible parties within a VO determine the trustworthiness of new markets and communities that are required to meet the circumstance? Are there particular controls that can be removed in order to optimise the process of operation on the basis of a “trustworthy environment”? Is it necessary for the VO members to reach consensus regarding policies and new partners? These are the issues we address through the integration of a planning concept (trust relationship planning) and a flexible credential management solution (hybrid PKI model).

From a solutions perspective, we have considered Trust Management to be a form of Relationship Management System. Other relationship management systems of which we possess functional and features knowledge are SRM (Supplier Relationship Management) and CRM (Customer Relationship Management) systems. These systems have evolved over time due a competitive market and customer demand. They are concerned with forging mutually beneficial, efficient and profitable relationships between a business, its suppliers and customers respectively. When reading marketing statements or technical white papers covering these products, support for activities associated with planning resources, production cycles, marketing, investment, and other strategic decisions are always the key system features. We found it practical to correlate these features with the perceived strategic needs for trust in VOs. The resources of a trust relationship are credentials and other forms of evidence (recommendations and reputation), with which the quality and productivity of a process can be certified.

The novel challenges of the VO come with the vision of computer-based automation. A key aim is therefore to make the tasks of establishing, monitoring and advancing trust between production systems more of a system-activity requiring minimal human involvement. The human's role in the management will be increasingly conceptualisation and parameterisation of business processes, while the system efficiently enacts the process without failing neither the expectations of the process stakeholders or the integrity of their assets and data. Our approach is to offer a baseline for automated trust management, equipping existing trust management approaches with a facility for utilization and integration in VO environments. Our vision is an application independent process model based on representing the states and ensuing lifecycle of dynamic VO relationships. Variant trust models can then be flexibly selected for use in discrete states of the VO relationships, based on the context, available knowledge and nature of resources.

3. Trust Relationship Lifecycle

Strader et al. [16] provide a general state-model of the complex VO relationships but do not explicitly discuss trust as an important driver that causes these states to transition. They describe the states of Identification, Formation, Operation and Termination of the VO. Nevertheless, the SECURE project proposes that trust itself may be abstracted into states, and defines the phases of *Formation* (establishing initial trustworthiness), *Evolution* (iterating the process of trust formation) and *Exploitation* (determination of behaviour on the basis of trust). When considering the semantics of these two state models, they appear to be complementary and transitionally related. That is, we can either view the trust state as the conditions under which a relationship is advanced, or, vice-versa, the relationship state as the context within which trust is advanced. This is represented in figure 1.

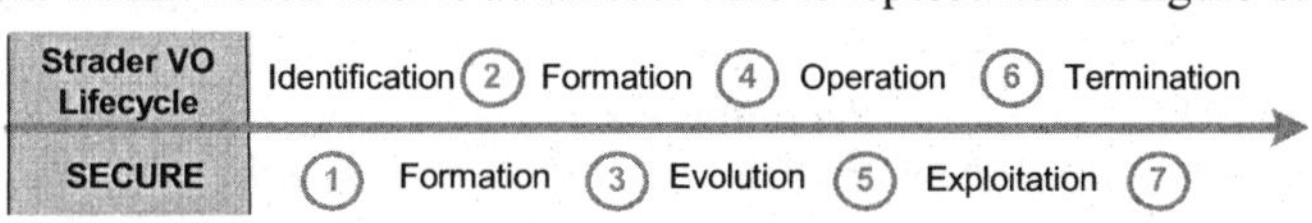

Figure 1. *Combination of VO and Trust Lifecycles [taken from 14]*

Considering these as accepted models, we contributed new designations for how we could describe their combined states and represent them in a single lifecycle for a trust relationship between at least two parties. We consider a party in a relationship as having a set of characterizing properties (e.g. legal identity, roles, group memberships, capabilities), a set of published resources (e.g. delivered products, white papers) and a set of protected resources (e.g. product recipes, internal processes). These are possible sources upon which the definition and value of trust within a relationship can be measured, consistent with the differentiation of reputation, recommendation and experience as mechanisms of trust building. In accordance with what we have depicted in figure 1, the advancement of trust in a relationship is considered a refinement process that advances until the relationship's objectives can be considered fulfilled or validity nullified. These phases are described below preceded by the designations we have derived, with respect to a relationship initiated by a party A with another party B:

(1) Existence: A has formulated an objective yet neither A nor B are aware of each other's characterizing properties, nor have accessed each other's published resources (moreover not each other's protected resources).

(2) Awareness: A has discovered a subset of the characterizing properties of B and/ or published resources.

(3) Intent: A contacts B by using a subset of B's characterizing properties and B therefore receives a subset of the characterizing attributes of A.

(4) Commitment: A and B decide on particular access to their individual protected resources, and come to an agreement on those that will be exchanged during their interaction.

(5) Operational - Active: A and B exchange protected resources and create new published resources.

(6) Operational - Inactive: A and B cease to exchange protected resources for either technical or contractual purposes

(7) Unrecoverable: A and B end the relationship but the created public and exchanged protected resources are no longer recoverable.

The goal of Trust Relationship Planning is to find a means of optimising these phases based on the parameters of the relationship objectives. The exchange and interpretation of previously unrelated data and semantics is a capability of the underlying system.

4. Evaluation

4.1 Informational Environment

Virtual Organisations can provide services and thus participate as a single entity in the formation of further Virtual Organisations. For example, in a Collaborative Engineering (CE) scenario, one of the participating suppliers could need to deliver an aggregated service to the VO planner of the CE scenario. For this purpose, this supplier may initiate a second VO, in which some other suppliers may deliver services for the aggregated service needed. Thus, we can have recursive VOs realizing hybrid scenarios.

We consider an informational environment in which a dynamic VO brings independent and autonomous service providers (SPs) together to deliver ad-hoc aggregated services to a customer. In such environments, in response to a customer requirement a bundle of services is composed on the fly to provide a composite service tailored to the customer's needs. The participating providers contribute with their core competence and thereby generate a "best-of-breed" construct in respect of required service.

More specifically, we consider a dynamic VO environment where the customers and service providers as suppliers are brought together by an aggregated service provider (ASP). The ASP is a third party provider with no organizational relationship to the customers and service providers. There is no fixed business relationships between the ASP and SPs. The SPs are evolving or dissolving based on market driven criteria. The participating entities remain independent of their peers, with the aim to satisfy abstract requirements that correspond to their core competence.

Furthermore, we observe following crucial points:

- Each entity in the VO is represented by (one of) its public key(s) and characterized by the assigned properties.
- A trusted authority or a server (e.g. ASP) itself assigns properties to public keys.
- A server follows a security policy that is expressed in terms of properties.

4.2 Problem description

The main goal of current SRM systems is to help organizations evaluate the capacity of suppliers all over the world to deliver high-qualified goods that match their specific needs as fast and efficient as possible. Strategic sourcing, as an important process of SRM systems, is the process of finding qualified sources to fulfil supply needs, negotiate agreements, manage contracts, and evaluate supplier performance. Looking at the state-of-the-art strategic sourcing process, we observe following steps: request for invitations (RFI), request for quotations (RFQs), reverse auctioning, and contract management. We argue that finding qualified and credible suppliers and evaluating their qualifications and capabilities can be a daunting task for many organizations.

What is the concrete problem? Whatever composed services an ASP has to offer, it may aim at contacting a wide range of potential qualified SPs, which are in general unknown in advance and may belong to heterogeneous and autonomous security domains. Why is the problem a problem? The conceptual challenge arising in this situation concerns how an ASP and service provider, potentially acting in different security domains, reach a common understanding of the meaning of properties, and how they establish trust that claimed properties are valid indeed. On the one hand, characterizing properties (e.g. certified and recognized supplier) are assigned to service providers in their autonomously operating security domains, in principle without knowing their later usage. On the other hand, the ASP independently defines its security policies in terms of these properties. What is the solution? In such situations the ASP wishes to be assisted to determine potentially qualified service providers. To reach potentially eligible service providers, an ASP could use a specific software agent which could map between the ASP's property-based security policy and service providers' characterizing properties which have been asserted by some trusted parties. Why is the solution a solution? Electronic business transactions will involve asserted commitments, properties, etc. from many parties and the participants of such transactions will, in general, not be in a position to understand or manage everything that is involved. To reach qualified suppliers, who might belong to remote, separate security domains, organizations acting as ASPs will need to trust mediating software agents as trust services providers (TSPs) (see section 4.3) having the required domain expertise as well as the relationships with the potential clients.

We argue that the basic assumptions of the current SRM systems are not valid in such dynamic VOs. An organization acting as a VO planner (in this case an ASP) need to quickly and effectively identify, select, and negotiate with the best partners to achieve the best portfolio of suppliers to optimize price, risk, and performance. In particular, organizations may not know all marketplaces (or catalogues) where potentially qualified suppliers are registered, and even if they know them, the VO planner may not be in a position to understand and verify the certified properties of the suppliers. In order to achieve the lowest total cost for an upcoming product development effort, the VO planner needs to find the optimal portfolio of suppliers that satisfy its supply requirements. By expanding qualified supplier base, a VO planner can also maximize the competition across suppliers and thus achieve the lowest total cost.

4.3 Integrating the Hybrid PKI Model into TRP Lifecycle

Due to the dynamic and open nature of VOs, it will be difficult for the participants of a VO to establish and enforce procedures for engaging safely in a heterogeneous VO. There are technologies available for specifying and enforcing security policies. However, it is not at all easy for non-specialist companies to use them and deliver services that would allow such companies to easily achieve the trust levels and protection levels they desire. Furthermore, the complexity of trust and security related tasks will increase the level of risks for VO participants. The risks will be passed to those specialist providers, which will have the expertise to understand the trade offs and handle the complexity. We argue that, in addition to main players of a VO including VO planners and main service providers (e.g. ASPs, SPs), we will have so-called "trust service providers" acting as neutral mediators or protecting the interests of particular VO participants. The hybrid PKI model provides necessary support for establishment of the relationships between the main service providers and trust service providers. We present this support by integrating the main tasks of the hybrid PKI model into the trust relationship lifecycle (see section 3).

The Hybrid PKI Model [2][3][5][6][7] has been developed to be used for specifying and enforcing credential-based access control policies in distributed computing systems. The hybrid model integrates, unifies and extends previous approaches, in particular X.509 [12] dealing with free properties (characterizing attributes of entities, including group membership) and SPKI/SDSI [11] dealing with bound properties (promises to get a specific service, including capabilities). The Hybrid PKI Model allows protocols that enable servers to permit access for strangers as clients only based on their approved characterizing properties. Speaking more technically: a client can characterize himself by showing properties that are assigned to him by potentially other entities and that are encoded in certificates and credentials; a server can either base access decisions directly on such properties, or first convert such properties into potentially conditional promises to be returned to the client for later use and then examine these promises on request; property conversion can also be delegated to mediating agents.

In all cases, at some step, whether explicit or implicit, a property conversion of free properties into bound properties takes place. Here the term "bound" is intended to express some kind of promise for a service and thus a relationship of the property holder to a server, whereas the term "free" is intended to indicate a feature of the property holder alone. The interpretation of properties as free or bound depends on the context, or more technically on the security domains where the properties are assigned. In order to cross domain borders, again property conversions might be necessary, and manageable indeed. As testbed for the design the authors analysed protocols dealing with some form of property conversion for secure mediated information systems [9][10].

Considering the aggregated services scenario outlined in Section 4.2, following steps will be needed in order to solve the problem exhibited in that section:

(1) a SP is a holder of some free properties (e.g. outstanding service provider of the year) in a domain A and offers a specific service. We assume that the SP has already collected his free properties and corresponding free property-certificates.
(2) an ASP is the provider and owner of aggregated services in a domain B and looking for qualified SPs. The ASP defines the services he is seeking, and its security policy expressed in terms of characterizing properties of potential qualified SPs.
(3) a TSP is a delegatee who has the expertise in interpreting the free properties of the SP and is able to map between the ASP's property-based security policy and SP's free properties which have been asserted by some trusted parties in domain A. We assume that the ASP knows already the TSP.
(4) The ASP expresses by a delegation credential that the TSP is entitled to assign a specific bound property (e.g. award-winning service provider), i.e., to grant corresponding credentials.
(5) The TSP defines its property conversion policy specifying which set of free properties an SP has to enjoy in order to obtain a bound property assignment.
(6) The TSP finds a suppliers pool and contacts a potential qualified SP having the services sought by ASP and sends an invitation request.

(7) The SP shows his certified free property-certificates and applies for a bound property from the TSP who is acting as a grantor on behalf of and in explicit delegation of a ASP.
(8) The TSP:
   a) verifies the submitted free property-certificates with the supporting licences,
   b) extracts the contents of the free property-certificates and interprets them as free properties,
   c) applies his conversion policy on the extracted free properties, and
   d) finally, if all checks have been successfully completed, grants a bound property-credential where the subject (grantee) is the same public key as in the submitted free property-certificates.
(9) The SP contacts the ASP and shows its bound property-credentials with supporting delegations.
(10) The ASP, after verifying the submitted credentials, follows its "reconfirmation policy" [8] for bound properties (as security policy aiming at confidentiality) to decide whether the SP is a qualified service provider or not, based on shown bound properties.
(11) In the positive case, the ASP performs a chain reduction process [12] and grants a reduced credential encoding the access rights that will be used by the SP in order to contact the ASP for further activities (e.g. contract formation).

Now, we can relate the steps shown above into the TRP lifecycle, as presented below:
Existence: Neither ASP nor SP are aware of each other's characterizing properties and security policies, nor have accessed each other's published resources (moreover not each other's protected resources). (See steps 1, 2, and 3)
Awareness: TSP has discovered a subset of the characterizing properties of B and published services (e.g. Web services). TSP has done this on behalf of and in explicit delegation of a ASP. (See steps 4 and 5).
Intent: TSP contacts SP, applies his property conversion policy by using a subset of B's characterizing properties, and B therefore receives a subset of the bound properties ASP. (See steps 6, 7, and 8). The SP contacts ASP and ASP checks whether SP is a qualified service provider or not.
Commitment: ASP decides on particular access to their individual protected resources, and grants a credential encoding necessary capabilities to the SP for its further contacts as a qualified service provider.

5. Conclusions

We considered an informational environment in which a dynamic VO brings independent and autonomous service providers (SPs) together to deliver ad-hoc aggregated services to a customer. We argued that finding qualified and credible suppliers and evaluating their qualifications and capabilities will be one of the challenges of dynamic VOs. As a solution we proposed a Hybrid PKI based approach. In this paper we made a contribution to the trust management aspect of dynamic VOs by evaluating our trust relationship planning concept against the Hybrid PKI model, and integrated the hybrid PKI model into the phases of the trust relationship lifecycle. As a future work, we plan to use the hybrid PKI as part of the underlying support for achieving interoperability between other components in the VO space as described in TrustCoM [1]. These include other trusted service providers like notaries for contract management and monitors for quality control.

References

[1] TrustCoM. A Trust and Contract Management framework enabling secure collaborative business processing in on-demand created, self-managed, scalable, and highly dynamic Virtual Organisations. http://www.eu-trustcom.com/.

[2] J. Biskup and Y. Karabulut: A Hybrid PKI Model for Access Control in Distributed Systems with Mediation. March 2004, submitted to a journal for publication.
[3] J. Biskup and Y. Karabulut: A Hybrid PKI Model with an Application for Secure Mediation. In 16th Annual IFIP WG 11.3 Working Conference on Data and Application Security, pages 271-282, Cambridge, England, July 2002. Kluwer Academic Press.
[4] Y. Karabulut: Investigating Trust Management Approaches for Trustworthy Business Processing for Dynamic Virtual Organizations. Special Session on Security and Privacy in E-Commerce within the 7th International Conference on Electronic Commerce Research, INFOMART, Dallas, June 2004.
[5] Y. Karabulut: Towards a Next-Generation Trust Management Infrastructure for Open Computing Systems. Security and Privacy Workshop within the 2nd Pervasive Computing Conference, Vienna, April 2004, to appear.
[6] Y. Karabulut: Developing a Trust Management Based Secure Interoperable Information System. Special Session on Security and Privacy in E-Commerce within the 6th International Conference on Electronic Commerce Research, INFOMART, Dallas, October 2003.
[7] Y. Karabulut: Implementation of an Agent-Oriented Trust Management Infrastructure Based on a Hybrid PKI Model. In 1st International Conference on Trust Management, LNCS 2692, pages 318-331, Crete, Greece, May 2003.
[8] J. Biskup and Y. Karabulut: Mediating Between Strangers: A Trust Management Based Approach. In 2nd Annual PKI Research Workshop, pages 80-95, Gaithersburg, Maryland, USA, April 2003.
[9] C. Altenschmidt, J. Biskup, U. Flegel and Y. Karabulut: Secure Mediation: Requirements, Design and Architecture. Journal of Computer Security, 11(3):365-398, 2003.
[10] Y. Karabulut: Secure Mediation Between Strangers in Cyberspace, Ph.D. Thesis, University of Dortmund, 2002.
[11] SPKI/SDSI. http://theworld.com/~cme/html/spki.html#1-SPKI/SDSI.
[12] X.509. http://www.ietf.org/html.charters/pkix-charter.html.
[13] Yu, T., Winslett, M., and Seamons, K. 2003. Supporting Structured Credentials and Sensitive Policies Through Interoperable Strategies for Automated Trust Negotiation. ACM Transactions on Information and System Security 6, 1 (Feb.), 1-42.
[14] J. Haller, R. Kilian-Kehr and P. Robinson. Towards Trust Relationship Planning in Virtual Organizations. 2nd International Conference on Trust Management, Oxford, March 2004
[15] Aca, Mejía, et. al. Integrated Product Development in Virtual Enterprises Supported by Web-Based Applications, pp. 361-368 Processes and Foundations for Virtual Organizations, Kluwer Academic Press, ISBN/SKU 140207638X, 2003.
[16] Strader, T.J., Lin, F. and Shaw, M.J. (1998), Information structure for electronic virtual organization management, Decision Support Systems, 23, pp. 75-94

eAdoption and the Knowledge Economy: Issues, Applications, Case Studies
P. Cunningham and M. Cunningham (Eds.)
IOS Press, 2004

Decision Support and Strategy Formulation in Supply Chain Management

Matthias SCHNETZLER[1], Andreas NOBS[2], Andreas SENNHEISER[3]
Center for Enterprise Sciences (BWI), Swiss Federal Institute of Technology (ETH) Zürich, 8092 Zürich, Switzerland
[1]*Tel: +41 44 632 05 34, Fax: +41 44 632 10 40, Email: matthias.schnetzler@ethz.ch*
[2]*Tel: +41 44 632 05 31, Fax: +41 44 632 10 40, Email: andreas.nobs@ethz.ch*
[3]*Tel: +41 44 632 05 25, Fax: +41 44 632 10 40, Email: andreas.sennheiser@ethz.ch*

Abstract: This paper outlines the application of the Axiomatic Design methodology to supply chain management for the formulation and implementation of supply chain strategies. After an overview of strategic supply chain management issues, the supply chain design decomposition SCDD is presented, which systematically distinguishes objectives and means. The SCDD is used to formulate and implement supply chain strategies, which are aligned with top-level business objectives in the sense of value-based management. This approach is framed into a decision making process. A short case study illustrates the application of the methodology.

1. Introduction: Issues in Strategic Supply Chain Management

Supply chain management (SCM) is a successful concept for the co-operation of enterprises in the area of logistics by connecting, aligning and coordinating processes in supply chains as well as flows of material and information between suppliers and customers. "Supply chain management is the coordination of a strategic and long-term cooperation among co-makers in the total logistics network for the development and production of products, both in production and procurement and in product and process innovation"[1].

While many concepts and best practices exist on an operational level of SCM, on the strategic level dealing with business objectives, the subject of supply chain strategies has hardly received attention [2]. Nevertheless, the interest of top management in SCM on a strategic level is growing due to its impact on business success as surveys show [3], [4]. Therefore, there is a need to close the gap between the strategic and operational level of SCM: The application of concepts and methods of SCM (e.g. vendor managed inventory) should be aligned with the business strategy in order to ensure the achievement of top-level business objectives (shareholder value, sales, profit, customer satisfaction, etc.). Strategic SCM deals with supply chain strategies and priorities and pursues the development of logistic capabilities for competitive advantages. The supply chain strategy itself can be described as a balanced set of appropriate measures for the development and exploitation of competitive capabilities and improvement potentials in terms of logistics and SCM in order to achieve logistics and supply chain objectives. These objectives usually cover the target areas of quality, delivery (lead time), flexibility and costs [1] and, additionally in supply chains, collaboration, coordination and transformability [5].

In literature, three main trends and issues concerning SCM on a strategic level can be identified: strategy focus, value based focus and performance focus. Strategy focus is about the strategic alignment of supply chain strategies with business strategies, which is considered crucial for business success (e.g., [6], [7]). The value based focus aims to align all management activities to improve the company value. Value based management (VBM) originates from financial management and is widely accepted and used (e.g., shareholder value, economic value added, economic profit, etc.). However, the adoption of VBM to logistics and especially to SCM is in an early stage. The pivotal questions of a value based SCM are: "How to derive means and ways from objectives in order to create value?", "How do measures contribute to value creation?" and "What are the value drivers of SCM?". Answers to these questions are the basis for the formulation of supply chain strategies. Research on the value drivers of SCM is not very profound since the relationships between objectives and means are not analysed in detail. As a consequence, the impacts of SCM on business objectives are not considered in a holistic way. In the area of the performance focus, the importance of supply chain performance is high and increasing [3]. Furthermore, there exist many concepts of performance measurement and management in SCM, e.g., performance indicators of SCOR etc. (Supply Chain Operations Reference model), benchmarking, controlling and monitoring as well as balanced scorecard. There intend is to quantify, measure and improve the logistics performance of supply chains.

2. Objectives and Context

The gap between strategic SCM and business strategy needs to be closed, so that SCM contributes to business success in a sustainable way in the sense of value based management. This will be achieved by aligning supply chain strategy with business strategy and measured and improved using performance measurement and management. This paper presents a methodology, which facilitates the formulation of comprehensive supply chain strategies based on overall business objectives. Furthermore, it provides supply chain managers with decision support for the improvement of supply chain performance. The Axiomatic Design methodology (to be introduced) forms the basis for this approach.

This subject is part of PRODCHAIN, an international research project with several academic and industrial partners co-funded by the European Commission IST programme (IST-2000-61205). The main objective of PRODCHAIN is to develop a decision support methodology to analyse and improve logistics performance of globally acting production networks. The outcome is a toolbox consisting of performance indicators, a benchmarking database, customer-supplier relationship processes (based on the PRODCHAIN generic model) as well as best practices of SCM [8]. The toolbox provides decision support for the improvement of logistics performance and the selection of appropriate best practices.

3. Methodology: A Decomposition of Supply Chain Design

Axiomatic Design is a scientific approach developed at the Massachusetts Institute of Technology for the generation and selection of good design solutions for products, processes and systems (see [9], [10]). It focuses on the identification of functional requirements FRs (what to achieve), i.e., objectives, and the selection of means for achieving them, i.e., design parameters DPs (how to achieve). By decomposing the design into several levels of objectives-means-combinations, a hierarchical causal model of the design is created showing the connections of an objective and the corresponding solution. In doing so iteratively, high level objectives and means are decomposed and concretised into lower level objectives and means until a level of detail is reached, which is sufficient for implementation. Axiomatic Design has been successfully applied in a large number of examples [10], among them for the development of manufacturing systems [11].

In PRODCHAIN, Axiomatic Design was applied to SCM; the result is the Supply Chain Design Decomposition (SCDD). The highest level of SCDD concerns strategic SCM and is set up in a value based manner following the concept of economic value added (EVA), which represents business success in the sense of value based management (VBM) [12]. EVA is net operating profit after taxes minus a capital charge, which depends on the total invested capital and the capital costs. The EVA concept is widely used and accepted; it can be transformed into other concepts of VBM (like economic profit, shareholder value etc.). The overall objective of an enterprise is to increase the EVA. The achievement of this objective can be facilitated by means of excellence in SCM.

The SCDD is set up in a systematic way as follows:

- The EVA concept is the root of the decomposition.
- First, the target areas of SCM regarding quality, reliability, flexibility, lead times, assets and costs are covered in this specific order.
- Second, in each target area the generic value-adding SCM processes "source", "make", and "deliver" are considered.
- Third, these processes are in turn differentiated according to the input factors capacities, information, and material.

Figure 1 shows the set up of the SCDD by means of an example path of decomposition.

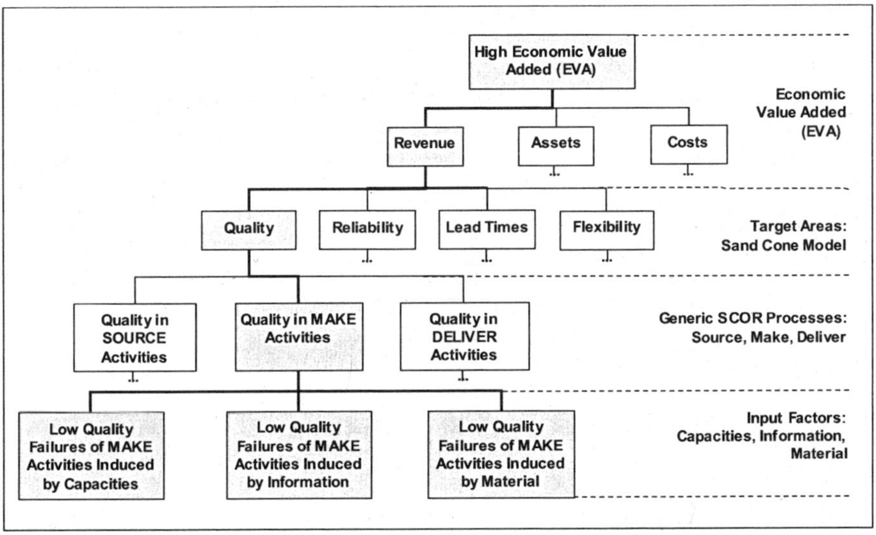

Figure 1: Set up of the Supply Chain Design Decomposition (SCDD)

The sequence of the target areas of logistics from left to right is intentionally chosen: It reflects the logical sequence of decisions and implementation of measures [11]: First, a certain level of quality has to be established—according to strategic priorities—prior to optimise reliability. The rationale behind: compromising quality would induce serious problems while optimising the reliability and lead times. If a certain degree of reliability is established, then lead times can be optimised and subsequently flexibility. This is the prerequisite for reducing assets and costs. This is in accordance with empirical findings [13] (so called sand cone model). See Figure 2.

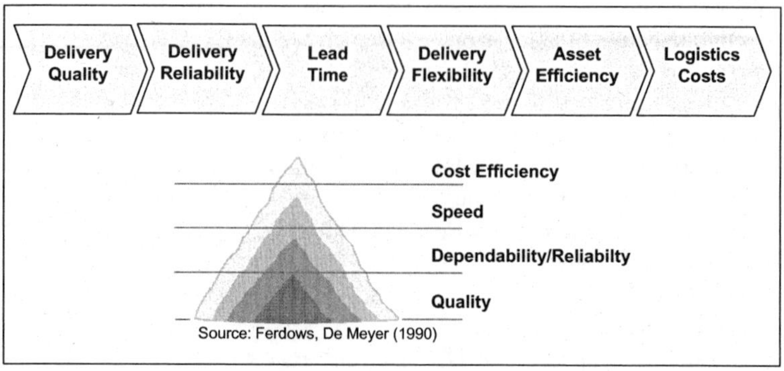

Figure 2: Order of Performance Target Areas and Sand Cone Model

Based on this order of performance target areas, on the principles of Axiomatic Design (separation of means and objectives) and structural set up (i.e., EVA, target areas, generic processes, input factors), the SCDD was elaborated. Figure 3 shows a small excerpt of the upper part of the SCDD tree, which consists of approximately 200 elements.

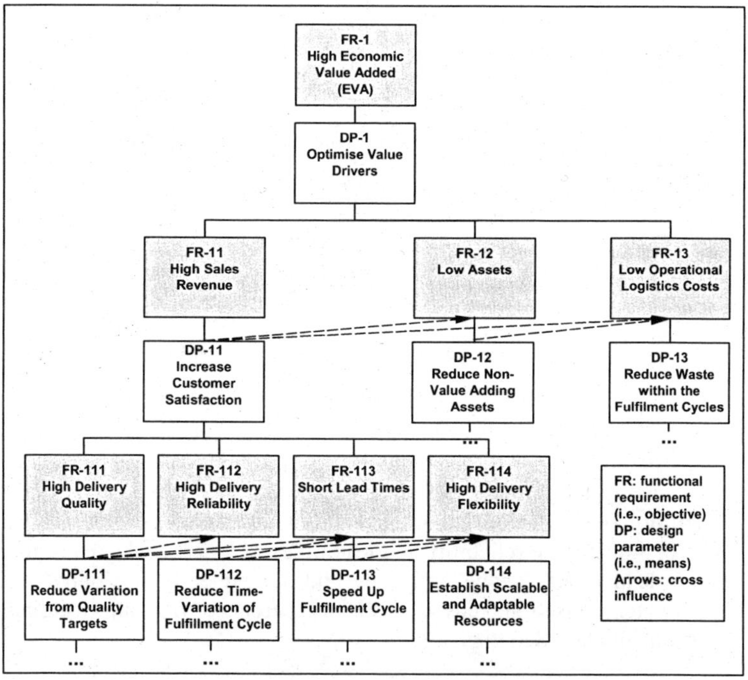

Figure 3: Excerpt from the Supply Chain Decomposition (SCDD)

The target of a high EVA (FR-1) is achieved by means of the optimisation of its value drivers in terms of logistics (DP-1). Therefore, the first decomposition of DP-1 consists of the value drivers: high sales revenue (FR-11), low assets (FR-12), and low operational logistics costs (FR-13). As means for FR-11, increase customer satisfaction (DP-11) is identified. It is further decomposed into the objectives of high delivery quality (FR-111), high delivery reliability (FR-112), short lead times (FR-113) and high delivery flexibility (FR-114). For each of these objectives, appropriate means are identified. These elements are further decomposed into objectives and means over several levels down to operational

SCM and corresponding best practices (e.g., vendor managed inventory). The same principle applies for the sub-branch of assets (FR-12) and costs (FR-13).

The main benefits of SCDD are the separation of objectives and solutions—which helps clarifying the inner logic of SCM and focusing on what is to achieve prior to thinking about solutions—and the systematic decomposition, which enables to concretise high level objectives stepwise down to operational objectives and means [14].

4. Formulation of Supply Chain Strategies

SCDD is the essential element of the PRODCHAIN toolbox, since it represents a causal model of SCM connecting objectives and means in a systematic way. Therefore, SCDD can be used for the formulation and implementation of supply chain strategies: The SCDD tree can be passed top-down concretising objectives and means step by step so they get more and more operational. This way, we search for the essential driver (DP) for each objective (FR), and then, relevant sub-objectives and their drivers, i.e. means, are identified. This decomposition is continued until the strategy is operational and best practices can be selected. In each step, the sub-objectives can be chosen and prioritised according to the business strategy and strategic priorities. Conflicts of objectives may arise when means influence the achievement of more than one objective. This is depicted in the SCDD by dotted arrows (Figure 3). Therefore, when selecting means and prioritising objectives, we have to take conflicts of objectives and side effects into account. Moreover, available resources and capabilities have to be considered as well.

This logic can be framed as a process of supply chain strategy formulation and implementation, following common decision making process phases [16] (see Figure 4):

1. Intelligence: Identification of opportunities and improvement potentials by means of an analysis of strengths, weaknesses, opportunities and threats, as well as performance indicators and benchmarking.
2. Design: Development of supply chain strategies as described above.
3. Choice: Selection of the appropriate supply chain strategy based on logistic competitive capabilities, achievement of objectives, priorities, conflicts of objectives, capabilities, resources, risks etc.; and furthermore, assessment of the feasibility.
4. Implementation/Review: The aforementioned implementation sequence, resource allocation according to the priorities, controlling of progress and development of logistic competitive capabilities, monitoring of possible side effects.

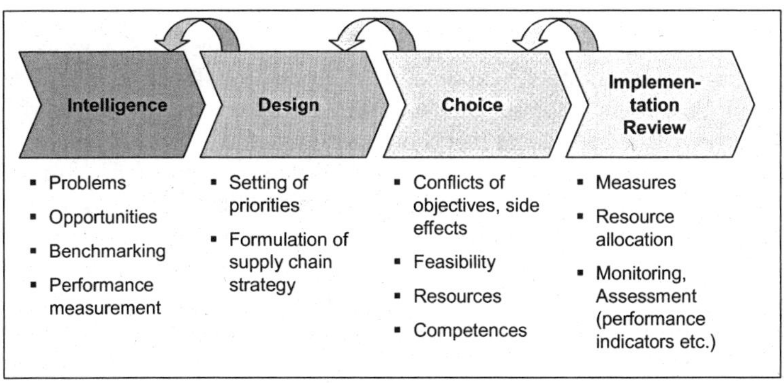

Figure 4: Process of Supply Chain Strategy Formulation

Logistic capabilities for competitive advantages can be developed and exploited by defining areas of operational excellence and setting priorities in the SCDD where this excellence is to be fostered.

This way, comprehensive and coherent supply chain strategies can be developed and their implementation started, and appropriate best practices can be selected. There are several benefits: The supply chain strategy fits into the overall business strategy since it is systematically derived from top-level objectives. This ensures that all measures are aligned and that they contribute to the creation of value in the sense of value based management. The strategy and the best practices are customized to the specific situation, though they are based on a common generic framework. The several levels of concretisation correspond to the different layers of the management in an enterprise; therefore, responsibilities and competences can be assigned. The underlying causal model facilitates the understanding of cause-and-effect relationships for decision makers.

5. Case Study

This section is dedicated to a short case study, which aims at illustrating the application of the Axiomatic Design in the field of SCM as described above. Dell Inc. is a very successful manufacturer of computer systems hardware, for which the efficiency of the supply chain can be perceived as the basis for its competitive advantage (see, e.g., [17], [18]). Dell is known for its operational excellence. Dell's business strategy focuses primarily on cash, profitability, and, third, sales growth. These priorities can be translated into the SCDD as follows: first, low assets (FR-12), second, F low operational logistics costs (R-12), and third, high sales revenue (FR-11).

Following the aforementioned implementation sequence, Dell has to ensure first the achievement of the objective of high sales revenue (FR-12), although this is the third priority according to the business strategy. The meaning is, that the achievement of FR-11 is not being maximised, but optimised to a certain degree. The rationale behind is, that the first and second priorities (assets and costs) should not be achieved at the expense of sales. The efforts and resources are dedicated according to the priorities of the business strategy.

Therefore, we first take a closer look at the objective of high sales revenue (FR-11). Figure 5 depicts the achievement of this objective and the priorities according to the business strategy. High sales revenue is achieved through increased customer satisfaction (DP-11), which in turn is concretised by means of high delivery quality (FR-111), high delivery reliability (FR-112), short lead times (FR-113) and high delivery flexibility (FR-114). Dell's priorities are short lead times and high flexibility of processes and resources. These objectives can be further decomposed until best practices can be identified and assigned as means, like for instance e-procurement, the Dell direct model as well as 3rd party logistics–here, strong logistics capabilities for competitive advantage can be developed (e.g., efficient and fast SCM processes). Analogous, the objectives of low assets and low operational logistics costs (FR-12 and FR-13) can be decomposed into sub-objectives and thus made operational (not shown in Figure 5).

Considering side effects, for example DP-11 (high sales revenue) has a strong influence on FR-13 (low operational logistics costs). This is depicted in Figure 5 by a dotted arrow. Therefore, especially an appropriate level of quality has to be established first, since delivery quality (FR-111) is an important driver of sales (DP-11): The level of quality as perceived by the customer should neither be too high (too costly) nor too low (putting customer satisfaction at risk). For that reason, the implementation sequence of measures is from left to right as discussed above.

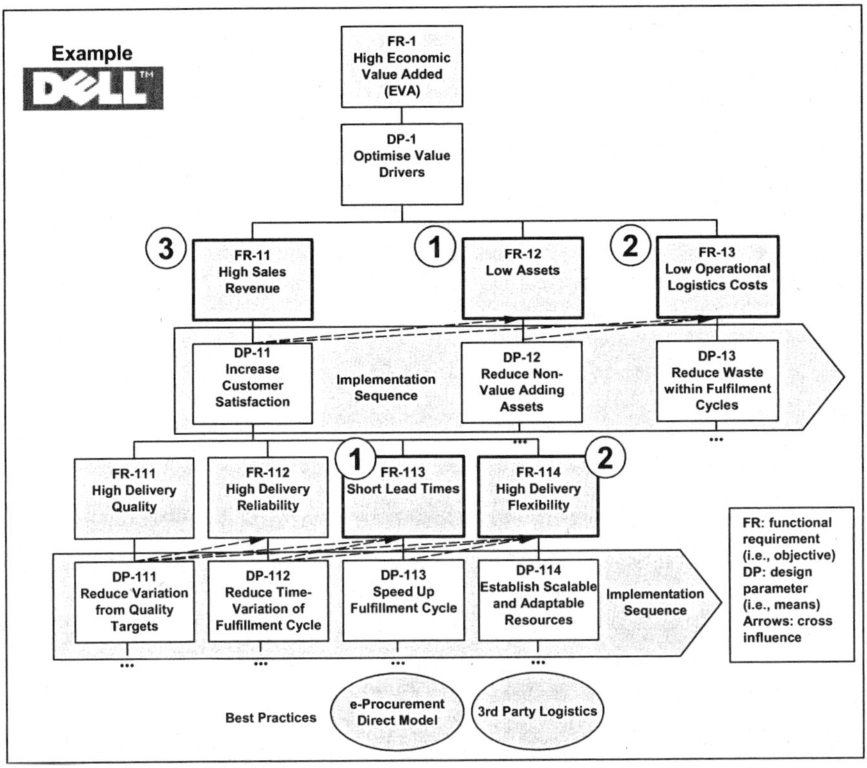

Figure 5: Example for the Formulation and Implementation of a Supply Chain Strategy

The supply chain strategy can be described as paths of prioritised and stepwise concretised objectives and means in the SCDD. It has to be assessed in terms of feasibility. For the implementation, the efforts and allocation of resources follow the priorities of the business strategy. Performance indicators can be defined for the assessment of the measures and the achievement of the objectives, e.g. order fulfilment lead time.

6. Lessons Learnt

Case studies conducted with industrial partners during PRODCHAIN in the area of make-to-stock and make-to-order products and equipment show the application of this approach is quite intuitive and leads to meaningful results. However, it requires some effort and expertise in SCM. To develop a supply chain strategy, managers along the supply chain (sourcing, procurement, production, warehousing, distribution etc.) and top management, business development and marketing have to be involved. For best results, this is done in workshops, which are guided by a person who is familiar with the methodology. Therefore, the target user group of this methodology are supply chain managers, managers of business development and consultants in the area of SCM. The principles of this methodology can be applied to other areas, e.g. supply chain risk management.

7. Conclusions

The Supply Chain Design Decomposition SCDD is a comprehensive causal model of SCM developed based on the Axiomatic Design methodology. It can be used for the selection of appropriate best practices as well as for the formulation and implementation of supply chain strategies in the sense of value based management. This way, it provides decision support for the improvement of supply chain performance. Objectives and measures are concretised and made operational in a systematic way. Further work will focus on a more detailed process and on additional case studies in order to gain more experiences and feedback from industrial application for improving the methodology.

In general, Axiomatic Design is of value in developing and implementing strategies and selecting appropriate means and solutions, for its consistency and systematic foundation.

Acknowledgement

PRODCHAIN (www.prodchain.net) is an international research project with ten industrial and four academic partners co-funded by the European Commission in the IST programme (IST-2000-61205) and IMS (IMS-99006). The authors wish to acknowledge the European Commission, the Swiss Federal Office for Education and Science, Prof. Dr. Paul Schönsleben and all partners of PRODCHAIN for their support.

References

[1] Schönsleben, P. (2003): Integral logistics management – Planning and control of comprehensive supply chains. 2nd ed., Boca Raton (etc.): St. Lucie Press

[2] Ross, D.F. (2000): Competing through supply chain management – Creating market-winning strategies through supply chain partnerships. 3rd printing; Norwell: Kluwer Academic Publishers

[3] Nienhaus, J.; Schnetzler, M.; Sennheiser, A.; Weidemann, M.; Glaubitt, K.; Pierpaoli, F.; Heinzel, H.; Negretto, U. (2003): Trends in supply chain management – Results of a study among more than 200 companies. ETH Center for Enterprise Sciences (BWI), Zürich

[4] ELA/Bearingpoint (2002): What matters to top management? – A survey on the influence of supply chain management on strategy and finance. ELA European Logistics Association / BearingPoint, Brussels

[5] Hieber, R. (2002): Supply chain management – a collaborative performance measurement approach. Zürich: vdf

[6] Gattorna, J.L. (1998): The drive towards strategic alignment in the supply chain. In: Gattorna, J.L. (ed.): Strategic supply chain alignment – Best practice in supply chain management. Hampshire: Gower, pp. 1-7

[7] Chopra, S.; Meindl, P. (2001): Supply chain management – Strategy, planning, organization. Upper Saddle River NJ: Prentice Hall

[8] Weidemann, M.; Nobs, A.; Stich, V. (2004): Guidance in SCM configuration - The ProdChain toolbox. In: Conference Proceedings of the e2004 - eChallenges Conference, Vienna (Austria), 27-29 October 2004 (forthcoming)

[9] Suh, N.P. (1990): The Principles of design. New York (etc.): Oxford University Press

[10] Suh, N.P. (2001): Axiomatic Design – Advances and applications. New York (etc.): Oxford University Press

[11] Cochran, D.S.; Arinez, J.F.; Duda, J.W.; Linck, J. (2001): A decomposition approach for manufacturing systems design. In: Journal of Manufacturing Systems, Vol. 20, No. 6, pp. 371-389

[12] Ehrbar, A. (1998): EVA economic value added – the real key to creating wealth. New York (etc.): Wiley

[13] Ferdows, K.; De Meyer, A. (1990): Lasting improvements in the manufacturing performance – In search of a new theory. In: Journal of Operations Management, Vol. 9, No. 2 (April 1990), pp. 168-184

[14] Duda, J.W. (2000): A decomposition-based approach to linking strategy, performance measurement, and manufacturing systems design. Dissertation Massachusetts Institute of Technology (MIT), Cambridge MA

[15] Sennheiser, A.; Schnetzler, M. (2003): Lean benchmarking with clustered company prototypes. In: Cunningham, P. et al. (ed.): Building the Knowledge Economy - Issues, Applications, Case Studies. Amsterdam (etc.): IOS Press, pp. 1349-1356

[16] Simon, H.A. (1977): The new science of management decision. Englewood Cliffs NJ (etc.): Prentice-Hall

[17] Dell, M.; Fredman, C. (1999): Direct from Dell – Strategies that revolutionized an industry. New York: Harper Collins

[18] Park, A.; Burrows, P. (2003): What you don't know about Dell – A look at the management secrets of the best-run company in technology. In: Business Week, No. 44, November 3, 2003

eAdoption and the Knowledge Economy: Issues, Applications, Case Studies
P. Cunningham and M. Cunningham (Eds.)
IOS Press, 2004

Profiling for Supplier Selection in the Context of the Extended Enterprise

Kate DUNNE, Jim BROWNE
CIMRU, NUI Galway, Galway, Ireland
Tel: +353 91 512293, Fax: + 353 91 562894, Email: Catherine.Dunne@nuigalway.ie

Abstract: Selecting the most suitable 1st tier supplier for an Extended Enterprise (EE) is critical to its success. A review of supplier selection literature found that the supplier selection process steps are often overlooked, and that very few support models for the initial preparation step are available. A number of industry case studies conducted confirm a gap in the planning and definition of requirements practices during collaboration initiation. Therefore, the objective of this paper is to gain an understanding of current supplier selection preparation solutions available in literature and industrial practices, and to propose a profiling method to support this step in an EE environment. The profiling method is based on the concept of a common source from which potential suppliers and Original Equipment Manufacturers (OEMs) can define their business, offers, and requirements to simplify the matching process, and to form the basis for a strategic relationship.

1. Introduction

The Extended Enterprise (EE) paradigm is defined by Browne et al [1], as a manufacturing company extending it's traditional boundaries to include all partners along the entire product life cycle, from material and component suppliers, manufacturers, assemblers, distributors, customers, customer service agents, through to end-of-life recyclers. Global and economic pressures mean a group of companies in an EE are stronger than an individual company and therefore, there has been a trend towards EEs competing against EEs rather than individual companies competing against each other. This results in an EE being based on long-term trust and mutually dependent relationships between the partners [2]. The integrated nature of an EE means the introduction of any new partner along the EE has consequences for all the other partners. In the context of purchasing, and OEM-supplier relationships, relevant factors not just for the Original Equipment Manufacturer (OEM), but also for the entire EE must be considered when selecting a supplier.

This paper will focus on the preparatory phase of the selection of strategic suppliers to be integrated into the EE. Literature indicates that the failure rate of supplier agreements is very high [3], [4], with inappropriate partners being cited as one reason for the failures. Following an extensive search in the area of supplier selection, the authors found that a significant amount of work has been published in the area of detailed final choice models, but the initial preparation phase has largely remained under researched. This paper reviews, from the point of view of the EE environment, the supplier selection processes and the supplier selection methods to be found in literature with particular emphasis on the initial preparation phase. Four industrial case studies provide an insight into the use of partner selection processes, and in particular the initial preparation phase. The following sections will argue that an OEM cannot expect to select the most appropriate supplier if the preparatory work is absent. In other words, the method used by an OEM and potential suppliers to define their needs or offers, and the content of the defined need and offer influence the chances of a successful match. The concept of a profile will be proposed, which can be used to represent the OEM/supplier requirements/offer needed to correctly match an OEM and a 1st tier supplier. A supplier selection process using the proposed generic profiling method will also be presented.

2. Background Research

With 80% of total product cost attributed to raw materials and components (Weber et al [5]), the importance of the purchasing function for an organisation's competitiveness is clear. Selecting the correct 1st tier suppliers leads to minimised purchasing costs and an increase in the competitive advantage of the organisation. Many researchers including [6], [7], [8], advocate the importance of selecting the right supplier to work with an OEM. This importance is increased when the selection of a supplier for the EE is considered. However, according to literature [3], [4], the failure rate of collaborations mentioned in the previous section, including supplier agreements, is as high as 50 percent. Many reasons have been attributed to this high failure rate, some of which will be discussed in the following two subsections through an extensive literature review and a number of case studies.

2.1. Literature Review

Based on the review it emerged that very few publications address supplier selection processes, which include preparatory steps such as the formulation of criteria and pre-selecting potential partners. The overwhelming majority of the literature available in this area was found to concentrate on final selection methods. Authors such as Weber *et. al.* [5], Holt [9] and Degraeve *et. al.* [10], consider the final choice phase to be the only step in the supplier selection process and use this step as the basis for their supplier selection review papers. de Boer *et. al.* [8] and Ghodsypour *et. al.* [6] do review available methods for decision-making steps prior to the final choice phase and for the final choice phase itself of suppler selection. de Boer *et. al.* [8] confirms the authors finding that research relating to the preparation phase is underdeveloped, and could not find any papers addressing problem definition and only two addressing criteria definition. The limited number of methods available to support supplier selection is echoed by Ghodsypour *et. al.* [6]. This preparation phase gap in supplier selection research means planning and requirements definition are at best carried out in an unstructured, ad-hoc manner and at worst are not carried out at all. Either way the chances of selecting the correct supplier are greatly reduced. If a company does not spend time considering why a supplier is needed and what exactly they need from that supplier, the role of any supplier selected is unclear and may be selected using incorrect requirements, while the actual requirements are overlooked. Long term, disagreements and misunderstandings will occur, and the relationship is more likely to fail.

Literature confirms the focus by researchers on the final choice phase by way of the availability of an abundance of comprehensive and well documented methods to support the final choice step. These methods may be captured into six categories including; categorical methods, linear weighting models, total cost of ownership models (TCO), mathematical programming models, statistical models and artificial intelligence (AI) based models. Details of these methods can be found in the supplier selection method reviews cited above by de Boer *et. al.* [8], Ghodsypour *et. al.* [6], Weber *et. al.* [5] and Degraeve *et. al.* [10]. However, regardless of how good these methods are they can only be as good as the input information, which if not developed properly will reduce the chances of the optimum suppler being selected. Lorange *et. al.* [7] warns, that without due consideration for the initial steps the probably of the supplier selected being unsuitable is high, regardless of how sophisticated or advanced the final selection method used is. de Boer *et. al.* [8] also confirms this point when he states the quality of the supplier selected is dependent on the quality of the steps prior to the final selection step.

Those few publications that recognise the need for additional steps in the final choice during a supplier selection process include de Boer *et. al.* [8], Presutti [11], Motwani [12], and Lorange *et. al.* [7]. Although all the processes cited above include a planning/preparation step they are only aimed at OEMs defining their requirements and do not provide guidelines for potential suppliers to define the products/services they wish to offer OEMs. This means even if an OEM utilises a structured method to define their requirements, the method applied by the potential supplier to define their offer may be different, leading to possible terminology and conceptual misunderstandings during the decision step and therefore, incorrect suppliers being selected. That there is an emphasis on supplier selection based predominately on product related information. Product related information such as product requirements, functionality, cost, delivery and quality are sufficient if an OEM is purchasing off the shelf items, but is not if the objective is to select a strategic partner such as a partner for an EE. In this case more detailed information relating to the production, technical and development facilities and capacity, credit rating, market position, performance history, etc. is needed. In other words the circumstances of procurement or supplier selection, and the resultant effects are rarely considered, which increases the chances of incorrect supplier being selected and the partnership failing. To the best of the authors knowledge the concept of an OEM and potential suppliers defining a holistic profile of their organisation using commonly defined terminology and concepts prior to engaging in supplier selection cannot be found in literature.

2.2. Case Study Findings

Dunne et al [13] applied a case study research methodology to a number of distributed organisations in order to obtain a deeper understanding of the current partner selection practices. By focusing on the partner selection practices in each of the cases an insight into how these organisations define their requirements, source and select partners and where improvements are required was developed.

Three companies were chosen to represent the collaboration cases of three distributed production organisations engaged in supplier agreements. They included a large European manufacturer, a large Chinese manufacturer, and a small Chinese domestic market manufacturer (Case A, Case B and Case C respectively). Table 1 illustrates a classification of the cases according to industry branch, type of production and collaboration type.

	Case A	**Case B**	**Case C**
Branch of industry	Automotive (cars and trucks)	Mechanical Industry (steam turbines)	Electronics Industry (computer monitors)
Type of production	Mass production	Batch production	Job shop production
Collaboration type	International supplier agreements	International technology partnership	Domestic supplier agreement
Location	Europe	China	China (SME)

Table 1: Classification of Cases

One of the major findings that emerged was that insufficient emphasis is placed on initial planning steps prior to engaging in the partner selection process by the three cases studied. A planning step was found to be absent from Case B's collaboration initiation process with requirements being defined during the final choice phase when a number of potential partners were already assumed. Case A includes a planning step at the start of their supplier agreement initiation processes. However, the planning involves the definition of a strategy and justification for forming a collaboration by relevant internal and external personnel, while assuming the requirements are known at the start of the process. The only case to include the definition of requirements in a formal planning step was Case C. Case C chooses a set of requirements according to internally defined attributes. It was unknown how the potential suppliers defined their offers and whether they used the same method or terminology. This confirms the authors' view that incompatible supplier partnerships may be formed due to seemingly matching requirements and offer attributes.

The sources and methods of sourcing used to identify potential partners were found to be limited and unstructured in the three cases. Steps to source partners were informal in Case A and not part of the collaboration initiation process in Case B. Case C rely on an agency to source partners. Case A uses trade fairs and catalogues to locate suppliers. Case B does not include a sourcing step in their collaboration initiation process, assuming all potential partners have already been identified. Case C uses an agency to source and initiate contact with potential suppliers. Although agencies represent a potentially large source of partners they are generally too expensive for Small and Medium sized Enterprises (SMEs), and their sourcing capability vary. Sourcing from limited sources reduces the possibility of finding the best partner and leads to settling for the best among limited sources accessed.

In relation to final selection Case A creates a matrix and applies weighting factors in order to rate potential supplier partners, along with a company visit. Case B defines requirements, develops a business and technology plan to support the selection step. Documents, technical drawings and the history of collaboration all support the definition of the requirements. Weighted criteria including competence, location, price quotation, service, and reputation are applied during evaluation to determine a suitability mark for each potential partner. Negotiations are the primary method used by Case C to evaluate the potential suppliers identified by the agency. The other two cases also use face-to-face negotiations between the two parties as part of their evaluation step. In the opinion of the authors, the final evaluation and selection decision of each of the three cases are adequately conducted. However, the quality of the input information for this step along with a number of potential suppliers needs to be assured, which in the authors' view is not in these cases due to the absence of a complete planning/preparation phase.

In summary, all the above cases applied their own in-house selection process, which included limited requirements definition and preparation steps. While requirements were defined no consideration was made for how potential suppliers would define their offers for matching purposes. Pre-selection of potential partners was not carried out. Overall they demonstrate the diverse use of heterogeneous methods and techniques during the early stages of supplier selection, which adversely affects the chances of the best OEM-supplier partnership being identified and higher possibility of an ensuing partnership failing.

3. Supplier Selection using Generic Profiling

The results of the background research demonstrate that a shift in focus in supplier selection is needed. OEMs must be committed to spending time on planning their need and requirements for a strategic supplier, and a supplier on defining their offer and expectations for working with a customer. It is important to recognise that a supplier selection process is a two-way process between an OEM and a potential supplier, and that both parties should be satisfied upon its completion. For the purpose of this paper any proposed changes to supplier selection will take into account that it is a two-way process and that any supplier selected will be integrated into an EE. Taking these factors into account the authors propose a revised supplier selection process framework as illustrated below in Figure 1. Each step of the revised supplier selection process will be discussed in terms of the need they address.

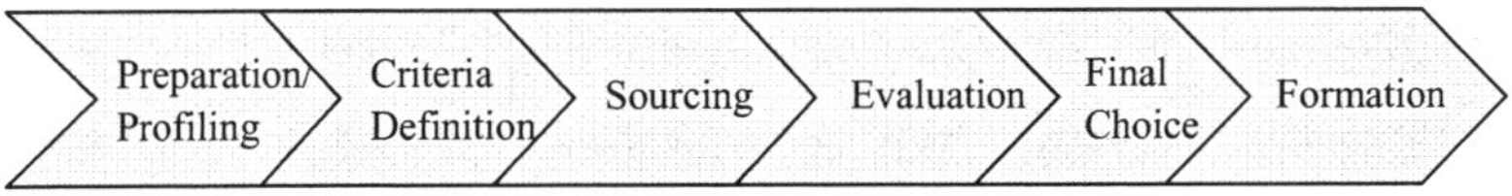

Figure 1: Supplier selection process

Preparation/Profiling - From the perspective of an OEM engaged in an EE, the purpose of the preparation/profiling step is to reflect on why they need to source a supplier, the expected supplier role and how they will be integrated into the company's EE. Firstly, the OEM brings together a cross functional team made up of representatives from the relevant functions right across the EE value chain partners. This team will take a strategic view of the EE and identify their core competencies, which make them competitive in one or more areas. Secondly, the team will analyse their competitors, current market and supply conditions, and identify future business potential as part of a market analysis. Based on this analysis a vision for the EE will be developed, and goals and metrics defined. At this point a profile of the entire EE will be documented. The profile includes product, core competency as well as strategic, tactical and operational information to capture a holistic view of the company. The emphasis in on an all-inclusive view of the EE since the successful integration of a supplier will need more than just product data. A profile only needs to be developed once and updated when changes occur within the EE, or when a decision of whether or not to source a new supplier is needed. The final planning step involves the EE comparing the competencies they have with the competencies they require to fulfil their vision, to identify the competencies/suppliers they need to source.

The selection situation also needs to be considered during this step since the approach to supplier selection will depend on the type of supplier. For example in the case of the EE a supplier fits the "Partner" type according to Kamath and Liker's [14] classification. A "Partner" type supplier is expected to fully integrate into the OEM's company and requires only rough specifications. Therefore, attributes to be considered during selection will be more holistic since the relationship will be strategic. de Boer *et. al.* [8] presents a supplier selection framework which would place a new EE supplier into the new task category, where importance is high and no previously used criteria are available and therefore, need to be all defined as part of the supplier selection process.

From the perspective of a supplier wishing to find new customers they also need to engage in a preparation/profiling step before advertising their offer(s). A supplier needs to identify their core competencies, conduct a market analysis to identify their target market and future vision, and to document their profile. In the case of a supplier their profile will tend to be less complex than an OEMs considering less diverse companies will be involved. Nevertheless the profile needs to be holistic as described for an OEM above and only needs to be developed once, and updated when necessary.

A generic profiling system provides a common database from which a company, either an OEM or a supplier, can define their profile. Both the OEM and supplier can navigate through the hierarchically organised database and select relevant attributes for their company to build up a profile. The profile can be divided into different views to cater for the diverse sets of information utilised by the different functions. A more complete discussion on the generic profiling system is presented in section 3.1.

Attribute definition - OEMs and suppliers need to move away from describing their offers and requirements using internal terminology and concepts, to building a request or offer from a common repository of attributes. The profile documented by the OEM and potential suppliers in the previous step forms the basis on which a set of attributes are defined. In the case of the OEM a request made up of a number of requirements attributes and their importance will be defined, while a potential supplier will define a number of offer attributes. A standardised mechanism to record a company's request and potential suppliers offers is provided based on a commonly defined knowledge base. Whatever selection method is then applied will have compatible input information from both the OEM and the potential suppliers. Since any supplier selected will be integrated into an EE, attributes should not be confined to product related specifications (product requirements, functionality, process requirements, and customer requirements), but should also address communication, levels of technology, geographical location, financial situation, organisational issues, industry position, attitude, performance history, vision and trust.

Sourcing - The Internet offers the best possibility for an OEM to source a suitable supplier from the widest and most diverse sources, and the widest audience for suppliers to offer their goods and services. Currently, the majority of information on the Internet is unstructured and searching mechanisms inefficient. Therefore, an automated searching service based in the generic profiling system is proposed. A single OEM request is matched against all available supplier offers. This involves applying a linear programming model to determine how closely matched the request attributes and offer attributes are. Each corresponding request attribute and a potential supplier's offer attribute with acceptable values are assigned a score based on the importance of the request attribute. When each request attribute has been searched for and a score for the potential partner assigned a total score for the particular is assigned. This matching algorithm is applied to each supplier's offer registered. A ranking of the supplier offers is presented to the OEM based on the overall scores achieved by each potential supplier. The search is applied to a central repository of registered OEMs and potential suppliers with structured requests and offers developed from the commonly defined attribute repository. Direct matching between request and offer attributes is possible due to the use of the common attribute repository by both the OEM and the potential suppliers.

Evaluation - The evaluation step is similar to those well documented in literature and therefore, have no need for further treatment in this paper.

Final Choice and Formation - The final choice and formation steps are similar to those well documented in literature and therefore, have no need for further treatment in this paper. It is worth noting that the authors view face-to-face negotiations and company visits as an important aspect of this step along with any automated support mechanisms

3.1 Realising Generic Profiling

The generic profiling method proposed borrows from classification theory and the Product Data Management (PDM) concept. Product classification systems provide a structured method for dividing all goods and services into commonly agreed industry sectors or classifications. The International Standard Industrial Classification (ISIC) of all economic activities was introduced by the United Nations in 1948. The European system, based on ISIC was developed by the European Union, and is called the "Nomenclature generale des Activites Economiques dans les Communautes Europeenes" (NACE). This classification system along with an attribute library forms the basis for the supplier selection profiling method as is illustrated in figure 2 below.

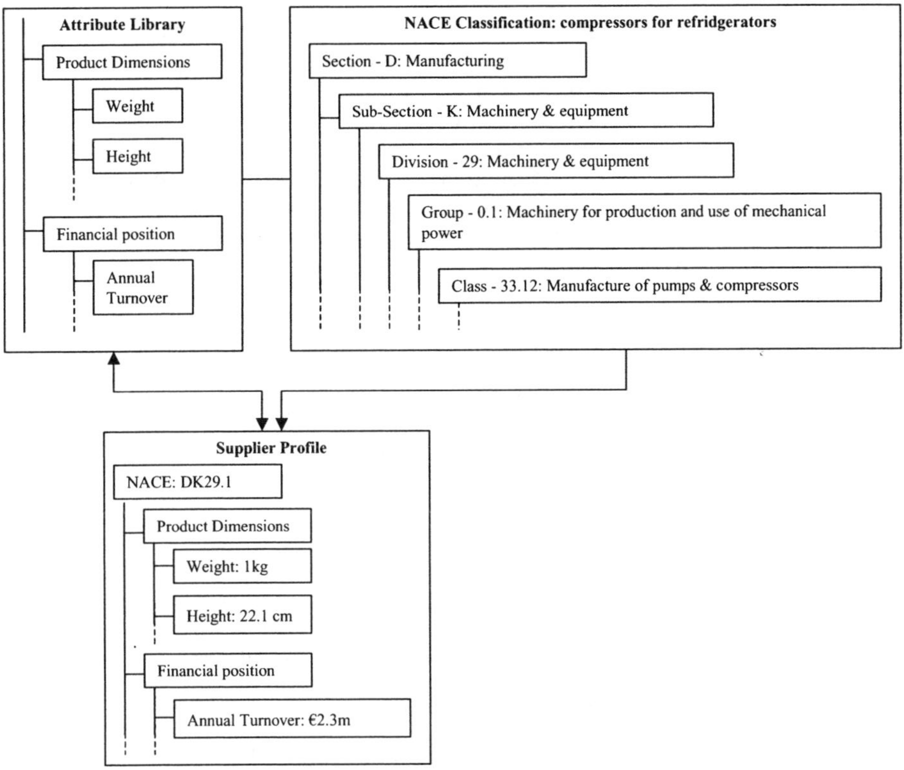

Figure 2: Generic Profiling Method

A company's core competency is linked to a particular product or service, allowing an OEM and potential supplier to use the NACE system to classify their core competency. NACE was chosen because all companies must use it to report their statistical data and it is internationally accepted. Adapting an existing standard will make it application/acceptance easier that an entirely new one. The attribute library provided includes a hierarchy of attributes which the OEM or supplier can add to if a particular attribute they require is missing. Attributes are associated with the product classification to build up a company's profile. The library can be divided into many categories to cater for the various views inside a company. This concept is found in PDM where different views relating to product data may be taken from a single repository of information relating to one product.

The generic profiling system is based on a single source of attributes which all companies use to describe their organisation, offers and requirements. This structure forms the basis for a potential supplier to define its offer attributes and for an OEM to define their requirements. All parties will have the same understanding of terms, which reduces misunderstandings. As both parties need to define their respective attributes it makes sense for them to do so from the same data repository. The data may be stored and used for future selection initiatives and to support the collaborative relationship.

4. Conclusion

The main finding of this paper was the identification of a shortfall in current supplier selection research and industry practices in the preparatory phase of the supplier selection process. Therefore, a generic profile definition system was proposed to overcome the identified gaps. OEMs and potential suppliers are advised to spend time preparing for supplier selection and to define a profile with a holistic view of their company, and not just the requirements or product/service attributes to guide the matching of appropriate OEM-supplier partners for the EE. The benefits of such a system include a clear understanding of need on both sides, consideration for a wide range of factors for building a strategic relationship, and assurance that request and offer attributes are defined utilising the same method. Therefore, the chances of selecting the correct supplier partner increased. Future research is needed to develop, implement and test the profiling method proposed. If validated, this solution could standardise the supplier selection process and increase the chances of OEM-supplier partnerships in the EE being successful.

Acknowledgements

This work has been co-funded by the European Commission and the Ministry of Science and Technology (MOST), China through IST Project DRAGON: *Development of an inteRActive enGineering Portal for Open Networks* (No. IST-2000-29366). The authors wish to acknowledge the Commission and MOST for their support, and all the DRAGON project partners for their contribution during the development of various ideas and concepts presented in this paper.

References

[1] Browne, J., Sackett, P.J., Wortmann, J.C., *Future manufacturing systems- Towards the extended enterprise,* Computers in Industry, 1995. **25**: pg. 235-254.

[2] Browne, J., Zhang, J., *Extended and virtual enterprises- similarities and differences,* International Journal of Agile Management Systems, 1999. **1**(1): pg. 30-36.

[3] Inkpen, A.C., and Ross, J., *Why do some Strategic Alliances Persist beyond their Useful Life?,* MIT Sloan Management Review, 2001(Fall): pg. 132-148.

[4] Dyer, J.H., Kale, P., and Singh, H., *How to make Strategic Alliances Work,* MIT Sloan Management Review, 2001(Summer): pg. 37-43.

[5] Weber, C.A., Current, J.R., Benton, W.C., *Vendor selection criteria and methods,* European Journal of Operational Research, 1991. **50**: pg. 12-18.

[6] Ghodsypour, S.H., O'Brien, C., *The total cost of logistics in supplier selection, under conditions of multiple sourcing, multiple criteria and capacity constraint,* International Journal of Production Economics, 2001. **73**: pg. 15-27.

[7] Lorange, P., and Roos, J., *Strategic Alliance- formation, implementation and evolution*, 1992, Oxford: Blackwell Publishers Ltd., pg. 273.

[8] de Boer, L., Labro, E., and Morlacchi, P., *A review of methods supporting supplier selection,* European Journal of Purchasing & Supply Management, 2001. **7**: pg. 75-89.

[9] Holt, G.D., *Which contractor selection methodology?,* International Journal of Project Management, 1998. **16**(3): pg. 153-164.

[10] Degraeve, Z., Labro, E., Roodhooft, F., *An evaluation of supplier selection methods from a Total Cost of Ownership perspective,* European Journal of Operational Research, 2000. **125**(1): pg. 34-59.

[11] Presutti, W.D., *Supply management and e-procurement: creating value in the supply chain,* Industrial Marketing Management, 2003. **32**: pg. 219-226.

[12] Motwani, J., *Supplier selection in developing countries: a model development,* Integrated Manufacturing Systems, 1999. **10**(3): pg. 154-161.

[13] Dunne, K., Browne, J., *Collaboration initiation practices- experiences from case studies*, *Proceedings of the 10th International Conference on Concurrent Engineering*. 2004. Seville, Spain: 14-16 June.

[14] Kamath, R.R., and Liker, J.K., *A Second Look at Japanese Product Development.* Harvard Business Review, 1994(Nov-Dec): pg. 154-166.

The Role of ICT in Reverse Logistics: A Hypothesis of RFID Implementation to Manage the Recovery Process.

Andrea PAYARO
University of Padova, Via Venezia 1, Padova, 35131, Italy
Tel: +39 049 827 6757, Fax: + 39 049 827 6716, Email: andrea.payaro@unipd.it

Abstract: Traditionally a product was developed to be manufactured and go through the supply chain to be sold to a customer. However, supply chains are steadily integrating more activities than those concerned with supply alone, like including service and product recovery. Here we will focus on the latter, and especially reverse logistics, i.e. the handling of products, components and materials during the recovery process (Revlog, 1998). Several forces drive reverse logistics, like, competition and marketing motives, direct economic motives and concerns with the environment. At present, in literature it is not present a model that describes which products can easily be recovered and what are the elements that determine the feasibility of recovery process. This study aims to define the product's characteristics that influence the adoption of reverse logistics and to suggest the use of information technologies to support the recovery process. Information and communication technologies have a main role in the recovery process of electronic devices. In this study we propose a solution with a radio frequency tag (RFID).

1. Reverse Logistics Processes

Supply chain management (SCM) describes the management of the flow of materials, information, and funds across the entire supply chain, from suppliers to component producers to final assemblers to distribution (warehouses and retailers), and ultimately to the consumer. In fact, it often includes after-sales service and returns or recycling [5].

A class of ‘reverse’ goods flows that has gained particular importance concerns the return of used products at the end of their lifecycle. Companies have been discovering used products as a valuable resource. A scale of recovery options, including refurbishing, remanufacturing, and recycling may allow for recapturing significant shares of the original value added and/or material value, thereby opening the route to extended profits [19].

Though the conception of Reverse Logistics dates from long time ago, the denomination of the term is difficult to trace with precision. Terms like Reverse Channels or Reverse Flow already appear in the scientific literature of the seventies, but consistently related with recycling [7][6]. Kopicky [11] defines Reverse Logistics analogously to Stock [18] (1992) but keeps the sense of direction opposed to traditional distribution flows. In the end of the nineties, Rogers and Tibben-Lembke [15] describe Reverse Logistics including the goal and the processes (the logistics) involved. The European Working Group on Reverse Logistics [14] defines it as: “The process of planning, implementing and controlling flows of raw materials, in process inventory, and finished goods, from a manufacturing, distribution or use point to a point of recovery or point of proper disposal”

The above definition is more extensive than the one proposed by Rogers and Tibben-Lemke [15]. We do not refer to “ point of consumption” nor do the products need to be returned to their origin, but may be returned to any point of recovery (e.g. collected computer chips do not go back to the original supply chain, but may enter another chain). In this way we incorporate more flows that naturally fit in the definition and which characteristics are the same as of other reverse logistic streams.

Recurrent reverse logistics activities include collection, inspection/separation, reuse, remanufacturing, recycling, re-distribution and disposal. The first stage in the process is collection, that is, all those activities that are necessary for reclaiming returned products, surplus or by-products and transporting them to a place, where they will be subjected to further examination and processing. Locating such products, purchasing, transporting them and storing them at a collection point, are all activities related to collection.

Remanufacturing is a series of steps necessary to transform a part or product that has been used into one that is usable again. Some typical activities in remanufacturing include cleaning, disassembly, replacement and re-assembly. However, remanufacturing is so product dependent that it can barely be characterized by typical activities. For example, restoration for a piece of old furniture may require artistic skill, whereas remanufacturing of a piece of heavy equipment requires advanced industrial infrastructure.

Re-use refers to cases where returned products have such a good quality that they can be re-used almost immediately in the same or an alternative market (e.g. reusable bottles, containers, most leased or rented equipment). It may also happen for surplus goods, e.g. spare parts that are left over after discarding the original equipment.

Finally, re-distribution refers to logistics activities required to introduce a product into a market and transfer it to customers (i.e. storage, sales and transportation). Efficient marketing of re-usable products requires protocols supporting clear, concise communication between interested parties and mechanisms to facilitate matching of offers with requests.

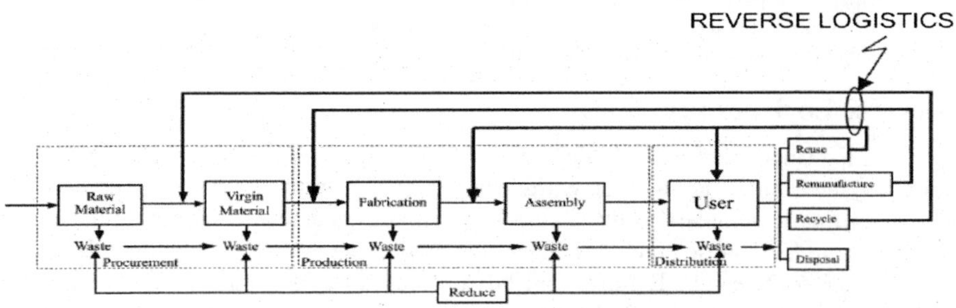

Figure 1: Functional model of an organizational supply chain with environmentally influential practices [17]

2. Product Characteristics and Reverse Logistics

Which products are suitable for reverse logistics? De Brito and Dekker [12] consider what is actually being discarded or returned. Three product characteristics seem to be relevant: composition; deterioration; use-pattern. As highlighted by Gungor and Gupta [8], product composition in terms of the number of components and of materials is one of the many aspects to keep in mind while designing products for recovery. Not only the number, but also how the materials and components are put together, will affect the easiness of re-processing them and therefore the economics of reverse logistics activities.

The presence of hazardous materials is also relevance, as it demands special treatment. Material heterogeneity of the product can play a role in recovery, where one tries to obtain separate streams of different materials that are as pure as possible (a problem for plastics).

Product size can also be a significant factor for recovery systems (e.g. the impact on transportation and handling). Tibben-Lembke [20] has studied the way that reverse logistics is impacted by changes in sales over the product's life cycle. In the product life cycle De Brito and Dekker introduce that there are the deterioration characteristics, which eventually cause a non-functioning of the product, but also determine whether there is enough functionality left to make a further use of the product, either as a whole or as parts.

The product use pattern, with respect to location, intensity, and duration of use, is an important group of characteristics as it affects the collection phase. It will make a difference if the end-user is an individual or an institution (bulk-use), demands different locations for collection or different degrees of effort from the end-user (e.g. bring to a collection-point). The use can also be less or more intensive. Time is not the only component describing intensity of use, but also the degree of consumption during of use.

The product characteristics are related to the type of product. Product type gives the first global impression on the potential states of the product when it reaches recovery. Fleischmann [5] distinguish the following types: spare parts; packages; consumer goods.

In another study, Rose developed a model to forecast End-Of-Life (EOL) product recovery and accurately predicted 86% of 37 case studies based on six technical product characteristics including product durability, rate of technological obsolescence, extent of product complexity, duration of a design cycle and reason for redesigns [16]. Further refinements to such theories would benefit both manufacturers and policy makers [21].

Ammons et al. [1] hypothesize there are two key product features that will help shape the structure of its reverse logistics system: 1) average and variability in frequency of product retirements, and 2) complexity both in materials and manufacture.

The frequency of product retirements is dependent on two further product features, the length of use and the number in circulation. However, consumer durable goods and occur in medium numbers, leading to a lower frequency of product retirement. The complexity in manufacture and materials content of products will impact reverse production system.

3. Product Characteristics Model

Literature proposes several characteristics that identify the "level" of recovery of a product. The precedent studies consider product characteristics and process characteristics at the same manner. In this study we divide product characteristics and process characteristics and we suggest an approach concentrated on the product. Following studies will take in consideration the processes related to the recovery of products.

The model we propose define the product characteristics for the recovery as a group of six parameters. The following figure represent the model we use in this study for a middle or small sized product. The product size; Volume of sale of products; Hazardous components; Design cycle and product life cycle; Product traceability; Product modularity

3.1 Product size

The size is the dimensions of the product and its weight. Large dimensions are a bound in the recovery processes. Consumer cannot transport the product to the collection center and the handling is very difficult. A product with small size is suitable for the recovery process.

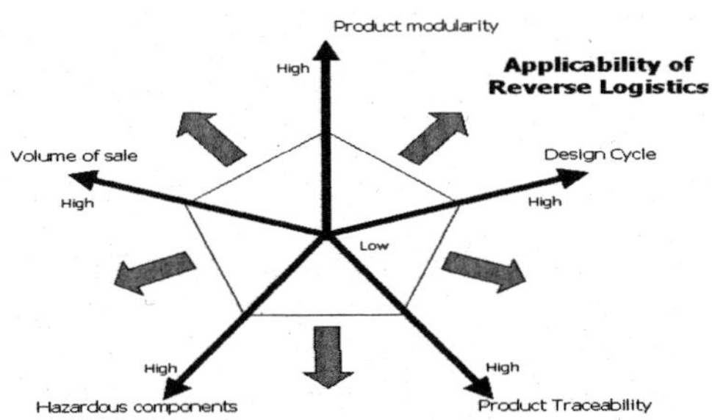

Figure 1: The Product Characteristics for a Middle or Small Size Good.

3.2 Product Traceability

Traceability systems are record keeping procedures that show the path of a particular unit or batch of product or component from supplier(s), through all the intermediate steps which process and assemble components into new products and through the supply chain to customers and consumers. A high-level of traceability allows to identify the consumer and to stimulate him to the updating of its product. This type of control makes it possible to increase marketing services and create an high level of fidelity through up-selling activities.

3.3 Volume of Sale

This parameter represents the number of products sold. A high number of products sold facilitate recovery procedures to achieve economies of scale. An inferior level of products sold can be recovered through collaboration with retailers. Recovering little diffused products is more complex as it needs to define one-to-one connections with the consumer.

3.4 Hazardous Components

A product contain hazardous components when it has a large environmental impact at end-of-life. Computers and other electronics are comprised of a large number of different materials, which makes disassembly and recycling difficult. Additionally, there are considerable amounts of toxic and potentially hazardous waste material in electronics [9]. The hazardous elements found in electronics require that the processing of recovered electronics be responsibly managed in order to protect the health and safety of the workers and to protect the environment where the processing occurs. A product with a high percentage of hazardous components must be recovered.

3.5 Product Modularity

Modularity is an approach for efficiently organizing complex products and processes [2], by decomposing complex tasks into simpler portions so they can be managed independently and yet operate together as a whole. From a system's perspective, modularity is a continuum describing the degree to which a system's components can be separated and recombined. It refers to the tightness of coupling between components and the degree to which the system architecture "rules" (or prohibit) component mixing and matching.

To enhance component reuse and material recycle, engineers must embed strategic modularity into the product and reduce the cost to the recycling organizations. Such effort will lead to overall improvement of industrial ecology through reduction of raw material use, energy use throughout the product life cycle, and solid waste [13]. In this study we consider the modularity like the ratio between the number of modules present in the product and the total number of its components. A product with a modularity near to one is suitable for the reverse logistics because we can reuse the modules in the forward logistics. [10].

3.6 Design Cycle and Product Life Cycle

The design cycle is the length of time between successive product generations. The design cycle is the frequency that a design team redesigns the product or designs a new product thus making the original product obsolete. A long life cycle permit to recovery the product, disassemble and check the components, and re-insert them in new products. If there is a short life cycle, the manufacturer introduces with high frequency in the market new products. This makes it necessary to innovate the components, causing high obsolescence.

4. RFID Support for the Recovery Process

The characteristics object of this study can be gathered together in three clusters: aspects relate to the structure of the product (dimensions and weight); the market (volume of sale and life cycle); and recovery (modularity, toxicity and traceability). While the manufacturer cannot change the physical characteristics of product and the market typology, the firm has to implement some solutions to improve the aspects related to recovery. First, the firm has to increase the modularity, developing the Design-for-Disassembly.

The products designed for disassembly and remanufacturing can deliver much greater savings than can be achieved through the remanufacturing of a product that was not designed with this intention. This finding supports the argument that design plays a key role in determining economic and environmental benefits of remanufacturing [3] [22].

The research and development needs many years to develop products with low level of hazardous components. We can think about the lubricants in the cars, the batteries in the cellular phones or in the PCs, the refrigerant liquids in the air conditioning systems, etc. At present, the firms can only develop product traceability to simplify the recovery processes.

Some products have a very long cycle of life (i.e. boilers), in some cases from the eight to ten years. This means that an individual will purchase on average 8 boilers during his existence. The manufacturing firm must estimate the value of a durable customer relationship management and must follows the product during all the life cycle phases until the end-of-life. If the firm loses the knowledge of the product when the product exit from the retailer, the firm loses many strategic information about the period of use, like the malfunctions. The firm must know what will happen to the product during its life. Otherwise, it cannot apply any direct marketing initiatives and will lose competitiveness.

It becomes strategic for manufacturers to manage all phases that follow product sale to the final customer. To follow the goods during their life will involve many advantages:

- to increase the services to the customer;
- to trace the life of the product and to gather information related to the life of the product (use behaviours, malfunctions, etc.) ;
- to maintain the contact with the customer, and increase the fidelity to the brand;
- to manage the activities of recovery in definite periods;
- to stimulate the up-selling;
- to check the defectiveness of the product;
- to check the state of the sales in real time.

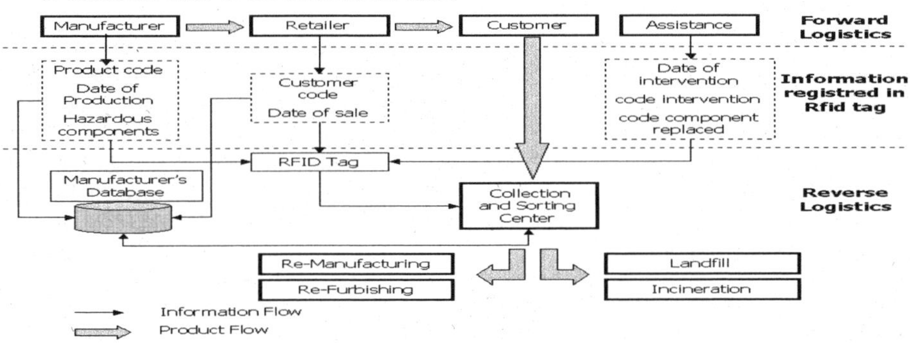

Figure 2: The Proposed Model

Product traceability is possible with RFID. In order to handle reverse logistics better, firms will need to improve their reverse logistics information systems. Automation of those processes is difficult because reverse logistics processes have so many exceptions. Reverse logistics is typically a boundary-spanning process between firms or business units of the same company. Developing systems that have to work across boundaries add additional complexity to the problem. To work well, a reverse logistics information system has to be flexible. Information systems should include detailed information programs about important reverse logistics measurements, such as store compliance, return rates, recovery rates, and returns inventory turnover. Some of the systems for controlling returns will obviously require significantly expanded and improved information systems.

RFID is similar in theory to bar code identification. With RFID, the electromagnetic or electrostatic coupling in the RF portion of the electromagnetic spectrum is used to transmit signals. An RFID system consists of an antenna and a transceiver, which read the radio frequency and transfer the information to a processing device, and a transponder, or tag, which is an integrated circuit containing the RF circuitry and information to be transmitted. One of the key differences between RFID and bar code technology is RFID eliminates the need for line-of-sight reading that bar coding depends on. Also, RFID scanning can be done at greater distances than bar code scanning. High frequency RFID systems (850 MHz to 950 MHz and 2.4 GHz to 2.5 GHz) offer transmission ranges of more than 90 feet, although wavelengths in the 2.4 GHz range are absorbed by water and therefore has limitations

A very small, low powered radio transmitter is installed in each product, broadcasting a very faint signal. The signal is strong enough, that it can be picked up by receivers in a warehouse. Each product can send a different signal. You could build 10 million computers, and install an RFID "tag" in each one, and each one could have a different signal.

Using RFID to assist in the management of returned boilers might be a good option. Placing an RFID tag on the machine at the time of manufacturing would take away the errors in the paper chain and assist in the life cycle management of the boilers.

RFID has the potential to aid reverse logistics operations in a number of ways. As mentioned, it may be helpful in keeping track of products inside the warehouse and outside in the collection phases of the recovery processes. The other way it may be beneficial is in gatekeeping. RF tags may be used in recording the ID of products when they are sold, and this information can be useful in determining which products to accept for return.

In this study, we consider the case of a large enterprise in the north Italy. The company manufacturers more than two million boilers sold in Europe, more than 1,700 employees, a streamlined sales organisation, an extensive network of service centres. The project is in the test phase. The boiler has a long lifecycle and, at this moment, the company is studying a reverse logistics model based on the RFID technology.

The information system needs a unique central database that collects the products code and the technical characteristics of goods. This database is updated when the product is sold via a Web-portal or using a GSM system. If the product needs assistance, technicians up-date data in the tag with the Personal Digital Assistant (PDS) endowed with RF transmitter. At end-of-life the product is brought to the Collection and Sorting Center (CSC), where the tag is read. The Center can query the manufacturer database via an Internet application. At this time, the center can know the modules that can be remanufactured or refurbished, the demand for remanufacturing of the firm, the toxicity of product and eventually the instruction for disassembly. The manufacturer update its database with the information contained in the tag and sent by the CSC. Finally, the Collecting and Sorting Center decides if the product will be remanufactured, refurbished or send to landfill on incinerator.

The strengths of RFID system are: to increase the recovered products; to simplify the operations of collecting and sorting; to simplify the operations of disassembling; and reduce the quantity of toxic components scattered in the environment.

The weakness for RFID system are: a unique identification system is needed; the system of coding has to be shared among all the manufacturers of a particular good; the firm needs an organizational change; products with an high level of modularity are needed.

5. Conclusions

The main problem that the firm has met in the realization of the project is the organizational change needed. The project will be operative in the first months 2005 However the presented model is suited for products with long cycles of life, with an elevated level of modularity and with middle dimensions. New studies will be done for analysing the processes related to the recovery of products with different characteristics.

References

[1] Ammons J.C., Realff M.J., Newton D. Reverse production system design and operation for carpet recycling, Submitted for publication consideration to *European Journal of Operational Research*, 1997.

[2] Baldwin, C.Y. and Clark, K.B. Managing in an Age of Modularity, *Harvard Business Review*, (September-October), 1997, pp.84-93.

[3] Clegg A, and Williams D. Production planning for companies with remanufacturing capability. In: Proceedings of the IEEE *International Symposium on Electronics and Environment*. IEEE, May, 1995.

[4] Commission of the European Communities. Proposal for a Directive of the European Parliament and of the Council on waste electrical and electronic equipment. June 13, 2000.

[5] Fleischmann M., Krikke H.R. , Dekker R. and Flapper S.D.P. A characterisation of logistics networks for product recovery, *Omega*, Vol. 28, No. 6, 2000, pp.653-666.

[6] Ginter P.M. and Starling J.M. Reverse distribution channels for recycling, *California Management Review*, Vol. 20, No. 3, 1978, pp.72-81.

[7] Guiltinan J. and Nwokoye N. "Reverse channels for recycling: an analysis for alternatives and public policy implications" in R. G. Curhan (ed.), *New marketing for social and economic progress*, Combined Proceedings, American Marketing Association, 1974.

[8] Gungor A., and Gupta S.M. Issues in environmentally conscious manufacturing and product recovery: a survey. *Computers & Industrial Engineering*, Vol. 36, 1998, pp.811-853.

[9] Industry Canada Environmental Affairs Branch. Computer Recycling Infrastructure in Canada. March 2001.

[10] Kerr W. and Ryan C. Eco-efficiency gains from remanufacturing. A case study of photocopier remanufacturing at Fuji Xerox Australia, *Journal of Cleaner Production*, Vol.9, 2001, pp.75-81

[11] Kopicky R.J., Berg M.J., Legg L., Dasappa V. and Maggioni C. Reuse and Recycling: Reverse Logistics Opportunities, Council of Logistics Management, Oak Brook, IL, 1993.

[12] Marisa P. de Brito M.P. and Dekker R. Reverse Logistics – a framework, *Econometric Institute Report EI 2002-38*, Erasmus University Rotterdam, 2002.

[13] Mikkola J.H. Modularity assessment of product architecture: Implications for substitutability and interface management, Paper prepared for DRUID's Nelson and Winter Conference Aalborg, Denmark June 12-15, 2001.

[14] RevLog, the European Working group on Reverse Logistics. http://www.fbk.eur.nl/OZ/REVLOG/, 1998.

[15] Rogers D.S. and Tibben-Lembke R.S. Going Backwards: reverse logistics trends and practices, Reverse Logistics Executive Council, Pittsburgh, PA, 1999.

[16] Rose C.M. Design For Environment: A Method for Formulating Product End-of-Life Strategies., Dissertation, Stanford University, 2000.

[17] Sarkis J. A strategic decision framework for green supply chain management, *Journal of Cleaner Production*, Vol. 11, 2003, pp.397-409.

[18] Stock J.R. *Reverse Logistics*, Council of Logistics Management, Oak Brook, IL, 1992.

[19] Thierry M.C., Salomon M., Van Nunen J., Van Wassenhove L. Strategic issues in product recovery management, *California Management Review*, Vol. 37, No.2, 1995, pp.114-135.

[20] Tibben-Lembke R.S. Life after death: reverse logistics and the product life cycle. *Int. J. of Physical Distribution & Logistics Management*, Vol. 32 No. 3, 2002, pp. 223-244.

[21] Toffel M.W. End-of-life Product Recovery: Drivers, Prior Research, and Future Directions, Conference on European Electronics Take-back Legislation: Impacts on Business Strategy and Global Trade Center for the Management of Environmental Resources, INSEAD, Fontainebleau, Oct. 17-18, 2002.

[22] Umeda Y. Key design elements for the inverse manufacturing. In: Proceedings of the IEEE *International Symposium on Environmentally Conscious Design and Inverse Manufacturing*. IEEE, February 1999.

E-Solutions for Planning Lifecycle-Oriented, Flexible Production Systems

Günther SCHUH[1], Carsten SCHLEYER[2], Nils WEMHOENER[3]
Dept of Production Engineering, Laboratory for Machine Tools and Production Engineering (WZL), University of Technology Aachen (RWTH), Steinbachstrasse 53, Aachen, 52074, Germany
[1]*Tel: +49 241 8027405, Fax: + 49 241 8022293, Email: g.schuh@wzl.rwth-aachen.de*
[2]*Tel: +49 241 8028199, Fax: + 49 241 8022293, Email: c.schleyer@wzl.rwth-aachen.de*
[3]*Tel: +49 241 8027388, Fax: + 49 241 8022293, Email: n.wemhoener@wzl.rwth-aachen.de*

Abstract: Increasing unpredictability, dynamic markets, and shortened product lifecycles tremendously increase business risks in particular industries investing in highly specific, capital intensive production systems. In this environment companies remain competitive by designing flexible and faster responding production systems across company boundaries. Hence, the authors introduce a methodology for lifecycle oriented planning of production systems on in-plant level as well as on network level. Based on this methodology e-solutions for supporting long-term planning and continuous performance measurement of production systems under high market uncertainties have been developed. They are presented in an in-plant and network oriented application procedure.

1. Introduction

Producing companies act in a highly unpredictable and competitive market environment. Product technologies change rapidly. Time spans between new innovations are becoming even shorter: lifecycles of products have decreased by 30% in the last ten years [1]. The number and complexity of product variants grow. The volatility in market demands increases. Thus, companies have to react to movements of the market for these products. In such an unpredictable and dynamic market, it is impossible for a company to proactively adapt to the market. Enterprises normally choose to *re*act, resulting in a continuing struggle for adaptation (Figure 1) [2] [3]. Many resources are bounded by the continuous adaptation of production structure and processes. Subsequently it makes steady long-term development of factories all but impossible, and therefore often leads to permanently suboptimal operation. By permanently trying to reach the ideal state the factory it is never optimally configured. Clearly, trying to constantly follow ever-changing markets is not a formula for success [4]. The challenge to cope with the illustrated business environment is to ensure sustainable competitiveness due to the capability of quickly and systematically adapting of production systems [5]. We propose a paradigm change for the planning of production systems to "factory on demand".

The paper shortly presents this paradigm change and stresses the detailed explanation of the supporting composition of e-solutions, which are developed in the research project LicoPro ("Lifecycle design for global collaborative production"). After explaining objectives and paradigm change in section two a methodology for lifecycle oriented planning in a dynamic environment is introduced in section three of this paper. Based on this the authors are currently developing an adequate approach for planning flexible production systems (section four). In section five, two different procedures are presented. Section six deals with the application. Finally section seven concludes this paper.

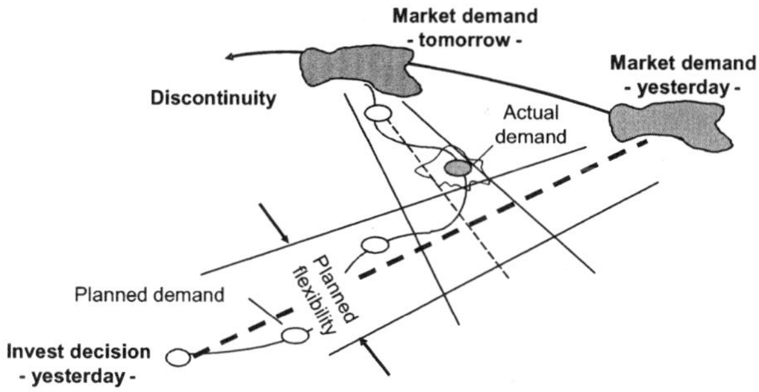

Figure 1: Reactive planning in dynamic markets

2. Objectives

The consideration to invest in highly flexible production systems or even production networks mostly ends at the point, when additional initial costs occur. This is caused by the inherent short-term perspective. The currently used approach of planning product systems is suboptimal and not based on a long-term perspective: product systems are planned for the lifecycle of a product and not for their own lifecycles. »Factories for upcoming products« arise. Flexibility is not explicitly planned: "Flexibility" exists in the form of authorised maximum additional idle capacity. These "factories for upcoming products" wreak high adaptation costs in the long run, because of shorter lifecycles and higher adaptation investments. The traditional flexibility planning only covers the establishment of new products under fixed conditions.

This leads to additional costs and reduces competitiveness. In the case of excessive capacity as well as in the case of unused capacity, costs arise: either opportunity costs arise because of loss of volume or any belated adjustments are necessary. Therefore, the full potential of adaptation to the lifecycle has not been tapped yet. Currently a decision is based on initial costs. (Initial costs mean costs, which arise during the production of the first product.) Additional costs, which arise during the production of subsequent products with the same production system, remain unconsidered. Therefore, the initial costs will be low, but the adjustment costs will be higher during the lifecycle of a product. It is not guaranteed that the most cost-efficient system will be selected. In some cases, it might be possible to obtain a substantial cost reduction by increasing initial costs. Based on this situation the paradigm change to the "factory on demand" has been developed: Competitiveness can be achieved by obtaining efficiency by designing flexible and faster responding production systems across company boundaries while using a method for lifecycle oriented design of production systems [6]. Obviously, factories cannot cover the complete fluctuations of the described market discontinuity in an efficient way. Instead, they have to collaborate with partners in value networks, so-called factories on demand.

3. Methodology for Lifecycle Oriented Planning in a Dynamic Environment

The approach of the "factory on demand" is not only to focus on in plant level, but to combine in plant and cross-plant aspects in order to configure a production system that delivers the required flexibility at the lowest cost possible. Such networks have to pursue the market and meet its requirements. In the view of the described market discontinuity and therefore demanded flexibility, this paper provides a methodology to configure production systems concurrently on in-plant and cross-plant level under lifecycle considerations with a special focus on uncertain market conditions. Accordingly, not individual factories have to follow market fluctuations directly but networks. This will lead to a process of constant formation, reformation, and disintegration of factory networks [7]. Single factories must be positioned so that they can easily integrate themselves into changing production networks. Therefore in-plant (single-factory) as well as cross-plant (network) level must be taken into account. In order to achieve this, two system levels are chosen as general approach (Figure 2).

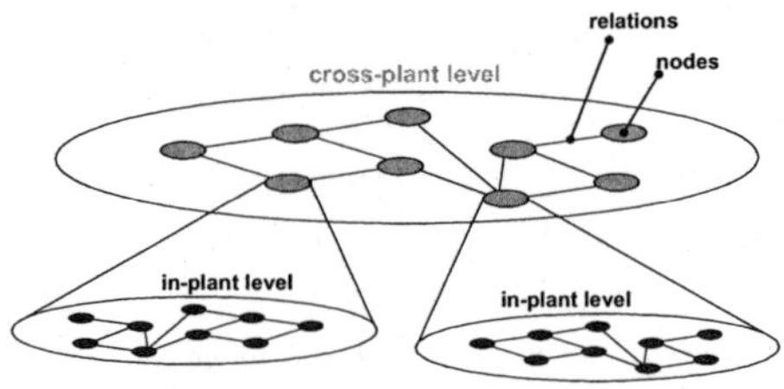

Figure 2: General approach with two system-levels

Both levels contain nodes and relations. By combining them, an in-plant or cross-plant production system arises. This methodology is a process sequential procedure of identical processes with different (level-specific) design objectives (Figure 3) [8].

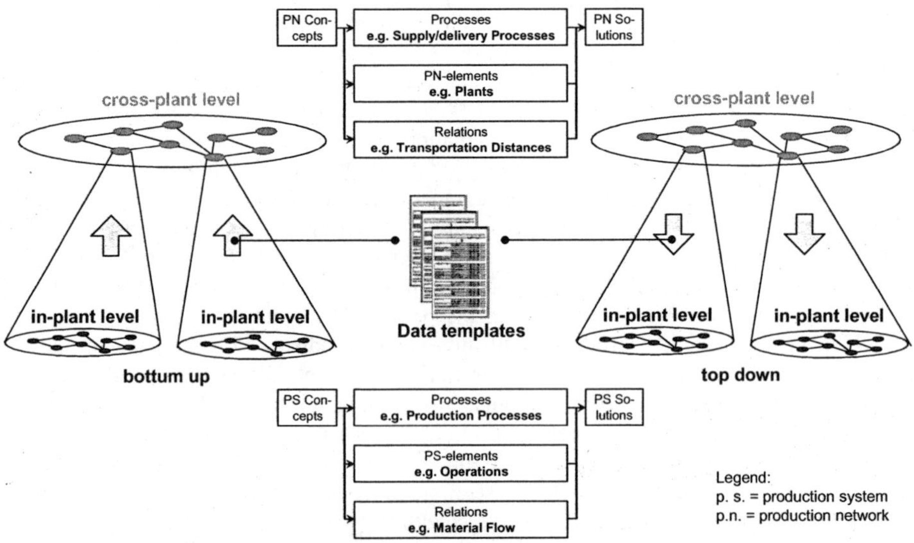

Figure 3: Process sequential procedure with level-specific design objects

Both levels can be described by using processes, production system elements and relationships. Production system elements on cross-plant level can be e.g. plants, while on in-plant level e.g. operations and for processes e.g. supply processes for cross-plant level and e.g. production processes for in-plant level. As cross-plant and in-plant level are described in an identical way, the data interchange can be realised more smoothly. This is important in order to ensure the integration of in-plant and cross-plant level. An in-plant production system acts as a node of cross-plant level and a node of cross-plant level can be seen as an in-plant production system, respectively. Thus, in-plant level has to deliver the data, which characterise the "nodes" and are necessary to configure and evaluate cross-plant production systems. On the other hand the data, which are created on cross-plant level for the nodes, must be available in a form that they can be used to describe an in-plant production system. In brief, a common data interface is essential. This common data interface allows for planning a production system by using a top down or bottom up approach (Figure 3).

Data templates serve as data interfaces between the cross-plant and in-plant levels. The data templates contain information about existing and desired flexibility of the production system. In the case of a cross-plant oriented planning process the data templates delivers information on missing flexibility. This desired flexibility is the input for the planning on in-plant level. On the other hand the information of the available flexibility of an in-plant production system is the input for cross-plant level. This input is used to combine adequate flexibility nodes in order to plan a production system network, which achieves the required flexibility.

4. Approach for Planning Flexible Production Systems

Drawn on the described requirements and the identified two levels of in-plant and cross-plant, a method for lifecycle oriented design of production systems has been developed [9]. It is based on a simplified systems engineering approach [10] and is structured into the three main phases: 1) Analysis of the current production system and market demands, 2) alternative configurations of production systems and 3) evaluation of the developed production systems [11]. Consequently, the approach contains three main modules: a) a strategy module, b) a configuration module and, c) an evaluation module. Its basic structure is shown in figure 4. As the objective is to configure and evaluate production systems both in-plant and cross-plant, the configuration and evaluation module exist for both levels. The strategy module however exists only once and can be used for both levels. Based on this approach e-solutions respectively software tools have been developed by the LicoPro consortium.

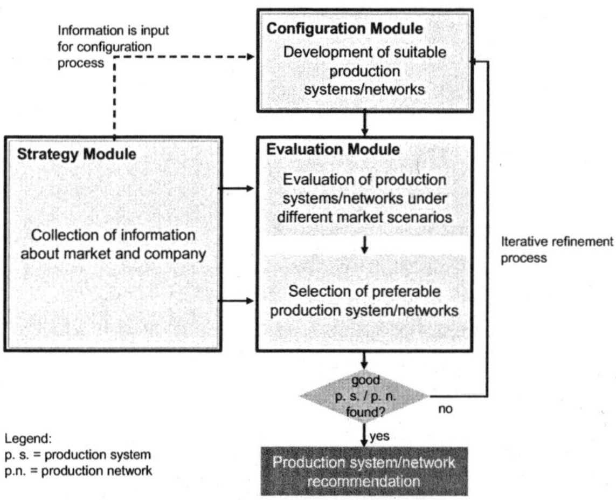

Figure 4: Interconnection between modules

4.1 Strategy Module

Presently, in the conventional planning procedure the strategic production planning department receives fixed demand curves of the products, which will be produced on the production system. These figures are the result of compressions of sales forecasts and market scenarios. The only task of the strategic planning department is to design production systems that can produce the required products in the required volumes. This procedure ignores the existence of dynamic markets and neglects uncertainties. This single demand projection is not able to mirror the reality in an adequate way. Especially uncertainties have to be considered and quantified in order to appropriately plan production systems for dynamic markets.

The underlying method can capture, model, quantify, and analyse uncertain market requirements. Firstly, all pieces of information about possible market developments that exist in the network or in a single factory are collected. These pieces of information can contain events that can influence the demand (i.e. their possible effects, their time and duration of occurrence, and the connected probabilities) and estimated sales volumes. This information are processed and condensed in the LicoPro project by a tool called ScenarioWizard. It delivers a number of possible demand scenarios over time with an associated probability of occurrence [12]. Monte Carlo simulation is used to keep the number of scenarios manageable [6]. Each scenario deals with not only for one product, but for all products and variants to be produced over the complete lifecycle. Therefore it is possible to model the fluctuations of products or the introductions of new products. The resulting information of the ScenarioWizard is used as input for the evaluation module. It will utilize it for evaluating production system alternatives. Summing up, the generated scenarios are based on assumptions and therefore the scenarios themselves are uncertain; how-ever, it is a way to guarantee that as much information as possible is considered for the system configuration and evaluation.

4.2 Configuration Module

Production system alternatives are conceived and modelled in the configuration module [13]. The underlying approach considers data about competences, capacities, and flexibilities of single production units or nodes. It can be machines or lines in the case of factory design or single factories when designing a production network. Thus, two tools are available both for design of production networks as well as for in-plant production systems. A list of enablers for in-plant and cross-plant guides the process of configuring. The outputs of the configuration module are descriptions of possible production system alternatives. These production system alternatives contain information about capacities, times needed for adjustments, and costs of operation, including initial investment costs and running costs (consisting of operation costs and changeover costs). They serve as input for the evaluation module.

4.3 Evaluation Module

The evaluation module is used for calculating the cost effectiveness of each production system alternative for its whole lifecycle on the base of the market scenarios (output of the strategy module). By doing this the alternatives can be compared and the most efficient one with adequate degree of flexibility can be identified. The adequate flexibility is not automatically the highest one. The cheapest alternative of a production system under lifecycle considerations might also be inflexible. It is only important that it optimally meets the needs of the company. In the evaluation tools each production system alternative from the configuration module is matched with every market scenario from the Scenario Wizard. It then delivers the lifecycle costs, including initial costs and operation costs, of each combination.

Finally, the calculated figures are aggregated into key figures, which characterize the cost effectiveness and risk of the production system. It can be shown that investment in flexibility lead to lower risk. The investments in flexibility can be considered as a premium enterprises have to pay to insure themselves against risk [6]. The risk awareness of the company determines the amount of this premium. The calculations are used to select the optimal configuration of the production system. It is calculated for each combination of a production system with a scenario. Net present value is favoured for use as a basic performance indicator for the evaluation. At the moment the LicoPro consortium works on the implementation of a sensitivity analysis that is able to characterise the sensitivity of the performance of a production system to market changes. The authors suggest to use the figure "value at risk" to evaluate risks associated with the implementation of different production system alternatives.

5. Procedure for Planning Flexible Production Networks

As mentioned above the start point for planning these production systems can be arranged top down or bottom up [8]. The top down approach starts to configure production system alternatives on cross-plant level. It is shown in Figure 5.

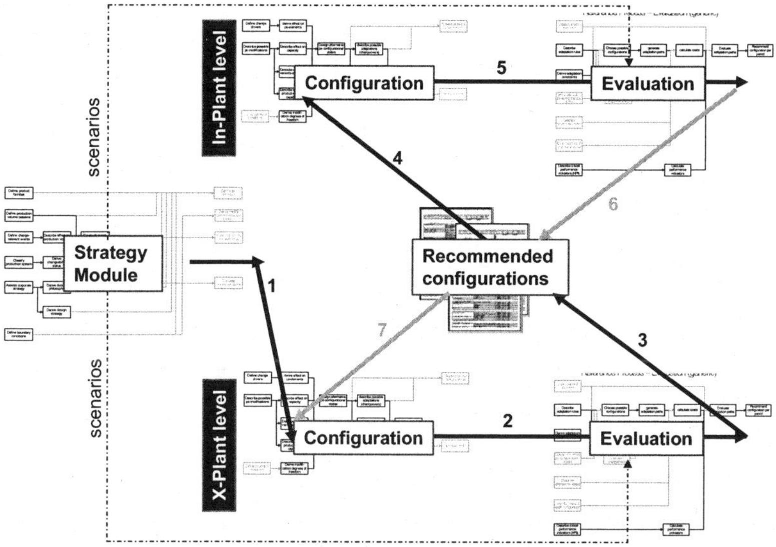

Figure 5: Cross-plant oriented top down procedure

These alternatives are compared with the demanded requirements of flexibility. If the requirements are not matched or the alternative is considered to be not sufficient, the nodes can be reconfigured in a second step. This means, that the production system will be configured on in-plant level accordingly to the missed requirements. The evaluation of different in-plant production system configurations leads to the best fitting alternative. This one will replace the previous node on cross-plant level. The methodology allows for an iterative procedure, if the first run will not provide suitable production system alternatives. The best alternatives can be modified and calculated in a second or third run.

This iterative procedure can be used for the bottom up procedure, as shown in Figure 6. Here the planning starts with a production system on in-plant level. This production system is configured according to the strategy module requirements. If the production task cannot be fulfilled with this production system configuration, it will be lifted on cross-plant level. There it emerges as a node. Then the configuration on cross-plant level will catch up the missing flexibility and provides several production system alternatives, which will be evaluated.

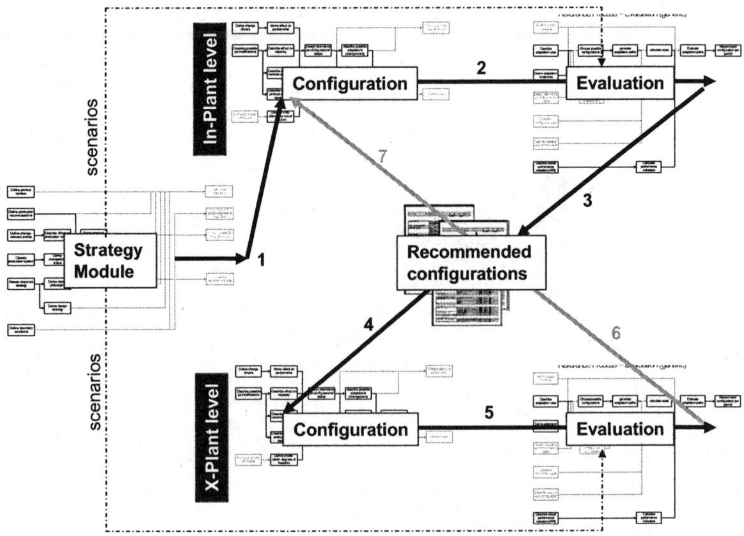

Figure 6: In-plant oriented bottom up procedure

6. Application Study

Currently, the described method is being implemented in an IT tool developed by the LicoPro consortium. First software prototypes are available for application and have been tested successfully by the industry partners in different areas, e.g. for a machining line, a welding cell in a body shop, multiple flexible welding lines, and a production network for manufacturing and assembly of a high volume motor and sub modules for stop lamps. Although the method is considered to be independent of any specific (producing) industry, the examples above have shown that there is a certain focus on automobile and automobile supplier industry.

In the case study "sub modules for stop lamps" the method and software tools were used to answer questions like how decentralized should a production be and one production plant for worldwide delivery? Following the presented cross-plant oriented top down approach firstly different scenarios have been derived. This has included all data the considered automobile supplier collected about market developments (e.g. market growth in China, market decreases in Mexico, stagnation in Europe, etc.) Six scenarios (including best and worst case scenarios) have been used as input for the evaluation module. In the second step important parameters for the configuration of the network have been identified, namely logistic figures like distances and transportation cost, production figures like capacity and changeability, cost figures like work costs and energy costs and external factors like interest rates, taxes, and official regulations like local content requirements, etc. By using these parameters different production network alternatives have been configured, such as a worldwide, a European, and a Chinese production network. Finally, these alternatives have been evaluated for the different scenarios. The evaluation results have been measured in figures like average production cost per piece (differences of 8.8%) and utilization of production resources (differences of 2.5 times).

7. Conclusions and Outlook

The explicit planning of flexibility is becoming increasingly important due to an increasingly dynamic business environment. Production systems that remain optimal on the long run become an essential competitive factor. The authors have provided a methodology and described an approach which helps companies to configure a production system with a long-term optimal degree of flexibility. Uncertainty and the evaluation of risk are explicitly considered. This approach supports well-founded investment decisions for production systems. It consists of a strategy module, a configuration module, and an evaluation module. The explicit planning of flexibility becomes increasingly important in markets with increasing discontinuations. Therefore the authors' intent was to support enterprises under these conditions with valuable design and decision tools, which are both powerful in supporting the decisions to be taken and easy enough to use in praxis.

Feedback from industry partners inside and outside the LicoPro consortium has shown that further research work is needed especially in the area of evaluation, adaptation paths and data integration. Further measures for economic evaluation and characterisation of profitability and risks of different production systems have to be elaborated, IT tools have to be developed that support the optimisation (or, in a second step, can perform automatic optimisation) of rules for adaptation of production systems, and means and methods for interaction and for data integration between production units inside a factory on demand have to be developed.

Acknowledgements

We extend our sincere thanks to all partners in the LicoPro („Lifecycle design for global collaborative production") research project, who have contributed significantly to the development of the results described in this paper. LicoPro is co-funded by the EU under the IST programme (contract number IST-2001-37603).

References

[1] G. Schuh.; N. Wemhöner; A. Kampker: Lebenszyklusbewertung flexibler Produktionssysteme. Wt Werkstattstechnik online 94 (2004).

[2] H.-P. Wiendahl; S. Lutz: Production in Networks. Annals of CIRP 51/2 (2002), pp.1-14.

[3] G. Schuh.; K. Millarg; A. Göransson: Virtuelle Fabrik - Neue Marktchancen durch dynamische Netzwerke. Carl Hanser Verlag, München, 1998.

[4] National Research Council (U.S.): Visionary Manufacturing Challenges for 2020. National Academy Press, Washington DC, 1998.

[5] H. Eicke: Modular Sourcing. Huss, München 1991.

[6] G. Schuh; N. Wemhöner; A. Kampker: The Factory on Demand: Lifecycle oriented Production in Networks. To appear in: WGP Annals XI 2004.

[7] E. Westkämper: Manufacturing on Demand in Production Networks. Annals of CIRP 46/1 (1997), pp. 329-334.

[8] J. Klink: Deliverable 2.4. EU research contract LicoPro, number IST-2001-37603, Brussels, 2004.

[9] W. Eversheim; G. Schuh; M. Sesterhenn; N. Wemhöner: LicoPro – Lifecycle oriented design for global collaborative production. ANNEX 1 to EU research contract number IST-2001-37603, Brussels, 2002.

[10] R. Haberfellner et al.: Vertiefung der Teilschritte im Problemlösungszyklus. In: W. F. Daenzer; F. Huber (eds.): Systems Engineering, Verlag Industrielle Organisation, Zürich, 1994, pp. 109-222.

[11] L. Gottschalk; N. Iliev: Designing and Evaluation Production Networks' Flexibility. In: Proceedings of the IMS-Forum, Cernobbio, 18th May 2004.

[12] J. Gausemeier; A. Fink; O. Schlake: Szenario-Management – Planen und Führen mit Szenarien. 2. bearb. Auflage. Hanser, München, 1996.

[13] A. Urbani: A method for life cycle cost analysis of manufacturing systems. In: Proceedings of the 2004 Japan – USA symposium on flexible automation, Denver, 2004.

P. Cunningham and M. Cunningham (Eds.)
IOS Press, 2004

GRID based Virtual Laboratory for Scientific and Industrial Collaboration

Geleyn R. MEIJER[1], L.O. HERTZBERGER[2]
[1]*LogicaCMG, P.O. Box 159, Amstelveen, 1180AD, The Netherlands*
Tel: +31 20 5033000, Email: geleyn@logicacmg.com
[2]*University of Amsterdam, Kruislaan 403, Amsterdam, 1098SJ, The Netherlands*
Tel: +31 20 5257464, Email: bob@science.uva.nl

Abstract: This paper and related presentation will address the impact of GRID based virtual collaboration environments on the way scientific and industrial business is conducted. As with many developments, the scientific community is leading in adoption of new ways of working, and GRID applications are in use in this community for some time. We consequently focus on the take-up of these technologies and methods by the industrial and services sectors and will discuss application areas where already now the impact of GRID based collaboration is making its footprint. These application areas are outsourcing, ICT services industry, software development and maintenance.

1. Introduction

The exceptional increase in computing power, storage capacity and network bandwidth of the past decades lies at the basis of a new digital revolution. Information is becoming the fuel of our knowledge society and our ability to digest this information, to understand and to share it will determine scientific, economic and social progress.

GRID technology, emerging since 1998 [1], enables large computing and data processing facilities among heterogeneous computer networks. GRID computing is a services oriented architectural approach that enables distributed computing using a heterogeneous collection of resources acting as one large collective computer system. There are organizations that deliver services on the GRID and organizations that use these services. One therefore speaks of virtualization of computing power.

In a GRID, all software components are defined as a service. There are, for example, low-level system and communication services, utility services, and high-level application services. These services work together in one or more applications, introducing a high level of interdependency. These services are delivered by multiple organizations, working together as a Collaborative Network Organization.

The promises of GRID computing are very appealing to these user communities and the market shows clear signs of hype around this topic. In short, these promises are:

- ICT support for sharing distributed resources such as processing power, data storage, capital intense devices and human knowledge
- Availability of service level agreements based on heterogeneous ICT systems and heterogeneous governance models.
- Computing services availability 'on demand' and at competitive prices

In the recent past, the subject of GRID computing has also started to get attention from the industrial, commercial and public services domains. Although these domains do not necessarily have a high need for data storage or processing power as in the academic domain, the promise to solve systems management in heterogeneous environments (as seen in for instance in the financial sector with many legacy systems), or the ability to deliver on demand services at a pay-for-use price (such as needed in Collaborative Networked Organizations) are considered of high potential. At this stage of maturity however, the GRID operating software is still at a basic level and it requires extensive ICT skills to make it effective and secure for the industrial, commercial and public domain.

We believe therefore that it is not GRID itself that will live up to the promises, but the applications and middleware build on top of it. Developing these applications and middleware is precisely the goal of the Dutch national research program Virtual laboratory for E-sciences (VL-e). We will describe this program and its research roadmap. Furthermore, we describe our approach in bridging the gap between scientific progress and the end-user communities with their high expectations.

2. Objectives of the VL-e program

The Dutch national research program Virtual laboratory for E-sciences (VL-e) [2] had its Kick-off in March 2004. Employing earlier work on virtual collaboration and support ICT infrastructure [3] [4], the VL-e project accumulates the know-how of academic, industrial as well as infrastructure and application experts.

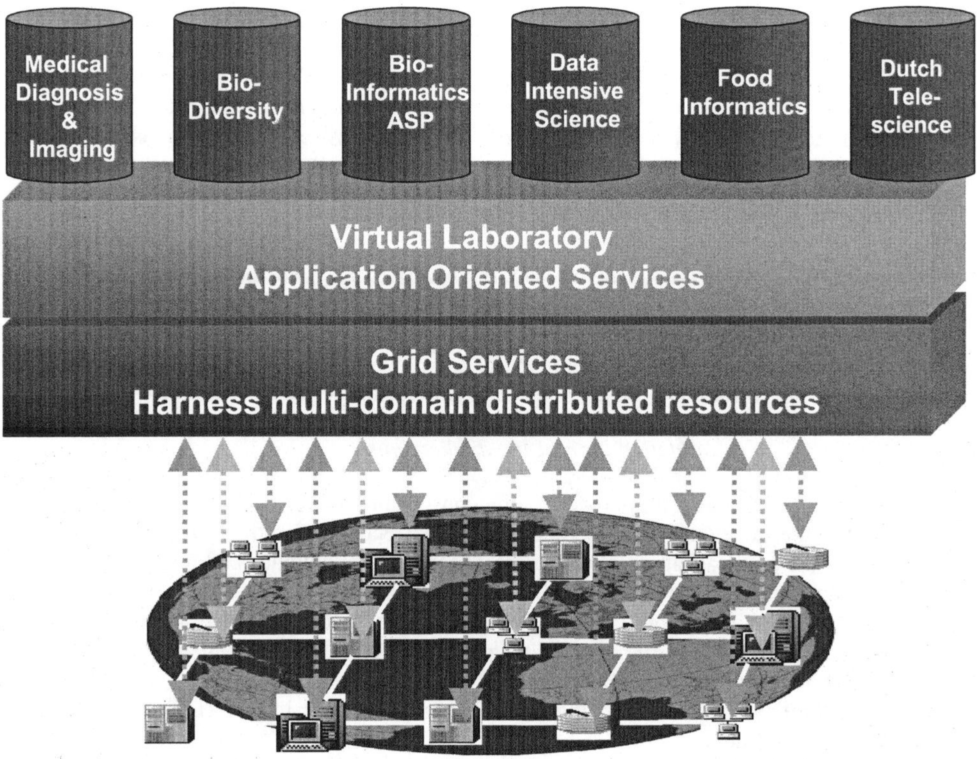

Figure 1: The VL-e program structure with the R&D application domains

The mission of the VL-e project is:

- To boost e-Science by the creation of an e-Science environment and doing research on methodologies.

And our strategy is:

- To carry out concerted research along the e-Science technology chain, ranging from applications to networking, focused on new methodologies and reusable components.

The essential components of the total e-Science technology chain are:

- e-Science development areas,
- a Virtual Laboratory development area,
- a Large Scale Distributed computing development area, consisting of high performance networking and grid parts.

Participants range from academic institutes as University of Amsterdam and Free University of Amsterdam to leading industrial actors as Philips, IBM, Unilever and LogicaCMG. The author/presenter is member of the management board of the program.

The total budget of the program amounts to 40 MEuro, of which 20 MEuro is funded from the national investment funds BSIK.

3. Methodology

To reach its mission the VL-E project has set itself the following four project aims.

3.1 Create scientific prototypes of application specific e-Science environments.

In order to verify the applicability of newly developed e-Science ideas, methodologies and techniques, scientific prototypes will be developed for a number of well chosen application domains. These application domains are all challenging in various aspects of the required methodologies and underlying technology. The key question that has to be answered is:

How can we create flexible collaborative e-Science environments providing time and location independent experimentation and allowing the processing, sharing and integration of data and resources from "in vivo" or "in vitro" and "in silico" experiments?

3.2 Develop a methodology for re-usable ICT components.

Reusability of ICT components (e.g. virtual laboratory, grid technology) is critical to improve R&D. This has an economic impact as it speeds up the R&D development cycle and broadens its range of applications. The corresponding key question is:

How can we provide a versatile basis for new R&D applications and improve the quality and speed for realizing them by using generic and re-usable software components?

3.3 Scaling up to & validating in 'real-life applications'

To emphasize the integral approach of the consortium, a considerable effort is planned in validating the developed ICT methodologies and technologies by scaling up. This gives insight in the applicability and robustness of these methodologies and techniques over the various domains. The corresponding key questions are:

Will it be possible to create a secure and reliable distributed hardware/software infrastructure base that can be used to provide access to grid computing, storage and visualization resources, instrumentation and information?

Will the developed methodology and resulting software in the VL-E project scale in real-life applications?

3.4 Build and transfer knowledge on realizing application specific e-Science environments

Transferring the acquired knowledge, both within the consortium and to society at large, is considered to be of great importance in the VL-E project. The impact of e-Science on the research world and society in general will more likely be achieved when the e-Science paradigm is adopted throughout the public and private research communities. Therefore a dedicated effort is undertaken to establish a 'Virtual Laboratory Knowledge Transfer

Center'. The next section explains more in detail its functioning by employing a Proof-of-Concept Environment approach.

4. Technical program description

This section describes the technical approach of the VL-e program. It consists of four lines. These lines structure the research and facilitate the dissemination of results:

4.1 e-Science in applications

This research program line has the objective of creating research prototypes of advanced e-Science application specific Problem Solving Environments (PSEs) in the area of

- food science
- medical science,
- telescience,
- data intensive computing
- bioinformatics
- biodiversity.

All cases are based on the VL-E generic part of the PSE and the facilities and functionalities it provides. The research prototypes are further developed towards proof-of-concepts and act as a driver for key research areas in the generic Virtual Laboratory program line, and as such provide suitable field tests.

4.2 Generic Virtual Laboratory methodology

This research program line develops the fundamental knowledge for the Virtual Laboratory. It focuses on generic methodologies for e-Science such as problem solving, adaptive information disclosure, visualization and user interface, information systems and systems integration. It applies them and tests them in the various applications, with the purpose to validate and improve the functionality and performance of the methodologies.

4.3 Large Scale Distributed systems

The focus is on knowledge development in the area of large-scale distributed computer systems, based among others on high performance networking and Grid technology.

4.4 Scaling up to & validating in 'real life applications'

This research line has the objective of doing field-testing for evaluation and scaling up of the proof-of-concept environments under several well-chosen real-life conditions. Two environments are developed for field-testing with the aim to evaluate the methods and tools developed in this project and to integrate methods and tools developed elsewhere.

Figure 2 shows the set-up of the scaling and validation activities. All initial developments and R&D testing of the GRID-networking implementations and the Virtual Laboratory Rapid prototyping takes place in the VL-e Experimental Environment. The researchers within the VL-e project use this environment.

Stable versions of the GRID-networking software are released to form the Proof of Concept (PoC) Environment. The software is maintained and kept under release management by a dedicated team of the VL-e project. Also the Virtual Laboratory software of the Experimental Environment is released in the PoC Environment to form the Virtual Laboratory Services. It is further extended with application generic services per application domain. The figure shows the applications that are developed within the VL-e project itself.

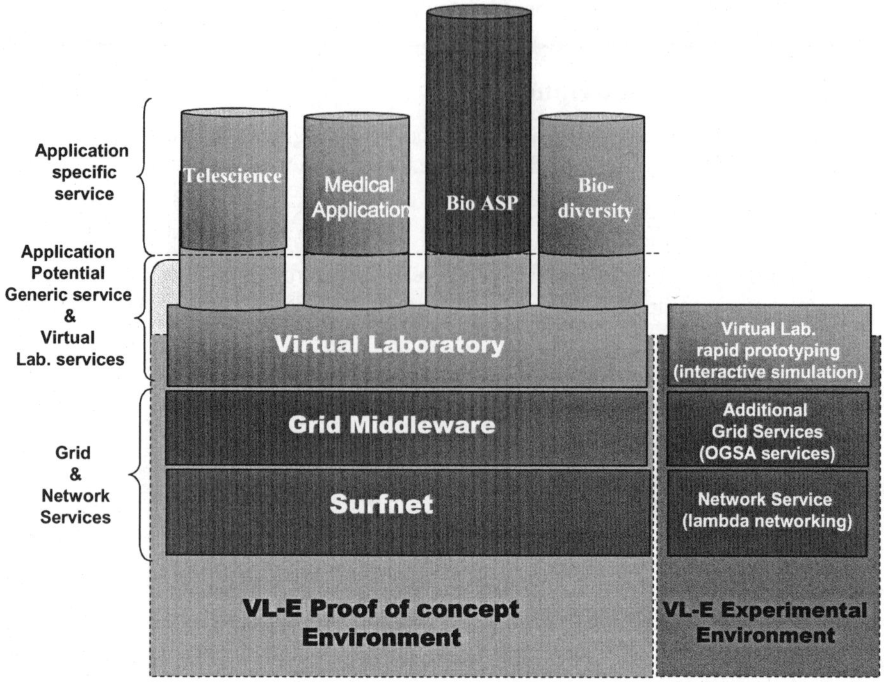

Figure 2: The Proof of Concept environment

The key purpose of the PoC environment is however, to serve the need from parties outside the VL-e project to experiment at an early stage with the potential of Virtual laboratory services based on GRID. Therefore a team of the project is engaged in serving this demand. Support is offered to get the know-how on used Virtual Laboratory services and users can connect to the PoC environment to start developing their own application support and implement their applications.

5. Industrial sample application

To illustrate the role of the PoC Environment in bridging the gap between the VL-e concepts and ideas and the end-user community, we consider the development of software maintenance of GRID based applications itself.

The structure and geographical spread of GRID systems poses new challenges to the ICT services industry. We believe that human intelligence and related skills are a central element in facing these challenges and see the emerging paradigm of virtual organizations as promising direction to realize the availability of these skills. In [5] Mulder and Meijer introduce the notion of squads as a mobile virtual organization consisting of human experts and support tools that operate in the field of software application development and application management.

The squads themselves need tools and instruments to allow them to collaborate, to exchange information and to diagnose and solve system malfunctioning. An architecture of these tools and instruments, called ASIS (adaptive squad information services), is proposed containing four elements: a transformation element (T), a history element (H), a prediction element (P) and an interaction element (I). Figure 3 gives an overview of ASIS.

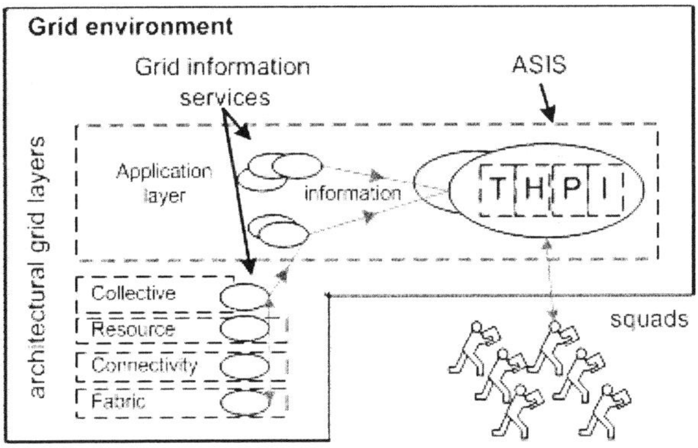

Figure 3: ASIS and their environment

ASIS uses standard grid information services to obtain actual information about the grid infrastructure, the traffic on the grid and the jobs running on it. These information services reside in various architectural layers of the grid. In the fabric and resource layer, for example, they provide information about the availability and capacity of the resources. They might also provide information about the jobs that are currently running or scheduled to run. In the application layer, various vendor-specific information services may provide application (or application-service) specific information. ASIS may use all these kinds of services and combine their information to inform squads.

All core elements are loosely coupled and have well-defined interfaces. In this way, it is possible to replace or extend them.

The next step in the development of ASIS is the experimental validation of the concept. For this purpose now, the VL-e Proof of Concept Environment is being employed. The industrial development team working on ASIS has connected its own development environment with the PoC Environment. In terms of figure 2, this means that an additional application column is added. The ASIS team is now able to employ all GRID-networking and Virtual Lab. generic services available in the current release of the PoC. When new services are released (after being developed and tested in the Rapid prototyping environment), the ASIS team can directly benefit from these developments.

In this way, the results of the VL-e project are becoming available to the external user communities right from the start of the project.

6. Conclusions

We have described the rationale and structure of a new prominent R&D project in the Netherlands that advances the use and applicability of the GRID computing paradigm. The strong interest of various non-computer-science academic research communities demonstrates the potential of middleware services. These middleware services will have to bridge the gap between the mechanics of the GRID software, being predominantly the domain of computer scientists and the application needs of the scientist working in their, non-ICT, domain. We described how the VL-e project approaches this challenge in three levels of activity:

- Research on e-Science in applications
- Development of a Generic Virtual Laboratory methodology
- Development of Large Scale Distributed systems

Although the program itself is in its early phase, industrial interest in the developments is already strong. This holds for the industrial R&D laboratories (as a natural partner of the academic R&D) but also for ICT departments in commercial and public organizations. These people are responsible for systems development and maintenance and ICT architects. Transferring the acquired knowledge to these new users is considered to be of great importance in the VL-E project. We described a dedicated effort to establish a 'Virtual Laboratory Knowledge Transfer Center'. The central idea is to establish a Proof-of-Concept Environment that offers testing and scaling capabilities and which can be used by external organizations.

The interest we observe originates from:

- ICT service providers
- Financial sector
- Maintenance and support providers

We described a particular industrial application that is adopting the Virtual Laboratory concept and is making use of the Proof of Concept environment. We expect to be able to accommodate a number of additional users before the end of the year.

References

[1] Foster, I., C. Kesselman, eds., The Grid 2: Blueprint for a New Computing Infrastructure, Morgan Kaufmann,. 2003, ISBN 1-55860-933-4.

[2] www.wtcw.nl

[3] H. Afsarmanesh, R.G. Belleman, A.S.Z. Belloum, A. Benabdelkader, J.F.J. van den Brand, G.B. Eijkel, A. Frenkel, C. Garita, D.L. Groep, R.M.A. Heeren, Z.W. Hendrikse, L.O. Hertzberger, J.A. Kaandorp, E.C. Kaletas A1, V. Korkhov, C.T.A.M. de Laat, P.M.A. Sloot, D. Vasunin, A. Visser and H.H. Yakali. "VL-E: A Grid-based virtual laboratory", Scientific Programming Journal Vol. 10, No. 2, page 173-181, 2002.

[4] A. Belloum, D. Groep, Z.W. Hendrikse, L.O. Hertzberger, C.T.A.M. de Laat, V. Korkhov and D. Vasunin. "VL-E: a grid-based virtual laboratory", Future Generation Computer Systems, Vol. 19, page 209-217, 2003.

[5] W. Mulder, G.R. Meijer. "Squads: Software development and maintenance on the grid by means of mobile virtual organizations using adaptive information services", PRO-VE'04 5th IFIP Working Conference on VIRTUAL ENTERPRISES, Toulouse, France 23 - 26 Aug 2004.

Section 5.2

Applications

Competence Profiling and Problem Solving in Virtual Networks

Christina EDELMANN[1], Kristina WAGNER[2]
Fraunhofer Institute for Industrial Engineering (IAO),Nobelstrasse 12, Stuttgart 70569, Germany
[1] *Tel: +49 7119702120 Fax: +497119702299, Email: Christina.Edelmann@iao.fraunhofer.de*
[2] *Tel: +49 7119702215, Fax: + 49 7119702299, Email: ina.wagner@iao.fraunhofer.de*

Abstract: Collaboration offers companies the opportunity to exploit new markets by increasing innovation capability and productivity. An important prerequisite hereby is the efficient support of personal knowledge exchange and problem solving in collaborative environments. The methodology and the software tool developed within the Eureka project TRUST, developed conjointly with industrial partners of the automotive industry, enables companies and their employees to provide demand-oriented and solution-driven necessary knowledge provided by actual competence profiles and problem solving processes within an integrated working environment. Employees are supported to access ad-hoc experiences, knowledge, and competences as well as to develop solutions for new problems in a structured way.

1. Introduction

The trend of globalisation and at the same time the need of being presented regionally lead to new forms of cooperation structures for enterprises [1], [7]. Enterprises confronted with these two trends are beginning to collaborate in virtual environments [6], [5], [8]. Solutions for being innovative in virtual environments are described in the following chapters. The approach is to support individual knowledge networks by using dynamic competence profiles and support individual problem solving processes in virtual environments.

2. Objectives

Analysis and interviews in the current research project TRUST (Use of regional potentials in respect of problem solving processes in production - EUREKA project Σ! 2736 factory) show that the change especially in the method of handling co-operations e.g. in the automotive sector, is characterised by the suspension of development competences. By reducing the vertical range of manufacture at the OEM an intense trend is notable that the system and development competence as well as the quality assessment will increasingly be deflected to the partner on the next tier-level, [13], [2].

This requires a supplier, which is capable of quickly identifying conflict situations, and has the potential to solve these efficiently. However, the manufacturer also faces new challenges. Increasingly, he misses the competence to evaluate and assess appropriately and target-oriented problems, changes and conflicts as well as to take the corresponding steps.

Companies and their network partners have to face higher requirements towards the management of the cooperation processes. Compared to classic procurement processes there are now higher degrees of independence in collaboration due to: the increased flexibility, the high amount of globally distributed network partners involved in the problem solution process, and closer, competence-driven relationships between globally distributed partners.

Thus the integration of distributed know-how and competences and the development of competences are core factors in the competitive environment. The goal-oriented use of suitable competences in problem solving processes is still a big challenge not only for enterprise but also for the researchers developing methods and tools to support the competence management. The systematically use and development of know-how hasn't played such an important role in the field of knowledge management as other research areas of knowledge management, e.g. document management [4], [12], [11]. Competence management of the enterprise and employees are important against the background of

- Stronger integration of organisation units company internal and external
  This fact emphasises the task spectrum of employees. They need in their daily work more and more additional know-how.
- New and modern organisational structures
  Project teams or competence centre lead to new distributions and structures of knowledge in an enterprise. Therefore new methods are needed to get transparency and the possibility to use the new knowledge networks.
- Reorganisation and cooperation
  New technologies and market demands lead to new enterprise strategies concerning the competences. Enterprise has to decide which core competences, complementary competences and periphery competences are important [9].
- Temporary of knowledge
  Most knowledge and know-how is task oriented and only useful in certain specific situations and problems. New possibilities showing the existing knowledge and know-how of the employees and the company are needed.

Faced with these challenges the aim of TRUST is to support the employee in the daily work by providing methods for competence development and problem solving

3. Methodology

The use and development of distributed know-how and competences was achieved by the approach of competence center in TRUST. The competence center enables and supports the know-how, idea and knowledge exchange among critical know-how owners [10]. In addition the problems lying in the allocation of the know-how owners were accomplished by a new form of virtual networks: virtual cluster [3]. This efficient form of cooperation in virtuality combines advantages of regional clusters with advantages of virtual networks [14]. The main characteristic of a virtual cluster is that members of the virtual cluster are focussing on core competences. The TRUST approach was to establish several virtual competence centres (VCC) in a virtual cluster. In TRUST a VCC is defined as a virtual organisational unit. In the VCC information, knowledge and competences are bundled and integrated under specific topics (e.g. quality, IT, mechatronics). The topics are prepared and edited decentralised within human network structures and provided again through services. One VCC represents one competence area of the participating companies.

Supporting the knowledge exchange and the problem solving within a VCC the following challenges are pursued:

- Definition and development of competence development in VCCs
- Definition and development of a topic tree
- Definition and development of problem solving

3.1 Competence development

A competence development actively supports the knowledge flow, idea exchange, and the discussion and exchange of experiences between experts. A competence profile links experts in one competence area. The main objective of the networking of experts is the creation of transparency of existing competences.

The focus of the competence profile in TRUST lies on one hand on the dynamic maintenance relating to the activities and interactions of a VCC member. On the other hand it focuses on the continuous assessment of different sources (Figure 1), which creates an actual expertise level to each competence field of a VCC member.

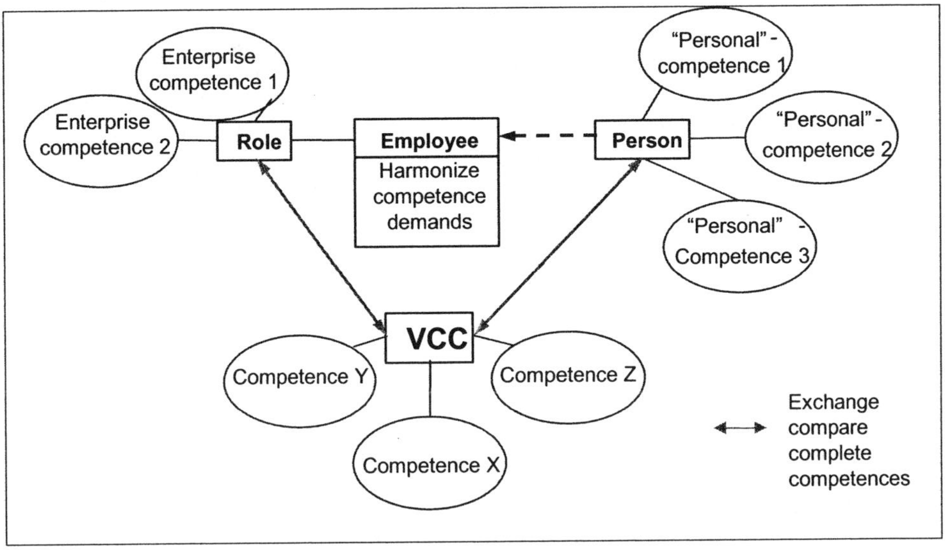

Figure 1: Competence sources and interactions

The advantages using the competence profile for each VCC member are that he or she could easily and quickly find a suitable VCC member for discussion or problem solving. The finding could be done on the one hand by reading the competence profile or on the other hand by searching an expert to a specific topic. Another advantage is the information pull through the software system itself. Additionally experts are linked together through the competence profiles. This reduces parallel development and dual work.

The advantages for the participating companies are, on the one hand, an employee neutral assessment can be done to identify competence gaps and trends. On the other hand the competence profiling supports the human resource management and the profiles could be used as a basis for discussions about career, job development and training.

The competence profile is the background and fundament of the virtual competence centre. For creation and maintenance there have to be done several organisational steps.

In a first step a topic tree has to be defined. The objective of the topic tree is the establishment of a consistent structure of all themes and topics throughout the VCCs. This leads to a high degree of transparency and comprehension in the VCCs. In a first stage the tree is build up from existing directories of each VCC. The topic tree links contents and topics. Therefore it connects and links members or employees.

3.2 Problem solving

The other main objective, supporting the knowledge and cooperation intensive business processes and knowledge-based problems, which occur within processes, is the systematic, methodically supported problem solving process.

When discussing problem solving in this context two aspects must be distinguished: preventive and ad-hoc problem solving. Situative problem solving aims at supporting the problem solver exactly in the situation when a problem occurs. Managing the symptoms often has a higher priority than exploring and eliminating the causes of a problem.

Preventive problem solving aims at avoiding the re-occurrence of a problem by adequate knowledge provision. This often implies a re-engineering of existing and involved business processes in order to remove the causes of a problem. Especially if a problem occurs more than once and if it additionally causes high costs, it is obviously necessary to prevent the problem on the long term by removing its causes. The TRUST approach supports both, the solution of a problem when it occurs, as well as the prevention of a problem.

The advantage of the TRUST approach for the problem solver lies in the increased transparency of knowledge and expertise in the field of the problem. By the systematic approach, the problem solver is enabled to develop solutions by him or in cooperation with others in a structured way. The result of the problem solving process itself is not only the documented solution, but also the transparency of the approach as well as of the necessary knowledge. By this approach the problem solving competence will be enhanced.

The technical implementation of these two approaches is described in the next chapter.

4. Realisation

In order to support daily working processes, these concepts were realised as two software modules. They are integrated in software for virtual clusters comprehending virtual competence center. In the following the two realised modules are described.

4.1 Realisation of Competence Profiles

In Figure 2 a part of a competence profile is shown. The competence profile is updated manual by the competence profile owner itself, semi-automatic by the users of the virtual competence center who rate the contents and automatically by the platform itself.

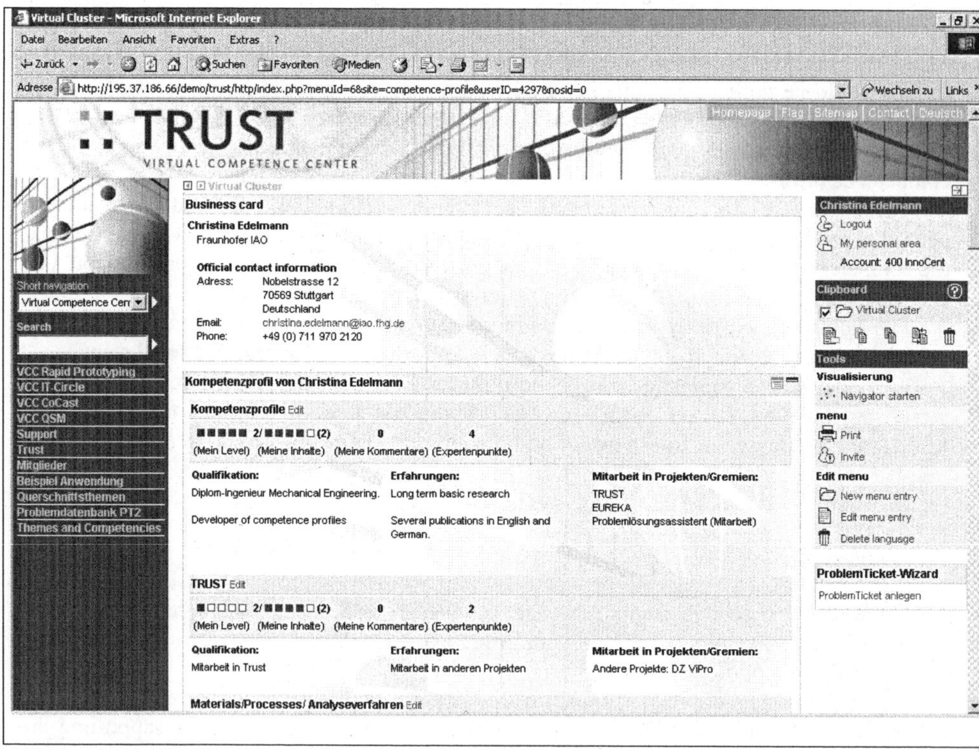

Figure 2: Competence profile

The four main fields of this competence profile are described in the following:

- Topics (e.g. in Figure 2: "Kompetenzprofile")
  The VCC member is able to choose topics out of the topic tree, which are interesting for him or in which he already works in. After filling out the qualification and the experience in this topic he or she is allowed to assess the topic on three expertise levels. This field shows the professional competences of the VCC member.
- Expertise level
  There are three levels defined in TRUST: interested, experienced and expert. These can be allocated by the VCC member itself, a VCC colleague, a superior and by the system. If the topic is assessed as "expert", the topic becomes a competence. The change from topic to competence is visualised at the topic tree. There the topic is highlighted.
- Networks (figure 2: "Mitarbeit in Projekten/Gremien)
  The field networks show the activities of the VCC member across the VCC boundaries. Therefore the profile allows a better insight of activities in projects, clubs, networks or unions etc.. This field shows a part of the personal competence of the VCC member.
- Content
  Stored content from the VCC member is shown in this part of the VCC competence profile. Content and owner are directly linked. VCC members can therefore easily find an expert either by searching through stored content, or by surfing through the competence profile of one VCC member and its assessed content.

4.2 Realisation of Problem solving assistant

IT-support accelerates the process of distributed problem solving in the knowledge network. A software tool was developed, which supports collaborative processes in the knowledge network and distributed development of problem solutions and (re-)use of existing solutions.

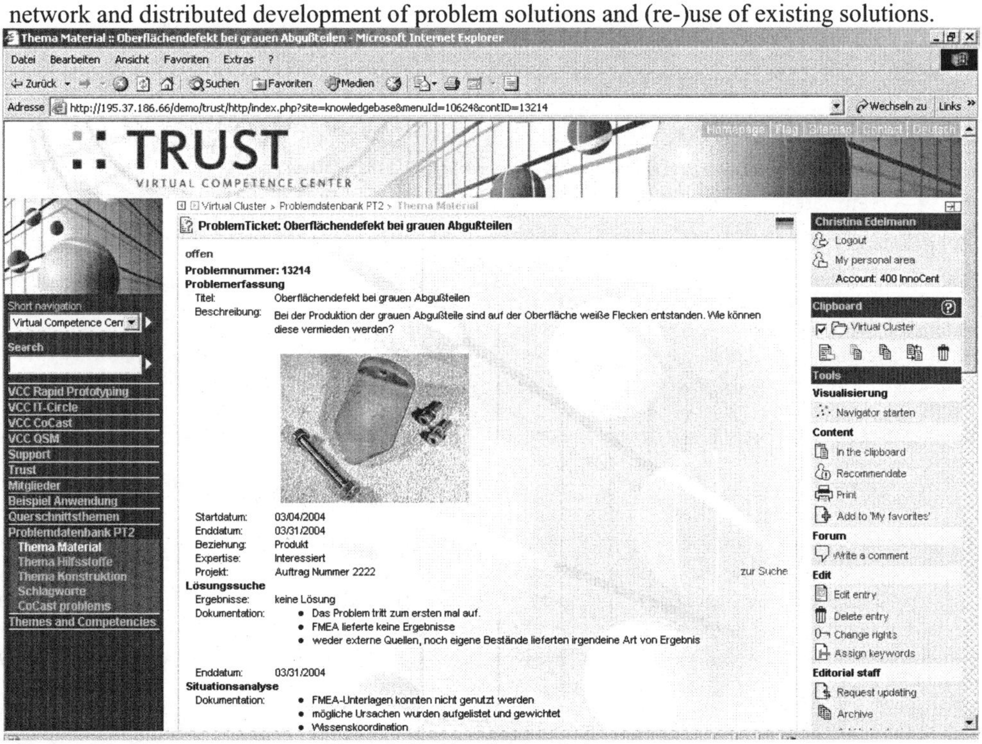

Figure 3: Problem Solving Assistant

The Problem Solving Assistant (PSA) aims to support the user in all phases of the problem solving process by providing extensive knowledge e.g. in form of checklists, methods, tips, examples or contact persons (see Figure 3).

The PSA will be integrated into a knowledge network and can be linked to software tools focusing e.g. on the problem prevention like FMEA tools or to other applications like project information systems, quality management systems etc.

5. Advantages and benefits

This approach results in an improvement of the individual working processes. Through the structured, guided instruction for the development of problem solutions, the systematic search for information and the structured answering of professional questions, the quality of the task processing, the processing logic, and the result itself will be improved decisively.

Furthermore, this approach supports and enhances the profound decision making process. For example the quality of decisions and the capability to make decisions of the involved experts is improved by quickly providing all necessary expertise for the problem solution. Also, shorter reaction times can be realised through the direct access to expert information and innovative consulting services.

In addition to this, work in the knowledge networks fosters the targeted development of innovative solutions, as decentralised expertise is available also beyond the project team. The linking of experts with similar professional background, working issues, and interests, supports the creation of an atmosphere, in which creative work is enhanced.

Efficient learning („learning on the job") through the global processing of topics allows a targeted, individual training and the development of individual competences according to the specific need. Thereby the experts have the chance to get to know each other intensively and to develop a common understanding for coherences.

On strategic level, complex knowledge domains can be developed through the department and project spanning collaboration within knowledge networks. Thus critical know-how can be acquired and secured. This in turn reduces the loss of know-how.

The transparency of distributed expertise finally helps to realise synergy potentials and to identify redundancies as well as to transform synergy effects into a target-oriented manner.

The virtual competence centres offer therefore

- Transparency (visualisation) and evaluation of existing competences
- Linking of distributed experts and competence carriers on various locations for the integration of e.g. technical know-how, partner or customer knowledge
- Profound, semantically linking content to a topic or a competence field (provision and administration of a knowledge basis)
- Services and support from experts for processing of specialised tasks & decision support
- Competence carriers and tools for the development of problem solutions

6. Conclusions

The management of distributed knowledge and its use for the efficient development of solutions is a big challenge for global acting companies and their supply network. By an optimal design of distributed problem solving processes immense innovation potentials can be realised, enabling the companies to realise advantages in global competition.

The company-spanning collaboration offers companies the chance to exhaust and explore new market potentials by increasing their innovation capability and productivity. An important prerequisite therefore is to optimally support knowledge networks and especially the corresponding knowledge exchange and problem solving processes.

In the context of the project TRUST an approach was developed to enable companies and respectively their employees on the one hand to provide knowledge needed for problem solving. On the other hand the employees have access within an integrated working environment to experiences, know-how and competences of the knowledge network to solve their specific problems, and to develop their individual domain competence. The TRUST approach shows how the individual problem solving and the professional knowledge development can be designed efficiently by the use of knowledge networks.

Acknowledgements

This paper describes results from the EUREKA Factory project TRUST "Use of potentials of regions for problem solving processes in production"(Σ! 2736). This project was realised by industrial companies and research partners from Slovenia, Italy and Germany.

References

[1] Altvater, E.; Mahnkopf, B.: Grenzen der Globalisierung; Ökonomie, Ökologie und Politik in der Weltgesellschaft. Münster: Westfälisches Dampfboot, 1996. ISBN: 3-929586-75-4.

[2] DIW 2000. Forschungskooperationen und Innovationscluster am Beispiel der deutschen Automobil-Zuliefererindustrie. Berlin: DIW, Mai 2000

[3] Edelmann, C.; Wagner, K.; Mirtschink, D.: Cooperation in virtual clusters. In Conference Proceeding of ICE 2003.

[4] Gebert, H.: Kompetenz-Management – Bewirtschaftung von implizitem Wissen in Unternehmen. Universität St. Gallen.

[5] Hirsch-Kreinsen, H.; Schulte, A. (Hrsg.): Standortbindungen. Unternehmen zwischen Globalisierung und Regionalisierung, Berlin: edition sigma 2000. ISBN 3-89404-480-2.

[6] IKB Information Dezember 2002. Bericht zur Branche Automobilzulieferer. URL: http://www.ikb.de/objekte/Branchenberichte/01_IKB_Brber_Automobil.pdf.

[7] Krätke, S.; Heeg, S.; Stein, R.: Regionen im Umbruch. Probleme der Regionalentwicklung zwischen "Ost" und "West", Frankfurt/New York, 1997.

[8] LOGIK. BMBF gefördertes Projekt. URL:http://www.isi.fhg.de/pi/projekte/logik.htm. 12.12.2002.

[9] Müller, T.: Virtuelle Organisaton Konzept, Theoriebasis, Möglichkeiten und Grenzen Nr. 21 (1997) Diskussionsbeitrag Oktober 1997. In: Virtuelle Organisation - Konzeptionelle Grundlagen, Möglichkeiten und Grenzen Management Forschung und Praxis. Universität Konstanz. Herausgegeben von Prof. Dr. Rüdiger Klimecki. URL: http://www.ub.uni-konstanz.de/kops/volltexte/ 1999/293/pdf/293_1.pdf.

[10] Neumann, R. et al: Changes and Risks of Knowledge Management Systems in interorganisational Competence Centers. (www.ifi.uni-klu.ac.at/IWAS/HM/eBusiness/doc/KM_ArtikelEng_CC_ECKM.pdf)

[11] Nonaka, I., Takeuchi, H., Die Organisation des Wissens, Campus Verlag, Frankfurt a. M., 19

[12] Probst, G., Deussen, A., Eppler, M., Raub, S., Kompetenz-Management, Gabler Verlag, Wiesbaden, 200097

[13] Saldern, von F. C. 2003: Transparente Prozesse im Supply Chain Management – der Schlüssel zum Erfolg. URL: http:// www.agiplanfl.de/pdf/auto-motive.

[14] Ticoll, D.; Lowy, A.; Kalakota, R.: "Joined at the Bit - the Emergence of the E-Business Community." Blueprint to the Digital Economy –Creating Wealth in the Era of E-Business, D. Tapscott, A. Lowy, and D. Ticoll, eds., McGraw-Hill, New York, 1998.

eAdoption and the Knowledge Economy: Issues, Applications, Case Studies
P. Cunningham and M. Cunningham (Eds.)
IOS Press, 2004

Guidance in SCM Configuration – The PRODCHAIN Toolbox

Martin WEIDEMANN[1], Dr. Volker STICH[2], Andreas NOBS[3]
Forschungsinstitut für Rationalisierung (FIR) an der RWTH-Aachen,
Pontdriesch 14/16, 52062 Aachen, Germany
[1]*Tel: + 49 241 47705 336, Fax: + 49 241 47705 199, Email: wei@fir.rwth-aachen.de*
[2]*Tel: + 49 241 47705 101, Fax: + 49 241 47705 199, Email: st@fir.rwth-aachen.de*
[3]*ETH-Zentrum für Unternehmenswissenschaften (BWI),*
Zürichbergstrasse 18, 8028 Zürich, Switzerland
Tel: + 41 1 632 05 31, Fax: +41 1 632 10 40, Email: Andreas.Nobs@ethz.ch

Abstract: Companies in nowadays economies are acting globally, integrated in supply chains and production networks. Caused by the very complex structure within production networks, the requirements for the cooperation and coordination between the involved partners are increasing continuously. Therefore, easy adaption without great effort to changing markets and customer requirements is only possible with customizable manufacturing resources belonging to different, economical and/or organizational independent partners. Although there are various advanced communication and data-base technologies to support such dynamic reconfiguration and customization, a major problem remains in the organizational ability of each partner and the network as a whole to link and detach from each other to form efficient networks [1]. Under these circumstances, the PRODCHAIN toolbox represents a useful tool supporting the reconfiguration of the supply chain based on networks characteristics and performances of the network and its partners [2].

1. Introduction

The main objective of the IMS project PRODCHAIN (IST-2000-61205) has been to develop a decision support technique and methodology to analyse and improve the logistic performance of globally acting production and logistics networks. The decision support technique incorporates how decisions of different levels are related to each other and which objectives are influencing these decisions.

The key questions, which have been answered by PRODCHAIN, are [3]:

- What measures can improve the logistic performance of a production network?
- How can current production networks be analysed in terms of logistic performance?
- How can customer-supplier relationships in production networks be modelled with regard to the processes?
- How can customer-supplier relationships be described and standardized?
- How can appropriate measures for the improvement of the logistic performance be derived for a specific customer-supplier relationship?

While pursuing the improvement of the logistic performance of globally acting production and logistics networks, the focus has been set on the measurement and improvement of inter-company logistic performance, i. e. the logistic performance of customer-supplier relationships and of the network itself, and not only the isolated performance of a single company.

The resulting decision support methodology has be implemented in a toolbox (the PRODCHAIN Toolbox), which allows operations managers to compare their supply chain's performance to such of other, comparable supply chains. It helps to identify the potential for improvement based on company characteristics and performance indicators and to find supply chain management concepts and best practices, which are feasible to improve the supply chain considering its current configuration.

2. PRODCHAIN Toolbox

The PRODCHAIN toolbox guides the user, like in a storybook through the decision making process. Within this "guided tour", the user selects its company characteristics and inserts its performance measurements. At the end, the toolbox gives suggestions of possible solutions, which shall improve the performance of the overall supply chain.

The core of the PRODCHAIN toolbox are frameworks for classified customer-supplier relationships combining objectives, design and performance measurements. These frameworks shall lead to referenced processes in the PRODCHAIN model [4] and drive standardization, resulting in an easier applicability for smaller companies with less financial resources.

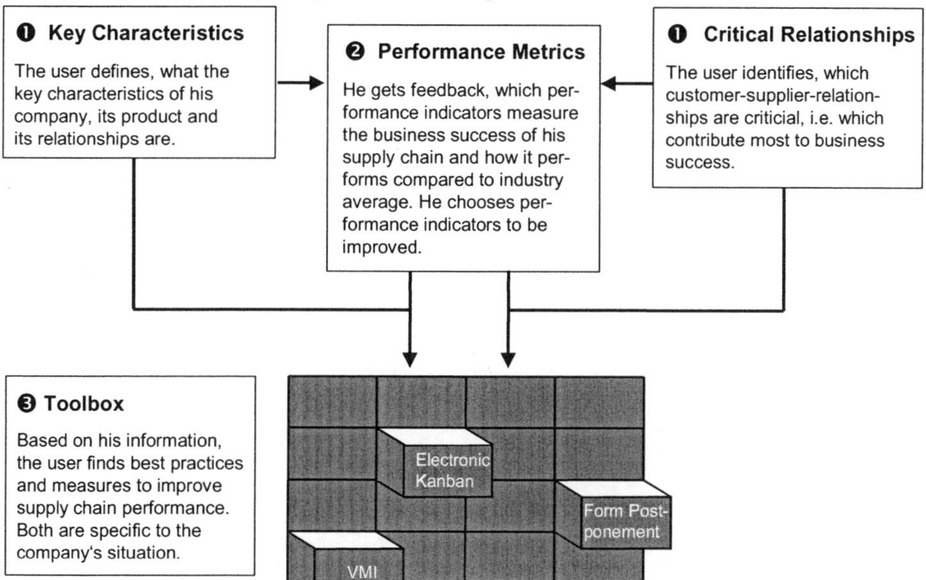

Figure 1: Concept of the PRODCHAIN Toolbox

It takes three steps to reach improvement with the PRODCHAIN Toolbox (see figure 1):

❶ The user, usually an operations manager, defines what the key characteristics of his company, its product and its relationships to customers and suppliers are. This investment guarantees, that the following steps yield results, which are specific to the current configuration of the supply chain.

❷ What is relevant for business success differs from supply chain to supply chain. While, for example, risk of obsolescence is a major threat for innovative companies, that manufacture products with a short life-cycle, it plays a minor role if a large amount of a product with a longer life-cycle is manufactured. The toolbox names the main drivers of business success with according performance indicators. Users can compare performance in the fields critical for business success to supply chains, which are comparable to theirs' according to the characteristics defined in step one. Finally, users select the field in which they aim to improve performance.

❸ The toolbox contains a documentation of approximately 60 different supply chain management tools. It is mainly based on applications of these tools in industry, especially within the PRODCHAIN consortium. From this superset the toolbox lists such tools, which are feasible according to the characteristics, defined in step one and affect performance in the fields chosen to be improved (see step 2) positively.

Alternatively, users name the process between their company and others, as well as the field, in which performance should be improved and again receive a number of tools, which are appropriate in their situation.

2.1 Determining the Type of Company (Step 1)

In the toolbox, the type of a supply chain is being determined by the values of a set of determinants, which are describing the key characteristics of the market, the production network and the company within the network. Depending on the value of these determinants, a company type can be allocated to a company cluster, which leads to a set of performance indicators appropriate for this type of production network.

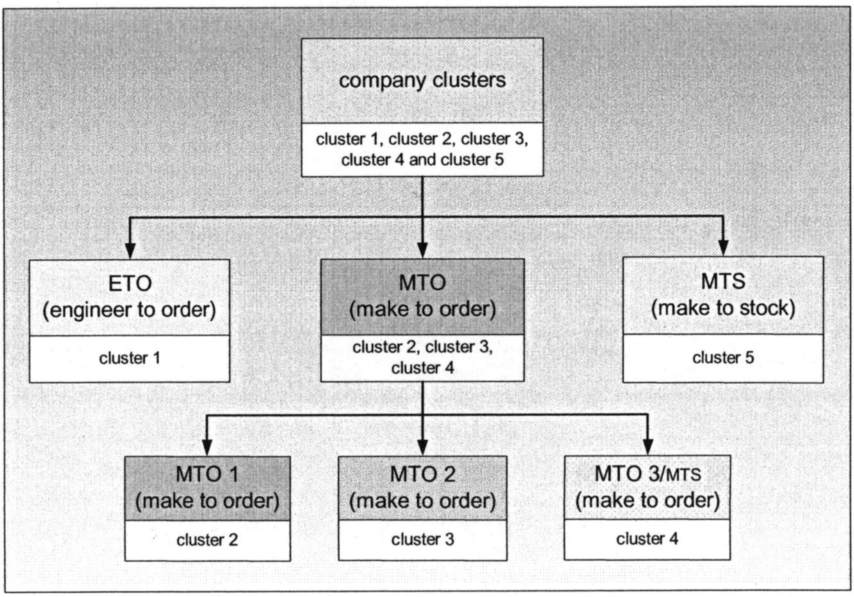

Figure 2: The Structure of the Company Clusters

Figure 2 shows the different types of companies, which have been derived by computing the frequency distributions of the determinants of a European wide survey. It was found that the determinant "production concept" was the only variable that did not vary within a cluster (except for cluster 4, which consists of Make to Order and Make to Stock companies). Therefore, the logistics-determinant "production concept" is used to give a first overview of the structure of the generated company clusters of the typology used in the toolbox. It can be seen that three main groups can be created by the cluster analysis. These production concept groups are: Engineer to Order (ETO); Make to Order (MTO); and Make to Stock (MTS).

The MTO group can be further divided into three subgroups (MTO1, MTO2 and MTO3), whereas the latter comprises also MTS companies. This picture of company clusters seems reasonable as companies with different production concepts are not usually comparable in terms of logistics. For example, with MTO, production is triggered by customer-orders before any delivery can take place. As products are usually delivered to customers immediately after production, expensive stock-keeping of end-products is dispensable. With MTS, production is triggered by demand-forecasts and customer-orders are then directly delivered from the end-product warehouse. Because the underlying process-structures differ significantly for different production concepts, the usefulness of comparing logistics performance indicators measured at benchmarking partners with different production concepts is very limited. In this respect, the outcome of the statistical analysis of the collected company data seems to be in line with theoretical considerations in logistics sciences of supply chain management.

2.2 Performance Indicators to derive fields of improvements (Step 2)

Depending of the allocated cluster, a set of performance indicators useful for this cluster is provided to the user. The value of the performance indicators will then identify the fields of improvement in the particular case due to a benchmarking approach. A benchmarking database has been build up for this purpose by PRODCHAIN. The user receives the benchmarking result immediately, as shown in figure 3, as support for determining his strategic objectives [5]. The strategic objectives, which basically state on which performance indicators need to be improved from the strategic standpoint of the company in the supply chain, serve as input for the selection of the suitable SCM concept and best practice.

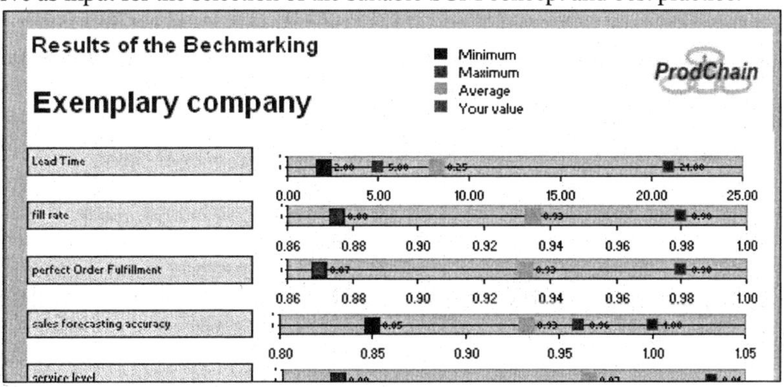

Figure 3: Screenshot of Benchmarking Results (Excerpt)

2.3 Selection of Suitable SCM Concepts and Best Practices (Step 3)

The toolbox developed in PRODCHAIN is intended to allow companies to systematically improve their performance according to their specific situation and strategic objectives. Therefore, relevant improvement areas have to be identified and measured, followed by a selection of optimal improvement measures. The significant contribution of the toolbox is a procedure to facilitate the selection of best practices based on a given set of weighted performance indicators (PIs), which represent the strategic objectives of the user. The software application of the toolbox is be able to identify and recommend improvement measures in the form of best practices based on a previously determined set of weighted PIs.

At the heart of the selection procedure lies the Axiomatic Design Framework (ADF), which are described in more detail in [6]. For the ADF to be applicable, it needs to be ensured that it adequately reflects reality, which is not necessarily the case. Usually, Axiomatic Design Frameworks represent ideal system designs, which are either decoupled or partially coupled [7]. This emphasizes the fact that system designs are artificial in nature. Moreover, the design of generally applicable systems is constrained insofar as situation-specific cause and effect relationships have to be accounted for. Three ADFs (cf. for example Figure 4) have been developed in PRODCHAIN, taking into account the specifics of MTO, MTS, and ETO.

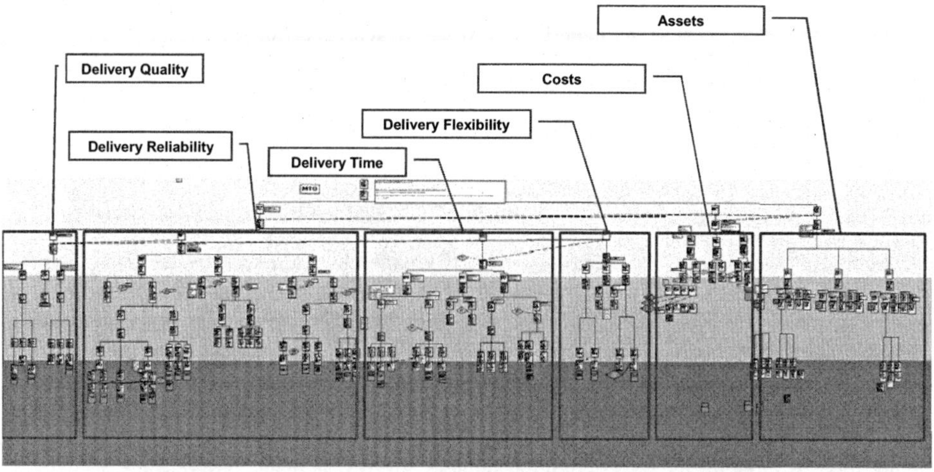

Figure 4: ADF tree for MTO

For the development of the selection procedure several aspects have to be taken into account. The initial situation of a company, for which the toolbox could be of use, is usually characterized by different specifications regarding

- the performance with respect to the fulfilment of objectives
- the strategic importance assigned to performance indicators.

While the actual performance indicates specific weaknesses and promising areas for improvement, the determination of appropriate best practices also needs to consider the strategic weight a company assigns to performance indicators. However, the results of previous research demonstrated that a priority of Functional Requirements (FRs)/strategic objectives exists, which results out of the complex interrelations between cause-and effect relationships. Measures for the improvement of performance indicators are interdependent and may influence several objectives at once. Moreover, several objectives may be influenced to a varying extent. This priority is reflected in the structure of the respective ADF trees and serves as an indication for the order in which a set of Design Parameters (DPs) should be implemented. The determination of best practices needs to account for these aspects.

The AFD trees are the major logical connections to identify best practices and supply chain measures given top level requirements. In other words, the ADF trees are needed to establish a causal connection between high level targets such as increasing on time delivery and the respective measures to achieve this. Therefore, these trees build the backbone of the Toolbox, allowing to map functional requirements (FR) (in this case targets) to design parameters (DP). To take into account the specific features of the three different production environments in PRODCHAIN (i. e. MTS, MTO, ETO), one ADF tree must be developed for each of the three different supply chain types, since the prioritisations of targets in the production environments differ as well as the solutions to fulfil the functional requirements (e.g. in an ETO environment stocking is not an option to increase the delivery time). The FR-DP pairs are broken down and concretized from high level FRs to low level DPs until process elements are identified bearing the DP to fulfil the last FR of the respective branch. Since PRODCHAIN is focused on the optimization of the interface processes between companies, the leaves of the trees are the process elements of the customer-supplier relationships identified earlier in the project [7].

Once an improvement field has been discovered, alternative solutions will be presented to the user out of the best practice repository. Furthermore, the requirements for introducing the best practice are given as well. The success of introducing the best practice is measured by process related performance indicators in terms of quality, cost, delivery and flexibility. This should result in a better achievement of these overall network and company objectives.

3. Technical implementation

From a technical point of view, the toolbox has a modular structure. It is built from modules, which partly have been completed in earlier phases of the project and which have been validated separately. Figure 5 shows the components of the toolbox.

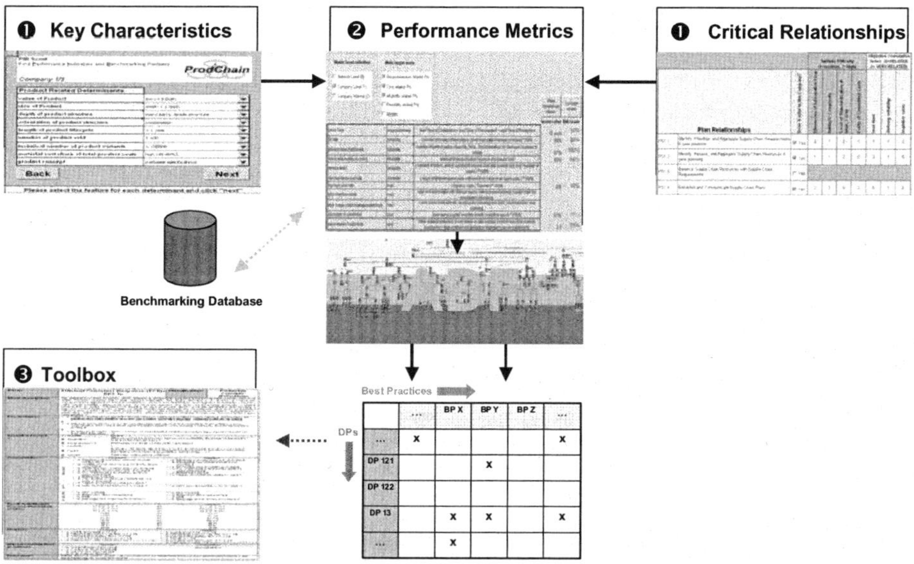

Figure 5: Modular Structure of the PRODCHAIN Toolbox (Screenshots)

The toolbox as such can only been used in its fragmented structure by those experts, who have developed it. Therefore, an additional layer integrates the components and guides the user through the procedure. This guideline also serves as a tutorial, which teaches the user on the various aspects, which need to be regarded when deciding on the implementation of a SCM concepts and best practices. This integrated version has been validated in case studies with the industrial partners of PRODCHAIN as well.

4. Discussion

Dealing with SCM and the implementation of SCM concepts is very complex, because of the nature of logistics. Improving logistics on one end, usually causes negative impacts on the other hand. The use of the Axiomatic Design Methodology has lead to more than 80 design parameters (DPs) on the lowest level. A best practice suitable for application in a specific case needs to contribute to those DPs, which have been identified as most important to fulfil the strategic objectives of the toolbox's user. Therefore, the user needs to determine its objectives. Within the toolbox, this can be done either through a direct selection and weighting of the performance indicators (PIs) to be improved or by determining the most critical customer-supplier processes. In the first case, the PRODCHAIN toolbox provides a typology and a benchmarking database as support, in the second case, a module called relationship manager helps to identify the critical collaboration processes and the complying PIs to be improved.

The approach of PRODCHAIN has been to develop modules, which have been elaborated and validated together with its industrial partners [9]. This way, PRODCHAIN ensured the practicability of these components. Using an additional layer to integrate these components opened up the opportunity to design a guide and tutorial for the user of the toolbox. Therefore, the toolbox does not only represent an assembly of tools, but a guideline to select the most efficient SCM concepts and best practices, which make the user understand, why a concept or best practice has been chosen.

5. Conclusion

Most SME do not have the time and the financial resources to inform and to reorganize their processes according to the latest developments and standards, in order to successfully participate in production networks. More and more global operating companies implement these standards and expect their suppliers to re-organize their processes accordingly. The PRODCHAIN toolbox can guide these companies in dependency of their company, product and supply chain characteristics, as well as its strategic objectives. A European-wide benchmarking study helps the user to determine its improvement potential and to set its strategic objectives. Based on these objectives and considering the company type the best practices most suitable are selected by the PRODCHAIN toolbox. The methodology itself is quite complex as well and a Java based tool needed to be programmed to calculate out of the ADF trees the most relevant DPs. The relation between DPs and best practices results in the selection of the SCM concept or best practice. Consequently, the tool can also inform the user on the fields of impact, if a specific best practice is chosen. Therefore, it represents a useful tool to support the reconfiguration of supply chains.

References

[1] Schumacher, R.; Weidemann, M.: Business Process Integration of Customer-Supplier-Relationships in Production Networks. In: Human Factors in Organisational Design and Management – VII. Editors: Luczak H., Zink, K.J., IEA Press Santa Monica 2003, pp. 287-292.

[2] Schönsleben, P.; Nienhaus, J.; Schnetzler, M.; Sennheiser, A.; Weidemann, M.: SCM – Stand und Entwicklungstendenzen in Europa. In: Supply Chain Management, No 1, 2003, pp.19-27.

[3] Stich, V.; Weidemann, M.: Supporting SME participating successfully in production networks. In: Building the Knowledge Economy. Editors: Cunningham P., Cunningham, M., Fatelnig, P., IOS Press Amsterdam, Berlin, Oxford 2003, pp. 1493-1497.

[4] Stich, V.; Weidemann, M.: Development of a Decision Support Methodology to Improve Logistics Performance of global Production Networks. In: Proceedings of the 1st International IMS Project Forum. Editors: Ferroni, B., Boer, C., Anderson, Ch. M., IMS International, Tokyo 2001, pp. 206-211.

[5] Sennheiser, A.: Lean Benchmarking with clustured company prototypes. In: Building the Knowledge Economy. Editors: Cunningham P., Cunningham, M., Fatelnig, P., IOS Press Amsterdam, Berlin, Oxford 2003.

[6] Schnetzler, M.: Decision Support and Strategy Formulation in Supply Chain Management. In: Conference proceedings of eChallenges conference 2004, to be published.

[7] Suh, N. P.: Axiomatic Design – Advances and Applications. Oxford University Press, New York 2001.

[8] Colombo, C.; Ferigo, S.; Pierpaoli, F.: A roadmap to improve the control of the supply chain: application to an Engineer to Order scenario, The 8th International Symposium on Logistics (8th ISL) - Logistics and Networked Organisations, 6-8 July 2003, Sevilla, Spain.

[9] PRODCHAIN: Development of a decision support methodology to improve performance in production networks. WWW page. http://www.PRODCHAIN.net

eAdoption and the Knowledge Economy: Issues, Applications, Case Studies
P. Cunningham and M. Cunningham (Eds.)
IOS Press, 2004

e-HUBs: e-Engineering enabled by Holonomic and Universal Broker services

Godfried AUGENBROE
Georgia Institute of Technology, ARCH 0155 Atlanta GA 30332, USA
TU Delft, CICAT, PO Box 5048, 2600 GA, Delft, The Netherlands
Tel: +1-404-894-1686, Fax: +1-404-894-1629, Email: fried.augenbroe@arch.gatech.edu

Abstract: A project planning platform for engineering partnerships is introduced. The focus is on partnerships that are remote, time-critical, volatile and limited to dedicated engineering services. The EU-funded e-HUBs project developed a web hosted set of services that enable such partnerships to be formed and executed efficiently through a so-called e-Hub. The new e-Hub business entity offers collaborative project planning (PP) services that focus on the type of collaborative, tactical decision making that goes into the formation, work planning, contracting and trust building on both sides of the e-engineering partnership.

1. Introduction

The paper reports on the work by a joint European and Latin-American consortium in the EU funded e-HUBs project (e-Engineering enabled by Holonomic and Universal Broker services). The project's target was to introduce a new breed of technologies and support environments for global engineering partnerships with focus on projects that are performed in so-called small "project windows", i.e. partnerships within a short time frame. Engineering companies recognize that global partnerships are critical to their future success. Ad-hoc partnering in project specific dynamic settings provides the agility that long term strategic alliance based partnering cannot guarantee. It is this realization that has companies looking for support to initiate and plan partnerships that are remote, time-critical, volatile and limited to dedicated engineering services. These partnerships necessitate a new generation of collaborative project planning (PP) methodologies and services. They must support the tactical decision-making that goes into the formation, work planning, contracting and trust building on both sides of the partnership. Although there are elements in this approach that resemble "outsourcing" practices, the two types of business partnerships are in fact very different. First of all, e-engineering is not driven by the need to "ship work" from one organization to the other; e.g. to lower wage countries. Rather its main purpose is to bring in expertise which is needed for the new product development but not part of the core expertise of developer organization. Another contrast is that there is no need to form strategic long term "service level agreements" as is current standard practice in outsourcing agreements. Rather, the contract is project specific, governed by the tactical needs of the project at hand. e-Engineering partners need platforms that enables them to "fuse" their processes rapidly, remotely and securely, limiting project failure risks to the minimum. This obviously requires adequate tools that enable partners to reach agreements about project requirements, work arrangements, process mediation etc.

Figure 1(a) shows a simplified view of the range of activities in a typical product development process. The process is managed by the client organization and includes different "actors" performing distinct activities in the design development process. The decision to involve an outside partner in an activity may be reached at a certain moment in the project. This may be up-front or at a later stage in the project life. Figure 1(b) shows different moments at which such a decision may be reached, e.g. at project initiation time (i.e. when the project team is prospected and formed), or at some later stage when the requirements of the engineering service are better defined. In all cases a project planning process needs to be initiated, going through stages of partner prospecting, selection, project planning, execution and eventually close-out. The first three stages of this process will be denoted here as e-Engineering project partnering and preparation (PPP). This PPP process may start at any time before the engineering service is actually required. Ultimate flexibility and reactive-ness could be achieved by Just in Time (JIT) PP but it is obvious that the demands on the PPP support environment will grow with the reduction in lead-time.

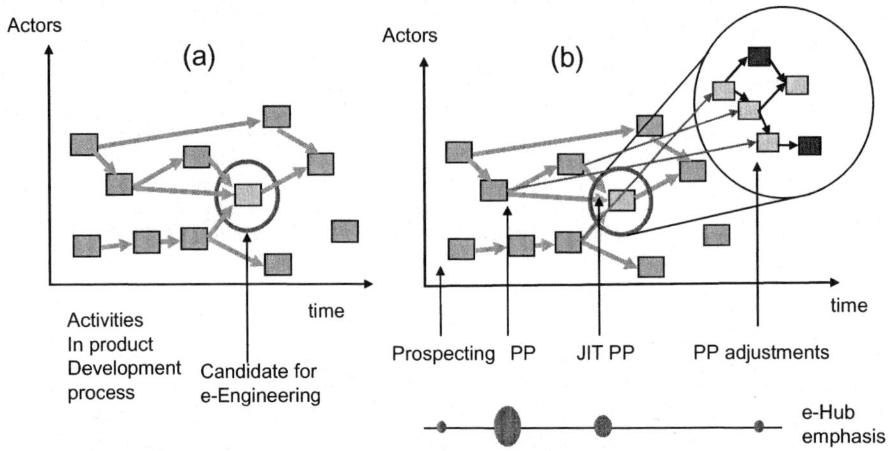

Figure 1: Project Planning life cycle stages

Partner finding and selection are already well supported by the current generation of B2B partnering sites. The e-HUBs project has therefore focused on the Project Planning (PP) phase. In fact it is expected that future agile e-Engineering partnerships will be formed through a partner finding and selection process at the start of the overall project whereas the actual project planning is left to the latest possible moment (JIT). The introduction of the e-Hub PP support functionality reflects this objective, as will be shown later.

Figure 1(b) shows that the PP functionality should present partners with the right tools to seamlessly merge procured engineering service into the overall project. They have to deal with risks, roles, responsibilities, schedules, deliverables etc. They may want to reflect all of the negotiated outcomes in a contract, which is of course part of the project plan.

Figure 1(b) also shows another important dimension of project planning: dynamic adjustments during project execution. This is unavoidable as project plans are just plans [1]. A good project plan will regard everything as dependent on the dynamics of the project environment. Dynamic adaptation will be greatly enhanced by a comprehensive project plan in which not only a work schedule is agreed but all assumptions, rationales, stated conditions, and prior discussions are captured, to provide a rich knowledge base to help the project managers react to changing circumstances and adapt their project plan accordingly.

Based on the arguments introduced above, the following sections will translate the need for flexible PP of e-Engineering partnerships into a set of objectives and describe the basic architecture and functionalities of a prototype e-Hub.

2. Objectives

As indicated in the previous section the project aims to develop a Project Planning platform that enables partners to make the tactical preparations of an e-engineering project. The PP service will be delivered through a web hosted project-planning platform. This PP platform is delivered as part of a new Business entity in the B2B arena and is expected to lead to the creation of a number of new e-Engineering hubs ("e-Hubs") in the market place. e-Hubs will start-off by providing only PP functions but will soon start becoming full PPP providers. This will occur when the market requests an increasing number of additional PPP services, both through the web hosted collaboration platform as well as through add-on services. The add-on services will consist of advice offered by affiliated human experts, e.g. in the form of consultancy services channelled through the storefront of the e-Hub. The hybrid mix of web hosted and human consultancy will over time be enriched by training and training, education and marketing services, primarily directed at SME's.

Three main business drivers of the e-Hub have emerged from an analysis of the current landscape of collaborative engineering:

- The strategic importance of efficient integration of engineering services on an ad-hoc basis into engineering projects for the productivity of engineering design consortia.
- The recognition that project preparation and planning adds to the business value and ROI on investments in current collaborative engineering platforms
- The fact that delivery of generic project planning functionality paves the way for a whole range of other services that enhance the productivity and competitiveness of companies engaged in new product development.

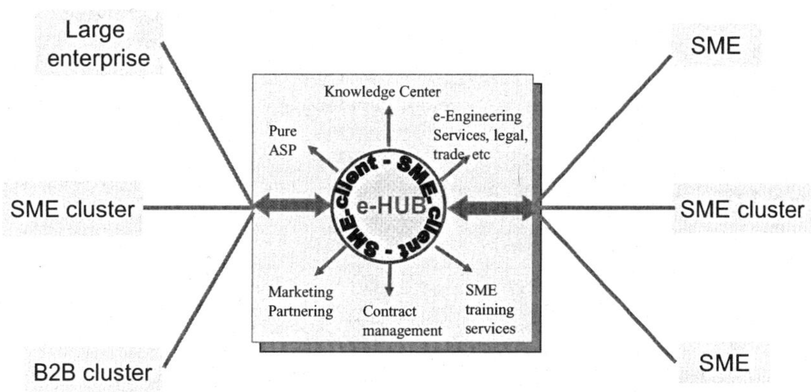

Figure 2: Future landscape of diversity of e-Hub functions

Figure 2 defines the potential functionality of the e-Hub in the future B2B landscape.

3. Methodology

Project planning is an activity that relies heavily on human intelligence, acquired skills, experience, creativity, a good sense of people and risk management. The introduction of e-Hubs is not intended to displace, automate or supersede these human skills. Instead they will augment them and add new functionality, especially when project planning involves two or more parties that have asymmetric knowledge of the involved engineering activities. It was decided to analyse the elements that constitute a good "project plan", and reverse engineer this into a set of communication templates and workflow models that supports its efficient and comprehensive generation. The starting point for this part of the study was the PMBOK [2], together with the analysis if typical engineering scenarios. This led to a set of PP processes associated with communication templates to capture and enhance the structured dialogues during generation of the project plan.. The modelling approach and its results are reported in another paper at this conference [3].

The support of PP functions must start with the analysis and codification of the semantics of project planning. It is surprising that project planning has received relatively little attention in the research literature. Previous studies such as [4] and existing commercial products deal predominantly with the mechanistic phases of project planning. In many cases the emphasis is on task scheduling, arguably one of the "easy" and predictable parts of project planning, and strictly speaking not a part of project planning but a follow-up of it. The current B2B space contains a set of "project planning" sites, either as stand-alone offerings or as add-ons to collaboration spaces (e.g. products from the major collaboration technology providers such as IBM, Lotus, Documentum and others).

These products exclusively offer support for mechanistic activities such as work breakdown and activity scheduling. A further drawback is that there is no distinction between strategic, tactical and operational decisions in project planning. We argue that this distinction is very essential. An e-Hub must reflect the different responsibilities for engineering projects at the three levels. This distinction has played a key role in the development of the e-Hub concept. Figure 3 depicts the role of the so-called project planning model (PPM), a formalized representation of the project planning process. The PPM goes through three different life cycle stages as it is defined at the strategic enterprise level, enacted at the tactical project planning level, and finally produces an operational project model as the outcome of its enactment. The PPM is defined at the strategic level by companies with the incentive to form e-engineering partnerships. A "marketplace" is the vehicle that an e-Hub may offer for that purpose. A market place is an open community within an engineering domain. It is there that companies (typically large clients on the one hand and clusters of small engineering service providers on the other) meet to "declare" and negotiate the business rules with which they re willing to engage in collaborative projects.

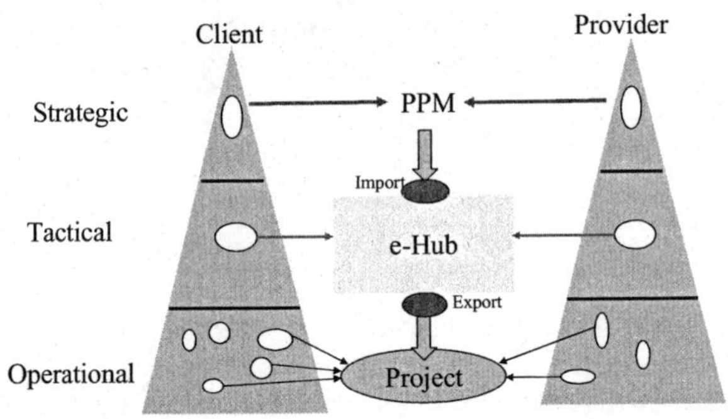

Figure 3: strategic tactical operation levels of PP "intelligence"

Negotiation about these rules will involve company executives and project managers, assisted by experts in contracting, trade rules, tax laws, standards etc.

The core functionality of the e-Hub is offered at the tactical level of the partnership. The basic mechanism that delivers this functionality is a web hosted collaborative project planning platform. The platform enables human project planners of registered e-Hub companies (the client, provider and potentially other (third) partners) to make tactical decisions about the execution of an intended e-Engineering project. The tactical collaborations are "directed" by the PPM that has been previously defined on strategic level. The end result of the tactical PP phase is a project plan consisting of a complete "work statement". It typically includes risk assessment, work breakdown structure, schedule, negotiation trail, contract and others. The next section shows how the core tactical functions are implemented in the prototype e-Hub.

4. Technology Description

As shown in the previous section, collaborative PP is viewed by the e-Hub as a process that transparently generates a set of comprehensive planning documents. The added value of the e-Hub is that the generation process is logically ordered and driven by structured content exchange. Both aspects are embodied in the PPM and are discussed below.

It has to be noted that the PPM is not one single model but a collection of models. Each of these models consists of a workflow model that incorporates the coordination logic of how project planners logically reach a resolution on each of the aspects that need to be tactically agreed. Each of the workflows operates on one or more content templates. A content template is an ordered set of fields with specific meaning. The WF model controls who has read or write access to which field. Figure 4 explains the basic set-up. All parts of the PPM are grouped in "packages", each of which may contain a set of (sub) process models. Each process model is defined as a workflow model that adheres to the WfMC standard [5]. In the project planning platform in the e-Hub the workflow models are enacted, initiated by the project planners. Depending on who is the owner of the workflow, different planners will have the right to launch the enactment a workflow.

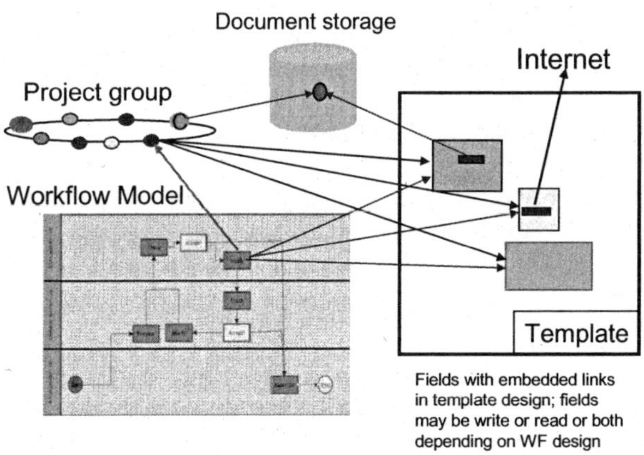

Figure 4: workflows and templates

Figure 4 shows a screenshot of a workflow model that defines that a task is to be assigned to a particular project planner (a member of the project group), while three fields of the template can be accesses by this task. At time of enactment, the project planner will fill fields with specific information. In doping so, he may use links to internal documents and external resources whenever appropriate. It is very important that workflows can be started at will and run concurrently, reflecting the multi-tasking and multi-threading working styles of real life project planning. Planners typically work on different issues concurrently (Figure 5). Moreover, any workflow can be aborted at any time thus avoiding the risk of the system being perceived as implementing a form of "process tyranny". It obviously increases flexibility and self-organization, both of which are regarded essential for knowledge intensive teamwork.

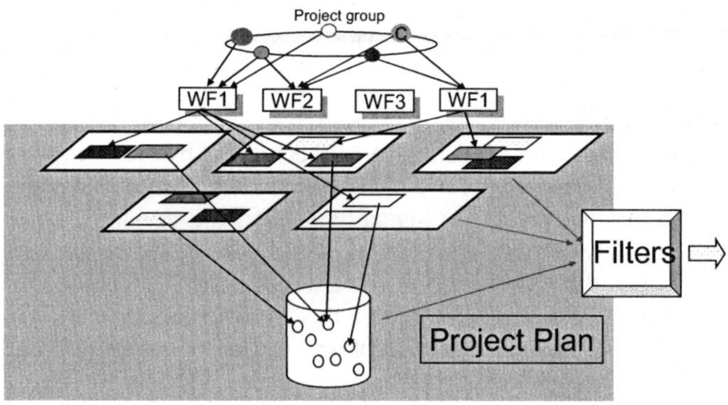

Figure 5: Workflows operating on a collection of templates

Figure 5 shows the typical situation where a project planning team deploys a PPM with four workflows. In this case three workflows have executed, or are executing concurrently (WF1, WF2, WF4). WF3 has been uploaded in the workspace but has not been executed, whereas WF2 is executing but has not yet reached the state where interaction with information templates has taken place.

In the figure it is assumed that the four workflows have been defined to interact with five different information templates. Each template has a set of fields and different members of the project team have inserted information in these fields as mandated by the logic in the workflows (the coloured fields). It is also indicated that fields may contain hyper links to stored documents and other fields thus making the space of project documents (the Project Plan) a rich information resource, which can be navigated in many different ways. It is now possible to define filters in the e-Hub workspace that transform the generated project information into structured reports, contract templates, project execution schedules, etc. for downstream use.

5. Developments

A prototype e-Hub has been developed on the substrate of an existing web hosted collaboration platform. The platform offers all the normal functions that one typically expects in a web hosted collaboration space, e.g. community building, team communication manager and document management. The PPP module operates on the basis of these functions but has two added functional modules: workflow management and project planning. The workflow management module offers a JAWE [6] based workflow modeller with which the PPM can be developed offline and uploaded onto the e-Hub. Workflow models are exported in the WfMC compliant XPDL format, based on a neutral process definition language XPDL [5].

The project planning module allows the selection of workflows to be instantiated in a given project space and enables project planners to launch the enactment of any workflow. Workflows operate automatically on templates (Figure 5) through a set of applications that are embedded in the e-Hub PPP module. All tactical project-planning activities are controlled by the enactment of the workflows. The sequential ordering of the workflows is in some case determined by so-called meta processes as part of the PPM, but in most cases the project planners can override this logic and enact any workflow at any time. Figure 6 shows a high level architecture of the e-Hub distinguishing the five major functional modules and how they operate on communities, document, workflow logic and templates.

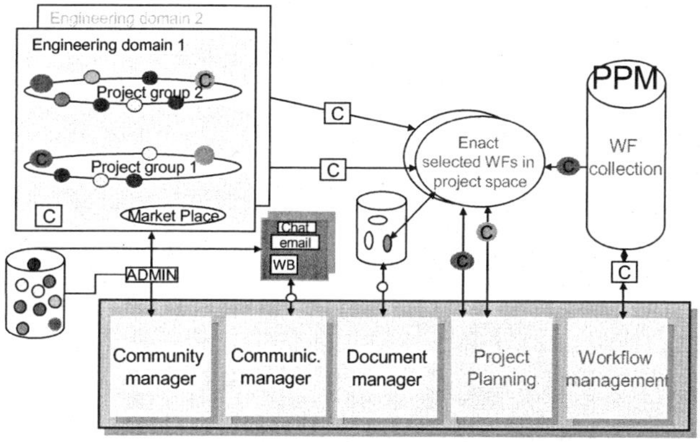

Figure 6: Functional Architecture of e-Hub prototype

The figure shows how the community manager module (managed by an administrator) maintains user identities, and assigns access rights to engineering domains and active projects within engineering domains (managed by a domain Coordinator). Every engineering domain has an open Market Place, to which registered users has access.

The communication manager module controls chat, email, web meeting and other events, while the document manager provides access to document. The workflow management module stores and manages the PPM, creates instances of workflows and exports instances to the WF run time environment. Project groups coordinators decide which PPM, or which packages within a PPM will be made available to the project team. The Project planning module enacts an instance of a workflow, allows the assignment of actual project partners to defined roles, maintains the link between WF variables and native e-Hub applications, and manages the link between WFs and information templates.

6. Results

The e-HUBs project has resulted in a first generation prototype with unprecedented project planning functionality. The prototype has been used in two demonstration test beds. The first test bed deals with the procurement of seismic risk assessment in a large construction project, the client being a Dutch design and the engineering service provider being an Italian SME. The second test bed deals with structural part engineering of a trailer. In this case the client is a steel fabricator and the engineering provider is an SME cluster in Mexico. Both test beds have been harnessed in a web hosted "demonstrator" which can be accessed through the e-Hub project site: www.e-hubs.org.

A series of "e-Hub clinics" has been conducted in Europe reaching out to the community of project planners in engineering and product development domains. A clinic is conducted as a half day session in which planners are walked through the functionality in order to engage them in an open discussion about acceptance level, usability and outlook on industrial implementations. In addition to the clinics a broad scale survey is being conducted among associated professional communities asking them to conduct live trails.

7. Business Benefits

The integration of engineering services into new product development projects is of strategic importance for the productivity and competitiveness of inter organizational work. From the provider perspective, the costs to engage in cumbersome negotiations and face to face meetings outweighs the potential benefits of going global with their services. Many companies see the lack of cost effective PPP as a major hurdle to become successful in e-engineering. This perspective is shared by client and providers alike.

The coordinated, rapid and transparent support of tactical project planning is an answer to both perspectives and is the core of the e-Hub business case. Recent surveys among large companies showed that the transparent management of in-house and outhouse projects is posing the major challenge for the next decade, when the number of external global partnerships is expected to grow exponentially. The role of the e-Hub as a gateway to SMEs, and a provider of program management functions (eventually playing the role of the "outsourced PM office") are huge opportunities that are ready to be exploited.

In addition, the delivery of generic project planning functionality is expected to pave the way for a whole range of other services that enhance the productivity and competitiveness of manufacturing enterprises.

8. Conclusions and Recommendations

The e-Hub development has created a first mover in a relatively virgin space in e-Engineering partnering. The resulting services are convincing from a project management perspective but human and organizational barriers for the acceptance of the technology are still perceived as high. The generation of a "near industry" prototype should be the next step in the development. Such development should test issues in "cultural and organizational ergonomics", develop a framework for PPM generation driven by strategic business goals, do large scale testing and embed the core PP functionality in a wider array of business value adding services.

References

[1] Suchman, Lucy A. Plans and situated actions: the problem of human-machine communication. Cambridge University Press, New York,1987.

[2] Project Management Institute. A guide to the Project management Body of Knowledge (PMBOK). ANSI/PMI 99-001-2000, PMI, 2000.

[3] Amaral Daniel Capaldo, Godfried Augenbroe, Régis Kovacs Scalice, Leonardo D. V. Ribeiro, Rafael G. Dias Netto and Henrique Rozenfeld. Using Enterprise Models for Defining a Web Based Collaborative e-Engineering Environment for Small and Medium Sized Enterprises. Proceedings eChallenges, Vienna, 2004.

[4] Goldmann Sigrid, Juergen Muench, Harald Holz. Distribited process planning with MILOS. International Journal of Software Engineering and Knowledge Engineering Vol. 10, No. 4 (2000) 511-525

[5] WfMC, 2002. *Workflow Process Definition Interface -- XML Process Definition Language*. Lighthouse Point FL: Workflow Management Coalition, (WFMC-TC-1025) Available from: http://wfmc.org/standards/docs.htm [Accessed 15 September 2003]

[6] Java Workflow editor (JAWE). http://jawe.objectweb.org/

eAdoption and the Knowledge Economy: Issues, Applications, Case Studies
P. Cunningham and M. Cunningham (Eds.)
IOS Press, 2004

Implementation of an Integrated Organisation and Process Tool for Engineering Design Co-ordination

Christophe MERLO[1], Raphael MICHEL[1,2], Philippe GIRARD[3], Pierre NOWAK[4], Lionel ROUCOULES[4]
[1]*LIPSI/ESTIA, Technopole Izarbel, Bidart, 64210, France*
Tel: +33 5 59 43 84 33, Fax: + 33 5 59 43 84 01, Email: c.merlo@estia.fr
[2]*ESTIA Innovation, Technopole Izarbel, Bidart, 64210, France*
Tel: +33 5 59 43 84 68, Fax: + 33 5 59 43 84 01, Email: c.merlo@estia.fr
[3]*LAP - UMR 5131 CNRS, Groupe GRAI, Université Bordeaux 1,*
351 cours de la Libération, Talence, 33405, France
Tel: +33 5 40 00 24 04, Fax, +33 5 40 00 66 44, Email: girard@lap.u-bordeaux1.fr
[4]*LASMIS - FRE 2719 CNRS, Troyes University of Technology,*
12 rue Marie Curie, BP 2060, Troyes, 10010, France
Tel: +33 3 25 71 56 71, Fax: + 33 3 25 71 56 75, Email: lionel.roucoules@utt.fr

Abstract: Co-ordination of engineering design is a major problem in very large design projects. In this paper we focus on the organisation and process point of view in order to improve the collaboration between designers in distributed companies. After proposing an integrated model, architecture of an information system based on components re-use is described and its first implementation is detailed.

1. Introduction

This paper deals with the co-ordination of engineering design. We focus on the organisation and process aspects to facilitate collaboration between designers working in distributed companies. The IPPOP project [4] fosters the co-ordination of design projects by integrating the product, process and organisation points of view. After having defined the integrated conceptual models of this integration, we focus on the implementation of a prototype showing the relevance of these concepts. The product development process can be viewed as the set of activities aiming to fulfil the design objectives. The design objectives concern mainly the product specifications. They are constrained by the company organisation and by the design steps and are influenced by technologies or human and physical resources. The review on engineering design focuses on product modelling, design process and coordination of design. Finally an information system to support these concepts is developed using software components architecture.

2. Engineering Design Co-ordination Context

2.1 State of the Art for Engineering Design Co-ordination

The organisational dimension of product engineering design needs to be taken into consideration because the design results depend not only on deadlines and budgets but also on efficient collaboration among the people concerned. The design teams are set up temporarily until a project is completed, then reassigned to other. The new challenge in product engineering design is therefore to manage virtual design teams [1]. Academic and industrial works on control processes are very active since long time. The last decade some results focus on controlling (i.e. conducting, piloting or coordinating) of design activity. Generally the objective of those works is to control tasks, exchanged and shared data of the design process. One of the original features of GRAI model is its capacity to model decision-making according to product and process considerations. The aim of GRAI model is to organise the engineering design departments according to performance objectives.

Generic tools for activity or process modelling are available. A basic survey can detail IDEFØ and IDEF3, Petri nets and GRAI nets [2]. IDEFØ provides a model for an efficient and simple use. It also offers a good representation of key elements of activity (input, output, control and mechanism). IDEF3 offers description of process flows, precedence and causality relationship of activities and their logical junctions which allow capturing the behaviour and performance of the process. Petri nets propose a structured description of process behaviour and allow performance assessment with associated mathematics tools. GRAI nets are based on three concepts: state or result, activity and support.

2.2 The Engineering Design System

In order to improve design projects co-ordination, the GRAI approach [3] proposes a conceptual framework to model the decision-making aspect of project management. It is based on a set of formalisms for the modelling of the design system used to improve the performance of existing design systems. The GRAI reference model describes the design system as 3 subsystems: the decision system, the technological system and the information system. Decisions are structured according two criteria: a time criteria defining the strategic, tactical and operational levels; and a functional criteria defining products or project-oriented decisions. At a specific decision-making level, several decision centres exist according to the functional criteria. Project managers from the decision centres control the technological system, which is broken down into design centres. A design centre is a local organisation, which has in charge a set of design objectives. It is the place for collaborative design work and it generates product and process information that must be taken into account by design centres in order to manage and to improve co-ordination.

In this paper we focus on the study of organisation information flows to ensure the co-ordination of the technological system by the decision system. While managers must structure the design centres and define design frames to define design objectives, they must also control the activities carried out by design centres based on process information flows.

3. Co-Integration of Organisation and Process points of view Proposal

We first formalise an integrated model for managing organisation and process information, based on UML formalism (figure 1). Concerning organisation modelling, enhancing performance in engineering relies on the ability to create design environments fitted to each design situation during product development. A design situation is defined as a state of the system to be co-ordinated, characterised by parameters related to product knowledge, engineering process, human and material resources or designer's skills. The aim is to set a design environment that is the most adequate to the situation and to the given objectives.

Concerning process modelling, the proposed design process model reuse the logical and temporal links from IDEF3, and the semantic of IDEFØ and GRAI. Of course those concepts are modified in order to fit to our needs. Industrial partners involved within the IPPOP project brought their analysis and needs on this topic. Then, the main key elements of the design process model are: task, constraints, maturity, milestones, product data, objectives, resources, status, transition, and trigger.

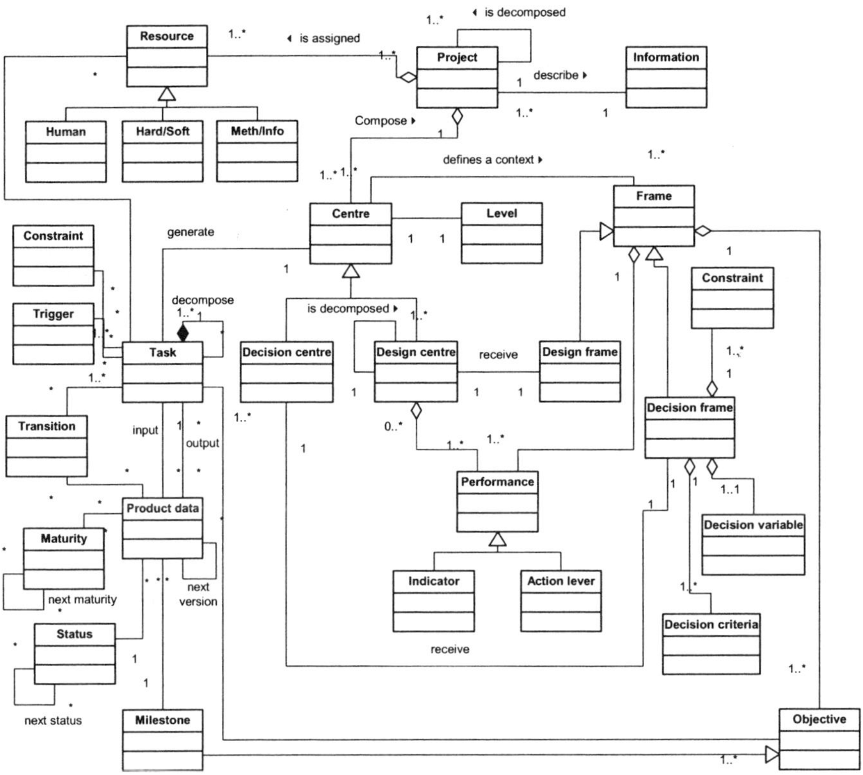

Figure 1 : Integrated Class Diagram

4. Results

The next phase is to implement a collaborative information system [5], [6] that allows users to co-ordinate engineering design according to the proposed concepts and presented in the last section. We first introduce the method used to transform engineering design co-ordination concepts into useable functionalities. Then we present the architecture of the information system and illustrate the first results of its implementation.

4.1 Specifications for an integrated tool

Our objective is to define the architecture of the collaborative information system. Previous co-ordination modelling integrating product, process and organisation point of views is considered as a 'business view' that gives requirements for an object-oriented approach based on UML [7]. First main decision for the definition of the collaborative information system deals with the choice of an architecture based on components re-use. Such an information system has to manage innovative concepts for engineering design co-ordination but also manages traditional concepts in order to be really useable. As an example the class diagrams (figure 1) introduces the "resource" concept: this means that we have to manage resources (human or not), their definition and their allocation Resource management can be a re-usable component as it is used by existing information systems such as groupware, ERP (Enterprise Resource Planning) or PLM (Product Life cycle Management) systems.

So we proposed to decompose the implementation approach into two phases [8], [9]:

1. a phase dedicated to the global analysis of the future information system in order to define technical specifications ensuring the integration of the whole system,
2. a phase of analysis, design and implementation of each defined component leading to the final integration and tests of the final prototype.

We use the Rational Unified Process [10] in its elaboration phase and we customize it in order to realise two phases from the analysis to the design of the prototype. In the first phase (figure 2), we use the 'business view' as user's requirements to characterise use case diagrams and activities diagrams in order to identify the generic functionalities. At the same time we define a first Human-Machine Interface (HMI) to validate the user's interaction. The combination of both activities diagrams and HMI allow us to characterise global sequence diagrams used as specifications preparing future integration of components.

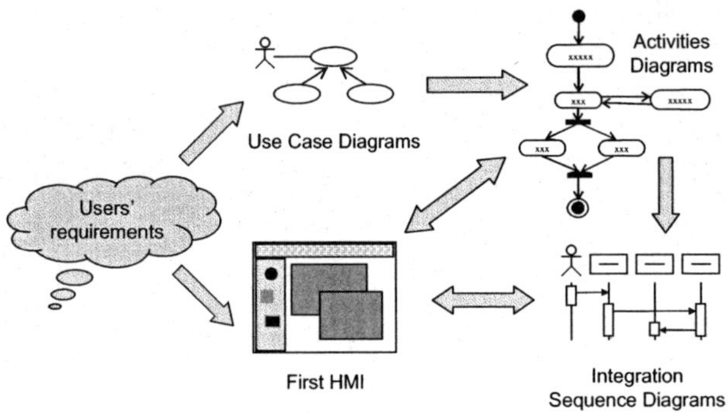

Figure 2 : Technical specifications phase

From user's requirements two UML actors are defined: the co-ordination actor responsible for defining the organisation and process and control its progress, and the design team member involved in the scheduled process. Figure 3 shows an HMI proposed to characterise the first screen of a co-ordination actor connecting to the IPPOP information system. This screen shows the organisation point of view and the list of projects he is implied in. He can create new projects, stop existing ones, and select an existing project to define the organisation and the design process (its design frame) of this project in order to select different tasks. A task allows a user to access to the product data that he needs.

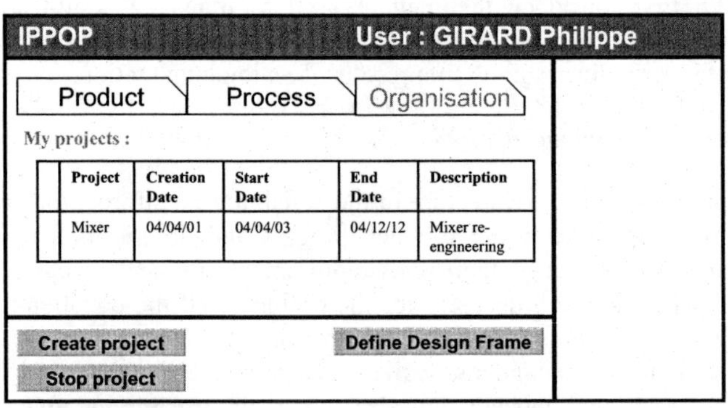

Figure 3 : HMI specification for a co-ordination user's first screen

The second phase starts with the definition of the architecture of the IPPOP prototype.

4.2 Architecture of the prototype

Web-based applications [11], [12] and distributed architectures [5] facilitate the evolution of an information system by allowing easily components replacements or new component integration. The second phase begins with the definition of the component architecture of the whole information system:

- first definition of necessary components,
- then identification of existing components to integrate and components to implement,
- finally evaluation of the difference between existing functions realised by the chosen components and the functions to be implemented in order to determine the "glue-ware" necessary for the whole integration.

When considering the organisational point of view, specific concepts require a specific component but several concepts can be re-used (e.g. project management and resources management). In the same way from the process point of view, task management and resources management can be re-used. As a consequence (Figure 4) MS Project was selected as a global "project management component" that integrates two specific sub-components "project" and "task". These sub-components must communicate with two to-be-implemented components "organisation" and "process" which allow users to manipulate the IPPOP specific concepts in correlation with MS Project functionalities and data.

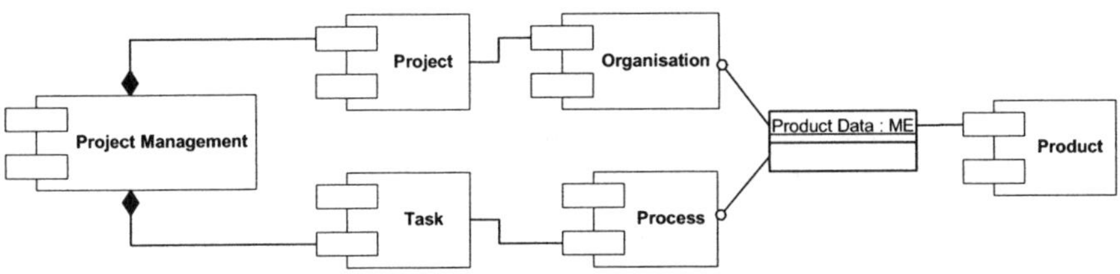

Figure 4 : IPPOP global architecture

To this core architecture is associated a Web portal for the users' interaction and expert applications that can be connected to the database of the information system. For example eMagim (Graisoft) software is dedicated to enterprise modelling and it can be used for the organisation aspects of projects definition and decision centres structuring. On the same way a CAD system can be configured to exchange information with the IPPOP kernel.

After the architecture and the re-used components are defined, the analysis and design steps are realised for each component. Figure 5 illustrates the impact of the defined architecture on the HMI implementation. The corresponding sequence diagram describes the action of the co-ordination actor in order to access to design process information. First co-ordination actor interacts with MS Project to select a project and to access to the corresponding Product Data Flow. This request initiates the "process" component and specific requests are executed with MS Project Kernel and with IPPOP kernel to display the Product Data Flow, i.e. input/output product data and transitions.

Second the co-ordination actor can also directly interact with MS Project to select a task and viewing its related Product Data Flow. By this way the integration between organisation data, process data and product data is carried out.

Such sequence diagrams specify the implementation to be done and characterise the API that will ensure the integration of all components.

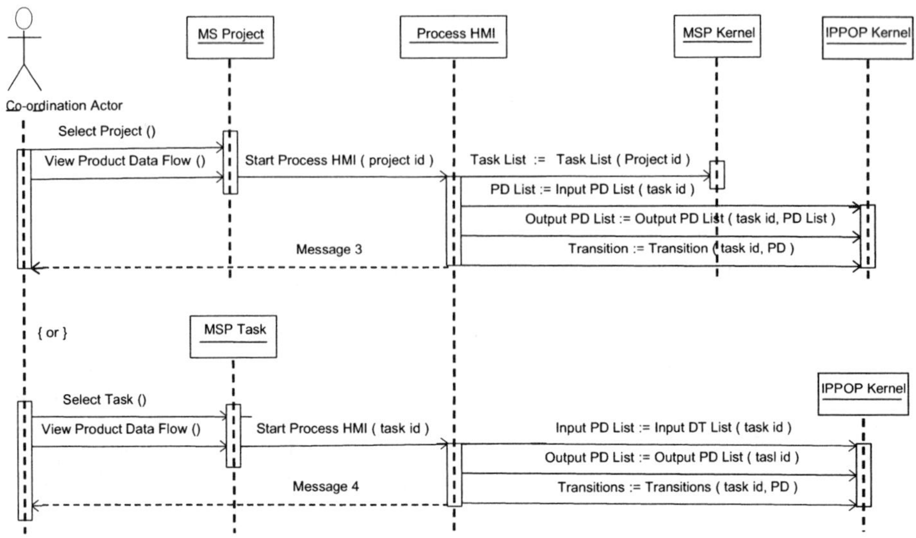

Figure 5 : "displaying Product Data Flow" sequence diagram

4.3 Results of the implementation

A first implementation is complete and being tested to be consolidated. Figure 6 illustrates how the HMI specification introduced in figure 3 is implemented through the Web portal.

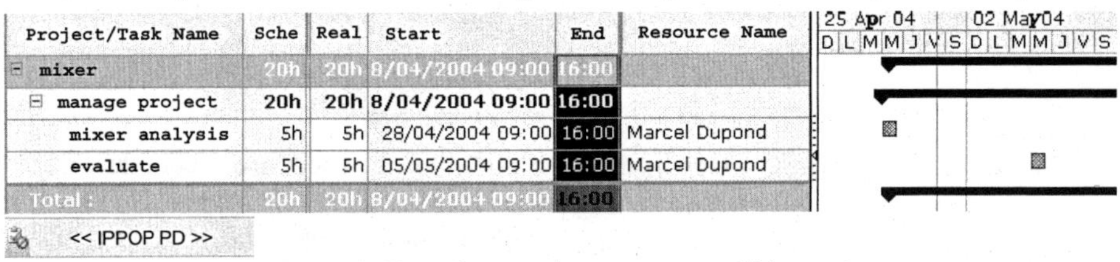

Figure 6 : View of project decomposition on Web portal

A co-ordination actor must structure his project through the "organisation" component according to the integrated class diagram and relevant GRAI concepts. Figure 7 shows the HMI of this component, showing the structure of the decisional system composed of decision centres at a specific level. He can access the co-ordinated design centres from the technology system in order to define them or modify them but also to control their results.

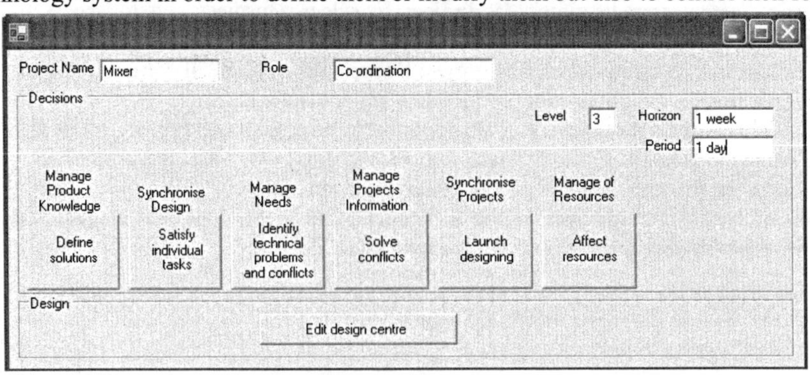

Figure 7 : View of organisation component

5. Conclusion

This paper deals with the co-ordination of engineering design. We focus on the organisation and process aspects and their integration to facilitate collaboration between designers working in distributed companies. Having defined the corresponding integrated conceptual models, the different partners focus on the implementation of a prototype of a collaborative information system: based on component architecture this prototype shows the relevance of these integrated concepts. Existing concepts such as resource or task management are based on re-usable components. First implementation has been performed. The evaluation of both models and prototype will be carried out by using academic and industrial case study in order to illustrate the proposed concepts [13]. As an academic example, we develop the design of the fixing between the rack-and-pinion and the support of a translation system of bowl on a mixer. The industrial case concerns the development of the aircraft pylon and the management of engineering data exchanges between multi-disciplinary designers working in a collaborative way. It will address in a unique and common understanding a collaborative design process modelling for enhancing project and engineering performance.

IPPOP project introduces new integrated concepts in the area of engineering design and allows the study of component-based development at both technical and methodological levels. IPPOP partners have heterogeneous scientific backgrounds: on design product modelling, on engineering design co-ordination, on software development or on component-based architectures. This situation leads to an important work of communication in order to have a shared understanding of proposed concepts before integrating them and of each partner objectives.

This situation influences collaboration between partners by the fact that we had to define a global methodology dedicated to the implementation of the integrated concepts. On one hand, partners involved in the development of the prototype needed information from academic partners and from industrial partners in order to define the needs and the specifications. The resulting methodology (4.1) requires a shared comprehension of UML formalism and a shared interpretation of the diagrams. This first requirement is necessary for academic partners to characterise useful information about the prototype specifications. Development partners also need to explain the proposed architecture and the resulting screens in order to convince all partners of the appropriateness of technical solutions.

Concerning technical aspects of the implementation of a component-based architecture, we encountered problems when analysing and evaluating the possible components to be integrated into the prototype, especially with Microsoft ones. Integrating a component requires to know precisely what are its input and output parameters but also the behaviour of its internal methods. These problems allow us to define a very specific axis of research concerning the requirements and the methods to apply when realising a component-based development. This work will be published in the next months.

The major problem in such a project is to co-ordinate the software implementation with the results of the research which are necessary to establish the specifications. If co-ordination fails the development may start too late to produce a well-consolidated development. This is the main lesson learnt during this project.

The realised IPPOP prototype must now be industrialised before being used in an industrial context, this can lead to the proposal of a new project.

Acknowledgements

The authors thank every participant of the IPPOP project for the results presented here. This project is funded by the French government (Ministries of Research and Industries) under the RNTL program (www.industrie.gouv.fr/rntl/). The consortium was formed in 2001 and is composed of 4 research institutes dedicated to the integration of product, process and organisation concepts; 2 industrial partners for development and 2 industrial-user partners. IPPOP aims at federating several research trends in the subject of product modelling, technological databases, design process modelling and engineering design co-ordination. For any further information, please visit www.opencascade.org/IPPOP/.

References

[1] Stough, S., Eom, S. and J. Buckenmyer, 2000, Virtual teaming: a strategy for moving your organisation into the new millennium, Journal of Industrial Management & Data Systems, 100/8, 370-378.

[2] Nowak P, Rose B, Saint-Marc L, Callot M, Eynard B, Gzara-Yesilbas L, Lombard M., 2004, Towards a design process model enabling the integration of product, process and organization, Proc of the 5th International Conference on Integrated Design and Manufacturing in Mechanical Engineering - IDMME'2004, Bath, UK, April 5-7.

[3] Girard Ph., Doumeingts G., "Modelling of the engineering design system to improve performance", *Computers & Industrial Engineering*, Vol 46/1 pp 43-67, 2004.

[4] Girard, Ph., Eynard, B., 2004, Integration of product – process – organisation for advanced engineering design, Perspectives from Europe and Asia on Engineering Design and Manufacture, Edited by Yan X.T., Jiang C.Y., Juster N.P., Kluwer Academic Publishers, Dordrecht.

[5] Kim, Y., Kang, S.K., Lee, S.H. and S.B. Yoo, 2001, A distributed, open, intelligent product data management system, International Journal of Computer Integrated Manufacturing, 14/2, 224-235.

[6] Xu, X.W., Liu, T., 2003, A web-enabled PDM system in a collaborative design environment, Robotics and Computer Integrated Manufacturing, 19/4, 315-328.

[7] Booch, G., J.Rumbaugh and I. Jacobson, 1999, The unified modelling language user guide, Addison-Wesley, (Boston, USA).

[8] Carney, D., 1997, Assembling Large Systems from COTS Components: Oportunities, Cautions, and Complexities, SEI Monographs on the Use of Commercial Software in Government Systems, Carnegie Mellon – Software Engineering Institute.

[9] Morisio, M., Seaman, C.B., Basili, V.R., Parra, A.T., Kraft, S.E., Condon, S.E., 2002, COTS-based software development: Processes and open issues, The Journal of Systems and Software, 61, 189-199.

[10] Quatrani, T., 2000, Visual Modelling with Rational Rose 2000 and UML, 2nd Edition, Addison-Wesley Object Technologies Series, Addison-Wesley Longman, a Pearson Education Company, ISBN 0 201 69961 3.

[11] Huang, G.Q., 2002, Web-based support for collaborative product design review, Computers in Industry, 48, 71-88.

[12] Rezayat, M., 2000, Enterprise-Web portal for the lifecycle support, Computer Aided Design, 32, 85-96.

[13] B. Rose, 2004, Industrial case of product design: towards specifications of a collaborative design tool, e-Challenges e-2004 Conference, 27 - 29 October, Vienna, Austria.

eAdoption and the Knowledge Economy: Issues, Applications, Case Studies
P. Cunningham and M. Cunningham (Eds.)
IOS Press, 2004

Specifications of a Collaborative Tool for Product Design

Bertrand ROSE[1], Muriel LOMBARD[1], Lilia GZARA[1], Luc LOSSENT[1]
Pierre-Antoine CLAUDON[2], Patrice LEBOEUF[2]
[1]*CRAN Automatic Research Center of Nancy, CNRS UMR 7039, University Henri Poincaré, Nancy I, Faculty of Sciences, BP 239,* 54506 Vandoeuvre-lès-Nancy - FRANCE
Email: {firstname}.{name}@cran.uhp-nancy.fr
[2]*ALSTOM Power Conversion, 4 chemin Rompure – 54250 Champigneulles - FRANCE*
Email: {firstname}.{name}@powerconv.alstom.com

Abstract: This paper presents static and dynamic specifications of a collaborative design tool dedicated to conflict handling. The solving process specified is applied on a real-life industrial case: a windmill stator sheet design. The design context of the artefact is exposed and the met conflicts are explained. Extracts of IPPOP demonstrator's Graphical User Interfaces, illustrating these collaborative aspects of the software application are then presented. They show the ability of the demonstrator to run the conflict solving process and various means to subscribe relevant actors in this process as well as filers to track pertinent past solutions suitable for the current problem.

1. Introduction

New Organizational frameworks for companies dealing with product development are required for the new market rules as much as for the increasing complexity of product and process development. Thus, the new stake is to examine new methods of leading the design activities: the cooperative design, dealing with the sharing of various interests and resources among various actors with the aim of reaching a common purpose. This purpose lay on the development of products by way of knowledge sharing and interactions with a certain level of coordination between these varied activities. Embedded into the IPPOP research project perspectives, this paper will focus on the particular collaborative situation of conflict management occurring during design activities. Therefore, it meets the IPPOP (Integrated Product Process Organisation for Engineering Performance) objectives of integrating product and process knowledge in order to improve the enterprise technological patrimony along with the coordination of design activities within a complete design environment [1].

2. Specifications of a framework for conflict handling

2.1 Static View

Collaborative design process consists of several stages alternating between definitions of new solutions and adapting old solutions. There is no longer a need to prove the capitalization of design historic with a re-use and time-saving perspective. However, its implementation remains difficult. Previous works on the design process field and more precisely on the conflict management field [2], [3] enables to apply the cybernetic loop protocol on this situation [4], [5]. We can therefore highlight the Observation phase of the conflict, a Decision stage about the solution to be adopted and an Information to be brought to the involved actors (forwarding of the solution). In order to keep trace of the conflict resolution process (in terms of actions chaining and knowledge exchanged), we define an

UML class diagram [6] built around the class called “Collaboration Activity” to refer to the various resolution processes held to resolve different conflicts. This class is a specialization of the “Activity” class defined in the IPPOP process model [7]. Figure 1 presents this class diagram and its implementation within the design process. Each “Collaboration Activity” (i.e. each conflict management process) is then composed of a set of “Iteration” classes. The “Collaboration Activity” class is instantiated to initialize the conflict resolution process. The “Iteration” class can handle several actions depending on the phase of the decision-process (arguing the actors’ choices, negotiating the proposed solutions, concluding the conflict…). The “iteration class” was therefore specialized into three sub-classes in order to facilitate the capitalization of the conflict management process by keeping trace of the different intervention:

2.2 Dynamic view

This section presents the running rules of the previously exposed model.

2.2.1 Collaboration Activity Creation

The instantiation of this class occurs upon conflict detection. Once a conflict is detected, a message is sent to the appropriate actor (the one who has first detected the conflict or an other designated actor) asking him to declare into the “collaboration Activity” class the key elements characterizing the conflict that he observed, i.e. the element of the product that is carrying the conflict, the conflict type, etc... In order to class collaboration activities by conflict type (for future reuse), an attribute “conflict category” is included. An ontology of conflict categories is proposed by the system to help actors instantiating this attribute.

2.2.2 Iterations Creation

An iteration is created every time an actor wants to react on the proposals or to bring information to the solving process. Different kinds of iteration previously presented are instantiated depending on the location within the solving process (Resolution iteration, Vote Request iteration, Vote iteration, Closure iteration). These various iterations are chained hence forth a temporal and a logical link. The “temporal next” link is specified in order to define the chronological succession of the diverse actors contributions (to link an iteration with the last one instantiated). This allows to represent the succession of iterations in a Gant chart. A “logical next” link is also implemented in order to obtain a logical tracking of the contributions while defining who has answered which proposal. This is undertaken with the aim of studying the rationale design leading a solution. A subscribers list specified with the “subscriber” class is attached to each instantiation of the iterations. It can be reconfigurable at each iteration instance since the level and the field of expertise may vary during the conflict solving process.

- Resolution iteration: The successive Resolution iterations allows to structure the exchanges during the solving process. During a “Resolution iteration” one actor can popularize and mediate a problem by explaining the problems he faced with the former proposed solution (“explanation” attribute), justifying or arguing the new solution (“justification” attribute) and proposing the solution (by filling the “solution” attribute and eventually associating a file to describe the solution with a CAD model, a Word document …). He can also just popularize the problem by explaining the problems he faced with the former proposed solution without giving a new solution or just give his agreement on the solution proposed by another. Then, the actor can fill one or all attributes of the iteration entity (explanation, justification and solution). Two cases have been identified while representing the logical succession of iterations: iteration with a new solution (the arborescence is developed vertically) and iteration without new solution (the arborescence is developed horizontally). At the end of the popularization mediation stage run through the resolution iteration, two configurations can happen: whether the conflict is solved and a viable solution is retained by the actors within the framework given by the organization (a closure iteration is then triggered) or the design framework does not allow the conflict resolution (timeframe and resources not adapted: a voting process is then launched).

- Vote Request iteration: In case actors do not agree on a solution within the time allowed by the project manager to resolve the conflict (N iterations or D period), the system or an other designated actor (project manager usually) requests all actors involved in the resolution process to vote for their favorite solution among the various proposed ones. They receive a warning message when login on the software.
- Vote iteration: This class is only instantiated if Vote Request iteration has been launched. The field "Solution" must be filled in with the most relevant proposed solution's index or the worst solution's index, in lack of an effective proposed solution in order to eliminate this one. A quorum of X% of subscribers must be raised as well as a minimum of X% of the votes in order to acknowledge a proposed solution.
- Closure iteration: This class is filled either when the concerned actors agree on a solution during the popularization/mediation (before the vote request) or when a vote process is performed and no consensus is made (many criteria can be defined to close a vote: all involved actors has voted, a number N of actors has voted or a vote delay D is elapsed whereas N and D are usually fixed by the project manager…). Further to a vote, actors may either converge into a common solution or diverge. In the latter case, the conflict is solved in a hierarchical way usually by appealing to a designated chief . Whatever the case, the "Solution" attribute must be filled in with the retained solution and a message must be sent to concerned actors to forward them this solution. The figure 1 illustrates the Conflict Management Process in the Decision phase.

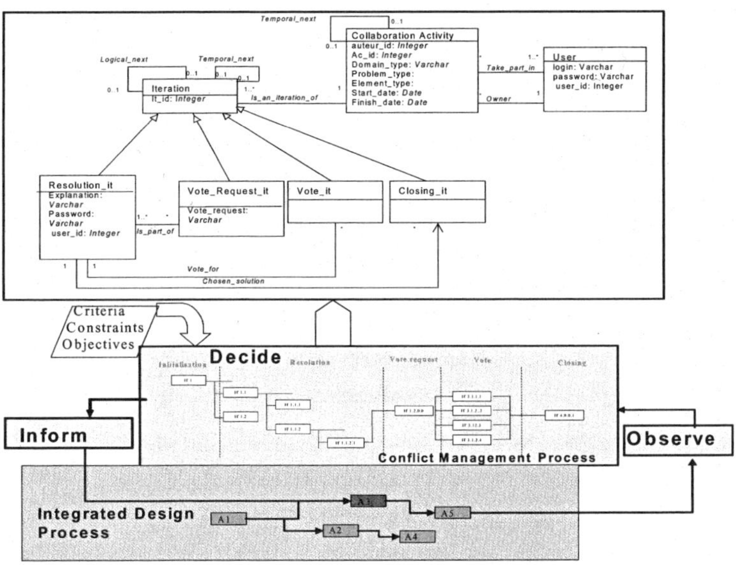

Figure 1: Dynamic and static view of the conflict management process

3. The E64 Stator Metal Sheet Design Study

3.1 Case Study Presentation

We applied this dynamic protocol and instantiated the data model for conflict management on a real case industrial project. The selected project deals with the design of a high voltage power generator at Alstom Power Conversion facility located in Nancy, France. This generator is tailor-made for off-shore and high power windmills. This project was carried out between March and September 2002.

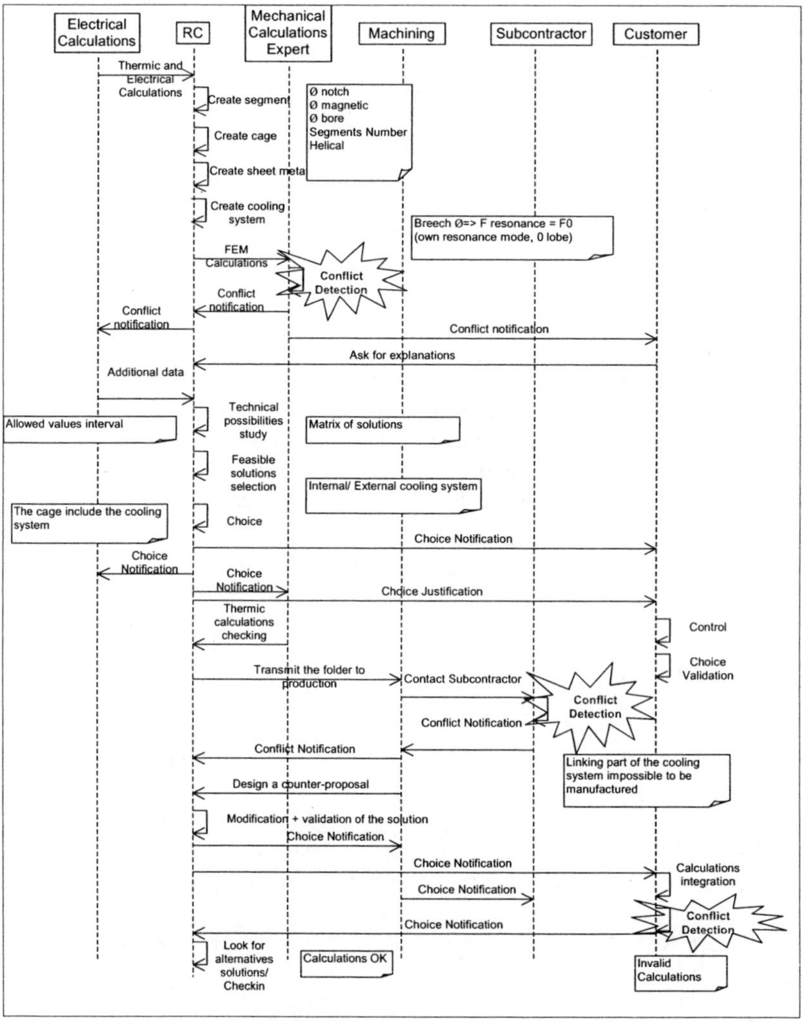

Figure 2: Alstom Stator Sheet Design Process

The benefits of such a study case are numerous:

- Elaborating from a technological viewpoint at first -this type being a novelty for the company- It can be clearly noticed that even with the use of the basic mechanical, electrical and electrotechnical concepts fostering the core competencies of the company, a lot of technical conflicts appeared during the various exchanges between the various involved stakeholders. These conflicts were mainly due to the product novelty combining the new technologies and methods used to achieve such a feature (cooling system positioning, technique for coil implantation…).

- Expanding to an organisational viewpoint -since this project is the first to be launched after major restructuring as after the redeployment of the Research Consultancy and Production means within the company, that, besides being the first experimentation of the new software suite of CAD/PDM Unigraphics©/Iman©. We can also notice that this project was the test rig for the software suite that allowed to define and parameter the workflows procedures for the PDM viewpoint; and the Calculation and Design rules of the 3D Volumes from a CAD viewpoint. Finally, this project was led within a context of extended enterprise: the components to be designed and produced were shared between the company and the principal; and between the company and the subcontractors. This implied a stronger collaboration between the company and the customer, who remains the master builder of the project.

3.2 Description of existing conflicts

We represent the chaining of the design activities of this product in an UML sequence diagram (Figure 2). This diagram allowed highlighting the various conflicts occurring during the design along with actions taken by the diverse stakeholders involved in the resolution of these conflicts. Our special interest is mainly focused on the appearance of conflicts from a technical nature. As an example, a problem occurred on a stator diameter dimensioning between the “Mechanical Calculations” expert, the “Research Consultancy” actor and the “Electrical Calculations” actor is studied. The customer was also involved in the problem solving. The problem deals with a calculation solution proposed by the “Research Consultancy” actor to the “Mechanical Calculations” expert.

4. Solving Process Applied on the Industrial Case

4.1 Conflict Solving Scenario

Based on the previous presented design process of the stator sheet we tried to extrapolate the result of such a design project with the help of software like the IPPOP demonstrator. Figure 3 presents the result of such a design project. The first conflict can be avoided by sending the calculated data to the system. The correlation with the internal rules allows the software application to process the loaded data in order to verify if the diameter range in the accepted tolerance to avoid resonance problems. The conflict notification is therefore quickly sent to the concerned design actors and allows some time saving by avoiding to run useless calculations. Besides, to capture the data to be processed by the software application requires a strict formalism. This improves the readability as well as the communicability of these results to the various project actors. The conflict handling is then run via the use of the software application as shown in figure 3 and 4. It must nevertheless be noticed that the actors are the only master final decision master. Various communication tools (emails, Visio conference, white board…) can be used during mediation and argumentation phases.

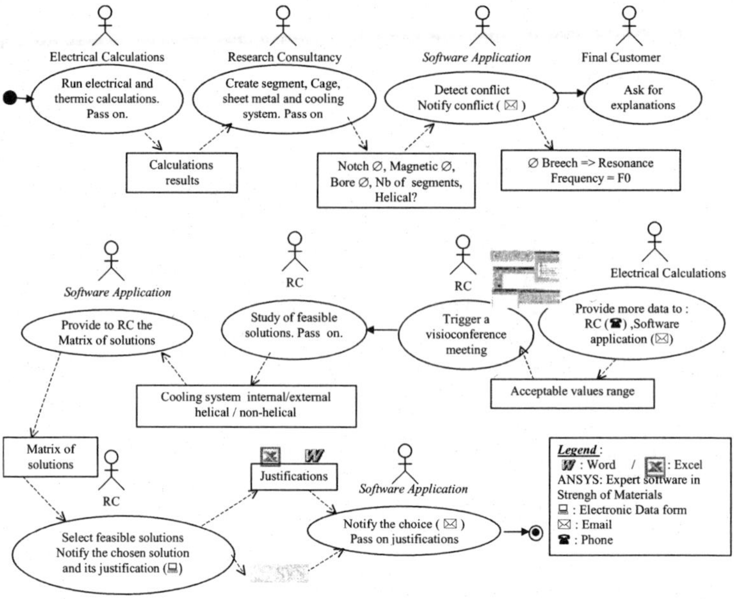

Figure 3: UML Activity Diagram of the Conflict « Resonance » on the E64 Stator Sheet

4.2 Graphical User Interfaces Presentation

We imagined to implement the previously evoked method on the stator sheet E64 study case. This consists in integrating the exchange protocol among the actors inside the IPPOP demonstrator, with the ability to manage the creation of collaborative activities as well as the passage from an activity to another.

Subscribers selection:

At first the subscribers selection is done by a preselection of the project involved actors. The demonstrator is supposed to help to refining this preselection by providing some performance indicators (table 1) susceptible to help the design actor or the project manager while defining the stakeholders to be involved in the project. These performance indicators are risen from the past project observations of implicated actors. They are supposed to precisely target the actors to register in the conflict list depending on their fields of competency. They also targets their ability to criticize and/or to propose new solutions in a given domain (regarding the keywords).

Table 1: Performance Indicators for actors subscribing

Name	Formulation	Context of use
Creativity by domain	Number of solutions given/name/keyword	Target the more dynamics design actors within a given domain
Level of competency in a given domain	Level of competency in a given domain /reference target in the field	Target the actor's field of competency
Personal indicator	Number of solutions leading to an consensus/name	Target the more efficient and pragmatic actors

The subscriber selection can also be risen in the eyes of an availability matrix in order to check the matching between the stakeholders supposed to enter the solving process with their current workload in their personal planning. It must be noticed that the chosen actors are subscribed manually by the instigator of the collaborative activity. Besides, the demonstrator will be able to manage the on-going as well as the past collaborations. It is also supposed to enable the management of iterations (creation, tracking of past iterations depending of the collaborative activity to whom it is bound). Some specific GUI will enable the actors to declare the conflicts and create the subscribers lists. This can be realised in scanning the potential Human Resources available in the project or in the company, depending of the competency level or the qualification level required.

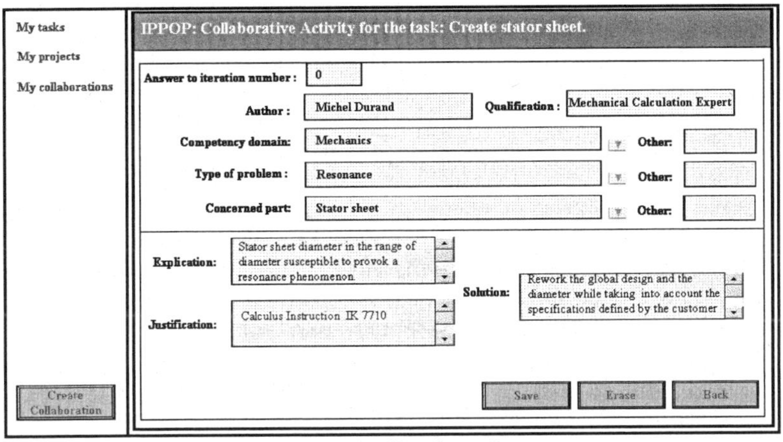

Figure 4: Example of Resolution Iteration

We implemented a mock up of these GUI on the Alstom Stator sheet example. Figure 4 shows various fields filled in by an actor during a conflict solving iteration. Such various filled in information will be stocked as attributes of instantiated iterations. This system therefore enables to maintain the tracking of the various adopted or rejected solutions on a specific project. It can be also enhanced by a research engines or the use of filters in order to select a conflict and the past collaborative activity related to this conflict as well as the chaining of iterations composing these activities (Figure 5). This can enables a quick and efficient access to the previously used solutions as well as the explanations and arguments motivating these proposals. The aggregation of these information is the basis of a real "collaboration memory" within the company.

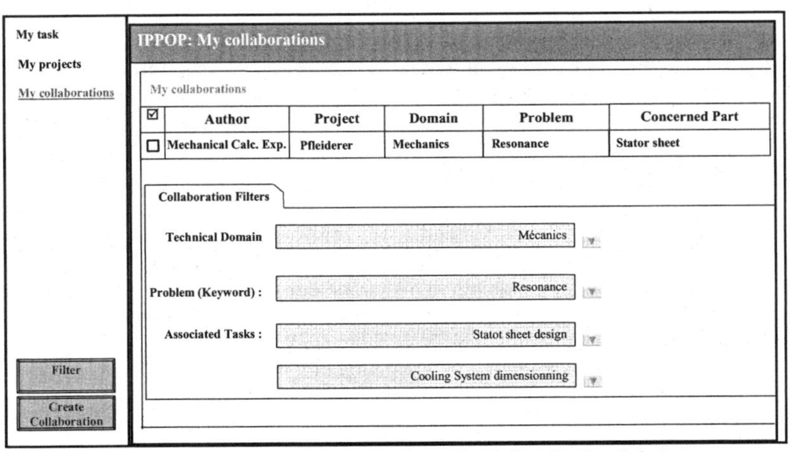

Figure 5: Collaboration Filters Examples to Track Past Project Solutions

5. Conclusion

The product design actors today evolve in a context of strong interactions and sharing of knowledge and competencies. The conflict management therefore appears in this context as the most constrained form of collaboration. This article presented a methodology and a dynamic protocol allowing to manage this situation in a formal way. The proposal have next been applied on an industrial case: the design of an ALSTOM stator sheet for a windmill generator. This example showed the importance of the exchanges structuring among actors both with the formulation of the collaborative knowledge in order to optimise the global understanding among the actors. This method has to be implemented within the IPPOP demonstrator now. It will have the aim to measure and validate its efficiency in an industrial real-life case while allowing a collaborative activity and run iterations to solve conflict with a list of subscribed actors. Besides, the demonstrator will be able to track the past collaborations and to propose suitable evoked solutions. The IPPOP demonstrator will have to meet these requirements while being complementary to other software solutions existing in the company. It replies to a real need at ALSTOM power conversion, The future works considering the collaborative perspective of the IPPOP demonstrator concern a relative automation of the conflict detection, the strengthening of the capitalisation asset of the software and the implementation of a set of performance indicators. These indicators must measure the relevance and the dynamic impact generated by the use of this methodology in term of delay and quality that it implies. To tighten the link with the organization perspective as initiated in [8] is also an issue of this on-going study.

Acknowledgements

IPPOP project is a French national project and encouraged by the industry and research ministry in the framework of the RNTL program. More information is available on the web site www.opencascade.org/IPPOP/.

References

[1] Robin, V., Girard, Ph, Barandiaran, D., (2004). A model of design environments to support collaborative design management., *5th International Conference on Integrated Design and Manufacturing in Mechanical Engineering,* April 5-7 2004, Bath, UK.

[2] Matta N. and Cointe C., Concurrent Engineering and Conflict Management Guides, *International Conference on Engineering Design ICED97*, Tampere. 1997.

[3] Klein M, Towards a Systematic Repository of Knowledge About Managing Collaborative Design Conflicts. *International Conference on AI in Design*, Boston, 2000.

[4] Eriksson, D., A Principal Exposition of Jean-Louis Le Moigne's Systemic Theory, *Cybernetics & Human Knowing Revue* vol. 4, no. 2, 1997.

[5] Rose B., Gzara L., Lombard M., 2004, Towards a formalization of collaboration entities to manage conflicts appearing in cooperative product design, in *Methods and Tools for Cooperative and Integrated Design*, ISBN 1-4020-1889-4. Ed. Kluwer Academic Publishers, pp 475-486.

[6] Booch G., Rumbaugh J. and Jacobson I., *The Unified Modeling Language User Guide, The Addison Wesley Object Technologies Services*, Addison Wesley, 1998.

[7] Nowak, P., Rose, B., Saint-Marc, L., Callot, M., Gzara-Yesilbas, L. and Lombard, M., Towards a design process model enabling the integration of product, process and organisation, *5th International Conference on Integrated Design and Manufacturing in Mechanical Engineering,* April 5-7 2004, Bath, UK.

[8] Robin, V., Rose, B., Girard, Ph., Lombard. M., Management of engineering design process in collaborative situation, *Cirp Design Seminar,* May 14-17 2004, Cairo, Egypt.

eAdoption and the Knowledge Economy: Issues, Applications, Case Studies
P. Cunningham and M. Cunningham (Eds.)
IOS Press, 2004

A Comprehensive XML-based Approach for Trust Negotiations

Elisa BERTINO[1], Anna Cinzia SQUICCIARINI[2], Elena FERRARI[3], Lorenzo D. MARTINO[2]
[1]*Dipartimento di Informatica e Comunicazione, Università degli Studi di Milano, Via Comelico 39/41, Milan, 20135, Italy and CERIAS Purdue University, USA*
Tel: +39 02 50316227, Fax: + 39 02 50316253, Email: bertino@cerias.purdue.edu
[2]*Dipartimento di Informatica e Comunicazione, Università degli Studi di Milano, Via Comelico 39/41, Milan, 20135, Italy*
Tel: +39 02 50316227, Fax: + 39 02 50316253, Email:{squiccia|martino}@dico.unimi.it
[3]*Dipartimento di Scienze Chimiche, Fisiche e Matematiche*
Università dell'Insubria, Via Valleggio 11, Como, 22100, Italy
Tel: + 39 031 2386377, Fax: + 39 031 2386119, Email: elena.ferrari@uninsubria.it

Abstract: In this paper we present Trust-X, a comprehensive XML-based framework for trust negotiations. The framework takes into account all aspects related to negotiations, from the specification of the profiles and policies of the involved parties to the determination of the negotiation strategy. We present the system architecture and describe the phases to which negotiations are executed.

1. Introduction

The establishment and operational management of secure collaborative business processes in dynamic Virtual Organizations require suitable mechanisms for establishing mutual trust between the parties and for policy-based access control to resources. In a conventional system the identity of subjects is known in advance and can be used for performing access control. This paradigm is not suitable for a Web environment, where the parties can be strangers. A promising approach for Web based interactions is represented by trust negotiation [1], according to which mutual trust is established through an exchange of digital credentials. Disclosure of credentials, in turn, must be protected through the use of policies that specify which credentials must be received before the requested credential can be disclosed. A number of approaches to trust negotiation have been recently proposed [2], [3], [4], [5], [6]. These approaches mainly focus on one of the aspects of trust negotiation, such as for instance policy specification, or the selection of the negotiation strategy, but none of them provides a complete solution to trust negotiation. In this paper we present Trust-X, an XML-based framework able to take into account all aspects of the negotiation. The paper focuses on the X-TNL Trust Negotiation language [7], the trust negotiation and disclosure policies, and on the proposed architecture of the negotiation system.

2. Trust-X Overview

Trust-X provides a language, X-TNL [7], supporting the specification of Trust-X certificates. These certificates convey information about the profile of the parties involved in the negotiation. The language supports the specification of both credentials and declarations. A credential is a set of properties of a party certified by a Certification Authority, whereas declarations contain information that may help the negotiation process (such as for instance specific preferences of one of the party) but do not need to be certified.

Disclosure policies are also encoded in XML [9]. A disclosure policy specifies the rules that regulate the disclosure of a resource by imposing conditions against the certificates the requesting party should possess. A resource can be a service, a credential, or any kind of data that need to be protected.

2.1 X-TNL

In this section, we summarize the key elements of X-TNL and X-TNL disclosure policies.

2.1.1 X-TNL certificates

In X-TNL a certificate conveys information about the profile of parties involved in the negotiation. A certificate can be either a credential or a declaration. A credential is a set of characterizing properties of a party. Each credential is digitally signed by the issuer Credential Authority, according to the standard defined by W3C for XML Signatures [9]. X-TNL simplifies the task of credential specification by providing a set of templates called credential types, which allow the specification of credentials with similar structure. A credential type is modelled as a DTD; a credential is an instance of a credential type. Figure 1 shows an example of credential, containing basic information about a library badge issued by the digital library Library_Badge; the degree of sensitivity of the information is denoted by the attribute SENS, while Element Issuer specifies the address of the Issuer's server.

```
<Library_Badge credID='12ab', SENS= 'NORMAL' >
    <Issuer HREF='http://www.DigitaLibrary.com' Title=DigitaLibrary_Repository/>
        <name>
                <Fname> Oliver </Fname>
                <lname > Stone </lname>
        </name>
    <address> Grange Wood 69 Dublin </address>
    <badge_number code=34ABN/>
    <e_mail> O.Stone@yahoo.com </e_mail>
    <position> Student </position>
</Library_Badge>
```

Figure 1 Example of a X-TNL credential

Declarations are sets of auxiliary data that collect personal information about the owner. They are not certified, are stated by their owner, and can help the negotiation process. A declaration named book preferences describes the literary preferences of a given subject. Like credentials, declarations are structured into DTD declaration types. All certificates associated with a party are collected into its X-Profile, which is organized into Data-sets. Each data set collects a class of credentials and declarations referring to a particular aspect of the life of their owner. Demographic_Data, Education, Working Experience are examples of data sets (we assume data set names are unique and registered through some central organization). Organizing certificates into data sets facilitates their retrieval during negotiation. Indeed, all the certificates collected in the same data set are logically related. Data sets can then be used to refer to a set of homogeneous declarations or credentials as a whole, and this can facilitate their evaluation and exchange during negotiation.

2.1.2 Disclosure policies

Each party specifies its own disclosure policies to regulate the release of local information and access to services. Disclosure policies state the conditions under which a resource can be released during a negotiation. Conditions are expressed as constraints against the certificates possessed by the involved parties and on the certificate attributes. Like certificates, disclosure policies are encoded using XML [7].

Trust-X allows each protected resource to be described by a set of attributes, specifying relevant resource characteristics. Attributes can be used when specifying disclosure policies too. To make easier resource management and protection, resources can be further classified into *simple* and *composite* resources. Intuitively, a simple resource is an atomic service or information whereas a composite resource R can be thought as the composition of several resources R_1, R_2,.., R_k. Resources R_1, R_2,.., R_k in turn, can be either simple or composite. An example of composite resource may be a theatre package, including a theatre ticket, the corresponding script, and a dinner at the restaurant of the theatre. Disclosure policies can be associated with either composite or simple resources. When a composite resource R is requested, the related disclosure policy is obtained by processing all policies for R, if any, and of R_1, R_2,..R_k. Figure 2 shows the template of X-TNL policy base.

```
<!DOCTYPE policyBase[
<!ELEMENT policyBase(policySpec)+>
<!ELEMENT policySpec  (properties, resource, type)>
<!ELEMENT properties (DELIV |certificate+)  >
<!ELEMENT resource EMPTY>
<!ELEMENT type EMPTY >
<!ELEMENT certificate (certCond*) >
<!ELEMENT DELIV EMPTY >
<!ELEMENT certCond (\#PCDATA) >
<!ATTLIST certificate targetCertType  CDATA \#REQUIRED>
<!ATTLIST DELIV  value CDATA \#FIXED 'DELIV' >
<!ATTLIST resource  target  CDATA \#REQUIRED >
<!ATTLIST type  value (CERT|SERVICE) 'SERVICE' >
]>
```

Figure 2 Trust-X policy base template

3. Trust-X Negotiation

A Trust-X negotiation typically involves two entities (or parties). The notion of entity includes users, processes, and servers. Each entity is characterized by a set of credentials, issued by Certification Authorities (CAs) and has a Trust-X profile of certificates, conforming to the syntax described earlier. The party requesting a resource will be referred to as Requester, whereas the party owning the resource will be referred to as Controller.

During a negotiation mutual trust is established between the Controller and the Requester, by means of the mutual exchange of certificates. Release of information is regulated by disclosure policies and by appropriate policies governing access to protected resources by specifying credential combinations that must be submitted to obtain authorization. Disclosure policies are exchanged to inform the other party of the trust requirements that need to be satisfied to advance the state of the negotiation.

A Trust-X negotiation is composed of the following phases: introductory phase, policy evaluation phase, certificate exchange phase. Each phase is executed only if the previous ones succeed; the sensitivity of the exchanged information increases during negotiation. Certificates are more sensitive with respect to policies; thus they are disclosed at the end of policy evaluation, that is, only when the parties have found a trust sequence of certificate disclosures that makes it possible the release of the requested resource, according to the disclosure policies of both parties. Multiple-phase negotiations result in a multilevel protection mechanism that avoids the release of unnecessary or unwanted information.

3.1 Negotiation introductory phase

The introductory phase begins when a Requester contacts a Controller asking for a resource R. Preliminary information is exchanged stating the conditions that must be satisfied to start the actual processing of the resource request. Such information exchange is regulated by the introductory policies of both parties. Introductory policies are used to verify properties of the counterpart that are mandatory to continue in the negotiation. They can also help in driving the subsequent phases of the process, by collecting information about the client preferences and/or needs. For instance, an online bookstore may ask the customer to submit the book_preferences declaration, if any, in order to satisfy his/her preferences. As a further example, consider a Rental Car Service. When a customer asks to rent a car, the negotiation starts. Possible prerequisites that the Agency may require during introductory phase are modelled by the following introductory policies. Policies are expressed in terms of logical expressions to simplify the comprehension of the corresponding semantics:

- Car_Rental_p -> Preferred_customer()
- Car_Rental_p -> Car_Preferences()

The first policy checks whether the client has the Preferred_customer credential, denoting a previous business relationship. The second policy asks the requester to submit the Car_preferences declaration, if any, in order to satisfy the requester preferences.

3.2 Policy evaluation phase

The policy evaluation phase is the core of the negotiation process. Its goal is to determine a sequence of Requester and Controller certificates that, when disclosed, enable the release of the requested resource in accordance with the disclosure policies of both parties. During each interaction of this phase, one party sends a set of disclosure policies to the other. The receiver party verifies whether its X-Profile satisfies the conditions stated by the policies, and determines a policy counter-request regulating the disclosure of the certificates requested. If the X-Profile of the Controller satisfies the conditions stated by at least one of the received policies, the Controller can adopt one of two strategies. It can choose to maximize the protection of its local resources replying only for one policy at the time, hiding the real availability of the other requested resources, or, it can reply for all the policies to maximize the number of potential solutions for negotiation. When selecting a policy, each party determines whether its preconditions are verified by the policies disclosed until that point, and, only then is the policy selected. By contrast, if the X-Profile of the Controller party does not satisfy the conditions stated by the Requester policies, the Controller informs the other party that it does not possess the requested certificates.

The counterpart then sends an alternative policy, if any, or halts the process if no other policies can be found. This exchange continues until both parties determine one or more sets of policies that can be satisfied for all the involved resources. No certificates are disclosed during the policy evaluation phase. The satisfaction of policies is only checked to communicate the possibility of going on with the process and how this can be executed [8].

3.3 Certificate exchange phase

This phase begins when the previous phase ends successfully, determining one or more sequences of credentials, encoded by certificates, to be disclosed. In this phase, each party discloses its certificates, according to the order defined in the sequence. Upon receiving a certificate, the counterpart verifies the satisfaction of the associated policies, checks for revocation, checks validity dates and authenticates the ownership (for credentials).

Eventually, if further information is needed for establishing trust, the receiver party has to check for new certificates using credential chains. For example, if a medical certificate was requested and the issuer is an unknown hospital, the receiver party has to check the validity of issuer certificate by collecting new certificates from the issuer repository. The receiver then replies with an acknowledgment message, and asks for the following certificate in the sequence, or if it has received all the certificates of the set, it sends a certificate belonging to the subsequent set of certificates in the trust sequence. If no unforeseen event happens, the exchange ends with the disclosure of the requested resource.

4. Trust-X Architecture

The Trust-X architecture, graphically illustrated in Figure 3, is composed by a Policy Base, storing disclosure policies, the X-Profile associated with the party, a Tree Manager, storing the state of the negotiation, and a Compliance Checker, to test policy satisfaction and determine request replies. The policy evaluation phase is mainly executed by the Compliance Checker, which evaluates the remote policies with respect to local policies and certificates (Certificates can be locally available in the X-Profile or can be retrieved through certificate chains) and the selection of the strategy for carrying out the remainder of the negotiation. To simplify the process a tree structure is used which is managed and updated by the Tree Manager. The module of Trust-X in charge of caching and suggesting the sequences is the Sequence Prediction module (not shown in Figure 3).

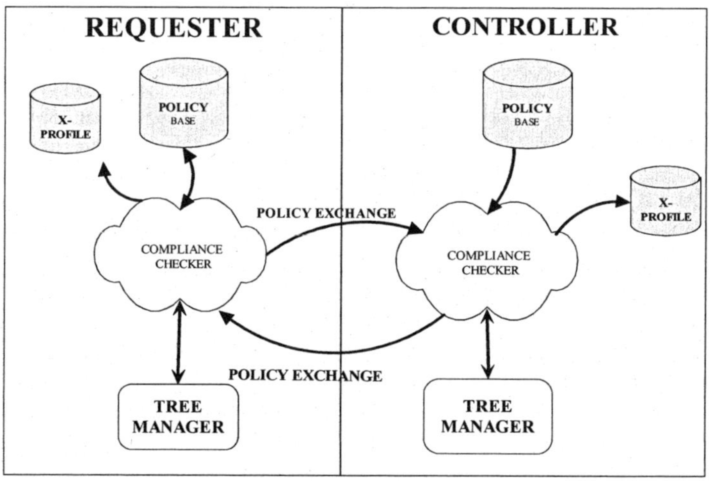

Figure 3 Trust-X Architecture

5. Additional Features of Trust-X

To speed up negotiation processes, Trust-X provides two additional features: negotiation of composite resources; and the possibility of caching the sequence of certificates.

5.1 Negotiation of composite resources

Each component of the composite resource is sequentially negotiated. The negotiation is executed evaluating first the policies for the root resource and then negotiating each component. Each time the policy evaluation phase of a resource component succeeds, the corresponding trust sequence is determined. Although it is possible to determine more than a sequence for the same resource, we now refer to the sequence on which parties agree.

Instead of immediately executing such sequence, both parties store it and start evaluating requirements for negotiating the next component resource. In this way the information obtained from the previous negotiation process can be re-used, thus avoiding asking for the same certificates or properties again. This simple strategy reduces the number of party requests and optimizes the number of exchanges. In addition, the Controller can choose whether to allow partial disclosure of some of the resource components or to deny the entire access. For example, during a negotiation of a composite resource (composed by three atomic resources, say), it may happen that a party results to be in order to obtain only two of the three resource components of the composite resource. This decision depends from the context and from the kind of the resources that the parties are negotiating.

5.2 Sequence caching

It is likely that an entity will perform some negotiations with different counterparts having a similar profile. In such cases it might be useful to keep track of the sequences of certificates most frequently exchanged, instead of recalculating them for each negotiation. Moreover, we expect that in many scenarios there will be standard, off-the shelf policies available for widely used resources (e.g., VISA cards, passports). In case of negotiations involving such common resources the sequences of certificates to be disclosed will be only regulated by such standard and predictable policies. In this case, certificates represent only a means to prove parties properties; thus, it could be possible to suggest the sequences at the beginning of the process. If the counterpart cannot satisfy the proposed sequence, the negotiation can continue by executing the policy evaluation phase or by suggesting another sequence.

6. Existing negotiation systems

A number of trust negotiation systems and research prototypes have been developed during the last years that use property-based credentials to manage trust. Up to now, the best-known trust management system is Keynote [6]. KeyNote provides a single, unified language for both local policies and credentials. KeyNote credentials, called assertions, contain predicates describing delegations in terms of actions that are relevant to a given application. As a result, KeyNote policies do not handle credentials as a means to establish trust, mainly because of the language intended use for delegation authority.

The Trust Establishment Project at Haifa Research Lab has developed a tool (TE) for enabling trust relationships between strangers based on public key certificates. A key element of the system is a Trust Policy Language (TPL) [4], specified using XML. TE extends traditional role-based access control systems by validating certificates and then mapping the certificates owners to a role. A policy, specified by the owner of the resource, states the rules mapping entities to roles. A role in TPL is a group of entities that represent a specific organizational unit (e.g., managers, doctors). Each role has one or more rules defining how a certificate owner can become a member of the role. The TE system also includes an intelligent certificate collector that automatically collects missing certificates from certificate repositories, allowing the use of standard browsers that can only pass one certificate to the server. However, it does not provide support for sensitive credentials. One of the TE's basic assumptions is that credentials can be disclosed whenever they are requested. Further, the TE system does not have the notion of sensitive policies.

The Internet Security Research Lab (ISRL) [10] at Brigham Young University developed TrustBuilder, a system supporting trust negotiation. (A number of references to TrustBuilder can be found in [10]). TrustBuilder currently represents one of the most significant proposals in the negotiation research area. It provides a broad class of negotiation strategies, as well as a strategy and language independent negotiation protocol that ensures the interoperability of the defined strategies within the TrustBuilder architecture. Each participant in a negotiation has an associated security agent that manages the negotiation. During a negotiation the security agent uses a local negotiation strategy to determine which local resources to disclose next, and to accept new disclosures from other parties. TrustBuilder includes also a credential verification module, which performs a validity check of the received credentials, a policy compliance checker, and a negotiation strategy module, which is the core of the system.

Researchers at ISRL have recently explored other issues in the negotiation area, such as support for sensitive policies, obtained by introducing hierarchies in policy definitions [11], or privacy protection mechanisms, obtained by introducing dynamic policies (policies dynamically modified during negotiation) into the trust negotiation architecture [12].

Privacy protection in TN is also the focus of [13] that proposes Unipro, a unified scheme to model protection of resources, including policies in trust negotiation. Unipro models policies as first-class resource and provides a fine-grained control over policy disclosure, giving subjects more flexibility in expressing authorization requirements.

7. Future Work

In this paper we have presented an overview of the features of the Trust-X negotiation language. Future work that will be carried out as part of the TrustCoM project includes extensions to both the language and the negotiation strategies of Trust-X (e.g. the possibility of specifying the credential submitter and support for anonymity and privacy, disclosing only portions of a credential during the negotiation process) and several other enhancements in order to support privacy-preserving negotiation strategies. We also plan to develop techniques and algorithms for credential chains discovery and for recovering from negotiation failures, and caching strategies to increase the efficiency of negotiation. Finally, we plan to investigate the use of shared ontologies to increase interoperability.

References

[1] K. E. Seamons, M. Winslett, T. Yu, B. Smith, E. Child, J. Jacobson, H.Mills, and L. Yu. "Requirements for Policy Languages for Trust Negotiation". International Workshop on Policies for Distributed Systems and Networks (POLICY 2002), Monterey, CA, June 2002.

[2] E. Bertino, S. Castano, E.Ferrari. "On Specifying Security Policies for Web Documents with an XML-based Language". Proc. of SACMAT 2001, ACM Symposium on Access Control Models and Technologies, Fairfax, VA, May 2001.

[3] T. Yu, M. Winslett, K. Seamons. "Supporting Structured Credentials and Sensitive Policies through Interoperable Strategies for Automated Trust Negotiation". ACM Transactions on Information and System Security, volume 6, number 1, February 2003.

[4] A. Herzberg, Mihaeli, Y. Mass, D. Naor, and Y. Ravid, "Access Control System Meets Public Infrastructure, Or: Assigning roles to Strangers". IEEE Symposium on Security and Privacy, Oakland, CA, May 2000.

[5] P. Bonatti, P. Samarati. "Regulating Access Services and Information Release on the Web". 7th ACM Conference on Computer and Communications Security, Athens, Greece, November 2000.

[6] M. Blaze, J. Feigenbaum, J. Ioannidis, and A. Keromytis. The KeyNote Trust-Management System. RFC 2704, September 1999.

[7] E. Bertino, E.Ferrari, A.Squicciarini. "X-TNL - An XML Based language for Trust Negotiations". Proceedings of Fourth International Workshop on Policies for Distributed Systems and Networks, Como, Italy, June 2003.

[8] E. Bertino, E. Ferrari, A. Squicciarini. "Trust-X A Peer to Peer framework for Trust Establishment". Accepted for publication in IEEE TKDE, to appear.

[9] World Wide Web Consortium, Extensible Markup Language (XML) 1.0, 1998. (www.w3.org)

[10] ISRL – Internet Security Research Lab, Brigham Young University, Provo, Utah. (http://isrl.cs.byu.du/)

[11] K. Seamons, M. Winslett, T. Yu. "Limiting the disclosure of Access Control Policies during Automated Trust Negotiation". Third International Workshop on Policies for Distributed Systems and Networks, Monterey, CA, June 2002.

[12] K. Seamons, M. Winslett et al. "Protecting privacy During On-line Trust Negotiation". 2nd Workshop on Privacy Enhancing Technologies, San Francisco, CA, April 2002.

[13] T. Yu, M. Winslett. "A unified scheme for Resource Protection in Automated Trust Negotiation". IEEE Symposium on Security and Privacy, Oakland, CA, 2003.

New Working Environments for Product Development - A Component Framework for CAx Application Development

Martin RICHTER
Department for Applied Computer Science in Mechanical Engineering (RPK), University of Karlsruhe, Karlsruhe, 76131, Germany
Tel: +49 721 608-4156, Fax: + 49 721 661138, Email: richter@rpk.uni-karlsruhe.de

Abstract: The scope of this paper is to show a new approach for CAx software development based on middleware components. It enables smaller software companies to develop innovative software solutions without being dependent on proprietary software systems from major CAD vendors by using such standardized software components. It is the first step against the threatening monoculture in CAx software development, comparable to the OS market.

1. Introduction

Conventional Computer Aided Design (CAD) systems are now widely used along the whole development process of complex products (cars, planes). Despite all efforts, these systems are not able to fulfil all requirements of the whole process chain used to design such products. However, concurrent and simultaneous engineering needed for shortening development time and improving companies' productivity require seamless interoperability between applications and continuous numerical flow between these applications. The practice of big industrial companies to cope with this situation is:

- to rely on one main monolithic CAD system,
- to require from subcontractors to use their CAD system, and
- to still rely on poor Data Exchange for domains not covered by main CAD systems.

For example in the automotive industry every OEM has a homogeneous installation of CAD systems. But a supplier must have every CAD system in house (with disadvantages like high costs for system and personal and low utilisation of the systems) or rely on neutral file exchange formats like STEP (data loss) in order to have the option on an order. If the software (e.g. NC code generation in CAM) used by the supplier is based on the 3D Workbench framework it would be interoperable with all OEMs CAD System. Original assembly/part data reside on the OEM server and the supplier connects online via the CAD Services to get original geometry data via internet. Custom Software development for the supplier would be more efficient because of the use of standardized software components.

2. Objectives

Distributed object oriented CAD systems consisting of components from various system suppliers accessed via a common standardised APIs is now accepted as a proven technology suitable to solve this need for concurrent and simultaneous engineering. It allows a seamless integration using "best of class tools" for every task without the constraint of using products of only one system provider.

The scope of the ITEA (Information Technology for European Advancement -Strategic EUREKA cluster) project 3D Workbench is to define, develop, maintain and standardize through the Object Management Group (OMG) software components for CAx software development. It is not about developing middleware techniques (e.g. CORBA, SOAP).

We can expect to rely by the end of year 2004 on tree major components, CAD Services, Visualization Services and PDM Enablers, which are the basis of any CAD/CAM/CAE system. The CAD Services were implemented and verified for the two major CAD systems on the market, which is CATIA V5 from Dassault Systèmes and Pro/ENGINEER from PTC. The Visualization Services were completely developed inside our department and will undergo the standardisation process inside the OMG by end of 2004. This component allows an immersive visualisation of 3 dimensional part geometry together with in information from the whole product development process. The third component, the PDM Enablers, allows integration with all common PDM systems.

2.1 Why open source CAD/CAM/CAE middleware components?

Major CAD/CAM/CAE software vendors are able to make large investments to establish their proprietary technology and gain market share. Smaller software suppliers, which are often bringing the most innovative solutions are more and more isolated and put out of the game not being able to follow the required high level of necessary investment.

The availability of standards based CAD/CAM/CAE middleware components providing the fundamental CAD/CAM/CAE functionality will allow those smaller software suppliers to concentrate on their know-how and to provide higher quality software fully interoperable with other systems. The development of such middleware components will minimise the entrance cost for new CAD/CAM/CAE application development while maintaining competivity pressure on monopolistic major CAD/CAM/CAE vendors.

The open source development model is recognised as a competitive approach to proprietary software in term of performance and quality. Linux has been widely accepted as a powerful, reliable Operating System able to compete with Microsoft Windows. It is increasingly supported by hardware vendors and is used by many applications (Internet, data servers), new distributions are improving the ease of use which become comparable to Microsoft Windows. Open source solutions addressing the office automation, comparable to Microsoft Office, already exist (e.g. StarOffice). The next domain to be addressed is the industrial world, particularly in CAD/CAM/CAE where no competitive solution exists.

The ITEA Project 3D-Workbench makes up a component based development platform for industrial applications independent of major CAD systems, addressing a solution to application interoperability through standards, and available in open source.

While CAD domain is the natural candidate for using such a development platform, it must be useful in many other areas such as:

- Product Data Management (PDM) and Computer Aided Process Engineering (CAPE) applications for visualising and manipulating geometrical data
- Applications producing illustrated part catalogues or illustrated training material will be able to easily access to 3D models
- On-line access to geometrical 3D data catalogues (e.g. e-maintenance, e-documentation)

3. Technology Description

The final goal is to build a standards based development infrastructure for industrial applications — a Computer Aided Design, Computer Aided Manufacturing and Computer Aided Engineering (CAD/CAM/CAE) middleware — and available in open source.

As 3D-Workbench is standards based, it allows the development of CAD/CAM/CAE specific applications independent from and interoperable with major generic CAD systems in a distributed environment, presuming these CAD systems implement those standards.

Direct users of 3D-Workbench are:

- Industrial companies developing dedicated industrial applications for internal use, using their internal resources or software development subcontractors.
- Software service companies basing their offer — consulting, support and specific development of industrial applications — on 3D-Workbench.
- Software vendors in the CAD/CAM/CAE area.
- Universities demonstrating and disseminate results in CAD/CAM/CAE research area.

Given that acceptance of this platform will depend on the standardisation of components it is made up of, this project:

- Includes participation to task forces answering to Request for Proposal (RFP) from the Object Management Group (OMG, organisation for standardising software). As such, CAxOPEN is voting member of OMG working on the CAD Services proposal — a component for accessing to the geometry and topology of CAD models.
- Bases its architecture on the Common Object Request Broker Architecture (CORBA) and its Interface Definition Language (IDL).

3D-Workbench also includes a Rapid Application Development environment (RAD):

- A ready-to-use application (Product Configurator) for experimenting with the middleware, demonstrating its components and prototyping applications.
- A Web Access Viewer for interacting with 3D models via the Internet, available as a stand-alone application and a component reusable for development of applications.
- A production environment providing tools for managing workspaces connected to a source code control system and dedicated to development of new CAD/CAM/CAE added value components.
- A virtual reality Product model explorer which enables the designer to visualize the product in an immersive way based on the Visualization Services. (VRview).

The diagram below illustrates the entire content and positioning of the 3D-Workbench product - the project proposed in this document is a subset of this - in which:

- Two components are already standardised by the OMG - PDM Enablers - or other organisations - IGES and STEP data exchange formats
- One component is currently under specification - CAD Services
- Two components have been presented to OMG to be candidate for future RFPs in bounds of OMG Manufacturing Domain Task Force (MfgDTF) roadmap - Design Algorithms and 3D Visualisation
- Other components are expected to be standardised later

This diagram also shows that:

- Many implementations of some components may exist - for example, Unigraphics/SDRC, NASA and TranscenData have also published their intention to implement CAD Services.
- End-user applications based on this middleware are interoperable.

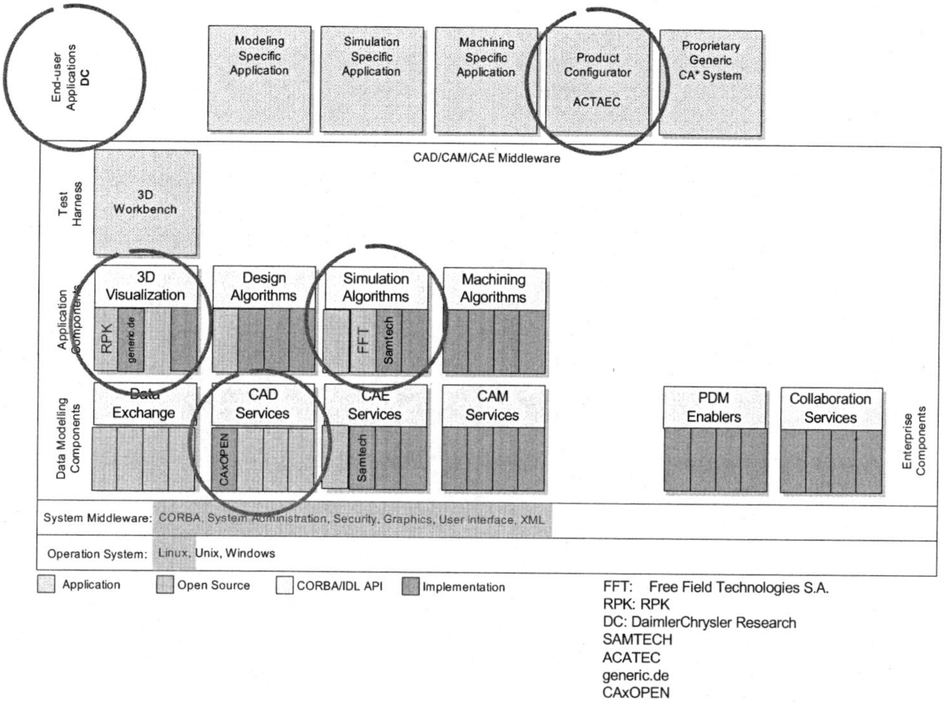

Figure 1: 3D Workbench CAx Framework and covered domains

4. Development Contents of the Project

The 3D Workbench project includes:

- The 3D-Workbench project includes the following 4 components:
- CAD Services (current Version 1.2)
- A first lot of Simulation Algorithms addressing Finite Element calculation
- 3D Visualisation (Figure 2)
- The 3D-Workbench RAD

Although 3D-Workbench targets Data Sharing, eventually through the use of PDM Enablers, it also will include existing implementation of Data Exchange component.
Components in the CAM domain are expected in the future. Also, enterprise components are out of the bounds of this project.

As 3D-Workbench is the first open source implementation of this CAD/CAM/CAE middleware, it is developed using currently available open source libraries such as:

- CAD Services for the geometry and topology
- The Finite Element kernel FEMTown for simulation algorithms
- OpenSG for the visualization
- QT for the user interface (open source on Linux only)
- MICO as default CORBA support to be CORBA implementation independent.

Although 3D-Workbench will also run on Windows and all major Unix platforms, the intention is to disseminate it through Linux distributions.

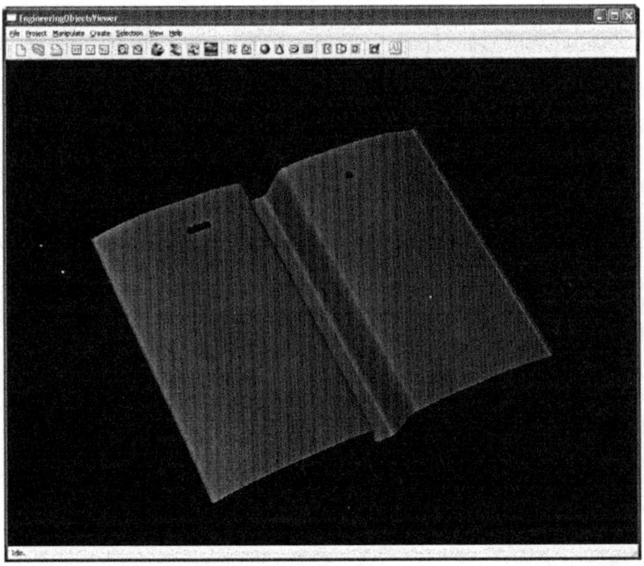

Figure 2: Example for the VRView component based on the Visualization Services

5. Benefits

5.1 Benefits for Software editors

- Facilitate applications integration through standardised components
- Decrease development costs by reusing existing components
- Allow added-value components (not necessarily open source) to be widely distributed
- Provide equal opportunities for all software suppliers, giving them access to the technology

5.2 Benefits for Industrial companies

- Facilitate on-line access to data, whatever their format, avoiding constraints due to data exchange based on file
- Improve interoperability between different supplier system
- Improve portability of application (consequently increase the longevity of company know-how because dedicated applications can be no more dependent on proprietary CAD systems)
- Increase competition between software vendors

5.3 Benefits for the open source community

- Provide access to CAD/CAM/CAE technology
- Will accelerate open source Project creation in the CAD/CAM/CAE domains
- Provide additional opportunity to build partnership between companies having a business model based on open source

5.4 Market relevance

Three vendors - Dassault Systèmes (CATIA), Parametric Technology (Pro/Engineer) and Unigraphics Solutions / Structural Dynamics Research (Unigraphics and SRDC I-Deas) - provide integrated systems which give access to design, simulation and manufacturing.
It is possible with such systems to integrate corporate know-how by either customising them or developing complementary applications using their Application Programming Interfaces (API's). This leads to a full integrated system able to answer to the company needs. On the other hand, such customisations and applications are not portable on other systems — a big investment entirely dependant on CAD vendors.

Suppliers such as Dassault Systèmes (ACIS), Unigraphics Solutions (Parasolid), Open CASCADE (Open CASCADE) and D-CUBED (DCM3D, DCM2D) provide software libraries used by CAD systems.

These libraries facilitate development of CAD and specific applications, but the resulting applications are still not portable across components from different competitors and are not interoperable with existing CAD systems.

The proposed CAD/CAM/CAE middleware makes up a real progress, thanks to:

- Standardisation of components supported by major vendors (already announced for CAD Services by Unigraphics/SDRC and Dassault Systems) which answers to the integration of applications on top of their system while guarantying interoperability and keeping developments portable
- Open source implementation of these standards giving access to the technology and its dissemination in the open source community

6. Conclusions

Although this project is a step into the right direction, there are still many "white spaces" in the CAx Development framework. Subsequent projects must fill this gap in order to make this framework fully operable. Especially extracting design functionality into a standalone module and make it accessible through standardized interfaces is a big challenge.

Interoperability is for sure a big advantage when software solution provider rely on this framework, but this approach could also be used making product-defining data residing in individual product modelling systems accessible along the whole product life-cycle. This would lead to a whole new generation of PDM/PLM (Product Lifecycle Management) systems which manage product defining data not only on file based information but allow a close integration of information residing in the files itself. Currently available systems for data integration (PDM, PLM systems) focus solely on the management of so-called meta-data that is used for the management of product-defining data.

In order to maintain the 3D Workbench platform a "spin off" company (www.caxplusplus.com) was founded at the University of Karlsruhe (TH). The URL of the project homepage is: http://www3dwb.mach.uni-karlsruhe.de.

References

[1] *Grabowski, H.; Anderl, R.; Pätzold, B.; Rude, S.:* The Development of Advanced Modelling Techniques – Meeting the Challenge of CAD/CAM-Integration, Computer Integrated Manufacturing Proceedings of the 4th CIM Europe Conference, Seite 119-138, CIM Europe, Madrid, May 1988

[2] *Grabowski, H.; Benz, T.:* Functional Modelling in Intelligent CAD-Systems, 2. Workshop on Intelligent CAD, IFIP WG 5.2, Cambridge, September 1988

[3] *Grabowski, H.; Pätzold, B.; Rude, S.:* Entwurfsmethoden auf der Basis technischer Produktmodelle, VDI-Berichte Nr. 610.1, Seiten 55-78, VDI-Verlag, 1986

[4] *Grabowski, H.; Lossack, R.; Kunze, H.*: Functional Modelling: Representation of dynamic aspects in function structures, Proceedings of the 12th International Florida AI Research Society Conference, FLAIRS, Orlando, Florida, May 1999

[5] *Grabowski, H.; Rude, S.; Benz, T.*: Integrierte Produktmodelle als Basis intelligenter CAD-Systeme, Wiss. Z. Techn. Univ. Magneburg, Band 33(4): Seiten 21-30, 1989

[6] *Grabowski, H. ; Anderl, R. et al.*: DIICAD: Integrated CAD/CAM System for Product and Progress Modelling. In F.L. Krause und H. Hansen (Hrsg.), Advanced Geometric Modelling for Engineering Applications, Proceeding of the IFIP WG 5.2, Berlin, 1989

[7] *Grabowski, H. ; Rude, S.* : Advanced Modelling Design by Features, CAM-I, European GMP Meeting, Karlsruhe, 1987

[8] *Grabowski, H. ; Rude, S.* :Intelligent CAD-Systems based on technical associated modelling, Vortrag internationale Konferenz "Theory and Practice of Geometric Modelling", Blaubeuren, Oktober 1988

[9] *Krause, F.L.; Tang, T.; Ahle, U.*: Innovationsforum Virtuelle Produktentstehung, Proceedings Blue Band Hotel Berlin 11.-12. Mai 2000

[10] Krause, F.-L.; Jansen, H.; Kiesewetter, T.: Breitbandkommunikation in CAD-Prozessen zur Optimierung der Produktentwicklung. In: Dietrich, U.; Kehrer, B.; Vatterott, G. (Hrsg.): CA-Integration in Theorie und Praxis. Springer, 1995, S. 223-240.

[11] *Meerkamm, H. / Schweiger, W. / Schön, A.*: A Common Design Language For Developing Mechatronic Products; in: Proceedings of 1st International Symposium on Concurrent Multidisciplinary Engineering (CME), Bremen, 17.-19.06.1998, S. 191-202.

[12] *Meerkamm, H./Schön, A. / Schweiger, W.*: Konstruktionsmethodik bei der Entwicklung mechatronischer Produkte; in: Gedenkband zum Gedenkkolloqium für Wolfgang Beitz, Berlin, 9. Juli 1999, S. 473-484.

[13] *Patron & Roßgoderer*: Planung hybrider Arbeitsplätze mit virtueller Realität. BAIKA Kooperationsforum "Virtual Reality", München 1999

[14] *Schulte, M.; Weber, C.*: The Relationship between Function and Shape. 9th International Conference on Engineering Design 1993 (ICED 93), Den Haag/Niederlande 17.-19.08. 1993. Schriftenreihe „Workshop–Design–Konstruktion", WDK 22: Proceedings of ICED 93 (herausgegeben von N.F.M. Roozenburg), Vol. 1, S. 9-20. Heurista-Verlag, Zürich 1993.

[15] *Spur, G., Krause; F.-L.*: Das virtuelle Produkt, Management der CAD-Technik. Carl Hanser Verlag München Wien, 1997

[16] *Weber, C.; Werner, H.*: Implizite und explizite Anteile des Produktmodells – Bedeutung für die Weiterentwicklung von CAx-Systemen. 10. Symposium „Fertigungsgerechtes Konstruieren", Schnaittach/Erlangen 14.-15.10.1999. Tagungsband, S. 1-6. Friedrich-Alexander-Universität Erlangen-Nürnberg 1999.

[17] *Weber, C.; Werner, H.*: Klassifizierung von CAx-Werkzeugen für die Produktentwicklung auf der Basis eines neuartigen Produkt- und Prozessmodells. 11. Symposium „Design for X", Schnaittach/Erlangen 12.-13.10.2000. Tagungsband, S. 126-143. Friedrich-Alexander-Universität Erlangen-Nürnberg 2000.

Section 5.3

Case Studies

Enhancing Presence and Context Awareness in Collaborative Settings

Henk de POOT[1], Joke KORT[2], David LANGLEY[2]
[1]Telematica Instituut, P.O. Box 589, Enschede, 7500 AN, the Netherlands
Tel: +31 53 4850485, Fax: + 31 53 4850400, Email: Henk.dePoot@telin.nl
[2]TNO Telecom, P.O. Box 15000, Groningen, 9700 CD, the Netherlands
Tel: +31 50 5857751, Fax: +31 50 3122415, Email: {j.kort,d.j.langley}@telecom.tno.nl

Abstract: For effective teamwork knowledge workers have to communicate and coordinate many different activities. In co-located settings this often happens during chance encounters and corridor talk. With respect to distant and mobile workers such presence awareness is currently not possible, so communication may take place at inappropriate times, or with undesirable means. In our research we investigate how communication between distant knowledge workers can be improved by better presence awareness and by a palette of available media. Here we describe the design and pilot test of our prototype service Live Contacts.

1. Introduction – the Knowledge Worker Problem

Knowledge workers have to communicate a lot ([1], [2]). But often interaction stops at the office building's boundaries. Distant co-workers and colleagues on the move are difficult to engage in conversations and ad hoc meetings. We believe that distance interaction would improve with a better support of ad hoc communication. So we must find forms of presence and context information that assist in contacting one another at the appropriate moment using the appropriate medium. While many studies have pointed at (lightweight) peripheral awareness (e.g., [3], [4], and [5]), recent evidence exists that ordinary communication and coordination tools such as Instant Messaging (IM) ([6],[7]) and the electronic calendar ([8] and [9]) already function as presence cues among knowledge workers. Therefore we try to build on their virtues to create presence awareness independent of someone's whereabouts.

To enhance presence and context awareness for those knowledge workers, we developed a communication "launching pad", Live Contacts, which combines several presence and context cues and helps users choose the most appropriate communication medium. The idea of adding presence and context cues has been proposed earlier, e.g. by [10]. The approach we took when developing Live Contacts was to have target group members decide what they want by inviting them to join a Creative Design Session. Next, the solution was built into a first prototype (mock-up), which we tested in a usability test. A redesign of the mock-up resulted in the final prototype, which was tested in a user pilot.

Our paper is structured as follows:

- In section 2 we describe the target group and the media they typically use.
- Section 3 gives some highlights from a Creative Design Session with our participants.
- Section 4 describes the service prototype after several iterations in the design process.
- Sections 5 and 6 present a pilot study we conducted with the Live Contacts service.
- In section 7 and 8 we discuss the main observations from our design and pilot study.

2. Target Group

Our target group are knowledge workers who are deskbound at times, and may travel a lot at other times. They may work independently for times and shut off all interruptions. They may even work at home. At other moments they could work in teams according to a very tight schedule, or engage in a beanbag brainstorm session. Knowledge workers mostly use a rich palette of communication media ranging from email and paper to forms of mobile and instant messaging and telephony. As a "de facto" archive email is gradually being seen as the formal workflow medium among co-workers. For timely communication face-to-face communication as well as telephone, Instant Messaging (IM), and, more generally, instant communication (such as Push to Talk), are more appropriate. Although some of these media address a recipient immediately, they are perceived as unobtrusive ([6] and [7]) because current culture allows one to leave such messages unanswered when unwelcome. This is much like walking into someone's room to ask a question. Other relatively new channels are the mobile telephone and mobile messaging (SMS and MMS).

We presume that our target group members may need some generalised presence management to help choosing the appropriate medium and time for a given contact.

3. Design Experiment

To develop and test our ideas in a collaborative setting we chose an existing research project team with participants from three organisations spanning four locations. Org1 has 103 employees, with 72 scientists and engineering staff and support staff of 31. The office is located in one place. Org2 has 350 employees distributed over two locations that lie 235 km apart. Org3 is a university Faculty with 350 employees and 1200 students.

We organised a "Creative Design Session", documented in [11] while following an iterative design approach inspired on [12, chapter 5] with 9 representatives from Org 1, Org2, and Org3. The main questions were: "What should the presence and context awareness service look like? Which information would a user like to have?" and "What should the user availability profiles look like". They focussed on a persona "Frits", a dynamic mobile worker.

Table 1: Examples of Static and Dynamic Context Information to decide: Can I disturb Frits?.

	Static	Dynamic
Recipient	• Is Frits bothered by being called at home during his free time in emergency situations?	• Is Frits driving on a highway, 140 km/h? • Is Frits in a meeting right now?
Initiator	• I like to handle formal or factual information by e-mail	• Is it an emergency?
Relation	• Frits is open for contact, no matter what time of day	• Is Frits in a happy mood?
Location	• Office location in building (my room, Frits' room)	• Is Frits in or out?
Content	• Private or work appointment?	• Urgency of subject

Table 1 provides examples of static and dynamic context information to help determine whether or not to disturb Frits. The associations that came forward fell into five partly overlapping categories concerning the recipient ("Frits"), the initiator (self), the (perceived) initiator-recipient relation, the location, and the content of the planned contact.

Next the group reflected on the context information necessary to reach Frits under various circumstances with messages of different importance. Table 2 gives an example of such a solution generated in this process. Note the emotional information. In our prototype service we chose not to include "emotional mood visualisers" (e.g., emoticons), but given its impact, this might actually be worthwhile trying in future.

Table 2: Example of a search strategy initiated from the workplace: How can I reach Frits in this case?

	Static	Dynamic
Recipient	• Available media/ preferences	• Status (on-the-phone,...)
Initiator	• My attitude toward disturbing people	• How does this activity fit in with my planning / mood
Relation	• Superficial?	• Recent matters
Location	• Do I know this location?	• Location of Frits
Content	• Who needs information from whom?	• Urgency

In third phase of the "Creative Design Session", participants were asked to design a solution to support the envisioned scenarios. An example is shown in Figure 1.

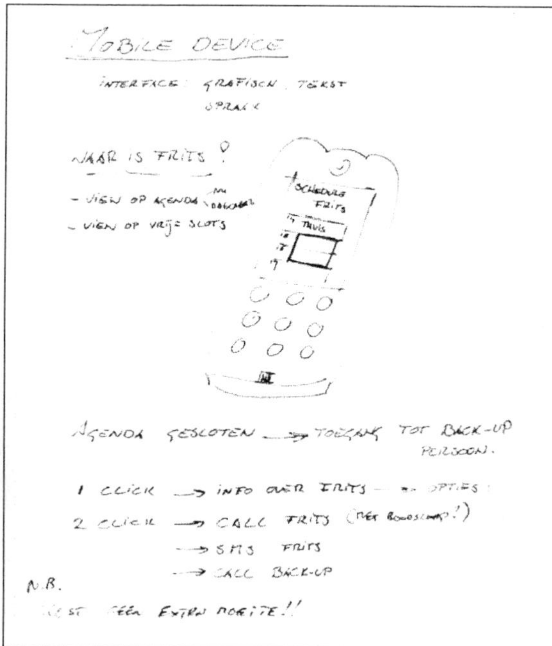

<u>Device designed for mobile use</u>

The interface combines graphics, text, voice

<u>Where is Frits?</u> at Home?
- view on agenda (now; daily overview)
- view on free slots

Agenda locked → access to backup person

First click: information about Frits should appear

Second click: one should be able to contact Frits by telephone or SMS or to contact his backup

Figure 1: Design of a mobile solution to locate and contact someone, original in Dutch (L) and the English translation (R)

4. Application Developed

The ideas and functional requirements generated in the Creative Design Session, were tested in a HTML mock-up feedback session [13]. 12 employees from Orgl and Org2 gave their feedback. They evaluated designs and answered questions to test the logic of the interface elements and interaction principles. This session led to several conclusions:

- Need to have? Participants saw the service as a nice to have, not a need to have. They expected it would not affect their ways of contacting others to a large extent.
- Colours: The first version of the Live Contacts service was considered to have "too much colour". The interface was redesigned accordingly.
- Calendar Participants preferred calendar information over Instant Messenger based information. We extended the main screen with current time calendar view.
- Basic information Calendar and IM based presence and context information affords users to form their own opinion on how to make contact. Communication preferences of contacts based on presence and context information is not trusted at first glance. In the default setting these preference icons were therefore moved one level deeper.

With these conclusions the actual application was designed. The service ran on desktop PCs and on mobile PC/Phones.

The final design, Figure 2 (here with fictitious names), provided real-time context information for a list of contacts including instant messaging status, current and near-future calendar appointments, location information (work, on-the-move, home), and colour-coded availability preferences for various communication media, depending on the type of calendar appointment and the instant messaging status. The service respectively supported work phone, mobile phone, home phone, SMS, IM, and e-mail (Figure 2, centre).

For our pilot we scrambled the Calendar appointment descriptions but preserved the location descriptions to ensure privacy across different organisations. Within organisations employees had access to the complete calendar information of their colleagues.

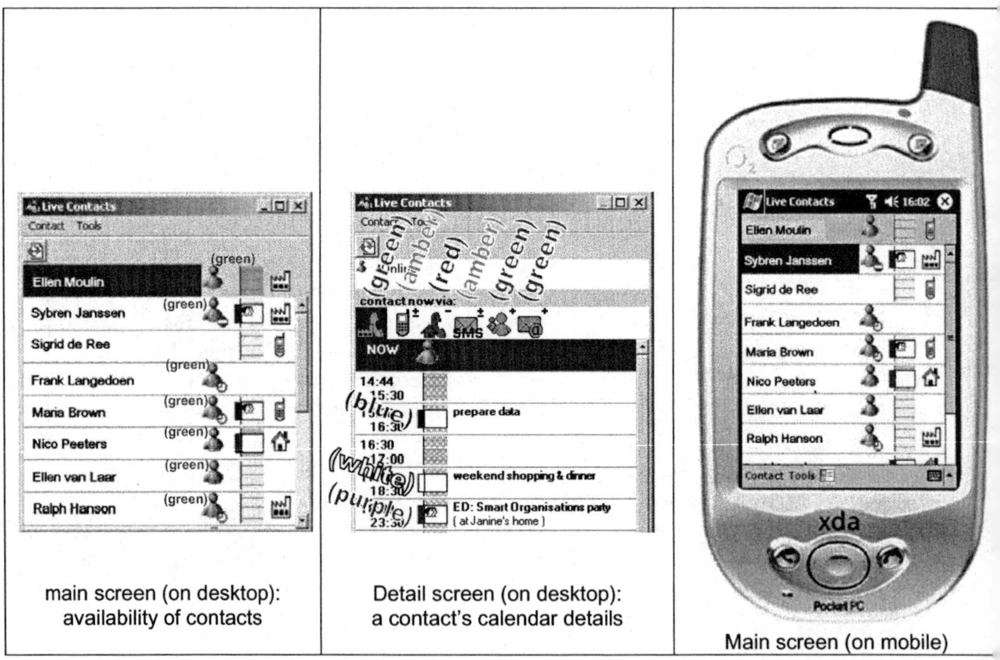

Figure 2: Live Contacts prototype service for the desktop and for handhelds: two clicks to contact.

5. User Study

The two organisations Orgl and Org2 (section 3) also participated our pilot study. They both used an online electronic calendar (Microsoft Outlook Calendar), so colleagues could check one another's agenda. The organisations used IM and telephone differently:

- 100% of the participants in Orgl and 35% of the participants in Org2 used IM.
- At Orgl power lay at the telephone recipient's side: desk phones had a "do not disturb" option and caller line identification. Unanswered external calls were redirected to a reception desk, and missed internal calls appeared in the telephone memory.
- In contrast, at Org2 the telephone initiator was much more empowered: colleagues carried a cell phone. They had a voice operated connection service at their disposal, a voicemail service was always available, and landline phone numbers were redirected to these mobile handsets.

The number of users with desktop applications and mobile clients was balanced among the organisations. In total 17 subjects used the Live Contacts desktop client (8 in Orgl, 9 in Org2), 10 subjects used a mobile client (5 per organisation), and 4 subjects (3 in Orgl, 1 in Org2) used a home client. 9 out of 10 mobile client users used a desktop client at work as well and 3 even used a home client. The pilot ran for 2½ months. We kept client and server data logs to analyse usage over time. At the end of the pilot participants were surveyed.

6. Results

Conclusions drawn from the log and survey data can be split into different categories: organisational differences, differences due to the Live Contacts client used (e.g. mobile Live Contacts client use versus the desktop client use) and differences between the experiences of users. The last category concerns largely subjective information and is measured with a survey. Table 3 summarises some of our findings from the log data, in the next section (section 7) the results of the survey are explained in more detail.

The *Selections* in table 3 are the total number of times a user selects another contact's detailed information (second screen) within the pilot period. The *Checks* refer to every time a selection or a refresh has taken place. The *Calls* indicate the number of communication sessions launched from the Live Contacts application. In the rightmost columns under *Media*, the type of communication medium has been counted. In the rows the Work client, Desktop client and Home clients are summarised, as well as the clients per organisation. Note the difference between the average use and "power use" in each category. As a result such power users weigh heavy on the results.

Table 3: Live Contacts usage over a 2½ months testing period.

	Selec-tions	Checks	Calls	Media					
				Work Phone	Mobile Phone	Home Phone	SMS	IM	email
Work	72	132	33.5	9.2	9.9	2.6	(2.0)	6.9	2.8
max	255	594	230	55	63	12	(13)	65	22
Mobile	116	226	44.7	12.3	10.7	2.4	4.3	10.3	(4.7)
max	257	496	143	29	24	10	15	72	(21)
Home	103	133	9.7	4	2.3	2.3	(0.0)	1.0	0.0
max	280	345	16	6	4	3	(0)	3	0
Orgl	128	236	46.1	9.8	9.1	2.4	2.4	7.6	3.1
max	280	594	230	55	63	12	15	72	22
Org2	46	81	22.0	7.9	7.4	0.9	1.9	2.3	1.6
max	139	200	51	29	20	4	6	11	9

In general the Live Contacts application leads to a rich and balanced media choice. Even unsupported media (indicated between brackets), such as SMS from the desktop and email from the mobile were selected now and then. There are quite some similarities between the activity patterns of mobile and deskbound users. Mobile users have a much-increased presence and context awareness view by getting Instant Messaging based status information and by having access to their contacts' calendar information. Obviously this inspires to choose the media for contacting someone with some care.

At an organisational level, differences in viewing frequency (Selections and Checks) are remarkable. At Org1 viewing frequencies are on average above 200, whereas these viewing frequencies did not exceed 200 views for any subject at Org2. For Org1 the number of calls is on average much lower than the number of views. The average #Checks/#Calls, 236/46.1>5.1, indicates that subjects use the Live Contacts application to see availability information rather than reach a contact immediately. At Org2 the average #Checks/#Calls is 81/22≈3.7. This might be seen as a form of self control, which respondents reported earlier for Instant Messaging: they use the presence information as a means to see who is around, and to see whether contact is appropriate. This may explain the higher rate of checks at Org1 compared to Org2.

We expected this awareness to work reciprocally: viewing the availability of colleagues, subjects could improve the articulation of e.g., their calendar events. Our preliminary analyses indicate they did not. Different labels to tell e.g., internal from external (and non-) appointments were used by 4(1)/10 before the User Study and by 5(2)/10 during the experiment. In the control group 3(0)/10 users differentiated between these labels before the user study, and 2(1)/10 did so 3 months later. These differences are only small.

Once subjects initiate a communication session, they may do so in accordance with, or against the suggestions given by the Live Contacts application, encoded in coloured media icons in the traffic light colours red, amber, and green. According to a simple algorithm, where a green light gives 1 point, an amber light gives ½ point and a red light gives 0 points, we computed the average "obedience score" in relation to IM based and Calendar based suggestions respectively. These scores may be the result of bad luck: your contacts are busy and leave you no alternative but to interrupt them. To measure this, we also computed the "obedience scores" if a chance process would make the media choices. So if a chance process would make 20 telephone calls in the given period, and 15 mobile calls, etc. what would its obedience score be? Table 4 summarises some statistics for the least and most "obedient" subject in our study.

Table 4: Subjects participating in the User Study.

Media Choice	least obedient	most obedient
Work phone	30%	37%
Mobile phone	40%	22%
Home phone	20%	3%
SMS	7%	5%
IM	3%	15%
Email	0%	18%
Obedience to IM based suggestions	20%	81%
Chance value	42%	49%
Obedience to Calendar based suggestions	10%	83%
Chance value	22%	41%

The differences in "obedience" as presented in Table 4 cannot be explained by mere chance behaviour. There seems to be a relation to media stickiness however. The "most obedient" subject seems to switch easily between communication media and uses the little intrusive IM and email media almost as often as the very intrusive mobile phone medium. The fact is that our "least obedient" subject did not even evade email or IM. In fact this subject was a heavy user of both media, but they were not launched via the Live Contacts application, so this happened outside the scope of our measurements.

Of course the role of the traffic lights is only indicative. In the mock-up evaluation session participants already expressed that they would like to stick to their own judgement and keep their own responsibility about contacting others. So the traffic light indications are being valuable for some, whereas others prefer their own interpretation of context.

7. Experiences and Survey

The following issues must be taken into account to appreciate the results presented in Section 6. After the User Study we conducted a survey, asking a. o. to give comments on the experiment and application and suggest improvement.

- Scalability and Consent
  Many respondents asked to extend the coverage of the application 10-20 to their entire contact list. In the current approach certain scalability issues would arise: The user study was impossible without explicit consent between individuals to share Instant Messaging and calendar information (especially across organisational borders). In an opt in sharing system [14] explicit consent can grow too complex. Respondents already complained that consenting procedures created so much fuss that they were shied off adding more persons to their contacts list.
- Mobile Device
  The mobile devices used had limitations, which may have influenced the experiment. Their battery had to be reloaded daily or the memory was erased and software had to be reloaded. The device was not meant to switch off like a normal mobile. However, the mobile client was useful for Instant Messaging while travelling or in a meeting
- Telephones
  In the design sessions and during the start of this study, the palette of work phone, mobile phone, and home phone was much criticised. Org2 used mobile phones as their work phone and respondents feared that a choice between telephones would make the application unnecessarily complex. Our findings show balanced use of the respective telephone media. Obviously the work telephone is seen as more location specific and less obtrusive than the person specific mobile telephone.

8. Conclusions and Discussion

Uniform presence awareness has been mentioned often as necessary condition for effective knowledge sharing. Our user study shows the practicality and feasibility of generalised presences awareness, which crosses organisational borders. Security issues have been dealt with in our working prototype, but the consent-related issues require more attention in future. The desirability to communicate more subtly and spontaneously had already been demonstrated for Instant Messaging. Employees often introduce the media of their liking to their work places. The interesting aspect of the Live Contacts approach is to introduce new forms of presence awareness while maintaining safety. This allows a better match between organisational policies and the knowledge sharing demands. It is still an issue for research how to deal with trusted information. In the pilot with two organisations participating, a tailor-made solution could be devised, but generic approaches are needed to allow growth.

Next to knowledge worker organisations, there are many other application domains where urgency, professionalism, and availability are pivotal. Among these are medical assistance, emergency and rescue work, but also business applications where time and expertise matter. In each domain the scope and scale of temporal and spatial information may differ. E.g., cab drivers or security personnel might need frequent context updates incorporating accurate location information, but they may have a shortened time horizon. On the other hand, the 24 h look ahead for knowledge work is already insufficient in many cases, when peers have a tight schedule and free time is rare. So, in some domains expertise weighs heaviest, whereas timely availability does in others.

In its current form the Live Contacts prototype has been specialised toward access to expertise (with calendar updates every 15 minutes, a large variety of communication media, simple location categories, and a reasonably large look ahead). Specialisations toward urgent real time availability could focus on a single medium (e.g. push-to-talk) and use highly accurate and up-to-date location information of fellow workers, agents, drivers, doctors, or engineers. These context issues will be investigated further in the Freeband project of which the current research has been a forerunner. For more information on context awareness research in the Freeband project, check http://www.freeband.nl.

Acknowledgements

This research presented here was part of the Dutch Freeband Impulse project B4U http://b4u.freeband.nl. For the design part we are indebted to Arlette Pikaart (TNO Telecom), Ingrid Mulder, and Henri ter Hofte of Telematica Instituut. The user study and surveys were carried out in cooperation Nico Pals of TNO Telecom. We would like to thank project manager Ferial Moelaert (Telematica Instituut) for her valuable comments.

References

[1] Brown, J.S. and Duguid, P. (2000) *The Social Life of Information*, Harvard Business School Press.

[2] Davenport, T.H. and Prusak, L (1998) *Working Knowledge: How Organizations Manage What They Know*, Harvard Business School Press.

[3] Dabbish, L.; Kraut, R. (2003) Coordinating Communication: Awareness Displays and Interruption *CHI 2003*, April 5-10, 2003, Ft. Lauderdale, Florida.

[4] Churchill, E.F.; Bly, S. (1999) It's all in the words: Supporting work activities with lightweight tools. *Proceedings of GROUP 99*

[5] Erickson, T. & Kellogg, W.A. (2000) Social Translucence: An Approach to Designing Systems that Support Social Processes. *ACM TOCHI*, Vol. 7, No. 1, March 2000, p 59-83.

[6] Herbsleb, J.D.; Atkins, D.L.; Boyer, D. G.; Handel, M.; Finholt, T.A. (2002) Introducing Instant Messaaging and Chat in the Workplace, Chi2002, April 2-=25, 2002, Minneapolis, Minnesota, USA

[7] Handel, M; and Herbsleb, J.D. (2002) What Is Chat Doing in the Workplace? *CWCW'02*, November 16-20, New Orleans, Louisiana, USA.

[8] Poot, H. de.; Hofte, H. ter, Kijl, B.; and Mulder, I. (2003) The value of presence at work and on the move In C. Stephanidis (Ed.), *HCI International 2003 Adjunct Proceedings* (pp. 191-192). Heraklion: Crete University Press.

[9] De Vos, H., Ter Hofte, G. H., & De Poot, H. IM [@Work] (2004) Adoption of Instant Messaging in a Knowledge Worker Organisation *HICSS-37*, Hawaii, USA, January 5-8, 2004.

[10] Milewski, A.E.; and Smith, T.M. (2000) Providing Presence Cues to Telephone Users *CSCW'00*, December 2-6, 2000, Philadelphia, PA.

[11] Mulder, I.; and Hofte, H. ter (2003). B4U Creatieve design sessie, *Telematica Instituut Internal Report*, TI/RS/2003/002

[12] Mulder, I. (2004). *Understanding designers, designing for understanding*, Chapter 5. Ph.D. Thesis, Enschede, The Netherlands, Telematica Instituut.

[13] Pikaart, A.; and Mulder, I. (2003) Presence@work and on the move, *Telematica Instituut Internal Report*, B4U/D2.2.a

[14] Grudin, J. A (1996) Case Study of Calendar Use in an Organization, *SIGOIS Bulletin*, Vol 17, No. 3 (December 1996) pp 49-51

eAdoption and the Knowledge Economy: Issues, Applications, Case Studies
P. Cunningham and M. Cunningham (Eds.)
IOS Press, 2004

Learning through Online Communities - A Study of Health Care Sites in Europe

Åsa SMEDBERG
DSV, Stockholm University/KTH, Forum 100, S-164 40 Kista, Sweden
Tel: +46 8 16 16 99, Fax: + 46 8 703 90 25, Email: asasmed@dsv.su.se

Abstract: Online communities have become common in most industries. In the health care sector there are many online communities for people to communicate, share information and learn about different diseases and bad habits. Although studies have been made to better understand the use of these communities, it remains unclear to what extent the communities manage to encourage people to change a bad habit. This paper presents results from a study of NetDoctor sites in Sweden, United Kingdom and Denmark. Online communities on overweight, smoking and alcohol habits were targeted. The results give examples of empathetic discussions, but they also present a conflict between learning a new behaviour, which involves questioning each other's behaviour, and the need to hold the community together.

1. Introduction

The definition of a traditional community is a place where groups and individuals who share the same interests, who want to cooperate and to satisfy each other's needs meet. An online community is a community that uses a computer system to mediate the interaction between the groups and individuals involved in the community. The computer system should be able to support the feeling of togetherness among the community members [7]. Online communities can also be regarded as virtual social networks useful for empathetic support, information sharing and problem solving [1].

Online communities have become common in most industries today. Service and product companies use them for different purposes. Support of group learning is one area for which online communities are used. The interest for this kind of online communities seems natural, since learning and communication are strongly related to each other. Learning involves drawing on our experience to help others see their own situation better, to help them interpret it [6]. Through questioning our underlying assumptions we can help each other to develop a new understanding, and to start to behave in a different way [2].

In the health care sector there are many patient online communities for learning purposes used on a daily basis by people with different physical and mental conditions. These online communities aim at helping people reflect upon their conditions and support each other. The participants are encouraged to share experiences and to give advice on how to cope with illnesses, such as heart diseases or asthma, but also to help each other change behaviour. Many of the online communities are about bad habits, such as bad eating habits and smoking. The discussions in these communities are on how to change one's behaviour, either in terms of giving up a habit, or to start a new and healthier way of living.

Impact on Communication Behaviour from Online Communities

Online communication differs in many aspects from traditional, face-to-face interaction. One positive effect of communicating online is that it can help to expand social circles [8]. This allows traditionally peripheral groups to engage in a social context. The community is held together by the common beliefs and values that guide the conversations [8].

There are also some negative effects when communicating online, such as a tendency to forget about the receiver of the message and to be unaware of the receiver's response [8]. Regarding online communities for people with certain physical or mental conditions, there are other potential complications. Even though people want to hear about the experiences of others as well as advice from doctors, there is a risk that participants neglect differences in reactions to treatments, pain tolerance, etc., when trying to help each other [7].

Furthermore, both face-to-face and online communities act according to group norms. The group norm of an online community has shown to be more adapted to when the members identify themselves with the group as a whole, and with its goals, instead of identifying themselves solely as individuals [3]. When online participants use a behaviour that does not agree with the norm, messages can be used to inform the offender to stop or change his or her behaviour. The others can also ignore members that are hostile or in another way deviate from the accepted norm, in order to eliminate their involvement in the community. A moderator can also be assigned to scan the discussion and to filter the discussion from unwanted messages [3].

Usage of Online Communities – Previous Case Studies

A previous study on constructing a typology for online messages presented a one-month long comparative study on two Usenet newsgroups on health issues [4]. The study showed differences in the way the members of the two newsgroups communicated. One of the newsgroups focused on a life-threatening physical illness, while the other one focused on an emotional disorder. The results showed that the group with an interest in a serious issue of physical health avoided flames. Instead, they sent messages mostly of collaborative and social nature. The group interested in a mental disorder, on the other hand, engaged often in conflicts. The study indicated that there might be differences between different types of online communities, but that future research needs to examine this issue further.

A case study of learning through an online community presented how kids and elderly worked together to build up a shared database of oral history [5]. The elderly people were interviewed by the young ones in order to help them learn about historical experiences. One thing that was learnt during the pilot work was that both the kids and the elders felt that they needed more information about those they were talking to. In-depth background information about the elderly felt especially important since the kids were to understand the life stories told by the elderly persons. In order to deal with this, profiles were created that provided information about name, age, location, and a photo of the member was also included. This information was stored and made accessible to the community members.

Although these previous studies provide us with new knowledge, they also raise questions. There is still a lack of understanding regarding how to encourage people to change a bad habit and to learn a new behaviour through the online communities.

2. Business Case

Trying to help others to cope with a certain condition is difficult, as Preece [7] has pointed out. However, an even more delicate task is to help others reflect upon and change a bad habit. Online communities for people with bad habits, such as smoking and eating problems, give examples of learning situations where behavioural changes are targeted.

The practical business case for the study presented in this paper has been the open online health-communities for public use in the NetDoctor sites in Sweden [11], United Kingdom [9] and Denmark [10]. In these communities hundreds of issues related to physical as well as psychological problems are discussed on a regular basis. In total, there are more than 60 online communities present today at the NetDoctor site in the United Kingdom, more than 350 in Denmark and about 230 in Sweden. The business case of this study is restricted to online health-communities for people who want to change a bad habit. These communities are open to anyone who wants to share his or her experience with others, ask for advice and help others to quit a bad habit.

Since some bad habits can later result in serious illness, encouraging people to change behaviour is of great importance to their future well-being and the health care sector. Using the Internet to help people change a bad habit is therefore an important challenge.

3. Method

The practical part of this paper is based on a study of different learning situations in European online health-communities. The focus of the study was online communities for modern health problems: overweight, smoking and alcohol problems.

The study included two NetDoctor communities on eating and exercising, one in Denmark and one in Sweden, and two on smoking and alcohol, one in Sweden and one in the UK. The communities were studied from June 2003 to April 2004. Discussion threads of the communities were observed in order to find out about different conversational patterns. Communication and learning aspects were used to analyse the discussions. In order to illustrate the characteristics of the discussions, quotations were extracted.

4. Objective

The aim of the study was to see to what extent existing online health discussions on bad habits encourage people to change behaviour, and to map out obstacles. This knowledge is helpful when trying to make online health-communities in Europe more effective.

For the health care sector, a benefit of having more effective online health-communities is that people are better informed. Finding out how to help people to change a bad habit can reduce the number of people likely to develop heart conditions and asthma, for example. A longer-term impact for the health care sector would then be to improve people's health and to prevent people from getting severe illnesses. As a consequence, this future impact can also reduce the burden on the European health care resources.

5. Results

When monitoring online discussions, different types of discussion are easy to detect. Frequently, individuals request people's experiences related to medical treatments, practices and use of medicines. Another common type of message is from people who want to share their experiences with others. In some cases warnings are delivered. Furthermore, many messages aim at encouraging others to continue their struggle for a change in behaviour, such as to quit smoking or to lose weight. For example, words of encouragement can be seen in connection with the description of experience. However, there are also examples of discussions that use a more aggressive and hostile tone.

The following sections are examples of learning situations in the NetDoctor health-communities. The first two consist of examples of online discussions on eating and exercising habits, discussions held in the Swedish and the Danish NetDoctor sites. The last two sections are about smoking and alcohol habits, showing discussions from the NetDoctor sites in the United Kingdom and Sweden.

5.1 Eating and Exercising Habits – Online Discussions in Denmark

In the NetDoctor site in Denmark [10] there are several discussion threads on overweight starting with a request for medicine advice, i.e., people asking for recommendations concerning diet pills, herbs, etc. Participants responding to these requests often express their own experiences, but they also give recommendations concerning change of life style. Some suggest smaller meals and regular exercising, often as a replacement for pills.

However, there are also examples of breakdowns in the communication. One discussion filled with a lot of advice on how to change life style was suddenly interrupted by an indignant response. The participant found the discussion to be condemning. This participant expressed his or her feeling in the following ironic way: “Or find a debate on slimness that is not full of condemned people who know everything about the “REAL” methods ;-).”, and continued by saying: "The NetDoctor site on how to get slim is for slim people who know everything about what we overweight people must do :-).” (The message was sent on the 4th of April 2004.) This was responded by a short and offending message asking if the sender wanted to remain fat. Another response to the ironic message expressed the stupidity of following the so-called magic cures presented by the industry.

Although some of the discussions use harsh words, there is also another type of discussion about overweight and habits that is more filled with compassion. One example could be seen in March and April 2004. The discussion started with a message from a woman having many different problems, and she expressed feelings of resignation using a header called “Lost Motivation”. In her message she related to different issues in her life, such as the loss of her father a few months ago, the struggle against childlessness and her back problem. (The message was posted on the 31st of March 2004.) Two community participants responded to this woman on the following day, expressing their compassion and understanding. One of the responders started her message by saying: “It seems enormously sad all that you are going through.” The rest of the message encouraged the woman to do some exercising activities that she thought felt good, which also could help the woman to ease the pain and to get her in a better mood.

5.2 Eating and Exercising Habits – Swedish Online Discussions

In the Swedish NetDoctor online discussions on overweight [11], there are both encouraging messages and messages that questioned other people’s behaviour and values. In one discussion focused on being overweight, the participants questioned the way a woman described her life, her eating and exercising habits. While the woman understood that she had overweight, the others thought she was exaggerating the training programme and that she ate too little and the wrong things. To one of the replies, the woman tried to explain her situation by saying that her clothes did not fit her any more, but the questioning went on. The dialogue continued between the 19th and 25th of October 2003, when the woman ended the discussion. With hurt feelings, one can assume, the woman left the discussion by sending a short defensive message with the heading “No more e-mail, please!” and the body text: “I don’t want any more e-mail messages.”

In the same overweight community there were participants who expressed their annoyance with the discussions, since they believed that the discussions were not about overweight but about normal weights. The following is an extract from one of the critical messages: “I suggest that we, who want to discuss real overweight and nothing else, simply don’t answer all messages that should be left out to the page for eating disorders.” (The message was sent on the 13th of October 2003.) Another message addressed this ongoing discussion on how to define weight problems: ”When you post your messages here, we, who really suffer from overweight, get sad and annoyed - We are not interested!”

Both the Danish and the Swedish discussions on eating and exercising habits showed that a shared empathetic understanding is necessary for people who want to communicate and learn together. When the participants could not relate to and sympathize with the ones they discussed with, breakdowns occurred in the interaction.

5.3 Smoking and Alcohol Habits – Swedish Online Discussions

Most of the discussions on smoking habits in the Swedish NetDoctor site [11] show compassion and understanding. Side effects of quitting smoking described in the messages are met with explanations, people’s own experiences and encouragement to struggle to get rid of the addiction. Health issues such as the loss of cilia and other problems with the throat, weight gain, etc., are ventilated. Empathetic responses are met with gratitude, and replies saying “Thank you” are common. There are also responses that include successful stories, such as those from ex-smokers who have changed their way of living.

One community message came from a person who had gained 4-5 kilos since they gave up smoking a year before. At the end of the message some questions to the other participants were posted: A quotation from the message: “[…] What are your experiences? How much of the increase in weight can be explained by metabolism changes? That food becomes a substitute for cigarettes? Other explanations? […]” (Sent on the 25th of June 2003). The responding message included this successful story: “I also stopped smoking one year ago and started at the same time to increase my bicycling exercise. I drove even in the wintertime, in all weathers, in snow and thaw. I feel great, and I have reduced 8 kilos since I gave up smoking. […]” (Sent on the 28th of June 2003) The message did not get any responses from the original sender.

Present in the community on smoking are also the discussions related to negative effects on the environment, and whether it is a human right to smoke or not. Some of these discussions got a bit heated, and the smokers who tried to quit defended themselves.

About alcohol habits, lots of messages can be seen that include long and personal descriptions about the situation of the sender. Sometimes it is the sender him/herself who is addicted to alcohol, and some other times it is a close friend or a relative. These personal messages are often met with understanding and advice on where to seek professional help. Since the community members answer each other quickly, urgent questions, such as how to avoid drinking during the Eastern holiday, were met with responses and encouraging words to hold back and be strong. Further, many of the members tried to help each other to interpret and explain underlying causes as well as the effects that a person with alcohol problems has on the rest of the family. Often, the responding members also related to and exemplified from their own experience.

5.4 Smoking and Alcohol Habits – Online Discussions in United Kingdom

As in the Swedish discussions on smoking and alcohol, the discussions held in the NetDoctor site in United Kingdom [9] consist of compassion and understanding. Many messages contain practical advice on how to deal with different social situations, and they often relate to the sender’s own experiences. Especially one community member (who used a real name that made it possible to identify recurrent messages from him) engaged in many of the alcohol discussions. He tried to interpret the life stories described by others as well as giving advice on how to struggle for a new way of living. The members who received advice from him often expressed their gratitude, and some also liked to use his name in their messages, letting the conversation be more personal.

Regarding the smoking discussions, at one occasion a community member responded in a hostile way to a person who had just stopped smoking. The responding member let the anxious person know that it was not because of abstinence from nicotine or side effects from using nicotine patches that caused distraction while he was driving. Instead, it was the fact that he was a lousy driver that put him in awkward situations on the highway. This message was met by a response from the first sender who said that he did not find it helpful at all. Also another member of the community started his or her response by correcting the hostile person, and the member continued then by giving information about health centres and help lines together with words of encouragement. The deviation from the group norm was thereby neutralized, and the exchange of advice and encouragement could take over.

6. Conclusions and Recommendations

6.1 Conclusions

The objective of the practical study presented in this paper was to see to what extent online health discussions encourage people with a bad habit to change behaviour and to present obstacles that were found. This section presents conclusions drawn from the study.

The results showed that most people involved in online discussions liked to share experiences and to give advice. Through empathy, stories and advice, many participants were able to find strength and motivation in the community.

However, the study also showed that the openness of the public online communities sometimes resulted in controversies related to different values and standards. These controversies caused communication breakdowns when users got annoyed and offensive.

The goal of many participants seemed to be to get confirmation of the difficulties they experienced and of the changes in behaviour that they suggested. This can be seen as an obstacle to learning, since questioning behaviour is an essential part of learning.

Furthermore, all participants could not manage to balance between questioning the behaviour of each other and showing empathy and togetherness. Even though questioning is essential for creating a new behaviour, participants of a community also need to consider each other's emotions in order to hold the community together.

Still another obstacle noted was that the complexity of and the differences between the participants could not be fully considered. It appeared to be difficult to respond to questions about weight in relation to height without knowing the other person, his or her physique and health status, for example. The discussions on the amount of sport activities in relation to how big meals and how many calories they had constitute another example.

Finally, community values seemed more accepted by the members of the online communities on smoking and alcohol than on eating. Most interactions on smoking and alcohol were sincere and often explicitly appreciated by the members. However, the findings of this study are restricted to a limited number of online communities. Further research in this area is needed in order to conclude about any differences.

6.2 Recommendations

When dealing with bad habits, the social and psychological background of a person is of importance to understand the specific behaviour. The complexity of the individuals should, therefore, be considered. To take care of this complexity the community would benefit from inviting medical trained people to monitor and participate in the discussions. Even though they will not get all relevant information about the participants, they are able to modify and balance the discussions, and to follow up discussions when necessary.

The virtual sessions can beneficially be combined with face-to-face meetings. This becomes obvious when discussing someone's weight, for example. A combination of online conversations and face-to-face meetings can reduce the gap of understanding.

Further studies on online health-communities are to be conducted in order to fully understand how to enable fruitful online discussions on changing a bad habit. Additionally, studies of online learning would benefit from being complemented by interviews with community members. This would let us know more about the background of the members, and it would also make us understand better what impact the online discussions have on their struggle for a new behaviour.

References

[1] Andrews, D.C. (2002) *Audience-specific Online Community Design*, Communications of the ACM, April 2002/Vol. 45, No.4

[2] Argyris, C. (1994) *Good Communication that Blocks Learning*, Harvard Business Review, July-August 1994, pp. 77-85

[3] Blanchard, A. (2004) *Virtual Behavior Settings: An Application of Behavior Setting Theories to Virtual Communities,* JCMC 9 (2), January 2004

[4] Burnett, G., Buerkle, H. (2004) *Information Exchange in Virtual Communities: A Comparative Study*, JCMC 9 (2), January 2004

[5] Ellis, J.B., Bruckman, A.S (2001) *Designing Palaver Tree Online: Supporting Social Roles in a Community of Oral History,* CHI, Vol. 3, Issue 1, 31 March – 5 April 2001

[6] McDermott, R. (2000) *Knowing in Community: 10 Critical Success Factors in Building Communities of Practice,* IHRIM Journal, March 2000

[7] Preece, J. (2000) *Online Communities – Designing Usability, Supporting Sociability*, Wiley & Sons, Ltd

[8] Sproull, L., Kiesler, S. (1995) *Connections – New Ways of Working in the Networked Organization*, The MIT Press

Websites:

[9] http://www.netdoctor.co April 2004

[10] http://www.netdoktor.dk April 2004

[11] http://netdoktor.passagen.se April 2004

Virtual Organisations in Healthcare: Organisation, People and Technology

Marjan GROOTVELD[1], Janine SWAAK[1], Rogier BRUSSEE[1],
Rianne HUIS IN'T VELD[2], Margreet MICHEL-VERKERKE[3]
[1]*Telematica Instituut, P.O. Box 589, 7500 AN Enschede, The Netherlands*
Tel: +31 (0) 53 4850485, Fax: +31 (0) 53 4850400, Email: Marjan.Grootveld@telin.nl
[2]*RRD, P.O. Box 310, 7500 AH Enschede, The Netherlands*
Tel: +31 (0) 53 4875740, Fax: +31 (0)53 4340849 Email: r.huisintveld@rrd.nl
[3]*University of Twente, P.O. Box 217, 7500 AE Enschede, The Netherlands*
Tel: +31 (0) 53 4894134, Fax: +31 (0)53 4892159, Email: m.b.michel@utwente.nl

Abstract: This paper describes a virtual organisation in healthcare, emphasising collaboration around a common task (organisational aspect), a virtual administrative domain spanning several information systems using communication technology (technological aspect), and the way this requires or causes changes in people's behaviour (social aspect). We give an inventory of the existing organisation, technology and communication patterns within a group of healthcare institutions in the Netherlands and then describe the design, development and validation of a mobile application to support the diagnosis of strokes. The pilot indicates that supporting virtual organisations is a vast challenge, but not necessarily a complex endeavour. This work shows the benefits of starting with a concrete case and the importance of understanding the working processes before identifying – together with stakeholders – possible adaptations in the working processes as well as the required technology support and security levels.

1. Introduction

Virtual organisations are loosely coupled, largely independent organisations cooperating in an ad hoc manner for a specific goal. These characteristics allow for switching between partners who can play a similar role. Mowshowitz [1] even considers the systematic use and management of this flexibility to offer services where and when they are most needed, as the fundamental aspect of virtual organisations. Even a virtual organisation requires individuals and organisations to exchange communication, information and resources (e.g. money) for various reasons such as synchronisation, agreements, to establish common goals and for redistribution of rewards and efforts. If we consider the existence of agreements as the essential aspect of an organisation, there is a continuum between real and virtual organisations: formal existing agreements between partners can be re-negotiated and new agreements can emerge on the fly in both real and virtual organisations. From this perspective, many human activities in commerce, healthcare, government and science involve a virtual organisation.

The goal of this paper is to describe the design and results of the TeleCare pilot project in which general practitioners and other healthcare professionals associated to the Stroke Service Enschede (The Netherlands) are given mobile and ad hoc access to patient records. We identify the stroke service as a virtual organisation with ad hoc collaboration around a common task, but with some existing formal agreements to facilitate the process. The pilot project provided a rudimentary virtual administrative domain centred around the patient that spans several information systems and crosses organisation boundaries (technological aspect). We discuss the changes in people's working practices caused or required by this technology (social aspect). The societal importance of this research is emphasised by the finding of a nationwide Dutch survey [2] that a serious number of medical mistakes results from incorrect or incomplete information in patient records and the lack of easy communication and collaboration agreements to check the patient files. This illustrates the urgency for improving support for virtual organisations in the medical field.

1.1 Organisation of the Paper

This paper combines an engineering approach with an empirical study. First we introduce the goal and the current organisation of the Stroke Service Enschede. Next we present the context in which the research took place – the TeleCare project – and the research objectives. We give an analysis of the existing organisation, technology and communication patterns within the Stroke Service Enschede and as well as the design, development and validation of a mobile application to support general practitioners and emergency room staff in diagnosing. We indicate the advantages of this analysis in terms of a better understanding of the current situation (i.e. existing organisation, technology, communication patterns and information exchange) and stakeholder involvement. Finally we present the results of the evaluation of the developed application in practice.

2. The Stroke Service Enschede

After a stroke or Cerebrovascular Accident (CVA) a multitude of neurological disorders sets in suddenly because of blood circulation failures in the brain. Due to the diversity of the remaining symptoms, a large number of healthcare professionals is involved in the care of the CVA patient. As a consequence, the risk of inefficient and inadequate care due to inadequate collaboration and coordination is high. A stroke service is a regional network of healthcare professionals giving competent coordinated transmural [3] care to patients in the event of a stroke and during the rehabilitation process in its aftermath.

The members of the network have a collective responsibility to transfer patients from one participating institution to another and for the quality of cure and care of the chain as a whole. The Stroke Service Enschede consists of a hospital, rehabilitation centre, geriatric centre, indoor and outdoor healthcare professionals such as home carers, general practitioners, physiotherapists and occupational therapists. These organisations and actors work together according to the Stroke Service Enschede guidelines.

The Stroke Service Enschede has a firmly established organisational basis for their work. At the same time, each patient requires a new informal "team" of healthcare professionals made up of the members of the Stroke Service. The team is a virtual team [4] in that available members of the Stroke Service are chosen on an ad hoc basis. Collectively the Stroke Service is able to rapidly respond to the patient's needs without the need for a permanently dedicated team.

3. The TeleCare project

In this paper we describe the work performed in the Freeband TeleCare [5] project. The objective of the project is to make the care process of the Stroke Service Enschede more effective and efficient by supporting and advancing medical decisions. The research goal of the project is to improve communication and information exchange in the Stroke Service Enschede by using integrated fixed and wireless networks. The main focus has been to give healthcare professionals mobile access to the medical file of stroke patients for a view on the patient's medical history. The TeleCare pilot validated an application that has been developed for the emergency situation after an ischaemic stroke. The project's goal was not to create a virtual healthcare organisation but to enhance the capabilities of an existing formal group of institutions to switch patient care tasks to members that are available.

4. Methodology I: research into the Stroke Service Enschede

The current organisation, existing technology and the communication and information exchange between the collaborating parties were analysed by means of

- questionnaires sent to all Stroke Service Enschede institutions (N = 62, response rate = 88.6%) [6], measuring the intensity and type of communication within and between institutions, and the attitude towards the role of IT for communication;
- interviews with representatives of nine professions involved (UseIT method [7]) and with stakeholders and decision makers in the institutions [8], assessing the primary processes and the role and use of information provision within the primary process;
- patient file analysis, focussing on the type and completeness of information in relation to the work agreements of the institutions.

5. Results I: communication in the Stroke Service Enschede

The analysis of the current situation showed among other things that communication and information exchange about patients is frequent, within and across institutions as well as within and across disciplines. Figure 1 is only an indication of existing information flows.

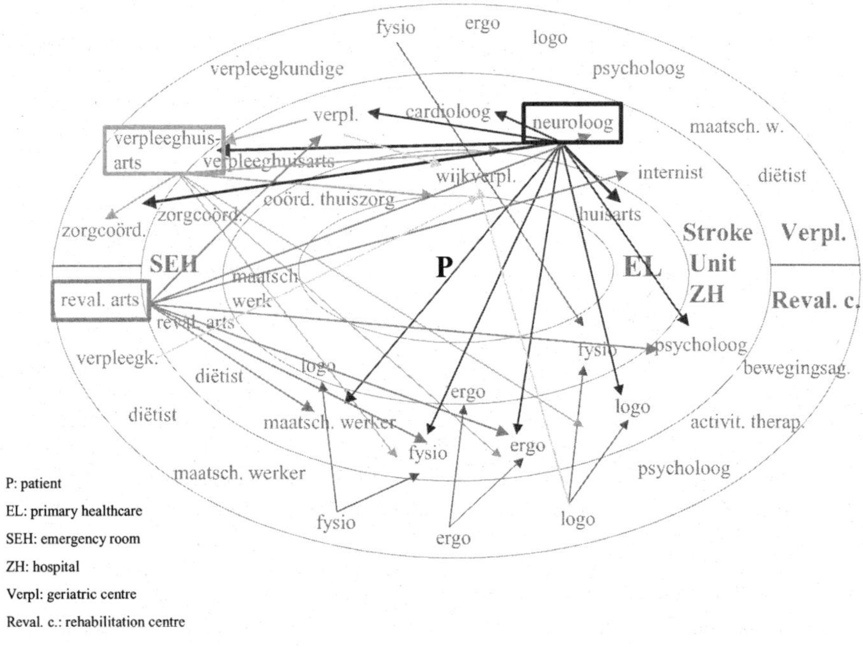

Figure 1. Indication of existing information flows in Stroke Service Enschede

The major part of communication and information exchange in the (para)medical community takes place through personal contacts, phone calls and letters. In other words, the members of this virtual organisation heavily rely on the availability of colleagues to contact each other and apply traditional technology. Another outcome, however, is the positive attitude towards information technology, as long as the information technology introduction trajectory fits the organisation and patient privacy is not at risk [9].

6. Designing a validation pilot

Having gained these insights the project partners agreed that an information technology validation pilot to support the Stroke Service Enschede should focus on a process, rather than a single institution or single professional group. Put differently, it was decided that the focal area should be transmural multidisciplinary healthcare. In close cooperation with external medical experts it was further decided to focus on the initial, critical phase of the Stroke Service Enschede, that is, the selection of patients for thrombolysis.

The focus on thrombolysis was chosen for the following reasons. A CVA can be caused by a blood clot blocking an artery in the brain (an ischaemic stroke) or a by an internal bleeding of a bursted vessel (a haemorrhagic stroke). The symptoms are similar and a definite diagnosis requires a CT or MR scan of the brain. Thrombolysis treatment of a patient suffering an ischaemic stroke requires blood thinners to be applied within three hours after a blood clot formed to prevent permanent damage. However, this treatment can be fatal in the case of a haemorrhagic stroke. Information about medical conditions such as hypertension or possibly previous strokes and about medication can give strong indications in favour of or against a certain treatment. Healthcare professionals in the stroke service indicate that patient information is frequently incomplete and not timely available. In particular the thrombolysis treatment can hardly ever be applied. Both on medical and on technological grounds (mobile access to patient files) diagnosis support with an eye on thrombolysis treatment seemed a challenging focus area. Moreover, all later processes in the healthcare chain benefit from improvements in data collection at the first stages.

7. Design issues

In a number of workshops with healthcare professionals – potential end users of the mobile application – analyses of the current working processes and user requirements for the intended application were achieved. These requirements were then translated into development specifications. Since the design decisions concerned various healthcare parties (general practitioners, central general practitioners' unit, emergency room staff; see Figure 2) it was crucial to involve them throughout the design process [10].

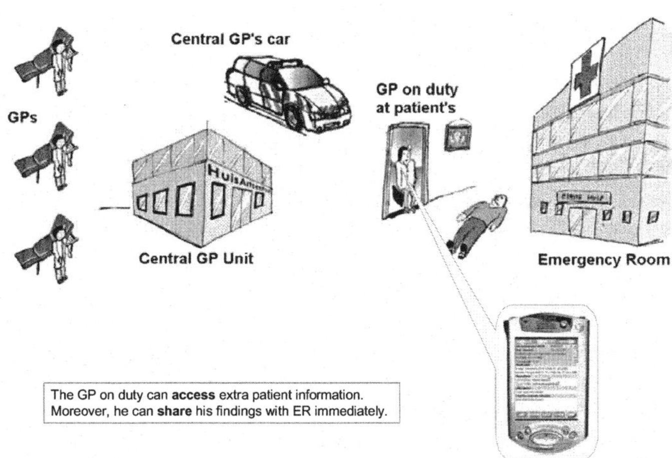

Figure 2. The virtual organisation in the validation pilot

The mobile application was to provide a (limited) virtual administrative domain. Typically, general practitioners on duty don't know their patients yet. Therefore stroke-relevant medical information is retrieved from the electronic patient's record system of the patient's own general practitioner. This information is presented on the personal digital assistant (PDA) of the general practitioner on duty. At the patient's home the general practitioner on duty adds his observations. The application can sum up possible indications against thrombolysis to support the diagnosing process. Finally, this information is forwarded to the emergency room before the patient arrives.

A primary concern in the design process is security. First, secure data storage and secure (internet) connections are required to respect a patient's privacy. As in any other organisation – real or virtual – confidentiality and data integrity [11] require authentication and authorisation. In line with the recommendations from Nictiz [12], the Dutch umbrella organisation for IT in healthcare, we set up a Public Key Infrastructure. GPs who participate in the pilot have individual certificates and must identify themselves by means of a password before they can see or add patient information. Data is transported using this certificate and Transport Layer Security (TLS, also known as SSL (Secure Socket Layer) [13]). This way, access to sensitive data is properly restricted.

Second, security can be understood as minimising the risk of disrupting the normal working process. For this reason the TeleCare applications do not run on the existing medical systems yet. Instead, all GPs whose patient record system is disclosed, as well as the central GP unit and the emergency room were provided with a project laptop with a firewall installed. The laptop communicates with the primary system. Only this parallel network of TeleCare laptops exchanges information with the TeleCare server through GPRS and ADSL. Since interoperability with the call management system at the central GP unit proved impossible within the timeframe of the pilot, the extra TeleCare laptop was more than a security measure. The application of wireless technologies in the healthcare domain is also challenging given the risk of electromagnetic interference with critical and life support medical equipment [14]. However, these risks proved manageable.

The privacy and authentication issue is relevant from both a technical and a legal point of view. Providing a GP who visits a potentially unknown patient with patient information is hoped to improve the GP's (confidence about his) diagnosis and to increase a patient's trust in this diagnosis, but ought not infringe on privacy laws. In designing a mobile application for GPs on duty we have taken care to comply with Dutch law [15].

8. Methodology II: evaluating the validation pilot

During a two months validation period 13 general practitioners, the central GP unit and the emergency room staff have used the applications in a real-life setting. Since the GP application on a Personal Digital Assistant (PDA) is the core of the three TeleCare applications, the evaluation methodology focuses on the PDA application.

The validation results were analysed by means of

- a choice-based Conjoint Analysis [16] (N = 13, response rate = 100%), determining preferences of healthcare professionals regarding a PDA application for a time-critical situation (it is important to note that informants are asked to compare fictional 'products', not to evaluate the actual application);
- a Software Usability Measurement Inventory (SUMI [17]; N = 8, response rate = 61.5%), measuring usability of the application;
- a simulation study with professionals (N = 4) who contributed to the main requirements workshop, assessing the level of CVA relevance of retrieved patient information;
- a record study of all CVAs during the pilot (N=3, plus 3 CVA incidents where the GPRS connection failed – in the latter case the patients were diagnosed and transferred in the pre-TeleCare way), measuring the elapsed time between the initial call from the central GP unit and the moment the information arrived at the emergency room;

- interviews with the GPs involved in the 3 CVA incidents (again with the UseIT method), assessing appreciation for and relevance of the PDA application.

9. Results II: the validation pilot

The TeleCare applications were used successfully in three CVA cases. This indicates that the TeleCare platform functions technically when connecting the central GP unit Enschede, the GP's and the emergency room. In all cases the patient information arrived at the hospital long before the patient did. In addition, the suitability of a wireless application was shown, since the GPs visited the patients at home and had no other means of connecting to the information systems. However, since three stroke incidents were missed due to failure of the wireless (GPRS) network, this technology proved not to be sufficiently reliable yet.

The validation application has a number of clinically relevant information attributes such as medical history, risk profile and medication, most of which were considered relevant in the simulation study. The choice-based Conjoint Analysis, which measured the trade-off between seven attributes, revealed that "insight in relevant medical history" is considered of high importance (25% relative importance). However, an even more important attribute is diagnosis support (44,7% relative importance). Although the actually implemented diagnosis support is limited, 61.5% of the respondents strongly agree that it is sufficient. Set-up and results of the Conjoint Analysis are described in more detail in [18].

As the SUMI questionnaire is a standardised method, the results of a particular questionnaire can be interpreted against a benchmark. The TeleCare median scores for the subscale "control" are on the level of the benchmark, whereas all other subscales (efficiency, affect, helpfulness and learnability) are above normal. Put differently, the GPs were satisfied about the usability. We may assume that this follows at least partly from the design process in which many intended end users have participated.

The PDA application obviously changed the process of informing the emergency room staff. The application did lead to a positive change in behaviour: it increased confidence, i.e., the availability of a stroke checklist reassured the GPs about the information they needed before calling the neurologist [19]. The interviews did not reveal any negative aspects of this change, such as stress induced by using a new device under time pressure.

10. Conclusions and Recommendations

Healthcare is a knowledge intensive operation that can involve many organisations and medical professionals. The TeleCare pilot project addresses the problem of data need in an acute situation by giving members of the loosely but formally organised Stroke Service Enschede mobile access to relevant parts of one another's patient data on an ad hoc basis.

The pilot participants found mobile access to patients data useful and were satisfied with the pilot application's usability, and we can recommend our approach to involve stakeholders in identifying necessary and feasible adaptations in the working processes as well as the required technology support and security levels. As in any pilot, not all went as well as was hoped for: We found that currently (2004), medical professionals cannot rely on the wireless GPRS network. In order to enhance the relevance of the pilot it should be extended to other disorders. Increased use of mobile access technology like PDAs is likely to improve the acceptance by a larger group of healthcare professionals. Upscaling the pilot will certainly stress the importance of interoperability, which we could partially sidestep since all medical file systems we disclosed on behalf of the pilot are of the same make, whereas throughout the Netherlands seven systems are deployed. Nevertheless, we believe this pilot is a good example of the advantages of standardising information. Patient data that are retrieved and added need not "stop" at the emergency room, but can be used throughout the whole healthcare chain. Understanding working processes, involving end users, standardisation and using the new possibilities of broadband technology are main ingredients for the creation of effective virtual teams centred around the patient. Greater flexibility to structure healthcare chains on an ad hoc basis has great potential for improving the efficiency in the whole healthcare sector.

Though (research on) supporting virtual organisations is a challenge – it needs to take into account technological, organisational and social factors – this work shows that it is not necessarily a complex endeavour.

References

[1] Mowshowitz, A. (1997). Virtual organization. Communications of the ACM, 40 (9): 30-37. Retrieved from http://portal.acm.org/ft_gateway.cfm?id=260759&type=pdf&coll=ACM&dl=ACM&CFID=20743510&CFTOKEN=71290819

[2] Retrieved from http://www.nictiz.nl/kr_nictiz/uploaddb/downl_object.asp?atoom=2593&VolgNr=5

[3] Rosendal, H. (2002). Comparative cohort studies in transmural care: three cases of structurally embedded practice in the Netherlands. Dissertation Utrecht University.

[4] Palmer, J.W., C. Speier (1997). A Typology of Virtual Organizations: An Empirical Study. Proceedings of the Association for Information Systems 1997 Americas Conference, Indianapolis. Retrieved from http://hsb.baylor.edu/ramsower/ais.ac.97/papers/palm_spe.htm

[5] The TeleCare research project is a Freeband Impulse project and looks into possibilities to develop and validate new technologies, especially the integration of fixed and wireless networks, in society. Institutes participating in TeleCare are the Telematica Instituut, Roessingh Research and Development, Twente University and Atos Origin. See for more information: http://telecare.freeband.nl/

[6] Huis in 't Veld, M.H.A., J.K.C. Bloo et al (2003). Resultaten van het onderzoek naar de communicatiepatronen van de Enschedese Stroke Service. Freeband/TeleCare deliverable 1.1. Enschede, Roessingh Research & Development. Retrieved from https://doc.telin.nl/dscgi/ds.py/Get/File-31929

[7] Michel-Verkerke M.B., R.W. Schuring, T. Spil (2003). USE IT or leave it: a model to reveal satisfaction of ICT support in health care processes ex post and ex ante. Hospital of the future conference. September 2003, Warwick, UK.

[8] Mitchell, R.K., B.R. Agle et al. (1997). Toward a theory of stakeholder identification and salience: defining the principle of who and what really counts. Academy of Management Review 22 (4): 853-86.

[9] Michel-Verkerke, M.B., R.W. Schuring, W.H. van Harten (2003). Needs, requirements, interests and impact of integrated wireless ICT in care. Freeband/TeleCare deliverable 2.2. Enschede, University of Twente. Retrieved from https://doc.telin.nl/dscgi/ds.py/Get/File-32131

[10] Hettinga M., R.J. Slagter, M.J. Grootveld (2004). Aligning communication in the stroke service. Abstract accepted for EACH 2004, Vienna, Austria.

[11] NEN (2002). NEN 7510:2002 Informatiebeveiliging in de zorg. Nederlands Normalisatie-Instituut.

[12] Nictiz (2004). Architectuurontwerp basisinfrastructuur in de zorg. Retrieved from http://www.nictiz.nl/kr_nictiz/uploaddb/downl_object.asp?atoom=2075&VolgNr=2

[13] http://www.ssl.com/

[14] Morissey, J.J. (2002). Communication industry perspective on compatible deployment of wireless equipment in healthcare facilities. Retrieved from http://www.mohca.org/presentations/JoeMorrissey.ppt

[15] Slagter, R., E. Tieman, M. Snijders (2003). Architecture requirements for a healthcare application. Freeband/TeleCare deliverable 2.1. Enschede, Telematica Instituut. Retrieved from https://doc.telin.nl/dscgi/ds.py/Get/File-31943

[16] http://www.sawtoothsoftware.com/

[17] Kirakowski, K., B. Cierlik (1999). SUMI Introductory Notes Version 2. Human factors group, Cork.

[18] Huis in 't Veld, M.H.A., M. Grootveld, M.M.R. Vollenbroek (2004). Preferences for wireless ICT applications in acute stroke care: a choice-based conjoint analysis. Freeband/TeleCare deliverable 6.1. Enschede, Roessingh Research & Development. Retrieved from https://doc.telin.nl/dscgi/ds.py/Get/File-41053

[19] Huis in 't Veld, M.H.A., M.B. Michel-Verkerke, M.M.R. Vollenbroek (2004). The usability of wireless ICT applications in acute stroke care. Freeband/TeleCare deliverable 6.2. Enschede, Roessingh Research & Development. Retrieved from https://doc.telin.nl/dscgi/ds.py/Get/File-41058

eAdoption and the Knowledge Economy: Issues, Applications, Case Studies
P. Cunningham and M. Cunningham (Eds.)
IOS Press, 2004

Managing Virtual Projects A Benchmark Study of Collaboration Tools

Bernhard KATZY, Gordon SUNG, Cecilia SERRANO
CeTIM at University Bw Munich, Werner -Heisenberg-Weg 39, D -85577 Neubiberg, Germany
Tel: + 49 89 55058 001; Fax: + 49 89 55058 009
Email: Bernhard.Katzy@CeTIM.org; Gordon.Sung@CeTIM.org; Cecilia.Serrano@CeTIM.org

Abstract: The role of projects in the organization changed from the early days of simple projects for managing specific tasks to today's matrix organisations with complex projects for cross-unit or even inter-organizational coordination. Such virtual projects are a new form that intensively relies on IT technologies for team communication and coordination. This study provides a selection guide for collaboration tools that is based on a project management framework. A market research lists and benchmarks existing tools. Most functionality needed for managing virtual project are well covered by existing tools, but different tools differently integrate them based on the often implicit assumptions about business processes and project organisation. An emerging new technology element is real time communication, which increases media richness for non-routine tasks and already is included in half the tools.

1. Introduction

Projects as a distinct organisational form steadily increases in practical relevance. In the beginning of the 1960's, projects were mainly used within hierarchies to support line managers for specific tasks. Later, projects were increasingly used for cross-unit coordination in matrix organizations. Today, under the pressure of high market competitions and customer oriented products and services development, many organisations extensively utilize cooperative or inter-organizational projects to quickly rally competences for product innovation and project based manufacturing. Projects are employed in a wide range ranging from EU research projects to the development of the new European jet fighter Typhoon or goods delivery in the supply chains of Dell or Cisco. Because of their distributed nature coordination and daily operation relies heavily on advancing IT and telephony technologies, so that we refer to them as virtual projects [6], [16].

Although many professionals and organizations are already practicing virtual projects in their daily routines, they still are regarded as high-risk and are little understood. Especially, there is no a well defined conceptual framework to guide the life cycle management of a virtual project. Most studies on collaboration technology and virtual collaboration are still very much focused on group level collaboration [1], [2], [3], [4], [8], [15], [16].

The objective of this paper is to extend the study towards the strategic and organizational level of virtual projects. We will focus on the analysis of information systems as artifacts that automate coordination of virtual projects. Advancing Internet and information technologies, such as video/audio/data conferencing, group calendar, on-line data repository, voice over IP, instant messaging, and so forth do offer modular functionalities that support the coordination, and daily operation of a virtual project [9], [5], [11], [10], [13]. Our special interest is how various collaboration tools offer different ways of integration, combination and arrangement of a quite standard set of modular functionality and what this tells about the type of project needs the developers had in mind.

The intended contribution of the paper for academic research is the development of a typology of different virtual projects and its empirical validation through an analysis of currently existing project management and collaboration tools. The contribution of the paper for project managers is a benchmarking approach and a benchmarking study of current systems that can serve as guidelines for the selection of such tools.

The remainder of the paper is structured as follows. We will set out with key management processes of a virtual project, break them down into activities and map those onto needed functionality. We will then turn to the overall view of existing tools (COTS) and their functionalities. Based on the identified virtual project management activities, we will continue with recommendations for their selection. We will complete the paper with an outlook on future research directions.

2. Benchmarking Approach for Virtual Project Management Systems

2.1 Virtual Project Management conceptual framework

All projects allocate resources from a network of distributed sites and organizations for limited duration only. We therefore define a project as a temporary management structure that is established to meet defined objectives under the constraint of limited resources [12]. Unlike traditional projects, management of virtual project strongly relies on information technologies for both routine (idea exchange/negotiation, conflict resolving, and decision making) and non-routine tasks (project planning, milestone tracking, and reporting).

If virtual projects are temporary, it is useful to structure their life span in different phases or a life cycle from early inception, establishment, and operation to completion and de-briefing. All routine and non-routine tasks occur randomly across the life cycle of the project, but these can be expected to differ in form and intensity. At the beginning of most of our research projects (take a typical EU project) intensive idea exchange, negotiation, and decision-making are needed to select, coordinate and engage potential partners for proposal writing and tasks allocation. Once the project goes into operation, routine tasks like milestone tracking and reporting get more dominant, unless conflicts occur. The need of information technology support therefore will vary across the life cycle of the project.

But projects normally introduce only one collaborative system during their life span. It does not come as a surprise that despite the insights of several studies showing how IT helps improve collaborative work performance [1], [2], [4], [5], that conventional e-mail and telephone are still the most frequently used media for communication and coordination.

This study starts with the key phases of the virtual project life cycle. Based on identified phases, key operation processes and corresponding management tasks were identified, which could be turned into the specifications of the IT functionalities. In several feedback cycles, we therefore reflected on the management tasks within virtual project as they are seen by vendors of collaborative systems that are available in the market. Success cases about performance increase of supported virtual projects lets assume that a FIT could be reached between the collaborative practices amongst the project partners in the virtual project and implemented software functionality. The approach of the benchmarking study therefore is to select collaboration tools that fit the need of future projects.

To this end we structure the overall life cycle of a virtual project in four broad phases: initiation, configuration, operation and completion. During the initiation phases, the main operation processes is setting up the project consortium. In one case a network community used a web-portal on which associated network partners constantly post new business opportunities. From there a project manager can take on the responsibility of contacting interested members, review their track records, price quotes, and resource availability. Such routine tasks were well supported by the collaboration system, but the non-routine task of the project launch decision was reserved to a physical meeting of all participating members.

At the configuration phase, detailed tasks breakdown, scope definition and tasks assignment are important operation processes. Take the case of a collaborative research project where the project proposal will be jointly be delivered by the members of the project consortium. At this stage, a collaborative document-sharing repository is often introduced, for routine tasks like keeping the different chapters of the proposal document and for general information sharing. Similarly member profiles with cost rates, capacities and contact details are introduced for the routine task of planning and budgeting. Non-routine tasks like idea exchange and joint decision-making often are reserved for face-to-face meetings and conventional telephone conferences. These have rarely been substituted by the existing early versions of low cost web-based audio/video/data conferences.

During the operation phase of the observed virtual projects, even the majority of routine tasks like project planning are currently managed through e-mails. Collaborative systems could increase productivity with status tracking functions and group calendar and automatic e-mail notifying functions. Non-routine tasks like joint work and decision making in most projects is still reserved for face-to-face project meetings and conventional teleconferencing. Occasionally web-based audio/video/data conferencing are being used. Non-routine tasks like resolution of conflicts of interests are still managing through conventional telephone phone calls. The choice of the right communication channel emerges as an important issue, which often decides over the amount of time needed to clarify issues and re-solve conflicts, especially when more than two members were involved.

Finally, at the completion phase, all the project documents, reports and deliverables will be stored within an archive data base for future referencing, which generally speaking is a forgotten functionality, both in technical systems and organizational routines.

Occasionally, knowledge management approaches are applied to capture project results and project learning for usage in other parts of the organisation or in later projects.

Table 1 summarizes the conceptual framework with the four main life cycle phases in the first column, key operation processes in the second column, and management tasks in the third column. Column four lists typical support tools.

Table1: Conceptual Framework for Virutal Project Management

Level I	**Level II**	**Level III**	**Support Tool**
Life Cycle	**Key Process**	**Management Task**	
Initiation	Acquisition	Checking the available tendering opportunities over the Internet	Customer contact / information database Central document repository Dedicated customer web-links web page
		Making initial contact with the funding bodies via e-mail or telephone	
	Customer requirement	Downloading the relevant tendering documents	
		Attending the tendering public information meetings	
	Network Information exchange / Feasibility Check	Posting information on the collaboration web portal	Public information web page Discussion thread Audio / video/ data conference equipments Partner contact/information/competence database E-mail / fax / telephone
		Creating topics discussion threads	
		Making virtual conference meetings or teleconferences	
		Log into the collaboration platform and checking the partner competences and availabilities	
	Partner selection	Making contact with the potential interested partners	
		Organising virtual meetings and Teleconference with the invited partners	

		Finalised partners based on competence, availability, and price	
Configur-ation	Task creation	Creating a dedicate collaboration project web-space , and assigns login and password	Group workspace (with the ability to allocate access permission, creating subfolders, uploading and downloading documents) Audio / video/ data conference equipments Working templates (proposal, task distribution) Public information web page Partner contact/information/competence database E-mail / fax / telephone
		Creating proposal template, and make it available on the Collaboration project web space	
		Organising virtual or teleconference meeting to brainstorm on the proposal ideas	
		Planning work packages and deliverables	
		Distributing the writing tasks via e-mail or posting on the collaboration web space	
	Task break down	Proposal writing partners post their contributions on the collaboration web space	
		Other partners cross check the contributions	
	Task allocation	Full partners meetings, and assign men months and responsibilities to each tasks	
	Contract and negotiation	Submitting the proposal via post or tendering web space	
		After acceptance of proposal, attending the budget negotiation meeting	
Operation	Project planning	Creating work packages and tasks subfolders in the project collaboration web-space, and assign responsibilities	Group calendar Group Voting Project planning (with milestone, delivery date, reviewing point) Status tracking Working templates (report , meeting minutes, review) Audio / video/ data conference equipments Partner contact/information/competence database E-mail / fax / telephone
		Making the timeline and milestone visible to the partners	
	Project status tracking	Regular virtual meeting and teleconference for status reporting	
		Checking the web-portal for availabilities of the deliverables	
	Project reporting	Posting the deliverables onto the dedicated work package folders	
	Conflict Management and task re-allocation	Making additional virtual/telephone conference	
		Organising project consortium voting meeting for decision making and reallocation of the tasks	
Complet-ion	Documentation/knowledge management	Archiving the deliverables and relevant project reports and documents	Achieve database
		Close the collaboration project web-space	

2.2 Diffusion / Usage of Information Technology in Virtual Project Management

The functionality of collaboration tools is made up of a fairly concise list of modules that is listed in figure 1. Information technology is used for the three purposes, to collapse time and space effects in collaboration, to substitute generalized for highly specific tasks and processes, and to capture and use organisational memory [14]. In conjunction with the wide spread of fast network connection, enhanced workstation speed & software, and distributed database, information technologies have been adopted by many of today's competitive organisations, either for improving the operation efficiency, facilitating the project coordination and control or gaining the strategic advantages.

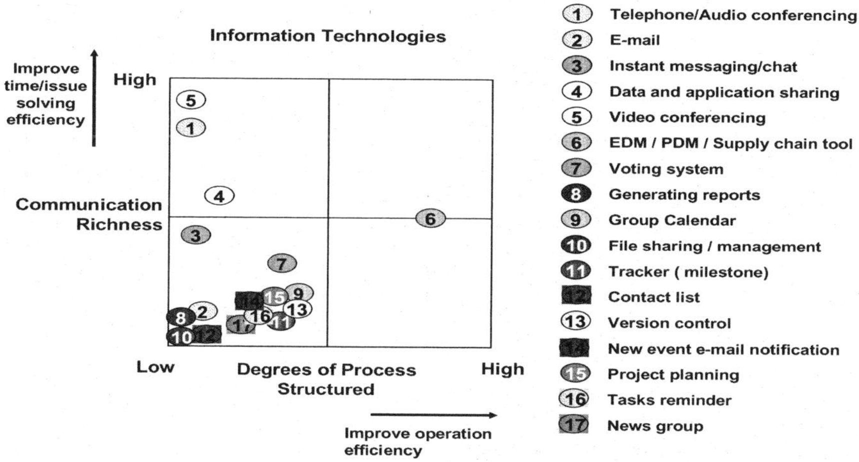

Figure 1: Information Technologies Position Matrix

In Lengel's and Daft's [7] study on selection of communication media, most of the reported high performing executives use high media richness (face-to-face, telephone, electronic media) for non-routine activities, while low media richness (computer reports, e-mail) for routine activities. Therefore, based on above findings, the existing information technologies can be positioned according to its communication richness and degrees of process structured as shown in Figure 1.

3. Key Benchmarking Results

The so far presented framework was developed for a benchmark study of the state-of-the-art collaborative systems especially offered for virtual project management. An Internet based search was undertaken with the key words "virtual collaboration tool", "project management tool", "groupware", and "distribute work management tool".

3.1 Key findings from the benchmarking study

We found a total of 26 commercialised products from which 23 design descriptions gave input to the development of the benchmarking framework. The detailed functionalities of each tool are available under http://www.ve-forum.de/Kooperationstools. Figure 2 gives an overall view of all the different functionalities offered by the 26 reported products.

There were three key findings from the benchmarking study undertaken.

First, functionality converges for all virtual project management tools as it becomes a modular technology. We expect this trend to continue with the increased availability of web services. For tool vendors, it is a competitive need to offer the full range of the identified functionality. Most functionality is of general purpose nature, such as calendaring, emailing, of document sharing. But simple standard project management routines such as group calendar, status tracker and project planning are available in most of the virtual project management tools. We expect this list of general functionality to extend quickly with a maturing project management tool market.

Functionality	Tools																											
	MainsGate	Flypaper Enterprise	TeamSpace (Flypaper)	eRoom Collaboration	Webplan 7	GROOVE WORKSPACE	PHProjekt	TWIG	phpBB	TUTOS	Teamware Pl@za® 3.5	Teamware Office™	Team Crossing 3.0	VCOM	Flash Com. Server MX 1.5	IBM LOTUS Workplace	IBM LOTUS Team	CeTIM CMS	Zeno 2.0	Webcorp	Microsoft SharePoint	IBM Lotus	Web Crossing 4.1	SiteScape Enterprise	eProject	onProject	ePeople	BSCW 4.1
1	√	√		√	√		√																					
2	√	√	√	√	√	√	√			√	√	√	√	√	√	√	√	√	√	√	√	√	√	√	√	√	√	√
3		√		√		√	√			√		√																
4	√	√				√	√	√		√			√			√												
5	√	√	√				√			√			√				√			√								√
6	√	√	√	√			√		√		√	√	√				√	√	√	√	√	√	√	√	√	√	√	√
7	√	√	√	√		√	√			√		√					√	√		√		√	√	√	√	√		√
8		√		√			√			√			√								√				√		√	
9		√				√	√	√		√		√	√			√					√		√				√	
10							√		√	√																		
11							√																					
12							√	√					√															
13			√				√	√																				
14		√					√																					
15		√		√			√		√		√						√	√	√	√	√	√	√	√			√	√
16	√	√	√			√	√				√						√											
17		√				√			√		√																	
18		√				√					√																	
19		√																										
20	√	√				√	√		√	√	√		√		√													
21		√		√			√			√	√		√															
22	√	√		√	√	√	√	√								√												
23		√											√															
24			√										√															
25								√																				
26		√	√								√				√	√	√											
27		√	√			√	√		√		√			√		√	√	√			√	√	√	√			√	
28			√											√			√	√			√	√		√			√	

1. Generating reports
2. File sharing / Management
3. Version Control
4. Contact list
5. Tracker (milestone)
6. Discussion Forum/group
7. Group Calendar
8. Voting system
9. e-mail
10. Multiple Languages Interface
11. Time card system
12. Bookmarks
13. Todo list
14. Tasks Reminder
15. Search system
16. Ability for integration to other system
17. Personalised profile
18. Survey and feedback
19. Access level based on role
20. Access Control/Security
21. New events e-mail notification
22. Project planning
23. Create and manage announcements
24. Post team announcements
25. News Group
26. Web Conferencing
27. Instant messaging /chat
28. Audio conferencing

Figure 2: Tool Functionality

Second, tools differentiate in the way they integrate and combine the standard functionality into operational and decision making processes. In most cases these processes are not explicitly stated or document (like it is often done with processes in ERP systems).

We therefore had to reflect on the implicit assumption about project processes and project organization for which they were built. Distinct types of projects and supporting tools emerge for example from the structure of the network as a peer-to-peer group of researchers, a hub-and-spoke network of a main contractor or a supply chain configuration with respective coordination needs. Project managers, who need to select a collaborative system, can use the network typology to select tools that best fit their project needs.

The VE-Forum Portal gives a more detailed list of concrete selection criteria (www.ve-forum.org/kooperationstools) with a mapping of 26 market available collaborative systems.

Third, Figure 1 shows that virtual technologies still mostly cover the lower left corner of the matrix for well structured process that require low media richness. The upper right corner of virtual team collaboration that is typical for knowledge workers or professionals remains much less developed.

4. Conclusion

This study shows that technology for virtual projects has matured to the breakpoint point where collaborative systems will become a serious business technology. For tool vendors this can result in increasing markets, if the current fragmentation can be overcome.

With decreasing differences between the available tools, project management routines and the organizational capability to manage virtual projects are key to successful collaboration in a virtual/distributed environments. It is clear that the challenge is to master the organisational and business issues rather than simply purchase yet more software.

References

[1] Benson-Armer, R. and T. Hsieh, Team work across time and space, Mckinsey Quarterly (4),1997.
[2] Bubshait, A. A. and G. Farooq, Team building and project success, Cost Engineering, (4), 1999, pp. 34-38.
[3] DeSanctis, G. and R. B. Gallupe, A foundation for the study of group decision support system, Management Science, 33(5), 1987, pp. 589-609.
[4] Iles, P. and P. K. Hayers, Managing diversity in transnational project teams, A tentative model and case study." Journal of Managerial Psychology 12(2), 1997, pp. 95-117.
[5] Jarvenpaa, S. L. and D. Leidner, Communication and trust in global virtual teams, Organization Science 10, 1999, pp. 791-815.
[6] Katzy, B., R. Evaristo, et al.,Knowledge Management in Virtual Projects.A Research Agenda,1999.
[7] Lengel, R. H. and R. L. Daft, The selection of Communication Media as an Excutive Skill, The Academy of Management, 11(3), 1988, pp. 225-232.
[8] Nunamaker, J. F., A. R. Dennis, et al., Electronic meeting systems to support group work, Communications of the ACM 34(7), 1991.
[9] Poole, M. S., An information-task approach to organisational communication, Academy of Management Review 3(3), 1978, pp. 493-504.
[10] Rasters, G., G. Vissers, et al., An inside look rich communication through lean media in a virtual research team, Small group research 33(6), 2002, pp.718-754.
[11] Rickards, T. and S. Moger., Creative leadership processes in project team development: An alternative to Tuckman's stage model, British Academic of Management 11, 2000, pp. 273-283.
[12] Shenhar, A. J., From theory to practice: Toward a typology of project-management styles, IEEE Transactions on Engineering Management 45(1), 1998, pp. 33-48.
[13] Watson Fritz, M. B., S. Narasimhan, et al., Communication and Coordination in the Virtual Office, 1998.
[14] Yates, J. and R. I. Benjamin, The past and present as a window on the future. The corporation of the 1990s, S. Morton, Oxford University press, 1991.
[15] Zigurs, I. and B. K. Buckland, A Theory of Task/ Technology fit and group support systems effectiveness, MIS Quarterly, 1998, pp. 313-334.
[16] Zigurs, I., J. Evaristo, et al., Collaboration Technologies for Virtual Project Management, Academy of Management, 2001.

Fostering Innovation in Extended Enterprises

Mikel SORLI[1], Dragan STOKIC[2], Álvaro GOROSTIZA[1], Ana CORREIA[2], Ana CAMPOS[2]
[1]Labein, Cta. de Olabeaga 16, 48013 Bilbao, Spain
Tel: +34 94 4892400, Fax: + 34 94 4892460, Email: sorli@labein.es
[2]ATB, Wiener Strasse 1, 28359 Bremen, Germany
Tel: +49 421 2209240, Fax: + 49 421 2209210, Email: dragan@atb-bremen.de

Abstract: The goal of the IMS AIM (Acceleration of Innovative Ideas into the Market) project is to develop a system managing the innovation process by supporting the collection of innovative ideas and relevant knowledge throughout the extended enterprise for new and existing process and product development. The AIM system supports the development of these ideas and knowledge into a means of fostering industrial innovations. AIM intends to optimise the innovation process in an industrial company by a combination of advanced methods for generating innovative ideas with "classical" methods for collection of knowledge on products/processes and their problems. The AIM system includes specific ontologies and WorkFlow tool needed to enable efficient exchange of ideas/knowledge between different experts/actors within the Extended Enterprise. In particular, the paper presents findings and achievements of the project up to date, including results of the validation by the industrial End-users enrolled in the AIM Consortium.

1. Introduction

In current Global Markets, it is generally assumed that one of the most critical factors for success in industrial firms is Innovation. Innovation is important for all companies, and just as important is the need to get innovative products to the market place quickly. People inside and outside the physical boundaries of the industrial organisation are an untapped resource for innovative ideas and knowledge.

This paper introduces the IST/IMS project AIM with the goal of fostering industrial innovations throughout the extended enterprise for new and existing process and products by supporting the collection of Corporate Knowledge and Innovative Ideas. These ideas and knowledge are later developed supporting industrial innovations. Such system provides a means to collect, store and use/develop innovative ideas over the extended enterprise, and it will "accelerate" innovation into the market. In addition, Team Work is enhanced by co-operation among manufacturers, customers and suppliers by means of the Internet facilities provided by the AIM System. The AIM system is described, focusing on the module for the assessment of ideas collected throughout the extended enterprise. In addition, the paper describes one of the technologies used to support this assessment, Case-Based Reasoning.

2. Business Cases

The project is based on three business cases, one from each end-user. These business cases are focused on innovations for product and process developments. The business cases will therefore use the AIM system in different ways, e.g. while some business cases are oriented to directly collect innovative ideas and knowledge, in some the motivation for collection of ideas is realised via identification of problems/potential improvements asking for innovative ideas. This will enable to develop and test the AIM system for different scenarios, ensuring its general applicability.

The first Business Case is focused on rapid product innovation in an SME by involving all actors, including field engineers working with customers to generate product ideas. This business case will focus on providing a structured and rapid approach to product innovation, so that the time to market is reduced. This is extremely important for most companies, particularly SMEs that have to produce innovative products for the marketplace, and where it is essential to have a minimal time to market.

The second Business Case is focused on process innovation in multiple manufacturing sites based on the identified problems and potential improvements. The end-user is a large multiple site company producing high volume products. Currently, many innovative ideas from employees are not used since there is no system to collect such ideas, assess them and deliver them to process designers. In order to collect information on problems in production, for which innovative ideas are needed, the integration and expansion of the IT-Systems implemented in production will be applied. The special challenge of this business case is that it will address manufacturing process distributed over multiple sites. Several sites will be involved in this business case. The goal is to collect problems/potential improvements and innovative ideas from these multiple site manufacturing plants, i.e. to provide means to put together ideas from actors in different plants. The teamwork on developing the ideas across the multiple sites will be supported by the AIM system as well.

The third Business Case is focused on procut and process innovations in a medium size company targeting industry, and strongly oriented towards sales, service, marketing and after-market. The company is working closely with their suppliers/partners. Therefore, a system for collecting innovative ideas from both employees and suppliers is an urgent need. The business case scenario will involve collection of ideas internally and at supplier sites. Specifically the benefits from collecting ideas at supplier site could be high, taking into account a high interest of suppliers to provide ideas to improve services with their products.

3. System Concept

AIM system includes methods and tools (modules) for collecting innovative ideas and knowledge on products/processes. The system also contemplates another important source of innovative knowledge coming from problems and potential improvements. The system also supports assessment on these innovative ideas and helps to manage them in order to provide the best way of using them for innovative product and process designs. These ideas and knowledge will later be developed into a means of fostering industrial innovations. It will enable organisational learning by providing means to collect, store and use/develop innovative ideas over the extended enterprise.

Main RTD challenges faced along it contemplate basically the combination of advanced methods for generating innovative ideas with "classical" methods for collection of knowledge on products/processes and their problems. It also includes the development of specific ontologies needed to enable efficient exchange of ideas between different experts/actors within an extended enterprise. The AIM system comprehends several modules, as presented in Figure 1.

- Innovation Repository: This repository classifies ideas by using an 'innovation' meta classification, and will store them for rapid access. The overall meta classification of the ideas and innovations will be defined as a basis for all AIM modules. The problem is how to enable appropriate classification for different specific products and processes, as well as within a specific company concept. This will include knowledge on products/processes, problems/potential improvements, (innovative) ideas and innovations.

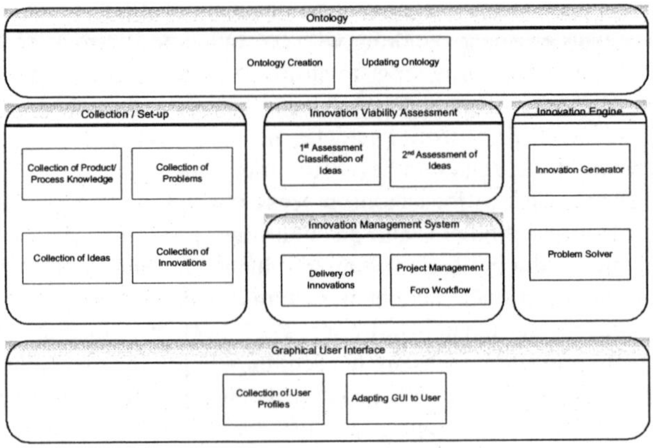

Figure 1: AIM System

- Collection of innovative ideas and product/process knowledge: This module is based on combination of 'classical' approaches/commercial tools together with new developments required to provide means to efficiently collect innovative ideas, but also to collect knowledge on product and process problems for which the innovative ideas are needed. This module includes an appropriate user interface to introduce ideas and knowledge on products/process and about the identified problems.
- Innovation Engine: This is a collection of methods oriented to finding innovative solutions following a systematic methodology. This facility provides a structured means for the development of ideas into innovation concepts, by sharing and working on these ideas in a structured framework. The ideas collected within previous module and stored in the repository will be further developed. The specific requirement is to provide robust solutions to be applied in the industrial environment. TRIZ methodology serves as a baseline approach for this module, where the in-depth analysis of technical requirements and manufacturing failure situations is performed, structured knowledge is delivered, and graphical aids for team working and creation of Concepts are provided.
- Innovation Viability Assessment: This facility provides a structure (based on rapid consulting within the company of evaluation of developments and risks, combined with a multi-criteria decision support) to assist users in assessing the feasibility of new ideas at the collection stage, and innovation assessment facilities for design teams. It is important to focus on feasible, good innovative knowledge, and develop this.
- Innovation Management System: This is a means of providing an efficient way for planning and monitoring the use of the innovation knowledge during design activities and a structured delivery of the innovations/ideas to the process and product Design Teams. This module will assist graphically the work of the Design Teams in designing new process and products in the companies.

This architecture has been finally deployed following a multi-level architecture based on Internet technologies. Integration with other tools inside each enterprise is carefully being studied and adapted to specific needs. Here the Innovation Viability Assessment module will be explained in more detail.

The Innovation Viability Assessment is the AIM module oriented to assist users in assessing the feasibility of new innovative ideas, developing them into concepts. Innovations that cannot be turned into reality, for technical, commercial or socio-economic benefits are of little use. The assessment is realised in two distinct steps, both supported by the AIM system (see Figure 2).

The First Assessment consists of a rough classification, identifying the type of the "Ideas" collected throughout the extended enterprise, classifying them according to a scheme defined by each user during the set-up phase of the system (e.g. improvement to product/process, cause for problems identified, new product/process etc.).

The Second Assessment comprehends a detailed study of the new "Concept" developed before implementation. This assessment is based on strategic policy, including: technical viability, implementation cost, materials to be used, equipment, profit expected, corporate efforts, Return on Investment etc.

This module is nurtured by the Innovation Repository where all ideas proposed are stored. The ideas collected must be related to the problem or product/process that intends to improve, or to other Ideas to which they are related. Later, these ideas are filtered focusing on commercial or socio-economic interest, possibilities for turning them into reality.

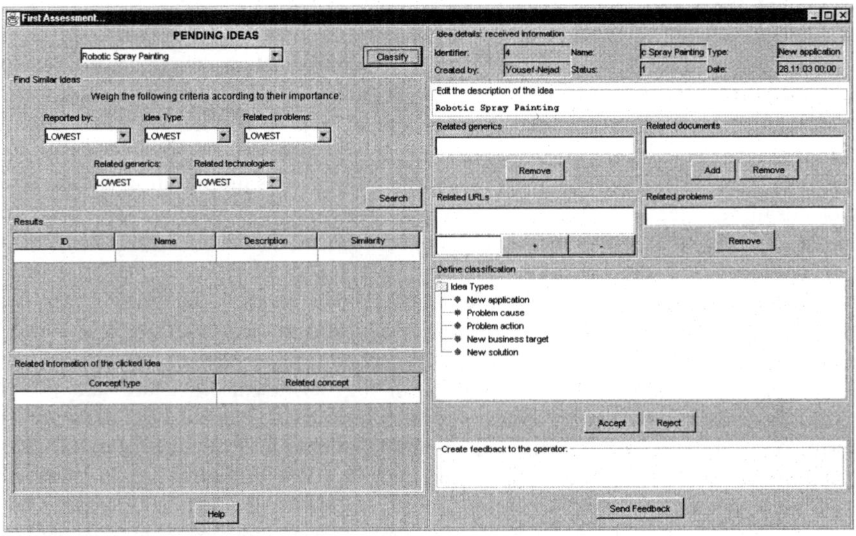

Figure 2: Assessment Screen Example

4. Technology and System Concept

The main asset of the AIM System is to provide means of efficient delivering Corporate Knowledge and Ideas (by integrating a WorkFlow Tool), collected throughout the extended enterprise (by offering web-based applications to customers, clients etc.) and stored in a structured repository. Therefore, the information and collective knowledge have to be structured in such a way that it is easy to access and re-use.

The AIM System combines existing tools and technologies in an innovative way, in order to fulfil the stated objectives. AIM fosters creativity by combining classical reasoning methods, Case-Based Reasoning (CBR) and Rule-Based Reasoning (RBR), which focus on the Company's Business Objectives with an innovation supporting method, Theory for Inventive Problem Solving (TRIZ), and graphical aids for combination of concepts, within the context of specific products/processes, formalised by the use of continuously adapted ontologies. Although the main technologies mentioned are available in the market, the results of the analysis of the state-of-the-art conclude that methods and tools for capturing and structuring knowledge and innovative ideas, over extended enterprise, in a way that enables product/process innovative practical means are missing.

CBR, for example, is used in three different modules of the AIM System: Collection, Innovation Viability Assessment and Innovation Engine. Therefore, the functionality of

CBR has to be flexible and adjustable to fulfil the functionality in the different modules. CBR is used to search similar problems and/or ideas. For each of these entities, cases have to be built, with the information that will be considered to evaluate similarity. The functionality will be used for problems, to identify the respective causes, and in ideas to support an effective collection of knowledge and appropriate assessment. One of the main challenges of the AIM project is the great variety of problems, ideas or situations the system should be able to deal with. In many CBR applications, the domain is bounded in the sense that all influencing conditions (attributes) and their ranges are known and it is assumed that all occurring ideas/problems could be described by these conditions. This assumption may not hold in AIM. The system may not need only to learn possible problem/idea situations and their causes but also to learn possible descriptions of problems or ideas. For this reason, the common structure of cases has to be more generic than in conventional CBR systems.

In conventional CBR systems, the description of a problem or idea (case) is given in a "flat" table. When information has to be entered into the structure, where no attributes are defined, the structure needs to be extended. The problem in AIM is that it is not known in advance which information is accessible in case of a problem or idea and how it is structured. Therefore, a more generic approach is also considered, based on object-oriented Design. The generic structure assumes that every case occurs during an operation which takes one or more objects as input, provides one or more objects as output and is performed by one or more objects as operators (human operator, machines etc.). In one case, all the objects could be instantiated as often as needed to describe the current situation. For both operations and objects, different conditions could hold. Neither the type of significant conditions nor its value is known in advance. Therefore, these conditions could also be instantiated by objects and operations as often as needed.

The simple structure described seems to be sufficient to store all possible problems/ideas, but it is being further elaborated and refined. In classical flat structures, the similarity between cases is computed via similarity functions, attribute by attribute, and a weighted mean value over all outcomes of the functions. The difficulty lies in determining the similarity functions and the weights for the mean value. Another problem arises especially in the selected object-oriented approach because cases do not only differ in the value of their attributes but also in the existence of attributes.

Similarity of ideas is based on five fields of information: Idea Type, User who reported the Idea, Involved Generics (processes, products and tools), Involved Problems, and Involved Technologies. Similarity of Problems is based on the following information: Generics involved in the problem (processes, products and tools), and Actual State Items defined for the problem (values). When two ideas/problems are analysed to ascertain their similarity, each of the fields is compared to check if the respective information is the same in both cases. The comparison of each field provides a result (in percentage), which is afterwards computed in a total percentage, representing the similarity of the two ideas/problems. CBR considers that an undefined value is more similar to a defined value, than two different defined values. The several parameters that constitute the similarity criteria of each entity can be adjusted by the user, each time CBR is used to obtain similar ideas/problems. This allows the users to perform a more flexible search, and obtaining appropriate results. The priority given to each field is a value within Ignore, Lowest, Below Normal, Normal, Above Normal and Highest (see an example of Interface for this search in the AIM System, in Figure 3). Furthermore, it is possible to filter ideas on the similarity comparison by selecting specific status that should be ignored (e.g. the user can choose to ignore in the analysis all the ideas marked as Invalid).

AIM uses the tool ReCall from ISoft for the implementation of the CBR module. This decision was based on the analysis of the existing market available tools for CBR, and on laboratory tests carried applying this tool, which provided positive results.

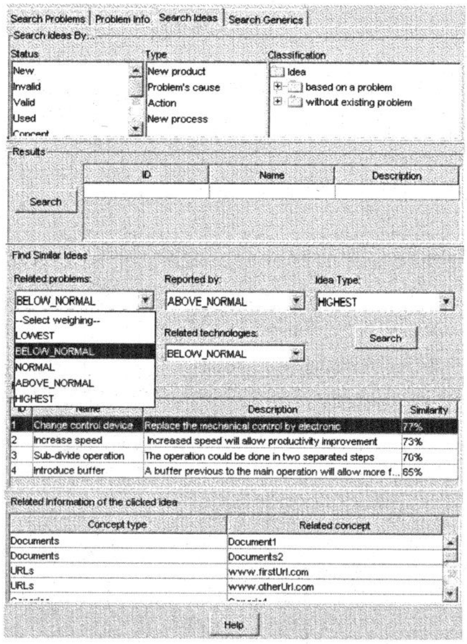

Figure 3: Searching Ideas Screen Example

5. Results

An early prototype of the AIM system has been developed and tested in the three business cases described. The Project is currently realising integration tasks of the modules already developed, so new results and feedback from the utilisation by the end-users of the integrated system are expected.

Related to the use of the CBR for efficient search of ideas and problems, through the Innovation Repository of the AIM System, the results from the tests performed indicated improvements needed. To test the developed CBR functionality, in Business Case 2 several problems occurred in the manufacturing processes were stored, as well as ideas, providing the system the necessary information to reason. CBR uses information from problems stored in the system to provide the results. For Business Case 2 the rather flat case structure is designed and filled with cases. The weighting for attributes has been specifically defined for each problem type. The same information was also filled in the generic structure. The objective was to prove that the generic structure does not yield a loss of accuracy. The list of problems from production was used to test the CBR module. An example of problems for one of the business cases is provided in Table 1. The problems were structured both in a specific structure and in a generic structure in order to enable a comparison of appropriateness of these two structures. The tests performed considered ca. 350 problems. The results obtained are sets of cases with a high similarity. When the specific structure is applied, CBR identifies the reasons of problems in more than 90 % correctly (even with incomplete information) and the similarity achieved in the range of 75-99%. In the case of the generic structure, the identified problem causes are correct in more than 88%, while similarity is between 83-99%. This indicates that the proposed generic structure is appropriate for the cases and that CBR approach is likely to efficiently solve more than

80% of problems in the companies (a conservative estimate, taking into account that the considered cases are very typical for the companies).

Table 1: Problems/Ideas

Error	Process Step	Product Part	State Items	Cause	Idea/Action
Broken can V-Crash	WIM, Coater, Decorator	Bottom of the can	manual check, where the damaged bottom is identified (no available measurement of the air pressure of the machines)	Coater/WIM too high Base deformed	WIM/Coater control/reduce
Falt Batwings/Line fold	used tinplate (supplier process)	tinplate	tinplate strengths; (problems with) the coil in the front end (cupper/wim)	Soft metal plate	Increase lubrication impulse Sedimentation in the plate
Falt Line fold	IBO	inside lacquer	visual inspection-> bubbles in the inside lacquer; temperature inside oven too high?	Temperature (inside oven) inner lacquerer	

6. Business Benefits

As a result of the tests performed, the following business benefits are registered.

The essential benefits expected within Business Case 1 were to increase the number of innovative suggestions on products from customers and suppliers by a structured link via Internet (50% achieved, 60% with large suppliers and customers), increase the number of innovative ideas on products from employees (field engineers), improving it by means of easy to use facilities (around 60% achieved up to now), establish a classification scheme for product/process knowledge to be used for further development, to increase the number of implemented innovation/new concepts of offers to customers (a 30% improvement achieved but it is expected to increase), to have a managed way of developing ideas into new practical concepts, shorten the time needed for collecting and implementation of new ideas, to reduce time and efforts for solving product problems (20% improvement achieved up to now but expected to increase).

The essential benefits expected within Business Case 2 were to establish a classification scheme for problems, problem causes and ideas and innovations to remove these causes and so improve the production process in the shop floor, to collect the Corporate Knowledge from the company and record and classify ideas, to shorten the time needed for collecting and implementation of new ideas in the manufacturing process, to reduce wastes and costs associated with problems, and support customers to reduce time and efforts for solving product/process problems (a 15% improvement was achieved up to now). This business case also expects to gain benefits from the focus given upon innovation in multiple sites manufacturing process based on the identified problems and in this way improve potential to foster the innovation process based on the experience.

The essential benefits expected within Business Case 3 were to set some goals in terms of expected benefits for their company. They are to increase the number of innovative ideas on products from employees and suppliers, improving it by means of easy to use facilities (50% achieved up to now), to increase the number of implemented innovation/new concepts of offers to customers (30% already achieved but more is expected), establishment of a classification scheme and IT based collection and evaluation for the problems, problem causes and ideas and innovations to remove these causes and to have a managed way of developing ideas into new practical concepts. Furthermore, benefits in a more general note can be expected. Among others they are to collect the Corporate Knowledge from the company, shorten the time needed for collecting and implementation of new ideas in the business process, reduce wastes and costs associated with problems, and supporting customers and to have a structure to record and classify ideas.

7. Conclusions

The overall objective of the AIM project is twofold: increasing innovation and accelerating its introduction to the Market. This paper presents the approach developed in the project to fulfil this objective.

After the preliminary assessment of the benefits expected and already achieved, the three business cases are unanimous in presenting positive results. One of the common benefits expected is the reduction of time and efforts for solving product/process problems which already has achieved an improvement of 20% (15% in business case 2) but all expect to further improve this value. Other specific achievements expected out of the full implementation of the AIM system are the development of means of stimulating the creation of innovative ideas and collecting them from people at the extended enterprise level involved with the products and processes, the development of ways of processing these ideas and storing them into a structured knowledge repository (to ensure that all the useful knowledge, innovative information, is saved), the development of means of analysing innovative knowledge to determine which is useful, and which is not (to enable the viability of ideas to be assessed) and the development of means of delivering the innovative ideas to product and process designers for maximum effect. The changes on the companies to reach these specific achievements are still ongoing and can not still provide specific numbers on the overall improvement of the company, the assessment so far has shown signals of positive results. This should lead to important business benefits on the fields of reduction of product innovation cycle-time (by at least 30%) and the improvement of process efficiency (by at least 15%) and reduction of wastes (by 12%).

In the future, it is planned to finish integration with legacy systems, continue with industrial testing and make respective measurements to have a full system assessment.

References

[1] AIM -- IST-2001-52222: Acceleration of Innovative ideas to Market.

[2] A. Blake, D. Mann, Making Knowledge Tangible. CMC and DuVersity, 2000.

[3] Knoblock, S. Minton, J. Ambite, N. Ashish, P. Modi, I. Muslea, A. Philpot, S. Tejada, Modeling Web Sources for Information Integration. In: Fifteenth National Conference on Artificial Intelligence (AAAI98), Madison, WI, 1998.

[4] V. Kohnhauser, Use of TRIZ in the Development Process. In: Triz Journal, 1999.

[5] Levy, A. Rajaraman, K. Ordille, Querying Heterogeneous Information Sources Using Source Descriptions. In: Proceedings of the 22nd VLDB Conference, 1996.

[6] M. Uschold, M. Gruninger, Ontologies: Principles, Methods and Applications. In: Knowledge Engineering Review, 11(2), 1996.

[7] R.J. Brachman, J.G. Schmolze, An Overview of the KL-ONE Knowledge Representation System. In: Cognitive Science, 9(2), 1985, pp. 171-216.

[8] M. Sawaguchi, Study of Effective New Product Development Activities trough Combination of Patterns of Evolution of Technological Systems and VE. 2001.

[9] M. Sorli, D. Stokic, A. Campos, A. Gorostiza, Accelerating Innovation in Practice in New Product Design. In: Proceedings of IEP Porto 2003 Conference (Portugal).

[10] M. Sorli, D. Stokic, A. Campos, A. Gorostiza, Acceleration of Innovative Ideas to Market. In: Proceedings of IMS Conference, 2004, Como (Italy).

[11] D. Stokic, M. Sorli, A. Campos, A. Gorostiza, KM System to support Incremental Innovation in Manufacturing Industry. In: Proceedings of CE Conference, 2003.

[12] A. Zlotin, A. Zusman: Managing Innovation Knowledge, 1999.

Virtual Integrated Design in an Intranet Environment

Zenobia WEISS[1], Jacek DIAKUN[2]
Poznan University of Technology, Piotrowo 3, Poznan 60-965, Poland
[1] *Tel: +48 61665 27 74, Fax: +48 61665 27 74, Email: zenobia.weiss@put.poznan.pl*
[2] *Tel: +48 61665 27 31, Fax: +48 61665 27 74, Email: jacek.diakun@put.poznan.pl*

Abstract: This paper presents an overview of the implementation of a product lifecycle management process within the academic environment of the VIDA Centre at Poznań University of Technology. The characteristics of modern manufacturing influencing this activity are outlined, as well as the scope of research included in the process, the assumed levels of integration, the requirements of a common collaboration platform and the processes involved in the early phase implementation of a selected solution for a design example. Finally, the general experiences and future plans in relation to a presented design environment are highlighted.

1. Introduction

The increasing impact of IT technologies in design and manufacturing areas, at all stages of the product lifecycle, is considerable. Recently, there has been a tendency to create virtual product models which are processed during the individual design stages until a product is achieved that fulfils the customer's requirements. In the case of work being carried out in different locations, work on a common project may lead to the creation of a virtual design team and, in consequence, the creation of a virtual design environment. This kind of activity requires a platform of collaboration involving both hardware (various kinds of computer networks mainly) and software. In the case of engineering design, an implemented collaboration platform, apart from ensuring such functions as data transfer, should also reflect the structure of the design team, the roles played by its members, and the characteristics of the design processes (for example, the functions involved in approving or rejecting documents or project stages).

The requirements of producers (on a legislative or economical basis) means that all product lifecycle stages (Figure 1) are managed. Not only are production and utilisation considered in the early phases of product design, but service and recycling are also taken into account.

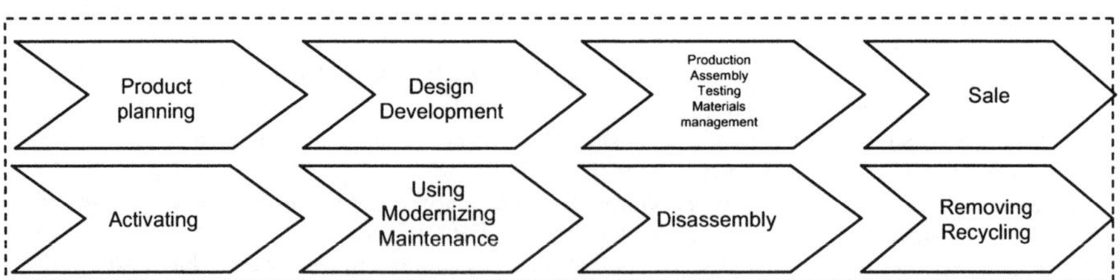

Figure 1: Product lifecycle [1]

The above trend influences the structure of an engineer's task – in the course of time more and more time can be spent on documenting and communication, mainly at the cost of the creative work (Figure 2).

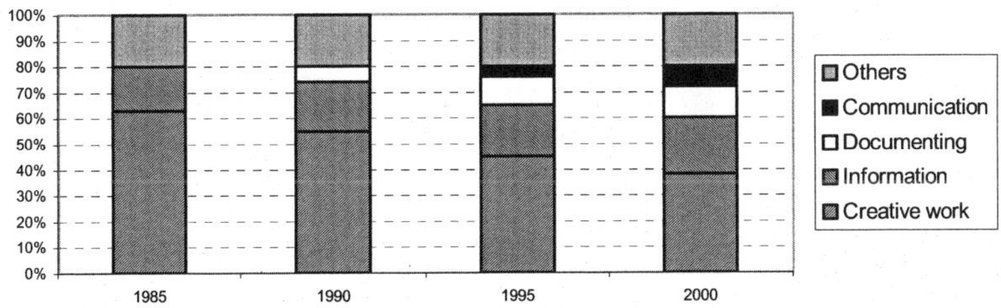

Figure 2: Changes in an engineer's task structure in the course of time [2]

The above trend should also be, in the opinion of the authors, reflected in the academic area and this paper presents the attempt to implement the product lifecycle idea within the academic environment of the VIDA Centre at Poznań University of Technology.

2. Virtual Design Environment of VIDA Centre

2.1 Objectives

Poland's access to the European Union raises a substantial challenge both for the scientific community and manufacturing companies. A key factor for high level achievement within the extended EU structure will be the ability to achieve and maintain current and future EU standards. One of these standards is the tendency to move design and manufacturing into virtual space and to create virtual design teams. The Virtual Design and Automation Centre VIDA [3] was created at Poznan University of Technology (Figure 3) supports this goal.

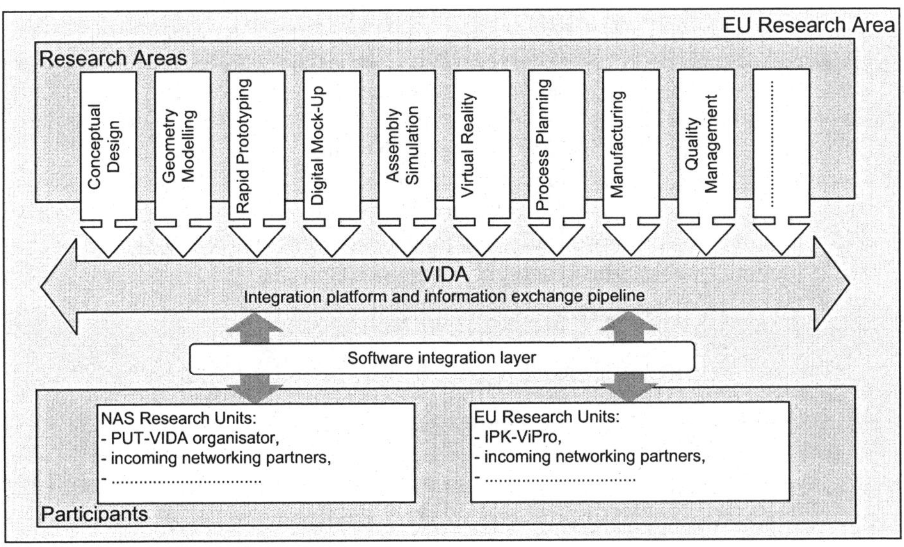

Figure 3: The role of the VIDA Centre as the integration platform for the Project [4]

2.2 Scope of Research

Units working within the framework of VIDA were previously involved in research which was related to particular stages of product lifecycle. However, these activities took place in various units of the Faculty. The scope of research encompassed the following areas:

- geometrical modelling,
- dynamical modelling of machine parts,

- concept studies in drive and units design
- Rapid Prototyping techniques,
- assembly design,
- manufacturing simulation, planning and control,
- quality management.

The reason for the dispersion was the lack of a common integration layer, both from an organizational and from a technical point of view. Particular units operated in a highly independent manner.

2.3 Levels of Integration

The creation of a virtual team may be perceived from various points of view. During the process of establishing the presented design environment it was assumed that the integration process would proceed on four levels:

- organizational, consisting of the structure of particular teams within the sphere of development project: their members (designers) and the roles played by individuals during the design process,
- data, based on a choice of document (file) format which is suitable for all participants,
- tools, seen as a common collaboration platform (tools and methods for collaboration),
- methods of product development, according to standard guidelines, eg. VDI-Richtlinen or Lemach.

2.4 Requirements for Collaboration Platform

In order to establish the virtual design team in the VIDA Centre there was a requirement for the implementation of a common collaboration platform. At the beginning of the selection process several assumptions were made, taking into consideration: (i) the broad scope of the research areas, (ii) the various computer tools and systems already used by teams, which include either commercial systems (CAD, CAD/CAM, CAE, etc.) or self-developed systems within the framework of particular research team tool requirements, and (iii) the dynamic structure of the design team. It was decided that the collaboration platform should:

- enable the organization of a team working within the framework of a particular project,
- reflect the structure of an organization (teams and their members),
- enable the simultaneous execution of different projects,
- reflect the roles of particular members within a team and project (e.g. designer, approver, etc.),
- reflect the characteristics of design information systems (i.e. approval or rejection of documents or project stages),
- aid in the utilisation of documents of different kinds and formats,
- use already existing IT infrastructures (Intranet),
- encourage the speedy implementation of project work within the system,
- organize data access and documents management in relation to the project,
- manage workflows,
- reflect the methods of particular team members (work within the established environment should be as close as possible to the already existing methods and tools),
- ensure the mechanism for data classification and search,
- deliver common services of data transfer between design stands.

2.5 IT Tools Supporting Design in Virtual Environment

During product design in the virtual environment, various IT tools and systems are used, and any number of applications may be utilised in supporting cooperative work and creating a collaboration platform for the establishment of a virtual team. The solutions consist of two main groups:

- commercial systems and tools [5], such as: Internet/Intranet service clients (e-mail, newsgroups, ftp, web pages), instant messaging, computer phone and fax, video conference, resource sharing (workspaces, applications, files), workgroup support (group calendars, project managers, etc.), EDM/PDM/PLM systems,
- experimental systems developed within the sphere of research projects [6] (e.g. iViP, MILOS, CPM, VICOPLAN, μWebFab).

The use of a particular solution depends mainly on time (synchronous or asynchronous), location (common or dispersed) and IT infrastructure factors (Intranet or Internet). At the moment, the use of popular net service clients is still the most common, in spite of the availability of advanced systems (Figure 3).

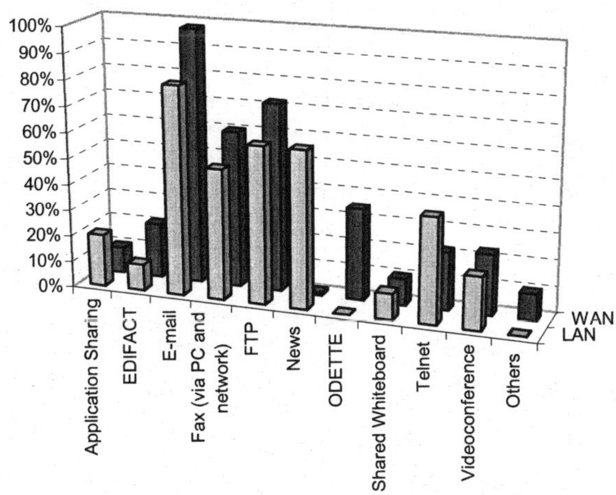

Figure 3: Using of IT tools during communication and collaboration [7]

During the process of selection, several systems were taken into account, but ultimately the PDM-class system collaboration platform was chosen as the optimal solution and the one best fitting the previously presented requirements (Table 1).

Table 1: Usage of PDM-class system as collaboration platform for presented design environment

Requirement:	**PDM functionality:**
organizing of design team	user management
reflecting the structure of design team	group/roles management
reflecting the roles of particular members within the team	group/roles management
reflecting of processes characteristic for design	approving/rejecting documents or project stages
enabling simultaneous execution of different projects	core functionality
using of documents of different kinds and formats	core functionality
using already existing IT infrastructure	functional integration with existing software (especially CAD)
organizing access to data and manage documents related to the project	document management
aiding of workflow	workflow management
ensuring the mechanisms of data classification and searching	core functionality
delivering common services of data transfer between design places	core functionality

3. Example Design Process in VIDA Centre

After the initial implementation phase of the selected collaboration platform, in order to test the core functionality of a chosen solution and to familiarize the users with the system, an initial test project was conducted. A water pump was chosen as the design product.

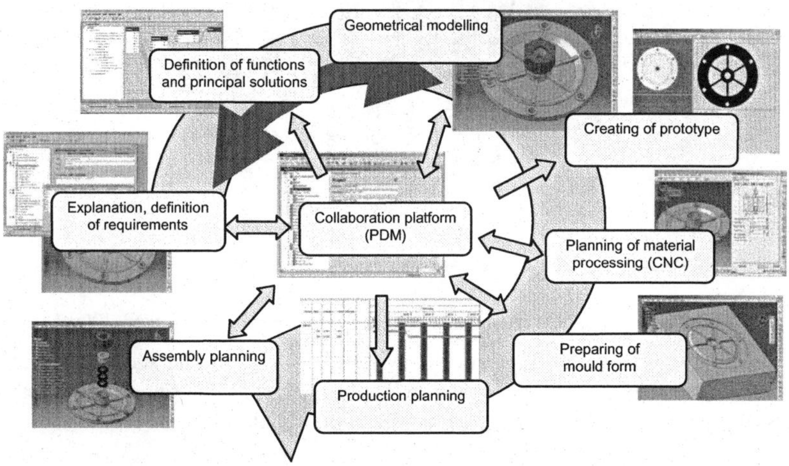

Figure 5: Execution of water pump design in virtual environment of VIDA Centre [8]

Appropriate teams and designers are involved in executing the project using computer workstations equipped with appropriate software, (mainly CAD/CAM Catia system, a functional oriented design FOD system [9] and other software). The basis for the design process is a geometrical model created in 3D CAD system. Product functions are modelled in an FOD system (Functional Oriented Design) and the cost is estimated, leading to the possibility of creating product variants that fulfil client's requirements. Finally, the product technical documentation is drawn up. According to the specificity of particular product parts, CNC programs are generated (using a CAM system) or mould forms are designed. The dimensions and shapes are optimised through the metal element fluid simulation during the pouring and self-cooling processes. A product manufacturing schedule is also provided, with the possibility for a simulation of an order execution (Figure 5).

Design teams and their members working on the common project are equipped with hardware (mainly computer workstations), and software, according to their competences and role in the project. The participation in the common virtual design environment is ensured by the PDM client being present on each workstation. Because of this the designers (as PDM clients) have the possibility of sourcing documents from the PDM server and of processing them or creating new ones.

4. Conclusions

The use of a collaboration platform usually changes the character of communication between team members (in the described scenario, the system implementation, before PDM, was based on communication mainly through spontaneous data and information exchange). Thanks to the internal system mechanism, the elimination of several minor tools is possible (this mainly applies to popular Intranet and Internet service clients). The implementation of PDM changes the method of organising IT infrastructural usage. Individual workstations become the location for data processing while data storage is handled by the PDM system. Users should be familiarized gradually with the functionality and specificity of the system and therefore implementation should be in stages.

Further activities within the presented environment are planned. Apart from carrying out new projects, these relate to expansion of the functionality of the selected collaboration platform (e.g. workflow and access from outside the Intranet in order to collaborate with partners from industry and other research institutions), including the methods of VR (Virtual Reality) and taking into account disassembling within the design process.

Acknowledgements

The results presented in this paper were achieved within the project No.GMA1-2002-72036 founded by the European Community under the 5. FW – GROWTH Programme.

References

[1] EHRENSPIEL K., „Integrierte Produktentwicklung", Carl Hanser Verlag, München Wine 1995
[2] EIGNER M., „Warum brauchen auch KMUs PDM-Technologie", Proceedings of DZ-ViPro Thementag „Einsatz von PDM-Technologien", Berlin, March 2003
[3] www.vida.put.poznan.pl
[4] Virtual Design and Automation Centre, Description of Work, Competitive and Sustainable Growth Programme, Project No. G1MA-CT-2002-04015 (internal document), Poznan 2002
[5] ALZAGA A., YALNIZ Z., „Collaborative Development of Tools and Dies in SMEs Networks", Methods and Tools for Co-operative and Integrated Design, Kluwer Academic Publishers 2004
[6] HAHN A., KERN E.-M., „Dynamic Peer-to-Peer Process Configuration in Virtual Engineering Organization", Proceedings of e-Work 2003, Bologna
[7] von LUKAS U., „Synchronous tele-cooperation in virtual product creation"; Proceedings of 1st VIDA Workshop; Poznan 05.12.2003
[8] WEISS Z, WEISS E, DIAKUN J., "Design environment of Poznan University of Technology VIDA Center", 4st Wroclaw Symposium "Manufacturing Automation", Wroclaw 2003 (in Polish)
[9] http://fod.cadsys.de

eAdoption and the Knowledge Economy: Issues, Applications, Case Studies
P. Cunningham and M. Cunningham (Eds.)
IOS Press, 2004

Digital Engineering and Supply Chain Management for Enhanced Toyota System

Satoshi KUROIWA
Chairman Planning Committee, Electronic Commerce Promotion Council of Japan (Former Toyota Motor Corp.)
Kikai Shinko Kaikan Bldg. 3F, 3-5-8 Shibakouen, Minato-ku, Tokyo 105-0011, Japan
Tel: +81 3 34367500, Fax: + 81 3 34367570, Email: skuro@ecom.jp

Abstract: This paper discusses structural changes to the automobile industry that were brought about by the advancement of ICT, as well as two major issues in the concurrent engineering and supply chain management, namely, "agile vehicle development and production preparation" and "agile production and delivery responding to customer orders." Information sharing with business partners through digital engineering is the first step in the application of ICT to automobile business processes like new vehicle development, production, and sales. Toyota is carrying out its concurrent engineering and supply chain management as part of the improvement activities on "human creativity" which is the basic principle of the Toyota Production System. The paper introduces some examples of the corporation's concurrent engineering activities, such as "V-comm," a collaboration tool, and "TLSC."

1. Introduction

The automobile industry is now entering a new epoch. Many auto manufacturers are merging and forming partnerships to create a new structure for the industry. The very survival of these manufacturers is at stake as they face many challenges, including environment issues, globalization and fierce competition. All these structural changes to the industry can be ascribed to advancing information technologies and use of the Internet. The Internet, enabling the distribution and sharing of information worldwide, is pushing businesses to grow more global, open-structured, and to further speedup their operations.

This paper first summarizes the current situation and trends relating to the structural changes in the automobile industry, which have been promoted by Information and Communication Technologies (ICT). Then, it will describe some examples of how we should develop our own supply chain management based on the Toyota Production System.

The paper will focus on two aspects of this issue, namely digital engineering in new vehicle development and Just-in-Time (JIT) system to the customer. This discussion stands on the proposition that the automobile industry is another kind of information processing business which utilizes human resources and ICT. It emphasizes that the Toyota Production System, which focuses on the creativity of workers and the vitality of the organization should continue to serve as the foundation of our supply chain management and concurrent engineering, even as ICT evolves further during this new century.

2. The Automobile Industry in the Age of ICT

2.1 Challenges Facing the Automobile Industry

The most serious challenge the automobile industry faces is its response to global environmental issues. Automakers all over the world are shifting their focus from gasoline, which currently accounts for some 30% of the world's crude oil consumption, to new zero-emission energies. Manufacturers are busy trying to develop fuel cells and other new energy sources. This technological competition is accelerating the formation of alliances among the world's automakers. The world's Original Equipment Manufacturers (OEMs) are required to secure the business resources needed to develop these environmental technologies and to handle their production capacity surplus. No doubt all these OEMs will resort to further M&As in their effort to survive in the future.

In this new century of ICT, what was formerly a business group united around physical organizations should evolve into a logical union based on an information-sharing networks. In other words, more and more businesses, including the automobile industry, should form such global alliances or Virtual Enterprises which share core technologies to carry their operations and organizations forward across chronological and geographical boundaries.

2.2 Structural Changes in the Automobile Industry Accelerated by the Digital Economy

A recent report issued by the U.S. Department of Commerce said that the expansion of the Internet and the digital economy are changing the very structure of industries. In the U.S. auto industry - referred to as "typical of all the manufacturing industries" in the report - GM, Ford, and other OEMs are no longer just producers of vehicles, but instead are transforming into providers of automobile-related services.

Today, OEMs producing finished automobiles create 25% of the total added value an automobile carries, while "upstream" component and material manufacturers create 30%. The remaining portion of the total value added, according to the report, is ascribable to services, including sales, accessories and insurance. It is only natural that OEMs, whose major business is designing and assembling finished cars, are now trying to reach out to their corresponding "upstream" and "downstream" operations. The modularization of car components is forcing some OEMs today to shift their operations to the "upstream" section. Also, the "downstream" section now covers not just automobile production and sales but the whole car related lifestyle, as suggested by the ITS (Intelligent Transport System).

2.3 Creating New Business Models

The expansion of the Internet has nurtured the rise of a new kind of venture business exploiting information networks. Autobytel has initiated a whole new trend in automobile sales. The emerging force of Internet businesses, often referred to as "dot com firms," no doubt stimulated the older ones, called "T (Traditional) businesses," in their respective industries. Some examples of this are Amazon.com and Barnes & Noble; Dell and HP; Autobytel and automobile OEMs. GM is now known for its IT-powered customer services to car owners. Those services, provided by systems named GM-Access, BuyPower and OnStar, Toyota is in no way lagging behind. Toyota is accelerating e-business initiatives and programs, as shown by Gazoo (www.gazoo.com), which is a Web site providing ITS and e-commerce services, available from mobile communication terminals and many other new features. The vehicle information service by Gazoo and GBOOK which is an on board system, will become one of Toyota's strategic information services in the age of ICT era. In terms of business reform, Toyota has been taking new steps in digital engineering to support concurrent one, supply chain management, and other e-commerce programs.

2.4 Deploying virtual enterprises

Japan's automobile industry is structured vertically. OEMs are positioned at the top of the hierarchy, with the primary, secondary, and other component providers placed below the OEM. Yet global competition is rendering such a closed, hierarchical structure meaningless, inefficient, and outmoded. Business practices and rules, peculiar to OEMs are no longer accepted. The whole auto industry is required to comply with the EDI or other standards of business, which are employed by the majority of the world's auto industry. The Japan Automobile Manufacturers Association is now deploying JNX, a Japanese counterpart to ANX, a Virtual Private Network (VPN) deployed by AIAG (Automobile Industry Action Group) in the U.S. This marks the first step of the Japanese auto industry's progress toward more open and global business models.

In recent years, we have been witnessing the emergence of B-B or B-C Web sites, selling products to consumers. A new electronic market place (E-MP) plan, called Covisint (www.covisint.com), was kicked off by the "Big Three" U.S. auto makers and other participants. Covisint lets participants procure automobile components over the Internet and tries to integrate all the corporate activities into an information system, covering component and material procurement through development, production, and distribution.

The author (now retired Toyota) participates in ECOM (Electronic Commerce Promotion Council of Japan) as a chairman of Planning Committee of ECOM, Japan's largest private sector driven NPO organized by METI. ECOM is (www.ecom.jp), (Toyota's president, CHO is a chairman), began its CALS studies (B-BEC) and EC verification on B-C in 1995 and is currently focusing on rule or guideline-making, standardization development related to EC on B-B, B-C, B-G such as ebXML, STEP and so forth, and dissemination of EC in Japan and information sharing globally.

3. Business Reform using ICT

3.1 Transformation of the auto industry

The expansion of the Internet and the digital economy are changing the very structure of industries. Structural changes in the auto industry will be accelerated as follows:

- Design, production, & sales activities on computer networks
- Creation of new business models (dell models, etc)
- New more open and global business rules
- Virtual enterprises that transcend company networks
- Switch to slim company organizations & industry structures and alliances of the strong
- Expansion of project scope to upstream and downstream areas, creation of new projects

3.2 Critical issues of Toyota's business process innovation

Toyota has four critical issues related to ICT for business innovation listed bellow:

1. Global management by information and data sharing
2. Better customer relationship management
3. Short lead-time of new vehicle development
4. Just-In-Time order to delivery

In the auto industry it has become more critical than ever to deliver the products that customer need on a timely basis. The first issues are agile product development and production preparation. The second one is agile production responding to customer demand. The business process of the first issues is product planning, design, development, production preparation, procurement and production prototyping. The second ones are sales, production planning, procurement, production, distribution and service. Figure 1 shows a business process of the automobile industry relevantly mapped Toyota's ICT systems.

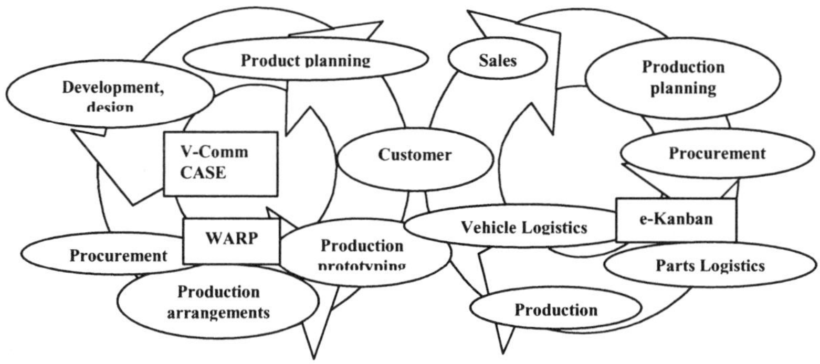

Figure 1: Business process of the automobile industry

The first stream (left circle in Figure 1), "From customer, product development and preparation to production" represents the new vehicle development. The lead-time of new model development at nearly all Japanese car manufacturers is less than 20 months. In this stream, it has become more critical to introduce digital engineering through data sharing and unification of development information among business partners to develop products and production processes. In this stream concurrent engineering is inevitable using V-Comm, CASE and WARP, which are Toyota's ICT systems explained later.

The second stream (right circle in Figure 1) represents customer order flows from the customer to production and delivery. The term "Supply Chain (SC)" or SC Management (SCM)" is usually used. At Toyota this stream from customers' order to production and delivery is executed based on the Toyota Production System (TPS). The term "SC/SCM" which was initially used in the U.S. from around 1990 originated in Just-In-Time as one of the basic concepts of the TPS. But SCM empowered by modeling and simulation technology is applied effectively as the planning stage of the business process rather than the execution one. To realize JIT, Toyota has been using pull production and logistics based on the Kanban system. But due to changes of customer demand, conventional Kanban system has been evolved responding to the change of manufacturing environment.

3.3 Collaborative Work and Digital Engineering with Business Partners

Toyota involve suppliers in the early stage of development and work with them closely to shorten lead-time and cut costs in the product development process. The manufacturing divisions and quality assurance divisions get involved in the development process early and prototype stages. Cross-divisional teamwork with supplier's engineers and designers to work out part designs and offer the required quality and performance while meeting cost targets. As one of ICT tools for BPR in this stage WARP (World-wide Automotive Real-time Purchasing systems) has been applied, which is based on the global common database with product number, item name, supplier, region, model and so on. It was developed and applied just a couple of years ago, which development aims are listed bellow:

- Centralization of information
- Support for strategic planning
- Order policy planning at concept stage
- Accumulation of global SE/production arrangement information
- Expansion of data transfer and sharing with business partners

In the product development process, it has become more inevitable to apply digital engineering as virtual communication, as well as physical one, such as face to face meetings. One of the digital engineering systems applied at Toyota is V-Comm, which stands for "visual and virtual communication", another is CASE (Computer Aided Simultaneous Engineering). V-Comm is applied to the vehicle body, CASE to the Parts. They allow the sending and reception of still/moving image and voice among each of concerned sites through the application of conventional TV conferences and visual communication services. It is useful for checking out in real time any problems that appear at remote sites, identifying the causes of the problems, and figuring out how to handle them. Then turn to our 3-D simulator, which converts and processes CAD data into clear relief images projected on three 100-inch screens. With the simulator, we can view simulations from a variety of angles showing final configurations as well as the movements of multiple components when assembled. For example, it will be possible for suppliers to make sales approaches based on the configuration data without the need to build prototype products. Figure 2 shows the concept of digital engineering at Toyota, which is inevitable ICT enhanced engineering especially to promote globalization of Toyota.

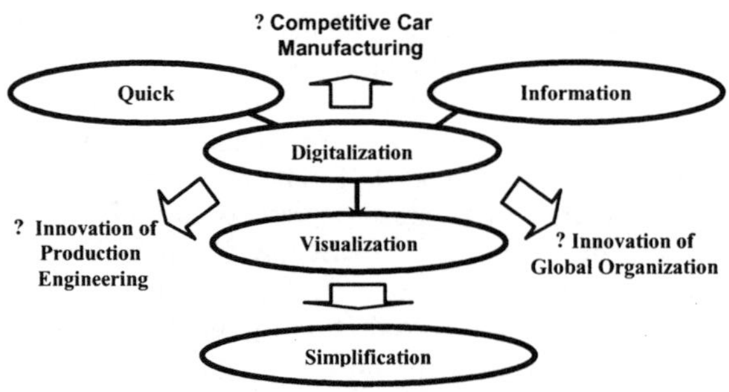

Figure 2 Concept of digital engineering

3.4 Agile Production and Delivery Responding to Customer Order

In this business process as production and delivery Toyota has established JIT based on the TPS. The basic philosophy of TPS will be constant even if the manufacturing environment changes in the future. But ICT has dramatically advanced since the establishment of TPS around 30 years ago. Now JIT activities are expanding globally from customer to suppliers based on human resources using advanced ICT.

When Toyota constructed a new assembly plant in Kyusyu (western island of Japan) to which parts were shipped from the general vicinity of Toyota's head office, we introduced a ICT enhanced Kanban system to realize the pull system with a long conveyance lead time. Now Toyota has introduced e-Kanban system (Toyota Parts Procurement System) keeping the basic principles of the Kanban system. The following technology was introduced:

- Logistic information system to realized an efficient mixed conveyance
- Parts ordering system with automated leveling of the number of Kanbans
- Electronic settlement of accounts with no written of parcel
- Automated issuing of Kanbans

After improving the first development system, e-Kanban system has been applied to almost all assembly lines. Newly developed systems feature real-time issuing Kanbans based on the sequence of customer orders at the assembly plant. From the view point of B-B EC systems, Toyota uses WARP for the vehicle development stage to select parts and suppliers and for the mass production stage, uses e-Kanban system to order volume based on the vehicle assembling sequence and consumed parts at the assembly line. But in order to gain better customer satisfaction and to realize "Build to Order" manufacturing in the near future, it becomes more critical to integrate data from customers' orders, production, suppliers' parts delivery, vehicle delivery and information sharing with business partners.

4. Best Practice in the SCM and CE

4.1 Toyota Production System (TPS)

Toyota's business activities are based on the TPS called 'lean production' in the US. It is also called Toyota's production philosophy, management philosophy, and Toyota's DNA. The basic philosophy of the TPS is putting the "Customer First" which consists of Just-in-Time and Jidouka (Autonomy). TPS arranges all the processes from raw materials to finished products in a single, smooth flow. It means continuous challenges to bring production systems and logistics of discrete-type machine industry close to the "continuous flow" effectively and efficiently. I introduce several ideas learned from the TPS as follows:

- Next process is your customer (Customer First)
- Elimination 7 Muda (wastes)
- Continuous small flows (Leveled production and logistics)
- One-piece-at-a-time production (Mixed flow production)
- Shortened process
- Remove intra-process distribution that does not add value
- Working is totally different from moving. (Jidouka)
- Elicitation of problems (Each worker can stop the line. No warehouses.)

4.2 ICT and the Human Role

We have experienced a big gap between the human-oriented system by Kaizen activities and ICT oriented one. The former is more accessible, flexible, changeable and more collaborative than the latter. Taking into account the basic factor of human nature, which says that people look for satisfaction in the jobs, we are pursuing ways to provide better working environment to make jobs more interesting and to motivate employees. Even in the ICT era Toyota will observe the basic principle of the TPS of which goal is that create teams and members who continue Kaizen activities always seeking for "To Be" ideal systems. TPS always focuses on human creativity as follows; first, "improve mechanism/operations"; then start on "automation (introduction of ICT)."

4.3 Business Process Visibility for Better Business Process

In order to improve the business process based on the TPS it is important to visualize related business processes for information sharing. Business process or manufacturing process are advanced and evolve with synergy of Kaizen and innovation. This synergy is provided by the creativity of people involved in business processes or manufacturing systems. In Japan, acronyms such as SIS, BPR, ERP, SCM and CRM are frequently used in the IT business. They sound like buzzwords of IT business strategy. In the era of ICT we must recognize that a man's or woman's role of business processes rely on not only the ICT or new concepts for BPR, but also human creativity itself. In Japanese industries we have experienced several unsuccessful examples of introducing ERP or SCM software packages. To be sure, SCM will become more important in the ICT era. But we should recognize that higher productivity and better business process can be realized through the synergy of Kaizen (continuous improvement) and innovation, in other words, the synergy of humans and ICT. Business process and manufacturing process are planned and executed by many relevant persons such as operators, maintenance staff and systems engineers, designers, managers, venders, as well as many organizations. In order to gain the creative knowledge necessary to improve or innovate the system it is essential to visualize business process.

Each organization or company has visualization methods, tools and modeling methodology. The expression methods and description procedures for visibility have many variations due to the multiple view-points of business process involving for example, materials, information, organization, resources, functions, locations, sequence, and time. In the manufacturing and logistics division at Toyota, TLSC (Total Link System Chart) has been utilized for more than 10 years. The TLSC named at Toyota enables all the relevant business partners to discuss and verify the system and enables the creation knowledge on just one chart. TLSC (Figure 3) expresses process-related items as follows in one format:

- Process control basic drawing: overall concept and diagram
- Process drawing: process plan and design
- Process control drawing: electronic circuit and equipment drawing
- Computer functionality drawing: information process design

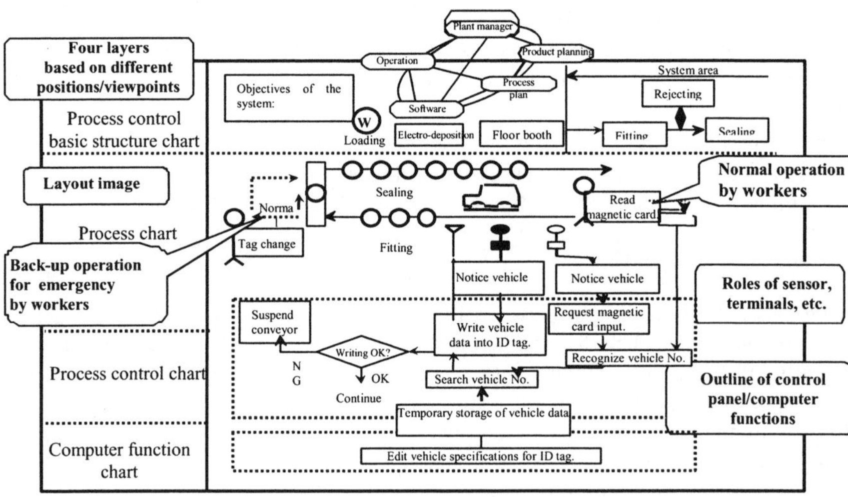

Figure 3 Outline of TLSC (Total Link System Chart)

Utilization of "TLCS" and other "information tools" is very effective, especially when it covers a large geographic area, a long time span, and involves many affiliated businesses. In such a case, the parties involved should be able to see a comprehensive part of the entire system, understand its objectives, and avoid having wrong presuppositions and misunderstandings about the system in analyzing it. At Toyota, the personnel concerned take the initiative in carrying out the process of reforming, from the investigation and analysis through the scenario creation and choosing of the final improvement and reform plans for implementation. In supply chain management, it will be increasingly important for the many people involved to develop creative ideas during the planning stage through information sharing and the utilization of information tools as a means of doing so.

5. Conclusions

The automobile industry consists of countless complex business processes, these include procuring the materials and components, the production and sale of finished products, services, and much more. Now, the advancement of ICT is introducing changes to the industry's structure and the way people work within the industry. It becomes more critical issues to share information with business partners and make the business processes visible. One principle of Toyota's SCM is "Just-in-Time," which is also one of the principles of the Toyota Production System. The goal of the Toyota Production System is to crate teams and members who continue Kaizen activities always seeking for “To Be” ideal systems. The focus of this production system including logistics is on the human creativity and their desire to improve. Today, the progress of ICT is enabling Toyota's production system (which is one kind of people centric ICT system) to evolve even further. The best practices in Toyota's digital engineering and supply chain management will make the most of ICT as a means enhancing the creativity of the corporation's human resources and their desire to improve. The Toyota Production System, whose principles include Just-in-Time, Jidouka (Autonomy), visible management, and others, should remain the keynote of the best practices in the corporation's concurrent engineering and supply chain activities.

References

[1] T. Ohono (1988), Toyota Production System, Productivity Press Inc.
[2] Kuroiwa (1994), Kaizen and Enhanced Kanban System at Toyota, Aachen, 27th ISATA
[3] Kuroiwa (1995), Approach to the computer integrated Toyota Production System, Israel, The 13th International Conference on Production Research
[4] Naito (1998), Development of a Just-In-Time and Production Preparation Support System for Automotive Parts Plants, Paris, FISITA98
[5] Kuroiwa (1999), Growing an open Environment from CALS, JIT and Supply Chain, Florence, 4th ISL

Applying Collaborative e-Business in the Automotive Electronics Industry

Jens ESCHENBAECHER[1], Nobert MEYER[2]
[1]*BIBA, Hochschulring 20, 28359 Bremen, Germany*
Tel: +49 421 218-5539, Fax: +49 421 218 5610, Email: esc@biba.uni-bremen.de
[2] *SIEMENS VDO Automotive AG, Siemensstr. 12, 93055 Regensburg, Germany*
Tel: +49 941 790-4870, Fax: + 49 941 790-4995, Email: meyer.norbert@siemens.com

Abstract: Collaborative e-business is considered to be the driving concept of enterprise evolution by many researchers and industrialists. The authors claim that cooperation within Collaborative Networked Organisations (CNO) will ensure more efficient collaboration along four dimensions of a collaborative e-business framework. The framework has been conceptually applied in the automotive industry to demonstrate challenges and lessons learnt. The case study has implications for the automotive electronic industry in Germany. The current state of the art indicates that practical implementation of collaborative e-business concepts is still very difficult.

1. Introduction

Collaborative e-business has been discussed by various authors [15, 16, 17, 19]. We define collaborative e-business as a set of electronically supported collaborative interactions between an enterprise, its suppliers, trading partners, customers and employees. Collaborative e-business utilizes the Web to create and maintain an interactive business community of employees, trading partners, suppliers and customers. By means of real-time Internet connectivity internal intellectual capital, human resources and processes can be shared throughout the collaborative community. The concept of collaborative e-business can be conceived as an extension of e-business in combination with the concept of supply chain management. As a matter of fact research studies clearly show that Collaborative Networked Organisations (CNO) will adapt the concept of collaborative e-business [1].

In practice companies are faced with a substantial failure rate of innovation processes in CNO (Table 1). Consequently multi-national companies such as Audi or BMW have established departments dealing with worldwide collaboration and innovation management [2]. The high failure rate forces the European manufacturing industry to think about new approaches and solutions that focus on the requirements of CNO's. Implementation of innovation processes often cannot achieve the desired profits. Many research studies show that 50 to 80% of innovation does not have any impact on organisational goals.

Source	Strebel, P.	Rothwell, R.	Hammer, M.	Jaikumar	Field, T.	Burnes, B.
Percentage	60 %	80 %	50-70 %	50-75 %	73 %	70-80 %

Table 1: Percentages of Failure for Innovation and Collaboration Projects [3]

Considering this situation, the role of collaboration has evolved during the last decade. Camarinha-Matos [1] clearly determines roadmaps for future evolution of networked organisations. Among others, Rothwell [4] argues that industry is currently facing the fifth generation of innovation management, focusing on "system integration and networking models". Thus, innovation does no longer take place within isolated companies or departments, but in widely distributed, collaborative organisations. Consequently, the authors propose the "collaborative e-business" approach integrating the entire range of collaborative processes in supply networks through web-based systems, ensuring more trust and confidence than nowadays e-business solutions.

The authors of this paper argue that the quality of collaboration (which is very difficult to measure) between CNO is one success factor for industry. This statement will be confirmed empirically by a Delphi study conducted in the EC co-funded COMPANION project (www.companion-roadmap.org) to which 60 experts made a contribution.

The role of collaboration in CNO is essential to create stable business processes between partners in order to improve the supply chain performance. The case study in the automotive electronics industry underlines the need for collaboration management system in the automotive Electronic Industry. The following research questions will be answered:

1. What are the main challenges for collaborative e-business in the automotive industry?
2. Does the concept of collaborative e-business adequately fulfil the needs for successfully managing supply networks?
3. Which lessons were learnt from the collaborative e-business case study?

2. Delphi study results

Studies currently discuss that the phenomenon of the new economy will not resurge, but rather the next economy is on its way [6]. The next economy puts a focus on values such as trust, confidence and collaboration between organisations. A key question for collaborative e-business is, whether companies do already collaborate with others or if they intend to do so in the future. A result of Innobarometers confirms this trend: Yet, 63% of the companies collaborate with others to prepare new products and services. The majority of that 63% already collaborates for a longer time whereas 18% is going to do so in the near future [7].

The results are summarised in Figure 1 and based on a Delphi questionnaire and a business case study done within the EC co-funded COMPANION roadmap project [5].

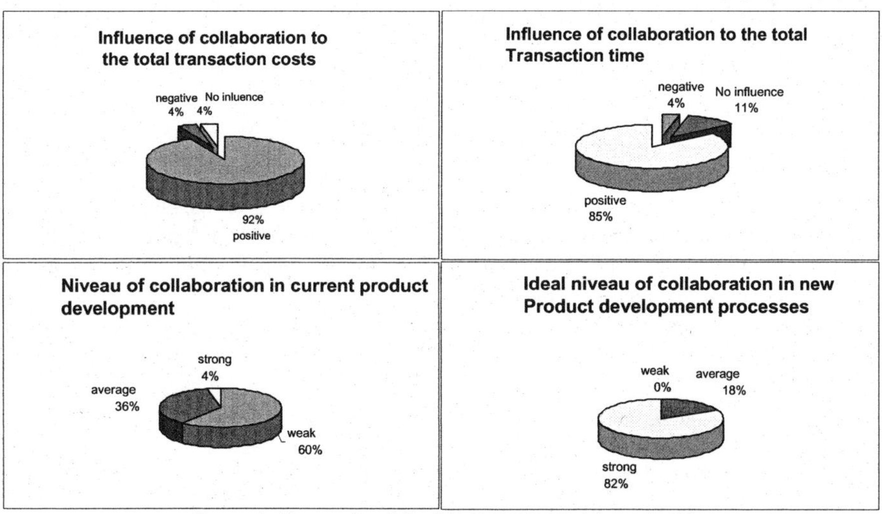

Figure 1: Key results of the COMPANION Delphi study [5]

The results of the assessment show a direct inverse relationship between the degree of collaboration and total transaction costs as well as transaction time of business processes:

- 92% of the experts judged that collaboration has a positive impact on transaction costs in networks, 4% state there is a negative influence and 4% that there is no influence at all.

- 85% judged a positive influence of collaboration on the total transaction time in networks whereas 4% say a negative and 11% no influence at all.
- In the development of new products 60% saw a weak usage of collaborative networks, 36% average and only 4% judged a strong usage of collaborative network technologies.

In contrast to that 82% claim that collaborative networks will become very important.

3. Collaborative eBusiness in Manufacturing

Manufacturing is currently facing a previously unequalled phase of outsourcing or even off shoring of business processes [17]. Multinational companies transfer their production activities towards China or the eastern European countries. Based on a sound framework, this chapter sketches the subject collaborative e-business. The concept is applied in a case study, bringing forth some findings and conclusions.

3.1 Building vision, benefits brought to enterprises by collaboration

The manufacturing industry of the future is characterized by a stricter correlation of products and services than today and even by merging of the two elements. That is why services have substituted the physical product in business considerations, completely in many cases, e.g. in mobile phones. This new concept of integrating physical products and related services to one single item is called extended product [8]. It has become evident that collaborative e-business in extended products manufacturing is the inevitable evolutionary path of the current business practice: Deloitte Consulting [9] affirms that more than 57% of US manufacturing companies manifested a strong interest in Collaborative e-Business, whereas a recent survey conducted by IBM Germany [10] shows that cost reduction, increase of flexibility, focus on the core business and service improvement are almost unanimously considered tangible benefits brought to enterprises by collaboration.

In spite of such a promising and shared business perspective, the current heavy presence of inhibiting factors has resulted in a very limited adoption of collaborative e-business in real extended product life cycle management so far. The reason is mainly a lack of a system approach – e.g. a collaboration management system - addressing collaborative e-business

3.2 Need for Collaboration management system

The collaboration management system is the outcome of a long discussion in which the dimensions of collaboration have been defined [11]. In all these dimensions, processes of communication, co-ordination or co-operation take place. The method sketched is a holistic, multi-dimensional, collaborative approach able to encompass four dimensions of collaboration management system (Figure 2).

The four dimensions were developed in the COMPANION project. A few partners have conceptualised the needs for organising collaboration in a proper way. The following points summarize these approaches:

- all stages of collaboration from the beginning to the end (initiation, management, operational life and dissolution),
- all phases of extended products' life cycle (conception, design, manufacturing, usage, maintenance, service integration and end-of-life),
- all forms of collaboration (ad-hoc, mediated and planned) and
- all enterprise assets in any type of business network (people, ICT-systems, processes and knowledge assets).

Stages of collaboration Initiation Management Operation Dissolution	**Collaboration over extended products' life cycle** Requirements, Design, Manufacture, Use, Maintain, End-of-life
Assets of collaboration People Process **ICT-Systems** Knowledge	**Forms of collaboration** **Ad-hoc** Mediated Planned

Figure 2: Dimensions of Collaborative eBusiness

The dimensions of collaboration ensure a holistic view of the collaboration management systems, and help to differentiate projects by allocation to a suitable category. The concept of a collaboration management system is widely discussed in the literature [12, 15, 16]. Many authors have evaluated 30-50 collaboration systems by using their own classification logic. As a result, they conclude that most systems look at single dimensions of collaboration instead of really focusing on managing the collaboration between companies.

3.3 Sketch of a collaboration management system

The methodological foundation of a Collaborative Management System (CMS) is based on a fully integrated and interoperable holistic view of collaboration shown by the dimensions of collaboration. This requires a multi-disciplinary and multi-sectoral perspective and interoperable ICT systems. The impact of adopting and demonstrating collaboration within enterprise manufacturing networks can be enormous [17]. It is needed to synthesize of scientific and technological approaches those results in a CMS and in its application to sample phases of product life cycles in several different industrial sectors and domains.

The major challenge is the creation of a customised adoption of the Collaborative e-business paradigm, well supported by specific suites of IT applications (the CMS platform, seen as a plug & collaborate platform) along all phases of collaboration. This will enhance traditional time-cost-quality performance indicators for any manufacturing industry. Adoption will facilitate and improve collaboration (measurement of specific collaboration performance indicators), which is often an important added value per se especially in innovation-driven activities, and also drive new business opportunities in general.

3.4 Collaboration life-cycle management

Justifying and discussing all the dimensions of collaboration is outside the scope of this paper. Indeed, the stages of collaboration have been defined by the COMPANION project as one of the major research challenges. In all of these stages, the objective is efficient delivery of extended products or sometimes the delivery of a solution. Most available solutions underestimate the complexity of managing collaborative e-business processes [17] which require a holistic approach. The system we envisage is supporting the complete fife-cycle of collaboration as shown in Figure 3. Extended products require a heavy IT support in order to make them attractive to the customer.

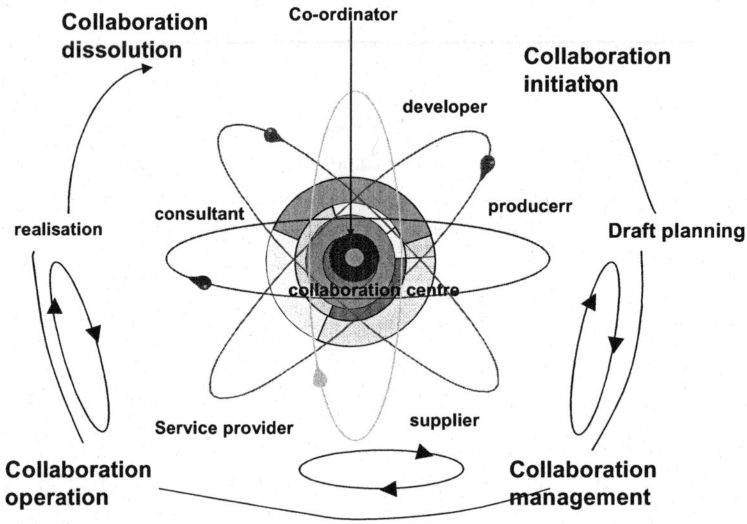

Figure 3: Collaboration life-cycle management

3.5 Applying Collaborative eBusiness in the Automotive Electronics Industry

Collaborative business is a new challenge for industry, which leads to a lack of empirical findings. The case presented in this paper has been used to analyse the importance of a collaboration management system for the automotive electronics industry. Many publications have already discussed interfaces between enterprise applications. Stevens et al [18] point out that most discussion focuses on XML base structures. However many industries are still trapped in mainframe solutions focussing on point-to-point EDI solutions. The business case used in this paper belongs to this old paradigm. As a matter of fact interoperability is needed to support the applicability of collaborative e-business.

From an organisational viewpoint governance and clear rules for collaboration driven by the OEM (e.g. BMW or VW) because of their dominating position within a network. Siemens VDO is in a complicated position. On one hand they act as a supplier network hub and on the other hand they are a system supplier to the automotive industry. Consequently, SIEMENS VDO must carefully organise their collaboration processes and intends to use collaboration approaches and technologies more intensively. Today there is no approach used which systematically supports collaboration life-cycle management. A totally collaborative environment integrating first and second tier suppliers enabled by a shared innovation process could change this situation dramatically and would prevent failures [12].

In an in-depth analysis of collaborative e-business with a particular focus on Demand Planning and Orders Visibility has been made. This information was used to investigate the needs regarding structure, governance and coordination. The following figure shows the as-is situation of collaborative e-business and the specific problem addressed in supply networks. The number of EDI-based systems (Figure 4) highlights the problem of creating inter- and intra-organisational collaboration at Siemens VDO. Different systems from the various supply network partner need to be integrated with ERP and web-based solutions.

Ideally, a collaboration management system can coordinate the various systems and business processes in a sensitive manner. Additionally, analysing the Siemens VDO case new requirements for transparency and collaboration become visible. The OEMs, which still coordinate their network mainly in a hierarchical fashion, have to take new customer requirements into account, which enhances collaboration.

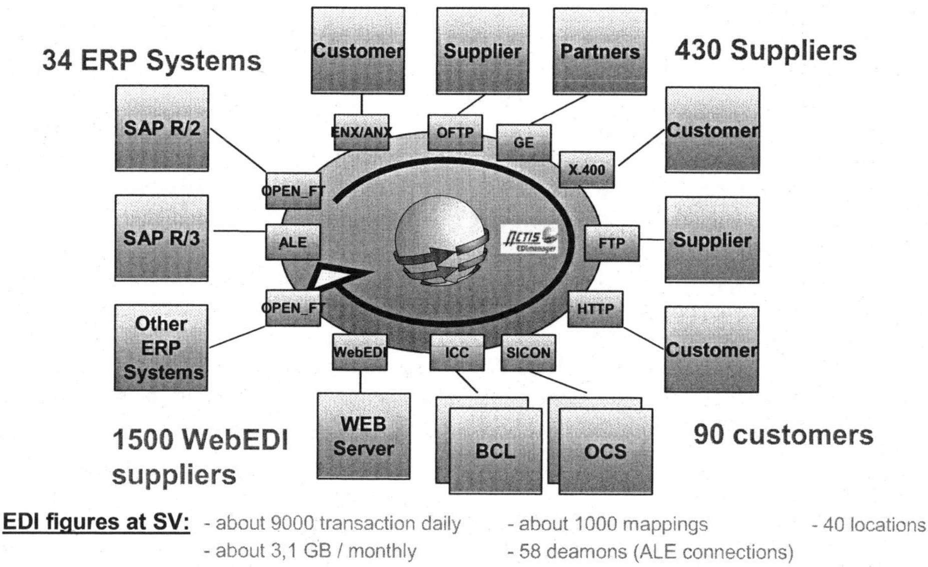

Figure 4: Current Siemens VDO collaborative e-business landscape [13]

The authors claim that collaborative e-business and acceptance of new methodologies supporting CNO is just in its beginning phase. More open collaboration platforms will improve supply chain collaboration. OEMs have the following requirements [13]:

- short lead-time (days)
- high flexibility for production changes (up to 30%)
- short reaction time for changes (information within hours)

Collaborative e-business in supply chains depend on the motivation of large companies as well as integration over the supply chain. The case shows the necessity of a collaboration management system in the automotive electronics industry in order to reduce complexity and make efficient management a realistic aim. All four dimensions shown in Figure 2 have a strong coordination need in order to achieve a successful collaboration.

4. Conclusions

The trend of closer collaboration between OEMs and their suppliers indicates that industry is facing a major challenge to become more collaborative. Companies such as SIEMENS VDO must enter into collaborations to create Win-Win situations for all participants. The usage of collaboration management tools could improve the transparency of the processes. An analysis of further case studies has confirmed the findings of this paper [14].

The dimensions of collaboration illustrate very clearly that there is a long way to truly enable companies to become collaborative. The case study illustrates both the technical (interoperability) and organisational problems (structure and governance) need to be addressed. As long as companies do have hundreds of EDI applications in place the issue of interoperability will remain a dominant problem. Consequently for efficiently implementing collaborative e-business the following prerequisites must be met:

- The OEMs initiate new business processes without integrating the wishes or ideas of suppliers because their own interest can be seen in the optimisation of their own cost position. This is not supporting collaborative e-business.

- Large suppliers of Siemens VDO are not at all as flexible as Siemens VDO towards the OEM. Risk sharing and a high transparency for smaller companies must be recommended. The OEM should make it more visible if parts or products are not anymore needed or if ramp up of new products are planned.
- The collaboration life-cycle management at the OEM and Siemens VDO exclusively takes place on the products side. A common process understanding or even better a common product and process definition would be most valuable for collaborative e-business.
- Common use of software tools such as CMS to improve collaboration is recommended. This process is complicated by the absence of standards.
- A common approach for collaborative e-business must include a stronger adjustment of tool usage, the integration of 1st and 2nd tier supplier wishes and a customer oriented approach focussing on an industry sector rather than expensive solutions for companies

The experience of Siemens VDO confirms the importance of applying a collaborative e-business concept. Ideally a commonly used information system ensuring transparency and governance will have a major impact.

References

[1] Camarinha-Matos, Luis: New collaborative organisations and their Research needs, In: Processes and Foundations for virtual organisations, Kluwer Academic Publishers, Boston/Dordrecht/London, 2004, p. 3-12.

[2] Schoen, A (2002): Innovationsmanagement at the BMW group. Presentation at the Technologiemanagement Kolloquium in St. Gallen on November 11, 2002.

[3] O'Sullivan, D.; Dooley, L.: Developing a software infrastructure to support systemic innovation, in: Int. Journal of Technological Innovation and Entrepreneurship, Vol. 23, No. 8, 2003, S. 689-704.

[4] Rothwell R. (1994): Towards the fifth generation innovation process, Int. Marketing Review, pp7-31.

[5] COMPANION project. URL: www.companion-roadmap.org

[6] Horx, M. (2003): Accent on the Future: Die Zukunftsstudie von Accenture und Matthias Horx, Wien 2003.

[7] Europäische Kommission (2002): Innobarometer 2002, www.cordis.lu/innovation-smes/scr/innobarometer2002.htm, 08.10.03.

[8] Hirsch, B.E., Eschenbächer, J.: Extended Products in Dynamic Enterprises: The IST Project Cluster EXPIDE; in Stanford-Smith, B. und Kidd, P.T. (Hrsg.): E-Business – Key Issues Applications Technologies IOS Press; Amsterdam 2000.

[9] Deloitte Consulting (jferreira@dc.com, lprokopets@dc.com, eschlumpf@dc.com): Going public to get private results. Survey about a study published on January 13, 2002 on www.dc.com), 2002

[10] Koch, W., Ulrich, M.: Warum kollaborieren. In: Logistik heute No. 1 2003 (p. 38), 2003

[11] Thoben, K.-D., Eschenbächer, J. (2003): Die Erweiterung des Produktbegriffs - Konzept und Praxisbeispiele. In: Industrie Management (19) 16, 4, S. 48-51, 2003.

[12] Bafoutsou, G.; Mentzas, G.: Review and functional classification of collaborative Systems, in: International Journal of Information Management, Ausgabe 22/2002, p. 281-305, Pergamon, Elsevier Science Ltd, 2002

[13] Meyer, Nobert: Supply Network Optimisation in the Automotive Electronic Industry. Presentation at the BRIDGES conference on September 9, 2003 in Phoenix, Arizona.

[14] Palacios, D. S.: Collaborative Business: New challenges for Distributed Innovation Management. Master thesis, Bremen 2004.

[15] Silberberger, Holger (2003): cBusiness . Erfolgreiche Internetstrategien durch Collaborative Business. Spinger, Berlin 2003.

[16] Röhricht, Jürgen, Schlögel, Christian: cBusiness (2001) . Erfolgreiche Internetstrategien durch Collaborative Business. Addison-Wesley, München.

[17] CapGemini (2004) Collaborative business experience. Position Paper April 2004. http://www.capgemini.com/collaborative/Business/why.shtml

[18] Stevens, Richard, Felice, Mauro, Gazotti, David, Paganelle, Paolo, Pepe, Antonio (2001) Supporting collaborative product and project life-cycle management in Network enterprises. Proceeding of the 8th International Conference on Concurrent Enterprising 17-19 June 2002, Rome, pp. 235-243.

[19] Thoben, K.-D., Jagdev, H., Eschenbaecher, J. (2003) Emerging concepts in E-business and Extended Products. In: Gasos, J., Thoben, K.-D. (Eds.): E-Business Applications - Technologies for Tomorrow's Solutions; Advanced Information Processing Series, Springer, 2003 (ISBN 3-540-44384-3).

Section 6

New Working Environments

Section 6.1

Issues

eAdoption and the Knowledge Economy: Issues, Applications, Case Studies
P. Cunningham and M. Cunningham (Eds.)
IOS Press, 2004

Getting Organisation and Human Ready for Information Systems

Ip-Shing FAN[1], Nel WOGNUM[2], Henrik BUHL[3]
[1]*Cranfield University, Cranfield, Bedford, MK43 0AL, United Kingdom*
Tel: +44 1234 750111, Fax: + 44 1234 750852, Email: i.s.fan@cranfield.ac.uk
[2]*University of Twente, PO Box 217, 7500 AE, Enschede, Netherlands*
Tel: +31 53 4893736, Fax: +31 53 4892159, Email: p.m.wognum@utwente.nl
[3]*Technical University of Denmark, Bygning 115 1 sal, 2800, Lyngby, Denmark*
Tel: +45 45 25 16 33, Fax: +45 45 88 55 82, Email: hb@byg.dtu.dk

Abstract: No matter if it is a small company or a large multi-national, historically over 60% of enterprise system implementations fail. Research has shown that many of these failures are due to organisations overlooking the preparation for the changes introduced by the new technology. Experienced consultants can tell that the same problems are repeated over and over again. The knowledge gained previously has either been forgotten or lost. The BEST assessment increases the likelihood of success by guiding the project team through others implementation experiences in a simple and approachable manner. The tool matches the causes of problems and effects in similar project situations. It also provides a list of improvement actions based on the assessment. This allows the potential risk and impact of not taking preventive actions to be properly evaluated. This paper presents the BEST research, the assessment tool and the engagement approach.

1. Introduction

Organisation and 'people' problems in the introduction of information technology are not new, there has been anecdotal 'complaints' from the early days of Management Information System (MIS) in the 1960s. Studies by social scientists, especially work psychologists have been published from these early days. Reports from the management schools and manufacturing systems disciplines are more widespread in the 1980s when the manufacturing industry started to introduce Material Resource Planning (MRP) systems in large numbers. Reports of project difficulties and failures continue unabated with the coming of age of Product Data Management (PDM) systems and other eCommerce related systems. In the government and defence systems acquisition community where project overruns are prevalent and public scrutiny has been increasing, the discipline of systems engineering has been established. Methodologies for best practice project management are developed and promoted in the attempt to strengthen project control and accountability.

Despite these developments, the IT system scene is still difficulty. The cost of implementation has become the largest part of IT project costs. Yet there is little guarantee that new IT systems will bring significant productivity gains and business benefits.

Improving the likely success in IT projects has been a matter of interest for a long time. The first significant set of guidelines to set up and run IT projects made available in the public domain is the US Air Force Military Standard on System Engineering Management MIL-STD-499 first issued 17 July 1969. This has been updated to MIL-STD-499A and spawned into many versions for military and civilian versions all over the world. This set of standards takes the viewpoint of a purchaser of complex systems [1].

The Carnegie Mellon Software Engineering Institute is a US federal funded organisation, with the vision of 'The right software, delivered defect free, on time and on cost, every time.' Its Software Engineering Capability Maturity Model(SE-CMM) is the golden standard to measure the capability of a software developing organisation. In addition to representing the capability standard from the software developers' point of view, the CMM introduces quality management concepts into the IT development world [2].

Within Europe, the largest body of work to guide project management to deliver successful IT projects is from the UK government. An early product of the UK work is the Structured Systems Analysis and Design Method(SSADM). It is currently at version 4 and is still the basis for the specification and delivery of IT systems for UK government projects. In addition to the rigour of system design, the UK contributed the PRINCE(Projects in Controlled Environments) Project Management Methodology. PRINCE 2 was launched in 1996 and is the approach for setting up and running projects, not only IT, in the UK public and private sectors[3].

Professional bodies of project managers, the Project Management Institute(PMI) based in USA and the Association of Project Management(APM) based in the UK, also contributed to the knowledge pool. The PMI PMBOK(Project Management Body of Knowledge) and the APM BOK(APM Body of Knowledge) are both industry standard resources for project management professionals to be examined and gain accreditation.

Apart from these public and high profile resources, there are a large variety of project management and executive guide book to recommend IT and project management techniques [4,5,6,7,8,9]. The recurrent difficulties in IT projects raise the question of why the wealth of material available to guide IT project management is not helping yet.

2. Objectives

Having identified that the human and organisation difficulties are the consistent problems in enterprise systems implementation, the BEST (Better Enterprise Systems Implementation IST-2001-35385) consortium intends to complement the existing tools with the organisation and human concerns which are missing in most of the current IT project management practice. The effectiveness of this additional help is highly dependant on the recognition of the need for the 'soft' changes and then doing the appropriate changes. BEST thus sees the interaction with the organisation in two steps.

The first step is to allow the organisation to determine if any changes are necessary. The step is called 'readiness assessment' and the consortium also uses the term 'benchmark' loosely to refer to this step that helps an organisation to gain an appreciation of the areas that improvements are needed.

The second step is the more detailed stage of identifying specific changes and the improvement actions to be taken. The consortium calls this step 'readiness diagnostic'. The BEST diagnostic is designed to help organisations to work through the options relevant to their situations and make a balanced judgement based on the practicalities of the situation.

3. Methodology

The research work to support the creation of the tool has two main components. The main intellectual challenge is to develop a coding system that can locate the relevant organisation and project stage context to provide the implementation help appropriate for the situation. This coding system is the classification framework. The second challenge is to accumulate the volume of implementation knowledge and provide them through the coding system.

Enterprise implementation project is a social activity. Compared with natural science, it is unlikely that any particular situation will exactly repeat itself. Even when the same organisation is implementing the same project with the same team at different times, it is highly unlikely that the exact same set of difficulties will arise. However, empirical experience suggests that there are repeating patterns. An experienced consultant can normally suggest high risk areas from understanding the situation of the project. The effectiveness of the BEST tool relates closely to the 'accuracy' of its advice. The 'predictability' of social science research is an issue rich with different viewpoints. The large number and complexity of the organisation and human issues suggests that a quantitative, statistical approach is not feasible. The effort needed to collect the number of case studies to provide statistical confidence is huge and not necessarily profitable. A qualitative approach to reach learning appropriateness is a viable alternative. Established qualitative research uses a variety of case study methods to develop theories of social science. The BEST research planning aims to arrive at an appropriate approach to deliver the research results needed to build the BEST tool.

4. Classification scheme for BEST

The classification scheme is the key to match the relevant organisation and human issues for a particular implementation project. From a superficial point of view, implementation projects of similar system and similar organisation should have similar characteristics. A classification system based on system and organisation parameters would suffice. However, organisations of similar industrial sector and size may have very different social behaviour and dynamics. There could be stronger similarities in social characteristics for organisations of similar command and control structure but of different industrial sector and size. There is a significant volume of management and social science research that propose a variety of theories to explain causal relationship of specific cases. From an application point of view, managers would have stronger confidence to learn from experience of organisations of similar business characteristics. The BEST tool would use a number of business parameters as part of the classification scheme.

The BEST consortium has adopted a reference framework to classify previous experience. The BEST Reference Framework consists of 3 dimensions and 6 aspects. The boxes in the reference framework are called focus cells, for example Business/Strategy & goals. The frameworks consist of 18 focus cells (see Table 1).

	Business	**Project Management**	**Enterprise System**
Strategy & goals			
Management			
Structure			
Process			
Knowledge & skills and resources			
Social dynamics			

Table 1: The BEST Reference Framework

To support the reference framework there are 3 cross cutting subjects: communication, training and change. The objective of the framework is to address and cover the significant aspects and dimensions in the 18 focus cells.

The reference framework is stable, not static. It is based on in-depth case studies in 8 European countries and consultants' experiences. The reference framework allows us to identify differences between 'social' characteristics in different situations. This becomes the context that must be taken into account when applying the BEST knowledge.

5. Building the implementation knowledge base

The knowledge is collected through a 'cause-effect-action-outcome' (C-E-A-O) construct. Collection of knowledge is done through a critical incident approach. For each Event, attempt is to be made to capture its Cause, the Action taken and then the Outcome of the action. From the collected material, analysis to identify the patterns of causes and events would allow the important issues or factors to emerge. Dominant 'issues' are expected to be effective social characteristics for the classification of similar implementation projects.

In Figure 1 the patterns of the C-E-A-O chains are depicted. An event can be caused by an action of an actor or a condition which causes the event. An event may lead to further action, but can also be perceived as a cause of a future event. Collection of chains is considered useful to improve future processes.

The C-E-A-O chains is captured and perceived by actors with different roles involved in an ESI process (e.g. a project manager, an end user, a key user, a senior manager, and an IT-person). The C-E-A-O chains identified through our case studies are expected to be different for different contexts. The mapping of causes of the C-E-A-O chains into reference framework has led to different clusters of C-E-A-O chains. Each cluster belongs to a focus cell in the framework.

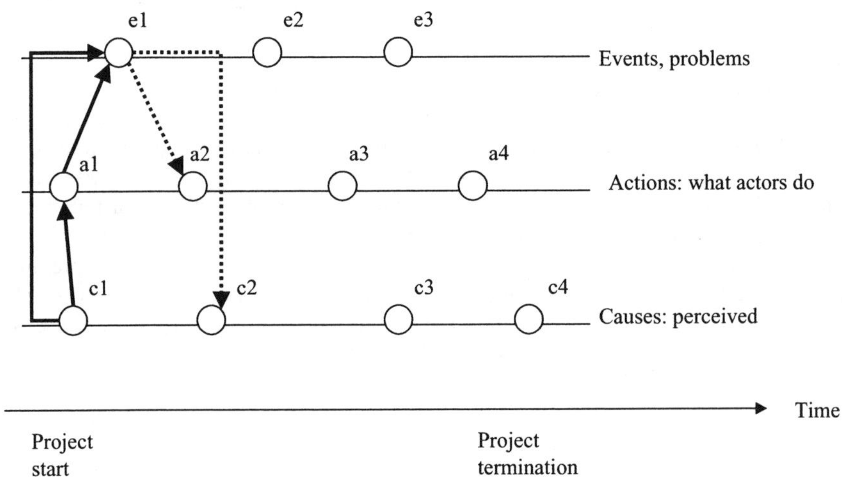

Figure 1: Cause, event, action map (adapted from Lanzara and Mathiassen (1995))

The wealth of the 'C-E-A-O' issues collected form the knowledge base that presents the possibilities of actions and previous case history. Worded as situational statements or questions, the Cause is used as the key to extract possible events and actions in similar implementation situations. Worded as incidents, the Event is used as the key to extract possible causes in a diagnostic mode or to extract the Action and Outcome for planning improvements. The success in the use of the 'C-E-A-O' construct as keys is heavily language dependent. The analysis and common agreement of the language used in the coding of the knowledge base requires discipline. The consortium has a central core team responsible for the analysis of the collected material.

The BEST consortium draws upon three sources for the development of the knowledge base. A first cycle used the experience of the consultant partners in the consortium. The captured C-E-A-O chains were used to develop and prove the BEST knowledge structure. A second cycle uses C-E-A-O chains collated from published literature. A total of about 250 chains were collected and this was used to inform the design. The use of literature cases is limited as most of the literature cases so not have the comprehensive information on the context of the project and do not record the cases to provide all elements of the C-E-A-O chain structure. The major concern in the attempt to use published cases centred on the research and philosophical perspective of the authors.

The main source of knowledge used was the industrial case studies that the consortium conducted. This is used as the primary source of knowledge as they were on-going or recently completed implementation projects. The research was done using the BEST case study protocol that provides the consistency of input. The first version of the BEST assessment tool contains 120 C-E-A-O chains.

The chains have been clustered into the different focus cells of the reference framework with respect to causes of issue. From this collection of issues the BEST Tool has been developed. The number of chains is expected to reach 400 when the BEST project funding finishes in November 2004.

6. BEST Assessment

The BEST assessment is delivered by a BEST practitioner using the knowledge base to help assess the 'readiness' of the organisation and people for the enterprise system (Figure 2).

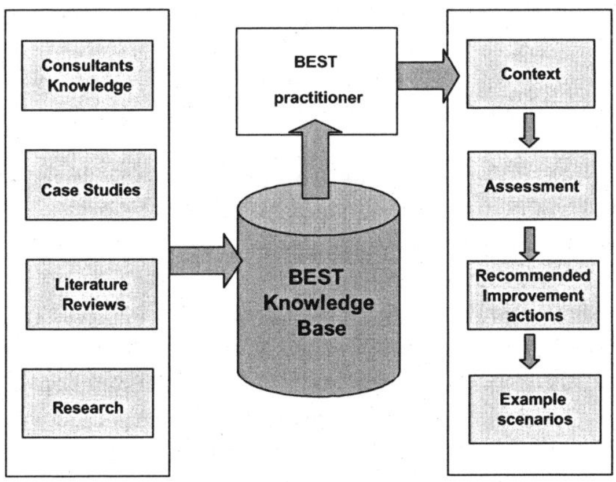

Figure 2 The BEST Assessment

There are four main outputs of the assessment. A BEST profile provide a graphical illustration of the size of the gaps in readiness based on the six aspects of the reference framework (Figure 3). This focuses the project team on possible areas for improvement.

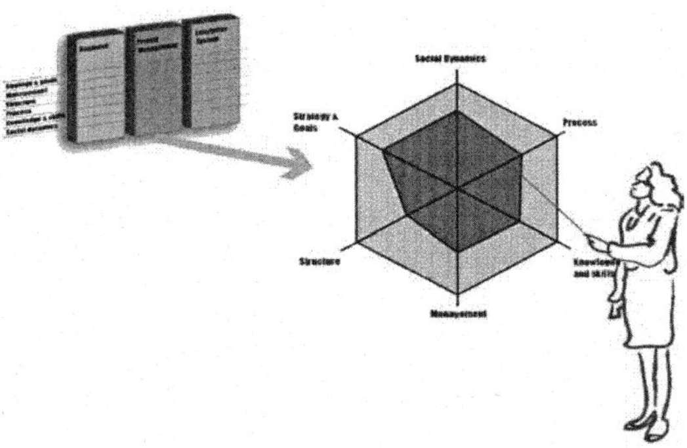

Figure 3. The BEST Tool readiness profile output

The second output is a collection of C-E-A-O chains that matches the project situation. This information allows the project team to learn from other experience and better informed about the strengths as well as potential risks. The learning about actions and outcomes prepare the team for future events if investment could not be made to effect improvements. The third outcome is a list of improvement actions appropriate to the situation. These improvement actions are related to the available actions that the team can take, or buy, and not historical actions in the cases. The fourth output is a collation of case studies that are in similar situations. The stories are useful to help the management team to visualise the possible courses that the project may take from the BEST readiness assessment.

7. BEST Engagement

As the BEST assessment is a learning process for the management team to learn from other peoples experience, the way that the assessment is delivered has been carefully designed from a socio-technical consideration. From an exploitation perspective, there would be variations in the exact delivery of the BEST engagement. From a system design perspective, the following steps represent the ideal engagement.

1. Getting to know the BEST on internet: www.best-project.com
2. Contacting a BEST provider
3. The initial meeting with the company. Presentation on BEST and the BEST method.
   Introduction of the BEST approach (context, assessment, improvement action)
   Reference framework
   This step ensures that all participants are familiar with the method and why it is being undertaken.
4. Run a CEAO workshop with relevant participants
   Context characterization. Questions in this step need to be answered to determine the characteristics of the company being assessed.
5. Context characterization. Questions in this step need to be answered to determine the characteristics of the company being assessed. This characterization has two goals:
   - Selection of assessment questions and answers applicable for the specific context.
   - Support of the consultant using the tool in formulating advice for the specific company
6. Performing the assessment of the readiness of the company to start an enterprise system implementation process. This step consists of answering the questions on the different dimensions and aspects of the reference framework. Each answer will be scored according to the predefined scores.
7. Presentation of scores in spider diagram. The spider diagram presented in the tool shows the dimensions and aspects that need attention. The scores will form the starting point of communication between the consultant and the company representative.
8. Presentation of c-e-a-o chains applicable to the situation assessed. The consultant will select chains from a list of chains linked to the dimensions and aspects that have been given low scores. The chains are used to discuss what could happen when the sub-optimal situation is not improved. The chains show what happened in similar cases.
9. What-if analysis. The consultant may also present information on previous enterprise system implementation processes from which the c-e-a-o chains have been selected as a basis for discussion with the company representative. This is used to support a what-if analysis of the situation assessed by referring to historical data from other companies.
10. Presentation of case information. The consultant may also present information on previous enterprise system implementation processes from which the CEAO chains and what-if analysis have been selected, for discussion with company representatives.

11. Selection of improvement actions from the repository of improvement actions. The repository can be adapted for individual consultancy practices. Select and agree on the improvement actions that need to be taken.
12. The company (supported by consultants) start to improve their situations and run a workshop on improvement actions. Presentation of the improvement actions from the repository of improvement actions. The repository is under construction and will be linked to the categories in the reference framework.
13. The company wants a follow-up assessment.

The process of using the BEST Tool is very important, the process is characterised with high degree of interaction, participation and reflections on the different subjects/topics while doing the assessment.

8. Application and exploitation of BEST

The first working version of the BEST readiness assessment tool was completed. The tool was demonstrated to a small number of consultants and user organisations outside of the consortium. This had yielded positive feedback and enthusiasm. These early tests included a Danish service provider, a Dutch independent consultant, a Dutch national public organisation and a large German industrial enterprise. The approach and framework for readiness assessment were considered very effective. The link between cause, event, action and outcome was considered very innovative and led the clients to plan for possible weaknesses. In the UK, BEST was demonstrated to K3, a UK software vendor focusing on manufacturing SMEs and also the regional IT adviser for SME business support. The UK consulting partner is using BEST as the approach to deliver the Microsoft Axapta SME ERP systems to their clients.

9. Conclusions

This paper has presented a methodology to gather and analysis knowledge from enterprise implementation processes. The knowledge has been translated into a prototype assessment tool as described in this paper. The innovative design of the BEST assessment can increase the likelihood of enterprise system implementation success by guiding the project team through others implementation experiences in a simple and approachable manner. The early results are already gaining significant exploitation uptake. Further work consists of adding additional knowledge and refining the tool to reflect the knowledge. An international community is envisioned to continue the work after the end of the EU funding.

Acknowledgement

The authors acknowledge the support of the European Commission through the BEST (Better Enterprise SysTems implementation) project, (www.best-project.com), IST-2001-35385. The contribution of consortium partners, Cranfield University, University of Twente, CeTIM, Technical University of Denmark, gedas uk ltd, KPA, ADEPA, Qualitech experts, SINTEF, CE Consulting, Fundecyt, Xpert Technologies, is also acknowledged.

References

[1] http://www.incose.org
[2] http://www.sei.cmu.edu
[3] http://www.ogc.gov.uk
[4] Markus LM, Tanis C (2000), The Enterprise System Experience: From adoption to success, in Zmud, R.W.(Ed.), Framing the Domains of IT Management: Projecting the Future through the Past, Pinnaflex Educational Resources, Inc., Cincinnati, OH, pp 173-207.
[5] Nah F, et al (2001), Critical factors for successful implementation of enterprise systems. Business Process Management Journal, Vol 7 No. 3 pp.285-296. MCB University Press, 1463-7154. USA. Roberts HJ,

Barrar PRN (1992), MRP II implementation: key factors for success. Computer Integrated Manufacturing Systems, Vol 5 No. 1, pp 31-8
[6] Robey D, Ross J, Boudreau M (2000), Learning to implement Enterprise Systems: An Exploratory Study of the Dialects of Change. Georgia State University. USA
[7] Rosario, JG (2000), On the leading edge: critical success factors in ERP implementation projects. Business World. Philippines.
[8] Sheth J (1981). Psychology of innovation resistance. Research in Marketing, Vol. 4, pp. 273-82.
[9] Stedman C (1998). ERP user interfaces drive workers nuts. ComputerWorld. URL: www.computerworld.com

eAdoption and the Knowledge Economy: Issues, Applications, Case Studies
P. Cunningham and M. Cunningham (Eds.)
IOS Press, 2004

Challenges of Work/Home Boundaries and User Perceptions for Ambient Intelligence

Rebecca ELLIS
Chimera, University of Essex, PP1 Ross Building, Adastral Park, Martlesham Heath, Ipswich, IP5 3RE, UK
Tel: +44 1473 632240, Fax: +44 1473 614936. Email: rellis@essex.ac.uk

Abstract: Current visions of Ambient Intelligence (AmI), as suggested by scenarios from advisory groups, challenge the way some of us currently lead our lives. These challenges principally arise from AmI's *de facto* blurring of work/home boundaries through its pervasive and 'always on' nature, and the projected manifestations of AmI devices which are subject to negative user perceptions. These challenges are explored in this paper, which reports on qualitative fieldwork from the Eurescom project 'PROFIT'. These challenges are shown to have significant business implications – from the need to have a greater ability to filter data and calls between people's work and home roles, to the necessity for a more sophisticated 'off' switch. Negative perceptions of AmI devices in terms of the independence of their advice also implies the need for collaboration with a trusted third party.

1. Introduction

Radical changes in the Information Society have opened a fast path towards a vision of "Ambient Intelligence" (AmI). Yet this AmI vision itself has some key underlying assumptions, which challenge the way some of us currently lead our lives and expect to live them in the future. These challenges principally arise from AmI's *de facto* blurring of work/home boundaries, and the projected manifestations of AmI devices - which are subject to negative user perceptions. These two challenges are explored in this paper, which reports on qualitative fieldwork from the Eurescom project 'PROFIT,' involving a collaboration of European ICTs researchers from Norway, Finland, Hungary and the UK.

1.1 Situating Ambient Intelligence and Work/Home Boundaries

To consider the theme of Ambient Intelligence at work, as is the focus of this session, increasingly involves exploring ideas of Ambient Intelligence at home. Existing telecommuting technologies such as laptops and mobile phones with Internet capabilities, and remote access to office servers, already blur the idea of work taking place both in a geographically separate office and during set working hours. Nippert-Eng's [1] classic study of the boundaries of work and home suggested telecommunications technologies are boundary-attenuating or modifying – they place pressure to integrate work and home. Considerable effort is needed if people wish to maintain work and home as separate domains. However, a vision of AmI devices which are ubiquitous, potentially 'always on,' and have 'intelligence' enough for work calls or data to 'follow you' towards many different devices in any location, potentially breaks down the notional boundaries of work and home to an even greater extent than in Nippert-Eng's study. The first objective of this paper is therefore to explore the key issues and implications of work/home boundaries for AmI.

Other authors have suggested people's work/home and public/ private boundaries as an important challenge for the AmI vision of the future. Aarts and Marzano [2] support this area as significant and suggest that AmI is important in the increasingly blurred boundaries between work and life. Riva *et al.* [3] note that AmI involves the integration of mobile technologies in a number of individual spaces - the body area network, the personal area network, the local area network, and the wide area network. The integration of these spatial layers inherently suggests a seamless integration across work and home. AmI also has tremendous monitoring and surveillance capabilities. This is due to an intelligent environment where people's everyday actions are monitored both on and offline [4]. Punie [4] suggests that Ambient Intelligence therefore makes the crossing of boundaries easier and more likely – between the private and public, and work and home. Ubiquitous computation is said to challenge facets of people's public and private lives – which will have them reaching for the 'off' button rather than 'always on' technologies. Punie's report [4] also posits that the home of the future could be a place where people are disconnected from too intrusive AmI devices – home then becomes a sanctuary. Yet although the issue of boundaries has been flagged as an important one for Ambient Intelligence, few pieces of original research have emerged which explore the pertinent issues.

One exception is Schlosser's paper [5], which provides us with some insights for AmI, and key issues of the present and future surrounding wireless handheld technologies. This primarily involves the negotiation of home and work identities through devices – such as a separation of social networks, work and home diaries and data, work and home phone calls and e-mails. The paper suggests that while mobile technologies will give us flexibility to juggle work and family aspects of our self-identities, they may also blur such traditional aspects of our sense of self. The study explored Rim's Blackberry – a pager and e-mail device, and mobiles with e-mail capabilities. Internet-enabled handheld computers have features which suggest further blurring of traditional home/work boundaries may occur. The 'always on' context, wearability and pervasiveness of the device may create the expectation of being on call all the time, leading to work-family conflicts. As such, the study shows how individuals regulate these boundaries between work and home while using handheld mobile devices. These activities include selective reading and responding, and leaving the device on, but putting it in a place where it won't disturb your sleep. Some felt their privacy was disturbed by the device. The devices presented problems in terms of home versus work identities - employees tried to separate home and work diaries on these devices due to their employer's ability to fully access the data.

Disciplinary boundaries themselves have mitigated against examining the challenge of work/home boundaries for Ambient Intelligence. The area of pervasive computing has traditionally been associated with exploring the computing technologies of the 'office,' but this focus has increasingly been critiqued by research on Ambient Intelligence and 'smart homes' which explores domestic spaces. Yet these two perspectives help maintain a dichotomy which prevents the holistic consideration of work, home and Ambient Intelligence. The Eurescom project therefore examined people's approaches to work and home as a whole - particularly whether they integrate or separate work and home and work/home identities, and the role of existing ICTs in this. Of particular concern was whether people liked and adapted to the integration of work and home enabled by pervasive ICTs, and if not, what existing coping mechanisms they used to maintain a separation.

1.2 User Perceptions of Ambient Intelligence

It is generally acknowledged that a user-centred approach is vital to the success of the Ambient Intelligence vision [4]. Yet existing AmI scenarios including those from ISTAG (Information Society Technologies Advisory Group) have been criticised for their unrealistic portrayal of everyday life. The fact that AmI devices can do 'mundane' things (such as housework) but that these are not included in AmI scenarios is noted in Punie's

EMTEL report [4]. The scenarios stereotyped user groups and featured ideal, successful users in a perfect world [4], whilst ignoring the struggles, irregularities and anxieties of existence. There are no technological malfunctions and the technology is mostly accepted without question [4]. User perceptions present societal challenges, which may be crucial barriers to the uptake of the Ambient Intelligence vision. The paper therefore secondly examines user perspectives on key elements of the AmI vision as identified in existing AmI scenarios from ISTAG and the WWRF (Wireless World Research Forum).

Punie's EMTEL report [4], through desk research alone, anticipated some negative user perceptions of Ambient Intelligence devices. The report notes that AmI technologies can easily appear to be controlling the user. Non-independence of AmI devices through business manipulation is also an identified risk of the AmI vision. Businesses may try and influence and manipulate consumers through AmI devices, such as through interactive, personalised marketing [4]. The EMTEL report also noted that there needs to be a relationship of trust and confidence between the user and device as agent for user acceptance – the device as agent would need to be at least as effective as the user in carrying out its tasks. Finally, AmI networks are noted to need a high degree of robustness and fault tolerance for the user to accept them [4]. The fieldwork element of the Eurescom project sought to explore such user perceptions through in-depth interviewing. The key elements of future AmI scenarios were presented to them verbally, and their initial views and feelings about the scenario were asked for.

2. Methodology

The research methodology involved semi-structured in-depth interviewing on work/ home boundary issues and user perceptions of AmI, followed by participants using diaries and disposable cameras to respond to research prompts on work/ home boundary issues. Two groups were studied - small business owners and the employees of large companies. These two samples were chosen because the literature suggested that they may have very different work/home boundaries, access to and usage of ICTs. In particular, small business owners are likely to integrate work and home by necessity of having few, if any, staff members; and shared work and home contact details. 47 individuals were interviewed across Norway (11), Finland (3), Hungary (15) and the UK (18), 13 of whom were self-employed or small-business owners and the rest were employees of government or business. Small business owners formed the majority of those involved in manual occupations in the study (such as plumbing and mechanics), although many were also involved in retailing (6). The UK sample included the most self-employed people (8), who were recruited through a small business association. All the other participants were recruited through the researchers' social networks. Employees interviewed were overwhelmingly white collar workers, with a good representation of those who worked for the state (doctors, teachers, social workers) as well as private business (analysts, consultants, website managers, finance managers).

This paper is presented with a number of caveats. It does not suggest that a sample size of 47 is adequate to generalise with certainty for a wider population. Indeed, the researchers' use of their own social networks led to an over-representation of knowledge workers and subjects like themselves – also involved in research and similar occupations. However, the extremely uniform repetition of responses across the European fieldwork countries gives a good indication of the socially constructed discourse surrounding Ambient Intelligence at the present time. These may or may not indicate barriers to the adoption of future AmI devices, and this is the second caveat of this paper. People's attitudes and perceptions of technology often change after they have used the technology, or after the technology has been introduced. Bagozzi, Davis and Warshaw [6] note that attitudes towards intending to use technology may be different from those formed after actual use, and may not be well informed.

3. Results

3.1 Work/Home Boundaries and AmI

Although AmI presents real challenges to work/home boundaries through being ubiquitous and 'always on,' it also has the potential device and systems intelligence to enable them to be re-established according to user needs and preferences. The qualitative fieldwork revealed a number of important work/home boundary concerns, which are relevant to the AmI vision. These involve firstly how ICTs currently break work/home boundaries that are unacceptable in people's everyday lives. Secondly, it is important to understand the key drivers behind wanting to keep work and home domains separate versus taking an integrationist approach, in order to help identify the subsets of people who may be taking these approaches. Whilst integrationists are likely to welcome a vision of pervasive and 'always on' AmI, separationists are likely to have special requirements of their AmI devices - and indeed may be more resistant to adoption unless it can support their approach.

ICTs break work/home boundaries in a number of ways at present. The self-employed are frequently interrupted by telephone calls 'after hours,' because they have the same contact details for both home and work, through landline and mobile phones. The use of the Internet in their businesses, and often the reliance on a desktop computer situated at home, means boundaries are broken through the need to respond to customer e-mails and to search for suppliers. Corporate employees have their work/home boundaries broken by calls to their work mobiles at home by their colleagues or their managers. Interruptions may also occur for corporate employees because work mobiles are used for both work and personal use. Personal calls creep into work time, or, more rarely, work calls into personal lives. Remote access also causes intrusions into home life or involves breaking down intra-work boundaries. Using remote access for whatever reason, such as to search the Internet, involves being diverted onto urgent work rather than the work planned. E-mails can create a trail of urgent work to deal with, which can disrupt the existing boundaries of work or home. Using remote access may also become a temptation for conscientious employees, where they cannot easily establish what their employers might expect of their usage.

There are, of course, many existing coping mechanisms to help prevent boundaries being broken. Caller display is used on both mobile and landline phones. Mobile phones may be turned off, put on silent mode or voicemail. Landline phones may be unplugged or use an answering service. In more extreme cases, the complete non-adoption of the technology or service may be used, or insurmountable barriers placed so that the service cannot be used. This was often the case with remote access in the study - obsolete laptops without Internet capability were taken home. But AmI can offer some more 'intelligent' solutions to such user needs, as discussed in detail in section 4 on business implications.

There are some specific sets of people who wish to keep work and home quite separate, based on key drivers, which are very important to their everyday lives. One of the principal reasons given for separation was that integration led to distractions and fragmentations in either one or both domains. Home and work domains may also be kept separate because people have strong philosophies that this is the way to maintain a certain quality of life. Work and home life is also kept separate as a result of responsibilities at home – people's children and partners. Certain types of employment can also lead to a separation of work and home domains. Mobile phones are forbidden in the health services because they interfere with machines and are a potential distraction. Work and home may also be kept separate, partly because this is the culture in a particular place of work. Another key reason to keep home and work life separate is to maintain a degree of privacy. This is especially true of small businesses, who both live and work at home. Finally, work and home domains may also be kept relatively separate in order to be able to impose some intra-work boundaries. This is especially true of ICT usage – work and home boundaries may be enforced in terms of ICTs to enable quiet, contemplative work to take place uninterrupted at home. People for whom these key drivers are important will not want 'always on' AmI devices to break their firmly established boundaries. It is important to have the ability to maintain such work/home boundaries – to stop or divert incoming messages or data from work at home or home at work. A form of 'off switch' is necessary for such devices, which is more sophisticated than just powering down – such as a do not disturb or sleep mode.

But the integration of work and home domains is already occurring due to a number of key drivers, and this increased blurring may make always on AmI devices acceptable to another subset of people. Integration may occur for those who are time pressured, and spend many hours in the formal work place. The integration of home and work may also occur out of preference for a way of working which gives individuals more control about when to work – such as when feeling creative or inspired. Those who integrate work and home to the greatest extent, and place no boundaries to protect their home lives, tend not to have demanding home responsibilities, such as their own home or children. Work and home may also be integrated because this is what is expected either by customers or by one's boss. This is particularly necessary for some small businesses who build a customer base through excellent customer service and having a reputation for it. Work and home may additionally be integrated in order to make work more 'social' or pleasurable. Integrating work and home may also be the result of a particular work culture.

It was postulated during the research that those who want to and are able to separate work and home are more likely to be employed by other people – since they can delegate responsibility to their colleagues during non-work hours which small businesses cannot. The fieldwork, especially in the UK, Finland and Hungary, showed employees were often more able to separate and that 'profit maximising' small businesses integrated work and home by necessity. However, the study also revealed the situation of work/home boundaries is more complex than anticipated. In the UK fieldwork, a subset of small businesses, 'lifestyle businesses,' also wish to maintain strict work/home boundaries since their businesses were formed to maintain a certain quality of life and lifestyle rather than profit maximisation. They tend to value demarcated home time as part of achieving a high quality of life. The Hungarian study also found that highly committed research workers, as a subset of the corporate group, were likely to be integrators.

3.2 User Perceptions of AmI

The responses to existing AmI scenarios presents crucial data for ICTs businesses in terms of key concerns which will provide barriers to the adoption of AmI devices and services and a challenge to the AmI vision. User perceptions of key elements of the AmI scenarios were surprisingly uniform across the fieldwork countries - Norway, Finland, Hungary and the UK, with the same responses being repeated across the countries. The user perceptions also confirmed many of the suppositions of the EMTEL report [4]. These key devices and elements were: a 'digital me' - a device which could control who accessed individuals by voice at a particular time and which calls would be ignored, a unified identity verification device, the 'guardian angel' system of health monitoring and advice, a vision where AmI devices adapted the environment and data for your tastes and preferences, and devices which acted as your 'agent' - such as Internet 'bots' or smart fridges.

Respondents were concerned that devices such as the 'guardian angel' health monitoring system, the identity verification device, and the device as 'agent' which can order things for you, will not be independent. For the 'guardian angel' and device as 'agent,' interviewees feared that the advice or results given would be used to encourage sales of particular items, rather than being optimal for their needs. There was also concern about data privacy. Such AmI devices are constantly monitoring you and gathering data, and questions arise about who owns this data, who can access it, and if it can be sold for marketing purposes. Equally, people felt the wide range of information on the identity verification device may be downloaded in total by firms in order to be used for marketing – rather than a small, specific piece of information necessary for a transaction. The identity verification device raised strong feelings about the need for data privacy, and many would be nervous about what business and government might do with such data. People preferred to have an identity verification device that only offered an extremely 'hollowed out' form of identity verification - just confirming who they are with simple biometric data, not being combined with other data such as financial details or a passport. Related to the privacy issues of data generated and stored on AmI devices, is one of security. In particular, the identity verification device which unified a number of data sources, promoted feelings of insecurity. Respondents felt that they might lose the device, or that it might be stolen or hacked into. Equally, the other AmI devices such as the 'guardian angel' contain sensitive data, and users will need to feel that such devices are totally secure.

Respondents were also concerned that AmI devices led to a loss of control, or were too controlling. They felt they would lose control of how their personal information was used, which is strongly related to privacy issues. However, AmI devices were seen as too controlling through their didactic qualities – telling others or their owners what to do. Both the 'digital me' and the 'guardian angel' share these qualities. The 'guardian angel' was particularly poorly received from this perspective by younger people – disliking the device potentially telling them what not to do because it may be unhealthy. The programming of AmI devices will need to make them seem less controlling and more advisory.

Although Ambient Intelligence devices have a form of intelligence where they can act autonomously and predict tastes and preferences based on programmed choices and previous behaviour, interviewees felt they weren't intelligent enough and never could be. Their tastes could not be defined mechanistically, and the device couldn't identify an important phone call from an unimportant one. The device could not anticipate their behaviour or moods well enough to make decisions as good as, or better than them at a particular time. Norwegian respondents were particularly sceptical about the issue of 'intelligence' - citing the Microsoft paperclip as an example of intelligent agents that weren't intelligent enough, and therefore became annoying. Other respondents feared that being surrounded by AmI devices would lead to over-reliance on the technology, which would cause tremendous problems if there were systems failures. AmI systems must be extremely robust, but also allow people to return to more conventional ways of doing things if necessary (such as dim lights or lock doors).

4. Business Implications

The challenges of work/home boundaries and negative perceptions of AmI devices have substantial potential implications in bringing AmI devices and services to market. However, such observations remain high level and largely hypothetical generalisations, due to the still largely unknown manifestation of AmI products in practice and production.

Maintaining work/home boundaries is significant for a subset of people for whom there are key drivers in their lives which make such boundaries important, such as the desire to prevent distraction or spending quality time with their children. AmI devices need to support work/home boundaries through sophisticated yet simple to use forms of diverting data and calls and 'switching off,' and support unmet needs people presently have in this area. Yet AmI devices must also accommodate the seamlessness expected and an integrationist approach that is present for others. Suppliers of AmI services need to offer a variety of service 'bundles' to accommodate separationist, integrationist and in between 'hybrid' approaches to work and home domains, and find a way to quickly determine and predict such user requirements - which often arise from particular home circumstances, attitudes and types of employment. There are some specific identified unmet needs in work/home boundary area. Most of these unmet needs already have technical solutions. However, they are often too expensive for the average user, not user friendly, too complicated or are not offered as a service 'bundle' - or by a particular supplier who the user is signed up with. Differentiated ring tones to identify work or home callers and better establish boundaries was one need. The need to maintain work/work boundaries was also an important research finding. This principally involved the need to have some way to better filter e-mails, so that e-mails which would cause a stream of work would not be immediately visible, but diverted into a priority folder. The easy and automatic filtering of e-mails into work and personal folders, and the ability to differentiate between bulk e-mails and e-mails just to oneself was also important. AmI devices, which break the boundaries of work and home through their pervasiveness and 'always on' nature, could, if they were so designed, ironically better support work home boundaries than is possible at present. It may be easier to have multiple phone numbers directed to a single device so that filtering of work and home calls is more possible. Mobile, robust, 'always on' AmI devices would also enable work-related e-mailing and Internet surfing to be reintegrated into work time for those who now have to use their home PCs 'after work.' AmI devices and services must be 'intelligent' in such subtle social ways in order to be accepted by the majority of people..

In this study, AmI devices were socially constructed in mostly very negative ways, with surprising uniformity across Europe, which is an important challenge to the AmI vision. Some of these negative social constructions have tangible business implications, which need to be addressed before AmI devices and services are introduced to the consumer. The issue of non-independence raises problems for AmI-related businesses. They are unlikely to be seen as independent, but to have a vested interest in selling details on for marketing, or for use within their existing businesses. They may need to have external verification by a trusted third party, such as a regulator or government, that they are giving accurate advice and not misusing data. Policies must be clearly established which maximise and define users' privacy. Security features must be emphasised, explained and highly visible. Finally, users must feel they are ultimately in control of such devices – from the data they produce, to being able to override them and cope with systems failures.

AmI devices were also associated with some positive qualities, which will need to be strongly emphasised in design, manufacture and marketing - AmI devices were thought to be extremely useful in taking over very mundane tasks which people find no pleasure in. This was said to reduce people's cognitive load and be time saving. Examples include turning off lights, compiling a shopping list, or looking for cheaper car insurance. AmI devices additionally gave some people back a feeling of control in certain circumstances. This is most true of the 'digital me' device and the device as 'agent.' The 'digital me' puts the owner back in control of who can contact them by voice at a particular time, and the device as 'agent' carries out the owner's wishes. AmI devices were also seen as useful in filtering much of the digital material that people do not want coming into their homes or workplaces – such as junk e-mails. AmI needs to be associated with undoing some of the more problematic aspects of existing ICTs to be accepted and not resisted as a more invasive, insidious and controlling form of what already exists.

5. Conclusions

This paper identifies some of the key challenges Ambient Intelligence presents for the way we lead our lives at present, and how such a vision would have to be modified for more widespread adoption of its key elements. While AmI has many positive features which can help people in their everyday lives, never has it been so pertinent to understand people's life worlds and how AmI devices could be usefully incorporated into them, if AmI itself is not to be challenged and resisted. This will help mould and shape how AmI devices, networks and services materialise in practice, reducing some of the current uncertainties and unknowns of this vision. Further research and bigger sample sizes of more varied subjects are needed to ascertain whether the user perceptions of AmI devices are indeed as uniform across Europe as they currently appear. Additionally, research is needed into whether user perceptions are likely to change after the *ad hoc* introduction of some AmI elements - such as identity cards with biometric data, as currently being trialled in the UK.

References

[1] Nippert-Eng, C. E. (1995) *Home and Work – Negotiating Boundaries through Everyday Life* (University of Chicago Press, London).

[2] Aarts, E. and Marzano, S. (2003) The *New Everyday – Views on Ambient Intelligence* (010Publishers, Rotterdam).

[3] Riva, G.; Loreti, P.; Lunghi, M, Vatalaro, F. and Davide, F. (2003) 'Presence 2010: The emergence of ambient intelligence,' *Emerging Communication*, 5, 59-82.

[4] Punie, Y. (2003) *A social and technological view of Ambient Intelligence in Everyday Life: What bends the trend?* Key deliverable, The European Media and Technology in Everyday Life Network (EMTEL).

[5] Schlosser, F. K. (2002) 'So, how do people really use their handheld devices? An interactive study of wireless technology use,' *Journal of Organizational Behaviour*, 23, 401-423.

[6] Bagozzi, R. P., Davis, F. D. and Warshaw, P. R. (1992) 'Development and test of a theory of technological learning and usage,' *Human Relations*, 46(7), 660-686.

eAdoption and the Knowledge Economy: Issues, Applications, Case Studies
P. Cunningham and M. Cunningham (Eds.)
IOS Press, 2004

Natural Multimodal Interaction for Design Applications

Els DEN OS[1], Lou BOVES[2]
[1]*Max Planck Institute for Psycholinguistics, Wundtlaan 1, Nijmegen, 6525 XD, Netherlands*
Tel: +31 24 352 1333, Fax: + 31 24 352 1213, Email: els.denos@mpi.nl
[2]*Radboud University Nijmegen, Erasmusplein 1, Nijmegen, 6525 HT, Netherlands*
Tel: +31 24 361 2902, Fax: + 31 24 361 2907, Email: L.Boves@let.kun.nl

Abstract: One of the open issues in multimodal interaction is the antagonism between proponents of the direct manipulation and the communication agent metaphors. In this paper we describe an experiment in which we tested a system based on the communication agent metaphor for a bathroom design application. We found that non-expert users have no difficulties interacting with the communication agent application, due to the fact that they were able to discover the mental model applied by the application designers. However, we observed the need for substantial improvements of the recognition technology needed to build conversational interfaces.

1. Introduction

One of the important open issues in multimodal interaction is the question whether the direct manipulation or the communication agent metaphor should be preferred. Some authors argue that direct manipulation is always best [1], while others provide evidence in favour of the conversational agent metaphor [2]. However, it is quite likely that the users' preference for the interaction metaphor depends strongly on their knowledge of the application domain and the functionality of the interface. In [3] it is shown that users do not appreciate the guidance of a conversational agent in completing the query form for a timetable information system. However, the authors suggest that the help and guidance that an agent can offer will be appreciated if users need to accomplish a task that they perform seldom, and that addresses a domain where they lack detailed technical and procedural knowledge. Architectural design –instantiated here in the form of bathroom design application- is probably a good example. Most customers buy a new bathroom only once or twice in their lifetime. Yet, designing a new bathroom requires substantial knowledge about existing options for tiles and sanitary ware, as well as of guidelines for how to arrange sanitary and select designs that go together well.

In principle, a task such as bathroom design can be implemented both in the form of direct manipulation and a conversational agent. In the COMIC project (www.comic.mpi.nl) we are working on the implementation of a conversational agent system for bathroom design [4]. Some companies have launched competing solutions based on the direct manipulation approach. In this paper we focus on our experiences with the design, implementation and test of the conversational agent approach to bathroom design. In doing so, we will address a number of technical issues that have a large impact on the users' appreciation. In addition, we will report on our observations of a number of subjects who used direct manipulation applications for the same task, as a stepping stone for a larger comparative analysis of the two approaches that is presently being carried out.

The information provided in this paper should be of immediate interest for scientists in the area of multimodal interaction for eCommerce and eWork services. In addition, it should help managers and investors to better assess the opportunities and risks involved in developing multimodal applications.

2. Objectives

The first step in bathroom (re-) decoration is to input the shape and dimensions of the room, and the location and dimensions of doors and windows. The best way to do this is by specifying a blueprint of the room, adorned with some annotation (for example for the height of window sills). In existing commercial software packages this information must be entered by means of drag and drop actions, combined with keyboard input. Figure 1 shows a snapshot of a screen as it may appear in such an application.

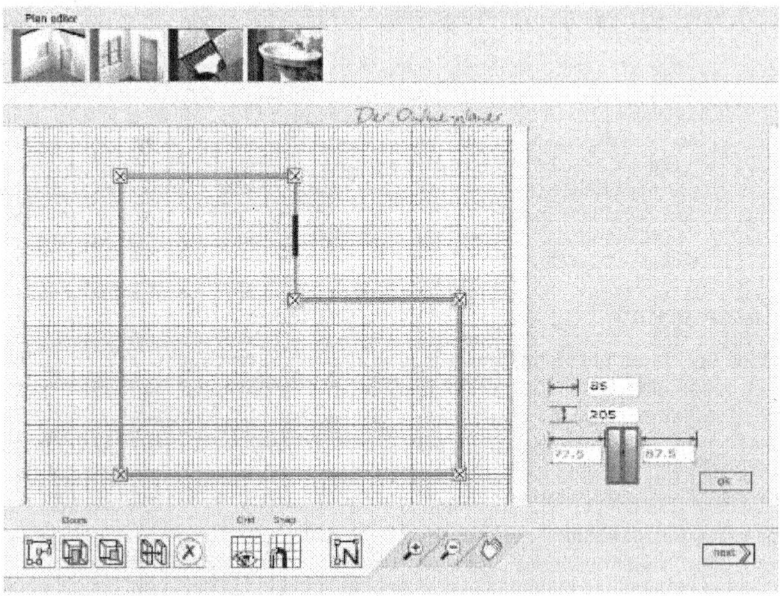

Figure 1: Snapshot of the direct manipulation tool. The outline of a room is shown, together with the location and the dimensions of a door. Icons at the bottom indicate objects. The digit fields at the right must be used to indicate dimensions.

Although expert sales persons can learn to operate this type of software packages in a training course, one must doubt whether non-expert customers are able to use this kind of applications, for example as a self-help tool to get a global impression of the possibilities for (re-)decorating their bathroom within given budget constraints. To investigate this, we observed six highly educated subjects while they attempted to enter a pre-specified blueprint with the ViSoft Websolution, a prototype GUI application for bathroom design and the Saniweb tool (www.saniweb.nl), an application for access by the general public.

Until now, few user studies with multimodal systems have been reported. The primary goal of this paper is to report on the results of an experiment that was designed to investigate the task completion and user satisfaction of the conversational system for bathroom design that is under development in COMIC. In doing so, we pay special attention to the performance of the pen and speech module as well as the fusion and Natural Language Processing module that are responsible for the recognition and interpretation of the users' input, since it has been shown repeatedly that this performance has a major impact on user satisfaction [5].

3. Methodology

The usability evaluation of the ViSoft Websolution was performed in the form of participating observation. The authors observed six colleagues while they tried to input a pre-specified blueprint with the two GUI applications. During and after the interaction the beliefs and opinions of the users were recorded in the form of unstructured question-answer conversations. The results of these interviews are presented in section 5.

The conversational agent system built into the COMIC project uses pen and speech for input, and two graphical screens and a loudspeaker for output. One screen is used to display an avatar that interacts with the user by means of synthetic speech and by head gestures (thinking, listening) as back channel information while the user is speaking or drawing. The second screen is actually a tablet computer, which renders the ink produced by the subjects, as well as the interpretation that the system made of the user's input. Figure 2 shows a user interacting with the system, wearing a headset and head mounted microphone.

Figure 2: The COMIC system is shown on the right. The left screen shows the flow of active models for demonstration purposes.

To evaluate the user appreciation of our system, we designed an experiment in which 28 subjects (20 females and 8 males) entered three blueprints, that of their private bathroom, that of their parents' and that of a friend or relative. The age of the subjects ranged between 20 and 37. All subjects were students or scientists associated with the University of Nijmegen or the Max Planck Institute for Psycholinguistics in Nijmegen. Thus, all subjects belong to the group the highest possible education level. After completing the three tasks, subjects filled out a questionnaire comprising 26 Likert scales, designed to measure their appreciation of the system. Examples of statements that we used are "It was easy to use the system", "I always understood what the system expected me to do", "I would be happy to use this system a next time", etc. Subjects had to indicate whether they totally disagreed (scale value 1), disagreed (scale value 2), neither agreed nor disagreed (scale value 3), agreed (scale value 4), or totally agreed (scale value 5) with the statements.

During the experiment all data pertaining to the interaction between the subjects and the system were logged and stored in a database. After each experiment the interaction data were annotated by hand. In this manner we added information about the recognition performance of the pen and speech recognizer, the Natural Language Processing and the Media Fusion modules to the database. Using the combined subjective and objective data of the 28 subjects, we conducted statistical analyses to search for interesting relations between the behaviour of subjects in response to the behaviour of the system.

4. Technology Description

The bathroom design system tested in this experiment has essentially the same functionality as the GUI system that it will eventually supersede: users can draw the outline of the room, specify the lengths of the walls with centimetre precision, and indicate the position and dimensions of the doors and windows. A subsequent version will also allow users to add sanitary ware to the blueprint, but this was not implemented in the tested version.

Pen input was acquired by means of a Wacom CintiQ 15X graphical LCD tablet. The pen input recognition software was developed at the NICI [6]. The recogniser is able to automatically classify pen input as deictic gestures (point-and-click), sketching or handwriting. This interpretation is helped by the expectation that is generated by the Dialog and Action Manager: after a request from the system to draw the shape of the room, it is reasonable to expect drawing, while pen input is much more likely to be handwriting after a system prompt to specify the dimensions of the room.

Speech input used a head mounted noise cancelling microphone. The speech recognition system is based on the open source Hidden Markov Toolkit (HTK). Both pen and speech input were fed into a Natural Language Processing module that is responsible for the semantic interpretation of the individual input channels. A Fusion module combined information from the two parallel input channels. During the experiment the Dialog Manager was partly simulated in the form of a Wizard-of-Oz design, but at the time of this writing is has been replaced by a fully implemented software module. Feedback of the system to the user was in the form of stylised graphical output. Finally, system guidance was provided by means of spoken utterances.

4.1 Multimodal Turn Taking

One of the important issues that came up during the implementation of the COMIC system was the concept of multimodal turn taking. The concept of turn taking originates from the theory of conversations between two or more persons. In an 'ideal' conversation at any one time only one person is speaking. It is also assumes that speakers convey clear signals to inform their interlocutors that a turn has ended, so that another person can take the floor. Moreover, it is assumed that the meaning of what a speaker just said when (s)he stops talking can be determined from the verbal contents of the message. In face-to-face interaction, where visual signals are exchanged in addition to verbal information, the simple concept of dialog turns does not hold. Visual and verbal information do not need to be synchronised. For example, a speaker can assume a posture that indicates an imminent end of turn well before the speech message is complete. But if two persons are talking about a bathroom design, and support the information exchange by sketching and pointing, it is quite possible that sketching continues after a spoken utterance is completed, and that the sketch is essential for interpreting the meaning of the verbal information [7].

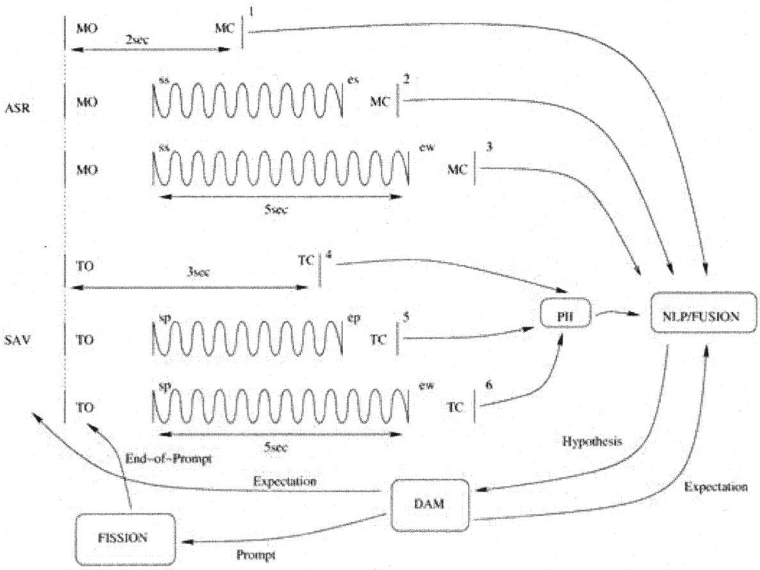

Figure 3. Definition of multimodal turns and end-of-turn synchronisation. Time is running from left to right. The leftmost edge represents the end of a system prompt.
MO: Microphone Open; MC: Microphone Closed
TO: Tablet input Open; TC Tablet input Closed

Presently, there is no computational theory of multimodal turn taking. But to build a multimodal interaction system a rudimentary version of such a theory must be formulated and implemented. In the COMIC system under test in this paper we opted for a definition of turns in which the verbal and gestural input channels are synchronised (cf. Figure 3). This enables the system to determine the end-of-turn and to make a definitive interpretation of the inputs. Strict synchronisation, as implemented in COMIC, has the advantage that it turns input processing and interpretation into a process that is manageable. However, it has the disadvantage that users must learn that speech or gestures produced after the end-of-turn detected by the system will get lost. Presently, we are working towards a less rigid definition of multimodal turn taking, in which the system still starts processing the input received up to a moment when both pen and speech contain a relatively long pause, but where speech and pen input produced after the pause are captured and stored for processing in the next user turn. However, the system's reaction to the first turn will not reflect the information provided after the pause that triggered the interpretation process. We are planning experiments to investigate under what conditions this behaviour that is different from what we expect in human-human interaction may confuse users.

5. Results

5.1 The GUI applications

The main observation we made form observing six users trying to enter a blueprint is that they all started with a different mental model of how the application expected them to input the data (walls with measures, doors with measures, and windows with measures). These mental models never matched the "default mental model" of the system. This caused a large number of repair actions that sometimes resulted in a perfect copy of the blueprint but most often did not. One user started drawing the room without looking at the right measures (she thought that she could adjust these later, which turned out to be rather complicated). Another user started inputting measures of the walls without first drawing them, and again another user was able to input all data, but was not able to position the window at the correctly. Only one subject discovered how she could change the width and height of a window in the easiest way. None of the users read the instructions; all just started to input data and some of the subjects tried to recover the instructions when they got stuck. This is a well known phenomenon for almost all applications.

It also appeared that the experience gained with one GUI application had a negative effect on the other, because they were based on different choices for the interaction protocol: one used the 'select object, then indicate action' protocol, while the other used 'select action, then select object' order. On the other hand, once the system had been explained to the users, they learned very fast how to use this system in an efficient way.

It was also evident that users found it very difficult, if not impossible, to get a good idea of the design options that were available for sanitary ware and tiles. This is due to the fact that browsing on the basis of thumbnail pictures is a very difficult task for users who do not know how to interpret tiny pictures. Adding short explanations to the thumbnails in pop-up windows does not solve this problem, because more often than not users are not able to understand the meaning of crucial terms in the explanations.

5.2 The Conversational Agent application

Twenty-eight subjects participated in the user test with the COMIC system, a medium-scale user test for multimodal systems. The data logs obtained in multimodal user tests are usually very large (Mbytes) and difficult to analyse automatically. This is because not all events that happen during a dialog can be classified and annotated automatically. For example, the performance of the speech and pen input recognisers can only be established by having a person compare the acoustic and visual input with the recognisers' output. All user data have been analysed by an analysis tool that was developed for this project [8]. In addition, the answers to the questionnaire have been analysed.

Log data analysis showed that, similar to the direct manipulation application, there was a learning effect: users were faster when inputting the third bathroom than when inputting the first bathroom. Mean turn duration decreased from 12.3s for the first bathroom to 11.5s for the third bathroom. The total number of turns (35) did not change. From the log analysis it became clear that recognition performance for handwriting and speech was far from perfect. Handwriting recognition was 83% correct, and speech recognition was correct only 56% of the time. This is because users have no way to know the types of input the system can handle (cf. [5]). The lack of application specific training data, especially for speech recognition, is responsible for the low recognition performance. Our user test provided valuable data that will be used to train the recogniser for this specific task.

We observed that most users showed the tendency to continue using the modality they started with, and only switched to the alternative modality after repeated recognition errors. Thus, when users used speech for inputting the measures of the walls, they often only switched to handwriting after three or more misrecognitions. Similar observations have previously been reported [9]. Apparently, changing modality requires conscious cognitive activity, which users are not able or willing to perform easily. This means that also for multimodal systems speech and gesture recognition performance should be high, and that one should not capitalise on the hope that one modality naturally acts as a back-up if another fails. It is also evident that users do not easily discover the most efficient and affective manner of using a mix of modalities.

The answers to the questionnaire made clear that the users found it easy to form a mental model of the system. The instruction was clear (mean scale value 4.2) and most subjects understood what they were supposed to do while using the system (mean scale value 3.5). They liked that they could combine pen and speech (mean scale value 4.1), and the feedback by the system was very clear to the users (mean scale value 4.3). However, they were not happy with the recognition performance and did not consider the system to be efficient (mean scale value2.5). There was a high correlation between the objective performance of the system and most subjective judgements.

From the answers to the questionnaires it can be deduced that the turn taking protocol that we implemented did not confuse the users, despite its difference from multimodal turn taking in human-human interaction. At the same time, however, an analysis of the timing of user and system turns suggests that this protocol has contributed to the impression that the system is quite rigid, and needs improvement.

6. Business Benefits

This user study suggests that at least for this type of design applications, an interface using a multimodal communication agent metaphor will provide user-friendly and intuitive user interfaces. Since users can more easily form a mental model of the application, this type of interface solves the problems that occur with the direct manipulation application in which users have to struggle to find out how to use mouse and keyboard. Moreover, the conversational agent metaphor makes it much more natural and easy to provide guidance and explanation to non-expert users during an interaction, compared to consulting on-line help systems when problems occur in interacting with a direct manipulation interface to an application that assumes that users have a considerable amount of domain knowledge. Intuitive interfaces are of course very important for offering eInclusion to the highest possible proportion of European citizens. However, this study also made clear that the basic technologies, like pen and gesture recognition, need to be improved and should be made more robust against all types of unexpected user behaviour.

7. Conclusions

The most important result of our experiment is that non-expert subjects are able to use the COMIC system to accomplish tasks that could not easily be completed with web-based direct manipulation applications. The multimodal communication agent metaphor makes it easier to form an adequate mental modal of the application. In addition, users like to combine pen and speech, because for them this is the most intuitive way to communicate design issues. In addition, the results of the user studies provide clear guidelines for further improvements of the recognition technology. Last but not least, the analysis of the interactions between users and the COMIC system suggests that the concept of turn taking in multimodal interaction needs to be revised and redefined.

The need for intuitive user interfaces is huge, given the aim of Europe to include as many citizens as possible into the world of electronic data exchange. However, many more user studies have to be performed with multimodal communication agent applications to fully understand how these interfaces can best be designed and deployed. In the final year of the COMIC IST project, we will perform additional user studies that should give more insights into the benefits and needs of this type of interface.

Acknowledgement

We thank all members of the COMIC team for their contributions to the work reported in this paper. The COMIC is co-funded by the EU, under the IST-2001-32311 contract.

Special thanks are due to ViSoft GmbH, one of the partners in COMIC, who made their experimental Websolution available for the research reported in this paper.

References

[1] Shneiderman, B. and Maes, P. (1997), "Direct Manipulation vs. Interface Agents, excerpts from the debates at IUI 97 and CHI 97" In: *Interactions of the ACM*, 4 (6), pp. 42-61.

[2] McGlashan, S. (1995), "Speech Interfaces to Virtual Reality" In: *Proc. of 2nd International Workshop on Military Applications of Synthetic Environments and Virtual Reality.*

[3] Sturm, J., Boves, L., Cranen, B. and Terken, J. (submitted) Direct manipulation or conversational agent: what is the best metaphor for multimodal form-filling interfaces? *Human Computer Interaction Journal.*

[4] den Os, E. and Boves, L. (2003) Towards Ambient Intelligence: Multimodal Computers that Understand Our Intentions. *Proceedings eChallenges 2003.*

[5] Kvale, K., Rugelbak, J. and Amdal, I. (2003) How do non-expert users exploit simultaneous inputs in multimodal interaction?, *Proc. International Symposium on Human Factors in Telecommunication*, Berlin, 1-4. December 2003.

[6] Van Erp, M., Vuurpijl, L.G., & Schomaker, L.R.B. (2002). An overview and comparison of voting methods for pattern recognition. *Proc. of the 8th International Workshop on Frontiers in Handwriting Recognition (IWFHR.8)* pp. 195-200.

[7] Lee, J. (1999) Words and pictures -- Goodman revisited. In: R. Paton and I. Neilson (Eds.) *Visual Representations and Interpretations*, London: Springer Verlag, pp. 21-31.

[8] Vuurpijl, L et al. (2004) Evaluation of multimodal dialog systems. Workshop on MMCorpora, in press

[9] Sturm, J. and L. Boves (submitted) Effective error recovery strategies for multimodal form-filling applications. *Speech Communication.*

eAdoption and the Knowledge Economy: Issues, Applications, Case Studies
P. Cunningham and M. Cunningham (Eds.)
IOS Press, 2004

Ambient Intelligence Vision: Exploring the Social Risks of its Construction

Irene LOPEZ DE VALLEJO,
UCL, The Barlett, Faculty of the Built Environment, Gower Street, London, WC1E 6BT, UK
Tel: +4402076781754, Fax: + 4402079161887, Email: i.vallejo@ucl.ac.uk

Abstract: This paper explores the social risks associated to the construction of the Ambient Intelligence (from now on AmI) vision. Starting with an overview of what is AmI, and how the social challenges posed by the vision are differently interpreted by research, industry and policy-makers, the author argues how difficult is today to visualize the implications that AmI realization has on our common future. Two main hypotheses are presented to the public and a research proposal is suggested to take actions to avoid the possible negative implications of the AmI vision.

1. Introduction

Since the AmI concept lacks clear and accepted definitions it is necessary from the outset to clarify terms. Throughout this paper the author refers to the "development of Ambient Intelligence", by this it's meant the multiple technological developments in areas such as pervasive computing, interface design and communications that are leading towards the creation of a truly intelligent environment.

Ambient Intelligence (AmI) will not be the outcome of any single technology or application; it is an 'emergent' property [1] that results from the parallel development and introduction of a large number of interrelated systems, sensors, databases and interfaces.

Policy makers and research community are starting to understand that the 'emergent' nature of the concept, its complexity and its actual manifestation in real life poses challenges for society as a whole. These concerns are clearly expressed by the ISTAG group who state "AmI needs to be driven by humanistic concerns, not technologically determined ones, and should be controllable by ordinary people" [1]

The research community interprets the social challenges posed by the development of the vision differently. Two main perspectives exist, the optimistic perspective, that sees mostly benefits instead of challenges and that hopes AmI will improve our lives, and the pessimistic approach, that perceives the challenges as risks, the risk of intrusion and loss of privacy, and of the emergence of an Orwellian 'Big Brother' society.

The author believes that neither position is sustainable and positions her in a posture that tries to reconcile these views. The deployment of AmI technology opens huge possibilities, though also huge risks to society. We have to be aware of both, chances and risks, and work for a balanced realization of the vision.

This paper focuses on the possible social risks attached to the AmI vision. One reason for focusing on negative aspects is that this is the right moment to do it, at an early stage when we are talking about how to make the vision real. The positive aspects, if they come out after the deployment of technology will be welcomed, but not the negative ones. This paper contributes to the debate on the risks that this technological future poses, identify and discuss a number of social issues and suggest actions to be taken to avoid them.

1.1 Social risks of the AmI Vision

The author understands that the above-mentioned developments will profoundly change the way that people interact with technology and possibly each other. Given the pervasive, or environment wide nature, of AmI the author believes that its development will have implications for the lives of all Europeans.

But the fact is that today, nobody knows certainly how it is going to materialize. We know that "everything will be connected to everything else," but "no one has any idea what all those connections will mean" [2]

This uncertainty can be understood at several levels. It can be taken as a criticism of the perceived lack of focus when it comes to AmI applications, or as a lack of understanding the consequences of its deployment in the real world: how will we use "smart things" in our everyday lives? When should we switch them on or off? What should smart things be permitted to hear, see, and feel? And whom should they be allowed tell about it?

It can also be taken as a simple statement of fact about the complexity of the future. The outputs resulting from the myriad interconnections required to create ambient intelligence cannot be read of a schematic or wiring diagram. Rather than predict what the consequences of these technologies will be we will have to observe them.

In this context, and taking the posture of the pessimists, it can be argued that the research community has no clear picture of what AmI is or what it implies for the future. They would also argue there is no transparency to the construction process and what is worse, there are no channels for society to give an opinion on the matter.

Society, in recent times, has showed a significant concern regarding the development of specific technologies such as nuclear and biotechnologies. Even what appear to be far less threatening technologies such as email, have generated unexpected security and privacy concerns. With regard to the nuclear and biotech industries these concerns have been widely reflected in interviews in the newspaper and in opinion polls. In the last few years the biotech industry in particular has suffered serious setbacks in Europe a result in part at least because of their failure to understand or address wider concerns in society regarding genetically modified foods. Researchers, designers, developers and policy makers concerned with realising the AmI vision have to take this fact very seriously into account.

Developers of Ambient Intelligent systems can profit greatly from a careful evaluation of the consequences of such technology within the framework of established concepts from the fields of sociology, economics, and jurisprudence [3].

Professor Ian Angell, a computer security researcher at the London School of Economics, said in a recent interview at a British newspaper that "modern software's complexity made it almost impossible to predict what will happen as different applications interact with each other" [4]. This comment matches Robert Lucky´s about the lack of understanding of the consequences of the connections made in an AmI environment. The upshot is that people are simply not in control of their software.

2. Objectives

The key questions therefore, of social and of sociological [5] concern on the deployment of AmI technologies in society are:

- How European society is going to participate in this process
- How are different stakeholders including the general public, policy makers and businesses, going to be involved, and
- Which are the effects of this imminent reality on the life of the people and the society

Objectives of this paper are to provide an idea on how society could participate on the construction of AmI and to identify what kind of social risks might arise on the process.

This paper sets out the following hypotheses and proposes a methodology for addressing them:

1. The participation of society in the construction of the AmI vision can place people in control of technology,
2. Social risks associated to the vision can be minimised through active involvement of society in the technology design process

3. Methodology

3.1 Barriers to social research

To put a single technology to the test from a social sciences perspective is sufficiently complex task in itself although there are many different techniques to do it. Trying to do the same with an as yet not realised technological vision is something different.

Today there are isolated instances of ambient (-ish) technologies, such as those on the lampposts in our cities that are sensitive to ambient light, and there are "popular ubiquitous technologies" [6], such as the Mobile phone, the Oyster Card or the recent London's Congestion Charging System. It is relatively easy to get feedback from the users to explore issues related to the daily use of those devices.

But how should we test the social consequences of an environment that is still a vision and that will not be real for 5-10 years. Today we have pilot projects that are working to build environments in which provide a truly ambient environment, but even those won't be ready in a couple of years time. What should be done today in 2004?

The ISTAG report says, "The AmI vision anticipates that ICT will increasingly become part of the invisible background to peoples' activities and that social interaction and functionality will move to the foreground resulting in experiences that enhance peoples' lives. This not only requires insight into the design of sophisticated distributed systems; it also requires a deep understanding of how user needs can be translated into functional requirements" and it remarks that "engineering requirements for Ambient Intelligent systems design can no longer be seen as a task that can be accomplished through the development of scenarios and the translation of use cases into system requirements. System functionalities that generate true user experiences can only be determined in a reliable way from feasible prototypes providing proofs of concept. New approaches to prototyping are likely to be key to the successful development of AmI products and services." [1].

So if we agree with the ISTAG we have to have the resources to develop a prototype to use with people, if we want to explore the social effects that technology will probably have.

The author believes that without a thorough understanding of the social, organizational, legal and ethical issues underlying the AmI technological development, to develop prototypes for the sake of doing it is never going to take us further, and will make us made the same mistakes once and again. Prototype development should always be conducted with a clear understanding of what issues the prototype serves to test.

3.2 Description of methodology

To test these hypotheses, the author has used the method of "triangulation". Triangulation is the technique whereby the researcher uses different approaches to test a theory. Each method enriches the other and can either reinforce and cross-validate conclusions if each corroborates the other, or reveal inconsistencies, which may indicate aspects not previously considered, or show that the research topic was not as straightforward as first thought [7].

The author has used three independent methods, literature review, personal interviews and scenario development, to plot where trends in the data lie.

The literature review and personal interviews were used to gain a broad perspective of what writers and experts generally believe constitutes AmI and to provide an understanding of the current trends being discussed in the ERA (European Research Area) at the moment.

The scenario development was useful to identify associated initial social risks.

The specific methodological focus of the study consisted therefore of a critical engagement with the discourses and claims that are made in the AmI vision building process and in AmI RTD projects and policies.

Table 1: Triangulation method

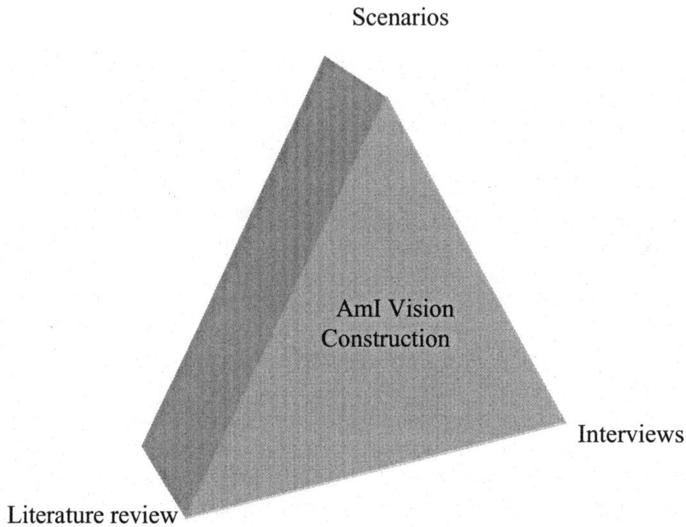

The literature review process consisted of reviewing books, articles, papers, research policies and initiatives and most important AmI projects worldwide. It involved searching for mentions of societal concerns, included legal, ethical and organizational issues.

Interviews and conversations have been held with experts inside the ERA, exploring their opinions and research on social issues, and views on the construction of the vision.

The scenario exercises have been conducted both at IST2003, where the author organised a networking session on "AmI and its effects on people", and inside Fundacion TEKNIKER with their Manufacturing AmI Knowledge Group. Knowledge was also gained through involvement in EU projects such as e-Locus http://e-locus.fundaciontekniker.com

3.3 Limitations of the methodology

On one hand, literature review is open to interpretation, and more in a field that has no established sociological references, and that is wide and multidisciplinary.

On the other hand, both the scope of the interviews and the scenarios have been located inside European territory. Only European researchers and experts have been included in the research. This might be censured as reductionism.

4. Results

The results obtained from the literature review, the interviews and scenarios can be summarized in the following conclusions:

- The research community is, generally speaking, confused about what Ambient Intelligence means as a concept, what implies in terms of technology and what kind of effects might have on Society. The concept is today too broad and more a vision of the future than a reality. The upcoming future will most likely be very different from the way it is predicted today.

- Future scenario building and iterations of the vision should treat AmI as an 'imagined concept" and not as a set of specified requirements. The scenarios proposed by different groups are a vision of the future that might not be realised. Researchers have to be careful and take this fact into account.
- The AmI concept is an emergent concept, it's not going to be the outcome of any single technology or application, it's going to result from the parallel development and introduction of a large number of interrelated systems, sensors, databases and interfaces. The emergent quality of the concept is about the convergence of technologies and the impossibility to predict the outcomes.
- To realize the construction of the AmI reality are needed shared long term visions addressed by broad international multidisciplinary consortia and a clear understanding of the demands and needs of consumers, users, workers and businesses
- The human-centred approach inner to the Ambient Intelligence vision has to be properly understood and interiorized by the different research groups working in this area. The resistance to involve end-users on the design process has to be overcome and new tools and approaches designed and put in practice
- The deployment of AmI technology opens enormous possibilities as well as risks. The promise of the technology has to be realised through social dialogue, multidisciplinary cross-cultural research and the daily involvement of European citizenry.
- Both technological and sociological issues run parallel in the construction of AmI systems. The identification of wider social issues underlying the development of AmI systems is a first and necessary step prior to its deployment in real life that has to be poured into the design process

5. Development: a research proposal

Building on these results, the author proposes a methodological contribution previous to the experience prototyping methodology mentioned by the ISTAG and described as "a form of prototyping that enables design team members, users and clients to gain first-hand appreciation of existing or future conditions through active engagement with prototypes" [1]. The author believes a deeper understanding of the social risks the realization faces, is previous work to be done before any real prototyping.

The hypotheses formulated suggest that, on one hand, if participation of Society on the construction of the vision is encouraged, this involvement can lead to a higher control of the technology. The author understands that higher control is about a better understanding of the design process and of the possible uses and implications of technology.

If a wide range of different people (with different professions, coming from different cultures, different social extract, etc) is given the chance to think about the vision and its construction, and to define it, they will feel in control of the technology for they will become prescriptors as well as end users.

On the other hand, along the paper is suggested that the social risks associated to the vision can be minimised through active involvement of society on the design process.

In this case, the author understands "people actively involved" as those individuals that, understanding the technology and the design process participate on the definition of the construction and are able to identify and beware of social risks. Once the risks are identified we'll learn how to avoid them.

To test these assumptions, three main steps should be taken:

- Identify the positive and negative aspects of AmI vision.

- Create AmI concepts.
- Test the concepts against general public.

The first step implies developing a methodology to identify positive and negative social aspects of technology. What does "privacy", trust, security mean. What does it mean in terms of technology and in terms of people. The objective is not to define a human centred vision of Ambient Intelligence but to identify what qualities any human driven vision of AmI should have. This first step is theoretical and personal research, and its outcome will be a methodology to identify positive and negative aspects of the vision and create concepts that will enable society to realize the "good" vision.

The second is about testing the methodology developed through private workshops in which groups of 5-6 people, each of them coming from different professional areas – computer scientist, sociologist, lawyer, product designer, architect, normal user, come together to discuss and create AmI concepts for "ordinary people", as the ISTAG suggests [1]. The results of the different workshops will be compared through qualitative analysis and as results we will have a battery of AmI concepts for "ordinary people".

The third is about testing the concepts developed with real users, the general public, in big numbers. The final objective will be to promote a consensus on a positive, human driven development AmI in EU.

Further research activities will comprise the dissemination of the results to the research community, industry and policy-makers and the development of a network of researchers and experts in the different disciplines involved, to continue with this line of thought.

6. Eventual Benefits

The emergent nature of the concept, the convergence of different technologies, the complexity of this process and its actual manifestation in real life poses a challenge for Society as a whole.

To conduct this research will provide the AmI research community, computer scientists, designers, architects, sociologists, psychologists, and legal researchers with a tool to test AmI proposals within Society.

Society will become a prescriptor and not an uninformed end-user in the process.

7. Conclusions

The promise of technology has to be realised. Nowadays we can't foresee how it's going to be the future, how the integration of technologies is going to be made, how people and society are going to be affected. Anything we say today can be laughable in ten years.

But we have the moral responsibility to try to make a better world, and to use technological advances in the best way possible.

This short proposal for a threefold study is a preparatory work for that future, what means that is not the panacea for all evil the so-called big brother nightmare might bring, but a reflection on the real possibilities and the real risks, as perceived for society and the general public, which should give the research, policy-making and industry communities a pretty good idea on what are the issues to be looked at and the simple mechanisms to be used when designing the technology applications.

This proposal is not about trust and privacy or trust and confidence neither about security and trust, titles too many times seen framing what along these paper are identified as the social, organizational, legal and ethical issues related to the construction of AmI.

The author believes the construction of a vision is not as simple as a matter of trust on a technology, because has been released by a certain company or about privacy because people are afraid of airing their identities. The implications run deep into society and are interconnected with social products such as organizations, laws and different sets of values that, depending on the geographical and cultural context vary.

It is clear that further work is needed. Whether this research is funded either by the European Commission, through different national research programmes or through private industrial funding is of small relevance. It is important that it is independent, multidisciplinary and multicultural. It should be open, flexible and articulated across the new EU. And it should conduct to, whenever possible, research at real environments to test how the vision works both from the technical realization and the social implications.

The wide range of social consequences that ambient intelligence may have certainly needs to be addressed in future social, legal, ethical, organizational, political and research debates. These challenges are of fundamental importance and will have a decisive influence on the large-scale acceptance of AmI technologies and environments.

References

[1] ISTAG report on Ambient Intelligence: from vision to reality. October2003

[2] Lucky R (1999) Everything will be connected to everything else. Connections. IEEE Spectrum, March 1999,

[3] Jürgen Bohn, Vlad Coroama, Marc Langheinrich, Friedemann Mattern, Michael Rohs, Social, Economic, and Ethical Implications of Ambient Intelligence and Ubiquitous Computing.In: W. Weber, J. Rabaey, E. Aarts (Eds.): Ambient Intelligence. Springer-Verlag, 2004

[4] www.guardian.co.uk

[5] It is a subject of study by sociology when it is detected an "individual and collective behaviour that is in need of study and understanding" International Encyclopaedia of Sociology, volume II, Fitzroy Dearborn Publishers, London, Chicago, 1995

[6] Naill Winters, London Knowledge Lab, Institute of Education, "Personal Privacy and Popular Ubiquitous Computing", presentation made at Ubiconf 2004, 19th April, London

[7] Robson, C. (1993). Real world research: A resource for social scientists and practitioner-researchers. Blackwell: Oxford.

Organisations as Multilayered Networks: the 'Space Syntax' of Ambient Intelligence

Alan PENN,
The Bartlett, University College London, Gower Street, London, WC1E 6BT, UK
Tel: +44 20 76795919, Fax: + 44 20 79161887, Email: a.penn@ucl.ac.uk

Abstract: Organisations of all kinds can be characterised in terms of the way that they construct interfaces and reporting lines between individuals and groups. It is this 'network' view that characterises most current thinking about organisational structures and in particular is of interest in the application of the sciences of complexity to the emergent forms of organisations. However, until recently one aspect of the modern organisation has not been brought within the network view – this is the built and ambient environment, which houses the organisation. This paper describes recent research, which addresses the issue of the role of the architecture of the work environment in the construction of the social and communication networks that characterise an organisation. We find that the spatial environment of the workplace plays a critical role in facilitating or inhibiting communication between workers. When new communications technologies are considered, these also work in tandem with face to face encounter and so the ambient environment must be included in analysis of the impact of new technology on the workplace.

1. Introduction

The study of organisations and management and the development of sociology as a discipline have gone hand in hand for over 200 years. Following Adam Smith's [1] observation that "the greatest improvements in the productive powers of labour, and the greatest part of the skill, dexterity, and judgement with which it is anywhere directed, or applied, seem to have been the effects of the division of labour." (p3), Emile Durkheim [2] characterised the progress of western society in terms of increased specialisation and an organic division of labour, while F.W.Taylor [3] defined scientific management in terms of just such a development of specialisms and the increased efficiencies these offered. Max Weber [4] and Henri Fayol [5] went on to advance theories of administration and bureaucratic organisation in terms of the roles and duties of a subdivided organisation. These were advanced in turn by Schumpeter's investigations of cycles of innovation, diffusion and his theory of organisation as evolutionary or emergent [6]. However, it is probably the second half of the 20th century that saw the greatest development in these fields, alongside the development of communications, and more recently computing technologies, themselves largely the products of pioneering technology corporations based on principles emerging from organisation theory. Elton Mayo [7] introduced in a systematic way the human dimensions of work organisation through his pioneering studies of productivity, and it was with these studies that the role of informal communication between workers finally took its place in management theory.

One characteristic of all these views of the organisation is that organisations can best be considered as networks. The specifics of the network vary – the process flow networks described by Gantt [8], the hierarchies of reporting and accountability described by Weber and Fayol, or Mayo's communication and social networks – however the common notion is that organisations are relational structures described by links between individuals, groups, roles or activities. The links can describe directed power relations, flows of information or temporal and process flows of goods or activities. In these terms organisations are configurations of elements in which relations between any two elements depend on their respective relations to other elements in the configuration. Strategic management is then seen as the design and operation of organisational structure, establishing the elements of the configuration and the definition and maintenance of relations between elements.

One aspect of the network description of organisational structure however, has always been less than satisfactory. This is the relatively abstract nature of the structures described, and the sense that these structures are defined in a 'top-down' fashion by management. Empirical studies of organisations often describe workers understanding of 'how the organisation is supposed to be' as distinct to 'how it really is'. This distinction between the organogram and 'the way things actually happen' is familiar, but it also raises a question: what is the origin of organisational structure? Or more precisely, how is it that organisational structures are generated, and how are they reproduced? Where, in effect, is the 'genetic code' controlling the reproduction and evolution of organisational forms, and their growth and development?

2. Space as a network and organisation as spatialised behaviour

In this context a novel body of theory, originating in the study of architecture and urban form, may help shed some light. During the 1980's a new body of sociological thinking was developed in the UK. Bill Hillier, Julienne Hanson [9] and their colleagues at UCL developed an approach to the theory of society in which the spatial environment in which people exist was neither a passive back-drop to society, nor just a product of social processes, but they argued an active component in the production and reproduction of social forms. The form of their argument is straightforward. There is one component of all social forms about which it is possible to be relatively objective. This is the physical – or, to be exact, the spatial – morphology of the buildings they build, the manner in which they inhabit them and the spatialisation of behaviours they exhibit within them. If one wants to understand a social form, then where better to start than with an analysis of the buildings they build and the manner in which they inhabit them. To this end they developed methods for representing patterns of open space in buildings and cities, first by their subdivision into discrete 'spaces' based on the local geometry of open space as this is defined by built form, and then by linking these spaces together into networks according to their inter-accessibility. Finally, the relational properties of these networks are quantified using simple graph theoretic measures, and these are used to control for the spatial environment variable in studies of patterns of space use and overtly spatialised behaviour. These 'space syntax' techniques have now been developed to cover a wide range of analytic and observational tools, and are widely applied in architectural research.

These methods emphasise the part-whole nature of buildings, considered as spatial systems, and have found that buildings can be considered in terms of the kind of interfaces that they construct between different classes of user. One function of a building considered as a spatial pattern is to create or control encounters between different categories of building user. Thus in a hospital interfaces need to be constructed between doctors and patients under a number of quite different conditions. In the consultants clinic the emphasis is generally on privacy and isolation of the meeting from other activity. In the ward, a quite different and often more public interaction is conducted. This is no accident. While the clinic is the doctor's domain, the ward belongs to the nurses. The nursing interface with the patient is mainly a supervisory and controlling one. The nurses' base within the ward tends to be located to control access to and from the ward, and to survey patients' beds. Within this environment, openness affords visibility and doctors must adapt their behaviour.

Similar, but if anything more subtle, variations in interface characterise the kinds of interactions that take place in the office environment. The relationships between individuals and groups of staff, managers and different kinds of professional are played out in office space in a multitude of different forms. Particularly recognisable are the association between high status and spatial isolation. Senior managers tend to locate in relatively isolated space. They often have cellular offices when more junior staff share more open plan space. The more senior manager will often have a PA or secretary in an anteroom to their office, further isolating them and in fact acting as an additional barrier to access. Even when managers are located in the open plan are often occupy relatively 'deep' parts of the space. However, at the same time these deep spaces are often located strategically from the point of view of surveillance.

These two dimensions; maintenance of status associated with isolation or spatial depth, and control associated with surveillance, especially of key access spaces; appear to be generic to many classes of social interface within organisations. They can be read from a building plan and analysed quantitatively using relatively simple measures of spatial networks. However, although an individual's workstation location is important both symbolically and functionally, it is a key characteristic of most organisations that people spend only a portion of their time (typically between 40 and 80%) at their workstation. During the remainder, they will be moving between other parts of the building, or engaged in meetings – either formal or spontaneous – with other staff away from their own workstation. During movement of this kind, spatial configuration affects the likelihood that people will be found in any given location.

Buildings appear to exert their most powerful influence on organisations through the probabilistic effects of spatial configuration on movement patterns. A great deal is now understood about these processes. Briefly, the network configuration of a buildings plan layout affects patterns of movement. Shallow locations in the network – that is shallow on average to all other locations – carry greater levels of through movement than deeper locations. However, buildings also carry movement to and from key locations and facilities. These include the photocopier, toilets and coffee room, but most importantly, the building entrance. As staff move around the building they are brought past others located in their offices or at their workstations in open plan areas. They are also brought into contact with others moving around the building. These patterns of contact are fundamentally stochastic – no one can predict when someone else will come past them, however, in spite of this, they appear to provide a vital resource in ensuring that an organisation maintains communication between staff. Backhouse and Drew [10], in an observational study of an open plan architects office found that up to 80% of all work related conversations took place as a result of these unplanned, and essentially unplannable, interactions. Although a meeting with a particular individual at a specific time cannot be planned solely on the basis of the chances he or she will move past, the likely location for meeting results directly from the spatial configuration of the building plan, and so can be used intentionally. It seems likely that people bias their routes in order to maximise (or minimise) encounters of this sort.

Two important factors follow from this. First, a mapping of administrative or group territories onto the building plan affects probabilities that random encounters will be predominantly within the group. It also follows that the workflow or information flow processes of an organisation, which lead to movement will have knock on effects on between-group interaction. The latter will affect not only the two groups with a direct programmatic need to interact, but also those located on the building circulation system that connects the two. Second, that movement into and out of the building through its entrances will create a specific type of movement pattern for visitors and those members of the organisation with external interaction. Organisations appear to vary to the degree that they separate externally related movement from internal movement around the building. This has particularly important implications for service organisations such as in health and education where the probabilistic interface between staff and clients is affected by the relation between internal and in-to-out movement patterns.

In view of these movement related patterns inherent in the structure of an organisation's activity there appear to be two main strategic pathways that can be used to construct a building's spatial layout. The first strategy is to aim to support the programmatic 'needs' of the organisation by reproducing the interdepartmental communication or information flow requirements ('what the organisation is supposed to be') in the layout of departmental or group adjacencies. Aiming for a correspondence between organisational structure and building layout is a common feature of modern building design and facilities management approaches and is supported by various software based optimisation models that aim to match departmental sizes and associations through blocking and stacking. In the most extreme form a building layout will be defined to exclude 'unnecessary' interruption by removing through movement from departmental areas. Tree like building configurations and card access security systems are used to achieve this. The second strategy is the reverse. Openness and inter-accessibility are the watchwords. Buildings designed using this approach tend to play down departmental boundaries in favour of plan layouts that stress the integrity of the organisation as a whole. Grids, streets and atria are often used to symbolise the intent, but many complex and apparently randomly aggregated or unplanned building complexes actually function in this way. At the extreme end of this spectrum some organisations have chosen to entirely eliminate departmental territories and focus on the provision of spaces to support the different functional requirements of all workers at different times by tailoring spaces to suit activity needs.

3. Space and communication

Most buildings and organisations lie somewhere between the two extremes of correspondence and non-correspondence of organisation structure and territorial layout. This continuum has allowed the evaluation of the effects of the spatial layout of buildings on patterns of communication between staff. In a series of studies of a wide range of knowledge-based organisations a standard questionnaire based method has been applied to elicit the strength of each individual's communications with others. A questionnaire listing all members of an organisation (or a 50% sample for organisations with over 500 staff) is administered to all staff. Each respondent is asked to place a tick on a 1-5 score against the frequency that they see each name on the list. They are also asked to tick those names on the list that they 'work with directly', and those they find 'useful in their work'. People they do not recognise by name they are asked to leave blank. The questionnaire is not anonymous and so the researcher knows each respondent's workstation location, status, group membership and job responsibilities. The relationship between the frequency of being seen by all other respondents and the number of respondents that find each individual useful in their work is then analysed. This analysis is repeated for specific departmental groups, status groups and for those that are not directly involved in working together at all.

The findings of this kind of analysis are direct: all other things being equal, frequency with which an individual is seen dictates the number of people who find them useful in their work (Figure 1). The finding is clearly subject to job and status specific effects. Senior management and certain technical staff are often found more useful than their frequency of being seen would suggest (Figure 2). This seems entirely natural given that they have 'whole organisation' responsibilities. However, even within these subgroups the dependency between perceived usefulness and frequency of being seen is maintained. It is also clear, at the whole organisation level, that being seen frequently is no guarantee of being found useful – there is a very marked increase in variance of usefulness as frequency increases shown in the triangular distribution of the scattergram in Figure 1. This means that individual attributes and knowledge come into play in people's assessment of those that they see frequently. The moral of this is that if you are never seen, people will not find you useful, but if you are seen frequently, how useful you are found to be depends on you!

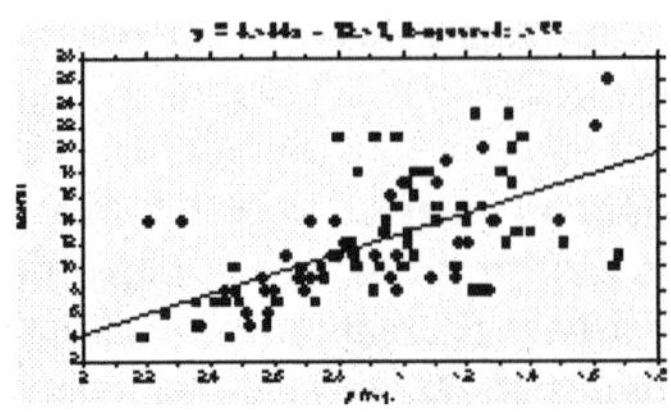

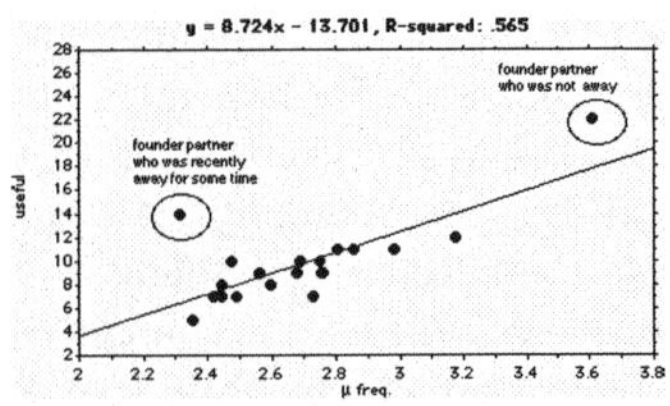

Figure 1. (left) the correlation between usefulness (vertical axis) and frequency for all individuals in an advertising organisation; Figure 2. (right) the same correlation for members of the 'creative department' – the two outliers are founding partners.

This set of findings suggests a mechanism linking the usefulness of human resources in an organisation to each other, to the spatial environment of that organisation, via the effects of the building layout in allowing people to be aware of each other's presence. Availability, as Backhouse and Drew found [10], is a prerequisite for unplanned, but work related interaction, and this interaction would seem to be a key component in establishing people's perceptions of other's utility. Strong support for this is found by comparing all the organisations we have studied to date on the basis of their mean 'shallowness' of spatial layout, measured using the space syntax methods described above, against the mean 'usefulness' of their human resources to each other, outside their immediate task related groups (Figure 3). The correlation is strong and very highly significant, and suggest that the ambient spatial environment acts as a key factor in achieving the most effective deployment of human capital in an organisation.

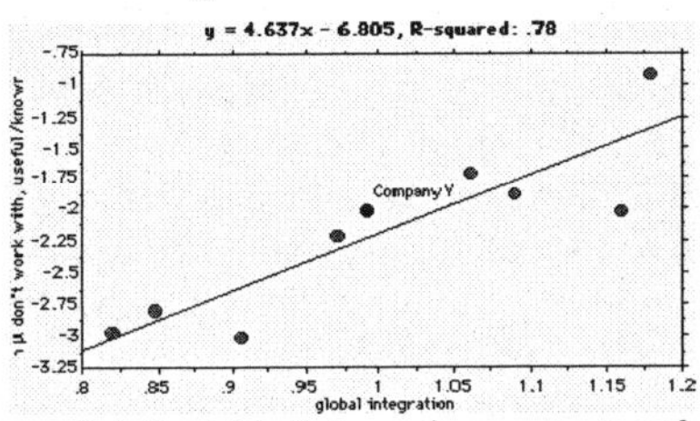

Figure 3. The mean usefulness of staff outside their workgroup against the mean global integration (a measure of spatial shallowness) for 9 organisations.r-.883, p<.001.

4. Organisational politics and culture

We now have the tools we need to begin to explain three familiar properties of work organisations, which are often described as intangible. The first is sometimes known as back stairs politics. This is a phenomenon with which many will be familiar in which the presence a particular individual in a part of a building in which they are generally not seen will be 'read' by those that see them as implying that 'something is up'. As people go out of their way to construct 'unplanned' interactions that are not part of their normal routine they will deviate from their usual movement patterns. This departure from routine carries in itself a signal, which is readable by those who are familiar with an organisation.

The second is the familiar notion of an organisational culture. Organisations are often recognised as 'lively' or 'deadly' depending on some aspect of their atmosphere that is almost instantly recognisable as one enters. The importance, as well as the notorious difficulty in pinpointing the origin of organisational culture, has led many to look for it and many more to become sceptical about its existence as an objective reality. However, the notion of availability and its importance in the construction of useful work related communications networks suggests that there are certain aspects of an organisation's behaviour that are both instantly readable by a visitor at first entry, and that are extremely important to the organisation's satisfactory function. As one steps through the door of a lively organisation one is met with a buzz of conversation and movement, and most important, as a visitor one is aware of this. This means two things, first that awareness of others is present, and second that visitors are made aware of the internal movement patterns. Both aspects are important aspects of an organisation's culture. The former in that it indicates low boundaries around departmental territory and so a readiness to change departmental boundaries in response to circumstances. The latter in that it indicates a readiness to create contacts with those coming in from outside the organisation, and so an ability to keep abreast of changes in the external environment. Contrast this with the atmosphere one experiences on entering a fossilised or dinosaur organisation. Here departmental boundaries are strongly defended, through movement discouraged and external visitors restricted to well-defined spaces of their own. Meeting with the organisation is conduced under highly controlled circumstances.

The last is the closely related notion of the generative or the conservative organisation. In the latter buildings appear to serve actively to conserve existing social networks and organisational forms – these may be characterised as conservative, and can often lead to the stagnation or fossilisation of an organisation type. Others buildings actively generate new social and organisational forms, and can be thought of as responsive to outside influences and unpredictability in the organisation's environment. These 'generative' building types are in turn characterised by openness and lower levels of spatial hierarchy, as well as by intelligibility of spatial layout. The most important property of these organisations is to be able to generate new social and organisational networks in response to changes in the business environment. This requires both a recognition of the social capital of the organisation, and an ability to relegate control structures to a second place in order to achieve innovation of social and organisational form. The approach of course carries risks. In an environment that is not subject to change new organisational forms can lead to inefficiencies in working and reinvention of the wheel. In these circumstances the conservative organisation may well be better suited to obtaining maximum efficiency.

5. New communications networks

Clearly, no organisation now exists based solely on face-to-face encounter for its communications. Since the invention of writing, records have been kept for organisational use, and the telephone, computer networks and email are now essential components of any organisation's communication infrastructure. The telephone and email offer a significant new source of information for the researcher since logs are kept of all communications, including in the case of the telephone unsuccessful attempts to call. In a series of studies of knowledgebased organisations Georgia Spiliopoulou [12] has developed analyses of email and telephone logs in association with studies of building plan layout and movement and behaviour patterns. Her findings with respect to telephone logs are particularly relevant. In modern phone systems internal and external calls have different ring tones. By looking at the relationship between internal calls received and internal calls answered, and external calls received and answered for individuals at different levels of seniority in an organisation she found that there were striking differences in answering rates for internal calls (but not for external calls) between junior and senior staff. The more senior a staff member was the less likely they were to pick up an internal call (Figure 4). Similar, results were found for email correspondence.

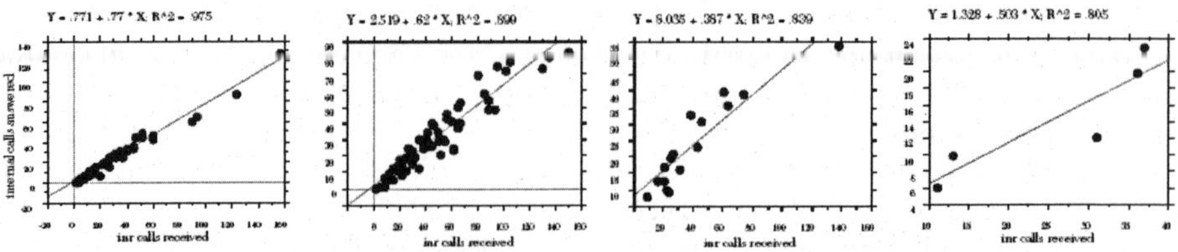

Figure 4. The correlations between incoming internal telephone calls and those answered for increasing levels of seniority in the organisation hierarchy from left to right.

These findings suggest that any new modality of communication serves at least two fundamental roles within an organisation. At an instrumental level it allows communication and information transfer. However, at a cultural level it facilitates access to an individual. In this second sense it becomes a part of the organisational configuration, in much the same way that spatial layout is, and it can be used to make statements about an individual's status within the organisational hierarchy. In the same way that a senior manager may isolate themselves spatially by selecting an office deep in the plan of the building, and can further isolate themselves using a PA to screen their availability, the telephone can be used in this way to preferentially deny access to internal callers. Email reply patterns suggest that these may also be used to distance seniority from the staff.

It would seem that any modality of communication, be it spatial, technological or human, can be exploited by individuals and organisations, either to conserve and reproduce the status quo by constraining access to the network to maintain existing power relations, or it can be used to generate new social forms by freeing access to networks to facilitate new interactions. Perhaps the clearest pointer to organisational culture lies in which of these strategic pathways a particular organisation pursues.

6. Industrial Significance: making time or the mythical man month

In any analysis of organisational structure, the issue of efficiency is clearly of central concern. It is increasingly the case that as organisational productivity rises and staff are asked to multi-task that they complain that there are too few hours in the working day. One immediate response is to employ more human resources. However, it is a paradox of project management, famously captured in Brooks' Law that "Adding manpower to a late software project makes it later". This results from the fact that the expected advantage of splitting development work among N programmers is proportional to N, but the complexity and communications cost associated with coordinating and then merging their work is O(N^2), that is proportional to the number of possible interactions in the group [13]. How then is it possible for an organisation to improve? One result of the analysis presented above is that there is an intimate relationship between space in organisations, and time expressed in terms of the deployment of human resources. By using spatial layout and communications media to increase availability and so to increase social density one can hope to reduce the transaction costs involved in communications between a given number of staff.

7. Conclusions

In considering the likely future of work organisation and the adoption of new technologies it is therefore important to understand recent advances in social theory of the workplace. In this paper a specific type of sociological study has been discussed in which the spatial and communications structure of an organisation and individual staff behaviours are observed and measured. The results suggest that the ambient spatial environment is an essential component of an organisation's operational infrastructure, and affects in a direct manner the cultural and political characteristics of the organisation. Spatial layout is complemented by communications infrastructure, but importantly all of these forms of structure can be considered to be configurational in that they form networks in which parts are related to the whole in a way that is not homogeneous, but is structured to strengthen local clusters of awareness and interaction, whilst eliminating or controlling other potential relations.

The hypothesis that follows from this is that the critical aspect of an organisation's growth, development and evolution over time lies in the way that the configuration of its multiple networks changes and responds to its changing environment. It suggests that it is the multi-layered configuration of networks that characterise organisations, and which actually serve to reproduce – and so conserve – organisational structure. However it is also these structures that bring individuals into contact who would not necessarily be expected or required to interact in the current form of an organisation. It is exactly these serendipitous contacts which generate the networks and information flows essential to the organisation's capacity to change. This is the power of the organisation: its ability to conserve structure and reproduce it over time by privileging certain contacts over others, at the same time as being able to adapt to new circumstances by using redundancy in social structure to provide capacity for new social forms. In answer to the question of where the equivalent of the genetic code for an organisation lies, one answer would be in these multi-layered configurations, chief amongst which is the spatial layout of the built environment.

As ambient intelligence begins to make the building responsive to the individuals and groups present, and their current state and activity, it becomes increasingly important to understand these multi-layered configurations in order to develop truly intelligent and responsive 'generative' ambient environments of the future.

References

[1] Adam Smith, (1776), An Inquiry Into the Nature and Causes of the Wealth of Nations, Book I, Chapter I.
[2] Emile Durkheim, (1893), The Division of Labor in Society.
[3] Frederick W. Taylor (1911), The Principles of Scientific Management, Harper Bros., New York.
[4] Max Weber, (1947), The Theory of Social and Economic Organization, tr. Henderson and Parsons, New York.
[5] Henri Fayol, (1930), Industrial and general administration, tr. J.A. Coubrough, London: Pitman.
[6] Schumpeter (1911), The Theory of Economic Development.
[7] Mayo, E., (1933), The Human Problems of an Industrial Civilization, Macmillan,
[8] H. L. Gantt, (1910), Work, Wages and Profit, The Engineering Magazine, NY.
[9] Bill Hillier & Julienne Hanson, (1984), The Social Logic of Space, Cambridge, CUP.
[10] Backhouse A., Drew P., (1992), The design implications of social interaction in a workplace setting, Environment and Planning B, Pion, Brondesbury.
[11] Penn, A., Desyllas, J. & Vaughan, L., 1999, The Space of Innovation: Interaction and Communication in the Work Environment, Environment and Planning B: Planning and Design, Vol. 26, 193-218, Pion, Brondesbury.
[12] Georgia Spiliopoulou and Alan Penn, (1999), Organisations as Multi-Layered Networks: face to face, e-mail and telephone interaction in the workplace, Proceedings of the Second International Space Syntax Symposium, Vol II, A1.1-1.23, University of Brasilia.
[13] Frederick P Brooks, (1975), The Mythical Man-Month: Essays in Software Engineering, Addison-Wesley.

Building Context Awareness into Physical Service Environments

Giovanni CORTESE[1], Fabrizio DAVIDE[2]
Telecom Italia Learning Services, Via A. Bono Cairoli 68, Roma, Italy
[1]*Tel: +039 335 8267704, Email: g.cortese@computer.org*
[2]*Tel: +039 06 55145120, Email: fabrizio.davide@telecomitalia.it*

Abstract: In the next few years, mobile computing, sensing technologies, and distributed middleware will combine to create a new generation of adaptive, context aware services. Context sensing infrastructures will be deployed in Physical Service Environments such as airports, conference centers, government agencies, and services. These infrastructures will use the wealth of information generated by sensors to better serve the needs of mobile users, including visitors and people or businesses operating in the physical environment. But, to make this vision succeed, we need to solve a number of technical and human factors problems. In this paper we discuss related technological and standardization issues.

1. Introduction

The deployment of a growing range of wireless connectivity technologies (WLANs, ad-hoc networking, 3G cellular networks) in private and public spaces, provides new business opportunities to offer services to users (including visitors and internal users) moving within their physical premises. Emerging sensing and semantic technologies make it possible to implement presence, identity and localization services. These in turn can serve as enablers for "Physical Service Environments" in which a range of intelligent services exploit context information to adapt to user and environment state. Examples of possible "Physical Service Environments" include airports, shopping malls, conference centers and hospitals.

Physical Service Environments provide services that are enhanced by knowledge of the physical environment. This may include information on the personal characteristics of users, their position, and the locations where they are working. A physical service environment seamlessly integrates services from a broad range of computing devices - embedded systems, network connected appliances and portable devices belonging to mobile users – as well as those supplied by application servers, running in a separate computer room or remotely in a computing grid. Users moving in this kind of pervasive computing environment will access services easily. User devices may also provide services to (and share data with) other components in the environment.

Context awareness adds a layer of intelligence to physical service environments. Environmental Context is information describing the current state of the environment. This includes sensed, dynamic context data, such as location information, information describing the presence and identity of people in the environment, and information describing specific situations. It may also include relatively static data such as a spatial model of environment, inventories of objects, and so on. Service environments gather, organize and 'publish' context information that applications can use.

Similarly, users share a range of information about themselves: a user profile, location and preference information, as well as information describing their plans, schedules and skills and their previous interactions with services. The local service environment exploits this information to deliver services that adapt to users' current status and needs.

1.1 Objectives of the paper

In this paper, we present a case study of a small-scale implementation of context aware services on our premises, and identify challenges that industry and research community must address as a prerequisite for ubiquitous deployment of context aware services.

2. Case study

Telecom Italia is currently engaged in a broad research program into Ambient Intelligence and Context Awareness. As part of this program we have recently implemented a testbed for context aware computing. The testbed is expected to provide insights into the maturity of enabling technologies. The results will be used as the basis for an initial assessment of services based on these technologies. The program is ongoing; in this paper we document the results of the first testbed and experimentation phase.

Currently, the testbed encompasses a 400 m^2 area in a Telecom Italia Learning Center, covered by 802.11b wireless connectivity. The sensing infrastructure consists of a WLAN-based indoor location system (Ekahau Position Engine), a network presence infrastructure (based on 802.1x technology) including WLAN connected devices, fixed workstations and a limited number of WebCams. The software infrastructure consists of XDM (a conteXt Data Management middleware), and a set of application services on top of the middleware.

At this stage, we have implemented, deployed, and tested the services with a controlled user base. In the next few months we plan to conduct more systematic usability tests, extending the testbed in terms of spatial coverage and user base.

2.1 Testbed Services and Target Users.

The testbed models two broad classes of physical service environment, both of which are relevant to our organization's business:

- public spaces such as learning or conference centers: the testbed is currently deployed on the premises of a Telecom Italia Learning Center with more than one hundred classrooms and large numbers of visitors attending training courses and events
- 'generic' office spaces

The target populations include Telecom Italia personnel and visitors to the center (e.g. teachers, course attendees and managers from supplier and customer organizations). The goal is to facilitate interaction between visitors and the facility. We have thus implemented:

- An indoor guide, to help users find a room, an event or a specific person
- A device leasing service, to provide visitors with access to computing facilities such as workstations and printers
- Monitoring of queues at facilities such as copiers, ATMs etc.
- Ad-hoc sharing of documents among a group of users (e.g. class participants)
- Remote monitoring and control of classroom facilities, allowing TILS personnel with mobile terminals, to monitor the presence of people in classrooms, lock/ unlock doors

Students and teachers entering the TILS learning center, with a wireless personal device (such as a PDA or laptop) use a login form to provide their identity to the service environment. The environment collects their profile and preferences (e.g. a user profile might define a list of the services to which the user subscribes, the willingness of users to make their location available to other users etc.), from the network and provides them with a personalized menu of available services, taking into account current context information.

Users without a personal device can lease a desktop PC. The presence service gathers profile information for the user (e.g. internal user, Telecom Italia student, external user), grants access to the IP network, and configures services appropriate to the profile. The point of attachment to the network is also used as coarse location information.

2.2 Architecture

To ensure that application services are available to as many users as possible, service provisioning uses Web protocols and no specialized middleware is required on the user device. A Tomcat web server is the container where services are deployed. Context aware provisioning of services makes it possible to dynamically adapt services and content to user needs, based on criteria such as position, time, and environmental conditions.

Applications use environment context information and user context information, to adapt their behavior to user needs. Environment context includes dynamic data and a context model of the environment. In the prototype, the dynamic context is represented by data representing the presence and location of users, and still images or video streams from WebCams. We also plan to include computer vision processing for scene analysis. The context model includes data representing the layout of the center, the location of rooms, corridors, printers, ATMs and other equipment, and providing descriptions of these objects.

Application access to context data is facilitated by the XDM middleware, which provides the following functionality:

- A context agent - for interfacing the applications with devices and sensors; this is implemented as a dynamically extensible, embedded Java-based platform running on a mobile device or embedded hardware
- Publish-subscribe style distribution of context data
- A policy engine supporting context aware provisioning of services
- Distributed user context manager

User context management is one of the original features of our implementation. User context, which includes user profile information, such as universal preferences, application or environment-specific preferences, session histories etc. is stored 'transparently' in the network using DHT-based middleware [9], and can be shared between the user (regardless of the terminal she is using) and service environment they are visiting.

A description of an early version of this prototype can be found in [1]. Work is currently in progress to extend the early prototype, to incorporate new ideas and to evaluate emerging research and industry middleware.

2.3 Results

This section summarizes lessons learnt from the test bed about technologies and applications, drawing on our own analyses and on interviews with users and management. A longer-term analysis and a discussion of research challenges is provided in Section 3.

The test bed provided us with a number of insights into the benefits and challenges of context aware services, which are discussed below.

Location based information services (e.g. indoor guide, context sensitive information push) are most appealing for organizations running a business in a public space (such as a learning center, an airport, a shopping mall). It is important that services should reach users equipped with a mobile phone (in addition to users with PDAs or laptops). Though it is conceivable that in the future virtually all mobile phones will have a browser and a flexible software execution environment, a number of issues in WLAN connectivity and WLAN-based localization are still open. Future services should take account of alternative access technologies e.g. Bluetooth (through gateways into the LAN) or UMTS.

Some of the services we envision do not lend themselves to a pure Web thin client approach, and require specialized middleware on each client (examples include services requiring advanced interactivity, such as collaboration and data sharing, multimedia conferencing etc). In the short term, advanced services should be targeted to internal users, whose mobile client is under the control of the company. In the medium and long term, it is desirable that mobile devices should be equipped with a standard middleware platform, allowing secure, dynamic component download. This would make it possible to implement a service-provisioning model where the terminal is reconfigured dynamically as it enters a service environment, and necessary software components are deployed on demand.

Leased device services (specifically leasing of PCs) received very high ratings from both users and management. Leasing a PC to a visitor requires the ability to personalize PCs so that users can recreate their own desktop and application profiles (e.g. browser favorites, email preferences). It would also be helpful if it were possible to create network mechanisms simplifying user access to Internet services, and to users' own intranets. We are currently working on this topic with our partners in the IST Simplicity project [13].

User location management is a critical component of the architecture. Most services under consideration depend on a scalable, affordable and widely available localization technology. Localization services should be sufficiently precise to correctly map the position of a user to a specific room. In our experiments, the technology worked effectively in ideal conditions but lost accuracy when current conditions no longer reflected those at the time the radio map was prepared. The creation and maintenance of radio maps for localization can be an extremely expensive activity.

In addition to providing network access control, information from the 802.1x infrastructure can be a valuable source for presence and location information, facilitating the personalization of services, independently of network access type (wireless or wired) and point of attachment. Currently, authentication to the network requires users to explicitly provide login and password information. The IST Simplicity project is currently working on the design of a device to store user preferences, identity and contract information, making it possible to provide transparent access and identification. Such a device could be a smartcard or USB device, physically plugged into the host device, or an external personal device, that uses wireless communication to exchange the same information. We plan to integrate the Simplicity device prototype into our testbed.

3. Architectural challenges for physical service environments

Drawing on the experience described above, we have dedicated the last year to the development of robust and manageable infrastructures for context aware services.

By generalizing our initial prototype, we have identified a number of challenges to be tackled by the research community. In the following section, we discuss these challenges together with possible responses.

3.1 A manageable, service-grade pervasive computing environment

Context Aware services go hand in hand with pervasive computing. If they are to take off industry must develop broadly accepted middleware architectures for pervasive computing.

The first challenge is to design a middleware architecture that provides communication, coordination (including transactions), discovery, and composition of services across the whole range of computing devices that may be operating in a physical service environment. These are likely to include J2EE application servers, embedded systems, and mobile devices with limited capabilities. Other key elements in such middleware include contract negotiation, possibly on the fly, and integration with payment/ billing infrastructures [2].

Existing service-oriented technologies including Web Services, OSGi, and GRID should be enhanced and integrated into a single, scalable framework, supporting development of industry-grade pervasive applications. In the long term, sensor networks should become interoperable components in this framework.

3.2 Context Information Management architectures

In pervasive computing scenarios, users and service environments participate in cooperative execution of services, within mixed initiative, distributed workflows. Context information is collected and stored both in user terminals (or wearable sensors) and in the infrastructure. Mechanisms are thus required to allow all components to advertise, discover and use available context information.

Standardized context information management architectures would make it possible to effectively decouple context acquisition from the use of context data. Though several research projects ([10], [11], [12]) have indicated possible directions for development, a standard architecture is required which a) allows vendors of sensors and semantic interpretation software to generate information based on well-known schemas b) let applications discover and use available context information to provide adaptive behavior. Sensor data generation, data fusion, the transformation of sensor data into reusable context information with clear semantics and the sharing of this information between producers and consumers should be organized according to standard interaction patterns and ontologies.

3.3 Technologies for context data sharing and distribution

Context data collection and distribution is inherently a peer-to-peer application. Publish-subscribe and data-sharing mechanisms are often used in implementations of context management infrastructures. In the VICom project [6] we adopt a context data management architecture based on a combination of Lime [4], which provides flexible data sharing mechanisms between peer components, and DHT-based middleware [7], whose scalability properties matches the need for large scale context data management infrastructures.

Privacy is a major challenge for context information management. Access control over sensed data should be in the hands of service users. It is important to devise methods for the controlled disclosure and use of this information by selected services.

3.4 User context

Mobile user context seamlessly extends from users' mobile devices into their personal computing environment. User context includes both physical context (such as position, emotional state – as shown by gestures, current activity) and digital context.

In a minimum application (such as the prototype used for the case study) the digital context consists of profiles and preferences for services accessed by users. We can think of user context as a set of metadata such as web browsing histories, and address books. As a final step, we can extend the concept to include the user's whole computing environment, including her desktop, applications and data. Though at first sight it may seem that this is stretching the concept too far, in real scenarios it is quite difficult to keep things separated. The literature on user context modeling often bunches these concepts together, reflecting the "fuzziness" of the dividing line. From a very practical standpoint, the vision of globally accessible, 'always-on', personal data and computing space, is a powerful one.

Middleware should ensure that data (such as documents and folders) of relevance to users' current activities should always be accessible to the mobile user, whether hosted on a home computer, office desktop or enterprise server. In the Simplicity project, we are exploring how to provide transparent, network-based storage of profile data and documents to a mobile user, by leveraging emerging technologies for P2P storage management [8].

3.5 Semantic interoperability

A key issue in dynamic environments (which include both the Internet and pervasive computing spaces, where components should work together without being designed for interoperability), is semantic interoperability. For pervasive computing, this is a Grand Challenge. But it is also a very specific challenge for context aware environments. Standardization of context ontologies can help (especially for 'low level context' such as user position and movement, environmental conditions e.g. sound and light levels). For higher level context information, uniformity in context representation will remain an open issue for a long time.

4. Conclusions

The development of such architectures would be facilitated by a strong vertical market focus. Today it is possible to deploy Physical Service Environments, providing context aware applications to people moving within a given physical area. We are now working on an Advanced Service Environment for Learning Centers. Similar environments could be implemented in airports and train stations. Full implementation of the concept will require new technology developments and above all, new standards.

In the short term, possibly the most urgent need is, easy to deploy localization technology. The technology required should be easy to manage and should be capable of handling large numbers of users (for example, each user carrying a mobile phone should be able to be located with enough accuracy for most applications). There are however a number of other issues that future projects will need to address:

- Effective context aware services require standard architectures for pervasive computing guaranteeing the interoperability between different system components (from mobile phones to servers) both in ad hoc and infrastructure based environments.
- Context information management requires industry agreement on standard architectures. Development would be much easier if it were based on a strong vertical industry focus. Any attempt to define a standard ontology has to deal with two opposing requirements, namely the need for generality and the need for specialization (to handle specific classes of application e.g. security, collaboration tools, entertainment, knowledge management, environmental control, building automation etc.). It is easy to see that conflicting requirements from different types of application make it difficult to create a single, general-purpose ontology for context information. In the approach we propose, different interest groups would take responsibility for developing their own application or industry specific models using a commonly agreed standard ontology language and framework (e.g. RDF, Owl). This is similar to what happened with network management based on the highly successful SNMP family of protocols.

In this paper we have focused on technological and standardization issues. We believe, however what research on context aware services really requires is an interdisciplinary approach, which take proper account of human factors. Approaches such as user-centered design, usability analysis and testing are highly relevant to the design. Analysis of social impact is also necessary. The benefits (which can be many – for example for the disabled) should be weighed against possible drawbacks including threats to privacy.

Acknowledgements

We wish to thank the following research partners who have contributed to the work described in this paper: the VICom consortium, the PHYSE consortium (including the Universities of Lancaster and Grenoble, Bull, IBM, ITC-IRST, Agent Oriented Software Ltd), the IST Simplicity consortium.

References

[1] G. Cortese, F. Davide, A. Detti "eCASA : an Easy Context aware System Architecture" IEEE Vehicular Technology Conference October 6-9

[2] Boddupalli, B., F. Al-Bin-Ali, N. Davies, A. Friday, O. Storz and M. Wu. "Payment Support in Ubiquitous Computing Environments". To appear in Proc. of 5th IEEE Workshop on Mobile Computing Systems and Applications (WMCSA 2003), Monterey Bay, U.S.).

[3] Dey, A. K. "Understanding and using context", Personal and Ubiquitous Computing, Vol 5, No. 1, pp 4-7, 2001

[4] Amy L. Murphy, Gian Pietro Picco, and Gruia-Catalin Roman. Lime: A Middleware for Physical and Logical Mobility. In Proceedings of the 21 st International Conference on Distributed Computing Systems (ICDCS-21), May 2001.

[5] N. Blefari Melazzi , G. Bianchi, G. Cortese, S. Kapellaki, K. Kawamura, C. Noda, S. Salsano, I. S. Venieris. "The Simplicity project: easing the burden of using complex and heterogeneous ICT devices and services - Part I: Overall Architecture". Submitted.

[6] VICom project – http://www.vicom-project.it/

[7] M. Castro, P. Druschel, A.-M. Kermarrec, and A. Rowstron. SCRIBE: A large-scale and decentralized application-level multicast infrastructure. IEEE Journal on Selected Areas in communications (JSAC), 2002. To appear.

[8] Kubiatowicz, J., Bindel, D., Chen, Y., Czerwinski, S., Eaton, P., Geels, D., Gummadi, R., Rhea, S., Weatherspoon, H., Weimer, W., Wells, C., and Zhao, B. OceanStore: An architecture for global-scale persistent storage. In Proceeedings of the Ninth international Conference on Architectural Support for Programming Languages and Operating Systems (ASPLOS 2000) (Boston, MA, November 2000), pp. 190-201.

[9] Rowstron, A., and Druschel, P. Storage management and caching in PAST, a large-scale, persistent peer-to-peer storage utility. In *Proceedings of the 18th ACM Symposium on Operating Systems Principles (SOSP '01)* (Oct. 2001).

[10] Panu Korpipää, Jani Mäntyjärvi, Juha Kela, Heikki Keränen, Esko-Juhani Malm Managing Context Information in Mobile Devices IEEE Pervasive Computing 2003

[11] Phillip B. Gibbons, Brad Karp, Yan Ke, Suman Nath, Srinivasan Seshan - IrisNet: An Architecture for a World-Wide Sensor Web To appear, IEEE Pervasive Computing.

[12] Anind K. Dey. Providing Architectural Support for Building Context aware Applications - PhD thesis, College of Computing, Georgia Institute of Technology, December 2000.

[13] http://www.ist-simplicity.org/

eAdoption and the Knowledge Economy: Issues, Applications, Case Studies
P. Cunningham and M. Cunningham (Eds.)
IOS Press, 2004

Understanding Innovation in the Mobile Workplace

Hans SCHAFFERS
Telematica Instituut, P.O. Box 589, Enschede, 7500 AN, The Netherlands
Tel: +31 53 4850418, Fax: + 31 53 4850400, Email: hans.schaffers@telin.nl

Abstract: This paper discusses frameworks for understanding innovation in mobile and multi-location work. The main perspective is their appropriateness in dealing with systemic change. Based on scenarios, the needs, requirements and bottlenecks in future mobile workplaces are identified. Example frameworks are 'transition management', 'national innovation systems', 'adoption dynamics' and 'economics of organisations'. All are dealing with specific aspects of innovation and do not cover the whole picture. Using them, we can better understand the success conditions for mobile workplace innovation. In doing so, more adequate strategies for designing mobile workplace testbeds and validation environments can be developed.

1. Introduction

This paper evaluates frameworks for understanding innovation in mobile workplaces and assesses them on the basis of their adequacy in coping with systemic change aspects in relation to innovation in mobile workplaces. This paper is part of the MOSAIC Specific Support Action (www.mosaic-network.org) that started March 1 2004 and has a key role in promoting workplace innovation and launching the Ambient Intelligence @ Work Communities activity of the European Commission. The over-all objective of MOSAIC is to accelerate innovation in new work environments in different sectors, establishing dialogue for innovation between stakeholders and developing roadmaps for change.

Section 2 discusses current forms and future scenarios of mobile workplaces. This enables us to identify major issues in the design of innovative work environments related to system change. These issues are intertwined and technological, organisational, human, and societal in nature. Section 3 discusses example frameworks like 'transition management', 'national innovation systems', 'adoption dynamics' and 'economics of organisations'. These are all dealing with particular aspects of innovation and do not cover the whole picture. However, the use of these frameworks as 'lenses' enables developers, end-users and policymakers better understanding the conditions for innovation in mobile workplaces, answering questions like: How to create large-scale lasting innovation? How to accommodate interests of different stakeholders? How to link innovation on different levels (societal, industry, organisation, task group, individual) using a holistic perspective?

2. Configurations of Future Mobile Workplaces

MOSAIC proposes four mobile workplace scenarios (Figure 1). These are structured along two driving forces, each having two extremes, 1. 'human attitude' (individualism or community oriented) and 2. 'organisational development' (hierarchical control or self-organisation). In the Contingent Workplace, human behaviour is individualistic in a context of self-organising; an example is a self-employed IT specialist relying on location-aware collaboration with others in temporary multi-site teams and in more long-term professional communities to develop competencies. Agile Workplace captures a community-oriented human attitude while the organisation is decentralised. An example is a group of SMEs in electronics manufacturing, collaborating in a self-coordinated network to design a new product. The Guided Workplace has human behaviour oriented towards individualism whereas the organisation is centrally coordinated. The example is a maintenance engineer working as individual, for several companies, under central coordination. Finally, in the Focal Workplace human attitude is pursuing community objectives and the organisation is hierarchical. An example is a manager of a global networked semiconductor company coordinating its supply network, solving emergency issues while working in changing, different locations or hotspots, and guided by experts in other locations.

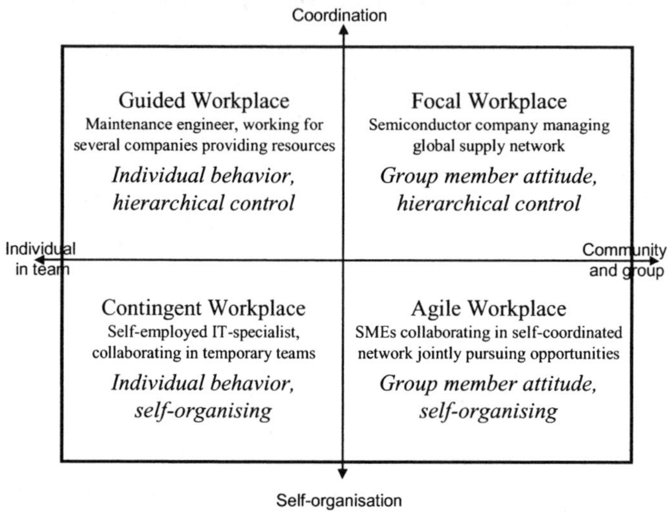

Figure 1: Workplace scenarios (based on COCONET [1])

Such scenarios enable us to recognise that mobile work must be considered at different levels: the worker, the workplace, the organisation and the organisational environment. Mobile work is a combination of technology, workplace organisation, (inter-) organisational procedures, and facilities and support systems allowing people to work at times and locations of their choice. Mobile work involves not only a traditional meaning of 'worker mobility' focusing primarily on multiple work locations including the office, home, hotspots, and on the move. Mobile work would broadly also include the mobility of the workplace and work organisation, increasingly following the needs and opportunities of the mobile worker and team irrespective time, place and other context-related constraints: the network may become the working place. The mobile workplace thus evolves towards a scenario of work organisation characterised by empowerment of workers and teams being part of ad-hoc temporary projects and organisations, and by awareness of context. Mobility services enable the worker to roam through arbitrary environments irrespective of network environments the user is in. Context awareness and context adaptivity exploit the relevant worker context variables to tailor applications, services, communication and connectivity to the workplace and workers' current situation and needs.

A very useful categorisation of five types of mobile work as currently found in practice is developed by Lilischkis [2] as part of the STAR project. On-site movers carry out work requiring movement around a certain site. Examples are workers in different places inside an office or on campus; security agents watching sites, and hospital doctors visiting patients. Yo-yos are occasionally working away from a fixed location, in temporary workplaces. Examples are work on business trips (in meetings), field work (e.g. interviews); working during travelling; working on emergency service, working on customer premises (mobile engineering and maintenance). Pendulums include alternate working at two different fixed locations such as the office and at home. This form would cover the classical forms of telework. Nomads refer to people who constantly are working at changing fixed locations, moving from one location to the other. Examples are: field sales forces, but also managers changing frequently to different locations. Carriers are working on the move transporting goods or people. Examples are train conductors and deliverymen. Emphasis in this typology is on the individual worker, whereas mobile and multi-site group work will be an important model for the near future. The yo-yo and the nomad type would be the forms most related to that. To reflect this evolution to mobile teamwork we combine the five types into three basic forms of mobile working: micro-mobility, multi-mobility and total mobility. Using an extensive list of criteria developed by Lilischkis [3] for distinguishing between basic types of mobile work and combining these criteria into two central ones, the number of work locations and the frequency of changing location, we get the simplified portfolio of mobile work overview of Figure 2.

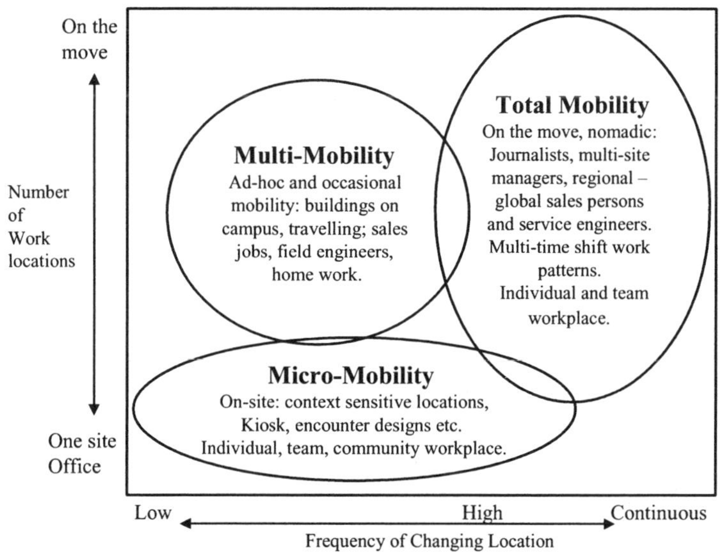

Figure 2: Portfolio of forms of mobile work (based on [2] and MOSAIC)

Based on this categorisation it is possible to analyse the future prospects and success conditions of each of the forms of mobile work and bridge the gap towards the more radical mobile work scenarios of Figure 1 setting out a roadmap implementing innovative mobile work solutions. This currently is elaborated in ongoing MOSAIC work.

3. Frameworks for Understanding Mobile Workplace Innovation

Work environments and work practice comprise various aspects: technology, skills, learning, worker behaviour, organisational processes and structures, societal conditions of legal and regulatory nature. If we wish to understand the patterns of work environment innovation, the success and failure factors and the strategies of designing successful innovations, we should capture these aspects in a holistic way. Below we discuss a number of frameworks dealing with specific aspects of mobile workplace innovation to see what we can learn.

A first basic framework for understanding success or failure of mobile working innovation is to analyse the underlying critical success factors inhibiting or stimulating learning processes. Applying the framework to workplace innovation can be based on recognising the different levels of analysis where different sets of critical success factors operate of societal, industry, organisational and human origin. In order to be of value, this basic model should be adapted to the case situation studied. Different types of critical success factors can be active in different parts of the innovation life cycle, from R&D to commercialisation. Also, specific critical success factors might be part of factors determining a national innovation system and could be described in terms of the dominant aspects of innovation systems. In this sense, the notion of "national innovation system" becomes valuable. Porter [3] has developed this concept to understand why a nation becomes the home base for successful national competitors in an industry. His "diamond" model has five determinants that are mutually enforcing and shape the environment in which local forms compete that promote the creation of competitive advantage: (1) factor conditions, (2) demand condition, (3) related and supporting industries, (4) firms strategy, structure and rivalry, and (5) government role. Together it creates the context for innovation and competitive advantage.

Applying this viewpoint to mobile working, it can be said that innovations in new work environments may contribute to strengthening such a national system of innovation in creating better conditions for innovation and competitiveness, and in realising transitions towards modernised work practices and work environments. The specific bottlenecks for introducing forms of mobile working can be analysed in using the critical success factors approach as a checklist. This could help in identifying the major bottlenecks and conditions for success. Figure 3 demonstrates the way critical factors operate on different stages of innovation in mobile working.

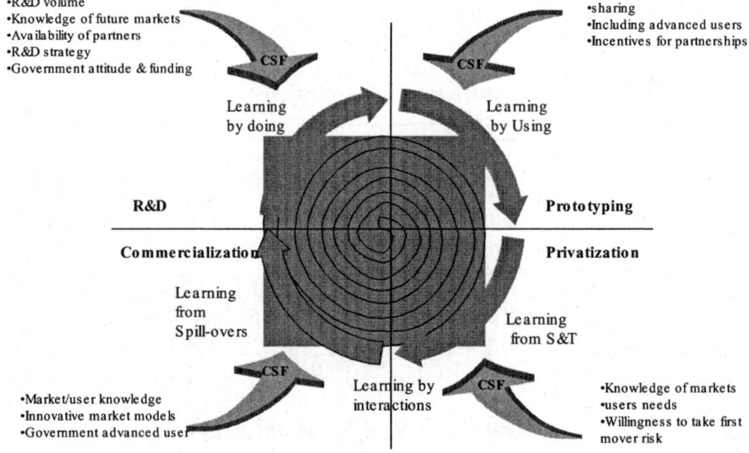

Figure 3: Critical success factors and the innovation system promoting learning

A second framework is provided by the literature of economics of organisations. Emphasis is on enabling us to understand organisational forms in situations of uncertainty, complexity, trust relations and information asymmetry. Malone a.o. [4] as presented in Figure 4 provide a theoretical framework based on evaluation of costs and benefits of communication and coordination in explaining the viability of particular organisational forms. In their three-stage model, in the first stage ('cowboys') communication costs are high and the best way to make decisions is via independent and decentralised decision makers. In the second stage ('commanders'), as technology causes communication costs to decrease, it becomes feasible to bring together decentralised information for coordinated, central decision making. Finally, in the third stage ('cyber cowboys'), communication costs have decreased to such a level that connected decentralised decision makers are more effective and combine local knowledge with the best information available elsewhere. This approach suggests that there are basically two factors determining the viability of an organisational form: (1) the decision situation (including also aspects of trust, location of decision relevant information, motivation, regulation, power distribution), determining the situational requirements of communication and coordination, and (2) technology, determining costs of communication and coordination.

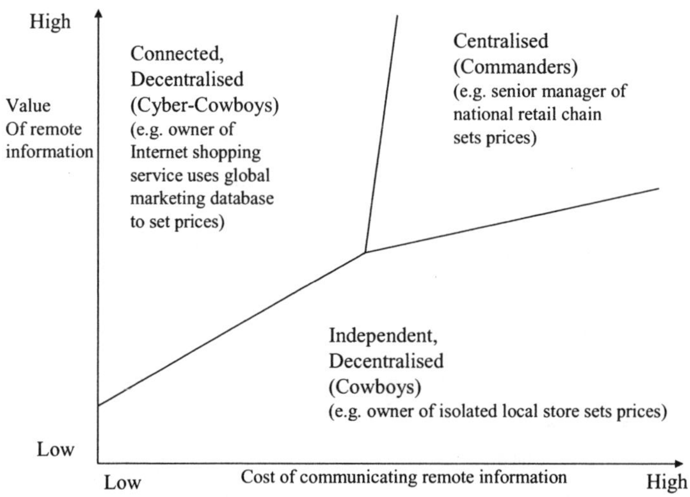

Figure 4: Desirable decision-making structures (Malone a.o. [4])

The value of this model is in taking into account explicitly the benefits and costs of using local information. It also points to the desirable level of making decisions: local or central, emphasising the importance of bringing decision power to where the most important 'sticky' information is located (example: owner of Internet shopping services using global marketing database to set prices). It also is describing aspects of trust and motivation that very well might change the outcome of the analysis if it would be based only on costs of communication. Applying the framework to mobile working it can be stated that mobile working will even more decrease the costs of communicating local information and increase the way local information can be used. Mobile ways of working will also enable new ways to gather and use local information.

The third framework is focusing on the dynamics of adoption. Approaches considering the adoption dynamics of particular technologies and products focus on markets, customers and on successful product introduction strategies in multiple stages of introduction, growth, maturity and decline. Often the innovation process is described as in terms of a family of technologies, each one succeeding the former with ever increasing performance characteristics. The general model for adoption dynamics is the well-known S-shape model. Shapiro and Varian [5] add factors inherent to 'network markets' such as network externalities, lock-in, the exploitation of positive feedback, and the development of critical mass. They also discuss different strategies for innovators as in network markets there are important choices between revolutionary and evolutionary innovations (with implications for compatibility) and choices between openness and control with respect to technologies (with implications for market size). Christensen [6] adds to this the aspect of undermining established markets and market players by disruptive technologies. Dominant established players often focus too much on their most profitable customers and businesses, ever increasing the quality and performance of their products, whereas disruptive technologies are simpler, more convenient and less expensive that appeal to new or less demanding customers. As soon as the disruptive technology is able to gain a foothold and attracts mainstream customers, an improvement cycle begins, winning in the end the attraction of more demanding customers. Moore [7] has developed an actor-oriented perspective to innovation, as in companies different viewpoints are active as regards innovation: technology enthusiasts and visionaries, but also pragmatists, conservatives and sceptics. In his view, innovation can only succeed if the different interests of stakeholders can be met (Figure 5).

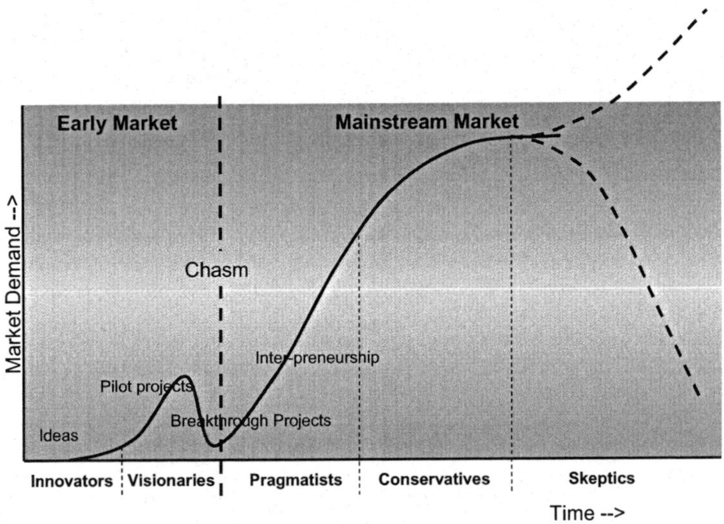

Figure 5: Crossing the chasm (Moore [6])

Applying the adoption dynamics framework to mobile work innovation, emphasis is on a number of highly important aspects of innovation, namely the positive feedback effects in network markets, and the issue of diverging stakeholder interests. Mobile work innovation in this view requires attention to stakeholders in work organisations and requires a strategy of introducing improvements step by step, developing and exploiting learning effects.

The fourth framework is the transition management approach ([8], [9]) focusing on longer term systemic changes in complex large-scale systems such as energy, water, healthcare and spatial development. The approach follows a multi-level description of innovation, distinguishing between 'niches' or protected experimentation spaces at the micro-level, 'regimes' at the intermediate level, and 'socio-technical landscapes' including aspects of infrastructure, culture and institutions at the macro-level. The approach assumes that innovation in complex systems requires transformation of 'regimes' of dominant technologies, practice and interest. It assumes a niche-based model of regime transformation starting in a protected environment. Also, the approach of transition management aims, as is called 'strategic niche management', to steer bottom-up niche-to-regime processes of transformation towards a pre-defined goal or vision (for example a low-carbon energy infrastructure). This theory, using a systems approach, provides a useful general framework of thinking in terms of systemic change and strategic analysis at a rather high level of abstraction and could be helpful for general policy and strategy development. It provides a set of useful metaphors like "transition" and "transition management", "network steering" and "arena". As regards mobile work innovation, the theory is not very discriminative. The approach is highly descriptive, although at the general level normative conclusions are proposed. It focuses on policy frameworks, not on industry sectors and business innovation. In mobile work the interests of the private sector and individual organisations and actors will be too dominant to expect that an approach with its roots in the existence of market inefficiencies would be successful. In some ways MOSAIC and the AMI @ Work families of communities are attempting to realise the transition management approach. This might be interesting to follow over the next few years.

A fifth framework focuses on learning networks. An example of this approach is the Hi-Res project [10] promoting the concept of "arenas of organisational change", a process of continuous learning, experimentation, adaptation and innovation. The value is that it brings together a collection of national models for workplace innovation and some comparative analysis. The project provides an analysis, a vision and an approach to workplace innovation based on case studies. The analysis results in a number of important challenges for policy makers and social partners. In some way this framework is highly complementary to the transition management framework, as the former could be considered very well as an operationalisation of the latter.

Table 1: Evaluation of innovation frameworks

Framework	Value in understanding and guiding mobile work innovation	Drawbacks in understanding and guiding mobile work innovation
Innovation systems and CSF: [3]	Raises the issue how mobile working affects the broader innovation system Focuses on interaction between key determinants of innovation Provides normative guidance at general level	Focus is on strength of organisational networks as a particular aspect
Economics of organisations: [4]	In broad terms providing insight in basic patterns of structural change Provides rational cost-benefit model for choice of organisational forms	Provides only very general normative guidelines for mobile work innovation
Adoption dynamics [5], [6], [7]	Focuses on introduction of products and systems in organisations and markets	Does not focus on broader societal issues regarding mobile work
Transition management: [8], [9]	Useful in analysing the "big picture" of transition Provides useful set of metaphors Useful to create awareness among policy makers and to design national strategies	Too unspecific to be of value in developing innovation strategies at business and industry level
Learning networks: [10]	Operationalises the challenge to develop policy-oriented transition strategies Focuses on policy development and policy experiments	Focuses on conditions for innovation, not on design principles

4. Discussion and Conclusions

Table 1 presents a comparative overview of innovation frameworks. There is not one single framework to help us to understand all aspects of innovation or to help us developing normative guidelines for innovation in new workplaces. Rather there are different frameworks coping with different issues in designing future workplaces. Mobile work innovation affects multiple layers: the mobile worker and his task, the workplace and the team, the organisation, surrounding workplace conditions, and the societal system providing regulatory conditions. Therefore holistic strategies for innovation need to consider all relevant layers in an integrated way. In discussing the five frameworks for understanding of innovation, it appears that emphasis is on (1) understanding a given situation of innovation, (2) providing guidance at a high level of abstraction. Not much concrete, specific guidance is given for designing robust mobile working environments.

Therefore it seems appropriate for policy makers and industries to focus more on the systematic creation of "conditions for learning through innovation". Experimental testbeds and validation environments in the area of mobile work can provide such learning environments, for the benefit of developers and users testing technologies, applications, work environments and business models and focusing on all aspects of user environments. This provides a vehicle to link interests of actors to initiate, design, engineer, validate and use workplace innovations. Testbeds and validation environments in mobile work thus could be catalysers of good practice. Also, it would provide a concrete approach on how to link different national proving grounds in national innovation programmes and to create critical mass and exchange of good practice.

Examples of such national testbeds as candidates for taking part in international "learning environments" would possibly be Freeband (Netherlands), BotniaNet, and Testbed Finland. Integrated Projects in Mobile work could combine resources and provide a new family of such a testing ground. Such testbed and validation environments on the other hand would strengthen their national systems of innovation and would enable these systems of innovation to integrate and create more international strongholds of innovation and contribute to value creation at the European level.

References

[1] COCONET, 'Context Aware Collaborative Environments for Next Generation Business Networks Research Agenda and Roadmap', 2003. See: http://coconet.telin.nl/ .

[2] Stefan Lilischkis (2003), 'More Yo-yos, Pendulums and Nomads: Trends of Mobile and Multi-Location Work in the Information Society'. STAR Project Issue Report N. 36, Draft.

[3] Michael Porter, 'The Competitive Advantage of Nations'. MacMillan Press, 1990.

[4] Thomas W. Malone, R. Laurbacher, M.S. Scott Morton (2003), 'Inventing the Organizations of the 21st Century'. MIT Press.

[5] Carl Shapiro and Hal R. Varian, 'Information Rules. A Strategic Guide to the Network Economy'. Harvard Business School Press, 1999.

[6] Clayton M. Christensen, 'The Innovator's Dilemma. When New Technologies Cause Great Firms to Fail'. Harvard Business School Press, 1997.

[7] Geoffrey A. Moore, 'Crossing the Chasm'. Harper Business, 1991.

[8] R. Kemp and J. Rotmans (2001), 'The management of the co-evolution of technical, environmental and social systems'. International Conference Towards Environmental Innovation Systems, Garmisch Partenkirchen.

[9] Jan Rotmans, 'Transition management. Key to a sustainable society', 2003. (in Dutch).

[10] Peter Totterdill, Steven Dhondt, Sue Milsome (2002), 'Partners at Work? A Report to Europe's Policy makers and Social partners'. Report of the Hi-Res Project funded by DG Research

eAdoption and the Knowledge Economy: Issues, Applications, Case Studies
P. Cunningham and M. Cunningham (Eds.)
IOS Press, 2004

Wearable Mobile Computing - a Paradigm for Future European eWork

Michael BORONOWSKY[1], Li GONG[2], Otthein HERZOG[1], Ingrid RÜGGE[1]
[1]Center for Computing Technologies (TZI), University of Bremen,
Universitätsallee 21-23, Bremen, D-28359, Germany
Tel: +49 421 218-7272, Fax: +49 421 218-7196, Email: [mb, herzog, ruegge]@tzi.de
[2]SAP Research, SAP Labs, 3475 Deer Creek Rd., Palo Alto, CA, 94304, USA
Tel: +1 650 320-3186, Fax: + 1 650 320-3766, Email: li.gong@sap.com

Abstract: "Mobile Solutions" as the future of Information and Communication Technologies (ICT) will influence all areas of life and work. Mobile office work is already common, and multimedia smartphones and PDAs are very popular. A large potential of this novel technology, however, lies beyond these mentioned areas in the support of mobile activities. The present article focuses on mobile work and business processes supported by wearable mobile computing technologies. It describes the current situation in this area and describes the potentials and the technologies to be developed. This paper also introduces a research framework for human-centred wearable system design considering a process that is organized along four different dimensions: modality, task and context, evaluation criteria and methodology. A human-centred and process-oriented approach is crucial for a successful introduction of wearable mobile computing technologies into the workplace.

1. Introduction

Wearable mobile computing can enhance the productivity of professionals by providing more seamless and effective access to knowledge at the point of work, collaboration and communication. This new technology helps many skilled individual professionals to act more flexibly, effectively and efficiently in the increasingly complex and challenging European work environment. It can be used to enhance jobs in industry and services to make them both more rewarding and effective and re-elevate the role of the professional at work. Economically, wearable mobile computing is becoming a core technology also for enabling the transition to a service-centred economy and can therefore significantly catalyse new job creation and economic growth in Europe. Europe should take the lead in exploiting this unique potential of job creation, job enhancement and economic growth. Currently a large consortium of industrial and academic partners is preparing an integrated European project to start in mid 2004: wearIT@work – Empowering the mobile worker by wearable computing. This project will address a broad spectrum of important aspects to make wearable mobile computing an application reality. It will span a bow from hardware issues, general software platform and infrastructures, clothing design, business potentials, application perspectives and most important, the user and his needs.

Wearable mobile computing can do for mobile professionals away from the desk what networked desktop computing has done for professionals in offices. Many industry and service work processes involve tasks where fixed ICT infrastructure is of limited use. Mobile work can take place at different locations, requires communication and access to online knowledge, binds the primary task and user's attention to the physical world, and is performed by professionals. The mobile solutions of today are not effective enough as they force the user to focus attention on the interaction with the computer rather than on carrying out the actual task at hand. Because the mobile computing solutions of today are still too complex, too obtrusive, and too demanding on the user to be seamlessly integrated into complex work processes, their usability and their acceptance by the workers is still limited.

The paradigm of wearable mobile computing takes the next important step of innovation in addressing this shortcoming. It aims to develop mobile platforms that support complex tasks with a minimum of human-machine interaction and thereby enable mobile professionals to focus on interaction with the work environment. It will broaden the scope of mobile applications to new areas such as the inspection of motorways, maintenance of large technical plants, emergency services, and the distribution of merchandise. It will have a long-term impact on organising individual and collaborative work.

To foster deployment of this new paradigm in professional environments it is important to develop methods and tools that allow delivering information and computing services to mobile workers based on their specific work situation and context, thereby furthering the European ambient intelligence vision. Because new tools often come in conjunction with new work processes wearable mobile computing puts the mobile professional at the centre and examines new methods to organize work such as knowledge sharing in collaborative teams. Another core driver is the "people first" vision explicated in the European ambient intelligence concept. To follow this vision, results of new developments must be tested and proven by realistic pilot applications in a number of practical and relevant application areas. To foster the development of these applications it will be important to follow a user-centred approach focused on the needs of the mobile worker. These new applications will result in an empowerment of workers in concrete work situations, but they will also have a long-term impact on the general organization of work and will drive the change and development of new effective work processes and work environments.

A real research challenge in this area is to set new European standards for mobile solutions in terms of wearable hardware platforms, necessary software and information infrastructures, and last but not least guidelines for how to successfully deploy wearable mobile computing solutions. These standards will allow companies to develop and produce highly innovative, marketable and yet sound applications and services for the mobile European professional, and it will allow the users to rely on proven concepts for adopting them. However, technology should not end in itself – technology is for people. Thinking about better systems requires thinking about the user or the worker that is expected to draw benefits out of technological solutions. Research in this area has to set a context in which the new paradigm of mobile wearable computing is going to be developed and tested and where the individual is put at the centre as core driver for organisational changes.

2. Motivation for the Need of a Paradigm Shift

Mobile service and knowledge workers are currently feeling pressure from two directions. On the one hand, tools, techniques and work practises change in an ever increasing rate, on the other hand, a constant improvement of productivity and quality is expected. This leads to the necessity to learn, remember and consider more knowledge in less time during the work process. Therefore innovative solutions to support mobile work and business processes are needed to strengthen European competitiveness by furthering the improvement of work conditions by capital investment for mobile work. The key to such solutions is the ability to deliver up-to-date information and collect data in situations in which the user needs to focus his/her attention and activity on the real, physical world.

Achieving the goal stated above requires rethinking of current (software) design principles. Rather than being technology-driven, the design of computer systems for mobile activities and work processes needs to be centred onto the work process and onto the competent human whose capabilities are to be supported and who is to be relieved of unproductive tasks. In particular, the system must not interfere with the user's ability to perform complex tasks in the real physical world. This implies strict constraints on the physical form factor of the hardware as well as on the cognitive load of the human-computer interface. Metaphors for such designs are the tutor, or the autonomous human assistant. In addition, mobile work and business processes cannot be supported with stand-alone solutions. Instead they must fit in smoothly with the already existing technological information infrastructure to make already existing knowledge and communication resources also available for mobile work. In the reverse direction it is necessary to integrate wearable mobile solutions into the existing infrastructure without a technological gap.

To discuss an example, we highlight some maintenance procedures that are typical for the inspection of large technical plants, motorways, buildings, or motor vehicles and aircrafts. The object in question (e.g., an airplane) must be inspected, examined, measured, tested, and evaluated on site. To support this work and make it more effective, a large number of information items must be accessible simultaneously, e.g., an assembly or operating instruction, inspection checklist, detailed information concerning individual components, drawings, or blueprints. In difficult cases, consultations with experts at different locations may be necessary. This collaborative effort can be made more effective if all involved parties have access to the same significant information. The results of each inspection will be permanently documented and serve as additional data at the next repair or inspection campaign. The environment and work processes make the use of conventional desktop computers impossible: there is insufficient space, the external (climatic) conditions are extreme, and the worker needs both hands to check, measure and grasp things.

In this situation, an ICT-system must not restrict the user in his/her freedom of movement. The explicit interaction must be minimal and must not interrupt the primary action. Also, it should fit in smoothly with the work process. The computer system should record most of the required data independently and screen the context with intelligent methods without the aid of user input. Its use should be simple and casual, comparable to automatically putting your hands into your pocket, taking out an instrument and testing for example a power circuit. The mobile support system should not make excessive demands on the cognitive resources of the user. It should only represent the information actually required and only request the input that needs human judgement. In its most restrained form, the support system should only make itself noticeable if the user seems to be at a loss.

The identified paradigm shift requires a European harmonisation in terms of research, development, standardisation, training, and exploitation. New user interaction methods are required to close the gap between usage requirements and the way in which technology is used to deliver the necessary information. Reducing this gap would mean that information could be delivered when and where it is needed.

3. Available Enabling Technologies

The concept of using integrated ICT to support users interact with the environment is of highest importance to the emerging field of wearable mobile computing. This approach has its roots in the work of Steve Mann [1] and Thad Starner [2] at MIT dating back to the late eighties, and has recently developed into a flourishing research field. Research into both fundamental aspects (e.g., 2Wear DC project) and specific (in particular medical) applications (e.g., AMON, SILC, LIFEBELT) has been funded in previous IST projects.

The first useable hardware and software components for wearable mobile computing have become commercially available only recently. This includes wearable CPUs as well as the respective input/output devices (like head-mounted displays; arm-mounted keyboards or touch screens with the appropriate virtual keyboards; wireless miniaturised loudspeaker/ microphone systems with robust voice recognition; speed acceleration mice and wearable GPS-modules). Currently, intensive research is being done on long-life batteries and new mobile energy sources. For a long time, different kinds of sensors have been used in control circuits, or are available as separate devices. The integration into a wearable mobile computer system, however, has not yet been realised. All components mentioned above still require further refinement, especially with respect to their modularization and easy integration into various wearable systems. The appropriate software systems to support such tools still have to be developed.

Currently, mobile solutions are applications that have proven to be successful as desktop solutions and exist on two levels: the computer program is transferred to a suitably powerful mobile device by installing the software on the mobile device without further changes or the program is reduced in functionality and adapted to less powerful hardware. An example is the development of functionally reduced office applications for PDAs.

The full potential of wearable mobile computing, however, can only be marginally exploited through these methods. To make full use of it, adaptations to the specification of the wearable computing paradigm as well as to the new possibilities of mobile activities have to take place. Still, there are a few research groups and companies who have been dealing with this subject for some time, resulting in the development of prototypes, e.g.,

- VUMAN 1, 2 & 3: Several wearable computer systems developed in 1990-1995 at the Carnegie Mellon University (CMU) to support industrial maintenance processes. One key element for interaction was a jog-dial like wheel for the selection of menu items [3].
- Symbol Wearable Scanning System WSS 1000: This is a commercially available computer worn on the forearm. It is used extensively by UPS to scan and decode barcodes in order to track parcels. It also has a wireless LAN connection [4].
- Winspect: This wearable computer prototype was developed in 1999-2002 at the TZI, University of Bremen. It is designed to support the maintenance of industrial cranes with checklists, a documentation browser and video conferencing. The computer as well as its input and output devices are completely integrated into the work cloths [5, 6].

All solutions and prototypes in the field of wearable mobile computing that have been implemented to-date are individual solutions for specific tasks. Common features have to be found in order to develop solutions for entire classes of application problems.

4. Towards Wearable Computing based eWork

"The worldwide market for wearable computers generated over $70 million in supplier revenues in 2001. The market will increase at a compound annual growth rate (CAGR) of over 51% through 2006, and grow to over $563 million. Wearable computers are providing higher employee productivity and improved customer service levels in a wide variety of market segments, and users in these markets are finding that purchase of premium priced wearable rather than other computing form factors to be money well spent. Improvements in related enabling technologies such as speech/voice recognition, head mounted and eyewear displays, and the continued miniaturization of components as well as increasing functionality and performance capabilities are major factors expected to fuel the anticipated explosive demand for wearable computers. In addition, the increasing adoption of wireless communications as a means to enhance operational efficiency and improve profitability is another factor that will help propel very robust demand for wearable computers through 2006 and beyond." [7]

Despite its massive growth, the market for wearable computers is still a niche market compared to the industrial use of desktop computers. Drivers of a stronger growth will be more standardised hardware and software platforms enabling the new work paradigms. To realize the full potential of wearable mobile computing, research is needed in three dimensions: 1) the technologies used, 2) the actors, tasks, and situations supported, and 3) the organizational and social aspects of the usage. Consequently, projects have to conduct research and produce empirically tested knowledge, methodologies and technological prototypes, e.g., in the following areas:

The foundation for development must be based on empirical research on appropriate mechanisms to support the competent situated activities of individuals or collaborating professionals. To make sure the new tools will empower the professional instead of leading to a loss of competence and responsibility, the risks of wearable mobile computing, such as reducing the professional to a human extension to a computer system, have to be given special attention. By understanding the importance of workspace quality, projects must make wearable mobile computing an accepted tool that brings added value to the worker.

The provision of appropriate context-dependent levels of assistance has to be achieved. Within different working contexts, not all communication channels and means of user-assistance may be appropriate or necessary. Finding the balance between what is possible and what is actually wanted in terms of user assistance will be crucial for usability and acceptance and the respective productivity gain of new tools.

Methods to derive process information from contexts, situations, and personalized information (e.g., individual task plans or workflows) have to be developed. This information will be used to configure the system for an optimal, context-dependent assistance of different work situations (e.g., to support single workers or the collaborative work of teams). It will also be used to optimize how this information is presented to the worker under specific circumstances, thus greatly reducing the "interaction cost". The different types of mobile assistance of individual applications and use cases have to be generalized to generic mechanisms covering classes of use cases. Standard processes and workflow templates that will support the analysis and introduction of context-driven information push to workers in specific work situations have to be derived.

New concepts for system architectures have to be designed which are based on the requirements of application areas. The integration of technology with a focus on functional and textile design ethics and health aspects has to be studied to integrate innovative technologies with a high comfort for the worker. Wearable mobile system architectures have to find a balance between using the computing power of the wearable device (providing a degree of autonomy from an intelligent environment), and resorting to resources offered by remote services (like complex video rendering).

New human-machine interfaces have to be developed. Changing the current paradigm of human-machine interaction and developing new ways for mobile workers to interact with wearable devices in a "casual" manner is a key component to the usability and acceptance of wearable mobile computing. Such interfaces will limit the necessary human-machine interactions to a minimum, providing a distraction-free environment in which for example a medical doctor is able to control complex medical devices during a surgery while being able to fully concentrate on his work and the patient.

These layers are multidisciplinary and complementary helping to build the "people first" ambient intelligence vision proclaimed by the most advanced research groups in Europe. It is important to base new working concepts like wearable computing on the requirements of the individual application domains and not on the technology. Existing workflows have to be reorganized demonstrating the tangible and intangible benefits of industrial wearable computing, e.g., for the productivity of the worker. Questions related to the future skills of workers, acceptance of the electronic support, social and ethic implications are inherent for a successful mobile solution.

Until now the individual has not been put at the centre of the research process, and this fact has become a main barrier in the implementation of the technological solutions. It is important to explore the implications of this changed perspective and develop a new concept of the design of mobile work environments in which the users are the key driver from the conception of the technology to the design of the application and to the implementation of the solution. Research in this area will have to conduct empirical social scientific and user-centred research on wearable technology at work, particularly focusing on the functionality and ease of use dimensions. Research will have to examine e.g. how people interact with wearable computing systems, regarding:

- modalities involved in the interaction because wearable computing systems are new;
- what functions or effects wearable computing systems provide against the background of workers' needs and contexts;
- ease of use of wearable computing systems.

The problem to solve is the lack of exploration on how individuals at work can be empowered by the new wearable technologies, and consequently how the use of these technologies may change organizational processes.

5. Methodology for a Human-centred Approach

One example is the consequent use of a human-centred design approach. This can be achieved by a research framework that is organized in four dimensions:

Dimension 1: Modality. Modality is a central aspect of users' interaction with wearable computers. How the input and output (I/O) modalities should be selected and combined in wearable technology has immediate and critical impact on users' interaction and requires sound and empirical analysis. A large body of literature comparing I/O modalities in human-computer interaction constitutes the basis for our investigation in the relatively new domain of wearable computers. Humans naturally use different or multiple modalities including visual and auditory modalities, touch, smell, and taste, in interacting with their surroundings such as computers [8,9]. Research, for example, has shown that speech is more effective for entering textual commands if speech recognition is robust, and gestural input such as pen or stylus is more preferred for spatial specification and manipulations [10,11]. Gong [12] observed that users tend to prefer using speech for entering textual data to the extend that they would keep trying in the case of speech misrecognition, while they prefer using stylus for clicking links and opening drop-down boxes on a PDA. Now for wearable computers which come unprecedentedly close to our bodies, the I/O modalities become the first and basic question of the study.

Dimension 2: Task and Context. Modalities cannot be assessed in a vacuum. The involved tasks and situations set the content and context. The workers' work context stipulates the environmental demand and constraints for wearable computing. In synergy with the mobile work, a typology of contexts can be collected and characterized by physical settings such as noise level and hazard level, and by social settings such as monitored vs. autonomous and shared vs. solo use. One way to achieve this will be ethnographic research to extract typologies of tasks and contexts in work situations, accompanied by field observations and interviews.

Dimension 3: Evaluation Criteria. Viable options of wearable technology and its modalities have to be identified and hypothesized to satisfy various work tasks and contexts. Then, social scientific assessments will have to be used to test such hypotheses and determine the functional effects and usability of wearables and wearable modalities. Empirical social scientific measurements will have to compare wearables against the control condition of not using wearables and compare different input and output modalities of wearables. The assessments and comparisons are made against four criteria: productivity, usability, likeability, safety

Dimension 4: Methodologies. To reiterate the proposed methodologies laboratory and field experiments have to be employed to measure productivity, usability, and workers' attitude, and field ethnographic research have to be conducted to collect and typify tasks and contexts and provide qualitative results of the use and effects of wearable computing systems. In addition, demographic variables of workers such as gender and education level will also have to be taken into consideration and measured.

6. Conclusions

Before exploitation in commercial products and services, the paradigm of wearable mobile computing has to be investigated in practical applications and subsequent development cycles have to be passed. This new paradigm covers multidisciplinary aspects involving experts from computer science, engineering science, cognitive science, ergonomics, design, psychology, and sociology. Wearable Computing comes along with a great economic potential and it will be an important step for Europe towards a knowledge based economy. This multidisciplinary approach addresses both technical and human challenges.

However, this progress should not be purely driven by technology. Research will focus e.g. on the definition of guidelines how to reorganise existing working structures taking maximum benefit of the new technology from an economic and a social point of view. To ensure the new tools will empower the professional instead of causing a loss of competence and responsibility, the risks of wearable computing and it's social ethical implications have to be given special attention. The wearIT@work project will be an important step in this direction – inherent for a successful deployment of this new paradigm.

Acknowledgements

We want to thank Paul Lukowicz, Markus Klann, Peter Knackfuss and Irene Lopez de Vallejo for the fruitful discussions and their support helping to shape this vision of wearable mobile computing supported eWork.

References

[1] http://wearcam.org/ last visit: April 30, 2004
[2] http://www.cc.gatech.edu/fac/Thad.Starner/ last visit: April 30, 2004
[3] Bass, L. et.al.: Constructing Wearable Computers for Maintenance Applications. In: W. Barfield; T. Caudell: Fundamentals of Wearable Computers and Augmented Reality. LEA Publishers, 2001. pp. 663-694.
[4] http://www.symbol.com/products/barcode_scanners/ barcode_wearable_wsc_wss1000.html last visit: April 30, 2004
[5] Boronowsky, M.; Nicolai, T.; Schlieder, C.; Schmidt, A.: Winspect: A Case Study for Wearable Computing-Supported Inspection Tasks. In: Proc. of ISWC'01, 2001, pp.163-164.
[6] Herzog, O.; Rügge, I.; Boronowsky, M.; Nicolai, T.: Potenziale des Wearable Computing in der Industrie - am Beispiel der Inspektion.- In: J. Gausemeier, M. Grafe (Hrsg.): Augmented & Virtual Reality in der Produktentstehung, 2. Paderborner Workshop Augmented & Virtual Reality in der Produktentstehung, 4. und 5. Juni 2003, Heinz Nixdorf MuseumsForum, pp. 21-39.
[7] THE GLOBAL MARKET FOR WEARABLE COMPUTERS: THE QUEST FOR KILLER APPLICATIONS, Tim Shea, Senior Industry Analyst, VENTURE DEVELOPMENT CORPORATION, August 2002.
[8] Bolt, R.: Put-That-There: Speech and gesture at the graphics interface. Computer Graphics, 14, 1980, pp. 262-270.
[9] McNeil, D.: Hand and mind: What gestures reveal about thought. Chicago, IL: University of Chicago Press, 1992.
[10] Martin, G.L.: The utility of speech input in user-computer interfaces. International Journal of Man-Machine Studies, 30(4), 1989, pp. 355-375.
[11] Oviatt, S.; DeAngeli, A.; Kuhn, K.: Integration and synchronization of input modes during multimodal human-computer interaction. In: Proceedings of Conference on Human Factors in Computing Systems (CHI '97), New York, NY: ACM Press 1997, pp. 415-422.
[12] Gong, L.: Multimodal interactions on mobile devices and users' behavioral and attitudinal preferences. In: C. Stephanidis: (Ed.), Universal access in HCI: Inclusive design in the information society. Mahwah, NJ: Lawrence Erlbaum Associates, 2003, pp. 1402-1406.

EDEL: Developing a Second Generation Night-Vision System

Carlo BELLOTTI[1], Francesco BELLOTTI[1], Alessandro DE GLORIA[1], Luisa ANDREONE[2], Dieter KOOSS[3], Michele MARIANI[4]
[1]*D.I.B.E., Via Opera Pia 11a, Genoa, 16145, Italy*
Tel: +39 0103532780, Fax: + 39 0103532780, Email: {Francesco.Bellotti, adg}@unige.it
[2] *FIAT Research Center, Strada Torino, 50, 10043 Orbassano (TO), Italy*
Email: luisa.andreone@crf.it
[3] *Universität Karlsruhe, Lichttechnisches Institut, Kaiserstr. 12, 76128 Karlsruhe*
Email: dieter.kooss@lti.uni-karlsruhe.de
[4] *University of Siena, Via dei Termini 6, 53100 Siena, Italy, Email: mariani@unisi.it*

Abstract: Accidents occurring at night and involving pedestrians represent a significant part of the total number of road fatalities. Thus, intelligent systems able to support night driving promise to have a significant impact on traffic safety. The second generation of such systems will provide semantic, symbolic information in order to effectively draw the driver's attention towards the actual danger source. This paper describes the requirements, the design choices and the system architecture of the EDEL European project. Moreover, we present the algorithms we use for detection of pedestrians and discuss early results. In particular, the implemented system provides recognition rates similar to the state of the art in daylight conditions, even if this requires a more in-depth analysis of the captured scene, with a consequent performance penalty in terms of response time. We finally discuss issues related to eye safety, which stem from the necessity for illuminating the scene with a NIR laser source.

1. Introduction

New generation cars feature an increasing number of electronic systems supporting safe driving. Typical Advanced Driver Assistance Systems (ADAS) functionality includes frontal and lateral collision warning, intelligent speed adaptation, blind spot detection, lane recognition, parking aid, etc. While early implementations have shown promising results, a further challenging research area is related to the support for night driving.

In fact, darkness is a major risk factor for driving. 90% of a driver's reaction depends on vision, and vision is severely limited at night. Depth perception, colour recognition, and peripheral vision are compromised after sunset. 62% of pedestrian/motor vehicle deaths occur at night, and visibility is a major factor [1]. Considering the psycho-physical point of view, "Motorists fail to appreciate the limitations of their visual functions at night" [2]. Accordingly, motorists may routinely behave in a manner that is not supported by their visual ability at night" [3]. Thus, reduced visibility crashes may be alleviated by systems that compensate for the drivers' inability to see adequately. In fact, in critical driving situations, the happening or prevention of an accident can be a matter of a fraction of a second. Studies indicate that about 60 percent of front-end crashes and almost one third of head-on collisions would not occur if the driver could react one-half second earlier [4].

It has been argued that "Night time driving is associated with the highest fatality rates. Night driving is generally accepted to be two to three times more hazardous than daylight driving per mile driven" [5]. Owens and Sivak [6] reported that: "For more than a decade, nighttime fatality rates, adjusted for mileage, have averaged more than three times higher than daytime rates ... if the night time rate were lowered to match the daytime rate, the number of road fatalities in 1993 would have been 35,9% lower, saving 15.092 lives". These studies confirm that implementation of night vision systems for automatic driver assistance is an important challenge in view of meeting the European Union's target of reducing the number of fatalities by 50% by 2010.

In the total of accidents within the EU, about 33% involve unprotected road users such as pedestrians and cyclists [7]. Analyzing statistics and studies about the victims of night-driving crashes it has been shown that pedestrians and cyclists are the most frequent victims [5, 8]. This is why a lot of research has been focusing on ADAS systems aimed at preventing accidents with pedestrians and other obstacles at night [9].

This paper presents the results from the EDEL project (Enhanced Driving in Poor Visibility Conditions), co-funded by the European Commission under FP5. EDEL involves CRF, Bosch, Jaguar, Hella, OSRAM and the Universities of Genoa, Siena and Karlsruhe. EDEL is aimed to develop a night vision system based on near infrared sensors and a novel illumination system based on multi-element array laser technology integrated in a newly designed vehicle projector headlamps. The design and development of an automotive night vision systems for mass production involves tackling a variety of issues, ranging from scene illumination to data collection and interpretation, from costs to usability and usefulness for the end user. In this paper we describe our approach, the system and discuss early results from the implemented simulators and prototype modules.

2. Designing a second generation Night Vision System

Relying on years of artificial vision research for road vehicles [9], the Japanese and USA markets already offer a number of night vision support systems. EDEL aims at offering on the market a second generation of night vision systems able to go beyond the existing "image centred" systems (i.e. systems presenting an enhanced representation of the scene) by providing an automatic interpretation of the images captured by the on-vehicle cameras.

Technological innovation and marketing needs are constantly pushing for the introduction of new devices in cars. However, it is uncertain whether such technologies will really improve the quality of the driving experience and the overall road safety. To ensure that these two aspects are taken into account throughout the whole project, EDEL adopted a user-centred design approach [10]. A customer benefit analysis performed in an early phase of the project, identified the following general critical situations in night time:

- presence of unexpected potential obstacles on the road (i.e. pedestrians, unlit cyclists);
- inappropriate use of headlamps;
- driving along unknown roads or familiar roads with unexpected events;
- driving at a speed greater or equal than 30 km/h
- driving on a single-carriageway, two-lane road far from any pedestrian crossing facility;

The following general system attributes/requirements were highlighted:

- simple representation to allow fast detection of hazards and reduce eyes-off-the-road time; an effective night vision system should primarily enhance the visibility of potential obstacles, not of the road itself.
- if a real scene is displayed (e.g. through a head-up display), potential obstacles should be tracked with key information (e.g. speed of an on-coming vehicle, angle, distance);
- the learning time required to correctly use the system should be non more than 1 hour;

When designing a new safety system, it is important to pinpoint possible drawbacks and side effects and tackle the related issues since the early phases of the design. We have identified the following main factors that may negatively impact the safety of the users.

- behavioural adaptation [11, 12]: the driver may behave in riskier ways as a result of a perceived increase in safety due to the EDEL support;
- traffic interference: Unsupported drivers may be surprised by the behaviour of drivers having the use of nigh vision systems;
- workload: the use of a night vision system may increase the mental and visual workload of the driver, in particular in the implementations that involve a direct, enhanced representation of the scene ahead (e.g. projected on the windscreen or the dashboard).

2.1 Systems for night vision

Two different types of Night Vision Systems are currently on the market or under development: systems based on Far Infrared Radiation (FIR), which have been on the market since the year 2000, and systems based on Near Infrared Radiation (NIR), which will be on the market around the half of this decade.

FIR systems exploit the radiation emitted by any warm object. In the resulting image, warm objects are displayed in white or light grey, while cold objects appear dark.

FIR images provide a type of information quite different from the images in the visible spectrum. While such information is not immediately comprehensible by a human observer, the high thermal contrast between the background and the foreground elements have spurred the development of algorithms for automatic detection of cars and pedestrians.

NIR sensors detect the radiation reflected by objects in the infrared range which is close to the visible light. This requires an active illumination of the scene through NIR light sources. The first NIR applications, around 10 years ago, were based on CCD cameras as they were becoming highly sensitive, smaller and cheaper. CCD sensors, however, are blinded by oncoming vehicles' headlamps. The recently developed highly dynamic CMOS sensors are able to reduce blinding effects by exploiting a nonlinear response. Rain or fog reduce the sight distance, penalizing the performance. In general, FIR systems have a greater sight distance. On the other hand, NIR sensors offer images that are quite intuitive to the viewers, since the spectrum is close to the visibility range of human eyes.

This property makes NIR images suited to be displayed directly to the driver. The EDEL system exploits such a property by implementing a "frontal-view mirror". This is an additional display the driver can blink at from time to time, when the external visibility is reduced. Tests in different European countries (e.g. within the DARWIN project) have shown that displaying only the FIR images of the scene to the driver in a complex scenario cannot offer the driver a substantial support since she/he needs time to interpret thermal images. Moreover – even for NIR images – the presentation of a continuous "movie" in driver's peripheral view is not able to attract the driver's attention in case of presence of sudden obstacles. As we mentioned above, the most substantial benefits to the driver come from an automatic interpretation of the image. NIR images are difficult to automatically recognize, since the contrast is smaller than in FIR images. Nevertheless, they provide more complete information (e.g. road lanes are now visible). Since the NIR images' spectrum is close to that of the human eyes, recognition algorithms typically rely on techniques similar to those of artificial vision in daylight conditions, even if luminosity is lower.

A good NIR illuminator should cover a proper range (up to 150 m) to substitute the high-beams – when they cannot be used - and to further enhance them. Up to now, the introduction of such a system on the market has been prevented by the fact that two oncoming vehicles, equipped with a NIR light source, would blind each other. This is the reason why EDEL specifically targets the problem of glaring by developing and testing a new illumination system synchronized with the camera. Another issue – we will discuss it later in the paper - concerns eye safety, as the human retina is vulnerable to thermal burns.

Some manufacturers and suppliers are studying the integration of NIR and FIR systems in order to benefit from the respective advantages. EDEL did not follow such an approach because the foreseen final costs are considered unsuited for mass production.

3. Algorithms for Night Vision

The EDEL night vision system involves two image processing modules. The first one concerns image enhancement, the second one image recognition. Both modules elaborate the pictures taken from the camera with different purposes: the first one is just to provide visual information, the second one to provide semantic information. The front-end for displaying the image to the driver. Two different implementations are foreseen: a Head-Up Display (HUD), installed on top of the dashboard in the distance of "far accommodation" of the driver's eyes, and an Active Matrix Liquid Crystal Display (AMLCD) replacing the current electromechanical instrument panels.

3.1 Image Enhancement

The scene image displayed on the HUD or the AMLCD exploits the intuitiveness of the NIR image. However, the source quality is low and needs enhancement. Thus, we have developed a histogram manipulation algorithm that, at each frame, spreads the information over all the available 256 levels (Figure 1). The algorithm adapts in real-time to the ambient light conditions and employs hysteresis to avoid disrupting the viewer with sudden jumps in the level mapping rules. Fig. 2 shows image elaboration in a lower ambient light condition.

Figure 1. Enhancement through histogram manipulation.

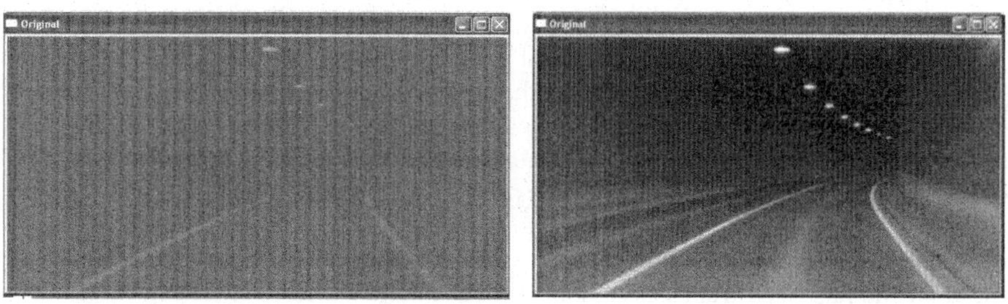

Figure 2. Enhancement through histogram manipulation in lower ambient light condition.

3.2 Image Recognition

The most important part of the image interpretation module – which includes also road detection and car and obstacle identification - is represented by the pedestrian recognition algorithm, which enables the EDEL HMI to provide the driver with a semantic warning. In order to identify pedestrians, we have adopted a machine learning approach based on a

Support Vector Machine (SVM) [13]. This technique has been proposed at the MIT, and successfully applied to daylight vision applications [14]. We have extended this approach to the night vision, drawn by the fact that NIR images have a similar spectrum as daylight images. Moreover, the SVM approach is very general and the system can be trained to recognize a variety of classes (e.g. obstacles, animals, etc.).

Figure 3. SVM detected pedestrian

The SVM's training set we have developed involves 700 pedestrian and 2,000 non pedestrian images. We foresee that the final database will include about 1,500 pedestrians and 5,000 non pedestrians. The images are processed with a Haar wavelet transform in order to guarantee low intra-class variability and high inter-class variability [15]. Analyzing the coefficients of our current database, we have extracted 58 most significant coefficients (i.e. coefficients encoding most of the differences between pedestrian and non pedestrian images). Considering only such coefficients, we managed to achieve a processing rate of 1Hz. The SVM has been trained so that it makes no errors on the available input videos.

We tested the SVM on 100 further frames representative of night driving conditions, with and without pedestrians, obtaining the Receiver Operation Characteristic (ROC) curve depicted in Fig. 4. The recognition's system overall performance (a false recognition rate of 0.03% with a true recognition rate of 60% - which is penalized by pedestrians taken in non frontal nor rear positions) is in line with the results presented in daylight conditions [14]. However, we pay the toll of reduced luminosity by increasing the number of coefficients to be analyzed (58 instead of 29), which penalizes the system's time response as the inner product of the coefficients is the execution hotspot of the SVM's computation.

The classifier was developed iteratively, resulting in significant improvements. First, we have increased the decision threshold above the default zero value, as false alarms are more frequent than misses. We carefully tuned the training set since the overall performance is quite dependent on the sample images. Finally, we have implemented a clustering algorithm which is performed at each frame on all the image areas where a possible presence of a pedestrian is detected, since the same pedestrian is often detected more than once in the same frame. This is because the SVM is trained to detect also parts of a pedestrian, in order to cope with danger situations where a pedestrian may be partially occluded.

Training the system with more images improves precision. However, this also increases the number of support vectors (i.e. the vectors that define the hyper-plan separating the pedestrian and non-pedestrian spaces) and consequently the frame processing times.

Thus, we are currently investigating several additional solutions (beyond improving the images' training set and optimizing the code) in order to increase the overall system performance. In particular, we are complementing the SVM detection with other techniques based on symmetry, shape and pattern matching. Finally, we expect a significant improvement by introducing a tracking module which exploits spatial correlations between subsequent frames, even if the car's speed impedes relying on a static background.

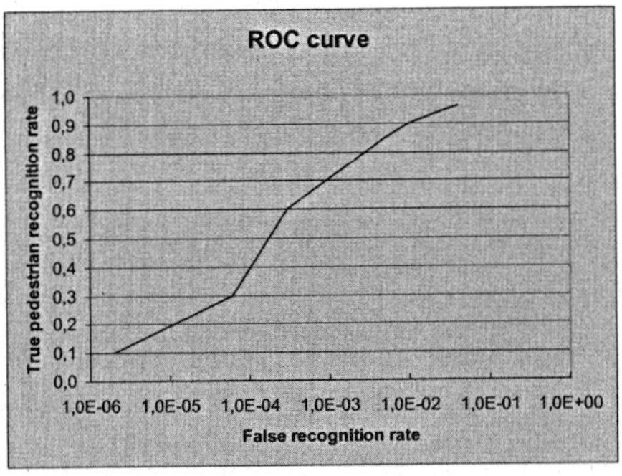

Figure 4. Receiver Operation Characteristic curve for the implemented SVM

4. Eye safety

An important aspect of EDEL involves eye safety, because of the need for a NIR laser source able to illuminate the scene ahead for about 150 m. with an illuminance of about 50 mW/m². We selected an 808 nm IR-laser from Osram Semiconductors and an optical system ad-hoc designed by Hella in order to illuminate the road like an automotive beam.

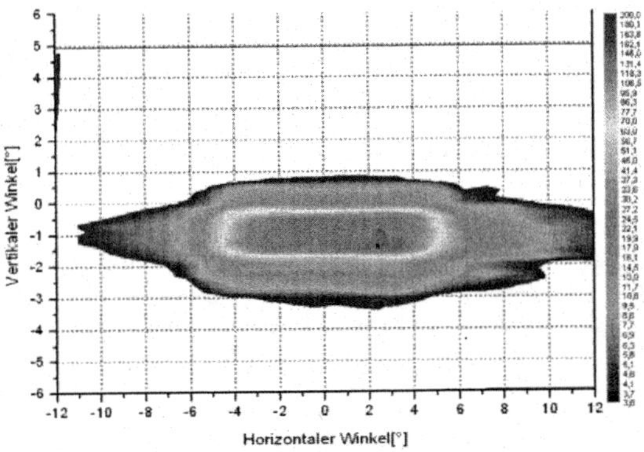

Figure 5. Light distribution of the illuminating system

Current measurements refer to a laser power of 20 W, pulsed with a frequency of 20 khz and a pulse duration of 1 to 10 μs. The apparent illuminating surface is about 3 mm x 30 mm. Considering the IEC 60825 specifications [16], this leads to a Nearest Optical Hazard Distance (NOHD) of about 18 m - the distance within there is a potential eye risk looking directly into the illuminating system. The goal during development of the optical system and camera system is to minimize this distance as much as possible. Fig. 6 shows the dependence of the NOHD with the pulse duration when observing the laser for 100s.

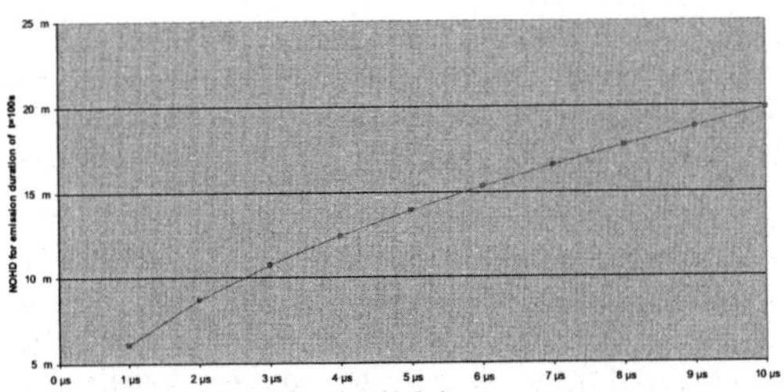

Figure 6 Dependence of the NOHD with pulse width

For a pulse width of 10 μs, the NOHD is 18 m., decreasing to 6 m. for a pulse width of 1 μs. The final system's pulse will be shaped according to the actual sensitivity of the camera system and in order to meet the existing safety regulations and recommendations [16, 17]. We can clearly already foresee the necessity of a risk management for the complete system (e.g. IR inhibition in case of break of the headlamp lens and switch off of the system at low vehicle speed and in other cases when the system is not really needed).

5. Conclusions and future work

Accidents occurring at night and involving pedestrians represent a significant percentage of the total. Thus, implementation of night vision systems for automatic driver assistance is an important research challenge for the next years. Developing an effective night vision system involves a number of aspects, ranging from illumination systems to human factors, from image processing to eye safety. The EDEL EU project has developed a system architecture which processes videos taken by a NIR system with a CMOS camera and display visual and semantic information to the driver. The core of the system is represented by image processing modules relying on existing algorithms, that have been adapted to the targeted night conditions. We have obtained results similar to the state of the art in daylight conditions at the cost of a more accurate computation. This raises performance concerns, in particular considering the limited capabilities of the hardware available for the in car deployment. Thus, the next steps of EDEL will be devoted to the integration and the tuning of the developed modules and to their mapping to a suitable hardware architecture.

Another issue concerns eye safety due to the use of a NIR laser source to illuminate the scene. While some procedures have been defined to reduce the danger impact, further investigation and algorithm optimization are needed to keep the average risk under control.

References

[1] http://nncf.unl.edu/eldercare/info/seniordriving/nightdriv.html Technical Report 6, Nebraska Highway Safety Program.

[2] Leibowitz H. W., Owens D. A. "We drive by night" Psychology Today, January, pp. 55-58, 1986.

[3] Ward N.J., Wilde G.J.S. "Driver approach behaviour at an unprotected railway crossing before and after enhancement of lateral sight distances: An experimental investigation of a risk perception and behavioural compensation hypothesis". Safety Science, 1-2, nn. 1-3, pp. 63-75, 1995.

[4] P. Knoll, "A NIR Based System for Night Vision Improvement", Convergence 2002.

[5] Blanco M. (1992). Relationship Between Driver Characteristics, Nighttime Driving Risk Perception, and Visual Performance under Adverse and Clear Weather Conditions and Different Vision Enhancement Systems. Doctoral Thesis. Faculty of the Virginia Polytechnic Institute and State University.

[6] Owens, D.A., and Sivak, M. (1996). Differentiation of Visibility and Alcohol as Contributors to Twilight Road Fatalities. Human Factors, 1996, 38 (4),pp. 680-689.

[7] Sala G. (2000). Accident Analysis. PROTECTOR EU Project IST-199-10107, Del. 2.1.

[8] Brown, I. D. Motorway crashes in fog-who's to blame? New Scientist, 48, 1980,

[9] M. Bertozzi, A. Broggi, M. Cellario, A. Fascioli, P. Lombardi, and M. Porta, "Artificial Vision in Road Vehicles", Proceedings of the IEEE, Vol. 90, No. 7, July 2002.

[10] Norman D. A. & Draper, S. W. User Centered System Design. Erlbaum: Hillsdale, NJ., 1986.

[11] European Transport Safety Council - ETSC (1999a). Intelligent Transportation Systems and Road Safety. European Transport Safety Council, Brussels.

[12] Smiley, A. (2000). Auto safety and Human Adaptation. Issues on Science and Technology Online, Winter 2000. Available at http://www.nap.edu/issues/17.2/smiley.htm

[13] V. Vapnik, The Nature of Statistical Learning Theory. Springer Verlag, 1995.

[14] C. Papageorgiou and T. Evgeniou and T. Poggio, "A trainable pedestrian detection system", In Intelligent Vehicles, pp. 241--246, October 1998.

[15] Mallat S.G., 1989, "A theory for multiresolution signal decomposition: the wavelet representation", IEEE Transactions on Pattern Analysis and Machine Intelligence, 11(7).

[16] IEC 60825-1: Safety of laser products, part 1: Equipment classification, requirements and user's guide

[17] ANSI 136.1 (American National Standards Institute) American National Standard for the safe use of lasers. Laser Institute of America, Orlando FL, 1986.

Section 6.2

Applications

eAdoption and the Knowledge Economy: Issues, Applications, Case Studies
P. Cunningham and M. Cunningham (Eds.)
IOS Press, 2004

Mobile Support for Communities of Practice

Elke HINRICHS, Wolfgang PRINZ
Fraunhofer FIT, Schloss Birlinghoven, 53574 Sankt Augustin, Germany
Tel: +49 2241 142442, Fax: + 49 2241 142084,
Email: elke.hinrichs@fit.fraunhofer.de, wolfgang.prinz@fit.fraunhofer.d e

Abstract: New ways to support communities of practice are required. Our approach is to provide situated support for community members depending on their work environments. In this paper, we focus on mobile work situations. Based on a requirements analysis, we identify four clusters of mobile support functionality and evaluate state-of-the-art target mobile platforms. The back-end system is based on a groupware system enhanced to support mobile communities. We describe the functional design and implementation of three mobile prototypes. Finally, we report on some problems encountered during prototype development and evaluation.

1. Introduction

For the scope of this paper, we define communities of practice as "an informal aggregation of people who share work practices and common experiences" [8]. Communities are thus social areas where knowledge is created and exchanged. They are characterized by spontaneous participation and by common needs and problems. Examples are knowledge workers of a globally operating company who exchange ideas on product marketing or on market analysis. Other examples are customer communities who share experiences with a product or ask for or give advice on bugs and features.

Communities of practice can be computer-supported by company portals, news forums, recommender systems, email distribution lists, etc, but as of now specific mobile and situated support for communities of practice is still underdeveloped.

Figure 1: MILK integrated solution

In the MILK project, we aim to provide situated support for community members depending on their (work) environments — meeting in their offices, in public places, or while being on the move: desktop environment, social environment, and mobile access environment [2] (Fig. 1). This paper concentrates on mobile aspects of community support.

2. Communities of Practice: Requirements

The ethnographic study during the first phase of MILK was the basis for the development of the three end-user environments and their back-end service. For mobile work situations, prospective users expected four main blocks of functionality:

- awareness in context: stay informed about what's new and important;
- search and browse: browse context related documents, based on keywords;
- access to documents: download documents to the supported mobile devices;
- person-to-person communication: stay in contact with other users and be aware about their communication features.

Our goal was to define an integrated and comprehensive system that provides users with a seamless work environment that addresses their needs in different situations. Naturally, users expect to share the same look-and-feel in all work environments independently of the underlying technology, though functionality may vary.

The technological challenges for mobile support were: restricted disk space and memory, low bandwidth, small displays with limited resolution and color capabilities. As our ambition was to make use of the latest mobile devices on the market and of state-of-the-art technology, we constantly had to deal with moving targets.

3. Approach

We are an interdisciplinary team of sociologists, designers, system developers, and end-users who continuously exchange their work. In particular, end-users were involved from the very beginning of the project. Requirement assessment, functional and interface design, and system development were done following the seductive design approach, which integrates two design approaches, one from the industrial design and the other from the information systems design [1]. We reserved six months for system evaluation at our user organzations: an Italian consulting company with a high percentage of workers constantly on the move and a German multi-media software company which resides on two sites.

In order to make our system available to end-users in a limited time span, we decided to base our system on an existing and well-developed groupware tool, BSCW (Basic Support for Cooperative Work). This allowed us to concentrate on mobile and community aspects rather than on the provision of a groupware infrastructure. An additional advantage of integrating community support into an existing and wide-spread tool is that people need neither change the tool they are used to nor the database they use for their daily work.

4. Core groupware system: BSCW

BSCW — Basic Support for Cooperative Work, [3, 4] — is a web-based groupware system based on the notion of a shared workspace, a joint storage facility that may contain objects such as documents, tables, graphics, spreadsheets, links to web pages etc. The members of a workspace cooperatively upload, edit or download documents and other objects.

Besides user and group management, the BSCW system maintains stored documents and applies access control mechanisms to shared workspaces. BSCW supports the concept of roles — workspace managers may define new roles and assign roles to group members. Version control, group calendars and discussion forums are other features that allow advanced group collaboration. Documents can be put under version control, thereby enabling distributed co-authoring of work-in-progress while keeping track of previous versions as well as of the changes made by each author throughout.

The BSCW system keeps group members informed about one another's activities in the shared workspace by means of event alerting, catch-up functions and reports. BSCW proved a powerful and scalable groupware system in several thousand installations. BSCW servers run on all major operating systems such as Windows, Linux, Solaris, etc.

However, BSCW's user interface is ill-suited for access from mobile devices due to the large size of its HTML output generated and a graphical interface designed for standard browsers with full capabilities. Moreover, BSCW supports shared workspaces for closed workgroups, but lacks specific support for flexible and informal communities.

5. Community Support in MILK

BSCW's notion of shared workspaces was extended by the new concept of BSCW communities. A community can be open or semi-open. Open communities are open for self-subscription. Subscription to a semi-open community requires prior consent by the community managers. In contrast to project workspaces where all members are treated equally, community members have restricted access rights by default — manipulating or deleting documents (and other data) of other members is not permitted. This helps protect the community's knowledge and takes into account the relative anonymity in a community.

Communities feed not only from BSCW's document store, but also from a recommender system interfaced to BSCW: Knowledge Pump (KP) [6] of Xerox Research Centre Europe. KP is a recommender engine that uses collaborative filtering to provide recommendations tailored to each user. Users may submit recommendations of URLs, local files, or text. A recommendation consists of a rating and a comment, along with the user's classification of the item into one or more communities of practice. Knowledge Pump calculates a personalized set of user recommendations for each community to which she belongs and sends individualized recommendations via various communication channels.

6. Mobile Platforms

MILK supports mobile users by a wide range of tools including portable computing devices, mobile phones (Fig. 2) and even stationary devices (e.g. a fax machine at a client's office or in a public place). We group mobile technology into four device categories:

- Mobile Web – access using PDA/laptop via HTTP/HTML/XML over GSM, GPRS
- Smartphone – access using Java MIDP application over HTTP
- Mobile Phone – WAP access (WAP/WML over GSM, GPRS…)
- "Switch of media" – Gateways to external services (fax, SMS, printers…)

MobileWeb supports PDAs or Laptops with Internet access. For this device category, the MILK system provides a front-end to mobile Web browsers taking into account network restrictions and display capabilities of mobile devices.

Smartphones represent a combination of a mobile phone and a PDA. MILK provides Java MIDlets for installation on J2ME-enabled mobile devices. The MIDlets will use HTTP (and higher level protocols) to connect to MILK services and display information to users.

Mobile Phones are simple phones with basic services such as SMS (short message service) and WAP (wireless application protocol). Mobile phones using WAP browsers.

Switch of media in MILK means the switch from a mobile device to a stationary device outside the MILK system. This may be necessary when a mobile user requests to send a document to a nearby fax machine or to a printer, or when the user interacts with large screens in meeting rooms etc. For the latter, available technologies such as Infrared and Bluetooth are being evaluated.

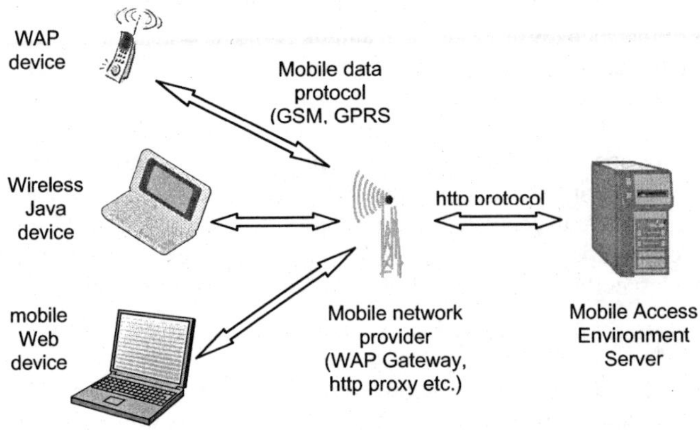

Figure 2: Data communication of mobile devices and server

7. Mobile Community Support

MILK's mobile access components give access to the MILK database from various viewpoints. At the user interface, a portal provides direct access to each view. The most recent and most important news are also directly shown in the MILK portal.

7.1 NewsBroker

In a mobile situation, the "What's new for me" aspect seems more important than the actual content of a document. Therefore, the NewsBroker is the primary view. It actively provides awareness about objects, people and their context and helps the user focus on important actions and information in the MILK system or whom to contact next. The NewsBroker pushes active notifications on MILK objects such as documents, links to the Web, appointments, discussion forums and annotations, tasks.

7.2 KnowledgeBrowser

While documents and their context play a crucial role in the desktop environment and — less so— in the social environment, in the mobile access environment, documents in their original form are of lesser importance.

7.2.1 Documents on mobile devices

Mobile devices are typically constrained by their input and output capabilities (e.g. missing keyboard, small screen) as well as by their available memory. For this reason —and also because of network constraints— download and display (or editing) of documents is usually not possible. This especially holds for WAP devices and wireless Java devices. For those cases the system will provide valuable meta-information on documents and a short document abstract which may be displayed on the device.

Other mobile devices with more memory and better output capabilities (such as notebooks and PDAs) are able to download and display documents. However, display of documents may be restricted to a fixed set of document types (depending on the available applications for document editing). The system may provide methods for document conversion in order to enable mobile access to these documents (e.g. conversion from MS Word to HTML). This latter case especially applies to the mobile Web device category.

Documents, links and bookmarks may be annotated with informal textual messages. Annotations can be shared by user groups and structured as threaded discussions. For mobile devices however, typically only very short textual messages will be used.

7.2.2 Browsing the system database

The mobile environment will only provide very limited document upload and download functionality. The mobile input and output restrictions and the restrictions in bandwidth and connectivity also prevent heavily browsing the system database. Nevertheless, it must be possible to browser folders and projects from time to time. A very simple browser, the KnowledgeBrowser (Fig. 4), is provided. It allows users to navigate folders and check documents and, if necessary and feasible, download documents or their abstracts or redirect documents to other media, e.g. a nearby fax machine. The KnowledgeBrowser provides only very limited user interaction facilities with the system database.

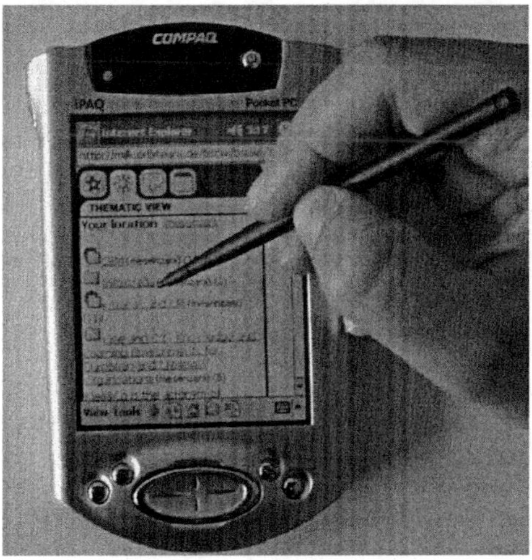

Figure 3: KnowledgeBrowser on a PDA

7.3 Bookmarker

Bookmarks are the glue between the three MILK environments and also they are the combining element of the different viewpoints of the mobile environment. Bookmarks are annotated links to any object in MILK, including documents, folders, projects, Web sites, appointments, tasks and even people. From all views, objects can be marked and added to the Bookmarker. A bookmark may be enhanced by an informal text message; this is useful to add short memory aids like “I have to read this document” or “Do not forget to talk about the meeting with XYZ”. The Bookmarkers’ list is private to each user and cannot be shared. A user can keep a bookmark on a mobile device for a later visualization and processing in the social or the desktop environment. Annotated bookmarks made in one MILK environment will always be available in the other two environments as well.

7.4 PeopleFinder

The PeopleFinder (Fig. 4) handles information about people. It provides awareness about who is active in the system, who is important in a context or for a community, who is available and how people can be reached. The interface is focused on representations of human users by their names, icons or faces.

To facilitate direct communication between users, the PeopleFinder proposes a list of prioritized communication channels for reaching a person and gives addressing information. The PeopleFinder proposes communication channels depending on the availability profile and the reachability profile.

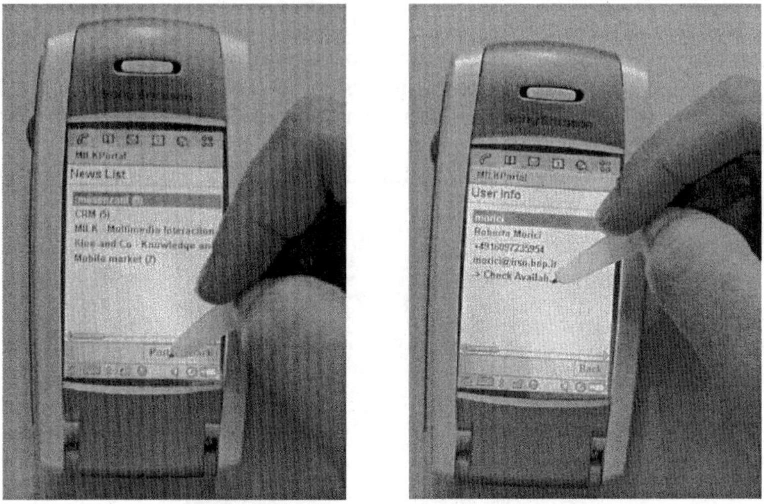

Figure 4: NewsBroker and PeopleFinder on a smartphone

Using the NewsBroker, PeopleFinder, KnowledgeBrower and Bookmarker components, we tried to match the functional clusters that the requirements analysis elicited.

8. Conclusions

In this paper we described how we addressed the goal of supporting communities of practice on the move. Starting from a requirements analysis, we identified four most important clusters of functionality in order to support mobile communities and designed an appropriate system architecture for the support of three mobile platforms. By now we have succeeded in implementing stable prototypes on various state-of-the-art mobile devices. Prototype evaluation in user organizations started at the time of writing this paper.

The decision not to start to develop a complex system from scratch, but to build upon an existing and well-developed groupware system proved wise, because we were able to concentrate on novel issues and on the demands of an ever-changing mobile base technology. Also, to involve end-user organizations from the very beginning was very helpful and reduced their reluctance to finally make use of our prototypes.

It should be noted, however, that communication und understanding between programmers, artists and end-users is not always easy. Many face-to-face meetings were necessary and after a short time it became apparent that a common glossary of terms was absolutely necessary to limit mis-understandings. We encountered a certain reluctance of users to deal with new technology or with demands to change the way they worked, supporting the observations of Bowers et al. [5]. This was in part due to users being under the pressure of their daily business which sometimes made it difficult to leave enough time for evaluation of research prototypes. Another reason is that devices still suffer from too small screens and limited document handling facilities. Often the user interface and interaction concepts are also different. Users can not simply map interaction techniques from a desktop interface to the mobile device. Thus the wide range of possibilities of mobile devices are often not utilized [7]. To overcome this problem users must become aware that mobile devices require an initial investment in training before they can be fully integrated and applied for sophisticated cooperation process. On the organizational side it is important that the mobile solutions do not remain as islands, but that they are fully integrated into the organizational processes.

Technically, the full exploitation of the developed solutions was restricted from a rather slow moving dissemination of recent mobile technology. UMTS is not yet fully available and GPRS is only now covering the whole of Europe. Software development platforms for mobile support that we had to use proved partly buggy and incomplete and featured frequently changing releases. On the other hand, our system was to be introduced in a real-work setting with real users. In short: developing a system while the base technology is a moving target is time-consuming and sometimes frustrating, both for the developers and the users. Having to build stable prototypes on emerging mobile technology was a challenge and continues to be so. This includes the use of new mobile platform software libraries as they become available. The low performance on mobile phones is still not sufficient for more complex cooperative applications. As a consequence we plan to expand and improve the MobileWeb prototype on PDAs to be present on the very promising WLAN market.

Acknowledgements

MILK is a joint research project co-funded by the European Commission — IST Project no. 33165. — Multimedia Interaction for Learning and Knowing. We would like to thank all our project partners for the friendly and fruitful collaboration: IRSO (Milan, Italy), Butera e Partners (Milan, Italy), Domus Academy (Milan, Italy), Fraunhofer FIT (Sankt Augustin, Germany), OrbiTeam (Bonn, Germany), PictureSafe (Hannover, Germany), University of Milano Bicocca (Milan, Italy), XRCE (Grenoble, France), XGS (Zurich, Switzerland).

References

[1] Agostini, A., et. al. (2000), From User Participation to User Seduction in the Design of Innovative User-Centered Systems. In: R. Dieng, et al. (Eds.), Designing Cooperative Systems: The Use of Theories and Models. Proc. of the 5th International Conference on the Design of Cooperative Systems, IOS Press, pp. 225-240, 2000.

[2] Agostini, A., Albolino, S., Boselli, R., De Michelis, G., De Paoli, F., Dondi, R. (2003), Stimulating Knowledge Discovery and Sharing. In: Proc. of GROUP'97, ACM Press, New York, 2003.

[3] Basic Support for Cooperative Work (BSCW), http://bscw.fit.fraunhofer.de/

[4] Bentley, R., Appelt, W., Busbach. U., Hinrichs, E., Kerr, D., Sikkel, S., Trevor, J., Woetzel, G. (1997), Basic Support for Cooperative Work on the World Wide Web. In: International Journal of Human-Computer Studies, 46, Special issue on Innovative Applications of the World Wide Web, 1997, pp. 827-846.

[5] Bowers, J., G. Button, et al. (1995). Workflow from Within and Without: Technology and Cooperative Work on the Print Industry Shopfloor. Fourth European Conference on Computer-Supported Cooperative Work: ECSCW '95, Stockholm, Kluwer Academic Publishers, 51-66.

[6] Glance, N., Arregui, D., Dardenne, M. (1998), Knowledge Pump: Supporting the Flow and Use of Knowledge in Networked Organizations. In: Information Technology for Knowledge Management, Eds. Borghoff and Pareschi, Springer, 1998.

[7] Perry, M., K. O'Hara, et al. (2001). "Dealing with Mobility: Understanding Access Anytime, Anywhere." ACM Transactions on Computer-Human Interaction (TOCHI) 8(4): 323-347.

[8] Wenger, E., (1998), Communities of Practice. Learning, Meaning and Identity. In: Learning in Doing: Social, Cognitive and Computational Perspectives. Cambridge University Press, Cambridge, 1998.

Sustainable eWork: an Online Self-assessment Tool for Organisations

Werner B. KORTE, Norbert KORDEY
empirica Gesellschaft für Kommunikations- und Technologieforschung mbH,
Oxfordstr. 2, 53111 Bonn, Germany
Tel: +49 228 985300, Fax: + 49 228 9853012, Email: Werner.Korte@empirica.com

Abstract: The eWork Sustainability Assessment Tool SAT is a self-assessment tool for organisations already practicing eWork, as well as those planning to do so. It allows them to carry out an assessment of the sustainability and viability of their existing or planned eWorking scheme along three dimensions: economic, social and environmental sustainability. Different applications of the tool in real-life eWork contexts have been carried out successfully. A case study is presented illustrating how the SAT provides solid and relevant measurements along the above three dimensions. This supports decision-making and strategy development especially by personnel, HR and organisation but also financial managers in organisations practising eWork or interested in doing so in the future.

1. Introduction

eWork has been of core interest to the European Commission in trying to make European organisations more competitive. The Commission has been successful in promoting the implementation of eWork. This is demonstrated by a sharp increase in terms of diffusion and penetration rates of different forms of eWork over the last few years. At a European level and taking all types of eWork together, it is now being used by 13% of the workforce with frontrunner countries like the Netherlands achieving figures of more than 25%.

The average annual growth rates of telework development from 1999 to 2002 are also impressive, reaching an average of 29% in the 15 old EU member states. However, the differences between the adoption of different forms of eWork are striking. Alternating and permanent home-based eWork is almost stagnating, while all other forms of eWork achieve annual growth rates of between 38 and 54%. One can conclude that while work is being carried out in more locations, there is no general shift of work from the office to the home.

When considering the potential of eWork (measured by the articulated interest of the workforce) it is apparent that the level of interest is considerable: 40% of the EU workforce express interest in permanent eWork, 52% in alternating eWork and 55% in centre-based eWork (see below). Nearly 66% are interested in at least one of these forms of eWork. While interest in alternating telework is somewhat higher, the number of workers interested in permanent telework is remarkable, given the low actual adoption of this method of work.

However, this potential has not been realised and put into practice. There are still large numbers of organisations shying away from eWork, especially SMEs and public sectgor organisations. Today, only 11% of European companies with less than 10 employees practice eWork, compared to almost 19% of those with 10 – 49 employees and over 50% in organisations with more than 250 employees (empirica 2002).

Table 1: Development of eWork in the EU 1999 – 2002

Type	in % of all persons employed		average annual growth (in %)
	1999	2002	
Alternating and permanent home-based eWork	2.0	2.1	2
Supplementary home-based eWork	2.0	5.3	39
Mobile eWork	1.5	4.0	38
Self-employed eWork in SOHOs	0.9	3.4	54
All eWork (excluding overlaps)	**6.0**	**13.0**	**29**

Base 1999: All persons employed; base 2002: All persons employed (N=5,100); both weighted by EU15 population

Source: ECATT 1999, SIBIS 2002 in: empirica 2003, p. 60

Most of those not practicing eWork still have doubts about its cost-effectiveness and efficiency. They also question its suitability for achieving a better family/work-life balance, although this is seen as the key motivation to eWork by almost 50% of European teleworkers (empirica, 2002, p. 38). These organisations need more than positive results from research projects showing various advantages of new and more flexible forms of work organisation. Ideally they must be able to assess a fictitious eWorking scheme they design for themselves, identify the best options and get some hand-on support and guidance for its implementation. Alternatively, those already practicing eWork may want to assess their existing eWork implementation, identify weaknesses and areas for improvement.

2. Objectives, Methodology and Implementation

2.1 Objectives and Approach

The SAT "eWorking Sustainable Assessment Tool" is a web-based tool to provide organisations with an online self-assessment opportunity for an existing or planned eWork implementation. It enables organisations to evaluate and optimise the economic, social and environmental sustainability of such projects. The underlying thinking of this tool is that the key to successful eWork and the achievement of both economic benefits and wider sustainability is an appropriate organisation, implementation and management of eWork in organisations which the online self-assessment tool supports. The tool has been developed by empirica as part of the IST project SUSTEL (Sustainable Teleworking) (www.sustel.org). The SAT objective is to provide and broadly disseminate freely usable material and guidance to allow organisations to assess and understand the relationship between eWorking and sustainable development. The SAT combines both a self-assessment–tool with a handbook. SAT puts the survey (self-assessment tool) in the foreground or centre and makes available extensive information for those users who want to deal in more depth with a particular topic (handbook). Included In SAT are checklists, recommendations, examples (results from the SUSTEL project surveys and case studies), links as well as materials developed within SUSTEL and the FlexWork (cf. below) project, which are made available for downloading. The service offer is complimentary to other offers already in the market such as the FlexWork portal (www.flexwork.eu.com). The authors of this paper were also involved in setting up the FlexWork portal and responsible for the development of the CBT Cost-Benefit-Tool for eWorking, a slimmed down version of which has become an integral part of the SAT. For the SAT and in the SUSTEL project in which this tool was developed, sustainability has been defined along three dimensions:

- Economic dimension: cost-effectiveness
- Social dimension: socially acceptable to workers, families and society
- Environmental dimension: environmentally sustainable.

SAT is aimed at decision makers and project leaders in organisations already practising eWork or wishing to introduce it. SAT constitutes a tool that can be used by organisations with different level of knowledge and sophisticated in relation to eWorking practices. The SAT focus is on eWorking from home (and mobile eWork) by employees.

2.2 Methodology and Implementation

SAT is designed as a questionnaire-based assessment tool. SAT assesses information that is both quantitative and qualitative in nature. Furthermore, the tool contains or refers to additional supporting materials that help organisations to design sustainable eWork solutions. SAT is designed to provide an assessment of an eWorking scheme (assessment tool) and to support learning how to implement sustainable eWorking (handbook and guidance part of the tool). The tool is available in five different languages (further ones are under preparation) and can be accessed at www.telework-test.org.

The eWork Sustainability Assessment Tool (SAT):

- enables users to quickly assess the economic, environmental and social impacts of a teleworking scheme using simple 'traffic light' measures (green = positive, red = negative etc) and quantitative ratings to provide an assessment
- provides ideas in relation to making schemes more sustainable
- provides useful background information about the relationship between eWorking and sustainable development (including links to other sites for more detailed material).

It is organised in three main sections, corresponding to the three pillars of sustainable development i.e. economic, environmental and social. Each section has five sustainability 'elements'. The table below visualises the elements of the three dimensions. Users choose the most relevant of six statements to assess the performance of an eWork scheme for each of these elements. Users can access more detailed information about the current state of knowledge about the element, and examples from the SUSTEL cases and other sources of what can be done to improve performance. SAT users can also access action checklists for many of the elements, summary and full versions of the SUSTEL cases, and links to other sites. Two further tools - an eWork cost-benefit tool and a transport tool - are provided as further self-assessment tools as an integral part of the SAT.

Figure 1: eWork Sustainability Assessment Tool (SAT) Overall Structure and Functionality

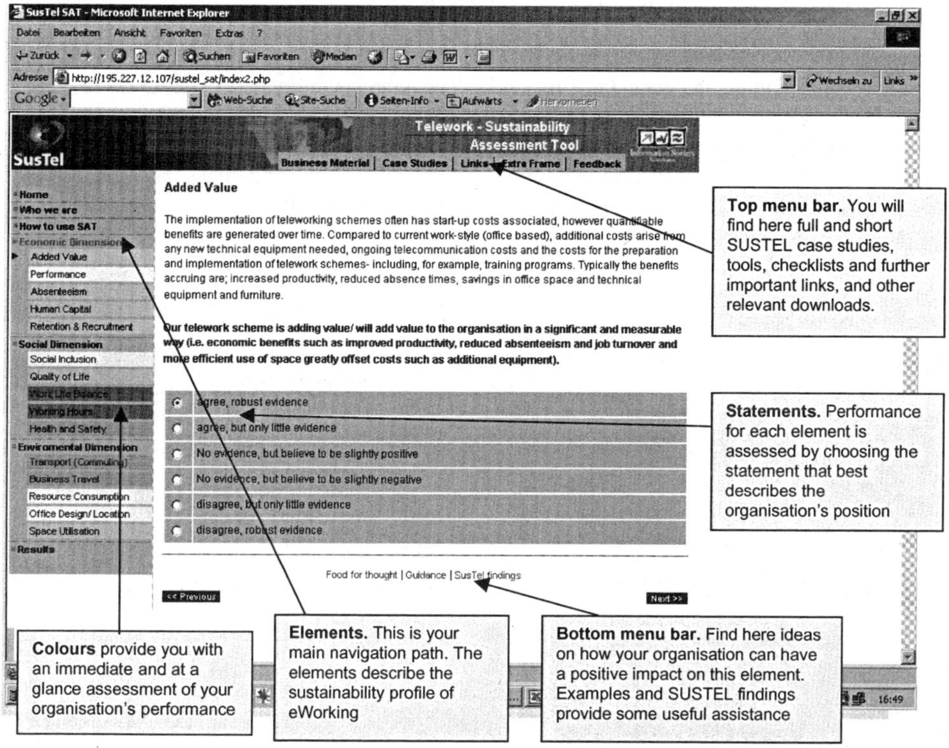

3. Results of a Real-life Application of SAT

In this section we present the results of a real-life application of the SAT in a medium-sized German software development and services organisation focused on the insurance industry. The organisation has 240 employees. It has started to implement home-based and mobile eWorking in the year 2000. Today 60 of the employees, which amounts to 25% of the company's workers, are either working as alternating home-based or mobile eWorkers.

After almost 4 years of eWork operation the SAT and the Cost-Benefit-Tool (which is also provided via the SAT) (cf. section 4) were used to evaluate and assess the sustainability of the present implementation of the eWorking scheme. Figure 2 presents the results of the sustainability assessment of the eWorking scheme. The results are structured in terms of fifteen sustainability elements – five for each of the dimensions of sustainable development (economic, environmental and social). The assessment is given as both a qualitative colour coding, and a quantitative score. The colour coding is:

- Green means that the eWorking scheme supports this aspect of sustainable development
- Red means that the eWorking scheme has very negative effects on this aspect of sustainable development
- Orange means either that the eWorking scheme has somewhat negative effects on this aspect of sustainable development, or there is uncertainty about its effect
- Yellow means there is uncertainty, but it is unlikely that the effects are very negative.

There are some difficulties with quantitative scoring of sustainability. However, some people find it useful so we also provide results in this form. Each statement is scored in numerical values: 5 for green, 2 for yellow, 1 for orange and 0 for red, allowing for a maximum of 75 points. The aim is to help stimulate improvement in the economic, environmental and social impacts of eWork schemes and gain insight on how this can be achieved. As can be seen from the results the eWorking scheme achieves 57/75, which is a good result. It is particularly positive on the environmental dimension with 22 out of 25 possible points, followed by the economic dimension (19/25) and the social dimension (16/25). In the latter some improvements are possible especially concerning the reduction of long working hours which eWorking seem to have resulted in in this organisation.

Figure 2: eWork Sustainability Assessment Tool (SAT) Result of a Real-life Sustainability Assessment

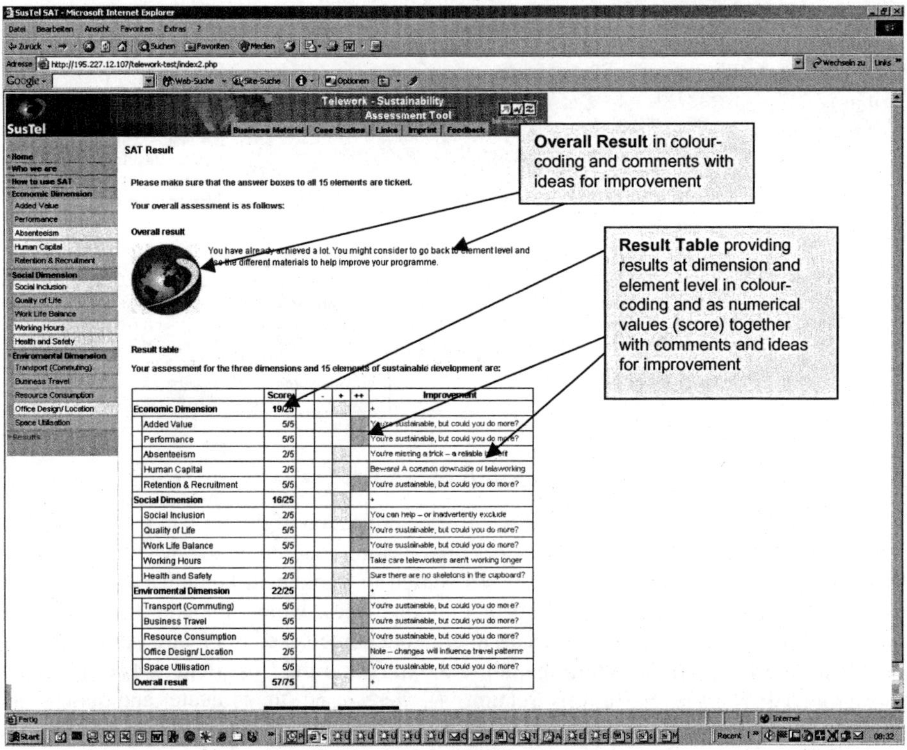

	Score	--	-	+	++	Improvement
Economic Dimension	19/25					+
Added Value	5/5					You're sustainable, but could you do more?
Performance	5/5					You're sustainable, but could you do more?
Absenteeism	2/5					You're missing a trick – a reliable benefit
Human Capital	2/5					Beware! A common downside of teleworking
Retention & Recruitment	5/5					You're sustainable, but could you do more?
Social Dimension	16/25					+
Social Inclusion	2/5					You can help – or inadvertently exclude
Quality of Life	5/5					You're sustainable, but could you do more?
Work Life Balance	5/5					You're sustainable, but could you do more?
Working Hours	2/5					Take care teleworkers aren't working longer
Health and Safety	2/5					Sure there are no skeletons in the cupboard?
Enviromental Dimension	22/25					+
Transport (Commuting)	5/5					You're sustainable, but could you do more?
Business Travel	5/5					You're sustainable, but could you do more?
Resource Consumption	5/5					You're sustainable, but could you do more?
Office Design/ Location	2/5					Note – changes will influence travel patterns
Space Utilisation	5/5					You're sustainable, but could you do more?
Overall result	57/75					+

Further support for improvement of an existing eWork scheme is provided by:

- The Food for Thought link on each of the element pages with ideas and insights gained from the SusTel case studies
- The Guidance link with one or more specific company examples of good practice with regard to the element
- The SusTel results summarises key project research findings about the element.

4. Business Benefits: Cost-Benefit Assessment of a Real-life eWork Scheme Using SAT

Also after 4 years of operation of eWorking the Cost-Benefit-Tool (which is also provided via the SAT) was used to assess the cost and benefits of the present implementation of the eWorking scheme. Access to this tool is provided through the top navigation bar of the assessment site which provides links to:

- Business materials such as checklists and tools to assess financial benefits and costs, and transport impacts
- Summaries and full versions of the 30 case studies
- Links to third party sites which should be useful if you need more material.

In this company, the eWorking scheme has been set up for 60 employees (26% of the workforce), who work either as alternating home-based or mobile eWorkers. The Cost-Benefit Tool uses the following indicators and figures for calculating the cost and benefits:

1. Information on the eWork scheme: number of eWork places, weekly working days at home, workplaces kept in central office, rent, personnel daily rates, recruitment costs, depreciation periods
2. Additional costs relating to the infrastructure at eWork place, central office infrastructure, organisation and management
3. Cost savings and financial benefits relating to savings on infrastructure, productivity and absenteeism, savings on leavers retained.

The eWorking introduction and implementation process was carried out with the support of a dedicated consulting organisation, which also conducted a mid-term and final evaluation of the scheme. The costs of this contract have been considered in the cost-benefit calculation under "organisation and management".

The Cost-Benefit Tool uses the inputs for these indicators provided by the organisation to calculate the one-off, annual and monthly running costs, savings and financial benefits along the above cost/benefit categories and the overall balance of these and provides information on the following relevant indices:

- imputed interest rate
- residual value
- capital value
- amortisation period
- internal rate of return.

In this particular case, the organisation has been faced with a one-off investment for implementing eWork for 60 eWorkers of around 800,000 €. The monthly running costs are around 4,000 €. The amortisation period has been calculated at only slightly more than one year, which is seen as a very positive result by the company directors.

The tool also provides graphical overviews of the annual running costs of the whole scheme and per eWorker according to cost and benefits/savings categories. It is apparent that the benefits outweigh the costs. The categories where the largest costs occur are support activities addressed to eWorkers, and infrastructure investment and maintenance costs. On the benefit side the productivity gains make up for the largest savings despite the very moderate productivity increases, which the company calculated at 10% on the days the workers are eWorking. Case studies show a wide range of productivity improvement from 10-50% depending on the job role, commuting time etc. It is therefore not unlikely that even further gains can be achieved in the future.

5. Conclusions

The eWork Sustainability Assessment Tool SAT is a self-assessment tool enabling organisations already practicing eWork but also those planning to do so, to carry out an assessment of the sustainability and viability of their existing or planned eWorking scheme along three dimensions: economic, social and environmental sustainability.

The eWork self-assessment tool can be accessed at: www.telework-test.org. The tool has been tested intensively in five different stages with different target groups including eWork and personnel consultants, expert researchers, representatives from the social partners as well as prospective users – particularly managers within organisations. Responses have been positive and some suggestions for improvement have been considered and already implemented in the presently available version.

Different applications of the tool in real-life eWork contexts have been carried out successfully. The case study presented in this paper shows that the SAT provides solid and relevant measurements along the above three dimensions supporting decision-making and strategy development especially by personnel, HR and organisation but also financial managers in organisations practising eWork or interested in doing so in the future.

Currently SAT is available in five languages: English, German, Danish, Italian and Dutch. Localisation to and implementation in further languages is simple and straightforward. The SAT is database-driven. This architecture means that existing SAT coding can be imported to a national or local server - via a CD supplied by the authors and developers of the tool - and that all national content is then uploaded to the database in a standard format. This process should not therefore require detailed PHP programming knowledge and only basic knowledge of the Microsoft Access database software.

The main task for a national organisation wishing to develop an SAT is translation of the main SAT pages, the examples, case summaries etc which are stored in the database. There is also the opportunity to substitute local examples etc. for the SUSTEL ones.

Acknowledgement

The SUSTEL project which developed the eWork Sustainability Assessment Tool (SAT) has been funded from 2002 – 2004 under the European Commission's Information Society Technologies (IST) programme. It was set up to:

- provide a more comprehensive assessment of the overall relationship between eWorking and sustainable development (which involves assessing its economic, environmental and social impacts)
- explore aspects of eWork which had previously been little researched (for example, whether eWork leads to greater involvement in local communities)
- integrate this new with existing knowledge in a form which can be useful for organisational decision-making.
- In order to obtain a variety of national and organisational perspectives, it has brought together seven different kinds of organisation from five countries, Denmark (Danish Technological Institute), Germany (empirica), Italy (avanzi), Netherlands (Telewerk Forum) and the UK (BT and University of Bradford).

References

[1] Cullen, K., Kordey, N., Schmidt, L., Gaboardi, E. (2003), Work and Family in the eWork era, ISBN 1 58603 310 7. IOS Press, Amsterdam, 2003.

[2] empirica (2000) Benchmarking Progress on New Ways of Working and New Forms of Business Across Europe. ECaTT Final Report, IST Programme, KAII: New Methods of Work and Electronic Commerce. Brussels: Commission of the European Communities.

[3] empirica (2002), Verbreitung der Telearbeit in 2002: Internationaler Vergleich und Entwicklungstendenzen. Bonn, September 2002.
[4] empirica (2003) Benchmarking Work, Employment and Skills in the Information Society in Europe and the US, SIBIS Topic Report No. 5, Brussels: Commission of the European Communities.
[5] Gareis, K., Kordey, N., Korte. W.B. (2003) 'Statistics on Trends in eWorking in Europe', in Commission of the European Communities (eds) Collaboration at Work – The 2003 Report on New Working Environments and Practices, 20-27, Brussels: Commission of the European Communities.
[6] Hanhike, T., Gareis, K. (2004), Modelling eWork – Towards a better understanding of information technology's impact on workplaces and work locations – Paper presented at the 22nd Annual International Labour Process Conference, Amsterdam, 5-7 April, 2004.
[7] SIBIS (2003), Measuring the Information Society in the EU, the EU Accession Countries, Switzerland and the US. SIBIS Pocketbook 2002/03.

Web sources

[1] www.telework-test.org: eWork Sustainability Assessment Tool (SAT)
[2] www.flexwork.eu.com: FlexWork - New Ways of Working in Remote Regions
[3] www.sibis-eu.org: Statistical Indicators Benchmarking the Information Society
[4] www.ecatt.com: Electronic Commerce and Telework Trends in Europe
[5] www.sustel.org: Sustainable Teleworking
[6] www.empirica.com: empirica Gesellschaft für Kommunikations- und Technologieforschung mbH

COMBINE-for-PACE: Performance Assessment of a Complex Enterprise

Nadezhda YARUSHKINA[1], Innokenti SEMOUSHIN[2]
[1]*Ulyanovsk State Technical University, 32 Severny Venec Str., Ulyanovsk, 432027, Russia*
Tel: + 7 8422 439089, Fax: + 7 8422 430322, Email: jng@ulstu.ru
[2]*Ulyanovsk State University, 42 L Tolstoy Str., Ulyanovsk, 432970, Russia*
Tel: + 8422 329224, Fax: + 7 8422 412340, Email: SemushinIV@ulsu.ru

Abstract: The solution strategy for a given complex enterprise performance assessment problem often depends on the experience and creativity of the assessor as well as the tools and computing resources that are available. In most cases, there are a number of different approaches using different tools, different data and even different variations of the problem formulation that could be employed in an attempt to solve the assessment problem at hand. This paper describes the development of a flexible assessment environment through an integration of expert system and decision making support system relied upon Zadeh's soft computing methodology.

1. Introduction

eBusiness is becoming an ever-increasingly complex activity involving numerous software tools, communication/transformation of data and collaboration among enterprises within a corporation. Among the new tasks that have appeared, assessing the performance of an enterprise involved in a large-scale collaboration in all phases of activity seems to hold the lead. The past decade has witnessed an obvious proliferation of software tools available for business managers and assessors such as knowledge bases, expert systems, rule-based dynamics analysis tools, decision making and support systems, cost estimation tools and others [1]-[3]. While this has resulted in greater accuracy and finer detail in the level of estimation, it also added to the complexity of the process overall. The mere existence of and local improvements in these individual analysis tools does not mean that they increase the productivity and efficiency of the business; in fact, the opposite may very well be true at a stage. The reason for this is that different tools are based on different principles. Moreover, they use different types of data: crisp or fuzzy, qualitative or quantitative. The multiplicity of ill-matched tools, heterogeneous data and polytypic approaches put obstacles in the way of placing eBusiness on a broad footing. This reflects the well-known principle of uncertainty by Lotfi Zadeh. According to this principle, accuracy and meaning start to conflict since some point of analysis [4]. The problem becomes even more overbearing if part of the assessing process involves contributions from partner teams in geographically disparate locations. Under conditions of geographical remoteness, lack of coordination is observed, firewalls create communication barriers, security is seen as a matter of utmost concern, and data transfer among tools becomes cumbersome and error-prone.

Considering all of these obstacles, eBusiness leadership and partnership, as well as isolated managers, auditors, performance assessors and consulting experts, are now keenly expecting to be provided with software tools that are intuitive, are easy to use, and that can interact with other tools involved in the process fairly seamlessly. The solution is not more or even better assessment tools – the solution is a framework that provides a solid foundation for overcoming these problems by combining different approaches, tools and technologies within a unified web based assessment environment.

The theoretical grounds for such solution have been prepared by many works in the field of fuzzy sets and systems [5], decision analysis [6] and analytical planning [7]. On the other hand, recent technological advancements enable noticeable improvements in distributed computing and have made it feasible to construct new web-enabled environments such as FIPER [8] and the Globus Toolkit providing a standard way for companies to publish their services for common use.

Recognizing the need for the aforementioned framework, Ulyanovsk State Technical University has teamed with Ulyanovsk State University, Russian Association of Artificial Intelligence, and a group of Volga Region enterprises in a three-year collaborative effort to develop a Component-based Integration Environment (COMBINE) for Performance Assessment of a Complex Enterprise (PACE), a project sponsored by the Administration of Ulyanovsk City and partly by Russian Foundation for Basic Research (RFBR). The COMBINE joint venture team is well into its second year of work, with the various team members and additional sub-contractors, investigating different aspects of the environment and components to be provided in it. The requirements for this project continue to be established as the problems and obstacles become more clearly understood [9]-[11]. The remainder of this paper provides a high-level overview of this environment including objectives, methodology and technology used up to this stage of work.

2. Objectives

For a more penetrating insight into our COMBINE-for-PACE solutions, we start from the very notion of and need for performance assessing.

When several enterprises pooled to form a partnership, every partner, wishing to succeed in one's business (and in their common business, as well), should (and wish to) be clear in one's mind about the main issues:

- How much is one's activity efficient?
- How much is a partner's activity efficient?
- What further effort should be mounted to increase the outcome of one's management activities and/or financial activities?

Solutions to the first and second questions mean that every partner should have a possibility to obtain the results of self-assessment and cross-assessment, correspondingly. The COMBINE tools must take into account all the data available from partners concerning their activities. Solutions to the third issue imply that the tool can present some positive recommendations to any partner who asks for them. Lastly, the COMBINE must fully exclude any chance for unauthorized access to the data.

This interactive system has been developed to serve as a plug-and-play framework for

– top managers to

- obtain the integrated express-estimates of their management activity, as well as financial activity of their enterprise, at a reasonable price and
- compare their enterprise performance indices with the mean level of the same indices existing over the set of all partner or similar enterprises

to continually improve their managing decisions and increase the company income;

– auditing firms to

- obtain a new sort of service that they may sell,
- attract new clients who can wish to order a complete set of auditing and consulting services after having an express-estimate from the COMBINE,
- accumulate knowledge about businesses' state within a market segment and
- verbalize their cumulative experience and formulate, on this basis, their own techniques and procedures for the enhanced performance analysis and assessment

in order to increase their client network; and for

– any individual consulting expert to

- automatically collect information about a market segment or business type,
- express his/her expertise in consulting business in the form of his/her own inference rule base and
- develop new components and publish them to the COMBINE Library

to raise the level of his/her skill and his/her value as a consulting professional.

3. Methodology

The main methods used in the paper (and in the project COMBINE) comprise:

1. Hierarchy analysis processing [7].
2. Object programming and object-oriented design [12].
3. Genetic programming and genetic algorithms (GAs) [13].

The COMBINE is a component-based system whose main components are:

1. Soft Expert System (SES) containing:
   - Fuzzy Neural Network (FNN).
   - Fuzzy Relational Data Server (FRDS).
   - Fuzzy Logic Inference System (FLIS).
   - GA for tuning parameters of FLIS and FNN.
2. Hierarchy Analysis Processor (HAP).
3. Decision Making Support System (DMSS).

One of the fundamental features of the system is that any experienced consulting expert or auditing firm can develop and propose their own components to be published (incorporated) to the Library. Any component is viewed as a wrapped tool exposing itself to the Library and other components exclusively through its inputs/outputs (formal procedure parameters). Thus, COMBINE is an extendable system capable of self-organization and enlargement of its functions. Its component-based nature is perfectly suited for such an assessing session in which multiple independent components need to be utilized in various ways throughout an expert diagnosis procedure.

The expert diagnosis procedure is realized by the SES, the intellectual heart of the system, while the others are realized as traditional data server and WWW-server. It is caused by the fact that usually the actual data available for an expert are crisp, precise values presented by time series. This input information is transformed by the expert into the fuzzy (qualitative) conclusions, forecasts and recommendations. Analysis of the real-world expert conclusions shows that up to 80 % of them are either qualitative judgments or estimates of data trends, and only 20 % are recommendations. Consequently, the workflow of expert diagnosis can be determined as the soft expert diagnosis procedure (Table 1).

The soft expert system is a fuzzy expert system possessing the following features:

- For data mining, the SES uses statistical data interpreting them as the learning samples.
- The SES represents knowledge in the form of linguistic variables (or membership functions, MF), fuzzy productions and the learned neural networks. Reduction of the set of fuzzy productions and tuning MF and the rule base are performed with a GA.
- The SES operates as a system of interacting components.

Let us characterize the main components of the developed COMBINE and methodology used to construct them (Table 1).

Table 1: Steps of the soft expert diagnosis procedure

The name of step	The question to be answered at the step	Mathematical approach used
Step 1. Transformation of the crisp time series into the fuzzy time series (FTS), – Fuzzification	What estimates should be assigned to the values of variables chosen to describe the object state?	Theory of fuzzy intervals [5]
Step 2. Estimation of the FTS trends	What are trends in the change in variables describing the object state?	Algebra of fuzzy intervals [5], neural networks theory [14]
Step 3. Forming the expert summary for a state of the object under analysis	What are general terms that characterize the object as a whole?	Fuzzy inference system [5], decision making support system [6], [7]
Step 4. Forecasting trend of developments	What is the prognosis of developments in the object state?	Neural network theory [14]
Step 5. Planning	What recommendations can be offered to attain the goal state of the object?	Decision making support system [7]

3.1 Fuzzy Neural Network (FNN)

Fuzzy time series is generated by Fuzzificator (Figure 1) as a series of linguistic terms (fuzzy labels of quality) such as: "excellent", "good", "adequate", "alarming" and so on. The FNN transforms the FTS into the wider concepts expressing trends such as: "rise", "decay", "stabilization", "fluctuation" or "chaos".

3.2 Fuzzy Relational Data Server (FRDS)

The FRDS has been developed as a set of triggers and procedures for data server Oracle 8i to save MFs, linguistic estimates and the data base containing fuzzy rules, crisp time series and fuzzy time series, and intermediate assessment results together with estimated states and trends. Because Oracle 8i does not have a means to save fuzzy data, a special repository has been developed.

3.3 Fuzzy Logic Inference System (FLIS)

The FLIS is implemented as a neural network able to learn to predict behaviour of a FTS and by virtue of this ability, to forecast the future state of object. Expert systems combining the traditional production inference mechanism and the learned neural networks, form the new class of expert systems called here neural expert systems.

3.4 Hierarchy Analysis Processor (HAP)

The Hierarchy Analysis Processor is intended to perform the multi-criterion decision analysis using criteria C_{ij}, aggregation operations Q_i, membership functions $\mu(.)$, comparative matrices of criteria, and variables x_i representing the real-world features such as the price, the size and so on. Also, it calculates the accordance index, accordance relation and local/global priority vectors sufficient to allow definite conclusions.

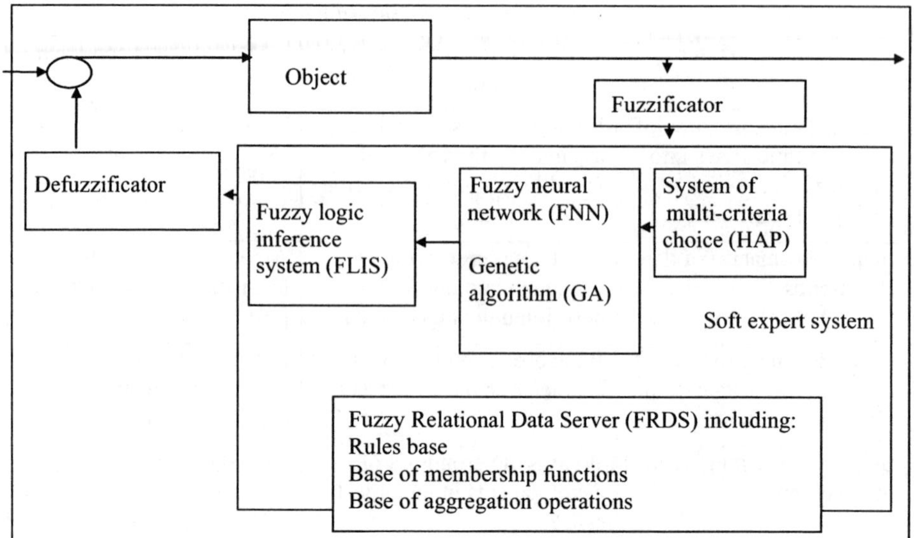

Figure 1: Integration of components in the COMBINE

4. Technology Description

By the statement that the COMBINE is a web-based consulting service intended to assess the performance of a complex enterprise, we mean that the following technology instruments exist at an end user's disposal:

- The IP-net supporting the base set of web services for data transfer with the unified numbering and routing policy under DNS.
- The allotted Web-server providing availability of hypertext documents through the IP-net in response on Web-client's request.
- Fuzzy relational data server providing storage and retrieval of large scale data bases.
- The intellectual processing component viz. the above considered Soft Expert System.

COMBINE is based on Client-Server technology and implemented by combining the FRDS (viz. MS/SQL) server and Web-server. The main operation – assessing – is the responsibility of the fourth component, SES, organized as a toolbox for MATLAB. It uses data from SQL server, forms the summary (resume) and transfers it to the web server. The web server transforms this result into an HTML code and returns it to relevant web-client.

5. Developments

In the expert systems traditionally used for economic analysis, visualization of results is performed by such means as verbal expert conclusions, line diagrams, histograms, circle diagrams, and/or three-dimensional diagrams. These traditional means of representing results require much time for understanding the information by the enterprise leader or expert economist. For this reason, it seems advisable to develop the Chernoff faces as an integral estimate expressed in a graphic image [15]. The constructive elements of the Chernoff are designed by using the images suggested earlier, which are adapted to special features of the enterprise economic state (see ahead, Figure 2).

The objects (enterprises under assessment) are usually of large dimension, i.e., their economic state is determined by a large number of primary economic indices recorded in the account books. Presently, the account balance plan includes about 90 account types.

Taking into consideration that some of the accounts are of regulation and control types, a new development in the project is made based on our assumption that there exist 10 to 20 basic indices for enterprises with various forms of property and various activities.

6. Results

The main result of this project has been implementation and testing the novel Internet service. By this, we put at client's disposal a collection of interacting components forming together an integral environment handy for making express (high-speed) analysis of economic and financial activity of a complex enterprise.

Implementation of express-analysis functions poses its own unique challenges. Data mining necessary for business performance assessment has been a major challenge. Such functions as: (1) "On-line formation of characteristic functions for qualitative estimates of economic data" and (2) "On-line formation of the knowledge base of linguistic terms", depend upon filling the knowledge bases by rules.

Another challenge has been software development. Experience leads us to conclude that good software requires consulting experts with a high level of professional skills.

Some functions such as: (3) "Generating linguistic estimates of the basic economic parameter values," (4) "Evaluation of linguistic estimates of the analytic parameter values," and (5) "Generating a linguistic description of data trend diagrams and their analysis," are difficult to test. In the course of project development we used two types of testing data: hypothetical and real life time series. By our experience, both of these types should be used. Real life time series can be obtained only from enterprises; this will entail great practical difficulties; more to it, such data are usually fragmentary. On the other hand, hypothetical time series being formed by designers are generated as a full set of possible trends based on a formal model. However, hypothetical time series do not describe all real life economic phenomena; as a result, some essential or prevalent case may become untested.

Service functions such as: (6) "Evaluating the state of the enterprise under performance assessment," (7) "Inference of a summary for the expert conclusion," and (8) "Forecasting the values of economic variables," necessitate, ways to adjust parameters of a business model to guarantee high quality business prognostication.

Function "Visualization of the analytical parameter diagrams," is very important for creating the interface well suited for the end user. We know from experience that habitual interface similar to that used on former occasions, turns out to be most successful. Here of prime importance is to preclude the presence of inner special terminology on the screen.

We used the COMBINE for assessing two Stock Corporations: "Volga-Dnepr" and "Nomatex". The analysis and recommendations have proven to be of great business benefit.

7. Business Benefits

Consulting services are very expensive. Of particularly high value are prices asked for full-scale assessment. Thus, the main benefit from the COMBINE is reduction of consulting costs. The benefit exists for consulting firms, too, because in one way or another the data server and web server exist and the COMBINE intelligent component is not very costly.

As may be inferred from Section 3, the SES relies upon the knowledge base containing the rules that are based on the interrelations between economic indices and able to link typical business situations and advisable management solutions. The SES analyzes the enterprise initial data, establishes the critical values of indices, makes a conclusion about the effect of particular factors on the economic and financial result, recognizes the characteristic economical situations and, finally, forms recommendations for enterprise management. As a result, the user obtains the WWW-response to his Internet request in the

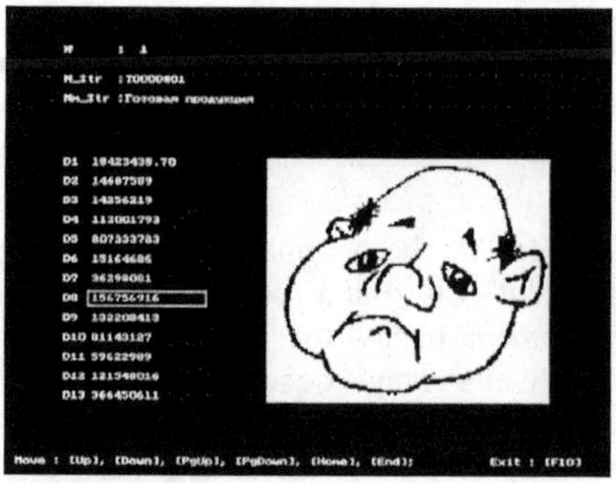

Figure 2: The resume by Chernoff face

form of a conclusion-resume. To illustrate the benefits from such a service, let us cite a fragment of the resume for the public stock corporation "Volga-Dnepr," (Figure 2). The resume follows: "Volume of business increases at a rapid pace thus testifying that the turnover rising trend is stable. Average annual rate of growth of airlift tonnage was 16 %, considerably lower than corresponding turnover rate of growth. Volume of business outside of the NIS was lower than within the NIS."

This fragment shows that the SES separates first of all the most significant economic indices and describes their dynamics. Next is selection of the typical situations for which the management actions may be recommended:

"The Stock Corporation "Volga-Dnepr" by the end of 1992 year is a company with high rate of growth. Skilfully and successfully, the enterprise made the use of the market factors and opportunities: drew additional income from the forming rate of exchange and borrowed funds. However at the same time, the enterprise has made some errors:

1. Profitability of main economic activity was weakly controlled that was a result of euphoria from the galloping fall in the ruble exchange.
2. The inflation factors remained out of control that allowed inflation "to eat up" the gain obtained from the exchange rate in the second half of the year.
3. Lack of attention was given to correlation between interest rate and borrowed funds that resulted in "eating away" up to one third of income.
4. Most likely there was not posed the problem of forming the own liquid assets that led to the quickened crises of solvency.

In this situation, the following steps should be taken:

1. Abandon the "common stock" practice of cost-flow assumptions.
2. Determine beforehand each contract payments profitability, was this a contract on air transport service, credit contract or otherwise."

8. Conclusions

In this work, the COMBINE-for-PACE team develops an advanced environment and middleware object-oriented components in response to the primary obstacles in existing individual analysis tools as described in the introduction of this paper. It enables eBusiness partnership to obtain access to a novel web-based service for assessing the performance of a complex enterprise in order to continually improve its performance and increase thereby the company income. On its merits, this rather complex intelligent system is placed at end-user-client's disposal in a relatively simple, easy to use, form and at a reasonable price. With the COMBINE, a new segment of consulting market emerges in the WWW-space as an essential factor of further eBusiness development.

The main lesson learnt is that complex technology and the architecture of the intelligent expert system can be hidden from the end user, while consumer benefits can be easily explained and exposed. Another important lesson is the critical role of a practicing consulting firm acting as indispensable team-mate with its experts and analysis techniques.

The ultimate outcome of the project is a commercially developed and supported Component-based Integration Environment for Performance Assessment of a Complex Enterprise, COMBINE-for-PACE. To bring this service to market, a further increase in quality of express-analysis is needed which requires the cooperation of a consulting firm. With luck and a good marketing strategy, this WWW-service can pass the way from a free "toy" able to brighten the consulting firm's site to an e-service of real commercial value.

Acknowledgements

This paper was submitted with the support of the ADMIRE-P project (№ IST-2001-35449).

References

[1] R. Askers, I. Bica, E. Kant, C. Randall and R. Young. SciFinance: A Program Synthesis Tool for Financial Modeling, AI Magazine, Vol. 22, No. 2, 2001, pp. 27-43.
[2] J. Nolan. An Intelligent System for Case Review and Risk Assessment in Social Services. AI Magazine, Vol. 19, No. 1, 1998, pp. 39-47.
[3] Sh. Chen and Sh. Chang. Fuzzy Economic Production Quantity Model with Quality Improvement Investment and Fuzzy Costs. In: Proceedings of the 10th IFSA World Congress, 2003, Turkey, Istanbul, pp. 523-527.
[4] L.A. Zadeh. A Theory of Approximate Reasoning. Machine Intelligence, Vol. 9, 1979.
[5] D. Dubois and H. Prade. Fuzzy Sets and Systems: Theory and Applications. Academic Press, New York, 1980.
[6] G. J. Klir. Architecture of Systems Problem Solving. Plenum Press, New York, 1985.
[7] T.L. Saaty and K.P. Kearns. Analytical Planning. The Organization of Systems. Pergamon Press, Oxford, 1985.
[8] M. Sobolewski. Federated P2P Services in CE Environments. In: R. Goncalves, R. Roy and A. Steigler-Garcao (Eds.). Advances in Concurrent Engineering. Proc. Intern. Conf. CE2002, Balkema, Lisse, Abington, Exton (PA), Tokyo, 2002, pp. 13-22.
[9] N. Yarushkina. Data Flow Distribution in Concurrent Engineering. In: R. Goncalves, R. Roy and A. Steigler-Garcao (Eds.). Advances in Concurrent Engineering, Proc. Intern. Conf. CE2002, Balkema: Lisse, Abington, Exton, Tokyo, 2002, pp. 735-743.
[10] N. Yarushkina. Application of Fuzzy Relational Data Server for Concurrent Engineering. In: J. Cha, R. Jardim-Goncalves and A. Steiger-Garcao (Eds.). Proc. Intern. Conf. CE2003, Book 2, Balkema: Lisse, Abington, Exton, Tokyo, 2003, pp. 87-93.
[11] N. Yarushkina. Soft Computing and Complex System Analysis. Int. J. General Systems, Vol. 30. No. 1, 2000, pp. 71-88.
[12] T. Budd. An Introduction to Object-Oriented Programming, (2nd ed.), Wesley, 1997.
[13] D. Beasley, D.R. Bull, and R.R. Martin. An Overview of Genetic Algorithms. University Computing, Vol. 15, No. 2, 1993. Part 1, pp. 56-58 and Part 2, pp. 170-181.
[14] A.N. Gorban, D.A. and Rossiev. Neural Networks on Personal Computers, Nauka, Novosibirsk, 1996.
[15] H. Chernoff. Using Faces to Represent Points in K-Dimensional Space Graphically. J. ASA, 1973, p. 68.

P. Cunningham and M. Cunningham (Eds.)
IOS Press, 2004

Gesprecons: An eSafety and Risk Prevention Platform

Jesús MOLINA, Manuel MARTINEZ, Ignacio GARCÍA
AIDICO, Benjamin Franklin, 17. Parque Tecnológico, Paterna (Valencia), Spain
Tel: +34 96 1318278, Fax: + 34 96 1318033, Email: jesus.molina@aidico.es
manuel.martinez@aidico.es, ignacio.garcia@aidico.es

Abstract: In this paper we present Gesprecons: a platform for collaborative work on safety and risk prevention. Gesprecons system provides support in the generation and application of the Health and Safety Plan for the construction sector. It provides the integration of on-site availability of the documents, activity plans, test data, inspections and results, that may have any relation with safety assurance in building and construction companies. For that, pre-structured context-focused quantity and quality test data, simple access to technical knowledge (standards, codes for practice, text books, co-operate company knowledge, contract specification and of course agreed alterations kept in multi-media notes, etc.) have to be provided in order to enable comparison according to best practice and state-of-the-art.

1. Introduction

The high rate of unfortunate accidents within the workplace is one of the main challenges faced by the construction sector. This is caused by three fundamental elements: The needs of specific organisational activities, lack of information related to industrial health and safety provided to contractors and other employees responsible for safety procedures, as well as related legislation regarding to risk prevention and finally the simultaneity of different activities with numerous companies at every stage of work.

This situation, combined with the intermittent participation of all the agents involved in each construction site creates a very complex situation to guarantee that labour risks information at every specific phase of the work site is enforced by the safety coordinator.

On the other hand, in today's competitive environment, differentiation is key for companies to achieve a leadership position. Safety assurance in the working environment in the construction industry is an issue that can help the companies to secure differentiation.

Safety on construction sites demands the close interaction of the construction-site players and public authorities, laboratories and project surveyors. Codes, standards, regulations as well as guidelines have to be quickly at hand, interpreted and understood in a common sense in order to ensure safety continuously. The right decision taken at the right moment can avoid serious accidents thus preventing from damages and even deaths.

Gesprecons defines a cooperation model among the different work construction representatives from the safety perspective: facultative guidelines, safety coordinator during building phase, constructors, subcontractors, personnel delegates, personnel designated by the companies in security matters (according to the prevention law), and the employees. This approach provides personnel dedicated to the control of health and safety and risk prevention at the construction site with a tool that allows decreasing the number of labour accidents existing within this sector. Therefore, it could guarantee the application and fulfilment of the current safety normative by the personnel in charge of assuring the achievement of the Health and Safety Plans (HASP).

In order to reach all subcontractors and agents involved in construction, the model is based on the use of mobile and static Internet technology, as well as SMS communication to facilitate contact with autonomous personnel. The system transmits information regarding labour risk prevention and safety alerts detected by the integration of data capture sensors in the construction site. At a higher level, the system is able to react to possible consultations the user might organise. This is accomplished by linking these consultations to a Safety Plan database and risk prevention database specific to building work activities.

In order to provide the different stakeholders with the updated information at every moment, a huge effort has been done in the part of the documentation for the information systems for Gesprecons. The information has been structured in two categories: construction labour and risk prevention. In both cases, current way of working, documentation, bibliography and experienced people have been consulted in order to provide the final users with the most useful information and as well structured as possible.

2. Objectives

The main objective in the development of Gesprecons platform is to offer a remotely accessible collaborative tool for the creation and subsequent application of the HASP. In more detail the list of objectives is the following:

- Decrease misfortune accidents at work.
- Promote the Health and Safety law fulfilment. Currently the preparation of most HASPs consists of copying from past projects and slightly adapting it to the new project. Later on, its application during work tasks is very low and difficult to control. Gesprecons facilitates the creation of the plans and supports its application.
- Increase construction companies (most of them SMEs) competitiveness taking profit of the advantages provided by technology.
- To exonerate from responsibilities. Gesprecons, by keeping register of all the transactions, contributions, warnings, alerts, will provide a legal framework to demonstrate his part.
- Ease coordination between the different stakeholders by means of collaborative work.
- Ease the communication flow amongst all the participants at the construction site.
- Give the safety coordinator a tool to concentrate the management of all the different construction sites he is working on.
- Provide a tool to establish and control workflows between participating stakeholders.
- To produce an application which users are likely to use. It is a difficult environment and the barriers to apply new technologies are very high. In order to get people using it the application must be very friendly and provide real help in the daily work.
- Promote the eWork in the construction industry. It is an industry naturally distributed, each company works on several sites simultaneously, an ideal scenario for eWork. By connecting the construction site, Gesprecons gives seamless connection to the workers.
- To be the first step towards the development of a platform for the collaborative work in the whole life cycle of building.

3. Methodology

The application has been carefully designed and developed based on the following steps:

- Information compilation.
- Process modelling.
- Data modelling.
- Web tool development.

3.1 Information compilation

Information compilation is a major issue within this kind of project. The group needed to gather all key information, and the project must improve and ease the current way of working and at the same time take into account all the legal compulsory issues.

In order to reach these objectives, it is crucial to have all the relevant information. In the project this information has been acquired from all the different involved sources: Firstly all the legal information [1,2,3], including normative, laws, procedures, have been analysed; then the main current software applications used in the sector with similar aims have been tested; also the most updated bibliography related to Health and Safety has been consulted [4,5,6,7] and finally and probably the most important, the potential users have been contacted and questioned about their expectations of such a system.

The Spanish Law Ley 31/1995 for Labour Risk Prevention, which transposes the European Framework Directive 89/391/CEE, establishes constructor obligations: To plan preventive action from initial risks evaluation, and evaluate the risks inherent in selected work tools, substances, and work places conditioning. This obligation is developed in chapter II, articles 3 to 7 of Real Decreto 39/1997, Regulations for the Prevention Services.

3.2 Process and Data Modelling

In order to develop an application that covers the Risk Prevention Tasks the actual processes have been modelled. To this end, all the compiled information has been analysed. Special attention has been paid to the comments from the potential users. This being so because they provide the real taste of the current processes.

A data model has been defined by analysing process information. This data model consists of the data structures needed to perform all the operations in the Risk Prevention.

3.3 Web Tool Development

The platform is a web accessible application to maximise remote access via an Internet browser. Application updates are dynamically available as no PC installation is required.

The application development aimed to achieve necessary performance, while reducing costs and maximising platform independence. The programming is in JAVA, using MS SQL Server as the database, and the applications server is Apache Tomcat which allows for encrypted connections through https.

4. Developments

This section describes the main functionalities offered by the application. One of the main issues taken into account was usability. For this reason the design of the user interface has been specially studied. The main criteria for the design have been:

- To offer access to most important functionalities in every screen.
- To reduce the number of steps to reach a determined function.
- To show the user the path he has followed to reach a function.
- To make the functionalities easy to use.
- Allow different profiles.

The development of the platform had two main parts: The database generation and the application implementation. In the following subsections these developments are detailed.

4.1 Information Database

As previously introduced, there has been a hard work in the side of the database contents preparation. Not only in the selection of that information, but also in its structuring.

The information is divided into two types: construction labour, and construction risks. The former is composed of the elements that describe a construction process: phase, activity, materials, machinery, and tools. The latter is composed of concepts related to safety issues: risk, prevention measure. Both types of information are interrelated, as any construction element may have several risks and each risk several preventive measures.

The diagram below shows the structure of the information database. The concept is that a construction work is divided into phases. Each phase consists of a set of activities. In each activity a set of materials and machinery are used. All of the construction elements (phase, activity, materials etc.) can trigger a set of risks. And finally a set of preventive measures must be applied in order to remove or at least reduce the risk.

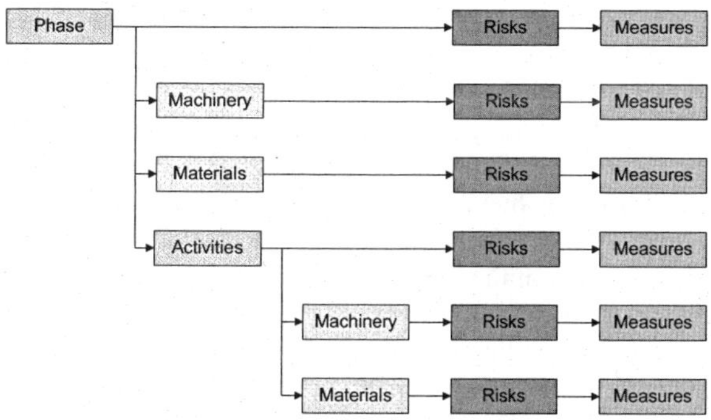

Figure1: Information system structure

All the information related to construction labour and risk management has been studied and fitted into the scheme shown above. The database is accessible and the system administrator can easily do changes, such as adding new items, deleting others or modifying the existing ones. So, once this structuring was agreed, the next step was to organise all the compiled information according to it.

The table below shows some representative figures about the database.

Table1: Database figures

Concept	Number	Relations
Phase	16	20 activities
Activity	250	7 materials 8 machinery 45 risks
Machinery	74	12 risks
Materials	36	7 risks
Risk	130	14 measures
Measure	1200	------

This shows the huge amount of work dedicated to the information system in the application. The first column of the table shows the different types of elements contained in the database. The second column shows the number of elements contained in the database for each type. And finally, the third column shows the average of relations that each element has with each of the other elements.

4.2 Application

The main objective of the application is to offer support to a user in the generation of the HASP for a construction site. Furthermore, the aim is to allow for the collaborative participation of several users in the creation and later treatment of the HASP.

Depending on the user id on login, the application addresses the user to a different interface, one is addressed to the system administrator, and another one to the normal user.

The system administrator maintains the system and sign up, delete or modify the data of the user companies. Information database maintenance involves the administrator can update the contents of the database including new elements or modifying the current ones.

The user interface provides access to the main functionalities of the system based on the user profile. The system allows for the users to access to different construction with different profiles. This way a user can be the main safety coordinator in one construction and only a participant in the Safety plan creation in another one.

The list of functionalities offered to the user is the following:

- Make the HASP in a collaborative way. The platform main aim is to allow the preparation of the Health & Safety Plan in a collaborative way. To this end, the system allows the users to define the hierarchy they want to follow amongst the different companies participating in the preparation.
- Gesprecons platform assists in the HASP execution. It can automatically send alerts notifying the affected workers of a hazardous situation at the construction site. It can send notifications about beginning or ending of phases, risks, etc.
- Gesprecons allows for a coordinated management of the construction schedule. This facilitates intra-company collaborative in a construction environment.
- The H&S coordinator checks fulfilment of the preventive measures in the construction site by preparation and fulfilment of the appropriate checklists. A checklist contains the set of conditions that each preventive measure must accomplish. Gesprecons assists in the preparation and later fulfilment of such checklists. Furthermore, it allows the user to access from the construction sites through mobile devices.
- Gesprecons allows users to regulations in Safety and Risk prevention remotely.

The figure below presents the user interface. On the left, the system provides the user with the most important information (pendant measures, recent alerts etc.) and access to functionality. On the right, the graphical visualization for the HASP schedule is shown. It allows the user to get a quick overview of global planning and provides access to the screen for modifying elements by clicking on the bar. Each element type is in a different colour.

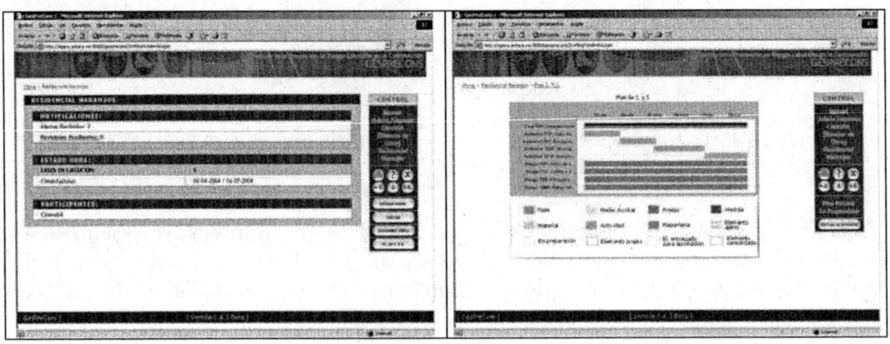

Figure3: User Interface detail

5. Business Benefits

The platform Gesprecons offers a list of benefits for different actors in the scenario.

For the construction companies:

- They can easily generate and apply the Health and Safety Plan.
- They can define the collaboration workflow with their subcontractors.
- They can reduce the invested money on the application of the HASP as the system detects overlapping preventive measures.

For the Safety assurance responsible:

- He can exonerate his responsibilities because the system keeps registry of his actions.
- He can consult and modify the HASP at any moment and anywhere with an Internet connection.
- He can easily know at every moment who is the person responsible for any activity, thus facilitating his communication tasks.

For the workers:

- They have a safest working environment.
- They can alert in case of emergency.

6. Conclusions

The application of these new work methods provides a significant improvement in internal management, documentation, and resource management.

This tool eases interaction between different agents and reduces the risk of accidents by facilitating health and safety management at the construction sites.

Following an initial trial, initial user feedback has been very positive and some constructive suggestions have been reported. In the next months, after taking into account the suggestions from the test users, the platform will start its exploitation phase.

Apart from modifications suggested by test users, a set of improvements is already planned, focused on the openness of the system. For instance to allow the application to import data from standard formats, to allow the calculations of budgets, etc.

Another improvement will be focused on the connectivity. This way the system will be done more accessible, i.e. through advanced mobile devices. To this end the application will be configurable, and the contents will be displayed depending on the connected device. The target devices will be mainly pocket PCs and third generation advanced mobile phones.

The final aim of the group is to develop a multi-discipline platform for collaborative work in the construction sector. Gesprecons is the first step. Following steps will add new functionalities to the platform, for instance to assure fulfilment of Quality procedures.

References

[1] Ley 1627 / 1997, Disposiciones mínimas de seguridad y salud en los lugares de trabajo

[2] RD 39/ 1997 de 17 de enero. Reglamento de los Servicios de Prevención

[3] Ley 31/1.995, de 8 de noviembre, de Prevención de Riesgos Laborales

[4] Manual Básico de Prevención de Riesgos Laborales. Cuadernos Cinco Días. Centros de Estudios Financieros.1999.

[5] Guía práctica para la prevención de riesgos laborales en obras de edificación. Generalitat Valenciana. Consellería de Economía, Hacienda y Trabajo.2003.

[6] Manual de Seguridad y Salud en la Construcción. Pedro-Antonio Beguería Latorre. Colegio de Aparejadores y Arquitectos Técnicos de Gerona. 1998

[7] Manual de seguridad y de riesgos laborales y de la protección del medio ambiente. Mutua Universal. CIE. Dossat 2000. 1999.

Spin-3D: a VR-platform on Internet ADSL Networks for Synchronous Collaboration

Dominique PAVY[1], Arnaud BOUGUET[1], Pascal LE MER[1],
Stéphane LOUIS DIT PICARD[1], Laurence PERRON[1], Gregory SAUGIS[1],
Christophe CHAILLOU[2], Samuel DEGRANDE[2]
[1]*France Télécom R&D, 2 av. Pierre Marzin, 22307, Lannion Cedex, France*
Tel: +33 2 96 05 23 82, Fax: +33 2 96 05 11 29, Email: dominique.pavy@francetelecom.com
[2]*LIFL USTL/CNRS/INRIA, Bâtiment M3, 59655, Villeneuve d'Ascq Cedex, France*
Tel: +33 3 28 77 85 46, Fax: +33 3 28 77 85 37, Email: {degrande, chaillou}@lifl.fr

Abstract: Various business activities are increasingly requesting Virtual Conferencing tools that enable distant team members to meet and collaborate around digital documents without travelling. In order to overcome the limitations of current offerings, France Telecom R&D and INRIA/LIFL have developed a new platform called Spin-3D based on a Collaborative Virtual Environment approach. This paper first describes its original interface and interactions specifically designed for strong real-time collaboration in small groups around 3D models and providing a high level of communication. The platform software architecture protocol, which allows Spin-3D to run on the Internet, is explained. Then Argonaute 3D, a cooperative planning surgical system built on top of Spin-3D, and its first experimentation are presented. Finally results and potential business benefits are discussed.

1. Introduction

According to economical forecasts, the collaborative software market will grow dramatically over the next few years. The main advantages are reduced costs, shortened product development cycle, increased innovation, improved communication, faster time to market, and increased productivity. It addresses business needs for internal and inter-enterprise teams in different processes: R&D, manufacturing, sales and marketing, client interactions, etc. Thanks to the capacities of high bit rate networks combined with the fast growth of PC power, Internet-based solutions are rapidly emerging. New synchronous collaboration tools, involving multimedia data over the web will start to be marketed.

One of the new strongest demands, arising from various sectors of activities using CAD tools (automotive, avionic, AEC, medicine, etc) concerns the possibility to collaborate in real time around 3D models. The only existing solutions rely on the screen sharing principle. However, this kind of "Virtual Conferencing" is still presenting some well-known drawbacks: learning how to effectively use the equipment, the lack of face to face interaction, the required bandwidth and the limited possibilities of the interactions (non symmetrical and exclusive). It also implies to lay out the generally expansive 3D CAD software on at least one of the PCs involved during the conference.

For several years, solutions based on a full virtual approach have been investigated by a number of laboratories. They take advantage of Virtual Reality (VR) techniques: real-time 3D computer graphics, spatial sound, immersion, simulation, input devices and direct interaction and more. Particularly, Collaborative Virtual Environments (CVE) that rely on VR and on telecommunication technologies enable new forms of collaboration and could be considered as very challenging alternatives.

2. Objectives

In this framework, France Telecom R&D and INRIA/LIFL carried out joint studies on the design and realisation of a new 3D CVE called Spin-3D. The aim is to create a synchronous collaboration application that allows strong collaboration by a small group of users, around virtual objects. The work is mainly focused on interface design and technical platform development involving human factors specialists, software architects and developers. The first main objective is to design a user-friendly 3D interface that facilitates ease of use, collaborative task interactions, and quality communication between the participants. The second main objective is to perform a technical platform supporting the management of collaborative applications running on standard PCs connected to the Internet via ADSL. The other main requirements of Spin-3D are the ability to accept 3D models coming from various origins and to offer a secured data transfer and hosting. In order to validate the interface's concepts and to test the technical effectiveness of the whole platform, several applications have been developed during the course of the project.

3. Interface and interaction design

As previously mentioned, we want to provide a virtual environment into which users are able to manipulate objects together, and communicate with other participants, implied in the realization of a common task. Those two main objectives were our leitmotivs when we defined each part of our Spin-3D platform: its graphical interface, the human-computer interaction mechanism, and the remote representation of inter-actors.

Usual 3D multi-user environments (e.g. Dive, Blaxxun Community) tend to provide a virtual representation of a realistic world: they transpose real 3D geometry constraints onto virtual objects, and transpose real ways of acting (displacement, manipulation…). Based on our two objectives, those virtual-reality concepts have several drawbacks. First, a user has to move frequently before being able to use an object, disrupting the user's concentration on the final goal. Secondly, the shared common geometrical representation of the world implies that two users cannot see each other while looking at the same part of an object. This can be a problem, for example, during a discussion about an object's design. Finally, current VR technologies are not able to analyze all human gestures in order to interpret and reproduce them, and, usually, virtual tools or effectors are provided to manipulate objects. Instead of focusing on the realization of their task, users have to concentrate on manipulating those tools. As a consequence, we consider that a standard multi-user virtual world is not a good starting point to provide a collaborative virtual environment. A CVE has to efficiently support collaborative tasks, by using a realistic homogeneous representation of objects, but without being constrained to any real 3D geometry, by providing simple interactions means, and by removing any useless actions.

After some studies of actual synchronous collaborative activities, we have observed that collaboration is effective when only a small number of people are actively working together on a small number of objects, the inter-actors being situated around a common place, usually a table, or at least inside a unique room. Moreover, in order to understand the performed tasks, each user needs to be constantly aware of any document's transformation, and thus no manipulation must be hidden. Based on those observations, the visual interface of the Spin-3D platform is built on a "meeting room" metaphor, within which all documents and avatars are displayed [1]: a rotating *band* around a table is a place holder for all the documents needed for a given task, and the central *table* is a manipulation area on which the users put the documents they want to interact with at a given time. In a collaborative activity, even if the goal is shared, each user has her/his own mental representation of the ongoing task, and needs to spatially arrange the documents in a way that reflects her/his mind. One feature of the Spin-3D interface is that each user organizes her/his environment independently of the others (see Figure 1): the *band* can be rotated, objects can be exchanged between the *band* and the *table, etc.* Spin-3D can thus be considered as a shared document manager, rather than as a multi-user virtual world.

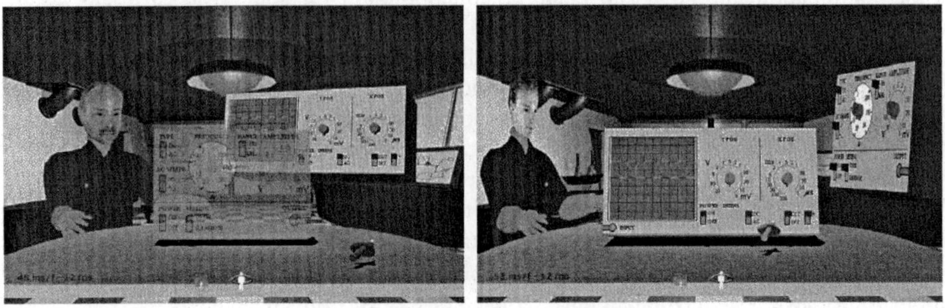

Figure 1: Two users working together, each one with a different object on the table, in a virtual laboratory-work scenario.

Spin-3D implements a two-phase bi-manual direct interaction mechanism. The dominant hand is first used for designation/selection of objects, with a 3D position tracker that controls a 3D virtual pointer. The other hand is then used for the object's manipulation, with a 6 degrees of freedom tracker (enabling 3D rotation and 3D translation). Some complex actions are however not directly related to the object's manipulation, but rather to the management of the 3D interface. For such actions, Spin-3D provides advanced metaphoric tools, such as a tool to interchange the position of two objects.

There are many ways to represent users in a CVE. Video technologies allow participants to be seen, but the data is almost impossible to manipulate (e.g. it is impossible to illustrate what a participant is looking at), and the camera angle has an impact on how users' gestures and attitudes are interpreted. Spin-3D uses 3D synthetic avatars, which are a realistic representation of users in terms of texture, morphology and animation [2]. Using avatars requires the recreation of non-verbal communication between users. Our avatar's model is based on four interaction modes (addressed and non-addressed expressive gestures, action gestures, and neutral gestures). Interaction modes are changed using an implicit detection of the user's gestures [3] and peripherals information. Facial animation [4], inverse kinematics [5], motion capture [6], and acoustic spatial localization are used.

4. Technology description

The Spin-3D platform is designed to run synchronous collaborative applications developed by third parties, involving a small group of co-workers. The platform integrates a set of functionalities common to any CVE, thus simplifying the task of the application developer.

4.1 Communication mechanisms

Most CVEs are built on a centralized architecture. However, such an architecture introduces latency in user interaction. Indeed, to manipulate shared data, the user requests the remote server and waits for the updated state. To ensure optimal interactivity, Spin-3D runs over a distributed architecture [7][8]. Each shared data is duplicated on each instance of Spin-3D present in the collaborative session, thus forming a *logical group* as proposed in [9]. Each user interacts with the local copy, and then the platform ensures the coherency of its logical group. Figure 2 illustrates the general architecture of the Spin-3D communication layer.

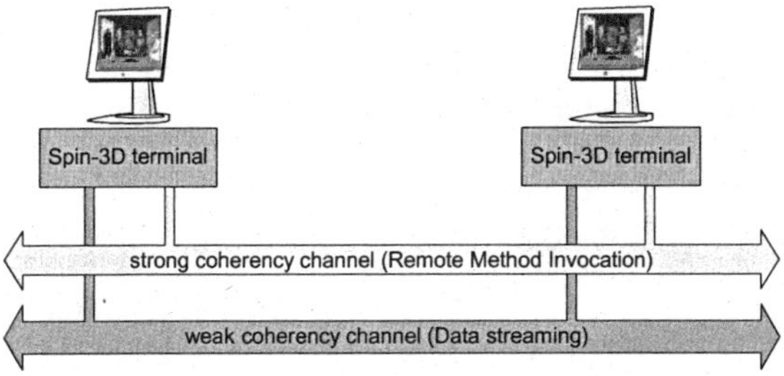

Figure 2: The Spin-3D communication platform

To support the co-operative activity, it is mandatory to ensure that all the distributed copies belonging to the same logical group are in the same state. The Spin-3D platform provides a strong-coherency channel for group communication using a reliable transport protocol, at some cost. This channel is typically used to transmit one-time events: a user enters the session, an object has been selected, etc.

However, in some cases, coherency can be relaxed: some intermediary positions a moving object goes through, or some frames of a broadcasted movie can be lost without harmful consequences. Spin-3D provides a second weak-coherency channel using an unreliable transport protocol. This channel should be used to transport streams of data.

Among different possible implementation techniques (distributed shared memory (DSM), low-level message passing (PVM), etc.) we have chosen the high-level object-oriented remote method invocation to implement the strong-coherency channel. We have elected the CORBA standard defined by the OMG [10]. In the classical use case, CORBA is designed for the client-server model. The Multicast Inter-ORB Protocol (MIOP) [11] introduces the notion of a logical group of objects over an unreliable multicast network. We have defined a new protocol preserving the notion of a logical group as defined in MIOP, but kept independent of the underlying transport layer, in order to provide various implementations for different kinds of networks.

The OMG has defined the Audio/Video Streaming Service standard [12], giving the ability to control multimedia streams, linking producers and consumers, in a CORBA environment. The stream control operations are done through CORBA remote method invocation, whereas stream data are transported through other means (e.g., low-level socket programming). For the implementation of the weak-coherency channel, we have adapted this service to run over our decentralized architecture.

In order to manage the virtual collaborative session, our platform relies on several services, namely a group service in charge of maintaining the list of the users in session, a lock service giving access to a shared data to one user at a time, and a persistency service providing the current state of shared data to a user joining the session. All these services have been specifically designed to run in a decentralized architecture.

Currently, we support two transport layers. First, we use a reliable/unreliable multicast protocol that naturally implements group communications. As IPv4 does not natively support multicast routing, we have developed a software bridge (using TCP/IP and UDP/IP) to run the Spin-3D platform on common networks (e.g. xDSL).

4.2 Application development

All tasks needed to support a virtual synchronous collaborative activity (user embodiment through avatars, voice transmission and spatial localization, 3D interaction, shared data management, objects layout) are hidden to application developers and automatically performed by the Spin-3D platform. Developing an application is limited to the creation of contents using the VRML97 syntax [13]: the 3D object geometry, the definition of the user interaction, the description for shared objects [14] and the related object behaviors. The sharing description includes the specification of communication channels to use.

The developers can write specialized display plug-ins that are loaded by Spin-3D, dynamically extending the capabilities of the platform (see Figure 3). Complex or already existing applications can also be plugged onto Spin-3D through an API very close to the VRML97 External Authoring Interface (EAI) [15].

Figure 3: The components of the Spin-3D core

5. A medical application: Argonaute 3D

The aim of Argonaute 3D is to overcome the difficulty of sharing 3D medical image between different distant users, in order to cooperatively plan surgery or simulate it. Argonaute 3D is based on the merging of a 3D Virtual Surgical Planning software (3D VSP) which has been developed by IRCAD [16] and Spin-3D.

5.1 Description of the application

3D VSP is software for reconstructing a 3D model of a patient's body from a CT-scan or an MRI and for planning surgical acts. It runs on a simple laptop or multimedia personal computer providing a 3D reconstruction of the body and its visualization (see Figure 4-a) [17]. It allows a practitioner to see organs in transparency, to interact on them, to navigate anywhere, to simulate any kind of cœlioscopy, to perform virtual resection and to automatically provide the volume of any visualized 3D structures.

The technical issue of Argonaute 3D consists in developing a version of the 3D VSP tool that can be manipulated cooperatively while using Spin-3D technology and preserving the functionality level of 3D VSP (see Figure 4-b and 4-c). Therefore, we have firstly developed an API to control virtual views, actions carried out by planning tools and the choice of organs affected by the various actions. Secondly we have adapted interaction concepts of 3D VSP to bi-manual 3D interaction concepts of Spin-3D using 6DOF input devices for pointing and manipulating.

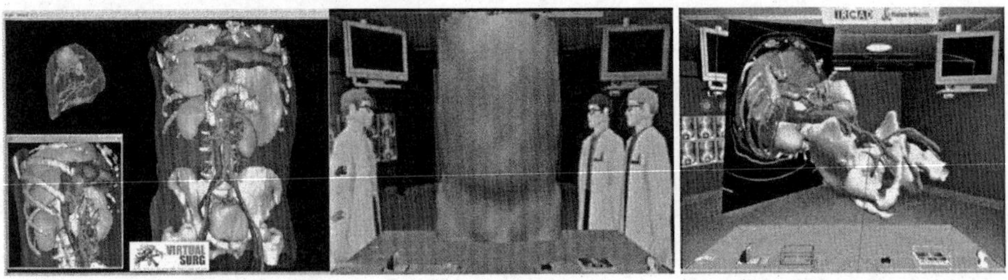

a *b* *c*

Figure 4: 3D VSP on a laptop (a) and Argonaute 3D collaborative interface (b, c)

5.2 Experimentation and results

In order to validate the interest of Argonaute 3D in the medical procedure and to test the effectiveness of the software, we have carried out experimentation from a real case of an anonymous patient file [16]. This patient, presenting four hepatic lesions, had undergone a surgical intervention planed from the 3D VSP software and carried out by a first surgical team. The Argonaute 3D experimentation was carried out afterwards by a second team (see Figure 5). This second team was composed of several practitioners (surgeons, radiologist, general practitioner) who were located on different sites and connected to the Internet network thanks to a standard ADSL type link (512 Kbits/s best effort).

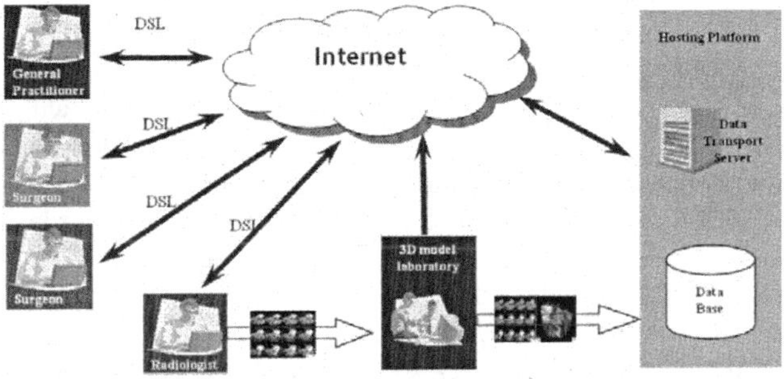

Figure 5: Network configuration of the experimentation

In relation to ergonomics, the system exploits the advantages of 3D VSP and adds an improved ease of 3D interaction thanks to the use of the SpaceMouse 6DOF input device, which was particularly well controlled by the radiologist and surgeons. The Spin-3D user interface appeared as being well adapted to the task. However, several developments have been requested such as a private space included in the 3D interface that would allow practitioners to locally test a strategy and then propose it to all actors.

Finally, from a medical point of view, we have compared the virtual surgery proposed by the two teams. In the case of the Argonaute 3D experience, practitioners had only very little information on the patient file, the major information being his medical imaging and its 3D model. In the case of the real surgical intervention, the surgical team had the whole patient file, his 3D representation, the 3D VSP software to plan the intervention and especially the patient, thus they could adjust their planning on the real patient. In both cases, the clinical examination revealed four identical hepatic lesions, and medical experts who have used Argonaute 3D have proposed the same therapy as the other team.

5.3 Business benefits

Although the Argonaute 3D prototype still requires routine clinical validation and some improvements in regards to ergonomic and technical issues, it seems promising on both technical and medical aspects. It speeds up therapeutic care, as network consultation between medical experts saves a considerable amount of time in pathology analysis and preparing for surgery. Real-time information exchanges offer a faster and more precise concerted diagnosis, and limit additional examinations and appointments for patients.

As evidence, such a cooperative working application can be extrapolated to many other business activities where a decision has to be taken collaboratively and as promptly as possible by several distant experts. It is especially designed for collaboration around 3D models such as project review meetings involving a Digital Mock Up. It could overcome the current limitation of existing tools while being cost effective thanks to: web access to the applications, easy deployment of the software, a typical xDSL network connection, running on conventional PC, and its compatibility with various CAD software.

6. Conclusions

We have developed a CVE platform called Spin-3D that enables collaboration in real time and in small groups about virtual objects through avatars or clones. Thanks to its original conception, not aiming at strictly reproducing the real world, Spin 3D allows users to focus on the cooperative task while providing high level communication. User representation by clones or avatars, combined with real-time oral communication, promotes more natural exchanges. The Spin-3D platform relies on a server-less communication layer implemented over innovative technologies (CORBA and multimedia streams). It has been designed independently of the transport protocol, therefore Spin-3D runs over multicast networks or unicast ones with a software bridge. The required network resources for data and voice flow are of about 64 Kb/s per user, making the Spin-3D software compatible with existing DSL-type networks. The software architecture hides problems due to the distribution of users in order to ease the collaborative application development with the Spin-3D platform. Moreover 3D visualisation modules can be integrated as plug-ins in order to display the various 3D models and to keep the benefits of our specific interactions.

A cooperative surgical planning application, Argonaute 3D, built upon the Spin-3D platform, has demonstrated that practitioners located at different places could well establish the diagnosis and define the best strategy for a surgical intervention without travelling. Anyway, various fields of activity could be addressed by such a virtual conferencing tool based on a CVE approach: from the industrial world to e-learning, trade, architecture, or online computer games and, more widely, in situations requiring the real-time intervention of several distant participants. Compared to the real world and conventional mediated tools (e.g. video-conference, screen sharing), the Spin-3D platform provides a new form of synchronous collaboration by exploiting low cost VR and Internet technologies. According to these results, the first industrial prototype of the Spin-3D platform is under development and therefore evaluations of the usability and user acceptance are in progress. More prospective investigations mainly concern: real-time avatar animation and rendering, new interface concepts, dynamic reconfiguration of the scene, application authoring tool design, and connection with external 3D or 2D applications.

Acknowledgements

We would like to thank Alain Bernard and Frederic Tendron from France Telecom, and also the IRCAD team that has contributed to the Argonaute 3D common project, and in particular Luc Soler, Johan Moreau and Pr Jacques Marescaux.

References

[1] C. Dumas, S. Degrande, G. Saugis, C. Chaillou, M.L. Viaud, P. Plénacoste: "Spin: A 3-D Interface for Cooperative Work", Virtual Reality, Springer-Verlag, 4, p. 15-25, 1999.

[2] P. Le Mer, L. Perron, C. Chaillou, S. Degrande, G. Saugis: "Collaborating with Virtual Humans", *People and Computer XV – Interaction without frontiers*: Proceedings of HCI 2001, Springer, pp.83-103, September the 12th 2001, Lille (France).

[3] S. Marcel, O. Bernier, J.E. Viallet, D. Collobert, "Hand recognition using input-output hidden Markov models, Int Conf on Aut. Face and Gest. Recogn., March 2000, pp456-461"

[4] K. WATERS, "A muscle model for animating three dimensional facial expressions", Proc. Computer graphics, SIGGRAPH'87, 21(4), July 1987, pp17-41.

[5] D. Tolani, N.I.Badler, "Real-Time inverse kinematics of the human arm", Presence, 1996, Vol 5 (4), pp 393-401

[6] S. Marcel, O. Bernier, D. Collobert, "Approche EM pour la construction de régions de teintes homogènes", Coresa 2000.

[7] S. Louis Dit Picard, S. Degrande, C. Gransart, G. Saugis and C. Chaillou, A CORBA-based platform as communication support for synchronous collaborative environments. In: Multimedia Middleware Workshop (M3W), ACM Multimedia, Oct. 2001, pp. 56-59.
[8] S. Louis Dit Picard, Plate-forme de communication distribuée pour les Environnements Virtuels Collaboratifs 3D à fort couplage d'activité synchrone. PhD thesis, Université des Sciences et Technologies de Lille, Nov. 2003.
[9] O. Hagsand, H. Herzog, K. Birman and R. Cooper, Object-oriented reliable distributed programming. In: Proceedings of the 2nd International Workshop on Object-Orientation in Operating Systems, Sept. 1992, pp. 180-188.
[10] OMG, The Common Object Request Broker: Architecture and Specification – Rev. 2.5. In: OMG Document Formal/01-09-01, Sept. 2001.
[11] OMG, Unreliable Multicast Inter-ORB Protocol. In: OMG Document Formal/2001-03-01, Apr. 2001.
[12] OMG, Control and management of Audio/Video Streams Specification. In: OMG Document Formal/2000-01-03, Jan. 2000.
[13] R. Carey, G. Bell and C. Marrin, Virtual Reality Modeling Language (VRML 97). In: ISO/IEC 14772-1:1997, 1997.
[14] S. Louis Dit Picard, S. Degrande, C. Gransart, G. Saugis and C. Chaillou, VRML data sharing in the Spin 3D CVE. In: Proc of Web3D 2002 symposium, Feb. 2002, pp. 165-172.
[15] S. Louis Dit Picard, S. Degrande, C. Gransart, G. Saugis and C. Chaillou, VRML97 Distributed Authoring Interface. In: Proceedings of Web3D 2003 symposium, Mar. 2003, pp. 135-145
[16] P. Le Mer, L. Soler, D. Pavy, A. Bernard, J. Moreau, D. Mutter, J. Marescaux, "Argonaute 3D: a real-time cooperative medical planning software on DSL network", Proceeding of MMVR12, pp 203-209, Newport, California, USA, January 2004.
[17] C. Koehl, L. Soler, J. Marescaux: "A PACS Based Interface for 3D Anatomical Structures Visualization and Surgical Planning.", *SPIE proceeding*, 2002, Vol. 4681, pp. 17-24, San Diego (USA).

Useful Semantic Product Properties in Virtual Worlds

Rainer MALKEWITZ[1], Gianni GADDA[2]
[1]*ZGDV – Zentrum für Graphische Datenverarbeitung e.V., Fraunhoferstr. 5, 64283 Darmstadt, Germany*
Tel: + 49 6151 155488, Fax: + 49 6151 155450, Email: rainer.malkewitz@zgdv.de
[2]*Democenter s.c. a r.l., V. le Virgilio 55, 41100 Modena, Italy*
Tel: + 39 (0)59 899611, Fax: + 39 (0)59 848630, Email: g.gadda@democenter.it

Abstract: This paper deals with the question how semantic properties of product items can be used to enhance their usability in virtual scenes. The underlying thesis is that more "natural" behaviour of virtual product models will make it more easy, especially for untrained users, to plan and work in 3D-applications – such as electronic catalogues, product configurators, and CAD-based planning systems. The following is a report on basic concepts, as well as mid-term results, from a European project called SpacemantiX, funded under the IST programme's "Semantic Web Technologies" action line. The focus here is put on the results of user requirements, and its transformation into application logic and data modelling.

1. Introduction

The SpacemantiX project aims at bringing natural semantics of product items into artificial 3D scenes (see www.spacemantix.org). By doing so, we expect to enhance the potential usability and usefulness (utility) of 3D graphics, at least in some types of commercial applications. The project work has tried to concentrate on such applications related rather to untrained users of interactive 3D, like decision makers, technicians, or even private end users (customers), ending up with target applications such as product catalogues, planning applications, or assembling instructions. The basic idea has been to combine the existing geometry model of a part or product with other information about it, which is referred to as "semantic product properties". Obviously, such information could often be useful during interactive manipulation of a 3D-model inside a virtual 3D scene (e.g., in the case of "insert", "move", or "rotate" operations): Imagine a part that "knows" where it can be placed in a given scene, or how it may be "plugged" together with other items. Such an object could almost magically snap into the right position and orientation, with only very simple drag-and-drop operations required from the user.

The following chapters will include specific examples of how such behavioural constraints in 3D-applications may help the user. Before that, we explain how these examples have been derived from the answers that users from the business domains involved in the project have given to questions during the user requirements collection. Finally, an overview will be given for the concepts used to produce our technology demonstrators, as well as the property model used to encode the relevant product properties.

2. Objectives and Related Work

In the past, manipulation and coding of 3D objects and scenes has been the subject of scientific research in many ways. Among other results, this has lead to the development of a widely accepted standard for the exchange of 3D-models over the Internet, namely the

"Virtual Reality Modelling Language VRML", ISO Standard 14772 [6], and its successor X3D that includes an XML-encoding for the VRML syntax [5].

Also, some valuable work has been done on modelling intelligent features (also referred to as "semantic constraints") into single objects and scenes, and their use in methods for intuitive manipulation, even with traditional 2D input devices. As examples, we point to the work of Stuerzlinger et al. (York University, Toronto) on "3D scene manipulation with 2D devices and constraints" [1] [2], and Bier (Xerox PARC, Palo Alto) [3] [4] about "snap-dragging in three dimensions". Among other results, their papers provide evidence that task completion times can be reduced dramatically through the introduction of "natural" constraints, especially such concepts like "grouping", "geometric alignment" and "key-surface-matching" showed some benefit. Furthermore, such reductions in task completion times – especially with untrained users – usually indicate a more intuitive understanding of concept and behaviour of the user interface. Thus, one can say, that the use of semantic constraints is basically proven to make 3D-manipulation more user-friendly.

On the other hand, it is found that the use of 3D-models as a means of presenting and exchanging product information in the main-stream business world has so far remained a domain-specific, if not even a proprietary method, related only to specific departments and computing tools. This has led us to the question: Why do companies not use to a larger extent three-dimensional representations in their internal processes and in the communication with their end customers?

Possible answers include matters of tradition in the way of communication between different departments, as well as a lack of compatibility between different CAD-systems, and other cost-related aspects. However, we believe these "hard fact" aspects are just one part of the story. The more general problem is that of limited usability and usefulness of today's 3D-models of products, namely: You have to be a specialist to produce useful results in almost any of today's 3D computer applications – an untrained person cannot use a 3D CAD system (see Figure 1). One reason for this is that most of the rules needed to know how to use a product's virtual model in a 3D scene, and the skill to produce "nice-looking" rendered images from a 3D scene, are so far treated as human expert knowledge, and not as regular product properties. Not surprising, the few 3D tools actually targeting private end-users, like architectural and furniture configurator "toys", embed all sorts of object constraints – in other words "product semantics" – to reduce the user interface complexity and to simplify the user interaction.

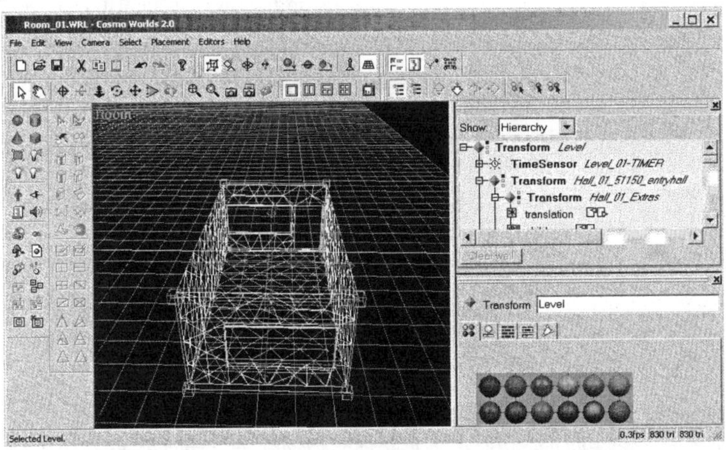

Figure 1: Even "simple" 3D tools, like COSMO Worlds (by Silicon Graphics, 1997), has a highly complex user interface and needs expert knowledge to be operated with success

3. User Requirements - Methods and Results

3.1 Methodology

To be as close as possible to real user needs, while on the other hand trying to remain independent of domain-specific aspects, it was chosen to collect, analyse, and prioritise requirements related to our "intelligent 3D models" approach from three different domains of application, which are: Interior design (architecture & furniture), mechanical engineering & automotive design, and the toy industry sector.

The methodology used for requirements collection was that of structured interviews, where an 8-page interview questionnaire was filled by the interviewer during the approx. 90 minute face-to-face interview. A total number of 33 persons have been interviewed.

The interview questions related to the user's profile (age, profession, gender, degree of computer knowledge etc.), working context (type of company, computing tools and networks used, general workplace description), and the typical workflow related to 3D working tasks (which CAD-tools used, hours of use per day, purpose of 3D work etc.).

Before the final part of the interview, several scenarios of use were introduced to the user by the interviewer. The proposed scenarios were related to the user's business domain, and should give a general idea about possible advanced features. The intention was to activate the user's power of imagination, not to restrict him to a fixed set of new features. In the end, the scenarios proved to be a valuable help, since many users reported they had not been able to imagine the concrete meaning and possible advantage of "semantically enhanced 3D-models" without some example scenarios given. To minimise the "self-fulfilling" effect of such scenarios, user feedback and suggestions were collected jointly for all scenarios, with hints to specific scenarios only noted where explicitly named by the users. To give the reader some idea about the scenarios, we give two examples here:

- From the domain of interior planning with furniture, one scenario was called "Guarded Distances", where the computer automatically controls the right orientation and distance between two or more related furniture items. The example given was to keep an office chair in front of a desk and to also guarantee enough empty space behind that chair enabling to move it backward for taking seat.
- From the automotive domain, one scenario was "Car Repair and Training", where the order of actions in replacement tasks should be visualised in 3D, along with the tools and techniques used to replace it. Like in some other scenarios, a mock-up user interface was shown.

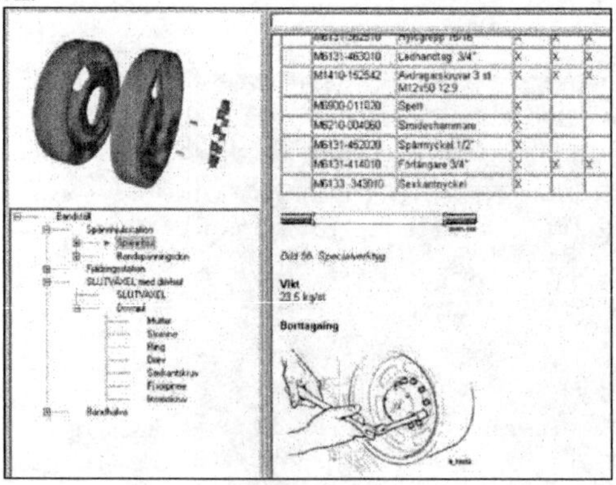

Figure 2: Mock-up interface for "Car Repair" scenario, as used in the user interviews

3.2 Analysis

After collecting user feedback, the data has been analysed in different ways. The statistical analyses showed that most users from our sample are only use 3D artefacts in a limited way when using computers. The second remarkable result was the big variety of 3D tools used: Even with more than 20 items given for selection, approx. 20% checked "other tools". This seems a good support for our hypothesis, that no solution related to only a limited number of even the most well-known CAD tools will be able to solve our target issue.

More meaningful and important than statistics has been reading and analysing all the comments and suggestions given with regard to the scenarios. In a first step, the user's utterances have been evaluated and categorised at a domain level, that is: One set for interior design, another one for mechanical engineering, and one for the toy sector.

The second step was to sum up similar ideas and comments and add up user priorities. The result is three short lists of prioritised common requirements, one for each domain.

3.3 Main Result

In a third step, the three lists were compared and similar issues identified. These requirements, appearing in all three domains, have finally been identified as the set of common requirements and have been re-formulated in the following short list [7]:

- Assisted generation of configurations: The possibility to create interactively a detailed configuration from base or empty start-configuration, with "alternative" (or "enhanced") possible choices suggested by the system.
- Advanced rendering quality: To have a good visual realism and "nice" look with possibilities of a "guided" distribution of accessories, camera views, and lights and possibilities of interactive rotating, zooming, dragging, and alike.
- Advanced connection to catalogues & part libraries: Quick access to databases of components (standard components, spare parts, product offers etc.) with possibilities of selecting and comparing them by automatically checking their properties against the requirements given by a the user's "target" configuration (3D scene). This should happen in "interactive time" and enable as well access to other technical descriptions, like technical details, prices, operation manuals etc.
- Property & requirement views: Simple visualisation, updating and reporting of properties and satisfied versus open requirements.
- Scaleable navigation and level-of-assistance: Step-by-step operations with assistance by virtual constraints for beginners and non-technical users, opposed to direct access to the appropriate information level for the experienced users. Ideally, there would exist a seamless transition between both extremes

Among these, the final one is clearly "out of scope" for our work, because the transition between "naive" and "expert" user interfaces is a very general and well-known issue, that is worked on by several approaches in the HCI research community and software industry.

4. Scenarios and Demonstrators

Based on the above set of requirements from the users, the scenarios (about 30 of them existed) were reconsidered. Which of them were most suited to demonstrate some advancements with regard to the user requirements? Which scenarios would be technically feasible with given effort? Which would lead to the most understandable and attractive technology demonstrators with regard to a broader audience?

Our plan has been, to first build several small "Demonstrators", each focusing on one specific aspect of innovative use of product semantics, followed by some "Prototypes", with broader set of functionality. Such a Prototype would demonstrate a more general scenario, like an online catalogue, or car configurator tool.

With the above questions guiding the decision, it was decided to address mainly the first three requirements: Easier generation of 3D-configurations (scene composition), easier image generation (view composition), and advanced access to catalogues and part libraries (product configuration and replacement). For the Prototypes, we wanted them to either represent advancements to typical tools, or to be entirely new in the target domain. Finally, the following examples were selected:

- Interior Space Planning (placing several furniture items in a room)
- Visual Online Configurator (interactive configuration of part assemblies)
- Interactive Maintenance Manual (interactive assembly and disassembly)

4.1 Examples from Interior Planning

From our Prototype tool for "Interior Space Planning" and addressing the requirement of scene composition, we pick here as an example the Demonstrator named "Table meets Chair", as shown in the following images.

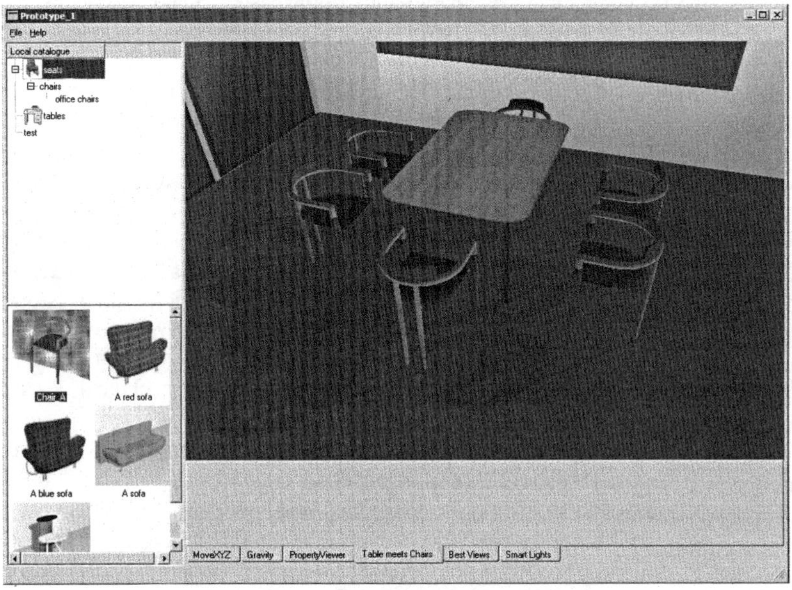

Figure 3: Screenshot of "Table meets Chair" Demonstrator, run as part of the "Interior Space Planning" Prototype

Compared to the tool shown in Figure 1, this user interface has few menus and no buttons carrying obscure icons. That is because all functionality is either drag-and drop, or automatic: When a chair is selected in the catalogue (left part of the interface) and its icon dragged into the 3D viewing area (upper right part) and dropped near the table in the scene, it automatically takes the right position and orientation relative to the table.

This "intelligent" behaviour is achieved by modelling the corresponding properties into the item's data models:

- The property data of this table has an entry about possible relations to up to 6 items of the kind "seating device; 1 user; home furniture", along with geometry-pointers to possible positions in space, where the chairs might be placed.

- The chair's data has entries identifying it as "seating device", "1 user", "home furniture", so that the relation with the table can be established.

Note, that no explicit encoding of dynamic behaviour has happened here. The table simply knows, which other items might become "neighbours", and where their default positioning should be. Anyway, for the user it looks like magic. (Remember: "Any sufficiently advanced technology is indistinguishable from magic", Arthur C. Clarke)

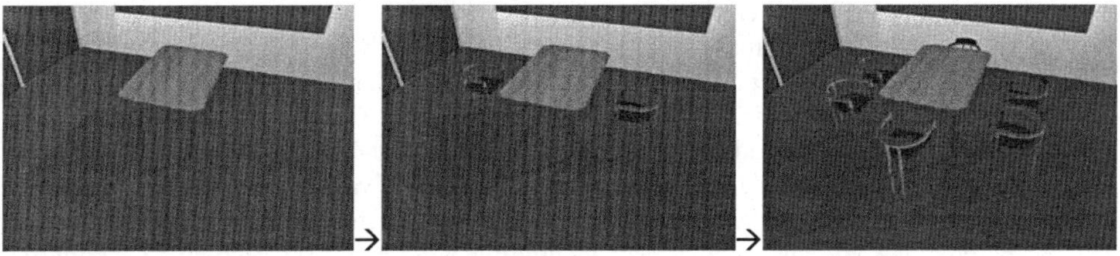

Figure 4, left to right: empty, incomplete, and complete configuration of a seating group. Note, that the two chairs in the middle are automatically "centred" with regard to the table

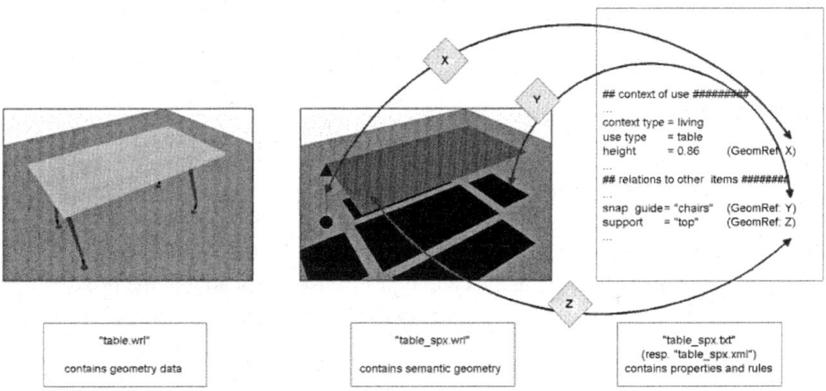

Figure 5: Semantic properties may include references to visible or invisible "ghost" geometry objects, like "snap areas" or "anchors [13]"

Other example Demonstrators also include issues related the other user requirements. For the composition of nice views, assistance for the positioning of the camera ("Best Views" Demonstrator) and for the distribution of light sources ("Smart Lights" Demonstrator) is provided, and for the easier access to catalogues, a Demonstrator called "Auto-Selection of new objects" has been implemented, where catalogue contents are filtered with regard to the existing scene (e.g. a table in the scene would make the program to look for chairs, in order to help the user to complete the configuration).

5. Modelling of Properties

At first glance, modelling of semantic properties is only a technical issue: the end user does not care how features are encoded, or where they are stored, whether within the data of a specific product item or hard-wired into program code. However, for the industrial user – manufacturer, dealer, or software provider – this is of interest: Will the semantic features be compatible between different software tools? Can they be bundled with the 3D models? Are these properties self-descriptive or proprietary? Are they human-readable or encrypted?

5.1 State-of-the-art analysis

To get a clearer view of possible existing solutions, an analysis of state-of-the-art methodologies and standards related to metadata and constraint management has been carried out [14]. Concerning metadata, analysis has been focused on standards conceived for the web (based on the XML syntax) and for the management of digital objects, including Dublin Core [9], RDF, LOM, and METS [10]. Regarding constraints, mainly rather academic formalisms have been found, conceived for the description of complex models and often dealing with difficult constraints satisfaction problems, such as the Object Constraint Language (OCL, that is also part of UML), Easy abstract Constraint Language (EaCL), Negative Semantic Constraints [1], and Topological and Geometrical Constraints [12]. Some slightly more intuitive and heuristic solutions were based on First Order Logic (FOL) and Articulation Rules [11]. Later in the project, with advanced knowledge of user requirements and technology demonstrators, the search has been concentrated on solutions that are based on XML and enable easy integration with open 3D geometry encoding standards (like X3D, or VRML97). At the same time, the encoding must be easy to understand and apply, as to be later accepted by a larger share of industrial domains. As a result, none of the approaches mentioned above provides satisfactory features. Thus, the project has developed a XML-schema for generalised product properties, mainly as a working shell for modelling our examples of semantic properties. Our schema is also open to integrate logical statements coded in any of the above mentioned constraint languages, as long as the corresponding processing model is known and interpreters are widely available.

5.2 Property model

During the development of Demonstrators and in many discussions with experts from the application domains, it has been found that the following categories of product properties seem to be globally relevant to characterise a product model for our purpose:

- Global Properties: The origin, owner (copyright) and identification of the data
- Usage Properties: About the domains and types of use applicable to the product item.
- Business Properties: About a product's manufacturer, price range, suppliers, warranties, delivery packaging, and about proprietary configurators and their interfaces.
- Presentation Properties: About geometry files, 2D images, thumbnail images, bounding volumes, surface appearances (incl. material sets).
- Relation Properties: About similar and complementary products, requirements (needs), offered features, matching accessories, and required tools.
- Variants: About existing variants, where a variant can be any subset of the total property model (subdivision of feature space)
- Initial Values: Possibility to specify "start-values" for all property values, useful when a new instance item is generated from the model. For instance, in the above example "Table meets Chair" (Fig. 3), we find 6 instance items of the same chair model.

While developing the XML schema for these general properties, these categories have been taken as highest level nodes. Being aware of the fact, that different property names and values may exist in different domains, and, even worse, the same words may be used with different meanings, the schema has been prepared to have domain specific extensions. The concept of XML namespaces, with the resulting prefixes is used to distinguish different domains in the final data. Thus, properties with the same name can actually be used with different meanings in the same dataset, because they have different domain prefixes: For a washhandbasin, "interior:height" may be 82 cm, while "sanitary:height" is 34 cm, referring to the water supply tubes, instead of the upper edge after mounting the basin on the wall.

6. Conclusions

By interviewing several users, we have identified there is good potential for enhancing the usability of 3D models by providing assistance to specific steps of work, namely the initial creation of a scene, the production of "nice" images, and the advanced access to currently "hidden" information, like catalogue data. Furthermore, we have shown examples of useful functionality that has been implemented in Prototype applications. Finally, an XML schema has been introduced, that is on the one hand able to map all relevant properties into a limited set of categories, while on the other hand it is very open and can be extended by any interested party with an extension schema. Thus, properties coming from different domains, companies, or countries can be kept together in the same product data model.

References

[1] G. Smith, T. Salzman, W. Stuerzlinger, 3D Scene Manipulation with 2D Devices and Constraints. In Graphics Interface 2001, Eds. J. Buchanan, B. Watson, 2001, Morgan Kaufman Publishers, pp. 135 – 142

[2] T. Salzman, S. Stachniak, W. Stuerzlinger, Unconstrained vs. Constrained 3D Scene Manipulation, Engineering for Human-Computer Interaction, Eds. M. Little, L. Nigay, Springer Verlag, 2001, pp. 207-219

[3] E.A. Bier and M.C Stone; Snap-dragging, ACM SIGGRAPH 1986, pp. 233-240

[4] E.A. Bier; Snap dragging in three dimensions, ACM SIGGRAPH 1990, pp. 193-204

[5] X3D framework & SAI — ISO/IEC FDIS 19775:200x; http://www.web3d.org/x3d/ specifications/ISO-IEC-19775-FDIS-X3dAbstractSpecification/index.html

[6] VRML97 Functional specification and VRML97 External Authoring Interface (EAI) International Standard ISO/IEC 14772-1:1997 and ISO/IEC 14772-2:2002

[7] N. Milic, S. Di Marca, R. Malkewitz, et al.; SpacemantiX - Common User Requirements Report; 2003; http://www.spacemantix.org/papers_set.htm

[8] A. Steinacker, A. Ghavam, R. Steinmetz; Metadata standards for Web-based resources; IEEE Multimedia, Volume: 8 Issue: 1; Jan.-March 2001; pp. 70 – 76.

[9] Dublin Core; IETF RFC 2413; http://www.ietf.org/rfc/rfc2413.txt .

[10] Library of Congress; METS, Metadata Encoding and Transmission Standard; http://www.loc.gov/standards/mets

[11] R. V. Guha; Context: A formalization and some applications; Ph.D. dissertation; Stanford University, Stanford, CA; 1991

[12] J. Lafon, Solid modelling with constraints and parameterised features; Proceedings of IEEE Conference on Information Visualization; 1998; pp. 102 – 107.

[13] E.A. Bier; Skitters and jacks: interactive 3D positioning tools; Proceedings of the 1986 workshop on Interactive 3D graphics; ACM Press; 1987; pp- 183 – 19.

[14] D. Krömker, L. Reum, C. Seiler, R. Malkewitz, et al.; SpacemantiX – State-Of-The-Art Report in Science and Technology; 2002; http://www.spacemantix.org/papers_set.htm

[15] R. Malkewitz et al.; SpacemantiX – Architectural Design Document; 2004; http://www.spacemantix.org/papers_set.htm

eAdoption and the Knowledge Economy: Issues, Applications, Case Studies
P. Cunningham and M. Cunningham (Eds.)
IOS Press, 2004

Virtual Reality Applications in the Energy Industry

Ricardo SALVE
TECNATOM, Avda Montes de Oca, 1. San Sebastián de los Reyes 28799, Spain
Tel: +34 91 6598789, Fax: +34 91 6598677, Email; rsalve@tecnatom.es

Abstract: This paper provides the author´s view on the role to be played by the Virtual Reality technology in the Energy Domain. Based on an analysis of some key features of this Industry Sector, it derives a list of potential areas of application (typical processes) of the technology; i.e. cases where Virtual Reality Technology can provide some added value to the present way of doing things. These cases are further illustrated with some specific real examples already developed as R&D projects, prototypes or commercial products. To conclude, some barriers that may prevent an extensive use of this technology in the energy domain are depicted

1. Introduction

Virtual Reality (VR) technology offers a good opportunity to improve and optimize typical processes in the Energy Industry. A vast amount of potential applications can be envisaged. While some of them may still fall into the R&D side (due to technological or cost barriers) many others are now possible satisfying cost - benefit criteria.

The steady reduction in associated costs and the increasing capabilities of this technology fosters its market penetration. This is especially true for so-called desktop VR.

2. Objectives

This paper presents a review of the potential fields of application of VR in the Energy domain. This industrial activity presents many features that make it especially suitable for the exploitation of the VR capabilities

3. Methodology

A generic top-down approach will be followed: A first and very generic analysis of the potential of VR along the lifecycle of a product is done. Then, an application of this analysis to the energy industry domain is shown. This provides a short list of areas that are matched to the "natural" or most common fields of application of the VR.

To further illustrate this generic exercise, a list of specific developments is then described. To conclude, some lessons learned coming from the development and application of these initiatives are extracted.

4. Business Case Description

A priori, it is not difficult to accept that VR can provide obvious advantages along the whole life cycle of a product in those cases where a shared perception of a complex scenario (mainly, visual scenarios) is a key factor of success.

During the designing phase, it is clear that VR is a tool that provides an ideal representation of the product to be developed that can be explored and modified in a very intuitive way so that the need for interaction between the customer and the developer (or among the developers) is diminished to a minimum. This has a positive impact on the development/construction phase, as the number of the required modifications is considerably lower, reducing costs and shortening times. For the same reasons, many manufacturing/development/assembling problems can be anticipated during the design phase, being the result the same: less costs, less time. Obviously, the same arguments used here for the design phase would be applicable to the decommissioning phase.

VR can be of benefit during the exploitation phase of the product:

- Planning of complex, dangerous or unforeseen tasks. The virtual representation of these tasks can help to plan them more efficiently and interactively. It is possible to test different alternatives and choose then the best one. Of course, in some cases this can also be achieved by "using" the real scenario but this is not always possible or affordable (cost, interference with the operation, involvement of many actors, etc).
- Training on procedures execution. VR is a powerful procedure design and training tool. Any kind of scenario can be represented; what if analysis can be easily performed and further validation is facilitated. Under certain circumstances, virtual mock-ups can replace physical ones, being cheaper to "manufacture" and modify. Besides they are "portable" (i.e. can be used anyware). This reduces errors, risks and costs.

To finalise, the product marketing activities can clearly benefit from such a friendly interface. Customers can easily perceive the product features and functionality, reediting of the marketing documentation is cheaper, information can be accessible via web etc.

Some features of the energy industry fit well in the scheme depicted above:

- The facilities are complex to design, operate and decommission. They involve many actors that need to interact each other: the owner, the operator (may be different), the main supplier, a myriad of "minor" suppliers, the architect engineer, the subcontractors during the operation, the regulator and, finally, the public
- A complex facility also involves a complex operation which, in turn, requires a large number of procedures
- Complex procedures (operation, maintenance, safety related procedures) with important implications in terms of cost and safety, unavoidably lead to the need of training.
- Typical operational conditions (high pressures and temperatures, chemical compounds, radiation) impose the need to protect the workers: there are hazardous tasks to carry out
- The safety and cost implications of the human errors give rise to the systematic consideration of the man-machine interface
- The existence of a regulator imposes the need of a continuous dialogue regulator-licensee that, in some way, may resemble the customer-seller dialogue.

While this is true for the oil, gas, and electricity sub-sectors, in the nuclear industry all of these aspects are magnified. VR can provide significant advantages in the fields of:

- Training: To train the staff or subcontractors in the execution of complex maintenance tasks (no mock-ups needed, enhanced didactic effectiveness); to train plant operators (simulators); to train in safety procedures.
- Procedures: For the design and validation of procedures (operating procedures, emergency procedures…)
- Engineering: For the design ex-novo or the design modifications, as a tool to keep the plant configuration control, for plant decommissioning, for the co-design with the customer or for the review by the regulator, for the design and review of man-machine interfaces in control rooms.
- Tasks planning: It can be used in the execution of task feasibility studies (v.g. analysis of interferences, human interventions), in the design and utilisation of special tools, in the fulfilment of the ALARA (As Low as Reasonably Achievable, applied to committed radioactive doses) criteria.
- Communication: To be used in the information centres and in the regulatory dialogue

5. Specific Examples of VR Applications in the Energy Industry

Bellow are briefly described some specific examples developed than can illustrate the way VR can help the main players (operators, services companies, regulators) in the optimization of processes described in the previous chapter.

The first three examples are clearly training related applications (5.1, 5.2 and 5.3). The same example 5.3 together with the fourth and fifth ones can be seen as applications belonging to a mix of training and procedural areas (maintenance procedures, 5.4 and emergency procedures 5.5). Application 5.6 falls entirely in the field of engineering, meanwhile examples 5.7 and 5.8 can be classified as part of the concept of task planning.

5.1 Radiological Protection Course

PRVIR is a Computer Based Course on Radiological Protection. This kind of training is mandatory before entering a Nuclear Power plant. The student receives training on the basics of Health Physics in an interactive way, including evaluation exercises after each module.

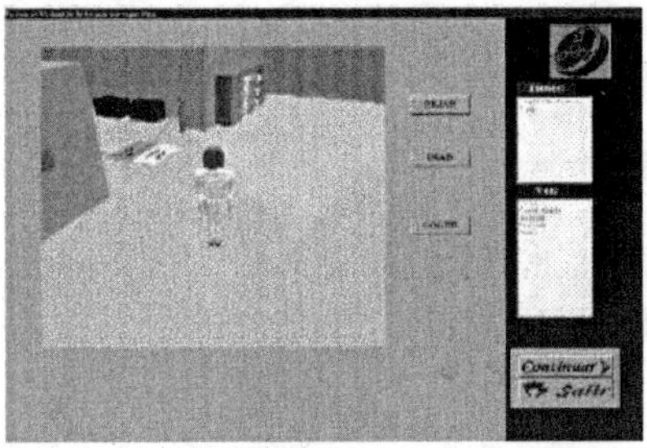

Figure 1: PRVIR

Some modules deal with specific procedures of a particular facility, showing the trainee these procedures in a VR environment (how to register, how to use protective clothing, how to use dosimeters, how to behave in restricted areas, etc). The exercises are also performed in a virtual environment representing the facility, providing that way the trainee an easy-to-understand framework of training. No special SW licenses are required.

5.2 Training Tool for Maintenance Procedures.

A Computer Based Course in VR named VIRMAN has been developed. It makes use of the Halden Virtual Reality Toolkit [1]. This prototype has been applied to a typical Nuclear Power Plant Procedure: vessel head and internals removal during an outage.

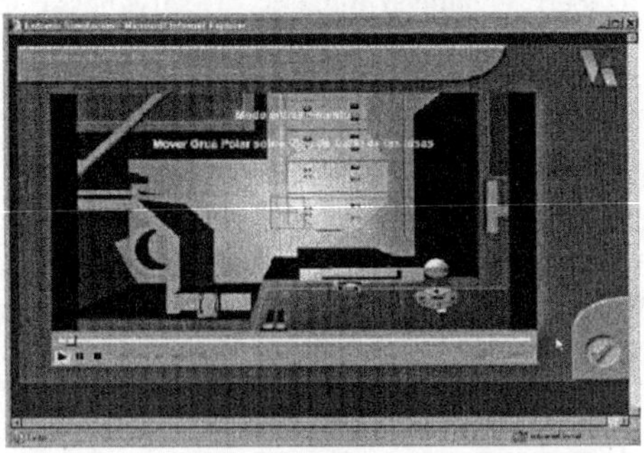

Figure 2: Virman

Using a client-server architecture, the trainee goes through each of the steps of the particular procedure (150 steps) following this sequence: first a 3D video of each step is shown, then the student can "flight & play" in the virtual environment trying to reproduce the right sequence of actions (some "clues" and additional information are available). Finally, the student is evaluated (by reproducing the procedure). The system is intelligent in the sense that it informs the trainee whether the action performed is correct or not.

5.3 Training Course on Particular Equipment

A prototype of web based course using html + vrml technology has been carried out. In this case, a Limitorque © valve actuator has been used as an example. This is a kind of "virtual manual" where the trainee can get information on the equipment visualizing its components, assembly and dismantling sequences and functioning.

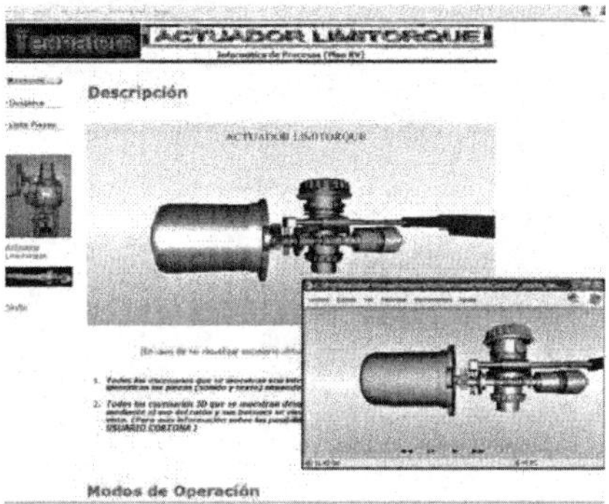

Figure 3: Training course on a valve actuator

Text plus 3D interactive images offers an unusual didactic potential compared to a traditional course (either paper based or just "conventional" web based course). The most relevant feature is that no special software or hardware is required, just an Internet navigator and a free plug-in to visualize vrml contents are needed.

5.4 Starmate

STARMATE [2] is the result of an European project (http://vr.c-s.fr/starmate/). It is an augmented reality device intended to help technicians in complex maintenance tasks.

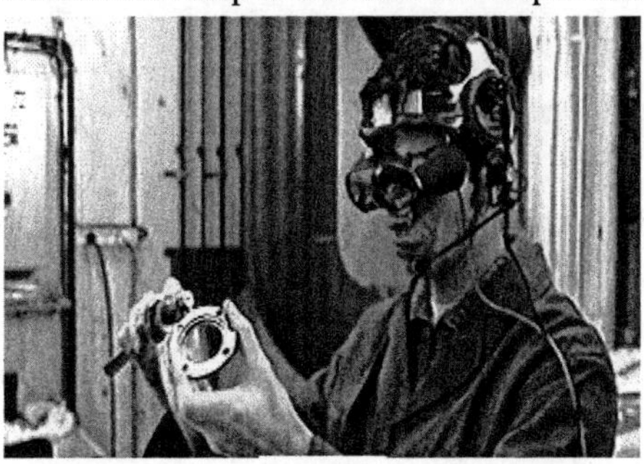

Figure 4: Augmented Reality. Starmate

The trainee uses the following equipment: semitransparent glasses, computers, a positioning system, a microphone and headphones. The user is able to see superimposed 3D images onto the real ones plus written, graphic and audio instructions guiding him through a maintenance procedure. He communicates with the system via voice recognition. The displayed information can be referenced to the equipment (as if it were a part of the equipment), to the operator (as if it were a part of the user) or to the world (as if it were a fixed part of the environment). One application has been made on a valve actuator.

5.5 Emergency Planning and Evaluation

ETOILE [3] was a European Project aimed at facilitating the training of the staff involved in the emergency management. The trainee plays its role in the virtual simulation of the emergency (responsible of the emergency, member of the operational crew, Administration representative...) and interacts with the other players who behave as intelligent agents according to predefined rules.

Figure 5: Emergency preparedness

He is requested to provide inputs to the simulation as he receives the pertinent information from it. Once the case has been run, the sequence of events is analysed in order to extract the lessons learned.

5.6. Control Room Modifications Design Applications

An interactive VR model of a Nuclear Power Plant Control Room (CR) has been developed. This is being used to start making modifications in the CR (physical layout, panels, etc). CR modifications (migration from analogue to digital) are driven by the obsolescence of the analogue technology and use to be a gradual process.

Figure 6: Control Room Modifications

Both the customer and the designer can test in the virtual model different potential solutions before freezing the design and start manufacturing the components. Man machine interface considerations can be taken into account more easily during the design phase and the reporting of the modifications is also facilitated. Again, a navigator and a plug-in are the only things required.

5.7 Online Monitoring and Simulation of Robotic Arms

SIROCO-3D is a VR based user interface to simulate and visualize the movements of robotic devices, for instance those used for the In Service (or Pre Service) Inspection of the main components of a Power Plant or in the aeronautics industry.

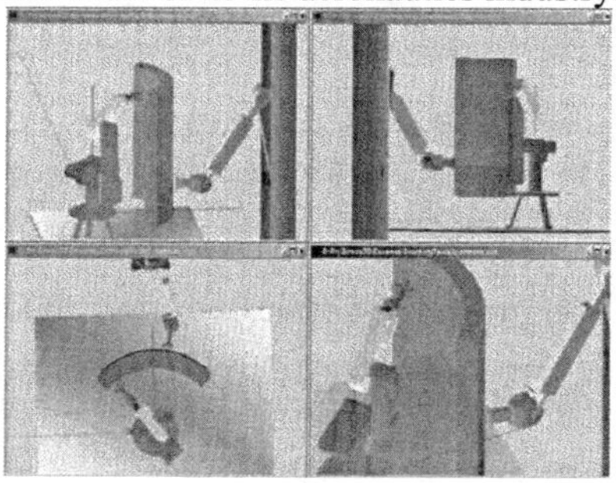

Figure 7: SIROCO 3D Simulation of robotic arms

The user can see the real robot movements on line (while performing the inspection) and navigate in the related 3D environment. He can also run off-line simulations to plan the intervention ex-ante.

5.8 Simu2

SIMU2 is a highly flexible software tool based on Virtual Reality (VR), which allows the simulation of human tasks in radiological environments, providing dosimetric information in all the points of the environment as well as the doses received by the workers during the simulated tasks performance.

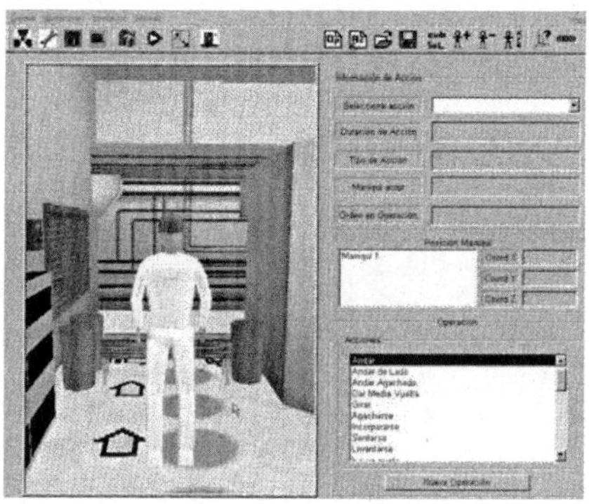

Figure 8: Human simulation SIMU2

Once defined the tasks, they can be replayed for the maintenance staff training.

5. Conclusions

VR has reached a level of maturity enough to make part of some typical internal activities in the Energy industry. Some examples belonging to several typical areas illustrate the way this technology can be successfully applied in this sector.

Planning tools and training related applications (all of them having to do with procedures) are probably the first candidates for commercialisation. "Communication" and engineering related tools are now probably the most accepted and easy to understand applications by the industry.

However, some barriers have been identified that difficult the penetration of VR in the energy industry: "psychological" barriers and cost-related barriers.

The first ones have to do with the fact that, probably, the first customers contact with this technology has taken place through the video games and this lead them to trivialize the application. This first impression is even enhanced when dealing with more complex systems like those used in Augmented Reality applications. It must be taken into account that, specially in the nuclear field, the average worker's age is relatively high.

Cost-related barriers are easier to understand: In a highly competitive environment like the recently deregulated energy market, cost considerations seems to dominate customer´s decision on the introduction of any new technology: VR is not an exception to this rule.

Following this reasoning, simplicity, flexibility and modelling are important aspects to take into account:

- low-level applications, meaning with this low cost and simply systems, are the best candidates for the commercialization of VR in this sector.
- case by case applications tend to increase the cost and represent a barrier for the introduction of this technology: therefore, tools flexibility and reusability are unavoidable requirements for any product to be developed.
- pre-existing 3D models of the facilities (plants) ease the introduction of VR. New plants with fully digitalized information are better candidates than the 20 or 30 year old ones.

References

[1] M. N. Louka, Software Toolkit for Implementing low-cost Virtual Reality Training Systems. OECD Halden Reactor Project, HWR-581, April 1999

[2] http://vr.c-s.fr/starmate/

[3] http://csalt.lancs.ac.uk/etoile/

Section 6.3

Case Studies

eAdoption and the Knowledge Economy: Issues, Applications, Case Studies
P. Cunningham and M. Cunningham (Eds.)
*IOS Press, 2004*1511

Visiting eWorkers' Homes - Three Stories for Designing eWork Homes and Furniture

Katja VIRTANEN[1], Tuuli MATTELMÄKI[1], Sirkka HEINONEN[2]
[1]*University of Art and Design Helsinki, Hämeentie 135C, Helsinki, 00560, Finland*
Tel: +358 9 75631, Fax: +358 9 75630345, Email: firstname.lastname@uiah.fi
[2]*VTT Building and Transport, P.O.Box 1800, VTT, 02044, Finland*
Tel: +358 9 4566288, Fax: +358 9 464 174, Email: sirkka.heinonen@vtt.fi

Abstract: This paper describes the results of the case study 'eWork at Home', which is focused on understanding the needs of eWorkers. Amongst the aims was to define requirements for the user-centred design of future eWork environments in a home-office or an apartment. The requirements are described in three real examples of eWork at home, which illustrate the current reality of eWork and attempts to balance work and home life. The understanding of subjective perspective can broaden the design requirements from simple visual or functional aspects by taking into account activities in social contexts, personal values and attitudes.

1. Introduction

eWork at home goes beyond the actual work tasks. The home is a private space where people relax, engage in personal interests, spend time with and take care of loved ones. However, increasingly the home is also a place for working. Working at home carries various meanings. One person considers eWork at home as a regular paid job; another might think it as working overtime, studying or taking care of business.

To offer sustainable solutions that help maintaining a work-life balance in this contradictory context, designers and other stakeholders need to learn about the needs and requirements of the real eWorkers. User-centred design offers tools for understanding eWorkers' needs holistically and also for learning about their subjective experiences. This is necessary because of the importance of understanding what, and especially how, needs and requirements are fulfilled. Thus, a combination of background research, expert interviews, quantitative marketing research and qualitative user study approaches provide a large scale of both objective information and subjective insights for design.

1.1. User-Centred Design

User-centred design aims at creating a dialogue between the designers/developers and the users starting from the beginning of the development activities continuing throughout the design project [1]. This dialogue allows iterative design of solutions.

User-centred design and participatory design have a long and strong tradition in Scandinavian design community [2]. Participatory design involves the end user as an active design member in the development of products, environments and services [3]. Recently, the attention has shifted from improving usability and ergonomic problems into wider perspectives such as experience in everyday life [4]. Tools, that are more focused on the subjective experiences, motivations and attitudes, have been introduced for application in design for user experience [e.g. 5,6,7].

One of the roles of user studies that precede design phases is to probe for design opportunities [8]. The goals include getting designers to learn to understand the people they are designing for, their experiences, motivations and actions and the context of these actions. Furthermore, the user study results provide tools for a team of researchers, designers and other stakeholders to create a common understanding of the users and to use that understanding for creating more sustainable and pleasurable solutions.

1.2. Case 'eWork at Home'

The case study 'eWork at Home' was conducted at the University of Art and Design Helsinki from July 2002 to June 2003. It was part of the three year research project Luotain – Design for user experience [9]. It involved people from Finnish furniture, real estate and design consultancy businesses and was supported by well-established eWork research.

The objective was to draw a broad picture of eWorkers at home. The main focus was on eWork spaces within the home building, furniture and tools as well as on the best practices in the eWork field. The aim was to support user-centred concept design in the three participating small and medium sized enterprises (SMEs).

The results of the case study included various visual descriptions of eWork activities, central themes, opportunities and challenges at home. Moreover, the collaborative process and the results provided a learning experience for the company participants.

2. Objectives

Usually eWork at home is treated from an organisational or management perspective [10]. In this paper eWork is understood as work in the midst of individual living. This refers to the idea that eWork takes place as an extra home activity, where primarily leisure activities take place. The availability of information technology and broadband telecommunication networks is increasing the interest in eWork and, thus, offering opportunity for increased flexibility in everyday work and life [11]. Since requirements for work and home life may have remarkably different factors, home as a workplace has special demands [12].

The objective of this paper is to illustrate the perspective of eWork and everyday life. The paper presents three stories of individual eWorkers and summarises research findings for designing future eWork environments at home. The summaries include individual motivations, needs and habits; social issues; and aesthetics, functionality and ergonomic requirements for the environment.

3. Methodology and Process

The case study applied UCD methodology, group work tools and the latest eWork research. The process comprised of four phases that included participatory sessions with users, researchers and company representatives.

3.1. Collaborative Research and Design Phases

In the first phase [See Figure 1], a background study of eWork was conducted in order to outline the issues to be addressed in the case study. The survey covered eWork as a developing phenomenon and existing home-office solutions and practices. Contextual inquiry of an eWork expert exposed the complexity of the phenomenon, but supported the focus of the user study.

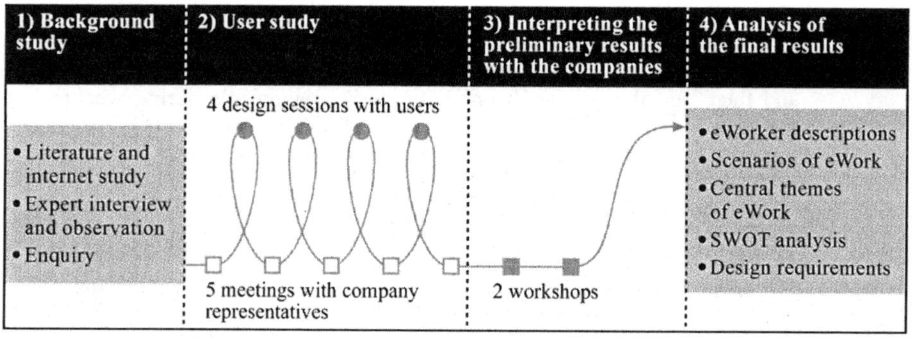

Figure 1: The four phases of the case study 'eWork at Home'.

The second phase, the user study, was the main research action in the case study. The user study aimed at understanding eWork at home with a broad interest in both concrete issues (e.g. ergonomics and electricity outlets), and more abstract issues including attitudes, activities and preferences. The focus was not on employer requirements or rules and regulations, but on the experiences of individual eWorkers. The user study lasted for ten weeks and gathered data about long-term experiences of eWork. The qualitative user study focused on five households in two newly completed apartment buildings. The households were chosen to cover various factors such as working tasks, apartment and family size.

The user study had two parallel activities: design sessions with users and their ongoing self-documentation. The design session included household-specific interviews and participatory design sessions that aimed at developing the ideal home-office furniture for eWorkers from existing modular furniture. The design consisted of 1) design of the home-office furniture based on the individual requirements and 2) redesign of the home-office furniture based on the use experience. In these design sessions, the users, company specialists and researchers were present. The users' self-documentation focused the design sessions by defining preconceptions of eWork and using the home-office.

3.2. Towards Results by Co-Operating with the Companies

The co-operation with companies played an important role in the case study. Several meetings were organized with company representatives between the design sessions to share the progressive understanding of eWork by presenting the latest user data and for focusing the user study when needed [See Figure 1].

In the third phase, the user data was interpreted into design requirements and future visions in workshops with multidisciplinary teams of company representatives and researchers. The results were further elaborated and documented into descriptions and visual summaries by the researchers in the fourth phase.

In the following chapters, three stories of eWork are presented to illustrate the results of the case study.

4. Story 1: Sam's Heavy eWork Family

Sam recently got married. The couple loves books and reading. They have collected books filling 46 metres of shelves. For them, the home is an investment for the future and a place for fulfilling their dreams. Sam's two grownup children visit him every other weekend. Work, studying and hobbies are important part of life in this active family.

The motivation for eWork at home is the ability to balance the active life for the benefit of the family. Another motivation is to be able to work in peace. Sam is the heaviest eWorker of the family. He works at home between two and four days a week. He does tasks for his work as a sales manager, runs his own business, studies for evening classes and prepares for his activities in local politics. Sam's wife finishes work documents at home every now and then, and the children work with study assignments during weekends at home. By working at home the busy family feels comfortably united with each other by being co-present. Efficient eWork hours also offer more leisure time.

Figure 2: Sam's family are active in work, studying, local politics and different hobbies. They are interested in an efficient and cosy home-office.

One room had been reserved for Sam's work [See Figure 2]. His visiting son sleeps in the room on a couch and shares the home office table with his father. The heavily equipped home-office offers Sam better facilities to work at home without the usual distractions off the office. He had purchased all the equipment needed, such as a PC, a printer, a scanner, a landline and Internet connection. Much space for organising and filing was also needed. Sam tries to keep his work material in the room and not to annoy the family.

Multiple activities guided the design of the home-office furniture in the heavy eWork family. A table with ergonomic screen-rack, shelves for frequently used items, multiple cupboards for filing, and drawers for miscellaneous items were chosen. The home-office furniture was designed to be placed next to the electric and Internet sockets. Some home-like solutions were also chosen: the ability to enjoy the scenery from the window and the space for the son's bed were taken into account. The decoration style of the apartment doors acted as inspiration for the home-office furniture.

In the redesign phase, functional and aesthetic improvements were made. As the sharing of the working space became an evident aspect during the study, more space was arranged at the table. Also, doors for some shelves were added to keep the look clean.

5. Story 2: Jan's and John's Multiple Interests

Jan and John are a young married couple. They enjoy going to the sauna after training outdoors, cooking and eating well, or planning the details of their next holiday. The home is the centre of life for them. They dream of a big single-family-house in a small town with all the possibilities for children, music, movies and maybe even billiards.

Home is not the primary work place for Jan and John. The motivation for eWork at home is because both are studying, Jan as an under-graduate and John pursuing a PhD. Presently, the only individually ergonomic environment for tasks that require peace and quiet is at home. Tasks related to reading, writing and preparation for seminars are done at home from two to five days a week, mostly in a separate study room. They underline that having a good relationship is a precondition to organising eWork flexibly.

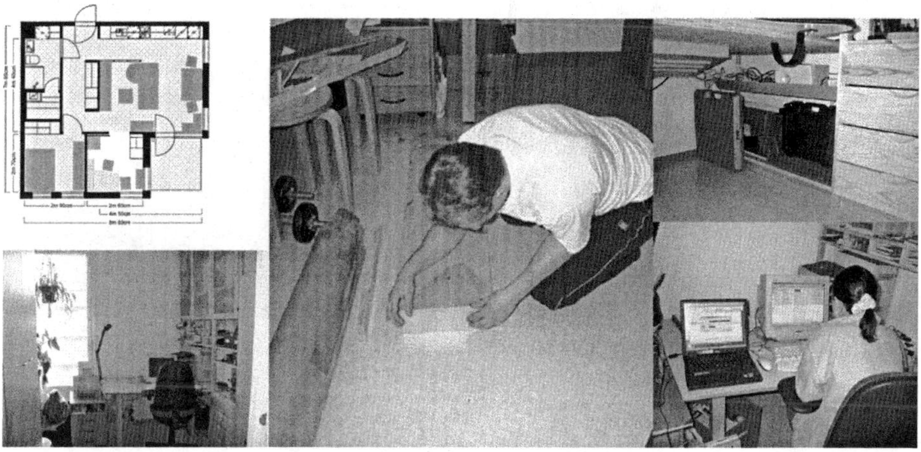

Figure 3: Jan and John are interested in many activities at home. They have a room for handcraft activities, storing hobby-related items and work, too.

Jan and John had reserved a room for studying, but also for other various interests [See Figure 3]. In the room, they do computer work with a PC and laptop by taking turns or next to each other. The original requirements led to quite traditional home-office furniture including a table with ergonomic screen-rack, shelves with pigeonholes for organizing frequently used items, cupboards for filing, and drawers for miscellaneous hobby-related items. The home-office furniture was set next to the electric and Internet sockets. Personalisation was made with light and youthful sanded glass doors. Also the scenery from the window and a place for potted plants were considered.

Later the multiplicity of the activities unfolded via self-documentation. For instance, Jan and John planned their next holiday trip to Mexico and sewed a wedding gown for a friend. Equipment for hobbies, such as sports clothes and running shoes or digital camera with all the accessories, was stored in the room.

The awareness of a multiplicity of activities guided the redesign of the home-office furniture to create more space for different activities. Some items were rearranged to create more space on the table, and more pigeonholes and drawers were added.

6. Story 3: Peter's Mobile Life

Peter is in his forties and lives alone, even though he is happily married. He regularly changes jobs and this involves living in different places. For the last three years he was in Asia and now the plan is to stay in Finland for a couple of years. Peter's wife lives and works in Rome, which is the location of their well decorated home.

The motivation for eWork is to ease life in practice. Peter's work as a manager includes many meetings that require mobility within capital area, inland and abroad. Often, meetings call for simple actions, such as writing memos, documents or e-mail. These tasks take approximately an hour, a couple of times a week or even daily, and are accomplished with a laptop. Peter wants to feel himself free to make his own decisions and eWork at home is a self-piloted way to help managing life in hectic business.

Figure 4: Peter lives in a small apartment. He is interested in light and stylish solutions that fit to his work-oriented and social ex-patriot lifestyle.

Peter's activities at home, such as sleeping, dining, watching television, socialising with friends and also working, are all located in one room [See Figure 4]. He has not reserved any specific location for work in the single-room-apartment. Since high aesthetic demands with a Scandinavian design style were set, simplicity with few and well-considered furniture were preferred when decorating the home. Peter had accepted only a bed, a sofa and a low bookcase in the apartment by the beginning of the case.

Since the current apartment is not a sustainable solution, a light, compact and easy to move home-office furniture solution was preferred. Peter's needs led to designing a home-office furniture including a table big enough for dining also, a few shelves for frequently used items, a place for a stereo set and a cupboard for storage. The home-office furniture was placed in a free space next to the kitchenette and the electric outlets. The Internet sockets are in the other side of the room. Personalisation was made with a stylish sanded glass door, and with the red-coloured table chosen to match the large wool rug.

In the redesign phase, some aesthetical improvements were made. Visual clarity and balance was created by adding pigeonholes in the shelves and an extra door of sanded glass.

7. Visions

These stories presented three very different eWork narratives from individual perspectives. The following table summarises the essential elements which should be addressed when designing future homes and furniture for eWork [See Table 1]. The elements are drawn from the three stories including eWorkers' needs, values, motivations, attitudes and experiences. They cannot be generalised as such. However, they are guiding design briefs into a more human and design solutions into more socially sustainable direction.

The eWorkers' homes and furniture need to fit into the high demand of combining personal lives and work into a sustainable, work-life balanced setting. In the case the participants' home-office furniture was combined from the existing modular solutions. Based on the findings of the study the ideal solutions could be quite different and more closely integrated with life situation, style, values and activities of individuals:

- Sam's family has a room where different tasks and interests are shared. This socially active family has guests often. A more suitable design solution would be a clapperboard like unit with cupboards to shelter private material. Instead of an openly untidy desk to be cleaned for guests, it would provide aesthetical and functional unit.

- Jan and John are mostly interested in leisure time activities but they also work at home. A room with modular furniture elements would configure the environment and support their current activities.
- Peter occasionally sends e-mail at the end of a long day on a business trip. He is interested in aesthetics and invites a friend sometimes for a glass of exquisite red wine in his small apartment. A table with stylish armchairs for socialising and eating, and a small cabinet with wheels next to his sofa for work would better fit his preferences.

Table 1: Summary of the essential elements from the three stories to be addressed when designing future eWork homes and furniture.

	Sam's Heavy eWork family	Jan's and John's Multiple Interests	Peter's Mobile Life
Apartment	4-room-apartment	3-room-apartment	1-room-apartment
Residents	2 adults and 2 adult children every 2nd week	2 adults	1 adult
Personal values	Well-being of the family, interests in many fields of work and leisure time	Family-centred, leisure time oriented with multiple interests	Work-oriented ex-patriot, self-piloted independence
Personal motivation for eWork	Work-life balance in family	External circumstances	Ease life in practice
Personal attitude to activities in home-office	Multiple work tasks	Varying tasks of multiple interests	Simple work tasks
Other requirements	Office-like furniture in home environment	Multi functional activity room	Aesthetic and light combination of work and dining

The concrete requirements identified in the case study related to equipment, transportation and connections, electrical and telecommunication accessibility, storage and working position can be used as a check list for design. The primary result is the illustrated stories of individual eWorkers everyday life situations, which can be utilised to support design empathy, inspiration and understanding the phenomenon.

8. Conclusions

In the presented case 'eWork at Home' holistic personal aspects of home and many overlapping and even contradictory activities were progressively unfolded. To the company representatives a new layer of understanding grew through their active participation. The company representatives stated the complexity of user segments when considering home context. Rather than crystallizing a stereotypical, average resident, user or eWorker, individual preferences were emphasised. Users are all individuals with varying needs and there is no sustainable or commercial sense in offering the same solutions for all of them. Thus, the most familiar office-like home-office is now seen as only one solution.

In fact, designing future eWork homes and furniture should emerge from lifestyles, activities, personal preferences and ways of working. Although ease of use and availability of technology are crucial, design emphasis should be on living at home and on activities, such as spending time together, doing hobbies or work. Home-office solutions should allow more variation also for social interaction. Apartment and furniture should allow flexible possibilities for re-configuration of environments according to the current life situations and activities and could be improved with ambient intelligent.

The future challenge is to grasp the novel understanding, and to use it as an inspirational starting point for designing homes, furniture and other related facilities for people working in the middle of living. Ideally, different aspects of the environment are developed with common visions. Co-operation should include user-centred approaches or participatory design with eWorkers, employers, building constructors, manufacturers, maintenance and others. Modular and configurable solutions created by the multidisciplinary design teams could enable individual eWork at home in a pleasurable and socially sustainable way.

Acknowledgements

We thank the case participants and companies for collaboration and co-workers at University of Art and Design for valuable feedback.

References

[1] Gould, John D. & Lewis, Clayton (1985): Designing for usability: key principles and what designers think. In Communications of the ACM, 28(3), 1985, 300-311
[2] Ehn, Pelle & Badham, Richard (2002). Participatory Design and the Collective Designer. In the Proceedings of the Participatory Design Conference PDC 02, 1-10. Malmö
[3] Kyng, Morten & Mathiassen, Lars (1997). Computers and Design in Context. The MIT Press, Massachusetts
[4] Sanders, Elizabeth B.-N. From User-Centered to Participatory Design Approaches. http://www.sonicrim.com/red/us/commune/papers/Canadapaper.pdf . 6.5.2003
[5] Sanders, Elizabeth B.-N & Dandavate, Uday (1999). Design for experiencing: New tools. In the Proceedings of the first international Conference on Design and Emotion, 87-92. Delft
[6] Mattelmäki, Tuuli (2003). Probes: Studying Experiences for Design Empathy. In Koskinen, I., Battarbee, K. & Mattelmäki, T. (Editors). Empathic Design – User Experience in Product Design. ITPress, Finland
[7] Buchenau, Marion & Fulton Suri, Jane (2000). Experience prototyping. In the Proceedings of DIS2000, 424-433. New York
[8] Mattelmäki, Tuuli (2003). VÄINÖ – taking user-centred steps with probes. In the Proceedings of Include Conference 2003. RCA, London
[9] http://smart.uiah.fi/luotain/eng_index.htm
[10] Heinonen, Sirkka (2000). Analysis of the Finnish Telework Potential. Ministry of Labour, Helsinki http://www.mol.fi/esf/ennakointi/raportit/telework.pdf
[11] Heinonen, Sirkka & Niskanen, Saija (2003). Etätyö työssä jaksamisen tukena. (Telework As A Bridge to Job Satisfaction, in Finnish with an English abstract). Working Papers 16, Ministry of Labour, Helsinki
[12] Lally, Elaine (2002). At Home with Computers. Berg Pub, Cornwall

eAdoption and the Knowledge Economy: Issues, Applications, Case Studies
P. Cunningham and M. Cunningham (Eds.)
IOS Press, 2004

Evaluation of an AmI Workplace

Andrew HARRISON[1], Pete STEGGLES[2]
[1]*DEGW, 8 Crinan Street, London, N16 0AJ, United Kingdom*
Tel: +44 207 239 7728, Fax: + 44 207 278 3613, Email: aharrison@degw.com
[2]*Ubisense, 1 Quayside, Cambridge, CB5 8AB., United Kingdom*
Tel: +44 1223 448170, Fax: + 44 448167 Email: pete.steggles@ubisense.net

Abstract: The Sentient Computing system developed by AT&T was used to investigate the possible impact of AmI based applications on social and functional aspects of the workplace. Key issues that were explored included the reaction of the building's occupants to the introduction of Sentient Computing throughout the building and a comparison of AmI based workplace evaluation measures with existing proprietary workplace evaluation tools. Users generally felt that the Sentient computer system had had a positive impact on people's work, particularly in the areas of teamwork, mobility within the office, talking with colleagues and telephone use. The majority of respondents did not report any concerns about privacy. It was also found that Sentient Computing can be used successfully for space use analysis, and provides information that can complement existing workplace evaluation techniques. Future research should consider privacy and trust issues in more detail and the development of European standards for location based applications.

1. Introduction

The 1990s have seen major changes in the way that space and time are used in many organisations. New Ways of working have allowed many organisations to integrate the physical work environment into the business process, to increase density of occupation within office buildings while at the same time creating effective work environments that encourage interaction and communication.

The current decade will see even greater challenges: both at the level of the individual trying to use the scarce resource of time more effectively and at the level of the organisation trying to manage a dispersed workforce while creating the spirit and teamwork necessary for organisations to continue to generate new ideas and thrive. Increasingly organisations will move outside of the physical container of their own buildings into larger organisational networks across cities, countries, the region or the world.

The implications of the distributed workplace were explored in detail through SANE (Sustainable Accommodation for the New Economy) in FP5 [1]. The focus of this project is on the creation of sustainable, collaborative workplaces for knowledge workers across Europe, encompassing both virtual and physical spaces. One of the core hypotheses explored by the SANE project was that as the level of remote working increases in an organisation it may not be desirable to house all types of workplace in the same location. Distributing workplaces around the city may allow staff to reduce the amount of commuting they need to do and allow the organisation to start using the attributes of the city to reinforce organisational culture and community. Organisations are increasingly incorporating semi-public spaces such as hotels, serviced office centres, airport lounges and cafes into their work environments. If this move away from owned organisational space is taken to its extreme it is possible to envisage an organisation where virtual work environments are used to house the organisation's knowledge and information resources and all physical work takes place in either individually owned space (for example, staff working at home) or in shared work environments booked on an 'as-needed' basis.

Shared workplaces have the potential to be large, anonymous workplaces where there is little interaction or sense of community. An airline lounge on a large scale, with people arriving, working and moving on without any sort of meaningful social experience.

It was felt that AmI applications can help to change this by making sense of the shared space, providing access to the spaces, services and people who inhabit the facility and to act as the catalyst for new types of interaction and communications between the occupants of the space. AmI can also act as the bridge back to the cultures and communities of the 'home' organizations of many of the users and will help these workers to continue to feel part of the organization, regardless of where they are physically located.

In 2000, the researchers at AT&T Labs Cambridge [4] created an AmI system that used ultrasonic technology to provide a location accuracy of about 3cm throughout AT&T's 1,000 m^2 building, making it the most accurate large-scale wireless sensor system in the world at that time. The research team implemented a distributed object model, which integrated location and resource status data for all the objects and people in the building, and an abstraction for expressing spatial relationships, allowing applications to detect spatial relationships between objects in a way that seemed natural to human users.

As part of the SANE project a validation exercise was undertaken at AT&T Laboratories in Cambridge [3] to explore some of the issues and the utility of AMI-based workplace measurement applications, using the Sentient Computing system developed by AT&T. This paper reviews the results of this exercise and presents the results obtained using AmI based workplace measurement tools and using existing time utilisation tools.

Since this work was done, the key members of the AT&T Labs research team have formed Ubisense [5], a company dedicated to making AmI a reality by making available a platform for location-aware 'Smart Space' applications. Such a platform has been made commercially feasible by the regulatory approval of UWB radio in the US (and hopefully soon in the EU). Ubisense's UWB location sensing system provides similar capabilities to the system at AT&T Labs Cambridge for a fraction of the cost. Several major international companies are currently exploring the feasibility of installing location awareness space measurement tools in R&D and other high value workplaces.

2. Methodology

The primary objective of this research was to explore the possible impact of AmI based applications on both the social and functional aspects of the workplace. Key issues that were explored included:

1. The reaction of the building's occupants to the use of AmI throughout the building
2. The reaction of potential end users to AmI workplace applications
3. A comparison of AmI based workplace evaluation measures with existing proprietary evaluation tools involving the use of observers and handheld computers
4. The development of scenarios for use of AmI in the workplace

To explore the potential impact of AmI applications on the workforce the research team used a number of methods involving both the staff at the laboratory and visiting designers and representations of large workplace occupiers

- Data collection on space use at the AT&T lab.
  - A Workplace Performance Survey (WPS) was given to all staff at the lab that explored their opinions about the work environment.
  - A one week long Time Utilization Survey (TUS) was conducted to measure how the spaces in the building were actually being used. In a TUS the emphasis is placed on observation by trained staff who interpret activity at a high level.

  - Anonymized data collected by the Sentient Computing system (during the same period as the TUS) was analysed. Here the emphasis was placed on how much data could be derived purely by automated analysis without a human observer.
- Workshops with AT&T researchers developing scenarios for use of AmI at work.
  - Data from TUS/ WPS was reviewed and workplace issues explored in more depth including the perceptions of contribution of AmI to the work environment.
  - The research team jointly developed scenarios for how AmI could be used in different types of work and learning environments.

3. Data Collection on Space Use at AT&T Labs

3.1 Workplace Performance Survey

The Workplace Performance Survey asks office staff for their perception of the importance and effectiveness of their office space - how well it supports the work they are doing.

Bar charts broken down by department or work group or job group show the average importance and performance of each aspect of the office environment. The analysis also provides information for each department/work group/job type such as:

- the performance of the most important items
- the worst-performing items
- the best-performing items

DEGW's standard Workplace Performance Survey (WPS) was modified to include specific questions related to AmI. For each of eight specified uses of the Sentient system, respondents were asked how frequently they used the system for this purpose and how easy to use the system was for this purpose. The overwhelming response was that introducing the Sentient Computing system had had a positive impact on people's work. The aspects of work which the highest numbers of respondents felt had been improved were:

- teamwork,
- mobility within the office,
- talking with colleagues and
- telephone use.

The aspects of work where a majority felt there was no impact were:

- using other electronic means of communication,
- communicating with colleagues when you are away from the office,
- information storage and retrieval and
- information sharing

The majority (almost three quarters) of respondents did not report any concerns about privacy. However, almost as many said that there were occasions on which they did not wish to be shown on the system. Examples of situations when they did not want to be shown included: lunch breaks (two people), times when they didn't wish to be disturbed / were trying to concentrate (three people), when in the toilet (two people), when not in the building (one person) and when dealing with confidential matters (two people).

3.2 Time Utilisation Survey

The Time Utilisation Survey is a method for quickly and cost-effectively obtaining quantitative information about how the office is used. Specific locations in the building are monitored closely by trained observers using hand-held computers. The data on the number of people and their activities at each location provide an objective picture of how the building is used throughout the working day and week.

The data are collected as the observers walk round a predetermined route through the building at regular intervals; this creates the minimum of disruption to staff and avoids giving anyone the feeling they are being watched. The programme of a Time Utilisation Survey is carefully planned to ensure that the working patterns observed are representative yet also take into account regular fluctuations in staff activities.

The Time Utilisation Survey covered 74 different spaces within the AT&T Laboratory at Cambridge; these consisted of 47 allocated workspaces plus a variety of shared ancillary (allocated to a team) and support spaces (shared by the entire population of the laboratory). These spaces were observed at half-hourly intervals over a typical working week.

The figure below shows the daily activity pattern (averaged across the whole study) in the 47 workspaces. It splits the observations (colour coded) into eight activities (when workspace is occupied) plus temporarily unoccupied (workspace is in use today but the user was not there at the time of the observation), empty (not in use today), and not obtainable

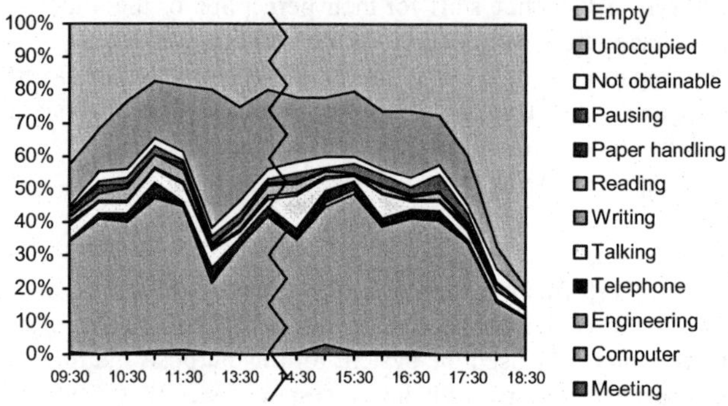

Figure 1: TUS analysis summary - Daily activity pattern in 47 workspaces

Approximately 20%-35% of workspaces were empty during each observation circuit (during the main part of the day). Around 20% of workspaces were temporarily unoccupied during each observation circuit, indicating that staff were elsewhere in the building ('internal mobility'). The predominant activity was computing and there were very few meetings at people's workspaces.

3.3 Space Use Measurement Using Sentient Computing

The sentient computing system was used during the same period to capture data about the locations of individuals.

The goal was to use sentient computing without additional information to enable a wholly-automated analysis of workplace use. The analytical steps taken were as follows.

1. Use the physical structure of the workplace setting and its furnishings to generate disjoint zones that have high-level architectural meaning.
2. Translate location data generated by the sensors into zonal containment data.
3. Record several complete days' sets of readings.
4. Create a zonal probability function for people to establish 'normal' building usage.
5. Use the zonal probability function and region data to characterise and measure mobility and interaction properties of regions automatically.
6. Categorise regions by looking at histograms of region mobility & interaction properties.

The key characteristic of this research is point (1) above. The space use measurement should be expressed in terms that are directly related to the kinds of decisions workplace designers make. Given the assumption that designers and users might want to reconfigure their buildings by redeploying furniture and partitions, it is appropriate to describe the spaces in the building in terms of these structural elements. One way of doing this is to give each structural element a 'sphere of influence', and so break the building up into zones each of which is associated with some structural element.

The analysis shown below breaks the building down into regions dominated by desks/tables and doors (which might be gaps between partitions). Initial linear 'seed' regions are created corresponding to the front of each desk/table and the line corresponding to each doorway. Where these seed regions overlap they are merged into one region (so that desks can be pushed together to create one work station); the regions are then grown at a constant velocity until the whole building is covered. This breaks the building up into a set of disjoint spaces that correspond well to the actual workspaces used in the building.

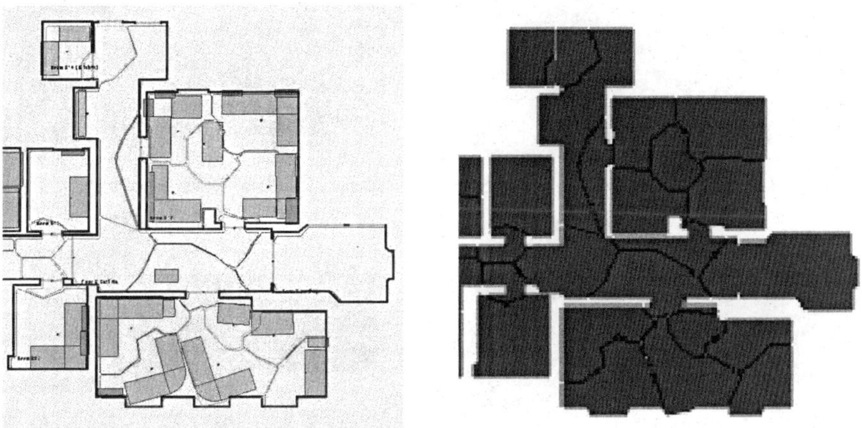

Figure 2: Automated region detection – furniture and doorways are used to automatically generate seed lines that are grown into a set of disjoint regions that cover the space. The resulting regions correspond well to real individual workspaces.

By segmenting the space into regions, it is then possible to use geometry monitoring to determine precisely the entry and exit times of individuals into and out of these regions.

This zone occupation information makes it possible to model normal building use. By dividing the total time person **p** spends in a given zone **z** by the data capture period duration, we get **(pdf p z)**, the probability of finding the person in that zone. By dividing the time person **p** spends in a given zone **z** by the time **p** spends in any zone, we get **(cpdf p z)**, the conditional probability of finding the person in zone **z**, if they are in the building.

Using the **cpdf** function, it is possible to characterise what it is for a person to be a stranger in a zone. Person **p** is a stranger in a zone **z** if **(cpdf p z)** is less than 0.25. In this way, it is possible to categorize individual regions based on the style of their occupancy.

Motion space. For each zone **z**, count the number of times that a person enters **z** and then leaves **z** within 10 seconds. Plotting a coloured map (Figure 3) of these zones shows spaces where people move (the redder the zone, the more motion going on). Unsurprisingly, in the AT&T building the corridors are the motion spaces. The results would be more interesting in an open plan design.

Owned space. For each zone **z**, consider the maximum value of **(cpdf p z)**, for any **p**. Plotting a map (Figure 4) of the zones, where red indicates a probability of 1 and blue indicates a probability of 0, highlights 'owned spaces', which are coloured red because some specific person is very likely to be found in each one. A large number of these spaces were identified in the AT&T building because the style of working there did not involve much physical mobility.

Space where one worker visits another. A zone is in this state if there is more than one person in it, there are no visitors present, and some but not all the people are a strangers in the zone. Plotting a coloured map (Figure 5) of these zones shows where it is more likely that a person visits another person who is based in the zone.

Space supporting based lone working. A zone is in this state if there is only one person in it, that person is not a visitor, and the person is not a stranger in the zone. Plotting a coloured map (Figure 6) of these zones shows where it is more likely that a worker will be working alone at his/her accustomed workstation.

Many such metrics are possible and several more are discussed and illustrated in [3], including the use of shared and communal spaces for individual work and interaction, and the frequency and activity of visitors by location.

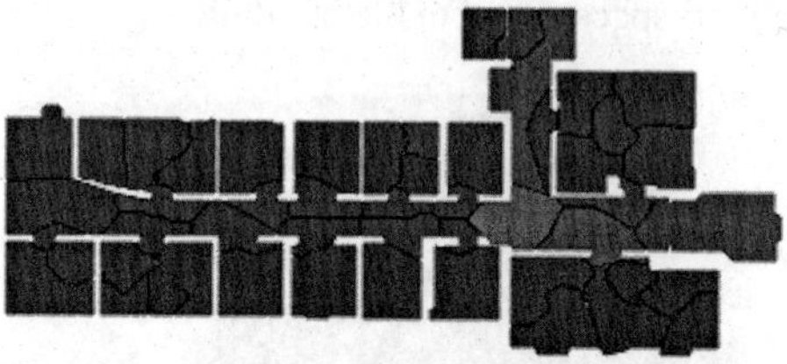

Figure 3: Workers move through a space

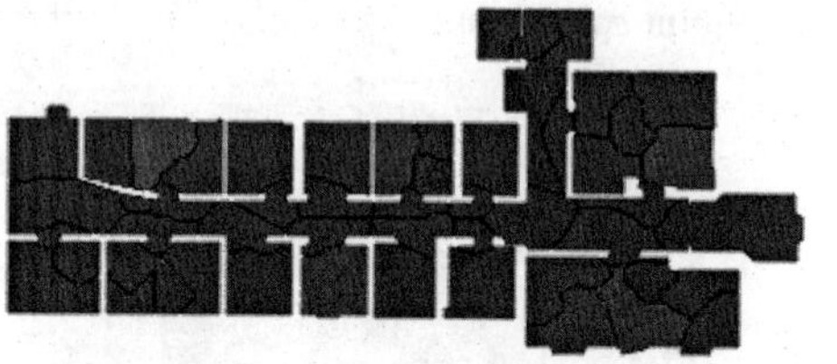

Figure 5: Worker visits owner of a space

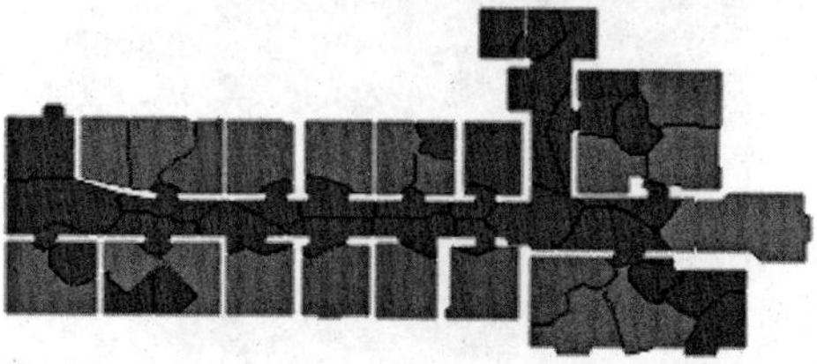

Figure 4: A single worker 'owns' a space

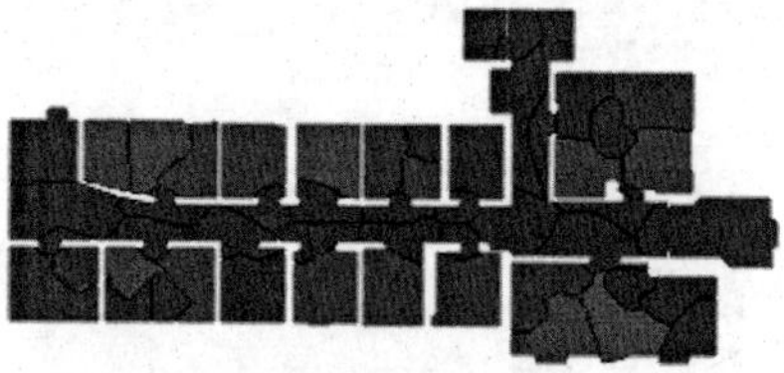

Figure 6: Lone working occurs in a space

Figures 3-6: Examples of Sentient Computing automated space use analysis: spaces are categorized using various metrics as described in the text above.

This technique seems to be quite successful for space use analysis: it is possible to automatically categorise zones, identifying which zones are used for which roles, and to measure exactly how much of each kind of activity occurs in each zone.

The analysis here looks at space in a context of complete anonymity. However by also using the identities of the individuals involved one can work out who works on each project, who supervises or liases between projects and so on. Without necessarily divulging this information, one could then feed it back into the space usage analysis to work out which projects use which spaces, how much interaction occurs between projects, which spaces are most popular for inter- and intra- project meetings and so on.

An obvious extension of this analysis is to consider the time that the events occurred: by building up probability functions over periods of time of varying lengths (longer and shorter than one day), by making more use time of day and duration in region state categorisation, and by seeing how our current categorisations change throughout the day.

Another area that has not yet been considered is equipment use data: who phones whom, and where; who moves their computer desktop where; who uses any given device, and where they do it; even, when applications are fully integrated with the sentient computing system, who chooses which option, and where they do it. This kind of data might be especially interesting when interactions between people, spaces and equipment are very complex, for example, in a hospital or complex manufacturing environment.

3.4 Comparing and Combining Sentient Computing and TUS

The Time Utilisation Survey focuses on the general patterns of activities in different kinds of spaces. It can also show group sizes. It cannot, though, provide information about *who* is doing what, where. Because Sentient Computing is person-oriented, it can provide information on people's habits, their appropriation of spaces, etc. It can indicate who collaborates with whom which could provide useful information on adjacencies for space planning. Conversely, because of its inability to establish *what* was happening in some zone, Sentient Computing is not strong on providing 'work process' information, but, if integrated fully with information systems, it may actually provide better (more detailed) information than the Time Utilisation Survey can, at some future stage (especially since the TUS is limited by what activities untrained outside observers can discriminate).

One potential avenue for further exploration is the combination of Sentient Computing and TUS analysis. By using Sentient Computing to guide the TUS researcher to those areas of the workplace where 'interesting' events are occurring, we could make best use of the interpretive abilities of the observer.

4. Other Scenarios for Use of AmI in the Workplace

The results of the user research and the comparison of AmI based workplace evaluation methodologies confirmed the research team's belief that AmI has a major role to play in the future workplace. This was further confirmed during the workshops and interviews with potential end users that formed the basis of the development of use scenarios. Application modules are envisaged to support a wide range of workplace applications.

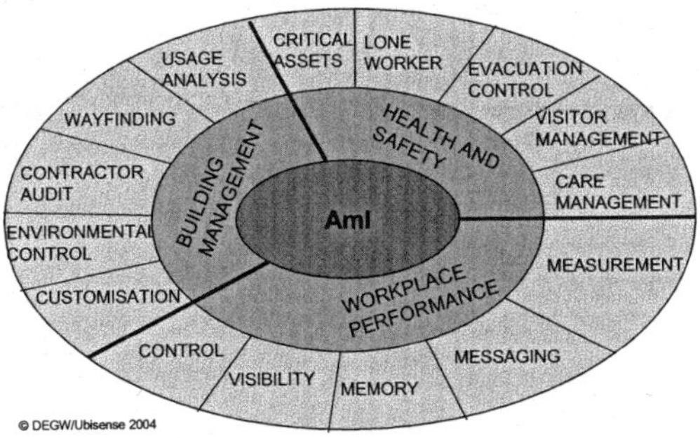

Figure 7: Potential AmI applications to support the distributed workplace

5. Conclusions

AmI has an important role to play in the future workplace and it will significantly change the way that space is procured, used and managed in many settings. Analysis of the use of the Sentient Computing system at the AT&T Laboratory in Cambridge found that the majority of system users believed that the system provided significant benefits for them and enhanced their working day. Further more the information collected by the Sentient Computing system can be used to analysis how individuals and groups of people use space over time. This analysis can be used to better understand how the workplace is functioning to support the business process and may also form the basis of a wide range of new workplace application in the future.

The introduction of AmI applications to the workplace raises significant concerns about privacy and trust issues. Concerns about the use of both external and internal positioning systems centre around the right to individual privacy and the fear that the information generated by the positioning system will be put to unauthorized uses such as monitoring employees or providing the information to external groups who could use it to aid criminal or terrorist activity.

These concerns are very real but relate to the negative use of such a system and discount the benefits that these same individuals may get from the system in terms of individual security and safety, increased community and connection to colleagues, and enhanced effectiveness.

Primary social research is required to understand in more detail what people's concerns are, to understand how the rights of individuals and organizations can be protected and to determine the types of contract or rules that must be in place if a locational system is to be used in a particular environment. The hypothesis to be tested by this research is that people will be willing to be part of a locational system if the benefits of the use of the system outweigh the negative consequences.

Further research is also required to support development of standards that will allow location sensor systems from different manufacturers to inter-operate and be easily integrated with location management platforms. These standards might also define how local positioning systems will work with other location and identification technologies, such as GPS/Galileo, RFID and mobile phone location services.

The first installations of Ubisense's UWB successor to Sentient Computing are now running at several sites including the University of Illinois, and the University of Cambridge. A system will also be running at DEGW before the end of 2004. It is envisioned that the DEGW installation will be used to support research in both these areas.

References

[1] SANE. SANE (Sustainable Accommodation for the New Economy) project funded by the European Commission, under Framework V ('New Ways of Working', contract nr. IST-2000-25257) with partners from DEGW (London), Ove Arup (London'), RHUL (London), Telenor (Oslo), IAT (Stuttgart), Institut Cerda (Barcelona) und FAW (Ulm).

[2] Harrison, A. et al (eds), The Distributed Workplace, E&FN Spon, London 2004

[3] SANE. DEGW Validation Exercise Cycle One: Extended report, WP4 internal deliverable, June 2002.

[4] Mike Addlesee, Rupert Curwen, Steve Hodges, Joe Newman, Pete Steggles, Andy Ward, Andy Hopper. Implementing a Sentient Computing System. *IEEE Computer Magazine*, Vol. 34, No. 8, August 2001, pp. 50-56.

[5] Ubisense Web site. http://www.ubisense.net

eAdoption and the Knowledge Economy: Issues, Applications, Case Studies
P. Cunningham and M. Cunningham (Eds.)
IOS Press, 2004

Citizen-centric Network of Professionals: Well-being Services @ Work

Niilo SARANUMMI
VTT Information Technology, PO Box 1206, 33101 Tampere, Finland
Tel: +358-3-316 3300, Fax: +358-3-316 3380, Email: niilo.saranummi@vtt.fi

Abstract: The Well-being Services @ Work Community seeks to innovate new working environments and new ways of working for health professionals, citizens and patients that provide better value services. The working method is based on scenarios and roadmaps. Scenarios are analysed based on identifying technological challenges and systemic factors that hinder or enable the diffusion of the new ideas in the health practice. An essential part of the process from idea to innovation is to show that the idea works in real-life situations, that it is benchmarked against existing work practices to show that it is cost-effective and efficient, and that it complies with the relevant legislation (the trust aspect).

1. Changing healthcare environment

National health systems in all countries have similar goals with regard to access, equity, quality and cost. The provision of health services is based on a varying mix of public, private and 3rd sector providers. Health systems are publicly regulated based on national legislation prescribing e.g. patient rights, terms relating to production of health services, funding / payment / reimbursement mechanisms, rights to practicing medicine (and other health professions), data protection and privacy of data (partly covered by an EU directive), and safety and security of health technologies (e.g. EU Directives, US FDA requirements).

Today healthcare systems experience pressure for change from inside and outside. From the inside, the continuing innovation in medicine and healthcare technologies expands the methods and tools available in healthcare. Combined with citizen empowerment the demographic changes of an ageing European population stretch the limits of what countries can afford to offer as services of their national health systems. Governments are confronted by the need to find means to limit the rise in healthcare costs. Consequently, at national level health policies, incentives and guidelines for payers and providers of health services are being adjusted to meet the national targets relating to access, equity, quality and cost.

Changes in the framework conditions have lead healthcare enterprises to investigate new ways to organise and deliver health services. They have been slow in embracing the possibilities offered by eWork and ICT to streamline processes and services, and to create new "business" opportunities, such as selling excess capacity or buying-in services. To some extent this is due to the fact that the incentives for healthcare organisations to step outside their established boundaries do not exist. At the grass root level however, eWork has gained acceptance. Healthcare professionals have in their domains of speciality adopted new technologies when these add value to their present work practises. In imaging services radiologists routinely access imaging studies from home through secure web interfaces. These remote services are part of the Picture Archiving and Communication Systems that many vendors offer today. Telemedicine is a broader concept where eWork is present.

The expectation is that national health systems will open up in the near future and health services will be traded across regional and country borders. Some of these services will continue to require a physical encounter between patients and healthcare professionals.

However, some of these services will be produced by virtual organisations. The important thing to notice is that the virtual healthcare provider has to operate in accordance with all relevant legislation and rules governing the practice of medicine, production of health services, reimbursement of services, and access to confidential patient data.

The traditional care and cure oriented healthcare is changing towards a more comprehensive approach where the citizen and patient also is expected to play an active role together with the healthcare team of specialised professionals. With the ageing population and current life styles chronic degenerative diseases are becoming more prevalent. The proper management of such conditions based on clinical evidence mandates active interventions to change life styles, diet and to increase exercise. Wellness management is seen as a highly important instrument to maintain an acceptable level of health. The role of the individual in carrying out these interventions is of course central for success. A further extension of health relates to facilitating by means of technology and technology based services the independent living of elderly in their natural surroundings.

All these changes call for new ways to organise and provide health and wellness services to the population, including patients. The health domain is generally viewed (see Figure 1) as being behind the business sectors in adopting and utilising technologies that enable new ways to organise, provide and pay for (health) services.

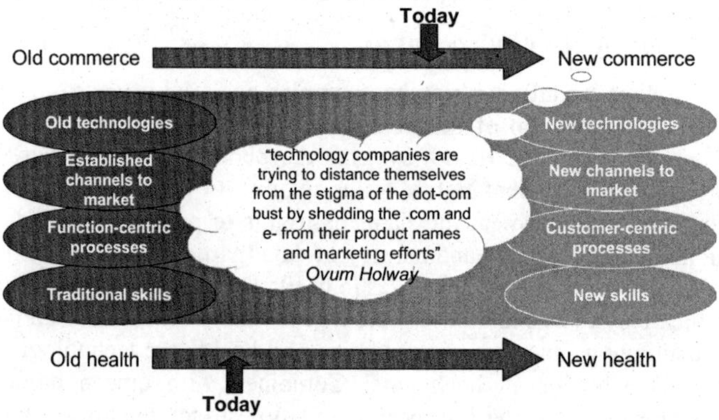

Figure 1: Comparison of the health and commerce domains in transition from "old world" to "new world"

ICT / Information Society Technologies have a central role to play in the reorganisation of the healthcare service delivery environment by facilitating and enabling new trusted and secure ways of working, collaborating and sharing of knowledge. The "eHealth dot.com bubble" a few years back, however, taught us an important lesson. As a rule, citizens and patients are not willing to pay for eHealth services directly. Instead they expect these services to be made available by existing health service providers and to be paid as part of the regular, normal, service. Therefore new health-related "eServices" need be seen as an extension and sometimes a replacement of the services healthcare organisations are already providing. They must be integrated with normal existing business (healthcare) processes in order to add value to existing services and to leverage the infrastructure. A proof-of-concept implementation in real life conditions is needed in order to create the evidence of cost-effectiveness and to argue convincingly how the costs can be reimbursed.

2. Characteristics of the healthcare working environment

The healthcare working environment has a number of distinguishing characteristics. First, the combination of knowledge, information and data is central in diagnosing, treating and monitoring patients. Second, it is a collaboration intensive environment where care is generally delivered by well-organised teams, and sometimes in acute cases by ad-hoc teams. Collaboration is typically via Peer-to-Peer communication along well-established procedures. Third, decision support by consulting colleagues and other experts for second opinions or by referring patients to other specialists or by accessing structured pieces of medical knowledge and clinical guidelines in textbooks, articles etc. are features of modern healthcare. Fourth, professionalism is a very strong feature in the practice of medicine and the master - apprentice relationship in on the job training is still highly important.

In addition to these profession centred features, the role of patients and their immediate family (interactive patient participation) has gained in importance with patient empowerment and a deeper understanding of the role of the patient (and her immediate family) in solving and managing health problems, especially chronic, degenerative conditions (such as the management of diabetes, asthma or hypertension). In addition to the need to manage illnesses more emphasis is being given to wellness management in all its forms. This starts with public health promotional issues (such as quitting smoking, use of alcohol and other substances), life style guidance (such as exercise and diet) leading to health monitoring based on wearable sensors and ambient intelligence technologies.

In the health care domain management approaches are gaining ground and the old administration, resource-usage focused approach is being replaced by concepts such as citizen-centred care and continuity of care. Care processes are being streamlined and production management concepts are being tried out. Although concepts such as workflow management and shared knowledge spaces (repositories) have been coined elsewhere, healthcare has been among the first to make use of these. The distinction, though, is that most of this is taking place without explicit usage of ICT.

3. Need for systemic innovation

ICT and Ambient intelligence (AMI) technologies on one hand and new organisational forms on the other are strongly intertwined. The traditional technology innovation viewpoint of new product development or new system development does not address this interdependence and needs to be replaced by a more integrated innovation viewpoint. Systemic Innovation refers to changes and adaptations in the integrated system of healthcare processes and services, institutional and organisational structures and products and technological systems. It is characterised as a combined effort of service and technology providers and other actors. These cannot be controlled or managed by a single actor but, instead, requires continuous dialogue and negotiation between the actors.

In general, innovation depends heavily on interactions between universities, academic medical centres and industrial companies where a dialogue must be created and sustained across numerous individuals with diverse perspectives. Such collaboration differs in nature from co-operation within organisations or between private companies. The former relationships are not mediated by hierarchy or by market mechanisms. It is more about negotiation between actors involving a wide range of issues such as the roles to be played by different participants and the nature of the problem to be addressed. Building trust and developing negotiation skills are definitive challenges for collaboration.

In the healthcare domain, existing services and technologies are embedded deeply in wider social and technological systems (Figure 2). These create economic, technological, social, cognitive, cultural and political barriers for innovation. The notion of "technological regime" has been introduced to explain why most innovations are incremental and why more radical innovations remain on the shelf. It explains why diffusion is especially slow in the case of systemic innovations that require changes in the context of the technology in question. Technological regime can be defined as the whole complex of user practices, scientific knowledge, symbolic meanings of technology and services, service characteristics, skills and procedures, infrastructure, organisational structures and policy.

The need for collaboration is confronted with several mechanisms that interactively tend to maintain the existing core capabilities. They relate to economics, politics of power and behaviour. Attacking core rigidities often means undermining the current economic foundations, managers and powerful experts are understandably reluctant to give up their political power, and organisational routines are ingrained. Changes in organisational procedures often call for changes in skills. Skills frequently become closely entwined with people's identity so that the requirement to switch skill bases is experienced as an attack on their very being. Organisational change is always a demanding and slow process. An organisation's core capabilities can become its core rigidities [1, 2].

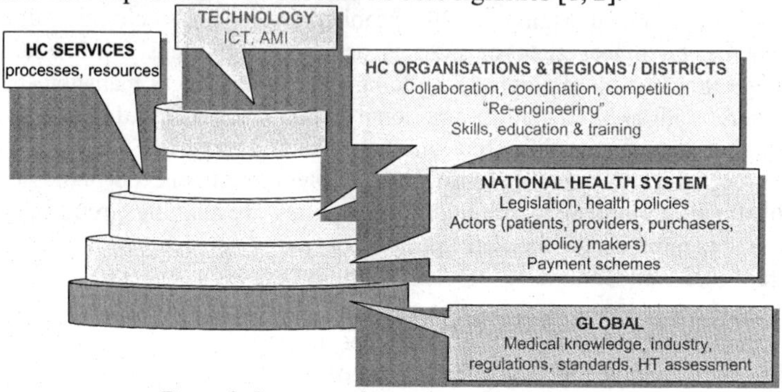

Figure 2: Interacting hierarchies of health systems

The challenge for systemic innovation in healthcare creates a strong need for documented evidence of success stories. The barriers for systemic innovation are multiple as explained above. The barriers and the need for systemic innovation also explain why so few of the new ideas on utilising ICT and AMI in healthcare have been successful in the marketplace. E.g. the EU Commission has over the years funded several ICT projects in the general area of diabetes management, many focusing on the aspect of facilitating the interaction of the various actors (incl. patients and their families) in the management of the chronic disease. The diffusion of the results and products of these projects in healthcare has been a disappointment to many, but can be explained by the lack of documented evidence of benefits to the patients, population and the health system.

The old paradigm of technology introducing and catalysing change is not working in the distributed healthcare environment. Therefore it needs to be replaced by value chain and service views complemented with an understanding of the actors (stakeholders) and their interests [3]. Figure 2 illustrates the healthcare innovation space and its interacting hierarchies. Various frameworks have been proposed to improve our understanding of the complexities involved. These include e.g. Strategic Niche Management [4, 5], Societal Embedding [6] and Transition Management [7, 8].

4. Ambient Intelligence Technologies and Well-Being Services@Work

The New Working Environments unit of DG INFSO has contributed towards the launching a number of self-organising communities in the European Research Area focusing on the impact of ambient intelligence (AMI) technologies on work and working environments. The formal launch event of the communities took place in June 2004. The proposition is that AMI technologies enable changes in organisational forms and organisational forms motivate changes in technology. The enabling technologies which interest the communities are foreseen to include for example: trust, security and privacy enhancing technologies; individually driven working; new work space designs; knowledge management in information dense and integrated, often media-rich working environments, including mobility and multimodality; collaborative work and organisations, ambient organisations, communities of practise and new organisation of work. The communities are organised into a kind of a "crossroads" format with half of them focusing on specific generic technologies and another half on specific sectors. The communities are expected to interact with each others in order to cross-fertilise ideas.

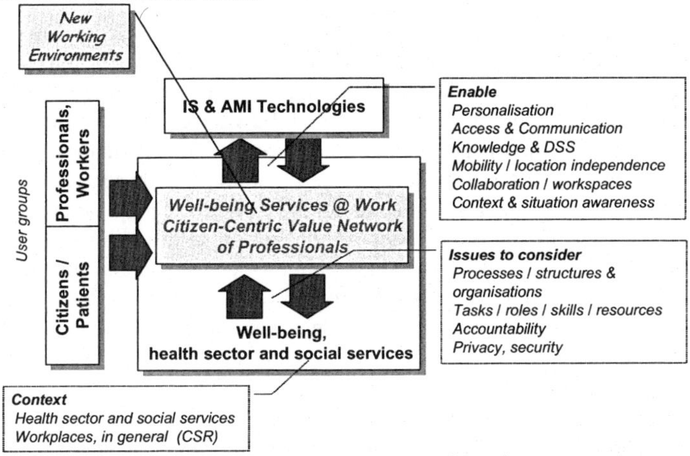

Figure 3: Scope of the Well-being services @ Work Community
(IS = Information Society, AMI = Ambient Intelligence, DSS = decision Support System, CSR = Corporate Social Responsibility)

Well-being Services @ Work is one of these eight communities and its interests cover the continuum of taking care of the sick and ill (the healthcare continuum) to prevention and health maintenance (wellness, health management). The focus of its activity (see Figure 2) is the interaction between AMI technologies, new working environments and, the organisational context. What is the impact of ICT and AMI Technologies? What are the technology demands created by new working environments, and how do they relate to the overall organisation and delivery of well-being, health sector and social services.

In this context, the concept of new working environments comprises physical locations (built environments) and virtual environments (location-independence), new ways to organise work through reallocation of responsibilities and accountabilities, tasks, resources, skills, and re-engineering of service processes that allow workers to carry out their tasks independently of time and location. It also includes mobility support for different user categories (e.g. fully mobile, mobile within a campus and desk-based) with the required level of privacy and security, and personalised, context and situation sensitive ways to communicate, workspaces to collaborate and to access knowledge and decision support.

The Community is not starting from scratch. The more than 10 year history of EU-funded projects in the ICT in healthcare domain combined with national and local activities form the baseline. This baseline comprises three "findings":

- An interoperable infrastructure is necessary for eHealth services to exist. This must be standards based, such as W3C web services combined with health specific standards such as Health Level Seven, DICOM and IHE (Integrated Healthcare Enterprise). Both enterprise level (EAI) and inter-enterprise integration (IEAI) issues have to be included.
- A structured semantic base must be created to facilitate the exchange of medical data and knowledge in an understandable context. Global agreements on medical terms and vocabularies are needed in electronic health record and decision support systems.
- Finally, in order to provide citizen-centric care, current service structures and processes will have to be redesigned. This touches the roles and functions of existing health

systems, organisations and professionals AND citizens (patients) and therefore calls for the systemic innovation approached outlined in the previous chapter.

5. Business cases, scenarios and roadmaps

The Well-being Services @ Work community is focused on identifying relevant scenarios and creating a roadmap charting possible paths towards working environments and new ways of working that would enable collaboration of healthcare professionals, patients and citizens to provide health services that have on impact on the well-being of a nation.

Several scenarios have proposed so far. The following example is discussed in more detail to give some insight to the challenges inherent to the domain. The basis of the scenario is a vision of a "trusted eMarketplace" to trade health services across country borders. The user categories that would be using the marketplace can be grouped according to their needs into eIndividuals (eCitizens / ePatients), eProfessionals (more generally eWorkers), eReach (consultation for second opinion between Peers) and finally eTeams (need to support collaboration among team members)

The use scenario for eCitizens could include sensors and ICT support to manage their health status and in the case of elderly people support of independent living in their normal surroundings through sensors that monitor daily activities and generate alarms when abnormal patterns are detected (context and location sensitivity) and personalised communication facilities. In the use scenario of ePatients can be characterised as "pervasive healthcare" allowing them to monitor their life styles and manage their diagnosed chronic disease, such as diabetes or hypertension, through measurements, personalised data stores, knowledge / decision support, and access to healthcare professionals when needed, and to support the appropriate use of medication (e.g. through alerts and reminders).

At the healthcare side eProfessionals (eWorkers) would have access to relevant case data and knowledge in order to identify the issues (diagnose) and plan for a strategy (therapy, care plan, workflow), with expected outcomes (monitoring / follow-up of progress). They would be supported by collaboration services (eReach). These enable requests for second opinions and include submission of relevant patient (multimedia) case history. The use of eReach services is needed when the eWorker feels that their knowledge/skills are not enough to solve the task and they need experts to provide advice or confirmation of a specific problem while still retaining the responsibility of the task. For eTeams virtual workspaces would be available to carry out tasks that need a multitude of skills by experts (including citizens) in complementary roles. Clear roles, sharing of data, information and knowledge in the correct context and the management of the workflow in problem solving are key ingredients in eTeam management.

The different use scenarios are created as business plans and are based on the usage of the eMarketplace as the virtual space providing the necessary means to broker service contracts and charge for services delivered with the required level of trust bridging and security between the participants.

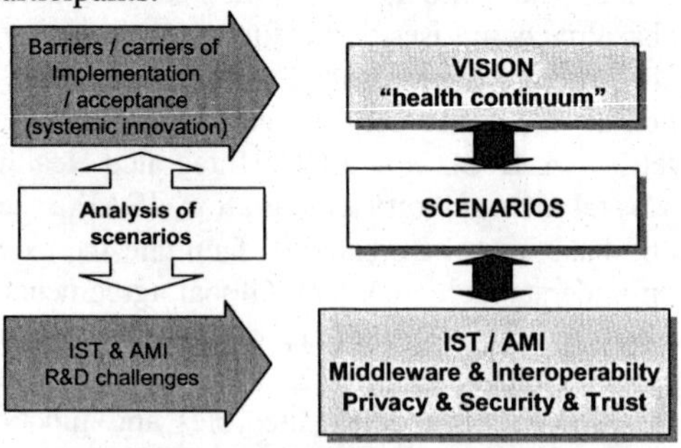

Figure 4: Analysis of scenarios

The scenarios will be analysed according to Figure 4. The aim is to identify from each scenario two sets of issues. The other relates to technological challenges in making the scenario a reality, i.e. what R&D measures are necessary to enable the technology required by the scenario. The other set of issues relates to systemic innovation aspects of the scenario. What are the issues that are in favour of the scenario becoming an accepted practice (carriers) and what are the issues that need to be solved or considered in implementing the scenario in order to be successful (barriers).

6. Conclusions

The work of the Well-being Services @ Work Community has only just started. The objective is to use scenarios to identify a roadmap for new ways of working and new working environments in the well-being, social services and healthcare domain. The work is based on a dual approach of identifying on one hand the technological challenges and on the other the systemic factors that hinder or enable the diffusion of the new ideas in the health sector. An essential part of the process from idea to innovation is to make sure that the idea can be shown to work in real-life situations, that it is benchmarked against existing work practices to show that it is cost-effective and efficient, and that it complies with the relevant legislation (the trust aspect).

Acknowledgements

The paper originates partly from work being done in the EU co-funded MOSAIC project (www.mosaic-network.org) and in one of the AMI@Work family of self-organising ERA communities, the Well-being Services @ Work Community (www.AMIatWork.com).

References

[1] Leonard Dorothy. Wellsprings of Knowledge. Building and sustaining the sources of innovation. Harvard Business School Press,1998.

[2] Christensen Clayton M., Bohmer Richard & Kenagy John. Will disruptive innovations cure health care. Harvard Business Review, 2002,September-October, pp.102-112.

[3] Eden C. The stakeholder/collaborator strategy workshop. In: Creating Collaborative Advantage, Chris Huxham (Ed.), Sage Publications, 1996.

[4] Hoogma R., Kemp R., Schot J. & Truffer B. Experimenting for sustainable transport. The approach of strategic niche management, Spon Press, 2002.

[5] Schot J. Towards new forms of participatory technology development. Technology Analysis and Strategic Management 13 (1), 2001, pp. 39-52.

[6] Kivisaari S., Lovio R. & Väyrynen E. Managing experiments for transition. Examples of societal embedding in energy and healthcare sectors. In: System Innovation and the Transition to Sustainability: Theory, Evidence and Policy, Elzen B., Geels F. & Green K. (Eds.), Edward Elgar (in print), 2004.

[7] Kemp R. & Rotmans J. Managing the transition to sustainable mobility. Paper for international expert meeting on "Transitions to Sustainability through System Innovations". University of Twente, 4-6 July, 2002.

[8] Geels F. Understanding technological transitions: a critical literature review and a conceptual synthesis. In: System Innovation and the Transition to Sustainability: Theory, Evidence and Policy, Elzen B., Geels F. & Green K. (Eds.), Edward Elgar (in print), 2004.

P. Cunningham and M. Cunningham (Eds.)
IOS Press, 2004

How to Speed-up the Implementation of eWork in the Health Care Sector

Uwe KIRCHHOFF, Dragan STOKIC, Harald SUNDMAEKER
ATB Institut für angewandte Systemtechnik Bremen GmbH,
Wiener Str.1, 28359 Bremen, Germany
Tel: +49 421 220920, Fax: +49 421 2209210, Email: kirchhoff@atb-bremen.de

Abstract: This paper covers results of the EU co-funded Team-Hos project (IST-1999-11567): METHODOLOGY AND TOOLS FOR WORLD-BEST TEAMWORK IN HOSPITALS. This paper presents a business process reengineering method enabling health care professionals to drive the introduction of optimal, ICT supported, new methods of work. The detailed results are outlined from one of five business cases applying the method to successful implementation of eWork solutions in hospitals. Presented are re-engineered business processes and implemented ICT solution, as well as business benefits achieved, indicating significant potential for performance improvements through the intensive use of eWork concepts in hospitals. Finally, the key lessons learnt about activities required to overcome the reluctance towards the introduction of eWork in the health care sector are summarised.

1. Introduction

The European health care system must be transformed into a modern, service oriented system able to optimally satisfy the needs of European citizens and the European economy (highest quality of service while minimising health care costs). Advanced Information and Communication Technologies (ICT) are essential to achieving these objectives.

In the past, the introduction of advanced ICT systems in hospitals primarily addressed the administration of hospital processes (e.g. admitting, nursing, housekeeping, billing etc.), rather than supporting the core activities of health care professionals. Support for optimising the planning and control of various patient treatment activities in a health care network, are presently insufficiently addressed. The actual day-to-day organisation of work in the health care network is based mainly on individual driven and experience based procedures, requiring a great deal of individual communication. This is often dictated by traditional organisational structures and boundaries, and ICT, which is not tailored to the needs of health care professionals. This causes extended queues for services, under-utilised resources, an overload for health care professionals and an immense efficiency [1].

It is incontestable that the health care operations environment differentiates when compared to an industrial business environment. However, the health care service has processes similar to those of business and are essential for the provision of an effective health care system [2]. In the scope of the Team-Hos project industrial business process reengineering methods and advanced ICT concepts have proven their applicability within the health care sector, enabling an effective introduction of industrial experience regarding advanced organisation of work supported by a new generation of ICT solutions (e.g. evolved ERP-systems, internet based B2B solutions, de facto industrial interface standards like XML, usage of open source/free software etc.) into the health care sector, aiming at the highest quality of services for citizens and also minimising health care costs [3, 4].

2. The Health Care Professional Driven Process Reengineering

When focussing on optimisation of patient treatment planning and control, in which patient treatment represents the key added value processes of a hospital, and comparing a hospital with a workshop oriented type of manufacturing process, from system engineering point of view there is a clear analogy between the manufacturing domain and health care sector. This is true for the basic process structures of "order handling" in the production domain compared the order to "treat a sick patient" in the health care sector, as well as in respect to QCS-optimising (Quality, Cost, Schedule) Best Practices from the manufacturing domain, to be implemented during process execution. For instance concerning the Best Practice "minimise intermediate buffers between production steps", analogy within the scope of patient treatment can be formulated "minimise the waiting time for the patients between subsequent treatment steps". Many other Best Practices are even identical.

In detail however, there are obviously different constraints to be considered (e.g. the dependence of treatment activities concerning treatment results, the required simultaneous optimisation of patient and resource oriented scheduling, the complexity of possible interaction between treatment steps etc.), requesting specific, sophisticated solutions customised for these specific health care environments and prohibiting a one to one transfer of solutions from the manufacturing domain to the health care sector.

Currently, within the health care sector there is as yet reluctance to change and a missing culture concerning process, performance and a cost oriented way of thinking, as well as missing qualification in respect to required system engineering techniques among the health care professionals. Furthermore the methodologies and tools required to support health care professionals through specification and implementation of new types of ICT supported new methods of work, also bridging the gap between the health care professionals and the ICT experts, are not state of the art within the health care domain. The key research objectives of the Team-Hos project were

- to adapt industrial business process reengineering methods and tools to the requirements of the health care sector,
- to validate the applicability of industrial best practices and principles to optimise health care processes and
- to transfer innovative eWork concepts (e.g. CRM, ERP, SCM) to health care processes.

These objectives were realised by three research partners (with strong background in industrial engineering as well as medical informatics) and five hospitals of different sizes based in three European regions, contributing the medical expertise and test bed scenarios.

The key approach of the methodology development was to transfer industrial so called "coaching oriented" business reengineering methodologies [5], due to their similarity of the reengineering targets as well as to overcome comparable reasons for innovation reluctance. The resulting BHP-Method (Best Hospital Practice), provides well defined working instructions (training material, BHP-Handbook, documentation templates etc.), which were applied by the hospital staff, involving all hierarchy levels, to reengineer their business processes and to specify required optimal ICT support from user point of view. This approach served as a verification and optimisation of the developed methodology. Furthermore, the specified ICT solution was developed and the eWork solution introduced into daily operation, enabling the assessment of the targeted business benefits.

The developed and validated BHP-Method provides easy learnable and detailed (cook-book like) working instructions for staff members regarding how to run the improvement process, based on a training on the job concept. The intensive involvement and qualification of health care professionals also guarantees an extensive acceptance of introduced solutions and initiates an innovation culture in the hospital. Furthermore the BHP-Method bridges the gap between the health care professionals and the ICT experts.

As presented in Figure 1, in order to benefit most from the improvement measures, the BHP-Method applies a goal oriented approach, focussing on introduction of improvement measures to overcome identified, most critical bottlenecks, jeopardising achievement of those hospital's objectives that deliver clear and measurable business benefits to hospitals.

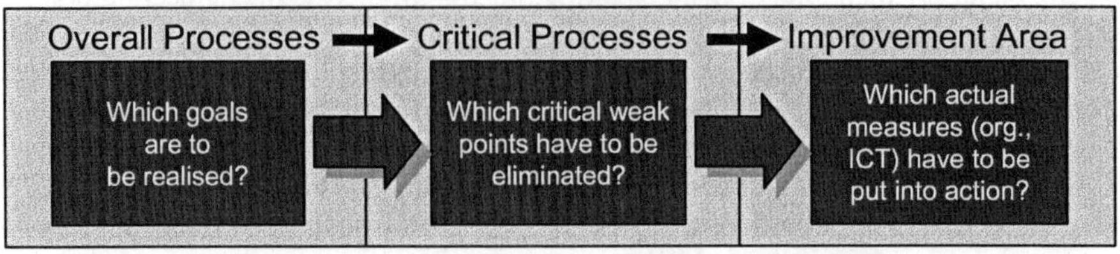

Figure 1: The goal-oriented approach of the BHP-Method

As presented in Figure 2 the BHP-Method covers all phases of an improvement life-cycle, guaranteeing full traceability of results between the different phases. All information is delivered required for management decisions, since management decisions drive the improvement process. An integral part of the BHP-Method is a cost/benefit assessment scheme creating essential information for sound management decisions. All required decision information is documented, enabling fast decisions to prevent any delays for implementing the improvements into day-to-day operation.

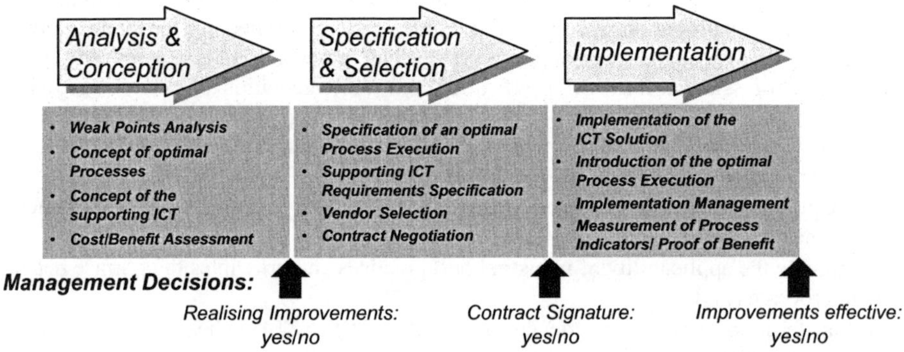

Figure 2: Life-cycle model of the ICT based business improvement

Experience tells us that, on one hand, the introduction of a software solution will not force an optimal tailored new organisation of work and, on the other hand, only a well defined and harmonised process execution based on a consistent information exchange can be optimally supported by ICTs. Therefore, the BHP-Method provides an integrated approach for redesign of the organisation of work and ICT infrastructure, in which design of new organisation of work precedes the specification of ICT requirements.

To guarantee that an ICT solution will optimally support the agreed process execution with the health care professional in their day-to-day operation, the BHP-Method covers an integrated approach for specification of organisational and ICT measures. The organisational re-design of the process execution drives the ICT design, which bridges the gap between the user's way of thinking – in a process world - and how software engineers think – in a software world. This approach provides a user driven ICT specification and implementation, based on a direct transition from process specification to the software specification, and ensuring intensive end user involvement in the ICT development process.

Furthermore this type of improvement life-cycle (addressing an improvement that is manageable for health care facilities to implement without putting operations or any patients at risk), represents one step of a continuous improvement process. The resulting evolutionary but continuous business process improvement must guarantee the achievement of a holistic hospital wide solution. In a "component based business reengineering approach" the BHP-Method supports, for a sequence of independent improvement steps, to achieve a consistent process flow and an integrated company wide information system.

3. Business Case - Geriatric Treatment Planning

During the project the prototype of the BHP-Method was validated and tested in five business cases in the pilot hospitals in three EU countries (Austria, Germany, Portugal). They addressed (1) optimisation of the geriatric patient treatment, (2) co-operation between the radiological area and other clinics, (3) co-ordination of the operation theatres, (4) paperless workflow for physicians and (5) optimisation of nursing tasks. For the business case of an optimisation of the geriatric patient treatment the results regarding the BHP-Method application is described in the following.

The business case required a reengineering of the cooperation between the geriatric department with other clinics (e.g. neurology, internal medicine, emergency surgery) and a well defined task allocation to the involved employees (nurses, physicians, geriatrics experts) along the treatment path, aiming at a reduction of the length of stay of the patients and an increased usage of the clinical resources.

Key objective of the process redesign was to guarantee an early identification of geriatric patients and a transition from primary clinics to the geriatric clinic without delay. As a result of the weak point analysis this required a redesign of the most critical processes "treatment order management" at the primarily treating clinics and "treatment order coordination" at the geriatric clinic. Previously different practised procedures in various clinics were substituted by well-defined procedures obligatory for all employees involved, supported by a tailored ICT solution. The key characteristics of process execution before and after introduction of the improvement measure are presented in Table 1.

Table 1: Process execution before and after improvement

Before	After
Potential geriatric patients are identified too late and many potential geriatric patients are not identified at all.	Registration of the Barthel-Index for all patients through the nursing service after 3-5 days following hospitalisation.
Consultation request was prepared too late and requires1-2 days to be forwarded to the geriatric department by internal mail.	Evaluation of Barthel results are evaluated by the ward physician according to defined exclusion criteria immediately and the consultation request is forwarded to geriatrics electronically.
After consultation a transfer date was defined (an average of 4 days waiting time).	After consultation in reference to the desired transfer date the final date is defined by the geriatrics (an average of 1,5 days waiting time), accessible by the clinics electronically.
Different procedures practised in different clinics with inadequate ICT support.	**Well defined procedures obligatory for all employees involved and a tailored, optimal ICT support.**

With application of the BHP-Method a solution is imposed covering clearly defined execution instructions for all staff activities relating to all the different areas involved (nursing, clinic doctors, geriatric expert) guaranteeing an efficient cooperation, creating an efficient co-operation, as well as an optimally ICT support (see Figure 3). The realised ICT solution, specified by the health care professionals, optimally supports the agreed process execution, such as taking over patient data from the HIS (Hospital Information System), automatic evaluation of geriatric indicators, management of communication (who to be informed and when), avoiding any type of redundant information input (e.g. patient and treatment data). Appropriate staff can access all information, via any hospital PC.

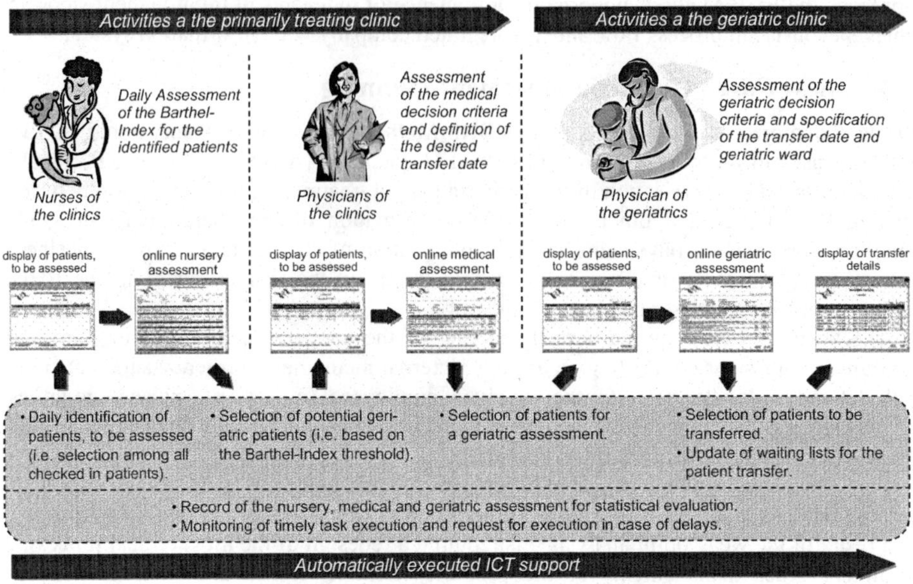

Figure 3: ICT supported geriatric processes

The introduced optimised process execution and supporting ICT solution is approximately since nine months in daily operation [6]. The measured process indicators clearly demonstrate significant business benefits achieved, even exceeding the targeted values:

- Increased efficiency and quality of geriatric patient treatment, reducing overall patients stay by 8-10 days, realised by: (i) a reduction of the mean patient waiting time from 8 days to 1,5 days and (ii) a reduction of required geriatric treatment duration by 29% achieving the same treatment results, due to earlier start of the geriatric treatment.
- Improved usage of resources in the primary clinics.
- The achieved smooth process flow and tailored software support significantly reduce labour efforts of employees for the handling of the geriatric assessment and treatment planning per patient by 60-70%.
- Improved identification of potential geriatric patients by 15% (i.e. no patients, which require geriatric treatment are sent home).
- The realised monitoring concept, providing a direct feedback to the affected staff, creating a high process quality and stable process execution (i.e. all patients were assessed not later than 2 days after the respective due date).

The developed software solution is based on a Free-Software concept so that no license costs are incurred to operate the software system. The application specific software is a Java based web-application linked to a MySQL database management system, with Linux as the server operating system. End-user access is realised via an Internet-Browser and communication between client and server via an Apache Web-Server. The realised software concept also enables to operate application specific software with commercial software products e.g. Oracle as a DBMS or MS Windows as an operating system.

The application specific software installed on a web-server can be accessed from any PC (client) in the hospital network via an Internet browser (compatible with MS Internet Explorer version 5.5 or above), requesting no additional software installation at the client.

For the purpose of a further required data analysis, there is the possibility to access the MySQL database by MS Excel or MS Access via an ODBC interface.

For actual software installation in the pilot hospital the software is linked to the Hospital Information System SAP IS-H*MED via an HL7-HCM interface. Patient data is continuously updated. The overall system architecture is presented in Figure 4.

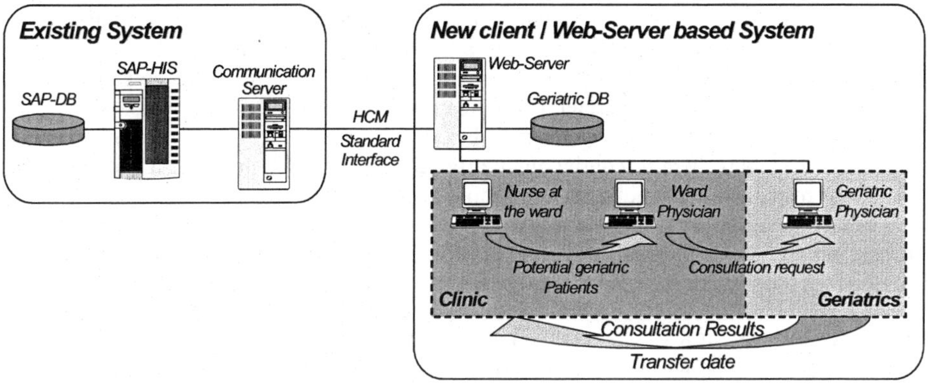

Figure 4: Overall system architecture

A German version of the eWork solution, covering the organisational procedures and the software system can be downloaded as Free-Software from the Internet via: (http://gerinet.atb-bremen.de/). This includes (i) a demo-version, (ii) a run-time software version, (iii) administration software, (iv) user and installation manuals.

4. Lessons learnt

A key lesson learnt in the scope of the pilot implementations of the Team-Hos project is that a well defined and efficient ICT supported new teamwork oriented organisation of work creates major benefits for all involved members of the co-operating health care areas and essentially contributes to a hospital wide stable quality of patient treatment, as well as to an increased utilisation of available resources.

The experience with the applied BHP-Method decidedly validated the clear advantage of coaching oriented approaches in all business cases. It becomes obvious that the tested coaching oriented BHP-Method allows time- and cost-efficient, as well as goal-oriented introduction of both organisational and technological measures, enabling hospitals to effectively establish an improvement process driven by health care professionals.

The coaching oriented approach of supporting health care professionals during a successful process improvement project, has been very effective in supporting the introduction of new ICT supported organisation of work in the health care sector.

The thinking in processes and process flows forced by the BHP-Method represents the key approach to overcome organisational barriers and the "thinking in kingdoms" it also creates a co-operation culture by convincing people instead of forcing them and by respecting people's opinion. Furthermore such an approach forces health care professionals to communicate individual experience, problems and knowledge concerning detailed process execution and problems overcoming existing barriers, which has never happened before without support of such a methodology. The holistic and process oriented view also creates, with project progress, a growing commitment of co-operation and team orientation from health care professionals, while becoming more and more aware of the win-win-situation created by such improvement processes for everyone involved. Through this approach using intensive involvement of all staff levels results in a very high user acceptance of the new organisation of work and ICT solutions. The approach to start with an ICT solution independent specification of the redesigned process execution and, based on this, accomplishing the ICT requirement specification from user's point of view, has proven to be essential for success of the implemented solution.

Critical for the success of improvement measures is the commitment and participation of staff on the operational level. The coaching oriented approaches demonstrated that especially on the operational level, initial typical reluctance changed to active commitment, as the employees become convinced of the advantages of the solution elaborated by the team. In particular the "pressure" to document results of brainstorming and discussion activities, enabling a tracing and referencing of agreements, is rated as very valuable.

The increased innovation competence of health care professionals achieved by the staff qualification, enables them to continuously drive the hospital's improvement processes on their own responsibility, requiring a minimal of external consultancy support. The participating hospitals are already extremely committed to progress with this improvement process. Initiated in the hospitals is a clear transition in the innovation culture, which can be characterised by: "Problems are not judged as problems any longer, but as challenges".

Even though advanced ICTs offer features that were unimaginable just a few years ago. Cost and availability of hardware and software products now allow the health care industry to deploy a fixed based or even mobile professional workforce, with huge market potentials. However, there are still many concerns such as issues of liability, cost, security and trust aspects, compatibility and insufficient workflow support, information availability, speed etc., which still impose reluctance by the health care professionals to adopt such advanced ICTs. These concerns represent central factors behind this lack of technology penetration regarding advanced ICTs in the health care sector. One additional major obstacle for moving forward is that there are cost, benefit and performance trade offs, which have not been made sufficiently obvious to potential customers.

To overcome the existing reluctance of health care professionals to use advanced ICTs, the gap between generic enabling ICT solutions and specific turn key solutions needed by health care professionals to support day-to-day operation must be bridged. This gap is still very big in the health care sector, implying high risks when developing specific health care oriented solutions. Thus, enhancing basic enabling ICTs to meet specific needs of the health care sector will not be achieved by market driven technology evolution.

To achieve a breakthrough in ICT penetration in the health care sector, application driven RTD activities are needed, oriented to bring together the required introduction of a new organisation of work and related enhancement and adaptation of basic enabling ICTs. This trend has further to be supported by demonstration of the explicit quantifiable business benefits achieved during daily operation of resulting solutions for the health care domain.

There is a Europe-wide missing awareness concerning huge optimisation potentials of treatment activities (i.e. planning and control of the execution of the sequence of required treatment activities on the patient) in healthcare networks, which nevertheless represent the key added-value processes. To overcome this situation, comprehensive Europe-wide activities are required such as extensive awareness campaigns, installation of networks of European showcases, qualification of medical staff in business process reengineering, etc.

5. Conclusions

There are enormous potential in the health care sector to optimise primary added-value processes concerning planning and control of the medical treatments. These improvement potentials may bring crucial benefits to patients as well as staff, by reducing costs and simultaneously increasing patient quality. Coaching oriented methodologies, like the BHP-Method represent promising approaches to introduce successful and efficient new, ICT supported, organisation of work in the health care sector optimal tailored to the needs of the health care professionals. Therefore, extensive activities are required to overcome missing awareness of the improvement potentials in the health care sector.

However, it will be difficult to overcome the lack of ICT penetration in the health care sector by providing solely cross-sectoral, basic enabling ICTs. Application driven RTD activities are required, providing holistic solutions to health care that take into consideration problematic areas not yet solved by this business sector. This will offer distinctively diverse and flexible solutions to efficiency in health care. This will not only enable health care to perform on a par with industry, but will also give health care extreme versatility, that industry currently does not enjoy, hence providing the health care system with an approach that goes beyond the capabilities of the current approach taken by industry.

References

[1] Bourke, Michael K.; Strategy and Architecture of health care information systems. Ber-lin 1994, Springer.

[2] Berwick, Donald M.; Godfrey, A. Blanton; Roessner, Jane; Curing Health Care: New Strategies for Quality Improvement; 2. Edition. San Fansisco 2002, Jossey-Bass.

[3] Kirchhoff, Uwe; The Importance of Process Improvement in the Hospital Area and Planning & Control Activity of Patient Treatment. IST2002 Conference, Copenhagen, November 06th 2002.

[4] team-Hos project – IST-1999-11567; Methodology and tools for world-best teamwork in hospitals. http://213.153.61.92/

[5] Kirchhoff, et. al. : How to Speed-up the IMSS Related Innovation in Manufacturing SMEs. International IMS Forum 2004, 17.-19.05.2004; Lake Como, Italy.

[6] Sgries, Bernd; Routinemäßiges geriatrisches Screening am Akutkrankenhaus. European Journal of Geriatrics Vol. 5 (2003) No. 3.

Section 7

SME Issues

Section 7.1

Issues

eAdoption and the Knowledge Economy: Issues, Applications, Case Studies
P. Cunningham and M. Cunningham (Eds.)
IOS Press, 2004

Using Enterprise Models to Define a Web Based Collaborative eEngineering Environment for SMEs

Daniel Capaldo AMARAL[1], Godfried AUGENBROE[2], Régis Kovacs SCALICE[1], Leonardo D. V. RIBEIRO[1], Rafael G. Dias NETTO[1], Henrique ROZENFELD[1]
[1] *São Paulo University (USP), Av. Trabalhador São-Carlense, 400, São Carlos, Brazil*
Tel: +55 16 2739433, Fax: +55 16 2738235, Email: numa@sc.usp.br
[2]*Georgia Institute of Technology, College of Architecture, Atlanta, Georgia, 30332-1055, USA*
Tel: +1 404-894-1686, Email: fried.augenbroe@arch.gatech.edu

Abstract: This article proposes the use of Enterprise Models to define a Web Based Collaborative environment for Small and Medium Sized Enterprises (SMEs). A four-layer model was created to describe the collaboration lifecycle between Engineering service providers and their clients, with the help of a web broker. The model is based primarily on three case studies. The whole model is presented in the Unified Modelling Language (UML). The model assisted in the identification of services and resource requirements that should add value to the broker's mechanism, and helped to identify the brokers' communication services. This article presents a critical analysis of the approach, describing the advantages and disadvantages of using Enterprise Models as a modelling technique for Web based collaborative eEngineering.

1. Introduction

The benefits of web-hosted information systems for enterprise collaboration are well known. Collaborative engineering tools are now mature and increasingly easy to use by enterprise staff.

Available tools are still too sophisticated for most day-to-day needs of Small and Medium Sized Enterprises (SME). Current tools are mostly high end and demand large infrastructure investments. To address this issue, a proposal was submitted to the European Commission in 2001, from a consortium comprising nine enterprises and universities from Europe (Greece, Netherlands, Germany, England, Belgium and Italy) and Latin America (Mexico and Brazil).

The goal of the consortium is to develop a B2B mechanism that (1) delivers a revolutionary set of web hosted collaboration services to aid e-Engineering activities; (2) allows low entry costs for Small and Medium-sized Enterprises (SME); (3) elevates the first generation of B2B services to more expressive forms of collaboration. The resulting system offers a "Holonomic and Universal Broker Service" through an "e-Engineering hub", or e-Hub in short.

The specification of these mechanisms started with the creation of SME's collaborative product development case studies. Two case studies focused on Construction Engineering and a third on a Mechanical Engineering project. The use of these cases gave the research team a basic notion of the negotiation process involved, as well as the development of partnerships. However, these case studies were not enough to define the necessary services of the e-HUB.

These cases were effective at showing a great diversity of barriers and needs through out the whole collaboration lifecycle. Nevertheless, there were difficulties to an effective comparison between the results of each case because of two main reasons: The projects had different areas of application (mechanical and civil engineering) and the researchers and professionals of the consortium come from different backgrounds, posing the usual conceptual and linguistic disconnects. Given these problems, the consortium had to face the challenge to generate the requirements of the software platform, to choose a set of e-HUB supported services and to develop the business and dissemination models, uniquely from the case studies description.

The solution encountered was the use of enterprise modelling concepts to create a model of the collaboration lifecycle, that is: a model to represent the creation, development and finalization of different kinds of collaboration, defining (sub) activities and most of all emphasising the services and software tool which could potentially be offered by the e-HUB.

This model represents the collaboration in five distinctive phases (discussed in Section 5). As the primary research scope of the project was project preparation after the initial partner selection phase the Project Planning Phase was prioritised for further analysis. To develop the model, many methodologies and modelling frameworks were analysed. As the e-HUB software platform would be developed using concepts of objects and web-services, a methodology was searched that, at its maximal level of detail, could satisfactorily represent such elements.

The result of this analysis led to the choice of the Unified Modelling Language (UML). This methodology was originally developed for software system specifications and has been discussed as an option in the modelling of business enterprises.

2. Objectives

This paper describes the development of a Project Preparation Model that can be used to support the project preparation phase of distant e-Engineering partnerships. The focus of this paper is the use of enterprise modelling concepts and UML to generate this model. Its use will be judged in relation to whether it is useful to build the kind of representations that enable the discussion and development of collaborative tools and services for e-engineering project planning platforms.

3. Bibliographical Background

This paper deals with three important research issues: e-Engineering collaboration, project management and enterprise modelling using UML.

3.1. Collaboration and Virtual Teams

According to Ostergaard & Summers [1], distant collaboration in projects is widely used and very popular, even though there is no common understanding of issues that may interfere with the process. While a multitude of tools have been developed to ease communication of ideas and information inside collaborative, geographically dispersed project teams, the information exchange requirements among such teams were not completely explored. Consequently, these tools might be inadequate or poorly directed for use in e-Engineering partnerships.

LARSSON et al. [2] made a keen compilation of the main factors affecting collaboration in dispersed team: time-fuse differences; cultural differences; lack of geographical proximity; conscience; delay on communication; mobility and heterogeneity, and distance from market. The authors conclude that the potential to apply collaboration to distributed product development is big, but in order to turn this potential into a reality it is necessary to intensify the research efforts.

One vital aspect of establishing collaboration through the Internet is the management of virtual teams. Cascio & Shurygailo [3] analyse the impact of the establishment of virtual teams on planning and management as whole. They conclude that during project planning, additional considerations must be given to the definition and attribution of tasks, mostly due to the geographical distribution of the team members and other resources. They also point to the great importance of trust among virtual teams and affirm that trust is based on the principle that the team members depend on each other and must deliver their promises. In the case of virtual team, trust is established only after the expectation of all team members are reached or surpassed.

3.2. Project Management

A project can be defined as a temporary endeavour to create a unique product [4]. Any collaboration performed through the e-HUB is unique and must be initialised, planned, executed, controlled and finished in a well organized manner, following the specific characteristics of each collaborative team setting. According to PMI, to correctly initialise the planning of a project it is essential to pay attention to its scope, time, cost and the integration of these elements.

3.3. Enterprise Modelling

As explained by Vernadat [5], an enterprise model is a set of complementary models describing many aspects of an organisation. The model has the objective to help one or more users in the enterprise to achieve something. It is the pre-objective to enterprise integration, which consists of breaking organisational barriers to improve the synergy of the company and, in this manner reaches more rapidly the business objectives in a productive and efficient way. In this context, the objectives of enterprise modelling could be defined as:

- Better understanding of the operational structure of an organisation (i.e. visualise enterprise embedded functions, activities, information flows and knowledge management patterns);
- Support the enterprise to (re)-engineering its existing or new parts, requiring support for analysis, simulation and decision taking;
- The creation of a model that can be used to control and monitor the enterprise operations, wholly or partly automated with the help of the model

There are many methods and specific frameworks for enterprise modelling. A method is a set of constructs and syntax rules that allows the representation of a specific dimension of the enterprise. Among the most widely known are the SADT (Structured Analysis and Development Technique)/ IDEF0 (Integration Definition for Function Modelling) and the EPC (Event-Driven Process Chain) A modelling framework can be defined as a set of methods and tools to conduct enterprise modelling in a given domain. An example of a full blown enterprise modelling framework is ARIS (ARchitecture of Integrated Information Systems) [6].

3.4. The Use of UML for Enterprise Modelling

The UML, according to Booch et. al. [7], is a graphical language to enable the visualisation, specification, construction and documentation of artefacts of software complex systems. UML was created to specify complex object-oriented software, from the preparation of software architecture planning to the specification of more concrete items, like classes written in a given programming language or database schemes and re-usable software components.

UML offers many constructs and methods that must be combined based on specific needs. Kim et al.[8] observed that enterprise-modelling languages like IDEF and CIM-OSA allow the representation of businesses, social structures, problems and solutions, and technical aspects.

Marshall [9] presents a proposal of UML utilisation in enterprise modelling efforts. To the author, enterprises are highly complex systems and therefore need models composed by various components, in order to make its representation possible. The author proposes the use of UML diagrams, discussing different possibilities of its use on enterprise modelling. Although the discussion and the examples demonstrate the viability of this approach, it doesn't show any evidence of real cases of application of UML to enterprise modelling.

BARBALHO et al. [10] analyse the use of UML in enterprise modelling through the inspection of advantages and disadvantages in terms of representing different visions of the organisation. As a result, it is demonstrates that, in contrast to the use of UML for software-development, the developments of state-diagrams is really the priority. The reason for this is that activities are the key to understanding a business process. Whereas in the modelling of complex software, this vision is important mainly when control or embedded systems are concerned.

4. Methodology for Developing the Project Preparation Model

The development of the Project Preparation Model (PPM) began with the study of various cases of collaboration between Small and Medium Enterprises (SMEs) on engineering, elaborated based on past experience of consortium partners and on extensive of the bibliography on reported project scenarios. Three of theses cases were explored in detail:

- Case A – a scenario where two companies involved on a construction project identify the need of seismic risk analysis. They contact the e-HUB and find a supplier of this specialised service. This case allowed the identification of a partnership, as well as some secondary roles that could exist during a multi-party collaboration (legal, technical, etc).
- Case B – a scenario where some issues of concept planning and development of the final product are more deeply detailed. This case demands a more elaborated planning phase, especially concerning the culture of partnering and contracting in the construction industry.
- Case C – more than just a single case, it presents a set of four supply methods of technological services supplied by a Mexican cluster of SMEs. The specific case concerns the development of mechanical products for the aerospace industry.

The three cases formed the basis for a more profound discussion about issues involving preparation of collaborative engineering and redirect the attention of the research group to many areas. The three cases were used to derive the general set of requirements to the e-HUB platform.

The first step to the development of the Project Preparation Model was the deep analysis of these cases to identify "standard stages" in the collaboration life cycle (refer to the next section). It also led to the identification of the basic entities, roles and functions in the PPM. Software and hardware resources, engineering services and the main actor's roles form these entities.

The roles defined in the collaboration process are:

- Client – Supplies all data about the requested project (description & detail) based on needs of the e-Hub and the ESP; plans the activities to fit in the overall, product development process
- ESP (Engineering Service Provider) – Evaluates the needs and requests for information about the project; plans the activities that respond to the requested engineering service
- (e-Hub) Broker – Provides templates, supplies the web communication platform, facilitates problem solving, offers tools to mediate and co-ordinate project changes and unsolved issues.

The modelling approach was used to represent all stages of the collaboration lifecycle, by reusing the basic model entities to describe specific aspects of the collaboration. By the end of the modelling process, it was possible to explore the requirements and actual implementation of every basic entity (actors, services and resources of the software platform), helping to describe the needs of hardware, the software functionalities and the services provided by the e-HUB.

5. Collaboration Stages – e-HUB's Engineering Partnering Process Model

The Engineering Partnering Process Model was created to cover the whole collaboration process:

- Stage 1 – project definition: the ESP or Client decides what to partner. The type of service offered by the e-Hub is a hybrid mix of business consultants and automated performance measurements of uploaded business processes.
- Stage 2 - finding the right partner: type of service: automated prospecting, online portfolios and expertise profiles… Human services are offered for legal and trade services on demand, pre-certification, validation
- Stage 3 - agreeing with selected partner what, how, with what and when to do, based on the following services: automated process negotiation, augmented by human services as required for legal support (contracting), dispute resolution, arbitration, banking/credit options
- Stage 4 - executing the process model developed in stage 3 through a "collaboration workspace": the output of level-3 is imported through a mapping interface that maps the project plan of stage 3 onto the set-up of the collaboration workspace

- Stage 5 - dissolving partnership: includes capture and storage of audit trails from collaboration workspace, aggregation of audit trails in partner rating, application of knowledge retention metrics.

6. Basic Types of Collaboration

One of the great challenges of this project lies on the scope of application of the e-HUB. The project's objective of being universal, serving as support mechanism to different kinds of collaboration at different sectors (civil, mechanical, etc), makes the identification of the generic needs and services hard, especially if one can only rely on studied cases. It is important to emphasize that this modelling approach can be easily used to model the collaboration of others industry sectors. Differences on the resulted models would certainly exist, most especially at the lower layers of the models, where sector-specific features are modelled in more detail.

It is important to capture generic collaboration characteristics regardless of industry sector differences. There was an attempt to identify these generic factors, based on two different dimensions, forming a "collaboration type matrix". The basic dimensions identified were:

- Interface Complexity: relates to the ease of project definition between client and engineering providers. This is related to the level of abstraction and complexity of parameters involved in the project execution. As complexity increases, the level of interactions required to understand related problems will increase, as will need for support of logic planning steps.
- Type of technologies that are fundamental to the collaboration project: Each type of technology has its specific characteristics in terms of project stages and necessary resources. In that manner, an engineering project or service that uses civil construction technology is different from a project containing mass manufacturing technologies.

With the identification of the basic types of collaboration the number of variants of project planning models could be kept to a minimum. This also insured that the analysis of the possible roles of the actors, resource needs in terms of hardware and software and the identification of services that could be offered by the e-HUB, could guarantee almost universality.

7. Description of the Project Preparation Model

The resulting layer structure of the model is shown in Figure 1. The first layer contains a representation of the generic collaboration lifecycle, describing the phases described in section 5.

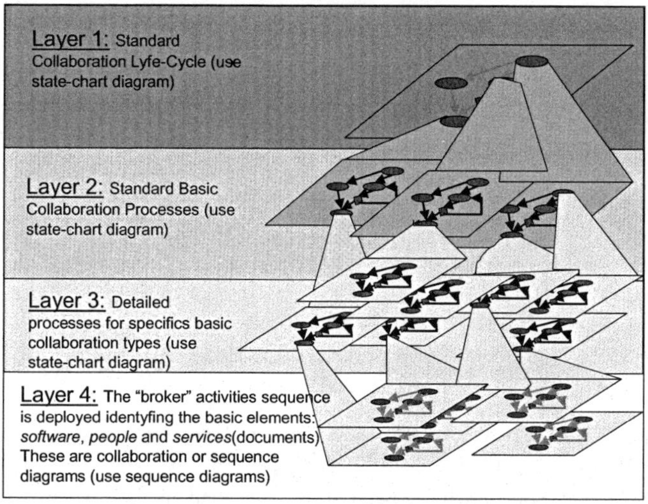

Figure 1: Project Preparation Model Layers

The second layer is also generic; it distinguishes different types of collaboration and shows the identified processes for each. Figure 2 illustrates the second layer of the third phase, i.e. project preparation, in which two other sub-processes are identified.

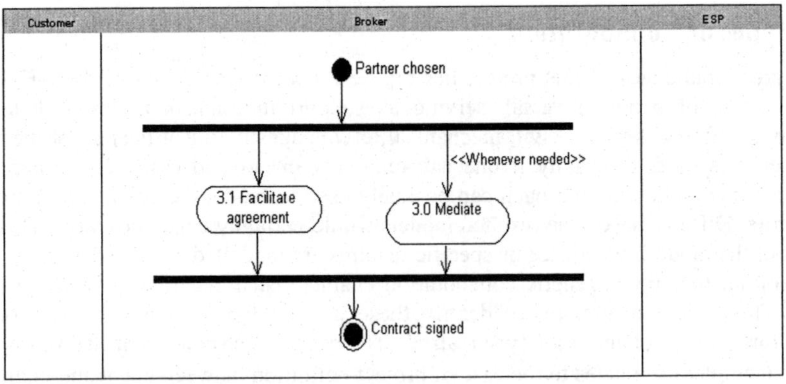

Figure 2: Project Preparation - Activity level 2 Diagram

The third layer of the model is composed by various diagrams, similar to Figure 3, detailing the two processes present at the upper layer. This refinement considers the four types of collaboration presented in Section 6. There is one diagram for the third layer for the process 3.1 in case the interface complexity of the collaboration is low and another diagram for the case the interface complexity is high; this is duplicated in the mechanical and civil engineering domains.

The last layer of the model (layer 4) contains a description of specific activities constituting the set of the model's basic objects. As an example, figure 4 presents the diagram for the activity "Request Project Charter", which is part of the activity "Define Project Charter" (layer 3), which, on its turn, is part of the generic process "Facilitate Agreement" (layer 2)

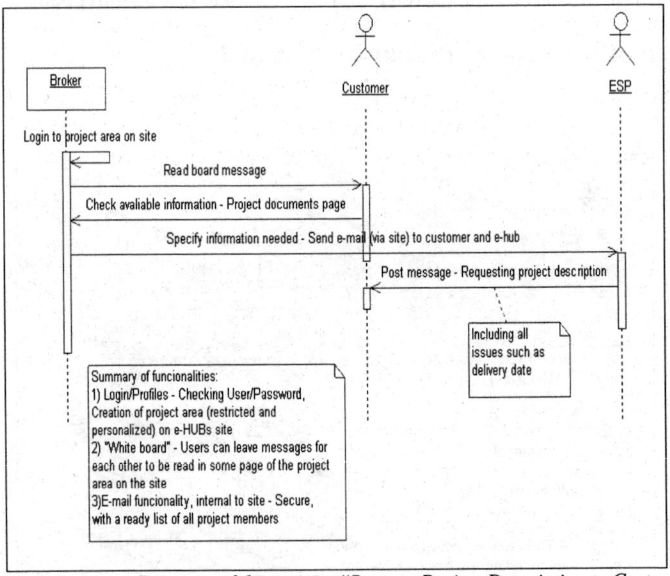

Figure 3: Sequence Diagram of the activity "Request Project Description to Customer" (part of mechanical-high complexity case).

Not all types of collaboration have been fully described in the current Project Preparation Model which was developed using the Rational Rose tool set, without which it would be nearly impossible to manage the consistency between the many different diagrams and objects.

8. Final Remarks and Recommendations

A Project Preparation Model was developed to assist the identification of services and resource requirements that should add value to the e-Hub mechanism. Through these diagrams it was possible to define the communication needs of the e-HUB, its possible uses and the services to be included. The model was very useful to orientate the works of the research consortium, facilitating the interaction between different internal research groups.

The same modelling approach described in this paper could be used by enterprises interested on the choice or specification of systems for collaborative engineering. The experience present at this paper makes also clear that the use of these enterprise-modelling concepts are extremely important to the development of applications in the field of collaborative engineering. Any software specification team, even very small teams, as usually found at technological based SMEs, can easily reuse the methodology presented here.

Regarding the benefits of using UML diagrams for representing the business process, the diagrams generated were more difficult to read than the models written in SADT or eEPC. During this research project, it was noticed that the communication between the development and the implementation team of the collaboration platform was greatly enhanced because the background of the researches was on the software development field. But, through the analysis of the model is possible to realise that it would be much more difficult if the majority of researches had different technical backgrounds. In such a case, an approach similar to that of KIM et al (2003), modelling the upper layers with a traditional methodology like SADT.

Another difficulty was found when generating a large number of possible collaboration types combinations. The reusability of the basic elements and models of the last layer and the description of the activities was difficult due to the barriers of generating reports at the modelling tool and due to the intrinsic effort necessary to increase the combination number.

The most important contribution of this research was to demonstrate this is a possible approach to consider all specification involved at the problem of collaborative engineering.

At present, different members of the consortium are creating two separate Test-Beds, from different industry sectors and countries, thus testing the e-HUB platform created through this methodology against a broad variety of business, engineering and also cultural criteria an needs. The result of this evaluation will be ready and available at the end of the project.

Another future researches could improve the modelling methodology with the introduction of new visions and creating specific resources inside other modelling tools.

References

[1] OSTERGAARD, K.J.; SUMMERS, J.D. A taxonomic classification of collaborative design. In: International Conference on Engineering Design, 14., 2003, Stockholm. Anais… Stockholm: Design Society, 2003.

[2] LARSSON, A. et al. Distributed team innovation – a framework for distributed product development. In: International Conference on Engineering Design, 14., 2003, Stockholm. Anais… Stockholm: Design Society, 2003.

[3] CASCIO, W.F. & SHURYGAILO, S. E-leadership and virtual teams. *Organizational Dynamics*. Vol.31, n.4, p.362-376. 2003.

[4] PMI (Project Management Institute). *Project Management Body of Knowledge*. 2002.

[5] VERNADAT, F.B. *Enterprise Modelling and Integration: Principles and Applications*. London: Chapman & Hall. 1996.

[6] SCHEER, A.W. (1998). Business Process Engineering: reference models for industrial enterprises, Heidelberg, Springer-Verlag.

[7] BOOCH, G. JACOBSON, I. RUMBAUGH, J. *The Unified Modeling Language user guide*. Addison-Wesley Longman, inc. 1999.

[8] KIM, C.H.; WESTON, R.H.; HODGSON, A.; LEE, K.H. The complementary use of IDEF and UML modeling approaches. *Computers in Industry*. Elsevier Science Ltd. N.50, p.35-56. 2003.

[9] MARSHALL, C. *Enterprise modeling with UML: designing successful software through business analysis*. Massachussets: Addison-Wesley. 2000.

[10] BARBALHO, S., AMARAL, D.C., ROZENFELD, H. Modelando processos de negócio com UML. In: *XXII Encontro Nacional de Engenharia de Produção*, 2002, Curitiba-PR. Enegep 2002.

eAdoption and the Knowledge Economy: Issues, Applications, Case Studies
P. Cunningham and M. Cunningham (Eds.)
IOS Press, 2004

Enabling Internet-based B2B Transactions through Application Interconnection

Yannis CHARALABIDIS[1], Vassilios KARAKOIDAS[2],
Stephanos ANDROUTSELLIS-THEOTOKIS[2], Diomidis SPINELLIS[2]
[1]*Singular Software S.A., 23rd Km Athens-Lamia Road, Ag. Stefanos, 14565, Greece*
Tel: +30 210 6267400, Fax: + 30 210 6267410, Email: yannisx@singular.gr
[2]*Athens University of Economics and Business, 76 Patission Str., Athens, 10434, Greece*
Tel: +30 210 8203370, Fax: +30 2108203664, Email: {bkarak, stheotok, dds}@aueb.gr

Abstract: The paper elaborates on an approach that will enable the typical Small and Medium Enterprise (SME) to carry out a large subset of its business transactions with other enterprises, the public administration or financial institutions over the internet, gaining significant resources that nowadays are wasted on editing, printing, transferring and re-typing business documents. The present approach can be characterised as a depth-first, pilot-oriented attempt to provide practical solutions to the Enterprise Application Interoperability problems of European SMEs and do so in a paradigm-building way. Part of the approach stems out of PRAXIS, a project co-funded by the 3rd Community Support Framework (CSF) under the Information Society Programme. The project, coordinated by Singular Software SA, brings together software vendors, research centres, public administration bodies, banking institutions and user companies in Greece, aiming to provide a solution that will allow the automation of the aforementioned transactions with significant productivity results for all the represented communities.

1. Introduction

As the functionality and complexity of modern Transactional IT Systems is rising to meet more advanced requirements, Enterprise Application Interoperability has become a key issue for most companies, in their quest for overall productivity, effective knowledge management and information security [1, 2]. Although various attempts have been made by large European organisations or Enterprises, usually addressing interoperability as a bespoke solution for legacy systems, very few attempts seem to address the issue from the aspect of a Small and Medium Enterprise (SME) or even of a Very Small Enterprise (VSE), companies that constitute the absolute majority of enterprises in the European Union [3]. What though may be the case for SMEs and VSEs in the context of making their Enterprise Applications more interoperable?

Nowadays, the typical European enterprise interacts on a daily basis with a multitude of external entities, which include the administration at local or European level (e.g. Ministries of Finance, Revenue and Tax Offices, Insurance Agencies, Statistics Agencies, etc), Financial and Banking Institutions, as well as other enterprises, mainly in the roles of Business-to-Business supplier or customer. In Greece alone, there exist 723,000 enterprises, including approximately 700,000 SMEs and VSEs, which constitute 97% of the total [4], the average European level being 93% [5].

Despite the rising pace at which Information Technology means are being deployed, the majority of several millions of daily transactions among the above entities are still carried out in the traditional manner: typically sending the various transaction documents through mail or fax, manually inserting data in Enterprise Resource Planning – ERP or Customer Relationship Management – CRM applications or, at best, manually filling in on-line web pages offered by Banks or Governmental Agencies. Based on the above inadequacy and on the absence of enlightening new approaches at the SME level, most of the companies waste significant effort and resources while not entrusting the Internet and current B2B (or even B2C) applications for their transactions. But then, why the application software vendor community does not succeed in responding to the need for really interoperable, application-to-application interconnected transactional software systems?

Recent evaluations and relative research [2] has showed that Interoperability problems may become very hard to tackle in case more than one of the following patterns characterise the problem domain: existing legacy systems that were not designed to work in common; applications belonging to a variety of different vendors; not well defined legal and statutory framework; a plethora of standardisation attempts in various levels of completion or adoption; certain cost and complexity limits – to name but a few existing in the interoperability domain. As a result of the above, one should not be amazed by the fact that most of the attempts whatsoever concern large enterprises and result in bespoke, project-oriented implementations that cannot provide a repeatable solution paradigm.

The present approach can be characterised as a depth-first, pilot-oriented attempt to provide practical solutions to the Enterprise Application Interoperability problems of European SME's and do so in a paradigm-building way.

2. Motivation and Objectives

The main objective of the presented approach is to develop and apply, at least in a pilot operational stage, the required processes and IT systems that will allow the typical Greek (or European) SME to carry out typical B2B transactions through the Internet, and in particular through the seamless interconnection of their Enterprise Applications with the corresponding applications of other enterprises, the public administration, and financial institutions. Other objectives include the following:

i. The creation and formal description of business processes, data transfer means and of a coherent overall architecture for the interconnection of transactional software applications.
ii. The adoption of the current legal and statutory framework but also the interaction with it in the form of substantiated proposals towards the responsible governmental bodies.
iii. The emphasis on security of the transferred data, on non-repudiation issues involving digitals means of signature, and on the protection of sensitive information of citizens and companies.
iv. The creation of an easily adoptable and financially feasible solution for the medium, small and very small enterprises, through hiding the complexity from the end-user – leading to the development of low cost, standardised solutions.
v. The pilot application at a proof of concept level of the resulting infrastructure, in typical users (enterprises, public bodies, banking institutions)

Part of the approach stems out of PRAXIS, a project co-funded by the 3rd Community Support Framework (CSF) under the Information Society Programme. The project brings together software vendors and e-business system integrators, universities, research centres and public sector bodies in Greece, banks, as well as typical SME's from the textile, food and services sector, aiming to provide a solution that will allow the automation of the aforementioned transactions with obvious results for all the represented communities [6].

The Potential benefits for the companies that will adopt such an approach for more interoperable enterprise applications will be: (a) A significant reduction in the required time and effort for carrying out the everyday transactions. It is estimated that, for a typical SME, this effort will be in the order of several man-months per year while the gain per transaction time is enormous – from days to seconds. (b) A significant reduction in the rate of errors that are currently made due to the repeated data entry and manual interventions in these transactions. (c) A major decrease in the cost of adoption of e-Business processes for SMEs, as such productised systems are bound to be made widely available at relatively small cost.

3. Background

3.1 European Legal Framework and Business Background

The evolution of the Internet and in particular the possibility to carry out Internet-based business transactions resulted in a series of legal issues that concerned the European Union as a whole as well as the independent Member States. The main issue that needed to be addressed with respect to electronic business transactions, payments and document exchanges was the lack of a clear legal framework within which such transactions would take place, common for possibly all the EU Members. The rapid rate though, with which technological developments followed one another did not allow for a timely legal response at an international and national level [7,8].

Various regulatory steps have recently taken place in Europe and in Greece in particular to address the above issues, as the European Union is gradually progressing in a coordinated approach to address the issue of electronic business transactions by creating a legal framework within which all transactions will be carried out, and which will be eventually adopted by the business world across Europe. Central to this approach was the Directive 2000/31/EC of the European Parliament and of the Council of 8 June 2000, which placed the foundations for the development of e-Commerce throughout Europe.

In Greece, as in most of the Member States and certainly in all of the 10 new Members, newly the local authorities are struggling to adopt the European Union directives, by adapting the local legal regulations accordingly and through constantly monitoring – but not driving – local needs.

3.2 Status of SMEs

In order to ensure the wide adoption of a system supporting transactions between SMEs, a realistic understanding of the current situation regarding the typical operation of its users is needed. As depicted in Figure 1, a typical European SME is daily making transactions with the following main groups of legal entities, in the B2B space:

- Enterprises acting as Customers, thus receiving goods or services and paying the price or fee, in an overall transaction characterised as "sale".

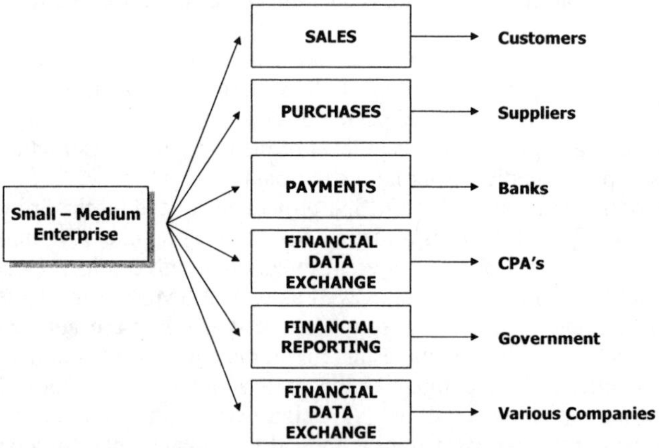

Figure 1: SMEs, their transactions and the interacting Legal Entities

- Enterprises acting as Suppliers, providing SME with goods or services, through a purchase process.
- Banking institutions, assisting in the management of the SME monetary assets and the processes of payments or receipts.

- Certified Professional Accountants that often offer services to SME's and also receive/send significant amounts of financial data from/to the enterprise, for book-keeping and tax-reporting purposes.
- The local Government, usually instantiated as a Tax/Vat Office or Ministry of Finance local authority, towards which both information and payments should be sent.
- Other Enterprises, among them SMEs, for various reasons leading to exchange of business and financial data.

4. Methodology

The methodological, paradigm building approach presented here and implemented within the PRAXIS project consists of the following steps:

i. Representation of the existing business processes relevant to the project, resulting in Computationally Independent Models (CIM) represented in various UML descriptions. More than 30 processes have been identified and described (actors, roles, flows, data, control, etc).
ii. Partial transformation of the previous models and representation of the to-be business processes, after the introduction of an A2A Interconnection System with Servers and Clients connecting with the existing ERP applications, resulting in a relevant Platform Independent Model (PIM).
iii. Formalisation of the data exchange, through further analysis of the business documents and the deployment of XML/B2B models, thus forming XSD/DTD descriptions.
iv. Formalisation of the needed behaviour of the system, represented in UML, as another PIM description.
v. Various design representations and model transformations at the level of Platform-Specific Model (PSM), for the system under development (client and server architectures and designs following the Service-oriented Architecture, SoA) [17], including the partial reverse engineering of already developed Enterprise Applications (commercially available mid-market ERP/CRM).

It has to be noted that the drafting of detailed specifications for the technological basis and architecture upon which the system will be based (including Web Services approaches, SOAP standards, .NET architectures, JAVA/J2EE architectures and various development environments) form a part of the on-coming steps of the approach.

5. Technology

The technological basis for the proposed system includes the currently available standards and solutions for modelling of business processes, the modelling and description of the information exchanged among the enterprise applications (including XML-based hierarchical languages) and the current technological standards for developing Server and Peer-To-Peer applications using Service-oriented-Architectures (SoA).

5.1 Data modelling and XML representations

When developing a solution for enhancing interoperability of existing systems, one has to choose between (a) instantiating one of the existing XML/B2B standards or (b) developing a tailor-made solution adhering to the standards, but also designed to provide the required flexibility while minimizing the system complexity – a set of characteristics very important to SME's.

Extending XML standardisation reviews [9], the currently available standards for business transactions can be categorised as shown in Table 1, according to whether their main focus is on business processes / message transactions or on business documents.

ebXML [10] is a standard proposed and maintained by the Organization for the Advancement of Structured Information Standards - OASIS. Currently supported by the

United Nations (UN) and other major bodies and organizations, ebXML covers business processes and message transactions, its strength certainly being the former.

Standard	Standardisation Body	Business Processes	Business Documents
ebXML	OASIS	✓	✓
RosettaNet	RosettaNet Org	✓	✓
xCBL	xCBL Org		✓
XBRL	XBRL Org		✓
ebisXML	BASDA	✓	✓
UN / CEFACT	UN/ECE		(✓)
UN / EDIFACT	UN/ECE		✓

Table 1: Categorisation of Business Standards

RosettaNet [11] is an emerging standard proposing a framework to securely exchange documents between businesses. The framework is based on XML and simplifies the transaction processes focusing only in security and transport. As a result we have a client-server model of work, inappropriate for large-scale applications.

ebis-XML is proposed by BASDA. It provides a suite of messages for conducting electronic transactions. Covering only the ordering / invoicing processes, it provides a quick and practical way for the exchange of the core business documents among enterprises.

xCBL (XML Common Business Library) [13] focuses on business documents. Supported by Microsoft, SAP, HP, Sun Microsystems and CommerceOne, it provides an XML-based, comprehensive collection of documents for conducting electronic transactions.

XBRL (eXtensive Business Reporting Language) [14] is a standard proposed from OASIS, in an attempt to describe financial information for reporting purposes. Formerly known as XFRML (eXtensive Financial Reporting Mark-up Language), XBRL is a technical specification that allows for the creation of business and financial reports.

UN / CEFACT [15] is the awaited XML-transformation attempt of UN / EDIFACT business documents. Still in progress, it is bound to use ebXML as the architecture definition, extending the various messages applying the EDIFACT experience.

UN / EDIFACT [16] is the oldest and most widely used standard in application-to-application interconnection, supported by numerous organizations and businesses. Included in the present review for completion purposes, it focuses mainly on business documents and provides for an EDI-based method for message transactions.

After the initial categorisation of the various XML/B2B standards, an evaluation "objective function" was created, based on the main objectives of the PRAXIS project. Among the important factors one will find: Expressiveness (span of existing processes and documents), Maturity (adoption by industry and international bodies), Compatibility (degree of coherence with other standards in the XML/B2B context), Applicability (easiness of embodiment, provision of material and support), Expandability (ability to include more documents/processes) and Royalties Independence.

The above evaluation framework concluded on the differences among the standardisations and their various scores according to different weighting scenarios. However, looking at the not-yet-converging requirements from United States, Europe and Greece and due to the fact that the types of transactions the PRAXIS system is bound to support are affected by the specific details of Greek business regulations, the complete adoption of any of the above standards would offer few advantages, and would considerably aggravate the implementation process. As a result, the adopted solution consists of modelling the transactional data in a manner similar, yet not fully compatible, to xCBL, while in parallel maintaining a detailed mapping of the alterations.

5.2 System Architecture

The PRAXIS system [12], as shown in Figure 2 consists of the PRAXIS Clients and the PRAXIS Server. The former provides end-users (SME's) with a way to access the system, while the later maintains the core business logic and the various documents exchanged.

Three types of clients are supported:

- The thick (or "Fat") Client, is a windows-based application that interconnects the PRAXIS system and existing ERP/CRM or relevant transactional enterprise application.
- The Thin Client is a windows-based application that provides the basic features of the system, able to work independently of existing ERP/CRM systems.
- The Web Client is a web-based, zero-client application used to access the PRAXIS server and create or view business documents.

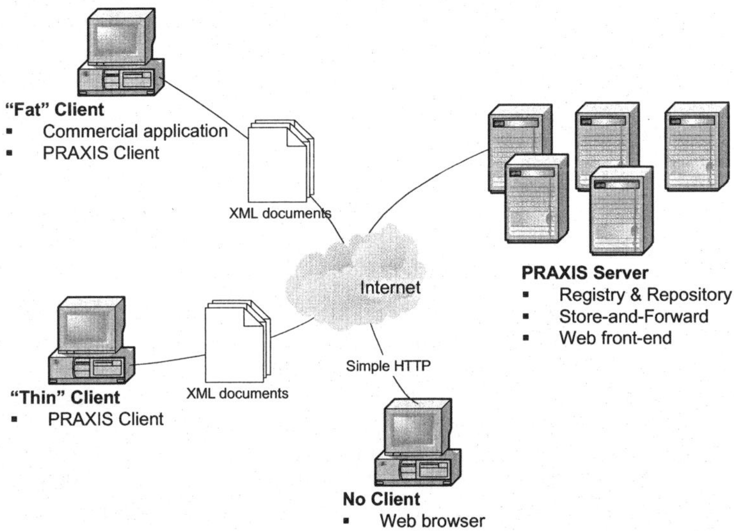

Figure 2: The PRAXIS Architecture

The PRAXIS Server implements three major functions:

i. Registry & Repository; supports creation and management of user profiles, storing and retrieving process descriptions, document templates and actual transaction documents.
ii. Store & Forward; provides a mailbox-style mechanism that receives, stores and sends the various business documents among the participating enterprises following certain time stamping, acknowledgment, security, encryption and performance requirements.
iii. Web Front – End; web-based interface for provide access to he PRAXIS Server (administrators, participating companies, candidate customers, public bodies, the public etc) each at the right level of security and permissions granted.

5.3 Protocols and Connectors

It is a vital specification for an interoperability-oriented system to be as open as possible to future extensions and interconnections. In order to comply with that demand, the system is designed so as to allow maximum flexibility in Interconnection Protocols and XML/ B2B Standards. Figure 3 shows the protocol stack of the system, where higher-level protocols (such as SOAP, CORBA or their ingredients) can be left transparent to the Server.

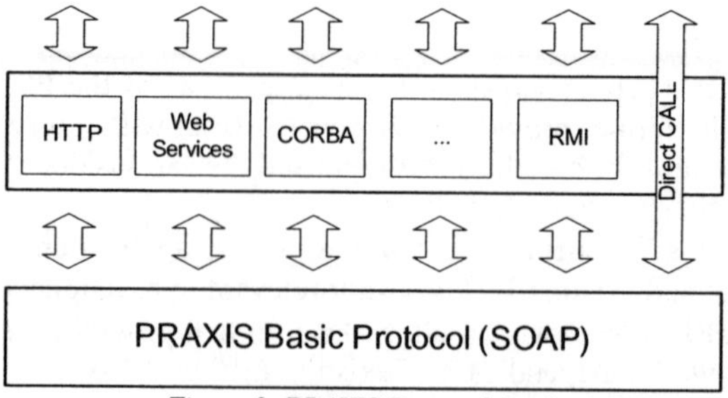

Figure 3: PRAXIS Protocol Stack

In an analogous way, as shown in Figure 4, in order to support XML/B2B standards to appear, a mechanism for the transformation of business documents will be implemented, using an XSLT (or XQuery) transformation engine for this purpose.

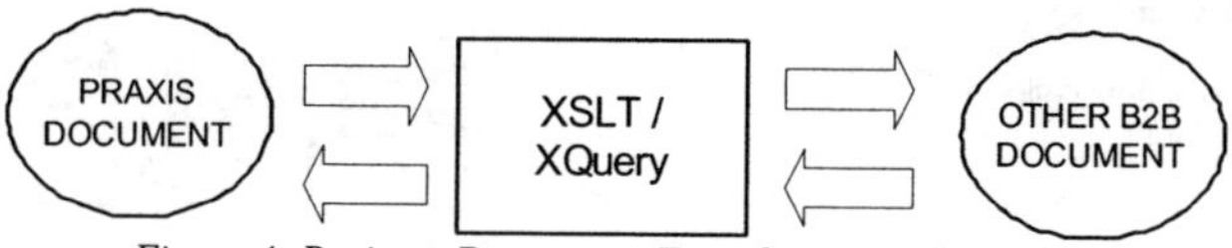

Figure 4: Business Documents Transformation Procedure

6. Conclusions

This paper presents an approach for making existing SME ERP/CRM applications interoperable over the Internet. Due to complexity, various methods and techniques are being deployed: Model Driven and Services Oriented Architecture (MDA / SoA) provide the methodological framework for research on B2B/XML schemas, assessment and deployment of existing and emerging standards and final creation of novel implementations – so standardised that will be affordable and easy to use by the typical European SME.

Although goal-driven approaches like the PRAXIS project will provide some practical, exploitable results, a legally compliant, standardised solution that will function easily within any EU Member State and any industry sector will not be a short term achievement. This will depend on the maturity of Legal and Statutory Frameworks, of Business Process and Documents Standardisation as well as of Information Technology capabilities.

Towards this direction, next steps to our approach include further analysis and formalisation of the MDA steps, classification and structuring of the various design decisions and patterns, as well as work on the ontological aspects of the paradigm.

References

[1] Interoperability Development for Enterprise Application and Software (IDEAS, IST project, 2002). www.ideas-roadmap.net

[2] M. Lenzerini, "Data integration: A theoretical perspective", in Proc. of the 21st ACM SIGACT SIGMOD SIGART Symposium on Principles of Database Systems (PODS), pages 233-246, 2002.

[3] The e-Business W@tch, European Commission, DG Enterprise, 2004. www.ebusiness-watch.org

[4] "VAT Statistics 2002 – 2003", General Secretariat of Information Systems (GSIS), Ministry of Economy and Finance, Greece, 2003. Available online at www.gsis.gov.gr

[5] "Information and Communications Technology (ICT) Yearbook", European Information Technology Observatory (EITO), 2003

[6] Y. Charalabidis, S. Pantelopoulos, Y. Koussos: "Enabling Interoperability of Transactional Enterprise Applications", Workshop on Interoperability of Enterprise Systems, 18th European Conference on Object-Oriented Programming (ECOOP), Oslo, 14–18 June 2004

[7] European Commission Enterprise Directorate General. Report of the expert group on B2B internet trading platforms, July 2003. http://europa.eu.int/comm/enterprise/ict/policy/b2b/wshop/fin-report.pdf

[8] "EU VAT legislation on electronic invoicing & electronic storage of invoices (overview of all the Member States)", PriceWaterhouseCoopers, Final Report to the European Commission, 2002

[9] Uche Ogbuji , "A survey of XML standards. The core standards - a foundation for the wide world of XML", IBM DevelopmentWorks, 2004. www-106.ibm.com/developerworks/library/x-stand1.html
[10] Mathew MacKenzie. ebXML messaging services specification v2.1. Draft, ebXML, March 2004. Available Online at http://www.oasis-open.org/committees/download.php/ 6130/wd-ebMS-2_1-04.pdf
[11] Rosetta Implementation Framework (RNIF): Core specification. Technical report, RosettaNet, March 2002. Available online at http://www.rosettanet.org/
[12] Diomidis Spinellis, Yannis Charalabidis and Vassilios Karakoidas, "Application Interconnection and Execution of Business to Business Transactions over the Internet", 20th European conference in Operational Research (EURO-XX), 4 - 7 July 2004, POSTER, www.dmst.aueb.gr/dds/
[13] XCBL (XML Common Business Language), available online at http://www.xcbl.org/xcbl40/xcbl40.html
[14] Phillip Engel, Walter Hamscher, Geoffrey Shuetrim, David vun Kannon, and Hugh Wallis. Extensible business reporting language v2.1. Draft, XBRL, December 2003. Available online at http://www.xbrl.org/
[15] UN / CEFACT: United Nations centre for trade facilitation and electronic business, www.unece.org/cefact
[16] United Nations Electronic Commision for Europe. UN / EDIFACT: United Nations directories for Electronic Data Interchange for administration, commerce and transport. www.unece.org/trade/untdid/texts/d100_d.html
[17] David Booth, Hugo Haas, Francis McCabe, Eric Newcomer, Michael Champion, Chris Ferris, and David Orchard. Web services architecture. Technical report, W3C, February 2004. www.w3.org/ws-arch/

Roadmap for SME Sustainable Profitability

Jorge FRADINHO OLIVEIRA, Alvaro de OLIVEIRA, Ermelinda FRADINHO
Alfamicro Lda, Alameda da Guia Nº192 A, Cascais, 2750, Portugal
Tel: +351 21 4866784; Fax: +351 21 4866752; email: mail@alfamicro.pt

Abstract: One year after the end of the European Commission co-funded SMARTISAN (IST-2000-26267) and SCOOP (IST-2000-25200) projects, this paper accounts for some of the eCommerce visions that simply did not take place as well as for a set of sensible and critical software engineering practices, which largely contributed to the success of both projects. Also, a recent analysis is presented on the continued and growing positive results of the digital business solutions implemented that are providing our "end users" with increasing differentiation and cost advantages over their competitors. Finally, picking up on our SME's existing momentum towards innovative eCommerce business practices, we also describe some of the concepts currently being researched for SMARTISAN 2, namely those of customer centric and extended enterprise strategies geared towards customer value co-creation.

1. Introduction

Over three years SMARTISAN (IST-2000-26267) and SCOOP (IST-2000-25200) attracted the attention of both academic and business environments and published several technical papers were published in dissemination activities [1][2][3][4]. These papers described the evolutionary methodologies and technological solutions adopted to accommodate the various industries in which our "end user" SME' were established, namely: textile and garment, automotive, food and beverages, retail and printing industries.

In the year following the end of SMARTISAN and SCOOP we provided post project assistance to SMEs and evaluated the impact of these projects. Before describing this new data, we present short project descriptions, followed by an overview of some of the envisioned Internet effects, which simply were not happening at our SMEs. This is followed by a list of software engineering practices and tools which in our view made a difference and are usually simply taken "as a given" or even ignored, ultimately hindering the chances of SMEs reaching sustainable profitability through eCommerce. We hope that these are taken as a useful guideline for others who venture in similar projects.

The final part of our paper brings together the proven successful concepts in both of these projects, ranging from knowledge management systems to dynamic supply chain configurations, towards strategies that support affordable product mass customization and customer value co-creation. These are to be implemented in SMARTISAN 2.

2. Project Descriptions

2.1 SMARTISAN

The SMARTISAN project aimed to provide SMEs with tools, processes and methodologies to support them adopting e-Business and collaborative e-Commerce. SMARTISAN developed a fully integrated Web-based e-commerce system, which integrates SMEs supply chains (business to business e-commerce with manufacturers), their retail activities (business to consumer), their involvement with accredited and approved consumer service providers (Artisans) and allow customers to track order progress to the point of delivery. Thus SMARTISAN offers new e-Commerce based value adding services making use of the latest technological developments and standardisation in the area of EDI/XML, as well as distributed component architectures (CORBA and JAVA), EAI and LEO (Low Earth Orbit) satellite services. These include solutions to support cooperation, flexible work, management and coordination planning and monitoring across the networked virtual enterprises and associated businesses processes. The end users from automotive, retail, food and beverages, formed a test bed to achieve these goals and to transport the benefits through their networks to the potential marketplace. A consortium of in eleven partners from research and development, academia, consulting and industrial users worked together from January 2001 to June 2003. A prototype system was implemented illustrating basic SMARTISAN concepts of powerful, affordable and integrated eCommerce solutions for SMEs. SMARTISAN empowers the customer with choice, allowing total transparency across the supply chain up to the manufacturers, and providing a full service. The level of transparency can be adapted to accommodate the specific nature of the relationships shared between entities in the supply chain. A common platform has been developed and customized for each end user including easy to use administrative tools. In the near future the commercial partners and end users aim to commercialise the SMARTISAN results and to incorporate most of the results, namely the virtual artisans into marketable product and services. For complete descriptions of system architectures, business plans and case studies please refer to our previous paper [4].

2.1 SCOOP

The threats to the traditional European garment industry can be overcome by a balanced use of IT technologies and business process re-engineering, together with an innovative business strategy. The SCOOP project addressed the problem of managing co-operation in dynamic SME networks using an innovative and advanced solution based on co-operative planning and control. The SCOOP solution is focused on the networked company needs, including those of SMEs', and provides a flexible, affordable and easy-to-integrate-solution, in line with the current market trends for business applications. Sustained competitiveness is achieved by improved productivity including production flexibility, outsourcing, creative design and efficient logistics and fulfillment supported by IT. Issues of integration, interoperability, brokering, knowledge sharing, and trust are supported by affordable tools based on Web technologies such as XML. For complete descriptions [5].

3. Building successful ICT strategies

SMARTISAN and SCOOP enabled us to crack the hard shell that sometimes SMEs on their own account isolate themselves. As we gathered, to blame was to a large extent the poor marketing strategy that major IT vendors adopted both during and after the ".com & .gone" era, whereby non IT proficient managers at SMEs became ever more cautious and dubious of the announced potential of electronic commerce for their operations.

3.1 Unfulfilled Internet Visions

Mass dis-intermediation and Customer Relationship Management solutions, were two slogans promoted by so called Internet visionaries, which we had to hear from our SMEs.

SMARTISAN showed the reality of existing relationships in some markets can be prohibitive and that quick profits through disintermediation are at best an illusion. We presented a manufacturing SME with the ability to offer his products directly to consumers, thus dis-intermediating distributors. The SME refused as it did not want to upset its distributor relationships. Its profit driver was based on designing better products and enhancing distributor relationships, rather than pushing existing products closer to market.

CRM is based on enhancing understanding of customer purchasing decisions by learning more about customers. Thousands of companies adopted the "CRM enabled" slogan. Data mining techniques were set in place. As an IT Manager put it, "we were flooded with new information on our clients' behaviour but had little ability to extrapolate real benefit".

In retrospective, much work was needed in bringing the involved SMEs up to speed with new business practices even before presenting them with the added transaction volume provided by electronic commerce and collaborative practices. In some cases, SMEs confided that SMARTISAN enabled them to see for the first time their complete internal operations in a clear manner and several bottlenecks were eliminated outright. The business process reengineering undertaken was twofold, in that efficiency improvements were achieved, but more importantly, our SMEs could evaluate for themselves that we were not simply trying to push them onto a bandwagon of our own.

3.2 Sensible and Effective Tactics

The following are individual factors that we believe combined to help reach successful results:

1. SME Champion: The reality is that it is difficult to persuade any organisation to fundamentally change some of their business processes. A key strategy was to get an SME Chief Commercial Officer to vouch for our project. Even in our absence they acted as Project Champion to the rest of the company board and employees themselves.
2. Managing Resistance to Change: The success of a system is largely determined by the acceptance of those who will use it on a daily basis in the organization. Despite holding discussion groups to gather requirements and make people feel part of the process (thus less likely to resist the actual system), we noticed some indifference from a Chief Industrial Engineer at some point. Following extensive discussions, he supported SMARTISAN. However, having listening to how he liked his paper based information layout, we replicated it exactly to his user interface on SMARTISAN. The lesson learnt is that one's efforts to include everyone from the start do not always work, yet there are simple workarounds to achieve the same result without jeopardizing the core.
3. Delivering Visible Results Early On: From the start SMARTISAN was set on delivering ambitious goals and the piloting phase started at month 24. However it was key to deliver visible results early on to capture organizational motivation and support for the project. On one occasion, a website that took into account the ideas of Sales, IT and Industrial key personnel was developed. We registered the site on specific search engines for the SME' particular market on different countries. In three weeks it received a RFQ from the Far East, from a 1st Tier supplier for Peugeot in France, and from a company in its own country not known to it previously! By focusing on collaborative development effort and delivering results, we gained SMEs support at an early stage.
4. Legacy Integration Methodology: SMARTISAN includes an integration module of its own that makes possible data exchange between various systems, including a simple GUI for setup purposes and a backend engine that automatically generates XML scripting and manages both local and remote integration processes (i.e. LAN, email, FTP, etc). However, SMARTISAN would gather online pre orders which had to be cleared by the SME' Commercial department and upon approval were automatically sent to the legacy production system. We faced the decision of forcing employees to use two separate systems concurrently, having to swap between them frequently to gather information and make decisions, or replicating extensively legacy interfaces onto SMARTISAN, thus meaning increased development effort and redundancy. In the end it was more cost effective to contract the legacy provider to implement new functionality directly into their legacy. These were successful ventures largely because the SME' had a good relationship with their legacy providers and we explained we were

not substituting their ERP legacy system but rather building on it. Also, a detailed spec and mock up shots were made, and then we had the legacy provider name its development price before even coding one line.

5. Content Management: One goal was to develop a system that reduced SME's dependency on third parties to maintain their business processes. Easy to use administrative tools were developed to handle content management, resulting in the dynamic content generation with visible results immediately on the website
6. Training: Following standard practices rolling out SMARTISAN and SCOOP included detailed user manuals with screen shot walkthroughs, detailed administrative manuals, and week long intensive training. We provided individual training to each SME' department head with regard to relevant functionality, and they taught subordinates. We provided individual training to IT heads for the whole system including the other user's system functionalities. Finally, we kept close contact with SMEs even long after the deployment making sure that they took full advantage of the available potential

4. R&D and Best Practice Co-existence Methodology Results

SMARTISAN and SCOOP have provided the opportunity to develop and test a methodology that allows for the co-existence of research and best practice in the same project. In this case the usual level of expectations of knowledge resources (universities, research organizations) and knowledge users (companies, etc) are raised significantly in their own domains creating additional ground for possible conflicts.

The most common example is the research objective to prototype a new idea and jump to the next one as opposed to the user objective of achieving a usable solution, simple if it must, that can enhance their profitability and bring quick tangible results.

Along the years we have developed a methodology to handle the process of innovation culture and the mechanisms to manage its implementation [6]. The degree of success of any of our Business Process Reengineering and outright technology R&D initiatives has largely depended on our efforts towards mentoring SMEs whilst providing them with the right level of knowledge within easy access and at an appropriate time.

This methodology is based on the trust built up, this meaning a close understanding and support to the developer and users which is more easily provided by an independent facilitator like ourselves than someone who has a potential conflict of interests [7].

We believe that our clear view of the overall scientific, technical and business architecture of projects together with our experience in managing their implementations were in the end the vital ingredients for our methodology's success. In the case of SMARTISAN and SCOOP added to overall SME efficiency increase due to installed system architecture interoperability, the following has been observed one year onwards:

1. "Pre Order" mechanism which allows for orders of previously engineered products reach up to six digits sales per order
2. Make to order company reduced up to 30% of its enquiry cycle with workflow system that integrates online environment with internal processes
3. Engineer to order company reduced up to 20% of its R&D costs with knowledge management system (with time and use, percentage is expected to rise even further)
4. Retail network simplified internal ordering process and improved delivering with tracking and tracing technology, meaning a 10% cost reduction
5. Garment production capacity flexibility increased by 40% with dynamic piecemeal subcontracting task management
6. Beverages manufacturer reduces transaction costs of ordering process and offers forward planning advice for small corner outlets, ultimately locking them in and meaning a new revenue source (still to be measured)

7. Garment resource waste reduction of 15% given increased and timely information on available internal and external production capacity

Generally, SME expectations were met in both SMARTISAN and SCOOP as a result of our harmonization of operations, adding necessary flexibility and creativity to their business processes. As a result, we are left with unprecedented motivation and commitment levels from the SMEs involved, who are from the start electronic commerce enabled, and thus ready and anxious to embrace the new business strategies we began unveiling towards the end of the project. In truth we achieved an add on effect of readying them to what we believe is the next step of sustaining competitiveness at a global level, namely cooperation, not just with their suppliers and distributors, but with their end customers themselves.

5. Future work… SMARTISAN 2

Globalization, delocalization and disintermediation are indeed realities of our increasingly competitive market. However, refraining ourselves from hard selling strategies, how then can we continue our mission of helping SMEs drive the European economy?

The knowledge intensive environment made available by the Internet no longer goes unnoticed by product and service providers, as increasingly they come across more demanding customers who are not simply focused in price differentiation. A networking effect built on common interests, needs and experiences has increasingly brought together consumer communities that by simple word of mouth are vastly more effective than corporate orchestrated advertising campaigns [8].

Global offering has come into play, whereby local dealers no longer host a selection of products able to accommodate the desires of their local customers who just got off the Internet looking for a brand new model sold 10000 Km away. Many studies acknowledge this customer inclination towards variety [9]. The hidden cost of this added offering capability has been an explosion in product offering that ultimately hinders the decision buying process of consumers. Customers are indeed more knowledgeable of what there is to buy, yet paradoxically find it more difficult to match their needs to available offers.

In future for Internet connected supply networks to compete there will be a need for the "instantaneous" transformation of information to knowledge and for knowledge to enhance new product development and operational excellence. In effect manufacturing needs to create Knowledge Supply Chains aimed at radically improving the supply and dissemination of knowledge throughout manufacturing organizations (see Figure 1).

SMARTISAN 2 will move from the strategies described as Business 2 Business (B2B) and Business 2 Consumer (B2C) to Consumer 2 Business 2 Consumer (C2B2C).

SMARTISAN 2 will provide extended innovative tools that allow SMEs to work closely with suppliers, clients and end consumers and position themselves as providers of added value services that extend their existing product range and encompass new information flows clients. We will go beyond so called "key customer indicators" which misinterpreted customers and neglected the intricate nature of business contexts. We believe that given the opportunity supplier and customer can work together to devise better products and services. It really isn't the matter of SME managers not worrying about their customers, but rather about not having clear and meaningful mechanisms that allow them to better and sooner understand their customer. Invisible perches on customer shoulders are not the way to go, but rather, empowering willing customers with an ability to provide feedback and new product requirements. Once such an understanding is in place the initial step may be confined to a re tinkering of a product offering strategy. However, much more can be achieved beyond that, such as reverse feedback cycles that influence product design and availability, nearing business as we know it to the concept of mass customisation.

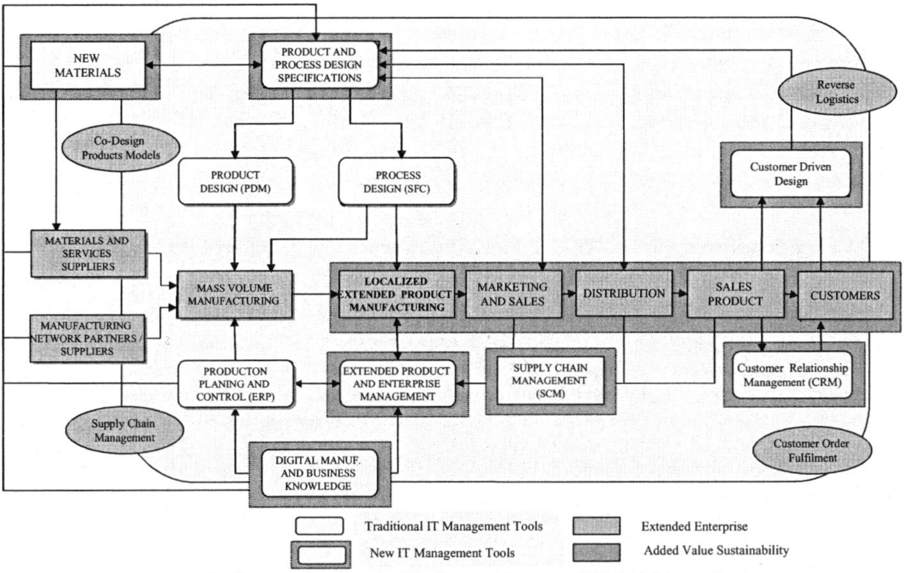

Figure 1 - Strategy for Sustainable Competitiveness of Global Digital Business (Extended Enterprises and Products)

The traditional supply chain will no longer be sequential or linear, as different suppliers may join or exit the chain depending on specific consumer preferences. Outright there are two major implications that determine SMEs capability to remain competitive, namely:

1. Balancing local customization and support with the cost efficiencies of standardization
2. Delivering high quality products and services amid changes in supply chain entities

"mass customisation" was first coined in 1987 [10] and since then an increased interest has been taking place as a natural extension of extended product and enterprise strategies together with the opportunities offered by Internet technologies. We ourselves have demonstrated the mass customization of the supply chain itself (SCOOP) or of a product requirements gathering process in an engineer to order environment (SMARTISAN).

We intend to make generally accessible to SMEs tools for dynamic product configuration and cost estimation through methods such as case based reasoning [11] and innovative routes that allow modelling of specific setting, evaluate cost/benefit of mass customization, and fine tune product/service families accordingly. Models of customer participation will be devised, measured, and engineered to serve as input into the supply chain. Research will be conducted on how to best support decision process of an SME to accommodate its customer in its supply chain and to understand how to best go about it according to distinctive product/service characteristics. Last but not least, SMARTISAN 2 builds upon its predecessor while remaining truthful to its promise of improved, innovative, flexible and affordable solutions for SMEs to take full advantage of electronic commerce.

6. Conclusions

SMEs that took part in SMARTISAN and SCOOP are now fully engaged in e-Business and exploiting new ways of e-Collaboration. They are also fully committed and have radically changed their approach to IT and their understanding about the benefits it can have on their business. Generally, their management are today very enthusiastic preachers of IT benefits inside and outside the company delivered by eCommerce strategies. Ultimately it must be said that we did not simply resort to leading technology or to a business bandwagon present at the time. Instead we looked for appropriate solutions that were fully understood by each of the SMEs and could provide effective returns. Also, we reported the good results achieved one year onwards after projects completion, and demonstrated that these largely depended on following sensible and effective tactics, including good software engineering practices and tools which more often than not are simply taken "as a given" or even ignored.

eCommerce is increasingly unlocking new potential for SMEs and very interesting avenues of research and application are before us for SMARTISAN 2 in Knowledge Supply Chains and exploring the concept of customers co-creating value.

References

[1] A. Oliveira, J. Oliveira and M. Oliveira, Moving E-Commerce to Extended Products. In: e2001 E-Business and E-Work Conference, IOS Press, Venice, October 2001

[2] J. Oliveira and A. Oliveira, Dynamic Management of Virtual Enterprises in the Textile/ Garment Industry. In: e2001 E-Business and E-Work Conference, IOS Press, Venice, October 2001

[3] M. Oliveira, J. Oliveira, F. Basto and A. Oliveira, SMARTISAN – The E-Business Solution for SMEs. In: Proceedings of e-Work Conference, IOS Press, Prague, October 2002

[4] J. Oliveira, A. Oliveira, M. Oliveira, J. Pinheiro, and D. Blake, Smartisan- Collaborative Services enabled by seamless integration of Virtual Artisans in dynamic networked organizations. In: Building the Knowledge Economy, P. Cunningham et al (Eds) , IOS Press, Amsterdam, October 2003

[5] A. Oliveira, J. Oliveira, and J. Pinheiro, SCOOP – Sustained Competitiveness in Dynamic Networked Organization Enabled by Innovative E-Work Processes. In: Building the Knowledge Economy, P. Cunningham et al (Eds) , IOS Press, Amsterdam, October 2003

[6] C. Edquist, Systems of Innovation: Technologies, Institutions and Organizations, ISBN: 185567453X, Pinter Publisher, 1997

[7] A. Oliveira, Global AICIME – An Integrated approach to support SMEs in the Global Electronic Commerce Environment. In: ISIP Conference Proceedings, 1997

[8] G. Silverman, The Secrets of Word-of-Mouth Marketing: How to Trigger Exponential Sales Through Runaway Word of Mouth, ISBN 0814470726. AMACOM, 2001

[9] R. L. Keeney, The value of Internet commerce to the customer. In: Management Science, 1999

[10] C. Davis, Future Perfect, ISBN: 020159045X, Addison-Wesley Pub Co, 1996

[11] J. Baumeister, A. Atzmueller, and F. Puppe. Inductive Learning for CaseBased Diagnosis with Multiple Faults. In: Advances in Case-Based Reasoning. Springer-Verlag, Berlin, 2002. Proceedings of the 6th European Conference on Case-Based Reasoning (ECCBR-2002).

Section 7.2

Applications

eAdoption and the Knowledge Economy: Issues, Applications, Case Studies
P. Cunningham and M. Cunningham (Eds.)
IOS Press, 2004

e-Services for Support of Robot Applications in SME-Networks

Ralf BERGER, Gerhard SCHRECK, Cornelius WILLNOW
Fraunhofer IPK, Pascalstr. 8-9, 10 587 Berlin, Germany
Tel: +49-30/39 006-129, Fax: +49-30/391 10 37, ralf.berger@ipk.fraunhofer.de
Tel: +49-30/39 006-152, Fax: +49-30/391 10 37, gerhard.schreck@ipk.fraunhofer.de
Tel: +49-30/39 006-173, Fax: +49-30/391 10 37, cornelius.willnow@ipk.fraunhofer.de

Abstract: The complexity of robot application is a considerable burden for small and medium enterprises (SMEs) when introducing and operating robots. For this reason, many SMEs cannot apply robots today. To improve this situation, specialized SMEs can provide process engineering, programming and diagnostics related services to SMEs using robots. To bridge distances between the SMEs, Internet e-services can be applied. The paper describes the methodology used to develop e-services for robot application by SME-networks, gives an overview on the developed services and tools, and presents services for process development in more detail.

1. Introduction

When introducing industrial robots today, small and medium enterprises (SMEs) are faced with the complexity of robot systems. While larger companies can afford specialist departments for planning and operation of robot applications, SMEs have only a small number of persons, and often only a single person, to perform all robot related tasks.

The introduction of a robot installation represents a large investment for a SME. Additionally it needs qualified personnel able to perform all tasks for the robot system. This often overtaxes the company and the personnel [1]. For these reasons, SMEs often hesitate to introduce robots, even if this is urgently required for productivity and quality reasons.

But a number of specialized SMEs have considerable expertise and skills for efficiently operating robot installations. SMEs specialized in process development, in product design for automation, in robot installations, in robot programming, etc. can support robot user SMEs by providing the required skills as services.

This cooperation, however, must be fast and efficient. Furthermore, the spatial distance between the SMEs must be bridged. Both can be supported by Internet e-services. The development of e-services for this area is, however, a challenge.

In pursuit of this approach, the EU CRAFT-Project "Small and Medium Enterprises - Robotics Service Inter-Network" (SME-Rosin), IST-2001-55039, was started [2]. The objective of the project is to develop concepts for services that simply robot application at small companies. The result of the project are methods and tools for providing engineering, programming and maintenance as services with Internet support.

In the following, the paper discusses the major challenges for the development of e-services for this area and the methodology used for tackling the challenges is described. Then an overview on the developed services is given and for illustrating the developed work procedures, examples for the area process design are outlined. Finally the paper closes with conclusions and lessons learned.

2. The Challenge

Robot application is a domain, in which personal on-site presence has been traditionally dominant and it is in many cases practically indispensable. The major reasons arise from the involved physical processes and their direct interaction with operators. Human-machine interaction often takes place with feedback frequencies above 1 Hz, e.g. when adjusting a welding current with a knob. At the same time, sensing modalities include vision, sound and vibrations with high spatial-temporal resolution. Also tactile information is important: a finger can sense surface structures that are not visible to the eye. Furthermore, manufacturing environments are often dangerous. Industrial robots are strong and fast machines and a remote operator may easily oversee a person in reach of the machine.

On the other hand, data transfer media that are required for providing services from remote, show certain strengths, but also certain restrictions. Telephone allows efficient verbal communication, but is limited mostly to speech. Facsimile allows to transfer graphical information, but has a low interaction rate. Internet allows to transfer any type of electronic data, including sound and graphical data. But, although considerable progress is made, it is still limited today for example in the response time, the field of sight of the cameras used, the transfer of haptic data and in interactive remote manipulation [3].

Nevertheless, activities can be performed from remote, when it is possible to efficiently transfer the needed data between the on-site and the remote location. For example, a proven set of welding parameters or a robot program can be transferred. Activities that need direct physical interaction have to be performed on-site, for example the commissioning of welding parameters and robot programs.

Consequently, when developing e-services for robot applications there must be a balance between what can be provided as a remote service and what has to be done on-site. Furthermore, proven work procedures should not be disregarded. Existing procedures must be considered to be an indispensable back-bone of expertise and practical needs.

Hence, the challenge consists, in a first step, in identifying activities that can be shifted from robot user SMEs to service provider SMEs. For these activities, the available communication technology has to enable the required company interfaces. In a further step, these remote activities have to be embedded into the over-all working environment.

3. Methodology

For these reasons, a domain focused and user driven methodology for the development of distributed work procedures is required. In the SME-Rosin project a proceeding consisting of the major steps listed in Table 1 proved to be adequate.

Steps 1 is of special importance for identifying and maintaining the domain specific back-bone of expertise. Step 2 is crucial for the optimal distribution of activities. Step 3 brings the 'step forwards', but considers the communication requirements of resulting company interfaces. Steps 4 and 7 ensure practicability.

To perform steps 5 to 7, the example SME-network formed by the industrial partners of the SME-Rosin consortium is used. It includes a supply chain for mechanical equipment extends from a wire-feeder manufacturer to a welding machine manufacturer and a robot system integrator to end user companies, and a supply chain for programming equipment that reaches from a programming system manufacturer over the system integrator to the end user companies.

Table 1: Methodology used for deriving distributed work procedures and services

Step	Activities
1. Current Work Procedures	Today's business processes during development and operation of robot installations are analyzed. This results in a 'map' of activities and their current distribution on companies.
2. Potential for Improvement	On this 'map' the suitability of the assignment of activities to companies is assessed with respect to the specific strengths and needs of the companies concerning available personnel, company skills, know-how and equipment.
3. Distribution of Work Procedures	Based on the identified potential for improvement, the current processes are re-arranged in consideration of needed data transfer. This results in the first design for distributed work procedures.
4. Feasibility and Efficiency Review	The re-arrangement is assessed with respect to feasibility and efficiency of the resulting processes. This second review results in the target definition of the future business processes for distributed cooperative work procedures.
5. Tool Implementation	The tools for the performance and the communication needs of the distributed processes are selected and, where not available, implemented.
6. Process Implementation	The business procedures are implemented in an exemplary manner in an example SME-network. Example installations are used for demonstration and verification purposes.
7. Improvement Cycles	Testing and improvement takes place in development-test cycles for verification of processes, e-services and tools in the example SME-network.

4. Overview on Service Areas, Procedures and Tools

For cooperation of SMEs in robot applications, the service areas, business processes and required tools in Figure 1 were identified and cooperation procedures developed [4].

The service area Production Engineering comprises procedures directly related to the technical processes, e.g. arc welding. This includes Product Re-design for automation, the design of suitable fixtures, as well as the development of processing tools and methods.

For the service area Programming, methods called 'off-line programming' (OLP) are used. OLP denotes the programming of robots on virtual computer models of the real installation. This stands in contrast to programming directly at the physical robot. Providing programming as an e-service requires OLP. OLP distinguishes Manual OLP, which requires the programmer to manually define robot motions and tool actions, from Automatic OLP, which allows an automatic programming system to derive robot programs from task specifications, e.g. CAD drawings of a product. To keep the virtual models consistent with the installation, processes summarized as Model Consistency are required.

The service area Maintenance includes procedures for obtaining process recording from the robot and the processing tool, procedures for visual inspection of manufacturing equipment and work pieces, as well a spare parts supply.

In practice, the service areas and their procedures are often executed in a combined, interwoven manner. For example, Production Engineering may use Programming for testing developments, procedures for Model Consistency are triggered by Maintenance when changes in the real installation have to be transferred to the virtual model, and Process Recording can be useful also during Production Engineering.

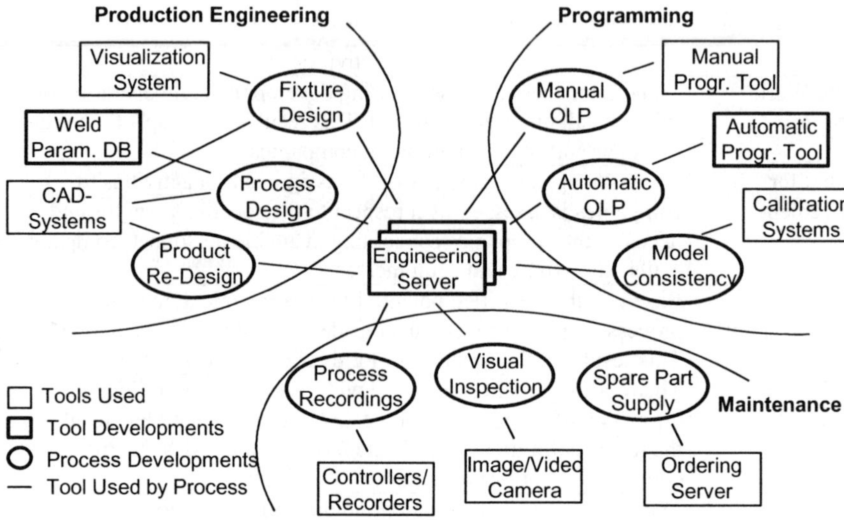

Figure 1: Service areas, business processes and involved tools

Furthermore, also conventional means like traveling to the site and communication via e-mail, telephone and fax are often more efficient or necessary. Hence, the services are carefully designed for enabling an almost seamless transition between conventional means and Internet based e-services. In fact the service procedures enable companies to freely combine conventional means with e-services in the most adequate way.

5. The Engineering Server

The main means for Internet communication of the participants of a service is an Engineering Server, as shown in the center of figure 1. It is developed in the project and tailored to the specific needs of SME-service networks. It supports and structures the exchange of data and documents such as CAD-drawings, measuring protocols and robot programs. Besides communication requirements like data exchange, event notification, archiving and project progress control [5], the major usability requirement for the Engineering Server is simplicity.

One has to keep in mind that small enterprises are already burdened with the complexity of robot installations. They should experience the usage of the Engineering Server as a relief. Therefore its usage has to be highly intuitive. Required internal complexity has to be transparent to users. This forms a considerable challenge and is achieved stepwise by the repetitive improvement cycles. Therefore, the functionality of the Engineering Server is restricted to what is actually needed. As a result, the Engineering Server provides easy oversight of its functions, and has become a slim and elegant tool.

6. Example

As an example, interaction schemes and work procedures of services are illustrated by the design of welding parameters. In the following section the relations between Tool Supplier, System Integrator and User are discussed. In the next two sections, distributed development of welding parameters and the organization of a knowledge community around a welding database are discussed.

6.1 Tool Supplier - System Integrator - User Relations

Analysis of current work procedures shows limited contact between tool suppliers and end users. This is illustrated in the interaction diagram (Figure 2a). Usually the tool supplier delivers tools to the system integrator, who integrates them into the installation, which is delivered to the end user. Further contact between tool supplier and end user is rare. The end users usually carry out tedious and costly welding processes by themselves. Today they have almost no access to the extensive knowledge of the tool supplier.

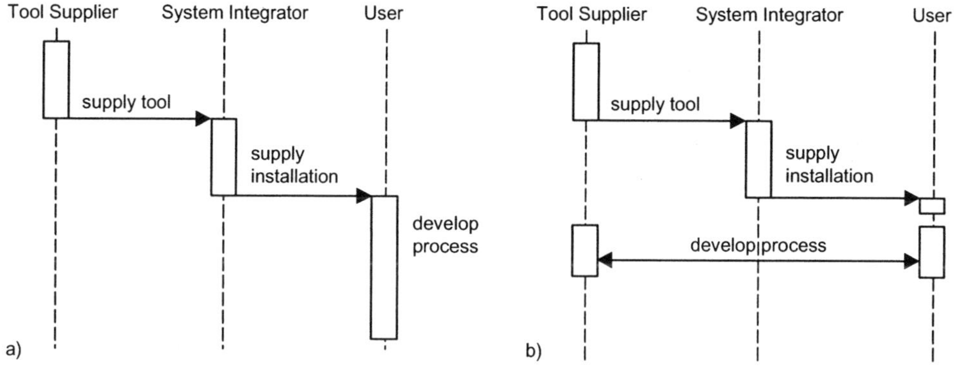

Figure 2: Current interaction (a) and cooperative interaction (b) between tool supplier, system integrator and robot user companies

To improve this situation, interaction has to be intensified and development support introduced (Figure 2b). The expertise of the tool supplier also shortens development times.

6.2 Process Development

The typical current work procedure for process design, e.g. for an arc welding process, is shown in the activity diagram in Figure 3a. It consists of selecting a set of welding parameters as a starting point. Then, in a test-modify-evaluate cycle, the parameters are improved, until the result of the welding process is good.

The principles of this current work procedure and the used tools and methods are proven. They are not subject to change. However, the location of the activities can be altered. A distributed work procedure is shown in Figure 3b. The tests are still done at the end user, since welding equipment, fixtures, work piece, etc., are physically located there. Yet it is the tool supplier who has the extensive knowledge about the application of the welding tool. Therefore, test results like photos, x-rays and process recordings are transferred from the user to the tool supplier. There, the experts evaluate the test results, propose new sets of welding parameters and send them to the user for the next cycle.

This work procedure is tailored to data that can be efficiently transferred via Internet, like photos, process recordings and welding parameter sets. To exchange these data, the Engineering Server is used. It supports a structured proceeding, notifies people when data are available, and archives the development process.

However, this procedure has to be considered as nominal. It can be altered or interrupted and resumed as practical needs demand. Other communication media like telephone can be included, or, when on-site presence is required, personnel of the service provider can travel to the user. In fact, it is assumed that from the currently needed 4 to 6 travels per process development, 2 to 3 can be substituted by remote activities with Internet support. This however, represents considerable savings in traveling efforts and the over-all duration of a development process.

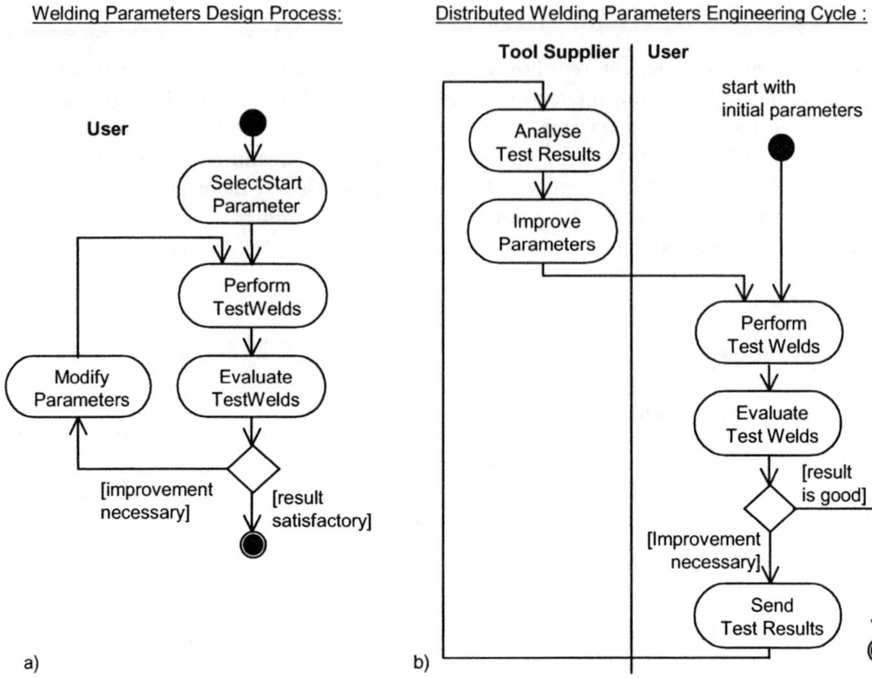

Figure 3: Current work procedure for welding parameter design (a) and distributed cooperative development loop (b)

6.3 Welding Data Base

To obtain sets of start parameters for the development of the welding processes, know-how can be collected at the welding tool supplier. It can be efficiently provided by an online Internet database. Such a database was developed and the work procedure for obtaining welding parameters from the database is illustrated as an activity diagram in Figure 4a.

The end user logs into the welding data base and defines the welding tasks by specifying material type and thickness, seam form, equipment used, etc. This specification is submitted to the database. The database associates the sets of welding parameters that match the task best and returns the parameter sets. The user then loads the parameters into its welding controller and starts the test-modify-evaluate cycle described above.

Since the development of welding parameters can be costly, they are worth being traded commercially. For this reason accounting mechanisms can be introduced. For the same reason, parameter sets developed by users can be returned to the tool supplier. This procedure enables the database to grow. The growth of the database is then guided by user applications, since users return parameter sets for the typical applications of the welding controller. Then, the tool supplier can monitor the actual usage of its controller and can use this feedback to optimise it.

The process of extending the welding parameter database is shown in Figure 4b. The user proposes a parameter set by placing the task definition and the parameter set in the 'support' page of the database server. The personnel maintaining the database fetches the parameters and evaluates and tests them. If the proposed parameter set proves valuable, it is integrated into the database and the user who developed it is remunerated.

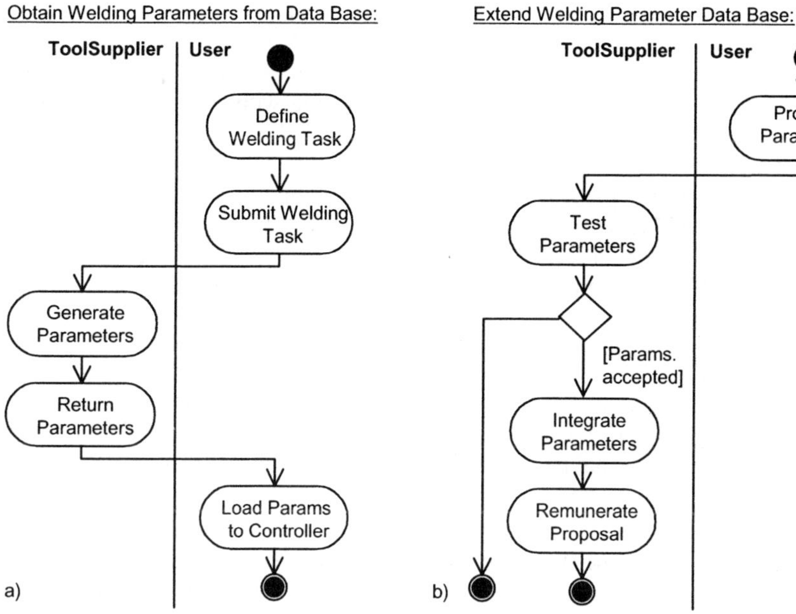

Figure 4: Work procedures for obtaining welding parameters from an Internet database (a) and for extending the database (b)

7. Business Benefits

Business benefits arise for three major types of companies involved in SME- networks:

SMEs that don't yet use robots are enabled to apply robots and they can benefit from the resulting improved quality and productivity. This improves their competitiveness. Further benefits are as for SMEs that use robots.

SMEs that use robots are relieved from robot related tasks like product design, process development and programming. They need less highly trained, costly personnel and they can concentrate on their core business. Their robots are applied more optimal what increases productivity and quality and reduces down-times. In summary, costs, efforts and risks of robot application are reduced.

Supplier SMEs like system integrators and equipment manufacturers profit from improved performance of their products. This adds value to the products and the threshold for potential customers to purchase the products is reduced. Both extends the market of the suppliers. Providing services along the supply chain to customers strengthens the contact to users of their products. This gives them better insights into actual user needs and improves customer loyalty. Furthermore, service provision is an additional business area.

8. Conclusions

The paper describes concepts for e-services that simplify the development, operation and maintenance of robot installations at SMEs. Major lessons learned include the following:

- The manufacturing processes and robot installations are related to physical processes. Many data about them can not be efficiently transferred via Internet.
- Consequently, on-site presence of personnel is often indispensable.
- Current domain work procedures are proven, well established and must be adopted.
- Several data like robot programs, welding parameters, CAD-data, and camera images, can be efficiently transferred via Internet.

- Several activities in the current work procedures can be performed based on data transferred via Internet.
- Based on these considerations it is possible to define service concepts and distributed work procedures that combine Internet communication with conventional means like telephone, fax and travel.
- Focus of the development are work procedures. Tools are only a means.
- The identified work procedures from the different service areas Engineering, Programming and Maintenance often have to be used in combination.
- In order to not restrict the flexibility of SMEs it has to be possible to seamlessly combine the different communication means and the different service processes with an adequate flexibility.
- For this reason only nominal distributed work procedures are defined. These procedures can be altered, interrupted and resumed as practical needs demand.

The defined services and work procedures are now continuously improved in development-test cycles performed of the project. For the future they have to be introduced into industrial practice for enabling the aimed at simplified application of robots by SMEs.

Acknowledgements

The SME-Rosin (Small and Medium Enterprises - Robotics Service Inter-Network) project is co-funded by the European Commission as FP-5 CRAFT Project IST 2001-55039. The project consortium was formed by the partners Industrieausstatter fuer Schweissen und Umwelttechnik GmbH (ISU) (Neubrandenburg, Germany), Visual Components Oy (Helsinki Finnland), Cooptim Ltd., (Erd (Budapest), Hungary), rs-technologies (Leipzig, Germany), Demar Laser B.V. (Hengelo, The Netherlands), MEBIA GmbH (Ossendorf, Germany) Fraunhofer IPK (Berlin, Germany) and ZDIS (Gliwice, Poland).

References

[1] IRF International Federation of Robotics, "European Robotics, A white paper on the status and opportunities of the European Robotics Industry", Prepared by European Robotics Forum (IFR ERF) & European Robotics Research Network (EURON), September 2001

[2] SME-Rosin Consortium, SME-Rosin Homepage, http://sme-rosin.ipk.fhg.de/, updated continuously

[3] Stanczyk B., Buss M., "Towards Teleoperated Exploration of Hazardous Environments: Control and Experimental Study of Kinematically Dissimilar Mater-Slave Structure", Deutsche Gesellschaft für Robotik, Robotik 2004, VDI-Berichte Nr. 1841, 2004

[4] SME-Rosin Consortium, "Infra Structure: Distributed Work Procedures", project documentation, 4 December 2003, publication planned

[5] Berger R., Hohwieler E., "Service Platform for Web-based Services for Production Systems", Proceedings of the 36th CIRP International Seminar on Manufacturing Systems, June 03-05, 3003, University of Saarbrücken, Germany

eAdoption and the Knowledge Economy: Issues, Applications, Case Studies
P. Cunningham and M. Cunningham (Eds.)
IOS Press, 2004

Traceability Service Centres Supporting Agri-Food SMEs

Paolo ONESTI[1], Matteo MATTIOLI[2], Massimo GARUTI[3]
[1]*Democenter Centro Servizi per l'Innovazione, viale Virgilio 55, Modena, 41100, Italy*
Tel: +39 059 899611, Fax: +39 059 848630
Email: [1] *paolo.onesti@democenter.it;* [2] *m.mattioli@democenter.it;* [3] *m.garuti@democenter.it*

Abstract: The European Directive 178/2002 established a new framework for EU food legislation, which must come into force in all the Member States on 1st January 2005. Under the directive any company operating in the agri-food sector must have the capability to track the source of nourishments or components entering the production process of foodstuffs, and to make traceability information available to the competent authorities. These new obligations represent a big challenge for small companies, who do not have the necessary instruments to implement the required traceability. In order to prevent agri-food SMEs from undermining the citizen trustfulness in the European wide agri-food production, new solutions are needed to support effective vertical integration of traceability data along the different steps on the way "from farm to fork" of any foodstuff. The paper presents a new methodology combined with a software architecture specifically conceived to meet this challenge for the agri-food sector.

1. Introduction

Europe is undertaking a unheard-of enlargement of its boundaries, giving reason to an epochal change bringing together societal, political and economical effects. Ten new countries joined the European Union on 1st May 2004, increasing the size of the Single Market by nearly 40% and the population by 105 million. The Single Market contains close to 500 million consumers and in the context of this paper, citizens who are anxious to trust European foodstuffs.

BSE and Foot and Mouth disease reduced the confidence of European customers in meat healthiness, resulting in a deep economical crisis of the related cows and swine sectors. Inside the enlarged Union, a big challenge exists related to the harmonization of national laws and the chance to effectively prevent and put under timely control any hotbed that may give reason to European wide crisis of the agri-food sector.

Enforcement of the European Directive 178/2002 is the starting point for the creation of the governmental and economical synergies necessary to strengthen the European wide framework for food legislation. In particular it evokes the concept of traceability and pushes its implementation along the agri-food value chains. Thanks to the enlarged Union and the harmonization process, extended value chains widely spread over Europe will also be subjected to traceability, favouring the control of deputed authorities and the rise of citizens consensus and confidence.

This very promising scenario has a weakness as a result of the disparity of skills and resources available to different sized agri-food operators, who have to adhere to the regulation coming into force. While big companies can ensure the traceability along their vertical value chain, leveraging their trademark to convince customers about the healthiness of products, small farmers and breeders may lack the capability to implement the due and expected traceability. This situation has the potential to evolve in an real crisis, since the media can influence the confidence that customers have in given foods, exaggerating sporadic disease hotbeds. In a worst case, unfitting traceability requirements, small companies may hamper the timely control of emerging hotbeds and this would result again in wide market side effects.

In the depicted scenario, a Collective Research Program involving entrepreneurial associations, large companies and SMEs from the swine value chain is aimed at implementing a methodological and technological approach to ensure vertical value chain traceability in one of the most complex agri-food chains. The approach is focussed on inter-company traceability and lean systems for small and very small agri-food operators.

Key success factors of the proposed approach is its flexibility, which does not impose any particular traceability instruments or method within a company, combined with a technical solution to support and automate the traceability of those missing internal traceability resources, with lowest costs. It also aims to avoid influencing farmers in relation to breeding habits. The result is a fast solution to track and trace material flows all along an enquired value chain.

Starting from the experimentation and tuning in the swine value chain, the approach is expected to be applicable for many other agri-food sectors. This paper describes the basis of cited approach.

2. Objectives

The approach to traceability of agri-food chains described in this paper is going to be implemented in the course of the P2P project [1]. As a matter of fact, it would not be feasible to aim to standardize the traceability systems within each stakeholder of the value chain. Each company has its own specific needs and therefore must choose the traceability system on the basis of the role it plays in the value chain. The final objective of the project approach is to define a Methodology (Trace Methodology) and a Software Architecture useful to solve the key issue of integration. It means to conceive and develop a solution aimed at supporting the quick collection of information from different traceability systems of companies belonging to a given agri-food value chain, resulting in traceability of the whole value-chain.

The methodology foresees the survey of the stakeholders taking into consideration the role they play in the value chain, the organisation model and the tools each company already has. The methodology also suggests the proper approach in order to share the information in a unified way.

The possibility to use a unified approach to quickly find and access information about a long and complex food chain will be the strong point of the purposed system, being able to avoid three dangerous risks:

1. Crisis of a whole national and international agri-food value chain due to alarming news about possible contamination of some foods;
2. Loss of consumer trust in products made by small producers, due to the lack of marketing capabilities of SMEs and to strong actions of large competitors, interested in increasing their market share.
3. Exclusion of small producers working in the food industry from market competition, due to the lack of financial resources to devote to development or purchase of complex traceability systems, that will be mandatory for European laws and strongly requested by the market.

The mission of the foreseen scheme will be the development of an harmonized system enabling all the people involved or interested in traceability matters (from national and international authorities to single citizens) to quickly find and clearly read updated information about pork products and swine breeding materials. This goal will have to be reached through a smart and not-invasive solution, in order to maintain the existing traceability systems and not to force small productive firms to buy, or develop and maintain, new complex data processing tools, nor to change their stated production systems or data management processes.

According to the purposed solution, all the traceability information will converge in real time on Traceability Service Centers placed in companies, in Industrial Associations or in dedicated companies as third parties. The tools supporting the Traceability Service Centers will be:

- A methodology to assure easily collection of information from companies;
- An Internet based and an open source software tool tailored for SMEs and supporting the easy collection, archiving and sharing of information and documents often from already existing information systems of the companies.

3. Methodology

A reliable traceability along the value chain depends on the traceability system of each company, but in particular by the capability to quickly collect information from different companies. The more the value chain is subdivided in phases carried out by small companies, the more traceability could represent a problem from the point of view of available data and timely response to inquiry.

This methodology assumes that all the companies have already implemented (or are going to implement) their own internal traceability system. The food value chain generally involves many small and micro companies. Even in the case where each company has its own traceability system, lack of homogeneity among the different systems makes it difficult for authorities to trace a product history all along the value chain. Only authorized officers with well-targeted audits all along the supply chain can trace the product history. It is an activity that takes effort and in particular a lot of time.

The methodology does not consider a unified traceability system as companies belonging to different levels of the value chain have specific needs and companies belonging to different agri-food sectors must respect specific rules, laws and standards.

The main objective of the methodology is to support the quick collection of information from different traceability systems, in order to obtain a global traceability and an unified way to automatically collect information from the traceability system each company has. "Quick collection" means that the automatic collection of the necessary information should take a few minutes, while the traditional collection of the same information and documents could take one week or more.

In this way each company can choose its own well targeted traceability system and, on the other side, customers, citizens and everyone else have a unified approach to automatically inquire via Internet that traceability system. Also, a proper access policy needs to be established so that to preserve the disclosure of private data, while customising the views available to different categories of users.

This methodology represents therefore the first step to uniform the automatic inquire of the traceability systems at European level. The main advantages gushing from the adoption of such a methodology will be:

- The confluence of many and different companies acting in the swine value chain to a standardized approach about data collection for traceability.
- The creation of a tight and reliable support system for SMEs concerning traceability; this external endorsement will help very small companies to reach the top level of the market and the legal instructions about traceability problems solution, so that they are not left alone to face such a complex materia.
- The foundation of a virtual network of companies acting in the same value chain, that are willing to put together relevant information in order to solve completely and with a

crystal-like approach problems related to traceability. The approach particularly used will mainly affect relations and data exchange among companies and third institutions, leaving internal organization and productive process unchanged and not affecting the treatment of legacy data.

4. Technology Description

The methodology outlined foresees a communication protocol to share the information, called Trace-XML. The Trace-XML protocol defines the minimum set of information to trace each batch and it represents the first step to define a standard to automatically access traceability information and documents of each complying company. The Trace-XML protocol defines different sets of information on the basis of the user profile and assures automatic collection via the Internet of the information, even if they are archived in different repositories. This approach does not require a unique repository and at the same time allows fast data retrieval.

The approach studied also implies the development of a software tool (Trace-Sw) supporting collection, archiving and management of information and documents related to the traceability. The Trace-Sw will have a twofold nature and implementation, as it could be installed in the single company or in a Service Centre, so that several companies might use it as an Internet service (ASP approach).

In this scope industrial associations could directly play the role of Service Centers or could support the constitution of new Service Centers (for example in collaboration with an Internet provider). Trace-Sw could also be customized by one company in order to manage its own supply chain. In general, the Trace-Sw could be used manually or it could be integrated with existing tools and/or with the legacy system.

The last element of the planned system is an ICT tool to browse the traceability information: the Trace-Browser. It is an open source software compliant with the Trace-XML protocol. Trace-Browser accesses traceability information collected in companies that have adopted the Trace-SW or that have tools with a new interface compliant with the Trace-XML. Trace-Browser automatically goes through the value chain collecting information in order to trace the history or to trace contaminated batches. The open source software guarantees the free adoption by each user and the opportunity to develop more complex software tools, tailored to the user needs and profile.

From the technical point of view, each kind of Trace-Sw implementation (or each implementation of generic tools supporting the Trace-XML protocol) will require an Internet web-server. It is envisaged that starting from the batch number of the product and the web address of a given company, the Trace-Browser will be capable of accessing the appropriate server and will collect traceability data concerning the target product batch. The collected data will also report links to the Internet web-servers of the other companies involved in the supply of goods related to the investigated batch, so that the Trace-Browser will be able to access these new servers and collect further information related to the traceability data of the suppliers. As the final result, the Trace-Browser will show a tree shaped hierarchical structure where the root is just the product and the leafs contain the set of information about ingredients, elements and semi-finished products.

As for data security, Trace-XML protocol requires the highly accessible form of public-key cryptography: the application of Secure Socket Layer (SSL) to the World Wide Web's http (the profiled combination of SSL and http is known as https). So, an https URL must be used to access the Trace-Sw. This system assures the trust in the information provided by the company.

Since the Trace-XML protocol foresees different sets of information on the basis of the user profile, the user needs a signing Key in order to electronically sign each query. The key is based on the Public Key Infrastructure (PKI). In this way the server can clearly identify the user and can verify if the user has the proper rights. If the user is authorised (for example from the healthcare public authority), the server answers to the query encrypting the information with the Public Key of the user. The owner of the information certifies the quality of the input data. As already happens with physical documents, the authorised public officers may audit the coherence among the published information and/or among published data and physical documents.

As a result of the background and previous experiences of the P2P partners, the technological risks are limited to the integration among the developed tools and the legacy systems. The lack of standard diffusion in the legacy systems must be compensated by a very high flexibility of the new tools in order to integrate the information flow.

5. Business Cases

The Trace-methodology will be tested using the following business cases:

1. Trace Service Centre: the companies will not be directly involved in the Trace-XML protocol matters. In this way the company will upload data in the Service Centre and all the Internet based queries of the different kinds of users (citizens, public officers, etc.) will be managed by the Trace Service Centre on the basis of the Trace-XML protocol.
2. In house case: this scenario is addressed to companies that are well structured from an organizational and technical point of view. In this case each company will install the Trace-Sw and will develop the "integration" with its own traceability system. Each company will autonomously answer requests for information coming from users on the basis of the Trace-XML protocol.
3. Supply Chain case: this scenario is focused on companies that play the role of the main contractor or leader of a supply chain. In this business case one of the companies will install the Trace-Sw. In general this company should be the main contractor of the supply chain and it would play the role of Supply Chain Service Centre with respect to the Suppliers.

It has to be stressed that the Industrial and Association Groups (IAGs) could play an important role as Service Centre on which will converge in real time all the information necessary to identify, monitor and register the material flows data that contribute to form the product. Such a "coordination node" will be the one authorised from the participant companies to coordinate and effect the data collection, verify the respect of the traceability rules, answer to the requests of information regarding the value chain, coming from clients, public inspection authorities, final customers or from authorised certification bodies.

Anyway each company will be free to buy the service or to buy the Trace-SW. IAGs will make the software and methodology available to SMEs, as well as offering consultancy support for introduction of traceability systems at SMEs. In this way Trace-Methodology will both represent an add-on that associations might sell to their associated and a new service that could be bought.

5.1 Potential Risks

Four type of risks have been identified for the purposed approach:

- Strategic: the basic idea is in conflict with companies' strategy.
- Cultural: lack of know-how.
- Operative: obstacle in the day-by-day operation of the company.
- Exploitation: difficult in become an official standard.

From the strategic point of view, the only companies that could be in conflict with the basic idea of the project are the owners of the most famous trademarks in the agri-food sector (leader companies). Their business approach could be:

- to buy unknown products at a low price imposing their tracking system;

- to pack those products under the logo of the famous trademark;
- to sell those products at an higher price.

In this case, the leader company might dislike that the supplier would be able to directly supply the products with its logo as a result of the *Trace-XML* protocol. In order to reduce this risk, it must be clearly highlighted that as a result of the P2P approach, leader companies will have the capability to change the suppliers looking for more competitive ones (in particular from the point of view of the quality/price rate) being sure that the traceability is not a problem.

The cultural risks are the most dangerous ones. In recent years a huge effort was undertaken in Europe to raise awareness about sectoral crisis risks and to define rules and methodologies for the traceability inside a company. Now effort must be spent in order to clarify how this information must be shared in order to obtain a reliable traceability system so that the users (mainly the citizens) can believe in the traceability systems. Otherwise the risk is that the users could not consider the information to be reliable and the huge effort spent to date would be redundant.

On the other side, the operative risks are several but not so dangerous. For example, one of the most diffuse risk occurs when the set of minimum information required for browsing the history and for browsing the contaminated batches is not available as electronic information. For example, the inbound procedure management in small companies sometimes results in only the physical document being manually archived. This means that some information may need to be manually uploaded into the Trace-Sw (manual data entry). There is also the risk associated with the adoption of new methodologies and tools within SMEs, who have low formalised organisation and few resources to address the adoption of new ICT tools. Taking into account the experience of its partners, the project will consider these risk factors from the beginning, addressing them with proper measures: a careful design of ICT tools, both in terms of adaptability to company systems and operative impact, and full support to end-users via the IAGs.

The main risk in the exploitation of methodologies and tools (which are based on new unified or standard schemas) is the capability of the promoter to impose the schema to the user. This risk was taken into consideration in the initiation phase of the P2P project. In fact the methodology, protocol and software tools could be applied only to a single company and it represents an important added value for that company. This means that the benefits from the results implementation begin with the first company. This also means that the return of investment of a promoter arise also in a limited market, for example:

- in companies associated to an Industrial Association,
- in companies placed in the same country,
- in companies belonging to the same value chain,
- in a company leader and in its own suppliers,
- in holding groups.

This characteristic assures a reliable exploitation of the P2P outputs even if they will not become an European standard for several years or if they never become an industry standard. Other important advantages will be reached if the P2P outputs are promoted at European level or supported by standard certification procedure or regulations at regional, national or European level.

6. Results

The main result expected by the P2P project is a good, profitable and vertical integration of all the members of the swine value chain. This is very important as "Vertical coordination accomplishes several purposes. Processors wish to control their supply chains more tightly to satisfy consumer demands for quality and safety. In the E.U., new regulations making large retailers liable for the quality and identity preservation of the food they sell impose a new set of problems that vertical coordination may alleviate." [2].

The purposed unified approach to supply information and data will represent a valuable substance for this motley economic environment, allowing all the involved companies to carry out the legal aspects about traceability and the market's request for information's brightness, food's integrity assurance, goods' origin control. ("Companies of a certain size have developed their own brands (private), guaranteeing the marketed product with their own reputation. On the other, also the use of geographical indicators has spread. Protected by a "public" guarantee, these brands refer to specific geographical spheres and/or production methods related to a superior product quality. Such is the case of the Protected Denominations of Origin (PDO), the Protected Geographical Indicators (PGI), the Guaranteed Traditional Specialties (GTS) and the Guarantees of Quality. Except for the GTS, all of them refer to a certain extent, to the geographical origin of the product. The European Union recognizes those products that have some kind of geographical name at a national level as Registered Denomination products." [3])

For SMEs who are facing many problems to assure traceability data and information, the designed system will represent a useful and profitable solution, in fact they will be supported in this difficult task without intruding any new and complex solution upon the legacy system. In this way companies could maintain their inner traceability system and will not have to change any internal habit, while the purposed system will attend all the aspects concerning relations with all the other involved companies, assuring a clear visibility to the several users interested to track products lifecycle.

7. Business Benefits

From a social point of view, the most important benefit, that the implementation of the Trace-Methodology will assure, is a relevant increase of customers' trust in the food industry and in its capability to assure the production of safe nourishment and to adopt all the necessary actions in case of critical situation, that could affect human health. The main business benefit created by this increase of trust will be a stronger image of all companies dealing with food production and shaping the swine value chain, with notable economic advantages for the singles enterprises and for the whole industrial sector. In the demanding business strategy of risk management, companies need to protect a valued "brand" by using more and more information about their purchased raw materials [4].

An important added value of the designed methodology will be the creation of a standardized approach to traceability in a complex industrial sector, full of companies with different features and dimensions: this standardisation will assure an important tool for new companies willing to enter steadily and quickly in such a market, guaranteeing a wider competition and, as a consequence, economical advantages for final customers.

From a legislative point of view the compliance with the Trace-Methodology will assure an important anchor for the plain respect of the future national and Community laws; the European Directive 178/2002 established a new framework for EU food law and it must come into force in all the Member States on 1st January 2005.

Furthermore the swine value chain represents a particular and complex environment featured by a high number of involved SMEs, many international relations, low value of the single animal, variety of transformation processes; all these features ensure that the experience and the results developed within the project and according to the Trace-Methodology could also be profitably used in other agri-food sectors. This possibility represents an important additional guarantee for the economic profitability of such a project that could be easily adapted and replicated in several food sectors.

8. Conclusions

This paper describes an effective solution for the traceability along the whole agri-food value chain, with a test bed in the swine sector. The methodology outlined in this paper will be tested and evolved during the P2P project [1]. In light of the fact that "pork is the most popular type of meat in almost every country in the European Union" [5], the successful adoption of such a new methodology is expected to assure important economical advantages in several European economies, while providing an effective solution to comply with regulations coming into force.

As a consequence of the purposed innovation in the traceability process of foodstuffs, animals and any other element entering the value chain it would be created a new favourable environment where:

- SMEs will ensure quick and easy traceability of foodstuffs, products and parts in the food industry; with this system they will represent a basic ring in the value chain for information communication and placing data at users disposal.
- Control authorities will have an additional instrument to perform their office effectively;
- The opportunity to check and trace all the life-cycle of several goods pertaining to food, their elements, origins, parts, producers and all the processes that contributed to create them, will be available for interested and permitted people, allowing producers to tighten their relations with customers and strengthen their marketing.
- The lead-time to perform a complete analysis of the whole story of a suspicious or contaminated food will be significantly reduced (this means that the automatic collection of the necessary information should take few minutes, today it could take one week or more).

The need for smart solutions to solve quickly and effectively traceability problems is also shown by some American studies that put high emphasis on this matter, on the need for an accurate analysis of related possible solutions and on compulsoriness of interventions by all the actors playing in the food industry. In this scope it has been stressed that "the ability to retrieve information within 48 hours of confirmation of a disease outbreak has been determined to be imperative to timely intervention strategies and effective recovery." "To protect the health of the U.S. herd, sound scientific principles indicate that being able to track and contain a disease event within 48 hours is essential. For the industry to maintain consumer confidence and protect its economic viability, the industry will need to demonstrate its ability to meet this standard" [6].

References

[1] P2P is an approved Collective Research Project under the first Call of the Sixth Framework Programme. This paper outlines the activities planned under this two-year project. The consortium represents relevant IAGs from four EU countries, SMEs and RTD Performers.

[2] Claude Ménard, Peter G. Klein in Organizational Issues in the Agri-food Sector: Toward a Comparative Approach

[3] R. L. "Rick" Sibbel in Identification and traceability in swine: business opportunities or cost of business? DVM Schering-Plough Animal Health

[4] Barcala, Diaz, Sanchez (University of Oviedo) in Quality assurance mechanisms in the agri-food sector: the meat sector case

[5] Livestock, Meat and Egg Statistics 2003, published by the Product Boards for livestock, Meat and Eggs (PVE).

[6] Mark J. Engle, (DVM Director - Swine Health Programs National Pork Board) in Living With Pig Traceability, The US Animal Identification Plan (USAIP)

Section 7.3

Case Studies

Results from an e-Business Strategic Framework Deployment in Micro-SMEs

Rui PATRÍCIO[1], Aires SILVA[2], Gonçalo RAMALHÃO[3], Luís CASTILHO[4]
[1,2,3] *Digital Partners, Rua Brito Capelo, 663 – 1º Esq., 4450-075 Matosinhos, Portugal*
Tel: +351 229351076, Fax: + 351 229352192, Email: [1] *rui.patricio@digitalpartners.pt;*
[2] *adsilva@digitalpartners.pt;* [3] *gramalhao@digitalpartners.pt*
[4] *UERN – União Empresarial da Região Norte, Rua D. Paio Mendes,*
156 – 1º, 4700-424 Braga, Portugal
Tel: +351 253261877, Fax: + 351 253261878, Email: luiscastilho@uern.pt

Abstract: This paper is based on the results of the deployment of an e-Business Strategic Framework (DIAGNET) in 150 Micro-SMEs under the RIAT TeamNet Project. The analysis of this DIAGNET deployment gives an important contribution for forthcoming ICT selection decisions, providing comprehensive guidance for Micro-SMEs that wish to invest in technology. Following the diagnostic phase (a cross-functional analysis of company's internal and external conditions to embark on the e-business), specific actions (covering processes, technology and people) were detailed to support the accomplishment of the Micro-SMEs business objectives. Results showed that the development of relevant recommendations for ICT implementation allows Micro-SMEs to reap the potential benefits of technology, such as productivity gains. However the extent of these benefits and the development of a competitive edge rely not only on the formulation of the strategy but also on the impact of technology on business processes.

1. Introduction

This paper is based on the results of the deployment of an e-Business Strategic Framework (DIAGNET) in Micro-SMEs clusters under the scope of the RIAT TeamNet Project. DIAGNET has been created by Digital Partners (a private company based in Portugal that provides e-business knowledge for strategic decision-making), who also conducted its deployment in 150 Micro-SMEs, located in North Portugal (NUT2) and mostly from the services sectors. The RIAT TeamNet project was promoted by UERN (a confederation of SMEs associations) and has been funded by Structural Funds from a wider national initiative, coordinated by the Portuguese government and called Digital SME.

Issues addressed in this paper include an observation of the project findings as well as an in-depth analysis of the topics that are critical for ICT implementation in Micro-SMEs. The target audience consists of Micro-SMEs managers who may wish to invest in ICT, in addition to many other SME support organisations, such as business advisors, consultants and industry & trade associations.

2. Objectives

There is often a lack of information on how a company should select the right technology and consequently outline its e-business plan. This paper aims to contribute to bridge a gap that often exists between what businesses require and the available ICT solutions, by describing the most critical e-business road map phases and providing comprehensive guidance for Micro-SMEs that wish to invest in technology. Section 5 provides a mapping of business process as they are today, and where they should or could be.

3. Methodology

The road to successful ICT implementation must be carefully planned and monitored in order to assure maximum return on investment. Therefore, SME managers shall start evaluating each ICT application category based on their business objectives and priorities and only afterwards search for *the technology that can support the process they want to implement: " ...once you've identified the solution that best meets your needs, evaluate the various deployments and pricing models and pick the one that's best for you*" [1]. However, problems may arise when SME managers do not have the resources and expertise needed to perform this evaluation process on a regular basis, and to determine what application makes more sense for their businesses.

DIAGNET helps business managers to incorporate ICT into their everyday business activities in a more efficient way, therefore lowering the inherent risks associated to this critical assignment [2]. Accordingly to the DIAGNET concept, the quadrants of the e-business positioning matrix [3] (see Figure 1) are portrayals of the Micro-SMEs e-business diagnostics. The positioning along the horizontal axis assesses factors such as the e-readiness of customers, suppliers and competitors, therefore depicting the Market conditions (external factors). The positioning along the vertical axis assesses factors such as the IT infrastructure and the availability and training level of the employees, therefore depicting the Company conditions (internal factors) [4]. Each Micro-SME is to be classified within four categories based on their positioning along the two axes (company and market conditions to embark on the e-business), namely, Development, Learning, Reactive and Pro-active.

Table 1: e-Business Positioning Categories

Categories	Type of Micro-SMEs
Development	Those that have strong company conditions and weak market conditions. Prepared to implement e-business solutions within the company and with its partners. However the market is not pressing for the use of such solutions.
Learning	Those that have weak company and market conditions. Not prepared to implement e-business solutions (within the enterprise) neither is the market pressing for the use of such solutions.
Pro-active	Those that have strong company and market conditions. Prepared, as well as the market, to implement e-business solutions. The main question is about process leadership.
Reactive	Those that have weak company conditions and strong market conditions. Not prepared to implement e-business solutions within the enterprise, but the market is pressing for the use of such solutions.

According to each Micro-SME e-business diagnostic and the nature of the relationship with its closest partners, an e-business strategy based on specific actions (involving people, processes and technology) is recommended. Through the implementation of this strategy the Micro-SME may remain in the same category, reinforcing the e-business diagnostic, or may be pushed into a different one that may have a better alignment with its business objectives and goals in going online.

4. Developments

In other comparable tools, the diagnosis is focused on the corporate functional areas, which is the case of "E-Commerce Readiness Assessment Tool" that assesses the readiness of a company to sell products directly over the Internet [5]. In other tools like the "Strategic Approach for Business-IT Alignment", focused on a Health Information Systems Project, the goal is to minimise the project risk and to achieve a continuously evolving information system, which is driven by the actual needs for process improvement [6]. DIAGNET is much more process-oriented, cross-functional and focused on the internal and external business relationship dimensions.

Besides the regular improvements continuously being made on the e-business diagnostic scorecards as well as on the e-business plan reports layout, a financial tool is to be added to DIAGNET so that Micro-SMEs managers will be able to measure the improvements and efficiency gains. Due to time and cost constraints, the first phase of the RIAT TeamNet Project did not include any kind of return on investment assessment.

5. Results

5.1 Business segments characterisation

The 150 Micro-SMEs involved have been grouped into 13 business segments. For the purpose of this analysis, only the first 4 business segments presented in Table 2, which include 70% of the total Micro-SMEs, will be considered.

Table 2: Business Segments

Segment	# Micro-SMEs	%	Average number per segment	
			Employees	Sales Revenues
Tax and Accounting	52	35%	7	215.654 €
Management Consulting	22	15%	5	171.655 €
ICT	15	10%	16	421.575 €
Trucking	15	10%	31	2.066.552 €
Industrial project management	14	9%	8	314.167 €
Advertising	11	7%	4	273.914 €
Education and training	7	5%	8	159.831 €
Construction materials distribution	4	3%	5	322.903 €
Media	3	2%	3	33.468 €
Travel	3	2%	3	2.566.457 €
Health	2	1%	37	6.814.893 €
Environment	1	1%	19	11.000 €
Real estate	1	1%	2	587.073 €
Total	150	100%		

The Tax and Accounting segment consists of firms that mainly provide tax and accounting services and may also provide Payroll, Finance and Insurance services. The Management Consulting segment consists of management consulting firms with expertises varying from the financial, quality and marketing to the human resources fields. The ICT segment includes service providers from the Information Technology fields, with special emphasis on software development, consulting and web solutions deployment. Finally, the Trucking segment consists of road transportation operators and logistics service providers.

5.2 Analysis of DIAGNET results

5.2.1 The Diagnostic Module

The diagnostic is based on two scorecards, one for the type of e-business positioning and another for the type of business partner's main relationships. Table 3 shows the results of the scorecard used to assess the type of e-business positioning based on the company and market conditions.

In relation to company conditions, all business segments with the exception of Trucking, achieved a score higher than 50%, indicating that they comply with the essential internal requisites to embark on e-business. As expected, the ICT segment leads the average scores, since most of its members are taking part in the e-business mainstream and, in one way or another are carrying out some process digitalisation projects.

Table 3: E-Business Positioning Matrix Axes

Segment	Average score per segment	
	Company conditions	Market conditions
Tax and Accounting	58,09%	33,26%
Management Consulting	57,74%	32,30%
ICT	73,10%	37,50%
Trucking	38,34%	32,72%

In general, all segments disclose a weak score on the external factors assessment, meaning that their partners and particularly their key customers are not e-ready. Although there may be other reasons, in the main this is due to poor economic conditions or lack of vision in relation to e-business potential.

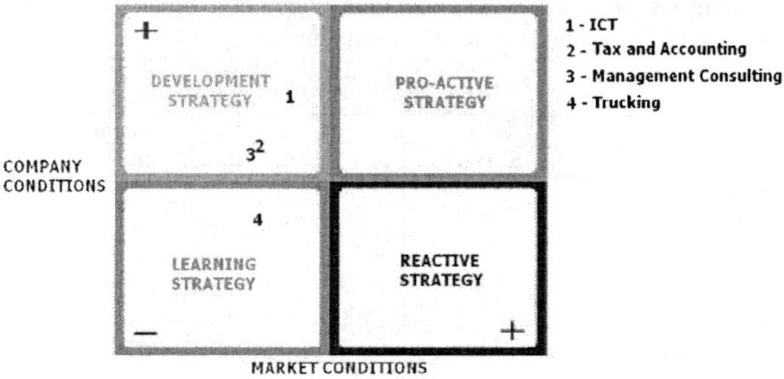

Figure 1: E-Business Positioning Matrix (Distribution per Categories)

Figure 1 shows that average scores of all business segments, with the exception of Trucking, fall in the Development Category. The Trucking segment falls in the Learning Category. The ICT segment is the closest to the pro-active category, in part because some of these Micro-SMEs are already pro-active in the development of e-business strategies with its channel partners. Both the Tax and Accounting and the Management Consulting segments are backing the ICT segment in company preparation and in general expressed interest in the implementation of e-business solutions with its key customers, therefore also assuming some pro-active behaviour.

Table 4 presents the average scores achieved by each segment on the scorecards used to assess relationships with business partners: confidence versus price, regarding relationships with customers, and cooperation versus competitiveness, regarding relationships with suppliers.

Table 4: Distribution per main relationship with partners

Segment	Average score per segment	
	Relationships with customers	Relationships with suppliers
Tax and Accounting	62,8%	56,1%
Management Consulting	57,5%	58,4%
ICT	56,2%	57,0%
Trucking	52,2%	54,6%

In the relationships with customers, Tax and Accounting scores the highest value due to the special degree of confidence required to carry out these business activities. All the Micro-SMEs that belong to this segment are strongly customer oriented and tend to develop long-term relationships with its customer base. The Trucking segment scores the lowest value because price is still the most important competitive factor in this market. As shown in the next module (e-business plan), these customer relationship patterns are very important to define the e-business strategies and action plans for each Micro-SME.

According to the DIAGNET methodology, the appraisal of the scores of type of relationships with suppliers should follow. However, in services sectors this appraisal lacks importance, and therefore we skip it, because most of the supplies are indirect goods that don't have a major impact on the service delivered to customers. In spite of this, and largely influenced by the subcontracting of other companies (or individuals) to participate in certain projects (e.g. in the management consulting segment), many of the observed Micro-SMEs are developing collaborative relationships with their suppliers.

5.2.2 The e-Business Plan Module

This module is about recommending sound e-business strategies and actions (Processes, People, and Technology) to each Micro-SME, based on the previous Diagnostics undertaken. The analysis of the most recommended e-business strategies and actions, according to segments, is now presented. It was assumed that, in order to achieve their strategic objectives, all the involved companies should use technologies as enablers to redesign their business processes, as well as to maximise the productivity of their employees. The recommended e-business strategy distribution per category does not diverge substantially from the distribution per category obtained on the diagnostic phase. Therefore, the segment's distribution per categories is about the same as depicted in Figure 1. Only a small number of companies were recommended to move to a different category, in most cases from learning to development or from development to pro-active. Tables 5, 6, 7 and 8 illustrate the most recommended actions that support the accomplishment of the Micro-SMEs business objectives.

Micro-SMEs belonging to the Tax and Accounting segment (see Table 5) should employ new technology applications in an effort to strengthen their closest relationship with customers. Providing customers with personalisation and new ways to acccss critical information in real time could help them to increase their loyalty and increase their competitiveness. However, this kind of differentiation can only be accomplished by redesigning traditional good business processes or developing and implementing new ones. Since these Micro-SMEs are being pressed to hook up into the e-government application that the Portuguese Finance and Tax Department is rolling out, it also makes sense to invest in the strengthening of the ICT infrastructure to respond to growing and demanding requirements.

Table 5: Tax and Accounting segment most recommended actions

Technologies	**Processes**	**Human Resource**
- Implementation of an automatic system of SMS alerts (critical information for customers); - Implementation of a consistent digital marketing campaign to promote Internet Presence; - Implementation of digital archive and content management applications specific for this segment; - Implementation of site improvements (extranet /private exchange applications that provide personal reports to the most e-ready key customers); - Participation in public e-marketplaces to purchase indirect goods (e.g. office supplies).	- Redesign of all the processes associated with the web interface of the Portuguese Finance and Tax Department; - New process design to support the implementation of the new technologies.	- Training of the operative staff in marketing, customer service and ICT deployment.

Taking into consideration the small number of employees involved in the Management Consulting Micro-SMEs (see Table 2), these companies (see Table 6) should implement web-based systems (intranets and customer self service) that enable them to easily manage the massive information and documentation workflow with a minimum of human intervention. Therefore it makes sense to invest in technologies that support all the processes associated with projects management, both internal and external workflow. However, similar to all the other segments, earlier investments in ICT infrastructures are needed to assist such a pro-active strategy.

Table 6: Management Consulting segment most recommended actions

Technologies	Processes	Human Resources
- Development of the hardware/software and network infrastructure (including the implementation of WLAN); - Implementation of a consistent digital marketing campaign to promote its Internet Presence; - Development of customer interaction features (for project follow up and report) provided through specific web applications or site improvements.	- Expert support on the selection of ICT application proposals; - Analysis of customer requirements for the development of online service features.	- Training of the operative staff in ICT deployment.

Micro-SMEs from the ICT segment (Table 7) should deploy pro-active strategies as soon as they identify good opportunities for it. The good performance of the ICT infrastructure enables this segment to concentrate its efforts on the business partners' process design along with the understanding of final customer's requirements. They should increase the online collaboration with their partners since all the related efficiencies will result in higher satisfaction and increase partner loyalty. Digital marketing is fundamental to support all the technology implementation and better integrate the web with other existing channels.

Table 7: ICT segment most recommended actions

Technologies	Processes	Human Resources
- Upgrading of the ICT infrastructure; - Implementation of a consistent digital marketing campaign to promote its Internet Presence (focus on final customers as well as on potential partners); - Implementation of extranet/private exchange applications oriented to its channel partners. The features include all the day to day processes related to the relationship with partners (marketing & sales, orders and account management, training, tech support, and many others).	- Expert support on the selection of management consulting service proposals; - New process design to support online collaboration with partners.	- Training of managers in e-business strategy; - Training of the operative staff in more specific areas: marketing and ICT legislation and security; - Hiring of new IT staff.

The Learning Strategy is the most recommended to Micro-SMEs from the Trucking segment (see Table 8). Most of these companies have to invest in basic IT applications like Fleet Management and Internet Presence. This trucking segment action plans are clearly influenced by the type of customer relationships. Since price is still the most important competitive factor in the transportation market, it is fundamental to shrink costs and expand the customer base. Companies should take advantage of online exchanges and redesign their daily processes to be able to provide more integrated applications (like online track and trace) as soon as their customers require them.

Table 8: Trucking segment most recommended actions

Technologies	Processes	Human Resources
- Implementation of fleet tracking and management applications; - Development of basic ICT infrastructure (including broadband connections, hardware and new web site development); - Implementation of a consistent digital marketing campaign to promote its Internet Presence; - Participation on the most important industry exchanges to track sales leads and optimise back loads; - Participation in public e-marketplaces to purchase indirect goods.	- Process redesign to support the implementation of the fleet management application; - Expert support for the Internet presence business case.	- Training of the operative staff in marketing, customer service and ICT deployment.

Table 9 shows the average level of investment per segment. The ICT segment alone is planning a total investment closed to 1.000.000 EUR in technologies, processes and human resources. For each of them a detailed action plan was prepared (providing a calendar and a budget for each line of investment) that resulted from a profound analysis of the several opportunities and constraints. All the recommended technologies are based in agile, scalable, open and modular application architecture to support the development of innovative business processes.

Table 9: Investment Distribution per Segments

Segments	*Average EUR investment per Micro-SMEs*
Tax and Accounting	25.244 €
Management Consulting	26.972 €
ICT	64.606 €
Trucking	41.121 €

5.3 Lessons learned

Findings from this study could be generalised across other European Micro-SMEs that fall into these market segments. While there are unique aspects related to the economic development stage and business culture of the Northern region of Portugal, many of the lessons learned hold true for virtually any European Micro-SME.

- One of the major adoption problems encountered in many Micro-SMEs was the general lack of perception of the role of ICT and e-business in particular. Taking the example of one of the companies from the Tax and Accounting segment, at the beginning of the project they were only interested in technology selection and integration. Only later did they realize the importance and the benefits of the diagnostic phase to best integrate technology investments with their day-to-day business processes. This lesson is reinforced by other research [7], whose results indicate that e-business must be pursued carefully as a strategic initiative rather than as an appendage to an existing organization.
- Micro-SMEs should look at the technology that can support the process they want to get to. For example, Micro-SMEs from the most paper-intensive segments (Tax & Accounting and Trucking) may benefit a lot from all the document-flow type applications.
- Micro-SMEs should also bear in mind that a step-by-step approach is fundamental. It lets them undertake a test and gives them more time to prepare themselves for a more complex technology implementation. It was observed that a company from the Trucking segment could not take advantage of the available track and trace technologies to deliver a higher level of service to their customers, given that it was not ready to manage such a wide-ranging internal and external process. As pointed out by other authors [8,] the development and implementation of complex technologies requires tremendous resources, a great deal of management time and energy, large organisation-wide changes, huge commitment from partners, and sophisticated technical infrastructure.
- All Micro-SMEs shall proceed investing in infrastructure technologies since most of the current technology needs a good network platform. In some cases, the internal ICT infrastructure is yet a major constraint, mainly for those located in less developed areas, like the case of a company from the insurance sector that couldn't get a broadband connection to enhance the deployment of the desired software tools.
- Micro-SMEs should not overlook people aspects. In many cases the intrinsic resistance of people to change revealed to be a major obstacle to progress of e-business. Whenever you take a manual process and decide to enable it with technology, there is a learning

curve, as observed by Mark Michener from Newell Rubbermaid's [1]. Other authors [9] also highlighted the role of management change and cultural readiness when adopting e-business solutions.

- Training was an essential factor for all the Micro-SMEs. Only by developing specific training programmes will companies be in a position to maximise the productivity of their employees and the successful integration of technologies. Even in knowledge-based segments, like the management consulting, the need for continuous training programmes was recognised.

6. Conclusion

As a result of the deployment of DIAGNET, the managers of Micro-SMEs achieved valuable insight on how to best integrate technology investments with their business partners and throughout their organisations. DIAGNET facilitates the implementation of business strategy through the deployment of most effective ICT solutions. The development of relevant recommendations for ICT implementation allows Micro-SMEs to reap the potential benefits of technology, such as productivity gains and optimisation of customer's interaction. However, the extent of these benefits and the development of a competitive edge rely not only on the formulation of the strategy but also on the impact of technology on business processes. It was noticed that companies could take full advantage of e-business when sharing day-to-day information with their closest partners, preferably directly between their back end systems.

Other potential projects in this area should keep in mind that ICT are just tools. Micro-SMEs should structure and design their e-business strategy in order to focus all their resources on the business processes that they want to enable by the employment of different ICT. Experience also showed that technology integration projects are not an easy assignment and some times take longer than expected.

The results obtained from such a massive deployment of DIAGNET in 150 Portuguese Micro-SMEs could be generalised across other European Micro-SMEs, in particular for the new EU Member States that are still in an early stage of ICT and economic development. This knowledge could be disseminated in many different ways such as the preparation of detailed business case reports for technology deployment. For all the above reasons, the outcome of the DIAGNET deployment could be used for the shaping of future actions in ICT promotion and implementation throughout Europe.

References

[1] L. Harps, Net Gains: The web helps companies gain visibility, flexibility, scalability - and affordability. In: Inbound Logistics, Vol. IV, No. 20, 2004.

[2] A. Silva; R. Patrício; A. Pires and L. Castilho, E-business strategic framework for Micro- SMEs - application in a regional initiative. In: Building The Knowledge Economy, Paul Cunningham, Miriam Cunningham and Peter Fatelnig, ISBN 1 58603 379 4. IOS Press, Amsterdam, 2003, pp. 1440-1445.

[3] R. Patrício; A. Silva; J. Magalhães and P. Higgs. In: E-marketplaces - Estratégias de selecção de portais B2B, IAPMEI, Porto, 2002.

[4] R. Patrício; A. Silva; J. Magalhães and A. Guedes, Strategies to Select B2B portals - The Portuguese Context. In: E-work and E-business, Brian Stanford-Smith, Enrica Chiozza and Mireille Edin (Eds.), ISBN 1 58603 284 4. IOS Press, Amsterdam, 2002, pp. 1532-1539.

[5] R. Wilson, E-Commerce Readiness Assessment Tool. In: Web Commerce Today, Issue 23, June 15, 1999.

[6] R. Lenz, and K. Kuhn, A Strategic Approach for Business-IT Alignment in Health Information Systems. In: Lecture Notes in Computer Science, Volume 2888, pp. 178–195, 2003.

[7] K. Chang; J. Jackson and V. Grover, E-commerce and corporate strategy: an executive perspective. In: Information & Management, Volume 40, Issue 7, Pages 663-675, 2003.

[8] S. Pant; R. Sethi and M. Bhandari, Making sense of the e-supply chain landscape: an implementation framework. In: International Journal of Information Management, Volume 23, Issue 3, Pages 201-221, 2003.

[9] C. Ash and J. Burn, A strategic framework for the management of ERP enabled e-business change. In: European Journal of Operational Research, Volume 146, Issue 2, Pages 374-38, 2003.

eAdoption and the Knowledge Economy: Issues, Applications, Case Studies
P. Cunningham and M. Cunningham (Eds.)
IOS Press, 2004

Is there an e-Business Digital Divide Among Firms? Evidence from a Multinational Pilot Study

Hans SCHEDL
Ifo Institute for Economic Research,Poschingerstr. 5, 81679 München, Germany
Tel: +49 89 92241366, Fax: +49 89 92242366, Email: schedl@ifo.de

Abstract: The aim of the e-Europe programme to make Europe the most competitive economic region by 2010 strongly relies on the diffusion of business-to-business (B2B) e-commerce activities throughout the whole economy. First results from the EU study B2B Metrics indicate that the realisation of this vision is still confronted with many problems. From the limited results of our pilot study we might tentatively conclude that there may well exist a digital divide regarding B2B application. We plead for a reorientation of supporting efforts from technology-oriented strategies towards more organisational oriented strategies.

1. Introduction

The aim of the e-Europe programme to make Europe the most competitive economic region by 2010 strongly relies on the diffusion of business-to-business (B2B) e-commerce activities throughout the whole economy. Initial results from the B2B Metrics [1] EU study (a joint project of the Ifo Institute for Economic Research, Munich, Nomura Research Institute, Tokyo, PREST, Manchester, RCS Conseil, Paris and VATT, Helsinki) indicate that the realisation of this vision is still confronted with many problems. There seems to be a digital divide among firms: those participating in B2B networks and those not participating. It may vary with sector, firm size and distance from the core of the value chain. The Net Impact [2] study suggests that the use of B2B applications is not correlated with enterprise size. Our interviews suggested the contrary.

At the time of writing (June 2004) the study was not completed. Only a limited number of individual data was available for detailed analysis due to data protection issues. The paper therefore is mainly based on the analysis of German interviews and survey data from the pilot study in the automotive value chain (from tyres and parts to distribution and service firms), and only in part on co-operative distribution centres and multinational distribution chains (due to a prevailingly wholesale oriented approach).

2. Objectives

The objectives of B2B Metrics were the measurement of diffusion and impacts of B2B e-commerce and the development of new indicators and survey toolkits. Special attention was paid to the development of use in small and medium sized firms and potentially inhibiting factors to development. The following text concentrates only on this aspect.

The task was difficult due to high non-response rates, especially among small firms, a limited availability of representative data from official, large-scale surveys and contradicting results from different studies – which were suffering from similar problems.

In order to achieve a more precise answer to our question, we used a theoretical model of B2B e-business development, linking application to the necessary complementary innovation. Complementary innovation includes standardisation, organisational adaptation, planning and controlling and the integration of processes. It is a precondition for successful implementation of B2B e-business.

3. Methodological questions

The study is based on data from face-to-face interviews and a mail survey. This mail survey was conducted in two steps; an initial two-page questionnaire with easily answered questions and a more detailed three-page questionnaire. The automotive sample of 1,200 firms led to 224 responses in the first and 84 responses in the second stage, the distribution sample of 372 led to 121 responses in the first survey; 72 firms were selected for the second stage of which 41 responded. Given the stage of B2B e-business development and the complexity of the matter the response rates and the numbers of responses are quite high [2]. The study not only measured B2B e-commerce application but also complementary innovation, e.g. in standardisation, systems integration and organisation. More detailed information is available at www.b2b-metrics.de.

3.1 Reliability of responses

Even though the German response rates in the selected segments were high compared to other studies dealing with B2B e-business [3,4,5], it has to be stated that 80% of firms in the automotive value chain and 70% in the distribution segment chosen did not respond to the first survey. This creates several problems for the interpretation of results:

- Are non-responding firms B2B users or not?
- Which consequences might be derived for size groups?

Only one percent of total turnover in 2001 in Germany was generated over the Internet [6], another three percent were generated over EDI. We might therefore assume that the majority of non-respondents are also non-users of B2B. Given our distribution of responses by employee size groups in the automotive chain we have very strong over-representations of our upper size groups and a very strong under-representation of the lowest size group. This indicates that non-users prevail in lower size classes and our responses tend to be unreliable here.

Table 1: Sample response distribution aberration

Size group by employees	Distribution of all enterprises in %	First wave response distribution aberration in %
1-49	30	-83
50-249	40	-16
250-1000	22	75
1000+	8	174

Source: DeStatis; B2B Metrics automotive survey 2003.

In order to get a clearer picture of a potential answering bias, we estimated development stages [7] - compound indicators based on the use of applications - and ordered them according to size groups. The hypothesis, based on interview data, was that an existing difference in use between small and large firms should be reflected by higher shares of SMEs in what we classified as "early" development and lower shares in "advanced". Our results for the automotive value chain are shown below. They indicate, that the majority of respondents had surpassed the early development stage and even lower medium sized firms

(50 to 250 employees) had mostly reached an advanced stage of development. Given the considerations on the reliability of responses we seem to have a strong bias in responses from users.

Development stage groupings and number of responding enterprises in sample by employment size groups

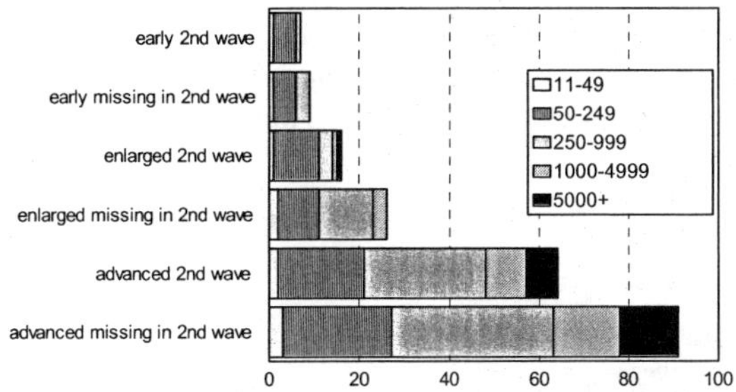

Source: Ifo automotive survey 2003

If we want to find a reliable answer to potentially existing development differences we have to take a closer look at the preconditions for application. For reasons of comparability we separated first and second wave survey responses as more detailed analysis, which will be referred to in the following section, is based only on responses from the second survey stage.

3.2 Measuring potential barriers to development

Theory [8,9] suggests that tangible impacts [10] of B2B use can only be expected when the necessary complementary innovation has been accomplished. Complementary innovation covers all preparatory steps for application, which could be seen as preconditions for successful implementation (or barriers to development): e.g. standardisation, organisational adaptation, integration of processes and the exchange of information with external partners. In order to measure potential barriers we selected responses to the following questions from our second survey (grouped by employee size) as indicators:

- Use of Product/ supplier standards
- Use of catalogue exchange standards with suppliers
- Use of catalogue exchange standards with business customers
- Does an institutionalised organisational structure for B2B implementation exist?
- Is e-business success subject to controlling?
- Is external processes information linked with accounting and planning system?
- Do suppliers have production and planning data access?
- Do business customers have production and planning data access?

In order to profit from the higher number of responses in the first wave we also used an indirect approach based on the number of collaborative B2B applications used, supposing that collaborative applications necessitate the implementation of complementary innovation. These results, though, have to be used with caution as we know nothing about the development stage of use – it can be an experimental stage or a developed application. It can be a system developed in the firm or introduced on the demand of a partner. The responses to the questions cited above, though based on a more limited number of responses, should generate more precise results.

4. Results

The use of collaborative B2B applications indicates clear differences between size groups: whereas smaller firms seemingly only use one or two of these applications, their use increases clearly with firm size. Based on these results, we could state a development lag of small enterprise but would not be able to deduce a kind of digital divide without additional assumptions on the large number of non-respondents. In order to circumvent this problem we decided to analyse the degree to which preconditions for B2B development were fulfilled: different levels of standardisation, the organisational institutionalisation of B2B and the information exchange with external partners. They all can be used as indicators for potential further development.

Use of collaborative B2B applications by employee size group

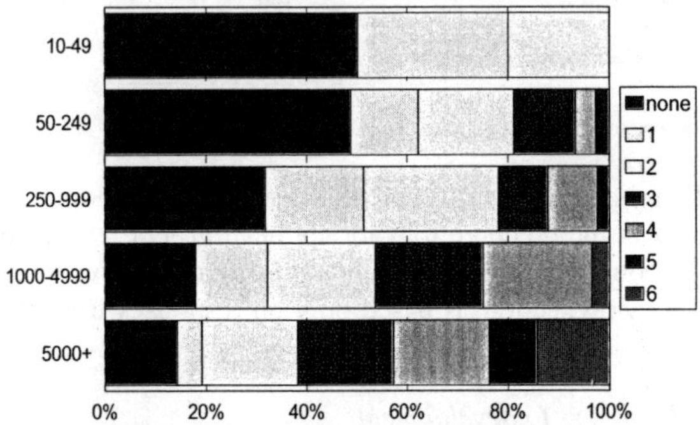

Source: Ifo automotive survey 2003

A different picture results if we have a look on the use of standards [11], which are one of the most important preconditions of B2B application. Here the smaller firms tend at best to passively use them, whereas bigger firms show wide use. This is true for the use of product/ supplier standards and even more for catalogue exchange standards, which imply active use.

Use of catalogue exchange standards with suppliers

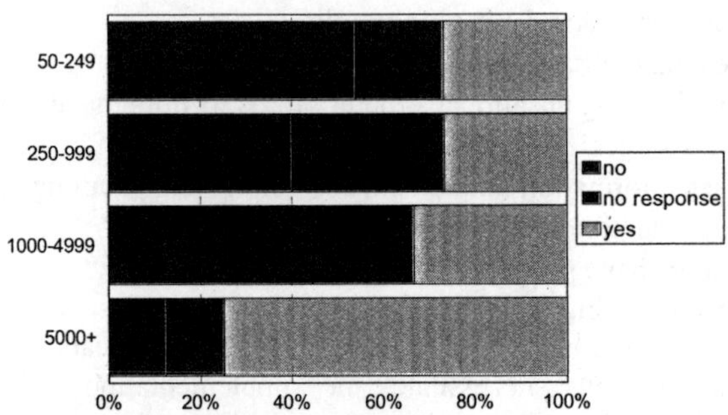

Source: Ifo automotive survey 2003

Similar trends can be found with the institutionalisation of organisational structures, the use of controlling with B2B applications and the systems integration from information related to external processes. An even more selective result is achieved with the question on planning data exchange.

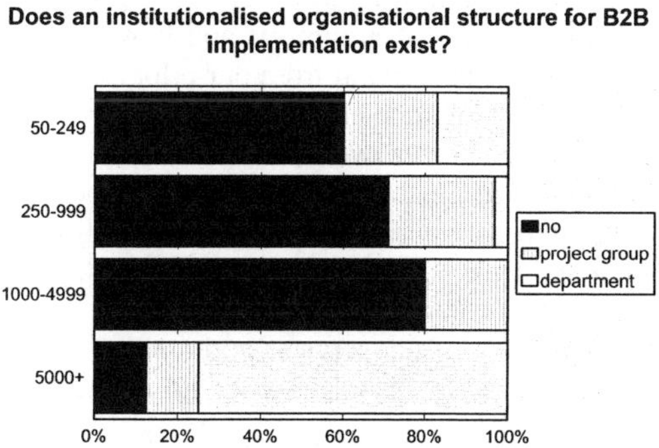

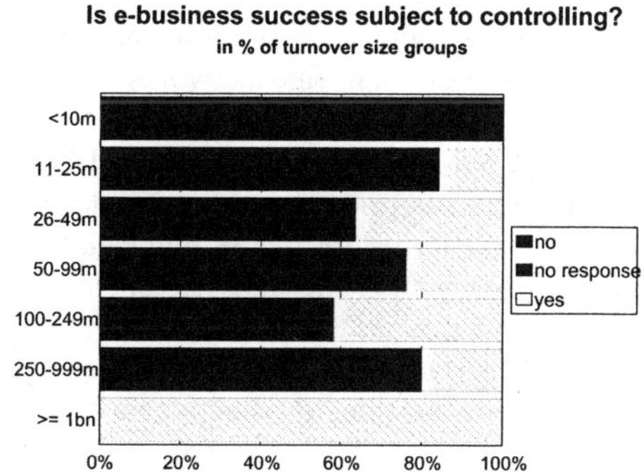

Source: Ifo automotive survey 2003

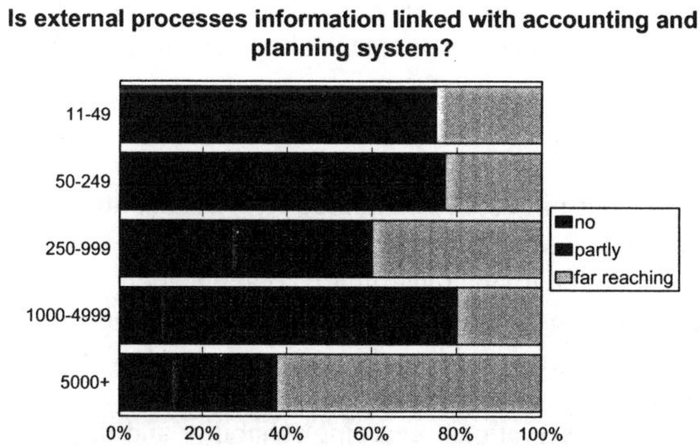

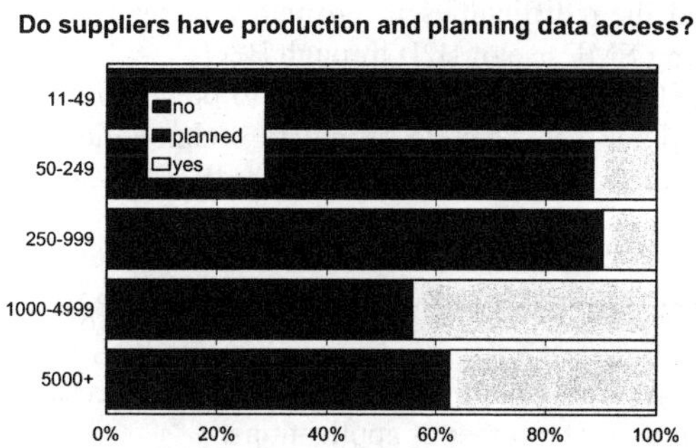

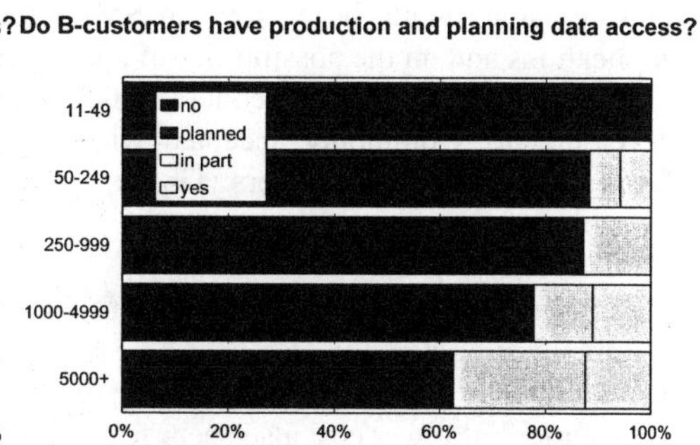

Source: Ifo automotive survey 2003

If complementary innovation is used as a criterion for differentiation a far greater lag between small and large firms is observable. Will this lag be closed within the next few years or is it more probable that different developmental pathways will co-exist? The latter is suggested by the interviews we conducted. At least two discernible pathways were discussed:

- The first will be aimed at an overall process integration including all firms with process-critical knowledge.

- The second will loosely link smaller firms through portal solutions of larger, central firms of the value chain.

It is still unclear what will happen in value chains where no firms with formative power exist, which could introduce standards and push for process integration. If and how self-organisation of small firm networks might work could not be derived from our pilot study. The only result visible from a comparison between a more hierarchically organised network as in the automotive value chain and a more self-organising network as in co-operative distribution suggests clear developmental advantages for hierarchical solutions: where around two thirds of the respondents from our automotive sample used collaborative applications, only one quarter of the respondents from our sample in co-operative distribution did.

It is also unclear if collaborative exchanges or the use of net-services and application service providers could offer a cost-efficient solution for small business in the medium term. For the moment, such a solution is not visible.

A "lean approach", too, so far was not sufficiently discussed. With a lean approach we refer to simpler B2B solutions, using lower band internet access (ISDN or DSL), simple and cheap standard software and the development of an easy to use XML standard which does not rely on IT specialists.

5. Conclusions

From the limited results of our pilot study combined with assumptions on non-respondents we might tentatively conclude that

- There may well exist a digital divide regarding B2B application.
- This may lead to developmental disadvantages of small firms and structural change.
- If the share of "peripheral" firms is high, this will probably lower the overall impact of B2B application (and the success of eEurope).

Given the initially made reservations regarding reliability and the limited scope of the pilot study we think that further and wider research is necessary to validate our findings. This research should be centred on SMEs and their difficulties in profitably using B2B applications and on the possibilities of stimulating SME use of B2B through B2G.

Let us assume that these conclusions are realistic. What could policy do to prevent this development? Commonly accepted wisdom so far has been to stimulate technological factors thought to be enablers: IT personnel, broadband deployment and B2B software technology.

Our study suggests that

- IT personnel and B2B development do not correlate (whereas institutionalised B2B organisation does).
- Broadband use seems to correlate positively with enterprise size, alternative access solutions at lower cost also seem feasible for a great number of applications.
- Not technology – complementary innovation is decisive for the success of B2B.

Preliminary conclusions for political action therefore could be to

- Study the situation of SMEs in different value chains in more detail.
- Switch incentives to B2B and organisation oriented approaches from a too strong technology orientation.
- Put more weight on lean approaches – other approaches may be self-promoting.

References

[1] B2B Metrics, Statistical Indicators for the Information Society. Measuring Forms, Content, Strategy and Impacts of B2B E-Commerce, to be published in 2004.

[2] B2B Metrics lead to 224 responses in the German automotive segment (response rate 18.7%) and 121 in the wholesale segment (32,5%), e-businesswatch to 100 each in transport equipment and retail (n.a.), DTI to 503 for all industries (response rate 2002: 10.7%), Net Impact to 200 for manufacturing, wholesale and retail, health care, financial services, service provision and telecommunications and other sectors in 2002 (n.a; a study in 2003 limited to the US achieved a response rate of 14%).

[3] Net Impact studies 2001 to 2003, www.netimpactstudy.com

[4] DTI Benchmark reports 1999 to 2003, www.ukonlineforbusiness.gov.uk

[5] The European e-Business Report, e-businesswatch, DG Enterprise, 2003.

[5] DeStatis, Informationstechnologie in Unternehmen, Wiesbaden, 2003.

[7] We defined three stages of development: early – consisting mainly of one way information exchange –, enlarged – including integration with other transactions – and advanced – including collaborative techniques with external partners.

[8] E. Helpman, M. Trajtenberg, A Time to Sow and a Time to Reap: Growth Based on General Purpose Technologies, NBER Working Paper No. 4854, 1994 (revised 1995).

[9] E. Helpman, M. Trajtenberg, Diffusion of General Purpose Technologies, NBER Working Paper No. 5773, 1996.

[10] E.g. Transaction, personnel and capital cost reductions, process/throughput time reductions.

[11] We analysed several levels of standards use: product/supplier standards, catalogue exchange standards, transmission standards and integration standards.

eAdoption and the Knowledge Economy: Issues, Applications, Case Studies
P. Cunningham and M. Cunningham (Eds.)
IOS Press, 2004

Coaching High-Growth Start-Ups: Integrating Online Intelligence Solutions and In-Depth Support

Estelle CHATARD[1], Dominique VIAN[2]
[1]*Newcastle City Council, 8th Floor, Civic Centre, Newcastle upon Tyne, NE1 8QN, UK*
Tel: +44 (0)191 2115665, Fax: +44 (0)191 211 4935, Email: estelle.chatard@newcastle.gov.uk
[2]*CERAM Entrepreneurs et Innovation, Rue Dostoievski – BP085, 06902 Sophia Antipolis, France*
Tel: +33 (0)4 93 95 45 42, Fax: +33 (0)4 93 65 45 24, Email: Dominique.vian@cote-azur.cci.fr

Abstract: Supporting entrepreneurship, technology transfer and the development of high-tech start-ups has become a priority in Europe in order to foster innovation and economic growth. Research shows that technology-based start-ups have specific needs to be addressed that require bespoke business support mechanisms. By adopting a Case Study approach, this paper highlights how the Teee-Inn consortium – The European Extended Enterprise for Innovation, Fifth Framework Programme – is combining in-depth business support activities with the use of an Economic and Technological Intelligence (ETI) tool to provide high-level coaching to innovative start-ups. The paper first explores how ETI is defined and its importance for coaching activities. It then presents a critical analysis of the tool and concludes with a list of Key Success Factors in using ETI tools for coaching purposes.

1. Challenges of Entrepreneurship Support Mechanisms

In a recent European Commission paper [1] "how to get more firms to grow" is highlighted as one of the fundamental challenges to be addressed in Europe today. The issue becomes even more complex when the needs of innovative high-tech companies are examined. The technology-venturing environment remains an imbalanced ecosystem where vital elements are missing. The idealised view of the entrepreneurial process where a driven individual can explore a new technology opportunity to the point where a commercial application is identified and venture capital is available is rarely as simple. Equity, access to information and partners, an appropriate network and skills are some of the fundamentals that, if mismanaged, may have negative effects on growth and sustainability. Consequently, successful high-growth ventures are a combination of well-defined processes that gather the right people and the right resources at the appropriate time.

In this context, the concept of high-growth start-up support becomes essential. Research is emphasising the importance of "conceptually integrated support" [2], and individually tailored support packages [3] to devise long-term solutions to early stage technology start-up needs. Across Europe, a number of good practices have been identified [4] from training and information, help with finance to incubation models.

This paper will examine the high-growth start-ups support tools and methods developed by The European Extended Enterprise for Innovation (TEEE-Inn), a consortium of five European partners, namely, Cambridge, Marseille, Newcastle, Sophia Antipolis and Turin. It will focus more particularly on the integration of coaching methods based on a market-pull approach to venture creation and the use of an online platform – enov@ction, first developed by the Nice-Sophia Antipolis Chamber of Commerce - to complement and inform the coaching activities. The project's paradigm is based on the necessity for start-ups to access relevant and timely information: "rapid-growth business owners want timely and appropriate information (...) in the just-in-time fashion required by these firms operating with very narrow windows of opportunity" [5]. Information is divided into three categories or Communities of Interest (COIs): Finance, Market and Technology and Commercial Partners. This is further explained in Figure .

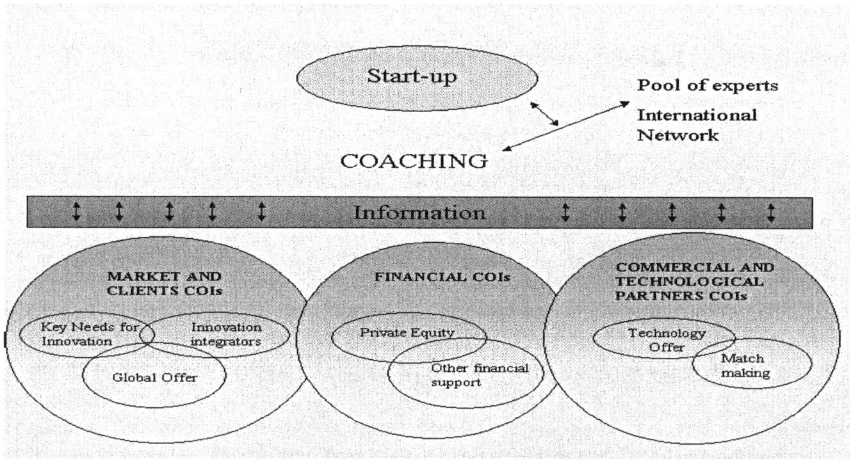

Figure 1: Three Communities of Interest

In depth and high-level coaching activities is now a well-mastered and relatively harmonised process within the consortium. However achieving integration of online tools to serve the coaching activities further, presents a number of challenges, difficulties and opportunities that will be described and analysed in more details in the rest of this paper.

2. Objectives

Many projects and business support groups in Europe have recognised the need for bespoke support packages to high-tech entrepreneurs and the "profound effect (of ICT) on the identification and delivery of business information and intelligence" [2]. There is a need to exchange best practice especially on projects that have strong trans-national characteristics. Consequently, this paper will aim at formulating a general framework on the challenges offered by the high-tech business support tools deployed by TEEE-Inn by examining the development, adjustment and exploitation of enov@ction.

Therefore, the objectives of this paper will be threefold:

1. In the context of the TEEE-Inn project, this paper will define online economic and technological intelligence and the importance of the coach in the design of the online tool to transform raw data into relevant and pertinent information for the entrepreneur.
2. The second part of this paper will analyse the opportunities and difficulties presented by enov@ction and the project management implications of developing a general economic intelligence product into an efficient support to high-level business coaching carried out in an international context.
3. The third part will aim at identifying the Key Success Factors in developing a dynamic high-growth start-up support mechanisms when using online resources.

3. Methodology

To achieve these objectives, a case study approach was adopted to allow in-depth analysis of the enov@ction tool's impact on business support. The case study approach is an effective way to gain insight into the dynamics of coaching methods using online economic intelligence platforms. The data sets collected were mainly qualitative.

The research was based on the partners' observations and analysis of the stages of development of the tool to be adapted to TEEE-Inn. It combines the results of secondary documentary research, exploratory interviews and field research carried out by the partners. A SWOT analysis was used to assess the attractiveness of the tool in its original format.

4. Definition of Online Economic and Technology Intelligence (ETI)

The TEEE-Inn project resulted from one main observation. Innovation transfer and creation of high-tech start-ups is a relatively well-developed process. However keeping start-ups alive during their first three years and addressing market needs is the real challenge. Entrepreneurs do not have the time and know-how to make sense of available information and simultaneously build the adapted strategy. As explained in Figure 1, the most important sources of information that must be regularly accessed and assessed are: information on customers, technical and competitive environments and on financial Communities of Interest (COIs). When using and exploiting information efficiently, a high-growth start-up becomes an 'Extended Enterprise' well-prepared to face market competition and opportunities. However, finding the right information management mechanisms that will genuinely support a high-growth enterprise also presents many difficulties. This part will therefore describe how ETI is characterised and achieved within the TEEE-Inn project.

It is important to define Economic and Technology Intelligence. ETI "concerns the set of concepts, methods and tools which unify all the co-ordinated actions of research, acquisition, treatment, storage and diffusion of information, relevant to individuals or clustered enterprises and organisations in the framework of a strategy" [6]. Within the TEEE-Inn project, the tool used to gather information is Enov@ction. Enov@ction is an Internet based ETI tool targeted at entrepreneurs, corporate organisations and consultants. Its objective is to deploy tools and methods for strategic information watch through the use of powerful search engines. Originally a European Fifth Framework programme project, it was developed with the expertise of Cap Gemini Ernst & Young. The tool is now self-sustainable and serves the needs of numerous organisations, projects and consortia such as TEEE-Inn. However, while the continuous development of technologies and networks have improved access to information, high-growth start-ups still need innovative approaches and answers to identify relevant sources of information, to analyse the collected information and to manipulate it for strategic decision-making. This is the reason why the TEEE-Inn partners are integrating the use of enov@ction to high-level coaching methods.

The TEEE-Inn coaching methods are based on the best practice of Cambridge Enterprise [7] and CERAM Entrepreneurs and Innovation [8]. These methods are shared among the partners and reviewed and improved regularly via workshops and seminars. In a nutshell, these methods combine individual coaching and small-team coaching activities.

- A coach is a professional – not employed or related to the client/enterprise – whose objective is the development, growth and success of those being coached. The TEEE-Inn coaches generally support 5 start-ups simultaneously. They have a high-level expertise in the strategic management and commercialisation of innovation and have a large network of contacts in the legal, industrial and financial arenas.
- Individual coaching is defined by an in-depth and bespoke support to an entrepreneur or a start-up whereby the coach and the client identify key needs and define a coaching mission – raising finance, targeting a first client, building the management team etc... Individual coaching represents around 30 days of support.

- Small-team coaching is also a bespoke service given to a small group of entrepreneurs or start-ups during a well defined timescale – e.g. for an international show, a partnering event – and for a specific mission: finding a partner or new customers, raising finance…

The ETI expertise and tool is a fundamental part of this process (see Figure). This combined coaching and ETI model is adapted to the needs of high-growth start-ups.

High-growth innovative start-ups need timely, relevant information and efficient systems to access this information to transform intelligence into action. Within the TEEE-Inn context, intelligence is defined into three Communities of Interest. To cope with the mass of information from the three COIs, it is vital to adopt a pragmatic and efficient approach to screen and select what is really useful to the decision-making process. This is achieved in TEEE-Inn by combining the role of the coach and the enov@ction platform.

The next part will describe some general attributes of the tools and analyse how enov@ction is used within TEEE-Inn focusing on how raw data are refined and analysed and then made available online.

5. Developments: from enov@ction to teeenov@ction

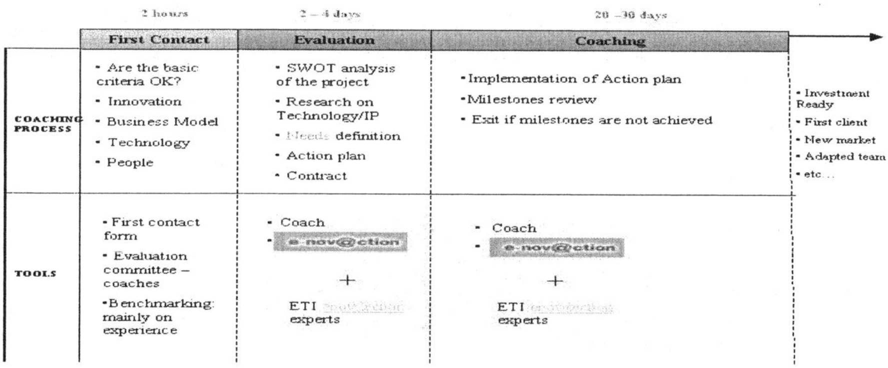

Figure 2 Coaching Process and Tools

5.1 Enov@ction SWOT analysis

Enov@ction is marketed as a "tailor-made and turn key competitive intelligence service" using competitive intelligence tools and methods. Enov@ction was developed to target specifically the SME market. The tool's business plan written in 2001 illustrates a competition analysis focusing on the French market. This analysis reveals that there was no real threat to the tool and that none of its competitors tackled Research, Consulting and Exploitation of Information at the same time. Despite this competitive advantage, the tool had to be adapted to the specificities and trans-national characteristics of the TEEE-Inn project. Figure 2 illustrates the initial assessment of the tool.

The first step consisted of addressing the tool's Weaknesses and Threats and exploring its Strength and Opportunities. The following part describes the results of this process.

5.2 Teee-nov@ction

The enov@ction tool is now available in English and has a separate zone dedicated to TEEE-Inn. Each partner has access to the tool online

The Teee-Inn consortium uses the tool both for Project Management and start-up coaching purposes. As it is made of five partners, three European countries and around 25 people, swift organisation, good communication and knowledge exchange and management are key success factors to the project.

As a result the tool offers two interfaces. One to be accessed by users – the TEEE-Inn partners and coaches - and one to be accessed by administrators – a Work Package leader, a coach, a project manager - to upload information, to organise and to update the system. It must be noted that the TEEE-Inn clients i.e. entrepreneurs and business start-ups do not have direct access to the tool yet.

Teee-nov@ction is now integrated to each TEEE-Inn partner's organisation and is used for information organisation, storage and exchange, research and for some business coaching activities especially market research and match-making between start-ups and potential clients and technological partners. There is still some work to be done to use the tool with different stakeholders in each region. However, the real value added of this tool is in the work that has been carried out to explore ways of transforming raw data into intelligence and this is explained in Section 5.3.

5.3 Transforming Raw Data into Intelligence and Action

Seventy per cent of the activities undertaken by the partners concentrate on improving understanding of the three identified Communities of Interest (COI): Finance, Markets and Partners. Although each partner is responsible for one COI in particular, partners are expected to contribute to the research and understanding of every COI.

The type of information gathered generally falls into three categories:

- External Information – on markets, financial institutions, technologies…
- Practical Guides and Information – e.g. how to register a patent, how to segment a market, etc
- Match making activities - start-up to partner/ start-up to clients

External information is obtained by desk and field research carried out by the Teee-Inn partners or external analysts. For this type of information to be relevant, it is always gathered in relation to a specific coaching mission and is tailored to the needs of a specific entrepreneur or a small group of start-ups.

Practical guides and advice are also the result of the research work. For example, on the work on Technological and Commercial partners, the consortium has produced the first version of a guide on "Forming an International Partnership for high-tech start-ups". This is the result of different questionnaires sent to companies, interviews with experts in legal issues, and the observations following practical work with start-ups.

In a global economy high-growth companies cannot survive unless they identify international strategic partners and clients. On a pilot basis, Teee-Inn is attempting to facilitate this process via the enov@ction tool. The partners have focused on three areas:

- Developing a Thesaurus
- Developing templates to harmonise information management across the consortium
- Developing Forms adapted to needs of the project

Using a common language is a key success factor to an ETI tool used by different partners on an international scale. The Thesaurus is based on Key Technologies and Key Words approved by all partners. The Thesaurus is a flexible list of key words that can be updated to satisfy the needs of the project.

The partners have also developed a set of templates – generally to describe a company's needs. To date the partners use a start-up description template and a partner search template. These are part of the tool and can also be updated when needed.

Key Words and templates and other relevant information are then gathered in four types of 'Forms': technology offer, key needs, media and standard.

The abovementioned points are illustrated in Figure 3.

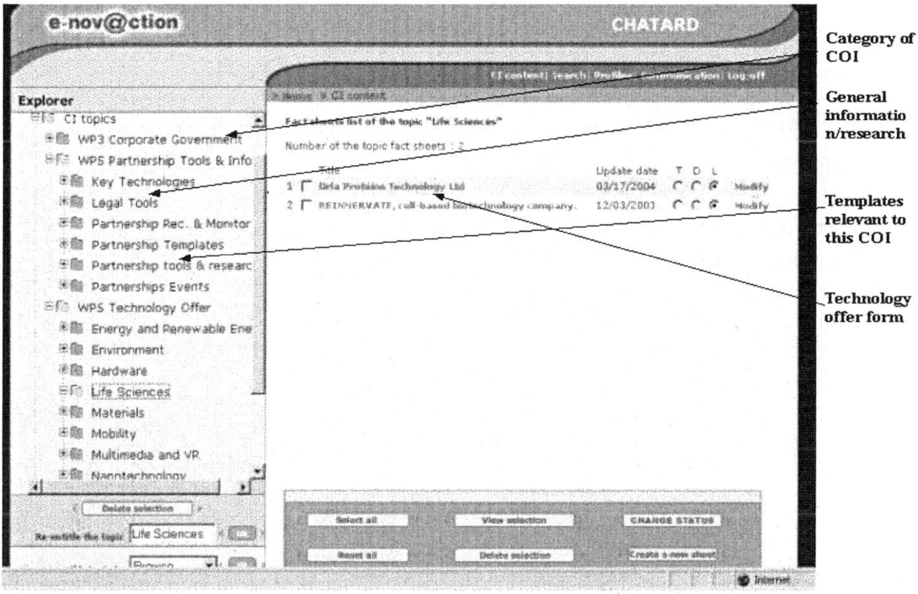

Figure 3 Data to Information in teee-nov@ction

The research work done by the consortium coupled with an appropriate organisation and management of the ETI tool provides an innovative platform to coach innovative start-ups and entrepreneurs. The consortium constantly examines the tool and how it can serve the objectives of the team but its actual features are adequate for the high-tech coaching services proposed by the project. There remain some less developed aspects of the product that will have to be addressed. These are linked to the commercial exploitation of the tool and are examined in the following paragraphs.

5.4 Towards Commercial Exploitation of teee-nov@ction

Originally, the licence agreement between enov@ction and the consortium only provided partners with access and some administrator's right to the tool. However, a fundamental aspect was missing. The Teee-Inn consortium did not include any analysts, as this was not originally their core professional activity. As a result a new agreement was negotiated to attach analysts' expertise to the product. Enov@ction analysts will now carry out "flash" type studies: market or technological reports relevant to specific individual coaching activities. This service is then invoiced to the TEEE-Inn consortium at a negotiated rate. However, the service is still free for start-ups and in order to be viable in the long-term, beyond the project's public funding period, a model will have to be adopted. One solution will be to invoice start-ups for the "flash" type studies at a percentage of the total cost and in a long term perspective to make the tool available directly to start-ups and entrepreneurs – using an access fee model – to encourage them to use it as an information platform.

However, Teee-Inn remains a pilot scheme that targets a small number of case studies. The emphasis is on the quality of the services provided and the results obtained through coaching as well the transfer of experience and the improvement of the use of the international network of contacts. In order to be fully operational and self-sustaining a tool like enov@ction relies on a certain quantity of data to be uploaded and updated regularly for the specific needs of the entrepreneurs. In addition ETI tools – or similar products – are being developed by many private and public organisations. Competition is a threat to the product if it has to become commercially viable. However, at the moment, the consortium is concentrating on the value-added that the tool can bring to their coaching activities and has been very successful in designing a platform adapted to their needs.

6 Conclusions

A number of Key Success Factors (KSFs) can be drawn from this case study analysis.

- KSF1: To choose or design a flexible ETI tools that can be embedded to a specific project's deliverables
- KSF2: To adopt a common language through thesaurus/key words and templates
- KSF3: To carefully take into account the international aspects: easy online access, same document management logic and language, combining the tool with Project Management facilities in order to store and manage information
- KSF4: To ensure that ETI is achieved – transforming data into knowledge and action – by using the expertise of analysts who are familiar with the tool
- KSF5: To always link online ETI with a 'human factor'. In the case of TEEE-Inn, a high-tech business coach.

Developing and using an ETI tool such as enov@ction provides consortia such as TEEE-Inn the possibility to disseminate knowledge and experience in a very effective and well-managed way. Because of its ease of access and the flexibility to design and organise information to serve the purpose of the project, it is adapted to expanded groups working from different locations. Although some aspects of the tool still need some further thought and development it supports business coaches in their mission to help high-growth start-ups grow. A number of recommendations and key success factors were identified. However, further analysis will be needed when the number of missions grows. Nurturing tomorrow's high-growth innovative businesses is currently very high on the European agenda. Delivering added-value services to entrepreneurs is a priority and this is what TEEE-Inn achieves by combining ETI tools to high-level coaching activities.

References

[1] Commission of the European Communities Communication from the Commission to the Council, the European Parliament, the European Economic and Social Committee and the Committee of the Regions, Action Plan: The European agenda for Entrepreneurship, 2004

[2] Commission of the European Communities Commission Staff Working Paper, Creating Top-Class Business Support Services, 2001

[3] Chrisman, James J., and W. Ed McMullan, A preliminary Assessment of Outsider Assistance as a Knowledge Resource: The Longer-Term Impact of New Venture Counselling, Entrepreneurship: Theory and Practice 24(3), 2000, 37-53

[4] European Commission, Enterprise DG, Helping Business Start Up, A 'good practice guide' for business support organisations ISBN 92-828-9316-2 (2000)

[5] Eileen Fischer and A.Rebecca Reuber, Support for Rapid-Growth Firms: A comparison of the Views of Founders, Government Policymakers, and Private Sector Resource Providers, Journal of Small Business Management 2003 41(4), pp. 346-365

[6] Vassilios Kelessidis Benchmarking and Economic Intelligence: http://portal.e-innovation.org/technique_overview.aspx?Cat=Benchmarking&Ch=4&Cont=51 ,2003

[7] www.enterprise.cam.ac.uk

[8] www.ceram.edu/cei

Understanding the Dynamics of e-Business Adoption by SMEs

Gordon LEE
Parallel 56 Limited, 69 St Vincent Street, Glasgow, G2 5TF, Scotland, UK
Tel: +44 (141) 572 3811, Fax: +44 (141) 572 3801, Email: gordon@parallel56.com

Abstract: This paper provides insight into e-business adoption practices, based on Europe's largest annual e-business survey. It identifies key trends while attempting to understand business behaviour and e-business support priorities. It may be unsurprising to learn that one sector has a higher level of e-business technology adoption than another. However, why should one region see a substantial drop in internet adoption between one year and the next? Technology adoption is now reaching unprecedented levels and yet awareness of e-business support and advice remains astonishingly low. This paper identifies three primary enablers for success that can be applied on a national or local scale and suggests that the "hype" is being replaced by something more than "hope".

1. Introduction

The Scottish E-Business Survey has been conducted by Parallel 56 on an annual basis since 2001. This paper reflects on the first three years results from this survey and the author's experience in this area, to explain a number of the critical dynamics of e-business adoption by SMEs. The Scottish E-Business Survey 2003 has been analysed and reported in a wide range of summaries and reports, which are available on the Scottish Enterprise website [1].

2. Background

The Scottish e-Business Survey 2003 was conducted by Parallel 56 Limited in association with MRUK Limited on behalf of Scottish Enterprise (SE) and Highlands and Islands Enterprise (HIE), Scotland's two main economic development agencies funded by the Scottish Executive.

The survey captures information from a representative sample of businesses on:

- The attitudes, barriers and enablers to e-business adoption
- The use of specific e-business technologies and Internet connection methods
- The use of customer and supplier interfaces (including the impact of e-commerce)
- The adoption of websites and e-business applications
- The awareness and impact of sources of support and advice
- The impact of e-business and the future optimism of organisations

This information has provided detailed market intelligence to track adoption, assist in the development of services and allow the measurement of impact.

3. Methodology

A telephone (CATI) survey of 12,636 Scottish businesses was conducted with organisations of the following employee sizes (Table 1):

Table 1: Number of organisations surveyed by size

	Micro (0-9 empl.)	Small (10-49 empl.)	Medium (50-249 empl.)	Large (250+ empl.)
Number of Organisations Surveyed	10,433	1,790	318	68

Source: The Scottish E-Business Survey, 2003

When re-weighted to be representative of the 144,076 VAT or PAYE registered businesses in Scotland, the number of organisations surveyed is (Table 2):

Table 2: Re-weighted number of organisations by size

	Micro (0-9 empl.)	Small (10-49 empl.)	Medium (50-249 empl.)	Large (250+ empl.)
Number of Organisations Surveyed	128,283	12,905	2,326	562

Source: The Scottish E-Business Survey, 2003

A questionnaire was developed with an interview length of between 10 and 15 minutes.

The sample was provided by the Scottish Executive using the 'Inter Departmental Business Register (IDBR)'. This database combines the former Central Statistical Office (CSO) VAT-based business register and the former Employment Department employment statistics. It covers all parts of the economy, but misses some micro businesses (self employed and those without employees and low turnover) and some non-profit making organisations. IDBR provides more than 99% coverage of Scotland's economic activity.

The Yellow Pages Business Database was used to fill any gaps in specified sample quotas, particularly micro businesses and under-represented sectors. Each interview was conducted with "the person responsible for making decisions about how your organisation uses information technology such as the Internet, e-mail & computers at this location?"

Survey results were accumulated to consider the trends and results as a whole (and by sub analysis such as size, region, sector, e-business adoption, etc). The survey methodology is statistically robust with the margin of error of $\pm$0.89% at national level and of up to $\pm$7.8% at Local Enterprise Company area level.

4. Key Findings

4.1 Sectoral Variances in eBusiness Adoption

eBusiness adoption varies significantly by industry sector. Industries such as IT, Creative Industries and Financial Services are leading the way and within these sectors, the relevance of e-business is well accepted. Lagging sectors, such as Retail and Construction & Quarrying could benefit from e-business but do not see its relevance. They have low adoption of most basic technologies, e.g. Internet connection, email and websites (Table 3).

This highlights the need to work closely with sectors that are of importance to the national economy such as Tourism, Food & Drink and Forest Industries. These sectors need to be constantly improving to compete successfully in international markets.

Selecting the optimum approach to initial engagement with a sector is critical for buy-in and Scottish Enterprise has adopted a flexible approach to each priority sector. The Tourism sector was engaged by focusing on online marketing, where benefits can be accrued quickly at low cost. Engagement with the Forest Industries sector was initiated through a focus on standardisation of electronic data exchange and supply chain management.

Table 3: Adoption of basic e-business technologies by sector

	Internet %	Email %	Website %
Software & e-Business	98	97	80
Financial Services	93	88	63
Creative Industries	91	89	70
Manufacturing	78	74	52
Food & Drink	76	75	48
Tourism	66	61	50
Construction & Quarrying	66	58	30
Forest Industries	65	56	34
Retail	62	54	39
Agriculture & Fisheries	60	54	17
All	72	66	43

Source: The Scottish E-Business Survey, 2003

4.2 Regional Variances in e-Business Adoption

Whilst the 2003 results for adoption of e-business technologies are very encouraging, there are significant points of interest in terms of regional comparisons. In more advanced adoption regions such as major cities, there is an increasing polarisation between those that see benefits from e-business and those that consider it less than relevant to their business.

Adopters in these regions are positive about the benefits they have had from e-business so far and are committed to further investment. In many cases they may not be fully aware of what their next stage of technology adoption will be, but they see it as an essential and permanent form of continuous improvement in their business.

Non-adopters in advanced adopting regions see e-business in a very different light. Although the proportion of non-adopters in these regions is lower than others, their views on the relevance of e-business are more extreme and more negative. More non-adopting businesses in these regions are 'convinced' that e-business is not relevant to their business and are much more definite in their opinions than non-adopters in low adopting regions.

There are stark differences between business attitudes of businesses in low adopting regions. They have been much more cautious in their attitudes towards e-business.

However, 2002 saw significant increases, 77% of organisations within the Highlands & Islands Enterprise region connected to the internet compared to 64% in 2001. Shetland (with 82% connected) and Inverness & Nairn (with 84% connected) showed impressive increases. This growth was heralded at the time as a critical moment in the advance of e-business and the general business competitiveness of these remote regions.

In 2003, the survey showed significant drops in connectivity within the Highlands & Islands Enterprise region where internet adoption fell from 77% in 2002 to 72% in 2003. Initial suspicion over the accuracy of the results was eased when the UK Department of Trade and Industry's International Benchmarking Study on the use of ICT was published in December 2003. This report, covering 11 countries, indicated that within micro SMEs, Internet adoption levels fell within 4 of the 11 countries surveyed, including the UK.

4.3 Disillusionment leads to Disconnection

These results indicate that there are businesses that have become disillusioned with the internet and, over the 12 to 18 months that they have been connected, they have not received sufficient benefit to justify continued expenditure. This highlights two key dynamics related to areas of low adoption:

- The businesses have delayed their decision to adopt primarily because they could not see the relevance to their business (Table 4). When they later 'get connected' their experience is like a 'self-fulfilling prophecy'. They didn't see where the benefits could come from, they used it for a period and it didn't change their business or their lives. Ultimately, they decided to cease the on-going expenditure.
- Their initial decision to delay getting connected was based on their lack of knowledge of what the Internet could do for their business. The action of getting connected does not remedy that lack of knowledge or improve their skills and abilities to capitalise on what the Internet has to offer (Table 4).

Table 4: Importance of e-business and levels of skills and knowledge of organisations without Internet access of website

Percentage of organisations without internet access or a website	Scotland 2003
e-business is essential, very important or important	18%
Staff do not have the relevant skills and knowledge	53%

Source: Non-Adopting Sub-Group of the Scottish E-Business Survey, 2003

The lesson learnt from this situation is that businesses that have been slow to adopt must be supported during their initial period of adoption to gain substantial and measurable benefits from the internet. Enterprise support agencies have a crucial role to play in this area, as have private sector e-business providers. In Scotland, Scottish Enterprise and Highlands and Islands Enterprise are currently reinforcing support to slow adopting areas that have had a disproportionate increase in connectivity over the past 12 months in order to avoid or lessen the potential drop-off in connection after 12 months.

4.4 Lack of Awareness of Sources of Advice and Support

A consistent result in each year of the survey has been the lack of awareness and use by businesses of sources of e-business advice and support. In fact, in each year of the survey, no more than 40% of businesses were able to name any source of e-business advice or support and this result is mirrored in a comparable survey conducted by Parallel 56 for Business link for London (Table 5).

Table 5: Adoption of basic e-business technologies by sector

	Scotland 2003	London 2003
Unaware of any sources of e-business advice or support	62%	67%
Do not use any sources of e-business advice or support	80%	80%

Sources: The Scottish E-Business Survey, 2003 and London e-Business Survey, 2003

As an example, software companies are only recognised as a source of e-business advice or support by 4% of businesses. In Scotland, the best-known source of e-business advice and support is the publicly funded enterprise support agencies where an awareness level was achieved in 2003 of 14% of all businesses.

This indicates that businesses have acted, in the vast majority of cases, completely independent of advice or support from e-business experts.

This suggests that businesses have been extremely self sufficient, it also highlights why so few companies have adopted the more advanced technologies and practices that can have a transformational impact on their business. As an example, even where businesses state that they "sell products and services through their website" only in a small minority of cases (9%) is this at a level above 30% of their total turnover.

4.5 Support Makes a Positive Difference

The 6% of businesses that used the enterprise support agencies for e-business advice and support in 2003 showed a significant improvement in their adoption practices compared to the average. Businesses that accepted this support have higher levels of adoption of basic internet technologies and higher levels of appreciation of the benefits the internet provides for their business (Table 6). For businesses using private sector advice (software companies, consultants etc.) the results were similarly positive.

Table 6: Comparison of Organisations who used e-business support/advice compared to those that have not

	Have used e-business support or advice	**Have not used e-business support or advice**
Have and use Internet	79.4%	67.7%
Have and use website	51.5%	39.1%
Allow customers to order products/services online	17.9%	12.1%
Make electronic payment to suppliers	23.6%	16.5%

Sources: The Scottish E-Business Survey, 2003

Support does matter and if higher levels of adoption of more advanced Internet technologies and practices are sought (e.g. e-commerce, wireless, systems integration), then the provision of appropriate support via the public or private sector should be a priority.

The worst assumption that can be drawn from the results of this survey is that by adopting an e-business technology without support and advice, the business understands the complexities and benefits of the internet. This would be a wrong and dangerous conclusion to draw. If more advanced use of e-business technologies and practices is the objective, suitable e-business advice and support must be available to businesses.

4.6 Broadband Brings Benefits

One of the more significant survey findings is the impact of faster Internet access speeds on the use of the Internet and the levels and types of applications that businesses use.

In Scotland there has been a threefold increase in the number of broadband connections during the period from May 2002 to May 2003. 13% of all Scottish businesses now connect using a broadband connection compared to 4% in 2002. Broadband within this survey is defined as Leased Line, Digital Subscriber Line (xDSL), Cable Modem, Satellite, Wireless Broadband and Other Broadband. The additional category of "Other Broadband" had to be added to the definition to accommodate those respondents that 'knew' they had broadband but did not know the type of connection they had. Nearly one third of companies with broadband (4.3% of all companies) fell into this category in 2003. This 'lack of awareness' of the type of internet connection is on the rise and is likely to increase as broadband becomes more common and definitions of connection types becomes more confusing.

The growing mass of less sophisticated broadband users has driven down the average adoption scores (of technologies such as such as e-learning or client extranets) of organisations that use broadband. However, it would appear this will improve as new broadband adopters become accustomed to the "always-on", fixed price, high-speed service and as the scope of their internet use increases.

A specific group of broadband users was identified in the survey that intend to upgrade to a faster version of broadband within the next 12-18 months. This group of 'mature' broadband users display a significantly higher level of advanced technologies and practices and perhaps indicate where the new broadband adopters will be in 1-2 years time.

4.7 Broadband Confusion

There are some inconsistencies with information on broadband. Many urban businesses still believe that they cannot access broadband - a perception that has been disproved in the majority of cases by the mapping of their postcode against the supplier data available on ADSL-enabled exchanges and coverage of cable broadband provision.

Not only do companies not know what type of broadband connection they have, the vast majority of organisations cannot state their internet connection speed (Table 7). This highlights a challenge that has been created through the consumer-type promotion of broadband services by ISPs and telecom providers. Businesses are happy to connect to what they understand to be broadband, but it is clear that in many cases they have connections with download speeds of less than 256 kbps (kilo bits per second).

Table 7: Awareness of Internet connection speed

	Scotland 2002	**Scotland 2003**
Connected organisations that don't know the speed of their Internet connection	53%	66%

Sources: The Scottish E-Business Survey, 2002 & 2003

Whilst this dumbed-down approach to marketing broadband has had an undoubted positive impact on uptake there is again a skills and knowledge challenge over the understanding of this fundamental e-business enabler.

If governments are keen to create high bandwidth connected business communities then it is important that businesses know the difference a faster broadband connection can make. Therefore communication, advice and support is needed to ensure that businesses appreciate what it is they have got and what it can and what it cannot do.

This also highlights the need, once the move to 2+mbps (mega bits per second) connections are deemed necessary, to consider a naming strategy that sets this type of connection apart from the sub 2mbps services.

5. Impact of Findings

Since the commencement of the survey in 2001, Scottish Enterprise and Highlands and Islands Enterprise has been very active in implementing initiatives that can address the issues identified by the survey.

These initiatives include e-business training and consultancy initiatives, wider distribution of information on the current status of e-business and working with e-business suppliers. In particular, the following initiatives have been successful:

- The development of a comprehensive e-business workshop and materials programme that has helped over 5,000 Scottish businesses learn more about how e-business could help them.
- Providing free and subsidised consultancy support to Scottish business to help them take action and implement e-business technologies.
- Engaging with e-business suppliers to improve their market focus, their business development and their quality of service to Scottish organisations.
- Establishing a Channel Partner Initiative that encourages organisations such as trade associations and intermediaries to become more actively involved in supporting member organisations to adopt e-business.
- Publishing the Survey data on an open access website (www.scottish-enterprise.com/ebusiness) that allows live interrogation of the data and provides a full range of reports by sector and by region.

6. Conclusions

The Scottish e-Business Survey provides detailed insight into many intriguing aspects of e-business adoption by SMEs.

Whilst sectoral and geographic differences provide obvious explanations for variances in adoption levels, there are a number of trends that have been highlighted by the survey that are cross-sectoral and independent of geographic boundaries.

There appear to be three primary enablers for change:

- Improved "skills and knowledge" within SMEs on how e-business can help achieve sustainability and growth.
- The existence of suitable "advice and support" for SMEs through either public sector agencies or private sector suppliers (it doesn't matter which) is crucial if slow adopting regions are to 'catch-up' and if advanced e-business technologies and practices are to be followed.
- Affordable "broadband connectivity" introduces SMEs to a more practical and valuable Internet experience and shows itself to be a springboard to advanced e-business adoption.

In summary, it is a 'wake up call' that e-business receives the same hard rules of business justification that any other form of business investment receives. Governments, enterprise support agencies and commercial providers must recognise that for e-business to transform the prospects of SMEs it must deliver tangible business benefits - fast - otherwise evidence suggests that they will simply switch it off!

References

[1] The Scottish e-Business Survey 2001-2003. Conducted by Parallel 56 Limited on behalf of Scottish Enterprise and Highlands and Islands Enterprise. www.scottish-enterprise.com/ebusiness.

[2] The London e-Business Survey 2003. Conducted by Parallel 56 Limited for Business Link for London.

[3] The 2003 International Benchmarking Study of Information and Communication Technologies by the UK Department of Trade and Industry www.ukonlineforbusiness.gov.uk/benchmarking2003/index.htm

eAdoption and the Knowledge Economy: Issues, Applications, Case Studies
P. Cunningham and M. Cunningham (Eds.)
IOS Press, 2004

Collaboration and Enterprise Networks: What about SMEs?

Manon VAN LEEUWEN[1], Kathryn CORMICAN[2]
[1]*Fundación para el Desarrollo de la Ciencia y Tecnología en Extremadura, Manuel Fdez. Mejías s/n, 2ª planta, 06002 Badajoz, Spain*
Tel: +34 924 014600, Fax: +34 924 001996, Email: manon@fundecyt.es
[2]*CIMRU, National University of Ireland, Galway, Ireland*
Tel: +353 91 512292, Fax: + 353 91 562894, Email: Kathryn.Cormican@nuigalway.ie

Abstract: This paper describes the research and analysis realised in relation to the creation of enterprise networks, based on the networked enterprise model, in European SMEs. It focuses on the barriers to inter-firm collaboration and on the skills and competencies needed by SMEs managers and employees in order to collaborate successfully with other SMEs and organisations. It describes the preliminary results of the Managing Enterprise Networks (MENS) project funded by the European Commission under the Leonardo Da Vinci initiative.

1. Introduction

The new economy is the result of the information revolution, of smaller, ever more powerful computers, and the emergence of an efficient, ubiquitous and invisible communications infrastructure. It is characterized by three distinctive attributes: it is global, it favours intangible things - ideas, information, knowledge, relationships, and it is intensely inter-linked. As more and more organizations prepare to "go digital", only few seem to recognize what implications this transition will have on their business processes and on the organization as a whole. The transformation involves much more than setting up a digital infrastructure and requires even more than the ability to enter into a virtual network or partnership with other organizations. Organizations must become "smart", i.e. knowledge driven, internetworked and dynamically adaptive to new organizational forms and practices. Furthermore, they must become agile in their ability to create and exploit the opportunities offered by the digital economy.

Globalisation has forged a shift from traditional corporate and big business conglomerate to an economy in which global and regional companies can be equally successful. Research suggests they must be part of an integrated network in which core competencies, localisation and customisation are achieved [1]. The networked economy has shifted the focus from wholly owned value chains (i.e. product development, operations, logistics and delivery), - to knowledge and relationships [2]. How should a business expand in today's knowledge economy? Various authors indicate that network building is a major source of competitive advantage and an essential regional, and indeed, global management requirement [3].

Our research found that many small organisations find it difficult to collaborate or network with other organisations. While Small to Medium Sized Organizations (SMEs) are lauded to be more flexible and responsive than their larger counterparts, they often lack the skills and resources to collaborate or network. The Managing Enterprise Networks (MENS) project was established to address this. This project team works with SME owner managers across eight

European regions in order address the restrictive issues of development and growth within the area of collaboration and networking. The purpose the project is to determine the extent of European SME collaboration and identify the barriers to effective collaboration. It is hoped that these findings will help to paint a clear picture of the state of play of SME collaboration in Europe. These results will then be used to develop a management framework supported by a training programme for SMEs. This will equip SME managers with the skills, structures and systems to collaborate effectively and thus increase competitiveness, sustained growth and profits. This paper aims to provide a better understanding of the nature of SMEs and collaboration and it reports on preliminarily findings from our research.

2. Collaboration and SMEs

2.1 SMEs and Large Enterprises

Small to Medium Sized Enterprises (SMEs) are an important source of employment and trade within Europe. According to the European Commission SMEs represent 99% of all enterprises in the EU and together with start-ups they are reported to create between one and two third of all new jobs within the EU. The majority of these companies employ less than 10 people. With this in mind, SMEs are a vitally important asset and must be specifically targeted to improve their effectiveness and competitiveness for development and growth. There is much debate as to what exactly defines an SME. The structural and behavioural characteristics of an enterprise often provides a great insight into an organisation. According to Storey [4] there are multiple definitions available for an SME each focusing on different business characteristics. Broadly speaking, small and medium sized businesses are characterised by relatively low levels of employment, turnover and balance sheet status (see table 1). However other behavioural traits that characterise an SME include; centralised management, lower level of skilled labour, low level of technology employed, reactive based planning and finally an increasing importance of human resources as the major asset in the daily running of the organisation [5].

Table 1. SME Definition (EU, 2003)

Category Size	No. of Employees	Turnover	Balance Sheet
Micro	< 10	≤ € 2 million	≤ € 2 million
Small	< 50	≤ € 10 million	≤ € 10 million
Medium	< 250	≤€ 50 million	≤ € 43 million

There are certain characteristics that are found in SMEs that help us to understand them better:

a. Management/Organisational Structure

SMEs managers can adopt different management strategies [6]. However many SMEs are managed by the company founder and adopt a personalised approach characterised by a desire to maintain control [7]. This can act as a major benefit as well as a limitation to the business. Owner managers are passionate, hard working and tenacious and often have a burning desire to succeed. Employees experience a sense of belonging and importance in such a family type set-up [8]. However, owner managers are often reluctant to relinquish power and control. Lack of empowerment can impede effective decision-making and prevent organisational development.

b. Financial Restrictions

Lack of finance is a significant characteristic of SMEs and is well documented as a major limiting factor for continued development [9]. SMEs often lack investors and suffer cash flow problems. Investment in as re-engineering, training, marketing and capital equipment is limited as purchasing of materials and day-to-day operations absorb most of the cash on hand.

c. Process and Planning

It is difficult to generalise about process and planning within SMEs as both depend on the type, the volume, specialisation and the flexibility of the product being produced. The one general characteristic of processes within manufacturing SMEs is the fact that they tend to be more labour intensive with lower levels of skilled workers than the larger manufacturer. This is mainly due to the cost of automated production. In relation to planning, SMEs tend to focus on the short term often with an emphasis on survival rather than strategy [10]. As is often the case the forecasting and planning is dictated by the larger enterprise within any given market.

There is a widespread perception that SMEs are entirely different from larger enterprises from a social, organisational and financial perspective with the SME in a subservient role to the larger enterprise[11]. There is also a view that the smaller firm exists in a complimentary rather than in a subjugated role with respect to larger firms [12], especially since the shift away from mass production towards the consumer market. In reality, the relationship between SMEs and larger enterprises is very much dependant on industry and market specifics. However there are significant structural, organisational and operational differences between the two. Table 2 illustrates the key differences between large enterprises and SME's.

Table 2 Differences Between LE's and SME's

Dimension	Large Enterprise	Small Medium Sized Enterprise
Workforce Size	Greater than 250 employees	Less than 250 employees
Management Structure	Rigid/Formalised/Decentralised	Dynamic/Informal/Centralised
Leadership	Board of Directors	Owner Management
Business Systems	Proactive	Reactive
IT Infrastructure	Fully Integrated	Basic Use of Computers
R & D	A Core Competency	Small Scale
Resources	Plentiful	Limited
Project Management	Implemented and Practiced	Ad hoc/ At Managers Discretion
Funding	Generally Abundant	Limited/Government Reliant
Training	Structured/Regular	Ad Hoc/Informal
Human Resources	Integral Part of Business Plan	At Managers Discretion

On examination of the table above we can see that due to the differences in scale, leadership and operations, an SME requires different support systems than their larger counterparts.

2.2 Collaboration

Collaboration at its simplest is a process in which two or more agents work together to achieve a common goal. In the business world collaboration is best defined as: "Collaboration is multiple enterprises working in concert to execute critical business processes while sharing responsibility, quality and accountability. It is key to greater efficiencies, better trading relationships and improved profitability" [13]. Collaboration is a business strategy that motivates partners with a common business interest to generate value through sharing information at all phases of the business cycle (from product design to development to delivery). The goal is to enhance profitability while satisfying ever-increasing customer demands. All members of the network benefit, by combining each of their core competencies in creating a new product or service that is of higher value than the sum of its components.

Enterprises have embraced the concept of inter-firm collaboration to remain profitable and enhance their market share. Research has show that the key drivers for collaboration include; the birth of the consumers market, the reshaping of today's ever changing global markets as well as the reform and reorganisation of local economies and industries to comply with global standards [14]. These changes have been accelerated by the development of information communication technology, the Internet and the growth of e-commerce.

Group processes through which collaboration operates include:

- Communication- intentional transmission of meaningful messages
- Coordination – the act of working together harmoniously
- Cooperation – the association of persons or businesses for common benefits
- Information sharing – group members can synchronously share and use information

These processes do not work independently but are usually intermingled and determined by each other. To facilitate effective collaboration, support must be provided for all sub processes.

Many SMEs find it difficult to collaborate or network with other organisations. While SMEs are often more flexible and responsive than larger organisations, they often lack the necessary skills and resources to collaborate. Collaboration takes place in a different business environment and has different requirements than large organisations, therefore approaches and systems for SME collaboration need to be designed specifically for their unique needs and requirements. For example, on the one hand it does not have the potential to dedicate large resources to experimenting within areas of collaborative work and innovation [15], but on the other hand the flexibility and the responsive nature have a positive impact on collaboration.

2.3 Barriers to Collaboration

The MENS project aims to identify and analyse barriers to enterprise collaboration and enterprise network creation in SMEs. To determine the key problems and challenges an open workshop was realised which focussed on the specific difficulties within the area of sharing information and knowledge for collaboration. It was targeted specifically at owner managers in the west of Ireland. It was facilitated in the National University of Ireland, Galway and a total of 16 SME owner managers actively participated in the event. The key findings from the workshop identified some of the softer "people" issues as the main barriers to successful collaboration. Specifically, four main obstacles to successful collaboration were recognised:

a. Semantics/language: There is a lack of a common language between representatives from different organisations and consequently there can be many different interpretations of the same statement. Therefore, information is often misinterpreted between its creation and incorporation. Furthermore, information is often incorrectly formatted in documents and files and people are unable to communicate effectively. These factors also impede effective information sharing. Therefore, a common and agreed language and format must be finalised from the outset in order to allow the members to understand each other.
b. Motivation: Many people are unclear of the benefits of inter firm collaboration. They do not know what are the drivers, advantages, rewards and returns of sharing information with others. Unless

mutual benefits to collaboration are established and communicated to all parties, people will remain unwilling to participate and reluctant to learn new procedures for information exchange.

c. Trust: SMEs often lack the confidence to share propriety information. They often fear that competitors will gain access to proprietary data if they share data such as sales forecasts, or promotional plans with collaborating partners. Nevertheless this kind of real-time sharing of vital operational information is essential if companies want to work together towards a common goal. Establishing trust is potentially the greatest barrier to overcome in collaboration, and it must be established from the outset to allow knowledge sharing.
d. Access: There is a lack of common standard to enable information access and transfer. Therefore SMES often do not know what information to share, where critical information can be found and how to transfer it to others. Software is a key enabler for collaboration and information sharing with the Internet playing a leading role. In the case of SMEs, access to sophisticated IT is often not necessary, however an adequate knowledge of the methods and mechanisms available for communication is important.

Most organisations are designed to work best within the four walls of the enterprise and basic business processes and technology architectures may be difficult to extend outside the company. Attention must be paid to redesigning and restructuring internal processes to support this new collaborative business environment. Successful initiatives require top management support and backing to overcome the natural resistance of organisations to change. Inter-firm collaboration may demand even greater leadership and support than previous internally focused initiatives. Leaders must focus on the specific, tangible business benefits of these efforts, and participants across collaborating organisations must understand and support those benefits. Such foundation building will be critical in overcoming the barriers to SME collaboration.

2.4 Successful Collaboration

There is a clear similarity between the barriers identified by the workshop and the success factors identified by Evens [16], both indicate that the major elements for effective collaboration include the following:

- There is a willingness and flexibility during the early stages of establishing a structure;
- Members have a stake both in the process and outcome;
- A shared vision with obtainable goals is necessary;
- Clear performance measures keep the vision and strategy focussed;
- The group develops clear roles for members as well as policy guidelines;
- Sufficient resources and funds with strong leadership and guidance;
- Effective project management is essential;
- Open ad frequent meaningful and informal communication structures are necessary;
- Vital membership characteristics include above all mutual respect and trust.

3. The MENS Findings

Much literature exists on collaborative business and training however there is little relevant material about SMEs. MENS applies a mixed method research approach to gain an understanding of the training needs of SMEs to improve collaboration. The workshop findings are used to contextualise existing material. Further to this a questionnaire has been developed to determine the relevance and level of current practice of the best practices contributing to effective collaboration and training within SMEs. The aim of the questionnaire is to ascertain (a) the extent of collaboration that takes place within the organisation; (b) the barriers experienced; (c) the structures and culture in place to support collaboration and (d) finally management skills that can be improved to facilitate effective networking and collaboration. It contains an explicit set of carefully chosen and justified statements. These statements have been formulated from best practice concepts that have been compiled from workshops and justified by extensive literature searches. The questionnaire employs a Likert scaling technique in order to identify the extent to which the interviewee agrees or disagrees with each statement and the relevance of each statement to his/her business. The Likert scale contains a rating scale (1-5) for each statement. This allows each statement to be quantified and analysed providing a set of results than can be summed up to give a total score or attitude.

The MENS study is targeted at the following population:

1. Owner Managers: main target audience as they make all the key decisions within SME's
2. Number of Employees: The companies that are mainly targeted are the SMEs that have less then 50. This is due to the fact that these SMEs tend to have less proactive mechanisms in place and account for the majority of SMEs in operation throughout Europe.
3. Level of technology: SMEs of less then 50 are characterised by low levels of technology. The use of the Internet and mail will be assumed to be the key resources of the audience.

A total of 160 questionnaires is being collected in 8 different European regions: Extremadura and Madrid in Spain; Friesland in Holland; Liguria in Italy; Athens area in Greece and the Western corridor in Ireland, with an average of 20 questionnaires per region. Preliminary results confirm the main barriers identified in the workshop, and identify two new barriers: the lack of knowledge on how to collaborate and lack of time. SMEs indicated that for them it is important to work together with their clients and suppliers, but in the day-to-day business this looses importance over other issues. Preparing SMEs for collaboration and providing them with the knowledge and tools to do so, can reduce many of the barriers identified, and help to put in place the conditions and factors for successful collaboration.

The preliminary results concerning the analysis of the training needs show a clear tendency towards the "softer" issues, mainly concerning people management, for example related to creating a basis for trust, such as the need for competencies regarding to emotional intelligence; or related to the improvement of the motivation for collaboration, for example by increasing the management skills and communication skill (both of management and the organisational members). Although this does not mean that the "harder" issues were not mentioned, the related competencies and skills that were considered important and needed for successful collaboration can be classified in three groups: performance (e.g. negotiating skills); structures (e.g. creating the legal structure of the collaboration) and finance (e.g. participating in shared results). The identification of the training needs will be based on the final results of the analysis, although it is clear that a training plan which is capable of providing the SME managers with the skills and competences for managing the extended networks of the organization on the one hand, and the ability to implement the networked enterprise model inside the own organisation on the other, will address the three groups mentioned above.

4. Conclusions

The collaboration process will ultimately be successful if there is an existence of appropriate systems and structures, open channels of communication, a strong sense of purpose and availability of the necessary resources. However, it must be noted that without a healthy interpersonal relationship including the existence of motivation, trust, loyalty and honesty between all members of the team then the collaborative process of doomed to fail. It is often the softer issues "people" issues that affects the success of the collaborative work. It is clear that SMEs need these skills to take maximum advantage of the opportunities offered by enterprise collaboration and the participation in enterprise networks. Much literature exists on collaborative business, however little relevant material exists in relation to SMEs. The setting up of the MENS project is a logical outcome of the above mentioned. The final objective of the MENS project is to provide European SME managers and their employees with the competences necessary for collaborating with other organisations and SMEs, and give the SMEs managers the ability to create and manage enterprise networks.

References

[1] J.Milton-Smith, The Value of Networking SMEs: The Asia-Pacific experience. In P.Formica and D. Taylor (Eds.) Delivering Innovation. Key Lessons from the World-Wide Network of Science and Technology Parks. Campanillas (Malaga): IASP 1998, pp 225-248.

[2] S.Davis, S.Meyer, Blur the speed of change in the networked economy, ISBN 0 201 33987 0, Perseus Books 1998

[3] S.Birley, S.Cromie, and A.Myers, Entrepreneural networks: their emergence in Ireland and overseas', International Small Business Journal, 1991 9(4), 56-74; D.Carson, S.Cromie, P.McGowan, and J.Hill, Marketing and Entrepreneurship in SMEs: An Innovative Approach. ISBN: 0131509705, Prentice Hall International, 1995; E.Shaw, The real networks of small firms, in D.Deakins, P.Jennings, and C.Manson, (eds) Small Firms: Entrepreneurship in the 1990s. London, Paul Chapman Publishing 1997; D.Lenoard-Barton, International communication patterns among Swedish and Boston-area entrepreneurs, Research Policy, 1984 13(2), 101-14.

[4] D.J.Storey, Understanding the Small Business Sector, ISBN: 1861523815, Thomson Learning, 1994

[5] S.Carter, and D.Jones-Evans, Enterprise and Small Business: Principles, Practice and Policy, ISBN 0201398524 ,Financial Times Prentice Hall, 2002.

[6] P.Chapman, Managerial control Strategies in Small Firms, International Small Business Journal, 1999 17(2)

[7] T.B.A.van der Wiele, Relative strengths and weaknesses of small firms in innovation, International Small Business Journal, 1998 16(3): 88-93.

[8] R.Holliday, Investigating Small Firms: Nice Work?, ISBN: 0415123054, Routledge Small Business Series, Edited by David J. Storey. 1995

[9] M.S.Freel, Barriers to Product Innovation in Small Manufacturing Firms, International Small Business Journal, 2000 18(2); P.M.Swamidass, Modeling the adoption rates of manufacturing technology innovations by small US manufacturers: a longitudinal investigation, Research Policy 2003 32(3): 351-366.

[10] Y.P.Gupta, Linking Small Business and Modem Management Techniques, Industrial Management and Data Techniques, 1998 13-19

[11] D.Hamblin, and J.Willcock, Assessing the likely effectiveness of the intervention programmes in small manufacturing companies. Proceedings of the 2nd International SME conference, Plymouth University, March 1999; S.Rahimifard, S.Newman, and R.Bell, Distributed autonomous real-time and control for small to medium sized enterprises, Proceedings of the Institution of Mechanical Engineers, 1999 213(B) 475-489.; C.H.S.Pollard, The changing face of information systems issues in small firms, International Small Business Journal, 1998 16(3) 70-77

[12] G.Bannock, Counting Small Businesses in P. Ganguly, (ed.), UK Small Business Statistics and International Comparisons, London, Paul Chapman, 1985

[13] P.Strzelec, Achieving the Potential of Network Collaboration (ASCET) Achieving Supply Chain Excellence through Technology 4, 2002.

[14] H.S.Jagdev, K-D.Thoben, Anatomy of enterprise collaborations, Production Planning and Control, 2001 12(5): 437-451.

[15] F.Bougrain,, B.Haudeville, Innovation, collaboration and SMEs internal research capacities. Research Policy, 2002 31(5): 735-747.

[16] E.Evens, Management Issues of co-operative ventures and consortia in the USA. Part one. Library Management, 2002 23(4/5): 213-226; G.E.Evens, Management Issues of consortia. Part two. Library Management, 2002 23(6/7): 275-286.

Section 8

Training & Education

Section 8.1

Issues

eAdoption and the Knowledge Economy: Issues, Applications, Case Studies
P. Cunningham and M. Cunningham (Eds.)
IOS Press, 2004

eInclusion of Sign Language Users

Franz DOTTER
Centre for Sign Language and Deaf Communication, University of Klagenfurt,
Universitaetsstr. 65-67, Klagenfurt, A-9020, Austria
Tel: +43 463 2700 2821, Fax: +43 463 2700 2899, Email: franz.dotter@uni-klu.ac.at

Abstract: An essential improvement of the access of deaf people to education can only be reached by comprehensive interdisciplinary applied research and the use of modern ICT. In order to guarantee an optimal development in this respect, two main conditions have to be fulfilled: First, the situation and needs of the sign language users have to be clearly acknowledged (especially in comparison to other hearing impaired people). Second, the intellectual, scientific, organisational, and political barriers for the necessary developments have to be brought to the attention of all decision-makers so that they can be removed. The paper recommends major changes and measurements in order to realise the very positive programmatic EU-declarations on inclusion optimally.

1. Introduction

This paper addresses the situation of sign language users (mostly deaf people) in the context of "eInclusion" and similar initiatives of the European Union. The first focus will be on the special situation of sign language users in contrast to the majority of hearing impaired, the second one on the reality of the initiatives, compared to the programmatic announcements sent out by the persons and institutions responsible for the respective initiatives. Experiences from previous surveys and projects (cf. [1], [2]) as well as from the last IST call will be analysed in order to develop recommendations for the subject under discussion.

2. Objectives

The objectives of the paper are to clarify the speciality of the target group addressed within eInclusion and to draw the necessary scientific, educational and organizational consequences from the given situation.

3. Methodology Used

This paper summarizes research and experiences from about 10 years' work. To reach the results, a mix of methods was used: Surveys, interviews, conferences, analyses of projects and project evaluation processes, interpretation of analysis results. In order to respect the principle of self-determined life, hearing and deaf experts have always collaborated.

4. The Special Needs of Deaf People

4.1 Acoustic Perception and Spoken Language

Compared to salient acoustic phenomena like a strong pulse or a loud noise, the perception of spoken language needs fine differentiation with respect to acoustic data: The differences in intensity between accented and non-accented syllables or words are big; the same is valid for intensity and frequency bands of different sounds. Therefore persons with a restricted hearing ability are in danger to miss some less salient sounds within words or some less salient parts of words, words themselves or even phrases. If a certain limit of this lack of perceptions is reached, the acquisition of spoken language may be negatively influenced: The respective persons acquire 'gaps' during their ontogenesis of language, which lead to a less complete mastering of their mother tongue than subjects with normal hearing show.

Many forms of a hearing restriction have less severe consequences and lead only to slight deficits concerning language or communicative competence. The situation is completely different if the hearing capability of a person is not sufficient in order to acquire spoken language via the acoustic channel (this is the practical definition of deafness).

While many of the hard of hearing only need adequate hearing aids to amplify acoustic phenomena, the acoustic channel is barred to the deaf so that all acoustic data have to be presented in a visual form in order to be accessible. This is also true for spoken language. Therefore practically all the deaf choose sign language as their preferred language.

4.2 Spoken and Written Language

Though it sometimes seems that written language represents language much better than the spoken one, we learn it the other way round, naturally: We have a good competence in spoken language by the time we begin to learn the written variant of our mother tongue. Although we should not say that it is impossible for a young child to learn a language first by its written variant, we all know that this would be unnatural. Human beings learn languages in realisations that can be quickly and spontaneously produced and perceived. For hearing people the acoustic mode is the best one for this enterprise.

We have to state another fact concerning language use: Our everyday spoken language is not identical with the standardised written language. Due to its production mode and our normal communicative behaviour, it shows some features we normally do not find in written language (we do not always 'speak as we write'), e.g. different registers and styles, breaks and new beginnings, or additional 'paralinguistic' information.

Due to shortcomings in deaf education yet existent in several countries, deaf people often lack a sufficient competence in writing and reading (as spoken language is the main basis for learning the written language). As a consequence, they are not only cut off from acoustically offered information but often also from written information. This is the reason why many sign language users need help with written language in spite of the fact that it is already in the visual mode.

As deaf people cannot hear spoken languages well enough to learn this way, they need a special form of bilingual education, where a sign language gives the linguistic and cognitive base and the national written/spoken language is 'anchored' to the first system (as a second language). There is the need for special research and optimisation of this sort of language learning. There is also the need to offer English as a third language in order to be able to follow the international communication, also in a form specially adapted for deaf people.

4.3 A False Analogy

The situation of deaf people with written language just described above explains why an appealing analogy falls down: Our experience shows that blind persons can easily read if they are offered a tactile version of written language (Braille). The reason for this is: They had no severe problem to learn the spoken language and can therefore acquire written language from this base like other hearing subjects. In this case the so-called compensation hypothesis applies: If an individual cannot perceive data from a certain sensory channel, these data have to be offered in another, accessible channel.

For deaf people the analogy would be: As they are unable to access the spoken language in the acoustic channel, we simply have to offer them spoken language via written language and all problems should be solved. Because this solution does not respect the natural learning sequence (spoken to written language) and because we cannot produce and perceive written language as simply and quickly as spoken language, the analogy does not work. Therefore we have to acknowledge sign languages as the languages chosen by deaf people for everyday use and instruction.

Written language is of great importance to deaf people if they want to be integrated into the hearing society and have written information at their disposal. The goal of offering them written language competence comparable to hearing subjects can only be reached if their respective instruction is considerably improved. ICT will play an important role in this task.

4.4 Sign Language Users as a Minority within the Hearing Handicapped

The first principle to be stated here, is that of self-determinacy: Everyone has the right to define the form of his/her life. Parents of a child with hearing difficulties have to decide for their young child, the child itself has to get more and more control over his/her language choices as it matures. Self-responsible adults have the right to get language and communicative contexts as they want them.

To describe the minority state of deaf people within the large group of hearing handicapped, let us look at some numbers: The standard estimation of the number of deaf people in any society is 0.1 to 0.2 per cent. The percentage of hearing impaired people as a whole varies from country to country, but with about 6-15 per cent it is at least sixty times the number of deaf people. From this fact it is understandable that the use of the generic term 'hearing impaired' in political or scientific discussion often leads to the consequence that only the needs of the overwhelming majority within this group, the hard of hearing, are considered. This fact is the reason that many scientific publications simply ignore the fact that there is an important divide within this group concerning language needs.

5. Technical Aids for the Perception of Spoken Language

5.1 Systems Amplifying Acoustic Stimuli

Before turning to the needs of sign language users, let me give a short overview concerning the aids for people who decide on the use of spoken language as their preferred language (mostly: the hard of hearing). They need all equipment which helps to strengthen the acoustic data in order to be sufficiently perceived for e.g. linguistic understanding. These are, in general, all amplifying systems, hearing aids and induction loops.

5.2 Systems Transforming Acoustic Stimuli

Here we have to differentiate between two very different systems, both rather new:

- Systems of manual or automatic transformation of spoken language into a written representation (i.e. sub-titling, manual writing services, and automatic speech recognition). These systems are useful only for persons who know a spoken/written language well enough to decode the meaning.
- Systems that transform acoustic stimuli into electrical ones for the inner ear, the so-called cochlea implant (CI). These systems are now recommended especially for deaf people whose deafness stems from an inability in the middle ear and whose inner ear nerves are working. They are generally working very well for people who had some experience of spoken language before becoming deaf; the rate of success in cases of deafness from birth being lower and subject of some controversies (cf. also section 10).

6. Technical Aids for Sign Language Users

The access of deaf people to communication and information has the following aspects:

6.1 Telecommunication between Sign Language Users

The transfer of visual information is necessary and modern ICT makes it possible. However, the quality needed for understanding sign language poses restrictions on the telecommunications used: While a double ISDN line provides a sufficient data rate, slower connections do not. Internet based video-telephony or videoconferencing are impossible for sign language users with a standard telephone connection. Mobile video telephony is sufficient within areas of UMTS service only. In all cases, the costs are a major problem.

6.2 Communication between Sign Language Users and Hearing Subjects

The most economic solution would be automatic translation in both directions. However, today human interpreters are necessary, the costs of which strongly limit their use. A good solution is represented by the so-called relay centres, especially those who offer written (= text) as well as signed (= video) access to their services.

6.3 Making Spoken Information Accessible to Sign Language Users

Two solutions are possible: The optimal one is real-time or delayed interpretation from spoken into signed language (for connected problems, cf. 5. 2.). The second solution is note-taking or captioning by humans or automatic speech recognition: the transfer of a spoken language from the acoustic into the visual mode, i.e. into written language. The EU-project VOICE is an example for such a system, but it has currently two major limitations: It forces the speaker to use a special sort of speech behaviour and the deaf person using it needs a good - often lacking - competence in written language (cf. section 4).

6.4 Making Written Information Accessible to Sign Language Users

Human interpreters are also needed if we want to have the information translated into a sign language. An example of good practice is the German Sign Language version of the German Government's "Sozialgesetzbuch IX" [3]. Concerning automatic transfer from written language to a sign language, the EU-project Visicast shows the state of the art: It converts frequent (written) phrases into fixed forms of a sign language produced by an avatar. This is no translation, but an important step towards more accessibility.

7. Examples and Experiences

7.1 The Web Accessibility Initiative (WAI)

The Web Content Accessibility Guidelines 2.0 (draft: [4]) give adequate recommendations, namely to use a written language, simple written language or a sign language in order to transfer acoustic information into a visual one. WAI also points out the importance of avoiding two different information tracks within one sensory area (e.g. for deaf people: watch an action <u>and</u> read the respective caption). But it represents the solutions as if they were equally applicable. It does neither make clear the connections between deaf education and different competence in written language nor the necessity to present content via sign language (maybe this is beyond the scope of WAI). WAI focuses on assistive technology, without telling us explicitly that some forms of this technology -especially those important for languages, including translations - are still not available. By this, the necessary understanding that the access of deaf people has to be provided not only by assistive technology but often needs direct human interactions is undermined. Additionally, it does not become clear that it is a human right to access information through a sign language.

7.2 EU Programmes

The inclusion of persons with special needs has a high priority in the European Union. Although there is no doubt that many fruitful developments have been instigated by EC programmes and initiatives, I see a few very strong obstacles to the expected success of all measures. I have to explain what I mean by 'expected success': Results of EC measures should provide solutions, which fulfil the demands of people with special needs for the whole area of the EU and in practice. To begin with the different programmes and their calls: Although there is a general coordination of all activities in the sense of the respective framework programme, there seems to be no control concerning the eventual overlapping of proposals delivered to different programmes (for LEONARDO it is even possible that different consortia deliver projects which share some tasks). There is no coordination, which should coordinate or relate such related projects in order to avoid double work.

The technology and economy orientation of programmes like IST have two facets, one concerning the development of proposals, the other concerning their review: Instead of searching rigidly for the demands and needs of people with special needs (though usability has a high value in evaluation), many projects emerge from what non-handicapped experts think that the handicapped persons would like to have. I do not wish to offend the reviewers as persons because they do a very hard job. But if the guidelines for a review say more or less explicitly that successful projects must promise either a high economic outcome (e.g. by integrating important companies) or a new technological result, one need not wonder when projects are rejected which do not show these properties but have a 'simple' overall improvement of the situation of people with special needs as their goal. It is really simple: Once you want to provide a working solution for handicapped people Europe-wide, you have to use established technology and you cannot promise a big profit. I know that the EC offers programmes in order to apply good solutions to all countries or new areas but these programmes are not sufficient in respect to finances and coordination.

7.3 The EC Initiative against Discrimination

The EC-Directive 2000/78/EC prohibits discrimination in the workplace and in other areas of society. This includes discrimination by disability. The Directive should be implemented in all the Member States' legal orders by 2 December 2003.

The situation for sign language users is as follows: In order to reduce their discrimination they have to get rights comparable to linguistic minorities using spoken languages. This means e.g. the acknowledgement of their language. Due to the ongoing violation of linguistic rights in some EU countries and their unwillingness to accept any change, the recognition of minority languages is still the sole responsibility of each Member State. This means that the EC is not able to act against discrimination on linguistic grounds in its own area. Therefore the sign language users suffer from the fact that some old European ethnic or linguistic conflicts are still not solved in a humane manner.

There may be a way out of this dilemma: One may argue that not providing adequate sign language rights and services to deaf people is a discrimination on grounds of disability. The disability of deaf people demands the use of a sign language. Deaf people cannot be compared to hearing people who can be forced to use another language against their will because they can hear both. Deaf people cannot choose, they have to be provided with a visual language if requested. As long as this question is not politically decided, sign language users will have to struggle with unjust regulations, missing rights & services [5].

7.4 Equal Opportunities Laws

These laws, forced by the above-mentioned EC-directive, try to offer some compromise between the official acknowledgement of sign languages like spoken minority languages and their ignorance (e.g. in Germany or in the respective Austrian draft under discussion now): They formulate the right of deaf persons to use sign language in many contexts. This includes the right to get interpreting financed. But - as they concentrate on equal rights at the workplace - they ignore the fact that the right of using ones preferred language is not very valuable if one cannot learn this language following the knowledge and standard of language acquisition. The result can be described as the following message: 'You may use you preferred language as an adult if you want to, but do not bother us by demanding an adequate education from the Early Years on or other services!'

8. Barriers to the eInclusion of Sign Language Users

In this chapter, I summarise points already mentioned and add a few perspectives:

8.1 The 'Brutality' of Statistics

As long as the deaf are subsumed under the big majority of hearing impaired persons who do not need or use a sign language, their needs simply do not appear in many publications or executive summaries, delivered to the politicians.

8.2 Adaptive Technology and Sign Language Users

Adaptive technology is an important instrument for deaf people. But it has to be developed to a status where it works stable (which is yet not the case for sign language synthesis and recognition) and it must not replace personal social interaction between deaf or deaf and hearing persons. Additionally, the potential users must be offered the competence to handle hard- and software (this means especially for deaf people that their knowledge of a written national language and written English has to be substantially improved).

8.3 Technology Orientation of EU-programmes like IST

Sometimes it seems that many technicians are not interested in a real eInclusion of groups of people with special needs if well-tried and tested technology is used. They are only interested in developing new technologies, ignoring the fact that these technologies cannot be applied to the eInclusion of a whole social group. In other words: Test beds are more interesting than services which cover the real needs of the people.

A practical example of a much more necessary task, using established technology, is the real inclusion of deaf people in the hearing society by extensive installation of relay centres [6]. To organise the improvement of standards according to the needs of deaf people is an equally important task of technology politics.

8.4 Costs per Individual Signer

As sign language users need their visual languages, they cause costs like any other acknowledged language minority or even more, because they often need interpreters in order to communicate with the hearing society. As they are low in number and spread all over the countries, the costs per capita are quite high. This fact often prevents them from getting the adequate service. If one proposes e.g. a EU-project with deaf collaborators, you have to take into account interpreters' costs which often cannot be covered by the normal project budget or are not understood or accepted by the reviewers.

8.5 Project Organization in a Developing Scientific and Educational Area

Understandably, sign language and deaf issues are only minor subjects in academic organisation. This means that - in contrast to established academic fields - even a lot of basic research needs funding through projects. Therefore many people working in this field depend on insecure and temporary limited finances. Some improvements fail to become sustainable because many projects simply end without further consequences, people leave, and the contents are lost.

9. Business benefits

The representative of the development department of a big electronics company told me two years ago that – due to the new orientation on share value - he is obliged to develop only those new ideas which promise a return of at least 10 per cent on the invested money. Everyone can calculate that this rule automatically excludes costly developments for small groups. As a consequence, eInclusion for people with special needs is an enterprise which needs a first impulse from public funding and some guarantee against deficits from the same source. If a respective initiative is provided professional counselling and looks for optimal solutions, it can certainly reach some sustainability or even a small profit - which has to be reinvested in the project, however. Therefore I plead either for non-profit organisations to carry out such projects or for a public-private partnership where the roles of each partner, the partially public funding, and the overall goals (which are those of inclusion and not those of a single company) are explicitly stated. With such constructions, the participation of private companies could become profitable for them in the long term, e.g. by gaining technological advantages or by fully utilising their capacities.

10. The Future: A Changing Sign Language User Population

With the invention of the cochlear implant, a big change began to take place: While the implants help almost all late-deafened adults, the implantation of deaf-born children is not so successful. Most important is that a cochlear implant does not mean that the respective person will identify always and only with the hearing society. This identification depends on the quality of understanding spoken language they reach with the implant.

The number of deaf people in the traditional sense may diminish, but the need for sign language will remain. It should be added, however, that this development is only valid for the rich countries. Starting from a number of about 6,000 millions of human beings, there are at least 6 millions of deaf persons worldwide for whom adequate measures of inclusion could bring about a higher quality of life.

11. Concluding Recommendations

An essential improvement of the access of deaf people to education can only be reached by comprehensive interdisciplinary applied research and the use of modern ICT. There are several equally important global measures necessary, namely building a "Deaf European Research Area" and a coordination network concerning deaf education.

In detail, sign language users

- must become a group specifically addressed by EU authorities in all questions of accessibility, education and vocational training. Without always questioning the necessity or the costs, this group has to be provided with equal opportunities in education from the Early Years on and at the workplace.

- have to be provided with information access in sign language as they want it;
- have to be provided with adequate education in written English & their home language
- There should be one coordinative institution or office for deaf issues (in connection with deaf representatives) to avoid double funding or repeating the same projects.
- Some money from EU funds has to be given directly to the deaf in order to enable them to release calls for projects on their own (like any other group with special needs).

References

[1] T. Dimmel. & F. Dotter & M. Hilzensauer & K. Krammer & A. Skant: Final document for the project "Steps Towards an Improvement of the Participation of Deaf Persons in the Information Society". Funded by the European Commission, Directorate General V under contract File Soc 98 100899, and the Austrian Government, Federal Ministry for Science and Traffic. 2 Vols., Ms. Klagenfurt 1999; http://www.uni-klu.ac.at/fzgs/

[2] Research Center for Sign Language and Communication of the Hearing-Impaired, University of Klagenfurt: Final document for the project "Preparing a European Deaf Network for Information and Communication". Project funded by: European Commission, Directorate General "Information Society", according to the Grant Agreement within the framework of the program PROMISE, and the Austrian Government, Federal Ministry for Education, Science and Culture. Ms. Klagenfurt 2000; http://www.uni-klu.ac.at/fzgs/

[3] Sozialgesetzbuch IX – Rehabilitation und Teilhabe behinderter Menschen (Social law book IX – rehabilitation and participation of people with special needs): http://www.sgb-ix-umsetzen.de/index.php/nav/tpc/nid/1/aid/221/sign/y

[4] Web Accessibility Initiative: http://www.w3.org/WAI/

[5] M. Bruce, Protection of sign languages in the member states of the Council of Europe. Doc. 9738; 17 March 2003, http://www.coe.int/T/E/Com/Files/PA-Sessions/April-2003/

[6] P. Roe, Comparative Study of Relay Services 1991-2001. http://www.stakes.fi/cost219/Procroerelay3.doc

eAdoption and the Knowledge Economy: Issues, Applications, Case Studies
P. Cunningham and M. Cunningham (Eds.)
IOS Press, 2004

eEurope-Plus: Digital Divide or Digital Inclusion?

Nerute KLIGIENE
Institute of Mathematics and Informatics and Vilnius Gediminas Technical University,
A.Gostauto 12, Vilnius, 01108, Lithuania
Tel: +370 5 2660386, Fax: + 370 5 2619905, Email: nerute@ktl.mii.lt

Abstract: Statistical techniques using a graphical display that simultaneously describes several important features of a data set, such as center and spread, has been applied to statistical data from 2002/03 that measures Information Society achievements in the 15 EU Member States and 10 Newly Associated States (NAS). This allows the results of any country of interest to be localized in the context of the enlarged EU or visualize the situation of that country in the defined areas. A simple measure expressing a digital inclusion of the NAS numerically has been developed in this paper, giving a clear picture of eEurope at a glance and enabling the identification of topics and areas where the NAS were dramatically behind the EU or where they had readiness and potential to reach the level of advanced EU countries.

1. Introduction

European integration and the enlargement of the European Union is a big challenge for all members participating in this process. A New Europe has become a new reality since May 2004. Consistent evaluation during a transition period is very important, not only in economics but also in ICT. The strategists of the newly emerged EU must know how ten new countries, often less advanced in Information Society (IS), affect the common results of EU and have to find the ways to convert a digital divide into a digital inclusion. Statistical analysis of data suggested here can help effectively in evaluating a situation.

This work analyzes the data elaborated and presented [1] as SIBIS (Statistical Indicators Benchmarking the Information Society) IST 5FP 2000 project results. The data includes 15 EU countries and 10 EU Newly Associated States (NAS), covering 84 statistical indicators, grouped into the areas: Basic Access and Usage, Information Security, e-Commerce, e-Work, e-Government, e-Health, Digital Literacy, Learning and Training, Digital Divides. The results in [1] are presented as data tables and charts on 84 indicators, some of them contain further differentiation by age, by gender of respondents or intensity of ICT usage. Therefore it is complicated to grasp the achievements of NAS and EU, it is difficult to compare them in different areas, and impossible to do statistically reliable conclusions.

The weighted averages of EU and NAS denoted as EU-15 and NAS-10 are the only summary characteristics used in [1] for EU and NAS countries groups. From a statistical point of view, the average is a poor observation characteristic. SIBIS has been extended by constructing a new handbook [2]. The new indicator system consists of 134 indicators. They come from the SIBIS project and from large variety of sources outside (such as Eurostat, Eurobarometer, and others). A general view of situation, focused on EU – NAS differences is badly needed, enabling motivated statistical inference indicating areas where NAS are far behind the EU level. Such data is also necessary for better understanding of whole situation and enhancing a policy making process in overall IS strategy.

The analysts of the Economist Intelligence Unit tried to fill the information gap by issuing a report on EU enlargement [3]. Its objective is to broaden understanding of the enlargement and to assess its likely impact on politics, economics and business. Some statistical data on economic factors are provided in [3] but a comparison of separate countries results is based on the averages EU-15 and EU-25 only, what is not sufficient from a statistical point of view. The open questions of a statistical inference will be covered below using medians and other statistical characteristics based on the spread of the data.

2. Objectives

The main goals of this study are:

1. To visualize a situation in the topics and areas defined in SIBIS to establish the position of each country in the context of the enlarged EU results;
2. To get at a glance a clear picture of eEurope in order to identify:
   - the areas where the NAS are dramatically behind the EU;
   - the topics in the enlarged EU where the IS development is not sufficient;
   - the areas where the NAS countries have a readiness to reach the EU level.
3. To develop a measure, expressing EU-NAS differences in separate areas numerically.

In this paper an example of proposed statistical techniques and data visualization are demonstrated in the areas of Basic Access and Usage, together with Information Security. Analogous study has been done in all areas where SIBIS has provided data. Results of these studies at a glance can be seen in the Fig. 5. The proposed approach can be applied equally to the new SIBIS data sets [2] or any other set of statistical data.

3. About Data and the Methodology Used for Deriving Summarized Data

3.1 Data Description

The main sources of data described in [1] deal with a target population - resident population (aged 15 and over) in private households representing EU and NAS in 2002-2003.

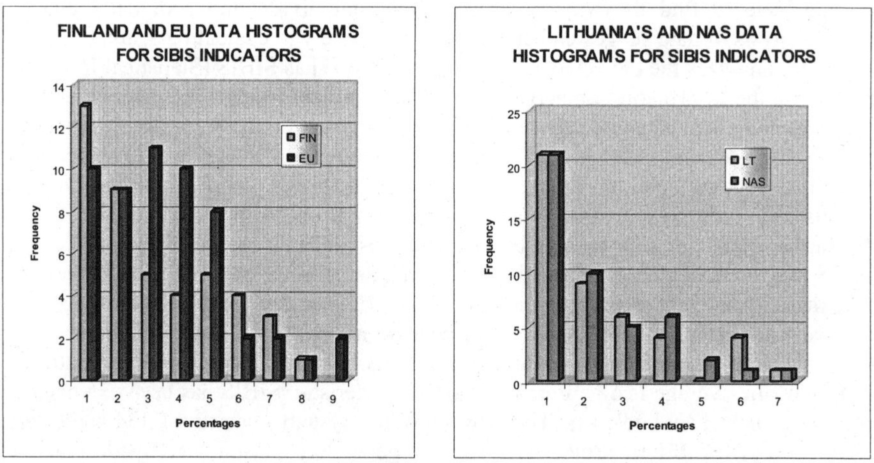

Figure 1. Histograms Representing Finland versus EU15, and Lithuania versus NAS – the Empirical Distributions of Percentages for 84 SIBIS Indicators with Bins of Percentages [0-10), [10-20),..., [80-90).

The survey fieldwork was carried out April-May 2002 and January 2003 resulting in two surveys: (1) General Population Survey (GPS) 2002, country coverage - EU15 plus Switzerland and USA (sample size 500-1000 per country); (2) General Population Survey NAS10 2003 (GPS-NAS), country coverage - NAS10: BG, CZ, EE, HU, LT, LV, PL, RO, SL, SK (with an average sample size 1000 per country).

Each data array from the statistical survey is a series of percentages of population, having a property investigated as a specified indicator in 27 countries. For example, the indicator No. 4 - Internet User Experience, is the array of 27 observations - percentages of Internet users with 2 and more years experience (versus target population) in each country.

The preliminary analysis of empirical distribution of any percentage data under consideration shows that none are symmetrical. the histograms are asymmetric and highly variable in shape (see Figure 1 and 2). The median and *IQR* (Inter-Quartile Range) are more suitable characteristics than conventionally used average and variance.

The eEurope-plus Action Plan [4] have similar objectives as SIBIS – to collect the data and to compare the relative position of the countries with respect to the general EU situation. However, a different classification, indicators, methodologies and different sets of countries have been used in [4]: 13 countries (Cyprus, Malta and Turkey added) considered instead of the ten NAS10 countries. This makes a comparison and common conclusions from SIBIS and eEurope-plus project rather difficult.

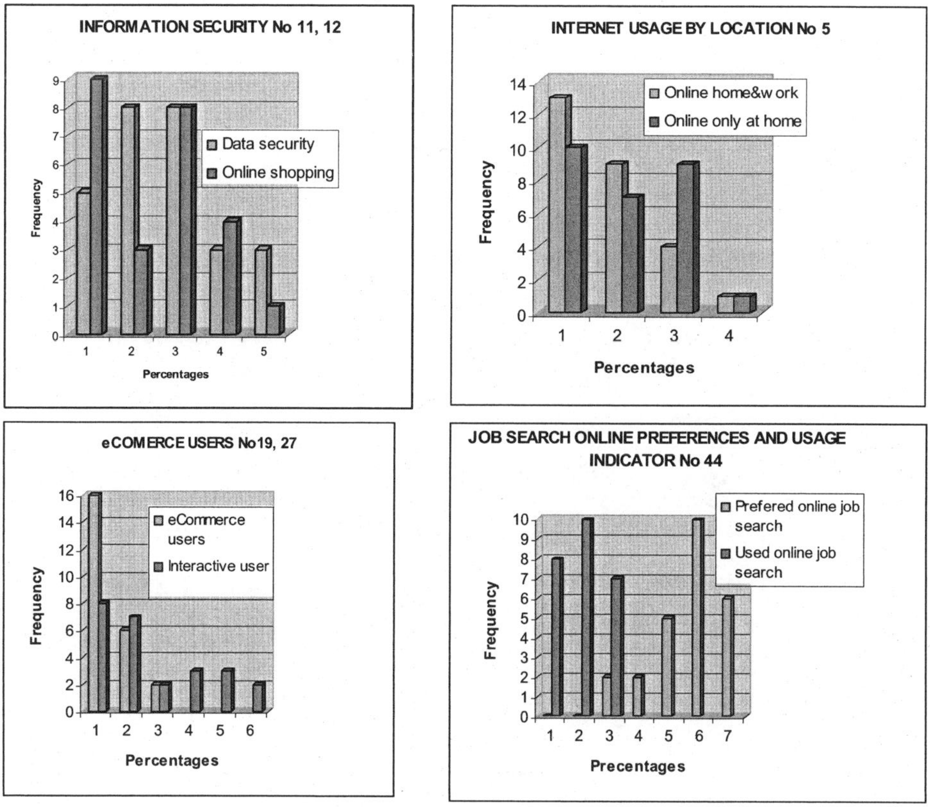

Figure 2. Empirical Distributions of Percentages over Countries in Several Selected SIBIS Indicators (Namely 5, 11, 12, 19, 27, 44) with the Bins of Percentages: [0-10), [10-20), ..., [60-70).

3.2 Methodology of Summarizing and Estimating Visually Data

The aim of our study is to compare the SIBIS results of separate countries or their groups in the context of data summary characteristics such as medians, EU-15 and NAS-10 averages, drawing the attention to the difference between them and the spread of data. For that reason the most informative statistical technique is related to the box plot – a graphical display that simultaneously describes several important features of a data set, such as center (median), spread (*IQR*), departure from symmetry. According to [5] the box plots are useful in graphical comparisons among data sets because they have high visual impact.

The Median, Inter-Quartile Range, denoted by *Me* and $IQR = Q3 - Q1$ (where *Q1, Q3* are the first and third quartile respectively) were used to discover differences and similarities in the data. The Median is a characteristic of location as well as a mean but median is more suitable for analysis of non-symmetrically distributed data like this.

Table 1. Figures of the SIBIS Areas: Basic Access and Usage, and the Information Security.

No	Indicator title	*Q1, Me, Q3*	*IQR*	*EU*	*NAS*	*D*	*Δ*
6	Intensity of online usage more 6h/week	7, 10, 13	6	13	6	7	**1,16**
5	Internet usage at work and home	4, 11, 17	13	16	4	12	**0,92**
12	Security concerns to e-shopping	6, 20, 28	22	28	6	22	**1,0**
11	Concerns online data security	11, 21, 28	17	26	24	2	0,12
4	Internet users (two and more years)	16, 26, 36	20	30	13	17	0,85
9	E-mail users, all intensities	16, 29, 45	29	37	14	23	0,79
8	SMS users	34, 43, 50	16	40	34	6	0,37
8a	Personal mobile phones ownership	54, 68, 76	21	69	44	25	**1,19**

Table 1 contains the summarized numerical characteristics of SIBIS indicators, the 3rd column of it is visualized in the pictures 3-4 below. We can compare the results of selected countries in the context of the enlarged EU; say Lithuania as a new member of EU25 and Austria as a member of old EU15.

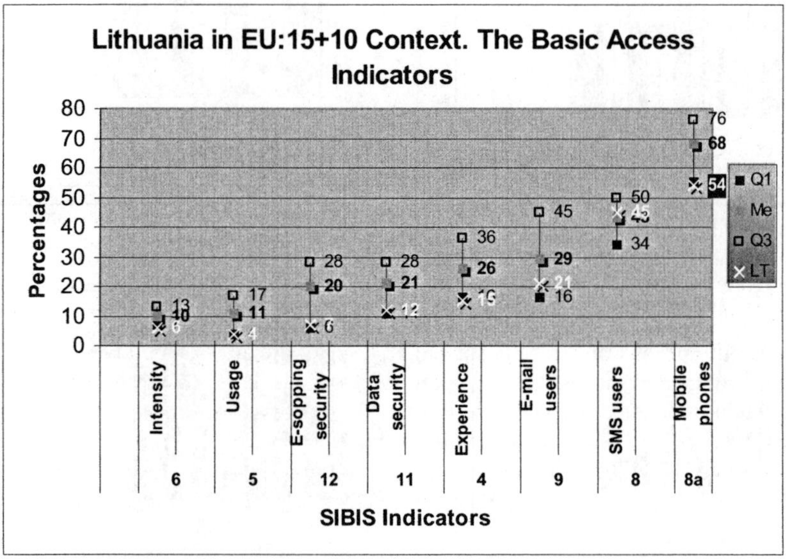

*Figure 3. Visualization of Summarized SIBIS Indicators and the Relative Position of Lithuania's Percentages (Marked by **x** and White Figures) in EU:15+10 Data Context.*

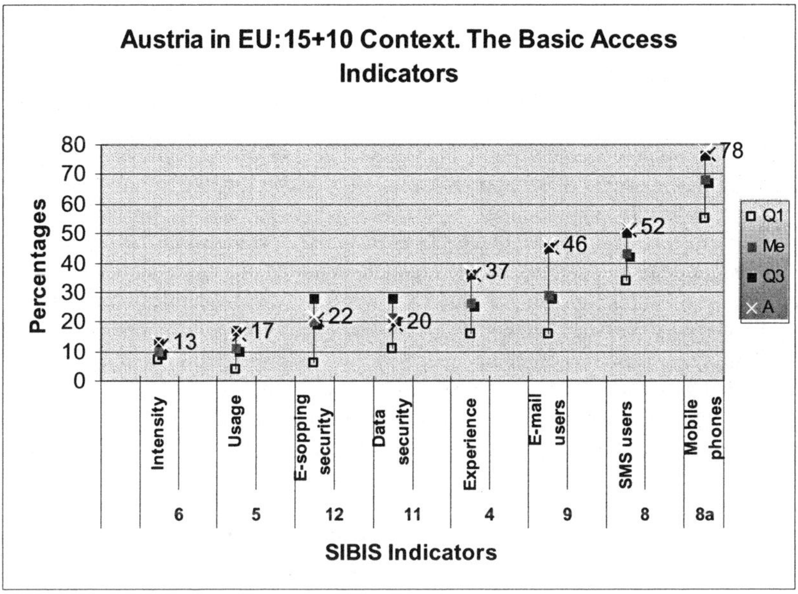

Figure 4. Visualization of the Corresponding Percentages in Austria and EU:15+10 Data.

3.3. Comments of the Summarized EU:15+10 Data in the Basic Access Area

Figures 3 and 4 illustrate the following facts:

- Internet usage by intensity and by location in the New Europe are around 10%, concerns on information security matters (indicators No 11, 12) are around 20%, and middle values of e-mail and experience of Internet users (No 4, 9) are almost 30%;
- Mobile technologies (No 8, 8a) are visibly different from other indicators and have the largest medians, illustrating extensive development of mobile IT;
- Data spread (*IQR*) is the largest in the e-mail usage and the security concerns (online shopping), and it is smallest in the intensity of Internet usage (over 6hrs/week intensity);
- Almost all indicators show departures from symmetry in data distributions;
- The majority of Austria's results presented in Fig. 4 are approaching *Q3* – the value of third quartile, what means that according to these indicators Austria is among the 25% best countries of the enlarged EU. Results on security problems in Austria are a bit lower - close to the median of a New Europe data;
- Lithuania in many indicators demonstrates quite good results – reaching or exceeding the first quartile *Q*, i.e. at least 25% of EU25 countries have worse results.

3.4. Deriving the Numerical Characteristics of Summarized New Europe Data

Introduce a difference between weighted averages of EU-15 and NAS-10 as $D = (EU\text{-}15) - (NAS\text{-}10)$ and divide it by *IQR* - the parameter of spread. Denote the result by $\Delta = D/IQ$. The values of Δ for selected eight indicators are represented in the last column of the Table1. Typically, in the data sets considered, Δ was ranging from 0.1 to 1.2. Rarely, when NAS-10 > EU-15, the negative Δ values do appear, seemingly indicating a difference in favor of NAS, but in reality expressing only too high expectations in NAS countries for digital technologies' usage. For example, negative values $\Delta<0$ emerged, when respondents answered the preference questions: "Would you prefer to use Internet for job search (No 44) or to fill the income tax return / tax declaration (No 43)?" The answers "Tried using it" demonstrate very low percentages, usually less than 5% in NAS countries. This property is clearly expressed in the last picture of the Fig. 2, where most respondents (around 60%) preferred online job search, but in reality their usages are centered around 20%.

If $\Delta>0$ is rather small – a little difference discovered between EU and NAS, if $\Delta>0$ is close to 1 – there is a big EU and NAS difference in the indicator under consideration. In this way each indicator, determined by SIBIS, has assigned the numerical value Δ, corresponding to the scaled difference in averages between the two groups of countries EU and NAS. The results are presented in the Table 1, where the No of indicator, corresponding to that used for SIBIS in [1] is in the first column, in the last column – the numerical values of scaled difference between EU and NAS, assigned for that indicator.

The display of the 3rd column of this data allows a clear graphical comparison of the results achieved as it was seen in the Fig. 3 – 4 and enables us to visualize a situation in the topics identified by SIBIS in order to see a position of any separate country in the context of the enlarged EU results or to get at a glance a clear picture of eEurope in any SIBIS topic. Investigating further we notice that four indicators in the Table 1, namely No: 6, 5, 12, and 8a have the values what seems to be significant. We are ready now to evaluate the significance of derived Δ values in the context of whole complex of available data.

We are seeking for more general results – to develop a measure of a digital inclusion expressing numerically EU and NAS differences in the wider areas such as Basic Access and Usage, Information Security, e-Commerce, e-Work, e-Government, e-Health, Digital Literacy, Learning and Training, Digital Divides, each of them composed of several indicators (ranging from 4 to 14 in considered SIBIS data 2002/03). Generalized results would have industrial significance for firms and companies developing ICT and potential benefits by indicating clearly and consistently the areas where the NAS were dramatically behind the EU, the topics in the enlarged EU where the IS development is not sufficient.

4. Measuring the New Countries Achievements in the EU25 Context

Let us develop a numerical measure of EU – NAS differences related to the area, having k indicators and represented by the numerical values: $\Delta_1, \ldots, \Delta_k$. An example of such data for the Basic Access and Usage area is provided in the Table 1. Some values of Δ_i are close to 1, some are not. To determine whether the contribution of any indicator was significant or not in the area of interest, we need to choose the threshold value λ. Theoretically the value of λ depends on unknown probability distributions of rather complicated statistics constructed from non-normally distributed (a departure from symmetric distribution is evident) sample data used for investigation here. It is difficult to relate λ to any theoretical significance level, therefore the selection of λ value can be done only empirically.

The proposed procedure is as follows: if $\Delta_i < \lambda$, we conclude the contribution of that indicator is small, if $\Delta_i \geq \lambda$, the contribution is significant. Say r values among k were satisfying $\Delta_i \geq \lambda$ in the considered area. Let us determine the measure of the NAS achievements compared with EU15 as

$$MARK = 1 - r/k.$$

MARK is a measure of digital inclusion. It has the numerical values between 0 and 1 and a clear interpretation: small *MARK* values means small NAS achievements compared to EU results, while *MARK*, approaching 1, indicates that NAS and EU15 had comparable achievements; *MARK* close to 0.5 means that approximately a half of indicators were significant, a half – not significant in that area. The measure *MARK* becomes more reliable if each area has more indicators, therefore the SIBIS New eEurope Indicator Handbook, describing 134 indicators, will provide more reliable background for numerical evaluation of situation using a proposed *MARK* approach.

Applying the described procedure in the areas defined in SIBIS project or other data sets, we obtain the numerical evaluation of a situation as a sequence of *MARK* values, related to the specified areas. For $\lambda = 0.9$, selected empirically, the *MARK* values, corresponding to the SIBIS areas give us a numerical evaluation of a situation in IS development presented in the diagram (Fig. 5). The empirical value $\lambda = 0.9$ was selected from several considered λ values as providing more stable results in evaluating a situation.

From the diagram below we conclude that the NAS are dramatically behind the EU in such areas as Learning and Training, e-Health, Digital Literacy, while seemingly in the e-Government area there is a readiness of the NAS to reach the EU countries level.

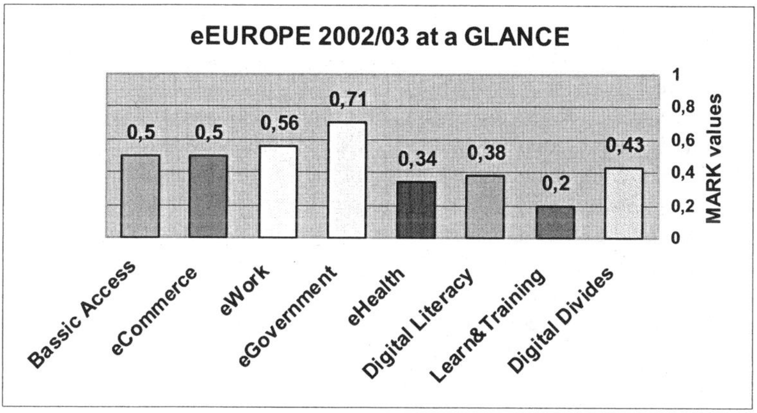

Figure 5. The MARK Values for Data in SIBIS Areas. (The values range from 0 to 1, the best possible is 1). The NAS are visibly behind the EU in Learning and Training, e-Health, Digital Literacy.

Topics similar to SIBIS were defined in the Action Plan eEurope 2000, where three objectives were declared: (1) Cheaper, faster, secure Internet; (2) Investing in people and skills; (3) Stimulate the usage of Internet. It is interesting to compare these objectives and their numerical evaluation using *MARK* measure, the results are presented below.

eEUROPE 2000 TOPICS	OBJECTIVES	*MARK* VALUES
Telecommunications, access	**[A cheaper, faster, secure Internet]**	**0.50**
Security and trust	**[A cheaper, faster, secure Internet]**	
Education	**[Investing in people and skills]**	**0.20**
Work, employment&skills	**[Investing in people and skills]**	**0.56**
Digital inclusion	**[Investing in people and skills]**	**0.43**
Digital literacy	**[Investing in people and skills]**	**0.38**
e-Commerce	**[Stimulate the usage of Internet]**	**0.50**
e-Government	**[Stimulate the usage of Internet]**	**0.71**
e-Health	**[Stimulate the usage of Internet]**	**0.34**

Numerical evaluation shows that a weak point while attaining these objectives is located at the investing in people and skills when compared with results of other two objectives of the Action Plan eEurope 2000.

5. Conclusions and Comments

How poor in terms of ICT development are the Accession Countries relative to the old EU members? Unfortunately there is no simple answer. Yet the answer matters: important decisions depend on it. One way of measuring relative ICT development level is by looking at statistical characteristics more elaborated than commonly used average values are. Rather simple statistical approach to cope with problems described in this paper and demonstrated on the SIBIS (Statistical Indicators Benchmarking the Information Society) data concluded:

1. A graphical display was applied in order to see a position of any separate country or a group of countries in the context of the enlarged EU.
2. A simple measure *MARK* expressing numerically a digital inclusion of NAS has been developed and applied to get a clear picture of eEurope at a glance and to identify:
   - the areas where the NAS were dramatically behind the EU, namely, as such were discovered: Learning and Training, e-Health, Digital Literacy;
   - topics where the NAS countries had their results closest to the EU countries' level. According to the statistical data available such area was e-Government.
3. Similar results could have industrial significance for companies developing ICT, by indicating the areas where the NAS were dramatically behind, and the topics in the enlarged EU where IS development is not sufficient developed currently.

Notice that in principle the results demonstrated here have an "optimistic" trend, because the data of EU – GPS 2002 survey must be compared with the NAS - GPS 2003 data, collected in SIBIS project almost one year later. In ICT development one year matters a lot, but regretfully, no data of the same year were available in SIBIS results for a correct comparison. The latest study of the enlarged Europe [3] considers analytically various aspects of EU enlargement: political, economical, business. The report [3] provides country profiles separately for Accession and candidate countries and former fifteen EU members but these results cannot be used for correct comparison purposes because there were no synchronous data again: from 1999 to 2002 data were used there in the charts comparing EU15 versus EU25. Four interesting scenarios (even with estimated probabilities to occur!) for the EU's future were considered and discussed in [3].

Further work and efforts of institutions responsible for data collection is required to develop unified approaches where data would be directly comparable and cross-referenced.

References

[1] SIBIS Pocket Book 2002/03. Measuring the Information Society in the EU, the EU Accession Countries, Switzerland and the US. Printed in Germany, 2003, 211 p. Available online [as 8 June, 2004] http://www.empirica.biz/sibis/publications/pocketbook.htm

[2] SIBIS New eEurope Indicator Handbook. November 2003. Available online [as 8 June, 2004] http://www.empirica.biz/sibis/files/SIBIS_Indicator_Handbook.pdf

[3] Europe enlarged: Understanding the impact The Economist Intelligence Unit, 2003. 104 p.

[4] 2001-2003 eEurope-plus Progress Report, February 2004, 52 p. / Report prepared by the Acceding and Candidate Countries (ACC) with the assistance of the European Commission.

[5] Douglas C. Montgomery, G. C. Runger. Applied Statistics and Probability for Engineers, J. Wiley and Sons, Inc., Second edition, 1999.

eAdoption and the Knowledge Economy: Issues, Applications, Case Studies
P. Cunningham and M. Cunningham (Eds.)
IOS Press, 2004

Initiating Transformational Change in Dynamic Environments

Ted O'KEEFFE
Waterford Institute of Technology, Cork Road, Waterford, Ireland
Tel: +353 51 302854, Fax: +353 51 302688, Email: tokeeffe@wit.ie

Abstract: Transformational change is now accepted as a sine qua non for business success and thus an integral part of learning organisations. Organisational wide learning programmes have constituted one of the corner stones of Japan's industrial success and many academics and industrialists agree that developing a learning organization approach is much more than another management fad. Learning organisations respond to the needs of the individual as well as the group, they understand that individuals initiate knowledge diffusion projects more often than functional groups. However, while much has been written on the importance of evolving a learning culture, less attention has been given to understanding in a practical way the characteristics of learning organisations and the ways in which companies can develop best practice throughout the organisation cost effectively.

1. Introduction

This paper has been developed from a study of 126 multinational companies with manufacturing operations in Ireland. The study explores the range of best practice programmes employed and identifies key learning characteristics that tend to be present in learning organisations. These characteristics on their own do not create learning organisations but stimulate companies to take better advantage of unique learning curve opportunities. A selection of the key quantitative findings will be presented as well as a new learning organisation model developed from the qualitative stage of the study. This new model allows organisations irrespective of size to identify organisational wide learning deficiencies instantly and cost effectively. It eliminates the need for expensive human resource development consultants to identify learning deficits, therefore more resources can be redirected towards training and development initiatives rather than expensive reports, full of recommendations but equally devoid of implementation initiatives in which said consultants take responsibility for agreed training deliverables.

A key finding from this research was that management consultants invariable are long gone before you really need them i.e. at the business end (implementation stage) of change programmes. Some commentators argue that the aspiration of becoming a learning organisation is not only necessary but also essential for long-term survival and the rate at which individuals and organisations learn [1] may become the only sustainable competitive advantage. The notion of effective knowledge diffusion and innovation champions as a long-term survival strategy is also acknowledged [2] as is the notion that transformational learning is no longer a choice but a necessity.

2. Transformational Change and Learning Initiatives

A narrow construct with regard to organisational learning will encourage learning within traditional boundaries only. To develop a powerful foundation for extensive learning, the organisation must provide the opportunity for generative learning by all stakeholders. Only those constituencies already possessing or developing competitive orientations and company wide learning initiatives have the potential to create superior customer value and competitive advantage. It could be argued that a learning organisation, with its focus on understanding latent needs, is inherently entrepreneurial. Organisations that value knowledge and innovation provide the necessary environment within which learning from exploration and experimentation is most likely to take place. The current, acceptance of organisational learning involves anthropomorphism as the known theory glosses over the, if and how organisations learn, which is far from self-evident. The argument that organisational learning cannot and should not be treated as an extension of individual learning has been made [3] despite the fact that learning organisations often produce knowledge that is at variance with what their members know, or understand. Although organisational learning occurs through individuals, it would be a mistake to conclude that organisational learning is nothing but the cumulative result of their members' learning. Organisations do not have brains, but they have cognitive systems and memories. As individuals develop their personalities and beliefs over time, so too will organisations develop their views and ideologies. Organisations select the stimuli to, which they respond because they typically face much more information than they can sensibly process [4].

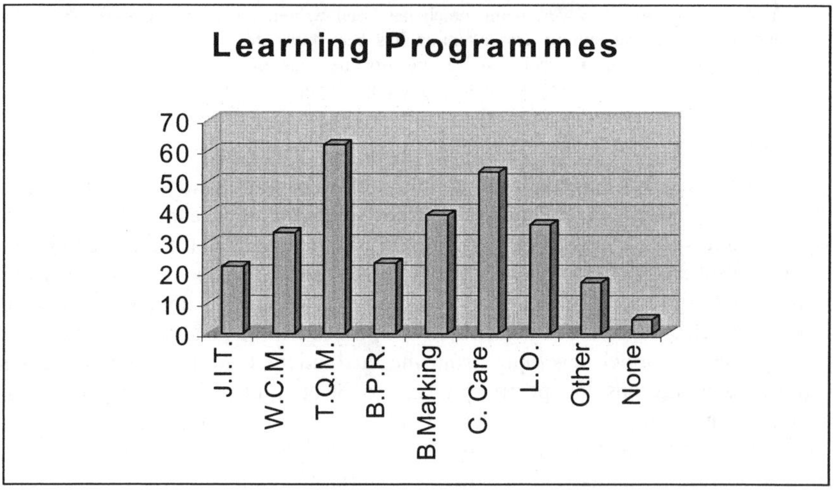

Figure: 1 Range of Learning Organization programmes

2.1 The Knowledge Economy

Up until very recently organisational resources were determined on the basis of buildings, equipment and capital. With the advent of modern technological developments, new management practices and systematic staff development initiatives, the importance of capital and land is diminishing in favour of intellectual capital. In more recent times intellectual capital has generated very powerful imperatives across all operating media but especially in the high technology sectors. Over the preceding decades the world's most prescient observers of societal change have predicted the emergence of a new economy in which intellectual prowess, not machine capability would be the critical resource [5] and while [6] has been credited with foretelling the downfall of capitalism, [7] established the organisational significance of each employee within a company irrespective of size. It is increasingly apparent that in excellent companies employees are identified as a key resource and that high performing organisations were above all, brilliant on the day-to-day operating imperatives [8]. In high-performing companies tools do not replace thinking. Intellect does not overpower wisdom. Analysis does not impede action. Rather, these organisations work hard to keep things simple in a complex world. They seek excellence at every opportunity while fawning on their customers. They listen to their employees and allow innovative product and service champions' enormous leeway, tolerate some chaos in return for enlightened customer responsiveness.

2.2 The Value of learning Organisations

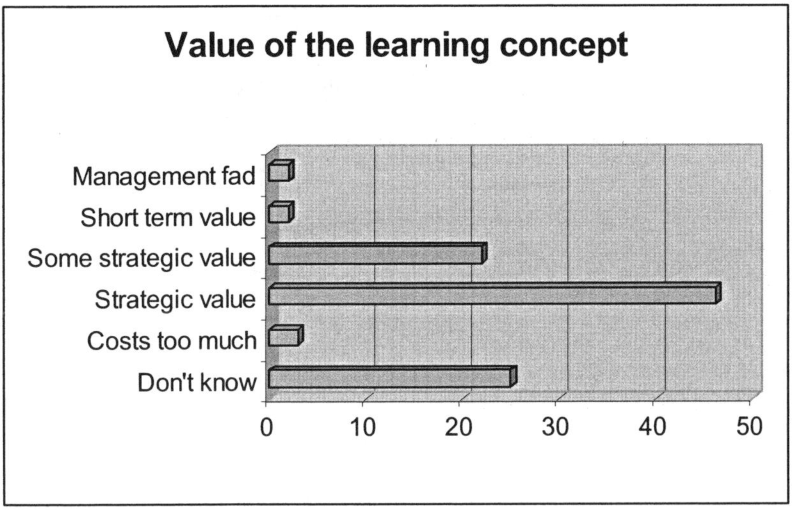

Figure 2: The Value of Learning Organisations

Learning organisation are attracting greater acceptance because they purport to overcome many of the concerns that have led to the discrediting of the traditional management paradigm, which has buckled under the strain of the ever-increasing pace of product and technological innovation. As the domain of operating environments continue to accelerate learning organisations are leading the way forward by becoming more nimble, flexible and responsive to customers needs and in many cases even before these same needs have been fully formulated. Trying to come to grips with the concept of organisational learning is like trying to explain the complexity of snow to someone who has never seen it, never mind the important role it plays in sustaining life and its destructive power when not in balance with its environment. The complexity of learning organisations is better explained by comparing the learning process to H_2O. Water has three main forms, solid, liquid and gas but has limitless combinations that are continuously responding to the changing forces interacting with it. A good example is sleet, which is formed from water vapour, has no definite shape yet it can form solid but never rigid snowflakes. Snowflakes, due to their mass, descend to earth, all the time changing shape until they fall as snow, sleet, rain or hail.

Just as one can never be certain of the exact form H_20 will take, the length of time it will continue at any one location or if a particular set of circumstances will result in drinking water unfit for human consumption for millions of people in one part of the world while at another location is can bring great enjoyment in the form of good snow for skiers. Yet good snow can create as much havoc if even one of the many critical characteristics needed to sustain it is undergoing rapid and undetectable transformation. So to with organisational learning one can never be sure what issues will come to the fore as an organisation drives down its own unique learning curve. However, key learning characteristics identified from the study are outlined in the learning model below.

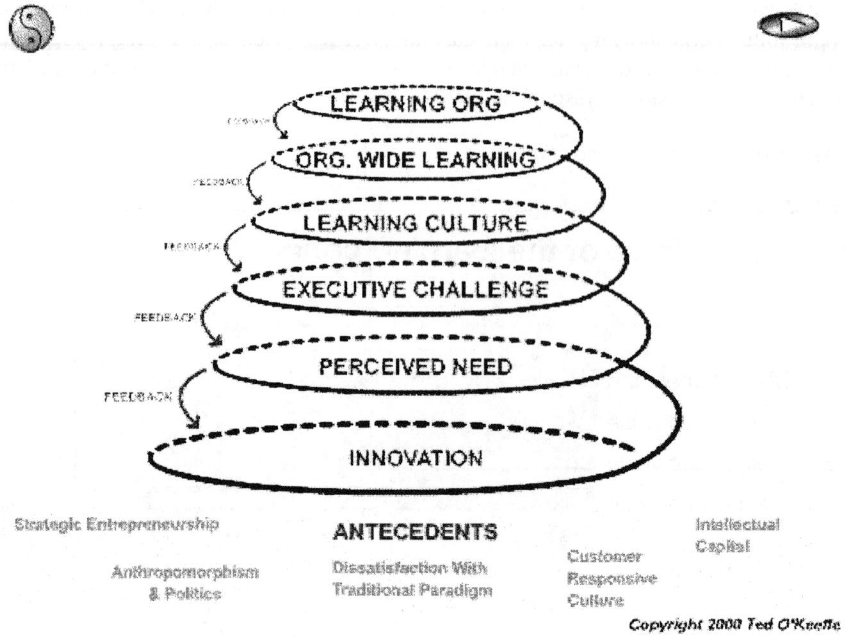

Figure 3: Learning Model

The real value of learning organisations is that they are better able to navigate across, around or over obstacles cost effectively, while less developed organisations may struggle for survival in similar circumstances. Contrasting H_20 with learning organisations is an effective way of surfacing the importance of organisational learning in delivering higher performance and greater longevity to companies. However, a learning organisation is nothing without effective knowledge diffusion initiatives in the same way that water, the lifeblood of all living things, can wreak havoc over large tracts of land if not dispersed quickly. Though rain is free, the ultimate cost is determined by the manner in which we use or abuse this gift. So too with learning organisations, the initial excitement and enthusiasm phase is free, the manner in which it is managed will determine its true cost, with competition for diminishing world markets growing more intense daily. The future battleground will focus on knowledge and intellectual capital rather than any other issue.

Companies are going to have to outdo each other to grow and prosper and a learning organisation is one such approach. Human beings are organisms in constant interaction with their environment, while members of learning organisations display a higher need for effectiveness, an essential prerequisite for long-term survival not all-learning organization members are capable of driving down their unique learning curve cost effectively.

2.3 Factors Facilitating or Impeding Learning

The importance of environmental change as a stimulus to learning continues to be emphasised. It has been argued that the greater the uncertainty in the environment, the larger the need for learning. However, on the question of change, some learning approaches particularly those that perceive it primarily as a response to environmental adjustment suffer from the reductionism tendency of behaviourism. Organisational learning cannot be created or eradicated by varying external stimuli. Indeed, the role of human agency and individual goals such as the drive for self-actualisation are almost completely ignored in many accounts of organisational adaptability.

This study found that organisational learning is stimulated both by environmental and internal factors in a complex and iterative manner as outlined in Table 1 below.

Table 1: Factors Influencing Organisations to Initiate Learning Programmes

Learning Triggers in Organisations	Ranking		
	1st	2nd	3rd
Need to Improve Productivity	27%	8%	11%
Innovation & Cost Reduction Imperatives	23%	51%	39%
Operational Crises	16%	25%	10%
Local Management Initiatives	14%	14%	11%
Corporate Directive	12%	0%	11%
Changing Work Environment	6%	16%	25%
Consultants	2%	0%	2%

Returning to the individual learning metaphor, [9] Social Learning Theory, for example, argues that people are neither driven by inner forces nor buffeted by environmental stimuli. Rather, psychological functioning is explained in terms of a continuous reciprocal interaction of personal and environmental determinants. By using the individual learning paradigm, the complexities in the relationships that encourage and constrain learning begins to be delineated. In addition to the levels of learning concerns there are further complications between collective and individual learning relationships as well as the organisation's interface with its environment. Developing facilitative structures that assist organisations overcome these particular problems is not easy.

Organisations purposefully adopt structures and strategies that encourage learning and proactively seek to influence the environment within which they reside. The relationship between strategy and structure and the role of strategic action as an intermediary filter between the environment and organisation has long been a focus of interest in the management literature. However, recent insights into the challenges faced by companies intent on creating organisational forms conducive to learning are reinforced by contemporary theories [10] i.e. that the nature of the firm is to be found in the economic, social, political and psychological mechanisms that the firm itself implements in order to achieve the necessary co-ordination of its individual members. The firm is seen as a co-ordinating institution and learning is one of the activities requiring co-ordination. The mechanisms used to achieve such co-ordination play a central role in tapping the organisational learning processes that determine learning outcomes.

2.4 Advantages of Learning Organisations

One hundred and twenty six company executive of senior managers were asked to identify and rank the organisational changes they perceived in their firms as a consequence of implementing learning organisation initiatives. The respondents were given nine options to rank in order of importance. The findings indicate that 39% of respondents ranked “competitive advantage” as the most likely outcome of learning organization initiatives. Some 21% of respondents ranked “improved customer service” as the most likely benefit. Another 16% of respondents ranked “higher productivity” as the most likely outcome of implementing organisational wide learning initiatives. These results confirm that a majority of respondents positively associate the learning organisation with achieving competitive advantage through higher productivity and improved customer service performance 76%.

In harmony with this finding a further 16% of respondents rated "competitive advantage" as the second most likely outcome of implementing a programme of company wide learning. Indeed, the results demonstrate that over half 55% of respondents ranked "competitive advantage" a first or second choice outcome from implementing learning initiatives across their organisations. Of further significance is the finding showing an additional 18% of respondents ranking "improved customer service" performance as the second most likely outcome of implementing a learning programme. These results suggest that just under two fifths 39% of the respondents view improved customer service relationships to be a first or second choice result of the effective implementation of a learning organisation programme.

Interestingly 5% of respondents ranked "fewer people more technology" as the most likely outcome of implementing a company wide learning initiative. Indeed 55 % of respondents viewed it as the most unlikely outcome of implementing the concept. Surprisingly, only 5% of respondents ranked "significant increase in training and development budgets" as the most likely outcome of learning programmes. A breakdown of the findings is outlined in Table 2.

Table 2: The Importance of Learning Organisations

Results of Learning Initiatives	Ranking		
	1st	2nd	3rd
Increased competitive advantage	39%	16%	11%
Enhanced customer services	21%	18%	12%
Higher productivity	16%	23%	18%
Staff empowerment	11%	21%	11%
More efficient work practices	4%	0%	21%
Shorter lead times	0%	11%	4%
Improved supplier commitment	0%	2%	49%
Less people more technology	5%	0%	5%

3. Learning Outcomes

The natural relationship between learning and context postulated above would more often than not indicate functional and supportive approaches yet such relationships can also be counterproductive and hinder performance. For example, using routine-driven learning in uncertain contexts might result in dangerous tunnel vision and inflexibility [11]. Moreover, organisational learning would be impractical where significant goal conflict exists. Interactive learning, on the other hand, might be unnecessarily inefficient in stable settings characterised by goal consensus because such contexts normally permit more economical kinds of learning. Hence, the further the learning modes stray from their typical contexts, the more organisational viability is likely to suffer. Although many different things can be learned from each of the modes, it is agreed that some outcomes may be especially typical i.e. that strategies are shaped by analytical learning, configurations by synthesis, procedures by structural learning, tactical accommodations by interaction, values by indoctrination and innovations by experiment. An important distinction among these outcomes is the importance of what is learned and the extent to which it underlies what the organisational members think and do [12].

Another distinction is the radical nature of what is learned, the degree to which it promotes a fundamental change in basic assumptions or orientations. A final distinction concerns the relationship between knowledge and behaviour. Learning always involves a continual interaction between these two elements but for some modes of learning, changes in behaviour usually precede changes in knowledge. For others it is the reverse and for still others, the two are too closely intertwined to know [13]. Upper echelons often use analytic learning in strategic planning and priority setting exercises, which can have an important impact on many aspects of organisational functioning. The use of methodical, deductive systems and the reliance on hard, quantifiable data may cause tunnel vision and leave fundamental assumptions unquestioned, thereby limiting the potential for radical change [14]. However, where deliberate gathering and analysis of information precedes action, feedback can be used to adjust behaviour.

Synthesis may be brought to bear on many issues, however as it often occurs at executive management level and pertains to overall strategy such learning tends to be of central importance. Also, the emergent, inductive nature of synthesis may allow creative managers to challenge fundamental assumptions and practices. Although synthetic insights may be fed by past actions, they can generate cognitive leaps that are not captured by any simple causal connection between knowledge and behaviour [15,16]. Normally, experiments are incremental; they concern competitive tactics and operating practices. Managers discover, which of their new efforts produce results and they tailor their offerings and practices accordingly. The results of most experiments will not cause major shifts in basic goals or strategies. Although in the short run, the limited importance of experiments may constrain any radical approach, there is at least the possibility of far-reaching reorientation occasionally where results are dramatically positive or negative.

Interactive learning takes place under many constraints. It has a local bias and is carried out mostly by middle managers. So its centralisation is limited, as is its ability to effect fundamental change. However, the political fragmentation that surrounds much interactive learning induces some organisational members to challenge basic assumptions. If these renegades can translate their scepticism into action, they may initiate the first steps towards significant transformation. Routine driven learning may concern local practices such as quality assurance, or it may pervade more fundamental things such as capital budgeting, innovation, marketing strategy. Routines deify assumptions and induce habitual, unreflective behaviour, thereby limiting the scope for radical changes.

Paradoxically, organisational routines sometimes provide equivocal experiences that lead to second order or step change learning [17]. They may, for example, indicate that performance is failing to meet aspiration levels and that some fundamental re-orientations are required. Organisations endeavour to indoctrinate members with values that are of central importance yet such indoctrination presumes that the elite have already formulated or embraced the values that they will be imparting to others. Hence, values at variance with the organisations strategy may already be reflected in the basic orientations at the apex of the organisation even before training is initiated.

4. Conclusions

Learning organisations are complex entities not widely understood by many, yet each one of us is a learning entity and will only cease to be so when and if we stop thinking for ourselves? As many people cannot distinguish between organisational learning from learning organisations it might be advisable to clarify the situation at this point in time. Both terms are broadly interchangeable yet organisational learning is something that an organisation does, in other words it is a process, while a learning organisation is an entity. In dynamic environments where the pace of change continues to increase there is a recognition that the only source of competitive advantage is in the untapped knowledge reservoirs within individuals. However such knowledge repositories often exist unknown to the organisation for a variety of reasons, one being unshared knowledge, which can be utilised as a bargaining chip in times of crises or a method of opening up personal development opportunities.

Organisations must understand that knowledgeable staff can vote with their feet any time they choose. It is imperative that companies with a long-term vision must seek individuals with leadership ability rather than management experience, individuals who are capable of driving down the learning curve more cost effectively than the competition particularly in a climate of turbulent change. The trend towards zero management learning organisations is the result of a confluence of circumstances, in which a set of circumstances have come together to create a market environment in which the drive towards zero management learning organisations is no longer a goal but an imperative.

References

[1] State, R., 1989. Organizational Learning: The Key to Management Innovation. Sloan Management Review, Vol. 30, Spring: pp. 63-74.

[2] Schein, E.H., 1993. "On Dialogue, Culture and Organizational Learning": Organizational Dynamics, Autumn.

[3] Argyris, C. & D. A. Schon, 1996. Organizational Learning 11, Addison-Wesley Publishing Company.

[4] Hedberg, B., 1983. How Organizations Learn and Unlearn: pp. 8-27 in P.C. Nystrom & W.H. Starbuck (Ed.), Handbook of Organizational Design. London: Oxford University Press.

[5] Graham, A. The Learning Organisation: Managing knowledge for business success. The Economist Intelligence Unit: New York 1996.

[6] Drucker, P. F., 1992. Managing For the Future: The 1990s and Beyond. Dutton, New York.

[7] Peters, T. J. & R. H. Waterman, 1982. 'In Search of Excellence Lessons from America's Best-Run Companies, Harper & Row: Publishers, New York.

[8] T. O'Keeffe A New Learning Organisational Model. Journal of European Industrial Training, MCB University Press 2002, Vol. 26: Number 2/3/4

[9] Bandura, A., 1977. Social Learning Theory: Englewood Cliffs NJ: Prentice Hall.

[10] Coase, R., 1937. Lowering Transactional Costs: The Social, Legal and personal Barriers that Impede Efficiency. In Kreitner 7th (Ed.) Management, 1998: 64.

[11] Miller, D., 1996. A Preliminary Typology of Organizational Learning Synthesising the Literature: Journal of Management, Autumn, Vol. 22: No.3: pp. 485-526.

[12] Tushman, M.L. & C.A. O'Reilly III, 1996. Ambidextrous Organisations: Managing Evolutionary and Revolutionary Change, California Management Review, Summer, Vol. 38, pp.8-30.

[13] Weick, K. E., 1991. "The Non-traditional Quality of Organizational Learning": Organization Science, Vol. 2, No. 1 pp. 116-124.

[14] Starbuck, W. H., 1985. Acting First and Thinking Later: Theory Versus Reality in Strategic Change: pp. 336-372 in J.M. Pennings and associates (Ed.), Organizational Strategy and Change: Jossey Bass.

[15] Miller, D., 1990. The Icarus Paradox: How Exceptional Companies bring about their own Downfall, HarperCollins: New York.

[16] Mintzberg, H., 1991. "The Innovative Organization", in The Strategy Process: Concepts, Contexts, Cases, 2nd Ed. Henry Mintzberg and James Quinn, (Ed.), pp. 731-746. Prentice Hall: Englewood Cliffs, NJ.

[17] Lant, T. K. & S. Mezias, 1992. An Organizational Learning Model of Convergence and Re-orientation, Organization Science, Vol. 3: pp. 47-71.

eAdoption and the Knowledge Economy: Issues, Applications, Case Studies
P. Cunningham and M. Cunningham (Eds.)
IOS Press, 2004

Developing European eSkills and Qualifications Frameworks

Burkart SELLIN
Cedefop European Centre for the Development of Vocational Training,
Europe 123, Thessaloniki, 57001, Greece
Tel: +30 23 10 49 01 21, Fax: + 30 231049 01 17, Email: bs@cedefop.eu.int

Abstract: This paper discusses requirements and pathways towards a European eSkills and Qualifications Framework. The paper focuses on how to achieve transparency, comparability, transferability and recognition of competences and/or qualifications between different countries and different levels. Current state of the art in credit transfer is presented and linked to current work on a European level by stakeholders. Particular attention is paid to the contribution and achievements of the Technical Working Group on Credit Transfer. The parallel activity on the eSkills reference frameworks will be briefly explained. More insight will be given at the workshop, because the latter is linked to final deliberations of the European eSkills Forum, which was established by the European Commission in spring 2003. [1]

1. Introduction

The European Commission's "Action plan for skills and mobility" from 2002 defines important objectives and needed activities to achieve enhanced mobility for the European workforce. Cedefop in support of the European Commission aims at establishing an European eSkills and Qualifications Frameworks to achieve comparability and transparency as well as transferability of competencies and/or qualifications.

This is an ambitious goal only achievable by collaboration of European stakeholders and an adequate public-private partnership at European level. Cedefop works on a practical solution in line with this objective set by the Commission in 2002 and defined as follows:
"The Commission will foster co-operation of the relevant authorities within Member States with social partners with a view to developing ICT and e-Business skills definitions. It will support the development, the maintenance and the promotion of European-wide standards as well as validation, accreditation and recognition schemes by 2005"(COM (2002)72 final).

In a resolution on enhanced European co-operation in vocational education and training (VET) approved in November 2002 by the Council of Ministers for Education [2], and the subsequent 'Copenhagen declaration' on the same subject (30 November 2002), adopted by the Ministers of 31 European countries gave a mandate to the European Commission to:
"[...] investigate how transparency, comparability, transferability and recognition of competences and/or qualifications, between different countries and at different levels, could be promoted by developing reference levels, common principles for certification, and common measures, including a credit transfer system for vocational education and training."

In this paper we discuss important initiatives, existing achievements, required activities and steps towards an eSkills European Reference Framework which, however, would have to be linked to the current effort to establish a European overarching qualifications' framework for education/training outcomes and respective definitions.

2. Objectives

The paper highlights important steps for a voluntary agreement on a European eSkills Framework. The potential purpose, use and benefits for such a framework is explained and further steps towards links with certification of ICT skills, the promotion of mobility and mutual recognition of outcomes of public and private training providers is being discussed.

3. Methodology

First, the paper presents state-of-the-art naming important initiatives and working groups dealing with the issue of European eSkills and Qualifications. Secondly, we outline possible pathways towards a European Framework. Therefore, requirements and implications for a future European Credit Transfer Framework are given.

eSkills was discussed by the European Commission's eSkills Forum under several headings: demand and supply, social aspects, outsourcing or off-shoring and public private partnerships. It was also the focus of a Cedefop study on a comprehensive European reference framework for eSkills and the work launched by CEN/ISSS within an ICT skills workshop to prepare an agreement on such a framework. The former is based on a study commissioned by Cedefop in 2003 on "ICT Skills on sub-degree and vocational levels" and on other bodies' proposals for a European wide approach to eSkills frameworks.

The purpose and benefit or use to be made by such a framework, which will describe levels of skills and present a typology of knowledge, skills and competences applicable on the European or International level will be explained [3]. The ambitious goal can only be achieved by an adequate public-private partnership. Thus, working groups in form of SIN (special interest networks) and forums are currently and will be established in the future to identify and discuss the needs of a European framework.

4. Towards a European Credit Transfer Framework

The European Commission set up in the following of the Copenhagen declaration on increased co-operation in VET inter alia a Technical Working Group (TWG) on Credit Transfer in VET in November 2002 to take forward this mandate.

The TWG is addressing this to develop

- a conceptual approach and general principles for Credit Transfer,
- proposals for reference levels frameworks or horizontal descriptors and
- common principles for certification

This is within the wider aim of developing a European credit (transfer) system for vocational education and training (ECVET) which, however, ought to be kept compatible with the European Credit Transfer System (ECTS) for Higher Education.

This ought to be inspired and kept compatible with the current ECTS system for HE. The discussions of the TWG have so far indicated [4] that the issues of credit accumulation and transfer, certification and qualifications levels frameworks are closely interlinked:

1. Credits can be considered as a basis for certification of (part) qualifications, or whole qualifications, linked to corresponding reference levels and sub-levels within a coherent qualifications level framework;
2. Credits are embedded in an institutional logic in terms of certification procedures, which lead to recognition of learning achievements between different training providers (public, intermediate or private providers);
3. The development of mutual trust and quality in a VET system using credits relies on efficient and credible certification and assessment procedures and on a basic agreement concerning reference levels or qualifications frameworks;
4. Learners with informal and non-formal learning experience, are expected to be motivated to have their learning activities formally recognised through certification;

5. Certification ought to be linked to agreed definitions of learning outcomes and achievements in terms of specifications of skills, knowledge and competences acquired along individual learning pathways on-the-job or off-the-job and ought in this context to encompass the bridging of formal and non-formal learning modes.
6. Modularisation and unitisation of programmes could ease accreditation of respective outcomes, an increasing of students' and trainees' exchanges and more generally a sustainable development of cross border cooperation in VET and LLL.
7. It is necessary to make certification procedures more independent from existing formal pathways. This will facilitate the assessment and recognition (both at home and abroad) of all forms of learning based on prior learning and achievements of the individual. The outcome could then be validated independent of when, where and how this took place.
8. It is probably necessary to agree the definition of generic job profiles, skills and qualifications frameworks and a sector specific typology of knowledge, skills and competences based on such broad profiles. The following definition is offered:

"A certificate is an official document, issued by an awarding body, which records the achievements of an individual following a standard assessment procedure"

5. Existing initiatives at political level

Work within the Credit Transfer Group is closely connected to the work and results of related working groups within the Education and Training 2010 work programme, e.g. Technical Working Groups on Transparency and on Quality, the Commission's Expert Group on non-formal learning (which has developed principles for validation of non-formal and informal learning), and current Leonardo da Vinci projects dealing with credit systems in VET and validation/accreditation of prior non-formal or informal learning (APL).

In taking into account the need to develop mutual trust between stakeholders, policy makers and practitioners in light of the increasing number of qualification systems and qualifications in EU Member states, it has been acknowledged that a common definition on the European level of reference levels or qualifications frameworks is crucially needed.

The Credit Transfer Working Group got a mandate to make proposals on common reference levels for VET. A study launched by Cedefop in 2003 made more detailed proposals for the TWG. However, the issue is of importance to a range of policy areas including the Commission's (DG Interior Market) Directive on recognition of professional qualifications tabled early 2002 and its potential implementation, which encompasses all levels of learning and qualifications. This Directive on the recognition of professional qualifications has now been accepted and will be published shortly on the Official Journal.

The framework discussion was also an issue within the Bologna process where a three levels "overarching" framework has been agreed for Higher Education. The discussion of equivalent frameworks in the VET and LLL area and the linkage to HE frameworks was a major topic in the recent Irish presidency conference held in Dublin on 8th of March.

The DG EaC Director General Klaus van der Pas summarised the discussion in stating that... "It is crucial to aim for a single qualifications framework for lifelong learning at European level. This is essential for the development of the European labour market. A comprehensive framework is of course more difficult to implement, but makes more sense in the long-run from the learner's point of view. In many countries stakeholders are calling for such a European framework in order to mobilise and guide reform and the development of new national frameworks, whilst not imposing on Member States responsibilities. The development of a European framework should draw on the experiences of those countries that already have national frameworks. The European framework should at least provide the skeleton on which national frameworks can build. This means that we need agreement on reference levels as a first step. Agreement by end of 2004 on common reference levels for VET, based on learning outcomes, is essential."

For this purpose the Commission is envisaging following van der Pas: "A specific working group, representing both higher education and VET within the Education and Training 2010 work programme, should be given the responsibility to develop a blueprint for the European qualifications framework as soon as possible."

The outcomes of the Cedefop study on reference levels and the deliberations of the TWG on Credit Transfer intends to assist the Commission in making substantial progress before the end of the year. In December 2004 a Ministerial meeting combined with a conference of stakeholders under the Dutch presidency will take place in Maastricht. Progress of the Copenhagen process will be discussed, including the proposal for common reference levels for VET, and new priorities will be set.

We all know that the Bologna Process on HE is more advanced. This Process, however, does not only include EU Member states but more than 40 Member states of the Council of Europe. The discussion in VET and LLL has a certain time-lag and started with a new impetus in 2002. It is expected, however, to produce equivalent results in due course. The three working parties mentioned above will report on their findings by the end of the year and new actions will be proposed for 2005 till 2010 in order to speed up the implementation of the current objectives set on policy level (see the recent report approved by the Council of Education Ministers in February 2004 on education and training in 2010).

6. Results

These initiatives and achievements contribute to the 2002 European Commission's "Action plan for skills and mobility" and supports implementation of the education and training objectives in the perspective of 2010 with a special focus at the Copenhagen process.

Parallel to the discussion on qualifications frameworks for VET and HE the eSkills Forum's recommendations on frameworks will promoted with the assistance of the European Committee for Standardisation (CEN). The CEN ICT skills workshop will suggest options for such a reference framework based on an analysis of different national approaches to such frameworks, e.g. Germany, Netherlands, Portugal and the UK.

7. Business Benefits

The benefits for business will be to better assess skills and qualifications in a strengthened European labour market, to allow for staff development and a human resource policy which takes into account European and International developments, to match demand and supply of skills and to better allocate their own training investments. It would benefit both sides of the industry, employers and employees and their organisations and assist them in innovating their staff and human resource policy.

8. Conclusions

The current discussion in the eSkills area steered by DG Enterprise in close cooperation Cedefop and the industry including social partners is a good testing bed for real progress in this increasingly important labour market segment.

The outcomes of the eSkills Forum and the eSkills Conference (20 - 21 September 2004) in Thessaloniki will certainly back up this dynamic and underpin developments also on the inter-professional level. The eSkills conference's results will contribute to the steering of policy interventions and actions at both levels, the national and the European level. Issues for further study will be forwarded and tools and instruments offered for implementing the ambitious objectives set by the European Union.

Cedefop and other interested bodies are engaged with CEN/ISSS to further promote the frameworks discussion on eSkills and will most likely take up the suggestions that arise from a workshop on certification. This took place in Brussels in March 2004 [1]. It launched several studies in 2003 on these more specific frameworks, which will be validated in this 2nd phase of the CEN-ICT skills workshop. Cedefop also launched a major additional study in spring 2004 on the issue of ICT certification in Europe.

Cedefop will ensure that both activities are matched and will continue to support DG Education and Culture in developing proposals for a real European Credits and Qualifications Framework. This will hopefully allow as stated in Dublin at an Irish Presidency conference in March 2004 to encompass both VET and HE as well as formal or non-formal learning achievements.

References

[1] These results, which include a number of recommendations, are available for consultation and comments of stakeholders at http://cedefop.communityzero.com/esf
[2] Official Journal C 013, 18/01/2003
[3] Information on a virtual community set up by Cedefop: http://cedefop.communityzero.com/CEN-ICT)
[4] Progress report from October 2003 http://cedefop.communityzero.com/credittransfer
[5] European Commission (2002): Action plan for skills and mobility (COM(2002)72 final
[6] Council resolution on The promotion of enhanced European co-operation in vocational education and training of December 19 2002
[7] Joint Interim report (2004) of the Council and the Commission on the implementation of the Lisbon Strategy, Education and Training 2010: the success of the Lisbon Strategy hinges on urgent reforms

Driving Informatics Competence in Europe: the EUCIP Programme

Paolo SCHGÖR
EUCIP Ltd c/o AICA, piazzale Morandi 2, 20121 Milano, Italia
Tel: +39 02 76455045, Fax: +39 02 76015717, Email: paolo.schgor@eucip.com

Abstract: After setting ECDL as a paradigm for measuring individual skills in using the most widespread types of information technologies (IT users), in 1999 CEPIS started a new project for the definition of a reference certification framework for IT professionals, now known as "European Certification of Informatics Professionals". In 2003 the first EUCIP Core certificates were released in Italy, Greece and Norway; currently several learning providers are deploying the programme in ten European countries. EUCIP contributes to a European standard classification of vocational paths & primary ICT professional profiles: it offers an independent and unified approach to the definition of professional profiles and to the certification of individual competences aligned with the needs of the labour market; its main feature is the ability to include university courses, IT vendor certifications and independent qualifications into one model that has been designed as the synthesis of contributions from a number of different countries.

1. Introduction

One of the main aspects in the e-Europe 2005 scenario is the increasing need for IT competence at various levels, starting from the e-citizen up to the experienced IT professional. Knowledge – and the ways to manage it within an organisation (KM) – are actually becoming a condition for success in most business sectors.

A practical way to address this need is to define new standards for individual knowledge & skills and to provide tools for measuring them – in a word: "certification".

This paper is going to focus on the concepts, goals and current achievements in various countries of the EUCIP programme promoted by CEPIS, the federation of the main European associations of IT professionals and owner of the ECDL.

Above all, this discussion should be interesting for today's and tomorrow's IT professionals, for companies searching IT-talents and for all those involved in IT training (e.g. technical universities).

Some aspects of this discussion can also be relevant for those who are working on vocational frameworks and standards and for policy-makers willing to facilitate the growth of e-Europe: at CEPIS we believe that certification of individual IT skills can really be a primary driver of informatics competence and thus support Europe in her progress towards a knowledge-based society as stated in the Lisbon declaration.

2. Certification of individual IT knowledge and skills

2.1 Different Ranges of Competence

As a result of the wide spread of Information and Communication Technologies, an increasingly large part of the population in developed countries has to have "some" knowledge of technical matters (e.g. the concepts of bit & bytes, JPEG format) to act effectively on their job or even during their free time: using a smart cellular phone with a digital camera, wireless headphones and diary functions is not easier than using a PC as a typewriter for simple documents, and requires some understanding of terms like "bluetooth connection" or "touchscreen calibration". Until 15 years ago, only specialists understood such technical concepts. Today's society is characterised by increasing general IT literacy.

However, it is more difficult today to evaluate the IT knowledge and skills in an individual and to distinguish between a skilled IT user, a specialist and an IT professional, as everybody knows something but no one can keep up to date with all new technologies. A network manager has little to do with a Java programmer or with a pre-sales support consultant showing demos of a specific CAD system: therefore, it is essential to cope with a higher specialisation and to find some shared criteria for classifying all the different professional profiles at the various levels of IT skills required.

2.2 Certification

Certification of individual IT competence is a way to measure a candidate against an agreed level of knowledge and skills. This requires:

- a precise and up-to-date definition of competence requirements (Syllabus);
- clear criteria and tools for measuring individual competences (QTB, CTT, ATES etc.);
- a certification body and a chain of trusted entities (e.g. ECDL-F, country-level licensee, test centres, quality auditors, publishers of accredited training materials etc.) involved in the deployment of the certification service.

2.3 International Certification Programmes Promoted by CEPIS

The Council of European Professional Informatics Societies (CEPIS) [1] is a non-profit organisation seeking to improve and promote high standards among informatics professionals in recognition of the impact that informatics has on employment, business and society; CEPIS unites 36 professional informatics societies over 32 European countries, representing more than 200.000 ICT professionals.

After setting the European Computer Driving Licence [2] as a paradigm for certification of computer users, in 1999 and 2000 CEPIS started two new projects for the certification of IT Administrators (the reference person for IT in a local unit) and IT Professionals. The EPICS project [3], partly funded by the European Commission through the eTEN programme in 2002-2003, also contributed to what is now called the EUCIP programme (i.e. European Certification of Informatics Professionals) [4].

3. The EUCIP Framework

The conceptual structure of EUCIP (Figure 1) is based on a Core level, an intermediate specialisation and a final certification at Professional level. The various EUCIP titles are defined in accordance with a vocational structure: this includes several profiles (e.g. Business Analyst, Information Systems Project Manager, Software Developer, Network Manager etc.) which correspond to typical ICT related roles within industry.

Three "Knowledge Areas" are defined:

A. Plan – Addresses the analysis of requirements and planning the usage of ICT. This area is tightly linked to business processes and defining ICT needs in terms of business strategies. Traditional business elements such as ROI, risk and financing are included.
B. Build – Encompasses the specification, development and acquisition of ICT. The crux of this area is traditional technical aspects of systems development, implementation and the ICT life cycle in general.
C. Operate – Addresses installation, supervision and maintenance of ICT. Typical domains are network management, upgrading, support functions etc.

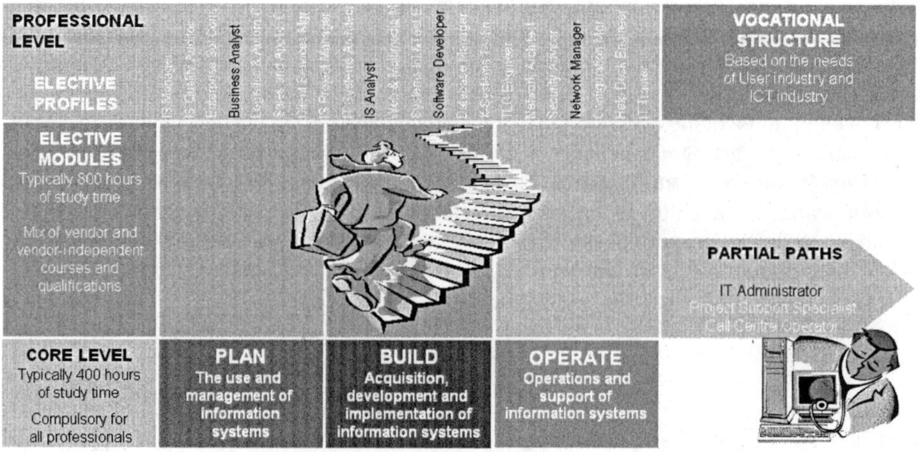

Figure 1: Knowledge areas and certification levels within the EUCIP framework

Each profile description specifies a complete set of competence requirements, which can show commonalities between different roles: for example, a Network Manager and an IT Administrator will share many common "blocks" within the Operate knowledge area.

Certification is based on various methods applying to different requirements per level:

- an automated testing systems (ATES) is used for theoretical parts, assessed through multiple-choice questions, especially at the Core level;
- practical exercises (especially for elective modules in the IT Administrator specialism) are performed partly through manual tests and partly through ATES providing a simulated operating environment;
- other elective modules are mainly external to the EUCIP scheme (e.g. university courses, vendor certifications) and are accredited with a certain number of EUCIP points (maximum 10 per module);
- final examination, resulting in a EUCIP Professional level certification, is based on evaluation of the individual "portfolio" (at least equivalent to 48 EUCIP points, see below for further details) and on a discussion / oral test in front of a panel of senior experts in the candidate's subject area; the members of this examination board are appointed by EUCIP and the local CEPIS member society.

3.1 Core Level

The core level of EUCIP provides a solid foundation for all types of ICT-related work. It gives a broad knowledge of the fundamental aspects of IT demanding approximately 400 study hours for a student at tertiary education level (i.e. during first university cycle).

The topics are evenly divided into the three knowledge areas described above, based on the main phases of the typical ICT lifecycle:

- A – PLAN knowledge area: the use and management of information systems;
- B – BUILD knowledge area: acquisition, development and implementation of information systems;
- C – OPERATE knowledge area: operations and support of information systems.

There are no formal entry requirements for this part of the scheme. Each student must pass all three modules to gain the core certificate, meaning the he/she will have to score more than 60% in each of the three exams (60 minutes for 40-45 multiple-choice questions extracted from the EUCIP Core Question & Test Base).

3.2 Elective Modules and Partial Certification Paths

An IT specialist can differ from a higher level professional in terms of greater need for practical skills in a specific field, than for breadth and depth of core level knowledge.

For example, an IT Administrator will not have a strong need for core knowledge in the area of Plan and Build, while topics related to operations and support of IS shall be deeper and more practical than in the core level. 500 study hours are estimated a reasonable norm for this profile. After passing 5 exams (each including MCQs and practical tests) the candidate gets the IT Administrator certificate and an exemption/credit for the Operate module if he/she is willing to apply for the EUCIP Core certification.

3.3 Professional Level and Final Certification

At the elective level a student may choose a combination of modules in different knowledge areas. The combination may consist of both vendor-proprietary and vendor-independent courses (with exams) and certifications. The total number of study hours is 800. The combination of elective modules will correspond to a recommended curriculum (elective profile) leading to defined vocational categories, e.g. IS Analyst or Security Adviser.

After accruing EUCIP points through accredited elective modules, the candidate shall present a portfolio showing his/her curriculum and samples of related project work. A EUCIP examination board will evaluate the portfolio and eventually admit the applicant to the final oral examination. Upon successful completion of this process, the candidate will be awarded a EUCIP Professional level certificate.

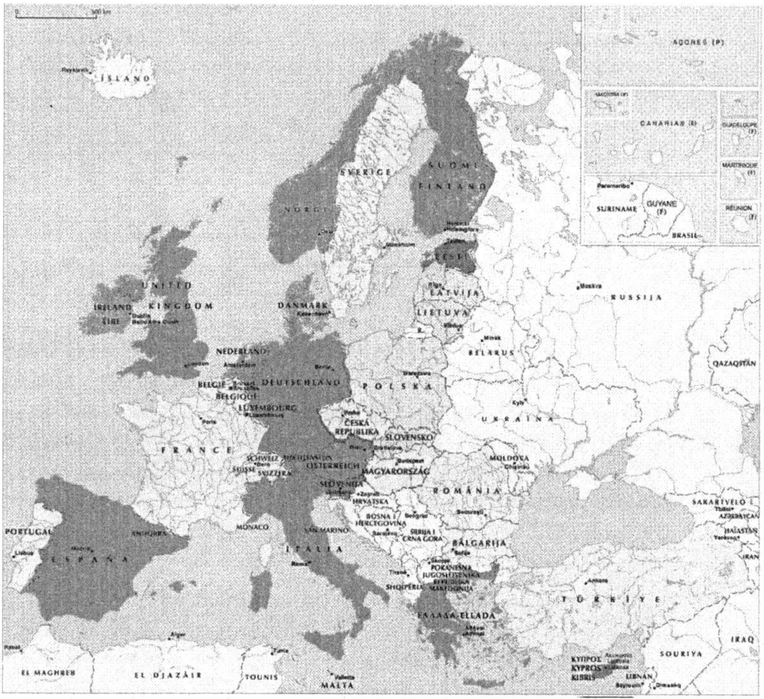

Figure 2: European Countries Currently Involved in EUCIP Activities (dark colour)

3.4 Accomplishments

In 2003 the EUCIP programme was officially launched: more than 400 tests were made at the Core level, plus about 150 for the IT Administrator profile. The first certificates were released in Italy, Greece, Norway and other countries to 60 certified individuals. In the first half year of 2004, over 2,100 exams were held, and there were over 80 accredited learning providers involved.

Apart from progress in the Core level, an initial set of profiles has been published, and the development of new profiles is in being co-ordinated with other external certification systems like the Irish ICS Skills Cert based on the Skills Framework for the Information Age (SFIA), and the Advanced IT Training System (so-called APO) promoted by the German Federal Ministry of Education and Research.

Current progress in dissemination is sensitive to local conditions: in general 8 countries (Norway, Finland, Estonia, Ireland, UK, Germany, Italy, Greece) have started their EUCIP activities and 6 more are actively involved in the process (Figure 2).

An important achievement announced in the UK is the possible accreditation of the EUCIP Core level by the national Qualification and Curriculum Authority (QCA) for Higher Education, meaning that the UK government should fund educational organisations that offer the EUCIP certification to their students.

EUCIP figures (as of 15/6/2004)		new centres		candidates enrolled		candidates certified		exams		pass rate %	
		<2004	2004 1H	<2004	2004 1H	<2004	2004 1H	<2004	2004 1H	<2004	2004 1H
Austria											
Cyprus											
Denmark											
Germany	Core	**1**		**6**				**18**		28%	
Greece	Core	**2**	**56**	**26**	**547**	**11**	**209**	**33**	**1687**	100%	76%
Estonia	Core	**1**		**2**	**53**	**1**	**12**	**6**	**120**	67%	53%
Finland	Core	**2**		**3**		**2**		**9**		89%	
Ireland	Core		**1**		**22**		**1**		**66**		41%
Italy	Core	**4**	**10**	**85**	**42**	**26**	**20**	**238**	**118**	59%	71%
	IT-Adm		**5**	**26**	**31**	**7**	**6**	**150**	**58**	65%	73%
Netherlands											
Norway	Core	**2**	**2**	**44**	**21**	**6**	**6**	**97**	**35**	51%	83%
Slovenia											
Spain											
UK	Core	**1**	**1**	**27**		**5**		**41**		88%	
Europe		**13**	**75**	**219**	**716**	**58**	**254**	**592**	**2084**	68%	73%
Totals		**88**		**935**		**312**		**2676**			

Figure 3: EUCIP Start-up Facts

3.5 Case Study: EUCIP in Italy

Three Italian associations are members in CEPIS: AICA is by far the most important, and is the local licensee for ECDL and EUCIP; AIP and ALSI, which are not interested in ECDL, are yet very keen to cooperate in the EUCIP programme.

Besides IT professional associations, a number of very different stakeholders is involved in a national "consulta" (panel) on ICT certifications: ministries, industry associations, trade unions, universities and various other entities. This broad commitment could be associated with the fact that our society is evolving from mere formality to a quality-based approach, i.e. from a state-driven system of professional orders, diplomas, licences and authorisations having legal value to a more liberal system of certifications proposed by independent bodies deserving public trust.

A general support to the concept of certification is facilitating the spread of EUCIP: in a few months, some training materials have been published for the Core level (e.g. a textbook in Italian [6]) and other are under development; AICA is aware of three different initiatives for e-learning modules on EUCIP, all of them initiated by universities.

Some candidates have gained the Core level certificate (46 people) and the IT Administrator (13), whilst some pilot projects are now starting UCIP Elective level courses.

A key partner of AICA in the deployment of EUCIP is CINI – Consorzio Interuniversitario Nazionale per l'Informatica, a consortium grouping the main and largest Italian universities: in 2003 CINI conducted a study on the correspondence between the EUCIP Core syllabus and the contents of university courses in Informatics and Information Engineering, and the results of this work were presented in a conference in Rome on 31/3/2004. The theoretical coverage results almost complete in all sites analysed, but in summer 2004 a wide test (10 different sites) on a sample of over 260 students of the third year who have not attended any EUCIP-specific course will actually show if reality corresponds. This "proof of concept" will provide a statistical base to be used for planning the next steps of a massive dissemination of EUCIP in IT-related university courses. A joint AICA-CINI project ranging over the period from June 2004 till December 2007 will enable all university students in the IT sector to access the EUCIP certification, targeting 7000 students in 30 scientific and technical universities throughout Italy.

Even under these facilitating circumstances, AICA – the local CEPIS member which is currently bearing all the costs through internal financial resources – is fully aware of the long time required for a complete maturation of a new ambitious certification programme: in spite of positive feedbacks and a very good general acceptance, up to date only a few people (including IT practitioners) are aware of the EUCIP concepts.

A clear EU endorsement of the EUCIP programme would speed up the dissemination process in Italy and other large countries; in smaller countries a strong support would be vital for giving equal access to a common system of ICT qualifications.

4. The Future

4.1 EU Standard Profiles

Standards are vital in order to allow both domestic and cross-border integration (just think of electric power plugs). A standard framework for classifying e-skills is not easy to define and maintain, primarily because competence is an intangible asset belonging to the individual or to an organisation. Moreover, some technical knowledge and skills can expire in a very short time, and the importance of each "pill" can vary in a few months due to rapid innovation of technologies.

In spite of all of the above mentioned obstacles, a standardisation process is going on, and some initial concepts towards a European framework of ICT skills have been defined by the European eSkills Forum [6], CEN/ISSS [7], Cedefop [8] and various other contributors. CEPIS is actively involved in this process: the EUCIP initiative gives an important contribution towards a European standard classification of vocational paths and primary ICT professional profiles; in addition to that, EUCIP profiles will definitely converge to these new recommended principles.

5. Conclusions

After the longest market crisis in the ICT history, the current year (2004) is showing a new increase in demand of products and services; in the meanwhile, technology is keeping the pace with a continuous evolution (e.g. more mature websites, ubiquitous computing etc.). The need for high skilled IT professionals is therefore high, and knowledge is actually becoming a condition for success in most business sectors.

The "supply side" in IT education is still very fragmented and influenced by:

- universities, very strong on theoretical aspects, but often weak on practice;
- training on specific technologies (typically vendor-proprietary courses & certifications).

It is really difficult to evaluate the actual individual competence both in the case of young people and for experienced professionals; moreover, different schemes are used in different countries, so that the mobility of IT workers is threatened by concerns about quality and risks for the employing organisation. The above mentioned mobility problem is very well known, and various EU-funded projects and entities are addressing it (e.g. eSkills Forum, Career-Space, CEN/ISSS, Europrofiles, Europass etc.) [9].

EUCIP offers an independent, unified approach to the definition of professional profiles and certification of individual competences; it includes university courses, IT vendor certifications and independent qualifications into one model that synthesises contributions from different national markets monitored by CEPIS Member Societies.

The EUCIP vocational scheme is open, and needs a continuous update to reflect evolving technologies and ever-changing market demand and supply. All existing profiles will be maintained and revised to achieve the maximum alignment between European and national frameworks like APO in Germany or SFIA in the English-speaking countries.

CEPIS, EUCIP and their joining societies are involved in a number of panels in order to achieve a real standard on IT professionalism throughout Europe. It is our mission to coordinate the efforts of different stakeholders in IT culture and to make the technologies easier to understand, to exploit (in a business sense) and to enjoy (for each one of us).

CEPIS initiatives are characterised by three elements:

- true vendor-neutrality, combined with a pragmatic approach deriving from a unique sectoral competence;
- the not-for-profit purpose of CEPIS and all of its member societies;
- the economic independence of the various programmes; this means that public funding is obviously helpful, but not prejudicial.

EUCIP is really the result of a trans-European project, and its future must be consistent with further steps towards eEurope: an endorsement by EU institution is vital for EUCIP, in order to keep IT professionalism aligned with official development policies.

References

[1] For more information on CEPIS visit: http://www.cepis.org
[2] For more information on ECDL visit: http://www.ecdl.com
[3] For more information on the EPICS project visit: http://www.cepis-epics.org
[4] For more information on EUCIP visit: http://www.eucip.org
[5] P. Schgör, F. Amarilli and R. Brambilla, Professione Informatica - Vol.I, ISBN 88-464-5382-4, FrancoAngeli, Milano, 2004.
[6] European eSkills Forum: http://cedefop.communityzero.com/esf
[7] European Committee for Standardisation / Information Society Standardization System visit: www.cenorm.be/cenorm/businessdomains/businessdomains/isss/index.asp
[8] European Centre for the Development of Vocational Training visit: http://www.cedefop.eu.int
[9] A comparison of different approaches in classifying ICT skills can be found in the article by (AICA), News - Certificazioni europee per le professioni ICT: lavori in corso. In: Mondo Digitale n. 4, dicembre 2003, pp. 82-84, AICA, Milano.

eAdoption and the Knowledge Economy: Issues, Applications, Case Studies
P. Cunningham and M. Cunningham (Eds.)
IOS Press, 2004

eLearning in European SMEs: the Challenge for Policies and Practice

Graham ATTWELL
Knownet, 6 Menai View Terrace, Bangor, Wales LL572LB, U.K
Email: graham@theknownet.com

Abstract: The paper reports on the work of three European projects examining the use of Information and Communication Technology (ICT) for learning in Small and Medium Sized Enterprises (SMEs). It starts by examining the definition of eLearning and of SMEs, suggesting that these raise important questions. It goes on to examine a number of issues for research and development including managers attitudes to learning, the cost benefits of the use of ICT for learning, and standards, technology and content. The paper suggests there is the need for new paradigms of learning and eLearning. In the final section the paper proposes some possible answers in terms of policy development to promote the use of ICT for learning in SMEs.

1. Digital Technologies and the Challenge of Lifelong Learning

Over the last twenty years, digital technologies have been a major driving force behind profound changes in work organisation, production and society. These changes have led to what economists call the knowledge-based economy, where individual and organisational knowledge is critical to innovation and economic and social development. While previously initial education and training were seen as providing the basic skills and knowledge required for work and participation in society, the new social & work forms require lifelong learning; continuous updating of personal and collective skills & knowledge.

Lundvall and Bórras [3] argue that the 'learning economy' is a more appropriate term than 'knowledge-based economy' in articulating today's agenda where specialised and codified knowledge has a very short lifespan. It is the capability to learn how to create new knowledge and adapt to changing conditions that will increasingly determine the performance of individuals, firms, regions and countries (Lundvall & Bórras, 1999: p. 31).

Just as digital technologies have been a key driver of economic and social demand for new knowledge, they have also been hailed as a means for developing a lifelong learning infrastructure. ELearning, the application of Information and Communication Technologies to curriculum and pedagogy, has been seen as providing universal access to information and as providing a new flexible and ubiquitous learning environment open to all.

Despite spawning a whole new industry, not to say numerous government and European sponsored initiatives and programmes, the reality has not been convincing. The development of eLearning has been dominated by the metaphors of the virtual classroom and virtual university, an obsession with technologies and a focus on distance applications of existing learning opportunities, rather than diffusion of learning in wider societal activities and forms. The term eLearning has become devalued to the extent where it might be often seen as a marketing word rather than a description of pedagogic and learning practices. There has been limited attention to vocational and occupational learning and the development of eLearning environments in less formal learning contexts. Research suggests most learning - for good or for bad - takes place in everyday life and work social situations [4]. In other words, most of our learning is informal learning taking place in a variety of social contexts. Furthermore anecdotal observations lead to a belief that eLearning may be at its most powerful in less formal and more situated learning environments.

Work carried out in various social settings and particularly in organisations plays a very important part in people's lives. Therefore, learning from an economic, human and social point of view has to be embedded in the fabric of all work organisations. If eLearning is to make a contribution to changing the learning paradigm, eLearning must be embedded in the work organisation. Many major companies have initiated programmes and environments for eLearning for continuous vocational training – and in particular for professional development – and to a lesser extent to support initial vocational education and training. However, eLearning has until now a limited application in small enterprises– and has tended to focus on providing networked access to virtual classroom type environments or to distance learning supported by computer based materials. At policy level European programmes and national programmes such as Go Digital have emphasized the importance of the Internet and of digital technologies for SMEs for e-commerce and for Business-to-Business (B2B) applications but have paid only limited attention to the use of ICT for learning. What little research there is, points to very limited uptake of eLearning by SMEs.

This short paper is based on three different projects. The first is two seminars sponsored by the European Commission DG Education and Culture which focused on the issues of pedagogies and evaluation for learning in SMEs. The second was a small pilot project organised by CEDEFOP which looked at the use of ICT for learning in SMEs in five European countries. The third is the work of an ongoing Leonardo da Vinci project, once more researching the use of new technologies for learning in SMEs. The work of all three projects can be accessed through a web site – www.sme-learning.org.

2. Definitions of eLearning and SMEs

The issue of what comprises an SME is not just a semantic issue. The needs of SMEs depend on a number of different factors of which one of the most important is size. The capacity for building the infrastructure and capability to develop appropriate cultures to support eLearning will be more different in micro enterprises (<50 employees) than in larger SMEs. Similarly, there will be differences between enterprises of 50 – 100 employees and those with between 100 and 250 employees. Our work suggests the greatest need for research and development is in the micro SME and in those with between 50 and 100 employees as these are the groups who have the most limited resources and thus experience the greatest problems in providing training for employees.

The definition of eLearning is very important in this context. The development of eLearning has been driven predominantly through the application of the virtual classroom paradigm for academic learning in the higher education sector. It has taken on many of the connotations of traditional learning in this environment. ELearning has tended to be seen as the use of digital media (including CD ROMs, the Web and intranets) for the delivery of structured programmes which are materials based. This definition is problematic.

Many SMEs make extensive use of digital media for accessing technical manuals and for web searches and increasing numbers are involved in business-to-business (B2B) e-commerce applications. This is often taken as evidence that they are engaging in eLearning. However, we would challenge the idea that the use of ICT for information storage and retrieval necessarily constitutes learning. Rather, we would contend that for real learning to take place, this new information has to be applied in a way which then develops new mental models and schema, be they tacit or explicit. For collective knowledge development to take place, these new mental models have to be made explicit and shared. There is no doubt that CD ROMs and the use of the web are useful and convenient ways of storing and retrieving information but unless that information is transformed through use it comprises neither learning nor knowledge development.

Nevertheless, eLearning in SMEs may be most powerful when it is integrated in company business processes through networks and systems for commerce and business development. The tools or software systems used in learning will often not be dedicated eLearning platforms but everyday business systems and software. In fact, email may be the most common learning tool for sharing information and new practices within the workplace, leading to knowledge creation. Critically, the learning materials may well not be bought in or prepared by eLearning specialists, software houses or multi media publishers but the products of employees' documented and shared enquiry into their own practice.

This requires a far wider definition of eLearning than is used currently. It means taking into account all the electronic and digital resources – both formal and informal – used by the enterprise as potential learning and knowledge development tools. It also means looking at the totality of business processes in designing the eLearning environment. In this respect, e-commerce may be a considerable driver for change. For example, even the smaller SMEs are increasingly using computers and software systems as part of their business organisation for a range of different tasks and processes, including the procurement of materials, logistic organisation, sales and marketing and process control. It is possible that eLearning may be most effective when it is integrated with these e-commerce practices and with the use of digital media, computers and networks within work organisations and structures as it then becomes part of the culture of the enterprise.

Such a perspective breaks down the divide between eLearning and what has been categorised as `knowledge management' or management development. Pedagogically, it integrates the acquisition and practice of skills and knowledge with work processes, developing what some researchers have referred to as work process knowledge [5].

Barry Nyhan [4] talks of "building organisations in which people have what can be termed 'developmental work tasks'." These are challenging tasks that 'compel' people to stretch their potential and muster up new resources to manage demanding situations. In carrying out 'developmental work tasks' people are 'developing themselves' and engaged in what can be termed 'developmental learning'." The challenge for developing eLearning in enterprises is the integration of ICT in such a way that it supports developmental work tasks, rather than merely electronically cataloguing routine roles and tasks.

Seminar participants said that eLearning is "Always combined with other learning". eLearning, whether in SMEs, large companies or schools cannot be viewed as an entity in itself. This is critical when it comes to designing SME learning environments.

3. Managers' Attitudes: the Most Decisive Factor

From our own personal experiences, SMEs want to break away from institutions and institutional based training. Despite the much-flaunted move towards flexibility in vocational education and training, VET institutions in general are still unable to meet the needs of SMEs. Managers are often looking for not `just-in-time' but `absolutely-last-minute' training. In order to provide this they need flexible learning materials and flexible methods of delivery. Current technologies and processes for developing and delivering materials are problematic in this respect. Arguably, this sort of training for SMEs is not a core function for VET institutions and we discussed the need for processes and systems, which allowed SMEs to develop and share their own materials (see below).

Thirdly, SMEs want to save money. They perceive eLearning as potentially cheap and effective. Given the present economic recession in many European countries and increased competition, many SMES say they can no longer afford face-to-face training. However, the perception that eLearning is cheap is not without problems.

The difference between `needs' and `wants' is critical in relation to SMEs. Few SMEs carry out systematic training needs analyses; neither do they have training officers. Few have full time qualified trainers. The Cedefop study [1] on eLearning and SMEs concluded that the attitude of individual managers is the single most decisive factor in influencing the development of ICT for learning in SMEs. Managers tended to be pragmatic in their wishes with regard to training rather than following any scientific method of assessing needs.

The Cedefop study found little support by managers for introducing eLearning. More surprisingly there was little support for SMEs or SME managers in developing eLearning in their enterprise. A number of the companies in the, admittedly small, sample were using eLearning because of their role in supply chains. In Italy, regional organisations were trying to stimulate the use of eLearning. In Birmingham, in the UK, the local government was promoting eLearning through an EU financed ADAPT project, In the Austrian Tyrol, the Chamber of Trade has some involvement. However, in each case the support available was both quite specific and quite limited. There was no natural point to which managers could turn for help, nor did the use of eLearning appear to be a major issue for the different support agencies and networks in which the SMEs were involved.

4. Cost Benefits

The question of who pays is perhaps the most pressing, unresolved and complex issue in the development of eLearning for SMEs. The issue is significant at a number of different levels. eLearning has been widely promoted as a cheap or cost effective answer to the policy issue of engendering and promoting Lifelong learning within SMEs. Yet, most researchers, and many consultants, are adamant that eLearning cannot be seen as a cheap solution. There may be economies of scale to be reaped in the future but even this is open to doubt. Despite the many ROIs – or Return on Investment Studies – it is unclear whether eLearning is at present competitive when compared with traditional learning methods. eLearning must, therefore, be justified in its own terms – in opening up access to Lifelong Learning or in providing richer learning environments for learning.

Whilst one task may be to develop the efficiency and effectiveness of eLearning and promote benefits to SMEs, it has been argued that as eLearning is too expensive for SMEs and is likely to remain so for the foreseeable future, the state should subsidise eLearning by fostering new ideas and supporting the implementation of new technologies in order to provide access to new learning infrastructures and cultures. A counter viewpoint is that, despite present low rates of take up, eLearning should be developed through the market.

5. Standards, Technology and Content

Access to learning materials is a major issue in the development and implementation of eLearning in SMEs. As the European Commission notes in a recent document: "the development of the `digital economy' and the wider use of the Internet and of computer and networking equipment has raised accessibility to multimedia to unprecedented levels, thus enhancing opportunities for producers and consumers... However, this rapid evolution does not seem to have been matched in the new educational content sector."

There is a lack of European educational multimedia content coming from institutional, professional and industrial sources in the education, publishing and educational software sectors. After an initial phase of enthusiasm, often described as "hype", there are growing doubts about the real demand for educational e-content, and about its relevance for improving learning"[6]. Our studies would, in general, bear out this assessment.

An examination of an extensive catalogue of eLearning materials available in Italy has revealed an extremely limited range of subject area provision. Most materials are for technologies, mainly the use of standard software packages, and for networking. The next largest category was learning materials for managers and for management activities such as marketing and thirdly, materials for language learning. Beyond this the provision is very limited. Obviously these materials are largely targeted at technical, professional and management employees (or white collar workers).

The situation is further exacerbated in Europe because of the diversity of languages. eLearning was pioneered in Europe in the university sector and most learning materials were provided in English. Whilst this may be acceptable in a higher education environment, most vocational learners require learning materials in their own language. Dondi and Zucchini [2] have drawn attention to the problems of market-led software and materials being provided in different language versions, especially those languages serving smaller population groups. Furthermore, whilst universities could draw on very broad discipline areas and on common discipline structures between countries, the learning needs of employees in SMEs are often quite narrow and very specific, with limited international (or even national) markets. There is a growing debate on the issue of globalisation and localisation in software and learning materials and the group agreed that the task of translating materials to different languages is not a straightforward technical issue but involves significant cultural transformations.

There have been many policy initiatives and measures to stimulate market provision of eLearning materials. A considerable number of projects have encouraged universities to provide learning programmes and materials for SMEs. However, it is open to question how effective these initiatives have been – and to the sustainability of project led developments.

One of the key debates revolves around standards, both for learning materials and learning platforms. Standards mean that learning materials and systems would be interoperable – and therefore more sustainable. Standards would enable and facilitate the development of learning materials within an individual enterprise or cluster of enterprises. Within a wider vision of eLearning, that is, eLearning as a contribution to knowledge management or collective knowledge development, a learning 'object' or discrete piece of learning material is seen as the fusion of the outcomes of learning together with the knowledge created, at all its different stages and in all its different forms. Learning objects or materials could be created by the learner themselves as a result of their engagement in business activities. The primary role of the computer based learning platform would not be in the delivery of the materials but in facilitating the transformation and communication of ideas as knowledge. The computer or ICT based learning environment would be primarily a process tool to support the creation and transformation of knowledge. The overwhelming advantage of this approach is it allows learning materials to reflect and support the different contexts in which learning takes place in SMEs.

6. New Paradigms

The real challenge is to stop thinking within existing paradigms of learning and eLearning.

One new paradigm to be addressed is the nature of informal (or tacit) knowledge as opposed to formal knowledge. eLearning has so far concentrated on formal learning and the reproduction of traditional courses through digital media. Yet most studies suggest that, at least for skilled work, it is tacit knowledge that is most powerful within SMEs. The question is how eLearning systems and architectures can be used to support the development and sharing of tacit or informal knowledge.

A second issue is the tension between individual learning, which eLearning tends to promote, and the social nature of more traditional learning. The social dimension is recognised as an important motivator and driver for many learners. A positive social environment can improve learning effectiveness and allow a wider range of methodologies.

Thirdly, if the sharing of existing knowledge and the generation of new knowledge are important future developments for SMEs and if eLearning or, better stated, e-resources are to be a medium for doing this, we need to look at the nature of the interactions in eLearning and to develop new processes and solutions. This requires moving towards a new paradigm of continuous learning based on the application of new working principles.

Fourthly, but arguably more fundamental, is the question of the nature of the problem that eLearning is trying to solve. Is it of benefit to SMEs at the present stage of technical and pedagogic development? Clearly SMEs are using ICT technologies for access to information, but they see that as very different to signing up for eLearning 'courses'. Some SMEs think they need eLearning, but they do not necessarily know why. In many cases they are being driven by the need to employ new information technologies, but the lack of any integration with eLearning is hampering progress.

Finally, there is a separate issue around how to persuade employees themselves, rather than their bosses, to use new technologies for learning, and to reconcile individual learning needs with collective ones. In other words, how can we resolve the PSP paradox – providing pleasure, sustainability and profit – all at the same time?

7. Possible Solutions

7.1 Promote a Culture of Learning

The most critical issue is to promote a culture of learning in SMEs. This entails taking actions to involve a wide range of stakeholders as well as SMEs themselves. This is a long-term strategy but one without which no amount of eLearning-directed initiatives will succeed.

7.2 Mobilise SME Managers

As part of such an approach, it is particularly important to mobilise SME managers through the development and support of sector networks, regional networks and regional learning networks.

7.3 Focus on Organisational Development

eLearning should not be viewed as an issue or aim in itself. In fact the present focus on learning and training can even be seen as unhelpful, particularly given the vague and unfocused nature of discourses on lifelong learning. Instead, eLearning has to be addressed within the context of organisational development, including more support for SMEs in introducing new forms of work organisation and new technologies within the workplace.

7.4 Support Networks as a New Developmental Paradigm

Networks should be seen as a new developmental paradigm. Present policy makers and planners' approaches to learning still reflect an 'industrial age model', with lifelong learning merely seen as "more of the same for more people".

7.5 Develop a Differentiated Approach

Such a new approach needs to be more culturally differentiated – "one size does not fit all". Due recognition of the different needs of different sectors and regions is necessary, rather than a blanket approach to introducing eLearning in SMEs.

7.6 Recognise Triggers for Change

It is important to identify the different triggers that act as a catalyst for change and to promote a learning culture. These vary between sectors and regions and over time. When these trigger points are recognised, structures are needed to allow immediate short-term actions to be taken to capitalise on opportunities.

7.7 Policy Support

There are many actions which could be taken by local, national and European policymakers to support the use of ICT for learning.

A change in present funding policies to promote and support larger numbers of small projects based on communities of practice, and running these projects more intensively over shorter time periods would be of benefit. Projects should focus on work-based learning rather than on the provision of distance learning courses or virtual classrooms, and should seek to develop and capitalise on informal processes of learning. Rather than looking to external learning materials developers or training bodies to supply learning programmes, they should focus on SME employees as providers (or senders) of knowledge. The development of competence in SMEs is predicated on the knowledge, skills and attitudes of the SME employees themselves.

At a European level, inter-regional networks and projects can be particularly valuable. Similarly, projects supporting clusters of SMEs offer great potential.

7.8 Research

Research is also important. Future research is needed into how SME managers and employees use ICT within their everyday work. The findings should then be used as a basis for developing environments and opportunities for eLearning. We also need to recognise an ongoing paradigm shift from eLearning to knowledge management, and to initiate research on knowledge. Finally, we need more research into social networks and SMEs and their impact on knowledge sharing, development and learning.

New forms of research – for instance the promotion of 'accompanying research' – with research taking place alongside developmental activities, could help overcome the present divisions between research and practice, and researchers and practitioners.

References

[1] Attwell, G. (2003) The challenge of learning in small enterprises: issues for policy and practice in Europe, Luxembourg: European Commission

[2] Dondi C. and Zucchini I., "Economic and Organisational Issues in the Trans-National Development and Delivery of ODL and eLearning Courses", in Research Perspectives on Open Distance Learning, SCIENTER, Bologna, 1998

[3] Lundvall, B-A. /Borras, S. (1997), The Globalising Learning Economy: Implications for Innovation Policy, EU.

[4] Nyhan, B,; Cressey, P.; Tomassini, M.; Kelleher, M.; Poell R. (2003) Facing up to the learning organisation challenge Volume I – key issues from a European perspective, Luxembourg: European Commission

[5] Rauner, F. & Bremer, R, (2001) Experten-Facharbeiter-Workshops als instrument der brufswissenschaftlichen Qualifihationsforschung' 'Mensch-Maschine-Inetraktion' Arbeiten und lernen in rechnergestuetzen Arbeitessystemen in Industrie, Handwerk und Dienstleistung, Eicker, Friedhelm A; Patersen W. (eds), Baden-Baden: Nomos

[6] European Commission Directorate-General for Education and Culture, Open invitation to tender No DG EAC 21/02 for the provision of services concerning the carrying out of studies in the context of the eLearning initiative.

From Hands-on Experience to e-Learning

Iskra POPOVA, Oliver POPOV
Department of Information Technology and Media, Mid Sweden University, Holmgatan 10, SE 85170 Sundsvall, SWEDEN
Tel: +46 60 148782, Fax: +46 60 148830, Email: iskra.popova@mh.se

Abstract: When a part of course curriculum consists of hands-on experience learning with real equipment then the design of a completely distance equivalent is accompanied with many impediments and caveats. The article describes the process of transforming the courses in data communications and computer networks from campus into completely distant courses. We present the decisions we have taken, as well as the development and the experience of running the first introductory course.

1. Introduction

The demand for on-line courses is growing as remote learning is extending and even slowly substituting traditional teaching methods. Indeed, numerous universities and schools have already embraced this trend. The faculty at Mid Sweden University has tried to create distance equivalents for the most of the current courses on campus with at least two major objectives: flexible way of learning, and producing a larger audience.

The area of computer networks on the undergraduate level is covered by six courses. The introductory course, "Internet and Data Communications", provides elementary knowledge in the area. "Network Programming" is an depth survey of the principal tools used in the design and development of programs that deal with datagram communications and remote procedure calls. The UNIX system administration course teaches the fundamental skills and hands-on experience for the day-to-day management and execution of the primary tasks needed to configure, setup, administer, and maintain UNIX systems.

There are three more advanced courses. In the first one, TCP/IP Internetworking, concepts like switching, multiplexing, naming, addressing, routing, quality of service, flow, and congestion control are explored through their implementation in TCP/IP protocol suite. Network Design focuses on design objectives and construction phases related to different types of networks, and their connection to the Internet. "Network Management and Security" comprises the issues concerned with the performance and security of the network.

All practical exercises for the courses are performed in the campus laboratory shown on Figure 1. The students are using equipment for measuring transmission media performance, work with switches and hubs and configure computers and routers. In addition, they use network analyzers to look at the structure of real packets, [1], software packages like network simulator to simulate diverse network behaviour, [2], and Boson simulator to configure switches and routers for various network architectures, [3]. The goal of the experimental work is to endow learners with a feeling for real network environment and the problems they can encounter as network designers and administrators.

Creating distant equivalents to all these courses involves intensive planning, starting with the guidelines that can be applied to all the courses and ending with the design of the teaching materials, assignments and laboratory exercises that can be given on distance, for each particular course. The next section of this paper describes the strategy chosen by the faculty in developing the distance courses. Section 3 is devoted to details concerning the development of the introductory course with the accent given to the laboratory exercises designed for it, while section 4 presents the lessons learned from its implementation. In the conclusions a summary of the current achievements, as well as the reflections on our work and plans for the future are presented.

Figure 1

2. Strategy

The two constrains imposed on our strategy from the very beginning were the following. First, we had to pursue the goal to attract more students, and second, we were advised to use the WebCT platform [4], educational software that supports e-learning, purchased and licensed by the University. When developing the general guidelines for transforming our campus courses into distance courses, it was vital to answer several questions.

2.1 Where to Start?

Based on the first constraint, whose goal is to entice and keep students in the Computer Networks profile, it was quite natural to start with an introductory course. The assumption was that the target group should span over not only students participating in some of the programs on the campus, but also many Internet users interested to learn what is happening when surfing the net. The second factor was the fairly small number of laboratory exercises associated with this introductory course, which made both the development and the verification phase rather feasible in order to have timely Proof of Concept (PoC).

2.2 How to Replace the Interactivity of Campus Courses?

The WebCT platform includes a discussion forum or bulletin board, where the instructor and students can write their messages and read postings written by the others. The private mail functions in the same way as the regular e-mail. The only difference is that the senders and receivers are limited to the participants in the course. While both of them provide asynchronous communication, the chat tool offers synchronous interaction. Two or more persons can "enter" a chat room and "talk" by using the keyboards on their computers.

2.3 How to Support Active Learning?

Present research shows [5], that the strategy "learning by doing" is giving very good results, especially in a distance environment. Hence, to provoke active learning, each course should have a number of individual assignments accompanied by a few group exercises. It is expected that collaborative work fosters group co-operation in which the majority of students are actively involved in the learning process.

2.4 How to Use the Offered Platform?

When it comes to the structure of the course and the appearance of the course pages our guideline was to keep it as simple as possible, yet to include all necessary information for the students. When entering the course, students can proceed reading more about the course, go directly to the lecture modules or use one of the communication tools.

The section that posits all the details consists of a tutorial on how to use WebCT platform and a learner's guide. The tutorial is devoted to explicating all WebCT tools used within the course and the way they should be exercised by the learners. The learner's guide consists of the short course description together with its objectives and goals, literature to be used, information about the instructor, a list of all the requirements for a student to fulfil along with a timeline, and the policy behind the student assessment and evaluation.

The lecture modules should explain the topics with text and pictures and provide a practice quiz at the end of each section. Animation applets are able to demonstrate complex relationships in networking [6], thus increasing the motivation to learn and enabling student to explore different aspects of the illustrated topics. Therefore, whenever suitable, the course content pages should include either applets developed by the designers of the course or links to sites providing animations. The practice quizzes are a mixture of multiple choice questions, and questions with short answers or matching phrases. Their purpose is to help students review and self-assess the acquired knowledge and prepare them for the real tests.

2.5 How to Organize Hands-on-Work-Experience Virtually?

Designing guiding principles for organizing virtually hands-on-experience work was one of the most difficult tasks to accomplish. It was almost impossible to establish a general guideline for all the exercises and all of the courses, most likely due to the domain specific requirements. Therefore, we have adopted a step-by-step strategy. Namely, practical laboratory exercises in each course should be treated separately.

So far, we have conclusions about how to organize the laboratory work for the courses in Computer networks and the TCP/IP internetworking. The assignments in the first one mostly consist of tasks that the students could perform on their home computers, while those in the second comprise experiments involved with configuration of routers.

When using their own computer, the only concern for students is the cost of the software needed to do the exercise. Free software was used whenever possible. Many distance students are using computers placed in the library or they have Internet access via other public places. In that case they are not allowed to install any new software. Hence, this problem should be addressed whenever the exercise requires installation of a program.

The configuration of the router's interfaces, building static routing tables and running different routing protocols are the core laboratory exercises in the TCP/IP internetworking course. To provide remote equipment access for the distance students we developed a virtual network laboratory [7], [8]. Special software running on the web server in the laboratory and connected to the routers were developed. It will manage the reservation scheme and provide access to the routers for the distance students. In addition, it should be capable to save students work and provide easy administration for the lab instructor. The actual implementation is expected to be done by our students as a final year project.

2.6 How to Make the Schedule?

There are two contradictory goals that need to be achieved when making the schedule. A fixed scheme contributes towards the synchronization in the work of all participants, promoting interactivity and discussion for the topic during the time planed for it. On the other hand, the flexibility in learning is lost. By default this is one of the main reasons for studying on distance. Removing this feature will constrain learners and impair the course.

To achieve the balance we proposed the “recommended schedule”, which sets dates for reading each section of the course content, working on and submitting assignments and group exercises and due dates for finishing practice quizzes and real tests. The schedule is published using the WebCT tool called Calendar and given to the students as a timeline of achievements in the Learner’s guide. Students should be advised to follow it closely, but they will have freedom to use the time in the most suitable way for each of them.

2.7 How to Make the Assessment?

As our goal was to make the courses completely distant, we felt obliged to have many different means for assessment. Besides assignments and group exercises that were primarily designed to provoke active participation, learning through discussion and exchange of experience, we thought it is necessary to include on-line quizzes. The two types of quizzes should be designed: practice quizzes that follow each section in the course modules, and real tests used to test student knowledge.

One obstacle when it comes to assessment was the authentication of the person doing all the work remotely. The user is authenticated by the WebCT platform with a standard user name and password. This kind of method does not provide real authentication and can be forged. The simplest solution to this problem was to introduce a classic exam at the end of each course. Fortunately, Sweden has a very well organised network of institutions that can offer examination services and provide authentication of the students all over the country. Hence, each student can choose the place for the exam. The only constrain is the date and the time for the examination.

3. Developments

Internet and Data Communications was the first course in the area of networking that was developed and has been offered to the distant students. The course design has followed the guidelines described in section 2. The first page of the course is shown on Figure 2.

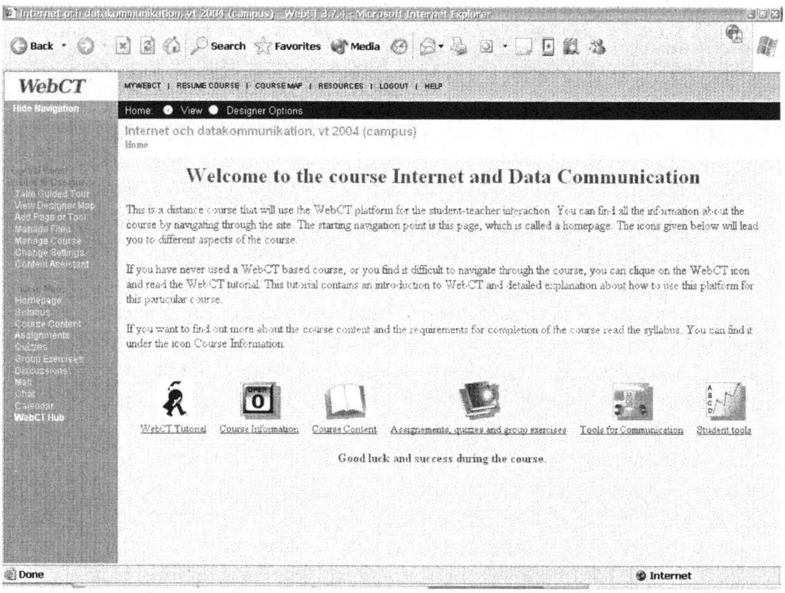

Figure 2

Under the Course Information icon, students can see and download the learner's guide and get acquainted with everything necessary for studying. The course content module presents the topics in an easy to follow way and is enriched with a lot of pictures and animations. The acquired knowledge and understanding is checked through thirteen individual assignments and four group exercises, eighteen practice quizzes and three real tests. In the text that follows, the development of the laboratory exercises will be described.

The course includes three practical laboratory exercises where students are using their computers and their Internet connection to do them. Some of them are a part of individual assignments while others are assigned as group exercises.

The objective of the first lab is to familiarize students with the concepts taught in the course, like host name, DNS suffix, IP address, physical address, subnet mask, default gateway, DHCP server etc. Students can obtain their own data by using a simple command on their machines, like the one shown on Figure 3. Their task is to explain the meaning of each of these terms, to associate the particular value they have obtained and the explanation about its meaning. In a similar way they can obtain and observe the routing table for the host. Their report should include description for all the entries in the table obtained accompanied by explanation about the functions and the necessity for each of them.

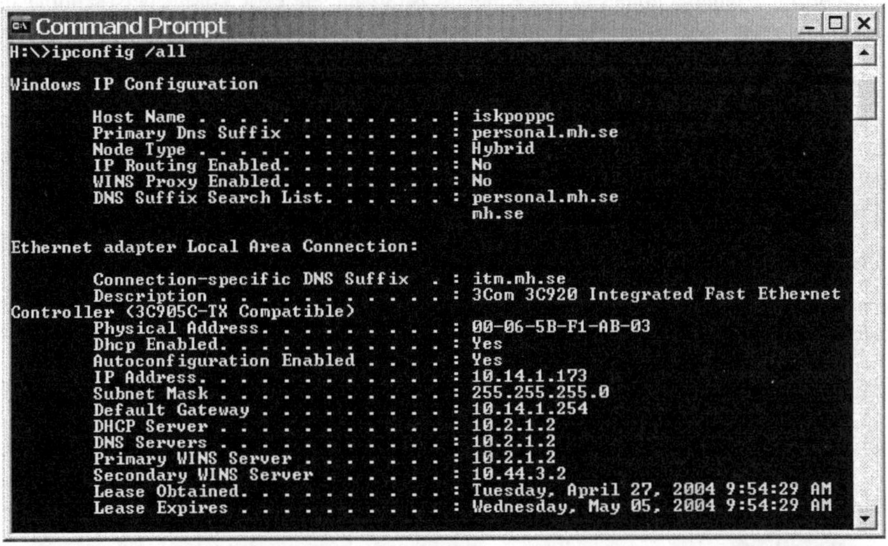

Figure 3

When this exercise is performed in the laboratory on campus it will give all the students similar output, because they are all using computers connected to a single local area network. However, distance students are accessing the Internet through different Internet service providers and therefore they usually obtain different outputs, which depend on the provider they are connected to. It is extremely useful when these exercises are done as a group work with a requirement that the students discuss with each other the values obtained and the different types of Internet connections they are using. The collaborative work helps them learn much more since instead looking at the data for one type of connection, they have the opportunity to analyse the data obtained from all the members in the group.

The second exercise is devoted to studying different times involved in a delay of packets sent between two hosts on the Internet, as well as the reasons for the delay being different each time a packet is sent. Students can observe hop-by-hop mode the packets travel to reach the final destination using the commands ping and traceroute. Both of them are built in the operating system and no additional programs or tools are needed on the student side. Furthermore, the publicly available servers running VisualRoute program provide a graphical user interface for the same command. When writing the report, students are asked to analyse the times and the hops obtained to different hosts located in different parts of the world, to analyse whether the path travelled in both directions is always the same and to make conclusions about the relations of the delay to the distance, number of hops, time of the week or the day when the measurements were taken.

There is no difference in this exercise in terms of the values obtained, when campus students and distance students do it. This means that campus students can obtain different outputs if they choose to ping or traceroute to different sites. Therefore, in the distance course this exercise was given as individual assignment.

The third exercise, which was also a part of an individual assignment, aims towards analyses of packets captured on a real network. The campus-based course used the demo version of the Shomiti network analyser for this purpose, [1]. However, based on the proposed set of guidelines given in the strategy, the distance course should use a publicly available program. Following others experience, [9], we have selected Ethereal network analyser, [10]. The exercise consists of offering students six sets of captured packets corresponding to six different network scenarios. They are supposed to analyse and recognise the types of packets and match each set of captured packets with the corresponding action. To do that the students need to download the Ethereal network analyser, install it on their own computer and use for packet analyses. The problem with students using public computers was solved in the following way. As they are not allowed to install the Ethereal network analysers, we provided for them pictures from the Ethereal analyser screen with the captured packets and all necessary fields opened. From the pictures they can see the same values as the students using the analyser and therefore are able to find out which set of packets was captured when a particular action was taken.

4. Results

So far the course Internet and Data Communications was offered as a distance course four times. It generated very high interest and the number of students was always over 80. This is a rather large number considering that the regular campus course was running during this time. As expected, we have attracted a lot of students working in the industry or being related to completely different area of study. However, it appears that the level of the course was possibly too technical and therefore very difficult for many of them, especially those coming without any or very little mathematical or engineering background. That was the reason we had a lot of dropouts mainly in the initial stage of the course.

To find out what was the students' opinion on the course, we have constructed an evaluation form and asked the students to fill it in. It was made up of 8 statements to which they were supposed to agree or disagree and two questions where they could write about the strengths and weaknesses of the course. All the students have either strongly agreed (50%) or agreed (50%) with the statement "The assignments and practice quizzes actively involved me in what I was learning". This was indication that they really liked the learning by doing approach. Most of the students thought that its greatest strength was the distance nature of the course and the flexibility they had to freely schedule their time.

To our greatest surprise many of the students thought that the greatest weakness of the course were the group exercises. The reason for this is in the best way expressed in the following statement from a student "...since all students have different motivation and priorities, the group exercises are a disadvantage. My feeling is that motivated students carry out the most in a group exercise because they want to proceed with the course. Less motivated group members use this fact to get a joyride".

Since we strongly believe that collaborative distance work can in the long term improve learning, arguably, we have kept the group exercises. However, the individuals that do not feel comfortable working in a group have the option of doing things alone.

5. Conclusions

It is evident that the transformation of a campus course to a distance equivalent is neither a straightforward nor a trivial matter. On the contrary, it has to overcome many challenges and caveats, especially if one of the main features and strengths of the campus course is based on intensive lab exercises using sophisticated hardware and software equipment.

Considering that the major goal of distance education is to become equivalent to face-to-face education, from a formal and administrative way, to the content and the knowledge generation part that produces in both cases the same level of competence, it is indeed a worthwhile effort and task to explicate, elaborate and resolve all the salient attributes of the campus courses and find their proper equivalents in the distance environment, since it is the only way to design, implement and run a successful distance course.

The work and the results presented in this article identify all the relevant problems in mapping campus courses in distance ones, propose valuable solutions and moreover verified in practices. It is our belief that the initial positive experience merits the need for further studies into the semantics of this transformation in order to produce some more general rules that will eventually form the basis of a transformational paradigm.

References

[1] Hall A. E., Internet Core Protocols, pp. 417-424 with Shomiti Surveyor Lite analyses tool.
[2] The Network Simulator ns-2, (www.isi.edu/nsnam/ns/)
[3] Boson NetSim, (www.boson.com/netsim/index2.htm)
[4] WebCT, (www.webct.com)
[5] Ramakrishna M. V., Learning by Doing Model for Teaching Advanced Databases, Proceedings of the Australian Conference on Computing Education, Melbourne, Australia, 2000, ISBN: 1-58113-271-9, pp 203 – 207.
[6] Holliday M. A., Animation of Computer Networking Concepts, ACM Journal of Educational Resources in Computing, Vol. 3, No. 2, June 2003, pp. 1-26.
[7] Liu S., Marti W. and Zhao W., Virtual Networking Lab (VNL): Its concepts and implementation, Proceedings of 2001 ASEE Annual Conference and Exposition, 2001, Session 3532.
[8] Zimmerli S., Steinemann M. and Braun Torsten, Resource Management Portal for Laboratories Using Real Devices on the Interenet, ACM SIGCOMM Computer Communications Review, Vol. 33, No. 3, July 2003, pp. 145-151.
[9] Mechtly B. and Decker J., Using Ethereal and TCPPortconnect in Undergraduate Networking Labs, The Journal of Computing in Small Colleges, Vol. 19, October 2003, pp. 289-298.
[10] Ethereal Network Analyzer, (www.ethereal.com)

eAdoption and the Knowledge Economy: Issues, Applications, Case Studies
P. Cunningham and M. Cunningham (Eds.)
IOS Press, 2004

A Methodology for Developing Quality e-Learning Systems

Katerina PAPANIKOLAOU[1], Stephanos MAVROMOUSTAKOS[2], Andreas S. ANDREOU[3]
[1]Cyprus College, 6 Diogenes Str. Engomi, 1516, Nicosia, Cyprus
Tel: +357-221713290, Fax: + 357-22590539, Email: apapanik@cycollege.ac.cy
[2]The Philips College, 4-6 Lamias Str., 2001, Nicosia, Cyprus
Tel: +357-22441860, Fax: + 357-22441863 Email: stephanos@philips.ac.cy
[3]University of Cyprus, 75 Kallipoleos Str., 1678, Nicosia, Cyprus
Tel: +357-22892700, Fax: + 357-22892701 Email: aandreou@ucy.ac.cy

Abstract: The importance of developing quality e-Learning systems and resources is crucial for the successful acceptance by the students. Most existing e-Learning environments though, are developed based on the Anglo-Saxon educational system ignoring the importance of human, social and cultural factors affecting the successful transfer of knowledge. In addition, these systems tend to miss those factors that affect the quality of a system such as the ISO standards. In this paper, we propose a methodology called e-MATHISI for developing quality e-Learning environments aiming at overcoming those drawbacks. E-MATHISI incorporates three axons: the Human, Social and Cultural Factors, the Quality Components, and the Pedagogy Requirements. Finally, the methodology is demonstrated through the development of an e-Learning environment.

1. Introduction

In the last few years we have experienced a huge increase in the development and usage of e-Learning systems, particularly by academic institutions. Among the greatest advantages of e-Learning to academics and students are accessibility, mobility and collaboration. These advantages address only one aspect of the learning process. Other factors that also need to be addressed are the incorporation of human, social and cultural factors in the e-Learning tools, the utilization of quality factors in the development process and the adoption of classical pedagogical methods to the new environment. The incorporation of these factors into the presented methodology will produce a quality E-Learning system. The efficacy of our methodology is demonstrated through the development of an E-Learning system.

2. Objectives

The objective of this paper is twofold: to identify and quantify the key factors needed for the development of a quality e-Learning system such as, human, social and cultural factors, quality components (e.g. ISO 9126), and key issues affecting the adoption of the classical pedagogical methods by the new e-Learning environment; and to present a methodology for developing quality e-Learning systems based on those factors.

3. Methodology

The development of the proposed methodology is done with the collaboration of three academic institutions. These institutions have a strategic interest in developing and implementing e-Learning systems. Their multicultural environment is ideal for the identification and study of the key human, social and cultural factors, their origin and importance [1]. Additionally, the experience acquired by these organizations through years of teaching experience in pedagogical methods is used in the adoption of classical pedagogical methods to the new environment.

Once these factors and their importance are identified, they are incorporated into the WebE methodology. Then, the utilization of these factors is described within the WebE process. Finally, the methodology is demonstrated thought a real case scenario.

The proposed methodology called e-MATHISI, is based on the Web Engineering (WebE) process introduced by Pressman [2], modified to include the requirements and peculiarities of designing and developing quality e-Learning applications. E-MATHISI is based on human, social and cultural factors, quality components & pedagogy requirements.

3.1 Human, Social and Cultural Factors

The importance of the development of e-Learning methods and resources addressing these aspects is proving to be very important. Numerous e-Learning systems are available serving the purpose of knowledge transfer and dissemination. These systems however, have been mainly developed and produced for the Anglo-Saxon educational environment. Despite the fact that most higher education is fairly uniform throughout the world there are still key differences that influence the learning process and critical requirements that existing e-Learning systems tend to miss. Human, social and cultural factors such as the learning background, the pedagogy practices used in the traditional education, the availability and acceptability of the use of various resources change from country to country even from area to area within the same country and make the need for differentiation even for the same application imperative if we are to support a successful e-Learning environment.

An e-Learning application must be tailored-made for each country, regions in the same country and groups of countries located in the same geographical area. In requirements analysis phase the emphasis should be placed on the specific characteristics of the countries targeted by the e-Learning application. These characteristics include [3]:

- Demographics - It is well known that human behavior varies depending on gender and age. These issues can affect system design and performance. The Web engineer or project manager must specify and design the application based on the target population.
- Social characteristics - The analyst/developer must examine the educational system, literacy level, and the languages spoken within the population, to design the e-Learning application in such a way that will accommodate diverged features. Religion plays a significant role in politics, culture and economy in certain countries. Thus, the analyst must investigate whether religion affects the system design and to what degree.
- Legal characteristics - The political system and legislation among countries vary; therefore one must investigate political stability and all the relevant laws prior to the development of an e-Learning application. National and international laws must be analyzed to guide the system towards alignment and compliance upon full operation.
- Technical characteristics - Identifying the technology level of each targeted country will help the Web engineer to decide on the technology and resources to use. Countries with advanced technologies and high Web usage are excellent candidates for an e-Learning application utilizing the full potential of the technology. Countries new to the Internet arena with primitive or basic technologies may need to design e-Learning systems, for low bandwidth networks and reduced communication capabilities.

Another important area the researcher must concentrate on is the timeliness of the content. Timeliness is examined through a cultural prism aiming at identifying certain human, social, and cultural needs in all three of its coordinates, as most of the e-Learning exhibiting a high rate of change often depend highly on ethos and customs of different people in different countries.

3.2 Quality components

Quality factors such as usability, functionality, efficiency, reliability and maintainability as defined in the ISO 9126 standard [4] together with web engineering quality components as presented in the research arena [5, 6] need to be addressed and incorporated into the methodology proposed leading to the successful design and development of quality e-Learning systems. Each component is decomposed into several features that must be separately addressed to fulfill specific user needs:

- Usability - Issues like understandability, learnability, friendliness, operability, playfulness and ethics are vital design factors that Web engineers cannot afford to miss. The system must be implemented to allow for easy understanding of its functioning and behavior. User-interface aesthetics, consistency and ease-of-use are attributes of easy-to-learn systems. E-Learning systems, by keeping a user profile and taking into consideration human emotions, can provide related messages to the user, whether this is a welcome message or a student customization page, thus enhancing the friendliness of the system. Playfulness is a key feature that should be examined to what extend the application requires this characteristic especially for young age students. E-Learning systems must reflect useful knowledge looking at human interactions and decisions.
- Functionality - The system must include all features needed to accomplish the required task(s). Accuracy, suitability, compliance, interoperability and privacy are issues that must be investigated in designing an e-Learning system to ensure the system will perform as expected. The e-Learning application must have all the capabilities in the traditional learning process, enhanced by the latest high technology features.
- System Reliability - Producing a reliable system involves understanding issues such as fault tolerance, crash frequency, recoverability and maturity. The system must maintain a specified level of performance in case of software faults. It must also have the ability to re-establish its level of performance. A system must consistently produce the same results, and meet or even exceed users' expectations. The e-Learning application must have correct link recognition, user input validation and recovery mechanisms.
- Efficiency – Students expect the system to run efficiently when utilizing an e-Learning environment. System response-time performance, and page and graphics generation speed must satisfy student needs. Fast access to information must be examined also throughout the system life to ensure that user requirements are continuously met on one hand, and that the system remains competitive and useful on the other.
- Maintainability - Some crucial features related to maintaining an e-Learning application are its analyzability, changeability, stability, and testability. The primary target here is to collect data that will assist designers to conceive the overall system in its best architectural and modular form, for a future maintenance point of view. With the rapid technological changes especially in the area of Web engineering, as well as the rigorous user requirements for continuous Web site updates, easy system modifications and enhancements, both in content and in the way this content is presented, are also success factors for the development and improvement of an e-Learning system.

3.3 Pedagogy Requirements

Transferring the dynamic nature of learning to the new e-Learning environment, maintaining student individuality and differentiation according to personal preferences and abilities, as well as motivating and inspiring students are key factors for the acceptance of the new learning environment [7, 8]. The key factors are identified as follows:

- The identification of learners' needs – The e-Learning environment should be shaped according to the predefined learners' needs and course required pedagogical outcome.

- The structuring of the pedagogical material – The pedagogical material should be constructed in a way that facilitates the successful transfer of the required knowledge.
- Enhancement of the e-Learning environment – The e-Learning environment can be used to compliment or in parallel with the real classroom environment. The e-Learning environment must adhere to the mechanisms and functions of the real environment. In the pure distance learning case this enhancement is even more imperative.
- The motivation for student participation – The transferring to the virtual environment is not always straightforward and easy. Students are not always willing to use the virtual environment for a number of reasons, such as the difficulty of the e-Learning tool, the non-intuitive nature of the environment, the provision of reduced interactivity, etc.
- The ability of the e-Learning environment to answer and solve student questions and problems. – It should be able to offer students a basic problem solving mechanism. Mechanisms such as on-line tutorials, instructor contact , reference to useful resources and even access to a technical helpdesk would offer students support and help.
- The establishment of collaborative mechanisms among students – In the virtual environment the student can be easily isolated from the rest of the class. This is usually avoided in the classroom and should also be avoided in the virtual classroom, by organizing and operating collaboratively so that students can interact and communicate.
- The utilization of the relevant tools and components for the support of any specific solution – Depending on the student audience and the required learning outcome the appropriate tools should be implemented and differentiated accordingly. Vocational training requires different solutions than educational training and undergraduate training has different pedagogical targets than undergraduate training. Tools and components can be utilized to enhance the e-Learning environment more efficiently.
- The right mix of the learning processes implemented – The most important learning processes are identified as follows: analysis, synthesis, reasoning, judging, problem solving, collaboration, simulation, evaluation, presentation and relation. These should be used dynamically for constructing the learning scene for each course and student.

3.4 The e-MATHISI Methodology

The e-MATHISI process includes six phases (see Figure 1): Formulation, Planning, Analysis, Engineering, Implementation & Testing, and User Evaluation:

1. Formulation – Defines the tasks and goals of the e-Learning application and specifies the length of the first increment.
2. Planning – Estimates the total project cost and associated risks, and sets a timeframe for the implementation of the first increment as well as the process of the next increments.
3. Analysis – Identifies all the system and user requirements together with system content.
4. Engineering – It involves two parallel tasks: (i) Content design and production, and (ii) Architectural, navigation, and interface design.
5. Page Generation & Testing – Development task using automated tools for the creation of the e-Learning application, applets, scripts, and forms.
6. Faculty/Student Evaluation – Evaluates each task and proposes new modifications and expansions that need to be incorporated to the next increment.

During the Analysis phase, the analyst following the classical approach studies the current system and processes and defines functional and non-functional requirements. The proposed three-axon approach is invoked next to obtain human, social and cultural factors as well as, pedagogy practices and requirements. These are then translated into functional and non-functional requirements. Requirements management follows, which deletes any duplication of the ones already found using the traditional method, or resolves conflicts resulting from contradictory requirements. After updating the system requirements, their final form is used in the Engineering phase to support the e-Learning application development. The Web engineer designs the e-Learning application's structure, the navigation mechanisms, the interface and content based on results from the previous phase.

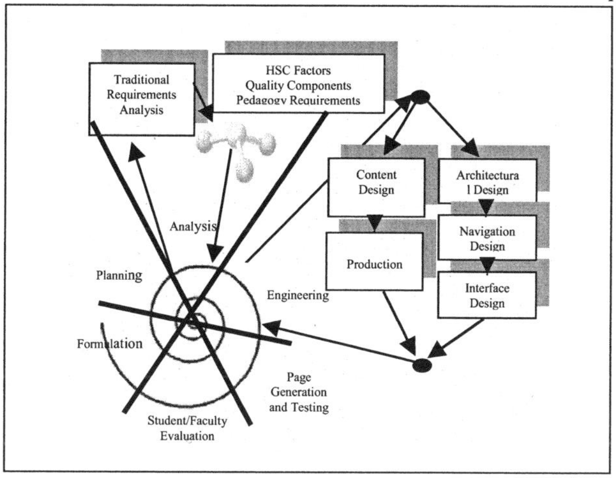

Figure 1: The E-MATHISI Methodology Diagram

4. Technology Description

The efficacy of our methodology is demonstrated through the development of an e-Learning prototype environment. While the proposed e-Learning platform comprises the common functions found in a typical environment it also includes the human, social, cultural factors, as well as, the quality components and pedagogy requirements already identified. In addition, it incorporates learning processes and templates for developing a dynamic e-Learning environment, and a requirements analyzer tool to identify new user requirements. Finally, the platform architecture uses open interfaces, protocols and technologies taking into account possible future needs and requirements.

The e-Learning system utilizes the open e-Learning platform Mentor for development. The reason was the flexibility that an open architecture provides, the cost-free availability of the software necessary in an academic environment, and the widespread adoption of the platform by academic institutions. The system is built on an Apache Web server and running PHP scripts and MySQL database. The architectural design of Mentor includes two main entities, the MySQL database and the Web application modules. The Web application modules are PHP scripts which interact with the Mentor users (students, teachers and administrators). These PHP scripts perform transactions on the database holding students and courses data. The conceptual architectural level of Mentor is used to create, store, assemble, and deliver personalized e-Learning content in the form of learning objects.

There are four entities defined in Mentor: a) Learning object repository, b) Automated authoring application, c) Dynamic delivery interface and d) Administrative application. The interaction between these entities is shown in Figure 2. The learning object repository is a central database in which learning content is stored and managed. From this point individual learning objects are either dispensed to users individually or used as components to assemble larger learning modules or full courses, depending on individual needs.

This application is used to create the reusable learning objects that are accessible in the repository. It automates authoring by providing templates and storyboarding capabilities that incorporate instructional design principles. To serve up a learning object based on learner profiles, or user queries, a dynamic delivery interface is required. This component also provides user tracking, links to related sources of information, and supports multiple assessment types with user feedback. This interface may be customized using Mentor. This application is used to manage student records, launch e-Learning courses from course catalogs, track and report student progress, and provide other administrative functions.

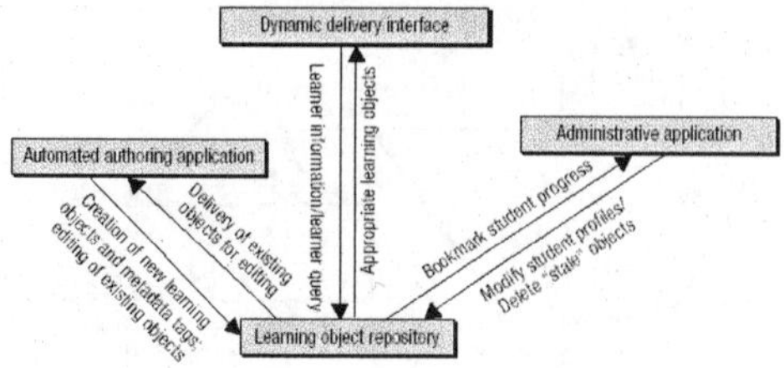

Figure 2: The 4 Entities of Mentor

5. Developments

Based on the functional and non-functional requirements revealed during the Analysis phase, the system provides the following main operations:

Class announcements, access to course material, assignments and case studies, online quizzes with a timer and a feedback mechanism, a virtual classroom with collaborative study groups and a discussion board utilizing synchronous and asynchronous communication. In addition, under the Personal Preferences, the system provides email, a progress report, a homework submission utility, access to classmates' public information, and the ability to view other courses while still logged in.

Finally, the Settings area includes an online help facility with access to the helpdesk administrator, a calendar for scheduling, a customization utility for specific preferences such as, the change of language, a requirements analyzer tool for suggesting new requirements, and external links to online databases and related material. In figure 3 a screenshot of the e-Learning platform is presented.

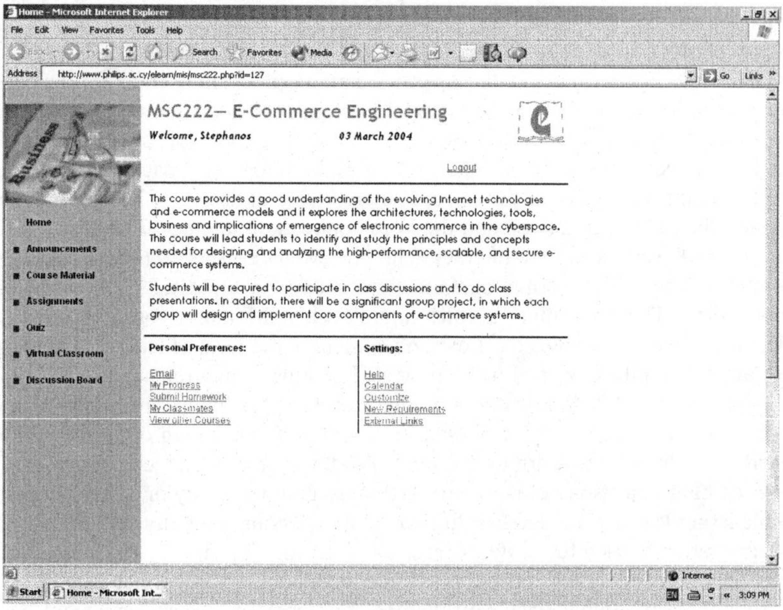

Figure 3: The E-Learning Platform based on Mentor

6. Results

The e-Learning platform developed using the e-MATHISI methodology was implemented in the academic environment. The aim was to help students to interact with instructors and other students and offer an efficient self-educational environment. The platform is fully functional offering four different courses to 92 students. Using the e-MATHISI methodology for the development we identified the key human, social, cultural factors and the pedagogy requirements. The available technology infrastructure was assessed and used to identify the key quality components. Once the key requirements were identified they were incorporated into the development process. An initial student evaluation showed that our methodology successfully captured the students and instructors needs and requirements.

7. Business Benefits

Equally effective systems can be developed for business utilizing the proposed e-MATHISI methodology. The particular business training requirements will be met since they will be identified in the analysis phase. Vocational training has different pedagogy requirements and these are identified in the analysis phase and incorporated in the development phase.

8. Conclusions

E-Learning systems offer several advantages to both academics and students such as, accessibility, mobility, collaboration, and the opening of the educational process for continuous and lifelong learning but mainly for the Anglo-Saxon educational environment. In addition, transferring the dynamic nature of learning to the new e-Learning environment, maintaining student individuality and differentiation according to personal preferences and abilities, as well as motivating and inspiring students are challenges that need to be met.

Revealing human, social, and cultural factors, addressing the quality components and their respective sub-components and examining pedagogy requirements are critical issues to be considered in the e-Learning development process. In this paper, we proposed a methodology called e-MATHISI that takes these issues into consideration when to develop quality e-Learning environments. This is demonstrated by development of an e-Learning environment. Currently, we are in the process of a detailed evaluation of the system by the students and the results will be analyzed for further enhancement of the system.

References

[1] A. S. Andreou, Promoting Software Quality Through a Human, Social and Organisational Requirements Elicitation Process. In: Requirements Engineering Journal vol. 8, No. 2, 2003, pp. 85-101.

[2] R. S. Pressman, Software engineering: A practitioner's approach, McGraw-Hill, London, 2000.

[3] A. S. Andreou, S. M. Mavromoustakos, and C. N. Schizas, Enhancing the Analysis Phase of E-Commerce Systems Development with Human, Social, Cultural and Organizational Factors. In: 2nd International Interdisciplinary Conference on Electronic Commerce ECOM-02, Gdansk, Poland, November 13-15, 2002.

[4] International Standards Organization, IEC 9126-1, Software Engineering – Product Quality – Part 1: Quality model, 2001.

[5] L. Olsina, D. Godoy, G. Lafuente, and G. Rossi, Specifying Quality Characteristics and Attributes for Websites. In: Proceedings ICSE'99 Web Engineering Workshop, Los Angeles, USA, 1999.

[6] K. Norton, Applying Cross Functional Evolutionary Methodologies to Web Development. In: Proceedings of the First ICSE Workshop on Web Engineering, ACM, 1999.

[7] M. D. Lytras, G. I. Doukidis, and T. N. Skagou, Value Dimension of the E-Learning Concept: Components and Metrics. In: Proceedings of the 20th ICDE World Conference on Open Learning and Distance Education, 2001.

[8] M. D. Lytras and A. Pouloudi, E-learning: Just a waste of time. In: Proceedings of the Seventh Americas Conference on Information Systems, (AMCIS 2001), Boston, Massachusetts, USA, August 3-5, 2001, pp. 216-222.

Development and Implementation of a Collaborative Environment for Education

Ignacio RIVILLA[1], Manuel CASTRO[1], Miguel ARJONA[2], Mar GONZÁLEZ[2], Juan PEIRE[1]
[1]*UNED, Juan del Rosal, 12, Madrid, 28040, Spain*
Tel: + 34 913 986 476, Fax: +34 913 986 028, Email: Manuel.Castro@ieec.uned.es
[2]*Altran SdB, Ramirez de Arellano, 15, 6th floor, Madrid, 28043, Spain*
Tel: +34 917 440 517, Fax: +34 914 152 457, Email: kiko@altransdb.com

Abstract: The application of new technologies to the distance education involves new problems that require new and innovative solutions from both pedagogical and technological points of view. The Ped-Care project has developed a new pedagogical methodology that improves and optimises the relationships between learners and teachers, by means of a more efficient use of new technology. This new methodology is called Learners Relationship Management (LRM) and it proposes new management methods for distributed groups of students, and new technologies and tools to facilitate the management of distance courses.

1. Introduction

Nowadays, teachers and education managers have numerous technologies available, at both infrastructure and application level, allowing them to support groups of students who are not physically present. The same systems that facilitate teacher-student communication provoke excessive demand on teachers. The usage of these technologies involves new problems that require new and innovative solutions from both pedagogical and technological points of view. Problems become more serious in the case of non-regulated education, since the degree of isolation of all agents is much higher than that of regulated education. Additionally, this impossibility of maintaining the personal communication flows between the group members makes it impossible to achieve an appropriate level of monitoring of the students by the teacher. Ped-Care proposes the application of a new pedagogical methodology that improves and optimises the relationships between learners and teachers, by means of a more efficient use of new technology.

The main result of the Ped-Care project, [8], is a new methodology called Learners Relationship Management (LRM). The LRM proposes new management methods for distributed groups of students and associated new technologies and tools. LRM has implemented intelligent tools based on an open and modular architecture that enables integration with most of the commercially available Learning Management Systems offering new and complementary services that will remedy significant needs.

2. Objectives

Certain needs arise from analysis of the current scenario in distance learning environments:

- To introduce a work method that revitalises current pedagogical techniques, adapting them to the technological platforms used and corrects deficiencies that said techniques contain due to the different time schedules and locations of teachers and students.
- To improve the communication processes between students and teachers and management of the relationship with students (pedagogical CRM, Learner/Student Relationship Management) through optimised processes. These may include e-mail

management and other communication tools using intelligent managers able to classify, re-address or answer them automatically, using semantic and syntactic analysis,.

- To improve the monitoring of students' activities during the course and evaluating them (surveys, exams, information on connections, access to the documentation, chats, etc.).
- To alleviate the disadvantages caused by the range of new mobile and customised services on offer through simple interfaces to the students. These accesses facilitate their connection with the group and teacher at any point and moment, increasing the information flow and the need to provide an answer to these flows.

3. Methodology

Ped-care started in June 2001 and ended in May 2003 [4][5], and its use and evaluation continues today. The work plan was divided into different phases, following a methodology called "Develop through incremental prototypes". The result of these development phases was a prototype on which the final users have tested in two experimentation phases.

The process followed during the two years of work within Ped-Care project, [3], to validate the proposed LRM methodology can be summarised in the following steps:

1. Study of the existent technological and pedagogical scenarios and their deficiencies from a technological and a pedagogical point of view (User Requirements).
2. Definition of a new pedagogical methodology able to solve these pedagogical detected deficiencies (LRM methodology, first draft).
3. Creation of tools to solve technological deficiencies supporting LRM in those areas that are not actually covered by the existing e-learning platforms (Ped-Care 1st prototype).
4. Application of the LRM methodology in education scenarios of end-user organisations participating in the Ped-Care project. Seven pilot courses were selected for this initial experiments involving real users –students and teachers– (1st experimentation phase).
5. From this first experimentation phase, several conclusions were extracted regarding the use of the new tools and the applied working method as well as suggestion for improving them (1st prototype experimentation report). Also, data about learning activities have been collected (use of communication channels, interaction with the platform and the teachers, use of mobile devices, etc.).
6. Optimisation of developed tools in the Second Prototype (incorporating new functionality when required) and refinement of LRM methodology (LRM second draft).
7. Planning and development of the second phase of experiments applying the updated LRM methodology and new tools to the same pilot courses (where possible) or similar ones, to compare experimentation data of the second phase with the collected in the first one and with the information with previous edition of the same courses.
8. Extraction of final conclusions from this second experimentation phase regarding the use of the LRM methodology and the new tools.
9. Validation of the LRM methodology in case these experiments provide expected results.

4. Developments

The Ped-Care project has developed intelligent tools, [1], [2], based on an open and modular architecture that enables integration with most of the commercially available Learning Management Systems offering new and complementary services that will remedy significant needs. The tools developed in the Ped-Care project are:

- IeMM (Intelligent e-Mail Manager): an Intelligent Agent, which captures questions addressed to teachers and, in most cases, can automatically answer them. The messages are received through different mediums (e.g. SMS, e-mail) and their content analysed in real time using Artificial Intelligent Semantic Analysis techniques to determine which ones are related to administrative or bureaucratic matters to be filtered and answered without the teacher contribution. With the IeMM tool, teachers will only receive those learner's questions that really require their special knowledge about the educational contents, avoiding the need of answering questions such as "When the courses begin?" or "How can I access the course contents?" which are often a waste of time.

- PCM (Personalise Content Manager): PCM facilitates the Internet access to learning contents, both to teachers and learners. It offers advanced searching services, based on metadata technologies, to select the most suitable documents that complement course's contents. That tool personalises the searched results depending on the learners' characteristics and behaviour using CRM techniques. Teachers can also use PCM to propose to students new learning contents that complete the course documentation.
- PPEM (Pedagogical Pursuit and Evaluation Manager): PPEM provides to teachers detailed information about the learners activity on each course (web accesses, sent questions, learning contents searches, use of the technology, etc.) allowing a continuous monitoring of their activity, their interests and their evolution in the courses. In this way, PPEM gives teachers the possibility of improving the learner's evaluation process based on the obtained qualifications, exercises and practical works and on the learner's behaviour (pro-activity, interest, motivation, progresses, etc.).
- IPSM (Intelligent Pedagogical Segmentation Manager): allows automatic classification of learners on different segments based on specific pedagogical criteria. This allows teachers to define different tasks or actions for each target group. For this segmentation it is necessary to use intelligent managers capable of gathering the maximum amount of data about students and their educational activities. Data currently being undervalued or less used should then make up an essential part of the segmentation system: the degree of involvement in face-to-face or deferred sessions, quantity and quality of the information access, e-mails received, forum participation, chats, news, etc.
- IPAM (Intelligent Pedagogical Action Manager): Its main functionality is to guide the requests and answers between the other components. Basically, when a service request arrives to the IPAM, it decides which will be the component (IPSM, IeMM, PCM or PPEM) that will answer the request made.

5. Technology Description

Ped-Care is based in a distributed architecture model with three different servers located in Spain (IeMM, IPSM, IPAM, SMS Centre), France (PCM) and Greece (PPEM). They are interconnected using Web Services and the SOAP protocol through Internet connections.

There are also, other external connections from those servers:

- PPEM server periodically connects to each end-users' Virtual Campus (UNED, Skeria, ACME and Fundación Directa) to import data regarding Learning Contents and Learners' Profiles. It uses the OAI metadata exchange protocol and the OAI Data providers developed and installed in each end-users' LMS. It's important to remark that PPEM got information from the Virtual Campus but it never updated it. Therefore, the additional information capture from Learners' activities was stored in intermediary databases accessible by the other components through the PPEM Web Services.
- PCM is able to connect to external Databases for searching LOM contents and also any kind of Metadata through the OAI protocol. On one hand, an agreement with Ariadne Foundation was reached having Ped-Care the possibility of accessing their LOM repository using Web Services (Ped-Care is the first external system that uses this service). On the other, the use of the OAI protocol lets PCM to access a wide range of external repositories compatible with OAI protocol. This new possibility offers PCM search facilities direct access to thousands of contents.

Altran SDB hosts the IPAM, IeMM and IPSM servers in Spain, with Data Providers (interfaces between LMS and Ped-Care system) to UNED, FD and Skeria's LMS (located in Spain and Sweden). Silogic in France locates the PCM server (including access to Ariadne Foundation "Knowledge Pool System" in Belgium). 01P locates the PPEM server and data provider to the ACME's LMS in Greece. (Ped-Care architecture Figure 1)

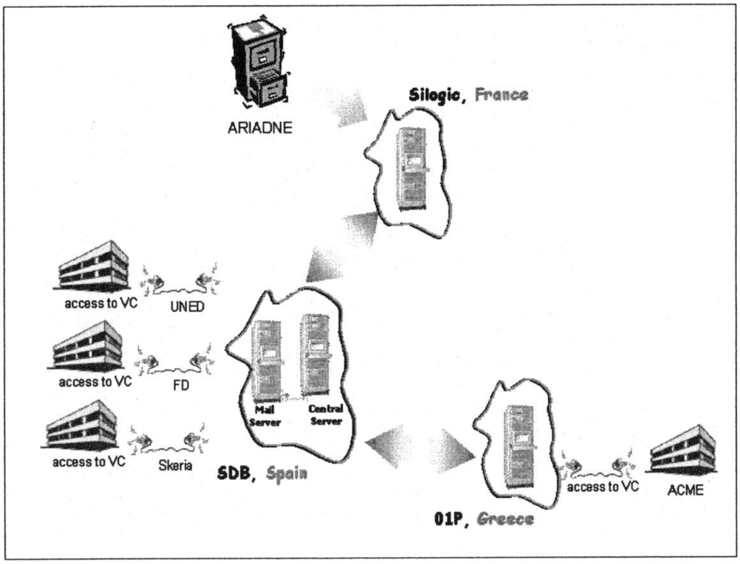

Figure 1: Ped-care Architecture Model

Combining Internet (HTTP for Web, POP3 and SMTP for e-mail), Mobile (WAP and SMS), metadata exchange (OAI) protocols and e-learning standards (LOM and LIP) allow us to create an effective distributed system over four countries (Spain, France, Greece and Sweden). In next future, the use of SCORM or IMS LD will give even more possibilities.

6. Results

Ped-Care project has introduced a work method that revitalises current pedagogical techniques, adapting them to the technological platforms used and correcting the deficiencies of said techniques due to the different time schedules and locations of teachers and students. Ped-Care has improved the communication processes between students and teachers and the management of the relationship with the learners (pedagogical CRM, Learner/Student Relationship Management) by introducing optimised processes. These processes have included e-mail management and other communication tools by means of intelligent managers able to classify, forward or automatically answer messages that are addressed daily to teachers.

Communication management tools based on semantic analysis techniques have demonstrated their suitability to relieve teachers from some of the work consequence of the high numbers of questions received in specific dates of the course (at the beginning, at the end or before the delivery of practices or exams). However, and especially in the case of questions received by e-mail, combination of syntax analysis techniques with semantic ones has to be explored in order to be able to manage complex messages including several questions and comments. Also, the analysis of received questions shows that their nature varies following the main course milestones being possible to anticipate most of them taking into account similar situations from previous editions of the same course or from other with similar subjects thus improving the algorithms effectiveness. In this sense, studying historical information make also possible to optimise the resource assignment management in the education centre anticipating the existence of specific periods for each course when a high number of request of information is expected.

Regarding the use of metadata searches in education (based on new e-learning standards as LOM) they have shown a great potential in our experiments specially for promoting the learning through discovering in the group. However, not enough of such kinds of repositories are available on the net. In our experiments we have offers different scientific repositories based on the OAI protocol with a good acceptation. Actually, we are also working trying to connect Ped-Care tools with other repositories as the Ariadne one using Web Services for doing the searches. Unfortunately, these services are not just available (we have made some tests but they are not stable). However, once the Semantic Web became a reality this kind of tools will make education to go a step forward always considering the necessity of providing learning contents in native students language.

Methodology and tools have also contributed to improve the process of monitoring students' activities during the course and evaluating them in the learning process being accessible through a wide range of mobile devices offering intuitive interfaces. In leaner-centred scenarios the learner teachers do not have too much information about students, so advanced monitoring tools based on segmentation techniques are of special importance. Moreover, segmentation have been developed without taking into account socio-economic or demographic indicators assuring in this way that no one will be excluded from education due to economic, cultural, ethnic or gender factors.

Another important advantage of these techniques is the ability to develop corrective actions when education gaps are detected and monitoring their effects in the learning process. In this way, information about the most effective corrective actions from previous editions of the course can provide confidence about their possible repercussion in the current one. Segmentation techniques will show their real potential when it will be possible to analyse historical data from previous editions of a course. From this information, it will be possible to detect from the beginning fails in the pedagogical approach that could provoke low motivation from learners. Successful corrective actions from previous years can be applied again with a reasonable estimation of their impact on the learning process.

The use of mobile devices and associated services is punctual in education due to economic and technical factors (GSM phones are cheap but have poor connection times and capabilities, GPRS phones offer better connection times and band-width but still having poor interfaces and a considerable cost). Only the use of next generation mobile devices as PDAs with integrated mobile phones features have proved their suitability for e-learning and have been welcomed by users. However, their cost is actually too high so their degree of penetration in the market is actually very low. Their effects in distance education will only appear once their use will be extended.

7. Business Benefits

The LRM methodology can be exploited by offering consultant services to customers interested in improving or revitalising current or planned learning processes. The implementation of the methodology in customer's organisations can be completed with developed tools. The heterogeneous target groups that tested the methodology ensure its suitability to a wide range of learning scenarios and a wide range of potential clients. Possible applications are for organisations that want to improve relationships with their learners and for those that want to improve their evaluation methods of students' progress or courses quality. Potential clients are large enterprises Human Resources Departments, education centres (private or public universities) and public administration.

It offers advanced added-value services to existing e-learning platforms. Potential clients are organisations with authoring Virtual Campus and e-learning providers taking advantage of the added value services to: improve management of communication channels with students, improve monitoring of students activities in the learning and evaluation process, or offering personalised learning contents and searchers. The independence of the tools from specific technologies ensures they will cover this potential market.

Ped-Care toolkit can also be offered to other business segments. CRM Systems, Knowledge Management Systems, Call and Data Centers, eBusiness portals would be benefit from some of PedCare developments as IeMM, PCM or IPSM. Semantic analysis and segmentation techniques are also useful for offering help-desk services in corporative Web Portals (Intranet or Extranet) of organisations interesting on improving their customer/employed services or on exploiting the available information from them. The Ped-Care tools combined together can be useful for companies when they comes to manage and take advantage of information that already exists. For example, the Ped-Care knowledge database can be configured to contain information about earlier projects and solutions to specific problems or to help newly employed people to be integrated in the organisation. IeMM and PCM would be used for answering questions about these new issues or for searching for personalised solutions to concrete problems just solved by other experts. The answer or the solutions can be tailored regarding the specific segment the user belongs (e.g. administrative staff can get different answer than engineers) Different access possibilities through mobile devices and multilingual services also give competitive advantages.

8. Conclusions

In traditional methodologies learner satisfaction was equivalent to accreditation (explicit motivation). Nowadays, it is necessary to ensure that the students are satisfied with the course and the education process itself. Ped-Care has not ever pretended to change those methodologies but adapting existing ones with innovative ideas based on CRM techniques as: personalisation of contents, use of advanced tracking and monitoring of students activities, segmentation of learners depending on available information, marketing actions to make feel the student part of the Educational Institution, etc. In LRM, personal treatment, motivation (attention, relevance, confidence, social and culture motivation), proactivity (participation, self-direction, leadership and responsibility), interactivity (communities construction, communication channels) and monitoring (segmentation, course tracking) are key issues to ensure the learner satisfaction.

The analysis of the use of the communication channels has demonstrated the correlation between the students interaction with the e-learning platform, the teacher, and the different learning activities planed during the course. The experiments, addressed to heterogeneous target groups with different culture, motivation, skill, preferences and relationship with the technology, have offered different values for these indicators in the different scenarios being, for example, more pro-active post-graduate students than industry workers.

The experiments have also contributed to highlight the importance of the application of an effective methodology in distance education. The course schedule including different activities for promoting the participation of the students in the e-learning process and corrective actions anticipating possible fails in the evolution of specific indicators is essential for the success of the course. Within them we can mention proposals for the participation in external events as conferences -or videoconferences- and practices based on discovering of new contents. Group Communication tools, as marketing campaigns management systems (including SMS support), are useful in this issue.

Finally, the application of the LRM methodology in education is based on the application of CRM techniques in which economic factors have been replaced by pedagogical indicators. However, we do not discard the combination of both kinds of indicators in the real world. We believe that the actual tendency of considering education centres more and more as a business in which customer satisfaction have to drive all the organisation processes will continue in the future. Therefore, economic indicators as enrolment, growth or profits cannot be discarded. Probably, LRM will act in this new scenario as a mechanism to ensure that the application of CRM strategies in education will not provoke exclusion of disadvantage or minority groups.

Acknowledgements

Ped-Care (Pedagogical Distributed Group Care) is a RTD project co-funded by the European Commission's IST Programme inside the Fifth Framework Programme. Ten partners form five European countries constitute the Ped-Care consortium: Altran SDB, [6], UNED, [7], Amena and Fundación Directa from Spain, Silogic from France, Qualital from Italy, 01 Pliroforiki and ACME from Greece, and ViewRope and Skeria from Sweden.

References

[1] M. Arjona et al, *"New Pedagogical Tools for Mobile Learning Groups"* IST MOBILE, Sitges (Spain), 2001.

[2] M. Arjona et al, *"Knowledge for Management Methodologies for a Global Distributed Organization"* 6th INTERNATIONAL ITF WORKSHOP & BUSINESS CONFERENCE. Amsterdam (Holland), 2001.

[3] M.Arjona, I. Fernández, M. González and E. Guardo, *"Information Systems for Pedagogical Distributed Group Care"* IST,. Teheran (Iran), 2001

[4] I. Rivilla, M. Castro, M. Arjona, M.González and J.Peire, *"Proyecto PedCare - Atención Personalizada al Alumno (Pedagogical Distributed Groups Care)"*, IV CONFERENCIA INTERNACIONAL SOBRE EDUCACIÓN, FORMACIÓN Y NUEVAS TECNOLOGÍAS (VIRTUAL EDUCA 2003), Miami, Florida (U.S.), 2003.

[5] I. Rivilla, M. Castro, M. Arjona, M. González and J. Peire, *"Experiencias del Proyecto PedCare - Atención personalizada al alumno (Pedagogical Distributed Groups Care)"* X ENCUENTRO IBEROAMERICANO DE EDUCACIÓN A DISTANCIA (AIESAD)., Costa Rica., 2003.

[6] www.altransdb.com

[7] www.ieec.uned.es

[8] www.pedcare.nu

ORGANIC - Continuous Organisational Learning in Innovation and Companies

Richard MESSNARZ[1], Romana Vajde HORVAT[2], Katja HAREJ[2], Eva FEUER[3]
[1]*ISCN GesmbH, Schieszstattgasse 4, A-8010 Graz, Austria*
Tel: +43 316 811198, Fax: + 43 316 811312, Email: rmess@iscn.com
[2]*CIT, Gosposvetska cesta 84, 2000 Maribor, Slovenia*
Tel: +386 2 228 2351, Fax: +386 2 35 5134, Email: cit@cit.si
[3]*MTA SZTAKI, Kende U. 13-17, H-1111 Budapest, Hungary*
Tel: + 36 1 279 6285, Fax: +36 1 279 5269, Email: eva.feuer@sztaki.hu

Abstract: This paper discusses different studies about innovation management, which have been performed between 1996 and 2003, and describes key success factors of innovative organisations. These factors are taken into account for the design of an innovation manager skill card in the EU Leonardo project ORGANIC (2003 – 2006, www.innovationmanager.org). The project results in a skills card, an online skills portal (MM 1032 project CREDIT, 1998 – 2001) which European managers can access to self assess their current skills and receive guidance about individual skills gaps in that area, and a trainer CD so that trainers can hold courses in the foreseen skills units. Recently a further complementary project SOQRATES EPI (Educational Partnerships in ICT) started which integrates the skills portal system with a set of large e-learning portals in different countries. This will allow that after receiving a learning portfolio automatically online courses can be entered.

1. Job Roles and Skills Cards in Innovation Management

Today there are many different innovation process models available which look at different process factors. Roles like process promoter, innovation champion, innovation team leaders, top managers are discussed and certain process steps are recommended. However, in reality the way innovation management works is dependent on the existing nature of business, the existing team and innovation structures, the skills and motivation of staff to deal with new requirements, etc. Copying a ready to use innovation management model to achieve innovation does not work, it requires rather the skills of an experienced innovation manager who can transfer the different models and (mostly university based and theoretical publications) concepts to his/her practical working environment.

This project focuses on the practical field studies from industry and does not try to create another theoretical process model. The project rather tries to analyse and identify the specific skills inside firms that made these firms market winners and innovative, and include these skills in an overall skill card against which innovation managers across Europe can assess their current skills online.

A skills definition concept (skill card) is an approach where by using standards (NVQ - National Vocational Qualification Standards) a common sense is created among different countries and institutions (as a collection of good practices and required skills) and illustrated in a standard skills description structure.

This will allow a benchmarking of required skills against a European proposed skills set and the establishment of learning portfolios to upgrade the skills of nowadays innovation managers to a higher efficiency. A description of some typical user scenarios is provided at the end of this paper.

2. Underlying Innovation Management Studies

The skills incorporated into the skills card have been derived from three large European studies, which analysed key competencies of market winning and innovative firms.

2.1 Best Regional Innovation Transfer Study

A study in 1998 (EU Leonardo da Vinci Project BESTREGIT – Best Regional Innovation Transfer, 1996 – 1999) analysed how innovative organisations operate and compared 200 organisations in Europe ([1], [5],[7]).
The study outlined that innovative organisations

- invest time and money in understanding of the fundamentals of the forces of change,
- understand the different cultures through personal contacts using personal networking,
- study trends and they are always up-to-date,
- concentrate their energy in areas where they excel or where no one else can operate,
- outsource all other non-core activities,
- are practical users of information technologies (IT) and have IT strategies in place .

This study illustrates the development in the mid 90s where organisations became more networked, the market became more global [10], and the learning and innovation is largely influenced by a networked learning society.

2.2 Team-Working and Team-Learning Study

In a project TEAMWORK ([5], [6]) with 13 partners from 7 countries (IST-2000-28162 TEAMWORK, 2001 - 2003) a generic platform has been developed that shall support these networked team-working and team-learning and tested this platform with teams from 59 organisations in 13 countries of Europe. The working behaviour of the users (team-working and team-learning members of the networked platform) has been analysed and a study with key success factors for social team-learning and team-working has been produced as a project deliverable. There were 42 different projects running through the system using the defined environment and managed by a virtual team leader. The team size of each project varied between 13 and down to 2 different organisations involved.

This study based on the situation at the end of the 90s where developments were carried out by a supply chain or a partnership of different companies integrating joint solutions. And these networked teams were multinational, multicultural, and consisted of members of different organisations. So the question was "How to manage the complexity of the distributed, multinational team-working and team-learning partnerships?".

The social experts team in the TEAMWORK project applied the social patterns analysis methodology [4] and also performed a set of interviews which were analysed to draw a number of conclusions concerning the social factors influencing team-working. This methodology analyses and selects typical patterns of behaviour. Some selected results of the 2003 study about organisations are presented below:

2.2.1 Management Style Related

- It was significant that people from universities, public service, and research centres were happy with the more democratic distributed team management and team learning style of a TEAMWORK environment. People from large enterprises were less happy.

- There was a significant difference between how managers from large enterprises and people from university, public service, and research centres responded to the ability of such a tool to enhance teamwork spirit. The former felt it reduced their influence.

The difference between research and large traditional companies was due to the fact that when involving a large organisation in a team it is necessary to define your agreed team-working processes and integrate existing hierarchies in the collaborating large organisation.

2.2.2 Innovation Related

- It was significant that people from university, public service, and research centres believed that a TEAMWORK environment encouraged an innovative approach to solving problems together, and creating new ideas together, people from traditional large enterprises believe it might interfere with existing procedures.
- It was significant that people from university, public service, and research centres believed that e-working helped them to improve the understanding of team roles.

It was an observation that larger organisations want to have more impact and decision power on projects and innovations, while the distributed team-working concepts (role based) only gave them equal weight among all team members (independent from their size).

Some selected results of the 2003 study about individuals were:

- Community of Trust - "If you are building a human networked organisation you must have a foundation of trust and respect for effective communication at levels deep enough to sustain growth."
- Work-Flows Inward – "If you want information to flow to the innovative producing roles in an organisation then put the developer at the centre and see that information flows toward the centre, not from the centre."

This means that innovation is carried out by a selected set of highly intelligent people (producers) who should not be hindered by hierarchies above them but become a central role in a networked organisation, to unleash the innovation power. The study produced some 200 criteria and proposed a list of 17 criteria to be considered by managers [3][6].

2.3 Innovation Management Study

While these first two studies were carried out with involvement of research centres, SMEs and to some extent by large companies, the third study was performed at 124 multinational companies and largely represents the viewpoint on innovation by large co-operations [8].

Large co-operations had the following expectations from learning organisations:

- Learn faster than competitors
- Balance teamwork with personal performance
- Reward high performers
- Develop ambidextrous thinking
- Transformational rather than incremental change
- Create and exploit new knowledge
- Ensure customer & company-wide diffusion of ideas
- Inherently entrepreneurial with a high risk tolerance

The favourite approach to implement innovation in a large corporation were

- Pilot programme with review 30%
- Company wide process with review 18%
- Systematic implementation 15%
- Project by project 14%
- Area specific 9%

- Benchmarking with competitors 5%
- Don't know 9%

And the drivers that influenced the success of an innovation were

- Executive management commitment 26%
- Supportive organisational structure 17%
- Positive culture with global reach 15%
- Young technically literate employees 13%
- Realistic milestones - fewer layers 6%
- Don't know 13%

The overall model for implementation of an innovation management programme contained seven phases:

1. Understanding learning antecedents (nature of business, anthropomorphism, dissatisfaction with traditional paradigm, customer oriented culture, intellectual capital)
2. Creating an environment of innovation
3. Analysing the perceived need and the required learning mechanisms
4. Executive challenge and implementing a learning processes
5. Including cultural and human factors and joint mission building
6. Organisational wide learning
7. Sustaining a learning organisation

In the first phase a number of parameters appeared which seemed to deal with factors that influenced the difference in opinion between large organisations and SMEs, research centres and universities in the study mentioned in section 2.2 of this paper.

A large co-operation focuses on the protection of the intellectual capital and global business opportunities and thus a networked learning and working across organisations needs additional controlling parameters to ensure the commitment from top managers. And as we see in the study the top managers by 26% have the largest influence on the success of an innovation in a large co-operation. (compare with results in section 2.2).

3. A Skills Card and Skills Portal for the Innovation Manager Role

The job role of an innovation manager (see Figures 2, 3) therefore is a specific position in an organisation who understands all these factors: networking, learning, organisational and social factors and is able to encourage, promote, manage, control, and disseminate innovation strategies in an organisation.

ORGANIC, the EU Leonardo da Vinci project followed the EU standards for skills cards [2] (see Figure 1) when structuring a skills set.

A **Domain**, contains
    Job Roles, which contain
        Units, which contain
            Elements, which contain
                Performance Criteria, which must be proven by
                    Evidences.

Figure 1: Basic elements of the skills definition model

In ORGANIC we identified 6 skills units and 24 learning elements for an innovation manager. These skills are available for online browsing and skills self-assessment.

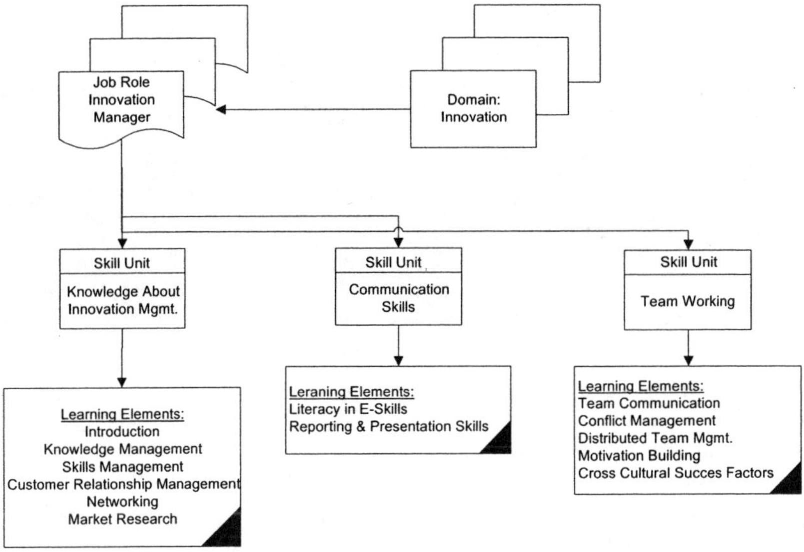

Figure 2: Skills Card of an Innovation Manager Job Role Part 1

Domain: An occupational category, e.g. childcare, first level management, engineering.

Job Role: A certain profession that covers part of the domain knowledge, e.g., domain = automotive, job role = automotive SW project leader

Unit (UK standards): A list of certain activities that must be carried out in the workplace. It is the top-level skill in the UK qualification standard hierarchy [9] and each unit consists of a number of elements.

Element (UK standards): Description of one distinct aspect of the work performed by a worker, either a specific task that the worker has to do or a specific way of working. Each element consists of a number of performance criteria.

Performance criterion (UK standards): Description of the minimum level of performance a participant must demonstrate in order to be assessed as competent. A performance criterion may have different relevant contexts.

Evidence: Proof of competence.

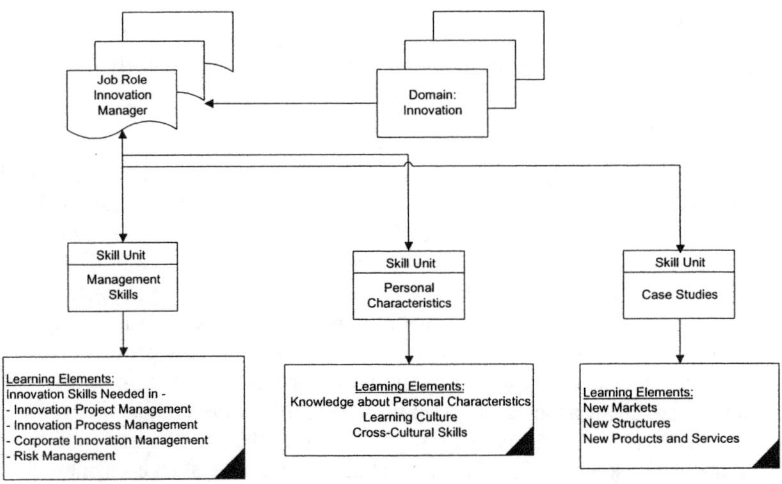

Figure 3: Skills Card of an Innovation Manager Job Role Part 2

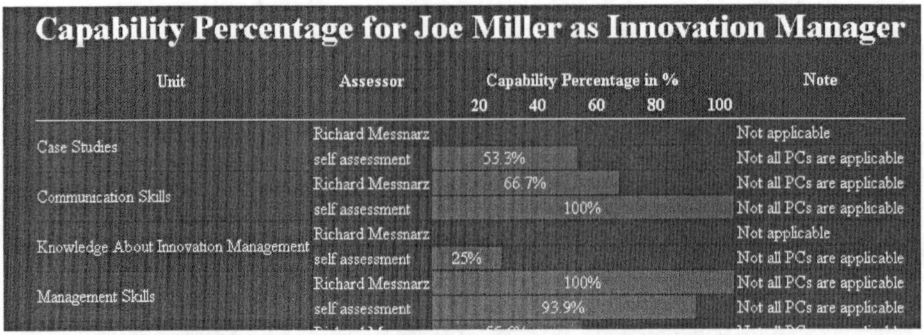

Figure 4: Sample Self-Assessment and Formal Assessor Profile

For each learning element ORGANIC develops a training module covering all relevant performance criteria listed in the skills card. A skills portal has been configured with the skills card and supports browsing required skills (Figure 5), self-assessment, formal assessment, evidence collection, skills profiles generation (Figure 4) and recommendations.

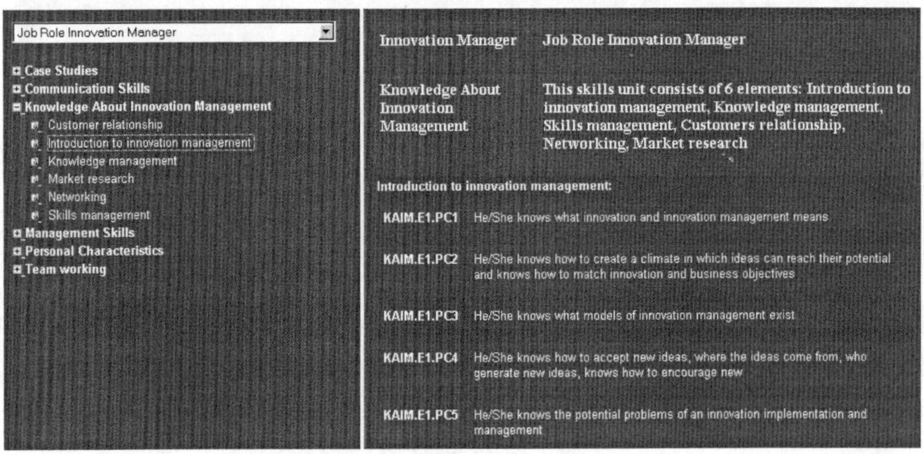

Figure 5: Online Skills Requirements Browsing

4. Typical Usage Scenarios

A skill card can be used to accredit training providers as well as to certify people.

4.1 Accreditation Scenario Examples

For the job role (skill card) certified software tester, for instance, represented by ISQI (International Software Quality Institute in Bavaria) and the Austrian Testing Board (ATB) for central Europe, accreditation is offered. Certificates have been issued since 2003.

Concerning e-commerce related job roles, two projects plan to merge their interest to offer 4 job roles, such as e-commerce engineer, e-business manager, e-strategy manager and an e-marketing manager. This way institutions from Hungary, Austria, Spain, Ireland, Germany, and Czech share the same content / skill criteria for these professions.

Through the skill card participating universities have used it to refine their study programmes to cover all aspects of the skill card and become comparable on a European level. In some cases, e.g. University of Valladolid, the development of a skill card influenced the establishment of a whole new study programme of an e-business manager.

For the certified innovation manager a similar approach is expected. The project will include a critical mass of training providers, and educational institutions and to establish a standard against which the training of an innovation manager will be benchmarked.

4.2 Learning Scenario Examples – Learning from the Work Place

While universities create study programmes focused on 4 to 5 year long learning schemes where students learn all skills related with general skill domains, industry must focus and tailor much towards specific skills sets and job roles (software architect, tester, etc.). And learning must become possible from the work place to upgrade skills for specific job roles.

The service portal of the ORGANIC project will allow managers to access the server online, browse the required skills, do a self assessment, print an individual (confidential) skills profile and receive a generated learning plan / portfolio.

4.3 Service Delivery Scenario – Virtual Competence Centers

In July 2004 for instance, a selected group of managers from China visited Europe and 20 managers attend the certified e-business manager course. This collaboration could be extended by offering accreditation between Europe and China through an e-portal with skills assessment and online course attendance. On completion of the SOQRATES project EPI this will be possible due to integration of the skills portal with e-learning systems.

Acknowledgements

We acknowledge the support for this paper from ORGANIC project partners [D. Ekert (ISCN), B. Wöran (Danube), K. Ennsfellner (IMC Krems), A. Gvishiani (EDNES), N. O'Shea (Tecnet), G. Velasco (FGUVA)] and EPI project partners [Miklos Biro (BUESPA) and Gearoid O Suilleabhain and Ray Coughlan (CIT-IRL)].

References

[1] M. Biro, R. Messnarz, A. Davison (2002) The Impact of National Cultures on the Effectiveness of Improvement methods - The Third Dimension, in Software Quality Professional, Volume Four, Issue Four, American Society for Quality, Sep-tember 2002

[2] Feuer E., Messnarz R., Best Practices in E-Commerce: Strategies, Skills, and Processes, in: Proceedings of the E2002 Conference, E-Business and E-Work, Novel solutions for a global networked economy, eds. Brian Stanford Smith, Enrica Chiozza, IOS Press, Amsterdam, Berlin, Oxford, Tokyo, Washington, 2002

[3] Feuer E., Messnarz R., Wittenbrink H., Experiences With Managing Social Patterns in Defined Distributed Working Processes, in: Proceedings of the EuroSPI 2003 Conference, 10-12 December 2003, FTI Verlag, ISBN 3-901351-84-1

[4] Project EASYCOMP (IST Project 1999-14191, homepage: http://www.easycomp.org/)

[5] Messnarz R., Stubenrauch R., Melcher M., Bernhard R., Network Based Quality Assurance, in: Proceedings of the 6th European Conference on Quality Assurance, 10-12 April 1999, Vienna , Austria

[6] Messnarz R., Nadasi G., O'Leary E., Foley B., Experience with Teamwork in Distributed Work Environments, in: Proceedings of the E2001 Conference, E-Work and E-commerce, Novel solutions for a global networked economy, eds. Brian Stanford Smith, Enrica Chiozza, IOS Press, Amsterdam, Berlin, Oxford, Tokyo, Wash-ington, 2001

[7] A Learning Organisation Approach for Process Improvement in the Service Sector, R. Messnarz. C. Stöckler, G. Velasco, G. O'Suilleabhain, A Learning Organisation Approach for Process Improvement in the Service Sector, in: Proceedings of the EuroSPI 1999 Conference, 25-27 October 1999, Pori, Finland

[8] O'Keeffe, T., & D. Harrington, 2001. Learning to Learn: An Examination of Organisational Learning in Selected Irish Multinationals. Journal of European Industrial Training, MCB University Press, Vol. 25: Number 2/3/4

[9] DTI - Department of Trade and Industry UK, British Standards for Occupational Qualification, National Vocational Qualification Standards and Levels

[10] Gemünden H.G., T. Ritter, Inter-organisational Relationships and Networks, Journal of Business Research, 2001

P. Cunningham and M. Cunningham (Eds.)
IOS Press, 2004

Future Educational Needs for Manufacturing Strategy

Asbjørn ROLSTADÅS[1], Bjørn MOSENG[2]
[1]*Norwegian University of Science and Technology, Department of Production and Quality Engineering, S.P. Andersens vei 5, Trondheim, NO-7491, Norway*
Tel: +47 73593785, Fax: +47 73597117, E-mail: asbjorn.rolstadas@ntnu.no
[2]*SINTEF Industrial Management, S.P. Andersens vei 5, Trondheim, NO-7465, Norway*
Tel: +47 73593797, Fax: + 47 73591299, E-mail: bjorn.moseng@sintef.no

Abstract: The main objective of the project Global Education in Manufacturing (GEM) is to develop a framework for a new curriculum in Manufacturing Strategy. The curriculum should fill the needs of the manufacturing industry. Therefore a survey of the needs of the manufacturing industry has been carried out using a questionnaire. A total of 556 responses from 22 countries were obtained. The competence needs is split on technological, humanistic and business competence. With respect to technological competence the survey shows a need for further education and training in clean products, intelligent manufacturing, simulation, cleaner production, sustainable manufacturing, enterprise modelling, extended enterprise design, extended enterprise operation, and end-of-life management. For humanistic competence the most pressing needs are within e-learning and multicultural skills and strategy. For business competence the major education and training needs are within e-commerce, benchmarking, and entrepreneurship.

1. Introduction

IMS (Intelligent Manufacturing Systems) is an international, industry driven research collaboration between Europe, North-America, Australia, Japan, and Korea. Its steering committee has discussed the need for education and training in the future manufacturing industry. It has come to the conclusion that existing curricula often tend to emphasise theory over process, and that basic education has not always met the needs of industry, producing graduates with often inadequate skills [4]. The committee argues that this necessitates a change in priorities and closer ties between industry and educational institutions. The curricula must reflect a mix between advanced manufacturing technology, economics and managerial topics, referred to as manufacturing strategy. To develop such specifications the Global Education in Manufacturing (GEM) project has been launched.

This paper describes the results of an industrial survey conducted to check what the perceived needs of the industry are concerning manufacturing strategy. The objective of this paper is to describe the results of the survey with main emphasis on digital business aspects. Universities will benefit from the results of this survey by being able to develop curricula that match the future needs of the manufacturing industry. The industry may benefit in a longer-term perspective by obtained human capital better trained to their needs.

The goal of the GEM project is to develop a framework for a new curriculum in Manufacturing Strategy [1, 2], based on modern pedagogic approaches to meet the training and educational requirements in extended enterprises [3, 4]. It will exploit e-learning.

The GEM project consists of five subprojects in Europe, Japan, USA, Australia, and Korea. In total there are 26 partners from 20 countries participating, and there are 75 industries associated with the project.

The GEM curriculum realizes that modern manufacturing business is global and requires e-work in order be competitive. The curriculum consists of a number of courses that fall within seven knowledge areas:

A. Development of extended products
B. Digital business along supply chain
C. End of life planning and operation
D. Business operation and competitive strategy
E. Intelligent manufacturing processes
F. Intelligent manufacturing systems design
G. Enterprise and product modelling and simulation

Course delivery will use multimedia technologies such as video, animations, games, text, etc. The curriculum should fill the needs of the manufacturing industry and to reflect the new way of work for this industry characterised by [5]:

- Working with digital tools for communication
- Working in a multicultural environment
- Working in interdisciplinary, multi-skill teams
- Sharing of work tasks on a global and around the clock basis
- Working in an virtual environment

Existing curricula in manufacturing do not sufficiently reflect these requirements. A survey of about 300 curricula around the world has documented this [6, 7]. In order to develop a curriculum responding to the needs of the industry, a survey amongst the manufacturing industry worldwide has been carried out [8].

2. Manufacturing Strategy Competence

The manufacturing industry is a key industry. The success of this industry is dependent on its ability to respond to accelerating pace of change in technology, short lead times, the need for "instantaneous" transformation of information to knowledge, business model changes resulting from outsourcing on a global scale, increasing customer expectations, constantly changing needs and market opportunities, and globalisation of markets and business competition. The manufacturing industry is one of the main drivers for industrial development [9] and how to develop and operate this industry is a key knowledge area for Europe. Challenging activities influencing competitiveness are connected to radical new way of operation (digital business) and to new products (extended products).

Competence needs for manufacturing was defined earlier. The US Society of Manufacturing Engineers (SME) has developed a skills taxonomy distinguishing between:

- Technological skills
- Humanistic skills
- Business skills

The SME must focus on traditional manufacturing and is not relevant for the GEM project. The skills taxonomy has been adopted as the basis for the GEM industrial survey. The competence needs have been split in three areas, then subdivided at a second level [8]:

- Technological competence
    - Product related topics
    - Production related topics
    - Business operation related topics
- Humanistic competence
    - Individual related topics
    - Company related topics
- Business competence
    - Business and economic related topics

- Management related topics

3. Methodology

The survey was undertaken in the manufacturing industry worldwide in order to get the industry's point of view on education for the development of an international curriculum. The design of the questionnaire is focused on measuring current needs and practices in the industry as well as getting an idea about future development.

556 companies from all regions have responded to the questionnaire (Europe 342, Japan 106, USA 14, Australia 7, and Korea 87). The European answers have come from 17 countries. In the analysis Europe has been divided into three sub-regions; North-Europe (95), East-Europe (188), and South-Europe (59).

The questionnaire consists of two parts. The first part covers general demographical information to be used as classification variables for the analysis.

The second part covers the seven competence areas (Example, figure 1). The companies are asked to rank the importance of the technological, humanistic, and business skills. Within each competence area they are asked to rate the importance of different pre-selected topics for their job performance today, within 5 years, and also rate the need for further education and training. The rating scale has six steps ranging from none to high importance.

PART 2:
MANUFACTURING STRATEGY COMPETENCIES

Manufacturing strategy is the purposeful management of change in manufacturing systems and operation towards the achievement of competitive advantage.

Instructions:
Please observe that there are no "absolute" answers to these questions. These questions are constructed to perceive your view, based on your personal background, when it comes to education and work-related experiences. If there are other important topics not mentioned in the list, please fill in the open fields.

1. TECHNOLOGICAL COMPETENCE

1.1. Product-related topics:	Rate the importance of competence for your job performance: Today (none <--> high)	In 5 years (none <--> high)	Rate the need for further education / training (none <--> high)
a. Product development in general			
b. Extended product development			
c. Simulation in product development			
d. Clean products			
e. Remanufacturable products			
f.			
g.			

Figure 1: Excerpt of Part 2 of the Questionnaire.

The companies are also asked to rate the importance of these topic groups for both their own company and for their industrial sector at large for today and in 5 years and also their needs for further education and training within the same groups.

The survey was accessible on the Internet to a contact person in each country. In addition a paper version was sent to the contact persons. The questionnaire was in some cases translated in order to meet language problems in different countries.

Based on the results demographic data has been presented and comparisons between importance of topics and the need for education have been done. Correlation analysis has carried out to find characteristics between regions, and between company size and importance of topics.

4. Results

From the demographic data the following respondents characteristics have been obtained:

- 50 % of the respondents have Technical background. Other main backgrounds are: CEO/admin 28 %, financial 17 %, and training 5 %.
- The majority of companies (29 %) belong to manufacturing and machinery industry. The remaining companies are representing 10 other branches (NACE classification).
- 45 % of the companies are a part of an international group.
- 47 % of the companies are SMEs (less than 250 employees), and large companies 35 % (more than 1000 employees).
- 53 % of the deliveries from the companies consist of physical products. Service, customer support, training, installation and other intelligent features cover 47 %.
- Communication with customers is still dominated by personal, paper based and telephone contacts. Only 9 % of the contact is performed by E-commerce techniques.

From part 2 of the questionnaire, the importance of each topic as well as the need for further training and education has been derived. Figures 2 – 4 show the results. In the diagrams the needs for each topic are sorted in descending order with respect to the importance of the competence today. The importance of competence today is given as black bars whereas the importance of further education and training is shown as light grey bars. The interesting findings are where the competence needs are low today, but where there is a large need for future education and training.

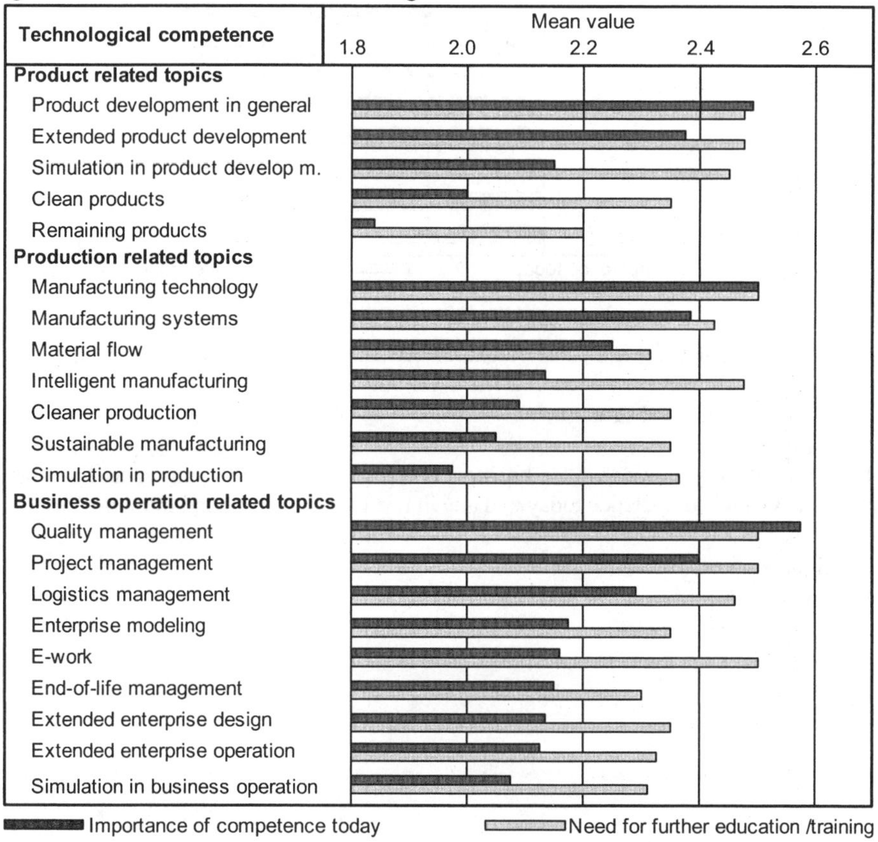

Figure 2 Industrial needs for technological competence.

Figure 2 shows that for technological competence, the following areas have been defined to have low competence today and a high need for education and training:

- Clean products
- Intelligent manufacturing
- Simulation
- Cleaner production
- Sustainable manufacturing
- Enterprise modelling
- Extended enterprise design
- Extended enterprise operation
- End-of-life management

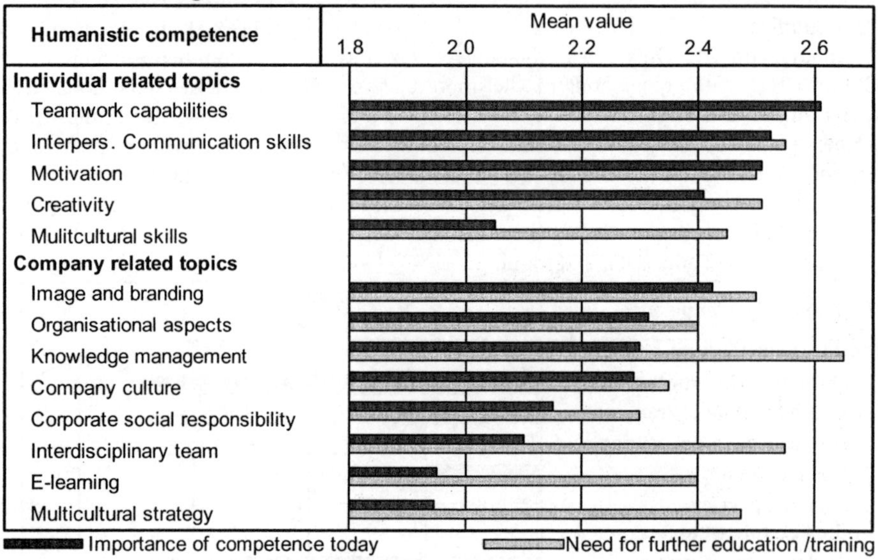

Figure 3 Industrial Needs for Humanistic Competence

Figure 3 shows that for humanistic competence, the following areas have been defined to have low competence today and a high need for education and training:

- Multicultural skills and strategy
- E-learning

Figure 4 (below) shows that for business competence, the following areas have been defined to have low competence today and a high need for education and training:

- E-commerce
- Benchmarking
- Entrepreneurship

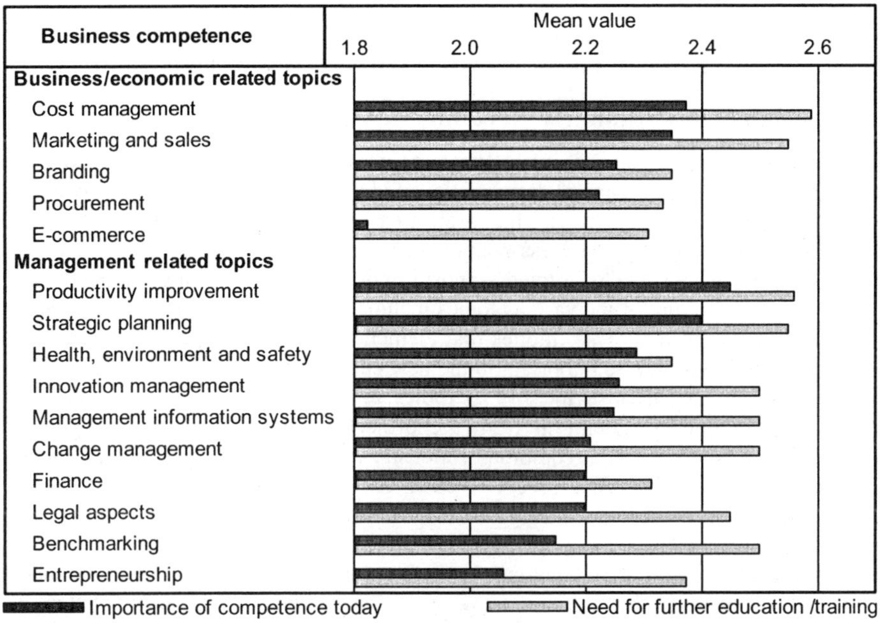

Figure 4 Industrial needs for business competence.

Correlation analysis has shown some differences between participating regions:

- Japan has more intelligent product features included in a typical delivery to customers than the average region.
- Japan has companies that offer more on-the-job training to their employees than the average region.
- Korea has companies that communicate more with customers by e-commerce techniques than the average region.
- Korea has a higher degree of service and maintenance included in a typical delivery to customers than the average region.
- Koreas has companies that offer less on-the-job training to their employees than the average region.
- USA has companies with less paper-based communication with customers than the average region.
- USA has companies that communicate more with customers by e-commerce techniques than the average region.
- Northern Europe has more intelligent product features included in a typical delivery to customers than the average region.
- Southern Europe has more external companies as main supplier than the average region.
- Southern Europe has a larger percentage of sales volume going to first tier suppliers than the average region.
- Eastern Europe has a higher degree of service and maintenance included in their product development than the average region.
- Eastern Europe has companies that communicate less with customers by e-mail and e-commerce techniques than the average region.
- Eastern Europe has fewer intelligent product features included in a typical delivery to customers than the average region.

Correlation analysis has also shown that there are some variations in the perceived importance of competence areas and topics based on company size. SMEs systematically tend to evaluate the competence areas as less important than large companies.

5. Conclusions and Summary Recommendations

An industrial survey was carried out to study the need of the manufacturing industry for future competence in technological, humanistic, and business related topics. There are only slight variations in needs between the three areas in terms of statistical means. The management-related topic of business competence and the individual-related topic under humanistic competence seem to be rated as most important both today and in five years.

For the overall picture of the various topics included in the three areas, all topics should be considered as important. This implies that elements from all competence areas and all topics should be considered as important in the new curriculum in manufacturing strategies. This is not surprising because the list of topics to select amongst in the survey was composed giving due consideration from the project to what they believed would be important. Obviously this met the opinion of industry quite well. It is interesting to observe that there are several topics that have a research focus today where industry claims low importance of their competence today. One would tend to believe that topics such as intelligent manufacturing, simulation, e-work, e-learning, multicultural skills, and end-of-life issues would score quite high. When this is the case, one explanation could be that the take of research results in this field is somewhat slower than what could be anticipated.

Also surprising is the small differences between regions with respect to the needs. One would tend to believe that the needs in for example Japan, USA, and Europe might be different. Correlation analysis has shown that here is a slight tendency that Japan and Korea consistently have opposite priorities. For the rest of the regions there are no systematic co-variances. Other differences are mainly on demographic data as explained above.

In listing the areas where the educational needs are highest (low importance of competence today matched with high importance of further education), it is possible to identify three major areas:

- Extended products
- Take up of e-business techniques and tools
- On-the-job training

Extended products can be split in "intelligent products" and "products with embedded services". For intelligent products there may be a slightly higher importance of competence today in Japan and North Europe, and a slightly lower importance in Eastern Europe. There is slightly higher importance in Korea and Eastern Europe for products with embedded services. For take up of e-business techniques there seems to be a slightly higher importance in Korea and USA, and a slightly lower importance in Eastern Europe. For On-the-job training there are slightly higher importance in Japan, and slightly lower in Korea.

The overall conclusion is that there is a need for education and training in the manufacturing industry with respect to operation by digital business and extended products as defined by the GEM project. The survey results has been exploited to define curriculum specifications and to develop a demonstrator. A number of European universities are forming an alliance for a virtual university to start offering such an education.

References

[1] A. Rolstadås: GEM – A Curriculum in Manufacturing Strategy Responding to the Needs of Industry. Paper at the IMS Forum 2004, Como, Italy, 2004.

[2] B. Moseng, F.O. Rasch, A. Rolstadås: Global Education in Manufacturing – GEM. Paper at the CIRP International Manufacturing Education Conference, CIMEC 2002, Twente, The Netherlands, 2002.

[3] D. Shunk: The Creation of a Competency-based, Anytime – Any Place Education System for Academia and Industry. Paper at the e-2002 conference, Prague, The Czech Republic, 2002.
[4] A. Rolstadås: An Example of an E-learning Solution for an International Curriculum in Manufacturing Strategy. Paper at the e-2002 conference, Prague, The Czech Republic, 2002.
[5] K. D. Thoben, M. Schwesig, J. Eschenbaecher: Global E-Business Education in Industrial Engineering-Meeting the Needs of the Networked Economy. Paper at the 2003 ASEE Annual Conference & Exposition June 22-25, 2003 Nashville, Tennessee, USA.
[6] D. O'Sullivan, L.E. Precuo, P. Duffy, S. van Dongen, S. Guochao: Survey of existing Manufacturing Curricula: GEM-EUROPE project report, Galway, Ireland, 2002.
[7] D. O'Sullivan, L.E. Precuo, P. Duffy, S. van Dongen, S. Guochao: Survey of Manufacturing Curricula from Around the World. Paper at the e-2002 conference, Prague, The Czech Republic, 2002.
[8] T. Kvernberg Andersen, T.B. Gjerstad, B.E Madsen, B. Moseng, A. Rolstadås: Training and Education Needs for Manufacturing Strategy. GEM-EUROPE project report, Trondheim, Norway, 2003.
[9] T. J. Duesterberg: U.S. Manufacturing: The Engine for Growth in a Global Economy Presentation at the Intelligent Manufacturing Systems ISC 16 Meeting, Monterey, California, USA, 2003.

The Suitability of an Irish Third-level Blended e-Learning Programme for Lean Competitiveness Training in SMEs

Liam BROWN[1], Eamonn MURPHY[1], Eamonn MCQUADE[1], Marie PAULI[2]
[1]*University of Limerick, Limerick, Ireland*
Tel: +353 61 331588, Fax: + 353 61 331589
Email: liam.brown@ul.ie, eamonn.Murphy@ul.ie, eamonn.mcquade@ul.ie
[2]*IVF, Industrial Research and Development Corporation, Mölndal, Sweden*
Tel: +46 317066000 Fax: + 46 31276130, Email: pauli@swipnet.se

Abstract: In this paper, we outline the major trends and thinking in e-Learning and in particular its applicability to an industrial audience. We present the results of our design, development and evaluation of a novel blended course for teaching university students. Evaluative feedback included Screen Design, Consistency, Terminology, Ease of Navigation and Explanations. We then outline the various issues that emerged in adapting, further developing and expanding the training material for use by an industrial audience – primarily Small and Medium Enterprises (SMEs). The main issues that were addressed were firstly the reasons and needs for the take-up in SMEs of the competitiveness or "Lean" methods and secondly the attitudes, awareness and expectations of the SMEs to eLearning course materials.

1. Introduction

1.1 Lifelong Learning and e-Learning

As Human Resource Development (HRD) practices shift away from training and towards learning, the notions of lifelong learning and electronic learning (e-Learning) are emerging in the growing HRD literature. Lifelong learning is defined by Brandsma [1] as a continuous process of personal development for everyone, whether in work or not, encompassing formal and informal activities, and making demands upon the social structures in which learning takes place. However, the OECD [2] suggests lifelong learning has broader objectives, including strengthening democratic values, cultivating community life, maintaining social cohesion, and promoting innovation, productivity and economic growth, and these are reiterated in recent EU publications [3].

Many European governments are encouraging lifelong learning for example the UK in particular [4] highlight the changing nature of work, the need for re-skilling as traditional industries decline and new technologies emerge, and the need for everyone to engage in ongoing learning. According to Sambrook and Stewart [4] one of the key reasons cited for aspiring to become learning organisations is the need to cope with technological change, to compete. A key government initiative in the UK was the launch of the University for Industry (UFI) now renamed "learndirect". This takes the form of establishing learndirect centres – located in public places such as libraries, local colleges and hospitals – and commissioning computer-based learning materials to be used in these centres. By providing such centres in local communities, existing and potential employees would be able to access personal and work-related learning, to enhance both their attitudes to learning and their personal knowledge and skills. At the European level, researchers are now critically evaluating the European policy for e-learning [5] (Attwell, 2002).

Electronic learning, often abbreviated to e-Learning, can be defined as any learning activity supported by information and communication technologies (ICT). There are debates concerning the labels, for example whether ICT-based learning is the same as computer-based learning, or is the same as e-Learning [6] (Figueira, 2003).

1.2 Learning – an Intrinsically Complex Phenomenon

Learning is inherently complex [7] (Stevens, 2002). One of the principal criticisms of many learning technologies, especially e-learning applications, is that they seem to be predicated on assumptions of learning that are overly simplistic. We can refer for example to many problematic attempts at using the Web or other forms of ICT to supplant or substitute face-to-face interaction between students and peers and tutors. [8] (Brown et al 2003).

The "Lean" e-Learning course was developed to support a competitiveness module, part of the Diploma in Quality Management delivered every spring semester to typically 200 students at the University of Limerick. Subject Matter Experts included leading academics in the field and experienced industry based "Lean" practitioners, typically from companies that had students enrolled on the course. These companies included Dell Computers, IBM Microelectronics, Analog Devices, Bausch and Lomb and Honeywell Engines and Systems. The technical development was undertaken by AMT (Advanced Manufacturing Technology) this development team was based at the University of Limerick. Key tasks included project management, instructional design, graphic design, quality assurance, technical development, iterative testing and user feedback. It is important to note that the design philosophy underpinning the development of the "Lean" e-Learning course was that learning is complex, and it is not sufficient, in educational or pedagogical terms, simply to put lectures online and expect fulfilling and transformative learning to happen.

The goal in designing the "Lean" e-Learning course was to create a novel combination of interactions, both offline and online thus creating a new and enhanced possibilities for profound learning to take place, which combined effective face-to-face with traditional third-level pedagogy alongside an interactive Web site. The principal aims for the course are: (1) to ground theoretical principles for students and to put these concepts into context for students; (2) and therefore make the material more relevant, authentic and meaningful for the students. (3) To reduce attrition rates in a difficult and demanding course, and (4) to engage students in an overall more compelling and motivational learning experience.

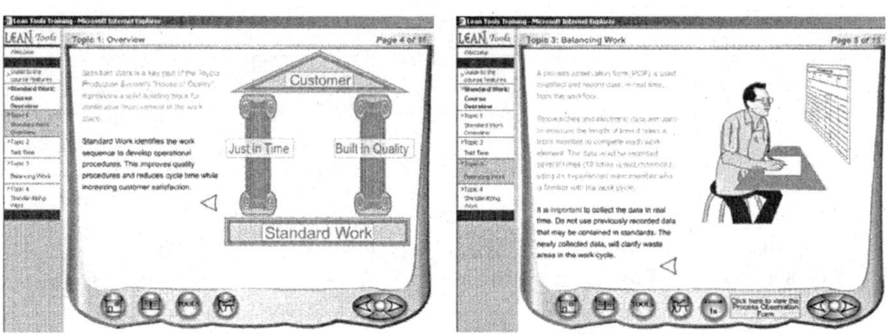

Figure 1. Screenshots, Online Animation Examples from the Lean Tools Training Course

The course combines online with offline interactions. Students can browse the Web site and complete interactive tutorials. These tutorials contain animations and also quiz the students, at regular intervals, as they traverse the site. The animations include for example engineers using statistics in conducting product quality reviews on a production line (Figure 1). Students can use a help facility often referred to as Dr. Dr. e-mail support to send urgent queries to the course TA, who will duly reply within 24 hours. There are also traditional course lectures and tutorials, but there are also intensive small-group tutorial and one-to-one tutorials with the course tutorial assistant.

2. Objectives

The overall rationale for the third-level course is to motivate and encourage 'more able' students, and to reduce attrition/failure rates by providing 'weaker' students with ancillary support. The motivation for developing the course arose from the understanding by the course design and teaching staff that, while traditional 'chalk-and-talk' instruction is problematic, posting lecture slides to the Web is not sufficient in supporting students; and that the goal should be to try to achieve an effective combination of novel online interaction and offline pedagogical and student support. The objective of the industrial version is to focus on adapting lean training to industry, in particular SMEs coupled with the use of highly accessible learning methodologies and finally to understand the issues involved in adapting training material developed for a third level audience to an industrial audience.

3. Methodology

The methodology used a proven design and development process as outlined below:

3.1 Description of content development process

AMT, University of Limerick use a formal product development process on all projects. Based on the Stage Gate philosophy, the development cycle has four separate phases (Proposal; Design; Development; Build and Test). These phases are depicted in Figure 2. Courses are typically broken down into a number of topics, which are self-contained units of learning. The Proposal and Design Phases refer to the product at a course level.

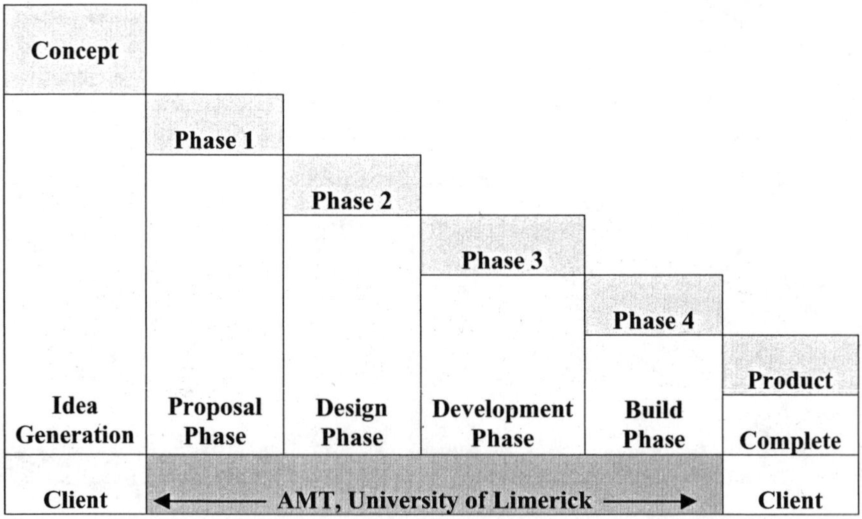

Figure 2. Phases within AMT, University of Limerick's design & development process

The Development and Build Phases refer to the course at a topic level. The purpose of this is to ensure that each individual topic may be reviewed and tested independently as opposed to waiting for the complete course. An independent gatekeeper controls each phase, which has a set of defined outputs that must be satisfied to guarantee the quality of the learning content. Upon project completion, we conduct a post project review meeting to learn from the experience of the project and to improve the robustness of our process.

3.2 Industrial applicability

The industrial version of the training course is LeanXeur (Lean across Europe) is co-funded under the EU's Leonardo da Vinci Programme. The purpose is to encapsulate best practice in LEAN education and training in a user based, on-line format for SMEs, coupled with highly accessible learning methodologies. The development methodology was more involved as it commenced with a survey of 100 SMEs in 5 countries across Europe (Ireland, UK, Sweden, Spain and Poland). The focus was on 3 sectors: component manufacturers (particularly polymers), the food sector and engineering products/sub-supply companies. These particular sectors are faced with a growing and relentless competitiveness challenge from both low cost regions and from over-emphasis on low value-adding activities.

The purpose of the survey was to investigate the infrastructure, cultural and other reasons why the LEAN approach to competitiveness improvement is poorly adopted by SMEs. In conjunction with the research into the adoption of "Lean", research was also conducted into the optimum ICT technologies to use in the delivery of training, bearing in mind the technical, financial and cultural restrictions within the general SME environment. This included pedagogical considerations, communication technologies, exercises, network support services and on-the-job facilitation. The third level material where possible will be adapted to fit into the developing industrial course. Iterative testing and feedback from the end users will also be encapsulated into the training material. Finally Promotion and dissemination is ongoing throughout the project – focusing on the goals and results with a view to promote uptake of the training material.

In summary, we have developed the material for the third level students using a professional and proven development process and have carried out an extensive analysis of this e-Learning material, primarily in terms of usability and benefits. We have also completed and analysed the survey of sample SME end users and are currently adopting the existing and developing further e-Learning material to suit the industrial user base.

4. Technology and Business Case Description

4.1 The Need for "Lean"

Research by the UK Engineering Employers Federation (EEF) highlighting the productivity gap between UK and US manufacturing, laid the blame on the slow take-up of Lean techniques. The report shows that the issues of Lean manufacturing, performance management, investment and skills are interrelated. Shortages of people with the required skills to implement Lean manufacturing were linked to lower profitability and lower productivity [9]. US research shows that knowledge of Lean has not trickled down to the last tier of suppliers - "Lean is totally unknown to the majority of small manufacturers" Research in Poland supports this: SMEs are slow to adopt new management techniques and new technologies [10]. The Swedish industrial organization, Bilkomponent Sverige, stated that suppliers don't have enough growing power to withstand competition from low cost regions. They identify a need for competence development through spreading Lean implementation to smaller businesses [11]. The Stockholm School of Economics concludes that Lean is applicable also to SMEs [12].

The goal is to address the productivity needs of SMEs and make Lean methodologies more accessible to SMEs. It will develop results that can be implemented in SMEs across several sectors. It will focus on 3 representative sectors to ensure wide applicability: component manufacturers, the food sector and engineering products / sub-supply companies. In the advent of globalisation these sectors face significant competitive challenges and have the greatest need to adopt lean tools and techniques. The project outputs will help meet the competitiveness goals of the Irish Precision Engineering sector [13]: (i) Increase annual sales per employee from €86K to €108K; (ii) Substantially improve competitiveness through adoption of world-class techniques.

4.2 SMEs and eLearning

Research on accessibility of training for SMEs in Ireland [14] identified the following barriers to access: Affordability (42%); Lack of local availability (25%); Too disruptive to release personnel (74%). Brock (2000) [15] notes that small firms use ICT more as tools to support organisational tasks like administration and accounting, rather than for formal, internal communications as in larger organisations. However, the size of the firm does not necessarily determine levels of ICT awareness, as very small firms can be highly IT sophisticated (Gray and Lawless, 2000) [16]. More recently there is evidence in Irish SMEs of increasing proficiency in e-commerce in general, with owner-managers the driving force (Barry and Milner, 2002) [17]. This may also be increasing in terms of e-Learning. It should also be noted in a European study, researchers found that online courses for managers in SMEs are only effective if there are collaborative links between educational providers and enterprises (Oberski et al., 2000) [18].

5. Results

In trying to assess the learning occurring for students taking the lean e-Learning course, we surveyed 200 of the students that had recently taken the course and had a response rate of 54%. We took elements from three disciplinary perspectives, from collaborative learning and work, HCI/usability analysis and instructional design. We had three concerns: (1) to assess the instructional effectiveness and usability of the course tool and interactive Website; (2) to get some sense of the overall pedagogical efficacy of the course. In addition we were interested in the collaborative work practices of the course designers and teachers, (3) with a view to generating some insights into how these practices might be better supported. The following illustrate how helpful, effective and instructional students found some of the elements of the course:

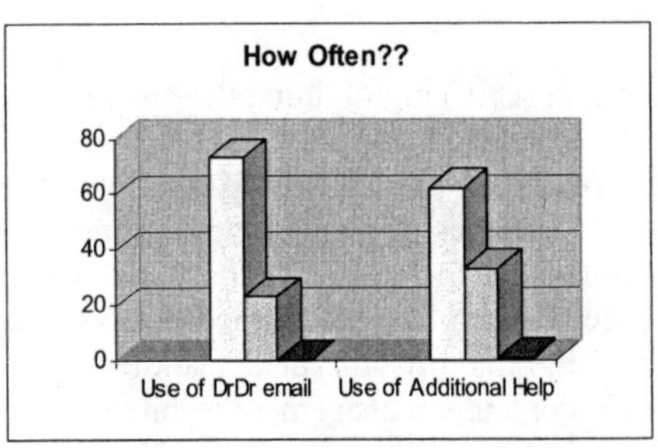

Figure 3. Frequency of students' use of Help

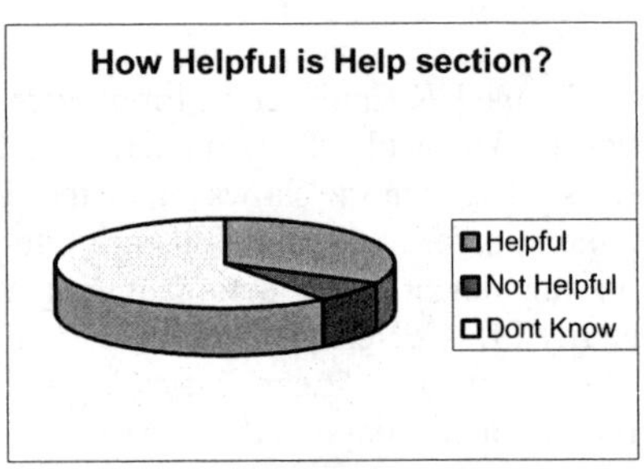

Figure 4. Perceived helpfulness of Web site help

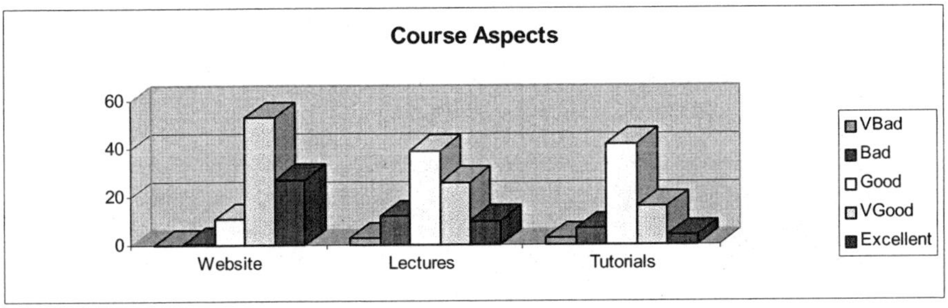

Figure 5. Student's General Ratings of Website, Lectures and Tutorials

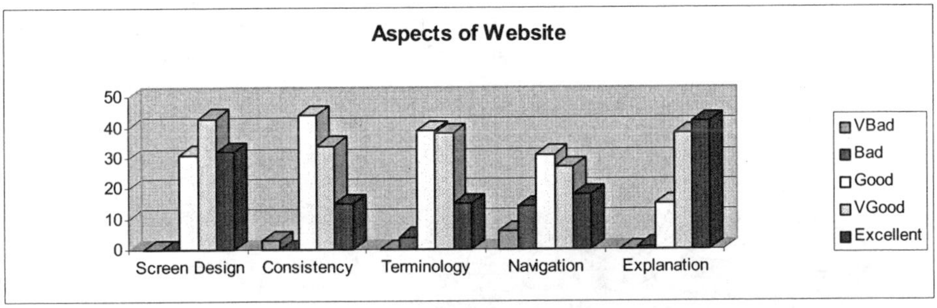

Figure 6. Students' General Ratings of Web and Instructional Design Elements

The following summarises the results from the survey of Irish SMEs on implementation of Lean and the effectiveness of e-Learning as a medium for supporting the implementation of lean. The primary driver for implementing lean was improved productivity, followed by improved customer satisfaction and reduced lead times as outlined in figure 7. Figure 8 shows that the main expectation from lean training is the ability to understand & be able to Implement Lean on work-floor, resulting in better work practices.

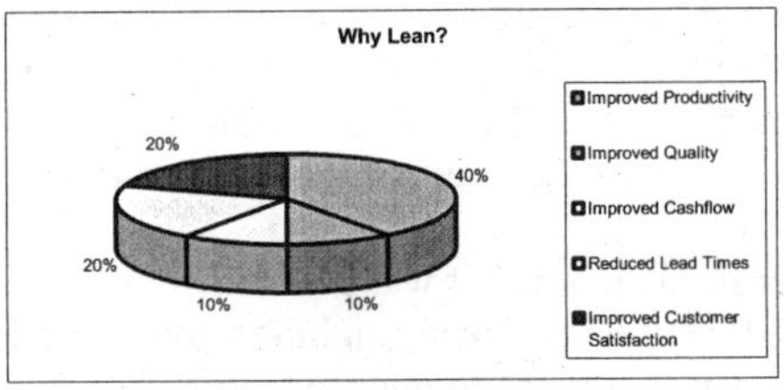

Figure 7. Why Lean

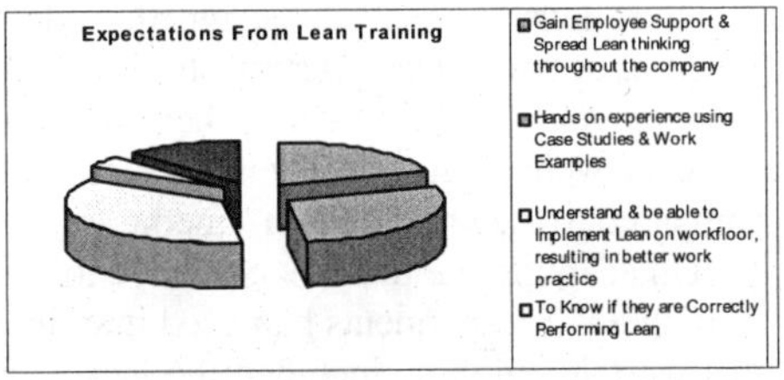

Figure 8. Expectations From Lean Training

Figures 9 and 10 show that only 20% of respondents have previously participated in Internet based learning courses but of those 50 % found them good.

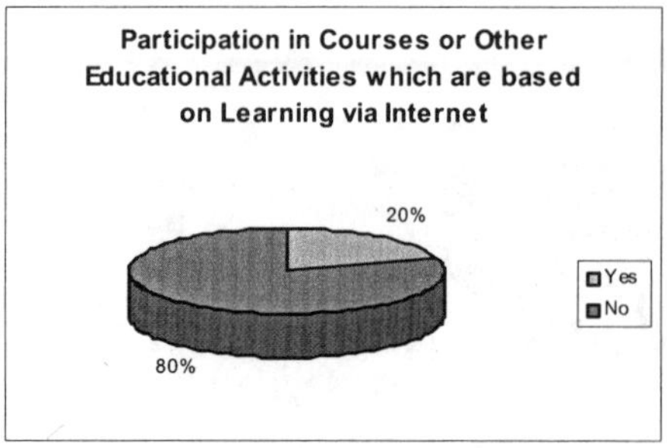

Figure 9. Participation in Courses which are based on Learning via Internet

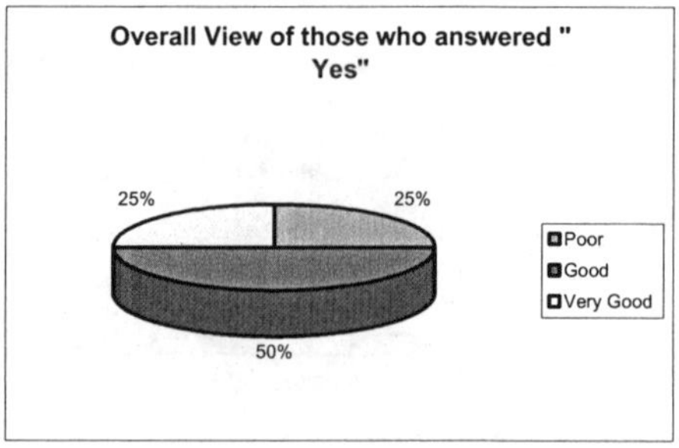

Figure 10. Overall View of those who answered " Yes"

As outlined in Figure 11, the main concerns highlighted with e-Learning courseware were:
1. Lack of immediate response to questions and trainer interactions
2. Concern about lack of personal motivation when left to do on their own

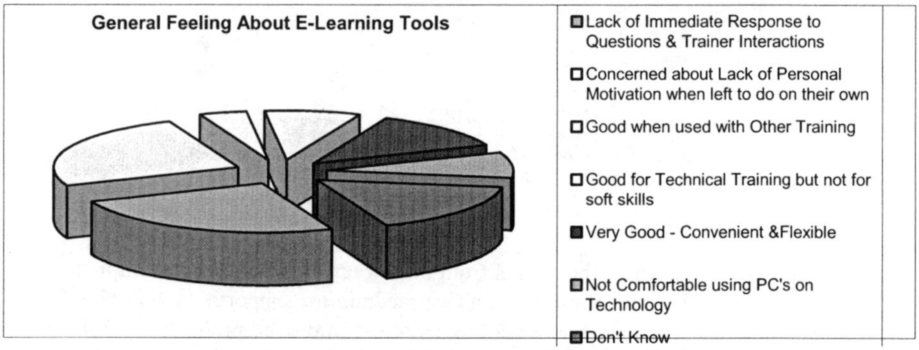

Figure 11. General Feeling About E-Learning Tools

6. Conclusions and Recommendations

The third level course was designed on the premise that learning is complex. In this paper, we have attempted to illustrate how a multidisciplinary approach to design, development and evaluation of a new course helped us to capture some of the complex learning in which students were engaged. The feedback from the course was very positive overall when compared to the other delivery methods.

On adapting the third level course to the industrial audience it was found that only 20% of Irish SME respondents had used internet based courses previously and the main concerns that were highlighted included the lack of immediate response to questions, lack of trainer interactions and the lack of personal motivation when left to undertake the course on their own. The studies from the other participating European Countries will be available in late 2003 when it is proposed to compare and contrast the findings. The SME version of the lean training will be available in early 2005 and at that stage it is intended to conduct an in-depth analysis of the effectiveness of the e-Learning material.

References

[1] Brandsma, J. (1997), Een leven lang leren: (on)mogelijkheden en perspectieven (Lifelong Learning), University of Twente, Enschede.
[2] OECD (1996), Lifelong Learning For All, OECD, Paris.
[3] European Union (2001), Memorandum of Lifelong Learning, available at: lifelonglearning@cec.eu.int
[4] Sambrook, S. (2000), "Factors influencing learners: perceptions of the quality of computer based learning materials", in Manning, S. and Raffe, D. (Eds), VETNET ECER 2000 Proceedings: Current Research in

European Vocational Education and Human Resource Development, Wissenschaftsforum Bildung und Gesellschaft e.V., Berlin.

[5] Attwell, G. (2002), "eEurope and e-Learning – is European policy working", paper presented to ELSEKEK: Hellenic Association of Vocational training Centres, 1st ELSEKEK conference, Athens

[6] Figueira, E. (2003), "Evaluating the effectiveness of e-learning strategies for small and medium enterprises", available at: www.theknownet.com/ICT_SMEs_seminars/papers/Figueira.html

[7] Stevens, R. (2002) Keeping it complex in an era of Big education. In *CSCL2 – Carrying forward the conversation*. (Eds. Koschmann, T., Hall, R., and Miyake, N.), Mahwah, New Jersey: Lawrence Erlbaum Associates, pp. 269-273.

[8] Brown, L., Hall, T., Bannon, L., Molan, C., Hogan, D., Murphy, E. (2003) "The design and use of a blended learning solution in Irish third-level education" Paper presented at EDTECH May 2003, Waterford, Ireland

[9] Unlocking our potential - supporting skills development, Engineering Employers Federation, *Nov 2001*

[10] Significant Opportunities for Lean Production in Small to Medium US Manufacturers - Experience collected in LMU Industrial Assessment Centre". A report on study carried out by Loyola Marymount University on 25 small companies (<500 employees) in the Los Angeles region for the US DoE's Industry Assessment Centre programme, Jan 2002

[11] "Bilkomponent Sverige", proposal to Swedish government to invest in the development of automotive suppliers, May 1999

[12] "A lean and global smaller firm", International Journal of Operations & Production Management, Vol. 17 No 10, 1997

[13] Precision Engineering: Sector Development Strategy 2001 - 2003

[14] Small Firms – The Training Imperative. Tansey Webster Economic Consultants. Report for Small Firms Association and Skillnets, Jan 2002

[15] Brock, J.K.-U. (2000), "Information and communication technology in the small firm", in Carter, S. and Jones-Evans, D. (Eds), *Enterprise and Small Business*, Harlow, Pearson Education, Financial Times, Prentice-Hall, Englewood Cliffs, NJ.

[16] Gray, C. and Lawless, N. (2000), "Innovations in the distance development of SME management skills", available at: www.nks.no/eurodl/shoen/Gray.html

[17] Barry, H. and Milner, B. (2002), "SMEs and electronic commerce: a departure from the traditional prioritisation of training?", *Journal of European Industrial Training*, Vol. 26 No. 7, pp. 316-26

[18] Oberski, I., Palomar, A., (2000), "Evaluating online work-based eudcation for managers in SMEs: some initial observations", *Industry and Higher Education*, Vol. 14 No. 3, pp. 200-3

Section 8.2

Applications

eAdoption and the Knowledge Economy: Issues, Applications, Case Studies
P. Cunningham and M. Cunningham (Eds.)
IOS Press, 2004

From Continuous Medical Education to Continuous Professional Development

Roberto NARDI [1], Giuseppe VENTRIGLIA[1], Jan HEYRMAN [2],
[1]*Società Italiana di Medicina Generale, via del Pignoncino 9-11, Firenze, I-50142, Italy.*
Tel: +39 055 700027, Fax: +39 055 7130315, Email: simg@dada.it Web: www.simg.it
[2]*Departement of General Practice, Katholieke Universiteit Leuven,*
Kapucijnenvoer 33 blok J, Leuven , B3000,Belgium
Tel: +3216337466, Fax: +3216337480, Email: jan.heyrman@med.kuleuven.ac.be

Abstract: Continuous Professional Development (CPD) is the new trend in the lifelong learning arena for healthcare professionals (HCPs). Most developed countries have put in place a credit system for attendance at educational meetings, to guarantee that professionals stay abreast of rapid developments in health care. CPD will require a new approach to recertification procedures. CPD provides a growing market for on-line educational services that are easily and regularly accessible to the HCP and can be focused to his/her needs and availability. The success of these services will rely heavily on their ability to bridge the flexibility of learning schemes based on individual requirements and preferences with the narrow criteria that usually govern any recertification scheme. The e-ProLearn concept, refined and trialled in an e-TEN Market Validation Project, defines a profitable business in e-learning in healthcare, by enlarging the scope from mainly knowledge transfer to practice development and health management.

1. The case for Distance Learning in the Health Care Domain

The rapid evolution of knowledge in all fields of activity, makes the risk of professional obsolescence both real and very significant, and sets a strong case for Continuous Professional Development (CPD). Nowhere is that more true than in the medical field where new knowledge must be transferred into real-day practice if healthcare systems are to fulfil their mission and offer the best available practice to their demanding customers.

1.1 Professional Recertification versus Continuous Professional Development

There is now a drive towards building recertification frameworks for healthcare professionals (HCPs) in many European countries. The aim is to ensure that they have a reasonably up-to-date array of both theoretical and practical knowledge.

However, recertification does not represent the whole of CPD for HCPs. It rather sets a base line. On top of this, each HCP is responsible for a never-ending process of updating his/her competences. CPD is therefore a broader concept than recertification.

CPD provides a growing market for on-line educational services. However, these must bridge the flexibility of learning schemes based on individual requirements and preferences with the narrow criteria that usually govern any recertification scheme. In addition, HCPs, and doctors in particular, have different CPD needs. These relate mainly to the specifics of their specialty or professional domain.

Increasingly, HCP Associations endorse the concepts outlined above.

1.2 e-Learning as a key instrument to foster Continuous Personal Development

Given the validity of the concepts identified above, any educational activity directed to medical professionals should therefore take into account the following items:

- The requirements of the new CPD schemes.
- The need to keep all the learning activities strictly linked to evidence.
- The need to provide learners with a selection of learning materials as precise and concise as possible, derived from a profiling of their effective learning gaps.
- The need to overcome organisational barriers preventing widespread implementation of proven learning techniques, to promote demonstrable behavioural changes in learners.

The ever-increasing volume of available knowledge, combined with the new CPD requirements, make traditional learning tools obsolete. This paves the way for new concepts to fulfil continuing education obligations, with a wide use of IT technologies. The requirement for continuing activities makes it impossible to rely on discontinuous learning schemes, such as those that compel learners to convene periodically in a separate setting.

Distance learning schemes (e-learning), where the pupil is empowered to access certified learning material remotely from his work and living environments, become in this perspective the most viable and almost painless way to provide would-be pupils with effective continuing education activities. However, the making of flexible, commercially viable e-learning seems to be a real challenge, especially for postgraduate professional learning. This is particularly true in healthcare, despite the large number of HCPs either potentially interested or required to be interested in postgraduate learning.

2. Objectives of e-ProLearn

The e-ProLearn project has been aimed at closing the gap described above between the almost unlimited potential of e-learning in providing effective tools for CPD and the scarcity of real world implementations.

e-ProLearn has been designed to deliver a set of learner-centred, commercially sustainable education services, aimed at the Continuous Professional Development (CPD) of various categories of medical doctors. These services are based, whenever possible, on an automatic profiling of users through the use that they make of the Electronic Health Care Records (EHCR) management software that they normally employ.

The e-ProLearn service offers a number of distinctive features. It allows individuals to identify their learning requirements. It sets up a personalised learning path, in collaboration with a tutor where appropriate. It reassures e-learners that they are part of a learning community of professionals. It provides a variety of learning methods (course based "pull method" and context sensitive "push method"). It monitors progress, enables measurement of learning and behavioural change impact on practice, and certifies the outcome.

The distance learning model that the service implements has a broad spectrum of applications. However, while the extension of the service to other categories of professionals will be evaluated in the future, the Market Validation and the Initial Market Development phases focus on the healthcare sector. This sector is particularly appealing and demanding for distance learning providers.

The healthcare sector is appealing, because the professional category of medical doctors is characterised by: a large number of individuals; an age range of some 40 years; an overwhelming need for permanent education due to rapid changes in technology and knowledge; and a marked geographical dispersion, as well as the difficulty of combining traditional classroom training with medical doctors' busy professional schedule.

A flexible system of distance learning is therefore the logical and natural solution to maintain or, even better, increase the ability of the medical profession to cope with today's demand for high quality and personalised care from EU citizens.

The healthcare sector is demanding, because medical doctors in general and GPs in particular have extremely stringent requirements for CPD. This is because: technology and knowledge grow more quickly in medicine than most other sectors; the role of medical doctors evolves over the time (e.g. the GP is now asked to become a real "manager" of his/her patients' health); and new legislation on accreditation which imposes on medical doctors the need to undergo training from providers certified according to quality criteria.

The approach to e-teaching chosen in e-ProLearn, is a well-balanced combination of user oriented, courseware based material, and real-time, context sensitive learning tools.

3. Methodology of Learning

3.1 Profiling

The competitive edge of e-ProLearn is the real-time personalisation of training to an individual's requirements through measurement of the training deficit, and the subsequent configuration of the courseware or learning nuggets to address this deficit. e-ProLearn also provides a framework for automatically evaluating the level of assimilation of the contents. Through error detection and management techniques, the system will ensure homogeneous knowledge/skill outcomes for a given group of professionals.

3.2 User oriented, courseware based (e-ProLearn pull mode)

The user oriented, courseware based e-ProLearn scenario provides the learner with the maximum degree of control over the educational material selection and study. It therefore entails a close interaction between the user and the e-ProLearn system to allow a strict adherence of the final educational proposals to the user's requirements.

The user oriented e-ProLearn scenario brings to the learner specific educational paths, mostly produced on the fly to suit the learning gaps to be filled. Since it is foreseen that the domains to be addressed will be relatively large (e.g. a disease, a process or a group of them), the educational material being produced resembles traditional distance learning courses, but with two main differences:

First, the e-ProLearn courses are centred on the identified learning gaps. E.g. a course focused on monitoring diabetes is proposed if this is precise need identified for a user based on profiling with the e-ProLearn profiling engine. Sections covering how to diagnose, treat and classify diabetes are also present, but their dimensions are kept to the minimum needed.

Secondly, the e-ProLearn courses are based on pre-existing atomic elements, and are built in a modular way based on acceptance of a profile proposed by the e-ProLearn system. As they are user specific, it is possible that each e-ProLearn user will receive a slightly different version of a course on diabetes, even if based on the same general framework.

3.3 Real-time, context sensitive (e-ProLearn push mode)

The context sensitive e-ProLearn scenario still uses the outcome from the profiling phase as an input for selection of the clinical domains to be considered. From this point onwards, however, instead of configuring and proposing to the user a learning path to be followed, the e-ProLearn system begins to analyse the clinical data residing in the user EHCR together with monitoring the behaviour of the learner when addressing the applicable clinical domain(s) during consultation with patients.

The e-ProLearn system is able to compare the data residing in the user EHCR and his/her behaviour with acknowledged standards for addressing the particular clinical domain. If a significant deviation is detected in one or more steps of the underlying clinical process, e-ProLearn will immediately produce a concise, logical and extensive set of educational material (learning nuggets) and send it to the user. The educational material will be shaped in a way to address the learning needs in a stepwise fashion, i.e. each step in the clinical process will be addressed by a unique set of learning material, tailored according to the identified user learning needs.

4. The e-ProLearn trials

Since March 2003, e-ProLearn is being trialled in three distinct environments. In Italy, a market representative of European public healthcare systems, approx. 100 Italian GPs who are users of the Millewin EHCR are using e-ProLearn. In Belgium, a liberal healthcare system, approx. 100 GPs use e-ProLearn based on the Clinidoc EHCR and MediBRIDGE network services. In the United Kingdom, Sweden, the Netherlands and Spain, some 200 respiratory specialists belonging to the European Respiratory Society (ERS) have begun testing e-ProLearn services provided via web browser application.

The trials are focusing on diabetes and chronic obstructive pulmonary disease (COPD), as these are the two most prevalent chronic diseases, which are associated with issues of misdiagnosis and mistreatment.

The high level objectives of the trials are to determine user acceptance of the e-ProLearn approach, acceptance by health authorities and accreditation bodies, impact on quality of training and behavioural change in practice, and economic feasibility.

5. Technology description

5.1 Architecture

e-ProLearn is enabled by an ICT solution with four core components:

- e-Learning service provider platform: the e-learning platform relies on a web-based architecture and comprises the following fundamental components:
  i. Content editing applications. Scientists and experts can create/modify learning objects.
  ii. Student administration application. Students can subscribe and create learning paths.
  iii. Learning Management System. This creates baskets of learning objects and for tracking e-learner activity such as questionnaire responses and the credits obtained.
  iv. Learning Profiler: Rules engine uses profile input to identify learning content needed.
  v. Learning Content Store: A simple storage server for media-rich learning content.
- Profiling Engine: a software tool to create a user profile by determining learning needs, either by self-assessment or objective assessment (using e.g. questionnaires or case studies) and analysis of the practice population of the learner if he/she uses an EHCR.
- Educational content selection: the user profile generated is used by a second tool to select appropriate learning materials (stored in the e-ProLearn educational database and called learning nuggets) to create a learning basket, i.e. a collection of multimedia educational content exactly meeting the learning needs as they have been outlined in the user's profile. The learner can modify his learning basket.
- Content Provision engine: The accepted learning basket delivers the learning nuggets to the user either during consultations (push mode) for highly specific items directly relevant to the consultation in progress, or at the will of the learner (pull mode).

The e-ProLearn solution is integrated with a Front End subsystem: typically the EHCR (in this case Millewin/Millenet and Clinidoc for GPs) and the web browser application. The key integrating components is a specific EHCR doctor's practice analyser: this includes the software components dedicated to the extraction of the physician's e-ProLearn profile. The structure of the profile has been defined during the project, based on XML format. The choice of using XML for exchange between the EHCR and the e-ProLearn service provider system makes e-ProLearn an "open" system: any EHCR, in addition to Millewin and Clinidoc, will be able to access to the e-ProLearn services if they respect the exchange format. The analyser extracts the EHCR data on the basis of a set of e-ProLearn practice behaviour rules that are defined on the entire patient population (rather than single-patient features): these rules have also been defined during the development of the project.

5.2 Implementation

On the software side, significant additions had to be considered. A whole new set of algorithms to detect the user's learning needs through assessment of clinical data stored into his/her EHCR has been developed and a unobtrusive way to present learning nuggets to the consulting physician has been designed. Moreover, the need to keep the user profiling mechanism updated with either new scientific knowledge or new CME requirements and the user educational database with the latest courseware productions, entailed the adoption of a VPN – like model for the distribution of both new algorithms and educational contents.

To evaluate different technical solutions and take into account the trial environments, the e-ProLearn services have been implemented using different technology and software tools by the service providers for Belgium, Italy and the respiratory specialists.

The solution implemented by the Belgium provider uses the SASS application, a client server assessment and e-learning product in the medical domain. As a full Java application, it is platform independent. The SASS application also supports the addition of additional languages, allowing any language to be plugged into the application.

In Italy, some of the services currently provided by the Millewin and Millenet GP EHCR applications supported a number of the e-ProLearn requirements. Other services have been extended or modified, including the provision of scientific material and the interaction with the e-learning environment, which uses Docent.

ERS provides the e-ProLearn services to its trial members in four countries in a web format supported by MediBRIDGE. As e-ProLearn integration with local EHCR market leaders becomes relevant for the specialists as well, collaboration with the EHCR vendor companies will be set-up. Collaborations will be initiated with individual National Respiratory Societies to translate and adapt the content to country local specifications.

6. Results

The software tools have all been configured, and the e-ProLearn solution has been implemented. In principle, the e-ProLearn developments are independent of individual learning platforms: this is essential to avoid unwanted dependency on any specific vendor. During March 2004, the Belgian and Italian pilots started with about one hundred users in each country. A complete user support system has been set up in both countries, thanks to the substantial contribution of the EHCR software vendors participating in the e-ProLearn Consortium. Another critical task carried out has involved the scientific partners of the Consortium; they have reengineered the existing paper based educational material in order to meet the often very different requirements of the new electronic environment.

A thorough evaluation of indicators will be carried out, to explore both the habits of the e-ProLearn trial users when using the system and their feedback about the e-ProLearn system's functionality and overall acceptability. The findings will be analysed and documented in an exhaustive report in October 2004. The deadline for preparing this paper (April 30th) prevents the e-ProLearn Consortium from including any trial results here. However, data from the pilots will be available at the time of the eChallenges conference and will be discussed during the oral presentation of this paper.

7. Economic Benefits, Quality of Practice Improvements and exploitation

7.1 Savings for the Healthcare Professional

The HCP is currently already investing important resources in his/her postgraduate education. The amount of credits to be obtained per year varies from 25 to 100 (in some countries even more). One credit point is generally linked to one hour of attendance.

In addition to the obvious time cost in attending, there are further associated costs: These include preparation time for some events, and the travel cost and travel time. There is a consequent opportunity cost, at least in countries with a free or liberal healthcare system.

The total investment cost borne by the individual GP learner can be estimated at between 2.000€ and 5.000€ per year. This is for a service that does not always satisfy the learner: inconvenient timing, inconvenient locations, not always a topic that interests the learner, and sometimes poor content and/or teaching. Costs for clinical specialists are estimated to be at least double this amount, and for more technical specialists, even more.

Allowing an HCP to replace say one third of his/her required credits by using an e-ProLearn enabled system can give him/her more benefit for less cost. It will increase the quality of his/her postgraduate investment, and enable him/her to save between 500€ and 1.250€ per year as a GP, and more than double this for medical specialists.

7.2 Health Authorities can affect and measure Quality of Practice

Because e-ProLearn focuses on the specific learning needs of the HCP based on actual practice behaviour, the impact on the quality of practice becomes direct and measurable.

For example, if a GP is in a consultation and the patient's EHCR does not contain his/her body-mass-index (BMI), e-ProLearn will push to the physician a learning nugget stating that determining BMI is an essential step in diagnosing diabetes. Each time this information is missing in a patient's EHCR, the nugget will be pushed. Over time, as the physician improves his/her practice behaviour in this area, i.e. records BMI for patients regularly, the number of warnings provided by e-ProLearn on this subject will diminish, constituting a measurable improvement. If one considers that approximately 50% of diabetes cases go undiagnosed for a long period of time, this type of learning and quality of practice improvement has a substantial value for the healthcare system.

7.3 Industrial significance

Given the amount of money that doctors directly or indirectly invest in their recertification schemes, it is clear that a market exists for a system that is designed along the structure of e-ProLearn. Tapping into such a market may be interesting for two major players: the publishing industry and the medical software industry. The publishing industry is already considering the production of distance learning tools for HCPs as a natural extension of its core business, while the medical software industry may be interested in extending the functionality of its products to cover their customer needs in the CME domain. A third player in this market could be represented by the telecommunication business, since an e-ProLearn based operation would surely emerge as a huge bandwidth consumer: a provider of Internet access may therefore see the e-ProLearn operation as a value added service to extend its basic service, in order to generate significant additional revenue.

7.4 Cost items

The experience drawn from the building of the e-ProLearn pilots shows that, at least initially, two items of cost emerge: the production of learning material which complies with e-ProLearn requirements, and the integration of the functionalities needed to support e-ProLearn into the pre-existing EHCR software.

The major item is learning material production (and maintenance). While the e-ProLearn enabled educational tools can be based on pre-existing traditional paper-based courses, adaptation to the new distance learning requirements entails a complete revision of the contents and a totally different arrangement of the subsections. This is needed to fully exploit the features of the distance-learning environment. For example, links can be inserted into the courses making it easier for the pupil to follow a logical trail connecting educational items that on paper may be separated by hundreds of pages; to obtain such a result, however, a painstaking activity of splitting the existing courses into atomic elements has to be performed, together with finding the appropriate multimedia tool for conveying the final product to the users in the most effective way.

The new software developments accounted for another significant amount of resources in order to put up an application for the pilots sufficiently representing the e-Prolearn CME content provision to the GPs testing the system.

7.5 Implementation models

A basic business model can be envisioned for selling a e-Prolearn based service to its potential customers. The e-Prolearn customers could be charged on either a fee for service or a flat rate payment basis. While the former could entail a "pay as you use" scheme perhaps more adapt to young professionals, the latter would target people with long professional experience (and with inherently higher learning needs) or professionals needing to get rather high amount of credits to comply with their own CME schemes. A mix of the above models could foresee a limited sum as an "entry fee" for some basic services (for example: profiling + educational material up to a fixed amount of CME credits). A fee for service scheme could be then used for additional options to be added on top of the basic platform (for example: a fixed amount of money for each CME credit exceeding the basic service)

Regardless of the business model used, the e-Prolearn service could be run by a telecom operator, a EHCR provider or a Publishing company. Considering the rather different skills needed for a comprehensive and efficient implementation of a service which spans across different sectors such as medical informatics, education for professionals and publishing, the best option could be represented by a Consortium built by different actors, each one of them bringing focused experience on one of the many different items to be addressed.

8. Conclusions

In healthcare, as in other domains, a shift is taking place from knowledge transfer through traditional means to Continuous Professional Development (CPD) that seeks to achieve and make measurable improvements in practice outcomes. There exists an increasing need for individualised, flexible and relevant training with a measurable impact on practice results.

As proven by e-ProLearn, ICT can enable distance-learning solutions that meet the functional and results requirements presented by health authorities and HCPs alike. If the latter will provide a appropriate regulatory framework, a new dimension of post-graduate education shall be added to traditional class-room training, allowing professionals to embrace the benefits that e-learning enabled by powerful ICT technology can offer.

Results from pilot trials are still to be gathered: a thorough discussion of the data collected in terms of user acceptability and economic viability of the services will be included in the presentation of this paper at the eChallenges conference. It is however already possible to draw some conclusions form the work done.

The experience derived from pre-tests conducted on a limited a number of doctors while setting up the pilots shows that e-ProLearn is likely to receive high marks under the user acceptability profile. The first set of users has made no significant remarks about obtrusiveness into daily practice when using the push mode functions. The usability of the pull mode functionalities has been also judged as good.

A much more difficult task will be to prove the efficacy and effectiveness of the e-ProLearn system in promoting behavioural changes in its users' daily practice. To explore this topic, significant studies will need to be conducted by the professional associations of the users, over an adequate time scale for the purpose.

References

[1] The good CPD guide. A practical guide to managed CPD - The open university Centre for Education in Medicine

[2] Continuing medical education and continuing professional development: international comparisons *BMJ* 2000;320:432-435

[3] Continuing Medical Education and Continuous Professional Development - Standing Committee of European Doctors - Brussels 1999

[4] McKay AJ Revalidation: the catalyst for change in continuing professional development? - 1: J R Coll Surg Edinb 2000 Apr; 45(2): 71-3

eAdoption and the Knowledge Economy: Issues, Applications, Case Studies
P. Cunningham and M. Cunningham (Eds.)
IOS Press, 2004

MetaCampus Marketplace and the Challenge for Next Generation eLearning Platforms

Solenn LE GOFF[1], Santi RISTOL[2]
[1, 2]*Atos Origin, Avda. Diagonal 210-218, Barcelona, 08018, Spain*
[1]*Tel: +34 93 486 18 18, Fax: +34 93 486 07 66, Email: solenn.legoff@atosorigin.com*
[2]*Tel: +34 93 486 18 18, Fax: +34 93 486 07 66, Email: santi.ristol@atosorigin.com*

Abstract: The challenge for the European Market in the domain of learning is to provide suitable training to European citizens to fulfil their lifelong learning needs, either to reduce their skill gap to reach new job opportunities than to improve their own personal development. The MetaCampus MarketPlace is the perfect answer to this need due to the fact that its main purpose is to guide the citizen in his lifelong learning by assessing the right training to the right learner with specific knowledge, needs and objectives. The strength of MetaCampus MarketPlace is to define the Learning Resource Catalogue as the Users Database with competencies. Thanks to this approach, the Training Consultant, which is the intelligent agent that prescribes and recommends learning assets depending on the learning citizen profile, is able to meet the user objectives and the contents with the user profile.

1. Introduction

The new information and communication technologies are having a deep impact on the way citizens obtain information, communicate and undertake training. The challenges they present for education and training are many, and affect highly diverse sectors of society [1].

If information technologies are to be successfully incorporated into education and training, then relevant and good quality services and contents must be available. The European educational multimedia industry, as well as being undercapitalised, lacks qualified manpower and needs to be strengthened, and closer links need to be established between this industry and the education and training systems. Moreover, the goal should be to develop and stimulate the European market for contents and services, which addresses the needs of the education and cultural communities and of European citizens.

Moreover, the capacity of the vocational guidance services should also be substantially strengthened so as to allow everyone to access information on initial and continuing training opportunities in the skills and qualifications required on the labour market and be able to plot or adjust their training and career pathways.

The MetaCampus Marketplace is based on an IST project (IST-2000-26314) that developed a user-friendly life-long learning portal to assist citizens in selecting and purchasing learning resources meeting their needs, preferences and profile. Co-funded by the eTEN Programme, MetaCampus REAL (510834) is performing the market validation in different domains: vocational learning, in-service training and home/personal learning.

2. Objectives

Since the Lisbon European meeting in March 2000, where the European Council invited the Educational Council to undertake a general reflection on the concrete future objectives of education systems, five main areas of goals have been defined [2]:

1. Raising the standard of learning in Europe, by improving the quality of training for teachers and trainers, and by making a specific effort on literacy and numeracy.

2. Making access to learning easier and more widespread at all times of life, through an effort to make lifelong learning easier to enter and more attractive, by making it easier to move from one part of the education system to another.
3. Updating the definition of basic skills for the knowledge society, in particular by integrating ICT skills, by concentrating more on personal competences, and by looking at shortages in specific skills.
4. Opening education and training to the local environment, to Europe and the world, through foreign language teaching, mobility by strengthening links with business and by developing education for enterprise.
5. Making the best use of resources, by introducing quality assurance into schools and training institutions; by better matching resources to needs, and by enabling schools to develop new partnerships to support their new, wider role.

The purpose of MetaCampus MarketPlace is to comply with these objectives as the expected outcome from the project is to validate:

That MetaCampus MarketPlace services already contribute to workforce reskilling and recycling professional CV's of working and unemployed population.

That professionals on specific fields (e.g. teachers, engineers, doctors, etc.) find in the MetaCampus MarketPlace services, a powerful tool for life-long learning in the form of In-Company training and/or specialized learning.

That personnel learning at home can be assisted by the MetaCampus MarketPlace system, by helping them to choose and find their targeted interests.

To reach these objectives, the competence approach is the key element because it allows for relationships to be established between learning resources, learning objectives and/or competencies, career considerations and learning citizen's training and education needs. The aim of establishing these relationships is to allow MetaCampus to facilitate the buying and selling of relevant education and training materials to meet individual Learning Citizens' needs and goals.

3. Methodology

To achieve these objectives, a market validation will be conducted simultaneously in three different countries. While the Spanish and Belgian pilots are focused in the vocational domain (workforce learning, in-company training and/or specialized learning), the German is focused in the home/personal domain.

The Spanish Pilot will be then focused of in-service learning by doing the validation with teachers already working who wants to improve their competences, change their way of teaching or changing of branch of education (i.e. a literature teacher who wants to use new technology in his class or want to be philosophy teacher). The Belgian pilot will more focus on jobseeker who want to improve their knowledge and skills to apply for a new employment (i.e. a secretary who wants to improve his knowledge in internet technology or office software). The German Pilot will be composed by students who want to improve their knowledge in general, without focusing especially in a specific job. These three different pilots will allow doing a complete validation market.

Each Pilot will be populated with courses coming from course providers that will provide the guarantee and the quality seal to the local target population. In addition to that, the training consultant expertise database is going to be populated with the job positions common for a specific region and industry segment.

Each pilot builds its own competency map by describing each certification, job positions and courses to be tested during the project. The map competence will be built in order to have common base within the three pilot and allowing specificity in function of the countries and sectors. Available efforts in terms of developing common descriptors and metadata, making them available in different languages (thesaurus), deriving validation strategies is also helping maximizing opportunities for cross-border operations.

Figure 1 shows the organization of the Consortium and the role of each partner.

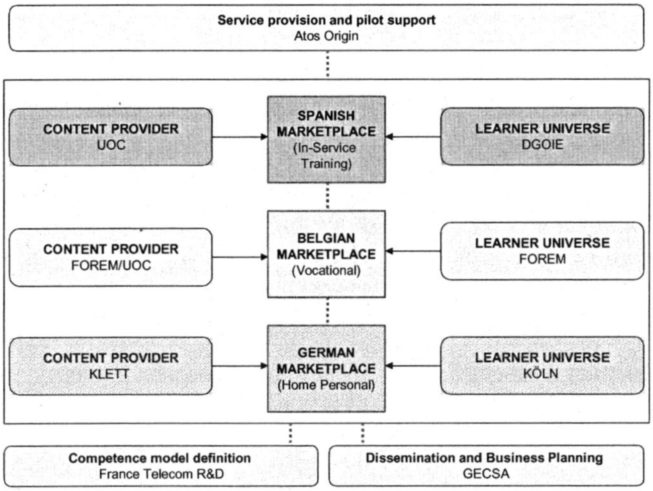

Figure 1: "The MetaCampus REAL Project Consortium Organization"

Figure 2 shows the different phases during the MetaCampus REAL Project:

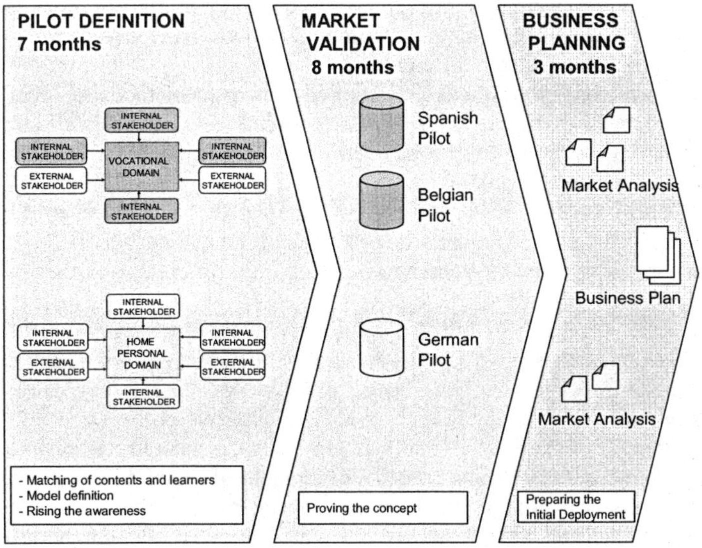

Figure 2: "The MetaCampus Real Project Methodology"

After completion of the Market Validation, the final project outcome is the Business Plan that will detail the Initial Market Deployment to be executed during the following two years. A first draft of Business Plan will be delivered at the beginning of the Project.

After the conclusions from the first Pilot Validation, a final version of the Business Plan will be issued. The final conclusions from the market analysis and the market validation will feed the elaboration of the final Business Plan.

The work items for this task are:

- Elaboration of a Exploitation Agreement
- Provision of a Business Plan
- Provision of a Deployment Plan
- Identification of the obstacles to tackle the market and the actions to overtake them

4. Technology Description

Unlike traditional educative portals, the services offered by the MetaCampus Marketplace are no longer a mere directory of resources from one single content provider. Instead, it consists of a set of guidelines for the transparent interoperation of learning digital dynamic objects and the use of an intelligent training consultant that can guide and recommend the best content choosing from a plethora of resources from different providers.

The platform is based on mature technology that offers the following linked services:

1. The Learning Resources Catalogue manages the database that defines all the learning resources available in the marketplace. The catalogue is dynamically updated by content providers that operate in the platform. Its definition is consistent with the current relevant e-learning standards and the supply format of content providers.
2. The Training Consultant is a key module as it is the intelligent agent that prescribes and recommends learning assets depending on the learning citizen profile. It is based on the knowledge of the learner (declared and inferred), the Learning Resource Catalogue, its own static expertise (the Training Consultant Expertise Data Base), and a solution searching strategy (embedded inference engine). Its functions include: allowing the learning citizen to check the required competencies for a job, guiding the learning citizen when reorienting his career; providing the learning citizen the path for obtaining certificates and proposing specific resources to help him improve his competences.
3. The Learning Content Assembler is a tool that allows the tailoring of contents by selecting learning assets from different resources.
4. The e-Payment System supports most popular payment methods in order to perform online commercial transactions (credit cards, direct debit and transfers). Accurate and timely information regarding the payment status is provided and available from the website of an associated banking entity.
5. The Authentication Broker is in charge of granting the security issues for the whole system. It is based on registration/certification processes and on single sign-on authentication: it enables the access to contents from different providers by registering only once in the marketplace.

To summarize, the value of MetaCampus Marketplace is based on its catalogues, the database where course descriptors (learning resource database), job descriptions (Training Consultant Expertise) and the learning citizen profiles (User Catalogue) are stored. Potential clients receive relevant answers to their training needs by querying the different catalogues in search of the best course that fits his/her needs. Therefore, having a well-populated catalogue is a key business goal. The strength of MetaCampus MarketPlace is to match these catalogues through the Training Consultant. During a search, the Training Consultant's work will be in three steps: (1) To match a given search to a knowledge state to achieve, (2) To determine the initial knowledge state of the learner and (3) To find the best resource(s) allowing to pass from one knowledge state to the other one, by following the learning path created by the Training Consultant.

To handle the task, it will rely on data about the initial knowledge state of the user, the knowledge state to be achieved and the prerequisites and preferences data stored in the user database and recommendations it has previously stored in it. Then the Training Consultant will interact with the Learning Resource database using the metadata (for example, the presence of exercises, videos in the resource, the availability of tutoring, etc.) and the competences associated to the course to match it with the user profile. When it has got all the data, for an assisted search, a path made of learning resources is created to allow the learner to pass from his initial knowledge state to the expected knowledge state. Moreover, when the real-time core has proposed its help (for the free browsing and the multicriteria search), the user can ask why some resources are advised by the Training Consultant [3].

All the chosen and developed components are based on open technologies and environments except for the database (Oracle was chosen just for performance and scalability reasons). However, due to the interoperability of the system, any other kind of product, including Open Source databases can be connected instead.

In fact, the full connectivity between the MetaCampus Marketplace and other products or services constitutes the basic approach of the platform and enriching the value proposition. The user database, the learning content standards, the security and certification issues, and the e-payment flexibility are clear examples of its interoperability.

5. Developments

MetaCampus' highly personalised services and its integrated software applications allow for relationships to be established between learning resources, learning objectives and/or competencies, career considerations and learning citizen's training and education needs.

The aim of establishing these relationships is to allow MetaCampus to facilitate the buying and selling of relevant education and training materials to meet individual Learning Citizens' needs and goals. This requires consideration of the intelligent use and referencing of competencies in learning resources, personal profiles and real world jobs.

Three main premises drove the MetaCampus' approach on competencies [4]:

1. The need to follow the many innovative and relevant undertakings regarding metadata standards, competency models and competency standards.
2. The need to create meaningful and practical software to meet the needs of Learning Citizens' education and skills training and maximize added value to enterprises in the knowledge economy, in particular Learning Resource and Content Providers.
3. The scope of the project, MetaCampus, which does not aim to define competencies or create a taxonomy or vocabulary for identifying learning resources and learning objectives. As such, the focus would be on developing a prototype workable competency model – one that will contemplate learning objectives (and competencies) and real resources, and also be replicable for other competencies and resources.

The decision to include competencies as an item to cover, to be contemplated in the metadata models for the MetaCampus brokerage and marketplace is directly linked to the project's goal of closing the triangle between Learning Citizens' training and education needs, the availability of clearly identified resources to meet those needs, and the specific, standardized needs of the employment market in the knowledge economy.

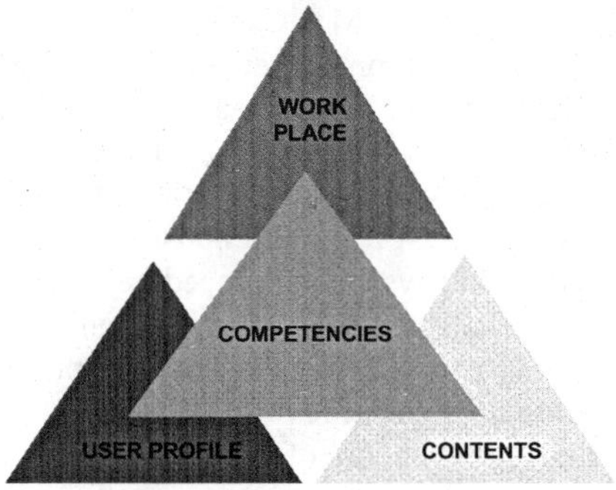

Figure 3: "The MetaCampus Model"

6. Results

MetaCampus REAL (MC REAL) project contributes to reduce the skills gaps of the European citizens (in particular practical training). This fosters social cohesion and helps citizens access better education and provides the opportunity to access better employment. MC REAL will contribute to this objective by enhancing practical skills for citizens and close the gap between market needs and professional skills. Despite the economic downturn, skills remain a crucial issue for the Competitiveness of European enterprises.

In this context, MC REAL e-learning platform will support the adoption of professional skills matching real market needs, based on access to existing knowledge of organisations.

MC REAL will have an impact in the building of e-skills, as defined in the document "eEurope 2005: An information society for all", The Commission and Member States should foster public-private partnerships and the co-operation of stakeholders with a view to developing European-wide e-skills definitions.

Furthermore, MC-REAL project will also:

Participate and support innovation in the professional education system: They will innovate in the implementation of new model in an area, the professional training, usually not beneficiary of the first technological development application.

Reduce public spending. By developing the MC-REAL learning process, the collectivity should be able to better target learning process. This is bound to have a positive influence on educational spending.

Offer equal opportunities of training. This will ensure no training gap from one centre to another and no facilities for real training from the urban environment to remote area.

MC REAL will have a positive impact on employment, as it will reduce the mismatch between demand and supply in the labour market. While in some economy sectors there is unemployment, some other needs workers and they are hard to find. This means that there are people whose competency profile are no longer relevant and require specific and well directed training. The objective is to reach the competencies required for the free positions and this must be granted by the training system. The reality today is that no training system is able to grant this. Clearly, the broad adoption of MC REAL platform and model would benefit this situation as the training actions would directly contribute to fill this gap and to position people at the competency level that is required today.

7. Business Benefits

Many content providers offer eLearning courses across Europe. European citizens can access to more and more eLearning content but the risk for him is to loose time to search for provider platform and the content provider challenge is to visible to most of potential buyer. The production and delivery of learning will increasingly utilize intermediaries that help in matching and facilitating the interaction between the suppliers and the customers of learning industry [5], that's the purpose of MetaCampus MarketPlace.

In this market niche, the competition to the services offered by the MetaCampus MarketPlace consists primarily of education portals, educational organizations offering products freely on the web. However, MetaCampus MarketPlace's competitors (a) focus more on e-commerce activities and less on supporting the learning/educational communities (support which is offered in the case of MetaCampus MarketPlace through its services, based on rigorous methodologies and systematic procedures), (b) are more 'institutional' in nature, (c) do not focus systematically on personalized training and educational needs, and (d) do not offer the unique services provided by the MetaCampus Marketplace.

In sum, the Unique Selling Proposition of the MetaCampus Marketplace can be described as the unparalleled combination of quality services and tools, which brings together learners and resource providers in a flexible and scalable environment, with vast possibilities for personalised learning and competence-based guidance.

The European Citizen will find in MetaCampus MarketPlace the added value of accessing a large offer and getting a good quality lifelong learning by the fact that he will be advised and follow-up in his choice during all his learning needs.

Private and public authorities will also benefit since they could cut their costs by:

- Replacing expensive off line courses by on line courses
- Exclusively delivering the specific education required by the learner (avoiding to deliver whole courses that usually provoke major absence of the learners)
- Controlling the performance, the usage and the impact on the learning citizen

The MetaCampus MarketPlace could be proposed as a global marketplace where any Citizen can access resources from any content Provider but could also be used by an organisation (private or public) to provide specific training restricted to specific users.

8. Conclusions

It is a major challenge for Europe is the development of an adequate supply of software, contents and services, which are suitable for the needs of European learning citizens. UE produces too little of the educational multimedia software, products and services available to serve training and education. The European educational multimedia industry is undercapitalised because of the high number of very small firms, while links between education and training systems and the industry are not strong enough to generate viable services which really cater for education and training requirements.

In the area of vocational training, there is a need for in-depth analysis of the competence models (qualifications and skills) required to give training to apprentices and workers in industry and services in the context of lifelong learning.

The MetaCampus Marketplace is ready to support the competence models that will assist and guide the citizen in his learning process, providing the connection for basic skills lifelong learning must provide, with the skills relevant to the new occupational profiles.

The MetaCampus Real Project can push initiatives from other projects in the domain of eLearning services focused on the customer care, by the fact that it shows that the real challenge in eLearning market today is not the development of Learning Management Systems, as the market is already fully supplied of them, but to help the citizen in its continuous apprenticeship and provide him good ways of selecting the best training that really fits his need. The work that will be done in the competence domain and its introduction in an intelligent agent which translates the user needs into learning path thanks to the matching of the user profile, the job description and the courses will be a good base for plenty of new work and market opportunities in Europe in the eLearning domain.

References

[1] Communication from the Commission to the Council and the European Parliament - "The eLearning Action Plan, *Designing tomorrow's education*" - COM (2001) 172 final - Brussels, 28.03.2001

[2] Report from the Commission – "The Concrete Future Objectives of Education Systems" - COM (2001) 59 final - Brussels, 31.01.2001

[3] Jean-Louis Macle (FTR&D) – "Deliverable 4.1: Training Consultant Specifications", MetaCampus IST-2000-26314 – 01.05.2002

[4] Nancy Grande (Scienter), Paul Fenton (UOC), Josep Canellas (UOC), Patrick Duclos-Montagne and Jean-Louis Macle (FTR&D) - "Justification of Competency Approach in MetaCampus" – 17.03.2003

[5] John Gordon, Director of Research and Strategy, Online Learning Ltd.; and Co-ordinator, NCEC Project, University of Paisley, Scotland & Prof Zhangxi Lin, Texas Tech University, USA – "The New Learning Industry" – 24.05.2001

eAdoption and the Knowledge Economy: Issues, Applications, Case Studies
P. Cunningham and M. Cunningham (Eds.)
IOS Press, 2004

Pilot Implementation of an Intelligent e-Learning Environment

Paul Dan CRISTEA, Rodica TUDUCE
Biomedical Engineering Center, University "Politehnica" of Bucharest,
Spl. Independentei 313, sect. 6, 060042 Bucharest, Romania
Tel: +40 21 4114437, Fax: + 40 21 4104414, Email:{pcristea, trodica}@dsp.pub.ro

Abstract: Intelligent e-Learning Environments (ILE) can increase the attractiveness of e-learning systems and their teaching efficiency by adapting to each learner's profile and by providing multiple support to the tutor. ILE components guide the trainee through the learning process, offer a platform for co-operative learning and knowledge discovery, customize the presentation to learner's preferences, interests and needs. The paper presents a pilot ILE and details aspects related to the learner profile and to the appraisal of learning.

1. Introduction

Despite impressive improvements [1-3], e-learning tools and platforms are still considered less appealing than traditional face-to-face teaching methods. Learners complain about the rigidity of e-learning systems that serve the same web pages to any user, without understanding their needs. Tutors spend significantly more time and effort preparing the teaching material, assisting students and assessing their advancement in learning, while "hiding behind a machine". On the other hand, the vast majority of the currently used web-based educational systems are powerful integrated systems, like Blackboard [4] or WebCT [5] that provide a large variety of support services to both learners and teachers, but lack adaptability, belonging to the class of Learning Management Systems (LMS).

Significant research and implementation effort has been dedicated to develop Intelligent Tutoring Systems [6] and Adaptive Hypermedia [7, 8], able to adapt to learner's objectives, interests, and preferences, i.e., to Learner Profile (LP). Currently, such systems offer remarkable adaptability, but only for specific tasks, lacking integration. Improved distributed architectures, centered on the concept of Intelligent Learning Environments, have been suggested to allow combining the efficiency of LMS with the flexibility of adaptive systems [9-11]. To implement the adaptivity feature, an ILE requires a quite complex structure, with several parallel version of the same learning item (LI), allowing many different learning paths to be selected in accordance with the LPs.

This approach requires considerable additional effort in elaborating teaching materials, may require several authors or institutional support, but is truly flexible and adaptable. A course is no longer a flat juxtaposition of learning items, but a multilevel structure with many parallel branches. The ILE recommends an optimal path for a user or class of users. As mentioned in [11], it has been argued that authoring learning material and building the structure of adaptive systems is too complicated for the average teacher. Correspondingly, portability – the ability to deploy system content on any other system, and reusability – the ability to search, retrieve and reuse LIs, including lessons, modules, exercises, activities, become necessary for efficient implementation of the ILE concept and for the woide scale implementation success of this approach. The problem has already been addressed for LMS: the DOD's Sharable Content Object Reference Model (SCORM) ADL initiative [12] aims to provide a comprehensive set of e-learning capabilities enabling interoperability, accessibility and reuse of Web-based learning content. Similar efforts are under way to provide a harmonized set of guidelines, specification and standards for Intelligent Tutoring Systems (ITS) and Adaptive Hypermedia (AH) systems [13, 14]. At the same time, significant changes in the basic methodology of teaching/learning is to be expected as result of the current advancement and convergence of cognitive psychology and computing science. Paradigms such as just-in-time learning, constructivist approaches, student-centered learning and collaborative approaches have emerged, and are being supported by technological advancements including simulations, virtual reality and multi-agents systems.

The paper presents the architecture of a pilot ILE and some of the tools used to evaluate and guide the students' advancement towards their learning goals. These tools can also be used to help in students' examination, but they are intended primarily to guide the trainee through the learning process, offer a platform for co-operative learning and knowledge discovery, and customize the presentation to learner's preferences, interests and needs. Preliminary work and partial results in the elaboration of the methodology and the implementation of the system have been reported in previous papers [15-18].

2. Elements of Methodology, Architecture and Implementation

The system is learner centered, all human and artificial agents being focused on achieving the learning-training tasks. Human agents include, aside the students, authors of teaching materials, tutors, course administrators, and system administrator(s). The pilot web oriented ILE has a server-client distributed multiagent hybrid architecture as shown in Figure 1.

The client side software and hardware requirements are minimised. Each human agent accesses the system via an intranet or internet connection, by using a standard web browser.

On the server side, each human agent is endowed with a personal assistant (agent) that inter-operates with the other artificial agents providing the system functionality. All personal assistants are linked to communication tools that facilitate the contact among human actors in the system, and provide support to the collaboration among the students. The learner personal assistant (LPA) controls, in the first place, the access to the agents providing the main functions – the Automatic Tutoring Tool and the Student Evaluation Tool, but also to the Learning Item (LI) Authoring Tool and Tests Authoring Tool – thus providing support to a participative learning approach. Students get credits not only for their results in the tests, but also for their involvement in the course development – by contributing with new versions to existing LIs, building new questions for tests addressing various LIs, etc. When submitted, the student contributions are stored in a buffer, waiting for tutor's validation to be introduced in the course and test databases. The contributions are marked similarly to the successful passing of regular tests. The LPA gives also access to the Registration and Personal Data Management Tool, and helps tracking student participation and results, passing the corresponding data to the Learner's Profile Eliciting Tool (LPET).

The tutor has also a Tutor Personal Assistant (TPA) that provides an interface to all system functionalities offered to a tutor: keeping track of class enrolment, following learners' progress in the training process, reading synthetic data on learners' profile, a.s.o. Authors and tutors have access to authoring tools, to update the course, tests and any other teaching materials. Course administrators have access to all relevant data about courses and students. The system administrator monitors the usage of the resources and takes care of the smooth functioning of the system. The distribution of the functional roles among human actors can be managed from an administrator platform accessed via root privileges.

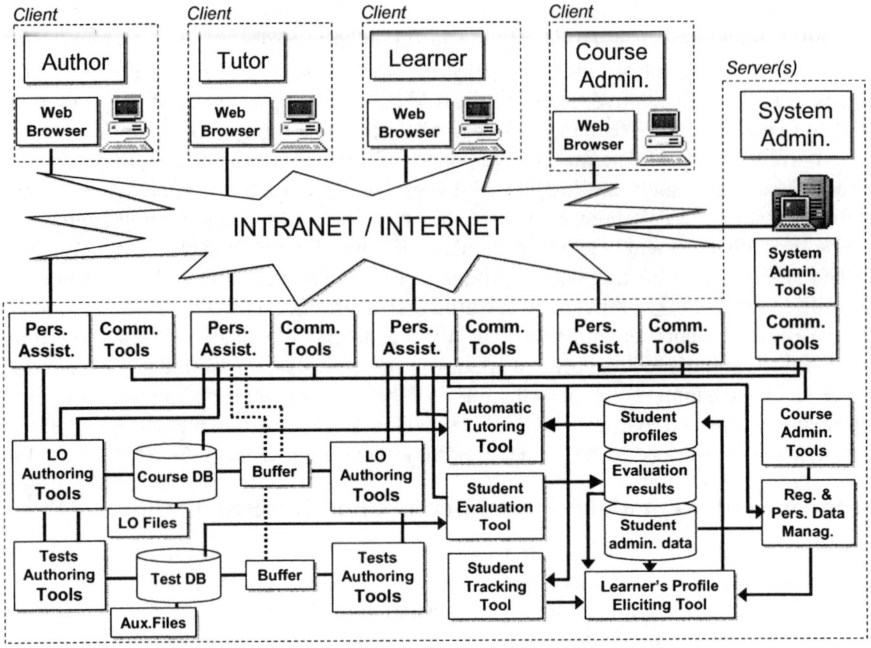

Figure 1: Architecture of the ILE Pilot

The server is an in-house developed J2EE compatible JAVA web-application, running on the Tomcat Apache Server and using the MySQL database server, both accessible and available on UNIX and WINDOWS. The modular approach allows easy restructuring of the system; e.g., a database change affects only the module controlling the database. Database access speed is increased by using a connection pool. Data access (some contained in the MySQL database, some in a system of related directory files) is made through interactive web pages implemented with Java Server Pages (JSP) and Servlets. Each JSP is controlled by a JavaBean which handles the security tasks and data manipulation. Every JavaBean within a module extends the class corresponding to an actor (learner, author, tutor, course and system administrator), being able to control authorized access.

2.1. Learner's Profile

In the pilot ILE implementation, the Learner Profile (LP) is simply an operational data record of a student, providing the information needed for the individualization of the content and presentation of teaching material. Nevertheless, in accordance to privacy protection legislation and rules, the LP file is treated as a private document, handled and used with due care. General conclusions, relevant to larger classes of students, without reference to individuals, are accessible to improve teaching, while individual data are encoded and used inside the system for adaptation purposes. Figure 2 presents a schematic diagram of the LP structure, as used by the LPET, showing its three basic components: Learning Objective (LO), Learning Modality (LM) and Knowledge Watch (KW).

The LO module specifies the basic requirements of the learning/teaching process. If the student is enrolled in aiming at a diploma, the study content and tests must satisfy some mandatory minimal acceptance conditions. The situation is different for complementary studies, when the content and study level are up to the learner. The modalities of training can largely vary depending on the LOs. An executive updating requires a dense digest-like presentation showing new opportunities, while avoiding going into technical details. A specialist up-grading must give a punctual in-depth presentation, building on learner's previous domain knowledge. For problem centered training, both content and tests must be structured around given tasks. The use of keywords allows flexible re-structuring of teaching material, in accordance with the LOs, sometimes quite different of the author's course structure. The input of LO module comes primarily from data provided by the learner in the registration form and, whenever necessary e-questionnaires, but can be amended with data from the Student Tracking Tool, tutors and course administrators.

The LM module is closely linked to the LO module, as the modalities of presenting the material are mainly determined by LOs. Still, there are aspects that must be explicitly specified in the LM module: predominantly descriptive or, on the contrary, including analytical details and proofs, stressing on theoretical or practical aspects, following the construction required by the inner logic of the field (actually, the domain theory), or based mostly on demos and examples. The LM module also takes into account the technical aspects of the user (client) platform, i.e. screen resolution, usable bandwidth, processing power, to adapt the presentations to the available resources.

The KW module provides the dynamic adaptability of the ILE based on the student's mastery of the course material. The data from the STT, the results of self testing and mandatory testing, as well as of the pro-active contribution of the student in supplying new LI, testing instrument, additional tests or any other contribution in the process of collaborative learning are also taken into account in defining the LP and in choosing the recommended path. The recommended path can simply be a re-ordering or a selection of the standard table of content, but can also imply a more elaborate choice of one of several parallel LI addressing the same subject in various approaches, depending on the priorities resulting from the LO and KW. The system is non-intrusive, as the student can follow either the recommended path or navigate along any path (s)he considers adequate. In the pilot implementation, part of the data about the student gathered during a learning session is processed off line, after the user logoff, to be used in the next session.

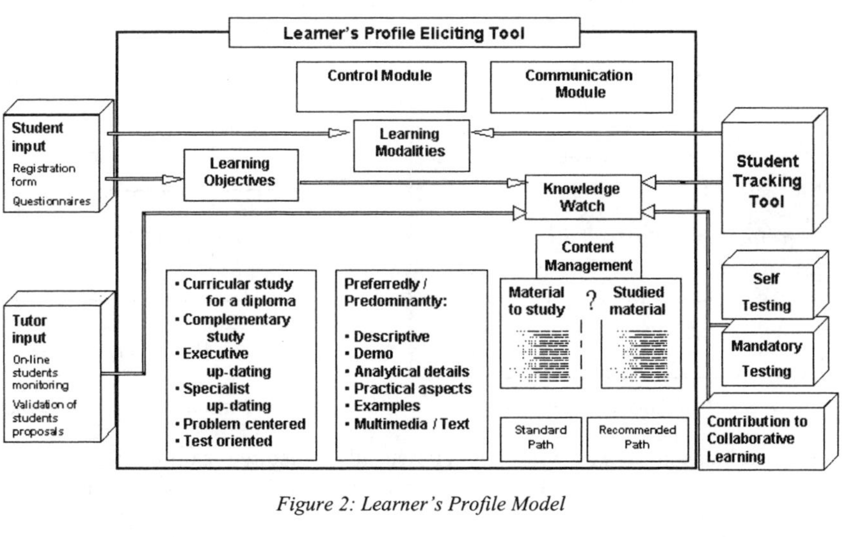

Figure 2: Learner's Profile Model

2.2 Learning Appraisal

Learning appraisal is based on both test results and the student involvement in proactive learning, including the contribution to the course continuous development. Care is taken to stimulate students to do more than just recognize textbook material when responding to tests. The proposed questions require finer distinctions between correct and nearly-correct statements, based not only on plain recognition, but also on deductive and inductive inferences, on analysis and synthesis abilities. Higher-order thinking questions make the content of the questions challenging for the students and help them to understand thoroughly the course. Students are encouraged to formulate themselves new questions and are given credits when their contribution is included in the question database (QDB).

We now describe the multiple choice questionnaires used as a testing tools for all the levels and learning items of a course. Figure 3 shows the three panels of the multiple choice test window. The upper panel comprises the identifier of the LI to which the test refers to, the number of questions that must be answered and an active table that keeps track of the current state. For self-testing, both the LI and the number of questions can be specified by the user. In the case of mandatory tests, these parameters are imposed by the system/tutor.

The questions can be seen either in sequence, relying on the default automatic sequential order of presentation used by the system, or randomly, by using the up/down arrows or by clicking the corresponding button in the active table. The background colors of the columns in this table are distinct for questions that have already been seen, the current question and the remaining questions. Current question content, text and figure, are displayed in the middle panel and the available options for the multiple choice are shown in the lower panel. The options can be made by clicking the corresponding buttons either in the upper or in the lower active tables. The corresponding field in the upper table is marked as checked. A previously answered question can be re-visited for changing the options before submission, by pressing again the selection button in the upper panel After submission, the checked marks are automatically replaced by the points obtained for each choice. The user can verify the result for already answered questions or for part of them, before submitting the whole test, by pressing the button "Points" or the field in the row corresponding to the question, but the options for these questions will be frozen.

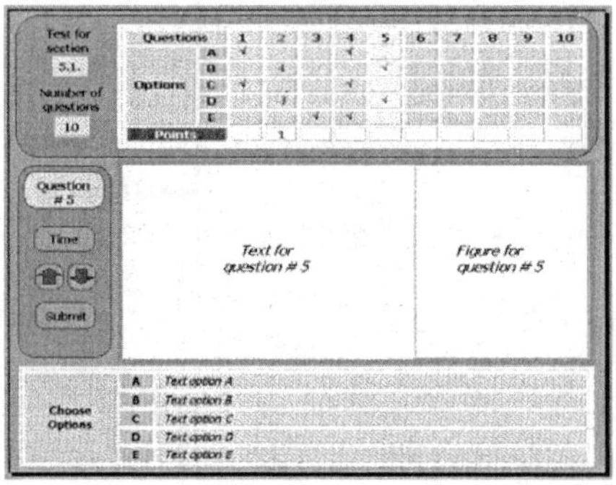

Figure 3: Multiple choice test window

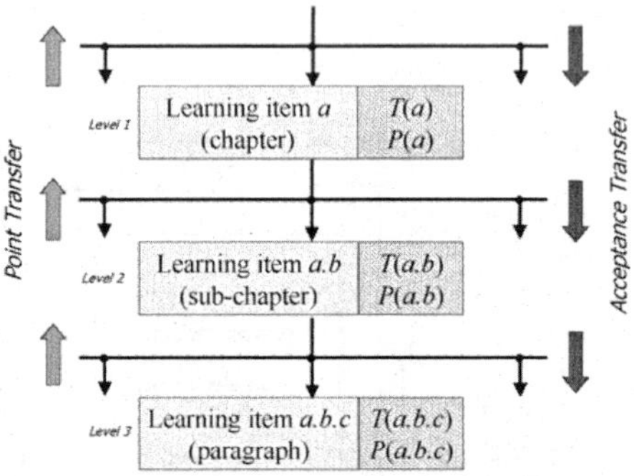

Figure 4: Point and Acceptance transfer

The questions are linked with the hierarchically structured learning item (LI) to which they refer, and various transversal structures, dynamically defined by adequate sets of keywords. Wrong choices for a question related to a certain LI, can signal errors relevant for another LI. To make the system closer to a classic examination that does not require the checking every item in a course, the passing of a higher level LI is not conditioned by the passing of all lower LIs it contains, but only by the sum of points exceeding the threshold for that level. The acceptance of a higher level LI gives credit for all LIs below it in the course structure. This results in an up-wards propagation of the awarded points and a downward propagation of the acceptance, as shown in Figure 4. The acceptance of an LI is irreversible, so that only warnings and advices are issued if later errors signal possible weaknesses in an already assessed LI. The tests are built by randomly choosing from the question database (QDB) a specified number of questions referring to the given tag (LI address or keyword). A test referring to a LI can comprise questions attached either directly to that specific LI, or to any LI placed below it in the course tree structure. The points obtained when making a choice C from the set of options O(Q) pertinent to question Q are recorded at the LI to which the question is attached and transferred upwards. The sum of points P(Q) for a question Q results by adding the points for all options selected at Q. Positive points obtained for a question are taken into account only when exceeding a certain minimum threshold. Such a learning appraisal aims at a robust understanding and proper using of the tested knowledge, by discouraging superficial and fragmentary learning. Each LI is not evaluated independently, but in the context of the course, in relation with the related LIs. The sum of points SP(LI) for a certain learning item LI consists not only of the sum of the points obtained for the questions Q referring directly to LI, but, also, of the sum of the points transferred to LI from its children – the learning items LI' placed one level below it in the course tree. The points obtained for a certain learning item are transferred upwards, to all LIs that are its ascendants, without double counting.

The points P(LI) acknowledged for a learning item LI depend also on the passing of a certain acceptance threshold T(LI), but, in this case, there is an award A(LI) for the successful completion of the study of LI marked by the passing of T(LI). At the same time, the status S(LI) of the learning item LI changes from 0 (pending) to 1 (passed), when its threshold, or the threshold of its ascendant, have been passed.

3. Results

To verify system usability and acceptance, the Pilot ILE described in this paper was used to teach several courses, from a simple "Introductory Java" course, requiring only presentation of text and checking of some code samples, to the "Anatomy of the surface of the brain by means of flat maps" [17], based on an elaborate graphical support. A new system of active images [18] has been experimented for a course on "Digital Circuits".

To partially assess and evaluate the results, usability and acceptance tests have been undertaken in six of the universities partners in the project. Figure 5 gives the results of an overall acceptance test carried out with a group of 32 undergraduate students taking a course on "Neural Networks" in the fourth year of study at the Faculty of Engineering Sciences of the "Politehnica" University of Bucharest. The test was run after students passed the final exam in that discipline, but were not anonymous, to correlate the opinion on the system with the marks of the students. Despite students noticing (and helping to remove) bugs in the current system implementation, the average acceptance rate was about 72%. There was little correlation between the time of usage of the system, as recorded by the *Student Tracking Tool*, the results of the acceptance test and the students' final markings at the NN course.

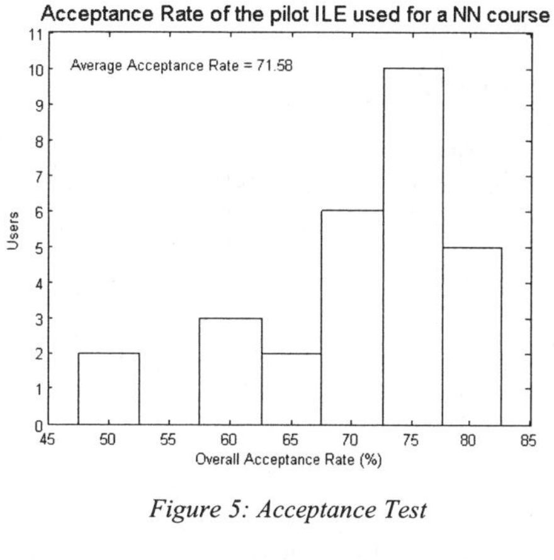

Figure 5: Acceptance Test

4. Conclusions and future work

A pilot Intelligent e-Learning Environment has been implemented and experimented to teach several university level courses. Attention has been given to the assessment of student knowledge, but only for the purpose of performing the adaptation tasks. Because of the difficulties related to a proper certification of the students, remote assessment of student's knowledge has not been used for marking purposes in this phase of the implementation.

The system was positively received by students, with an average overall acceptance rate of over 70%. In fact, the experiments with the pilot implementation showed that full cooperation of the students is necessary for the successful use of an ILE system.

The drawbacks of the increased system complexity and the larger organizational framework are offset by the true flexibility and adaptability. The system holds the potential for future improvements and will be used on an increased scale. Current research and development efforts are oriented towards several goals: (1) refinement of the Learner's Profile Eliciting Tool and the Automatic Tutoring Tool, primarily to make better use of the growing data bases with student profiles and diversified learning items, (2) development of content compliant to standards, to support interoperability, accessibility and reusability, whenever possible, (3) integrated communication facilities, to increase system availability. A co-operation with a commercial company is being sought to develop a marketable version of the product. The large scale implementation of the ILE approach requires the creation of an adequate organizational framework, including a proper accreditation system of learning items and methodologies, in accordance to widely accepted quality standards.

Acknowledgment

Part of this work was supported by the Socrates Minerva project 87574-CP-1-2000-1-RO-MINERVA-ODL "Artificial Intelligence and Neural Network Tools for Innovative ODL" (www.dsp.pub.ro). The content of this paper does not necessarily reflect the position of the European Community, and involve no responsibility on part of the European Community.

References

[1] D.A.Norman, J.D.Spohrer, Learner-centered education, Comm. of the ACM, 39(4), 1996, pp. 24-27.

[2] M.J.Wooldrige, N.R.Jennings, Intelligent agents: Theory and practice, The Knowledge Engineering Review, 10(2), 1995, pp. 115-152.

[3] J.Grudin, Computer-supported Cooperative work: History and Focus, IEEE Computer, 27(5), 1994, pp. 19-26.

[4] Blackboard Inc, Blackboard Course Management System, http://www.blackboard.com/

[5] WebCT, Course Management System, http://www.webct.com

[6] C. Frasson, G. Gauthier (editors), Intelligent Tutoring Systems - At the Cross-roads of Artificial Intelligence and Education, Ablex Publishing Corporation. Norwood, New Jersey, 1990.

[7] De Bra, P., Aerts, A., Berden, B., De Lange, B., Rousseau, B., Santic, T., Smits, D. & Stash, N., AHA! The Adaptive Hypermedia Architecture, Proc. of ACM Hypertext Conference, Nottingham, UK, August 2003, pp. 81-84

[8] P. Brusilovsky, Adaptive hypermedia, User Modeling and User Adapted Interaction, Ten Year Anniversary Issue (Alfred Kobsa, ed.) 11(1/2), 2002, pp. 87-110

[9] P. Brusilovsky, Student model centered architecture for intelligent learning environments, Proc. of Fourth international conference on User Modeling, 15-19 August, Hyannis, MA, USA. User Modeling Inc, 1994, pp. 31-36

[10] O. Conlan, C. Hockemeyer, V. Wade, D.Albert, D., & M. Gargan, An architecture for integrating adaptive hypermedia service with open learning environments, In Proc. of ED-MEDIA 2002, vol. 1 of World Conference on Educational Multimedia, Hypermedia & Telecommunications, pp. 344-350.

[11] P. Brusilovsky, A Distributed Architecture for Adaptive and Intelligent Learning Management Systems, Proc. of AI in Education (AIED2003), vol.4., Workshop towards intelligent Learning Management Systems, Sydney, Australia, July 2003.

[12] Advanced Distributed Learning (ADL) Initiative, Sharable Content Object Reference Model (SCORM), http://www.adlnet.org/

[13] A.I. Cristea & A. De Mooij, Designer Adaptation in Adaptive Hypermedia Authoring, Proc. ITCC'03, Las Vegas, US, IEEE Computer Science, 2003, pp. 444-448.

[14] D. Dicheva, L. Aroyo, Alexandra Cristea, Collaborative Courseware Authoring Support, Proc WEB-CATE 2002 – Computers and Advanced Technology in Education, Cancun, Mexico, 2002, pp. 52-57.

[15] P. Cristea, Rodica Tuduce, Test Authoring for Intelligent e-Learning Environments, Proc. IASTED Intl. Conf., Web-Based Education, Innsbruck, Austria, 2004, pp. 402-407.

[16] P. Cristea, Rodica Tuduce, Ioana Savescu, C. Gorgorin, D. Tomozei, V. Gradinescu, C. Rangu, Prototype Implementation of an Intelligent e-Learning System, Proc. IASTED International Conference, Web-Based Education, Innsbruck, Austria, 2004, pp. 441-446.

[17] R. Deklerck, M.Suliga, E. Nyssen, An intelligent tool to aid in understanding cortical brain anatomy visualized by means of flat maps, Proc. IASTED International Conference, Web-Based Education, Innsbruck, Austria, 2004, pp. 474-479.

[18] E. Nyssen, H. Patrascu, T. Yan, M. Suliga, and R. Deklerck, Active images - a tool for interactive and participative web-based learning, Proc. IASTED International Conference, Web-Based Education, Innsbruck, Austria, 2004, pp. 453-457.

eAdoption and the Knowledge Economy: Issues, Applications, Case Studies
P. Cunningham and M. Cunningham (Eds.)
IOS Press, 2004

The Virtual Laboratory as an Active Learning Environment

Mikhail MOROZOV, Andrey TANAKOV, Alexey GERASIMOV, Dmitry BYSTROV, Valery CVIRKO
Multimedia System Laboratory of Mari State Technical University, pl. Lenina, 3, Yoshkar-Ola, 424000, Russia
Tel: +8 362 68-60-90, Fax: + 8 362 41-08-72, Email: morozov@marstu.mari.ru

Abstract: The critical success factor in an effective e-learning strategy is the use of an active learning environment instead of the simple "page-turning" content. The aim of this paper is to present the virtual chemistry laboratory, a power tool of active e-learning, and a new approach for creating active learning environments. The virtual chemistry laboratory includes a great number of experiments, which are accomplished through the use of real-time 3D graphics and pre-rendered animation. Interactive laboratory activities are able to enhance a student's understanding of chemical processes and practical skills. In order to make human-computer interaction more enjoyable and productive, an animated pedagogical agent was added to the interface of the laboratory. The cost-effective approach based on the application of a presentation engine – NATURA – with scripting language for the development of virtual learning environment is described.

1. Introduction

There is some conflict in the development of e-learning materials between the manner of content representation and basic ideas of current learning theory. Most e-learning materials are still developed as a network of static hypertext pages, sometimes with Flash animation. At the same time current learning theory suggests that students' learning is increased when the educational resources incorporate a greater deal of interactive and multimedia content in the active learning environment.

The existence of this conflict can be partly explained by the fact that the production of educational hypertext is a simple and cheap process, while the design and implementation of an active learning environment is a difficult task, more time-consuming and costly.

Meanwhile many researches prove that simple forms for representation learning material are not effective for teaching [1]. Moreover, in [2] Prensky states that learners of the "videogame generation" are oriented on high interactive and multimedia-rich learning environment. Simulation and virtual reality software meet the above-mentioned requirements in the best way. Therefore, simulation products that can be used to support and extend the active learning processes have recently attracted a great deal of attention. In the natural sciences such as Chemistry, Physics and Biology, virtual laboratories can simulate real-world behavior in an engaging and intuitive graphic environment to assist students acquire new knowledge and skills through learning by doing.

This paper presents virtual chemistry laboratory for school education developed at the Multimedia System Laboratory MarSTU. The Virtual Lab includes a great number of experiments, which are accomplished through the use of the real-time 3D graphics and pre-rendered animation. The cost-effective approaches for the development of virtual learning environment are described.

2. Objectives

The significance of virtual experiments and their many benefits have been recognised by a number of researchers. For instance, in [3] it is noted that virtual experiments can be used to acquaint students with laboratory techniques and procedures prior to their laboratory sessions, so that they can be better prepared to conduct the same or similar experiments in a real-life chemical laboratory. It also allows students to collect and assemble the items of apparatus, as well as familiarize themselves with laboratory techniques and procedures. It should be emphasized that virtual chemistry experiments are safe even for novices.

Learners can carry out such experiments that might be dangerous and/or expensive in a real laboratory. In [3] it is pointed out that the performance of virtual experiments could help students achieve the skills in recording, reporting and interpreting data in a lab notebook. Besides, virtual experiments could potentially develop skills related to manipulative and instrument use. Moreover, computer simulations in a virtual chemistry laboratory encourage students to experiment and have some fun [4].

3. Methodology

Various approaches are used in the development of virtual laboratories. These approaches can be differentiated first of all by delivery methods - WEB-based and CD-ROM-based learning environment, - and also by the type of representation – two-dimensional and three-dimensional graphics and animation. In [5] virtual laboratories are classified according to two categories, depending on how they gain their knowledge. Fact based virtual laboratories have a limited set of preprogrammed facts in simulation. This is the way that the majority of virtual labs currently work. Derivation based labs allow the learners to proceed with the experiments beyond those preplanned before. The results obtained are based on a mathematical model solution of the experiments.

In a Virtual Chemistry Laboratory at Carnegie Mellon University there is Web-based delivery and it can be distributed as a self-contained CD-ROM. In this laboratory there is representation of two-dimensional graphical scenes and mathematical model of chemical experiments [6]. Virtual Chemical Lab (Brigham Young University) uses three-dimensional representation, fact-based simulation and CD-ROM delivery [7]. Oxford University Virtual Chemistry Laboratory applies WEB–based video for the experiments presentation [8].

Potentialities of simulation are generally determined by the method of delivery. It is evident that two-dimensional graphics is more suitable for WEB-based delivery, while for CD-ROM, 3D graphics and animation can be used without resource constraints. It is worth mentioning that pre-rendered 3D animation and video provide realistic representation and good visual quality. Real-time animation allows more opportunities to create 3-D virtual reality environments aimed to mimic real-life laboratory. Accordingly, a combination of both pre-rendered animation and real-time three-dimensional animations provide a realistic representation of both the visual environment as well as the learner's manipulation of chemicals in conducting virtual experiments. This very approach was chosen for the implementation of virtual chemistry laboratory described in this paper. Chemical equipment, apparatus and complex chemical processes are presented with pre-rendered 3D animations, but for simulation of glassware, chemical solutions and the activity of learners in the real laboratory (pouring from one vessel into another, putting chemicals in a test tube, retrieving a solution from the shelf) real time animations are used to simulate.

4. Development of virtual chemistry laboratory

In a virtual chemistry laboratory developed at the Multimedia System Laboratory there are more than 150 chemical experiments included in the school chemistry curriculum. The chemical experiments are carried out in a three-dimensional simulated laboratory, which contains all the necessary chemical equipment, glassware and chemical reagents. In order to prevent overloading of the visual space of the computer screen, the set of the lab equipment and chemicals available to learners is placed depending on the chemical experiment to be conducted. In some experiments – these are just bottles with chemical solutions, in others - complex chemical apparatus (Figure 1).

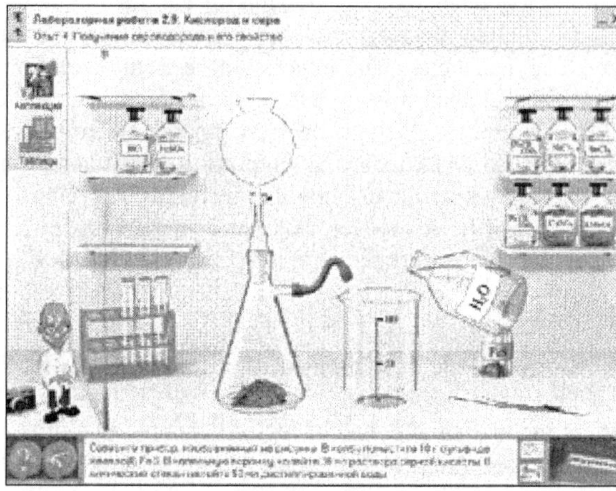

Figure 1. Virtual Chemistry Laboratory

Experiments are modelled using real-time animation techniques and a learner can interact with virtual equipment in a similar way to the real lab procedures. Learners can set up chemical apparatus and carry out virtual experiments. It is possible to make the required measurements by means of virtual measuring instruments or to change the parameters of the experiments. When performing the experiment the learner can record observations in the form of snapshots with the help of virtual photo camera, and report and interpret data of the experiment in the Lab notebook. It is possible to watch the enlarged images of the ongoing chemical processes in a special lens window. A learner's steps through the lab procedure are monitored by the program. The pedagogical agent, the animated character «Chemist», gives necessary comments and guidelines in the speech or a text-based form. To ease the recording of formulas and equations in the Lab notebook a special program «Editor of Chemical formulas» is realized using Macromedia Flash technology.

A "Molecular builder" for manipulating three-dimensional representation of organic and inorganic molecules is included as a part of the Virtual Chemistry Laboratory (Figure 2). The use of 3D modelling of molecules and atoms to illustrate phenomena in chemistry teaching is required to ensure all three chemistry understanding levels: micro, macro and symbol [9]. In order to make the behavior of substances more understandable for learners we introduce molecular models as means help visualize what learners cannot see.

A "Molecular builder" displays shaded colour models in a wire frame, ball-and-stick, and space filling spheres format. The molecule may be rotated in real time by direct mouse drag. Several user-friendly features of the builder allow learners to add and delete atoms and bonds by simple clicks of the mouse. To extend the use of molecules model in chemistry teaching the builder provides the visualization of various electron orbital. Created by learners model of molecule can be exported out to VRML format if required and then viewed in a web browser.

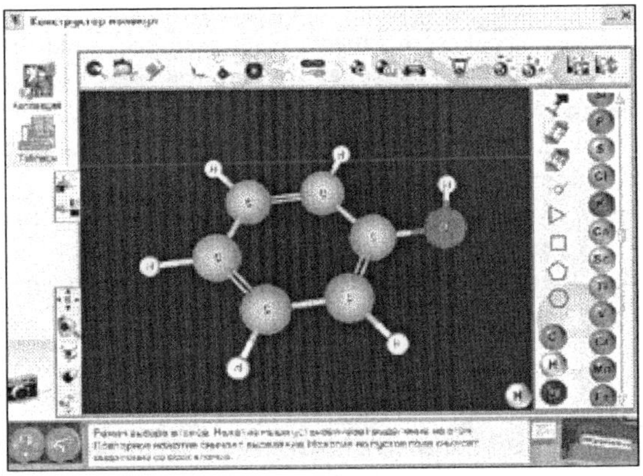

Figure 2. Molecular builder

4.1. Interface of Virtual Laboratory

The design of a valid interface for the Virtual laboratory is a challenging and responsible task. It is important to provide direct manipulation for collecting items of chemical apparatus and performing of laboratory procedures, as well as to offer a learner a suitable control and navigation elements. It would be interesting to place all the objects in the sole 3D scene within a common interface metaphor. Since in a virtual laboratory it is necessary to have a lot of glassware, chemicals and equipment to conduct experiments, placing additional 3D objects for navigation and control will lead to the overloading visual space of a computer display screen. Therefore, in the interface design of our virtual lab only those control objects are placed into 3D scene, which are necessary while performing experiments (for example, a photo camera to record the observations). All the rest navigation and control elements of the interface are removed to 2D space, which is placed on the borders of the screen. It allows us to increase the effect of presence when learners are practicing in the virtual laboratory.

Figure 3. Pedagogical agent

Many claim pedagogical agents, lifelike animated characters, represent an important concept in the new generation of learning environments [10][11]. Pedagogical agents attract the learner's attention, guide the leaner through the presentation and convey additional conversational and emotional signals via facial expressions and body movements. Pedagogical agents enable computer interfaces to become more human or "social".

This evidence prompted the inclusion of pedagogical agents in the interface of the Virtual laboratory. A Life-like character "Chemist" is realized in a real-time 3D animation.

"Chemist" monitors the learner's actions in the laboratory and helps out when problems arise. Sometimes the pedagogical agent participates in conducting experiments himself.

It is noted that believability is a key feature of animated agents for learning environments and can increase students' motivation and time spent with the educational software [12]. To increase believability and create the personalized appearance of a pedagogical agent, the program is able to generate expressive body movement by modifying the animation of synthetic character in real-time. Postures, agent's head's movements, facial expressions and hand gestures are included in the behavior of the pedagogical agent. It helps to make a better social contact with the learner and consequently provide more effective and engaging learning environment.

4.2. Script-based approach

How was it possible to develop cost-efficient learning environment, which contain more than 100 virtual experiments with high-level interactivity, a huge amount of complex 3D objects (glassware, chemical solution and equipment), and also containing a real-time animated character? To do so two recent approaches for development of full featured multimedia rich applications were used. The script-based approach is used for representation of high-impact multimedia content and interactivity. This approach provides extended tools to define the desired structure of content and user interaction with objects in the virtual environment, as well as giving it maximum flexibility for multimedia production. The script of the presentation is written in the high-level object-oriented language NML and is executed by the engine NATURA, described in [13].

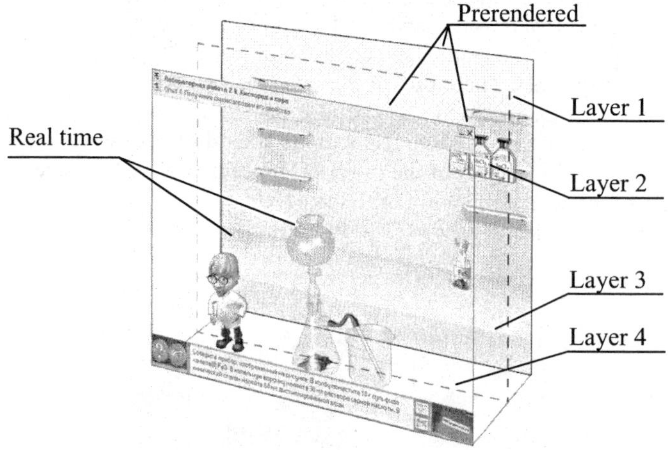

Figure 4. "Sandwich" of layers

4.3. Mixed real-time and pre-rendered animations

To visualize the content we used the approach based on the idea that various 2D and 3D objects in the scene are placed in different layers similar to the layers of a "sandwich" (Fig. 4). Different graphical objects including pre-rendered and real-time animation can exist in every layer. When the final image is created in the "sandwich" layers are blended with each other taking in account the transparency.

Special algorithms were developed to minimize the calculations to update the screen. It has considerably increased the speed of rendering dynamic scenes. This is important for modeling chemical procedures and for animation of the pedagogical agent.

One of the main difficulties in laboratory simulation is visualization of processes in chemical solutions. To simplify the process of development a special tool "Liquid modeler" was created, that helps to change the colour and transparency of the solution, as well as sediments and boiling parameters, etc.

4.4. Other Virtual Labs

The approach defined in this paper can be easily applied to creation of virtual laboratories for other subjects in the school curriculum. In the case of a Virtual Biology Laboratory, high-quality 3D graphics and animation allow the development of realistic simulations of state-of-the-art scientific equipment to expose students to the tools and techniques of modern biology. Similarly, the presentation engine NATURA can help to simulate an interactive 3D visualization of students' activities during the conduct of experiments in Physics. Students will use this virtual lab when physics experiments are too expensive, risky, or complex. Also it would be interesting to develop a virtual laboratory for ecological education, where students will be able to explore and experiment with ecosystems, something which can never be possible without computer simulation technology.

At the universities, virtual laboratories are important for education in Science, Engineering, Electronics, Robotics and other disciplines. In these areas the ability to test theories or perform experiments is crucial to knowledge formation and assessment, and virtual laboratories make it possible to visualize complex and tedious experiments.

Our approaches can also be used for the development of active learning environments for professional training. We developed the interactive multimedia environment for initial professional training of electricians in maintaining, troubleshooting and repairing electric equipment with the help of 3D simulations. The students can work with virtual electric equipments similar to the way they would in the field.

5. Conclusions

Creating an active and engaging learning environment is an essential part of a successful e-learning strategy. Active e-learning software can offer learners the opportunity to explore science through discovery and experimentation. Interactive simulations facilitate the acquisition of a higher level of understanding by the learners than passive learning. Moreover, all of these learner-centered characteristics of an active learning environment contribute to learner motivation and engagement.

Like the virtual laboratory considered in this paper, active learning environments are often based on content-rich multimedia simulation. Technical complexity and the high cost of development are primary obstacles in the way of a massive expansion in the use of virtual learning environments. New approaches are needed in order to solve this problem. To create such a system we suggest in this paper the approaches based on an application of the presentation engine NATURA, with scripting language as well as mixed real-time and pre-rendered animations. As has been shown, the approaches described allow us to create a virtual laboratory that is both engaging and effective. We believe that this approach can be useful for the development of other engaging learning environments.

Acknowledgements

This work has been funded by the National Training Foundation (Russian Federation) and this paper was submitted with help of EU project ADMIRE-P (IST-2001-35449).

References

[1] "Theory and Practice of Online Learning", Terry Anderson, Fathi Elloumi (eds.), Athabasca University, 2004

[2] Mark Prensky, Digital Game-Base Learning, McGraw-Hill, 2000.

[3] Barney Dalgarno, Andrea Bishop and Danny Bedgood, “The potential of virtual laboratories for distance science education teaching: reflections from the initial development and evaluation of a virtual chemistry laboratory”, Proceedings of the Improving Learning Outcomes Through Flexible Science Teaching, Symposium, The University of Sydney, October 3, 2003, pp. 90-95.

[4] Dan Carnevale, “The Virtual Lab Experiment”, Chronicle of Higher Ed, January 31, 2003, p. A30

[5] Jamie Robinson, “Virtual Laboratories as a teaching environment: A tangible solution or a passing novelty?”, 3rd Annual CM316 Conference on Multimedia Systems, based at Southampton University. http://mms.ecs.soton.ac.uk/papers/5.pdf

[6] Yaron, D., Freeland, R., Lange, D., Karabinos, M., Milton, J., and Belford, R., “Uses of Flexible Virtual Laboratory Simulations in Introductory Chemistry Courses”, CONFCHEM 2001.

[7] Brian F. Woodfield, Merritt B. Andrus, Virtual ChemLab for Organic Chemistry , Prentice Hall, September 2, 2003.

[8] Virtual chemistry, www.chem.ox.ac.uk/vrchemistry/

[9] Dori, Y.J. and Barak, M. (2001), “Virtual and Physical Molecular Modeling: Fostering Model Perception and Spatial Understanding”, Educational Technology & Society, 4(1), pp. 61-74.

[10] A. Nijholt, “Agents, Believability and Embodiment in Advanced Learning Environments”, Proc. IEEE International Conference on Advanced Learning Technologies (ICALT 2001), T. Okamto, R. Hartley, Kinshuk & J.P.Klus (eds.), 2001, pp. 457-459.

[11] W. Lewis Johnson, Jeff W. Rickel, James C. Lester, “Animated Pedagogical Agents: Face-to-Face Interaction in Interactive Learning Environments”, International Journal of Artificial Intelligence in Education, 2000, N 11, pp.47-78.

[12] J. Lester, J. Voerman, S. Towns, C. Callaway, "Cosmo: A Life-Like Animated Pedagogical Agent with Deictic Believability," in Notes of the IJCAI '97 Workshop on Animated Interface Agents: Making Them Intelligent, Nagoya, Japan, 1997, pp. 61-70.

[13] M. Morozov, A. Tanakov and D. Bystrov, “Pedagogical Agents in the Multimedia Natural Sciences for Children”, Proc. IEEE International Conference on Advanced Learning Technologies (ICALT 2003), Vladan Devedzic, J. Michael Spector, Demetrios G Sampson,Kinshuk (eds.), 2003, pp. 62-65.

Section 8.3

Case Studies

eAdoption and the Knowledge Economy: Issues, Applications, Case Studies
P. Cunningham and M. Cunningham (Eds.)
IOS Press, 2004

The Impact of Low Computer Literacy in the Information Society

Fulvia SALA
AICA, Piazzale Morandi 2, Milano, 20052, Italy
Tel:+39(0)276455026, Fax:+39(0)276015717, Email: fulvia.sala@aicanet.it

Abstract: Italian business underestimates the importance of learning how to use IT tools. Many Italian companies are reluctant to arrange training programmes for many employees. A main aim of the study, conducted by AICA and Bocconi University, was to quantitatively assess the cost which IT illiteracy can have on companies and the Italian economy; the research discovered that the annual economic impact of a delay in ensuring that a workforce is computer literate, in Italy exceeds 15 billion euros. The study also involved quantitatively assessing the ROI of users' basic IT training. The researchers discovered that a basic "ECDL like" preparation can help slash the cost of computer insufficient training by dramatically increasing the efficiency of staff who use computers; in fact acquiring computer skills results in increased productivity, annual savings being estimated at round 15 billion euros.

1. Introduction

The term "Information Society" refers to an economic-social context where new information and telecommunications technology (ICT) plays a pervasive role, capable of impacting both the economy and individuals' behaviour. The adoption of ICT in business has meant changing and enhancing many in-house and intercompany projects.

The European Union has been shown to deliver much attention to Information Society. In fact a European policy is being implemented in this respect, national policies being supposed to adjust to it. Human resources in general, and enhancing human capital and investing in developing skills in particular, mean a hot issue of EU policies: spreading information technology alone is insufficient to exert a positive effect on economic and social changes, as strategically pursued by the European Union. Information technology should be supported by European citizens' "digital" cultural development – that is, individuals' ability to effectively use technology, seizing any relevant opportunities.

A report drawn up by the European Commission states the following:
"The worker and workplace in the Information Society will be very different from those we are familiar with today. In the Information Society an increasing number of people work in jobs centring on information and knowledge and will make use of Information Society tools and services. Workers in the digital age therefore need to be ICT literate, highly skilled, empowered and ready for continuous training (lifelong learning)".

Thus, under the new model of development, human capital plays a crucial role in terms of innovating skills, creativity, quick, suitable response; as a result, training is of paramount importance, as a tool for enhancing such capital and, within the new economic-social context, generalized literacy about Information Society technology.

Under such circumstances, it is only natural to wonder whether Italy is ready to deal with the changes induced by spreading ICT and, in particular, whether in Italy people have been trained to use new technology.

2. Objectives

AICA, in partnership with SDA Bocconi, conducted a survey [1] – meant for the business world and public bodies - to quantitatively assess the cost of computer insufficient training ; that is, how much inadequate human resources, in terms of the workforce's late literacy about information technology, costs the Italian economy. In addition, the study was aimed at empirically assessing whether basic training, as provided, for example, by ECDL [2] courses, can reduce such lack of training and to what extent, thus helping slash the cost of computer ignorance. The study took place in Q1 2003.

3. The Need for Computer Training

What dimensions is workforce training taking on in Italy?

According to a survey conducted by SDA Bocconi, in 2003, about 50% of the working population in Italy uses computers in the workplace (Figure 1).

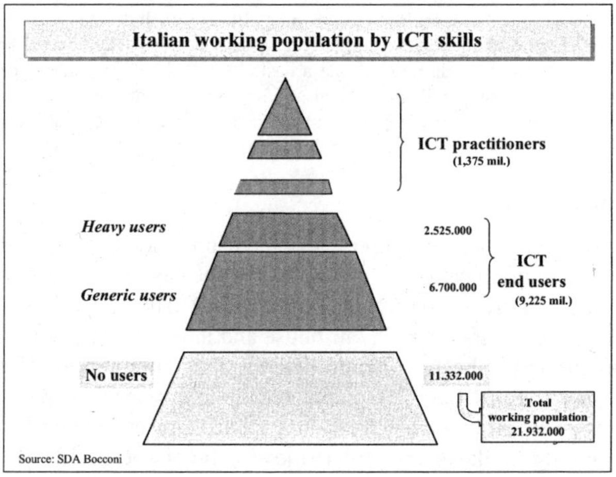

Figure.1: Italian Working Population in Relation to ICT Skills

Basically, the problem is how to train so many people to use ICT and PCs. In this respect school education and training in the workplace are proving largely inadequate. There is evidence that Italy is very late compared to the most advanced European countries.

It should first be pointed out that, as regards school education, information technology is not part of any secondary school curricula, except for a few technical schools.

Furthermore, among Italian-based businesses, as suggested by the data supplied by the European Commission in 2001, training has a definitely poor incidence: in Italy no more than 18% of the workforce has received basic training, vs. 28% in Europe, although the latter figure has been defined by the European Union as a dreadfully poor result.

However, the need for digital literacy is clearly understood by Italians. Over the last few years the acquisition of "computer skills certifications" has grown exponentially (+ 70% in 2003). This provides a reliable, measurable indicator of the level of literacy, and the importance individuals attach to computer training in the current working environment.

It should also be emphasized that, due to inadequate school education and workplace training, individuals often acquire required skills in their own time and at their own expense. This is based on a survey conducted by AICA in 2003 on people who had achieved ECDL certification. The survey involved matching data in AICA's databank with a sample analysis of the target population. It was shown, for example, that almost 75% of those who achieved ECDL certification (86% in the private sector) had invested in achieving certification without having been urged by their employers.

It seems as if the business world is underestimating the importance of learning how to use IT tools. Because expenditure on training does not provide immediate, tangible return on the period involved, many companies are reluctant to arrange training programmes for many of their employees, thus confining training to individual choices, subordinating it to individuals' desire to get up-to-date, to their personal effort. However, lack of suitable training may result in hidden costs as arising from people's lower productivity (results produced vs. working hours), or, in more severe cases, in wrongly used IT tools.

4. The Cost of Insufficient Computer Training

To assess how much lack of ICT related training costs the Italian manufacturing sector, AICA-SDA Bocconi referred to a survey conducted by the Norwegian Statistical Institute.

The Norwegian interviewees (800 users) estimated their time as absorbed, every week, by problems arising when using IT tools – that is, PCs, individual software, Web services, including e-mail and the Internet, and legacy applications – . According to the data supplied by the Norwegian Statistical Institute, every week users spend, on average, 24 hours out of 40 theoretical working hours per week in front of the computer. This accounts for 60% of working time, which has been absorbed by interaction with ICT systems. The survey also suggests (Figure 2) that 171 minutes per week, namely 2 hours and 51 minutes, are unproductive as the result of difficulties preventing work from being regularly done.

Thus the Norwegian survey (that is, the only one available so far) suggests how much time is, on average, lost every week as the result of any problems connected with computers, in a highly computerized society. It can be reasonably assumed that, in such a country as Italy, where the standard of IT knowledge is not as high as the European average in general and the Norwegian average in particular, the Norwegian data means an estimate, by approximation to the nearest number below, of the equivalent Italian data, and can then be relied on to estimate the cost arising from insufficient knowledge of IT tools.

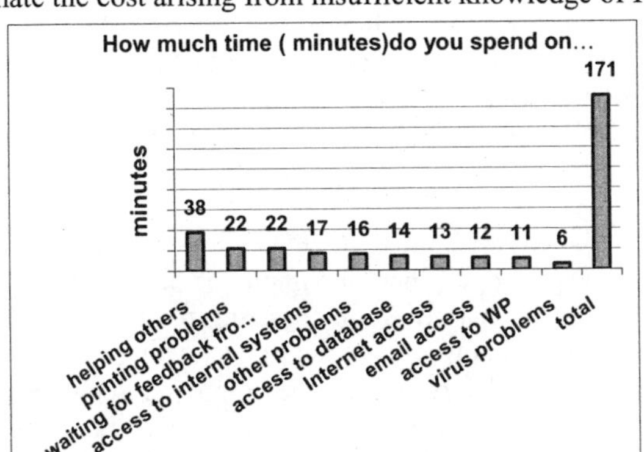

Figure 2: The Norwegian Survey

Norwegian survey data	Italian context		
Time lost per week	Number of generic IT users (Bocconi, 2003)	Working weeks per year	Mean labour cost per employee/per day (source:CNEL, 2001)
2h51min	6.700.000	48	€ 136.6

Table 1: The Norwegian Survey Results and the Italian Context

Inferring Italian values from the data collected in Norway produces impressive results. Considering only generic users (Table 1), as heavy users are believed to be better trained, the loss of productivity can be estimated as follows (Table 2):

Time lost per week (in Italy)	2h51m x 6.700.000 users = **19.095.000 h/week**
Time lost per year (in Italy)	19.095.000 x 48 weeks = **114.570.000 working days**
Annual cost per italian economy	114.570.000 x € 136.6 = **€ 15.6 billion**

Table 2: Loss of Productivity Estimate

€15.6 billion, is so significant that, even if it should be considered as a general indicator, a problem is posed: how can it be reduced? Investing in training is among the measures that should be taken in Italy with increased determination.

5. Correlation between Training and Productivity

The first stage of the survey was aimed at assessing the cost of computer insufficient training; whereas the second stage involved quantitatively assessing the correlation between training and productivity. Specifically the survey tried to quantify the Return on Investment (ROI) of users' basic computer training with a view to ECDL certification.

In this respect the researchers selected a stratified sample of about 200 subjects, including both university students at faculties not specializing in ICT and employees of large and medium size businesses (>100 employees). Although it would have been better to have a larger (and more representative) sample available, people willing to take part in such a long-term test could hardly be found. However, the sample is large enough to provide the information needed in terms of increased productivity.

The participants took the same test, before and after attending a course training them to achieve ECDL certification; the test comprised 37 questions concerning the solution of problems in individual IT environments.

For this sample the analysts estimated both the changed amount of time spent on dealing with problems and the scores achieved in the tests before and after attending the course. Obviously enough, the score is an indicator of the level of knowledge or mastery of the subject. It should be pointed out that most of those people were not totally illiterate about information technology – that is, they had a fairly good knowledge of IT tools, which may have resulted from daily use.

To assess the improvement in the level of knowledge, to which increased efficiency in using the computer may be ascribed, the following indices were used:

- Relative increase in knowledge, where the improved score is compared with the initial score. This index is useful mainly in emphasizing the level of literacy these courses provide people with a poor knowledge of the subject with.
- Absolute increase in knowledge, where the improved score is compared with the maximum possible score. This index is more useful in estimating the level of consolidation these courses provided people who were already familiar with the subject with, thus allowing them to get close to the maximum score that could be achieved.

Improved knowledge as – correlatively – increased productivity seem to be significant, whatever index is considered: +47%, in mean terms, compared with the initial level; +20% compared with an absolute scale of optimal knowledge (Figure 3).

This means:

- Carrying out jobs that could not be done
- Carrying out jobs that used to be unsatisfactory better
- Potentially reducing the amount of time unproductively lost in front of the computer as the result of lack of ICT skills.

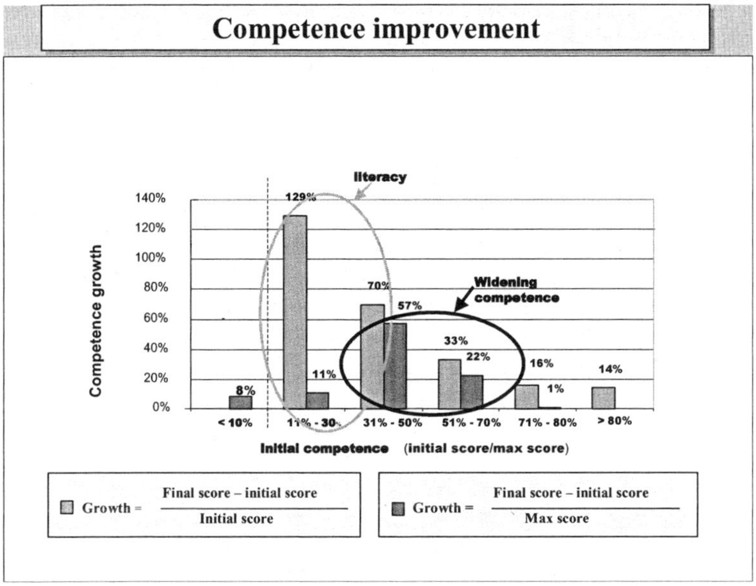

Figure.3: Competence Improvement

How can return on investment in training be calculated?

The amount of time spent, on average, before the computer accounts for 60% of the theoretical working time (as suggested by a survey conducted by the Norwegian Statistical Institute), namely 24 hours per week.

The survey carried out by AICA – SDA Bocconi suggests that the peoplc who attended training courses to achieve ECDL certification reduced the amount of time needed for the tests by 7% to 12%. Therefore, it can be estimated that the decrease in the amount of time required for any job to be done on the computer, among those who were not specifically trained vs. those who attended the courses, made up, on average, round 10%. No doubt this is a conservative estimate, as practice and expertise are actually needed to save time – that is, time can be saved after what has been taught at the courses has been metabolized.

On the basis of the foregoing, the productivity of anybody who has been trained to use IT tools can be estimated as shown in Table 3

R. O. I

❖ **Productivity increase connected with the time saving basic assumption: 10% reduction**

Working time spent on using computer	***24 h/w***
Time saving (after training)	***10% = 2,4 h/w***
Annual productivity increase (48weeks)	***115,2 h***
Annual productivity gain (in €)	***1967€***

Table 3: The R.O.I in Basic IT Training: Productivity Increase

It should be remembered that the ROI of training is connected with the opportunity for any company to cut costs arising from the users' lack of computer training. Here, as elsewhere, the data collected by the Norwegian Statistical Institute can be relied on. Apart from the items which are not impacted by training to achieve ECDL certification (technical failures, viruses, legacy systems), the other causes of inefficiency may result from a decrease in the amount of time lost. To assess to what extent the remaining items can be reduced, the analysts estimated the increase in absolute knowledge, namely that individual items may be subjected to a proportional decrease in the amount of time (Table 4). For example, as far as the Word Processor is concerned, the increase in absolute knowledge was estimated at 24%; this might mean that the amount of time lost due to any problems concerning this application may be subjected to a proportional reduction.

R.O.I

Items affected by training	*Min. lost per week*	*Competence improvement*	*Saved time (min)*
Help others	38	20%	7,6
Printing problems	22	13%	2,86
Waiting for help	22	20%	4,4
Internet access	13	16%	2,08
Problems with mail	12	16%	1,92
WP problems	11	24%	2,64
Minutes/week	*118*	*18%*	*21,5*

Hours/year = 17,2 ⇨ Days/year =2,15 ⇨ **294 €/year**

Table 4: The R.O.I. in Basic IT Training: Competence Improvement

Using the data on mean labour cost per employee in Italy (€ 136.6/day) and adding the two effects (increased productivity and cutting costs as arising from computer insufficient training) with each other, a saving of € 2,261 is achieved for each employee receiving training to achieve ECDL certification. If the whole population of Italian generic users (6,700,000 people) is considered, overall savings exceed € 15 billion (Table 5).

R.O.I

Return on Investment (per person) : 2261€ yearly

Productivity gain:	***1967€***
Reduction of hidden costs:	***291€***
Total:	***2261€***

Total Return on Investment : €15.1 billions yearly

2261€ x 6.700.000 generic users

Table 5: The Total Return on Investment in Basic IT Training

Clearly, this value should also be taken into account only as a general indicator; nevertheless, it suggests that basic training allows efficiency to be enhanced and, correlatively, highly significant savings – or, at least, savings that largely make up for any incurred costs – to be achieved, which is the case mainly in the medium-long term.

However, as emphasized, Italian-based businesses do not seem to be aware of the importance of computer training. A survey conducted by SDA Bocconi on a sample of 58 manufacturing companies showed that among 71% of businesses overall expenditure on training is lower than 0.05% of the turnover; whereas among the remaining 29% of businesses the incidence ranges from 0.05% to 0.5%. In addition, expenditure on computer training accounts, on average, for no more than 20% of overall expenditure on training, some companies reporting nil expenditure in this respect.

6. Conclusions

Although one out of two people in the working population in Italy uses a computer in the workplace, only 18 percent of the workforce has received basic training, compared with an overall European figure of 27 percent. The results of the research are revealing. They offer further proof that while a lack of core computer skills can impact a nation's economy, training that leads to ECDL certification offers clear solutions.

This study will help the Italian market to gain increased awareness of the correlation between productivity and training, as the result of both the emphasis placed on the results of the survey in newspapers and the interest shown by the Italian government; the extent to which this may actually translate into a change in current business mentality, mainly among small and medium size businesses will be ascertained as late as in the medium term.

However, the survey has provided the government authorities with significant data, which can be relied on to support politics and promote the spread of IT knowledge.

In addition, the increasing popularity of ECDL is also helping address this skill gap. Following an agreement with the Ministry of Education and the Headmasters Organisation of Italian Universities, most first year university students will undertake the ECDL, a development expected to lead to a sharp increase in core computer skills throughout the Italian workforce. The main problem lies in allowing those who are already part of the working world to adjust their skills.

What are the next steps to take?

- AICA, in partnership with Bocconi University, is going to keep monitoring the cost of computer insufficient training, developing the survey, year by year, in the Italian market, according to line of business: in particular, in 2004, the survey involved the health system [3]. It is among AICA's priorities to get public and private enterprises to consider IT training as an investment, rather than as a cost, with both an economic return, as the result of increased productivity, and a return in terms of adjusted professional skills.
- In addition, CEPIS (Council of European Professional Informatics Societies) is willing to extend this study to the whole of Europe, thus allowing the European cost of IT illiteracy, in relation to the gap between the current level of computerization and the strategic guidelines recommended by the European Union, to be quantitatively assessed.

References

[1] Il costo dell'ignoranza nella Società dell'Informazione- RCS libri-2003

[2] The European Computer Driving Licence (ECDL) is the world's leading end-user computer skills certification programme. Outside of Europe, the ECDL is known as the International Computer Driving Licence (ICDL). For further information: http://www.ecdl.com

[3] L'ignoranza informatica: il costo nella sanità – McGraw Hill- 2004

The Employability of ICT Professionals - A Study of European SMEs

Dora SCHOLARIOS[1], Esther VAN DER SCHOOT[2], Beatrice VAN DER HEIJDEN[3]
[1]University of Strathclyde, Department of Human Resource Management,
50 Richmond Street, Glasgow G11XU, Scotland
Tel: +44 141 5483135, Fax: +44 141 5523581, Email: d.scholarios@strath.ac.uk
[2]University of Twente, School of Business, Public Administration and Technology,
PO Box 217, 7500 AE, Enschede, the Netherlands
Tel: +31 534895366, Fax: +31 534892159, Email: E.vanderSchoot@sms.utwente.nl
[3]Maastricht School of Management, PO Box 1203, 6201 BE Maastricht, the Netherlands
Tel: +31 433870810, *Fax:* +31 433870800, *Email: Heijden@msm.nl*

Abstract: The present paper examines the management of employability of ICT professionals by small- and medium-sized enterprises (SMEs) in Europe. Employability can be defined as the extent to which employees have skills regarded as attractive by the market and employers, and is of increasing importance for the ICT sector, especially SMEs. The paper uses secondary data to characterise the ICT sectors in seven countries representing a range of markets, from highly developed to small and emerging, and presents a qualitative study of managers' in ICT SMEs attitudes towards employability and its management. The findings suggest an ad hoc and informal approach across countries towards assessing and developing existing employees' competencies, despite acknowledging skills gaps and the criticality of certain technical and non-technical qualities for meeting market demands.

1. Introduction

The paper describes a study conducted as part of the Indic@tor project co-funded by the European Commission (IST-2000-31070). The study examined the employability of ICT professionals and its management by small- and medium-sized enterprises (SMEs) in Europe and was conducted against the backdrop of a turbulent ICT sector, in particular at a time where there was a significant downturn in the market (2002-2003). Employability can be defined as the extent to which employees have skills regarded as attractive by the market and employers. The development of technical and professional workers is of high priority for governments concerned with creating an adequate supply of skilled labour and fuelling economic growth. For SMEs, there is concern about the supply and utilisation of ICT skills, high turnover of experienced staff, and the lack of qualified new entrants into the profession [1][2][3]. It is argued here that, despite the considerable retraction in the labour market evidenced at the time of the present research, the notion of employability enhancement remains a significant concern for both employers and policy makers in this dynamic sector.

Employability has become importance as the nature of employment and work patterns, particularly in knowledge-intensive industries, has changed. Discontinuous forms of employment (e.g. temporary contracts, increasing subcontracting), mean that employers are viewed increasingly as providers of the necessary knowledge and skills which enhance employability rather than secure employment [4] [5]. This highlights a tension between the role that should be played by organizations and individual employees in continuously updating knowledge and skills to enhance professional development. Employers generally do not take full responsibility for eliminating perceived skill gaps in their companies either through strategies for retaining highly qualified staff or through the provision of expensive training, mentoring or other development strategies. They may be reluctant to invest in the development of skills which make their employees more marketable while employees themselves may develop expertise which is too narrow to stay employable in the long run and keep up with technological and scientific developments. In difficult business conditions, training is unlikely to be of high priority for employers, although it may increase in importance for employees faced with a more competitive labour market.

Highly qualified employees may also face declining re-employability when entering later stages of their career. Consideration of age-related issues in career development is relatively recent but there is growing concern about guiding individuals' professional development by facilitating life-long learning approaches [6]. Given the ageing working population (i.e., the increasing proportion of older people coupled with decreasing proportions of young people in the labour force) and the tendency for older employees, working in middle and higher-level functions, to become immobile and overspecialised in narrow occupational domains, the need to ensure employability throughout the working career is apparent. Yet, the extent to which either management or employees themselves are actively engaged in furtherance of the professional career noticeably declines as employees age. For individuals, there may be serious consequences for older employees whose function becomes obsolete and who are unable to adapt to changing requirements.

2. Objectives

Despite the increasing importance of employability for governments, employers and employees, there has been little scientific study of how employability is acquired and how it can be developed and sustained over a career, especially in the relatively new ICT sector and for smaller employers with limited resources. The present study attempts to address this gap by examining employability of ICT professionals in different European countries and the management of employability by ICT SMEs. The paper has three objectives:

1. To examine the nature of employment in the ICT sector in seven European countries (Germany, Greece, Italy, the Netherlands, Norway, Poland, and the UK), each of which is expected to represent different employment conditions for ICT professionals.
2. To explore the perceptions of ICT SME employers in these countries in relation to the importance of employability and their concerns in managing this quality of employees.
3. To consider the implications of the study findings for sustaining employability across Europe, particularly in terms of the expected role of employers and the development of professional expertise through all career stages. Issues impacting SMEs in the ICT sector during the economic downturn of 2003, in particular, will be highlighted.

3. Methodology

The empirical focus of the paper involves analysis using secondary data sources and qualitative interviews of ICT SME managers. An analysis of the ICT sector in the seven countries based on cross-national and national data sources provides a summary of the key features of the ICT sector, including its contribution to economic growth, and a description of the high-skilled ICT workforce (e.g., demographic characteristics, labour market supply and demand for ICT professionals, the nature of companies employing ICT professionals).

The second approach was to conduct in-depth interviews with a group of managing directors, CEOs or managers in ICT SMEs who were representative of the population of ICT companies identified in the sector analysis. This explored employers' understanding of occupational expertise of ICT professionals, and the extent of practice addressing employability issues (e.g. dealing with skills gaps, performance assessment, or career planning). Interviews were conducted in all seven countries from April 2002 to February

2003 and aimed for five companies in each of three SME size bands: 10-49 employees, 50-149 employees, and 150-249 employees. A common semi-structured interview protocol was used covering three themes: employability (13 items), ageing (8 items), and future developments and requirements (13 items). The final number of interviews conducted was 107; numbers by company size in each country are shown in Table 1.

All final interview transcriptions were analysed by researchers in each country using a common coding scheme. This was constructed on the basis of three Dutch interviews by subdividing the data into core labels (variable categories), dimensions of core labels, and loadings [7]. There were three core labels: employability, ageing, and future developments and requirements, each of which was assigned several dimensions. For example, the core label employability included the dimension 'employability management'. A loading represents a group of similar statements given by respondents which are indicative of a certain dimension. Researchers at the national level were able to add additional categories to this general framework for each item. Comparable answering patterns were aggregated in the cross-cultural analysis to produce an overall frequency table of responses.

Table 1: Number of Interviews Conducted by Size of SME

Country	*No. of employees*			
	10 – 49	50 – 149	150 – 249	Total
Germany	3	7	5	15
Greece	13	2		15
The Netherlands	10	2	3	15
Norway	5	5	5	15
Italy	10	3	2	15
Poland	6	6	6	18
United Kingdom	8	5	1	14
Total	55	30	22	107

4. Results

4.1 The ICT Market in the Seven Countries

The European Information Technology Observatory's (EITO) 2003 overview of the ICT sector across Europe shows rapid growth during the 1990s and decline since 2000. Market evaluations for 2002-2003 indicated zero growth in Europe in 2002 and the prospect of limited development in 2003 (growth of 2.5%)[8]. However, strong growth in Internet penetration and broadband connections (DSL and cable) is expected. The EITO has forecast 3.1% growth in the total ICT market in western Europe in 2004 with some market segments (particularly software products and carrier services), showing stronger performance [9].

Comparisons across the seven countries showed key differences in the development and distribution of ICT activity. At the high end of development, the UK and Germany represent the largest IT software and services markets in Europe. In 2000, the UK contributed 9% and Germany 6% of the overall OECD ICT sector employment (by comparison, amongst OECD countries, only the US and Japan have higher country shares on both measures) [10]. They also represent a sizable proportion of Europe's overall employment in high technology [11]. Growth in the ICT sector for both countries is currently around 10% per annum and they each employ close to 1 million people.

Italy is the fourth largest ICT market in Europe (after Germany, UK and France) with a growth rate of 12% per annum. It is ranked sixth in terms of OECD share of ICT employment (after the US, Japan, the UK, Germany and France) and fifth in terms of country share to the total OECD value added of the ICT sector (after the US, Japan, Germany and the UK). It employed over 700,000 people in around 108,000 companies.

The ICT sector in the Netherlands, although representing only 1.2% of the OECD's total ICT sector value added and 1.6% of total OECD ICT employment, has seen rapid economic growth, growing from 9% to 13% of national GDP between 1996 and 1998. In 2000, the sector employed almost 270,000 people in 27,000 companies.

Norway is a small ICT market relative to other countries in the project, employing about 84,000 people in 10,000 enterprises, but in 2001, the ICT sector grew 7.7% from 2000. This represented 4% of total employment and 6% of the economy. Norwegian ICT employment and value added are dominated by consultancy services, which accounted for 45% of all employment in the ICT sector in 2001 and unlike the other industries within the ICT sector showed significant growth between 1995 and 2001.

Poland saw rapid growth, exceeding 22%, in its ICT sector through the 1990s, which began to retrench in 2000 falling to 8%. The Polish computer market was estimated at $2,500,000 in 2000, a 10% increase over 1999. This largely reflects the deteriorating economic situation and slower rate of development of the Polish economy in general.

Finally, although Greece has the smallest market in our sample of countries (ICT sector accounts for over 4% of Greece's GDP, 9.4% growth rate in 2002) there is a faster growth in telecommunications. The Greek telecommunications market (including telecom services, equipment, and systems) is driven by the growth in mobile telephony and deregulation of the industry. The ICT industry in Greece is expected to grow about 5.6% in 2004.

4.2 The ICT Professional Workforce

In all countries, ICT professionals (IT practitioners whose job involves "designing, developing, producing, installing, managing, maintaining or supporting systems for other people to use" [12]), are employed by both ICT-suppliers and ICT-users (i.e., organizations whose primary business is in another sector of the economy, such as telecommunications or manufacturing). There is a strong emphasis on ICT services in all countries, with the majority of enterprises classified in 'Computer and Related Activities' and 'Other ICT services' according to Revision 3 of the International Standard Industrial Classification (ISIC)). The subsector 'Software consultancy and supply' accounts for approximately 40% of all ICT employment in Italy, the Netherlands, Norway and the UK. Combined with other ICT services, over half of employment is in ICT services. Only in Germany does ICT manufacturing comprise a relatively larger share of total ICT employment.

Common job titles for ICT professionals include application developers, technical developers, software engineers and computer analyst/programmer. The growth in high-skilled ICT-related workers has been greater in Germany, the Netherlands and the UK. The EU average of high-skilled ICT workers as a proportion of total employment was 1.7%. This compares to the highest share of high-skilled ICT workers which was in the Netherlands (3.2%) and the lowest, which was in Greece (0.6%). The demographic profile of ICT professionals suggests a common pattern across all countries; more likely to be male (circa 70% across the seven countries); aged between 25 and 40 (again over 70%, although software engineers tend to be even younger); and better qualified than the workforce as a whole (i.e., more likely to be university graduates, particularly in computer science).

4.3 Labour Market Demand and Supply

The increased activity in the ICT sector during the 1990s, partly due to liberalization of the telecommunications sector, the authorization of new mobile telephone providers, and the level of internet and new media diffusion, has resulted in an increased demand for labour with ICT skills in both ICT supplier sectors and end-user sectors [13]. Since 2000, however, there has been considerable retraction, as is evident in the analysis for all countries. There is also a gap between the skills of current and future workers and the needs of firms. Studies carried out by International Data Corporation estimated skill demand and shortages in the EU-15 countries, Norway and Switzerland. ICT skill shortages in particular areas (internet-related activities, IT-supported business activities and host-based, distributed and applications environments) were expected to reach 13% of total demand in 2003 [14]. The demand for these ICT specialists was found to vary across countries, being particularly high in the Netherlands, where ICT has one of the highest weights in total employment, and low in Greece, where supply and demand are more balanced. The skill shortage in the UK was just above the Western European average, while the level of skill shortage for Norway, Germany and Italy was below the average.

Policy responses to shortfalls in supply of ICT specialists vary between countries, particularly in the role played by higher education, and the impact on ICT recruitment and training policies. While employers may look to government for a response (e.g. by expanding the supply of labour from higher education, as is the case in the UK [15]), one implication of the present study is to consider the role of employers in generating a larger pool of highly skilled ICT employees (e.g., through work-based training and development). This issue is addressed further in the qualitative study and final discussion of employability.

4.4 Analysis of ICT SME Needs

Our interviews show that most ICT managers have an interest in employability matters concerning the whole organization. However, attention is often ad hoc due to the influence of the market in the ICT sector which tends to dictate the required competences for ICT professionals. Flexibility is needed in order to maintain adequate accreditation for new software and as a result strategies tend to be ad hoc to fit with current demands. Employability management, where it is present, tends to be directed towards assessment and development plans, mainly in order to keep ICT professionals up-to-date. Management also tries to enhance employees' commitment towards the organization and to a lesser degree to optimize the full utilization and development of competences. Responsibility for employability matters tended to rest with the director/management team, the human resource manager, or the manager of the department concerned.

An aging population did not cause problems for the SMEs in this sample. Confirming the relatively young profile identified in the industry analysis, ICT professionals were found to function at senior levels, (e.g. as managers or directors of SMEs at around 35 years of age). Seniority was related more to competences which match the requirements of the market than age borders. However, some ICT managers thought young ICT professionals were more ambitious, mobile, and eager to learn than older professionals (over 40).

The present and future effects of the economic depression were mentioned by most ICT managers, and survival, especially for SMEs, was a major issue. Some companies where interviews were conducted have already gone bankrupt. Technological developments have meant that updating of technical knowledge and expertise, as well as communication and consultancy competences has become more significant; yet, this is unaffordable in times of crisis. Nevertheless, ICT professionals have to be flexible generalists often without the help of real organizational structures to stimulate and maintain learning. For the majority, these issues, as well as the problems of combating and/or preventing skill 'obsolescence' or of increased demand for ICT professionals, were not priorities.

In short, the analysis found that, although there is an interest in employability matters among SME ICT managers, actual policy and action lag behind. In this respect the current economic depression and the developmental stage of the ICT sector in each participating country have a strong impact. The development of ICT professionals' employability is not a top priority, but a luxury item on which little time and effort can be spent.

4.5 Implications for the Management of Employability of ICT Professionals

Despite management interest in their workforces' employability, there was little evidence of action to stimulate employees' further growth and development, flexibility or versatility in any participating countries. Our analysis of the state of the ICT sector provides a strong indication of why this may be the case; the economic slowdown affecting the ICT sector since 2001 has meant a considerably less dynamic labour market for ICT professionals compared to the 1990s, implying less competition for skilled professionals and simultaneously fewer resources for companies to invest in developing their own employees.

Despite the difficult economic conditions, our sector analysis also showed that there are continuing skills shortages in some areas (primarily internet-related activities, IT-supported business activities and host-based, distributed and applications environments). The demand for such ICT specialists is especially acute in the Netherlands, and less of a problem in Germany, Greece, Italy and Norway. Nevertheless, this shows that technological developments are still likely to dictate the required competences of ICT suppliers and hence require continuous updating of technical knowledge in key areas of the market. Moreover, amongst the small ICT suppliers who make up the majority of the sector in all countries, we found that managers consistently identified 'soft' skills, such as communication, flexibility, teamworking and consultancy competencies, as important for dealing with client service interactions in addition to technical software or systems development skills.

Interviews suggest that SME managers and employers in all countries, while acknowledging the importance of these competencies for the survival of their companies, could not afford to invest in developing their employees in this way in times of crisis. They seemed unconcerned with formally gathering data on existing levels of competence or with taking strategic action to prevent 'obsolescence' and meet expected future needs.

Such a short-term, instrumental approach to managing employees characterises well the increasingly temporary nature of employment relationships, which as we have seen, has been intensely felt in the volatile ICT sector. The need for rapid reaction times may also preclude managers from more strategic planning. They also may be unwilling to enhance the employability of their employees if they are likely to take these new skills elsewhere. Yet, a sizable proportion of managers across our seven countries also mentioned the importance of employee commitment to the organization, especially in a depressed market when an SME's survival may depend on specific expertise possessed by one or two individuals. Some writers have argued that employees, in fact, are more likely to commit themselves to an organization that invests in broader competence development and enables career development and professional growth e.g., [16].

The existence of a human resource specialist may increase the chances of companies developing career programmes for their employees or of being aware of development issues, but for SMEs, a separate HR function is rare. The present results showed that it is more often the managing director or line managers who take responsibility for performance assessment and development. This is consistent with literature which describes smaller firms' competence development and acquisition as improvised and informal, e.g., [17].

On the basis of the present findings, ageing and dejuvenization of the population is not expected to cause any problem for SMEs, most likely because of the already young age profile of the sector at all career stages. There was some suggestion that younger workers display greater adaptability to changing market demands, for example in accreditation for new software, but the majority of managers interviewed claimed that promotions were based on possession of competence in areas driven by market-need and this was not age related. It may be that the more direct communication and flatter hierarchy possible in SMEs means that managers are less likely to be led by age stereotypes than in larger organisation with more formal hierarchies.

5. Business Benefits

The study has shown that managers in ICT SMEs take an informal and ad hoc approach to the employability of their employees, despite the pressures imposed simply to survive in a highly competitive and, at present, depressed market. By investing in the employability of their present personnel, however, many authors have argued that companies can facilitate the flexible deployment of staff and provide a binding force for IT practitioners who may be more likely to remain in organizations where they can keep learning and where their market value is sustained. Investing in existing staff also improves the recruiting power of the organization, making it more attractive for potential employees. This is a critical feature in tightening labour markets.

Ageing as a problem for employability was not recognised in most interviews. In the relatively young ICT sector, however, it is possible that ageing of the workforce will present a challenge in the future for ensuring and promoting the employment of people over forty years of age, as this group was acknowledged by some to be less likely to possess the required adaptability in technical competence required in the ICT sector.

Changing career direction or acquiring new competencies is to be expected in the dynamic ICT sector, where reorganisations or market changes are frequent. Employees with limited expertise will find their prospects reduced. Individuals may have to accept more responsibility for their skills development and marketability and management would benefit from ensuring that highly qualified employees remain committed to the organisation.

6. Conclusions

Despite the diverse ICT sectors represented by the seven countries in the present study, interviews with managers of SME ICT companies revealed remarkable similarity in the concerns expressed with respect to issues of employability. SMEs in all countries, from the well-developed markets in the UK and Germany to the emerging Polish ICT sector and tiny Greek market, expressed concern with their own survival in the current economic conditions. There also was a general interest in attracting and keeping ICT professionals with key technical and general consultancy skills, but a relative absence of formal management systems for optimizing the competencies of their existing employees in the form of enhanced employability. Employee development practice and strategy in these ICT SMEs tended to be ad hoc, informal and short-termist.

The study fills a gap in HRM research generally with respect to SMEs as most HRM recommendations are based on studies conducted in large firms. Moreover, there has been little research on expertise and employability in the ICT industry, especially with respect to the role of management rather than other stakeholders, such as government and higher education, in expanding the supply of skilled workers. In addition to identifying the general lack of SME management of employability enhancement, the study addresses debates that individuals are increasingly expected to take responsibility for their skills development and marketability. While the paper confirms the relatively hands-off approach of management, the identification of continuing skills gaps and the potential resurgence of the ICT sector from 2004 each suggests that ICT SMEs also would benefit from ensuring that highly qualified employees remain both employable and committed to their companies. It can also be argued that the same applies under more buoyant market conditions than those encountered within the ICT sector at the time of the study. Ensuring the employability of workers enables organisations to meet fluctuating demands more effectively, particularly if attitudinal factors, such as adaptability and self-management, which are key dimensions of employability, are nurtured in addition to valued technical skills.

Although the ICT sector is of strategic importance for Europe, it continues to suffer from structural deficiencies, including insufficient supply of qualified human capital at both basic and higher skill levels. The present study supports proactive employer strategies in dealing with skill development, training and retention, even in economic downturn; it suggests further direction for policy-making for educational and training opportunities to enhance ICT careers in particular areas of skilled labour shortage and enhance entry into high skill occupations; and, finally, it shows that issues of ageing – and hence diminishing employability - during the life-cycle of an ICT career may become more of an issue in subsequent years for employers as well as individuals themselves.

References

[1] P Cappelli, Why is it so hard to find information technology workers?, Organizational Dynamics, 2001, 30(2), pp.87-99.

[2] R Hill and J Stewart, Human Resource Development in small firms. Human Resource Development International. Enhancing performance, learning and integrity, 1999, 2(2), pp.103-123.

[3] ITNTO/AISS Skills 99 – IT skills summary. IT National Training Organisation and the Alliance for Information Systems Skills (AISS), Report to DTI and DfEE, 1999.

[4] M B Arthur, K Inkson, and J K Pringle, The New Careers: Individual Action and Economic Change, Sage, London, 1999.

[5] P Capelli, The New Deal at Work, Boston: Mass., Harvard Business School Press, 1999.

[6] K Kwakman, B I J M Van der Heijden, J Streumer, A Wognum and S Van Zolingen, Current HRD trends in the Netherlands: conceptualisation and practices. International Journal of Human Resource Development and Management, 2002, 2(3/4), pp.358-378.

[7] D B Baarda., M P M De Goede and J Teunissen, Kwalitatief onderzoek [Qualitative research], Houten: Stenfert Kroese, 1995.

[8] European Information Technology Observatory (EITO) 2003

[9] European Information Technology Observatory (EITO) Update 2003. Available at http://www.eito.com

[10] OECD, Measuring the Information Economy 2002, Paris, 2003.

[11] I Laafia, Regional employment in high technology, Statistics in Focus, Theme 9, Eurostat, 1999.

[12] CEPIS, Information Technology Practitioner Skills in Europe, 2002.

[13] European Competitiveness Report, Annex. III.1 European skill shortages in ICT and policy responses, European Union, 2001.

[14] IDC, Europe's growing IT skills crisis, London, 2000.

[15] H Steedman, K Wagner and J Foreman, The impact on firms of ICT skill-supply strategies: An Anglo-German comparison, Centre for Economic Performance, London School of Economics, 2003.

[16] J Gaspersz and M Ott, Management van employability. Nieuwe kansen in arbeidsrelaties [Management of employability. New opportunities in labour relations]. Assen: Van Gorcum/Stichting Management Studies, 1996.

[17] C Hendry, M B Arthur and A M Jones, Strategy through People – Adaptation and Learning in the Small-medium Enterprise, London, Routledge, 1995.

TRAIN-IT: Turning e-2004 Technologies into Business

Ingo HUSSLA[1], Helga BECHMANN[2]
Gesellschaft für Technologieförderung Itzehoe mbH, IZET Innovationszentrum Itzehoe, Fraunhoferstrasse 3, 25524 Itzehoe, Germany
[1]*Tel: +49 4821 778600, Fax: +49 4821 778500, Email: hussla@izet.de*
[2]*Tel: +49 4821 778520, Fax: +49 4821 778500, Email: bechmann@izet.de*

Abstract: Key objective is stimulating an entrepreneurial spirit among e-2004 participants encouraging them to harvest their product and service ideas. With the international business plan training TRAIN-IT, IZET Innovationszentrum Itzehoe has established a support mechanism for technologists seeking to bring their products and services to the market. The contribution explains how the entrepreneurial training works, analysing results of six years activity. In case studies of currently active companies, different financing routes, business models and strategies are presented to outline possible paths and serve as motivation for e-2004 participants.

1. The Challenge: Entrepreneurial Training for e-Technologists

e-2004 related projects and R&D activities generate an excellent output of innovative e-technologies, solutions, services and products. However, the initiative to turn such potential into commercial activities is all too rarely taken due to insufficient business knowledge and lack of competent advice. The key to the transfer of technology into business is hands-on training and coaching in business planning, developed for the specific needs of technologists becoming entrepreneurs. The TRAIN-IT course was designed to meet a challenge for innovative technologists worldwide: how to turn technology into business.

Originally EU-funded, TRAIN-IT has assisted technologists involved in European R&D projects to move towards commercially exploitation of research results. This is in line with EU policy to support innovative technologies with a view to pan-European economic growth and job creation. TRAIN-IT received the EuroTraining Quality Label 2001-2003.

1.1 Methodology

TRAIN-IT is an optimised entrepreneurial training with a proven curriculum, active since 1997 [1]. Basis of the training activities is a one-week intensive course in business plan writing, complemented by a follow-up phase of up to 12 months. The approach of TRAIN-IT is practice-oriented and not to be confused with the academic research field of entrepreneurship studies. The TRAIN-IT content focuses on central business planning issues, which are specifically prepared to fit the informational needs of technologists:

- Business strategies and business models
- Market research and competitive analysis
- Financing strategies and options, financial planning
- Marketing and sales
- Intellectual property rights and patent issues

TRAIN-IT participants develop a business plan in one week. Although possible, it is not expected as a rule that participants finalise their business plans during the course week. In order to keep the entrepreneurial momentum and to ensure that business plan drafts will be completed successfully, the participants are given follow-up support. This includes mentoring through the TRAIN-IT team and international expert network, providing further information and advice, as well as mediating contacts to investors or business partners. The development and realisation of the planned ventures is closely followed and assisted.

The hands-on individual approach focusing on one-to-one coaching is a central aspect of the TRAIN-IT course. Key features of the TRAIN-IT course are:

- Lectures, hands-on training and individual coaching from high profile international experts and experienced entrepreneurs
- Business plan writing at individual PC stations, current literature at hand
- Presentational training: iterative "elevator pitch" exercises with video analysis
- Follow-up support until finalisation of the business plan
- Connection to business and financial networks during and after the course
- Establishing a world-wide TRAIN-IT community
- Special events such as information days and workshops
- Training activities are supported by specially developed materials, such as Business Plan Guidelines and Template, Internet links on all aspects of entrepreneurship and start-up and access to entrepreneurial literature.

2. Results and Analysis of Effectiveness

Between 1997 and 2003, 421 participants from 23 countries were trained in 47 courses. Tangible results are: 85% of the business plans are finalised, 90 start-ups and spin-offs are founded, with a further 130 currently in the planning stage. 60 business plans were implemented in existing companies as a form of intrapreneurship.

Between 2000 and 2003, 156 participants (20,5% female) from 22 countries participated in 15 courses. Main fields of activity reflected in the 133 participant business cases are:

Software development 22%	Communication, telematics and logistics 16%
Internet platforms and services 15%	Multimedia 10%
Software consultancy 8%	Life sciences and medicine 6%
e-learning 8%	Microsystem technologies 8%
e-business and e-commerce 5%	Technology transfer 2%

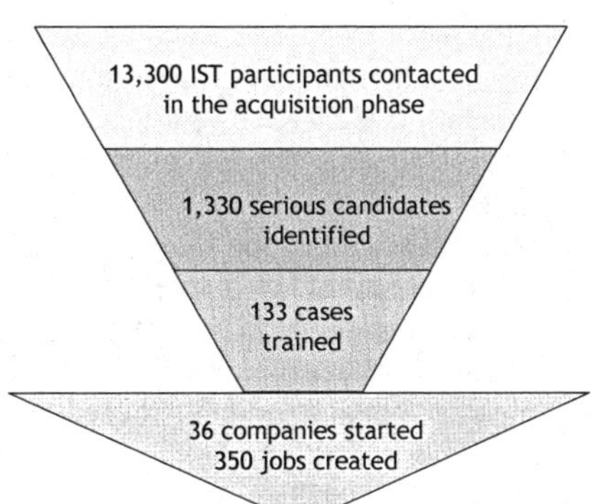

Figure 1

The 133 business cases trained have so far created 36 companies and 349 jobs – i.e. on average, 9-10 jobs were created per company. It was clearly seen that the course helped them focus and structure their business idea, fill informational gaps with expert knowledge and support, and accelerate the business plan writing and implementation process. To put the figures in proportion and visualise the impact of TRAIN-IT, the following approximation was developed, giving rounded numbers of participants contacted and serious contacts made, to simplify an average impact overview:

The following percentages are thus visualised:

→ 10% of the contacts made were serious and committed

→ 10% of the serious contacts actually took part in the course

→ 27% of the participants have reached a status of measurable success at this point.

The remaining business cases constitute 16 cases of intrapreneurship, as well as a future outlook of 33 planned start-ups and spin-offs and 29 cases of planned intrapreneurship. There is thus a potential of 86% successfully realised business cases (114 out of 133 cases). Notably, 90% of the successful business cases took advantage of the follow-up support.

These results show a significant rise in the percentage of success from 10% in the comparatively passive area of disseminating course information through to 27% in the active, hands-on training and particularly the future outlook of 86% effectiveness of the training. This proves the importance of a hands-on and personal intensive training and follow-up leading to optimal exploitation of the potential and therefore optimal results.

3. Success Factors and Business Benefits

The TRAIN-IT activity 2000-2003 had set itself the goal to produce at least 15 success stories. At the outset of the project, these were imagined as fast growing VC-financed companies ready for an Initial Public Offering (IPO) in the near future. However, the aftermath of the New Economy required significant reviews and adaptations of the approach, expectations, and definitions of success.

Chances of external investment decreased in parallel to the chances of a new start-up growing at high speed. Accordingly, more participants resorted to self-financing. A good business plan has been confirmed to be the first viability proof for which a potential investor will ask, which emphasises the importance of business plan training today.

A shift was made to lecture and coaching on the different sources of available financing.

A return to old economy rules and values was observed and reflected in course lectures.

The definition of a TRAIN-IT success story was revised: smaller scale achievements are valued, taking into account that most TRAIN-IT start-ups and spin-offs are early stage.

The course opened up to the alternative of intrapreneurship as a valid route of successful business plan implementation and TRAIN-IT success story potential.

Regarding the characteristics of finance-seeking among TRAIN-IT participants, the following observations were made:

27% of the business cases have been financing themselves out of private resources as well as revenue generated in their companies. 23% percent, also the same figure as in 2002, are financed by a mother company or institution. This applies to the categories of spin-offs and intrapreneurial activities. Since private resources and mother company resources are easiest to come by, it is not surprising that participants proceed on these modes of financing as long as they do not need higher amounts of funding.

Public funding (22%) has become significantly more important than business angels and strategic capital (15%). This shows that more young companies have realised that, though attractive, business angels or other strategic investors are hard to find and to commit. They therefore seek sources of financing in regional, state or EU funds.

11 business cases have received external funding following course participation so far:

4 participants have received a VC investment of EUR 500,000 (seed capital), EUR 750,000, EUR 1.3 million and EUR 1.625m (second round of financing) respectively.

4 business cases have received public funding of EUR 20,000, EUR 38,200, EUR40,000 and EUR 300,000 respectively.

2 cases have received bank credits of EUR 25,000 and EUR 60,000 respectively.

One participant received a combination investment of bank, state/government still loans and business angel capital amounting to EUR 2.5m.

6 further cases are promising candidates for external investment in the near future.

4. TRAIN-IT Business Success Stories

The following company profiles are taken from the brochure TRAIN-IT Success Stories 2000-2003, published in March 2004.

4.1 Axetel Consulting

Eduard Tric and Elena Zvarici took part in the TRAIN-IT course in February 2003. They needed a business plan to push forward a company that had started up in 1997, and to prepare the marketing of a new open source software which had been developed in the IST project EUPKI – European Libre Software Public Key Infrastructure (IST-2001-34340).

Axetel Consulting is a private IT services and consultancy company with locations in Romania and France and a team of currently six programmers. They are specialised in the field of electronic signature, encryption and security. They have positioned themselves as an ambitious player on the PKI market by initiating EuPKI, the first open source public key infrastructure with an industrial vision. This flagship product allows them to diversify their offer in the field of outsourcing and IT services consulting. The design and implementation of EuPKI is modular, allowing an easy integration with other commercial components: directory, ocsp responders, key archive, application servers and databases.

EuPKI open source PKI has attracted interest from the developer community and has started to receive code contributions from programmers around the world. The need for strong encryption, timestamping and authentication of sensitive data exchanges over the Internet is increasingly recognised by public administrations, banks and certification authorities. Customers from the public and banking domains are showing interest in EuPKI.

Having updated and optimised their business plan through the TRAIN-IT training, Eduard and Elena participated in two European Investment Fora organised in Prague and Milan in 2003 and presented their project results at the contemporaneous IST 2003 Event in Milan. The product was one of five presented by the Commission to eGovernment VIPs all over the world. Demonstrations were given for government representatives of South-Africa (Minster of Technology), India (Ministry of Trade), Slovakia (Tax payer office), Romania (Ministry of Research and Education). The business model was exposed in a panel on e-government and identity, together with Microsoft, Sun, HP and British Telecom.

Axetel was recently selected by Sun, St Microelectronics and Axalto (Schlumberger) to present Eupki at their worldwide java smartcard contest.

EUR 1m is required to expand operations in Western Europe. The business is profitable, with a low burn rate and constant growth. The capital will be invested in European marketing and sales and transform Axetel into the leader of open source security.

4.2 mimori technology group

Marc Mausch participated in the TRAIN-IT course in February 2002 in order to write a business plan for a start-up company. Based on the IST project SABRINA – Secure Authentication by a Biometric Rationale and Integration into Network Applications (IST-

2000-26273), he and his collaborators had developed a biometrical authentication methodology which they sought to commercialise.

Marc Mausch founded mimori technology group in January 2003 from private resources. The company is going to be registered as a GmbH in the near future.

mimori technology group are active in information/mobile technology and e-government solutions. Their focus is on Internet security, especially authentication issues, with a software on e/m-voting and a database access software. Their unique selling points are higher security and an integrated view of online and offline environment.

mimori anticipate an annual turnover of up to EUR 300,000 over the next 3 years. In parallel, they see a potential for creation of 5-10 jobs. Their envisaged market position is that of "edge end visionary". Partnerships with Sun Microsystems and Alcatel are to be signed shortly. mimori technology group are currently seeking EUR 700,000 in funding.

4.3 ConfigWorks Informationssysteme & Consulting GmbH

Markus Zanker took part in the TRAIN-IT course in April 2002. He joined the course to write a business plan for a university spin-off to market an innovative technology. In particular, he sought to learn about how to assess market size and competitor situation in a young, developing market. The company ConfigWorks evolved out of the IST project CAWICOMS – Customer-Adaptive Web Interface for the Configuration of Products and Services with Multiple Suppliers (IST-1999-10688).

ConfigWorks GmbH was founded in March 2003. The company is a spin-off from University of Klagenfurt, currently incubated in the academic start-up centre BUILD!

ConfigWorks provide e-sales advisor systems, supporting businesses in transforming their corporate sales knowledge into personalised handling and servicing of customers via various distribution channels - the Web, sales force, branch offices and call centre. The innovative "virtual sales consultant", enabled by the CW AdvisorTM software, guides online customers through the product selection process, facilitating decision support and significantly increasing e-commerce success. The software is based on artificial intelligence methodologies and has been awarded with the international TOPCALL Innovation Prize and the Innovation Prize of the state of Carinthia (Kärnten) in 2003. ConfigWorks is further nominated for the Austrian state Prize for Innovation 2004.

The initial financing required to get ConfigWorks started was EUR 150.000, provided through the founding members. Having launched their first product on the market in 2003, ConfigWorks expect to start generating revenue in their second year, increasing from an anticipated EUR 150,000 to EUR 400,000 in year 3.

ConfigWorks currently employ a team of 5 and expects to create 15 jobs over the next 3 years. ConfigWorks aim to become a specialised solution provider for virtual advisor systems and market leader in German speaking countries. They have made an excellent start with key customers won in Austria and Switzerland. They have a co-operation partner in Munich and are now seeking reference customers in Germany.

4.4 Duplicon

Martin Mißfeldt took part in the TRAIN-IT course in April 2002. He planned the start-up of a new company out of an existing one which was facing bankruptcy. Trusting in his own competence as well as the know-how and customer contacts established in his former company, Martin Mißfeldt joined the course as an employee and left it as an entrepreneur: "The decisive learning achievement was that TRAIN-IT enabled me to view my own business through the eyes of a competitor or a customer. This perspective vision has become the basis of business decisions taking us forward."

Duplicon was founded in June 2002. Martin Mißfeldt established Duplicon as a privately owned company without external financing and runs it through profits. He plans to grow his company organically, considering a limited company formation at a later point. Duplicon´s focus is regional, as Martin Mißfeldt believes in proximity to his customers. He is striving towards expansion within Northern Germany.

Duplicon is a full-service e-culture multimedia provider. Focused on presenting cultural content, they develop and produce multimedia art. In their business strategy, Duplicon are pursuing a clear profile in transfer of cultural content and expecting stronger investments in this sector from cultural institutions in the future. Out of the projects on which they currently work, they aim to develop long-term maintenance contracts.

Duplicon currently employ three freelancers, one of them long-term. They expect to raise their annual revenue from EUR 80,000 to EUR 150,000 over the next three years.

4.5 ESTeam AB

Gudrun Magnusdottír participated in the TRAIN-IT course in July 2002. She is the CEO of ESTeam AB, founded in 1995 in Sweden, and joined the training to write a business plan to market their product ESTeam Translator®. ESTeam AB was involved in the IST project MUMIS – Multimedia Indexing and Searching Environment (IST-1999-10651).

ESTeam Translator® is a multilingual translation software product, which integrates Translation Memory (TM) and Machine Translation (MT) technology to produce full translation in multiple languages. The MT already supports translations in any direction between all the European Union languages and Norwegian. The ESTeam Translator® is unique on the market, due to its technology, language coverage and customisability. The product is the subject of an IDC Report and nominated for the IST Prize 2004.

ESTeam AB have been funding their development from sales and currently have their second product on the market. They have already won large clients such as the EU, Olympics 2004 and Thompson Corporation. Their aim is to win further large clients and become market leader in corporate translation software. The small global budget in translation tools is currently estimated at EUR 30 m. ESTeam AB expect an annual turnover of EUR 2 m over the next three years. Currently working with 15 employees, Gudrun Magnusdottír estimates that staff may be doubled within the next two years.

4.6 Centrica s.r.l.

The company Centrica s.r.l. was founded in June 1999. Marco Cappellini, CEO of Centrica, took part in the TRAIN-IT course in November 2001 to write a business plan to develop the young start-up and launch a new product. Centrica have been involved in several European R&D projects, such as the IST project TRADEX – Trial Action for Digital Object Exchange (IST-1999-21031), which supported the development of their products.

Centrica started out as a service activity in web and multimedia development and digital imaging, mainly in the cultural heritage sector and in territory valorisation. On this basis Centrica developed their proprietary image server XLimage®. Unique features of XLimage® are enabling very high resolution images over Intranet/Internet and 3G mobile networks (GPRS, UMTS), and integrating IPR management through digital watermarking. For the innovative technology, Centrica were selected among 420 IST companies from 28 countries as one of the IST Prize Nominees 2004. In November 2003 Centrica received the Il Sole 24 Ore Prize for Premio Impresa e Cultura (Enterprise and Culture Prize) with high press coverage, especially in Il Sole 24 Ore, which is the most important economic newspaper in Italy and one of the most important in Europe.

XLimage® is being used by Italian companies and government agencies like Scala Group, Fratelli Alinari, Uffizi Gallery, A.C. Milan, Tuscany Region, ICCD, National

Library in Florence. The image server is being recognised as a reference technology for Internet imaging in Europe being the technological basis for many European Projects. Centrica have proved XLimage® potential also in 2,5G environment (GPRS) with mobile operator WIND and Tuscany Region - a prototype is available at www.imageflorence.com. Through EU project involvement, Centrica have established a network of international potential customers. First non-Italian customer is the Royal Library in Brussels.

Centrica aim to become a major player in Internet imaging software with EUR 2m turnover in 2006 (EUR 550,000 in 2004, 1m in 2005) and expect to be acquired by a larger company. Currently employing 7 people, Centrica expect to create two further jobs in 2004 (one commercial and one technical), and to reach the number of 12 employees in 2006.

5. Conclusions and Future Perspectives

In conclusion, it can be said that the hands-on and intensive TRAIN-IT course produces high quality business plans and significantly accelerates the processes of business plan writing and company start-up. Overall success factors of TRAIN-IT can be derived from the above described results and company profiles:

TRAIN-IT provides a tailored training concepts based on individual requirements and adapted to trends in the economy and business world.

The hands-on intensive course enables verification of business viability in the early stage, allowing corrective steps based on experts advice.

Consequently, participants save time and money through accelerated processes of business planning and implementation of business plans in entrepreneurial and intrapreneurial activities: start-up, spin-off, expansion of existing businesses.

Participants become part of an international network of experts, financiers, and entrepreneurs. Mediation of contacts to potential investors and business partners is provided to assist participants beyond the business plan stage towards realisation of their ventures.

Further, criteria for entrepreneurial success were identified which need to be competently addressed in the business plan:

- The quality of the business model and strategy
- Complementary competences of the management team
- Thorough and ongoing market and competition analysis
- Coherent marketing and sales strategy
- Proof of concept (key customers, turnover), significant USPs (Unique Selling Propositions) and customer benefits
- Intellectual Property Rights (IPR) ownership of the company/entrepreneur etc.

The individual features of the TRAIN-IT curriculum were extensively analysed and verified as to their effectiveness and relevance, resulting in a transferable European course model. The TRAIN-IT course has been made available for licencing at international level.

A first licence was successfully implemented by NITAP, the Northern Ireland Technology Assessment Programme (www.nitap.com). First results show that the model is transferable and flexible for adaptation to individual business needs and cultural requirements. Entirely positive feedback was received from NITAP course participants.

A regional version of the TRAIN-IT course in German is being prepared for August 2004 as part of the SPIN OFF Schleswig-Holstein business support initiative. Members are the regional business promotion corporation, financing institutions, and technology centres.

In support of these activities, TRAIN-IT organiser IZET Innovationszentrum Itzehoe is currently benchmarking TRAIN-IT against other entrepreneurial training measures available throughout Europe as part of the tasks of the EU-project START – Start-Up Related Know-how Transfer [4].

On a European level, IZET strongly recommends to give entrepreneurial support to e-technologists and researchers to exploit their findings in order to create impact on the economic growth and job creation. The potential on the part of the technologists is there. What is needed are structured support mechanisms beginning at awareness creation level and carrying potentials through to business take-up through hands-on accompaniment.

Acknowledgements

Funding by the European Commission of the EU projects outlined below is gratefully acknowledged.

References

[1] IST Business: TRAIN-IT was an Accompanying Measure in the IST (Information Society Technologies) Programme of the European Commission. The project fed on experiences gained in a TRAIN-IT pilot action conducted 1997-1999, as well as in the validation project Start-Up Support for Entrepreneurs 2000-2002. Thus, TRAIN-IT has been active since 1997. TRAIN-IT received the EuroTraining Quality Label in 2001.
Project details:
- TRAIN-IT pilot project 1997-1999 Training of IT Innovators, EP 25756, funded by the European Commission.
- Start-Up Support for Entrepreneurs, IPS029012PR, IPS Programme of the European Commission in the specific research and technological development programme "Promotion of Innovation and Encouragement of SME Participation. Project lifetime: September 2000 – February 2002. www.startup-support.net
- IST-Business: TRAIN-IT, IST 1999-29055, funded by the European Commission DG Information Societies. Project lifetime: September 2000 – August 2003. www.train-it.org

[2] HUSSLA, I. and A. THIEMANN (1999). TRAIN-IT – Training of Information Technology Innovators. In Advanced Materials, No 11, p. 701-705.

[3] HUSSLA, I. and A. THIEMANN (1999). Think BIG – Think Business, Innovation and Growth. In E-business: Key Issues, Applications and Technologies (STANFORD-SMITH, B. and P. T. KIDD Eds.), p. 262-267, IOS Press, Amsterdam, 2000.

[4] START – STArt-up Related know-how Transfer: Thematic Network of PAXIS II – The Pilot Action of Excellence on Innovative Start-ups, managed by the European Commission´s Directorate-General Enterprise under the 6th Framework Research & Innovation Programme. www.cordis.lu/paxis/src/start.htm

eAdoption and the Knowledge Economy: Issues, Applications, Case Studies
P. Cunningham and M. Cunningham (Eds.)
IOS Press, 2004

Noisy Reform or Silent Revolution in Higher Education? A Hungarian Overview

András GÁBOR - Zoltán SZABÓ
Budapest University of Economic Sciences and Public Administration
Department of Information Systems, Fővám tér 8., Budapest, Hungary, 1093
Email: gabor@informatika.bkae.hu - szabo@informatika.bkae.hu

Abstract: The necessity of radical changes in the Hungarian higher education sector was realized in the early 1990's, and several initiatives were launched to transform the sector. The central question is now how IT information systems can support or even facilitate institutional reform. It can be both an accelerating factor and a major enabler or, on the other hand, a major inhibitor of changes. New methods (eLearning), new management structures and styles, extensive monitoring and control systems, new administrative and collaborative systems are necessary. In this "turnaround" situation information strategy planning and IT governance plays a crucial role in the utilization of the IT potential for improving competitiveness and transforming organizations. The key element of IT Governance in the academia is the process focus.

1. Introduction

The structure and internal organisation of Hungarian higher education (HE) is rather conservative and outdated. Apart from the fact that the academia is conservative in nature, the need for renewal is more than a must. The reasons why higher education should change are the following: in a knowledge society it is assumed that the knowledge of the workers has a special, or at least different type of knowledge than 50 or 100 years ago. The lexical knowledge is of rather less importance, but the problem solving ability, and the creative and innovative character of the knowledge workers is more valuable. Second, the technology of learning/teaching will change radically in the next few years, the massive e-learning and distance teaching methods, tools and digital content need a much better organized administration. The educators need different skills. The third argument is associated with a long term decreasing demographic demand and a massive and growing overcapacity in the higher education will emerge. Not considering the forming of the European Research Area (ERA), these discrepancies emphasize the importance of competitiveness.

Hungarian higher education achieved a very high standard of excellence in the past, and as a result enjoyed an excellent reputation throughout the region and the entire world. However, Hungarian higher education is still not well prepared to meet the challenges that are emerging at the beginning of the 21st century. The necessity of radical changes was realized in the early 1990's, and several initiatives were launched to transform the sector [1]. One of the most influencing but, unfortunately, abandoned projects was the Higher Education Reform Project financed in part through a loan from the World Bank and in part by the Government of Hungary. The program was innovative, although its termination resulted in the break of local reform activities; it served as the basic conception framework of the next initiatives. One of the most crucial issues, the integration of the fragmented HE sector (small, overspecialised and isolated institutions) was handled administratively, without realizing any actual improvement in the efficiency and effectiveness of the sector. Now we are in the 24th hour of starting and implementing the reforms. Nowadays new legislation has focused on the higher education institutions (HEIs) to introduce new financing and governance model, based on a new legal framework.

During the preparation phase of the reform, several concepts were developed and discussed in a wide area of the academia. Public administration knows how to introduce new concepts on a regulatory level: laws, orders, and regulations. This is a typical cat and mouse game: the more decisive the administration in pushing through reforms, the better the counter-interested academia management resist avoiding the "efficiency" traps and calming down the hectic administrators. How can one then push through radical changes?

There are numerous practical and scientific publications that discuss the strategic importance and business transforming power of information technology (IT) [2]. If we look at only the agenda of IT fairs, the brochures of IT companies and the sales arguments of management consulting firms/EU institutions we see an idyllic scene. Nevertheless, the question remains whether Hungarian HE organizations have understood these possibilities, and if they have, to what extent they are able to realize IT-based innovations.

The central question is how IT information systems can support or even facilitate institutional reform. Whether, it can be both an accelerating factor and a major enabler or, on the other hand, a major inhibitor of changes.

2. Challenges in the Hungarian Higher Education

The Hungarian higher education system was rigid and unresponsive to the demands of the market economy, especially the world of labour. The system was inefficient and wasted enormous resources. It is generally accepted, that in order to profit fully from globalisation and integration, the sector has to be further developed.

The major problems are the following [3]:

- Lack of responsiveness (structural rigidities and overspecialisation, unresponsiveness of enrolment to market needs)
- Inefficient use of resources (high non-teaching costs, fragmentation, emphasis on high-cost disciplines, low student/faculty ratios, rigid state budgeting procedures, lack of transparency and institutional control, lack of fiscal discipline, lack of sophisticated governance and management practices)

Until now only small improvements have been achieved, although the sector has to deal with problematic challenges. These challenges can be classified into 3 major categories:

1. Academic challenges: demand-driven, flexible, EU-compatible, quality-orientated and competitive HE sector must be established. This is the need for effectiveness.
2. Financial challenges: as a result of the unfavourable demographic trends and the economic restrictions, financial problems must be managed by improved fund-raising activity, intensive R&D activities, marketing, PPPs.
3. Organizational challenges: internal efficiency, requiring professional management, efficient business processes, and implementation of a virtual university model.

The above mentioned challenges are interrelated and require a systematic solution: new methods (eLearning), new management structures and styles, extensive monitoring and control systems, new administrative and collaborative systems are necessary.

During 2004 a higher education reform will take place covering academic, organizational and financial relations. In the academia the introduction of the Bologna process is in the focus (linear structures, transparent educational systems, etc.). From an organizational point of view the structure of the academia does not fit to the requirements, i.e. inflexible, very little organizational relations with the world of labour, weak signals from the labour demand side, a high possibility of badly structured overproduction of young professionals. The new structure should be more flexible, innovative and adaptive. Financially speaking: the money is not enough. Indeed, it is never enough. But how much money do the universities need? Financial reform on a normative basis tries to allocate the minimum amount of the necessary funding; the rest is the institutions' responsibility.

3. Modernization Opportunities and Chances

The concept of "virtual university" is not far from the concept of virtual organization. The extensive utilization of a high quality IT infrastructure in the HEIs of developed countries renders IT-based applications a crucial role in the value creation process including the operative and managerial activities. IT is now a critical factor in developing and maintaining organizational core competencies, making IT essential for the survival of HEIs.

A future orientated company considers IT as a strategic resource, and a HEI is not an exception. To ensure competitiveness organizations plan according to their business targets and, on the other hand, invest in it generously. A modern HEI uses integrated Enterprise Resource Planning (ERP) to meet its standardized data processing and reporting needs and relies on MIS or even Online Analytical Processing (OLAP) tools for more complex analyses. In order to streamline the business process it deploys workflow and groupware systems. Internal communication and collaboration is facilitated by intranet, and extranet makes available its educational and administrative services. Its IT-based control mechanisms cross over the organizational borders of the HEI, on the customer side with Customer Relationship Management (CRM, as a tool of measuring customer satisfaction, managing alumni activities, etc.). It utilizes sectorial procurement applications, marketplaces, and the electronic public procurement. All these are performed in a state-of-the-art infrastructure, that is, in client-server architecture relying on up-to-date operating and database management systems, and 4GL development tools. In case the HEI wishes to conform to present trends, it entrusts – in outsourcing contracts – an external supplier to perform the operation of some or all of its systems.

Similarly to any private or public organization IT has become the major facilitator of value-adding activities. This emphasizes the importance of IT governance, which targets the alignment of information and communication technologies with organizational objectives [4]. The spread of new IT is a real challenge for HEIs, but also an opportunity for expansion. The necessary alignment is best achieved when cross-functional, collaborative information systems are instituted. This allows IT to become the agent of change, facilitating organizational transformation in a robust and nimble manner [5]. The top management of the HEI, the academic and the administrative staff, the IT function and the external providers should work together to have the new information technologies contribute in the strongest possible way to the growth in HEI value.

The crucial role of IT in Higher education can be observed in two fields. IT has critical a function in supporting and enabling the realization of sectorial and institutional objectives and needs. On the HEI level, IT can generate real intangible benefits such as reputation, trust, "product leadership", improved time-to-market, and tangible benefits like increased market-share and cost reduction. On the HE sector level the flexibility, the free movement between HEIs, the sectorial and academic control requires suitable systems to monitor, collect and exchange information. In addition to this a robust IT infrastructure (administrative support systems) should be put into operation (campus management, ERPs, intranets, student registration systems, etc.).

Unfortunately, the real penetration rate of the cutting-edge applications in the Hungarian HE sector is very low. Hungarian HEIs are now at the 1st level of the Venkatraman's framework [6], and they are far from the 2nd level. To achieve the goals of the reform, they have to implement 3rd or 4th level innovations.

In this "turnaround" situation [8] information strategy planning (ISP) plays a crucial role in the utilization of the IT potential for improving competitiveness and transforming organizations. In the organizations of developed economies, ISP appears as an independent function and for many organizations the parallel articulation of business and information strategy or a strict coordination between the two is the path to follow [9]. The question is how much care is taken about this in Hungarian HE organizations, or on sectorial level. The importance of IT is generally accepted. However, in fact, only a few HEIs were able to develop a more or less comprehensive IT strategic plan.

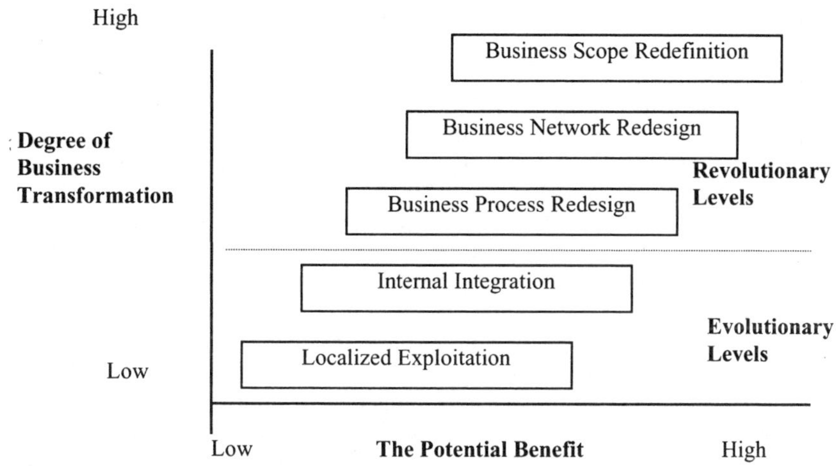

Figure 1: Venkatraman's Five Levels of IT Enabled Business Transformation [7]

The information strategy in higher education stands on four legs: a higher education (virtual) portal will collect information from the world of labour nationwide and Europe wide; will collect and redistribute the mobility opportunities; will give information about the final year students (carrier portal), will distribute digitised content (e-learning portal). The second leg of the strategy is linked to the institutional information systems: student registration, finance, R&D monitoring and facility management. These four subsystems cover all the important areas of a higher educational institution, special systems, like medical information systems for the university clinics, etc. will be added to the core systems. The third element concerns the academic relations: quality assurance in higher education and mobility tracking assumes central management (and also databases). This element addresses accreditation, credit transfer and quality control issues. The fourth element of the strategy covers the eager data needs of the Ministry of Education. An executive information system that sits on the institutional ones almost automatically, and in a well-controlled manner, collects the relevant and only essential data (this is information).

In the above information architecture the institutions will have an integrated system providing sufficient executive and controlling information in order to decide what branches are manageable or what and how to cross-finance, how expensive a diploma is, or in contrast, how cheap it is (competitive slack). Clear accounting and controlling procedures will result in a sound basis for decision support, in a different style, as it is usual on a faculty meeting. The legacy systems linked to the HE portal (via the university or college portal) will efficiently redirect the academic focus if it is necessary and the owner will have a clear view of the financial and human resource needs, as well as the infrastructure development requirements. Hence, the necessary changes will take place without a word. A bottom up approach will enforce the institutions to change their behaviour. However, this will not happen automatically. Only a combination of process improvement, process management (if you like BPR or BPM) and professional information system implementation can achieve the expected improvement in efficiency and, competitiveness.

4. Modernisation strategies

There are two strategic options of modernising the sector. One is focusing explicitly on the management, the academic, the financial structures and the organisation. In this approach the IT has very little, only supportive role, all inclusions finishes with the stereotypical echo of eLearning. The well elaborated sub strategies than will be fine-tuned via a series of conflict resolution meeting, event and policy making bodies (professional and political as well). (In Joining the Higher Education Era Program several concepts had been developed and detailed. In the last two years university rectors, several other organisations discussed more than 10 variants. Finally, due to the many compromises, everybody is unsatisfied.) The final compromise will be the solid basis of the legislation and when it is passed through the parliament, by the order of the law it will be in effect, the reform will take place.

The second strategy, in contrast with the first one, put the stress on the active role of IT. IT is emphasized, not only, and far not in the first place in technological sense, but as a major facilitator of organizational change, academic, financial and business innovation. The IT development cannot lack the solution all the above-mentioned organisational, academic, financial and management problems, hence it cannot be only a pure technical performance. IT has developed into a key factor in strategic planning. Harmonization of the corporate strategy, structural capabilities and IT is a central topic of information management: the issue of strategic alignment. According to a generally accepted axiom, an organization's competitive position and supporting administrative infrastructure must be aligned, and consistency between decisions concerning external and internal domains is necessary [10]. Organizational structure and competencies must be suitable for implementing strategy and for enabling efficient and effective operations. In other words: the real and effective driver of the changes is the IT based development and the efforts through strategic alignment will comply with the academic reform's requirements.

Strategic alignment was originally defined as concerning the inherently dynamic fit between external and internal domains, such as the product/market, strategy, administrative structures, business processes and IT [11]. The strategic alignment model developed by Henderson and Venkatraman [12] is based on the need for strategic choices in the external domain and the internal domain to be consistent and on the need for integration between the IS function and the organisation. In university environment the strategic alignment will be the strongest base of the university governance.

5. Alignment scenarios

Hungarian HEIs are faced with this alignment problem. No real organizational change can be implemented without the support of IT, and no IT investments are fruitful and beneficial without organizational changes. There are two possible scenarios.

5.1 Evolution – worst case scenario

A conservative step-by-step process is to "go up the stairs". The speed of both development and radical changes adopt a trial-error approach. Organizations learn from their own failures. The widespread use of eLearning can be institutionalised in this way: HEs have only limited experience, the infrastructure is not generally suitable and the educational culture should be changed – this is a long procedure. In front of this the administrative support systems, the sector-level MIS and web-based systems are inevitably necessary to implement the urgent reform-related changes. The lengthy process of experimentation with the above mentioned relatively matured technologies would lead the sector into a hopeless situation: the collapse and loss of competitiveness unavoidable. Unfortunately, there are many impediments. For example, for HEIs the requirement to provide an economical service that is reliable, consistent and of the highest quality is very difficult to fulfil. Amidst the outsourcing campaign of developed countries, the Hungarian HEIs seem relatively unmotivated by or unaware of IT outsourcing. Difficulties of redesigning internal processes can be another critical issue.

5.2 Revolution – it is a must or a nightmare

A more risky but more promising approach is to utilise IT, as the major facilitator of organizational and sectorial changes. ERP and process management must be implemented according to this strategy.

There are several implementation scenarios. The cheapest and most professional solution is the application service-providing (ASP) model. An ASP using economies of scale can be very competitive in prices and costs, and technically very professional at the same time. The analyses provide efficient proofs, although the individual investment is very expensive and, in a university environment provide very low efficiency. However, the BPR and the user management should remain university responsibility. In consequence the ASP specific in higher education is always on two-levels. Technical management is outsourced, user-management is insourced. There are two options that come from this dichotomy. First, there are ample areas for public-private partnerships. Second the HE institution can access and the industry can gain more profit from high-level knowledge transfer.

The above-mentioned scenario and strategy, which one can call the "organisational through technology enabler" paradigm is not a by-product of wishful thinking. Although it is not exactly as the reality is. In a first attempt 6-7 months ago an ASP concept was introduced in some of the universities, the reaction was total refusal. (The explanation seems to be more of psychological nature than technical, the learning curve could not been overtaken. On short term the lead-time and bureaucracy of the public procurement will be a significant incentive to choose ASP instead of separate investments. On longer term the competitiveness, reliability, risk management, etc will influence the decisions.)

In a second attempt university consortiums were organised in order to start BPR activities under the framework of human resource development of the EU structural and cohesion funds. As a result of an earlier pilot project, in Hungary a centrally available process model supports HE institutions to reorganize their processes and rearrange their organizational structure to derive the functional specification of their information systems. The joint model ensures the maximum uniformity but still gives ample opportunity to add local specialties to the model. This model is a key element of success if both the supply and demand side accept its use. International examples (e.g in Germany and Austria) prove that significant IT development without BPR cannot be successful.

Such a mapping serves several purposes. First, it forces the organization to think through exactly how it should do such a process in an ideal world. Second, it provides a benchmark against which to measure how well a particular system can support that process.

This should begin with some kind of vision of how the new institution will be structured organizationally. For example, what will be the nature of a faculty/school, how many will there be, how will the central administration be organized, where will be the principal points of financial control, etc.? Once the broad outline of the new organization is developed, then there will be the need to develop the business processes, as noted below, and to begin to integrate these processes into the organizational structure.

6. Conclusions

Radical reform of the HEI in Hungary is an unavoidable must. There are several approaches to carry out the reform. The scale starts from very strict administrative measures and ends with a soft, timely organic adoption process. Opening the national market the HEI should improve their competitiveness as well. External and internal motives force the strategic thinking and the strategy formulation. The IT both in the management and in the core business approved its unavoidable nature; hence the alignment of strategy is not just a side effect but can be the silent facilitator of the organizational changes. Adopting and practicing IT governance in the academic environment will result in a smooth, but quick adaptation process. The key element of IT Governance in the academia is the process focus, the coverage of all the core processes, value delivery, performance measurement, and quality control. Due to the nature of higher education, no single (isolated) system can meet the requirements, accreditation, quality control and supply-demand information flow, and many other interactions assume inter-organizational solutions. It will be the acid test of the strategic awareness of the institutions, whether cooperative systems will be developed under administrative pressure or will be the product of self-organized development.

References

[1] Staff Appraisal Report. Republic of Hungary Higher Education Reform Project. World Bank Human Development Unit, Report No. 16536-HU, 1998

[2] Scott Morton, M. S. (Ed.) (1991): The Corporation of the 1990's- Information Technology and Organisational Transformation. Oxford University Press.

[3] Staff Appraisal Report. Republic of Hungary Higher Education Reform Project. World Bank Human Development Unit, Report No. 16536-HU, 1998

[4] Bourdariat, J. (2001): Corporate Governance and ICT: A Marriage of Reason. Information Systems Control Journal, Volume 6.

[5] Guldentops, E. (2004): Key Success Factors for Implementing IT Governance. Systems Control Journal, Volume 2.

[6] Henderson, J. C.; Venkatraman, N. (1992): Strategic Alignment: A Model for Organisational Transformation Through Information Technology. In: Transforming Organisations, Oxford University Press, 1992, ed.: Useem, M.; Kochan, T. A.

[7] Venkatraman, N. (1994): „IT-enabled Business Transformation: from Automation to Business Scope Redefinition", *Sloan Management Review*, Winter. pp.73-87.

[8] McFarlan, W.F.; McKenney, J.L. (1983): Corporate Information Sytems Management. Homewood, Ill.: Richard D. Irwin.

[9] Earl, M.J. (ed.), (1996): *Information Management*. Oxford University Press, Oxford

[10] Chandler, A.D. (1962): Strategy and Structure: Chapters in the History of the American Enterprise, Cambridge, MA, The MIT Press.

[11] Venkatraman, N. (1994): „IT-enabled Business Transformation: from Automation to Business Scope Redefinition", *Sloan Management Review*, Winter. pp.73-87.

[12] Henderson, J. C.; Venkatraman, N. (1993): „Strategic Alignment: Leveraging Information Technology for Transforming Organisations", *IBM Systems Journal*, 32(1), pp.4-16.

eAdoption and the Knowledge Economy: Issues, Applications, Case Studies
P. Cunningham and M. Cunningham (Eds.)
IOS Press, 2004

Adopting Groupware for Collaborative E-Learning: A Blackboard '*Groups*' Case Study

Alan HOGARTH
Division of Business Information Management, Glasgow Caledonian University, Glasgow, Scotland, UK
Tel: +44 141 331 3943, Fax: +44 141 331 3193, Email: A.Hogarth@gcal.ac.uk

Abstract: Group working is becoming more common not only for businesses, but also in the educational environment. Employers want graduates who can communicate and collaborate, and they expect universities and colleges to provide training in these skills. As such in an attempt to prepare students for a business environment that emphasises collaborative work skills, universities are increasingly including groupwork in their programmes. However, research suggests that there is little formal recognition and value attached to the acquisition and development of collaborative skills in higher education institutions. Added to this, new technology is becoming central to higher education, as new e-learning materials are developed and Virtual Learning Environments (VLE) such as Blackboard are implemented. This paper considers the social and cultural changes that collaborative technologies may bring about in the university environment. A case study was carried out with undergraduate 'campus based' students to elicit their views on VLE technology (Blackboard 'Groups') for student project work.

1. Introduction

Currently one of the most popular organization innovations is the transformation of traditional hierarchical organization to a flat structure of self-managing, participative teams or work groups [3]. While the number of businesses that have adopted group working techniques reflects the depth of this penetration into the business world, even more important is the need for teamwork to be encouraged at university level in an attempt to prepare students for a business environment that emphasises teamwork skills.

However, despite this, research suggests that there is little formal recognition and value attached to the acquisition and development of collaborative skills in higher education institutions [14], [12]. Employers want graduates who can communicate and collaborate, and they expect universities and colleges to provide training in these skills [12]. Kuiper [18] suggests that teaching total quality management (of which teamwork is an essential component) exposes 'students to practices they are likely to experience when they enter the work force' and that the praxis of teamwork concepts in the classroom 'can empower students to take a more active role in the teaching/learning process'.

Other authors recommend the use of electronic mail to facilitate teamwork in classrooms: 'Email can help make group projects more practical and effective by allowing individuals to interact continuously independently with one another' [1]. Whereas, Ciborra [8] suggests that the use of groupware, of which electronic mail is one component, enables teachers to 'help their students adapt to a workgroup environment'. He further suggests that, in order to prepare students for participation in the business world, tutors should facilitate 'frequent collaboration among persons in a work group', and should promote 'techniques and procedures requisite to being effective team members and leaders'. Teamwork must be taken seriously as it can alter the culture and social structure of some university classrooms affecting the very ways in which knowledge is conveyed.

Furthermore, new technology is becoming central rather than peripheral to higher education, as new e-learning materials are developed and further change is inevitable.

Indeed, the Dearing Report [11] into higher education in the UK emphasises the need for 'communication and information technology' to be the new framework on which to build the 'learning society'. This paper will consider the technological, social and cultural changes that collaborative technologies may bring to the university environment. To progress this investigation a case study was carried out with a group of 3rd year undergraduate 'campus based' students at Glasgow Caledonian University to elicit their views on group technology for learning. The Blackboard VLE 'Groups' facility was used.

2. Objectives

The objectives of this research are twofold; review the literature in this area to clarify and understand the research background to this paper; and use a case study to establish how collaborative technology may help facilitate the student group project experience.

2.1 Engendering Collaborative Working Skills in the Educational Environment

The terms collaborative learning and cooperative learning are important for this research. However, defining the differences could prove difficult, but an attempt should be made in order to clarify aspects of this paper in regard to group working in the educational environment. Panitz [20] states that, 'Collaboration is a philosophy of interaction and personal lifestyle whereas cooperation is a structure of interaction designed to facilitate the accomplishment of an end product or goal'. Whereas, Myers [19] asserts that, 'Supporters of cooperative learning tend to be more teacher centred... collaborative learning advocates distrust structure and allow students more say in forming friendship and interest groups'. Rockwood [21] states that, 'Most importantly, in cooperative, the authority remains with the instructor… in collaborative, the instructor, once the task is set, transfers all authority to the group. Many authors have debated this issue; however for the purposes of this paper this author proposes the following working definition of collaboration: 'Collaborative learning respects and highlights group members' abilities and contributions.

The underlying premise of collaborative learning is based upon consensus building through co-operation by group members. The interpersonal and interactive nature of small groups makes them a challenging vehicle for engaging students in their own learning. Furthermore there is strong historical evidence from some students that they benefit from and enjoy the experience in a range of different ways [18][15]. These issues are emphasised in the Dearing Report into higher education and by Cubie when he states that 'across all sectors employers do highlight weak communication skills, lack of commercial awareness, poor team work, lack of motivation… as the major weaknesses of graduates' [11]. As Cubie shows, group skills such as collaboration, reliability and creative problem-solving are seen as important and relevant by students and employers, yet research by Rust (ed.) [22] and Hogarth [12], [13] indicates that students and lecturers must be persuaded and assisted in giving academic credit for such skills. It is surprising how few universities train students to work in groups or train academic staff to manage student project groups. The next section considers issues associated with group working and technology.

2.2 Group Working with Collaborative Technology

How is group working automated? Is it merely the adding of technology to the application of those traditional group theories and approaches to group work advocated by such authors as Belbin [4], [5] and Katzenbach [16]? There are many perceived views of what exactly is collaborative technology: is it e-mail, the Internet, video-conferencing or groupware?

Defining how collaborative technology functions can be difficult. However, a common definition of Groupware is computer software designed to facilitate the work of groups. Brinck, [7] highlights the most common reasons people use Groupware technology and Coleman [9] simplifies this when he defines groupware as 'computer-mediated collaboration that increases the productivity or functionality of person-to-person processes'. The emphasis on technological aspects when introducing groupware has remained paramount, with social and cultural aspects still being a secondary consideration. Research is showing that those organisations which introduce groupware systems while considering social and cultural impact as well as technical aspects are more productive than those who do not [12][13]. This emphasis on technical aspects is also reflected in educational establishments where Virtual Learning Environment (VLE) packages such as Blackboard and WebCT are being introduced in an ad hoc basis with little regard as to how these may affect the learning environment. However as the next section will demonstrate the pressure is on universities to implement these VLEs as speedily as possible.

2.3 Collaborative Learning with Virtual Learning Environments (VLEs)

VLEs are essentially tools, which are being encouraged for teaching and learning in a technological environment. The groupware element of VLEs allows students to work on projects in small, collaborative groups; engage in classroom discussion; access their own discussion board and virtual or real-time chat facilities e.g. Blackboard Groups facility; access reference materials and meet their instructor for individual conferences. This opens up the potential for collaborative projects and communications between different groups of learners. Despite the emphasis on the technological aspects of VLEs they are now recognised as a key component within any learning and teaching strategy in Higher Education. However they are not without their problems.

2.3.1 Problem of VLEs

Classroom teaching is structured both spatially and temporally the lecturer's presence and voice are powerful devices for focusing attention and directing activity. However, on-line tutors do not have the automatic structure that regular classroom meetings have and the unity that comes from meeting in the same physical cannot be recuperated in a distance setting. There are a number of reasons as to why VLEs have been utilised in many institutions. Ever increasing student numbers is one aspect of Higher Education where it is claimed VLEs can help. In terms of widening participation VLEs can provide support and resources to say, part time students who can't always travel to the campus.

However there are also 'political'motivations in using these products. The British government is willing to fund VLE technology to increase the use of ICT for learning. However, they are often purchased without much consideration of how they will be actually implemented. Thus many institutions use products such as Blackboard or WebCT as mere repositories for lecture 'handouts'. What appears to be lacking are proper requirements studies, resources for staff and follow up training for staff and students on how to use these products [6][7]. To choose a VLE a list of requirements and benefits must be drawn up. Unfortunately in most cases this requirements process seems to be being ignored.

2.3.2 Possible benefits of Using Groupware (in VLEs) for Student Project groups

Student groups may experience perceived benefits when they use Groupware (e.g. increased group efficiency through communication). Group members may share problems they encounter during a project at any time, not just when they meet physically. In addition keeping group members aware of the project's progress in real time may lessen the consequences of problems. Group members may be more likely to succeed at group tasks if difficulties are easily shared and requests for help are considered by all group members eg. group members who might not be willing to ask a question in a meting might be more willing to ask via Groupware; group members who might not be willing to share their knowledge in a meeting might be more willing to help out via Groupware. All of these potential benefits make the concept of Groupware for students very appealing.

However, while exposure to new technologies such as Groupware is expected to be helpful to students, the extent to which it decreases group problems in a classroom setting depends on whether or not students embrace the technology. The results of the following case study indicate that not all students are convinced by this technology. The next sections will introduce Blackboard and then discuss and analyse the results of the groupware technology survey based on students' views of the technology.

3. Methodology/Technology

In parallel with the literature search review, a case study survey has been carried out with a group of 'campus based' 3rd Year Business Information Management Students from Glasgow Caledonian University. This survey is part of an on-going PhD thesis undertaken by the author. This survey now considers the effect of groupware technology in an educational setting (Blackboard 'Groups'), specifically for managing and developing a coursework task. The survey questionnaire is designed to elicit information on technology (hardware/software) access, availability and usage; group working experience; experiences in using groupware technology. As such a qualitative approach will be taken. The results discussed and analysed in the full paper are both informative and interesting.

3.1 BlackBoard 'Groups' Facility Case Study: Glasgow Caledonian University

The Blackboard VLE was introduced to Glasgow Caledonian University over the past two years. It is mainly used as a repository for lecture notes, seminar material and assessment material. Staff can attend a number of training courses. To date the Groups facility has not been used extensively nor have any student views been elicited on this group technology until now. A case study survey has been carried out with 27 'campus based' 3rd Year Business Information Management Students from Glasgow Caledonian University who previously had been surveyed in a case study on 'traditional' group working with students [15] and group working and group working technology with business [14].

This survey is part of an on-going PhD thesis undertaken by the author. The sample comprises 3 males aged 18-25; 21 females aged 18-25; 1 female aged 26-34 and 2 females aged 35 and above. This breakdown reflects the overall population of the degree course. This survey now considers the effect of groupware technology in an educational setting (Blackboard 'Groups'), specifically for managing and developing a coursework task. The survey questionnaire is designed to elicit information on technology (hardware) access, availability and usage; group working experience; experiences in using groupware technology ('Groups') and was completed at the end of the coursework project.

4. Results and Discussion

The following is a summary discussion of the results of the aforementioned case study and are depicted in Table 1,Table 2 and Table 3. A qualitative approach to the survey was undertaken. Initially 25% of the students state that they did not find working in groups a beneficial experience at all. When asked how the group contacted each other during the project there was a mixed response. However the majority, 22, said they met in person, with 16 saying the contacted members by text message. It was interesting to note that only 8 used e-mail. When they did meet in person their preferred times were mid-morning, 16, and early afternoon, 20. These responses appear to indicate that the groups met when they had free time between formal classes. When asked if they had difficulty arranging meetings only 4 students said they had, 5 students stated they had difficulty finding time to meet with their group and 7 felt they had difficulty finding a place to meet. The majority of students obviously felt happy about the above situations, however if even one student has problems with these issues then that could lead to problems within the group. It is for these students that the use of 'Groups' could be beneficial.

Table 1: Summary Findings of Section 1 of Questionnaire

'Section 1a: General questions Response

	Yes	No
1: Have you worked on Group projects before	24	3
2: Was it beneficial?	20	7

Section 1b: Questions Related to MBIS Coursework

3: How did you normally contact group members?

In person	Phone Calls	Texting	e-mail
22	6	16	8

(Some groups used more than one means of contact)

4: When was the best time for the group to meet?

Mid morning	Early afternoon	Evenings	Weekends
16	20	0	0

(Some groups met on both morning and afternoon)

	Yes	No
5: Did you have difficulty arranging meetings with other members?	4	23
6: Did you have difficulty finding a common meeting time?	5	22
7: Did you have difficulty finding a common meeting place?	7	20
8: Did you find it difficult to exchange files?	2	25

Table 2: Summary Findings of Section 2: Use of Blackboard 'Groups'

Section 2: Access to/time spent on Blackboard 'Groups'

9: How do you gain access to a computer?

Home PC	Computer Lab	Laptop	Other
21	23	4	0

(Some groups used a combination)

	Yes	No
10: Did you use e-mail to contact group members?	10	17
11: Until this coursework project had you ever used any groupware products such as Blackboard 'Groups' for group project work?	20	7
12: Did you have difficulty getting access to a computer in order to use Blackboard 'Groups'?	20	7

13: How often did you use 'Groups'

Regularly	Daily	Weekly	Monthly
11	4	9	3

In Section 2 of the questionnaire the students were asked about the technology and the procedures pertinent to their use of Blackboard 'Groups'. A variety of responses were given to question on how they accessed a computer for their group coursework. The majority, 23 students, either used the Computer lab or a Home PC, 21 students, or both. The computer lab usage tends to bear out that the groups met or worked on their coursework between formal classes. However the fact that 21 had access to a Home PC might have indicated they may have found 'Groups' useful. However only 10 students in total indicated that they used e-mail to contact group members while the majority, 17 students, did not.

When asked if they had used a groupware product before for project work, 20 said yes, but 20 also responded that they had difficulty getting access to a computer in order to use 'Groups'. This seems to contradict the earlier responses where the majority of students claimed to have either access to a computer lab or a Home PC. (All students are attached to Blackboard for their modules and are allocated lab time so access should not have been a problem.). When specifically asked the frequency of use of 'Groups' 11 students used it as required, 4 on a daily basis, 9 on a weekly basis and 3 on a monthly basis. The next part of the questionnaire concentrates on 'Groups' facilities. Only 33% of students said they used Discussion Board. However most of them, 8 out of 9, did think it useful. Only 8% of respondents, 2 students, said they used Virtual Classroom', but again they found it useful.

Table 3: Summary Findings of Section 3 of Questionnaire: Use of 'Groups'

Section 3: Use of Blackboard 'Groups' Facilities	Yes	No
14: Did you use '*Group Discussion Board'* for coursework project?	9	18
Useful?	8	1
15: Did you use '*Group Virtual Classroom'* for coursework project	2	25
Useful?	2	25
16: Did you use '*File Exchange'* for coursework project?	4	23
Useful?	4	23
17: Did you use '*Send e-mail* ' for coursework project?	14	13
18: Overall did you feel comfortable meeting with electronically?	18	9
19: Did you feel comfortable using Blackboard 'Groups'for your coursework project?	15	12
20:Do you feel that 'Groups' helped the group communicate better when carrying out the coursework?	16	11
21: Did using 'Groups' specifically alleviate the problems associated with arranging meetings at specific times in specific physical locations?	11	16
22: Do you think 'Groups' should be used more for Project work in the university?	22	5
If No why not? (See comments later).		
23: Briefly Summarise what you perceive to be thebenefits or pitfalls of using 'Groups' for group project work? (See comments later)		
24: Do you think Groupware enhances student group working	21	6
25: Would you want Groupware technology to replace face-to-face student group meetings?	3	24
26: Do you think training in 'Groups' would be beneficial?	24	3

It is surprising that as many as 25 students did not use this facility as it is core to 'Groups'. One reason could be that, as most respondents stated earlier, they mostly contact each other face to face or by texting. In response to the use of File Exchange only 16% of students said they used it. Again this could be because they meet physically to exchange material. Oddly enough when asked if they used 'Send e-mail' over 50% said that they did. Despite the lack of usage of some of the facilities 66% of students felt comfortable meeting other group members electronically. However, that does leave a sizeable minority, 33%, who were uncomfortable with this medium. Furthermore less students, 56%, felt comfortable. Whereas a slight increase, 44%, felt uncomfortable using 'Groups'. Despite these responses it appears that a majority, 59%, of students felt 'Groups' helped them communicate better. In regard to eliminating the problems of physical location and times for meetings the majority 59% felt that 'Groups' did not particularly help.

The next question asked students whether 'Groups' should be used more for student project work. Given some of the earlier responses it was surprising to note that 81% of the students replied that it should. When asked why not 19% commented that it should not. This set of responses to Q22 (Figure 1), appears to correspond to the earlier responses in relation to time and place of meetings. Essentially if students see each other regularly on campus then they do not see a use for facilities such as 'Groups'. The next question asked the students to summarise what they saw to be the benefits and pitfalls of using 'Groups'. Some comments are shown in Figure 2. The set of responses to Q23 in Figure 2 sheds some light on the earlier yes/no answers. In general the students appear to think that 'Groups' is a good thing particularly for communication when members may be ill or unable to attend face-to-face meetings. However, as most of these students are 'on campus' they do not see the need to use 'Groups' extensively as they are in contact with other group members on a daily basis. Difficulty in getting access to computer equipment is also seen as a pitfall.

The next question asks if they felt that groupware enhances student group working. 78% of respondents felt that it did, but when asked if they would want groupware technology to replace face-to-face student group meetings only 11% viewed this favourably. The majority, 89%, was against this idea. Nonetheless when the students were asked if training in 'Groups' would be beneficial. The majority, 89%, replied that it would be beneficial.

Comments:	Comments:
1' Our group preferred meeting face-to-face' 2 'If you are in the same classes as your group members then you have the same time off to meet up. The only reason it could be useful is if one member was off for a long period of time'. 3 'The main (Blackboard) discussion board is more helpful, as you have feedback and discussion from the entire course of student than just the limited group who meet regularly anyway. Blackboard is useful as a means of gaining coursework and discussion boards, 'Groups' not as useful.' 4'Find meeting face-to-face more productive.' We (the group) didn't use the groupware as we saw each other on a daily basis.' 5 ' I found the use of 'Groups' very good. I was unable to meet up with the group due to illness however, I was still able to be part of the meeting, by using my PC at home.'	1Not seeing people face to face, met up everyday didn't need virtual classroom, couldn't always find a computer to do the work.' 2Used to meeting personally in same classes so we might not need iCan be difficult to use 'Groups' when your not used to itCould be good when people can't meet' 3'Positive – if not able to meet in person, groups a good way to exchange info. Negative - when group members do not know how to access and operate ' 'groups!' 4'Easy to communicate; Not many people know how to use it so you are better arranging face-to-face meetings' 5'I think it could be beneficial for groups who do not see each other on a daily basis. However as we were saw each other every day we did not feel the need to use 'Groups' very often.'
Figure 1: Sample Responses to Q22	*Figure 2: Sample Responses to Q23*

5. Conclusion and Recommendations

The problem in conceptualising group learning is to identify and maximise the pedagogical possibilities that distinguish it from traditional group work in the classroom. This is also the challenge in using VLEs such as Blackboard for group working: to avoid replicating the traditional group environment and focus on realising the teaching and learning experiences that VLEs make possible. Encouraging students to use VLEs, particularly groupware elements, cannot be taken lightly. The students must see a need for this type of technology. If they do not they will not see its worth and refuse to use it. Further, introducing technology into an unstable group working environments may make things worse.

The results of the above case study have demonstrated that students are not averse to technology such as 'Groups' being introduced, but again they must see a need for it. However, it is also evident that this might not be the best technology for 'on campus' students. Essentially VLEs and collaborative learning technologies are neither substitutes for nor a complete departure from the traditional classroom or traditional student groups, but an extension and development of that architecture and its pedagogies.

The argument posed by this paper is that not only technological but also social and cultural developments are important to the collaborative learning environment. and are critical to effective implementation of educational groupware. Group or team working practices and experience must also be present prior to groupware implementation. In addition, personnel (students and staff) must be educated in both group working practices and groupware technology. Minimum action that academic institutions must take prior to introducing such technology is to carry out a requirements study with those students that they wish to utilise the technology. Consequently, the author would expect the next step of his research to be the construction of a guidance framework for introducing collaborative technologies into the educational environment.

References

[1] Baker, M. J. (1994). A model for negotiation in teaching-learning dialogues. *Journal of Artificial Intelligence in Education,* 5(2), 199-254.

[2] Baker, M. J. (1994). A model for negotiation in teaching-learning dialogues. *Journal of Artificial Intelligence in Education,* 5(2), 199-254.

[3] Barker, J.R. (2000), *The discipline of teamwork.* Sage Publications, London

[4] Belbin, R.M. (1981). *Management teams: Why they succeed or fail.* London, Heinemann.

[5] Belbin, R. M (1993). *Team roles at work* London: Butterworth, Heineman

[6] Biggam, J. (2003). 'Identifying and capturing knowledge for website usage: a platform for progress', *International Journal of Electronic Business*, ISSN: 1470-6067, 1(3)..

[7] Brinck, T. (1998) online at. http://www.usabilityfirst.com/Groupware/intro.html.

[8] Ciborra, C. U., (1996), *What does groupware mean for hosting IT?* In C.U. Ciborrra (ed.), Groupware and Teamwork, Wiley, Chichester.

[9] Coleman, D. (1998), Groupware the changing environment, online at, http://www.collaborate.com/publications/section1.html

[10] Cubie, A. Glasgow Herald Article, Sept 7th, 2002)

[11] Dearing, R (1997). Online at. http://www.leeds.ac.uk/educol/ncihe/

[12] Hogarth, A (2003). Change Management and Collaborative Technologies: An Industry Survey, In *Proceedings of IADIS WWW-Internet Conference, Algarve, Portugal.*

[13] Hogarth, a (2002). Adopting Socio-Technical Concepts for Eliciting Groupware Requirements in the Educational Environment, In *Proceedings of ETHICOMP 2002,* Portugal.

[14] Hogarth, A. (2001a). Managing the social and cultural consequences of introducing groupware technology into the group learning environment. *Education and Information technologies,* 6(3).

[15] Houston, S K and Lazenbatt (1996). A peer-tutoring scheme to support independent learning and group project work in Mathematics, *Assessment & Evaluation in Higher Education*, 21(3).

[16] Katzenbach, J. R., & Smith, D. K. (1993). *The wisdom of teams: Creating the high-performance organization.* Boston: Harvard Business School Press.

[17] Kuiper,S (1999).*Transition into Business,* editor. NJ: Prentice Hall,

[18] Luker, R. . (1989). *Effective Teaching in Higher Education.* London: Routledge

[19] Myers, J. (1991).Co-operative learning in heterogeneous classes. *Co-op. Learning,* 11.

[20] Panitz, T (1996). Getting students ready for co-operative learning. *Co-op learning and College Teaching,* 6(2).

[21] Rockwood, R. (1995). Co-operative and collaborative learning. *NT &L Forum*, 4(2).

[22] Rust, C. (Ed) 2003 *Improving Student Learning 10: Improving Student Learning Theory and Practice 10 years on. Proceedings of the 2002 10th International Symposium.* Oxford.

eAdoption and the Knowledge Economy: Issues, Applications, Case Studies
P. Cunningham and M. Cunningham (Eds.)
IOS Press, 2004

eLearning Knowledge Representation by Interactive Formal Models & Virtual Worlds

Oleg MOUKHINE[1], Kirill MUKHIN[2]
Perm State Technical University, Regional Centre Informatization, Modelling Laboratory, Stratum Modelling Group
Off. 321, 29-a, Komsomolsky Avenue, Perm, Russia, 614600
Tel. +7 (3422) 198-308, Fax. +7 (3422) 121-147, E-mail: {oim, km}@pstu.ac.ru

Abstract: Well-known systems of distant learning exercise functions of storing, navigation of knowledge and its translation along the channels, maintain communication between the teacher and the student. Modern e-Learning should also contain the interpreter of the knowledge represented in the form of models. A model is a formally calculated description of the properties of the studied object. Models possess behaviour; interact with each other and the student through interface. Modelling environment allows the student to use the knowledge, to get intellectual reaction from the system, design the virtual world out of models, the world that interacts with the student and allows him to master the subject. The subject represents a system of related models. Interactive course provides the students with supervised demonstrations, exercises, laboratory works, tasks, training aids, tutors, tests, virtual stands for modelling. Methods and forms of teaching in e Learning are classified from the point of knowledge modelling.

1. Introduction

Teaching is one of the most difficult ways of thinking organisation. In the process of teaching the student's thinking and the teacher's thinking interact. Both of them should correspond to the objective contents of the studied subject. The process of teaching is more effective if thinking is properly organised.

In the system of e-Learning we cannot rely on the undeveloped students' thinking (as it is not formed yet) and on the teacher's thinking (as the teacher is separated from the student). Thus, up-to-date approach to the system of e-Learning should provide allowance for waste when organising the student's thinking by means of new IT.

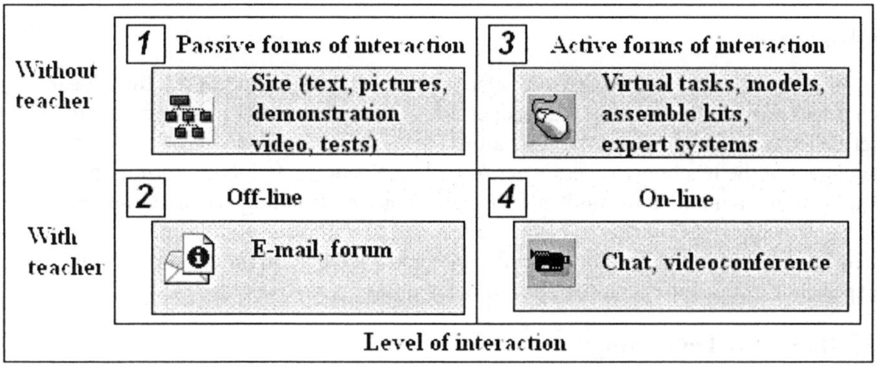

Figure 1: Four components of the system of e-Learning

Interactive object models of the studied subject help to solve this problem. The student solves given tasks on the model, actively manipulating task elements. Based on this interaction the student gains necessary skills. The computer plays the role of knowledge interpreter, assemble kit, virtual world of the studied subject, simulator, expert system, training aid. The knowledge should be presented by models, interpreted based on formal rules by the computer, and active interface provide feedback while teaching (Figure 2).

This method of teaching will be effective if the teacher himself designs models. For that reason it is necessary to have a certain information modelling technology for the end user.

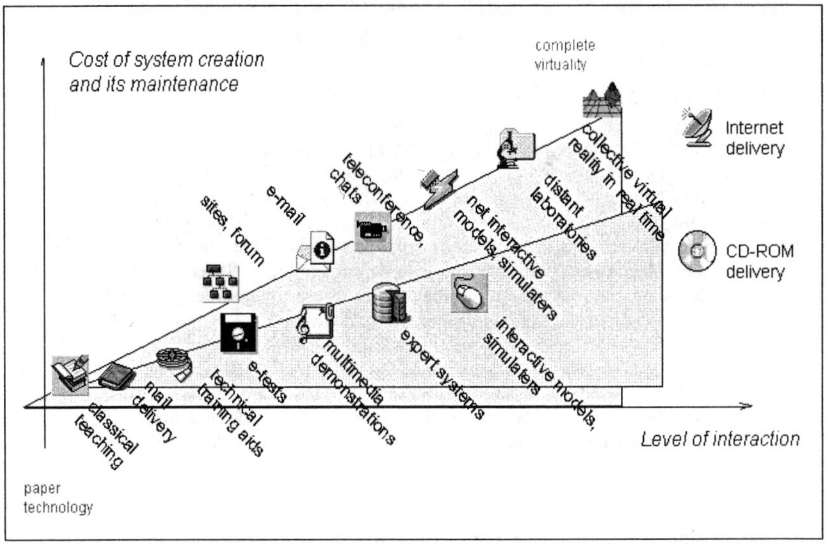

Figure 2: The Process of Distance Learning System Development

This paper describes the technology developed in Perm State Technical University. It helps improve the quality of e-Learning education thanks to interactive models that represent knowledge with which the student can interact when learning. This technology helps the student to master the subject as it gives a possibility to use the models in different methodic ways. The technology is provided with the tools and the ways for their design, it is easy to use and can be used together with other well-known systems of e-Learning.

2. Objectives

Our aim is to classify and design the system of tools and technologies for e-Learning, which could provide the student and teacher with a complete set of interactive courses and model collections for support. We also aimed at building the concept of monitoring and management of the teaching process when knowledge is presented in the form of models.

Application of interactive models for the purpose of teaching technical subjects in e Learning: to work out libraries of basic models and to work out highly interactive courses on their basis, to build the control system of interactive education process. We intend to use the experience of our European partners while creating interactive courses.

3. Method and Technology

3.1 Basic Principle

The teacher can choose the form of the lesson – a lecture, a seminar, a laboratory work, a practical work, a term paper, a test-paper, a consultation, etc. The experienced teacher uses these forms according to the situation and gains the required results.

When the material is transferred from the classical system to the system of distant education the teacher looks for adequate means and needs the suitable tools. Having analysed all well-known systems of e-Learning we have worked out the table for the teacher with the help of which it is possible to find correspondence between the classical traditional lesson and e-Learning lesson and to use it in practice (Figure 3). It is natural that each form of the e-Learning lesson needs special tools.

Classical technologies		*Distant learning technologies*
Computer support of forms of lessons:		Computer support of forms of lessons:
- lectures	→	- sites, Web-design, multimedia, demonstrations
- laboratory works	→	- computer controlled models
- practical works	→	- models-assemble kits, expert systems
- full-scale computer stands	→	- distant laboratories
- training aids	→	- computer training aids, simulators
- independent work	→	- e-shops, models-assemble kits
- work in the library	→	- e-libraries,e-search
- testing	→	- e-testing
- business games	→	- net business games by means of models
- course design	→	- term paper design, modelling, simulation
- individual consultations	→	- e-mail, chats, forums, conferences
- group seminars	→	- conference
- identification	→	- videoconference
- magazines	→	- distant data bases
- raiting	→	- students' monitoring
- students' monitoring	→	- curriculum, instructions
- curriculum, instructions	→	- e-payment
- payment		

Figure 3: Technologies of Learning Process Electronic Support

We have not noticed complete correspondence in the analyzed systems (for example, Hypermethod eLearning Office 3000, WebTutor, ReadyGo, Lotus Learning Space, WebCT, Moodle) and it is a considerable drawback. It means that the teachers do not implement all their possibilities and the students don't get corresponding quality of educational facilities. For example, widely used computer technologies (editors and multimedia) provide no more than 15 % of the needs of the educational process and are not always effective, whereas systems of e-Learning use them in more than 95 % cases.

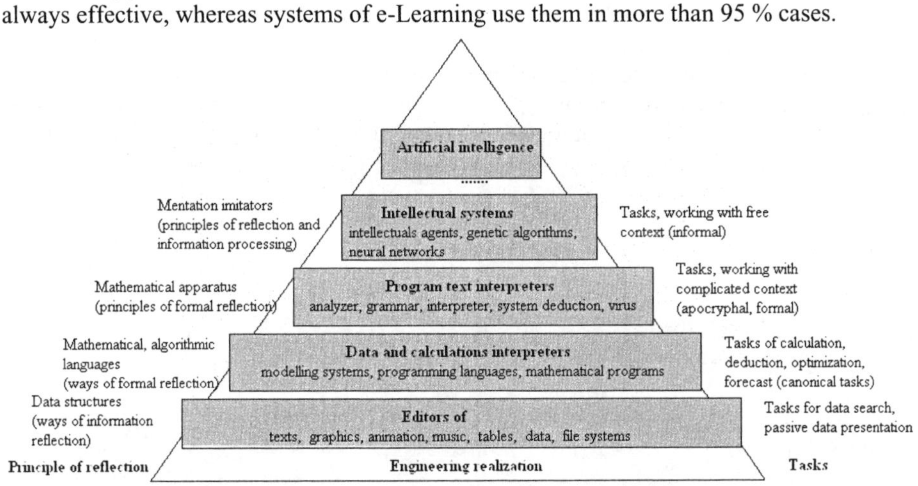

Figure 4: Hierarchy of Technological Means of Modelling and Design

Having used a number of such technologies in e-Learning (Figure 4) we found out they form a certain hierarchic system based on the functions provided. Text or graphic editors don't provide training. For that we need technologies of the second level, i.e. we need tools that can interpret the data according to a formal description (algorithm, method, model). This technology uses the data interpreting them with the help of models.

If we use the third level technologies it is possible to develop students' design skills. Design assumes the environment interprets apocryphal but formal task context manipulating with standard models. On this level it is possible to design a virtual world of the subject using dynamic model interaction. The fourth level technologies interpret tasks in the free context and design models based on the problem description using knowledge base [1]. On this level it is possible to use intellectual training aids, tutors, expert systems.

3.2 Technological Aspects

From the technological point of view a model is a mathematical structure, whose properties and behaviour are observed through a graphic interface. The object whose properties are simulated has the image (2d and 3d), sound, text of the model, links to other objects, a set of variables, etc. It is a complex creation [2]. The user can influence the model through a graphic image, data, text or structure and thus any variables at any moment of time.

Since model construction is quite a responsible and expensive process, the teacher needs a suitable means for quick model construction [3]. In our technology the teacher only needs to construct models out of basic objects, which are studied in a particular applied discipline. Then it is possible to combine models making links between them.

Our experience shows that the teacher can make up a new model version just before the lesson. So, a model is a system made of elements and links. A complex model may consist of other connected models, may have its structure. The interpretation of interacted models causes their behaviour. The interface allows the student to manipulate with the images and links and thus influence the simulated system and solve various problems, which help him to master the material. As the experience shows the material is mastered much quicker in comparison with mental experiment, which traditionally takes place in the student's head.

Formulating questions to the model it is possible to obtain the required result because the interpreter calculates the combined equations regarding to the required variables. You can formulate an unlimited number of questions to the model and thus solve a great number of problems. The model remains unchanged but the number of tasks, which could be solved on it, is unlimited. That's why every discipline is presented by a collection of basic models.

Solving problems the student can imitate properties of objects and systems, study different processes and phenomena. The model visualizes the results on the screen. The student can change parameters and variables with the help of active interface and he can manipulate, control the system and get the required results. It is easy to use dynamic controlled demonstrations, laboratory works, simple simulators, test systems (Figure 5).

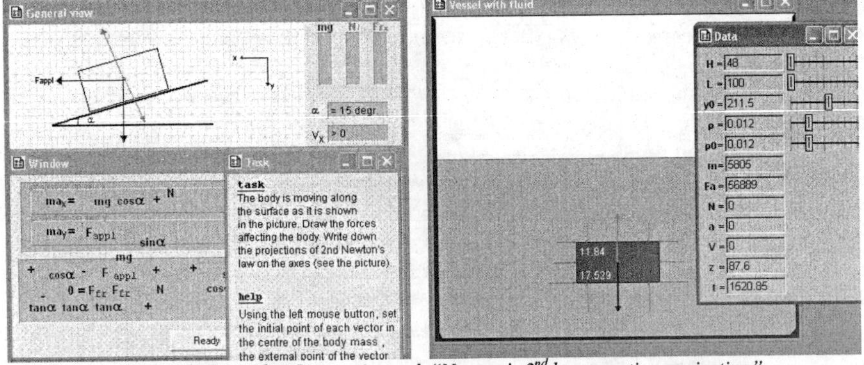

Figure 5: Examples. Interactive task "Newton's 2nd law equation projecting", Laboratory work "Archimedean law"

The task represents a chain of transformations and includes a number of models connected with each other in series, hierarchically and in parallel.

3.3 View of Teaching Methods

From the point of view of teaching methods any chain may play the role of a demonstration, test, simulator, laboratory work, exercise, tutor [4]. It depends on the interface formed by the teacher. Using interactive models the teacher can vary the teaching process, control it indirectly being separated from the student.

The models are presented to the student as a virtual world in which he has to make decisions. The education process is more dynamic as the student gets experience Observing, designing, controlling and solving problems and acquires knowledge and skills.

On the first stages of learning the student, observing the system behaviour, also tries to understand the texts, which are given to him. Having mastered them he may then control the model using a number of variables artificially limited by the teacher, and it allows him to specify principles of the studied discipline. Gaining experience he gets more freedom of model control from the teacher, gets more abstract results thanks to the solution of more complicated problems. For instance, the teacher may set the aim in such a way that the student could gain intermediate aims. The more often the teacher sets intermediate aims on the way to the main aim, the stiffer the education process is, the more seldom control points are set, the more creative the education process becomes. In such a technology the teacher can control the complexity of tasks, aims of education, making the student move from simple tasks to more complex ones in his subject [5].

With the help of the assemble kit the student can solve complicated problems using models from different sections. It develops his skills in design and creative abilities.

The model is obviously the next and a more advanced means of communication between the teacher and the student, which is different from on/off-line methods used nowadays. The teacher and the student find themselves in the virtual world of the discipline and interact with each other through it. The model becomes a powerful means of communicators' thinking organization.

As soon as they obtain enough number of interactive tasks, on the third level the teachers create the map of the discipline, which allows them to understand how its notions and laws are connected with each other. With the help of this map we can generate tasks and supervise the student's progress in the discipline.

3.4 Learning Process Control and Management

From the point of the learning process control and management it is necessary to provide parallel work of the expert system during manipulations with the model. The system will note the student's operations and the reactions (results) of the controlled model. During manipulations with the model the expert system evaluates the student's knowledge and skills. In case of mistake the expert system corrects the student. The expert system also makes statistics about the student mistakes. The mistakes made by the student are classified according to their types. The teacher has to make up a reference book of mistakes. Later the statistics will show what typical mistakes students make. All this allows to build the system of individual supervision over the student's progress in the discipline.

It is worth noting that on any level of the environment usage in order to design the task it is enough to make up a chain of models, transforming input and output. If the task is simple, the chain is short. If the task is complicated, the chain of transformations includes a number of models connected with each other in series, hierarchically and in parallel.

Thus, formulating lists of decision and fixed variables it is possible to vary the task complexity for the student making the chain shorter or longer. Every student is given an individual task – generators of random numbers vary values of variables, list of variables and model structure. As the chain of models for every task is different, the computer calculates the answer, which is not kept anywhere.

Besides, the environment gives a possibility to look through the answers, both final and intermediate. If the student finds it difficult to do something on a certain stage of the transformation chain he can see the answer calculated by the computer. If he cannot solve the task at all he is able to see the whole chain of transformations. Intermediate results are also possible, so the student can get help any time he needs it.

If the student cannot cope with the task solution, the chain is divided in half (dichotomy method) and the student is given two simpler tasks to solve in series. If the student fails to solve a certain task he has knowledge and skills gaps. To identify the gap it is possible to keep dividing the task and, consequently, the model in half. So it's possible to measure how well the student masters the material and what gaps in his knowledge he still has.

The students go from one model to another and gradually master the knowledge represented by them. The system makes notes of the studied sections and gaps in the knowledge on the map of the discipline made by the teacher. So it is possible to determine sections for individual learning and order of new material presentation.

4. Application

The model may appear in any forms of material presentation, always increasing their interactivity and may be used in any form the teacher prefers. It has been proved that the student masters the material better if he has a possibility to visualize the material, to experiment, to design knowledge. It helps to intensify the teaching process, to improve its quality and profitability and to spend less time on subject learning.

The aim of the laboratory is to increase interactivity of the training courses, which are used in education and industry, to offer technologies and services to design models, assemble kits and virtual worlds. The collection of models may be found in the Internet and can be used by teachers of European higher schools together.

For instance, the system of e-Learning in PSTU has the biggest in the world collection of models for technical subjects. Virtual Physics has 6 assemble kits (20-40 objects in each, more than 3000 interactive tasks), the course of electronics contains 120 objects with the help of which it is possible to solve any task, course of information studies includes 8 assemble kits with 200 objects, etc. This technology can be easily used in any existing e-Learning systems.

5. Business benefits

This approach helps the teacher to improve the quality of teaching, to improve the methods of material presentation due to its visualization and interactivity. It will allow them to work out new ideas on teaching methods, to increase the intellectuality of the tasks solved. It will be possible to keep track of the results and operations of the students, their mistakes that were not possible to observe before.

The technology allows the universities, educational centers, colleges to increase competitiveness, to provide a better quality of the studied materials, to make education accessible, to use e-Learning more widely thanks to home education with the help of CD. The technology can be used with other systems of e-Learning and popular data format. It provides research methods of teaching specialists.

For students this technology allows to illustrate complex processes and notions, to develop their research skills, to liven up the work with the material, to accelerate the process of learning, to make the process of getting knowledge more comfortable.

Application of the technology in the sphere of book publishing provides it is high investment appeal and can help to make up a new department of media-production. Publishing of interactive instructions on CD will help to make complex high production distribution more efficient. For business purposes it will be interesting to build a profitable service for production of interactive educational courses for European universities. It is also possible to use this technology for quick development of simulators in industry.

6. Conclusions

e-Learning should provide students not just with texts and pictures, means of information delivery and contacts with distant teacher, but it should also give an opportunity of active interaction with the objects of studied discipline thanks to interactive models.

The technology of distant learning at Perm State Technical University has laboratory works, guided media demonstrations, interactive tasks, exercises, simulators and training aids. Models may be not only interactive but also intelligent. So, according to the type of chosen interface, intellectuality and interactivity e-Learning has different levels. At present in PSTU there is a four-level system of distant learning for 50 technical disciplines. The experience shows that students work with models with pleasure. The teachers enlarge the collection of models (the size of the collection is more than 5000 models). Models with feedback allow to improve the knowledge and the skills no less than for 30 %.

Teachers who use distant learning should pay special attention to ordering of methods and use the unique base for their implementation described above.

We are planning to improve the technology, to expand the model base, to detail the models of technical subjects, to set them in the Internet in order to spread them and exchange the best samples with e-Universities. The laboratory is running experiments to transfer the technology to humanitarian subjects and non-standard tasks.

Acknowledgements

This paper was submitted with the support of ADMIRE-P (IST-2001-35449) EU project.

References

[1] Moukhine O. Knowledge representation by formal model language and its automatic interpretation by computer modeling environment Stratum-2000. / In: Cunningham. P et al (Eds) Building the Knowledge Economy: Issues, Applications, Case studies, IOS Press, 2003. Pp.1259 – 1264.

[2] Hill D. R. Object-Oriented Analysis and Simulation, Addison Wesley Publishing Company, Inc., 1996.

[3] Bayandin D.V., Kubishkin A.V., Moukhine O.I. The Usage of "Stratum Computer" Tool Software as the Technology of Man - Computer Interaction to the Model and Prototype Systems // East - West: interaction of the human being and computer: 2th International Conference EWHCI'96. - Moskow, 1996. - p. 207 - 219.

[4] Moukhine O.I., Shelemekhov A.A., Noskov V.A. High-leveled program enviroment intended for operation with technological objects in P-NET network. // 6th International Conference on the P-NET, Vienna, VUT, ICT, P-NET, Centre of Excellence for Fielbus systems, 1999. p. 17-21.

[5] Bayandin D.V., Kubishkin A.V., Moukhine O.I., Ryabukha A.A. The Usage of "Stratum Computer" Tool Software to Creation of Unified Multisub-Ject System of Model Knowledge and Set of Active Educational Structures // Proceedings of the second international conference on distance education in Russia: open and distance learning as a development strategy ICDED'96. - Moskow, AIE, 1996. V.2. - p. 413 - 415.

eChallenges in International Education

Hans DE RUITER, Baqun DING
Delft University of Technology, Section of Resource Engineering,
Mijnbouwstraat 120, Delft, 2628 RX, Delft, the Netherlands
Tel: +31(15) 278 5001, Fax: +31(15) 278 2836
Email: j.j.deruiter@citg.tudelft.nl; b.ding@citg.tudelft.nl

Abstract: For over eight years, a collaborative mineral education program has been running in Europe. This program now involves 10 universities, 60 students of 10 nationalities, 45 courses and 25 supporting companies. The experience has shown that e-techniques are essential for organising a complex joint education program. Immediately from the beginning e-techniques in various areas, such as web based registration of students, virtual learning environment, course evaluation, etc, were implemented as the most important part of the system. These techniques help not only to reduce the central management support requirement and therefore the program cost, but also to improve the system efficiency by allowing different parties to access the central database for on-time updates. The central organsition is carried out by only 0.5 fte staff member of Delft University of Technology and 0.25 fte secretarial support, whereas the high education quality has been achieved, which resulted in the "2003 Best Teaching Award" of the Rheinisch Westfaelische Technische Hochschule in Aachen Germany.

1. Introduction

Changing circumstances, since the seventies, led to new challenges for the universities, the industry and society in the organisation of the education in the field of mining and minerals engineering. At the end of the eighties it became clear at many of the European Universities that, in order to continue a high quality program, it was necessary to look for innovative ways. In order to optimise and enhance the quality of education the universities of Delft, London, Helsinki, and Aachen took the decision to investigate the feasibility of a joint curriculum during the final year(s). The general thought was that each partner would concentrate on subjects in which it was already strong. Thus a joint, high quality, curriculum was realised. The concurrent effect was that each university did not have to maintain the entire curriculum, which in turn yielded cost reductions [3][4][5].

Undergraduate students spend the first part, the bulk, of their university studies at their home university. There they obtain the basic engineering skills and a fundamental understanding of mineral science and engineering. However, during the fourth year, before commencing with the M.Sc. thesis work, the students of all 4 universities spend, as a group, two months at each of the four partners to study the various specialisations (figure 1). In addition, also exchange students of universities in North, South America and other parts of Europe were admitted to the program.

The success of the EMC has led to the development of the European Mineral Engineering Course (EMEC) in 1998 and the European Geotechnical and Environmental Course (EGEC) in 2003[1]. The number of organising universities has now increased to 10 [3][4][5].

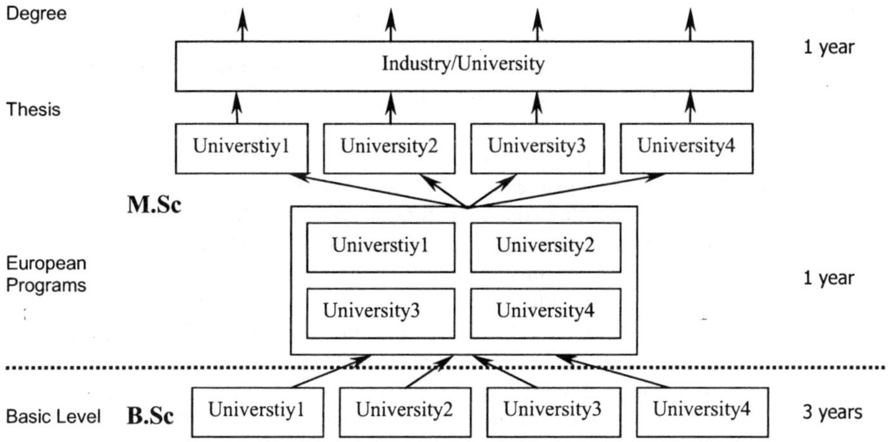

Figure 1 Structure of the Program

In 1999 a legal organisation was established: the Federation of European Mineral Programs (FEMP). Partners are the organising universities and 25 major companies. The industry contribution supports the cost of accommodation for students while abroad.

Because of funding constraints it was not realistic to establish a staffed "organising office". The solution was to build an e-based structure to run the complex organisation of courses and students. This was established over 2 years by involving a part time student.

2. Objectives

The objective of the e-system was to organise and rationalise the following matters which are essential for a well organised program:

1. Registration of the students and generation of the massive amount of paperwork related to the exchange of students among various universities.
2. Organisation of an alumni community for ex-students who participated in the programs.
3. Organisation of the 45 courses, offered in the program
4. Communication between staff and students
5. Evaluation of the 45 courses by some 20 students each.
6. Administer exam results and generate the official transcript forms

In addition, the system was aimed to take into account that ODL techniques would be introduced into the system at a later stage.

3. Technical Description and Methodology

It was decided to use standard software and application packages used at TU Delft. The following technology is used:

- Access databases for data about Course subjects and student and alumni information.
- Excel for various applications
- BlackBoard for the virtual learning environment [2]
- Sensor, the TU Delft developed course evaluation system
- Gallery for the picture archives
- Webpages for application and registration

The choice was made not to develop a totally integrated system written by a commercial company specifically for the programs, but to use existing software and link as much as possible of the applications. Another important point was that the staff at various locations had to be able to do most of the routine "update" work instead of sending their material to a central organisation for processing. The programs grew relatively slowly over the years and therefore the e-system was developed step by step. The co-ordination of the programs was being carried out by Delft University of Technology (TU Delft) and therefore the common programs, databases, websites and databases were placed on the university's server. The challenge was to minimise the central roll of TU Delft with regards to the maintenance of the systems, but have the staff and students at the various locations do this.

The first step was to streamline the registration. All universities involved needed to have various forms for each student to be completed and sent among the partners. The total package counts at least 5 pages per university or 20 pages per student in case 4 universities are involved. Many forms require information, which has also been entered on other forms (like name, address, date of birth, etc.). Students worldwide can register from their home.

An Access database was designed and connected to an Active Server Page on the websites of the programs through which future students could register. Several checks were built in to make sure that the format of the information was consistent. Also information is collected which is used to construct a standardised curriculum vitae. The database also contains the information of the participating universities, the marks of the students and a link with the database in which all courses are described. This makes it possible to construct and print the European Credit Transfer Sheets (ECTS), as required for exchange programs. The elimination of manual transfer of information minimises the chance for mistakes.

The second step was to set up the virtual learning environment. The main purpose was to have a central location for all course information, which could be kept up to date by the instructors at various locations. One important feature of this was to keep general information at one place and have each location update its own relevant items. For example, a total time schedule for the academic year (in the form of a spreadsheet) is kept up to date by downloading, changing and saving it on the BlackBoard. Hyperlinks with the webpage make the schedules also accessible to visitors of these sites.

The third step was setting up the course evaluation system. In the beginning the evaluation of the 15 courses per program was done on paper by the students, resulting in some 300 evaluations. These evaluations were manually summarised in order to get a usable result. The Sensor system of TU Delft was chosen for this purpose. Sensor collects the information from the students through a number of pre-defined questions. The answers can be in the form of marks (bad to good) or written comments. At the end of the academic year a summary report of the courses is automatically generated by Sensor in Excel form. The link used by students for input is included in the BlackBoard system for each course.

The fourth step was the organisation of exam results. For each of the exams percentage points, local grades and European Credit Transfer Standard grades are registered.

These grades are entered by the staff into the BlackBoard system and subsequently transferred into the central database. The Access program then generates the required official ECTS sheets for the administration of the participating universities and the Grade Point Average sheets for the students.

It was considered important to maintain a database with the addresses of those who had participated in the programs. Originally a spreadsheet was used, which could be downloaded through BlackBoard [2]. Changes had to be forwarded to the co-ordinator in order to be processed into the spreadsheet. Recently a web-based interactive database for the alumni has been established. Alumni can see the information of the other alumni and they can update their own information as well as e-mail addresses of their colleagues.

Figure 2 shows the flow of information between the programs and the participating universities and students.

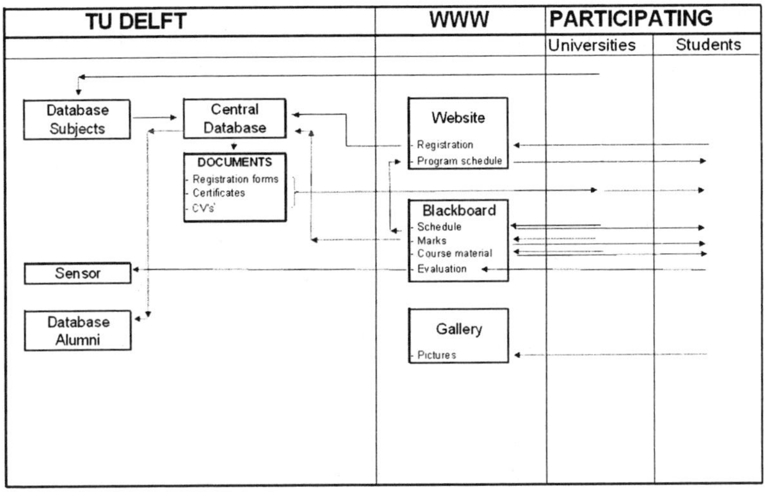

Figure 2 Information flow in the System

4. Developments

Since the start of the Mineral Engineering Programs there has been a great interest of the industry, other students and other universities either to participate as a student, or to offer courses for the program. Unfortunately the logistical limits of the programs did not make this possible. One of the limits is that we cannot accommodate more than 20-25 students per program and another is that we cannot expand the number of universities to be visited within a time period of eight months.

In the future the organization, infrastructure and e-learning techniques (BlackBoard) already in place with the programs will be used as a base for developing e-learning courses in the field of Minerals Engineering. This will be in addition to the current programs.

Associated universities will be invited to join the new network. This results in a true worldwide international distant learning program. The target participant students are from:

- Students with a B.Sc. who wish to complete a M.Sc.
- Students who wish to update or expand their knowledge through specialized courses.
- Companies which wish to upgrade their employees to a M.Sc.
- Companies that like to get their non-mining employees familiarized with certain aspect of the mineral business.
- Students from Developing countries, through International development programs
- Students who wish to complete a M.Sc. will choose a participating universities as their "base". The thesis project will have to be completed with guidance from this university.

Students will have to spend one or two periods of a few weeks at the university, but the rest of the courses will be completed through distant learning, during regular employment.

It is also envisaged that each of the universities will supply one or more courses that in total will form a "menu" from which the students can choose. This will be in consultation with the university concerned, in case the student plans to complete a M.Sc. Due to the complexity of the organization (various partners in different countries) and the new techniques required it is necessary to use external expertise and additional manpower.

5. Results

The implementation of the various applications started after the first year (1996) of the first program (EMC). The results have been very satisfactory and it is clear that without this system it would be very difficult (and expensive) to run the current 3 programs efficiently. The success is to a large extent because of the step by step approach in developing it and the modular structure.

6. Business Benefits

The development of the system was mainly carried out by one student assistant, working for 1 day per week, during a period of 2 years. Part of that was the initial time spent to set up the applications; the remainder was used for data handling. Currently an estimated average of 2 hours per week is needed for routine work.

Without these e-applications a secretary would have to spend at least 2 – 3 days per week to carry out the administrative matters, which are being dealt with by the system. A big advantage is also that the required work can be carried out on a decentralised basis by the staff of the partner universities.

7. Conclusions and Recommendations

It is practical approach for an education program to run collaboratively among several universities. Such program enables the curriculum to provide high quality education by taking in specific expertise of different universities, and helps the participating universities to avoid the cost for offering full-scope courses to limited number of students. To run a complicated joint education program among different universities in different countries, the administration can be a big challenge to the central administration of the program. The challenge comes not only from the requirement for an expensive support system, but also from the difficulty in keeping the information from different sources integrated and up to date if e-techniques are not applied.

The main reason that the European Mineral M.Sc. Programs, developed by 10 European universities, have been running very successfully is to a large extent because of the high level of e-applications for the organisational matters. This has made it possible to keep the operating cost down, and enhanced smooth and effective information flow. The practical and step-by-step development has avoided major problems during the operation of the programs. Further development will focus on the introduction of e-learning techniques in order to make the courses available to outside students.

This practice can be extended to other similar fields at educational institutes and research institutes. The research institutes, for example, might need to work together on a large research project to integrate different expertise possessed by each. In such case information exchange might be a bottleneck to the collaboration of the system. The e-applications will help to establish a cost effective and smooth-run communication system to keep the information up-to-date. Software package specially designed for a project is of course an option, but it can be extremely costly. It might be a good approach to make full use of the available software and construct the e-system in a step-by-step way.

References

[1] www.emc-edu.org, www.emec-edu.org, www.egec-edu.org

[2] http://blackboard.icto.tudelft.nl

[3] Ruiter, J.J. de; Towards a worldwide network of education in mineral engneering. In: Proc. 36th Annual Meeting of the Canadian Mineral Processors, 20-22 January 2004, Ottawa, Ontario, Canada, p. 3-14.

[4] Ruiter, J.J. de; Federation of European Mineral Programs (FEMP). In: Natural resource, Mijnbouwkundige Vereeniging, Vol. 5, No. 2, 2003, p. 26-27

[5] Ruiter, J.J. de; Die Internationalen Studienangebote EMC, EMEC und EGEC. In: Proc. Medzinárodný Seminár – Geotechnológie a Environment, Banská Štiavnica/Košice, Slowakije, 13 November 2003, p. 11-20.

eAdoption and the Knowledge Economy: Issues, Applications, Case Studies
P. Cunningham and M. Cunningham (Eds.)
IOS Press, 2004

A Client-Server System for Mass Recruitment to Secondary Schools in a Metropolitan Area

Cezary MAZUREK[1], Maciej STROIŃSKI[1], Andrzej P.URBAŃSKI[1, 2]
[1]*Poznań Supercomputing and Networking Center, ul. Noskowskiego 10, 61-472 Poznań, Poland, Tel: +48618582001, Fax: +48 61 8525954, mazurek@man.poznan.pl*
[2]*Institute of Computing Science, Poznań University of Technology, ul. Piotrowo 3a, 60-965 Poznań, Poland,*
Tel. +48 602 125 075, Fax: 48 *61 8771 525, andrzej.urbanski@cs.put.poznan.pl*

Abstract: There are many real-life problems, which in a small scale can be efficiently solved using traditional processing of paper documents or even with electronic documents, but with direct human decision making. Until now it has been in practice with for instance many recruitment problems in education. However, when more data have to be processed in shorter time, problems become unsolvable without computers and software for case-specific processing. We discovered such a case in educational recruitment when at the same time many candidates apply to almost the same set of schools. We describe such an almost catastrophic event, sketch our first solution and describe the objective of this paper in section 2. A more detailed description of a centralized solution proved in practice is shown in section 3. Experiments with a completely new solution based on distributed agents are presented in section 4. In section 5 we mention other work in this area. We finish with conclusions and further research directions in section 6.

1. Introduction

There are many real-life problems, which in a small scale can be solved using traditional processing of paper documents or even electronic documents, but with direct human decision making. Until now it has been the practice with, for instance, many recruitment problems in education. However, when more data have to be processed in shorter time, problems become unsolvable without computers and software for case-specific processing.

We discovered such a case in educational recruitment when at the same time many candidates apply to almost the same set of schools. We describe such an almost catastrophic event, sketch our first solution and describe the objective of this paper in section 2. A more detailed description of a centralized solution proved in practice is shown in section 3. Experiments with a completely new solution based on distributed agents are presented in section 4. In section 5 we mention other work in this area. We finish with conclusions and further research directions in section 6.

2. Motivation and Objective of this Paper

2.1. Dramatic Event as a Motivation

Since the early 1970's, Polish secondary schools have recruited new students based only on their certificates. Each school can have slightly different rules to compute the number of points from marks on the certificates. From all applicants, each school admits no more than the number of free places of those candidates having the highest number of points.

In 2002 Polish Ministry of Education changed the rules of recruitment to secondary schools extending simultaneous entailment from a single to an unlimited number of secondary schools at the same time. That year it led to total chaos in the recruitment process in many secondary schools in Poland, especially in big cities where thousands of students look for a place in up to a hundred schools and many try to enroll in as many as ten schools. The best students were admitted in every school they applied to and consequently locked places, which prevented others being accepted. This created great frustration over several weeks, during which places gradually became unlocked as better students selected a school.

2.2. Summary Solution

This event immediately led us to the idea that a centralized information processing system for all recruiting schools from the whole metropolitan area would address this problem. At the start we discovered that the main engine should be a simple sorting algorithm working on data containing a number of points and a list of preferences for each candidate. But instead of simultaneous school enrolment, a list of preferred schools must be declared by each candidate, where the first one is the most preferred, the next is less preferred and so on. A different algorithm for each school that computes qualification points based on the the certificate complicated the basic recruitment algorithm.

We implemented a demonstration system running the right algorithm in September 2002. Demonstrations received interest from the educational authorities of our metropolitan area. In cooperation with these clients and experts in secondary schools qualifications, we specified a computerized mass recruitment system and implemented it in six months.

The subsequent recruitment process in Poznań in 2003 was a great success. Candidates could provide their certificates and preferences by Friday afternoon and received the final results on Tuesday of the following week On the Sunday, a super-committee of all school principals worked together in order new educational places where possible and needed, and close classes of no interest to candidates. As a result, each student was admitted to only one educational place. More than 90% of students found places in this phase of recruitment. The rest did not because they had not provided a long enough list of preferred schools.

2.3. Paper Objective

Our objective is to show that efficient and fair mass recruitment (many candidates and recruiting units) requires coordination, which prevents situations such as occurred in 2002 reducing the efficiency and fairness of the recruitment process. In Section 3 we present a centralized coordination model (proven in 2003 and prepared for June 2004 recruitment) and a distributed multi-agent-based solution for future research is outlined in Section 4.

3. Commercial Solution

3.1 Architecture of Nabor 2004

The analysis of the workflow mechanisms employed in 2003 has been used to build a new edition – Nabór 2004. System components in this version have been defined very clearly, as well as roles and tasks of individual users groups and next steps for training. This produced a model of a strong, dependable, safe and flexible elastic solution, which is easy to use.

All user groups accessing the system have different rights. The "Inspector" oversees and administers of the whole process of recruitment, starts and finishes its individual phases, having access to all data. The software allows the drafting rules of clauses and personalization of the procedure for the region to be defined. The "Curator" answers essential problems related to the recruitment; this person has access to all data stored in the system and also the statistic reports. The "Operator", as an employee of a specific high school, answers the input to system all school data as well as data of candidates who are willing to attend that school; the "Candidate" is a pupil of the last junior high school class who competes for acceptance to at least one of the schools in the region. The "PSNC Service" controls all components of the recruitment systems from the administrative perspective; it oversees transmission and realizes technical assistance for all users groups.

3.2 Secure Data Access and Management

The "Inspector", "Operator" and "Curator" own access to the system only and behind the assistance of a stand-alone application supplied by Poznan Supercomputing and Networking Center, prepared on the Java software platform. In order to meet security norms, a restrictive version of the "NaborOS" operating system (based on Knoppix, one-disk distribution of Linux) was used; an application started up in this system is signed with a unique digital key. The server supports detailed access control and storage of history changes of the entire database. Such a solution increases the credibility of the system; anonymous system operation is not supported. The "Public" access to data (for candidates) on the server (separated from the rest of the system) is achieved using an Internet browser. General reports and reports on the recruitment of specific candidates are available.

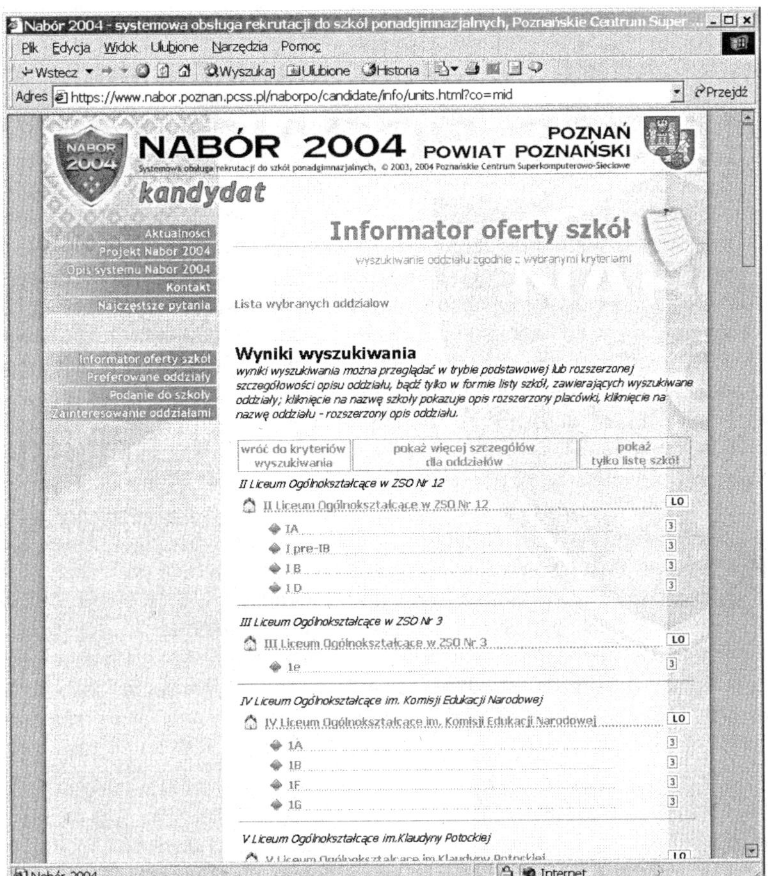

Figure 1: User Interface for Candidates in Nabor 2004

The system has a central server, to which data from all schools, departments and enrolment candidates are sent. Internet enabled computers (located in high schools, the local council and the Curator Office) are used to connect to the system's head office via the Internet by means of the Polish National Research Network POL 622/PIONIER, spare access to the central server is provided through additional dial-up connections, which can be used by all systems' clients in case of unexpected shortage of the Internet connections.

An obvious advantage of the Nabor system is access to the Curator Office and Department of Education, which makes getting information of the recruitment course possible. For a high school candidate, the most important feature is allowing a long-list of preferences, to be accepted to one of the chosen schools; the system is an excellent source of data also for schools, allowing them to tailor educational courses to current requirements.

3.3 Current Deployment Status

The process of recruitment is performed in the following steps: information on schools and departments enables for the introduction and creation of candidates' Internet informer (Fig.1); certificates, the results of tests and preference lists of an individual department choice supplied by candidates are added to the database. On their bases reports of preliminary imposing are created, which, after being published on WWW pages, enable making possible changes in candidates' preferences. The last step is a school principals' meeting, the start-up of the recruitment procedure and solving conflict situations. The result of this meeting constitutes ready reports for schools about the accepted candidates, candidates accepted to other schools, unaccepted candidates, and available free places.

In 2004 we are organizing installations of the Nabór system in five regions: the City of Poznań and its administrative district, Zielona Góra, Szczecin, Białystok and Kalisz.

The first phase of the system has been implemented and training courses for all system Operators (schools) and Inspectors (departments of education) in individual localities have been organized. At the same time, an installation disc for Inspectors was created, allowing them to enter information on all schools and regional departments in specialized applications, create accounts for Operators in individual schools, enter obligatory models of all rules of the grading scale for candidates' achievements and additional tests. Schools have received installation discs with applications and a printed version of the Nabór system User Manuals. After connection tests and verification of proper use of the software, all schools enter expanded data of departments, descriptions, instructed languages and cycle of education. Based on that data, a web application for candidates was built; pupils can receive information on the course and recruitment process for senior high school candidates in 2004, and interactively view a school educational offer informer and create a preference list of schools and departments. After filling and printing a high school application form, they have to take it to the "First Choice School" – in first position on their preferences list.

The second phase of development has begun. Candidates will be able to fill in school preference lists, the web application presents candidates' interests in departments, as a number of candidates' applications with a given department on the first position of the list, in relation to a maximum number of available candidates in this department. Simultaneously, helpdesk and technical service has been activated for the resolving of all system operation problems, mostly in the Operator's and Inspector's application.

4. Multi-Agent-based Approach

Many years ago Artificial Intelligence researchers developed a concept of solving problems using advanced programs, so-called agents, which cooperate efficiently. When applications using Internet in cooperation have been possible to develop this approach became much more attractive. We can now build complex open systems coupled from independent agents, where each one plays only its own role and is relatively simple.

In recruitment, we can distinguish some sorts of agents. The most significant is probably the agent, which represents the candidate in recruitment. Another one is the agent representing the recruiting unit. Sometimes it may be useful to add the agent representing the promoting unit. A simple agent-based algorithm is shown in Fig.2

```
proc AddToSchool(Cand,School);
SortedQueue[School].Add(Cand,Rank(Cand));
if SortedQueue.Oversized
then begin
   AddToSchool(SortedQueue[School].LastCand,
   SortedQueue[School].LastCand.NextSchool);
   SortedQueue[School].RemoveLast;
end;
end (* AddToSchool *);
```

Figure 2. Simple Algorithm for Agent Representing Candidate

From a list of 123 multiagent environments of Europe's Network of Excellence for Agent-Based Computing we have chosen - The MadKit Project (a Multi-Agent Development Kit see Figure 3), which is characterized as being easy to use:

- MadKit is a Java multi-agent platform built upon an organizational model. It provides general agent facilities (e.g. lifecycle management, message passing, distribution), and allows heterogeneous agent architectures, communication languages and customization.
- MadKit communication is based on a peer-to-peer (p2p) mechanism, and allows developers to quickly develop distributed applications using agent principles.
- MadKit is a free software based on the GPL/LGPL license.

We use it to develop a simplified equivalent of the recruitment system. In Figure 3 and Figure 4 the candidate agent is presented.

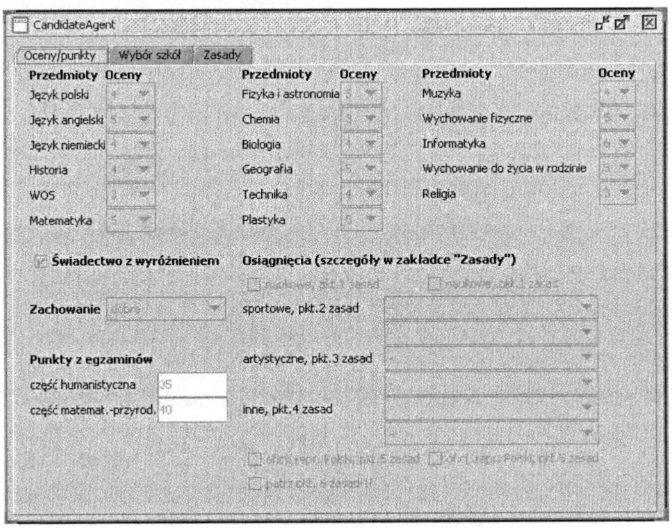

Figure 3: Candidate Agent in MadKit – Page for Marks Insertion

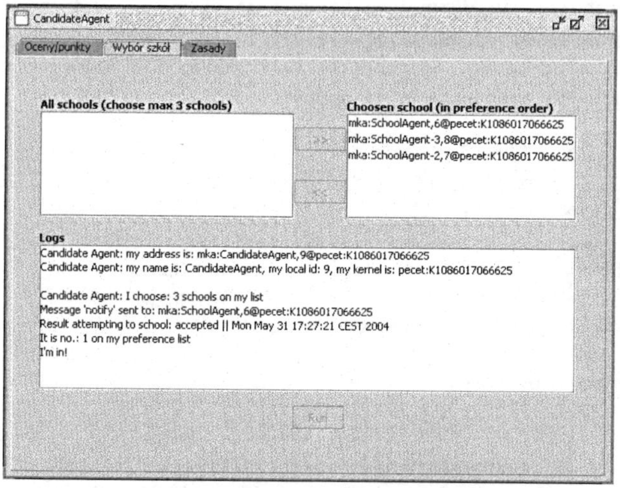

Figure 4: Candidate Agent in MadKit – Page for Declaring Preferences

In Figure 5, both candidate and school agents are presented.

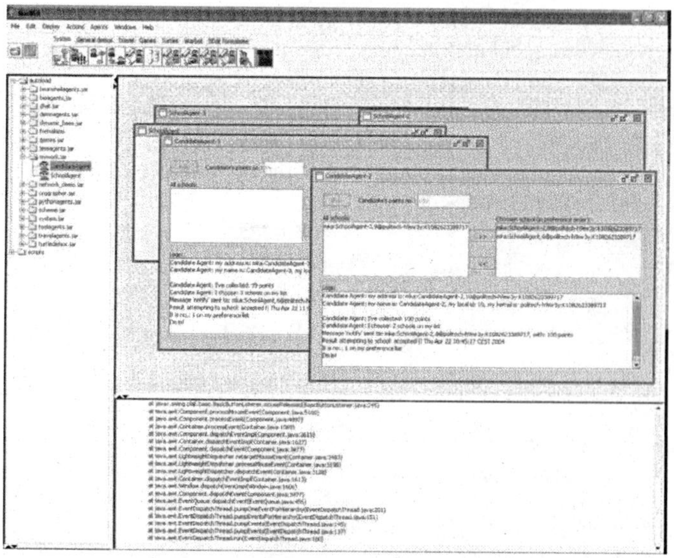

Figure 5: Recruitment Agents in MadKit Environment

There is, however, a serious problem in developing a useful and practical agent-based recruitment system. The reason is that persistent agents are not available in MadKit or any other known agents' environment. It means that solving our tasks require to have all agents in random access memory all the time, which is not practically possible for such a long job.

The solution is to use the agents' environment, which could save working agents' in a database, but until now it should be prepared by recruitment system developers. However, the agents' approach is fruitful and inspired for future versions of the recruitment system.

5. Related Work

The same event inspired another Polish company to develop the recruitment system in Warsaw. However, in 2003 the system did not work for the whole metropolitan area, but only for a small fraction of schools in two logically different recruitment subsystems.

The system used for massive recruitment in 2004 is called 'Nabór Optivum'. As one can read from the official sources published by the system's distributor 'Vulcan' and from the system's Web page, the system is being deployed in two different configurations:

- with Windows applications installed in gimnasiums(junior high schools),
- only with a WWW application.

In both cases, there are individual accounts for pupils created in the system. The individual account allows a pupil to choose the preferred units and watch the process of enrolment. However, different people enter their data to the system in different configurations. In the first case the personal data and scores of the pupil are entered by a gimnasium's employee. In the second case, all the data is entered by the pupil via a WWW module and verified by an employee of the high school to which the pupil intends to enroll.

It is important to note that even in the first case there is a group of pupils who enter their data into the system individually. These are pupils who study in gimnasiums in which the system had not been installed. For example, these are non-public gimnasiums or gimnasiums from outside the city in which the system had been deployed.

There are three main components of the system:

- a Windows application installed in gimnasiums ('Rejest Uczniów Optivum'),
- the WWW application available via the Internet browser,
- the central database ('Kseon 2000+').

The first application is installed on a local machine and allows for:

- creating pupils'accounts,
- entering pupils' scores .

There is no evidence that this application requires connection to the Internet apart from sending data to the central database. It does not require any intelligent database synchronization as it serves only as a data-entering terminal. The system is based on PHP technology for application programming and some database or persistence-layer backend. The system uses the HTTPS protocol for secure transfer of data. There is no evidence of usage of other security-related technologies and solutions. However, it is possible that they are used in the communication between schools and the system.

The central data-gathering database is a completely invisible component. There is no information available about the technology used to create this module, and no information about how this component communicates with other components of the system.

For recruitment in 2004 both companies have been contracted with about 15 big towns to sell commercial systems like the one described in section 3 and this section.

In other countries there were no such dramatic events as in Poland, because educational authorities are much more conservative. For instance, in the USA pupils can propose only three preferences – i.e. schools they wish to attend. However, our preliminary research has shown that it does not guarantee the fairness of the recruitment process, because it strongly depends on the right evaluation of pupil's chances to be accepted by the school. We believe that almost an unlimited number of preferences in accordance with a computer system, as in Polish solutions, will guarantee fairness in a much higher level.

6. Conclusions and Future Work

At this stage of research and development we can say that there is no way back to the educational recruitment in secondary schools without an integrated computing system. We believe that in a few years all Polish big cities will buy such a system, which is useful in many dimensions: guaranties fairness and efficiency of the recruitment process, and immediately provides statistic data necessary in the recruiting offices.

Our vision of the future of such systems is sketched only in section 4. In our opinion it requires much more research with funds from both commercial and scientific sources.

References

[1] Rychlewski J., Weglarz J., Starzak S., Stroinski M., and Nakonieczny M., "PIONIER: Polish Optical Internet", Proceedings of ISThmus 2000 Research and Development for Information Society conference, Poznan, Poland, 2000, pp. 19-28

[2] Płóciennik, M. "Solving recruitment problems in an agent-based environment", M.Sc. Thesis proposal, Poznań University of Technology, Poznań, 2004.

[3] Urbański, A.P., Nawrocki, J. „Algorithms for fair and efficient educational recruitment", EDI-EC, Łódź, 2003.

[4] http://nabor.psnc.pl/

[5] www.nabor.poznan.pcss.pl

[6] www.vulcan.edu.pl

[7] www.agentlink.org

[8] www.fipa.org

[9] www.madkit.org

Author Index

Abels, S. 460
Adam, O. 833
Akkersdijk, V. 604
Aleknevičienė, V. 537
Amaral, D.C. 1547
Ambrosino, G. 478,940
Andreone, L. 1448
Andreou, A.S. 1679
Androutsellis-Theotokis, S. 1554
Antona, M. 619
Apostolou, D. 1133,1156
Appelgren, E. 499
Arjona, M. 1686
Arredondo, M.T. 75,854
Attwell, G. 1665
Augenbroe, G. 1285,1547
Aunola, M. 335
Ballon, P. 12
Barbini, F. 453
Barceló, J. 940
Battaglino, A. 793
Bayer, F. 233
Bechmann, H. 319,1766
Behrens, H. 249
Bellotti, C. 1448
Bellotti, F. 141,1448
Benamou, N. 670
Berger, R. 1571
Berta, R. 141
Bertino, E. 1309
Bettoni, S. 1175
Biasiotti, M.A. 745
Biggiero, L. 134
Biró, M. 847
Bitran, I. 1115
Bjørnholt, M. 639
Blind, K. 264
Boero, M. 478
Bohlin, E. 12
Boi, S. 414
Bokma, A. 1051
Boronowsky, M. 1441
Borthwick, L. 732
Boscolo, P. 365
Bouguet, A. 1486
Boves, L. 1403
Brady, A. 42
Breu, R. 646
Brodt, T. 50
Brown, L. 1708
Browne, J. 1239
Bruno, C. 379
Brussee, R. 1340
Buhl, H. 1387
Bunduchi, R. 287
Busson, A. 693
Buyse, D. 155
Bystrov, D. 1742
Cabrera, M.F. 75
Callot, M. 1183
Camacho, M. 982
Campbell, S. 460
Campos, A. 1354
Cardoso, J. 1123
Carey, K. 42
Castilho, L. 1589
Castro, M. 1686
Cave, J. 188,760
Chadwick, D. 1216
Chaillou, C. 1486
Charalabidis, Y. 1554
Chatard, E. 1604
Chionsini, V. 94
Cho, H. 551
Cipriano, P.-A. 825
Claessens, J. 1208
Claudon, P. 1301
Conde, A. 982
Conlan, O. 42
Conn, S. 1115
Conso, N. 917
Contenti, M. 453
Cormican, K. 1618
Correia, A. 1354
Cortese, G. 1426
Cristea, P.D. 1734
Cullen, K. 611,624
Cunningham, M. 1035
Cunningham, P. 1035
Curwell, S. 654,974
Cvirko, V. 1742
D'Atri, A. 453
Dandi, R. 134
Danielson, M. 1004
Danilushkin, I. 102
Davide, F. 1426
Davies, A.J. 109
de Gloria, A. 141,1448
De Leastar, E. 28
de Oliveira, A. 1562
de Poot, H. 1325
de Ruiter, H. 1796
Deakin, M. 654
Degrande, S. 1486
del Hoyo-Barbolla, E. 854
del Río Rodríguez, A. 400
Demestichas, P. 20
Demyanenko, R. 102
den Os, E. 1403
Diakun, J. 1362
Dias Netto, R.G. 1547
Dickinger, A. 127
Dimitrakos, T. 445,1191,1199
Ding, B. 1796
Dirlenbach, H. 295
Djordjevic, I. 1191
Dogac, A. 522
Dotter, F. 1629
Dunne, K. 1239
Edelmann, C. 1271
Edelmann, N. 961
Edström-Frejman, A. 343
Ekenberg, L. 1004
Ellis, R. 1395
Enlund, N. 327
Eriksson, L. 327
Eschenbaecher, J. 1376
Evans, B. 109
Eynard, B. 1183
Falcão e Cunha, J. 543
Fan, I.-S. 1387
Feeney, K. 42
Fenoglio, E. 777
Fernandes, M. 543
Fernández, V. 982
Ferrari, E. 1309
Ferretti, E. 141
Feuer, E. 1693
Filipazzi, S. 700

Filos, E. 571
Finger, M. 662
Fodor, O. 407
Folmer, E. 394
Forsgren, O. 862
Fradinho Oliveira, J. 1562
Fradinho, E. 1562
Fragidis, G. 909
Frechette, S. 551
Fröschle, N. 724
Frosini, P. 940
Gábor, A. 847,1774
Gadda, G. 1494
Gadda, L. 1175
Gaeta, M. 445,1191
Gagliardi, R. 414
Gangemi, A. 1093
García, I. 1480
Gareis, K. 611
Garg, A. 295
Garretti, L. 825
Gartmann, R. 437
Garuti, M. 386,1579
Gaspari, M. 1069
Georgolios, P.-P. 1133
Gerasimov, A. 1742
Gerst, M. 287
Geuer-Pollmann, C. 1208
Gini, S. 940
Ginty, K. 1051
Giordano, S. 94
Girard, P. 1293
Glaser, E. 167
Göckel, M. 1044
Golby, D. 1199
Goliński, M. 869
Gong, L. 1441
González, M. 1686
Goossenaerts, J. 225
Gorbunov, V. 1101
Gorostiza, Á. 1354
Götzl, I. 631
Grill, M. 351
Grootveld, M. 1340
Guarnieri, D. 670
Gudergan, G. 249
Guidi, D. 1069
Gzara, L. 1301
Hackl, M. 407
Hafner, M. 646
Haller, J. 1223
Hamilton, A. 654,974
Han, J. 311
Han, Y. 437
Hansen, L. 65
Harej, K. 1693
Harrison, A. 1519
Hawkins, R. 485
Hecht, A. 351
Heinonen, S. 1511
Heitmann, M. 50
Hemilä, J. 429
Hemmerich, R. 155
Henriksen, H.Z. 901
Hertzberger, L.O. 1262
Herzog, O. 1441
Heyrman, J. 1719
Higel, S. 42
Hinderer, H. 394
Hinrichs, E. 1457
Hoeck, H. 249
Hogarth, A. 1781
Hollosi, A. 968
Holtkamp, B. 437
Hori, M. 708
Horvat, R.V. 1693
Huis in't Veld, R. 1340
Husmann, E. 1029
Hussla, A. 319
Hussla, I. 319,1766
Huveneers, C. 485
Igl, G. 685
Ivezic, N. 551
Jackson, P. 947
Jakobs, K. 241
Jansson, K. 429
Jardim-Goncalves, R. 211
Jatkūnaitė, D. 537
Jennings, B. 35
Jeong, B. 551
Johnson, M. 1140
Jones, A. 551
Jones, P. 1133
Jonsson, A. 499
Jucevičienė, V. 537
Kabak, Y. 522
Kafentzis, K. 1133
Kamps, T. 1085
Kang, K.S. 174
Karabulut, Y. 1223
Karakoidas, V. 1554
Katzy, B. 1347
Katzy, B.R. 685
Kearney, P. 1199
Keravel, A. 693
Kirchhoff, U. 1534
Klepal, M. 80
Kligiene, N. 1637
Knudsen, W. 639
Kő, A. 847
Koch, M. 1108
Kölmel, B. 147
Kolpaschikov, S. 102
Kooss, D. 1448
Kordey, N. 1464
Kort, J. 1325
Korte, W.B. 611,1464
Kosmopoulos, A. 751
Koumpis, A. 1051,1059
Koutsouris, N. 20,87
Kubitschke, L. 624
Kühn, H. 233
Kulvatunyou, B. 551
Kuroiwa, S. 1368
Kutsikos, K. 559
L'Abbate, M. 1085
Laleci, G. 522
Langley, D. 1325
Laria, G. 445,1191
Le Goff, S. 1727
Le Mer, P. 1486
Leboeuf, P. 1301
Lee, G. 1611
Leli, A. 785
Lennstrand, B. 491
Lewis, D. 42
Li, G. 437
Li, M. 256
Liberato, A. 478
Liehmann, M. 968
Lim, A.S. 530
Lissner, T. 639
Logi, F. 478
Lombard, M. 1301
Lopez de Vallejo, I. 1411
Lossent, L. 1301
Lotti, S. 893
Louis Dit Picard, S. 1486
Lowe, C. 597
Mac Randal, D. 445,1191
Macintosh, A. 739,997
Mahler, T. 180
Mäkinen, S. 335
Malkewitz, R. 1494
Mantovani, S. 670
March, D. 109
Margarone, M. 141
Mariani, M. 1448
Marques, A. 841
Marsh, J. 1009
Marshall-Ponting, A. 974
Martin, M. 724

Martinez, M. 1480
Martino, L.D. 1309
Maslennikov, A. 102
Mathews, S. 196
Mathur, R. 80
Mattelmäki, T. 1511
Mattioli, M. 1579
Mavromoustakos, S. 1679
Mazurek, C. 1801
McQuade, E. 1708
Meijer, G.R. 1262
Mekras, N. 279
Mena, J. 982
Meriluoto, J. 1140
Merlo, C. 1293
Merlo, L. 422
Messnarz, R. 1693
Meyer, N. 1376
Meyer-Reim, U. 319
Michel, R. 1293
Michel-Verkerke, M. 1340
Milone, L. 785
Mirad, J.I. 400
Mitrou, N. 87
Molina, J. 1480
Möller, A.K. 365
Monari, P.D. 460
Monks, N. 582
Montaletti, G. 724
Morozov, M. 1742
Moseng, B. 1700
Moukhine, O. 1789
Mukhin, K. 1789
Murphy, E. 1708
Murphy, J. 127
Murzek, M. 233
Muzzi, C. 134
Naber, L. 968
Nahum, F. 379
Nannucci, R. 745
Nantel, J. 167
Naranjo, J.C. 75
Nardi, R. 1719
Navarro, X.A. 400
Ni Fhloinn, A. 715
Nobs, A. 1231,1278
Nóvoa, H. 543
Nowak, A. 646
Nowak, P. 1183,1293
Nowicki, B. 1077
O'Donnell, T. 42
Ó Foghlú, M. 28
O'Keeffe, T. 1645
O'Sullivan, D. 42
Oberto Tarena, M. 809
Ohashi, M. 708
Olsen, T. 180
Onesti, P. 1579
Osterlund, D. 217
Ostyn, G. 940
Papadopoulou, L. 20
Papadopoulou, S. 1156
Papanikolaou, K. 1679
Park, S. 311
Parycek, P. 961
Paskaleva-Shapira, K. 654
Passantino, F. 1009
Patrício, R. 1589
Pauli, M. 1708
Pavlou, I. 1059
Pavy, D. 1486
Payaro, A. 1247
Peire, J. 1686
Penn, A. 1418
Perdoni, V. 1175
Peristeras, V. 909
Perron, L. 1486
Persson, C. 491,1148
Pesch, D. 80
Peters, R. 990
Petrucci, A. 1069
Pfister, J. 303
Picci, L. 1069
Pigulevsky, I. 372
Popov, O. 1672
Popova, I. 1672
Pöyry, P. 1140
Prandoni, C. 414
Prem, E. 1021
Prinz, W. 1457
Quadt, A. 295
Quinn, K. 42
Ramalhão, G. 1589
Ramos, C. 1123
Ramos, N. 543
Ratti, R. 1051
Raviolo, P. 809
Reichstaedter, P. 590
Reimers, K. 256
Renton, A. 997
Ribeiro, L.D.V. 1547
Richter, M. 1316
Ristol, S. 1727
Ritrovato, P. 445,1191
Rivilla, I. 1686
Robinson, P. 1223
Robinson, S. 196
Rodrigues, F. 1123
Rolstadås, A. 1700
Romano, N. 1191
Rose, B. 1301
Roucoules, L. 1293
Rowe, D. 932
Rozenfeld, H. 1547
Rügge, I. 1441
Rupp, C. 885
Sage, J. 1029
Saint-Marc, L. 1183
Sala, F. 1751
Salve, R. 1502
Sammarra, A. 134
Sanchez, O. 203
Saranummi, N. 1527
Saugis, G. 1486
Savoldelli, A. 670,700,1175
Scalice, R.K. 1547
Schäfer, M.-F. 1133
Schaffers, H. 1433
Schedl, H. 1597
Schgör, P. 1658
Schleyer, C. 1254
Schnetzler, M. 1231
Scholarios, D. 1758
Schreck, G. 1571
Schubert, L. 445
Schubert, P. 1044
Schuh, G. 1254
Sebastian, V. 841
Seboeck, W. 961
Sellin, B. 1653
Semoushin, I. 1472
Sennheiser, A. 1231
Serrano, C. 1347
Shahin, K. 893
Sigrist, B. 1044
Silva, A. 1589
Simmons, S. 768
Simonov, M. 1093
Sinigaglia, S. 809
Sinir, S. 522
Smedberg, Å. 1333
Sokolov, D. 507
Sorli, M. 1354
Soroldoni, M. 1093
Soubra, S. 654,974
Spinellis, D. 1554
Squicciarini, A.C. 1309
Stanbridge, P. 1029
Staniszkis, E. 1077
Stavroulaki, V. 20,87
Stefanou, A. 909
Steggles, P. 1519

Steiger-Garcao, A. 211
Stephanidis, C. 619
Stich, V. 1278
Stockhammer, C. 303
Stokic, D. 1354,1534
Strignano, O. 453
Stroiński, M. 1801
Sturm, F. 1169
Succi, G. 678
Sundmaeker, H. 1534
Sung, G. 1347
Swaak, J. 1340
Szabó, Z. 1774
Tambouris, E. 909
Tamm, H. 817
Tanakov, A. 1742
Tarabanis, K. 909
Tektonidis, D. 1051
Tepandi, J. 924
Terzidis, O. 469
Theologou, M. 20
Thiel, U. 1085
Topham, S. 365
Torkkeli, M. 1115
Törlind, P. 116
Torres, M. 841
Tric, E. 359
Trninic, D. 271
Tuduce, R. 1734
Tumer, A. 522
Turner, J. 654
Uppgård, T. 499
Urbański, A.P. 1801
Valeri, L. 188
van den Hoven, J. 685
van der Heijden, B. 1758
van der Meer, S. 35
van der Schoot, E. 1758
van Leeuwen, M. 1618
Vankeisbelck, R. 974
Värlander, S. 514
Vas, R. 847
Ventriglia, G. 1719
Verhoest, P. 485
Verhoosel, J. 604
Viamonte, M.J. 1123
Vian, D. 1604
Vieira, H.M. 211
Viherä, M.-L. 58
Villalar, J.L. 75
Virtanen, K. 1511
Viukari, L. 58
Vlachakis, J. 394,460
Wade, V. 42
Wagner, K. 1271
Wallin, E. 491
Warr, A. 559
Weber, B. 646
Weidemann, M. 1278
Weiss, Z. 1362
Weissenberg, N. 437
Wemhoener, N. 1254
Werth, D. 833
Wesner, S. 445
Whelan, M. 801
Wikström, S. 514
Wild, B. 478
Willnow, C. 1571
Wilson, F. 990
Wognum, N. 1387
Wolf, P. 1169
Wustinger, J. 955
Wylegalla, J. 5
Xenakis, A. 739
Yarushkina, N. 1472
Yildiz, A. 522
Yudashkin, A. 102
Zamboni, S. 422
Zamolotskikh, A. 1035
Zangl, F. 833
Zinkevičienė, D. 537
Zobel, R. 571
Zuliani, P. 678
Zwahr, T. 662